The United States Army in
Operation IRAQI FREEDOM
May 2003—January 2005

ON POINT II:

Transition to the New Campaign

Dr. Donald P. Wright

Colonel Timothy R. Reese

with the
Contemporary Operations Study Team

Combat Studies Institute Press
US Army Combined Arms Center
Fort Leavenworth, Kansas

Library of Congress Cataloging-in-Publication Data

Wright, Donald P., 1964-
  The United States Army in Operation Iraqi Freedom, May 2003-January 2005 : on point II : transition to the new campaign / Donald P. Wright, Timothy R. Reese ; with the Contemporary Operations Study Team.
    p. cm.
  Includes bibliographical references and index.
  1. Iraq War, 2003---Campaigns. 2. United States. Army--History--21st century. 3. United States--History, Military--21st century. I. Reese, Timothy R., 1959- II. Title.

  DS79.76.W73 2008
  956.7044'340973--dc22

                                                            2008016252

First printing, June 2008.

CSI Press publications cover a variety of military history topics. The views expressed in this CSI Press publication are those of the author(s) and not necessarily those of the Department of the Army or the Department of Defense. A full list of CSI Press publications, many of them available for downloading, can be found at http://usacac.army.mil/CAC/csi/INDEX.asp.

For sale by the Superintendent of Documents, U.S. Government Printing Office
Internet: bookstore.gpo.gov Phone: toll free (866) 512-1800; DC area (202) 512-1800
Fax: (202) 512-2104 Mail: Stop IDCC, Washington, DC 20402-0001

ISBN 978-0-16-078197-1

Foreword

This is the story of the American Army and its Soldiers during a critical period of Operation IRAQI FREEDOM—the 18 months following the topping of the Saddam Hussein regime in April 2003. *On Point II: Transition to the New Campaign* provides a contemporary historical account of the United States Army in Operation IRAQI FREEDOM from May 2003 through the Iraqi elections of January 2005. As its title indicates, the book depicts the transition of the Army from conventional combat to full spectrum operations in support of building a new, free Iraq.

One of the great, and least understood, qualities of the United States Army is its culture of introspection and self-examination. American Soldiers, whether it is the squad leader conducting a hasty after action review of a training event or the senior leader studying great campaigns from the past, are part of a vibrant, learning organization. The CSI motto—*The Past is Prologue*—neatly captures the need for this study. Publishing the recent history of the United States Army's operations is a key part of the TRADOC mission to develop adaptive, innovative leaders who are flexible, culturally astute experts in the art and science of the profession of arms, and who are able to quickly adapt to the contemporary operating environment.

On Point II is a comprehensive, balanced, and honest account of the Army's role in this particularly significant period in Operation IRAQI FREEDOM. It is neither triumphant nor defeatist. *On Point II* provides Soldiers and other military professionals with a means to understand important and relevant lessons from the Army's recent operational experience. The story of the Army in this period of Operation IRAQI FREEDOM is one filled with many transitions, with many successes, and with significant challenges. *On Point II* is dedicated to the outstanding men and women of the United States Army who have sacrificed so much and who remain "on point for the Nation" in the defense of freedom at home and abroad.

Victory Starts Here!

William S. Wallace
General, US Army
Commanding General
US Army Training and Doctrine Command

Acknowledgments

The completion of a project as vast in scope as *On Point II* is the work of hundreds of people, each of whom deserves individual recognition but which are too many to single out. The Contemporary Operations Study Team (COST) in the Combat Studies Institute (CSI) was formed in late 2005 within the US Army Combined Arms Center at Fort Leavenworth, Kansas, to begin the project. General (Retired) Kevin Byrnes, then the Commander, US Army Training and Doctrine Command, and General William Wallace, then the Commander, US Army Combined Arms Center, had the vision to initiate and resource the project and the team. When General George W. Casey Jr. became Chief of Staff of the Army in 2007, he made himself available for an interview. General David Petraeus, during his tenure as CAC commander, also assisted the *On Point II* team in many ways, to include a thorough review of the entire first draft. The Director of the Army Staff, Lieutenant General (Retired) James Campbell, helped us greatly with the Department of the Army review process. The Chief of Army Public Affairs, Major General Anthony Cucolo, also shepherded the study through the review and public release processes.

The individual members of the COST accomplished the hard work of visualizing the project, finding documents, traveling, scheduling and conducting interviews, and writing first drafts of each chapter. Major James Tenpenny deserves special recognition for being the temporary chief of the COST in 2005 and early 2006 and overseeing the creation of the team and the first months of its work. Staff Sergeant Ernst J. Amelang's initiative and technical skill provided the team with its office and information technology (IT) equipment and support. Ms. Catherine Shadid Small served as the team manager and skillfully orchestrated thousands of details while conceptualizing the overall structure of the study. Mr. Dennis Van Wey, a US Army Reserve Civil Affairs officer who served in Iraq in 2003 and 2004, brought his expertise and experience to the chapter on reconstruction operations. Mr. James Bird, a retired Army officer, worked on the chapters concerned with combined arms operations and Soldier well-being. Dr. Peter Connors, also a retired Army officer, concentrated on the study's analysis of Army governance operations. Ms. Lynne Chandler Garcia focused her efforts on understanding and explaining the Coalition's program to establish new Iraqi security forces. Ms. Christine Curtin, Ms. Angela Bowman, and Ms. Angela McClain all contributed to the heavy editorial work on various versions of the manuscript, and transcriptionist Ms. Kim Sanborn expertly transcribed the hundreds of interviews conducted with participants in the campaign. Archivist Ray Barker imposed order on the vast amount of documents and interviews that were gathered and made them accessible to the researchers and writers. Ms. Robin Kern, assisted by Major Channing Greene, collected or created all the visual images in this book. Major Chad Quayle and Major Jeffrey Holmes reviewed drafts of the study and provided research assistance while working at CSI.

Many organizations and individuals helped us gather primary materials and provided us with invaluable feedback after reviewing early drafts of the study. Mr. Frank Shirer and Ms. Chris Koontz at the US Army Center of Military History (CMH) helped us collect a large amount of documentary material from their voluminous archive. Mr. Kevin McKedy provided excellent access to the records of US Army-Europe and V Corps. Mr. Hamric Ellis, the 3d Armored Cavalry Regiment historian, provided a large number of documents about the regiment's operations in 2003 and 2004. We also owe a debt of gratitude to many others who assisted with the scheduling of interviews with participants in OIF. Brigadier General Michael

Linnington, former brigade commander in the 101st Airborne Division, not only sat for two interviews but helped us coordinate interviews with many other Soldiers who served in Iraq.

Dr. Alexander Cochran, Historical Advisor to General Casey, offered critical insights that greatly improved the study. Dr. Richard Stewart, Lieutenant Colonel Shane Story, and other reviewers at the CMH provided excellent advice for revisions. Colonel Marc Warren (Retired) and other officers at the Department of the Army Office of the Judge Advocate General took the time to carefully review chapters 5 and 6, focusing us closely on doctrinal and legal issues. Major General Barbara Fast, former commander of the US Army Intelligence Center, also provided critical input on these important chapters. Colonel William Darley, Chief of *Military Review*, and Colonel (Retired) Paul Tiberi helped us sort out the conceptual and doctrinal issues in chapter 7. CSI historian Mr. Matt Matthews provided valuable input to chapter 8 about Operation AL FAJR based on his book about the battle. CSI historian Mr. John McGrath reviewed chapter 8 and provided outstanding support with the order of battle, chronology, and analysis about the Iraqi Armed Forces in support of chapter 11. Armor Branch Historian Dr. Robert Cameron and Transportation Branch Historian Mr. Richard Kilblane each assisted with issues concerning armor and transportation operations. Major General Charles Fletcher provided very useful comments on chapter 12. Dr. Sanders Marble, Major Richard Prior, and Major Lewis Barger at the Office of Medical History in the Office of the Surgeon General provided invaluable input and reviews of chapter 13. Dr. Brian Linn, Professor of History at Texas A&M, and Dr. Adrian Lewis, Professor of History at North Texas State University, also provided important comments on the study.

Many Department of Defense (DOD) organizations and unit historians provided input and reviewed portions of the manuscript in their areas of expertise, including National Guard historian Ms. Renee Hylton; US Army Reserve Command historian Dr. Lee Harford; US Central Command historian Dr. John Q. Smith; US Special Operations Command historian Dr. John Partin; US Army V Corps historian Dr. Harold Raugh; Major Frank Gilbertson from the 1st Armored Division; Captain James Page from the 101st Airborne Division; Mr. Adam Elia, historian with the 25th Infantry Division; and Lieutenant Colonel Adrian Bogart from the 4th Infantry Division. Special thanks to Major Scott Znamenacek, the 1st Infantry Division historian, for providing extraordinary assistance with his unit's archive and in reviewing this study.

Dr. William Glenn Robertson, CSI Deputy and CAC Command Historian, mentored the COST, ensuring that the team stayed on course during the long periods of research and chapter revisions. CSI editor Ms. Elizabeth Weigand deserves special recognition for her extraordinary efforts to turn the manuscript and visual materials into printable form.

We are indebted to all those who agreed to be interviewed for the book about their roles in OIF. From Soldier to Sergeant to General to senior civilian, each one gave their time in support of the project. Finally, for every Soldier and civilian who has served in Iraq or supported OIF, this is their story and we have tried to honor their hard work and sacrifice by telling it accurately and honestly.

In spite of all the assistance and support, we are well aware that readers will find errors of fact and judgment in this project, for which the lead authors take full responsibility.

Dr. Donald Wright   Colonel Timothy Reese
Chief, COST   Director, Combat Studies Institute

Contents

Part II. Transition to a New Campaign

Part III. Toward the Objective: Building a New Iraq

Part V. Conclusion

Figures

Call Out Boxes

Introduction

On Point II: Transition to the New Campaign is the next volume in the US Army's series of studies focused on its operations in Iraq. The first volume, *On Point: The United States Army in Operation Iraqi Freedom,* showcased Army operations in the decisive maneuver phase of Operation IRAQI FREEDOM (OIF) through April 2003. *On Point II* begins with President George W. Bush's announcement of the end of major combat on 1 May 2003 and follows the Army's operations through the January 2005 Iraqi elections. In many ways, *On Point II* is a book the Army did not expect to write because numerous observers, military leaders, and government officials believed, in the euphoria of early April 2003, that US objectives had been achieved and military forces could quickly redeploy out of Iraq. Clearly, those hopes were premature. Like the first volume, *On Point II* will focus on the US Army within the context of a combined joint campaign and will also chronicle and analyze the Army's efforts across the spectrum of conflict to create a secure and prosperous Iraq.

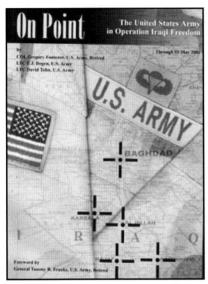

Figure 1. The first comprehensive study on OIF.

These two volumes share the crucial purpose of telling the US Army's story in OIF, a task that is challenging because of the contemporary nature of the events under scrutiny. As the authors of the first *On Point* stated in their Preface, "Interpreting history is difficult; interpreting ongoing events is even more difficult."[1] Additionally, just as *On Point* was not the definitive history of the first phases of OIF, *On Point II* is not the seminal history of the Army's struggle to transition from decisive combat operations to a new type of campaign in Iraq. More will be written in the future, and readers will come to understand the events of OIF better as time passes; however, for those Soldiers engaged in future campaigns involving full spectrum operations, *On Point II* will provide initial insights into the Army's experience in OIF. The authors of the first *On Point* stated their goal was "to kindle the discussion on what happened and why."[2] Ultimately, that is the goal of *On Point II* as well.

The idea for this study emerged in 2005 when General Kevin Byrnes, commander of the US Army Training and Doctrine Command (TRADOC), and Lieutenant General William Wallace, commander of the US Army Combined Arms Center (CAC), realized the Army had no means in place to capture the contemporary understanding of OIF in any comprehensive way. Both leaders found this troubling. Wallace knew that the Center for Army Lessons Learned (CALL) offered the Army expeditious analyses of current operational issues in the form of tactics, techniques, and procedures (TTP) and Initial Impressions Reports while the Center of Military History wrote the Army's official histories 10 to 15 years after the fact. Both Wallace and Byrnes envisioned a historical work that would close the gap between the analyses of TTP and the official histories. Wallace stated that this type of study would not be a "definitive history," but "an analyzed, researched chronicle of the events that says, 'here's what happened and here are the implications thereof.'"[3]

To fill this vacuum, Wallace directed the Combat Studies Institute (CSI) at Fort Leavenworth, Kansas, to research and write the Army's immediate history of the Global War on Terrorism. Since 1979 CSI has conducted original, interpretive research on historical topics relevant to the current concerns of the US Army and published this research in a variety of forms, including Leavenworth Papers and, more recently, Global War on Terrorism Occasional Papers. In late 2005 CSI formed a team of researchers, writers, and editors to create this study.

While writing *On Point II,* the authors were very aware of the pitfalls that, since the era of Herodotus and Thucydides, face those attempting to write contemporary military history. Among the most daunting of these challenges is the lack of perspective that clouds the historian's full understanding of events and their implications. The authors also faced the related problem of using sources that are, depending on the topic, too few or too many, classified, or problematic in other ways. To overcome these potential obstacles, the authors of *On Point II* relied on a broad foundation of unclassified primary and secondary sources, though the researchers and writers also reviewed many classified documents that provided context. The research and writing team conducted 200 oral interviews and a large number of discussions with many key political officials and military commanders, including most of the division and brigade commanders who participated in OIF between May 2003 and January 2005. The study also used thousands of unclassified documents, such as briefings and reports, which shed light on US Army operations during this period. While much of the material generated by the Army in OIF remains classified, the authors believe they have based this study on a solid foundation of sources composed of unclassified documents, oral interviews, and secondary accounts. In fact, one of the project's greatest challenges was to use even a small percentage of the primary materials gathered.

On Point II takes up where *On Point* left off. The authors of the first volume viewed their mission as recounting the Army's history in OIF from the planning stages through the toppling of the Saddam regime in April 2003. It focuses on Soldiers conducting conventional combat operations, though doing so with unusual boldness and speed. Accordingly, the key conclusions are closely related to the Army's future role as an institution that conducts conventional warfare, albeit in a new, dynamic environment replete with changing technology and emerging threats. Because of its scope, however, *On Point* did not address the Army's transition to the new campaign. The summer of 2003, the time *On Point* was written, was clearly too early to assess subjects such as the American response to the rising insurgency. In its conclusion, the authors of the first *On Point* recognized the need for subsequent studies that would closely examine the rest of the campaign, especially how the Army made the transition to the postconflict phase of the operation.

On Point II begins in May 2003, soon after President Bush's announcement of the cessation of major combat operations. The study does not progress chronologically, but instead takes a thematic approach. Many, if not most, works of military history recount the history of conventional campaigns in which the end result is known and the historian can discern a chronological framework for the progression of the war. Perhaps the best example of this methodology is the widely used approach that shapes historical accounts of the US Army in the European theater during World War II. That approach makes use of a generally accepted narrative that begins with the invasion of North Africa (or Normandy) and ends with the fall of Berlin. Using such a narrative, the historian can demonstrate progress toward the final objective, regardless of the many obstacles that slowed and diverted the effort.

On Point II takes a thematic approach for two reasons. First, this study was written in 2006 and 2007, long before the Coalition terminated its operations in Iraq. Thus, the authors do not know when and how the campaign will end. Second, the 18-month period under study does not lend itself easily to a narrative approach. To be sure, Coalition forces achieved major political and military milestones during this time. Events such as the capture of Saddam Hussein, the establishment of the Interim Iraqi Government, and the elections of January 2005 were significant successes and shaped the campaign in important ways. Because of this, the authors have tried to capture the general chronological structure of the May 2003 to January 2005 period in an overview chapter to provide some understanding of the major events, decisions, and crises that shaped this period.

However, for the US Army, operations in Iraq were not progressive in the sense that, over time, terrain was won from the enemy allowing forward movement toward a geographic objective, such as a capital city, followed by a surrender agreement and the establishment of peace. Nor was the nature of those operations compartmented in that they proceeded sequentially from peacetime buildup and preparation, to decisive offensive operations leading to victory, to brief and benign stability operations, and finally to a transition of authority and redeployment home. Instead, units conducted multiyear operations that were multifaceted and directed across what Army doctrine described as the full spectrum of conflict with the amorphous goal of establishing the conditions for Iraqi self-rule.

The concept of full spectrum operations provided the foundation of the US Army's doctrine in 2003, though few grasped the practical implications of the concept as OIF began. Field Manual (FM) 3-0, *Operations*, the Army's 2001 capstone manual, described a continuum of conflict that began on one extreme with major theater wars for which the Army would primarily conduct conventional combat operations, to military operations other than war (MOOTW) on the other extreme that featured stability operations and peacetime missions such as security assistance. FM 3-0 mandated that Army units *at all echelons* have the capacity to mount operations along this entire continuum or spectrum. Moreover, doctrine stated that Army units must be prepared to "combine different types of operations simultaneously and sequentially to accomplish missions in war and MOOTW."[4] Doctrinally, all units had to have the capacity to conduct a simultaneous mix of offensive, defensive, stability, and support operations, changing the relative weight of each of these four categories of operations depending on the nature of the conflict. In early 2003, however, few Army leaders had fully internalized the tenets of full spectrum operations. In addition, many national and military leaders incorrectly equated the types of operations (offense, defense, support, or stability) with the type of conflict (conventional war, irregular war, small-scale contingency, or peacetime engagement).

In March and April 2003, OIF began as a traditional, though very bold, conventional military offensive directed toward defeating Iraq's military forces and removing the Saddam regime from power. Following the accomplishment of this goal, most commanders and units expected to transition to a new phase of the conflict in which stability and support operations would briefly dominate and would resemble recent experiences in Bosnia and Kosovo. This phase of the conflict would require only a limited commitment by the US military and would be relatively peaceful and short as Iraqis quickly assumed responsibility. In this mindset, full spectrum operations would occur sequentially over time as one type of operation finished and another began. Few commanders foresaw that full spectrum operations in Iraq would entail the simultaneous employment of offense, defense, stability, and support operations by units at all

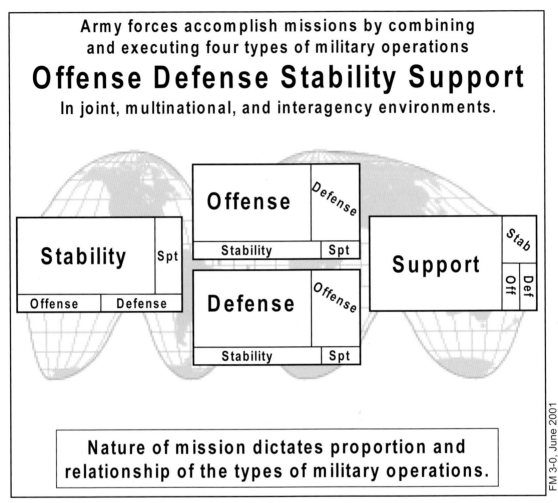

Army forces accomplish missions by combining
and executing four types of military operations

Offense Defense Stability Support

In joint, multinational, and interagency environments.

Offense

Defense

Stability   Spt

Stability   Spt

Offense

Defense

Stability   Spt

Support

Stab

Off

Def

Nature of mission dictates proportion and
relationship of the types of military operations.

FM 3-0, June 2001

Figure 2. Full spectrum operations, US Army doctrine, 2001.

echelons of command to defeat new, vicious, and effective enemies. Nor did they anticipate that it would require US and Coalition military forces to take the lead in providing security, reconstruction, and governance for Iraq for years. Certainly, few if any military or national leaders foresaw the beginning of full spectrum operations in Iraq as marking the Army's transition from its traditional role as a military force unequalled in the fighting of conventional wars, to a force engaged in an irregular war in which a variety of enemies would nullify many of the technological and organizational advantages enjoyed by American Soldiers while creating many advantages of their own.

Nevertheless, the US Army did become engaged in a new campaign in Iraq after April 2003, a type of campaign that required its units to conduct full spectrum operations in a manner unprecedented in complexity and comprehensiveness. Indeed, after the toppling of the Saddam regime, it became common to find combat arms battalions conducting intelligence, reconstruction, governance, combat, and information operations, while simultaneously training Iraqi Security Forces and sustaining these efforts with basic administrative and logistics support. This complex set of missions was not directed at any one, concrete, easily measurable objective, but toward less tangible achievements such as the erosion of the power held by a shadowy insurgent network and the garnering of popular support for the Coalition and the emerging Iraqi Government.

Accordingly, the authors concluded that a thematic approach would best address the broad and complex aspect of this campaign. Following this **Introduction** and the **Prologue,** which summarize the events that brought the United States and the Coalition into the conflict in Iraq in early 2003, the study is broken into parts, each encompassing chapters that discuss a specific category of operations and efforts.

The first part is titled "Setting the Stage" and includes the following chapters:

- **Chapter 1, Overview of Operation IRAQI FREEDOM: May 2003 to January 2005:** This chapter provides a chronological narrative of major military and political events, including major policy shifts and operations that shaped the overall campaign between May 2003 and January 2005.

- **Chapter 2, The US Army's Historical Legacy of Military Operations Other Than War and the Planning for Operation IRAQI FREEDOM:** The US Army has a long history of conducting what were commonly, if imprecisely, called stability operations. This chapter reviews the Army's experience with these operations in the years before OIF, including a discussion of doctrine, training, education, and relevant historical experiences. The discussion concludes with an analysis of the prewar planning for Phase IV, the postinvasion phase, of OIF and how the US Army's history with stability operations shaped those plans.

- **Chapter 3, The Rise of the Iraqi Insurgency and the US Army's Response:** This chapter is a review of the insurgency's rise after May 2003, the insurgent groups that made up the threat network, and their most common tactics. The discussion then shifts to how the Army units understood the insurgency and generally shaped their responses to that threat.

In the second part, "Transition to a New Campaign," the first chapter examines the command transitions that took place and the evolving responses chosen by US Army units to counter the growing insurgency threat. Each of the chapters that follow focuses on a distinctive set of missions, such as intelligence or detainee operations. Taken as a whole, these actions became the critical components of full spectrum operations designed to foster the growth of a new Iraq and counter a growing insurgency.

- **Chapter 4, Leading the New Campaign: Transitions in Command and Control in Operation IRAQI FREEDOM:** This chapter examines the major transitions of command and control during the period under study, focusing on the creation of Combined Joint Task Force–7 (CJTF-7), the evolution of that headquarters, and the shift to Multi-National Force–Iraq (MNF-I) and its subordinate elements.

- **Chapter 5, Intelligence and High-Value Target Operations:** Many American Soldiers have emphasized the critical role of intelligence in full spectrum operations, especially those focused on countering an insurgency. This chapter examines how the Army collected, analyzed, and disseminated information, including the use of interrogations in that overall effort. However, its focus is on the emergence of human intelligence (HUMINT) gathered at company and battalion levels as the main source of actionable intelligence and how that imperative shaped unit operations in Iraq. The chapter closes with a discussion of the operations that sought to capture or kill key individuals from the remnants of the Saddam regime and the emerging insurgent network.

- **Chapter 6, Detainee Operations:** This chapter covers the emergence of the detention mission as a critical part of the larger campaign in Iraq. The discussion covers a wide range of detainee operations in Iraq, from the problems at the Abu Ghraib Prison to the detainee operations conducted at the tactical level by units unprepared and untrained for this difficult mission.

- **Chapter 7, Fighting the Battle of Ideas in Iraq:** Because generating support among the Iraqi population for the Coalition's vision for the country became critical, the US Army became engaged in a competition of ideas. This chapter looks at information operations in the larger campaign and the role public affairs and the media played in those operations.

- **Chapter 8, Combined Arms Operations in Iraq:** By the end of the 20th century, the US Army had become adept at synchronizing the actions of various types of units such as infantry, artillery, aviation, and engineers to achieve mastery of the conventional battlefield. This capability also played a role in the new campaign in Iraq as the Army found ways to employ its skills in combined arms warfare in counter-improvised explosive device (IED) missions and countermortar operations. This discussion will look at the combined arms aspect of these missions and then consider four of the large-scale combined arms operations mounted between May 2003 and January 2005. These four actions demonstrate how and why Army leaders in OIF during this period focused their considerable conventional combat power against enemy forces when they believed major offensive actions were critical to achieve key goals in Iraq.

"Toward the Objective: Building a New Iraq" is the title of the third part. Certain aspects of the reconstruction of the country were tangible, such as the building of schools, hospitals, and infrastructure. Others, such as the establishment of new forms of governance and the creation of indigenous security forces, were more abstract. All of these efforts became critical elements in the larger campaign to attract the support of the general population for Coalition goals in Iraq.

- **Chapter 9, The US Army and the Reconstruction of Iraq:** American Soldiers became heavily involved in a wide range of reconstruction projects in Iraq. This chapter looks at the broad Army campaign to rebuild the country and deals specifically with civil affairs operations and the role of tactical units in nation building.

- **Chapter 10, A Country United, Stable, and Free: US Army Governance Operations in Iraq:** This chapter looks at how American Soldiers became involved in assisting Iraqis in the establishment of new governing institutions at a variety of levels.

- **Chapter 11, Training the Iraqi Security Forces**: The US Army's effort to train Iraqi forces became a critical facet of the new campaign. This discussion will encompass the Coalition Provisional Authority's early program to create a new national army as well as the CJTF-7 efforts to build the Iraqi Civil Defense Corps. The chapter will also highlight the establishment of the Multi-National Security Transition Command–Iraq and its new program to enhance the fielding of Iraqi Security Forces.

Part IV is titled "Sustaining the Campaign." The US effort in Iraq was large and complex, requiring a great deal of support of various kinds. The two most critical areas of sustainment—materiel and human support—are the focus of this block.

- **Chapter 12, Logistics and Combat Service Support Operations**: Sustaining the larger campaign in an increasingly dangerous environment became a major challenge for American Soldiers. This chapter addresses how US Army units sought to sustain its operations using both traditional and innovative techniques and technology.

- **Chapter 13, Taking Care of Soldiers**: This broad chapter touches on the overall issue of sustaining the Soldier's well-being during war. To fully engage this topic, the discussion ranges from medical treatment and casualty reporting to issues concerning families and morale.

In the "Conclusion," the final part of this book, **Chapter 14, Implications,** and the **Epilogue** will provide an assessment of how American Soldiers handled the challenges during this period of OIF and how the campaign will affect the Army in the future.

A central theme emerging from this work is transition. Out of necessity, the US Army made an astonishing number of transitions between May 2003 and January 2005. In fact, one could easily state that the US Army essentially reinvented itself during this 18-month period. There is, of course, the most critical transition that took the Army from major combat operations to the postinvasion phase that featured full spectrum operations. However, that larger transition encompasses a multitude of smaller yet no less dramatic changes. A series of important political transitions took place in Iraq during this period. At the same time, in June 2003, the military's theater-strategic and operational-level headquarters reorganized and, a year later, reorganized again. Many of the units that began the campaign in May 2003 returned to their home stations in the spring of 2004, to be replaced by units that had no experience in Iraq. The security environment required transitions as well, demanding that units conduct a wide variety of missions for which they were untrained. That environment likewise required Soldiers to give up their positions as field artillerymen and tank crewmembers to become multipurpose warriors, adept at the wide variety of missions necessary in a campaign that took place across the spectrum of conflict.

Other more profound transitions also altered the lives of American Soldiers. The campaign took hundreds of thousands of Active Duty, Reserve, and National Guard troops away from their families and placed them in an incredibly difficult environment. A large number of these men and women returned to their loved ones after being wounded in the effort, and some made the supreme sacrifice by giving their lives. Those involved in writing this study also recognize that members of the Coalition forces, the Iraqi Security Forces, and, most of all, the Iraqi people, have all paid a high price in the campaign to create a free, stable, and prosperous Iraq. This has driven the authors to present an accurate and meaningful history of the overall campaign, both for its participants and for those who might face similar challenges in the future.

Notes

1.   COL Gregory Fontenot, US Army Retired, LTC E.J. Degen, US Army, and LTC David Tohn, US Army, *On Point: The United States Army in Operation Iraqi Freedom* (Fort Leavenworth, KS: Combat Studies Institute Press, 2004), iii.

2.   Fontenot, Degen, and Tohn, iv.

3.   Lieutenant General William S. Wallace, CAC Commander exit interview by CAC History Office, digital recording, Fort Leavenworth, KS, 8 September 2005.

4.   Headquarters, Department of the Army, FM 3-0, *Operations* (Washington, DC, 14 June 2001), 1-47.

Prologue

Major combat operations in Iraq have ended. In the battle of Iraq, the United States and our allies have prevailed. And now our Coalition is engaged in securing and reconstructing that country.

—President George W. Bush, 1 May 2003[1]

In early April 2003, Coalition forces led by the US Army overwhelmed the Iraqi Army, captured the ancient city of Baghdad, and toppled the Baathist regime that had controlled Iraq for over 30 years. Many perceived the US forces' swift and stunning victory over Iraqi dictator Saddam Hussein as the end of hostilities. President George W. Bush reinforced this feeling when, standing aboard the USS *Abraham Lincoln* under a large banner proclaiming "Mission Accomplished," he congratulated Soldiers, Sailors, Airmen, and Marines for their success in Operation IRAQI FREEDOM (OIF). Unfortunately, ousting the dictator failed to bring peace and stability to Iraq. In reality, the President's speech signified the end of the beginning. The campaign's larger objectives—securing and removal of weapons of mass destruction (WMD) and the creation of a stable, democratic state in Iraq—would require much more time and effort. What followed the major combat phase of OIF was the start of a new campaign—an effort described by Secretary of Defense Donald Rumsfeld as the "long, hard slog" to stabilize and reconstruct Iraq.[2]

The United States' conflict with Iraq had been growing and intensifying for over a decade. America first took direct military action against Iraq after Saddam Hussein invaded Kuwait in August 1990. With the condemnation of Saddam's aggression through United Nations (UN) Resolutions 660 and 662, and the demand for his withdrawal from Kuwait by 15 January 1991, the path for American intervention was established. President George H.W. Bush enforced the two resolutions by issuing National Security Directive (NSD) 54 on 15 January 1991 authorizing US Armed Forces to initiate military action against Iraq. As a result, American forces and a large Coalition of international troops already occupying defensive positions in Saudi Arabia began preparing for offensive action against Iraq. The air war component of the Gulf War campaign began on 17 January and continued to destroy Iraqi targets until ground forces initiated their attack on 24 February. Coalition forces liberated Kuwait City and, in the 100-hour ground war, destroyed much of Iraq's military in the area. Kuwait's liberation seemed to establish Operation DESERT STORM as an unequivocal success.[3] However, many questioned the American President's decision not to direct his forces north to remove Saddam Hussein from power.

The ease with which the Coalition destroyed most of Saddam's army revealed the military weakness of the Baathist regime. Nevertheless, Saddam did keep his grasp on the levers of power within Iraq, partly because of the perception that dethroning him would bring too many difficulties. In a rather prescient statement, given the events of the summer of 2003, then Secretary of Defense Richard Cheney summed up the rationale for not overthrowing the Baathist regime in 1991:

> If we'd gone to Baghdad and got rid of Saddam Hussein—assuming we could
> have found him—we'd have had to put a lot of forces in and run him to ground
> some place. He would not have been easy to capture. Then you've got to put

a new government in his place and then you're faced with the question of what kind of government are you going to establish in Iraq? Is it going to be a Kurdish government or a Shia government or a Sunni government? How many forces are you going to have to leave in there to keep it propped up, how many casualties are you going to take through the course of this operation?[4]

Many in the first Bush administration assumed that the Gulf War had so gravely weakened Saddam that an offensive against Baghdad would not be necessary. Saddam's regime already seemed on the brink of collapse when revolts broke out after the Coalition victory between the Shias and the Baathists in the south of Iraq and between the Kurds and the Baathists in the north. As a precondition to an armistice, Saddam agreed to the provisions of UN Resolution 686 (2 March 1991).[5] Then, UN Resolution 687 established additional terms on a defeated Iraq. The latter resolution re-imposed on Iraq a host of previous resolutions that Saddam had ignored with regard to Kuwait. It was this agreement that contained the seed of future conflict between the United States and Iraq. Resolution 687 laid out strict prohibitions on Iraq in terms

Figure 3. Map of Iraq.

of development of nuclear, biological, and chemical (NBC) weapons. Saddam's defiance of Resolution 687 was one of the reasons the later Bush administration used to justify its invasion of Iraq.[6] Saddam seemed impotent, and with the Kurds rebelling in the north and the Shias in the south, Saddam's reign of terror in Iraq appeared to be tottering on the edge, ready to topple into oblivion.

Assumptions about Saddam's demise proved to be premature. The Iraqi dictator maintained control of his army and used it to brutally suppress the uprisings. The United States watched the course of events unfold, but provided little direct military support to either the Shias or the Kurds. Instead, Coalition forces intervened with humanitarian assistance for the Kurds in the north and by creating no-fly zones over both Kurdish and Shia areas to prevent further repression by the Iraqi Army. Saddam clung to power even as Iraq was transformed into an international pariah state that defied a host of UN sanctions.[7]

The United States and the United Nations attempted to contain Saddam between 1991 and 2003. After internal uprisings failed to depose the leader, President George H.W. Bush worked through the UN to implement a policy of isolation, using trade sanctions and weapons inspections to keep Saddam from acquiring WMD. Bush's successor, President William (Bill) Clinton, essentially followed the same policy. The United Nations Special Commission (UNSCOM) assumed responsibility for ensuring Iraq did not obtain WMD during this period. Conflict continued in the form of Iraq's obstruction of inspection efforts through constant harassment, intimidation, and threats against the UNSCOM teams. Despite these significant obstacles, the teams did uncover and dismantle significant NBC weapons programs. Throughout this period of sanctions, however, Saddam maintained a tight hold on power.

Diplomacy was not the only instrument of power used by the United States against Iraq in this period. By creating the northern and southern no-fly zones in 1991, the US military, with help from its British partner, contained Iraq's Army and Air Force to regions inside their own country. Many believed this policy would place further pressure on the Baathist regime, yet Saddam actually used his military forces several times in the decade following Operation DESERT STORM to threaten Coalition forces. In 1994 the Iraqi Army began mobilizing units near the Kuwaiti border, causing the deployment of 54,000 US troops to Kuwait to repel a potential attack.[8] When Iraqi forces quickly backed down, the United States began developing its military infrastructure in Kuwait, preparing bases and pre-positioning combat equipment that could be used to deter future Iraqi aggression.

After the 1994 incident, Saddam limited his actions to periodic surface-to-air missile attacks on British and American aircraft patrolling the no-fly zones. Serious conflict erupted in December 1998 when American and British forces launched a 3-day campaign of cruise-missile attacks and air strikes on key Iraqi military installations.[9] This offensive, known as Operation DESERT FOX, was mounted in response to Saddam's disruption of UNSCOM's WMD inspection efforts. Operation DESERT FOX punished the Saddam regime, but fell short of forcing it from power. The Iraqis responded by forcing the UNSCOM inspectors to leave. Just days after the last Tomahawk missile struck its target, Iraqi antiaircraft batteries again commenced firing at US warplanes policing the no-fly zones.

US frustration over Saddam's diplomatic cat-and-mouse games with UN inspectors grew. Many in and out of the US Government began to believe a golden opportunity to topple the Iraqi dictator in the first Gulf War had slipped away. To provide the groundwork for a remedy to this problem, the US Government made the overthrow of Saddam part of its official foreign policy with the *Iraq Liberation Act of 1998* (H.R. 4655). The act directed the President to support the overthrow of Saddam through a variety of ways, including funding domestic and external opposition groups. It also pledged that the United States would promote democracy in Iraq and in the region and catalogued a litany of violations of various UN resolutions, especially Resolution 687. Thus, by the end of 1999, US frustration with Saddam had been simmering for almost a decade.[10]

At the start of the new century, few means of mitigating tensions between Iraq and the United States seemed to exist. To some Americans, the situation was indefensible and simply could not continue indefinitely. The catalyst that ultimately shifted the dynamics of the conflict originated not in Iraq but from a shadowy terrorist organization called al-Qaeda, which launched a deadly terrorist attack aimed at key targets inside the United States on 11 September 2001.[11] Shortly thereafter, President George W. Bush launched the Global War on Terrorism (GWOT) to eradicate al-Qaeda and other terrorist organizations sympathetic to their cause. Because al-Qaeda was not a nation, Bush faced the dilemma of determining where to strike. With no mailing address, al-Qaeda proved an elusive foe.[12]

The Bush administration decided to attack the terrorist group by targeting the nations actively sheltering al-Qaeda operatives. The most active supporter of al-Qaeda, the Taliban regime in Afghanistan, provided Osama bin Laden a safe haven, money, recruits, and training grounds. The President wanted to send a clear signal to states sponsoring terrorism that the United States would not tolerate any support for al-Qaeda or its infrastructure. This major shift in strategic policy led to Operation ENDURING FREEDOM (OEF) in Afghanistan, which began on 7 October 2001. Using a combination of air power and land forces, a United States-led Coalition evicted the Taliban from Afghanistan's major cities. Perhaps the most striking feature of the campaign was the highly successful partnership of American and Allied special operations forces (SOF) and anti-Taliban forces from the Afghan Northern Alliance—an innovation that led to the relatively easy capture of the capital city, Kabul. Within 2 months, Taliban and al-Qaeda forces were driven into the mountains on the Afghanistan–Pakistan border, and a new Afghan interim government took power in the liberated capital.

With the Taliban removed from power and al-Qaeda on the run in Afghanistan, President Bush turned his attention to Iraq. Saddam Hussein's behavior following the 1991 Gulf War had established the dictator's willingness to flout international law. Saddam continued to obstruct the weapons inspectors (who had become known as the UN Monitoring, Verification, and Inspection Commission and returned to Iraq), bragged that he would use WMD on Israel if he possessed them, and maintained contact with Islamic terrorist groups.[13] In light of the terrorist attacks of 11 September, the possibility of a nuclear-armed Saddam passing WMD or related technology to terrorists, or actually using WMD, could not be permitted by the United States. The Iraqi dictator's obstructionist tactics and maltreatment of Hans Blix's team of weapons inspectors provided further cause to view him as a serious threat.

The Bush administration deemed Saddam the next significant target in the GWOT. On 29 January 2002, President Bush delivered the "Axis of Evil" State of the Union address, in which he singled out three rogue nations as particularly dangerous: Iraq, Iran, and North Korea. He also enunciated his policy of preemption: "We'll be deliberate, yet time is not on our side. I will not wait on events, while dangers gather. I will not stand by, as peril draws closer and closer. The United States of America will not permit the world's most dangerous regimes to threaten us with the world's most destructive weapons."[14] This clear policy statement might have caused Saddam Hussein to reassess his behavior toward UN weapons inspectors. The President articulated America's intent to take dramatic steps unless the Iraqi dictator altered course.[15] Yet the relationship between the United States and Iraq remained tense.

Throughout 2002 the Bush administration continued to argue for unseating Saddam. This claim rested on two main assertions: first, Saddam flouted international law by willfully ignoring UN resolutions requiring him to disarm and relinquish his WMD; and second, Saddam maintained ties with al-Qaeda. Further, the *Iraqi Liberation Act of 1998* made it official US policy to depose Saddam. Vice President Richard Cheney stated on 26 August 2002 at the Veterans of Foreign Wars national convention: "There is no doubt that Saddam Hussein now has weapons of mass destruction."[16] On 12 September, the President addressed the UN General Assembly urging the UN to enforce Iraq's disarmament obligations.[17]

While the Bush administration continued to lobby for international sanctions against Saddam, it began building domestic support for regime change through military action. In October 2002, with strong encouragement from the administration, Congress passed the *Joint Resolution to Authorize the Use of United States Armed Forces Against Iraq*. This measure gave the Bush administration the authority to use force against Saddam Hussein to uphold UN mandates and prevent terrorism. Having garnered this critical approval at home, the administration moved forward in its preparation for the impending conflict.[18]

Figure 4. Vice President Richard Cheney (right) talks with Secretary of Defense Donald Rumsfeld.

Most of the planning for war against Iraq occurred within the Department of Defense (DOD) at US Central Command (CENTCOM). These planners concentrated on defeating Saddam's army in battle (focusing primarily on what was doctrinally known as Phase III of a military campaign—Decisive Operations). As these preparations matured, the Bush administration made one of its most significant prewar decisions by placing principal responsibility for Phase IV of the campaign, the Transition Phase that included stability operations, squarely on the shoulders of the DOD led by Secretary Donald Rumsfeld. Charged with this mandate, Rumsfeld created an organization called the Office of Reconstruction and Humanitarian Assistance (ORHA) and, in late January 2003, chose retired Lieutenant General Jay Garner as its head.[19]

ORHA, with less than 3 months to organize itself and develop plans, faced the enormously complex task of restoring basic services and governance to a post-Saddam Iraq. To meet the timeline, Garner relied on his contacts in the military. ORHA eventually entered Baghdad several weeks after the Army with a senior leadership comprised mainly of retired generals and other senior officers who were adept planners experienced in conducting stability operations. The State Department and other organizations within the Government provided Garner with additional staff members. Despite this combined expertise, ORHA's senior ranks lacked significant depth in diplomatic experience and had limited understanding of the Middle East.[20]

As ORHA gradually coalesced in early 2003, preparations for the pending conflict accelerated. In early February 2003, Secretary of State Colin Powell briefed the UN Security Council about the grave threat posed by an Iraq that had developed and stockpiled WMD. In that address, Powell forcefully argued that Saddam continued to defy UN resolutions, possessed WMD, and was in league with al-Qaeda.[21] This diplomatic initiative supported the large-scale movements of Soldiers and equipment into the theater of operations. By mid-March one brigade of the 82d Airborne Division (82d ABN) and most of the 101st Airborne Division (101st ABN) had arrived in Kuwait, joining the 3d Infantry Division (3d ID), which had been in theater since late 2002. These forces would make up the major combat power of the US Army V Corps commanded by Lieutenant General William S. Wallace.

By early March the 1st Marine Division (1st MARDIV) and most of the 1st United Kingdom (UK) Armoured Division had arrived in Kuwait. By this time the US 4th Infantry Division (4th ID) prepared to open a northern front in Iraq by coming ashore at Turkish ports in the Mediterranean and transiting through Turkey to the Iraqi frontier. On 1 March 2003 Turkey's Grand National Assembly rejected the United States' request that 4th ID use Turkey's land corridors en route to Iraq, and American planners rerouted the division to Kuwait. While this upset the US plan, Army commanders believed they possessed enough combat power in theater by mid-March to conduct a successful campaign against Iraq. On 17 March 2003 President Bush gave Saddam Hussein an ultimatum to leave Iraq within 48 hours or face invasion. Two days later, the United States launched a "decapitation" attack on Saddam at Dora Farms in southeast Baghdad. This strike failed, but the message was clear—America was ready and willing to forcibly remove Saddam from power. The next day Coalition forces breached the berm on the Kuwaiti–Iraqi border and entered Iraq.[22]

The campaign, now called Operation IRAQI FREEDOM (OIF), was unique in a number of ways. When developing the operation, American planners designed Phase III of the campaign to achieve one strategic objective and two supporting operational objectives. The strategic objective was to destroy the Baathist regime: Coalition forces would attack Iraqi military and political targets and topple Saddam's government.[23] With this priority in mind, Coalition planners regarded the capital, Baghdad, as the enemy's center of gravity. Thus, while combat with Iraqi units in the south would be necessary, more critical was the need to get to Baghdad and destroy important military and political pillars of the regime. Coalition forces assumed the additional task of hunting down regime officials, often referred to as high-value targets, to prevent their escape or their going underground to lead an armed resistance. In many ways the plan proved to be bold and unconventional in that Coalition forces avoided combat with some frontline Iraqi forces, choosing instead to focus on other elements of Saddam's government as their primary targets.[24] The two operational objectives supporting the larger strategic goal were (1) the discovery and elimination of any WMD to prevent their future use against Coalition forces or other countries, and (2) the preservation of the Iraqi oil infrastructure to avoid a repetition of the disaster in 1991 when Iraqi forces inflicted massive damage on Kuwaiti oil wells. This latter objective was particularly significant for Iraq's postwar recovery because many in the Bush administration viewed Iraq's plentiful oil reserves as the source of funding for the reconstruction of the country.[25] War planners hoped to achieve all three of these objectives with minimal loss of human life.

The conventional combat phase of OIF essentially unfolded according to plan. The Iraqi military and government were subjected to a "shock and awe" display of the Coalition's uncontested control of the skies. Coalition air forces attacked a wide array of political and military targets in support of the overall mission shortly before the land component struck on 20 March 2003. Once ground operations began, air forces shifted their mission to close air support of Coalition land forces.[26] The audacity of the plan to invade Iraq with a relatively small ground force that totaled five divisions created debate inside and outside of the US Government and the military—debate that continues to this day.

OIF ground operations began 24 hours ahead of schedule when reports came in that Iraqis were sabotaging the oil wells. In examining captured Iraqi documents and postwar interviews with senior Iraqi leaders, however, it appears that Saddam did not order the destruction. Apparently the dictator did not want to be known as the man who destroyed Iraq's wealth.[27] In the first few days of the campaign, Coalition forces surged into Iraq and accomplished three tactical goals: they breached the berms on the Iraqi–Kuwaiti border, seized Tallil Air Base, and isolated the city of As Samawah. The berm separating Iraq and Kuwait required a coordinated and complicated action that would allow attacking forces to fan out after making their way through. 3d ID captured the Tallil Air Base on the outskirts of An Nasiriyah after a 140-kilometer attack; the air base ultimately became the Combined Forces Land Component Command (CFLCC) forward operating base for further operations into the Iraqi interior. Other units followed as Coalition forces isolated An Nasiriyah and met Iraqi paramilitary forces for the first time in substantial numbers. This was the first clear sign Coalition forces would not be warmly welcomed by all Iraqis.[28]

To secure Iraq's oil fields, US Marines, supported by US Army artillery, moved quickly around the southern oil fields west of Basrah. This maneuver, as well as a robust psychological operations (PSYOP) program, prevented Iraqis from defying Saddam's orders and sabotaging their own facilities. Coalition SOF also conducted operations in the Persian Gulf to secure offshore oil rigs. The combination of Marine Corps forces supported by Army artillery, PSYOP, and SOF was remarkably successful.[29]

The Coalition's advance continued to Baghdad despite short delays caused by extremely bad weather. While rolling toward the Iraqi capital, the Coalition paid close attention to securing ever-lengthening lines of communications (LOCs) by isolating and eventually securing the city of An Najaf, which lay along the axis of advance. The logistical difficulties of keeping Coalition forces supplied over a 450-kilometer road network from Kuwait to Baghdad were monumental. In fact, the need to safeguard the LOCs forced V Corps to commit the 101st ABN and an 82d ABN brigade combat team with divisional enablers and a division command post to provide route security and to defeat enemy paramilitary forces in cities such as An Najaf, As Samawah, and Karbala. The surprising amount of resistance from Iraqi paramilitary forces in these cities led Lieutenant General Wallace to comment to the *New York Times*, "The enemy we're fighting is different from the one we war gamed against."[30]

As the mechanized units approached Baghdad from the south, other Coalition forces occupied critical areas in the west and north of the country. The American members of the

10th Special Forces Group and other Coalition Special Operations Soldiers joined to make up Combined Joint Special Operations Task Force–North (CJSOTF-North), which infiltrated into northern Iraq to link up with Kurdish military forces called the Peshmerga. Once CJSOTF-North established its presence, one part of the task force combined with Kurdish troops to mount a successful assault on Ansar al-Islam, a terrorist group that operated from a base in the mountainous area of northeast Iraq near the Iranian border.[31] The other main element of CJSOTF-North focused on helping the Peshmerga attack and pin down the Iraqi Army units in position around the cities of Mosul and Kirkuk, preventing them from moving south to meet the main Coalition land offensive. Working with both the US Army's 173d Airborne Brigade that had parachuted into the area and Coalition air power, the Kurds and their special operations advisors began attacking these enemy forces. By the first week of April, Iraqi resistance crumbled under the combined assault of these forces, opening a path to these two crucial northern cities.[32]

In western Iraq, a second special operations force began deep reconnaissance missions and operations to thwart the Saddam regime from retaliating against the Coalition by launching Scud

Figure 5. Maneuver of V Corps, 1st MEF, CJSOTF-West, and CJSOTF-North.

ballistic missiles at the state of Israel. This force, known as Combined Joint Special Operations Task Force–West (CJSOTF-West), included American forces from the 5th Special Forces Group and Coalition special operations units. As they spread across the desert wastes, the special forces teams provided critical intelligence on Iraqi forces in the western area of the country, secured the critical military sites in this region that could have been used in strategic attacks against Coalition interests, and destroyed the small enemy elements that chose to fight.

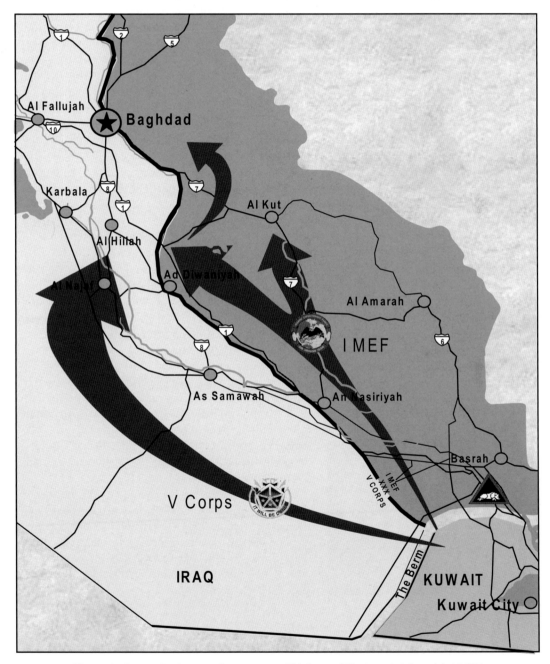

Figure 6. General scheme of maneuver of V Corps (Western Axis) and 1st MEF (Eastern Axis) toward Baghdad.

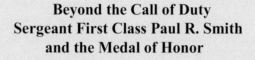

Beyond the Call of Duty
Sergeant First Class Paul R. Smith
and the Medal of Honor

On 4 April 2003, the 3d Infantry Division attacked to seize the Baghdad International Airport located on the western edge of the Iraqi capital. As part of that operation, Task Force 2-7 occupied a blocking position to prevent an enemy counterattack. While preparing to meet a possible Iraqi attack, the Soldiers of B Company, 11th Engineer Battalion, attached to TF 2-7, received orders to build a temporary prisoner of war compound in the area. Sergeant First Class Paul R. Smith, platoon sergeant for 2d Platoon, B Company, began to direct the construction of that site.

Paul Smith, a native of Tampa, Florida, joined the US Army in 1988 and became a combat engineer. During the 1990s, he served as an engineer in Kuwait, Bosnia-Herzegovina, and Kosovo. By the time he deployed to Iraq with the 3d Infantry Division in 2003, Smith was an experienced platoon sergeant as well as a husband and a father of two children.

Once Smith's platoon received the mission to build the compound near the airport, he began organizing his Soldiers, collecting materials, and preparing the site. Quickly, however, the Soldiers in his platoon sighted approximately 60 Iraqi soldiers armed with small arms and mortars approaching their position. Smith immediately began organizing a unit defense by establishing squad sectors and positioning three M113A3 Armored Personnel Carriers (APC) and a Bradley Fighting Vehicle on his platoon's perimeter to take advantage of their firepower.

As the enemy attack began in earnest, Smith directed the fire of his unit's weapons. He led by example by moving among his men and personally using both hand grenades and an AT-4 against advancing Iraqi soldiers. As the enemy ranks drew nearer, three members of the platoon fell wounded when an APC took a direct hit from a mortar round.

After supervising the evacuation of the wounded, Smith climbed behind the .50 Cal machinegun on the top deck of an APC, a position that was vulnerable to enemy fire. The official citation written in support of his award describes what happened next: "in total disregard for his own life, he maintained his exposed position in order to engage the attacking enemy force. During this action, he was mortally wounded. His courageous actions helped defeat the enemy attack, and resulted in as many as 50 enemy soldiers killed, while allowing the safe withdrawal of numerous wounded soldiers." Smith's courage turned back an assault that endangered not just his platoon but other task force units, including the battalion aid station where the wounded were located.

On 4 April 2005 at the White House, President George W. Bush posthumously awarded the Medal of Honor to Sergeant First Class Paul R. Smith for his actions on that day in Baghdad. In that ceremony Paul Smith became the first Soldier to receive the Medal of Honor for actions in Operation IRAQI FREEDOM.

Sergeant First Class Paul Ray Smith, posthumous Medal of Honor recipient with B Company, 11th Engineer Battalion, 3d Infantry Division.

http://www.army.mil/medalofhonor/smith/
(accessed 12 March 2008)

In the south along the axes of the main attack, Coalition forces moved so quickly that within 1 week of the start of operations, Iraqi resistance became confused and disorganized. This final phase of the operation in the south included the forcing of the Karbala Gap—a natural chokepoint where American intelligence officers expected Iraqi resistance to be fierce—and the crossing of the Euphrates River. On 1 April elements of 3d ID successfully pushed through the Karbala Gap. While some Iraqi units chose to fight near the town of Karbala, the American mechanized units quickly defeated them and secured crossings over the Euphrates. With the road to Baghdad open, the 3d ID continued its lightning push to the capital. On 4 April, after a tough but lopsided fight that dealt significant damage to Iraqi Republican Guard units, the division captured Saddam International Airport. This event signaled the final days of Saddam's hold on power.[33]

Understanding that the campaign's ultimate prize was in sight, Wallace, the V Corps commander, and Major General Buford C. Blount III, the 3d ID commander, aggressively pierced the Baghdad defenses with "Thunder Runs"—raids launched by the tanks and Bradley Fighting Vehicles of the 2d Brigade Combat Team of the 3d ID into the heart of the city. These forays began on 4 April and proved remarkably effective against a dazed and surprised enemy. The Iraqis resisted, but Republican Guard, paramilitary forces, irregulars, and armed civilians were no match for the tanks and Bradleys that streaked down Baghdad's streets. By 9 April organized resistance ceased and the Americans appeared to be in control of the Iraqi capital. Also on that day, US Marines helped Iraqis overturn Saddam's statue in Firdos Square, an event meant to symbolize the apparent implosion of the Baathist regime and the end of Saddam Hussein's dictatorship.[34] The Coalition's plan to oust Saddam had been an overwhelming success. Its rapidity and audacity moved military historian John Keegan to describe the offensive as "a lightning campaign" that was "unprecedented" in its speed and decisiveness.[35]

This stunning victory led President Bush, with the encouragement of his top military leaders, to announce the end to major combat operations on the deck of the USS *Abraham Lincoln*. While viewed by some as tantamount to a declaration of victory, in reality, this announcement merely marked the point where the campaign transitioned from combat to the next phase of operations focused on the reconstruction of Iraq. The US Government and Coalition military forces alike found themselves unprepared for what came next. At this point, policy formulated in Washington, DC, and in London began to shape operations far more than plans made by CENTCOM or even the actual conditions on the ground in Iraq. The Coalition's strategy for removing Saddam had been painstakingly conceived, rehearsed, and successfully prosecuted. Military victory over the Saddam regime had only been the first step toward success in Iraq however. Indeed, the next step—winning the peace by stabilizing and rebuilding Iraq—would become another campaign altogether. Few, if any, in the White House, Department of Defense, or the US Army foresaw the impending struggle to create a new Iraq in place of the Saddam regime as the greatest challenge of OIF.

Notes

1. "President Bush Announces Major Combat Operations Have Ended: Remarks by the President from the USS *Abraham Lincoln* At Sea Off the Coast of San Diego, California," *Whitehouse.gov*, 1 May 2003, http://www.whitehouse.gov/news/releases/2003/05/20030501-15.html (accessed 1 February 2006).

2. Donald Rumsfeld, War on Terror memorandum, 16 October 2003, http://www.usatoday.com/news/washington/executive/rumsfeld-memo.htm (accessed 9 March 2006). This memorandum was originally leaked to *USA Today*. Mr. Rumsfeld acknowledged the veracity of the memorandum in an interview on 2 November 2003, http://www.defenselink.mil/transcripts/2003/tr20031102-secdef0836.html (accessed 14 April 2006).

3. Lawrence Freedman and Efraim Karsh, *The Gulf Conflict 1990–1991: Diplomacy and War in the New World Order* (Princeton, NJ: Princeton University Press, 1993), 85–109; *Operation Desert Storm: Ten Years After,* National Security Archive, http://www.gwu.edu/~nsarchiv/NSAEBB/NSAEBB39/ (accessed 22 February 2006).

4. Freedman and Karsh, 413. The original quote came from BBC Radio 4, "The Desert War—A Kind of Victory," 16 February 1992.

5. Freedman and Karsh, 407; UN Web site, "Resolution 686," http://www.un.org/Docs/scres/1991/scres91.htm (accessed 12 September 2006).

6. UN Web site, "Resolution 687," http://daccess-ods.un.org/TMP/7258258.html (accessed 12 September 2006).

7. Freedman and Karsh, 425–427; UN Web site, "Resolution 686."

8. "Chronology: From DESERT STORM to DESERT FOX," *DefenseLink,* http://www.defenselink.mil/specials/desert_fox/timeline.html (accessed 20 April 2006).

9. "Chronology: From DESERT STORM to DESERT FOX."

10. "Iraq Liberation Act of 1998," Public Law 105-338—Oct. 31, 1998, *www.FINDLAW.com,* http://www.news.findlaw.com/hdocs/docs/iraq/libact103198.pdf (accessed 12 September 2006).

11. Williamson Murray and Robert H. Scales Jr., *The Iraq War: A Military History* (Cambridge, MA: The Belknap Press of Harvard University Press, 2003), 33.

12. Murray and Scales, 38–41.

13. On the connection between the Saddam regime and Islamic terrorist organizations, see Kevin M. Woods, Project Leader, with James Lacey, *Iraqi Perspectives Project, Saddam and Terrorism: Emerging Insights from Captured Iraqi Documents,* 5 vols. (Alexandria, VA: Institute for Defense Analyses, 2008).

14. "President Delivers the State of the Union Address," *Whitehouse.gov,* 29 January 2002, http://www.whitehouse.gov/news/releases/2002/01/20020129-11.html (accessed 23 February 2006).

15. "State of the Union Address," 29 January 2002.

16. David L. Phillips, *Losing Iraq: Inside the Postwar Reconstruction Fiasco* (Boulder, CO: Westview Press, 2005), 242; "Vice President Speaks at VFW 103d National Convention," *Whitehouse.gov*, 26 August 2002, http://www.whitehouse.gov/news/releases/2002/08/20020826.html (accessed 12 September 2006).

17. Phillips, 242.

18. "The Iraqi Liberation Act: Statement by the President," 31 October 1998, http://www.library.cornell.edu/colldev/mideast/libera.htm (accessed 27 February 2006); "H.R. 4655 Iraq Liberation Act of 1998," http://www.iraqwatch.org/government/US/Legislation/ILA.htm (accessed 27 February 2006); House of Representatives, Report 107, "Authorization for Use of Military Force Against Iraq Resolution of 2002," 7 October 2002, http://www.iraqwatch.org/government/US/Legislation/hirc-hjres114report-100702.pdf (accessed 27 February 2006).

19. Phillips, 242.

20. Phillips, 242; Larry Diamond, *Squandered Victory: The American Occupation and the Bungled Effort to Bring Democracy to Iraq* (New York, NY: Henry Holt and Company, 2005), 30–31.

21. "US Secretary of State Colin Powell Addresses the UN Security Council," *Whitehouse.gov,* http://www.whitehouse.gov/news/releases/2003/02/20030205-1.html (accessed 27 February 2006).

22. The "Coalition of the Willing" involved 30 nations: Afghanistan, Albania, Australia, Azerbaijan, Bulgaria, Colombia, the Czech Republic, Denmark, El Salvador, Eritrea, Estonia, Ethiopia, Georgia, Hungary, Italy, Japan, South Korea, Latvia, Lithuania, Macedonia, the Netherlands, Nicaragua, the Philippines, Poland, Romania, Slovakia, Spain, Turkey, United Kingdom, and Uzbekistan. Not all of these nations sent troops, but they did aid the war effort and later the reconstruction effort in some way. Steve Schifferes, "US names 'Coalition of the Willing,'" *BBC News*, 18 March 2003, http://news.bbc.co.uk/2/hi/americas/2862343.stm (accessed 13 September 2006).

23. General Tommy Franks, *American Soldier* (New York, NY: Harper Collins, 2004), 389.

24. Joint Chiefs of Staff, JP 3-0, *Joint Operations* (Washington, DC, September 2006), III-19 to III-21.

25. Murray and Scales, 90–91.

26. COL Gregory Fontenot, US Army Retired, LTC E.J. Degen, US Army, and LTC David Tohn, US Army, *On Point: The United States Army in Operation Iraqi Freedom* (Fort Leavenworth, KS: Combat Studies Institute Press, 2004), 86–87.

27. Kevin M. Woods et al., *Iraqi Perspectives Project: A View of Operation Iraqi Freedom from Saddam's Senior Leadership.* Joint Center for Operational Analysis (Norfolk, VA: US Joint Forces Command, 2005), http://www.cfr.org/publication/10230/iraqi_perspectives_project.html (accessed 12 September 2006), 98–99.

28. Woods et al., 86–89.

29. Woods et al., 95–97.

30. Woods et al., 141–150, 184–221.

31. Charles H. Briscoe, Kenneth Finlayson, and Robert W. Jones Jr., *All Roads Lead to Baghdad: Army Special Operations Forces in Iraq* (Fort Bragg, NC: US Army Special Operations Command History Office, 2006), 194–198.

32. Murray and Scales, 188–195.

33. Murray and Scales, 195–209.

34. Murray and Scales, 210–218.

35. John Keegan, *The Iraq War* (New York, NY: Alfred A. Knopf, 2004), 1.

Part I

Setting the Stage

Chapter 1

Overview of Operation IRAQI FREEDOM: May 2003 to January 2005

In April 2003 the US Army in Iraq transitioned to the new campaign without much fanfare or recognition. For at least some Soldiers, the combat operations that characterized the march from Kuwait to Baghdad remained the norm. In the latter part of April, isolated pockets of organized resistance still existed in Baghdad and other parts of Iraq. By early May most of the conventional combat had ended, a fact President George W. Bush recognized when he declared an end to major combat operations on 1 May 2003. American Soldiers and their commanders immediately began to assess the situation in which they suddenly found themselves. Over the course of the next 18 months, the US Army gradually gained clarity on this situation and developed cogent responses to political decisions made by Iraqi and Coalition policy makers, and to an emerging insurgent network that threatened the American enterprise in Iraq.

This brief overview of that 18-month period seeks to highlight the major political, military, and socio-economic decisions and events that shaped the Army's transition to the new campaign. All of the key leaders, occurrences, and actions emphasized here will be addressed in detail in the topical chapters that follow. Nevertheless, it is critical early in this study to offer a chronological framework for the campaign between May 2003 and January 2005, even if that framework strains at times to place order on what was often chaos.

A Decisive Month—May 2003

In retrospect, some may be surprised to discover that the decisions made and actions taken in May 2003 proved pivotal to the 18 months that followed. However, during this month the Coalition made critical choices about the nature of political power in Iraq—how this power related to the various groups within the Iraqi population and how this authority would treat the institutions of the former regime. May 2003 was equally important for US military forces. That month Coalition leaders at the Department of Defense (DOD), US Central Command (CENTCOM), and Combined Forces Land Component Command (CFLCC) determined the size, disposition, and command and control of the force in Iraq.

Relative to the invasion that preceded it and the insurgency that followed it, May 2003 was rather quiet as Iraqis attempted to comprehend the sudden toppling of the Saddam regime and the arrival of Western armies in their homeland. Looking back, some Americans and Iraqis described the period between May and August as a window of opportunity that could have been exploited to produce the conditions for the quick creation of a new Iraq. Instead, several events and key decisions quickly shut that window. Perhaps the most important factor in that process was the escalation of looting, crime, and general disorder that began in late April.

The institutions held together by Saddam's reign had collapsed along with his regime, furthering Iraq's descent into chaos. Long suppressed political, religious, and ethnic conflicts bubbled violently to the surface. The incredibly decrepit state of the Iraqi infrastructure became apparent once the veil of Saddam's tyrannical rule was lifted, and was made worse by unprecedented looting and destruction. Some Iraqis began to sense an absence of authority in their country, and, many, while happy to see Saddam Hussein removed from power, watched events unfold with increasing anxiety; other Iraqis saw an opportunity to pursue their violent goals. American units beginning to fan out across the country initially had no orders to halt the looting or serve as a general police force. These units had not trained for those types of missions, though some Coalition forces did take general actions to prevent the situation from descending into complete anarchy. At the same time, violent Islamist groups began targeting US and Coalition forces in Iraq as part of their larger terrorist campaign against Western interests.

For the Coalition, May 2003 was also a period of transition characterized by disorganization and an attempt to begin the reconstruction effort. Most important was the Bush administration's decision to create the Coalition Provisional Authority (CPA), which became the sovereign political power in Iraq. The CPA, headed by Presidential Envoy L. Paul Bremer III, a career diplomat who arrived in Iraq in early May, replaced the Office of Reconstruction and Humanitarian Assistance (ORHA) headed by Lieutenant General (Retired) Jay Garner. ORHA had arrived in Iraq in late April with a mandate to deal with the expected humanitarian crises, to restore Iraq's essential services, to oversee the reform of the Iraqi military, and generally to set the country on a very rapid path toward democratic self-government. But Garner had only been in Iraq for approximately 3 weeks when Bremer arrived to replace him and his organization. The CPA eventually grew into a large bureaucratic organization charged with the strategic mission of guiding Iraq to a new future; yet, in early May, the men and women of the CPA were just getting settled and beginning to make connections with the Coalition's military commanders and potential leaders of the new Iraq.

Ambassador Bremer arrived with the Bush administration's charge to dramatically reshape Iraq, a mandate which led to two major decisions that May. On 16 May Bremer issued CPA Order No. 1 (appendix A), "De-Baathification of Iraqi Society," which removed from public life those Iraqis who had held the top four ranks in the Baath Party and subjected to review members with lesser ranks who held significant positions in the civil bureaucracy.[1] CPA Order No. 2 (appendix B), "Dissolution of Entities," quickly followed on 23 May and disbanded all of Saddam's military and intelligence institutions, rendering hundreds of thousands of Iraqi soldiers jobless.[2] These orders, designed to signal the end of Saddam's tyranny and the beginning of a new era, removed thousands of Sunni Arab Iraqis

White House Photo

Figure 7. President George W. Bush and Ambassador L. Paul Bremer.

from political power, creating the perception that Sunni Arabs would have limited power in a new Iraq, fostering a huge unemployment problem, and leaving Iraqi institutions without bureaucratic or technical leadership. Many Coalition military figures believed at the time that these important CPA decisions created a pool of disaffected and unemployed Sunni Arabs from which a growing insurgency could later recruit.

That month also saw the CPA begin preparing for the establishment of an interim Iraqi governing body. Many Iraqi politicians, especially expatriates who were influential in the decision to intervene in Iraq, had expected the Coalition to form a provisional Iraqi governing entity soon after the military victory over Saddam. However, in the middle of the month, Bremer reversed Garner's plans for an early turnover of political power and announced the indefinite postponement of the formation of an Interim Iraqi Government. Instead of a temporary Iraqi sovereign body, the CPA would continue to serve as the chief political authority and the Coalition armed forces as the military arm of that authority. This decision, in the eyes of many Iraqis, transformed the intent of United Nations (UN) Resolution 1483, which recognized the United States and Great Britain as "occupying powers" and urged the two powers to promote the welfare of Iraqis and to administer the country until Iraqis were capable of self-governance.[3] The resolution appeared to formalize the sense that the Coalition powers were acting like occupiers rather than liberators, and this perception fueled the disaffection of some in Iraq.

Military Transitions in Spring 2003

During the 6 weeks following the toppling of the Saddam regime, as the CPA arrived and ORHA departed, Coalition military forces quickly established their presence in the capital city and throughout Iraq, preparing for what came next. Still, the role of the United States' and the United Kingdom's military forces in the next stage of the campaign remained unclear. During the initial planning that led to Operation IRAQI FREEDOM (OIF), General Tommy Franks, the CENTCOM commander, tasked Third Army/CFLCC to lead the postinvasion phase of the campaign known as Phase IV, Transition, in joint doctrine terminology, which CENTCOM believed would be relatively short. Once CENTCOM concluded its postconflict operations, CFLCC would pass responsibility for the longer, more complex reconstruction and stabilization effort to a combined joint task force (CJTF). The DOD gave this joint task force a variety of names, designating it first as Combined Joint Task Force–Iraq and later as Combined Joint Task Force–7 (CJTF-7). However, planners at the DOD and CENTCOM had focused on Phase III, Decisive Operations, of the campaign and, consequently, had invested only a limited amount of time and resources in the organization and manning of this joint task force.

In April the Third Army had been serving as the CFLCC, the headquarters responsible for Coalition land forces in Iraq under CENTCOM. General Franks told his subordinate leaders during a 16 April visit to Baghdad to be prepared to conduct an abbreviated period of stability operations and then to redeploy the majority of their forces out of Iraq by September 2003. In line with the prewar planning and general euphoria at the rapid crumbling of the Saddam regime, Franks continued to plan for a very limited role for US ground forces in Iraq.[4]

Following Franks' intent, CFLCC planners started preparations to redeploy, and soon the 3d Infantry Division (3d ID) and the 1st Marine Expeditionary Force (1st MEF) received orders to begin their own preparations for leaving Iraq. In fact, the desire to reduce US forces in Iraq was so strong that after listening to Secretary of Defense Donald Rumsfeld voice concerns about deploying the 1st Cavalry Division (1st CAV), already loading its equipment in the United States for movement to Iraq, Franks recommended to the Secretary in late April that the division stay stateside.[5] This decision stemmed from the belief, at the national level, that 1st CAV's Soldiers would not be needed to stabilize Iraq.[6]

Figure 8. General Tommy Franks.

Franks also wanted the Third Army/CFLCC out of Iraq as soon as possible and returned to its normal role in support of land operations throughout the CENTCOM area of operations (AO), which included Afghanistan. By the second week of May, V Corps commander Lieutenant General William Wallace received confirmation that his headquarters would serve as the core of CJTF-7, the Phase IV military headquarters tasked to replace Third Army/CFLCC in Iraq.[7] In late April Wallace learned that he would be replaced as commander of V Corps by Major General Ricardo Sanchez, then commanding the 1st Armored Division (1st AD), heading to Iraq from Germany. No new CJTF headquarters would be coming to Iraq after all. V Corps, which would not be officially designated as CJTF-7 until 15 June, was to operate under the political guidance of ORHA and Jay Garner. ORHA also expected to have a short lifespan, turning over political power to a new Iraqi Government by the end of the summer.

In late April CFLCC remained in charge of Coalition ground forces, but was beginning to transfer responsibility to V Corps and preparing to redeploy to the United States. It provided only limited guidance to the tactical units that fanned out across Iraq. Even without a detailed mission and guidelines on how to conduct the next phase, by the beginning of May US Army divisions took positions across the country and began executing a variety of operations. The 101st Airborne Division (101st ABN) established itself in the northwest of the country around the city of Mosul. To its southeast, the 173d Airborne assumed responsibility for the city and environs of Kirkuk. In the area between Kirkuk and Baghdad, a region known as the Sunni Triangle, the 4th Infantry Division (4th ID) set up a sprawling presence. In Al Anbar province, to the west of the Sunni heartland, the 3d ID and the 3d Armored Cavalry Regiment (3d ACR) began operating in cities such as Fallujah and Ramadi. The 1st AD, soon to be augmented by the 2d Armored Cavalry Regiment (2d ACR) and the 2d Brigade Combat Team (2d BCT) of the 82d Airborne Division (82d ABN), moved into Baghdad to begin its operations in the Iraqi capital. (See Appendix C, Map of Unit Areas of Responsibility, 2003–2004.) Across these areas of responsibility (AOR), the special operations Soldiers of the newly established Combined Joint Special Operations Task Force–Arabian Peninsula (CJSOTF-AP), created when CJSOTF-North and CJSOTF-West were combined, began conducting reconnaissance, psychological operations, and the hunt for high-value targets.

Of course the US Army was not alone in this early stage of postinvasion operations. To the south of Baghdad, the 1st MEF took up positions in the region around Karbala and An Najaf. In the southeastern corner of Iraq, centered in the city of Basrah, the British 1st Armoured Division established its AOR. At the end of May 2003, approximately 160,000 Coalition troops had spread out across Iraq to begin postconflict efforts.[8] Eventually, as more Coalition troops entered Iraq in the summer of 2003, CJTF-7, the Coalition military headquarters established in June 2003, redesignated all areas of operation as multinational division AORs. By the fall of 2003, CJTF-7 had divided Iraq into six AORs: Multi-National Division–North (MND-N),

Figure 9. CFLCC initial battlespace for PH IV operations.

Multi-National Division–North Central (MND-NC), Multi-National Division–Baghdad (MND-B), Multi-National Division–West (MND-W), Multi-National Division–Central South (MND-CS), and Multi-National Division–Southeast (MND-SE). (See Appendix D, Map of Theater Structure, 2003–2005.)

An Uncertain Summer: June–September 2003

In June 2003 the United States made a dramatic change in the Coalition's command structure. This transition began informally in late May when General Franks told both Lieutenant General Wallace, the outgoing V Corps commander, and the newly promoted Lieutenant General Sanchez, the inbound commander of V Corps, that CFLCC was pulling out of Iraq to refocus on its theater-wide responsibilities. Franks ordered V Corps to become the nucleus of the senior military command in Iraq designated as CJTF-7. This move was sudden and caught most of the senior commanders in Iraq unaware. Sanchez and V Corps (an Army headquarters focused on ground operations at the tactical level) would now have to become a joint and combined headquarters, responsible for the theater-strategic, operational, *and* tactical levels of war.

Sanchez assumed command of V Corps on 14 June 2003. On 15 June this informal transition became formal with the activation of CJTF-7. The process was complicated because the V Corps staff was not configured for the types of responsibilities it received. In retrospect, Lieutenant General Wallace stated:

> You can't take a tactical headquarters [V Corps] and change it into an operational [level] headquarters [CJTF-7] at the snap of your fingers. It just doesn't happen. Your focus changes completely, and you are either going to take your eye off the tactical fight in order to deal with the operational issues, or you are going to ignore the operational issues and stay involved in the tactical fight.[9]

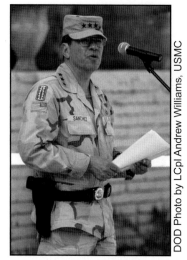

Figure 10. Lieutenant General Ricardo S. Sanchez, Commander, CJTF-7.

DOD Photo by LCpl Andrew Williams, USMC

To lead at all these levels, Sanchez designed a new staff that incorporated officers from the Navy, Marine Corps, and Air Force, as well as from the various Coalition forces. He also needed to add more Army officers to his staff if he hoped to guide postinvasion operations at all levels. Many of the military units in Iraq prepared to redeploy to their home stations, which complicated the task of bringing new officers into CJTF-7. CENTCOM and CFLCC quickly took their staffs back to Kuwait, Qatar, and MacDill Air Force Base in Florida. Within the V Corps staff, many officers received orders transferring them to new units and scheduled Army training courses. Sanchez found this transition to be particularly problematic for the staffing and support of his new organization. He stated, "CENTCOM had pretty much shut down its operations [in Iraq]. Most of the key people were back in CENTCOM [headquarters] in Tampa, Florida. For CFLCC, the barn door had been opened and everybody was in a mad dash to get back home. So we . . . knew, even by that point, that we had an issue."[10] Although CJTF-7 gradually added officers from the four American military services as well as from Coalition nations, the process moved slowly and posed significant challenges to command and control in the summer of 2003.

While Sanchez struggled to create a viable combined and joint staff immediately after taking command of CJTF-7, he issued broad guidance to his tactical commanders who were dealing with practical challenges across Iraq. Each commander was then free to develop and implement specific plans, particular to their AOR, within this general framework. By July 2003 Sanchez articulated that guidance in the form of the following mission statement:

> Conduct offensive operations to defeat remaining noncompliant forces and neutralize destabilizing influences in the AO in order to create a secure environment in direct support of the Coalition Provisional Authority. Concurrently conduct stability operations to support the establishment of government and economic development in order to set the conditions for a transfer of operations to designated follow-on military or civilian authorities.[11]

This statement essentially called for full spectrum operations, a doctrinal term that directed military forces to conduct a combination of combat and stability operations simultaneously in

Figure 11. CJTF-7 patch.

support of the CPA and new Iraqi political institutions. In July the plans officers in the CJTF-7 CJ5 section met with the planners from the divisions; collectively, the group developed a draft campaign plan for CJTF-7. This plan further emphasized the need for a full spectrum approach in Iraq by directing subordinate units to channel their operations in five directions. These five lines of operations were security—to include combat operations and training Iraqi security forces, governance, economy, essential services, and information operations. CJTF-7 designed these lines of operations to directly support the CPA's overall effort to create a stable and secure Iraq.[12]

The mission statement offered flexibility to the tactical commanders facing a diverse set of conditions and threats in their unique AORs. For some units, the threat appeared to be relatively insignificant. In northeast Iraq, for example, the 101st ABN, led by Major General David Petraeus, was quickly able to achieve relative security in its AOR, allowing it to focus its energy and resources on reestablishing Mosul University, rebuilding broken infrastructure, and fostering local self-government. However, just to the south in the Sunni Triangle, the 4th ID, under Major General Raymond Odierno, came up against a more structured threat comprised mainly of ex-Baathist organizations. Consequently, the division launched a series of large-scale offensive operations in June and July that sought to disrupt and destroy what remained of the Saddam regime.

Figure 12. Major General David H. Petraeus, Commanding General, 101st Airborne Division (Air Assault).

As the summer progressed, the political situation at the national level appeared to be stabilizing. In July the CPA presented Iraqis with its strategic vision of establishing "a durable peace for a unified, stable, and democratic Iraq."[13] Instead of a quick turnover of power to an unsteady Iraqi Government, the CPA announced a multiyear process of constitutional development and sequential elections leading to a new Iraq. The Coalition's role in Iraq was now, both de jure and de facto, that of an occupying power.

Additionally, the CPA began laying the foundation for Iraq's new security forces that included a new professional army and a skilled police force. To lead this critical effort, the CPA established the Coalition Military Assistance Training Team (CMATT) and the Coalition Police Assistance Training Team (CPATT). Both CMATT and CPATT existed only on paper in May 2003, and in July both were struggling to stand up and begin working with Iraqis. On

13 July 2003 the CPA took its first step toward including Iraqis in the political transition by appointing the Iraqi Governing Council (IGC), a semi-autonomous entity designed to help the CPA transfer full political sovereignty to Iraq.

Figure 13. Major General Ray Odierno (left) and Lieutenant Colonel Steve Russell on patrol in Tikrit.

Measured governmental progress in the summer of 2003 appeared to be matched by modest advances in creating a secure environment across Iraq. While military units reported continued resistance from enemies characterized as "former regime elements" or "non-compliant forces," most attacks were limited to small roadside bombs or sporadic mortar fire. American commanders remained optimistic and generally judged the threat as anemic and uncoordinated. The 101st ABN's operation with Special Forces Task Force 20 in Mosul that killed Saddam's sons Uday and Qusay in late July also seemed indicative of broader success.

But July also brought uncertainty. The Iraqi Survey Group (ISG) continued the extensive search for Saddam's weapons of mass destruction (WMD). By the middle of the summer, however, the group had not uncovered the expected stockpiles of chemical and biological weapons.[14] More unsettling was the concern growing within CJTF-7 and the US military about the sporadic attacks on Coalition forces. On 16 July General John Abizaid, who had recently taken command of CENTCOM from General Franks, stated in a press conference that he believed Coalition forces faced "a classical guerrilla-type campaign," mounted by ex-Baathist organizations such as the Iraqi Intelligence Service and the various paramilitary formations that had been under Saddam's control.[15]

Until that date, none of the Coalition's senior commanders had offered this kind of overt recognition that an insurgency appeared to be forming in Iraq. However, Abizaid's statement reflected the growing reality that faced many American Soldiers in some areas of the country. In June 2003 approximately 250 attacks occurred against Coalition forces. In July that number doubled to roughly 500.[16] Two devastating attacks the next month clearly signaled a major change in the security environment. Terrorists using a vehicle bomb attacked the Jordanian Embassy on 7 August 2003 killing 11 people. On 19 August 2003 a massive truck bomb was driven into the UN compound in the eastern part of Baghdad and detonated. The suicide bomber took the lives of 22 people, including Chief UN Envoy Sergio Vieira de Mello. For all intents and

Figure 14. General John Abizaid, Commander, CENTCOM.

32

Figure 15. Secretary Colin Powell with members of the Iraqi Governing Council after their meeting. Pictured from left to right: Abdul Aziz Al Hakim; Dr. Adnan Pachachi, President, Iraqi Governing Council; Ambassador Paul Bremer, Presidential Envoy to Iraq; Secretary Powell; and Dr. Ahmed Chalabi.

purposes, the bombing forced the UN to leave Iraq. These attacks signaled the rise of a coordinated terrorist threat in Iraq, one capable of strategic strikes targeting the larger political effort that could fracture the Coalition. Ambassador Bremer told his staff after the bombing, "We're in trouble here. The terrorists have arrived in a deadly serious way and we've got to be just as serious."[17]

Despite these setbacks, as the fall of 2003 began the Coalition appeared to be making limited progress across its political, military, and economic lines of operations. The CPA and the Coalition had begun rebuilding Iraq's decrepit infrastructure, establishing limited local governments, and training the first Iraqi Security Forces (ISF). CJTF-7 had also made progress in its military operations, directing its units to shift from large-scale offensive operations that were common in some AORs to a broader effort that mixed smaller, more focused attacks on the insurgent threat with operations designed to win support from the populace.[18] These operations led to the capture of Ali Hassan al-Majid, also known as Chemical Ali, and other important members of Saddam's regime who were believed to be part of the emerging insurgent network. Critical to the task of building popular support was the introduction of the Commander's Emergency Response Program (CERP). This program allowed CJTF-7 to begin funneling millions of Iraqi dinars and US dollars to units to fund local reconstruction projects. By the fall Army brigades and battalions were heavily involved in using these funds to improve the lives of the Iraqis in their AORs.

Despite these successes, the violence continued to mount. Insurgent attacks against Coalition forces increased again in September 2003. In addiition, Coalition troops were no

DOD Photo by MSGT James M. Bowman, USAF

Figure 16. Long shot wide-angle view showing damage to the UN Headquarters building in Baghdad, Iraq, following a truck bombing that destroyed a portion of the building.

longer the only targets. Sectarian, religious, and ethnic violence became intertwined with the anti-Coalition insurgency and with terrorism. In late August a car bomb outside the Imam Ali Shrine in the city of An Najaf exploded, killing 95 Iraqis including key Shia leader Muhammad Bakr al-Hakim. Almost a month later, assassins attacked and killed Dr. Aquila al-Hashimi, an Iraqi diplomat and the only ex-Baathist serving on the IGC. The situation in Iraq was still far from stable and the myriad causes of that instability were only beginning to be understood.

Peaks and Valleys: October 2003–March 2004

Photo Courtesy www.globalsecurity.com

Figure 17. Muqtada al-Sadr, Shia cleric.

As the summer heat began to fade, the situation in Iraq remained very unstable. There were new opportunities for the CPA to grasp as it attempted to formulate a winning combination of reconstruction, new governance, and military action to create a secure Iraq. Yet as 2003 waned, one of the squandered opportunities in the period after the fall of Saddam's government came back to haunt the CPA in the form of a radical young Shia cleric named Muqtada al-Sadr.

In the spring of 2003, al-Sadr had seemed merely a troublesome figure to the Coalition officials; but they had underestimated him. Al-Sadr's father, the Grand Ayatollah Mohammed Sadiq al-Sadr, and two of Muqtada's elder brothers had been assassinated in An Najaf in 1999, presumably on Saddam's orders. Muqtada al-Sadr exploited the tremendous respect the Shia community held for his late father, and, using his own charisma, began building a large following, including a militia called the Mahdi Army. US military intelligence recognized that al-Sadr's rhetoric at times threatened the Coalition's vision of the nature of post-Saddam Iraq and that his militia had been seeking larger numbers of small arms. Bremer and the CJTF-7 commander, however, differed over how best to defeat al-Sadr. By August Coalition military headquarters had developed plans to arrest al-Sadr, but the CPA called off any aggressive moves against the Shia leader to avoid inflaming his followers, hoping instead to discredit or co-opt him.

In October al-Sadr continued his aggressive anti-US rhetoric through sermons and his newspaper, *al-Hawza,* demonstrating that Coalition efforts against the radical cleric had been unsuccessful. At the same time, the Mahdi militia continued its expansion throughout Baghdad as the overall security situation deteriorated. The Mahdi Army became increasingly belligerent and challenged the CPA's authority to govern in certain parts of the countryside and the capital city, especially in the huge Baghdad slum called Sadr City—named after Muqtada al-Sadr's father.

Al-Sadr's Mahdi Army was not the sole reason for the increasingly turbulent situation on the ground in Iraq. Insurgent and terrorist organizations across much of Iraq were stepping up the number and sophistication of their attacks. The number of attacks on Coalition forces increased each month that fall, a period that included the Muslim holy month of Ramadan

DOD Photo by MSgt Robert R. Hargreaves, USAF

Figure 18. Colonel Richard Dillon, USA, Head of USA Mortuary Affairs, and Colonel Dennis Ployer, USAF, Commander, 447th Air Expeditionary Group (AEG), secure a UN flag over the transfer case of UN Chief Ambassador to Iraq, Sergio Vieira de Mello, prior to a memorial service at the Baghdad International Airport. Sergio Vieira de Mello was a victim of a homicide truck bombing at the United Nations Office of Humanitarian Coordinator in Baghdad, Iraq.

(26 October through 24 November 2003). In November the Coalition recorded approximately 1,000 insurgent attacks. They included a growing number of attacks on Iraqi infrastructure, the ISF, and the Iraqi Civil Defense Corps (ICDC), the latter a group of paramilitary organizations trained and equipped by Coalition military units to assist in the worsening environment.[19] The downing of a US Army Chinook helicopter by a shoulder-fired surface-to-air missile on 2 November 2003, an attack that killed 16 US Service personnel and wounded 20 more, was only the most striking example of the insurgents' increasing capability. That incident proved to be the worst single-day loss of US Soldiers since May 2003.

If Coalition forces met increasing armed resistance across Iraq in the fall of 2003, Coalition leaders faced another type of opposition from Iraqi politicians. Grand Ayatollah Ali al-Sistani and other Shia leaders were pressuring Bremer and others to hold elections in the near future and to quickly transfer sovereignty to the Iraqis. Kurdish and Sunni Arab leaders also sought a quick transition of political power. However, the Kurds and Sunnis were adamant that their country establish a constitution before it held elections. Only an established constitution, they believed, would guarantee their rights in the Shia-dominated state that would likely result from the electoral process. For their part, Bremer and Coalition leaders maintained serious doubts about speeding up the transition of sovereignty. Bremer himself had agreed with the Sunni Arab and Kurdish politicians, arguing that the Iraqis needed a constitution before they could create a government, but he believed that both processes would take years.

Despite these concerns, in October 2003 President Bush ordered the CPA to devise a plan to turn over full political authority to an Iraqi Government no later than 30 June 2004. Bremer then began negotiating with the critical Iraqi groups and by mid-November had finalized an agreement that committed the United States to build an Iraqi caretaker government to govern the country until the Iraqi people could approve a constitution. The so-called November 15th Agreement stipulated that the IGC would draw up the outlines of a transitional government with a specific bill of rights by 28 February 2004.

Ambassador Bremer's timetable was, by necessity, ambitious. The IGC would establish regional caucuses and, after gaining the CPA's approval, those caucuses would select the Transitional National Assembly (TNA), a body that would appoint a government and by January 2005 would conduct elections for delegates to a constitutional convention. By 31 March the plan called for the IGC to negotiate an agreement with the Coalition forces that clearly laid out the role of the latter with regard to security issues. Thus, by April 2004 Iraq would be asserting its sovereignty as the country progressed toward the 30 June 2004 transfer of power. As December 2003 began, it appeared that the CPA had paved the way for a peaceful transition to Iraqi sovereignty.

While a political settlement emerged in late 2003 and early 2004, Coalition military forces appeared to be making progress in their campaign to provide a safe and secure environment in Iraq. Tactical-level units became more familiar with their AORs and refined their approaches to engaging local populations and insurgents that operated in those areas. The significant decrease in insurgent attacks in this period suggested that Coalition forces had finally begun reaping the benefits of their efforts.[20] The capture of Saddam Hussein on 13 December 2003 was another apparent indicator of this progress. Saddam's detention resulted from months of careful intelligence work by the CJTF-7 staff, US Special Operations Forces, and especially the Soldiers of 4th ID who were operating in the Sunni heartland, the area where reports placed the fugitive dictator. In an operation called RED DAWN, the division's 1st Brigade Combat Team (BCT) and Task Force (TF) 120, a special operations team that had been hunting high-value targets in Iraq, surrounded the village of Ad Dawr near Tikrit and, after a careful search, found Saddam hiding in a spider hole.

The Bush administration, along with CPA and CJTF-7 leaders, believed that Saddam's capture would be a significant turning point in the Coalition's campaign in Iraq. Clearly, when Bremer excitedly announced, "Ladies and Gentlemen, we got him" to Iraqis and Coalition leaders in Baghdad, many perceived the event as a major triumph.[21] As long as he eluded capture, members of the former regime could take heart and hope one day that Saddam would return to power and restore all Baathists to their former positions. The capture of Saddam ended that dream, but it did not end the Sunni Arab insurgency nor lessen the Shia demands for dominance in any future government. Still, the former dictator's capture appeared to temporarily disrupt the Sunni insurgency. The number of insurgent attacks in the winter of 2004 dropped to approximately 600 per month, significantly below the number for the Ramadan period.[22]

The early spring heralded another positive event: the drafting of the Transitional Administrative Law (TAL), which promised to move Iraq closer to self-government. The negotiation over the provisions of the TAL proved to be a tortuous process for both the Iraqis and

Figure 19. Iraqi Governing Council (IGC) members (left to right): Dr. Rajaa Habib Dhaher Khuzai, M.D., Adnan Bajaji, Samir Shakir Mahmoud (at the lectern), an unidentified council member, and Dr. Mowaffak Al-Rubaie, M.D., hold a press conference to announce that the IGC had unanimously agreed to the Transitional Administrative Law (TAL) that will serve as an interim constitution and allow an Iraqi-led government to take control from the US-led Coalition.

the CPA. Getting Kurds, Sunni Arabs, and the Shias—not to mention the smaller blocks within those divisions—to agree on a temporary constitution to govern Iraq taxed the Coalition's patience. After much wrangling, shouting, walkouts, and hard negotiations among the various groups, the Iraqis approved the TAL on 8 March 2004.

Approval of the TAL appeared to be a major step toward a new Iraq. Perhaps most importantly, the law provided for regional governments, a decision that helped assure many Sunni Arabs that the new constitution would help retain their political position in Iraq by preventing the Shias from using their superior numbers to electorally swamp the Sunni Arabs.[23] The TAL would serve as the working constitution of Iraq until the body elected in January 2005 drew up a long-term constitution. The bitter infighting waged by the various groups during the negotiations indicated that the idea of minority rights was not fully accepted by all groups. However, by the beginning of 2004 Iraq seemed to have reached a political rapprochement that solved a number of the country's thorniest issues and set the nation on the road to a representative government and stability.

The Caldron Boils Over: April–June 2004

The Coalition's growing optimism was suddenly extinguished when the insurgency that had simmered throughout the previous year boiled over in April 2004. In that month Sunni Arab insurgents and Shia militia launched violent assaults in many parts of Iraq. Despite the drop in insurgent attacks in the months after Saddam's capture, the Sunni Arab-led portion of the insurgency had not permanently dissipated. Instead, at least some insurgent groups seemed to use that time to reorganize and consolidate in the Sunni heartland, especially in the city of Fallujah. Similarly, the advent of spring had emboldened the Shia leader Muqtada al-Sadr, who led his militia in attacking Coalition and Iraqi governing institutions in Shia-dominated cities southeast of Baghdad.

The explosion of violence in April came at a particularly inauspicious time for the Coalition's military forces. CJTF-7 had used the winter to begin the transition to OIF II—the deployment of a new set of American forces to Iraq and the redeployment of units that had been in Iraq since early 2003. (See Appendix F, US Army Units in Operation IRAQI FREEDOM, Order of Battle, May 2003–January 2005.) While Lieutenant General Sanchez remained in command of the joint task force, on 1 February 2004 the III Corps staff based at Fort Hood, Texas, formally replaced the V Corps staff that had served as the core of CJTF-7 headquarters since June 2003. At the tactical level, the 1st AD began turning over its responsibility for Baghdad (MND-B) to the 1st CAV in March; the 4th ID handed over responsibility for the Sunni heartland (MND-NC) to the 1st Infantry Division (1st ID) that same month. Also, the 101st ABN transferred responsibility for MND-N to TF *Olympia*, a composite unit that included the Stryker-equipped 3d Brigade of the 2d Infantry Division (2d ID), an air cavalry squadron, an aviation battalion, two engineer battalions, and other support elements.

In the middle of these transitions came an especially abhorrent attack on the Coalition. On 31 March 2004 insurgents in Fallujah murdered four American contractors who worked for the Blackwater security company and mutilated their corpses, hanging them from a bridge and broadcasting the barbaric scene around the world. In reaction, the US National Security Council and the CPA ordered CJTF-7 to take control of the city and to bring those who killed the Blackwater contractors to justice. Sanchez tasked the 1st MEF, which had just taken over responsibility for that area in Iraq from the 82d ABN, to conduct the attack.

1st MEF launched Operation VIGILANT RESOLVE on 4 April with two infantry battalions assaulting into the city. Marine forces made modest progress in clearing the city and killed hundreds of insurgents in the first week of the offensive. The Sunni Arab insurgents, however, fought back with a deadly effect and demonstrated a much higher level of tactical skill than Coalition forces expected. As a result, the 1st MEF ordered two more battalions into the city. In the course of the fighting, both sides inflicted heavy damage to Fallujah's infrastructure and the city's civilian population suffered greatly. The Marines also ordered the 2d Battalion of the new Iraqi Army to join the fighting in Fallujah. However, while en route to the city, a crowd stopped the unit's convoy and confronted the Iraqi soldiers about the impending operation that would force them into combat against other Iraqis. The 2d Battalion's soldiers refused to continue the movement to Fallujah, claiming they had not enlisted to fight their countrymen. On 9 April the IGC reached the brink of collapse over its opposition to the Coalition's attack on Fallujah and the civilian casualties incurred by the city's population. CPA Chief Paul Bremer reversed his earlier direction and ordered CJTF-7 to suspend the Marines' attack. The 1st MEF declared a unilateral cease-fire and agreed to allow the so-called Fallujah Brigade, an ad hoc Iraqi Army unit led by one of Saddam's former generals, to take control of the city.

While the CPA and CJTF-7 were attempting to reestablish control in Fallujah, Coalition leaders found themselves facing a potentially larger threat in the form of Muqtada al-Sadr's forces. In late March 2004 al-Sadr's virulent rhetoric and anti-Coalition actions prompted the Coalition to take action. The CPA ordered al-Sadr's newspaper, *al-Hawza,* to be shut down, and on 5 April Bremer declared al-Sadr an outlaw.[24] At the same time, an Iraqi judge issued an arrest warrant for al-Sadr in connection with the murder of Shia cleric Abd Al-Majid al-Khoei on 10 April 2003.

Al-Sadr reacted by ordering his forces to move against the Coalition. Beginning on 4 April violence erupted in Sadr City and in the Shia-dominated cities of An Najaf, Kufa, Al Kut, and Karbala. In Al Kut the arrest of one of Muqtada al-Sadr's lieutenants, Mustafa al-Yacoubi, prompted the Mahdi Army to take over the local television and radio stations and overwhelm the CPA compound, the local government buildings, and the Iraqi police station. Mahdi Army militiamen launched attacks on local police stations and government buildings in other cities as well.[25] In Sadr City the attacks against American units were particularly deadly. In that part of the capital, the Mahdi Army ambushed elements of the 1st AD and the 1st CAV, killing seven Soldiers and wounding dozens of others.

The Coalition response was swift and deadly. The 2d ACR began operations against the Mahdi Army in Sadr City, immediately occupying police stations that had been taken over by al-Sadr's forces. At the same time, the 1st AD, which was in the process of turning over authority for the Baghdad area to the 1st CAV, stopped its redeployment home and launched an offensive against al-Sadr's forces in the southern cities. In what the division called the "Extension Campaign," the Soldiers of the 1st AD crushed the Shia uprising. On 4 April the division sent elements of its 2d BCT to help the multinational troops in An Najaf secure CPA facilities in the city. The division then ordered the 2d BCT, newly designated as Task Force (TF) *Striker*, to move to Al Kut where Sadrist forces had taken over the CPA headquarters and a local radio station. Working with the Ukrainian forces in the city and with reinforcing elements from the 2d ACR, TF *Striker* moved into Al Kut on 8 April, and by 11 April had secured its objectives and suppressed the militia in the city.

The actions in Al Kut were the beginnings of a larger campaign that would involve most of the 1st AD as well as a BCT from 1st ID, a Stryker vehicle-equipped battalion from the 3d Brigade/2d ID operating in Mosul, and other CJTF-7 assets. As April progressed, the 1st AD

The Harsh Realities of Full Spectrum Operations
The 2-5 CAV in Sadr City
4 April 2004

In March 2004, the Soldiers of the 2d Battalion, 5th Cavalry Regiment (2-5 CAV), a part of the 1st Cavalry Division, arrived in Iraq and began taking over responsibility for the Sadr City section of the Iraqi capital from the 2d Armored Cavalry Regiment. By 4 April, the battalion's units were conducting full spectrum operations throughout the densely populated neighborhood dominated by Shia Iraqis. In the short time they had spent in Sadr City, most Soldiers in 2-5 CAV had patrolled the area and conducted what many labeled as stability operations—those noncombat missions designed to enable local government, reconstruct infrastructure, and give humanitarian assistance to local populations.

This was precisely the type of operation that the Soldiers of C Company, 2-5 CAV found themselves doing on the late afternoon of Sunday, 4 April. One platoon from the company had spent the day in their HMMWVs escorting waste trucks through Sadr City in an effort to remove sewage from the streets. Before returning home, the platoon leader received orders to lead his group of vehicles past the headquarters of the Sadr Bureau, Muqtada al Sadr's radical political organization that dominated the neighborhood. Near the bureau, the platoon found a large number of young men in the streets and on the buildings. Suddenly, the Soldiers came under fire from small arms and rocket propelled grenades. The platoon fought back fiercely but quickly suffered a number of casualties and had to move off the main avenue into a building where they established a defense.

2-5's commander mounted an immediate rescue but the units sent into the city were also ambushed and took casualties. Only after nightfall, when a column of M1 tanks penetrated deep into Sadr City was 2-5 CAV able to extricate the besieged platoon from C Company. By that time, six Soldiers from the 1st Cavalry Division and one Soldier from the 1st Armored Division had been killed. Over 60 other Soldiers had been wounded, many severely.

The ambush and subsequent rescue efforts in Sadr City reveal the difficulties underlying the Army's doctrine of full spectrum operations. Throughout Operation IRAQI FREEDOM, Soldiers had to conduct a mix of operations that required them to transition from nonlethal missions such as escorting waste trucks to high intensity combat operations in the blink of an eye. In 2003 when the US Army arrived in Iraq, it was the world's preeminent conventional fighting force. The situation in Iraq forced the Army to face a new reality in which excellence in combat operations was just one of many skills required to turn the military victory of April 2003 into an enduring success for the Coalition and the Iraqi people.

Based on material in Martha Raddatz,
The Long Road Home: A Story of War and Family
(New York: G.P. Putnam's Sons, 2007).

reorganized for combat and launched Operation IRON SABRE, a methodical set of actions intended to clear Sadrist forces from the towns of An Najaf, Kufa, Al Kut, and Karbala. Even though the last major action in this operation was at Karbala in May 2004, al-Sadr's forces continued to offer sporadic resistance to Coalition forces in An Najaf for another month. It was clear by that date that 1st AD and the other Coalition forces had defeated al-Sadr's attempts to lead an uprising designed to elevate him to power. Al-Sadr announced a unilateral cease-fire and ordered his militias to disband in late June 2004. It proved to be only a temporary setback for the Shia leader.

During the al-Sadr uprising, US forces demonstrated they could wield military power in a decisive way to suppress insurrection. However, neither the 1st AD's Operation IRON SABRE nor 1st MEF's Operation VIGILANT RESOLVE destroyed the forces that were intent on thwarting the Coalition's efforts in Iraq. The Mahdi Army would again strike out at American forces in the near future; undefeated insurgent groups in Fallujah became only stronger, transforming the city into a fortified sanctuary for Sunni Arab extremists; and insurgent groups in other parts of Iraq continued to mount small-scale attacks against Coalition troops. Exacerbating the situation throughout Iraq in late April and May was the public release of photographs depicting the abuse of Iraqi detainees by American Soldiers at the Abu Ghraib Prison. The Coalition had put the lid back on the caldron but the waters continued to boil.

Transitions of Command and Sovereignty: June–July 2004

Despite the instability in Iraq, the Coalition continued making progress toward two critical transitions in the spring and summer of 2004: the transfer of political sovereignty to the Iraqis and the major reorganization of the Coalition's political and military command structure to make way for that transfer of political power. In the spring, serious political problems had emerged that ultimately reshaped the 15 November agreement. Iraqi politics and UN pressure forced Bremer to abandon the original plan of provincial caucuses that would elect the TNA. Instead, the process would be slower with the CPA, UN, and IGC choosing the interim government that would lead Iraq until national elections for the TNA were held in late 2004 or early 2005. The UN codified this new roadmap on 8 June 2004 when it passed Resolution 1546, a measure that endorsed the creation of a new sovereign entity called the Interim Iraqi Government (IIG), recognized the need for the continued presence of Coalition military forces in Iraq, and proposed the timetable for the IIG to follow to move Iraq toward a more democratic government. While these political transitions occurred, Coalition military leaders reorganized the command structure in Iraq to create a new strategic-level military headquarters that would free the corps headquarters of theater-strategic responsibilities and allow the corps commander to focus on the conduct of tactical operations.

The IIG's main function was to act as a caretaker government until the elections scheduled for late January 2005 could be held and a new constitution drawn up. However, determining the structure and the membership of the IIG proved to be no easy task. UN Special Envoy Lakhdar Brahimi selected the IIG members and then nominated them to Ambassador Bremer, who held the responsibility of approving or rejecting them. Brahimi wanted a government comprised of skilled technocrats who were not strongly affiliated with the major political parties in Iraq. Getting the Iraqi political parties to go along with this idea was nearly impossible. But after much scheming and maneuvering, Bremer approved Ayad Allawi, a secular Shia politician, to be the IIG Prime Minister, and the CPA formed the new government in June 2004.

Coalition forces in Iraq underwent major high-level structural changes in preparation for the handover of sovereignty on 30 June. President Bush selected John Negroponte to be the first ambassador to the newly sovereign Iraq. DOD complemented the creation of the new embassy in Iraq by redesignating CJTF-7 as Headquarters, Multi-National Force–Iraq (MNF-I) on 15 May 2004. Lieutenant General Sanchez served temporarily as the commander of MNF-I and transferred his command to US Army General George Casey Jr. on 1 July 2004.

MNF-I's chief function was to provide theater-strategic and operational-level planning and command for Coalition military forces in Iraq while working closely with the US Embassy and the IIG. MNF-I's major subordinate commands consisted of the Multi-National Corps–Iraq (MNC-I), the Multi-National Security Transition Command–Iraq (MNSTC-I), and the US Army Corps of Engineer's Gulf Region Division. MNC-I planned and conducted operations at the tactical level of war. MNSTC-I coordinated the programs to train and equip the ISF, thus taking these responsibilities from the CPA. The Gulf Region Division coordinated and supervised the American reconstruction effort in Iraq after mid-2004.

Each of these subordinate commands played a key role in how General Casey, the new MNF-I commander, envisioned the campaign in Iraq. In 30 days, Casey and his staff created a new campaign plan that characterized the Coalition military effort in Iraq as full spectrum counterinsurgency operations. In this type of campaign, MNF-I, the senior military headquarters, would coordinate and synchronize the political and economic elements of counterinsurgency operations with the Iraqi Government and Coalition political representatives, especially Ambassador Negroponte. MNC-I, MNSTC-

Figure 20. US Ambassador John D. Negroponte (left) shakes hands with Iraqi Prime Minister Dr. Ayad Allawi at an American Independence Day celebration where the Ambassador made a toast dedicating this July Fourth to the Iraqi people and to their independence.

I, and the Corps of Engineers Gulf Region Division became the commands responsible for implementing the military-led aspects of the counterinsurgency campaign.

The staff structure of MNF-I also reflected the significant challenges faced by Coalition forces in detainee operations. After its public acknowledgment in April 2004 that US Soldiers had abused detainees in Abu Ghraib in late 2003, DOD made a number of significant policy and organizational changes, including the addition of a two-star general to the MNF-I staff who was designated the deputy commanding general for detainee operations. The deputy commanding general established policies for Coalition forces and oversaw the burgeoning detainee system that held and questioned Iraqis suspected of insurgent activities.

Figure 21. General George W. Casey Jr. (left), Commander of Multi-National Force–Iraq (MNF-I), walks with Polish Armed Forces Major General Andrzej Ekiert, Commander of Multi-National Division–Center-South (MND-CS) during a visit to Camp Babylon, Iraq.

The Sunni Arab Challenge: August–November 2004

While the Coalition had transferred sovereignty to the Iraqis and restructured its military command, insurgent and militia organizations had begun increasing their activity against Coalition forces and the ISF. In August 2004 the number of attacks against the Coalition, the ISF, and Iraqi civilians exceeded 2,500, making that month the most violent since June 2003.[26] The bulk of the violence resulted from the Mahdi Army's renewed campaign against Coalition forces centered in An Najaf. Muqtada al-Sadr had begun flexing his muscles again and MNF-I had responded by sending both US Marine and Army units to counter his attempts to gain control of that important city. The Coalition's combat proved decisive by the end of the month. However, the MNF-I commander had worked closely with the IIG to include ISF in the An Najaf fight, and directed Civil Affairs units into the city immediately after hostilities had ended to begin repairing damages caused by combat operations. This combination of combat power, ISF participation, and integrated reconstruction operations became the core of the Coalition approach in dealing with other cities in Iraq where Sunni insurgents had gained sway and threatened to undermine the legitimacy of the IIG and the upcoming elections scheduled for January 2005. Most important were the cities of Samarra and Fallujah, which by the summer of 2004 had become insurgent safe havens.

Samarra would be the first objective. In early 2004 the 4th ID had attempted to clear out insurgent cells in the city and enjoyed some success. But Coalition forces, with the exception of one US Army Special Forces team, had withdrawn after the 4th ID's operation and, by the middle of 2004, the insurgents had returned to the city and reestablished their control. The mission to clear the city and reinstate Iraqi Government control fell to the 1st ID, the unit that had taken responsibility for the Sunni heartland from the 4th ID in the early spring. By late summer the 1st ID had begun planning Operation BATON ROUGE to accomplish this objective.

Between late July and late September elements of the 1st ID began using a mix of information operations and other activities to shape the situation in Samarra. Working in concert with the ISF, the division planned to slowly isolate the city and then establish footholds first on its perimeter and then near its center. By late September Iraqi and American forces had made gains, but had not yet wrested control from the insurgent and criminal groups in the city. In fact, continued insurgent violence and intimidation spurred the Coalition to act in a more direct way. On 1 October 2004 Coalition forces launched a rapid large-scale attack and search operation and methodically cleared the city over the next 2 days. Following these successful clearing operations (during which approximately 125 insurgents were killed, 60 wounded, and 128 detained), the 1st ID and the ISF remained in place to conduct security, reconstruction, and information operations designed to stabilize Samarra and make the city less vulnerable to a return of the insurgents.[27]

With the Sunni Arab guerrillas evicted from Samarra, the Coalition turned its attention toward Fallujah. After the CPA called off the Marine offensive to destroy the Sunni insurgents in April 2004, Fallujah had once again become a sanctuary for Sunni Arab insurgents. The Fallujah Brigade, the Iraqi force that replaced the US Marine presence in the city, had dissolved within weeks, many of its soldiers joining the ranks of the insurgents. Increasingly confident, the insurgents inside Fallujah began instituting very conservative religious strictures and preparing for the next Coalition attack. By October 2004 intelligence estimates suggested that approximately 4,500 insurgents occupied the city of Fallujah.[28]

For the Coalition and the IIG, the idea of holding elections while a large city near Baghdad remained in enemy hands was untenable. To rid Fallujah of the insurgents, MNF-I worked with the Iraqis in planning Operation AL FAJR (known to US units as PHANTOM FURY), which not only incorporated US Army and Marine Corps forces but Iraqi Army units as well. AL FAJR was a three-phase operation, the first of which focused on shaping the battlefield environment. Iraqi Prime Minister Ayad Allawi, in a show of cooperation with Coalition forces notably absent from Operation VIGILANT RESOLVE in the spring, declared most of Iraq to be in a state of emergency. US and Iraqi forces then surrounded Fallujah, instituted a curfew, and warned Iraqis not to carry weapons. Coalition forces sealed off the city and urged all noncombatants to leave. One account of the battle estimated that "less than 500 civilians" remained in the city when combat operations began.[29]

Once the Coalition had isolated those remaining in Fallujah by establishing blocking positions around the circumference of the city, the second phase of the operation began. Two Marine regimental combat teams, each task-organized with a US Army mechanized battalion and several Iraqi Army formations, assaulted the city from the north on 8 November 2004. For months the insurgent forces had been constructing extensive defenses inside Fallujah's many buildings, and these fortifications allowed the small enemy groups to resist the Coalition attack using small-arms fire, improvised explosive devices, and rocket-propelled grenades. US forces employed their superior firepower and mobility using tanks, Bradley Fighting Vehicles, artillery, and helicopter gunships to destroy the insurgent resistance. After 2 weeks of hard fighting, Coalition forces had established control over Fallujah and began phase three of the operation which featured reconstruction missions. US and Iraqi forces killed 2,000 insurgents and captured approximately 1,200. But the tough house-to-house combat inside the city claimed the lives of 70 US Soldiers, Sailors, and Marines and 7 Iraqi soldiers. An additional 600 Coalition and Iraqi participants were wounded in the operation.[30]

Toward the New Iraq: December 2004–January 2005

With the Sunni Arab insurgent challenge in Samarra and Fallujah checked, the Coalition and the IIG prepared for elections they hoped would bring the nation together. The Bush administration viewed the emergence of a democratically elected government in Iraq as crucial to American security and the reshaping of the Middle East. Coalition leaders also hoped that a freely elected Iraqi Government would undercut some of the claims of the many insurgent groups operating in Iraq and reduce the level of violence. However, mounting free and fair elections in a country that had no democratic traditions in the midst of an insurgency presented unique challenges. If the Coalition and the IIG were to hold successful elections for the TNA according to the agreed-on schedule, security was of paramount importance and the ISF would need to play a large role.

To organize for the elections, the IIG created a nine-member commission to oversee the process. Thousands of Iraqi volunteers supported the commission by serving as election commissioners. The men and women volunteers successfully registered over 14 million Iraqi voters in the months leading up to the elections. To provide security for voters and for polling places, Coalition forces went to great lengths to keep a low profile, hoping to remain as unobtrusive as possible. Iraqi military and police forces provided security in the days prior to the elections, with American Soldiers remaining in the background, ready to react against insurgent plans to disrupt the voting.

In the days and weeks leading up to the elections, Coalition forces and their Iraqi partners were very busy—and very effective. The sheer scale of the task was such that even under

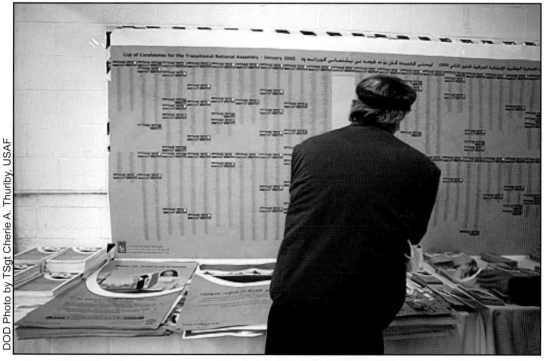

Figure 22. Najim Chechen, formerly of Baghdad, Iraq, looks over the list of Iraqi candidates for the Transitional National Assembly before casting his absentee ballot at the New Carrollton, Maryland, voting station, 28 January 2005, just 2 days before Iraq's national election.

peaceful conditions, Iraqi and Coalition organizers would have faced a major challenge in mounting the elections. Nevertheless, on election day, 30 January 2005, millions of Iraqis voted at approximately 6,000 voting centers all across the country. They chose from among 19,000 candidates, representing a wide variety of political parties, for the 275 seats in the TNA.[31] The voter turnout was approximately 60 percent of eligible voters, although the large majority of Sunni Arabs boycotted the elections.[32] Still, this was an astonishing percentage considering the very real dangers facing the voters. Lieutenant General Thomas Metz, MNC-I commander in January 2005, remembered that day with great clarity: "My command sergeant major was at a polling site when a mortar round came in. It killed two people and wounded four. The people got out of the polling line and did the right thing by the deceased, helped the wounded, but they got back in line."[33] The courage that many Iraqis displayed in expressing their political right to vote amazed Metz. He stated that the image of the Iraqi voters defying the insurgent attacks remained with him: "I always challenge every American audience, 'Would the people in your hometown get back in line?'"[34]

The elections were a success despite scattered insurgent attacks that took the lives of 26 Iraqi civilians, 8 members of the ISF, and 11 Coalition Soldiers. Iraqi forces performed quite well during this first, nation-wide test of their abilities. They played a large role in not only getting out the vote, but also ensuring that not a single polling place was destroyed. Days after the elections, Lieutenant General David Petraeus, commander of MNSTC-I, attributed a large part of the electoral success to the Iraqis and their security forces:

> The bottom line . . . is that considerable momentum has been achieved in the effort to help Iraq develop its security forces. We saw this most vividly on [30 January 2005]. Democracy was on the march in Iraq on January 30th, and that march was secured by Iraqi soldiers and police. Certainly the backup by Coalition forces was of enormous importance. However, it was Iraqi security forces that prevented terrorists from penetrating the security around any of the more than 5,000 polling sites, and it was Iraqi police and soldiers who gave their lives to prevent several suicide vest bombers from blowing up large numbers of those standing in line to vote.[35]

The elections of January 2005 were an important milestone in the history of OIF, and they mark the endpoint of this study. The elections inspired millions of Iraqis and helped move Iraq closer toward the US goal of creating a stable and prosperous country, led by a representative government able to prevent its territory from being used as a base for terrorism and regional aggression. Few in MNF-I headquarters or the military units under its command expected the elections to fully transform Iraq or to put an immediate end to the terrorism, insurgency, and increasing sectarian violence plaguing the nation. Still, as the polling stations closed on 30 January 2005, American Soldiers could acknowledge that they had made significant strides toward their objective during the first 18 months of the US Army's tenure in Iraq.

Notes

1.   Coalition Provisional Authority Order No. 1, "De-Ba'athification of Iraqi Society" (16 May 2003), http://www.iraqcoalition.org/regulations/20030516_CPAORD_1_De-Ba_athification_of_Iraqi_ Society_.pdf (accessed 14 September 2006).

2.   Coalition Provisional Authority Order No. 2, "Dissolution of Entities" (23 May 2003), http:// www.iraqcoalition.org/regulations/20030823_CPAORD_2_Dissolution_of_Entities_with_Annex_A. pdf (accessed 14 September 2006).

3.   UN Security Council, "Resolution 1483" (22 May 2003), http://daccessdds.un.org/doc/ UNDOC/GEN/N03/368/53/PDF/N0336853.pdf?OpenElement (accessed 14 September 2006).

4.   General Tommy Franks, *American Soldier* (New York, NY: Harper Collins, 2004), 392–393 and 528–531.

5.   General Tommy Franks (Retired), interview by Contemporary Operations Study Team, Fort Leavenworth, KS, 23 June 2006, 7–9.

6.   L. Paul Bremer III, *My Year in Iraq: The Struggle to Build a Future of Hope* (New York, NY: Simon & Schuster, 2006), 105–107.

7.   In April 2003 the commander of V Corps had received indicators that his headquarters would likely form the core of the follow-on joint task force. On 14 May CFLCC held a briefing that made the transition to V Corps official, naming the new headquarters CJTF-7 and scheduling the transition to take place no later than 15 June 2003. General William S. Wallace, Memorandum for Director, Combat Studies Institute, Subject: Review of On Point II Draft Manuscript, 20 December 2006, 1.

8.   John J. McGrath, *Boots on the Ground: Troop Density in Contingency Operations* (Fort Leavenworth, KS: Combat Studies Institute Press, 2006), 126.

9.   General William S. Wallace, interview by Contemporary Operations Study Team, Fort Leavenworth, KS, 22 May 2006, 8.

10. Lieutenant General Ricardo Sanchez, interview by Contemporary Operations Study Team, Fort Leavenworth, KS, 14 August 2006, 5.

11. V Corps and CJTF-7, *V Corps–CJTF-7 Transition and Challenges* Briefing, 30 September 2004, slide 5.

12. Lieutenant Colonel Wesley Odum, interview by Contemporary Operations Study Team, Fort Leavenworth, KS, 17 March 2006, 7, 16.

13. Coalition Provisional Authority, *CPA Vision Statement* (13 July 2003), 5.

14. Lieutenant General Keith Dayton, interview by Contemporary Operations Study Team, Fort Leavenworth, KS, 14 December 2005, 3–4.

15. "DOD News Briefing—Mr. Di Rita and Gen. Abizaid," *DefenseLink*, 16 July 2003, http:// www.defenselink.mil/transcripts/2003/tr20030716-0401.html (accessed 18 September 2006).

16. US Government Accountability Office, GAO Report GAO-05-431T, "Rebuilding Iraq: Preliminary Observations on the Challenges in Transferring Security Responsibilities to Iraqi Military and Police," 14 March 2005, 10.

17. Bremer, *My Year in Iraq*, 142.

18. See Lieutenant General Ricardo Sanchez's comments in Michael R. Gordon, "To Mollify Iraqis, US Plans to Ease Scope of Its Raids," *New York Times* (7 August 2003), 1.

19. GAO Report GAO-05-431T, see Figure 1, "Violent Incidents Against the Coalition and Its Partners, by Month, June 2003 Through February 2005," 14 March 2005, 10. This official unclassified report of the number of attacks, which will be used throughout this study, closely resembles unofficial reports such as those in the Brookings Institution's Iraq Index that derived its statistics from a variety of sources, including press reports. While there are differences between the reports in the precise number of attacks in specific months, the general trends in the number of attacks over time in the GAO report closely resemble those documented in the Brookings Institution's Iraq Index. For comparison, see Michael E. O'Hanlon and Adriana Lins de Albuquerque, "Iraq Index: Tracking Variables of Reconstruction and

Security in Post-Saddam Iraq, Updated April 18, 2005," The Brookings Institution, http://www.brook.edu/fp/saban/iraq/index20050418.pdf (accessed 18 December 2006).

20. GAO Report GAO-05-431T, 14 March 2005, 10.

21. Bremer, *My Year in Iraq*, 253.

22. GAO Report GAO-05-431T, 14 March 2005, 10.

23. See Transitional Administrative Law, http://www.cpa-iraq.org/government/TAL.html (accessed 11 December 2006).

24. "Bremer brands Moqtada Sadr an Outlaw," *Middle East OnLine*, http://www.middle-east-online.com/english/?id=9514 (accessed 30 August 2006).

25. 1st Infantry Division, 135th Military History Detachment, "Stryker Scimitar: The Battle for Al Kut, 8 April 04–11 April 04," CD, Fort McNair (Washington, DC: US Army Center for Military History).

26. GAO Report GAO-05-431T, 14 March 2005, 10.

27. Major General John R.S. Batiste and Lieutenant Colonel Paul R. Daniels, "The Fight for Samarra: Full-Spectrum Operations in Modern Warfare," *Military Review,* May–June 2005, 3.

28. Lieutenant General John F. Sattler and Lieutenant Colonel Daniel H. Wilson, "Operation AL FAJR: The Battle of Fallujah—Dousing the Bright Ember of the Insurgency," *Marine Corps Gazette,* July 2005, 14.

29. Sattler and Wilson, 16.

30. Matt M. Matthews, *Operation AL FAJR: A Study in Army and Marine Corps Joint Operations* (Fort Leavenworth, KS: Combat Studies Institute Press, 2006).

31. "Iraqi Elections, January 30, 2005," US State Department Web site, http://www.state.gov/r/pa/scp/2005/41206.htm (accessed 4 September 2006).

32. Anthony Shadid, "Iraqis Defy Threats as Millions Vote," *Washington Post Foreign Service,* 31 January 2005, A1.

33. Lieutenant General Thomas Metz, interview by Contemporary Operations Study Team, Fort Leavenworth, KS, 13 December 2005, 12.

34. Metz, interview, 13 December 2005, 12.

35. "Special Defense Department Briefing on Iraq Security Forces," *DefenseLink,* 4 February 2005, http://www.defenselink.mil/transcripts/2005/tr20050204-2083.html (accessed 17 October 2006).

Chapter 2

The US Army's Historical Legacy of Military Operations Other Than War and the Planning for Operation IRAQI FREEDOM

The US Army's history during more than two centuries of service to the nation has significantly influenced the way modern American Soldiers see themselves and the way they understand their missions. Throughout its history, the US Army often fulfilled its role of securing the nation by preparing for, conducting, and winning conventional wars. In 2001 the Army reinforced this understanding of its mission by stating in its capstone doctrinal work, Field Manual (FM) 3-0, *Operations,* "Fighting and winning the nation's wars is the foundation of Army service—the Army's non-negotiable contract with the American people and its enduring obligation to the nation."[1] This emphasis on conventional warfighting is driven by the fact that the United States has repeatedly required its Army to organize, train, and deploy large numbers of forces; to conduct conventional combat operations across great distances and for long periods of time; and to defeat the uniformed military forces of other nations.

The heavy demands of conflicts such as World War I, World War II, the Korean war, and the Vietnam war make this focus on conventional warfighting understandable. Indeed, the Army's efforts during the last 100 years have been focused on preparing for and fighting major conventional wars. It is clear the US Army's attention to and preparation for conventional conflicts were critical factors in its most recent successes in conventional warfighting—the victory over Iraqi forces in Operation DESERT STORM in 1991 and the lightning campaign against Saddam Hussein's regime in early 2003. However, in May 2003 when Operation IRAQI FREEDOM (OIF) became a "full spectrum" campaign that required the simultaneous use of lethal and non-lethal measures in an attempt to achieve US national objectives, the US Army found itself in a conflict for which it was less than well prepared. (For a complete discussion of full spectrum operations, see the Introduction to this study.)

During its lifetime, the US Army has fought eight foreign wars, one civil war, and the War for Independence. These conflicts traditionally garnered the most attention from Soldiers as well as from the American public due to the critical security issues and foreign policy goals at stake. Remarkably, since 1798 the American military forces have also conducted approximately 320 operations that cannot be characterized as conventional wars.[2] Put simply, the American military establishment in general, and the US Army specifically, have a long, well-established, and multifaceted history of conducting missions that do not feature conventional combat. These conflicts, taken as a group, have dominated the Army's historical record, even though they have not dominated its culture and training focus.[3]

In 2003 both the Department of Defense (DOD) Joint Doctrine and the Army's FM 3-0 described these conflicts using the term "military operations other than war" (MOOTW).[4] In the past, American Soldiers have identified these types of campaigns using a variety of other names, including small wars, contingency operations, and low-intensity conflict. Regardless of their official classification, MOOTW normally included one or more of the following missions: peacekeeping, peace enforcement, security assistance, humanitarian assistance, foreign internal defense (including counterinsurgency), and counterterrorism.

This chapter will examine the Army's experience in these conflicts, using the term "stability and support operations" to describe the wide variety of noncombat tasks conducted by

Soldiers within those conflicts.* Stability and support operations are two of the four categories of military actions that together comprise full spectrum operations, the others being offensive and defensive operations. These four types of actions are employed in varying sequential or simultaneous combinations to accomplish the mission, while a single type may predominate in particular places or times.[5] The discussion that follows will focus on important historical examples (including those from the recent past) to understand the attitudes, experiences, and preparation American Soldiers brought into the new campaign in Iraq. It will also look closely at the evolution of US Army doctrine, training, and planning for these types of missions, ultimately explaining how all of these factors shaped the planning for postinvasion operations in Iraq.

Historical Antecedents

The US military's experience in conflicts other than conventional warfare essentially began as the young nation started pushing its frontier to the West in the late 18th century. For most of the 19th century, the Army conducted a variety of operations along the frontiers, most involving the Native American people living in those areas. In the 20th century, the US military's focus changed as American foreign policy became more interested in asserting power outside of the United States. For the US Navy and Marine Corps, this meant a sudden upsurge in stability and support operations in the Caribbean basin. Perhaps the best example of this type of mission was the Navy and Marine Corps campaign to rebuild and democratize the nation of Haiti that began in 1915 and continued for the next 18 years.

The US Army's most formative experience with MOOTW in this period came not in Latin America but in the Pacific Rim. In 1898 the United States declared war on Spain and quickly mounted operations against Spanish colonial holdings in the Caribbean and the Philippines. Conventional operations on land and sea concluded rather quickly, leaving the Army as victors and occupiers in Cuba and the Philippines. By early 1899 Army units found themselves fighting an insurgency led by Filipino nationalist Emilio Aguinaldo who sought to bring independence to his country.

For the next 13 years, the Army conducted a variety of operations to counter a Filipino enemy that had a variety of faces. To defeat these insurgencies and stabilize the Philippines, the US Army relied on widely dispersed company-size units that pursued a complementary two-pronged approach featuring conciliation and coercion. US authorities hoped conciliatory policies would attract Filipinos away from armed opposition by using a combination of civic action and humanitarian aid programs that included the establishment of democratic institutions, the construction of schools and roads, and the introduction of vaccinations and other public health programs.[6] To assist in securing these improvements, the Army organized and trained a Filipino Constabulary and other native auxiliaries.

The second approach, coercion, promised punishment for those Filipinos who served in or supported the insurgency. Major General Arthur MacArthur provided the foundation for this policy in 1900 when, as military governor of the Philippines, he declared martial law over the

---

*Because of its common usage in recent years, changes to doctrinal definitions, and its importance to understanding and assessing Operation IRAQI FREEDOM, the precise meaning of the term "stability and support operations" will be further examined in the section that covers planning for OIF.

Figure 23. Soldiers and civilians intermingle in the Philippines.

islands and issued General Orders 100, first used in the United States during the Civil War, stating "Combatants not in uniform would be treated like 'highway robbers or pirates' and, along with civilians who aided them, they could be subject to the death penalty."[7] Following this approach, American Soldiers fought the insurgents and their sympathizers by imposing fines, destroying or relocating villages, and detaining those they suspected were part of the armed opposition.[8]

By 1913, the year most American Soldiers left the island of Mindanao, the US Army had accumulated a great deal of experience conducting stability and support operations in the Philippines. Officers published accounts of the war in professional journals and some of the tactical lessons from the campaign appeared in textbooks used at military schools.[9] Nevertheless, most of what American Soldiers learned about conducting stability and support operations in the Philippines remained in the memory of veterans, and this collective knowledge continued to shape how the Army approached similar operations for the next two decades.[10]

Between 1917 and 1945 the preparation for and waging of conventional warfare dominated the history of the American Army. During this period, the US Marine Corps was responsible for most of the stability and support operations required by US foreign policy, while the Army concentrated on defeating the conventional threats posed by Germany and Japan. In the immediate aftermath of World War II, however, American Soldiers once again found themselves conducting stability and support operations in those countries they had occupied. The US Government had done a great deal of planning for the occupation of Germany, Japan, and other liberated territories. For example, Army officers had begun work on Operation ECLIPSE—the plan for the stabilization and reconstruction of Germany—in 1943, 2 years before the Nazi surrender. Similar planning took place for the eventual occupation of Japan as well. In addition to creating plans, the US Army established the School of Military Government in Charlottesville, Virginia, in 1942, where Soldiers attended courses on the administrative and logistics challenges posed by the tasks of peace enforcement, stabilization, and reconstruction.[11] Other courses in this period trained Army officers in foreign languages and cultural studies as preparation for their future roles as civil affairs (CA) officers in postwar Germany and Japan.[12] The US Government took the further step of bringing civilian experts in governance, economics, and other fields into the planning process and sent some of them to Japan and Germany to assist in governing and rebuilding projects focused on establishing peaceful democratic nations after their defeat.

In 1945, when it came time to occupy Germany and Japan, the US Army enjoyed the advantages of both this preparatory work and the lessons Soldiers had learned in conducting stability and support operations in North Africa, Italy, and other territories liberated before the surrender of the Axis powers. This mixture of planning and experience contributed greatly to the very successful occupations that stabilized and began reconstruction in Germany and Japan. Even so, the success of the occupations also required time and resources. Between 1945 and 1951 hundreds of thousands of Soldiers performed the myriad duties integral to the stabilization and rebuilding of both countries. These operations took place inside nations and among populations that had been severely hurt by years of war and had surrendered unconditionally to the Allies as well as in the context of an unprecedented US commitment to rebuild the economies and political structures of its former enemies.

In the debate that surrounded the planning and execution of OIF, some observers and policy makers proposed the American occupations of Japan and Germany after World War II as models for Coalition postinvasion operations in Iraq.[13] However, postwar conditions in each of these countries were unique and any effort to employ these occupations as historical analogies should be made with caution. As previously noted, the American operations in both

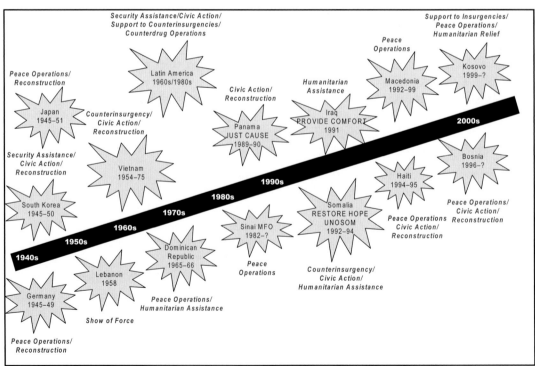

Figure 24. US Army stability and support operations, 1945–present.

Germany and Japan demanded a great amount of manpower, money, and time, even though the population in neither country mounted an armed opposition to US operations. For example, the occupation force for Japan, a country slightly smaller than Iraq, initially numbered more than 400,000 Soldiers.[14] Even though the number of troops would decrease as Japan became more stable, the US Army maintained at least 150,000 Soldiers in the country until 1951.[15] Also critical to the understanding of American success in Japan is the factor of culture. Japanese society was largely homogeneous, devoid of any serious ethnic or sectarian divisions. Once the Japanese emperor and his government surrendered unconditionally to Allied forces, this largely unified society submitted obediently to the occupation.[16] Despite the advantages of manpower, money, and culture, the American occupation of Japan was neither easy nor quick.

The advent of the Cold War forced new requirements on the US Army. American Soldiers struggled to adapt to the changes posed by nuclear weapons and their implications for conventional warfare. The nature of the conflict between the West and the Communist bloc also created situations in which the US military had to project power and conduct stability and support operations. The Army, in particular, conducted foreign internal defense operations in South Korea between 1948 and 1950, peacekeeping in the Dominican Republic in 1965, and civic assistance and foreign internal defense in El Salvador and Honduras in the 1980s, to name just a few of these operations.

The campaign in Vietnam dwarfed all of these conflicts and still stands out as the Army's most formative experience during the Cold War. From 1955 to 1973 American Soldiers in South Vietnam conducted security assistance, counterinsurgency, civic assistance, and reconstruction operations. In 1965 the US Army added conventional combat operations to its responsibilities and increased the tempo and number of these operations over the next 4 years as more American units flowed into South Vietnam. Nevertheless, throughout the two decades of American involvement in Vietnam, US Soldiers continued to conduct missions beyond conventional combat that focused on stabilizing South Vietnamese social and political structures, rebuilding infrastructure, and preparing the South Vietnamese Armed Forces to defend against the threat posed by the Viet Cong and the North Vietnamese Army. While this brief discussion of American stability and support operations cannot fully capture the size and complexity of the operations in Vietnam, it is important to summarize their general evolution and offer some detail concerning the extent to which American Soldiers were involved in missions other than conventional warfighting.

US military involvement in Vietnam began in 1955 as the French Army withdrew its forces after suffering a humiliating defeat to the Communist Vietminh forces. After the subsequent peace agreement divided Vietnam into a northern Communist state and a nominally democratic republic in the south, the US Army began conducting security assistance operations in South Vietnam. For the first 5 years, these operations focused on providing materiel support and technical advisory assistance to the new South Vietnamese Army (ARVN). Nevertheless, by 1961 as the threat from the domestic insurgents grew, American efforts shifted to the mission of foreign internal defense, which meant assisting the ARVN in training its units for conventional and counterinsurgency operations and providing advice to ARVN commanders during tactical operations. By 1965 the US military headquarters in the country, known as Military Assistance Command, Vietnam (MACV), included over 6,000 Army officers and enlisted Soldiers who served as advisors to the ARVN or in American units that supported the advisory effort.[17] Most of these men assisted conventional ARVN units in their conflict with the insurgent Viet Cong enemy. The MACV also included US Army Special Forces Soldiers who used their specialized training in counterinsurgency warfare to build and train irregular units in South Vietnam's remote areas, especially along its border with Laos.[18]

Through the advisory program, some American Soldiers became involved in civic assistance and reconstruction programs and other aspects of the counterinsurgency campaign. Additional US Government organizations such as the US Agency for International Development (USAID), the Central Intelligence Agency, and the US Information Agency were responsible for many elements of the larger effort to suppress the insurgency, stabilize the Vietnamese countryside, and build support for the South Vietnamese Government by improving the country's infrastructure. This decentralized approach led to problems, and by 1967 it was clear to the US Army and American officials in Vietnam that the efforts to pacify the countryside and create popular support for the South Vietnamese political structure were failing.

To bring unity of effort to the campaign, MACV worked with other US agencies to create the Civil Operations and Rural Development Support (CORDS) program. This new entity served as the coordinating body that linked and deconflicted the actions of the military forces with the various agencies involved in pacification and reconstruction. Because of its interagency nature, the CORDS program consisted of both civilian and military personnel. For the US Army, the new program meant increasing the number of advisors at the district and provincial levels of government. By 1970 approximately 8,000 American Soldiers served as part of CORDS.[19] These men made up small advisory teams that concentrated on the training of regional and local militia units and advising these units in operations against insurgents.

Most US Army advisors in CORDS became involved to some degree in the civic assistance and reconstruction aspects of the campaign as well. MACV and other US agencies designed CORDS so that small groups of US officials—both civilian and military—worked with the South Vietnamese throughout the country, setting up programs designed to win Vietnamese peasants over to the South Vietnamese Government's cause, and to destroy rural support for Communist forces.[20] Among other things, this program entailed the establishment of a national police force and the construction of a wide variety of projects such as schools, clinics and hospitals, highways, and farming cooperatives. To begin and sustain these initiatives, CORDS recruited and sent thousands of agricultural experts, doctors, nurses, teachers, engineers, intelligence agents, and civilian advisors to the rural areas of South Vietnam.[21]

As the Nixon administration's policy of Vietnamization slowly gathered speed in 1970 and 1971, US Army stability and support operations in Vietnam subsided. The number of advisors in ARVN tactical units and the CORDS program rapidly decreased. By 1972 MACV had shifted the small advisory effort to assisting the ARVN and the South Vietnamese Government with technical and logistical matters.[22] In many ways, US stability and support operations in Vietnam had come full circle, ending where they had begun in 1955 as a series of programs designed to improve South Vietnam's defense infrastructure.

Of course, much of the optimism that had accompanied early US involvement in Vietnam had dissipated by 1972. Even so, the conflict in Southeast Asia was not completely forgotten. During and after the Vietnam war, the Army rigorously examined its performance and its role within the broader context of American foreign policy. Army studies concluded after the war that many of its initial plans and assumptions required change and application of new concepts. The Army did put into practice many new ideas during the Vietnam war and, arguably, gained some measure of success. For example, the precepts of unified military and civilian effort and command, careful attention to cultural issues, the need for conventional military missions and stability and support operations to complement one another, and the close cooperation with the host-nation government became guiding principles during the conflict. The length and changing nature of the war had given the Army (and other US Government agencies) time to learn and put into practice those lessons.

While the US Army had shown a growing competence in its conduct of a variety of stability and support operations, the ultimate American defeat in Vietnam combined with a lack of domestic support for the war led many American Soldiers to reassess the Army's role in conflicts like the Vietnam war. Some Army leaders would conclude after the war that the Army needed to reassert its primary role of conventional warfighting. As a later section of this chapter will illustrate, this change in attitude would have a profound effect on Army doctrine, education, and training.

Recent Military Operations Other Than War, 1989–2000

By the end of the Cold War, the US Army as an institution had built a strong legacy in the conduct of MOOTW. Relatively few Soldiers who entered Iraq in 2003, however, had been participants in these Cold War operations. Instead, if these Soldiers had any practice conducting nonconventional missions, they earned it in the last decade of the 20th century. This section briefly examines the US Army's experience with stability and support operations since 1991. These missions took American Soldiers to Panama, Somalia, Haiti, Bosnia, and Kosovo; the experiences in these countries significantly influenced the Army's understanding of and preparation for stability and support operations in Iraq.

The first of these missions was the brief but complex campaign in 1989 that ousted Panama's authoritarian leader Manuel Noriega from power. The US military's actions in Panama, called Operation JUST CAUSE, included both a decisive operations phase that featured combat missions and a transition phase in which US forces conducted humanitarian assistance and other stability and support operations. A joint US force that included the 193d Infantry Brigade, elements of the 82d Airborne Division, the 7th Infantry Division, and the 75th Ranger Regiment went into combat against the Panama Defense Forces (PDF) and Noriega's paramilitary organizations. Within 2 weeks Noriega and the PDF had surrendered to US forces.

The overthrow of the Noriega regime, however, did not end the operation. While the decisive phase had been successful, parts of Panama suffered through a period of looting and general lawlessness in the wake of the collapse of the Noriega government. The looting alone is estimated to have cost the Panamanian economy close to a billion dollars.[23] American Soldiers did transition to the next phase, restoring order and conducting stability and support operations, but most had not been trained for these missions before the invasion.[24]

The shortcomings in the planning for posthostilities operations in Panama resulted from the US Army's historical emphasis on conventional combat operations and lack of focus on what followed combat in campaigns such as Operation JUST CAUSE. The staff of US Southern Command (SOUTHCOM), the joint headquarters responsible for the planning, devoted few resources to developing a detailed concept for that final phase of the campaign, and when the overall plan for JUST CAUSE changed in the fall of 1989, the new commander, General Maxwell Thurman, focused solely on combat operations.[25] In the period leading up to the US intervention, Thurman never received a briefing on the plan for stability and support operations.[26]

When it came time for US forces to execute Thurman's plan for Operation JUST CAUSE, most tactical commanders understood their objectives in the combat portion of the operation; yet, few knew what their roles and tasks were after the combat ended and had not trained for the missions they were expected to accomplish. Perhaps the most glaring problems caused by SOUTHCOM's lack of attention to the planning were the shortages of military police, CA, and other specialized units in Panama that are critical to the posthostilities phase of a campaign. SOUTHCOM's poor planning for CA operations, for example, appears now to have caused some disarray in the early attempts to establish a new Panamanian government.[27] To be sure, American forces in Operation JUST CAUSE achieved the great majority of their operational objectives. But, because of the tendencies of commanders and planners to focus on conventional combat operations, the posthostilities phase did not go as smoothly as the Army desired. The lack of planning for this critical phase of Operation JUST CAUSE was indicative of the deeply-held biases within the Army—attitudes that would persist and play a role in the planning for OIF.

The US military conducted its next major MOOTW in the Horn of Africa. By 1992 the country of Somalia was in a crisis with much of its population suffering from years of violence, political instability, and food shortages. The United Nations (UN) decided to intervene with humanitarian aid, hoping to cultivate a peace that could lead to a new, stable, and legitimate government. US forces, including thousands of Soldiers from the 10th Mountain Division (10th MTN), deployed to provide security for the UN organizations arriving in Somalia to distribute food. However, US military leaders quickly broadened the parameters of what became known as Operation RESTORE HOPE. In early 1993 US Army units were involved in the training of Somali police and civic action projects, such as resettling civilian groups and fostering local political institutions, in addition to the security mission.[28] When Somali militias began to threaten the success of these efforts, US Army units expanded security operations to include the conduct of counterinsurgency operations against key warlords. In October 1993, after the attempt to seize the militia leader Mohammed Farah Aideed ended with dozens of American casualties, support for the mission within the US population dropped sharply. Over the next 6 months, the Clinton administration scaled back military operations and US forces departed Somalia in March 1994.

For a short time, "No More Somalias" became a catch phrase within US military circles. The debacle there strengthened previous arguments made by Secretary of Defense Caspar Weinberger in 1984 after the abortive intervention in Lebanon in 1983, and later reinforced by General Colin Powell as Chairman of the Joint Chiefs of Staff in 1990–91, during the prelude to Desert Storm. The so-called Weinberger and Powell doctrines held that US forces should only be committed with overwhelming military force in support of a vital US national interest, with domestic US support, to achieve clearly defined goals, and with a clear exit strategy.

Less than a year later, however, American Soldiers were once again conducting stability and support operations, but this time in a location much closer to home. Political crises in Haiti had led to the creation of a UN-sponsored multinational force whose mission was to conduct a forcible entry into the island nation, stabilize the situation, and create an environment in which democratic institutions could set down roots. When the United States launched Operation

UPHOLD DEMOCRACY in the fall of 1994, an armed invasion became unnecessary after the junta that ruled Haiti decided not to oppose the intervention.[29] The US element in the effort consisted primarily of Marines, US Army Special Operations Forces, and Soldiers of the 10th MTN, many of whom were veterans of Somalia. By the middle of October, two brigades from this division established bases in the urban centers of Haiti and began conducting stability and support operations.

For the next 18 months, US forces created a stable environment with a combination of patrolling, civic-action projects, and campaigns designed to prepare the Haitian population for democratic politics.[30] US Soldiers trained the Haitian police, repaired the electrical infrastructure, inspected health facilities, and assisted governmental ministries in the transition to democracy. Over time, the level of violence among Haitians declined. When the UN took responsibility for the mission in Haiti and replaced most of the American troops in 1995, UPHOLD DEMOCRACY appeared to be a success as the new government prepared for national elections.

Soon after the end of the mission in Haiti, events in the Balkans redirected the attention of American civilian and military policy makers. The multiple crises in the region formerly known as Yugoslavia had been brewing since the late 1980s. By 1995 attempts by the UN, North Atlantic Treaty Organization (NATO), and other international organizations had failed to deter aggression by forces intent on fomenting ethnic strife and redrawing territorial boundaries. This failure—combined with the fact that by 1995 the warring ethnic factions were exhausted militarily—led the Clinton administration to attempt to find a diplomatic solution to the problems in the region. This diplomatic offensive succeeded in gathering the interested parties in Dayton, Ohio, where US representatives facilitated the creation of the General Framework Agreement for Peace (GFAP), an agreement that created a new territorial status quo and forms of protection for the various ethnic groups in the conflict.

Critical to the success of this process was the Clinton administration's commitment to send US ground forces into the region to implement the GFAP. The American operation to enforce the GFAP accords became known as Operation JOINT ENDEAVOR and consisted primarily of the 1st Armored Division (1st AD), which deployed in late 1995 from Germany to Bosnia where its 18,000 Soldiers joined approximately 40,000 peacekeepers from other NATO member states already in the region in a show of overwhelming force. The UN approved the creation of this new entity and christened it the Implementation Force (IFOR). For the next year, American Soldiers in IFOR served as peace enforcers, implementing the GFAP through-out Bosnia. The mission required operations focused on patrolling the zones separating the Serb and Muslim forces and enforcing other aspects of the GFAP. US Army leaders in Bosnia viewed peace enforcement as a tactical mission and were always prepared to use armed force if necessary.

Nevertheless, as the situation calmed, some American units began conducting other types of stability and support operations. One American brigade, for example, initiated efforts that reduced ethnic tension by improving a local market where different groups came together to conduct business.[31] Additional units provided security and other assistance in support of Bosnian national elections in September 1996. By the end of 1996, when IFOR's mission ended, American Soldiers were involved in hundreds of projects that relied far more on negotiating abilities and coordinating nongovernment organizations (NGOs) than on combat skills.[32]

In fact, Army leaders began to emphasize—in unequivocal terms—the importance of solving problems without using the force of arms. For example, Colonel Gregory Fontenot, the commander of the 1st Brigade of the 1st AD, told his troops that the firing of a weapon was equivalent to a tactical defeat.[33]

Despite the success of the multinational force in Bosnia, the region was still not politically stable when IFOR's mandate ended in December 1996. The UN renewed the charter of the mission, renaming the effort Stabilization Force (SFOR). Building on IFOR's success, SFOR would prevent the outbreak of hostilities between the ethnic groups, create a peaceful environment and, within means, provide assistance to civilian organizations involved in stabilizing Bosnia. The US Army continued to play a major role in Bosnia, but its commitment to SFOR dropped to 10,500 Soldiers when elements of the 1st Infantry Division (1st ID) replaced 1st AD in November 1996. Reductions continued after 1996 as SFOR made greater strides in establishing stability.

In 1998 the Clinton administration renamed the US effort in Bosnia Operation JOINT FORGE and made the US commitment to SFOR semipermanent. The American presence would remain in Bosnia even as the number of troops dwindled. In 1999 that number dropped to 4,000, and 5 years later fewer than 1,000 American troops remained in the multinational force in Bosnia.[34] More important than the numbers is that during Operation JOINT FORGE a large number of Active, National Guard, and Reserve units rotated through Bosnia on 6- or 12-month tours. The thousands of Soldiers that were part of JOINT FORGE gained experience in the conduct of a wide array of stability and support operations while they maintained the peace so that the people of Bosnia could recover from years of war.

Unfortunately, SFOR's success did not lead to the end of ethnic conflict in the Balkans. In 1998 the President of Serbia, Slobodan Milosevic, began a campaign to suppress and expel the Kosovars, the people of Albanian origin living in the Serbian province of Kosovo. To ensure that Milosevic did not succeed in violently "cleansing" Kosovo of this ethnic group, NATO intervened, first with diplomacy and then with an air campaign that in 1999 forced the Serbian Government to accept the deployment of a multinational peacekeeping force to Kosovo.

NATO built this new force, called Kosovo forces (KFOR), around the reinforced 2d Brigade of the 1st ID.[35] Taking up positions in the eastern region of Kosovo, the 7,000 US Soldiers of KFOR began peace-enforcement operations designed to ensure that all Serb military forces left the province, and to prevent new ethnic hostilities from erupting. In the first 18 months of the mission, the US command in Kosovo supported these imperatives with patrolling and other security-oriented operations. However, after the first year NATO began shifting the focus of the mission to the establishment of a stable political and social environment that would allow for the return of Kosovars who had fled the province or had been forced out by Serbian soldiers. The American brigades that began rotating through Kosovo for 6-month periods after 1999 adjusted to this new objective by providing logistical assistance for elections, forming and training the new police force (the Kosovo Protection Corps), and even conducting minor civic-action projects such as road repairs and the construction of sidewalks and bus shelters.[36]

Like the NATO presence in Bosnia, KFOR has become a semipermanent force. While the US Army still serves as a major component of KFOR, operations in Iraq and Afghanistan have taken priority over the peacekeeping effort in Kosovo. With OIF and Operation ENDURING FREEDOM (OEF) placing great demands on Active Duty units, the American commitment to

KFOR has shifted to the US Army Reserve and the National Guard. Since 2003 four brigades from the Reserve Component have provided the American manpower for KFOR.

The Army's experience in Haiti, Bosnia, and Kosovo between 1994 and 2003 demonstrated an undeniable capacity to succeed in MOOTW. This growing skill, coming so soon after the overwhelming victory in 1991 against Iraq, demonstrated the Army's flexibility in conducing different types of campaigns. It is important to note that, with the exception of Somalia in 1993, these operations were relatively peaceful. Looking back, some analysts have tried to understand the factors that led to American successes in these campaigns and many have focused on the issue of troop density—the ratio of troops to inhabitants—as a critical determinant in missions such as peacekeeping in the Balkans. At its peak strength under the IFOR in 1996, NATO deployed 15 soldiers per every 1,000 Bosnian inhabitants. In 1999 NATO deployed just over 21 soldiers per inhabitant when it occupied Kosovo with KFOR. In comparison, both of these figures exceeded the troop-density figures for the occupations of Germany and Japan after the end of World War II. The KFOR figure nearly matches the troop-density ratio of 24.7 troops per 1,000 inhabitants employed by the British at the peak of their victorious counterinsurgency campaign in Malaya from 1948 to 1956.[37] US and NATO accomplishments in the Balkans in the 1990s seem to owe some credit to the idea articulated in the Weinberger and Powell doctrines that overwhelming force is critical in military operations of all kinds.

As successful as these missions were, in neither Bosnia nor Kosovo did the population—or a segment of the population—significantly challenge the authority or objectives of the US Army. Certainly no insurgency ever formed in these situations to challenge Army operations and the legitimacy of the US mission. Thus, the Army's growing experience with MOOTW in the 1990s did not include counterinsurgency operations or major counterterrorism missions.

Doctrine, Training, and Education

Unfortunately, the US Army's experience with stability and support operations in the Balkans, Haiti, Somalia, and numerous other locations did not lead American Soldiers to internalize these types of operations as a core mission. As stated earlier, US Soldiers tended to view conventional warfighting as their main purpose, and the Army has traditionally reinforced that mindset. Some observers, both within and outside the Army, characterize this tendency as troubling and believe it explains why the Army sometimes had difficulties transitioning to these types of operations.[38] John D. Waghelstein, a US Army veteran of stability and support operations in Vietnam and El Salvador, contends that the Army has been "institutionally preoccupied with the 'big war'" and has shown "habitual disdain for studying 'little war' requirements."[39] He attributes this weakness to a permanent institutional mentality rather than the product of experience and careful analysis, writing, "There is something in the Army's DNA that historically precludes it from preparing itself for the problems of insurgency."[40]

In reality, how the Army as an institution makes decisions about its role and the corresponding nature of its doctrine is complex. The Army does not develop its doctrine in a vacuum based solely on its own understanding of its mission or its own whims. Instead, doctrine is based on federal law, guidance received from the National Security Strategy and the National Military Strategy of the United States, Joint Doctrine, and other forms of strategic and budgetary guidance from the DOD. Obviously, the Army brings to the process its own historical, cultural, and institutional views of what it can and ought to do. Among those is the belief that victory in a conventional war is a matter of national survival and, therefore, the primary purpose of the

Army. In the 20th century, the US Army has had a unique international role as the guarantor of freedom for the United States and its allies as a result of its conventional military prowess. Both are good and sound reasons for focusing on conventional conflict.

While Waghelstein and other observers have carefully documented the US Army's preference for viewing itself as an institution that fights conventional wars, it is incorrect to state that American Soldiers have historically ignored stability and support operations, failed to provide doctrine for these types of operations, or been unwilling to train for them. Indeed, the US Army's attitude toward stability and support operations has been complex, ambivalent, and subject to change based on a myriad of external factors, such as the development of technology, national military strategic goals, and the evolution of the geopolitical landscape.

The Army's doctrine for stability and support operations has evolved over time, and these changes have influenced the preparation of Soldiers in Army education and training institutions. Within the US Army, the term "doctrine" is defined as "the concise expression of how Army forces contribute to unified action in campaigns, major operations, battles and engagements . . . [and] also describes the Army's approach and contribution to full spectrum operations on land. Army doctrine is authoritative, but not prescriptive."[41] Traditionally, field regulations, textbooks used in Army schools, and other official guidance made up the body of works recognized by most Soldiers as their doctrine. However, this set of guidelines was rarely static and never became the sole source for directions on how to conduct operations. In fact, informal guidelines—developed by individuals and units based on their experiences—often played a significant role in how the Army operated. Still, written doctrine carried with it the official sanction of the institution, and greatly influenced how the Army used resources, designed school curriculums, and established training programs.

Historically speaking, formal doctrine for stability and support operations is a recent phenomenon. Despite the fact that the US Army has conducted stability and support operations since its inception, doctrine for these operations was a rarity until the middle of the 20th century.[42] Instead of using written guidance, Soldiers tended to pass on the accumulated wisdom derived from campaigns on the Western frontier and in other theaters in informal ways. As historian Andrew Birtle has shown, the American Army often relied on a unit's older, more experienced Soldiers to teach the younger members how to mount counterinsurgency operations or civic-assistance efforts.[43]

Formal doctrine for stability and support operations would not emerge until World War II. As the US Army began preparing for peacekeeping and occupation duties in Germany, Japan, and other liberated countries, Army officials began to set down the principles and methods required for success in these types of missions. The basic doctrinal guidelines appeared in 1943 in FM 27-5, *United States Army and Navy Manual of Military Government and Civil Affairs*. This single manual served as the doctrine for nonconventional operations until the outbreak of Communist-led insurgencies in the first decade of the Cold War led the Kennedy administration to push the American military establishment, especially the Army, to adopt counterinsurgency operations as one of its most important missions.[44] This change signaled less of a turning away from conventional warfighting than a realization by the Army that it must react to the realities of new strategic objectives and challenges in a reconstructed geopolitical environment.

The recognition of counterinsurgency as a core mission had a major impact on US Army doctrine. In the 1962 version of the Army's keystone manual, FM 100-5, *Field Service*

Regulations–Operations, doctrine writers directly addressed nonconventional operations for the first time with chapters devoted to "Unconventional Warfare," "Military Operations against Irregular Forces," and "Situations Short of War."[45] Two years later, the Army expanded its guidelines on these types of missions by publishing FM 100-20, *Field Service Regulations–Counterinsurgency*. The next major statement of the Army's general direction and objectives came in 1968, at the height of US involvement in Vietnam, and reflected the Army's focus on operations in that country. This new doctrinal manual, FM 100-5, *Operations of Army Forces in the Field*, included an expanded section on unconventional warfare and introduced guidelines on how to conduct "Cold War Operations" and "Stability and Support Operations," the Army's newest term for counterinsurgency and related missions.[46] More detailed manuals such as FM 31-23, *Stability Operations*, and FM 31-73, *Advisor Handbook for Stability Operations*, both of which were unprecedented when published in 1967, further documented the shift in the Army's general doctrinal outlook and its commitment to nonconventional operations.

This commitment weakened dramatically as the Vietnam conflict came to a close in the early 1970s. In doctrinal terms, the first hint of this change in attitude emerged in the 1972 version of FM 31-23, *Stability Operations*, that stated the Army's role in these missions should be "primarily advisory," and warned American Soldiers to avoid becoming heavily involved in the politics and civilian institutions of the countries where these operations were conducted.[47] By 1976 the Army had completed its retreat from stability and support operations by publishing a new version of its capstone manual, FM 100-5, *Operations*, which focused exclusively on fighting conventional battles in Europe. While this manual emerged just 3 years after the end of the US involvement in Vietnam, it contained no mention of irregular forces, counterinsurgency, unconventional warfare, or stability and support operations. The Army's focus clearly reflected the nation's focus on the overwhelming Soviet military threat to US and NATO interests. For the next 15 years, the Army continued to emphasize its primary mission as high-intensity combat. Army doctrine reflected this core mission with little attention paid to unconventional operations.[48]

The demise of the Soviet Union and the Warsaw Pact in 1991 dramatically altered global international relations and consequently caused a reexamination of US security policy. Naturally, the end of the Soviet threat and the emergence of new threats significantly disrupted how the US Army viewed its purpose. With the dissolution of its main conventional adversary, the Army began to recast its role in American security policy. The most significant change in Army doctrine after 1991 was the reemergence of stability and support operations as missions the Army might have to perform in the post-Cold War era. The 1993 version of FM 100-5 devoted an entire chapter to operations other than war, a term that included humanitarian assistance, peacekeeping operations, and support for counterinsurgency.[49] Doctrine writers then gave greater structure to the Army's understanding and conduct of these operations in manuals such as FM 100-23, *Peace Operations*, published in 1994.

Less formal doctrine concerning stability and support operations appeared in the 1990s in a variety of formats and supplemented the Army's official guidelines for these missions. These works often resulted from after-action reviews or similar reports produced by units that served in Somalia, Haiti, or the Balkans. A good example of this supplemental doctrine is the handbook created in 1998 by the 2d Battalion, 5th Cavalry Regiment of the 1st Cavalry Division (1st CAV) for the unit's rotation to Bosnia as part of SFOR. Titled simply *Peace Support Operations*, the book offered great detail on how to conduct a wide array of tasks, from patrolling and vehicle searches at checkpoints to giving interviews to media representatives.[50] The Army published this document and many others on the official Center for Army Lessons Learned (CALL) Web site, a database that offered Soldiers worldwide access for use in preparation for and conduct of stability and support operations.

The experiences of the 1st CAV and the other units conducting stability and support operations between 1993 and 2001 contributed to the publication of two important doctrinal works that established the Army's thinking about these missions at the beginning of the 21st century. As described in the introduction to this study, the 2001 edition of the Army's capstone manual, FM 3-0, *Operations,* stated unequivocally that, because of the new post-Cold War geopolitical setting, American Soldiers had to be prepared to conduct a variety of missions along what it called "the full spectrum of operations." This spectrum certainly included major combat operations. In fact, FM 3-0 reinforced the Army's preeminent purpose as "fighting and winning the nation's wars." In addition, the full spectrum also encompassed stability and support operations. In support of this concept, FM 3-0 devoted two chapters to the discussion of how the Army approached stability and support operations. More definitive, however, was the publication of FM 3-07, *Stability Operations and Support Operations*, in February 2003. Issued just 1 month before the beginning of OIF, this manual became the Army's most comprehensive statement about stability and support operations since the end of the Vietnam war. Arriving after the terrorist attacks of 9/11 and the start of the US campaign in Afghanistan, FM 3-07 reasserted that the geopolitical environment of the 21st century would demand that the US military have the capacity to conduct stability and support operations and that "Army capabilities are often the best choice to meet the requirement" of this new strategic environment.[51] The new doctrine addressed general planning principles and offered guidance on a variety of stability missions such as peacekeeping, counterinsurgency, counterdrug, and counterterrorism operations.

The US Army that entered Iraq in March 2003 accepted stability and support operations as operational requirements, and could even refer to published doctrine that established a formal approach to those operations. However, doctrine has limited influence if it is not disseminated and practiced through the means of education and training. To determine how well the Army prepared its Soldiers to conduct stability and support operations, one must examine the historical place of this subject within the curriculum of the US Army school and training systems. Not surprisingly, the last four decades have shown that the classroom and training resources assigned to the subject of stability and support operations depended directly on how Army doctrine portrayed these missions and on the Army's operational requirements at the time.

The best starting point for this survey is the late 1950s. Before the middle of the 20th century, the Army did offer a limited amount of instruction on stability and support operations, but it was confined primarily to schools such as Fort Leavenworth's Command and General Staff College (CGSC), which served the officer corps.[52] As counterinsurgency evolved into one of the Army's main missions and as Vietnam heated up, formal preparation for stability and support operations in general expanded within the school and training system. By 1966 the Army had developed several courses that focused solely on counterinsurgency operations and, perhaps more importantly, had integrated counterinsurgency lessons into the curriculums of Reserve Officer Training Corps (ROTC) units, the United States Military Academy at West Point, and officer schools at all levels. Similar efforts added primary lessons on counterinsurgency to the program of instruction for recruits at basic training. The Army also mandated that maneuver units add counterinsurgency operations to their yearly training calendar. Following this guidance, many divisions held full-scale exercises, often in civilian areas near military posts where they could practice civic assistance, negotiation skills, and other counterinsurgency tasks.[53]

While never eclipsing instruction on conventional operations, this emphasis on stability and support operations in the Army's education and training systems remained prominent throughout the Vietnam years. In the wake of the Vietnam war, doctrine turned decisively away from stability and support operations, and the Army began reducing the amount of resources committed to the teaching and training of counterinsurgency operations.[54] By 1979, for example, the US Army Infantry School at Fort Benning had completely eliminated counterinsurgency from its curriculum for junior officers. Field grade officers who attended CGSC that same year only received 8 hours of instruction on stability and support operations over the entire 10-month course.[55] In line with the nation's general aversion to unconventional conflict and its focus on the Soviet military threat, the Army's education system maintained its emphasis on conventional warfighting skills and operations well into the 1990s.

After victory in the Cold War, the Army began to broaden its training focus to include stability and support operations. In the 1990s, the Joint Readiness Training Center (JRTC), located at Fort Polk, Louisiana, became the Army's premier site for the training of nonmechanized units. Each year 10 brigades (each consisting of approximately 3,500 Soldiers) from the Army's Light Infantry, Airborne, Air Assault, and Special Forces units deployed to JRTC to improve their skills in conducting a range of missions that included stability and support operations and conventional combat. Typical rotations to the training center forced combat maneuver units to engage actors who played the roles of civilian refugees, members of NGOs and the media, insurgents, and terrorists.[56] Soldiers learned to deal with problems posed by these civilian players by employing CA teams and human intelligence (HUMINT) collectors to negotiate with civilians, providing civic assistance, and developing sources of information that could help prevent attacks on US troops in the exercise. The training scenarios punished the units that performed these operations poorly by allowing mock terrorists to attack US forces. Those units that conducted these missions well avoided the debilitating terrorist assaults.

Beginning in 1997 the Army expanded its training for stability and support operations in response to the real demands of Bosnia and Kosovo. JRTC and the US Army Combat Maneuver Training Center (CMTC), located in Hohenfels, Germany, became sites that provided tailored training for units preparing to deploy to the Balkans. These units participated in structured mission-rehearsal and mission-readiness exercises that placed Soldiers in terrain and situations closely resembling what they would encounter in Bosnia and later in Kosovo.[57] The training area included mock villages populated by specific political, religious, and ethnic groups. JRTC and CMTC also placed NGOs in the training areas and created scenarios in which units had to coordinate with these organizations, negotiate with village leaders, support civic-assistance missions, and conduct more routine peacekeeping missions such as convoy operations and force-protection activities.

While not all of the Army's units attended the JRTC or the CMTC to prepare for stability and support operations, by the end of the 1990s the Army had developed doctrine, education, and training for these missions. This effort, combined with the individual and collective experience gained in conducting actual stability and support operations during the 1990s, created a solid base of practice and theory. There were, of course, major gaps in the Army's preparation for stability and support operations. Doctrinal guidelines for these operations were not perfect or comprehensive. For example, few units had conducted counterinsurgency operations since the Vietnam war, and until 2003 the Army committed relatively few resources to the updating of doctrine or training for counterinsurgency. Overall, the largest practical shortcoming was that despite the training and doctrine, individual and unit experience with stability and support operations across the Army was uneven at best.

Soldiering in Stability and Support Operations: The Legacy of 1991–2002

When full spectrum operations in Iraq began in earnest, the US Army could and did make use of the real base of experience with stability and support operations that had coalesced within its ranks. Colonel Joseph Anderson, the commander of the 2d Brigade, 101st Airborne Division (101st ABN) in 2003, emphasized the importance of this knowledge base saying that when it came time to conduct stability and support operations in the city of Mosul, he relied on "pure experience."[58] Describing his brigade's missions to stabilize Mosul in 2003, Anderson added that he "did the same in Panama; did the same in Kosovo; did a little bit in Haiti; and now [in Iraq]."[59] For Anderson, success in stability and support operations in Iraq depended partly on "trial and error, and a lot of instinct."[60] However, he added, "The more experience you had coming into this thing, the better off you were going to be. And that could include from the training centers or anywhere else, but that's what was going to give you the background to do the job."[61]

The Army's experiences in Somalia and Haiti, and its ongoing rotations in Bosnia and Kosovo, created a core group of officers and noncommissioned officers (NCOs) like Anderson with experience in conducting various types of stability and support operations. Indeed, by the end of 2002, tens of thousands of American Soldiers had participated in either SFOR or KFOR. This fact is important to the understanding of the US Army's approach to operations in Iraq after May 2003. While not all of the Soldiers in OIF had served in Bosnia or Kosovo, many of the senior leaders in Iraq had deployed to the region. For example, both Lieutenant General Ricardo Sanchez, the commander of Combined Joint Task Force–7 (CJTF-7), and Major General David H. Petraeus, commander of the 101st ABN, had served in the Balkans. Sanchez felt his experiences with peacekeeping in Kosovo as well as supervising US counterdrug operations in Central and South America provided him useful experience in joint, interagency, and Coalition operations.[62] Petraeus stated that his time in Bosnia, combined with his earlier experience with counterinsurgency and reconstruction in Latin America and Haiti, helped him considerably when it came time to conduct operations in Iraq after the fall of Saddam.[63] Often, experience in Bosnia and Kosovo played a direct role in how commanders and staffs understood and planned stability and support operations in Iraq. For example, in 2004 when Multi-National Force–Iraq (MNF-I) began planning elections for Iraq's National Assembly, the task force purposely used IFOR's involvement in the 1996 Bosnian elections as a case study to help them understand how to assist the Iraqis in the electoral process.[64] The words of Major General Thomas Miller, who served as the chief of operations (CJ3) for CJTF-7, sum up the benefits of having previously conducted stability and support operations. Crediting his time in Somalia and Haiti as the best preparation for his duties during OIF, Miller stated, "It was the general experience of dealing with uncertainty and having to develop consensus in working with the interagency activities, etc., that [helped me most] once I got to Iraq."[65]

Perhaps more important than the experience of the senior commanders and staff were the experiences many of the NCOs and officers who led small units in Iraq had conducting stability and support operations in Bosnia or Kosovo. This shared experience assisted units to transition to the new campaign after May 2003. For example, Major General Buford C. Blount III, commander of the 3d Infantry Division (3d ID) in Iraq, strongly believed that his Soldiers' experience in the Balkans gave them a great deal of preparation for the shift to full spectrum operations after major combat operations ended in April 2003. Blount stated that his units conducted basic postinvasion operations on arrival in Baghdad because "most of my guys had been in Bosnia and Kosovo and had done the peacekeeping mission, so they knew how to do that."[66] Other officers in 3d ID echoed Blount's thoughts about the Army's previous experience with stability and support operations. Major Darryl Rupp, an intelligence officer who served in 3d ID's Division Artillery, describes how he had been impressed by "how quickly the team, squad, and platoon-level Soldiers transitioned from combat operations to stability and support operations."[67] Rupp attributed the 3d ID's success to his unit's experience in Bosnia:

> They had done that mission [SFOR] and they knew what it meant to do a 'presence patrol,' . . . They knew what it was to go in and do a bilateral meeting with a councilman or a tribal leader. Even from the lowest levels, from company and platoon on down, those guys were great and the transition was incredible. You could see it, from one day to the next, the change of the information that was being reported.[68]

Numerous Soldiers from a variety of units offered similar explanations of how previous deployments to the Balkans improved their ability to conduct stability and support operations in Iraq. Chief Warrant Officer Bryan Gray, an intelligence specialist who served with the 10th MTN in Kosovo, gained significant experience during his KFOR deployment in the gathering and analysis of HUMINT, a form of information that is critically important to stability and support operations. Gray then deployed to Iraq with the 4th Infantry Division (4th ID) in 2003 and used the HUMINT skills he developed in Kosovo to help locate and capture Saddam Hussein in December of that year.[69]

Gray's time in Kosovo and the experience of several other Soldiers in the Balkans assisted many units with the shift to postconflict operations. However, as Anderson implied earlier in this chapter, not all American Soldiers and US Army units in OIF had the same amount of familiarity with stability and support operations. The Army's uneven experience with postconflict operations, combined with a lack of detailed planning and training for those missions, ultimately made the transition from decisive combat operations during the invasion of Iraq to full spectrum operations much more difficult.

Planning for Stability and Support Operations in Operation IRAQI FREEDOM

As the previous section has shown, the US Army entered Iraq in March 2003 with a significant amount of experience in the conduct of stability and support operations. To understand how the Army employed this base of knowledge to prepare for full spectrum operations in Iraq, it is important to examine how the Army's legacy with stability and support operations affected its general approach to planning large-scale campaigns like OIF. The term "stability and support operations" had two meanings in 2003. First, stability and support operations were included within the category of MOOTW on the spectrum of conflict. These included such operations as humanitarian assistance, military training exercises, peace operations, and foreign internal defense which could include counterinsurgency. In this meaning of the term, stability and support operations were a type of action, campaign, or conflict that was less violent and intense than full-scale conventional or major theater war against a nation-state.

But stability and support operations were also defined as those specific military tasks that were not strictly offensive or defensive combat actions directed against enemy forces. In this meaning, stability and support operations could be performed at any time in any type of conflict whenever military units took nonlethal action to support their overall objectives. Guarding key infrastructure, providing aid to civilians, and supporting indigenous governing bodies are examples of these types of tasks.[70] In common practice, most Soldiers conflated these two definitions and used the term "stability and support operations" to refer both to conflicts that did not include combat against a conventional enemy force and to describe all noncombat military actions in a conflict.

Many Soldiers gave the term a third meaning when combining it with campaign planning. In 2002 and 2003 military planners divided campaigns into four phases: Phase I—Deter/Engage, Phase II—Seize the Initiative, Phase III—Decisive Operations, and Phase IV—Transition. Phase IV (PH IV) is critical to military campaigns because it is during this period that military success is used to finalize the achievement of the national goals that serve as the overall objectives of the campaigns. This meant that PH IV often focused on the establishment of law and order, economic reconstruction and civilian self-government, and the redeployment of most or all military forces out of the area of operations.[71] Unfortunately, many Soldiers used the terms "stability and support operations," "postconflict operations," and "PH IV operations" synonymously. This practice created the incorrect belief that stability and support operations took place only after major offensive or defensive combat had ended, and that full spectrum operations meant the sequential use instead of the simultaneous use of offense, defense, and stability and support operations during a campaign. This misunderstanding has also led to the mistaken belief that stability and support operations were somehow less difficult and required less planning and preparation. These ambiguities and assumptions affected how military planners thought about the design and conduct of OIF.[†]

Despite the importance of PH IV in successfully achieving the strategic objectives of a military campaign, the Army and the US military's tendency in general has been to spend the lion's share of its resources on the first three phases of a campaign. In the past, this inclination has had two related and detrimental consequences for the planning of PH IV. First, planners have often lacked the time and personnel to focus on the final phase of the campaign and thus left it undeveloped; and second, because of the understandable emphasis on combat operations, campaign planners, like those that designed Operation JUST CAUSE, allowed PH IV plans to develop in isolation, thus hindering the establishment of critical linkages and smooth transitions between combat and postcombat operations.[72]

[†]The 2008 version of FM 3-0 has removed this confusion and stability and support operations now refer only to military tasks designed to establish a safe and secure environment in support of a host-nation government or as part of an occupation. Stability and support operations are no longer a type of operation in the spectrum of conflict.

When preparations began for an invasion of Iraq in the fall of 2001, the US military based its operations on a plan known as Concept Plan (CONPLAN) 1003. This plan was the result of years of work at US Central Command (CENTCOM), the joint headquarters responsible for military policy and operations in the Middle East. On 27 November 2001 Secretary of Defense Donald Rumsfeld directed CENTCOM commander General Tommy Franks and his staff to develop a plan to remove the Saddam regime from power in Iraq. Franks first discussed the plans with President George W. Bush on 28 December 2001, and he and his staff immediately began reviewing the existing war plan for operations against Iraq that had been written in 1998.[73] Over the course of 2002, Franks directed a major recasting of these plans. Many of these changes resulted from concerns of both the Secretary of Defense and General Franks that the 1998 plan did not reflect either the US military's new capabilities or the reduced capabilities of Iraq's Army after a decade of sanctions.[74]

Specifically, the CENTCOM commander viewed the earlier plan as too unwieldy and inflexible in its demands for approximately 380,000 troops that would require months to deploy into theater and prepare for combat.[75] Franks sought to reduce the size of the force required for operations against Saddam's regime and to take advantage of new special operations forces (SOF) and precision-strike capabilities, which offered the CENTCOM commander speed and firepower. These capabilities allowed Franks to insert flexibility into the plan through the provision for a "running start," the initiation of major combat operations as soon as the requisite force package required for the beginning of combat arrived and was prepared to enter Iraq. The running start concept meant that other forces would continue to flow into the theater, but they would do so after combat began. Franks described the running start in the following way:

> We don't know what the force needs to look like for Phase IV, so we can't and we won't design a force of 250,000 or 350,000 people. What we will do is we will begin to move forces into the region and when we reach the point where that force is sufficient to remove Saddam Hussein, we will just start running. So it took on the name 'running start.'[76]

With this option, Franks could seize and retain the initiative. Further, the concept would allow conditions on the ground, rather than the schedule in the plan, to dictate when CENTCOM began combat operations.

Franks participated in numerous discussions with the President and his top advisors about modifying the original CONPLAN 1003. The CENTCOM commander described those sessions as an open, iterative process in which the President ended each session with the same question, "Well, are you satisfied with the plan now?"[77] While he and his staff refined the plan during the course of 2002, Franks' answer to the President's queries was "No." In January 2003 he was finally able to tell President Bush that the revised plan met his concept and requirements and that the plan now reflected his personal vision for the operation. According to Franks, at no time did the DOD or any other authority force any parts of the plan on him or CENTCOM over his opposition or that of the Armed Services.[78]

The plan that Franks and CENTCOM ultimately finalized in January 2003 was built around the so-called "hybrid" option, which combined the flexibility of the running start concept with a more traditional approach that planners labeled "generated start." The hybrid 1003V brought approximately 210,000 troops into the Iraqi theater, but CENTCOM built in enough flexibility to allow Franks to begin operations before this entire force was on the ground. The concepts behind the plan—a reliance on speed and air power, smaller and more agile forces, a rapid deployment without long buildups, as well as the desire to avoid lengthy and costly occupations like those in the Balkans—were all ideas debated since DESERT STORM by officials and critics in and outside of the US military. The rapid defeat of the Taliban regime in Afghanistan in 2001 by only a token US ground force lent some measure of credibility to those concepts.

The plan called for a two-pronged invasion of Iraq—from Kuwait in the south and from Turkey to the north. Franks envisioned a rapid assault that would quickly reach the heart of Saddam's regime in Baghdad. After the war, however, Franks stated that as early as January 2003 he knew the Turks would never allow 4th ID to invade Iraq from their territory. He kept the division in the Mediterranean until after the ground invasion began to deceive the Iraqis and tie down their forces.[79]

Not everyone favored Franks' ideas that formed the core of CONPLAN 1003V. Secretary of State Colin Powell told the CENTCOM commander at a September 2002 Camp David meeting that he thought too few troops were envisioned in the plan.[80] Powell disagreed with Franks' belief that a lightning strike toward Baghdad could succeed and that it was impossible to anticipate the number of troops needed in Iraq after Saddam was toppled. Others such as the V Corps staff and the Service Chiefs expressed their concerns and offered advice during the development of the plan throughout 2002.[81] Franks, nevertheless, was determined to prevent voices from outside the joint chain of command from injecting what he considered to be parochial issues into his plan. In his recollections of the planning process, Franks variously described the Service Chiefs during this period as "Title X bean-counters," "narrow-minded," and as "fighting for turf" to maintain their "end-strength and weapons systems," along with other, more colorful names.[82]

The credibility of the Joint Chiefs and others who had argued for more robust force levels had been significantly weakened during the planning and execution of operations in Afghanistan.[83] The controversy over Army Chief of Staff General Eric K. Shinseki's 25 February 2003 testimony to the Senate Armed Services Committee in which he stated it would take "several hundred thousand" troops to occupy Iraq after Saddam was deposed was the most open example of the professional differences CENTCOM's plans generated among the Services and within the DOD and the administration.

Some observers have claimed, incorrectly, that the Joint Chiefs were opposed to the CENTCOM commander's plans. General John Keane, who, as the Army Vice Chief of Staff attended almost every session in the Pentagon's secure planning room, stated:

> The Joint Chiefs asked questions, but when Phase III, Major Combat Operations [*sic*] went to the President it had the thumbprints of the Joint Chiefs on it, as well as Phase IV. That is another thing that is not fully understood. People attacked it as Rumsfeld's troop list and he kept the size of the force down. It was Tommy's [Franks] plan and the Army supported it. That is the truth of it.[84]

Keane also agreed with Franks' assessment that the US military had become much more effective since 1991 while Saddam's army had become greatly degraded:

> We knew this enemy for 12 years, we knew him cold, we knew what his limitations were, we certainly knew what his vulnerabilities were, we knew that we

had considerably better skill, we knew we had better will, and Tommy thought that he could achieve tactical surprise. The bold part of the plan was the size of the force. The brilliant part of it achieved tactical surprise. . . . I thought both of those were just brilliant pieces of work. He and his people deserve the lion's share of the credit for that.[85]

To many, the 1003V plan was a significant improvement over the original and took advantage of new US capabilities.

CENTCOM's plan designed a campaign around a joint multinational force. Franks delegated the development of the most critical part of 1003V—the ground forces plan—to the US Third Army, which had been designated as CENTCOM's Combined Forces Land Component Command (CFLCC). This joint doctrinal term designated the headquarters that planned and commanded the operations of the US Army, Marine Corps, and Coalition ground formations in the CENTCOM area of responsibility (AOR). In late 2001 CFLCC began work on revising the ground operations portion of 1003V, and by early 2003 its planners had produced four different versions of the plan, the last of which—a version called COBRA II—became the operative plan for the actual campaign on 13 January 2003.[86]

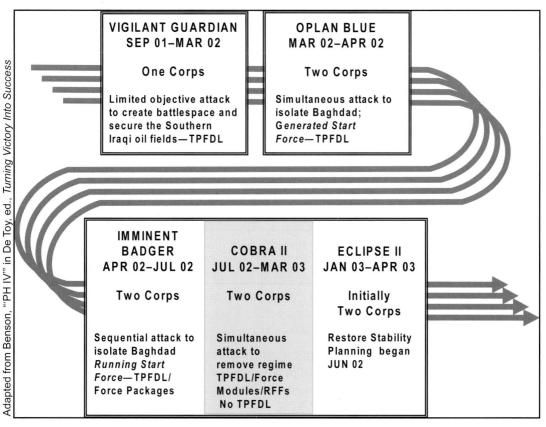

Adapted from Benson, "PH IV'" in De Toy, ed., *Turning Victory Into Success*

VIGILANT GUARDIAN SEP 01–MAR 02 One Corps Limited objective attack to create battlespace and secure the Southern Iraqi oil fields—TPFDL	OPLAN BLUE MAR 02–APR 02 Two Corps Simultaneous attack to isolate Baghdad; *Generated Start Force*—TPFDL

IMMINENT BADGER APR 02–JUL 02 Two Corps Sequential attack to isolate Baghdad *Running Start Force*—TPFDL/ Force Packages	COBRA II JUL 02–MAR 03 Two Corps Simultaneous attack to remove regime TPFDL/Force Modules/RFFs No TPFDL	ECLIPSE II JAN 03–APR 03 Initially Two Corps Restore Stability Planning began JUN 02

Figure 25. Evolution of the CFLCC OPLAN.

The Planning for Phase IV—Operations after Toppling the Saddam Regime

In January 2003 President Bush issued National Security Presidential Directive 24, which formally gave the DOD primacy in the postinvasion effort in Iraq.[87] This directive granted the department authority to assert leadership in the planning for operations after the Saddam regime was toppled. What had emerged in 2002, even before the directive, was a series of planning initiatives at various levels in the DOD that reflected a variety of attitudes and approaches toward the overall concept of American involvement in postinvasion operations. On the level of strategic policy, the DOD's approach to Iraq was significantly shaped by the Bush administration's overall wary attitude toward what was sometimes called nation-building. Bush had taken office in 2001 having campaigned on his dislike for nation-building projects, such as those in the Balkans that had absorbed a great deal of American military resources in the 1990s.[88] For some military theorists at the time, the US Armed Forces existed to fight and win wars and should not have its strength dissipated in missions like SFOR and KFOR.

This stance enforced Secretary Rumsfeld's desire to transform the military into a more agile force that could deploy quickly on a global scale. This vision of a transformed American military implied avoiding commitments to ponderous, troop-heavy, logistics intensive, open-ended, and costly stabilization and reconstruction campaigns. It would be wrong to attach this aversion solely to Rumsfeld or to the Office of the Secretary of Defense. These and other related views about the nature of war in the future and the need for the reinvention of military power were supported by many thinkers in and out of the US Government and the Armed Services in the 1990s. The US Army's much-debated transformation efforts launched by Army Chief of Staff General Shinseki were in some ways an outgrowth of this debate and preceded Rumsfeld's initiatives.

Despite the misgivings about nation-building, the DOD did commit resources to the planning of postinvasion operations. In retrospect, however, the overall effort appears to have been disjointed and, at times, poorly coordinated, perhaps reflecting the department's ambivalence toward nation-building. Within the department, most of the responsibility for the planning would fall on the shoulders of CENTCOM, the combatant command responsible for the overall campaign. And Franks' planners did prepare for operations after the fall of the regime.

Still, given the short time it had to prepare CONPLAN 1003V—and the fact that the command was simultaneously prosecuting the war in Afghanistan—the CENTCOM staff dedicated most of its planning effort to the invasion itself. Also, despite guidance about CENTCOM's role in PH IV of the campaign, Franks did not see postwar Iraq as his long-term responsibility. He later wrote that he expected a huge infusion of civilian experts and other resources to come from the US Government after CENTCOM completed the mission of removing the Saddam regime.[89] Franks' message to the DOD and the Joint Chiefs was, "You pay attention to the day after, and I'll pay attention to the day of."[90]

The Joint Chiefs of Staff, understanding that CENTCOM was focused on winning the conventional portion of the campaign, decided to assist in the planning for PH IV. To do so, in December 2002 the Joint Staff created an organization called Combined Joint Task Force–IV (CJTF-IV) (also designated as CJTF-4) to lead its planning effort for post-Saddam Iraq. Established by Joint Forces Command and headed by Brigadier General Steve Hawkins, CJTF-IV's relationship to CENTCOM and CFLCC remained unspecified, except that it would help design and prepare the joint task force headquarters that would take over PH IV operations from CENTCOM after the removal of the Baathist regime.[91] Though Hawkins' organization completed some initial planning before the war, its work did not influence CFLCC planning and by early April 2003 it slowly disbanded as its personnel drifted off to join other commands in and out of the theater of operations.

Around the same time CJTF-IV began to organize, the Secretary of Defense established his own organization for the civilian portion of the stabilization and reconstruction effort. By the end of January 2003, Rumsfeld had chosen Lieutenant General (Retired) Jay Garner as the head of what became known as the Office of Reconstruction and Humanitarian Assistance (ORHA). Garner earned his reputation as a smart planner in his work with the Iraqi Kurds during Operation PROVIDE COMFORT in the aftermath of DESERT STORM. While Garner and ORHA officially became the DOD lead for postwar planning, staff officers in CJTF-IV, CFLCC, and CENTCOM continued to develop their own PH IV plans. One reason for this lack of coordination was Garner's struggle to create ORHA from the ground up. He had 61 days between the announcement of ORHA's creation and the start of the war to build an organization, develop interagency plans across the administration, coordinate them with CENTCOM and the still undetermined military headquarters that would assume the military lead in post-Saddam Iraq, and deploy his team to the theater. It proved to be an almost impossible set of tasks.

The short period of preparation was not the only problem facing ORHA. Garner was supposed to give his organization an interagency character and, to some degree, he had success. For example, a significant number of officers from the Department of State, including four active ambassadors, would eventually join ORHA before its deployment to Iraq, although many of these diplomats and experts did so at the last minute.[92] However, Garner relied most on Active Duty and retired military officers as the core of an organization that grew to almost 300 staffers by the beginning of March 2003. Because some officials within the DOD opposed creating a full-scale interagency effort within ORHA, Garner was not allowed to accept all of the experts on Iraq offered by the Department of State.[93]

This general friction within the interagency process also prevented some ORHA officials from working with other government agencies to prepare for specific problems in post-Saddam Iraq. For example, Paul Hughes, a retired Army colonel who worked for ORHA, recalled that when he tried to create a political-military concept for PH IV operations and coordinate that plan with agencies outside the DOD, Undersecretary of Defense Douglas Feith rebuffed his attempt to gain interagency input.[94] Former Secretary of State Powell, who led the State Department between 2001 and 2004, has acknowledged that, in his opinion, these attitudes within the DOD hindered the overall planning process for PH IV operations. Powell stated that the Bush administration made the right choice in giving the DOD the lead in planning for post-Saddam Iraq, but the overall effort "would have been better served if [the DOD] had asked for more help from people outside."[95]

In retrospect, the ORHA planning effort appears to have suffered from this lack of interagency support. Garner has written that in January and February 2003 his staff reviewed various studies of post-Saddam Iraq completed by a number of Government agencies and tried to find the resources to achieve the objectives outlined in these works. Based on the findings in these studies, ORHA created its own plan that focused on preparing for the four most likely crises to occur in Iraq after the toppling of the Baathist regime: oil field fires, large numbers of refugees, food shortages, and the outbreak of epidemics.[96] None of these problems would emerge once Baghdad actually fell in April 2003.

Of all the organizations involved in the planning of OIF, CFLCC conducted the largest and most comprehensive effort in preparation for PH IV. COBRA II, CFLCC's plan for OIF, featured two relatively simple concepts: a quick invasion and the rapid ousting of Saddam Hussein. However, according to Lieutenant General William Webster, who served as CFLCC's deputy commanding general in late 2002 and 2003, the finalization of the details that brought these concepts to life consumed the efforts of the command's senior leaders and staffs, making it difficult for planners to commit much energy to PH IV of COBRA II. Webster recalled that policymakers in the Office of the Secretary of Defense made constant changes to the forces allocated for Phase III, modifications that forced the planners at CFLCC to keep their focus on adjusting the plans for Phase II and Phase III.[97] According to Webster, this left little time or energy for PH IV preparation: "Phase IV was always something we were going to get to when we got Phase III well under way and we knew what forces we were going to have available for this fight. Up until right before execution, we were still jacking around with the troops available and, therefore, were back into Phase III."[98] Given these pressures, the CFLCC deputy commander asserted that "there was seriously not anything but a skeleton of Phase IV until very late."[99]

However, in the 18-month planning process that led to COBRA II, the CFLCC planners were always cognizant of the requirement for PH IV operations. COBRA II's mission statement reflected that understanding: "CFLCC attacks to defeat Iraqi forces, to control the zone of action and to secure and exploit designated sites, and removes the current Iraqi regime. *On order, CFLCC conducts post-hostilities stability and support operations* [emphasis added], transitions to CJTF-4."[100] The CFLCC Chief of Plans, Colonel Kevin C.M. Benson, emphasized that this mission statement had remained the same since CFLCC began drafting plans for the land war in 2002.

CFLCC's vision of how the Coalition forces would transition to PH IV operations differed slightly from the one offered by CENTCOM. According to CENTCOM's Operation Plan (OPLAN) 1003V, Phase III, Decisive Offensive Operations, would take 125 days and PH IV would not begin in full until the Coalition completed Phase III.[101] Once PH IV did begin, the CENTCOM planners saw postinvasion operations divided into three subphases. In Phase IVa, CFLCC forces would serve as the lead authority and would focus on creating a stable environment and providing basic humanitarian assistance to the population of Iraq. Once stability was achieved, CFLCC would transition to Phase IVb, transferring its authority to a new combined joint task force and redeploying most of its forces. In this second subphase, the new CJTF and its stability and support operations would fall under the authority of ORHA. Phase IVc would begin only when a new representative Iraqi Government was prepared to accept full responsibility for the country. The Coalition would turn over authority to the Iraqis, maintaining a small number of military units in the country to support the fledgling state.[102]

Once Benson and his planners received the mission and intent statements, they began to develop a list of problems and issues that CFLCC would face once PH IV operations began. The list grew and included major challenges, such as general lawlessness, humanitarian assistance, and assessment of the oil infrastructure. After careful analysis to include wargames that tested US actions in the most likely scenarios of PH IV, Benson concluded that this phase was growing so complex it required its own separate plan. On 20 March 2003, the day Coalition forces crossed into Iraq, Lieutenant General David D. McKiernan approved the creation of a

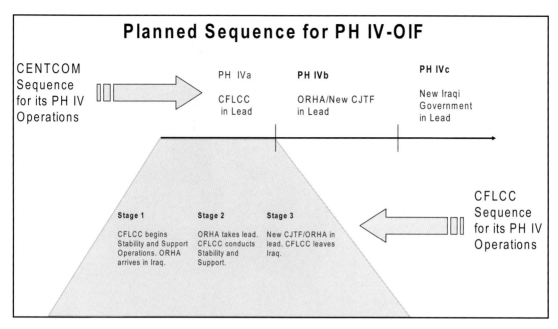

Planned Sequence for PH IV-OIF

Figure 26. CENTCOM/CFLCC phasing for PH IV.

new plan, and Benson's planners began work on what was called ECLIPSE II, after the original Operation ECLIPSE that served as the plan for the occupation of Germany after World War II. This new plan, really a sequel to COBRA II, would be published on 12 April 2003, almost a week after Coalition forces entered Baghdad.[103]

ECLIPSE II added depth to the earlier CFLCC plan by establishing the specific mission statement, assumptions, objectives, and phasing that would govern unit operations once Coalition land forces entered PH IV. In the plan's mission statement, CFLCC clearly stated its intent to conduct stability and support operations to create a secure environment in which the command could transition to the follow-on headquarters, then designated as Combined Joint Task Force–Iraq (CJTF-Iraq).[104] CFLCC assumed that while conducting stability and support operations there would be asymmetric threats to Coalition forces, that other elements of the US Government such as the Departments of Energy and Justice would reinforce the military efforts, that US forces committed to OIF by the 1003V plan would continue to flow into Iraq after major combat operations ceased, that the bulk of the Iraqi Army would be recalled to duty at some point, and that policies and definitions of the end state to the campaign would likely change over time.[105] While the planners did envision a variety of threats to Coalition forces, including sporadic resistance by Saddam loyalists, they did not assess the likelihood of an insurgency as very high.[106]

Based on these assumptions, the CFLCC planners developed a set of objectives for ECLIPSE II. This list included the completion of the Iraqi Army capitulation process, maintenance of law and order, security and destruction of Iraqi weapons of mass destruction sites, detention of terrorists and war criminals, and coordination with NGOs and other agencies for support.[107] To ensure it could achieve its PH IV objectives, Benson and the CFLCC planning staff prepared a troop-to-task analysis, a process that generated a minimum number of forces

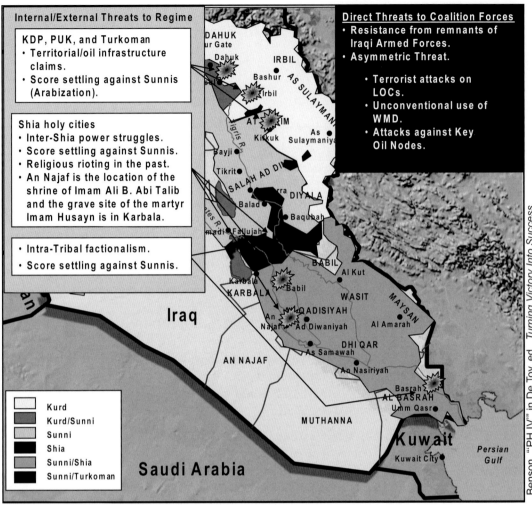

Figure 27. CFLCC/ECLIPSE II assumptions of PH IV flash points and threats to Coalition forces.

required to conduct a set of missions. Envisioning the central mission of Coalition forces in PH IV as constabulary in nature, the planners used information from law-enforcement institutions as a template to help them determine the proper number of troops required to secure Iraq and prepare for additional missions.[108] This analysis yielded a requirement for 20 combat brigades and their supporting logistics units, a force that would approximate 125,000 combat troops and as many as 175,000 noncombat support personnel.[109] In other words, Benson's planners were recommending a force of approximately 300,000 Soldiers that, given Iraq's estimated population of 25.5 million, would have fielded approximately 11 Soldiers for every 1,000 Iraqi residents.[110] Benson's suggested force would have given the Coalition a military presence almost twice the size of the force deployed by the British Army during its successful counterinsurgency campaign in Malaya, but less than half the density relative to Iraq's population. The CFLCC planners envisioned the majority of these troops taking positions in or near Iraq's cities where most of the country's population resided. Under this plan, six brigades would become the stabilization force for Baghdad.

Governance	Unit REQ	Comments
Baghdad	6 Bdes	Score settling, capital of Iraq, large population, SSE
Al Basrah/Maysan	2 Bdes	Rumalia Oil Field, score settling, border crossing with Iran, SCIRI
At Tamim/Irbil	3 Bdes	Kirkuk Oil Field, KDP/PUK intentions, border crossing with Iran
Salah ad Din	2 Bdes	Tikrit, SSE sites
Ninawa	1 Bde	Mosul, KDP/PUK intentions, border crossing with Syria
As Sulaymaniyah	1 Bde	Al-Qaeda enclave, PUK
Al Anbar	1 Bde	Border crossing with Jordan/Syria, SSE sites, LSA Copperhead
Babil	2 Bns	Population merge with Baghdad, SSE sites
An Najaf	3 Bns	Shia Holy City, LSA Bushmaster
Karbala	2 Bns	Shia Holy City
Dhi Qar	1 Bde	An Nasiriyah, SCIRI, LSA Adder
Wasit	2 Bns	MEK, border crossing with Iran
Diyala	1 Bn	MEK, border crossing with Iran, SSE sites
Dahuk	1 Bn	Border crossing with Turkey
Al Qadisiyah	1 Bn	
Muthanna	–	
Total	**20 Bdes**	

Adapted from Benson, "'PH IV'" in De Toy, ed., *Turning Victory Into Success*

Figure 28. CFLCC PH IV, troop-to-task analysis, minimum units required.

Finally, ECLIPSE II established a framework for the progression of postinvasion operations in Iraq. According to Benson, CFLCC's plan for what they termed "post-hostilities stability and support operations" was nested under CENTCOM's Phase IVa.[111] The CFLCC planners further separated those operations into three stages. In the first stage, CFLCC would position its forces across Iraq and begin working with ORHA to establish the foundations of a stable environment in Iraq. This period would give way to stage II in which CFLCC would focus fully on stability and support operations while allowing ORHA to emerge as the lead Coalition authority for postinvasion operations. Finally, in stage III, CFLCC would transition its authority for military operations to CJTF-Iraq and redeploy most of its forces. ORHA would remain as the lead Coalition agency, providing direction to CJTF-Iraq and its units.

Assessing Phase IV Plans for Operation IRAQI FREEDOM

Clearly, the PH IV planning efforts by ORHA, the Joint Staff, and CENTCOM attest to the fact that many within the US Government and the DOD community realized the need to plan for operations after the fall of the Saddam regime. CFLCC's ECLIPSE II represents the most detailed of these efforts. Nonetheless, as in the planning process for Operation JUST CAUSE, the emphasis within the major US commands, as well as within the DOD, was on planning the first three phases of the campaign. As stated earlier in this chapter, the Office of the Secretary of Defense focused the CENTCOM and CFLCC staffs on these phases. The CENTCOM staff spent a greater amount of time on the preparation for the staging of forces in Kuwait and initial offensive operations than it did on what might happen after the toppling of the Saddam regime.[112] At the CFLCC level, Benson, the chief CFLCC planner, asserted that he was not able to induce McKiernan to spend a significant amount of time on the planning for stability and support operations. In discussing how the planning process for OIF could have been improved, Benson stated:

> I would have made a much stronger case to my [commanding general] that he should have been more involved with phase IV planning during Phase III execution. . . . General McKiernan, to his credit, recognized that he only had so much energy because we were all getting really tired. He felt he needed to get through Phase III before we got into Phase IV.[113]

Not surprisingly, Benson felt somewhat overwhelmed by the task of PH IV operations given the lack of resources he had. He underlined the problem created by Army planners who gave most of their attention to conventional operations, saying, "We were extraordinarily focused on Phase III. There should have been more than just one Army colonel, me, really worrying about the details of Phase IV."[114]

Another symptom of this tendency to concentrate resources on the first three phases of the campaign was the broad acquiescence among high-ranking officers of the incomplete planning for PH IV. Both CENTCOM and CFLCC viewed their involvement in PH IV as temporary. Colonel Michael Fitzgerald at CENTCOM and Colonel Benson at CFLCC had developed a phasing scheme in which, at some point relatively soon after the cessation of major combat operations, CFLCC would hand off authority for large-scale stability and support operations in Iraq to another headquarters.[115] As previously noted, CFLCC clearly articulated this transition in the mission statements of both COBRA II and ECLIPSE II. In the former plan, that follow-on headquarters was called CJTF-Iraq; in the latter, CFLCC had renamed it CJTF-7. Yet, neither of these plans nor CENTCOM's 1003V stated with any clarity what organization would form the core of the headquarters that would have the responsibility to reconstruct Iraq.

In fact, as April 2003 began, no one at CENTCOM or CFLCC had any concrete understanding of how and to which headquarters the campaign would be transitioned. Staff officers at CENTCOM had attempted to clarify the issue and were reportedly assured that other elements of the US Government would handle the larger issues involved in planning for and executing PH IV operations.[116] And to some degree, clarification arrived with the establishment of ORHA and the coordination ORHA accomplished with the CFLCC staff in the month before the invasion began. However, Colonel Fitzgerald explained that ORHA's arrival in Kuwait in March 2003 raised as many issues as it solved.[117] Fitzgerald contended that neither ORHA's mission nor its relationship to CENTCOM was well defined. More importantly, ORHA was not resourced to provide the type of planning and oversight required in Iraq during PH IV.

In any case, the emergence of ORHA did not address the other critical question concerning CFLCC's posthostilities phase: What military headquarters would accept responsibility for PH IV once CENTCOM and CFLCC pulled out? The planners at CFLCC had conceptualized this transition and even developed a set of concrete criteria that would mark the point when it could transfer authority for military operations to the follow-on CJTF.[118] Nevertheless, in the spring of 2003 all US plans were devoid of any detail about military operations in Iraq once CENTCOM and CFLCC redeployed their forces.

Attitudes, tendencies, and unaddressed issues that shaped planning at the theater-strategic and operational levels had a direct impact on the tactical-level preparation for OIF. As in Operation JUST CAUSE, the focus on conventional operations shaped how tactical headquarters designed their training and conducted overall preparation for war. Despite the fact that the CFLCC plans directed units to conduct a rolling transition to stability and support operations—which implied that at some point in the campaign tactical units conducting combat operations would transition to stability and support operations—few if any of the Soldiers in these units seemed to understand what this meant or were aware of the general CFLCC concept for PH IV operations. One telling example is the experience of Lieutenant Colonel Steve Landis, executive officer of the 1st Brigade Combat Team, 3d ID. Landis knew that a plan for PH IV operations existed at levels above the division headquarters, but even after those operations began in April 2003, he stated that neither his headquarters nor, in all likelihood, his division headquarters, received a copy of that plan.[119]

Part of the problem was that 1003V and ECLIPSE II lacked the specific taskings and guidance that would have gained the attention of staffs and commanders before the beginning of hostilities. As Fitzgerald later reflected, "You can certainly argue whether the detail was there in time to be effective and [to garner] all the resources, not just the military resources, for Phase IV."[120] Another problem was that the OPORD was formally published in April 2003, after ground operations had begun. By then, CENTCOM forces were entirely consumed with fighting their way to Baghdad, and ORHA was just beginning to deploy to Kuwait. It is not surprising that CFLCC, V Corps, and most of the Army units on the ground in Iraq and Kuwait did not exert much effort preparing to execute ECLIPSE II.[121]

For many tactical commanders, the lack of detail in the plan for stability and support operations was a problem caused partially by the focus on the initial tactical challenge—overthrowing the regime. As the commanding general of 101st ABN, Major General Petraeus recalled, the CFLCC plan for PH IV was "relatively general," and that it contained "very general themes, which seemed to be sound in concept, but the meanings and the operationalizing of those themes, particularly beyond the Army and with programs and organizations and resources, again beyond the military, were not very evident to us."[122] Petraeus added that, from his perspective, the planning effort focused "primarily on the fight to Baghdad . . . and the ensuing fight that was anticipated to take place in Baghdad."[123]

For those commanders who did have concerns about PH IV, the plans and rehearsals for OIF rarely provided peace of mind. Colonel Thomas Torrance, commander of 3d ID's Division

Artillery, contended that the disconnect between the planning for postinvasion operations and the real requirements of PH IV emerged several months before the war:

> I can remember asking the question during our war gaming and the development of our plan, 'Okay, we are now in Baghdad, what next?' No real good answers came forth. I remember being at a V Corps exercise in Germany in late January and early February of 2003, I forget the gentleman's position but I know he was a colonel who was a member of the V Corps staff, and he essentially asked the questions, 'Who is responsible for economic development? Who is responsible for a judicial system? Who is responsible for a monetary system? Who is responsible for health care?' I was, in my own mind, always sort of personally questioning, 'What next? What now? Now that we are here, what now?'[124]

This statement captured a general truth about the lack of detailed plans. However, not all on the V Corps staff had completely ignored PH IV operations. Indeed, after the corps' VICTORY SCRIMMAGE exercise in Germany in January 2003, Lieutenant General William S. Wallace, the corps commander, directed some of his staff officers to convene an informal conference to discuss the probable ramifications of the Coalition's transition to the role of occupying power after the fall of the Saddam regime.[125] Working with members of the 1st AD's staff, the V Corps staff made assumptions that forecasted serious problems with looting, rioting, and general civil disorder in post-Saddam Iraq. To prepare for these potential problems, in January the corps' Staff Judge Advocate (SJA) created draft ordinances establishing policy for scenarios in which looting and other disruptions broke out. Several of these drafts became the bases for V Corps fragmentary orders (FRAGOs) issued to subordinate units during the march to Baghdad.[126]

This type of staff work remained at relatively high levels. In the meantime, tactical units were preparing for war. Certainly, ECLIPSE II would provide greater detail about PH IV plans after it was published in April 2003. But for units like the 3d ID that were training for and then conducting offensive operations against Saddam's army in this period, it seems there was little time or direction to prepare for the transition to PH IV.

Indeed, the Army units chosen to take part in OIF appear to have conducted little or no training for these operations. There were exceptions. The 2d Brigade Combat Team of 1st AD, for example, exercised with psychological operations (PSYOP) and CA units before it deployed to Kuwait.[127] However, this brigade conducted the training based on its own mission analysis rather than because of specific taskings. Far more representative of the norm was the experience of Major Rod Coffey, the operations officer of the 2d Battalion, 7th Infantry Regiment, which served with 3d ID. The battalion commander and his staff realized their Soldiers might be involved in operations to counter looting and other civil disturbances once PH IV began, but did not redirect its critical prewar training efforts to prepare their troops for this possibility.[128] Lieutenant Colonel Troy Perry, the operations officer of the 1st Battalion, 68th Armor Regiment of 4th ID, had a similar experience. In preparation for the campaign, his unit conducted a great deal of training at the National Training Center, as well as at their home station in Fort Hood, Texas. Perry stated, "None of [the training] included stability operations."[129] Deployment issues and preparing for the rapid attack to Baghdad and overthrowing the Saddam regime with a very small force against overwhelming numbers consumed nearly all the effort of joint and Army leaders at every level.

In retrospect, assessment of the planning for OIF must focus on the way the set of assumptions made by US Government officials and military commanders about the postwar situation in Iraq shaped the planning process. All military plans rest on a set of assumptions to a greater or lesser degree, and the famous dictum that "no plan survives contact with the enemy" would clearly apply in the spring of 2003. While planners can never expect their conjectures to be wholly accurate, they are supposed to make lucid, well-reasoned assumptions based on intelligence, commander's guidance, doctrine, and policy.

In the case of OIF, the postwar situation in Iraq was severely out of line with the suppositions made at nearly every level before the war. The V Corps commander, Lieutenant General Wallace, asserted that the assumptions made by planners about the Iraqi infrastructure and society after the conflict were particularly damaging to the PH IV plan:

> I believe the things that we assumed would be in place on the ground that make Phase IV operations extraordinarily easy if they are there or extraordinarily hard if they are not had most to do with Iraqi institutions and infrastructure. We made the assumption that some of those institutions and some of that infrastructure would be in place upon our arrival, regardless of the presence of the regime or not. The criticality of those assumptions was such that when the regime ceased to exist or ceased to dominate the areas in which we were operating, then all of those institutions and all of that infrastructure ceased to operate at the same time.[130]

Wallace succinctly concluded, "We had the wrong assumptions and therefore we had the wrong plan to put into play."[131]

General Keane echoed Wallace's analysis, highlighting the US Army's inability to predict the regime's course of action after the loss of Baghdad: "The essential problem with Phase IV was we never ever seriously considered that leaders of the regime would not surrender. If we occupied the capital and took down his military capability, essentially having physical and material control, we did not consider it a realistic option that they would continue to attack us indirectly. And shame on us for that."[132] Colonel Fitzgerald stated that the expectations about the security environment and the role of the Iraqi Army after the removal of the Baathist regime further complicated PH IV operations:

> We made an assumption in the original OPLAN that there would be some level of [Iraqi] security forces, both Army and police, that could be leveraged to provide immediate local security and that it would form a core for the rebuilding of an Iraqi Army. [CPA Order Number 2, 'The Dissolution of Entities'] . . . pretty much scuttled that and our ability to do that, in addition to the fact that standing [Iraqi military and police] elements just disintegrated.[133]

The issue of what would happen to the Iraqi military after Saddam's removal is one example of assumptions not being shared or understood across the Government and the military. This study will explore this decision by the Coalition Provisional Authority (CPA) more fully in the next chapter. For this discussion, it is important to establish that, at the CFLCC level, Colonel Benson and his planners assumed in ECLIPSE II that some form of the Iraqi Army would exist and be used by the Coalition in PH IV. ORHA chief Jay Garner also believed the Iraqi Army would remain and be employed. In fact, both he and Douglas Feith, the Under Secretary of Defense for Policy, have independently stated that the plan to retain the Iraqi Army was briefed to and approved by the National Security Council in March 2003.[134] Garner therefore protested the decision to dissolve the Army when he heard about it in Baghdad the day it was announced by Paul Bremer, the CPA Administrator. Yet, Bremer stated in his memoirs that beginning in early May, he and senior members of the Pentagon staff, including Deputy Secretary of Defense Paul Wolfowitz and Feith, began discussing the dissolution of the Iraqi Army.[135] Bremer further noted that he briefed the decision to officials at CENTCOM and CFLCC in mid-May before announcing it publicly on 23 May 2003. Still, numerous US military and civilian leaders in Iraq at the time have written about their surprise when that announcement came.

The lack of synchronization among the many military and civilian arms of the US Government—so dramatically illustrated by the problems in coordinating the policy toward the Iraqi Army—led planners at the major commands to make inaccurate assumptions that ultimately weakened their ability to prepare for the postinvasion phase of OIF. On the most fundamental level, it is clear that during their preparation for operations in Iraq, CENTCOM and CFLCC staff officers did not plan in an environment that allowed them to coordinate and nest their work in the larger context of a shared strategic and integrated vision of the end state of the campaign. Put more simply, the US Government's strategic end state for Iraq did not drive military planning in the way that Joint and Army doctrine prescribed.

Conclusion

As an institution, the US Army in 2003 had the experience, training, and doctrine to deal with many of the challenges posed by PH IV operations in Iraq. The Army's experience with unconventional missions in the last decades of the 20th century had prepared many American Soldiers for the type of chaotic and decentralized stability and support operations that characterized most unconventional campaigns. To be sure, these recent experiences did not include the mounting of a major counterinsurgency campaign, and that would lead to difficulties in 2003 when it became clear to many Soldiers that operations in Iraq would not closely resemble the missions in Bosnia or Kosovo. Nevertheless, there existed within the American Army a strong base of knowledge and practice that provided the basic foundation for operations after Saddam's regime fell.

Despite its extensive history with stability and support operations, this chapter has shown that the Army has often given less emphasis to stability and support operations than is prudent. The institutional tendency to focus on the conventional aspects of a campaign at times led to the creation of plans for PH IV operations that were poorly conceived and poorly coordinated. Many of the same shortcomings that weakened the plan for postconflict operations in Panama in 1989 emerged in the preparation for OIF. In the planning for Iraq, that tendency affected how much effort CENTCOM and CFLCC placed on the creation of the PH IV plan as well as how much attention tactical commanders and staffs were directed to give to the postinvasion phase of the operation. Had some of the considerable energy, focus, and resources of the overall prewar American effort been redirected toward preparing for PH IV, it is possible that CENTCOM, CFLCC, and the US Army could have been better positioned once major combat ended to begin the exceedingly difficult mission of creating stability, fostering legitimacy, and rebuilding a shattered nation. Moreover, had the US military's planning and preparation for PH IV in Iraq been more complete, the Army would have been able to leverage its powerful collective campaign experience in Panama, Haiti, Bosnia, and Kosovo much more fully, and almost certainly reduced the difficulties in the transition to full spectrum operations.

Notes

1.   Headquarters, Department of the Army, Field Manual (FM) 3-0, *Operations* (Washington, DC, 14 June 2001), 1–2.

2.   Richard F. Grimmet, "Instances of Use of United States Armed Forces Abroad, 1789–2004," Congressional Research Service Report RL30172, as posted by the Naval Historical Center, http://www. au.af.mil/au/awc/awcgate/crs/rl30172.htm (1 of 41) (accessed 16 April 2005).

3.   For a survey of US Army historical involvement in operations other than conventional warfare, see Lawrence A. Yates, *The US Military's Experience in Stability Operations, 1789–2005* (Fort Leavenworth, KS: Combat Studies Institute Press, 2006).

4.   FM 3-0, 14 June 2001, 1–14. See also Joint Publication 3-0, *Doctrine for Joint Operations* (Washington, DC, 10 September 2001), 20.

5.   FM 3-0, 14 June 2001, 1–14 to 1–17.

6.   John M. Gates, *Schoolbooks and Krags: The United States Army in the Philippines, 1898–1902* (Westport CT: Greenwood Press Inc., 1973), chapter 7; Brian M. Linn, *Guardians of Empire: The U.S. Army and the Pacific, 1902–1940* (Chapel Hill, NC: University of North Carolina Press, 1997), 12–18, chapter 2; Andrew J. Birtle uses the terms "Policies of Chastisement and Attraction" to describe the US Army's two-pronged approach in the Philippines. See Andrew J. Birtle, *US Army Counterinsurgency and Contingency Operations Doctrine, 1860–1941* (Washington, DC: US Army Center of Military History, 1998), 119–126.

7.   Max Boot, *The Savage Wars of Peace, Small Wars and the Rise of American Power* (New York, NY: Basic Books, 2002), 116.

8.   Birtle, 126.

9.   Birtle, 138.

10.   Birtle, 139.

11.   Earl F. Ziemke, *The US Army in the Occupation of Germany* (Washington, DC: US Army Center of Military History, 1989), 7.

12.   Ziemke, 19.

13.   Conrad C. Crane and W. Andrew Terrill, *Reconstructing Iraq: Insights, Challenges, and Missions for Military Forces in a Post-Conflict Scenario* (Carlisle Barracks, PA: Strategic Studies Institute, 2003), 15.

14.   Crane and Terrill, 15.

15.   John J. McGrath, *Boots on the Ground: Troop Density in Contingency Operations* (Fort Leavenworth, KS: Combat Studies Institute Press, 2006), 30.

16.   Crane and Terrill, 15–16.

17.   Jeffrey J. Clarke, *Advice and Support; The Final Years, 1965–1973* (Washington, DC: US Army Center of Military History, 1988), 56.

18.   Clarke, 69–74.

19.   Clarke, 373.

20.   Marc Leepson, "Most USAID personnel in Vietnam, including State FSOs, labored in obscurity; here are some of their stories," *American Foreign Service Association,* http://www.afsa.org/fsj/apr00/leepson.cfm (accessed 6 February 2006).

21.   Leepson.

22.   Clarke, 452.

23.   Anthony Gray and Maxwell Manwaring, *Panama: Operation Just Cause* (Washington DC: National Defense University Press), 6.

24.   Lawrence A. Yates, "Panama, 1989–1999: The Disconnect Between Combat and Stability Operations," *Military Review* 85, May–June 2005, 51.

25.   Yates, "Panama, 1989–1999," 46–52; John T. Fishel, "Planning for Post-Conflict Panama: What it tells Us About PH IV Operations," in Brian M. De Toy, ed., *Turning Victory into Success:*

Military Operations After the Campaign (Fort Leavenworth, KS: Combat Studies Institute Press, 2004), 169–178.

26. Fishel, "Planning for Post-Conflict Panama," in De Toy, ed., *Turning Victory into Success,* 173.

27. Yates, "Panama, 1989–1999," 51.

28. Robert Baumann, Lawrence A. Yates, and Versalle F. Washington, *My Clan Against the World* (Fort Leavenworth, KS: Combat Studies Institute Press, 2004), 91.

29. Walter E. Kretchik, Robert F. Baumann, and John T. Fishel, *Invasion, Intervention, "Intervasion:" A Concise History of the US Army in Operation Uphold Democracy* (Fort Leavenworth, KS: Combat Studies Institute Press, 1998).

30. Kretchik, Baumann, and Fishel, 122–132.

31. Robert F. Baumann, George H. Gawrych, and Walter E. Kretchik, *Armed Peacekeepers in Bosnia* (Fort Leavenworth, KS: Combat Studies Institute Press, 2004), 101.

32. R. Cody Phillips, *Bosnia-Herzegovina: The US Army's Role in Peace Enforcement Operations, 1995–2004* (Washington, DC: US Army Center of Military History, 2004), 31.

33. Baumann, Gawrych, and Kretchik, 126.

34. R. Cody Phillips, *Bosnia-Herzegovina,* 37.

35. Headquarters, US Army Europe, *Joint Guardian After Action Report* (2000), III-5-7; see also, R. Cody Phillips, CMH Pub 70-109-1, *Operation Joint Guardian, The U.S. Army in Kosovo* (Washington, DC: US Army Center of Military History, 2007).

36. Headquarters, US Army Europe, KFOR 3, *After Action Report, June 2001–May 2002* (2003), 21, 30, 38; see also, Phillips, CMH Pub 70-109-1, *Operation Joint Guardian.*

37. McGrath, *Boots on the Ground,* 91–109.

38. See, for example, Yates, *US Military's Experience in Stability Operations.*

39. John D. Waghelstein, "What's Wrong in Iraq or Ruminations of a Pachyderm," *Military Review* 86, January–February 2006, 112.

40. Waghelstein, "What's Wrong in Iraq," 112.

41. FM 3-0, 14 June 2001, 1–14.

42. Birtle, introduction, chapter 1.

43. Birtle, passim.

44. Russell F. Weigley, *The American Way of War; A History of United States Military Strategy and Policy* (Bloomington, IN: Indiana University Press, 1973), 456–457.

45. Headquarters, Department of the Army, FM 100-5, *Field Service Regulations–Operations* (Washington, DC, 1962), chapters 10 through 12.

46. Headquarters, Department of the Army, FM 100-5, *Operations of Army Forces in the Field* (Washington, DC, 1968), chapters 11 through 13.

47. Headquarters, Department of the Army, FM 31-23, *Stability Operations* (Washington, DC, 1972), 4–3.

48. The Army did publish FM 100-20, *Low Intensity Conflict,* in 1990, which defined and described in some detail the variety of missions renamed in 1993 as "operations other than war." However, these operations did not gain formal acceptance as core Army missions until the 1993 version of FM 100-5, *Operations.*

49. Headquarters, Department of the Army, FM 100-5, *Operations* (Washington, DC, June 1993), chapter 13.

50. Task Force 2-5 CAV, *Peace Support Operations,* 1998.

51. Headquarters, Department of the Army, FM 3-07, *Stability Operations and Support Operations* (Washington, DC, 20 February 2003), 1–12. This field manual continued the practice of defining stability operations both as a type of conflict and as a set of steps taken by military forces in a variety of types of conflicts.

52. Birtle, 256–257.

53. Birtle, 369–370.

54. Birtle, 656–659.

55. John D. Waghelstein, "Post-Vietnam Counterinsurgency Doctrine," *Military Review* 65, May 1985, 44.

56. Major Michael Eyre et al., "Civil Affairs (CA) Integration at the JRTC," *CTC Bulletin* 98-12 (Fort Leavenworth, KS: Center for Army Lessons Learned, 1998); "Intelligence BOS," *CTC Trends* 98-20 (Fort Leavenworth, KS: Center for Army Lessons Learned, 1998).

57. On the Mission Rehearsal Exercises (MRX) scenarios, see Captain Robert S. Rigsby, "Kosovo Bound," *Army Logistician* 33 (July–August 2001): 30; and, Captain Mark Stammer, "Peace Support Operations Rehearsals at the CMTC," *Stability and Support Operations Newsletter 98-11* (Fort Leavenworth, KS: Center for Army Lessons Learned, 1998).

58. Colonel Joseph Anderson, interview by Contemporary Operations Study Team, Fort Leavenworth, KS, 4 November 2005, 9.

59. Anderson, interview, 4 November 2005, 9.

60. Anderson, interview, 4 November 2005, 9.

61. Anderson, interview, 4 November 2005, 9.

62. Lieutenant General Ricardo Sanchez, interview by Contemporary Operations Study Team, Fort Leavenworth, KS, 14 August 2006.

63. Lieutenant General David H. Petraeus, interview by Contemporary Operations Study Team, Fort Leavenworth, KS, 17 February 2006, 3.

64. Major Mark Black, *Military Support to Elections: The Balkans Experience and the Implications for Future Planning* (Fort Leavenworth, KS: Center for Army Lessons Learned, 27 February 2004).

65. Major General Thomas G. Miller, interview by Contemporary Operations Study Team, Fort Leavenworth, KS, 25 August 2006, 2.

66. Major General Buford C. Blount III, interview by Operational Leadership Experiences Project Team, Combat Studies Institute, Fort Leavenworth, KS, 15 February 2006, 17.

67. Major Darryl Rupp, interview by Operational Leadership Experiences Project Team, Combat Studies Institute, Fort Leavenworth, KS, 15 February 2006, 11 January 2006, 10.

68. Rupp, interview, 15 February 2006, 11 January 2006, 10

69. Chief Warrant Officer 3 Bryan Gray, interview by Operational Leadership Experiences Project Team, Combat Studies Institute, Fort Leavenworth, KS, 17 November 2005, 11 January 2006, 4.

70. FM 3-0, 14 June 2001, see chapters 1, 2, and 9.

71. JP 3-0, 2001, III-1–III-21.

72. Yates, *US Military's Experience in Stability Operations,* 22–23.

73. General (Retired) Tommy Franks, interview by Contemporary Operations Study Team, Fort Leavenworth, KS, 23 June 2006, 3.

74. General Tommy Franks, *American Soldier* (New York, NY: Harper Collins, 2004), 349.

75. On the pre-2002 plan, see Michael R. Gordon and General Bernard E. Trainor, *Cobra II: The Inside Story of the Invasion and Occupation of Iraq* (New York, NY: Pantheon Books, 2006), 138. For Franks' thoughts on the necessity for revising the CENTCOM plan, see Franks, *American Soldier*, 349.

76. Franks, interview, 23 June 2006, 4–5.

77. Franks, interview, 23 June 2006, 5.

78. Franks, interview, 23 June 2006, 4.

79. Franks, interview 23 June 2006, 6.

80. Franks, *American Soldier,* 393–394.

81. Gordon and Trainor, 42–54.

82. Franks, *American Soldier*, 207, 277, 278, 383, and 545.

83. Franks, *American Soldier*, 274–275.

84. General (Retired) John Keane, interview by Contemporary Operations Study Team, Fort Leavenworth, KS, 29 June 2006, 3.

85. Keane, interview, 29 June 2006, 3.

86. Kevin C.M. Benson, "'PH IV' CFLCC Stability Operations Planning," in De Toy, ed., *Turning Victory into Success*, 179.

87. Gordon and Trainor, 141.

88. For an example of George W. Bush's statements on nation building during the 2000 campaign, see Terry M. Neal, "Bush Backs into Nation Building," *Washington Post,* 26 February 2003, http://www. washingtonpost.com/ac2/wp-dyn/A6853-2003Feb26?language=printer (accessed 27 September 2006).

89. Franks, *American Soldier*, 423.

90. Franks, *American Soldier*, 441.

91. Gordon and Trainor, 144.

92. Jay Garner, "Iraq Revisited," in De Toy, ed., *Turning Victory into Success*, 256.

93. Secretary of State, General (Retired) Colin Powell, interview by Contemporary Operations Study Team, Fort Leavenworth, KS, 25 July 2006, 7.

94. Colonel (Retired) Paul Hughes, interview by Contemporary Operations Study Team, Fort Leavenworth, KS, 1 March 2006, 6.

95. Powell, interview, 25 July 2006, 6.

96. Garner, "Iraq Revisited," in De Toy, ed., *Turning Victory into Success,* 259.

97. Lieutenant General William G. Webster, interview by Contemporary Operations Study Team, Fort Leavenworth, KS, 11 December 2007, 11–12.

98. Webster, interview, 11 December 2007, 13.

99. Webster, interview, 11 December 2007, 13.

100. Benson, "'PH IV' CFLCC Stability Operations Planning," in De Toy, ed., *Turning Victory into Success,* 181.

101. Colonel Kevin C.M. Benson, interview by Contemporary Operations Study Team, Fort Leavenworth, KS, 6 February 2006, 6.

102. Colonel Michael Fitzgerald, interview by Contemporary Operations Study Team, Fort Leavenworth, KS, 10 January 2006, 3-4.

103. Fitzgerald, interview, 10 January 2006, 3.

104. For a paraphrasing of the CFLCC mission statement, see Benson, "'PH IV' CFLCC Stability Operations Planning," in De Toy, ed., *Turning Victory into Success,* 185.

105. Benson, "'PH IV' CFLCC Stability Operations Planning," in De Toy, ed., *Turning Victory into Success,* 184.

106. Benson, "'PH IV' CFLCC Stability Operations Planning," in De Toy, ed., *Turning Victory into Success,* 189.

107. Benson, "'PH IV' CFLCC Stability Operations Planning," in De Toy, ed., *Turning Victory into Success,* 186.

108. Benson, "'PH IV' CFLCC Stability Operations Planning," in De Toy, ed., *Turning Victory into Success,* 187.

109. Benson, "'PH IV' CFLCC Stability Operations Planning," in De Toy, ed., *Turning Victory into Success,* 198.

110. McGrath, *Boots on the Ground,* 163–165. McGrath does not include indigenous security forces in calculating these particular ratios.

111. Benson, interview, 6 February 2006, 5.

112. Quoted in Gordon and Trainor, 139.

113. Benson, "'PH IV' CFLCC Stability Operations Planning," in De Toy, ed., *Turning Victory into Success,* 196.

114. Benson, interview, 6 February 2006, 15.

115. Benson, "'PH IV' CFLCC Stability Operations Planning," in De Toy, ed., *Turning Victory into Success,* 181.

116. Fitzgerald, interview, 10 January 2006, 2; Gordon and Trainor, 139.

117. Fitzgerald, interview, 10 January 2006, 4.

118. Benson, "'PH IV' CFLCC Stability Operations Planning," in De Toy, ed., *Turning Victory into Success,* 188.

119. Lieutenant Colonel Steve Landis, interview by Contemporary Operations Study Team, Fort Leavenworth, KS, 21 December 2005, 9.

120. Fitzgerald, interview, 10 January 2006, 3.

121. Wallace, the V Corps commander, stated V Corps was never tasked with postwar responsibilities. See General William S. Wallace, interview by Contemporary Operations Study Team, Fort Leavenworth, KS, 22 May 2006.

122. Petraeus, interview, 17 February 2006, 2.

123. Petraeus, interview, 17 February 2006, 2.

124. Colonel Thomas Torrance, interview by Contemporary Operations Study Team, Fort Leavenworth, KS, 1 November 2005, 7.

125. Colonel Marc Warren, interview by Contemporary Operations Study Team, Fort Leavenworth, KS, 15 March 2007, 6–7.

126. Warren, interview, 15 March 2007, 7.

127. Colonel J.D. Johnson, interview by Contemporary Operations Study Team, Fort Leavenworth, KS, 4 November 2005, 2.

128. Lieutenant Colonel Rod A. Coffey, interview by Contemporary Operations Study Team, Fort Leavenworth, KS, 8 December 2005, 12.

129. Lieutenant Colonel Troy D. Perry, interview by Contemporary Operations Study Team, Fort Leavenworth, KS, 11 May 2006, 3.

130. Wallace, interview, 22 May 2006, 4.

131. Wallace, interview, 22 May 2006, 4.

132. Keane, interview, 29 June 2006, 4.

133. Fitzgerald, interview, 10 January 2006, 6.

134. Garner stated in 2006, "[T]he other big mistakes we made the first 90 days were number one, the decision to disband the Army. . . . I had even briefed the President on bringing back the Army and he agreed with me. I briefed Condoleezza Rice every week on it and she agreed. I would bring it up with Rumsfeld every time I talked with him and he agreed with it. Wolfowitz and Feith agreed with it, and the President agreed with it." Lieutenant General (Retired) Jay Garner, interview by Contemporary Operations Study Team, Fort Leavenworth, KS, 6 June 2006, 16. For a more complete description of how and why US plans for the Iraqi Army changed between March and May 2003, see Douglas J. Feith, *War and Decision: Inside the Pentagon at the Dawn of the War on Terrorism* (New York, NY: Harper, 2008), 366–368, 428–433. See chapter 3 of this study for more discussion of the effects of this policy on the military campaign.

135. L. Paul Bremer, *My Year in Iraq: The Struggle to Build a Future of Hope* (New York, NY: Simon and Schuster, 2006), 54–55.

Chapter 3

The Rise of the Iraqi Insurgency and the US Army's Response

For nearly all of the American Soldiers who arrived in Iraq in the spring and summer of 2003, the most unexpected aspect of the campaign was the emergence of an organized and lethal insurgency. The surprise exhibited by both the Coalition military leadership and the Soldiers in Iraq stemmed from widespread assumptions about probable Iraqi reactions to war and liberation. Before the war, few United States (US) Government officials had expected this type of resistance in the absence of the Baath Party's rule, and that consensus ultimately contributed to the attitudes of military planners tasked to design the overall war plan.

American military doctrine in 2001 defined an insurgency as "an organized movement aimed at the overthrow of a constituted government through use of subversion and armed conflict."[1] As this chapter will discuss, this definition was broader than the more traditional understanding of the term derived from decades of dealing with the Marxist insurgencies during the Cold War. That earlier conception defined insurgencies as highly structured organizations motivated by a single ideology and guided by a central leadership that coordinated actions and purpose. The newer, less restrictive definition of the term aptly described the type of enemy that, despite the presumptions made by American officials, emerged in Iraq beginning in the summer of 2003. Throughout the remainder of 2003 and into 2004, the Iraqi insurgency grew in size and diversity to become the major obstacle to the Coalition's objectives in Iraq. This organized opposition was never a monolithic movement—united under one set of leaders and armed with a single ideology. Instead, the Iraqi insurgency consisted of a constantly changing constellation of groups and leaders who espoused a variety of purposes and ideologies and used a myriad of techniques in their opposition to the Coalition, the Iraqi Government, and the Iraqi Security Forces (ISF). While this chapter will focus primarily on the network composed of Sunni Arab insurgency groups, other organizations such as Shia militias and violent criminal gangs also became active during this period, mounting serious operations against Coalition forces and, at times, collaborating with the Sunni Arab network.

To face this evolving and complex threat, American Soldiers began conducting full spectrum operations designed to directly and indirectly engage the insurgent enemy. This response is the subject of the second part of this chapter. At times, US Army units launched focused combat operations—often described using the unofficial term "kinetic operations"—to destroy insurgent forces and capabilities. However, from the very beginning of the full spectrum campaign, US forces also mounted broader efforts to build popular support for the new Iraqi Government and the Coalition project in Iraq. These operations, sometimes called "nonkinetic" operations, concentrated on the reconstruction of the Iraqi infrastructure, the establishment of representative government, the training of ISF, and general efforts to improve the quality of life for the population.* Without relying on doctrine or experience, US Army units transitioned to a practice of full spectrum operations that, by the end of 2003, followed many well-established principles of counterinsurgency warfare.

---

*The 2008 version of FM 3-0, *Operations*, uses the terms "lethal" and "nonlethal" actions instead of "kinetic" and "nonkinetic."

Prewar Assumptions about Postconflict Threats

As the United States moved closer to confrontation with Iraq in 2002 and early 2003, the US Government began conducting a series of studies intended to help understand what might occur after a military defeat of the Saddam regime. None of the organizations involved in this effort came to the conclusion that a serious insurgent resistance would emerge after a successful Coalition campaign against the Baathist regime. The US Department of State (DOS), for example, launched a study in late 2001 designed to predict the landscape of a post-Saddam Iraq and anticipate the institutions and policies that would be required by the new Iraqi state. For this effort, known as *The Future of Iraq Project*, the DOS employed 17 working groups consisting of Iraqi expatriates and American experts focused on different aspects of a post-Baathist Iraq. One of these bodies, the Transitional Justice Working Group, looked closely at the legal and judicial challenges a post-Baathist state would likely face. This group did suggest that the period immediately following a regime change might offer an opportunity for criminals to loot and plunder while other groups in Iraqi society might seek revenge for past wrongs.[2] However, these experts did not predict the rise of any organized insurgency or armed resistance.

A similar study in late 2002 by the National Defense University reached a comparable conclusion. The authors of this study, a group of over 70 academics and policy experts from US agencies and private institutions, determined that the probability for unrest in post-Baathist Iraq was great, and the United States and its allies should be concerned about the possibilities of a civil war.[3] The work identified Baathist security and intelligence organizations as well as militias of various types that had been armed by Saddam as the most likely threats to post-conflict order.[4] Nevertheless, the study did not anticipate a broad insurgency and suggested the United States concentrate its resources on creating security after the regime collapse so it could avoid the worst of these possible threats.

Similar concerns about a post-Saddam Iraq grew out of a conference of officers and civilians from the Department of Defense (DOD) community held at the US Army War College in December 2002. This forum focused discussion on the military aspects of securing post-Saddam Iraq. Two participants in the conference, Dr. Conrad Crane and Dr. Andrew Terrill, then summarized the critical points discussed in a study titled *Reconstructing Iraq: Insights, Challenges, and Missions for Military Forces in a Post-Conflict Scenario*. The analysis emphasized that Iraqi society was complex and fractured along both ethnic and sectarian lines.[5] US forces that might become involved in postconflict operations had to be aware of multiple flashpoints, which could lead to instability in Iraq. The study argued that a mass uprising was unlikely, but might occur if, in Iraqi popular perception, the occupying force began to behave like an imperialist power. A far more likely threat was the use of terrorist attacks by various groups to damage the reconstruction effort and provoke violent reactions from Coalition units. Military crackdowns by US and other Coalition forces might then lead to growing resentment and a corresponding growth in the number of Iraqis willing to conduct terrorist actions.[6] Although the authors of the report did not predict the materialization of insurgent forces and never employed the term "insurgency," they did suggest that Coalition forces operating in Iraq after the regime change faced instability and the possibility of increasing levels of organized violence.

An equal amount of concern about instability and armed opposition in a post-Saddam Iraq existed among those charged with the direct planning for postconflict operations. Within US Central Command (CENTCOM), the Plans section of the Combined Forces Land Component

Command (CFLCC) struggled to understand what Iraq would look like after the fall of the Baathist regime. In the months leading up to the war, CFLCC planners reviewed a large amount of research on Iraq, including a portion of DOS's *The Future of Iraq Project* and Crane and Terrill's assessments in *Reconstructing Iraq*. According to Colonel Kevin Benson, the chief of the CFLCC planning effort, these two studies greatly aided his planners' understanding of Iraq and the tasks required in the postconflict phase of the campaign. Out of this research came the recognition that instability and violence were probable after Saddam's fall. In this environment, the planners considered the rise of an organized insurgency as a possibility, but according to Benson, they did not "rate it very likely."[7] If any resistance did emerge, Benson and his colleagues believed it would come from scattered groups of former high-level Baath Party loyalists who saw no future for themselves in a post-Saddam Iraq. Instead of planning for an insurgency, CFLCC focused on preparing for humanitarian crises, securing weapons of mass destruction (WMD) sites, and the general lawlessness that might break out after the regime fell.[8] Despite this effort by CFLCC to forecast the possible outcomes of a post-Saddam Iraq, most Coalition units did not train or otherwise prepare for postconflict operations. Thus, when faced with the actual problems of looting and lawlessness, the Coalition did not react in a coherent, well-rehearsed manner. This lack of preparation ultimately contributed to the emergence of the Iraqi insurgency.

Origins of Iraqi Discontent

In the weeks that followed the implosion of the Baathist regime in April 2003, the absence of organized violence created a period of relative calm. In many Kurdish and Shia regions of Iraq and even in some of the Sunni Arab areas, Coalition troops were indeed greeted as liberators as some American officials had predicted. As US units fanned out in Baghdad and other cities in the west, south, and northern regions of Iraq, they also found themselves in the middle of a political vacuum left by the collapse of the Baathist regime. The swiftness of the Coalition's advance and the apparent evaporation of Saddam's authority concurrently stunned the Iraqis. In retrospect, American Soldiers as well as many Iraqis have come to view this period of calm as a "window of opportunity" when Coalition forces had a chance to create a secure environment that might have forestalled the growth of any organized opposition. Those with this view suggest that this window of opportunity shut some time in mid-2003, largely because the Coalition was unprepared to conduct immediate, large-scale, postconflict operations that might have prevented the conditions in which inchoate anger could grow to form an insurgency.

Many Soldiers serving in the first units that reached Baghdad shared an acute sense of an opportunity lost. Colonel David Perkins, commander of the 2d Brigade Combat Team (BCT) of the 3d Infantry Division (3d ID), was one of the first senior officers to arrive in the Iraqi capital. His views on this early period are representative of this collective attitude:

> Right after we got into Baghdad, there was a huge window of opportunity that if we had this well-defined plan and we were ready to come in with all these resources, we could have really grabbed a hold of the city and really started pushing things forward. By the time we got a plan together to resource everything, the insurgents had closed that window of opportunity quickly. What we started doing in September [2003] was probably a good idea to have done in April 2003.[9]

Lieutenant General (Retired) Jay Garner, the head of the Office of Reconstruction and Humanitarian Assistance (ORHA), thought similarly. After meeting with a number of Iraqi civilian leaders in early April 2003 in southern Iraq, he began pressuring CENTCOM to allow ORHA into Baghdad to begin operations before this window closed. On 17 April 2003 Garner told General Tommy Franks, the CENTCOM commander, that inside Iraq there were "too many vacuums that are filling up right now with things that you and I don't want them to fill up with."[10] Franks then allowed Garner to travel to Baghdad and northern Iraq to begin assessing the situation on the ground. However, weeks passed before ORHA established itself and began operations in these critical parts of Iraq.

In this period just after the 3d ID and other Coalition elements arrived in Baghdad, Saddam's army, the Iraqi police, and other institutions of authority dissolved. Concurrently, looters began stealing from buildings and facilities across the capital. Captain Warren Sponsler, a company commander in the 3d ID, described being in Baghdad and witnessing the chaotic nature of the situation in the days just after the deposition of the regime:

> My company was going up the big north/south highway going to the center of the city and I remember seeing all kinds of people walking up and down the highway dragging all kinds of stuff all over the place. There were American units that were securing the routes, but it was so overwhelming that there really wasn't much they could do about it. There were guys dragging bathtubs, construction equipment, or you name it.[11]

Sponsler was amazed at how brazen many of the looters were in the chaotic environment that prevailed in the capital:

> We had a palace right on the corner where the big reviewing stands are that we were actually going to occupy for my company. We went in and did a recon to make sure everything was all right and it had been touched a little bit. When we went back 12 hours later, it had been completely gutted. This was right on the edge of our perimeter. They would just swarm. It definitely wasn't organized, but folks, I think, would find a particular hot spot and they would swarm and take everything down to the wires out of the walls.[12]

While units did make an effort to secure some buildings in Baghdad, the enormity of the mass looting prevented the protection of all facilities. Soldiers quickly had to discern which of the museums, government buildings, weapons caches, and other facilities could be covered adequately.[13] Because of the relatively small number of Coalition forces on the ground in April 2003, it was impossible to protect all or even most of these sites. Further, Soldiers on the ground who had been engaged in combat less than 24 hours earlier, and in some cases were still engaged in combat, were not immediately prepared to stop the actions of these Iraqi citizens. Soldiers are trained to use lethal force very judiciously, and firing on looters was outside the rules of engagement (ROE) established for the invasion of Iraq. Colonel Daniel B. Allyn, commander of the 3d BCT, 3d ID, offered insights into the thought process of his Soldiers in Baghdad at this time:

> If they faced a hostile threat, they took hostile action to defeat it. If there was an ability to mitigate the situation with means less lethal than hostile action, they took those steps. I think probably the most challenging situation for them,

quite frankly, was when the populace began to take advantage of their own people in terms of looting. That put our Soldiers in a position of forcing them to be policemen, which we clearly had not done a lot of training on.[14]

The looting witnessed by Allyn and his Soldiers would take a huge toll on the Iraqi economy. One Coalition Provisional Authority (CPA) study estimated the looting in this early period caused $12 billion in losses.[15] This damage included the significant destruction of several of Saddam's palaces and government buildings, many of Baghdad's sewage treatment centers, and numerous military and police facilities, as well as important cultural landmarks such as the Iraqi National Museum.

As bad as the physical damage was to the Iraqi infrastructure, the harm inflicted by the looting on Iraqi attitudes toward the Coalition was even greater. The vacuum generated by the regime's collapse was far more vivid to Iraqis, who often did not comprehend why Coalition forces would not immediately fill that void. One Iraqi officer, Lieutenant General Nasier Abadi, who served as a senior Air Force officer in Saddam's armed forces and would become a key leader in the new Iraqi military after 2003, pointed to the glaring gap in authority in the immediate aftermath of Baghdad's fall. Abadi stated:

> There was no contingency plan for something going wrong such as an outbreak of public disorder, looting, and crime and revenge killings. Neither was the Coalition prepared for the virtual disappearance of the police and in effect all public order forces. The Coalition had no plan for the total lack of public order forces in the wake of the success of the Coalition forces and the disappearance of the Iraqi Army. The vacuum that resulted was enormous.[16]

Another Iraqi, Faruq Ahmed Saadeddin, who had served Saddam as a diplomat, told an American journalist that "[i]f it had gone smoothly from the first day, honestly, I believe this a 100 percent: 95 percent of the Baathists, the registered Baathists, would have cheered, hailed America." However, the disorder following the arrival of the Coalition forces changed his mind: "When we saw the burning and looting, that was like raping the city, that was like raping my country. I cried when I heard the news on the radio. I was pissed off. And I cried. That was the golden opportunity to win the people and they messed it up."[17]

Part of the problem was rooted in Iraqi expectations of what would occur after the Coalition forces arrived. Many Iraqis were impressed by American technology during the war and thought that American skill would completely transform their country. Instead, some became bewildered by the disorder that erupted immediately following the demise of the Saddam regime. One Iraqi complained, "Saddam had ruled for nearly 25 years, behind the scenes for far longer; the Americans had toppled him in less than three weeks, and relatively few of their Soldiers had died in the task. How could these same Americans be so feeble in the aftermath?"[18]

For many Iraqis, the looting and disorder became signs of the Coalition's inability or unwillingness to maintain order. From the start, some Iraqis assumed Americans did not care about the looting, or that they even welcomed the destruction. One cleric told a journalist, "I simply cannot understand how your soldiers could have stood by and watched. Maybe, [the Americans] are weak, too. Or maybe they are wicked."[19] American Soldiers became intensely aware of the rising pessimism among the Iraqi population. Major Rod Coffey, who served in the 3d ID in Baghdad, believed he understood why many of the Iraqis began to doubt the intentions of the Coalition:

> The looting creates the perception that 'my country is being destroyed' to an Iraqi. The looting feeds all those myths that the Americans are here and they just want to take all our oil and they want us to be weak. That was certainly a perception on the street on the part of some Iraqis, or at least grappling with the doubt, 'Well, maybe this is the way the Americans want it. All of us looting and going at each other in chaos. This is what they want. This is to their benefit.' You can't let that perception develop and it did.[20]

The absence of authority and the growing cynicism about Coalition objectives helped foster an environment in which an insurgency could grow. Lieutenant General Abadi described the situation in the following way:

> With the [Iraqi] Army not in place, this left a big vacuum and the Coalition did not think that there was a necessity after they succeeded in defeating the Army to have people providing security. But they did not bring enough troops to do the policing job. We had fence sitters in Iraq who did not know what to do. At the beginning they thought there was going to be investment and money, and this came bit by bit. At the same time the insurgents came and were spending a lot of money and recruiting a lot of people to go against the Americans.[21]

Abadi concluded that the situation in Iraq that spring "was not a healthy atmosphere."[22]

De-Baathification and the Disbanding of the Iraqi Army

The policies of the new Coalition Provisional Authority (CPA) contributed to Iraqi unease. Indeed, many participants in OIF identified the CPA's decision in May 2003 to de-Baathify Iraqi society and disband the Iraqi Army as critical factors contributing to the emergence of the insurgency. Abadi's statement, quoted above, alluded to the key economic consequence resulting from these two decisions that caused significant unemployment and a great deal of uncertainty among those Iraqis—especially Sunni Arabs—who suddenly found their social and economic status threatened. Colonel Derek J. Harvey, a US Army Military Intelligence officer and Middle East expert, also viewed these two acts as critical to the growth of the insurgency in the Sunni areas of Iraq in the summer of 2003. In 2004 Harvey served as the chief of the Coalition's Red Team, an organization staffed with experts who focused exclusively on the Iraqi insurgency. Harvey contended that after talking with insurgent leaders and studying the first year of Coalition operations, he saw the CPA's decisions on de-Baathification and the Army as pivotal because Saddam's military organizations and the Baath Party had been dominated by Sunni Iraqis. Thus, for decades Sunni Arabs had enjoyed political, social, and economic dominance in Iraq. The policies of de-Baathification and the disbanding of the Iraqi Army, according to Harvey, "flipped the social, economic, and political order on its head."[23] The large number of unemployed soldiers, officers, and government officials created a mass of politically and economically disenfranchised individuals who viewed the Coalition with suspicion and felt they had little future in an Iraq shaped by outside forces. Many of these men became the fence sitters who, over the summer of 2003, were vulnerable to those advocating the use of armed force to oppose the Coalition and return Sunni Arabs to power.

While banning high-level Baath Party members from public employment and disbanding the Iraqi Army were the first two official orders of the CPA, these policies were not part of the DOD's original design for the reconstruction of Iraq.[24] ECLIPSE II, CFLCC's Phase IV

(PH IV) plan, assumed that after the removal of Saddam, the Coalition would recall the Iraqi Army to help with both the maintenance of order and the reconstruction of the country while removing only the highest echelon of the Baathist leadership.[25] In fact, CFLCC's deputy commander, Major General William Webster, recalled that the CFLCC commander and staff assumed that one of its most immediate tasks in PH IV would be to coordinate with the leaders of the Iraqi Army so their forces could begin assisting the Coalition in reestablishing security.[26] Lieutenant General William Wallace, the V Corps commander, and Jay Garner, the ORHA chief, made similar planning assumptions about the role of Saddam's army and a very limited removal of Baathist officials after the defeat of Saddam.

These assumptions had led key Coalition military and civilian authorities to begin making decisions about the Iraqi Army and the Baath Party as major combat in Baghdad subsided. On 16 April 2003 General Tommy Franks issued an order that outlawed the Baath Party, but did not direct or imply the removal of all Baath Party members, including Army officers, from continued public employment.[27] Around the same time, CFLCC's staff began negotiations with senior officers in the Iraqi Army to prepare the way for the army's position in post-Saddam Iraq, especially its immediate role in establishing order.[28] Wallace had anticipated that some purging of the Baath Party was likely, but he and his staff hoped to minimize its worst side effects. On its own initiative, the Corps developed a policy for the de-Baathification of Iraqi society focused on retaining critical public officials—judges, police, teachers, municipal workers—in their positions to ensure that essential services continued after the ruling regime fell.

Colonel Marc Warren, the V Corps Staff Judge Advocate, authored the policy basing it on the idea that members of the Baath Party should be judged on their conduct or actions while in the party rather than on their status as a party member.[29] Warren believed that because the Saddam regime forced many Iraqis to join the Baath Party as a condition for their employment, Coalition policy should not seek a wholesale dismissal of all party members from public service. Instead, the V Corps policy required the members of the Baath Party to sign a renunciation form in which they would disavow their association with Saddam Hussein and would swear "to cooperate fully with the Coalition Provisional Authority in serving the people of Iraq and building a new Iraqi government."[30] Coalition authorities would vet high-level Baathists and investigate those suspected of committing crimes. However, the V Corps policy created a streamlined process that allowed police officers, teachers, and mid- and lower-level bureaucrats who had been compelled to join the Baath Party to play a role in the new Iraq. Wallace authorized the de-Baathification program, directed his staff to print thousands of copies of the renunciation form, and had the forms distributed in early May 2003.

Garner agreed with the V Corps policy and folded it into his larger plan for postconflict operations, which he based on the assumptions in ECLIPSE II. His plan relied heavily on the involvement of Iraqis in the political and physical reconstruction of the country. In early May Garner began working to bring the old Iraqi Army units back and had even arranged for the US Government to pay the salaries of 300,000 soldiers, 12,000 police, and up to 2 million public servants.[31] Lieutenant General (Retired) Jared Bates, ORHA's Chief of Staff, recalled, "The first idea was paying them just to get them to stand by, with more to follow. Just to keep everything calm in the first days and weeks of the occupation."[32] Both V Corps and ORHA thought the Iraqi citizens, including officers and soldiers of the Iraqi Armed Forces as well as civil servants who had been members of the Baath Party, would play a critical role in constructing a new Iraq.

While ORHA, CFLCC, and V Corps took the initial steps necessary to implement their policies, Bush administration officials began to make new plans for a post-Saddam Iraq that would supplant the assumptions made and work done by Garner and the military headquarters. Ambassador Paul Bremer, head of the CPA, described arriving in Iraq in May 2003 with a mandate from the administration to remove the topmost layer of the Baath Party from public life.[33] To Bremer and key members of the administration, this policy was a decisive act, designed to show the Iraqi people the Baathists had been removed from their country forever. Bremer would later write that the goal of the de-Baathification order was to "quash the impression that the Coalition had toppled Saddam only to hand power to the next level of Baathists."[34] If this impression persisted within Iraqi society, some Bush administration officials believed it might quickly provoke the Shia and Kurdish elements of the Iraqi population who had suffered under Saddam, and scuttle the planned transition to a new democratic Iraq.

With the goal of establishing a new political order firmly in mind, Bremer announced CPA Order No. 1, "De-Baathification of Iraqi Society," on 16 May 2003 (appendix A).[35] The new policy, which the CPA had not coordinated with either the CFLCC or V Corps staffs, officially dissolved the Baath Party and excluded those Iraqis with full party membership in the top four levels of the Baath organization—regional commanders, branch members, section members, and group members—from future employment in the public sector.[36] The CPA order also directed that other individuals holding positions in the top three levels of government ministries and other official institutions were to be screened, and if found to be full members of the Baath Party at any level, were to be expelled from their positions. Bush administration officials recognized that membership in the Baath Party was required for many nonideological Iraqis who had sought social and economic advancement within the government. To deal with these lower-level members who were not complicit in the crimes of the Baath Party leadership, the CPA policy allowed for a review process that would decide the fate of individuals on a case-by-case basis. Bremer also explained how in early May 2003, as the administration was deciding to order de-Baathification, he and other DOD officials were already moving toward dealing with the Iraqi Army in a similar fashion.[37] Bremer made this policy official on 23 May 2003 when the CPA issued Order No. 2, "The Dissolution of Entities" (appendix B), which disbanded the army and other branches of the Iraqi armed services as well as Iraqi governmental ministries and other organizations related to the Baath Party.[38]

The decisions to de-Baathify Iraqi society and eliminate the old regime's army caught Coalition authorities by surprise. As documented in the previous chapter, the US Government had not coordinated these policies with either ORHA or CENTCOM. Jay Garner, the ORHA chief, recalled that he first read the de-Baathification policy in Iraq and because it "went too deep" into the strata of society, he immediately tried to get Bremer to reconsider.[39] Lieutenant General McKiernan, the CFLCC commander, was equally caught off guard by the CPA policies. Major General William Webster, deputy commander of CFLCC, remembered that CFLCC was heavily involved in negotiations with senior Iraqi Army generals when he and McKiernan heard the news about the CPA's intent to dissolve the old army and prevent senior Baath Party members from serving in the institutions of the new Iraq. In fact, that news arrived when the CFLCC commander invited Ambassador Walter Slocombe, the CPA's senior advisor for defense and security affairs and Bremer's point man for the new Iraqi security forces, to a meeting with several Iraqi generals who had volunteered to serve in the new forces. After briefing Slocombe on CFLCC's initial plans for the new Iraqi Ministry of Defense, Webster recalled the CPA representative stating, "No, you are not doing that," and then explained to both men the outlines of the CPA's de-Baathification program.[40] When McKiernan and Webster protested, arguing that Iraq's new forces required a trained and experienced cadre of senior leaders, Slocombe countered that the Coalition would have to grow new leadership from the junior officers that remained after the de-Baathification took effect.[41] Webster noted that at that moment, "We were surpised, shocked."[42] He added, "Lieutenant General McKiernan and I had established relationships with [the Iraqi generals] and had started to give them guidance and they were excited."[43] Webster asserted that he and the CFLCC commander immediately started to think about the unintended consequences of Bremer's new policies, finally concluding, "The officers who supported Saddam loyally for a long time were going to resist us. This fight would turn into something long and hard. That was a terrible night. Lieutenant General McKiernan and I walked around in the dark and talked about this a long time, about what that meant down the road."[44]

There was real reason for this level of concern. Saddam's army, numbering approximately 400,000 officers and soldiers, had been a key institution in Iraq. Order No. 2 rendered these men jobless and made their immediate economic prospects look bleak. Additionally, the way the dissolution was conducted offended many Iraqis who saw it as disrespectful of their most respected institution. However, the administration based its decision to disband the armed forces on a reasonable premise. Saddam's army had been a brutal institution in which a dispro-portionate number of Sunni officers exploited and mistreated the mostly Shia conscripts. Added to this was Saddam's historical employment of his army in the repression of Shia and Kurdish populations. In Bremer's mind, these facts overrode concerns about temporary unemployment. In his memoirs, Bremer recalled telling his staff, "It's absolutely essential to convince Iraqis that we're not going to permit the return of Saddam's instruments of repression—the Baath Party, the Mukhabarat's security services, or Saddam's army. We didn't send our troops half-way around the world to overthrow Saddam to find another dictator taking his place."[45] Bremer and others in the CPA held the conviction that retaining the old army would hinder their plans to move Iraq toward a future in which all ethnic and sectarian groups shared equally in the economic and political life of the country.

Compounding the problems surrounding the role and structure of Saddam's army were the practical difficulties involved in any potential recall of that army in May 2003. During and immediately after the initial invasion, Saddam's army had simply disappeared. Many administration and CPA officials believed no real institution even existed to be recalled to duty. Additionally, many military facilities had been damaged in the war or rendered useless in the looting that followed. Still, Bremer and other administration officials must have been conscious of the fact that Iraqi soldiers expected to be recalled and would suffer economically once CPA enacted Order No. 2. This realization led to Bremer including clauses in Order No. 2 that announced the issuance of a one-time termination payment to soldiers and other government officials who had been employed by any dissolved institution. Further, the order stated the CPA would ensure veterans, war widows, and other Iraqis who had been receiving pensions from the Baathist state would continue to receive their payments after May 2003. Later measures would expand on these promises of financial support by introducing a system of stipend payments for most of the former Iraqi Army career officers and enlisted soldiers. Clearly, these efforts sought to ameliorate the economic hardships imposed on much of the Iraqi population by the CPA's first two orders. Nevertheless, the order maintained a rigid anti-Baathist stance in its exclusion of all senior party members and officers with the rank of colonel or higher from the termination and pension payment scheme, and 4 weeks would elapse before the CPA announced plans to pay stipends beyond the termination payment.

The policies of de-Baathification and the disbanding of the army were largely successful on the level of national politics. The major Shia and Kurdish groups became strong allies of the CPA in its campaign to reshape Iraq's political structure. The consequences of both policies, however, on the emerging security environment were less salutary. As one Iraqi emphasized, the Baath Party "had become part of the fabric of Iraqi society, a complex, interrelated pyramid of economic, political, religious, and tribal links. . . . But to dismantle the Party, the Army, and the other structure of the state was only to replace them with chaos."[46] Key officials in the ministries, schools, and other government institutions had been members of the party. But, after Order No. 1, these functionaries could not serve in their former positions without a review by the Coalition, and full members in the senior four ranks of the party, according to the policy, could never return. In the spring and summer of 2003, US Army units often found it impossible to find officials and technicians to take their place. One example of this problem was the challenge faced by the engineer brigade of the 1st Armored Division (1st AD) that, after struggling to reestablish basic sewer and electrical services in Baghdad in May 2003, finally decided to commit a considerable amount of its own resources to find the ex-Baathist bureaucrats and technicians and place them back in their jobs.[47] The 4th Infantry Division (4th ID), which was operating north of Baghdad in the Sunni heartland, similarly struggled to retain thousands of teachers and police who had been low-level members of the Baath Party. Eventually the division was successful, but not before the CPA cut the pay of these teachers, consequently damaging American relations with the Sunni community in the area.[48] Lieutenant General Wallace, who was serving as the V Corps commander in the early summer of 2003, highlighted the basic problem de-Baathification posed to American Soldiers on the ground: "The de-Baathification meant that the bureaucracy that made Iraq work was no longer allowed to help make Iraq work. Regardless of whether you thought they are good people or bad people, they were running the country until we told them they couldn't."[49] Wallace added that the CPA policy hurt even those far away from the apex of Baathist political power:

> This particular regime, over the course of 30 years, had permeated every fiber of Iraqi society. It wasn't just Saddam in his castle. It was the teachers in the schools. It was the cops on the street. It was the bus drivers. It was the guys that ran the electrical infrastructure. All of those folks were Baathists or were somehow affiliated with the Baath Party. So when you proclaim that the Baath Party is now disbanded and illegal, all of those people immediately perceive that they are out of work, and not only are they out of work, but they are not available to the new government, the CPA, or the emerging Iraqi Government to help it run.[50]

Of course, for many Sunni Arabs, the policy meant the end of their ability to feed their families in a literal sense. One young Iraqi clerk, a Baath Party member, bluntly stated his view on the CPA policy: "We were on top of the system. We had dreams. Now we are the losers. We lost our positions, our status, the [economic] security of our families, stability. Curse the Americans. Curse them."[51]

Ambassador Bremer had ostensibly created the CPA's de-Baathification policy with enough flexibility to allow the electrical workers, teachers, and clerks who had been Baath

Party members to renounce their affiliation and become productive members of society again. Even so, Order No. 1 did not initially establish the details of its review process and the CPA itself had only a very limited capacity to screen and approve those Baathists who petitioned for exception to the policy. As a result, it was almost always up to the US military commanders in the field to make this review process work, and to some degree, the process moved forward at a sluggish pace in the summer of 2003.

Major General David H. Petraeus, who commanded the 101st Airborne Division (101st ABN) in 2003, struggled with the effects of the de-Baathification policy on Iraqi society in the northern city of Mosul and its environs. Petraeus noted that the city was home to Mosul University, an important intellectual center, and that the faculty of the university included a sizable amount of Baath Party members. However, these individuals, according to Petraeus, "were not necessarily Saddamists. They didn't necessarily have blood on their hands."[52] To reestablish the university and reemploy its faculty, Petraeus and his staff had to obtain permission from the CPA to begin a screening process. With the personal approval of Bremer, the 101st ABN assisted with a review of former Baathists and helped the Iraqis build a list of approved faculty to operate the university.[53]

Across Iraq, American units created processes to vet tens of thousands of ex-Baathists. But this work was slow and tedious, and did little to regain support from the Sunni population that was growing increasingly disenchanted in the summer of 2003. The situation only worsened in the fall when Bremer turned over the conduct of the de-Baathification program to Mr. Ahmed Chalabi, a Shia member of the Iraqi Governing Council (IGC) who, according to Bremer, expanded the policy beyond its original intent.[54] Chalabi's zeal for the widespread de-Baathification of Iraqi society made it very difficult for any former members of the Baath Party to regain their jobs. In many areas, Chalabi's interpretation of the policy undid everything American commanders had accomplished in redressing Sunni grievances about the original order. According to Petraeus, by the fall of 2003 the effect of the overall de-Baathification program "was that tens of thousands of former party members were unemployed, without any salary, without any retirement, without any benefits, and therefore, to a large degree, without any incentive to support the new Iraq."[55]

The CPA policy ordering the disbanding of the army and other official institutions had a more direct connection to the genesis of the insurgency. Once Bremer enacted the policy, Iraq was inundated by hundreds of thousands of unemployed men who had some military training and knowledge of the numerous weapons caches hidden across the country. In many parts of Iraq, former servicemen voiced their disapproval of Order No. 2 in the immediate aftermath of its announcement. On 26 May 2003, for example, 5,000 officers and soldiers demonstrated in Baghdad against the policy and the presence of Coalition forces. The group's spokesman demanded the recall of the old army, the payment of military salaries, and the formation of a new government.[56] One month later in Mosul, officers and soldiers became violent during a protest over the failure to provide the financial assistance promised by the CPA in the "Dissolution of Entities."[57]

On 23 June, 4 weeks after the proclamation of Order No. 2, the CPA attempted to address this issue by announcing the introduction of financial support for former members of the Iraqi Armed Forces. The new plan affirmed the CPA's strategy to issue a one-time termination payment to those conscripts serving in Saddam's army at the time of the regime's collapse. More important, however, was Bremer's decision to pay a monthly stipend to "former Iraqi career soldiers" and "long service enlisted personnel."[58] The policy applied to those who had served in the regular Iraqi Army and Republican Guard, but explicitly excluded those soldiers who were senior Baath Party members, officers in Iraq's internal security forces, or those accused of human rights abuses. The CPA determined that the stipends should match their pay as active officers in the old Iraqi forces.

On 6 July the CPA announced further details, including the amount of the stipends and the dates and sites for the disbursement of the payments.[59] In that month, some Army units became involved in distributing the stipend funds. The 3d Armored Cavalry Regiment (ACR), for example, reported that it paid former Iraqi officers and soldiers approximately $100,000 in July.[60] The 101st ABN reported that in the same month its officers disbursed $2.2 million to 35,131 qualified Iraqi Army veterans.[61] In August, the division issued a 3-month payment totaling $6.6 million to roughly the same number of recipients, and November brought a similar disbursal. By March 2004, one CPA document stated that the Coalition had paid a total of $45 million in stipends to former members of the Iraqi Army.[62]

The CPA also hoped to mitigate the effects of Order No. 2 by quickly establishing new security forces that would provide many former soldiers employment.[63] Still, Bremer's organization arrived in Iraq with only a rudimentary plan for the new Iraqi military and police forces and few resources to create those institutions.[64] As chapter 11 of this study will show, these shortcomings meant that the construction of new security forces moved very slowly in 2003 and employed only a relatively small number of Iraqis.

The CPA had alleviated the short-term economic concerns of those Sunnis who had been career officers and enlisted soldiers in Saddam's army, but other Sunni Arabs grew increasingly concerned about their long-term prospects in a post-Saddam Iraq. In this environment some Iraqi men, especially those who had been serving as conscripts in the military and security forces, became vulnerable to the appeal of the budding insurgency. Lieutenant General Wallace described the situation in the summer of 2003 as follows:

> The dissolution of the Iraqi Army meant that we put five hundred thousand [*sic*] military age people out of work instantaneously. . . . That created an instantaneous unemployment problem that might have been avoided. Now you had all these kids and young men who had families who were standing on the street corner wondering where their next meal was coming from. That was a big deal. And, as far as they knew, this was permanent, so their obligation to their family was to figure out how they were going to support their family.[65]

Wallace then noted the connection between the unemployment and the potential for the rise of insurgent groups in both the Sunni and the Shia communities:

> [The obligation to support their family] made [the unemployed soldiers] appropriate fodder for just about any criminal organization, insurgent organization, dissenting organization, Shia militia, or you name it. You are going to gravitate to whoever can meet your needs and that was where they gravitated to during this very interesting month or two.[66]

The judgment of Colonel (Retired) Paul Hughes, who served with ORHA and was working with the old Iraqi military in April and May 2003, is more succinct. Hughes called the decision to abolish the Iraqi Army a "strategic blunder."[67]

The Emergence of the Iraqi Insurgency

The Iraqi insurgency that evolved in the spring of 2003 was extremely complex in nature. Its disparate elements (all of which will be discussed in greater detail later in this chapter) gave it a diverse quality that militated against an easy categorization of the Iraqi opposition as an insurgency. In many of the general studies of insurgency and counterinsurgency, theorists tend to define an insurgency in narrow terms. Much of the literature on the subject refers to Mao Zedong's theories of revolutionary warfare and his model of an insurgency as the basic templates to be used in understanding insurgent motivations and methods. In this model, derived from Marxist-Leninist theory on the subject, as well as Mao's experience leading guerrilla groups in China in the 1930s, an insurgency is one tool in the revolutionary party's struggle for political power.[68] Mao's well-known model features an insurgent organization that benefits from both unity of command and unity of purpose, and offers a prescriptive set of operational phases through which the organization escalates the conflict and ultimately gains political control of a country. The multiple insurgent organizations in Iraq—with their various sectarian and ethnic identities, diverse command structures, and differing goals—did not easily fit into this well-established understanding of insurgencies.

As noted in the introduction to this chapter, US military doctrine in 2003 described insurgencies more broadly than traditional definitions, characterizing them as organized movements "aimed at the overthrow of a constituted government through use of subversion and armed conflict."[69] This description could be used to describe the wide variety of groups—former Baathists, secular nationalist organizations, Islamist terrorists, sectarian militias, criminal gangs and others—that made up the insurgent network in Iraq. Despite the broader scope, the DOD's doctrinal definition of insurgency retained traditional assumptions about command and intent, viewing an insurgent organization as operating under the command of an identifiable leadership and moving toward one overarching objective. However, this type of unified command structure was not present in the days just following Saddam's collapse and emerged slowly in the Iraqi insurgency in the summer of 2003. Nor was there any single political goal that defined the end state for all the insurgent groups fighting Coalition forces in this early period. American commanders who attempted to discern a unified purpose and command in Iraqi attacks found only vague political and religious statements and small-scale attacks, coordinated, at best, at the local or regional level. This view led to the widespread American conclusion that the violence was the work of small, isolated groups of Saddam's paramilitary formations (Fedayeen) and recalcitrant Baathists, albeit inspired by some central concept of resistance to the Coalition invaders.

The American assessment in the summer of 2003 was accurate in part. Ex-Baathists, sometimes called former regime elements (FRE) by US commanders, appear to have been behind the small number of attacks on Coalition forces during this timeframe. However, most Coalition commanders did not realize the small groups comprising the Iraqi opposition that summer expended most of their energy and resources on organization and making connections rather than on overtly attacking the Coalition. Initially, these individuals were almost exclusively Sunni and were drawn together because of anger and dishonor over their unemployment and resentment of the occupation. Disenfranchised individuals began leveraging pre-existing party, professional, tribal, familial, or geographic—including neighborhood—networks to create the foundation of their insurgent organizations.[70] Subsequent action revolved around defining the cause and recruiting followers.[71] Former Baathist officials often took the lead in these efforts, combining their military and intelligence skills with knowledge of the location of vast weapons stockpiles and money hidden for the defense of Baghdad.[72]

Still, the early Sunni insurgent groups were not simply Saddamists fighting to restore the Baathist Party and its ideology. Instead, the insurgency in Sunni areas grew because of concerns about political status in general. Colonel Harvey, the US Army officer who led CJTF-7's Red Team, suggested that the groups within the Sunni insurgency were always focused on retaking the political power they had enjoyed in the Saddam regime. In Harvey's estimation, the CPA policy of de-Baathification had been tantamount to "de-Sunnification" and the Sunni Arabs, "the old oligarchy, the old leadership, the clerics, tribal leaders and others, [were] focused on regaining their power, influence and authority in whatever form that is relevant."[73]

These Sunni leaders used a variety of means to recruit and focus members of their organizations. One study conducted by the International Crisis Group (ICG) contended that Sunni groups often appealed to the population with patriotic and religious themes while relegating Baathist ideology to only a minor role.[74] Thus, there existed within the growing insurgent network a strong sense of religious identity and an obligation to oppose Coalition forces that could be characterized as infidel invaders. While the Baathist regime was secular in nature, Saddam Hussein had fostered the practice of Islam during the 1990s to unite Iraqi society and enhance the regime's legitimacy. Ahmed Hashim, a professor at the US Navy's Postgraduate School, looked closely at the origins and structure of the Iraqi insurgency and found the role of religion within the Sunni insurgent groups to be significant. As an example, Hashim quoted a middle-aged insurgent named Abu Mohajed as stating, "We fight the Americans because they are nonbelievers and they are coming to fight Islam."[75] For some religious Iraqis, the actions and policies of the Coalition forces were irrelevant. Simply by entering Iraq they had become enemies of the Iraqi people. One cleric in Mosul contended, "In invading a Muslim territory, the objective of the infidels has always been to destroy the cultural values of Islam. . . . We have been delivered of the injustices of one man [i.e., Saddam Hussein] but this does not mean we must accept the American–British domination."[76]

Despite the rising importance of the religious factor in 2003, foreign jihadis played only a minor role in the day-to-day operations of the insurgent groups. The judgment of General John Abizaid, CENTCOM commander, was that in July 2003 there were "not significant numbers" of foreign fighters flowing into Iraq.[77] The ICG report on the insurgency concurred, but noted that this changed as the insurgency matured: "The impact of foreign jihadis grew over time, but during the early stages of the insurgency it appears to have been negligible, and al-Qaeda in particular was absent."[78] Colonel Harvey's assessment of the role of foreign fighters generally agreed with these assertions. Harvey argued that even as the number of foreign fighters grew after the summer of 2003, their presence in the insurgency remained disproportionately small while their use of large-scale terrorist acts earned them a great deal of attention.[79]

Between August 2003 and January 2005, the Iraqi insurgency continued to grow and diversify. Spectacular attacks against the Jordanian Embassy on 7 August and the United Nations (UN) Compound on 19 August 2003 clearly signaled the emergence of a larger and better-organized threat. In these two acts, CPA and Combined Joint Task Force–7 (CJTF-7) officials began to discern an organized Sunni insurgency amid the inchoate actions of Saddamists, foreign fighters, and others, who chose targets carefully to have the maximum political effect. The sharply increasing level of attacks between August 2003 and January 2005 also indicated a growing insurgency. In August 2003 the insurgents launched approximately 500 attacks on

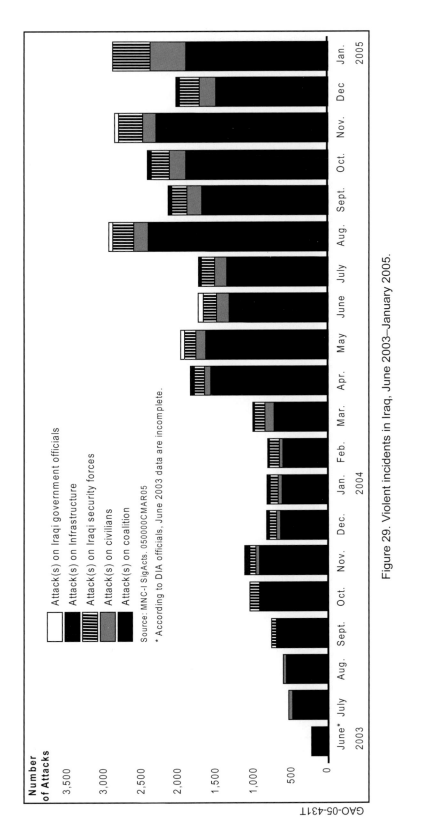

Figure 29. Violent incidents in Iraq, June 2003–January 2005.

Coalition forces, and in December 2004 this number roughly tripled to 1,500 attacks.[80] The capture of Saddam Hussein in December 2003 led to a brief respite between January and March 2004 when the attacks decreased. Still, a number of observers have noted that in the long term the removal of the Baathist leader may have actually intensified the insurgency. According to the ICG report:

> Saddam's capture in December 2003 helped rid the insurgency of the image of a rear-guard struggle waged on behalf of a despised regime. Paradoxically, his incarceration gave the insurgency renewed momentum, dissociating it from the Baathist regime and shoring up its patriotic, nationalist and religious/jihadist credentials. By the same token, it facilitated a rapprochement between the insurgency and trans-national jihadi networks, which had been hostile to a partnership with remnants of a secular, heretical regime and whose resources (monetary and human) could now be fully marshaled.[81]

While the first 3 months of 2004 witnessed fewer attacks on Coalition soldiers, this interval was only a temporary lull that saw insurgent forces consolidating in cities such as Fallujah and creating broader networks.

The events of April 2004 stand out as a jarring shock as both Sunni insurgent groups and Shia militants rose up in armed defiance of the Coalition. These events demonstrated that the capture of Saddam had not unhinged the Sunni-led factions of the insurgency. In that month, the number of attacks jumped precipitously, reflecting insurgent reactions to the US Marine Corps assault on the city of Fallujah and the insurrection mounted in Baghdad and the southern cities of An Najaf, Kufa, and An Nasiriyah by the Shia Mahdi Army (Jaish al Mahdi) under the control of Muqtada al-Sadr. The Coalition's decision to end the assault on Fallujah and enter into political negotiations with the Iraqi elements in the city had a particularly profound effect on the Sunni insurgency. Hashim argued that the insurgents viewed it as "major political and military victory" because they had endured the US assault and remained undefeated.[82] In a similar fashion, the Mahdi Army uprising gave strength to Shia organizations by demonstrating that they too could use violence to provoke a reaction from the Coalition and achieve specific political goals. The insurgents benefited from these events, using them to increase recruits, expand training, and improve the arming of their organizations. For the remainder of 2004, attacks against Coalition forces remained at the high levels achieved in April of that year.

As the insurgency became larger and more lethal, it also diversified. While the opposition had begun as a loose association of ex-Baathists operating more or less independently, by the spring of 2004 it had become a multifaceted and cohesive network. Because of its complex and evolutionary nature, it is difficult to describe the details of the structure of the insurgency with a high degree of certitude. However, it is possible to depict the insurgent network as a constellation of groups that cooperated but also shifted positions and loyalties as their motivations and actions changed. This constellation included the major Sunni groups made up of former Baathists, tribes, Islamist parties, and eventually terrorist organizations like Abu Musab al-Zarqawi's al-Qaeda organization. Shia groups and criminal gangs occupied positions within the constellation as well.

The key to understanding the network, according to Colonel Harvey, was the connections that key ex-Baathists leaders forged with the other groups in the insurgent constellation. Before 2003 the Saddam regime had established intelligence and paramilitary organizations such

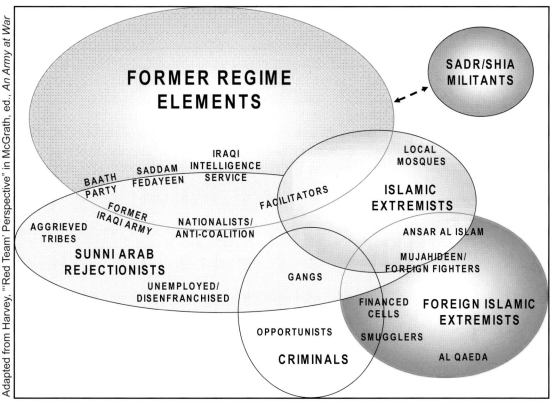

Figure 30. Iraqi insurgency, 2004.

as the Al-Quds Army and the Fedayeen Saddam in every Iraqi province to secure the Baath Party's political power.[83] These organizations had established safe houses and weapons caches in large cities. They had also prepared to use specific mosques as covert bases for operations against Shia or Kurdish insurrections or any other opposition that might threaten regime power. These groups benefited from the widespread and immense arms caches Saddam had dispersed throughout the country in the years leading up to the war.[84] The US victory in the spring of 2003 did nothing to dismantle these Baathist organizations, their infrastructure, or the significant relationships they had forged with tribal and religious leaders within Iraq. It was this set of Baathist institutions, Harvey asserts, that after May 2003 made up the central set of organizations in the constellation and provided general guidance and resources to other groups by leveraging their established relationships. Indeed, there was overlap between these groups, with some individuals active in more than one type of organization. This understanding of the network helps elucidate how and why former Baathists—secular in orientation— used tribal connections to establish a working relationship with Islamist terrorists affiliated with al-Qaeda in Iraq.[85]

Figure 31. Wanted poster for Abu Musab al-Zarqawi.

At the tactical level, these organizations used a cellular structure to mount operations against Coalition forces. To a large degree, this cellular structure was based on the framework of the Baathist paramilitary and intelligence systems. Specialized and compartmented cells, however, were characteristic of many insurgent organizations, such as the Algerian National Liberation Front (FLN) and the Viet Cong, and were not unique to Iraq. Iraqi insurgent groups employed cells that procured weapons, cells that constructed bombs, cells that provided command and control, and combat cells—the small groups that actually conducted the attacks.[86] One example of an organization with this type of structure was the Army of Muhammad, which operated in the Sunni heartland and claimed to have a number of specialized cells headed by an officer who had served in Saddam's army. The role of the Baathist network in the group, however, was diluted by the presence of the large, powerful Sunni Dulaimi tribe, to which many of the group's members belonged.[87]

While this diverse network was unified in its opposition to the Coalition, other overarching political objectives that might have provided cohesion were more difficult to detect. Most theoretical works on insurgency warfare make the assumption that an insurgent fights for something greater than military victory. The US military's doctrinal understanding of insurgencies certainly assumed that larger political goals, like the revolutionary seizure of power or the establishment of a particular ideology such as communism, have provided the impetus to modern insurgencies. Events in Iraq in 2003 and 2004 forced some to reconsider this definition, suggesting it remained too narrow and positing the existence of insurgencies without clearly articulated and widely accepted political goals. The Iraqi insurgent groups shared no common goal, having instead multiple political agendas. Some insurgent groups sought dominance in a particular area for their tribe. Many elements of the insurgency simply wanted their ethnic or sectarian group to have political control of Iraq when the dust settled. This latter goal was one of the most important motivating factors behind many Sunni groups and the militant Shia organizations.

Certainly religion played a role in the political objectives of Islamist groups. Al-Qaeda in Iraq and other Salafist groups based their actions on the desire to establish an Islamic theocracy. The Salafist Ahl al-Sunnah wa al-Jamaah Association, for example, openly demanded the founding of an Islamic state in Iraq.[88] Some Shia groups such as the Mahdi Army at times articulated a similar version of this politico-religious end state. However, it is critical to emphasize that religious figures were not always radical Islamists and not all Islamists sought a theocratic government in Iraq. In fact, some of the religious figures that used Islamist rhetoric and have roles in the insurgent network appear to have wanted a more limited goal of greater political power for their organizations in an essentially secular post-Saddam Iraq.[89]

The varying political objectives did not necessarily preclude cooperation between the many insurgent organizations. In fact, the force holding the insurgent constellation together was the central motive of opposition to the Coalition. This motivation was expressed in some groups in secular terms, a patriotic duty, and in other groups in religious terms, a Quranic duty, to expel infidels from Muslim lands. Hashim argued that for some insurgents, the expulsion of the infidel occupiers became the political objective with little thought to what Iraq should be after the Coalition is pushed out. He quoted one Sunni insurgent as stating, "Our main aim is to drive the Americans out and then everything will go back to normal, as it was before."[90]

Major Insurgent Groups

No brief survey of the major groups within the insurgent network can be complete, but it is important to offer a general summary of the organizations that provided the bulk of the energy and resources that established the network in 2003 and then expanded it in 2004. While each group is discussed as an independent entity, it is critical to recognize that these organizations often collaborated and their membership often overlapped with individual insurgents operating in a number of different groups.

Sunni Arabs

For much of the 18-month period under study, the Sunni Arab insurgency served as the primary opposition to Coalition military forces. These Sunni Arab groups, active primarily in Baghdad, Al Anbar province, and the provinces that made up the Sunni Triangle, had grown up around the support framework initially provided by members of the Baathist military and intelligence services that had gone underground after April 2003. In fact, for many Coalition leaders the role of the Baathists was so prominent as late as mid-2004 that some still identified the Sunni groups as offshoots of Saddam's regime. General George W. Casey Jr., who became the commanding general of Multi-National Force–Iraq (MNF-I) in July 2004, recalled that on taking command, his initial assessment of the various threats in Iraq focused on these Sunni groups whose core he identified as former regime elements.[91]

While the Baathists may still have made up the core of the Sunni insurgency, by mid-2004 the number of groups within the larger network had grown and diversified. Within the complex structure of this constellation, however, some analysts have discerned several basic groups or clusters. Amatzia Baram, a historian who has written a lucid explanation of the Iraqi insurgency for the United States Institute of Peace, contended that there were three major factions among the Sunni insurgents: secular/ideological, tribal, and religious/Islamist.[92] One unifier among traditional Sunni Muslims and Baathist or non-Baathist secular Sunni Arabs was the privileged status they enjoyed under Saddam's Baath Party regime. According to Baram, "Most Sunnis, whatever they thought of the Baath Party, were beholden to Saddam and were often connected to the regime through relatives or close friends."[93] Baram continued, "Men with strong tribal connections and bound by tribal interests, values, and norms are just as likely to define themselves as Islamists, Saddamists, or, to varying degrees, both. Still others define themselves as 'nationalists.'"[94]

While there were different motivations driving the Sunni insurgency, most insurgents could be further lumped into two categories: those who opposed the Coalition presence but were willing to work with the new Iraqi Government and those who rejected any cooperation with the new Iraqi state. The former category included all other secular and ideological groups, tribes, and even some religious organizations. "Insurgents in the latter category," according to Baram, "include the ultraradical Salafi and Wahhabi Islamists, ex-Baathists who have either committed crimes against humanity or are otherwise convinced there is no place for them in the new system, and hardened ordinary criminals."[95] Only the most radical Islamists, such as the Wahhabis and Salafis, were likely to state any criticism of Saddam.

The number of Sunni Arabs in the latter category—those not willing to work with the new Iraqi government—grew in late 2003 and 2004, because of the notion that Americans disliked

Sunnis or wanted to create an Iraq in which Sunnis were disenfranchised. Some of this was an outgrowth of the policy of de-Baathification and some of it resulted from the more general perception that the Coalition sought to deny the Sunnis their rightful role as rulers of the Iraqi state. Saddam Hussein had assured the Sunni Arabs, a group that composed approximately 20 percent of the population, that they represented the majority of the Iraqi population and thus had the right to rule the Shias, the Kurds, and other groups. After May 2003 it appeared to many Sunnis that the Coalition was overtly punishing them by granting the Shias and Kurds an inordinate amount of political power. For some Sunnis, this change suggested they might not only lose political power but also become dominated politically, economically, and socially by the Shias and the Kurds.[96]

Sunni disaffection increased in 2004 not only because of the factors mentioned above but also as a result of the Coalition's large-scale offensive operations in Sunni cities such as Fallujah and Samarra that appeared to target the Sunni heartland. This loss of Sunni support showed glaringly in January 2005 when relatively few Sunni Arabs participated in the national legislative elections. Hashim quoted one particularly important Sunni official, Adnan al-Janabi, Minister of State in the Interim Iraqi Government, as stating, "[the Americans] made every single mistake they could have thought of to alienate the Sunnis. The US is behaving as if every Sunni is a terrorist."[97]

Secular Ideologues: Baathists and Arab Nationalists

As mentioned earlier, Baathist groups are critical to understanding the foundation on which the insurgent network was built. These organizations were largely motivated by economic, ideological, social, and secular interests.[98] Baathists defined themselves as both pan-Arab nationalists and Iraqi patriots. They used these ideologies to gather followers and mobilize them against Coalition forces and the new Iraqi Government. However, according to Baram's report for the United States Institute of Peace, there were sectarian motives driving at least some of the Baathist insurgent groups:

> Adherence to pan-Arab nationalism in the new Iraq . . . has different functions . . . it provides a respectable ideological legitimacy to the effort to return the Baath regime to power or to return the Sunni Arab community to a position of supremacy through other means. This is essentially a sectarian quest to reverse the ascendancy of the Shia and the Kurds following the war.[99]

Adherence to a pan-Arab ideology also brought the promise of financial, political, and military support from other Sunni Arabs throughout the world, especially from those in the Middle East who objected to any increase in Shia influence.[100] The strength of these insurgent groups was based on their entrenchment in Iraqi society; their biggest weakness was that few people believed in the Baath ideology anymore. These groups were further hampered by their inability to state that they were fighting to return a popular leader to power.[101] If there was a geographic center for these groups, it was located along the Tigris River north of Baghdad, in the cities of the Sunni heartland near Saddam's hometown of Tikrit.

According to interviews conducted by the United States Institute of Peace with Baathist officials turned insurgents, there were other motivations for carrying out military operations against Coalition forces.[102] Many were no longer supporters of Saddam, but their grievances were centered on the loss of patronage jobs that provided economic security and prestige, and a sense of humiliation they felt both as a community and as individuals for being dishonored by the United States. Baram also detected a deep concern about the future of Sunni power among these individuals:

> Many senior and mid-level Sunni Baathists believe that only they know how to conduct the affairs of the Iraqi state, and that the Shia, and particularly the Shia clergy, are totally incapable of doing so. In some cases there is evidence of a genuine fear for the very existence of the community. An interview with a few armed guards at one of Iraq's most important Sunni mosques, the Abu Hanifa mosque, further illustrates the fear of growing Shia power. Speaking the day Saddam's capture was announced, one stated bitterly: 'We don't have any future.' They insisted they were no longer fighting for the privileges they had enjoyed but, rather, for the survival of their community in a Shia-dominated state.[103]

Baram described how many of the Baathist organizations took names that were essentially secular, such as the Kataib Thawrat al-Ishreen (1920 Revolution Brigades), al-Awda (The Return), al-Islah (The Reform), Jabhat al-Muqawama (The Resistance Front), al-Qiyada al-'Amma Li-Jaysh al-'Iraq (The General Command of Iraq's Army), and Munazzamat al-Tahrir al-Iraqiyya (The Iraqi Liberation Organization).[104]

Sunni Tribes

Often intertwined with the Sunni secular groups were hundreds of tribe and subtribal groups, some of which combined to compose 10 large tribal federations. The largest two tribal federations were the Dulaim and the Shammar Jarba, which had more than one million members each.[105] Baram explained, "The most meaningful tribal components . . . were the much smaller units, mainly the fakhdh (a subtribal unit numbering a few thousand) and the khams, a five-generation unit responsible for blood revenge and for the payment of blood money, or diyyeh."[106] Tribal affiliations were very strong and tribal membership served as a source of pride for many Iraqis. Most of these tribes also had a traditional reluctance to submit to any strong central authority. They preferred to rule themselves without outside, especially Coalition, interference.[107] A key tribal value was the emphasis placed on the warrior and the respect and social status one gains from being a soldier, a norm that Saddam Hussein made great use of in creating ties between the tribes and his regime.[108] Baram explained how the Iraqi leader took advantage of the tribal code of the warrior to mount his war against Iran:

> [Saddam] believed their Arab pedigree guaranteed their loyalty in any war against Iran, and their tribal background guaranteed that they would not turn their backs to the enemy, because they were bound by the tribal code of honor (al-sharaf). As a result, during the Iraq–Iran War, young tribesmen were promoted in the armed forces at breakneck speed, filling the ranks of the Mukhabarat.[109]

Baram also noted how promotion in the Baathist military built greater loyalty to Saddam, "For modestly educated country boys this was the fulfillment of a socioeconomic dream, and they were staunchly loyal to regime and leader."[110]

Tribal hostility toward the Coalition was then partially a result of the loyalty of the many tribal groups to Saddam. But this hostility was often exacerbated whenever US Soldiers, usually unaware of the intricacies of Arab and Iraqi culture, treated tribal members in dishonorable ways. Many tribes turned against the Coalition because of these perceived insults to tribal honor and pride. Sheik Hamad Mutlaq of the Jumali tribe said, "The hatred toward the Americans was heightened when they started to arrest the sheiks and insult them in front of their people—even in front of women."[111]

Opposition to the Coalition increased when Iraqi civilians died mistakenly during combat operations. In April 2003 in Fallujah, for example, Soldiers from the 82d Airborne Division (82d ABN), believing they had been fired on, began shooting into a crowd, killing and wounding a number of Iraqis. (The actual number is still in dispute). Tribal culture demanded compensation for the deaths of innocents and often sought to redeem the dishonor of the killings by seeking revenge. To avoid this process of redeeming the honor of the group meant that the family and clan would earn the disrespect of other groups and might result in a loss of social position.[112] While the US Army eventually paid compensation to the families of the victims in Fallujah, this type of amelioration did not always occur, leading some tribal members to seek revenge for the killings on US troops.

The only way to avoid tribal violence in these cases was to pay blood money to the family of the victim by the aggressor, in this case the US military. After many attacks, the US Army did offer some Iraqi families compensation for deaths, injuries, and damage to property. However, Baram's research suggests that this did not always lead to winning the tribes over to the Coalition's side: "While payment of this blood money led to a lessening of resentment and anger, they did not disappear. In effect, US success on the battlefield, while deterring some insurgents, encouraged others to perpetuate the insurgency."[113]

Religious Groups

Because the Baath Party claimed to be a secular, pan-Arab, socialist organization, in the early decades of his regime Saddam largely ignored Islam and activities in Iraqi mosques. But, the Islamic faith was an integral part of Arab life and in Iraq, even nonobservant Muslims identified closely with Islamic culture. Those who did attend the mosques found the sites as sanctuaries for those in search of alternatives to the Baath Party to gather and discuss forbidden ideas, such as the ousting of Saddam. As noted earlier in this chapter, the situation changed in 1993 when Saddam instituted the Faith Campaign (al-Hamlah al-Imaniyyah) to encourage popular devotion to Islam. In an effort to appear pious, Saddam directed the media and the educational system to put heavy emphasis on Islamic identity. A spiritual resurgence in the Islamic world coupled with a weakened Baath Party ideology led the Iraqi leader, according to Baram, to use the new religious campaign as a way for "young Iraqis to remain politically inactive in a regime that threatened their lives if they crossed a certain line, while providing them with a sense of value and mission."[114] After the Coalition decided to eliminate the Baath Party, Islamist activity in both the Shia and Sunni communities expanded dramatically.

Ultraradical Salafis and Wahhabis

The Salafist sect within Islam offered a reactionary version of the faith to its followers. Salafism grew out of an interpretation of Islam based on the literal reading of the Quran combined with a belief in restoring an older, more pure form of the faith. Those Iraqis who became Salafists in the 1990s had no love for Saddam. Baram emphasized that Salafists viewed the secular Baath state "as a return to jahiliyya, the pre-Islamic era of barbarism and paganism" and noted that the Salafists believed it was their duty "to use violence to remove such a secular regime from power."[115] As opposed as they were to non-Muslims, many within the Salafist sect viewed other forms of Islam, including Shia Islam, with suspicion and antagonism.

Some of the Salafis were also Wahhabis, followers of the 18th-century teachings of Muhammad Ibn 'Abd al-Wahhab. Like the Salafis, the Wahhabis sought a return to the Islam practiced by the Prophet Muhammad and his early followers and rejected Western ideas and influences. Wahhabis were also theologically opposed to Shia Islam because they saw idolatry in the Shia veneration of religious figures such as the Imam Ali. The Salafists and Wahhabists, who often made up the membership of the most radical insurgent groups in Iraq such as al-Qaeda in Iraq, Jaysh Ansar al-Sunna, and Ansar al-Islam, were committed to the armed struggle against Coalition forces.[116] Baram contended that for the ultraradical Sunni religious groups, this mission was paramount:

> While many insurgents might one day lay down their weapons and become integrated into the new state system, this does not apply to the Salafis and Wahhabis. For them, the only options are victory, death, prison, and the continuation of the armed struggle. There is no way that the Salafis can be dissuaded from continuing their terrorist activities. To please them, any future government would need to be both viciously against the United States and rabidly for Taliban-style Islam.[117]

These insurgent groups claimed they would never stop fighting until their extreme religious view of government was realized in Iraq.

Shia Groups

Most Shia Iraqis were happy to see Saddam Hussein removed from power. But in the spring of 2003, a number of Shia clerics made it clear that because the United States had accomplished its overarching goal—the overthrow of Saddam—Coalition forces had to leave Iraq immediately. A growing number of young clerics helped mobilize the Shia masses into political groups, which often had militia units attached. While Sunni insurgents sought to maintain or regain privileges, Shia groups sought to acquire power that had previously been denied to them.[118] During 2003 and 2004, most Shias stayed out of the armed resistance to the occupation forces, but some proved willing to join Shia insurgent groups that targeted Sunnis.

The most vocal of the young Shia leaders was Muqtadr al-Sadr, who emerged as one of the new faces of Shia politics in post-Saddam Iraq.[119] Often bitter and anti-American, al-Sadr gained a reputation as a young and dynamic cleric who seized the opportunity to emphasize Shia demands in an attempt to win popular support among the people. Al-Sadr's father, Muhammed al-Sadr, had been a senior ayatollah who spoke out against the Baathists and gained widespread respect in Iraq. In 1999 the Baathist regime killed him and two of his sons for this criticism.

In 2003 Muqtada al-Sadr claimed the downfall of Saddam was due to divine intervention rather than a US-led invasion. Asked about his ambitions in an interview with *Middle East* journal, al-Sadr stated, "Personally I'm not looking to claim any power or to be a member of any government, neither now nor in the future. I'm just striving to apply the Sharia law. Beyond that I have no ambitions."[120] This statement seemed in direct contrast to his call for the creation of an army to fight the occupation and the Sunni Arabs. In 2003 thousands of men from the Baghdad neighborhood of Sadr City and the Shia-dominated cities of southern Iraq joined al-Sadr's militia, the Mahdi Army (Jaish al Mahdi). In April 2004 this militia rose up in armed insurrection in Baghdad and the southern cities, forcing the Coalition to fight insurgent groups in Baghdad, the Sunni heartland, and the Shia south.

The other major armed force within the Shia community was the Badr Corps. Officially aligned with the Supreme Council for the Islamic Revolution in Iraq (SCIRI), a Shia umbrella organization that opposed Saddam, the Badr Corps served as a clandestine paramilitary organization that had at times been in armed conflict with the Saddam regime. The group allegedly consisted of thousands of former Iraqi officers and soldiers who defected from the Iraqi Army and other Iraqis who fled the country and joined SCIRI. While its activities were difficult to document in 2003 and 2004, many Iraqis believed that organizations associated with the Badr Corps often used violence against Sunni groups.[121]

Al-Qaeda and Other Foreign Groups

The role of foreign insurgents in the greater Iraqi insurgency is difficult to assess with a high degree of accuracy. According to some US military leaders, foreign fighters played a relatively minor role in 2003 and 2004. For example, General Abizaid, head of CENTCOM, estimated in late September 2004 that the number of foreign fighters in Iraq was below 1,000.[122] Analysts at the Brookings Institution concurred with Abizaid's assessment, estimating that the number of foreign fighters in Iraq between May 2003 and January 2005 never exceeded 1,000.[123] Abizaid did not dismiss the threat posed by these insurgents, but he did not want the Coalition to lose focus on the groups that formed the core of the Iraqi resistance: "While the foreign fighters in Iraq are definitely a problem that have to be dealt with, I still think that the primary problem that we're dealing with is former regime elements of the ex-Baath Party that are fighting against the government."[124]

The most obvious expression of foreign involvement in the Iraqi insurgency belonged to the organization called *Tandhim al-Qaida fi Bilad al-Rafidayn*, otherwise known as al-Qaeda in Iraq. Led by the Jordanian Salafist Abu Musab al-Zarqawi, this group quickly became the best known terrorist group in Iraq.[125] Al-Zarqawi's political aim in Iraq was to liberate the country from US occupation and at the same time possibly provoke a civil war between Sunnis and Shias in Iraq.[126] Although doubted by analysts of the Iraqi insurgency, the group claimed to have 15 brigades or battalions operating in Iraq. For al-Zarqawi, the Iraq conflict had two fronts: one against Coalition forces and the other against the Shia, who al-Zarqawi believed were heretics and should be killed.[127] However, while its use of suicide attacks gained al-Zarqawi headlines, its overall role in the Iraqi insurgency was unclear. The ICG report on the insurgency contended that al-Qaeda's importance in Iraq has been clearly overstated by both the Coalition and other insurgent groups looking to credit al-Zarqawi for the most controversial attacks, especially those on Iraqi civilians.[128] That report also argued that al-Qaeda in Iraq "was more a loose network of factions involving a common 'trademark' [rather] than a fully integrated organization"[129] While never a large organization, *Tandhim al-Qaida* gained publicity in 2004 by relying on suicide attacks, truck bombings, and hostage beheadings. At the same time, in 2003 and 2004 reports suggested that al-Zarqawi enjoyed relatively little popular support among Iraqis, some of whom believed the al-Qaeda leader was using the fight in Iraq for his own purposes.[130]

Insurgent Tactics

As the Iraqi insurgency matured in 2003 and 2004, the various elements within the network began to use a handful of similar tactics. In general, there was a tacit understanding within the network that the various groups did not have the firepower or organization to win a *military* victory against Coalition forces and the increasing number of Iraqi Government security forces. When insurgent groups did try to oppose Coalition forces using conventional tactics, such as the Mahdi Army's defense of An Najaf and Karbala in April 2004 or the Sunni defensive operations in Fallujah in November 2004, American firepower, air support, and organization proved too strong.

Instead, the insurgency adopted tactics designed to attack the Coalition's political, economic, and social program for Iraq and shake the Coalition soldiers' willingness—and the enthusiasm of their home nation's population—to prosecute the campaign in support of that program. Ahmed Hashim contended that the insurgents' overall tactical objective was "to make the occupation of Iraq so untenable and uneconomical that the Coalition will have no option but to withdraw."[131] Insurgent groups of all types did employ ambushes, mortar attacks, and other types of direct assaults as methods of attacking Coalition resolve. Perhaps the best known examples are the Mahdi Army's use of ambushes against US Army units in Sadr City in early October 2003 and April 2004. However, one of the largest of these direct attacks came in the Sunni-dominated city of Samarra in December 2003 when between 60 and 80 insurgents unleashed a well-coordinated ambush on an armored unit from the 4th ID. The American tanks and Bradley Fighting Vehicles (BFVs) caused dozens of casualties and disrupted the ambush.[132]

Because attacks of this type often resulted in heavy casualties for the insurgent groups, the insurgent network largely abandoned them in favor of more effective tactics that employed relatively simple technology: the roadside improvised explosive device (IED) and the vehicle-borne improvised explosive device (VBIED).[†] While the insurgents first used crude IEDs against Coalition forces in July 2003, it was later in the year when the IED became the insurgency's weapon of choice. The IED was cheap, easy to manufacture and use, and held little risk for the attacker. The fact that Iraq was covered with ammunition caches replete with large artillery shells and other types of explosives only aided the insurgent IED effort. By November 2003 insurgent groups were hitting US Army units with IEDs on a regular basis. In Baghdad, for example, the 1st BCT of 1st AD experienced 38 IED attacks between August and mid-October 2003, and most of those attacks were on convoys moving around the city.[133]

Not surprisingly, IEDs supplanted rocket-propelled grenades (RPGs), rockets, and mortars as the leading casualty producers among Coalition forces.[134] The insurgents continued to get better at building bigger, more lethal IEDs and smarter in their placement of them. By 2004 IEDs had become a routine threat facing US Soldiers on daily patrols in settings as diverse as the urban neighborhoods of Baghdad and the rural areas of the Sunni heartland. One report

---

[†]The discussion of IEDs in this section is limited based on the 24 April 2006 memorandum from Gordon England, Deputy Secretary of Defense, regarding the "Policy on Discussion of IED and IED-Defeat Efforts in Open Sources."

Figure 32. Aftermath of IED explosion.

by the US Army War College placed the total number of IEDs used against Coalition forces between 1 April 2003 and 30 November 2004 at 9,876, causing over 4,500 casualties.[135] At times, the insurgents combined RPGs and small-arms fire with the IEDs to inflict more casualties. The insurgent use of VBIEDs showed a similar increase. The first suicide attack in Iraq occurred on 29 March 2003 when a bomber drove a taxicab to a US military checkpoint in An Najaf and detonated a bomb, killing four Soldiers.[136] Suicide attacks continued, amounting to 25 throughout the course of 2003. In 2004 VBIED attacks increased to 133.[137] Most of these suicide attacks were car bombs driven into a target, but some represented a variation that featured a single attacker wearing an explosive vest. The most infamous of these explosive vest attacks came in December 2004 when a single suicide bomber killed 22 American and Iraqi soldiers in a US Army dining facility in Mosul. Insurgent attacks using VBIEDs were accurate, difficult to prevent, and deadly.

The Iraqi population was not immune from insurgent violence. Indeed, the insurgent network made a concerted effort in 2003 and 2004 to target the country's civilian population, security forces, and infrastructure as a way of preventing Iraqis from supporting the Coalition cause. Perhaps the most troubling aspect of the insurgent campaign was the decision by groups like al-Qaeda to direct suicide attacks against civilians and Iraqis serving in the security forces as a way of turning the Iraqi population against the Coalition. Young men lined up outside police and army recruiting offices proved to be particularly vulnerable targets. From September 2003, when these attacks began in earnest, until January 2005 the number of monthly assaults on Iraqi government officials, civilians, security forces, and infrastructure increased at a steady rate.[138] The toll of these attacks was high with over 1,300 Iraqi civilians killed and approximately 4,300 wounded by IED attacks.[139]

The Coalition Response to the Iraqi Threat

The US Army units that entered Iraq in April 2003 had not been trained to combat the type of insurgent forces that developed over the summer of that year. This lack of preparedness had as much to do with US assumptions about the situation in Iraq after the toppling of the Saddam regime as it did with the actual capabilities of Army units in Iraq at the time. As this chapter has demonstrated, few in the American Government had expected an insurgency to emerge in post-Saddam Iraq, and the US Armed Forces had done little to prepare for such an event. Most of the American Soldiers in Iraq in 2003 had trained to fight conventional wars with conventional weapons. Although Army doctrine held that all units had to be ready to conduct full spectrum operations, which included stability and support operations as well as combat missions, most units had not prepared to do so in Iraq. Moreover, with the exception of US Army Special Forces, very few Soldiers had experience in conducting counterinsurgency operations. To be sure, many American Soldiers had conducted stability operations in the previous decade in Bosnia and Kosovo and were familiar with the operational requirements of peacekeeping and rudimentary nation building. Reconstruction programs, psychological operations (PSYOP), intelligence activities, and civic action efforts accomplished by US Soldiers in the Balkans and elsewhere were missions the Army expected all units to be able to conduct under its over-arching doctrine of full spectrum operations. More significantly, counterinsurgency theorists generally consider these noncombat missions—reconstruction, PSYOP, civic action—as requisite elements of any comprehensive and effective counterinsurgency campaign.

However, the security environment in the Balkans had been relatively benign. No insurgent force had risen in Bosnia or Kosovo to challenge the might of the US Army and its partners. Only the UN mission in Somalia in 1992 brought US forces into a situation where they faced an armed irregular force willing to use a variety of measures, including organized insurgent operations, to end the US effort. American Special Operations Forces did mount a small number of counterinsurgent operations to meet this threat, but conventional Army units in Somalia remained largely uninvolved.

Given this lack of experience in combating insurgencies, it should not be surprising that US Army counterinsurgency doctrine and training had withered in the decade after the end of the Cold War. When al-Qaeda launched its attacks on the United States in September 2001, the Army's counterinsurgency doctrine had not been updated since 1990. That doctrine, included in FM 100-20, *Military Operations in Low Intensity Conflict*, described in broad terms the goals and methods of insurgencies and then offered a series of basic principles and organizational guidelines to American commanders who might become involved in fighting an insurgency. Nevertheless, FM 100-20 lacked critical detail and the conventional focus of US Army training in the 1990s did not provide lessons that might have filled this gap. The US Army thus entered the Global War on Terrorism without detailed training for or broad experience in conducting the type of complex operations necessary to defeat insurgent forces.

Instead of relying on institutional experience or well-established doctrine, each American unit in Iraq in the summer of 2003 tended to focus on their immediate challenges and ultimately each took a unique approach to the problems it perceived in their area of responsibility (AOR). In many cases, the commander's perception of the threat became the most important factor driving the unit's approach. Understanding the threat was central because of the common assumption among Army leaders that security was required before the population could be engaged more broadly. In this early period, establishing security often meant a focus on offensive operations that targeted the insurgent network. At the same time, it is critical to emphasize that all the units examined for this study used a full-spectrum approach to their operations in Iraq, integrating into their campaigns efforts to recruit and train ISF, rebuild infrastructure, and introduce new governance. The commander and staff of CJTF-7, the tactical and operational headquarters guiding the American divisions in Iraq in 2003, recognized the local character of each unit's campaign and, as will be described in more detail below, crafted a campaign plan that allowed for a great deal of flexibility and initiative at the unit level.

American Perceptions of the Threat

In 2003 and 2004 the American understanding of the Iraqi insurgency evolved as the insurgency matured. By the middle of 2004, US commanders at all levels of war would benefit from the relatively detailed and nuanced analysis offered by the CJTF-7 Red Team. Even so, this sophisticated picture of the threat was possible only after a prolonged period of operations in Iraq. In the summer of 2003, Iraq was an enigma to almost all American Soldiers. As early as July 2003, however, some commanders began to discern the beginnings of an insurgency. In July the CENTCOM commander, General Abizaid, stated publicly that he believed he was witnessing the beginnings of a "classical guerrilla-type campaign."[140] Abizaid suggested that terrorist groups like Ansar al-Islam and perhaps al-Qaeda were operating in Iraq, but believed the enemy cells involved in attacking Coalition forces were composed of "mid-level Baathists, Iraqi intelligence service people, Special Security Organization people, [and] Special Republican Guard people" but not under central control.[141] Neither Abizaid nor any other American official had at this point directly linked the Baathist network with disaffected Sunnis at large and a more broadly-based insurgency.

Over the summer and into the fall of 2003, the American understanding of the threat deepened as the attacks became more numerous, more lethal, and more sophisticated. Initially, American officials described the insurgents with terms such as "former regime loyalists" or the broader "former regime elements." During this period, American commanders continued to place importance on agents of the Baathist regime even as they debated the exact nature of those forces mounting attacks on Coalition troops. Major General Steven Whitcomb, the CENTCOM Chief of Staff in 2003, recalled deliberations about the enemy:

> There was a lot of discussion during the fall time period about using the term counterinsurgency or insurgency . . . on what are the classic signs of an insurgency, and what are the characteristics. As we kind of looked at those, we didn't necessarily think that it was an insurgency. We still thought it was primarily the former regime elements that we were fighting, and we started to see a bit of the foreign fighters coming in through Syria.[142]

For Whitcomb and others, assumptions about members of the Saddam regime forming the core of the insurgency were well founded. As the suicide and IED attacks escalated in mid-2003, Whitcomb remembered that those beliefs about the enemy remained essentially static, "We really attributed [the mid-2003 increase in attacks], again, to primarily former regime elements, because (1) they had military-aged males from the dissolved Army, so they had the knowledge; and (2) Iraq was a horrendous ammo dump. It [ammo] was just every place."[143]

By 2004, however, it had become obvious that former Baathists were not the only forces involved in the insurgency. Lieutenant Colonel Wesley Odum, one of CJTF-7's chief planners in 2003 and 2004, described how the Coalition understanding of the threat evolved:

> [I]f you look at the different labels that we have stuck on the enemy over time, clearly in August 2003, the label was former regime elements. We lumped everyone together that was conducting attacks against the Coalition or a disruptive element that was causing insecurity and instability in the environment and labeled them as former regime elements. As time went on, you started to see other threats emerge like the Mahdi Army and other Sunni groups that weren't necessarily tied to the former regime but were clearly anti-Coalition. So it is interesting if you track how we labeled the enemy or the threat in Iraq over time. It starts off as former regime elements, moves into anti-Coalition forces, and now we have the label of Anti-Iraqi Forces (AIF). If you track that migration of labels, it indicates the different views of the threat.[144]

The term "Anti-Iraqi Forces" certainly came to include the foreign fighters and the emergence of Abu Musab al-Zarqawi's al-Qaeda organization. The result was a picture of a threat that almost all American Soldiers would describe as diverse, complex, and difficult to comprehend.

Still, most units focused not on the national insurgent network but on those elements active in their AOR. Numerous threat assessments from divisions, brigades, and even battalions reveal how units sought to capture a definitive picture of the insurgent forces in their areas. In late 2003, for example, a briefing by the 1st AD documented the primary threat in Baghdad as "former regime 'powerbrokers,'" but recognized the growing diversity of groups in the city that included Salafist and Wahhabist groups as well as the Shia Mahdi Army. The short analysis in this briefing closed with a warning about the local threat and the challenges this posed for US forces: "Defeating this threat requires precision. There is no 'template' that fits over the 88 neighborhoods of Baghdad."[145]

On lower levels, assessments of the threat did have more precision. For the Soldiers of the 4th Battalion, 27th Field Artillery (FA) Regiment, assigned to the 2d BCT of 1st AD, the understanding of the enemy in their AOR grew more detailed over time. The 4-27th FA had responsibility for the Al Karkh district of Baghdad located near the International or "Green" Zone, and the unit's leaders initially believed the main threat to be the vague network of former Baathists who lived in the district. After 6 months of operations in this part of the city, the Soldiers of the battalion had a more nuanced view of the enemy. Evaluation of the insurgent network in their district pointed to one particular extended family of brothers who had been very powerful in the Saddam regime and were financially supporting other elements within the network, including a small number of Wahhabist groups that had emerged in the fall of 2003.[146] This sharper picture allowed the unit to focus its offensive missions while broadening its other operations designed to win the support of the population in Al Karkh.

In the city of Tikrit, the 1st Battalion, 22d Infantry Battalion of the 1st BCT, 4th ID, achieved similar precision in its September 2003 assessment of the threat. Tikrit is located in the Sunni heartland and was the birthplace of Saddam Hussein. The Baath Party had been powerful in the city and the leaders of the 1-22d Infantry saw most of the insurgents in its area as either "stay behind cells" from the regime or "malcontented ex-members of the Baath Party and of the Iraqi military" who supported these clandestine groups. However, by September 2003 the staff of the battalion had detected the presence of "religious zealots" in their area and had also identified black-market weapons dealers as part of the larger insurgent infrastructure in Tikrit.[147] Like the 4-27th FA in Baghdad, the officers and men of 1-22d Infantry gained greater clarity on the actual threat and could focus their combat operations against those elements.

Full Spectrum Operations and Counterinsurgency: The US Army's Evolving Response to the Iraqi Insurgency

Much has been written on insurgencies and the best approaches to defeating them. As noted earlier in this chapter, much of this literature originated in the period of the Cold War and assumed that Communist ideas about revolutionary warfare and its methods would continue to be the driving force in insurgent warfare. For theorists writing during this period, an insurgency was ultimately a method of gaining political power and the proper response of the counterinsurgent was to defeat the insurgent in the arena of politics. Among the most prominent theorists were David Galula and Roger Trinquier, French Army officers who had fought insurgents in Algeria in the 1950s and 1960s. In their writings, both men stressed the need for broad counterinsurgency campaigns that engaged an insurgency in a comprehensive way. Trinquier contended, "The *sine qua non* of victory in [insurgent/counterinsurgent] warfare is the unconditional support of the people."[148] The task was to use a variety of political, economic, social, and military measures to increase the legitimacy of the counterinsurgent force's cause in the eyes of the population while ensuring those same measures—especially combat operations—did not backfire and erode popular support. For this reason, Trinquier, Galula, and other counterinsurgency theorists stressed the need to create unity of effort in the campaign by closely coordinating all anti-insurgent operations and ensuring they are focused on the political end state.[149]

However, neither Galula nor Trinquier suggested ridding the counterinsurgency campaign of its military component. Indeed, both officers stressed the need to conduct focused combat operations aimed at disrupting and destroying the insurgent organization. For Galula, insurgent warfare was "20 percent military action and 80 percent political."[150] The army conducting counterinsurgent operations had to prosecute a multifaceted campaign in which the ability to gather intelligence, train indigenous security forces, conduct psychological operations, and guide political actions, such as the preparation of the population for elections, were more important than the ability to mount conventional military operations.

While relatively few American Soldiers in Iraq in 2003 were familiar with counterinsurgency warfare and its theorists, it did not take long before many of the basic concepts of counterinsurgency made their way into US Army planning and operations. This process was indirect and based on immediate requirements rather than experience or doctrine. After April 2003 when it became clear to many Soldiers that the Coalition forces were essentially the only organizations immediately available to conduct postconflict operations, US Army units simply transitioned to full spectrum operations without much in the way of detailed guidance or special resources. In the spring and early summer, most Soldiers assessed the situation in their AORs and designed responses they believed were critical to address the unique political, economic, and military challenges in those areas.

This response was immediate in many units. One of the best examples of this was the approach taken by the 101st ABN in northern Iraq. Once the division arrived in its AOR, which included Nineveh province and the city of Mosul, Major General Petraeus decided the unit could not wait for higher headquarters and other US agencies to present a detailed blueprint for the next phase of the operation. Petraeus argued that if the Soldiers of the division did not immediately get started with a broad program of what he called "nation-building," they would begin to see a threat emerge:

> The bottom line is we were going to have to do a lot and a big part of it, believe it or not, in the beginning, was just accepting or embracing the fact that we had to get on with [nation-building] because we are, in reality, going to do it—no one else is coming to do it. There may be very little help, if any, and so let's just get on with it because it is a race against the clock.[151]

To begin their campaign, Petraeus and his commanders immediately began making contacts within the community, and those actions led to a series of important efforts:

> We really launched into it in Mosul right away. We had some basic thoughts that guided us, among which were that we needed to get Iraqi partners as soon as we possibly could. We needed that partnership to include the spectrum of the society in our area of responsibility . . . we had to get workers back on the job. We had to then help them clean up, rebuild, and re-establish basic services for the Iraqi people. We had a keen desire to establish or achieve normalcy again.[152]

For the 101st ABN, combat operations against the perceived threat, which they defined as former regime elements, were just one part of a larger and simultaneous full spectrum campaign that would create security and build popular support for the Coalition, thus precluding the growth of the enemy.

The 2d Armored Cavalry Regiment (ACR), which took responsibility for the Baghdad district of Sadr City in May 2003, began work to win support among the Shia population in that neighborhood in a similar fashion. Major George Sarabia, the executive officer of one of the regiment's squadrons, described how his unit first sought to figure out what the people in Sadr City needed, stating, "One of the things that 2d Squadron, I think, did a very good job of was getting out and engaging the local population, trying to find out what's going on and gaining situational awareness, and later on, situational understanding. Who are these people? What do they want?"[153] He added that in May 2003, his unit, like the 101st ABN, sought to reestablish a peaceful environment. To do so, the 2d ACR implemented a variety of programs to provide jobs, essential services, and security: "What we wanted to do was return things to a sense of normalcy as quickly as possible. So that became our number one key task: to provide a safe and secure environment for the people of Sadr City. And we felt if we can do that, then all else follows."[154] To the west of Baghdad, in Al Anbar province, the commander of the 2d Squadron, 3d Armored Cavalry Regiment (3d ACR) created a comprehensive approach in May 2003 to engage the primarily Sunni population of that region. The squadron's plan had six keys to success: (1) Provide security, which included patrolling and focused combat missions against specific threats; (2) Restore rule of law, with Iraqi police, laws, and courts in place; (3); Enable the emergence of an Iraqi Government and administration; (4) Facilitate infrastructure recovery, including $1 million to repair the sewer system; (5) Support humanitarian relief and assistance; and, (6) Promote change in perception, which included winning support of local sheiks and clerics.[155] In late April, 3d ACR Soldiers had pursued this type of multifaceted campaign in the city of Ramadi, and in May they planned to use this type of approach to win the support of the population in the cities of Fallujah and Habbaniyah.

While units occupied their AORs and began initial operations in the spring and early summer of 2003, higher echelons began the creation and publication of campaign plans that gave guidance and set objectives for what became the full spectrum campaign. Although no cogent insurgent network had yet coalesced, these higher-level staffs designed plans that, in retrospect, incorporated many of the key concepts of counterinsurgency warfare. Like the Soldiers in the 101st ABN and the 2d ACR, few of the planners understood the campaign as counterinsurgency. Instead, these officers viewed their mission as emphasizing offensive operations against known enemy targets while ensuring their combat missions were complemented by stability and support operations, sometimes called nation-building efforts in these early months.

Important to the military planning process was the strategic guidance offered by the CPA. On 13 July 2003, the CPA issued its Vision Statement in which Mr. Bremer and his staff set out their mission to establish a new, free, and democratic Iraq that was "stable, united, prosperous, at peace with its neighbors and able to take its rightful place as a responsible member of the region and the international community."[156] To do this, the CPA directed overall Coalition operations in six main directions: security, essential services and civil society, economy, preparing for democracy, governance and sovereignty, and information.[157] With these objectives in mind, CJTF-7 began working on its preliminary campaign guidance in the summer of 2003. (The next chapter will recount the formation of CJTF-7 and its planning efforts in greater detail. The discussion that follows focuses on CJTF-7's role in shaping the initial American response to the security challenges in Iraq in the summer of 2003.)

In June the US military had formed CJTF-7 out of the core of the US Army V Corps headquarters and established it as the senior Coalition military headquarters in Iraq. The task force commander, Lieutenant General Ricardo Sanchez, had directed the task force planning section (CJ5) to begin planning immediately and established the following mission statement for Coalition forces:

> Conduct offensive operations to defeat remaining noncompliant forces and neutralize destabilizing influences in the AO in order to create a secure environment in direct support of the Coalition Provisional Authority. Concurrently conduct stability operations to support the establishment of government and economic development in order to set the conditions for a transfer of operations to designated follow-on military or civilian authorities.[158]

Sanchez was tasking the tactical units he commanded to do two things simultaneously: conduct combat missions to establish security and begin operations that would foster political and economic stability.

Armed with this mission statement, the CJTF-7 staff began to establish other important parts of its draft campaign plan.‡ Major Wesley Odum, one of Sanchez's chief planners, described how the CJ5 Plans section of the new joint task force began constructing the plan based on a

---

‡CJTF-7 did not publish its campaign plan until January 2004. Between July and December 2003, the draft plan served as the basic guidance for all of CJTF-7's subordinate units.

foundation laid by the CFLCC and V Corps staffs.[159] That preliminary work had established objectives, lines of operation (LOOs), and key tasks for CJTF-7. These fundamental concepts served as the point of departure for the CJ5 section when in July 2003, it convened a meeting in Baghdad attended by officers who planned operations at the division level.[160] Over a period of several days, these planners agreed on a number of guiding themes for Coalition operations. Perhaps most important was determining the center of gravity and the LOOs, both critical elements in campaign planning. The concept of the center of gravity is derived from the writings of 19th century military theorist Karl von Clausewitz who defined the center of gravity as the "hub of all power and movement on which everything depends . . . the point at which all our energies should be directed." US Joint doctrine adopted the idea, further explaining it as a key "source of moral or physical strength, power, and resistance" that is often embodied by individuals, forces, or other entities that have a decisive influence on a military force or its adversary.[161] In his campaign plan, Sanchez identified the Coalition center of gravity as the popular support of the Iraqi people.[162]

To focus the overall military effort on gaining the support of the people, CJTF-7 developed the LOOs that would guide its forces. In conventional campaign planning, LOOs are physical features, usually depicted on a map, that connect a base of operations, such as Kuwait, to an objective, such as the city of Baghdad. In nonconventional campaigns, planners often use

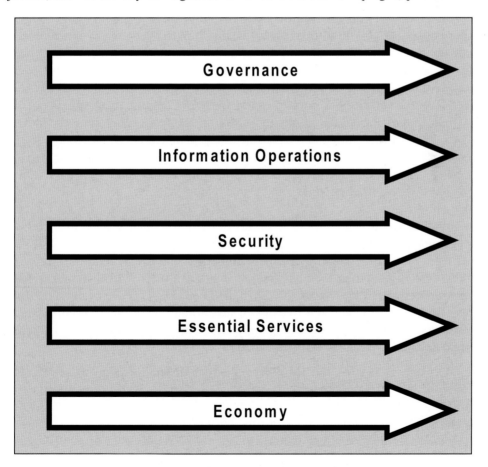

Figure 33. CJTF-7 lines of operation.

"logical" LOOs that are thematic or conceptual rather than geographic because the conflict is not geographic in nature.[163] These logical LOOs collect critical functions together in conceptual groups.

In the case of CJTF-7's draft campaign plan, the CJ5 section established five logical LOOs that spread across the full spectrum of operations—governance, security, economy, essential services, and information operations.[164] Most important for military units was the security LOO that not only ordered the US Army to conduct combat missions if necessary, but also directed them to get involved in the training of Iraqi police and military units. The governance LOO included the creation of a new national government for Iraq, but at the tactical level this primarily translated into Soldiers facilitating the creation of local and regional governments. The economic and essential services LOO similarly directed Coalition units to assist in repairing infrastructure and establishing organizations that would enhance the growth of commerce and employment. Finally, the information operations LOO drew attention to the need for Soldiers to find ways of using ideas and information to win support within the Iraqi population. These lines became organizing principles for tactical commanders to follow in the planning of their own operations.

The planners also began thinking about how the campaign would develop over time and the overarching objective it was designed to achieve. Using the Army's concept of full spectrum operations, the CJ5 created a four-phase campaign, with each phase emphasizing a different category of operation.[165] In its first phase, the plan emphasized offensive operations against noncompliant elements of the former regime and other armed opposition, but recognized that units would simultaneously be conducting defensive, stability, and support operations. Lieutenant General Sanchez viewed the first phase of his plan as essentially a continuance of Phase III—Decisive Operations from CFLCC's COBRA II, because in the summer of 2003 the CJTF-7 commander believed the instability in Iraq prevented CJTF-7's forces from moving into the next phase, which would de-emphasize offensive operations.[166] Indeed, in the CJTF-7 plan, Sanchez's focus on offensive operations led to this first phase becoming known as Phase III—Offense. The second phase, labeled as IVa–Stability, would come after the Coalition had created a secure and stable environment and would feature stability operations, especially those that supported the establishment of Iraqi political and economic development. The transition to Phase IVb–Support would shift the emphasis of Coalition operations to focus on what the plan called support operations and would concentrate efforts on training the ISF. Over the course of these phases, the number of Coalition units would not be removed from Iraqi soil until in Phase IVc–Deterrence, the fourth and final phase, a very small contingent remained to advise and support Iraqi forces in the defense of their country. CJTF-7 planners envisioned the campaign reaching its ultimate objective or end state when Iraq became a secure state, free of active terrorist organizations, in which the army and police could protect the population from any internal or external threats that might emerge.

The CJ5 planners and the division planners agreed on the fundamental principles of the draft plan at the July meeting in Baghdad. When the division planners returned to their units in early August 2003, they used these principles to shape their unit's campaign plans (discussed below). The CJTF-7 staff amended the original draft plan several times as the security situation changed in the summer and fall of 2003. In January 2004 the Coalition published a revised version of the original draft as the official campaign plan, but the mission statement and LOOs remained the same.§ The plan as a whole served as a broad statement of purpose, entailing a full spectrum approach to securing political, economic, and social progress as well as military success in Iraq.

At the tactical level, division commanders and their staffs produced campaign plans that were nested with the early drafts of the CJTF-7 plan. This process provided an amount of unity to an effort that differed based on the unique qualities of the local areas in which the divisions operated. The plan crafted by Task Force (TF) *All American*, a division-size unit commanded by the 82d ABN's headquarters, provides an excellent example of this process. TF *All American* took over operations in Al Anbar province in the fall of 2003 and quickly defined its overall objective as winning the "support of the Iraqi People."[167] Major General Charles H. Swannack Jr., the division commander, and his staff then created a plan that focused the task force's operations on this objective by channeling the effort into four LOOs: security, governance, essential services, and economy.[168] The security LOO included American operations against insurgent organizations in the province, but also the use of the task force's units to train the Iraqi Civil Defense Corps (ICDC) and the Iraqi police. Governance entailed actions by Civil Affairs (CA) and Psychological Operations Teams to foster local forms of democratic government, place greater authority for change in Iraqi hands, and assist with the conduct of elections. Operations along the essential services LOO sought to use reconstruction projects to improve Iraqi lives and demonstrate the Coalition's resolve to create a better Iraq. The economy LOO focused the division's attention on improving the environment for business and employment.

The 4th ID, operating to the east of Al Anbar in the Sunni Triangle, developed four LOOs similar to those in the TF *All American* plan.[169] The military LOO included offensive combat operations as well as the training of Iraqi Army units. The governance LOO directed subordinate organizations, including combat units, to build relationships with Iraqi community leaders and facilitate the establishment of a local government. Like the 82d ABN, the leaders of the 4th ID hoped to use the economy LOO to improve employment and foster a stable business climate. Finally, the infrastructure LOO involved unit Soldiers in the restoration of essential services and infrastructure improvements.

The 4th ID's campaign plan illustrates the broad, multifaceted approach taken by the unit's leaders in mid-2003. Establishing this fact is important because several widely-read accounts of OIF have asserted that from its arrival in the Sunni Triangle in April 2003, the division relied too heavily on large-scale combat operations, actions that alienated the population in the region and turned many Iraqis into enemies of the Coalition.[170] Certainly, the division's operations in the early stages of its deployment in the Sunni Triangle did feature large-scale combat missions such as PENINSULA STRIKE, an operation that tasked two combat brigades and supporting elements to conduct large cordon and sweep operations in the Sunni heartland. One important reason for the emphasis on these types of operations was that the region north of Baghdad, especially the cities of Tikrit, Samarra, and Baqubah, had not seen major combat actions during the invasion of the country and only relatively small US Marine units had occupied the area until the 4th ID arrived in April 2003. Baathist networks in the Sunni Triangle thus remained intact and active that spring and summer, mounting serious attacks on US troops with mortars,

---

§The CJTF-7 Campaign Plan remains classified as of the writing of this study.

small arms, and IEDs. The problem with operations like PENINSULA STRIKE was that in their attempt to remove the threat, the units conducting the cordon and sweeps often detained a large number of Iraqi men, not all of whom were associated with the insurgency. It is reasonable to assume that these actions disaffected at least some portion of the Sunni population in the division's AOR.

By August 2003 CJTF-7 had curtailed most of these large-scale operations. Iraqi leaders had convinced Lieutenant General Sanchez that because of their potential for alienating Iraqis, the operations were counterproductive. In early August Sanchez stated, "I started to get multiple indicators that maybe our iron-fisted approach to the conduct of [operations] was beginning to alienate Iraqis. I started to get those sensings from multiple sources, all the way from the [Iraqi] Governing Council to average people."[171] Sanchez directed his units to avoid large-scale operations like PENINSULA STRIKE and rely instead on more limited, highly precise raids on verified insurgent targets. The combat operations mounted by the 4th ID in the months following Sanchez's directive were much smaller in size than PENINSULA STRIKE.

By the time Sanchez directed the cessation of large-scale cordon and sweeps, the 4th ID was in the midst of conducting actions across their LOOs. In fact, as early as the middle of June, at the same time the division was conducting PENINSULA STRIKE, the 4th ID had already launched a variety of reconstruction and governance operations. The division commander, Major General Raymond Odierno, stated on 18 June 2003 that the 4th ID was involved in establishing a multi-ethnic representative government in the city of Kirkuk, opening a police training academy in Baqubah, re-opening 15 judicial courts and 37 banks in the area, and providing salaries to a large number of Iraqi civil servants.[172] The journal of Major Christopher Bentch, a police officer from Kansas City who was serving as a Reserve CA officer in the 4th ID, supports Odierno's description of the division's operations. Bentch described how, by the third week of June, he and his team were spending a large amount of money on a broad variety of reconstruction projects. The CA officer further described how the leadership in the 3d BCT directed him to work closely with brigade planners to ensure reconstruction programs were integrated closely into the plan for the sequel to PENINSULA STRIKE, a large-scale operation called DESERT SCORPION.

For the Soldiers of the 4th ID, a gradual shift in operational emphasis became more pronounced as summer faded into fall. Lieutenant Colonel Troy Perry, a staff officer in the division's 3d BCT, recalled that once the division eroded the insurgent networks in the Sunni Triangle and reduced the attacks on US units, his brigade began placing more resources in training the ISF, rebuilding the infrastructure, facilitating local government, and holding elections.[173] Perry asserted that by January 2004, roughly 65 percent of his brigade's operations were reconstruction, governance, and other noncombat missions. The remaining 35 percent were combat operations, but highly-focused missions designed to engage specific insurgents or insurgent groups in the AOR.[174] Thus, from the time of its entry into the Sunni Triangle in April 2003, the 4th ID had been conducting full spectrum operations. What evolved, however, is how battalion and brigade commanders in the 4th ID emphasized specific types of operations to meet the objectives of their unique AORs.

This issue of balancing the operational approach affected all units and was one of the thorniest challenges facing commanders in 2003. If the unit focused on aggressive combat operations that directly attacked insurgent networks, it might alienate the population. On the other hand, if that same unit concentrated the majority of its resources on reconstruction, fostering representative government, and training local security forces, it might lose the initiative and allow insurgent groups to grow and gain legitimacy within that population. Lieutenant Colonel Greg Reilly, commander of the 1st Squadron, 3d ACR, struggled with this dilemma as he directed operations near the city of Al Qaim in Al Anbar province in the summer of 2003. In September 2003 Reilly used a written assessment of his squadron's performance to express his frustrations in achieving proper operational balance:

> *My daily struggle, what I spend most of my mental energy on, is figuring out how to gain the initiative against the threat without causing increased dissention of the population. This situation is frustrating; it's a classical catch 22 situation* [emphasis in original]. I could aggressively go into built up areas on search and attack missions to destroy the threat, but the trade off is the collateral damage that will occur; the perception that security is getting worse; the loss of US soldiers as the risk increases and the risk of not achieving the objective at all.[175]

For Reilly, the solution to this problem seemed to lie in the establishment of local ISF that would create security and foster the rule of law. Nevertheless, this solution generated its own concerns: would the Iraqi forces be willing and able to engage insurgent forces and build the proper environment? While noting that the Iraqis themselves seemed to hold the key to creating stability, Reilly displayed a measure of unease: "The Challenge is the risk associated with allowing Iraqis to begin performing functions on their own and Coalition forces disengaging over time."[176] Many American Soldiers in Iraq shared this apprehension.

The local character of the insurgency and the measures required to counter it made close coordination of the overall campaign in Iraq difficult at times. Major General Thomas Miller, the chief of CJTF-7's Operations staff section (CJ3), likened Iraq to "a mosaic of different agencies, enemies, peoples, tribes, coalition differences and different conditions—each deserving a response of its own."[177] However, a full spectrum campaign focused on supporting the construction of a new Iraq while countering an increasingly complex threat had to maintain unity of effort in its operations or it would likely not achieve its overall political goals. The nesting of the division's campaign plans within the larger framework of the CJTF-7 mentioned above was one important means of creating unity of effort in OIF. Miller described the CJTF-7 campaign plan as laying out "cardinal directions" for the divisions to use as a general guide for their own operations.[178] The Coalition quickly adopted another process—the daily and weekly coordination meetings between CJTF-7 and its subordinate headquarters. In a nightly conference call, Sanchez, the commanding general of CJTF-7, and his major subordinate commands including Special Operations units, shared information and coordinated operations. The CJTF-7 staff also held weekly campaign plan synchronization meetings with Sanchez to ensure all of the command's efforts were focused on the larger objectives.[179]

As the campaign progressed, US Army planning and preparation for full spectrum operations became more deliberate and detailed. This was especially true for those units that deployed to Iraq in 2004 as part of the OIF II rotation. The commanders and staffs of these organizations had watched events in Iraq closely during the preceding year, had coordinated with the units they were relieving, and enjoyed the benefits of deliberate planning and training for the campaign—an advantage most units in Iraq in 2003 did not have. The 1st Cavalry Division

(1st CAV), for example, arrived in Baghdad in March 2004 to replace the 1st AD. The 1st CAV trained carefully in the United States for the type of broad mission set that the 1st AD and others had learned to do in Iraq. Major General Peter Chiarelli, the commander of 1st CAV, had looked closely at the CJTF-7 campaign plan and developed a broad campaign concept for his division that he clearly characterized as full spectrum operations.[180] Based on the same principles emphasized by counterinsurgency theorists such as Galula and Trinquier, Chiarelli's campaign plan set down six LOOs: combat operations, train and employ ISF, essential services, promote governance, economic pluralism, and full spectrum information operations. The division commander believed these six themes, if properly followed, would move his forces closer to political success by creating legitimacy for the Coalition and its Iraqi partners. Likewise, his subordinate units adopted the same LOOs to guide their own operations in various parts of Baghdad.[181]

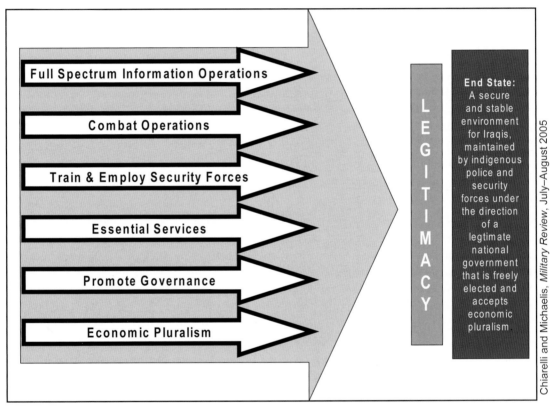

Figure 34. 1st Cavalry Division lines of operation and end state.

While limited combat operations might be necessary to deal with intransigent threats, Chiarelli focused more on winning the support of those Iraqis who were not yet actively supporting the insurgency but also not working actively on the side of the Coalition. These "fence sitters," as Chiarelli characterized them, could be alienated by unfocused Coalition combat operations. But they could also be convinced to support the Coalition through carefully planned noncombat operations, such as projects that rebuilt the infrastructure and provided employment. Chiarelli instilled these principles in his staff and his subordinate commanders:

The key is trying to get [Soldiers] to understand the need to in fact look at those nonkinetic lines, the reconstruction line, the governance line, the economic pluralism line, and the information operations line, and the key and critical role that they play in a fight like this. . . . I think I was bound and determined to go over with an emphasis that said we were going to look at the nonkinetic lines as important, and in some instances more important than the kinetic lines, to getting us closer to mission accomplishment because you run into some real serious issues over here with this culture and this society when you apply those kinetic lines without an understanding of how that affects people over time.[182]

For Chiarelli, the US Army's goals in Iraq were far better expressed using concepts like "political legitimacy" and "essential services" than in traditional military definitions of success derived from the experience and doctrine of conventional warfighting.

Chiarelli's emphasis on nonkinetic operations led to unique approaches to the problems of insurgency in and around Baghdad. Two of his division's battalions—the 2d Battalion, 12th Cavalry (2-12th CAV) and the 4th Battalion, 5th Air Defense Artillery (4-5th ADA)—both operating near the international airport, began to work closely with local tribal leaders to understand their grievances and reach a consensus about common goals that could be attained with Coalition assistance.[183] Using this approach, sometimes labeled by observers as "constructive engagement," American Soldiers listened closely to local leaders to understand how their tactics and behavior at times clashed with Iraqi cultural norms and how they might decrease tensions. Through this process, the local sheiks came to see the American units as the strongest, most influential players in the local political setting and negotiated to achieve what they wanted in exchange for aid in identifying insurgents and pushing them out of the AOR. In the experience of 2-12th CAV and 4-5th ADA, the launching of infrastructure improvement projects satisfied local needs, addressed unemployment problems, and granted greater status and influence to local Iraqi sheiks within their tribes, all of which helped create greater security. Indeed, one report suggested that the dramatic decrease in the number of insurgent attacks on American Soldiers in 2-12th CAV's AOR was largely a result of the approach taken by the unit's leaders.[184]

The transition to MNF-I in the summer of 2004 formalized the shift to a deliberate and well-defined full spectrum counterinsurgency campaign in Iraq. When General Casey took command in July, he and Ambassador Negroponte directed the creation of a Red Team and then used the findings of that team's research in conjunction with the MNF-I staff's efforts to develop a new campaign plan. According to Casey, the Red Team gave him detailed confirmation that "we were fighting an insurgency, that the primary threat to the accomplishment of our strategic objectives at that time was the former regime element insurgency."[185] For the MNF-I commander, it was imperative that he unequivocally define the enemy: "At my level, I felt it very important to be able to articulate to the command what the nature of the war was, and in my mind, there was still too many folks here that thought this was just the aftermath of a conventional war."[186] This understanding of the enemy led him to issue a new mission statement that described the Coalition's military purpose as "full-spectrum counterinsurgency operations." According to Colonel William Hix, who served in the Strategy, Plans, and Assessment (SPA) section of the MNF-I staff in 2004 and was heavily involved in developing the new campaign plan, Casey chose the term "full spectrum counterinsurgency operations" for his mission statement to stress that the Coalition was engaged with an insurgency and Coalition military forces had to simultaneously conduct a range of operations to deal with that enemy.

Casey's emphasis on the political and economic aspects of the campaign led him to integrate his own military staff with that of the US Embassy, led by Ambassador John Negroponte, which the US Department of State (DOS) had established after the transition of political authority to the Iraqi Interim Government (IIG). By the end of 2004, the MNF-I commander had also successfully forged a close relationship with Prime Minister Ayad Allawi, further strengthening the political aspects of the Coalition effort. Hix recalled that MNF-I's conception of the campaign in the summer of 2004 embodied Galula's assertion about the primacy of politics in counterinsurgency warfare. Indeed, the plan's four LOOs—governance, security, economy, and strategic communications—all focused the Coalition effort on the January 2005 elections and assisting the IIG to assume more authority in an effort to build greater legitimacy.[187]

The MNF-I campaign plan, published in August 2004, served as only a temporary guide. Casey began to re-conceive the plan in the fall 2004, bringing in counterinsurgency experts from the RAND Corporation and the Naval Postgraduate School to help him and his staff gain insights from counterinsurgency campaigns of the past. This initiative and others led to the emergence of new thinking about the counterinsurgency campaign in Iraq and bred ideas such as the creation of the Military Transition Teams (MiTTs) to assist in the training of the ISF.[188] Ultimately, Casey included these ideas in the modifications made to the campaign plan after the January 2005 elections established Iraq's new political environment.

Reorganizing for the New Campaign

The degree to which the US Army recognized the need to mount a new type of campaign in Iraq can be seen in the striking amount of reorganization that its tactical units underwent after May 2003. On one level, there were critical changes to task organizations for the new environments and missions that units faced. One type of reorganization was the increase in the number and types of units under a commander's authority. For example, after assuming command of all forces in the Baghdad area on 5 June 2003, the commander of 1st AD added the term "task force" to the division's name, signifying its major reorganization for the difficult challenges of securing the capital and conducting full spectrum operations there. To do these missions, the division added major combat units—2d ACR and 2d BCT, 82d ABN (2-82d)—to its already large complement of three maneuver brigades and other supporting elements.

The division then executed an extensive task organization to give each of its combat brigades a balanced mix of forces. The armor-heavy 1st and 3d Brigades each received light infantry battalions—the 3d Battalion, 124th Infantry from the Florida Army National Guard's 53d Infantry Brigade, and the 1st Battalion, 325th Parachute Infantry from the 2d Brigade, 82d ABN, respectively. To give it increased armor and mobility, the 2-82d received an attachment of troops from the division cavalry squadron. The 2d Battalion, 37th Armor, a unit armed with M1A2 Abrams tanks, was detached from the 2d Brigade and reported to the 2d ACR, which had converted to a wheeled light cavalry regiment organization and no longer had tanks. The division commander then attached the 3d Squadron of the 2d ACR, equipped with high-mobility multipurpose wheeled vehicles (HMMWVs), to the 2d Brigade for the task of securing the "Green Zone" in central Baghdad.[189] Later in the campaign, the division attached the 2d Battalion, 504th Parachute Infantry to the division artillery (DIVARTY), a command functioning as a maneuver element instead of its normal role as the provider of fire support to the division.

Reorganization to meet the campaign's requirements often meant huge growth in the number of commands under divisional authority. At one point, 1st AD added the 937th Engineer Group and the 18th Military Police Brigade, giving it the equivalent of 9 maneuver brigades and almost 39,000 Soldiers. The division accepted further reinforcements, such as a CA brigade, a chemical company, PSYOP companies, and an aeromedical evacuation detachment.[190] Every division in theater underwent its own version of organizational transition as they rapidly adapted to the requirements of the new campaign in Iraq.

More radical transformations that included significant changes in fundamental missions and capabilities occurred at brigade and battalion level. The most dramatic of these transformations was the conversion of field artillery and armor battalions to general maneuver units that conducted full spectrum operations instead of the primary combat missions for which their Soldiers had trained. Often this meant parking many of their combat vehicles and conducting patrols and other operations on foot or in wheeled vehicles such as HMMWVs. However, a new mission set also required new training and new organization. For example, the 4th Battalion, 27th Field Artillery, a unit in the 1st AD that became a maneuver battalion in Baghdad in May 2003, faced significant changes once the leadership realized their Soldiers would be conducting full spectrum operations in the Iraqi capital. After arriving in theater, the battalion commander reorganized his staff and began training his artillerymen in basic infantry tasks such as movement techniques, clearing buildings, and cordon and searches.[191]

Units that deployed to Iraq in 2004 often experienced similar transformations, but had more time to prepare and train their Soldiers than units such as the 4-27th FA. Before its deployment to Iraq, the 1st CAV converted its DIVARTY command into a maneuver unit called the 5th BCT, 1st CAV. This new brigade was built around the core of two converted field artillery battalions and one converted air defense artillery battalion. The new unit also included one light infantry battalion and at times two cavalry squadrons.[192] While they enjoyed some preparation time, brigade leaders still had less than a year to retrain their staffs and Soldiers for missions that were very different from their traditional role as the provider of indirect fire support to the division. The new maneuver brigade deployed to Baghdad in the spring of 2004 and established its AOR in the Al Rashid section of the capital. There, it began conducting the complex set of full spectrum operations laid out by the division commander, Major General Chiarelli. The newly formed BCT would eventually increase the size of its organization by taking command of two Iraqi Army battalions and for a time, even had the 2d Battalion, 24th Marines, a United States Marine Corps (USMC) Reserve unit from St. Louis, Missouri, under its operational control.

The broad array of unconventional tasks required by the new missions and environments also led to more novel types of reorganization. Army doctrine and practice assigned responsibility for reconstruction and governance missions to CA units. However, the scope of the campaign in Iraq forced units of all sizes and purposes to become critical players in these aspects of the campaign. The reorganization of the 101st ABN provides a good example of this. Once the division headquarters was established in Mosul, Major General Petraeus tasked his subordinate units with a series of new missions. He gave the division staff responsibility to assist in organizing elections for the interim provincial council, as well as those that would choose the governor,

---

Courage and Commitment in the New Campaign
2-5 Artillery in Al Anbar Province

In April 2003, the 2d Battalion, 5th Field Artillery deployed to Iraq planning on delivering indirect fire support to the 3d Armored Cavalry Regiment (3d ACR). Once the 3d ACR began full spectrum operations in Al Anbar province in late April, however, there was no longer a great demand for artillery support. Instead, the battalion transformed into a maneuver unit operating under the command of the 3d ACR, responsible for a large area of operation measuring 6,500 square kilometers. The artillerymen of 2-5 FA began conducting a broad array of missions, including working with the World Food Program to deliver humanitarian assistance, reestablishing Al Anbar University, training Iraqi security forces, and mounting raids, cordon and searches, and other security missions.

Another of the battalion's critical missions, the destruction of captured Iraqi munitions, provided the setting for a selfless act of courage by several of the unit's Soldiers. As Iraqi contractors worked in an ammunition bunker at a large Saddam-era Army base, a fire inside the bunker threatened to engulf the Iraqis and the American Soldiers supervising them in a huge explosion. Staff Sergeant Tim Huangs, Private Akai Johnson, Corporal Ryan Waters, and Captain Tim Godwin, all from 2-5 FA, repeatedly entered the bunker to help the injured Iraqis escape the fire. Once they were outside, unit medics provided first aid and loaded one terribly burned Iraqi worker on an ambulance. Staff Sergeant Huangs also extinguished the fire inside the bunker, preventing a catastrophic accident. After the incident, Huangs stated that his actions were simply the result of his commitment to the men—both Iraqi and American—that were under his charge. Huangs explained, "Why'd I run into [an] ammo bunker that had just had an explosion? You just do it. The Army trains you to take care of your Soldiers. I was responsible for those Iraqi workers; I was their supervisor."

LTC David C. Hill and MAJ Shaun E. Tooke,
"2-5 FA: A Ground Maneuver Force for the 3d ACR in OIF,"
Field Artillery (September-October 2004): 24-29.

---

vice governors, and assistant governors for the surrounding Nineveh province.[193] Other task-ings based on obvious functional linkages aligned the Division Surgeon's Office with the local offices of the Iraqi Ministry of Health, the communications staff section (G6) with the offices of the Telecommunications Ministry, and the engineer brigade with the Ministry of Public Works. In other cases, the linkage was not so direct, but the novelty of the mission the same. Petraeus tasked the 159th Aviation Brigade, a Blackhawk-equipped helicopter unit, to help the Iraqis reopen Mosul University and get its 35,000 students and faculty back into the classrooms. He also assigned the Division Support Command (DISCOM) and the Corps Support Battalion to assist the Ministry of Education and the Ministry of Youth and Sports.[194]

Before the beginning of OIF, the 101st ABN had not planned to conduct missions such as the reopening of a university or the staging of provincial elections. In any event, Petraeus' division and other Army units brought a number of assets and capabilities to this type of campaign, which CA units, NGOs, the CPA, and the UN simply could not provide. Among the most important were the ability to plan and monitor operations with disciplined staff processes, unequaled mobility on the ground and in the air, and huge amounts of well-trained and organized manpower. As Petraeus explained, he relied on the ingenuity of his Soldiers to release and direct the latent capacity of the Iraqis:

What you do is you get a general concept, you get some organizing principles, you explain it all as clearly as you can, and then you unleash the productivity of the people, if you will, our people and then their people, and get on with it because there was an enormous capability in the Iraqis as well. There were thousands of trained, certified engineers, just in northern Iraq alone. There is a huge legal community. There is a huge educated class and so forth. It was just a matter of getting them going again, engaged and enabled somewhat with resources, because of course the [national] ministries weren't yet doing that.[195]

By the middle of 2003, these types of taskings and missions were commonplace as the American Soldiers attempted to create a secure environment in which the Iraqis—with their Coalition partners—could gather their substantial resources and capabilities and begin re-establishing their state.

Conclusion

The shift made by many units in 2003 and 2004—from the mentality of an Army that prided itself on its prowess in conventional combat operations to one that conducted full spectrum counterinsurgency operations was challenging. Many of the dramatic changes required by this transition have been emphasized in this chapter, and they and other aspects of the full spectrum campaign in Iraq will be documented in greater detail in the remainder of this study. While the new campaign was unexpected, it would be a mistake to characterize the Army as wholly unprepared for the new missions, threats, and objectives it faced after May 2003. In most cases, Army leaders and Soldiers made that transition in a relatively smooth fashion, despite the fact that they had not trained for the types of operations required in the new campaign. Petraeus, for example, contends that the key factor in making this shift was the mind-set of the leader and that the great majority of his battalion and brigade commanders made the transition to the new campaign with little hesitation.[196] The same was true for the majority of the junior officers, noncommissioned officers, and enlisted Soldiers who, in their daily efforts in difficult circumstances, made the new campaign a reality.

The chapters in Parts II and III of this study provide a more detailed examination of the new full spectrum campaign by looking closely at the types of operations that became the core components of the larger Coalition effort. The next five chapters (Part II)—Leading the New Campaign, Intelligence and High-Value Target Operations, Detainee Operations, Fighting the Battle of Ideas in Iraq, and Combined Arms Operations in Iraq—focus on the US Army's evolving command structure in Iraq and its efforts to disrupt and destroy the insurgent network. The three chapters (Part III) that follow address reconstruction operations, governance operations, and the training of ISF to examine those missions designed to attract the fence sitters to the side of the Coalition and build legitimacy for the new Iraqi Government. Ultimately, these chapters describe how, with little fanfare and almost no preparation or planning, American Soldiers in the spring and summer of 2003 launched a broad, complex, and sophisticated effort to assist the Iraqis in the recreation of their nation.

Notes

1. Joint Chiefs of Staff, Joint Publication (JP) 1-02, *DOD Dictionary of Military and Associated Terms* (Washington, DC, 12 April 2001), 213.

2. US Department of State, "Transitional Justice Working Group," *The Future of Iraq Project* (Washington, DC, 2003), 29.

3. US National Defense University, "Iraq: Looking Beyond Saddam's Rule," *Workshop Report* (Washington, DC: Institute for National Strategic Studies, 2002), 10.

4. "Iraq: Looking Beyond Saddam's Rule," *Workshop Report,* 21.

5. Conrad C. Crane and W. Andrew Terrill, *Reconstructing Iraq: Insights, Challenges, and Missions for Military Forces in a Post-Conflict Scenario* (Carlisle Barracks, PA: Strategic Studies Institute, 2003).

6. Crane and Terrill, 37.

7. Kevin C.M. Benson, "'Phase IV' CFLCC Stability Operations Planning," in Brian M. De Toy, ed., *Turning Victory Into Success: Military Operations After the Campaign* (Fort Leavenworth, KS: Combat Studies Institute Press, 2005), 189.

8. Benson, "'Phase IV' CFLCC Stability Operations Planning," in De Toy, ed., *Turning Victory Into Success,* 183.

9. Brigadier General David Perkins, interview by Contemporary Operations Study Team, Fort Leavenworth, KS, 23 January 2006, 20.

10. Garner, "Iraq Revisited," in De Toy, ed., *Turning Victory Into Success*, 256.

11. Captain Warren Sponsler, interview by Contemporary Operations Study Team, Fort Leavenworth, KS, 7 December 2005, 4–5.

12. Sponsler, interview, 7 December 2005, 4–5.

13. Colonel J.D. Johnson, interview by Contemporary Operations Study Team, Fort Leavenworth, KS, 4 November 2005, 15.

14. Colonel Daniel B. Allyn, interview by Contemporary Operations Study Team, Fort Leavenworth, KS, 4 November 2005, 4.

15. George Packer, *The Assassins' Gate: America in Iraq* (New York, NY: Farrar, Straus and Giroux, 2005), 139.

16. Lieutenant Colonel David J. Conboy, *An Interview with Lieutenant General Nasier Abadi, Deputy Chief of Staff, Iraqi Joint Forces* (Carlisle Barracks, PA: US Army War College, 2005), 14–15.

17. Anthony Shadid, *Night Draws Near: Iraq's People in the Shadow of American's War* (New York, NY: Henry Holt and Co., 2005), 326.

18. Shadid, *Night Draws Near,* 140.

19. David Rieff, "Who Botched the Occupation?" *New York Times Magazine,* 2 November 2003, 44.

20. Lieutenant Colonel Rod Coffey, interview by Contemporary Operations Study Team, Fort Leavenworth, KS, 8 December 2005, 11.

21. Conboy, 13.

22. Conboy, 13.

23. Colonel Derek J. Harvey, "A 'Red Team' Perspective on the Insurgency in Iraq," in John J. McGrath, ed., *An Army at War: Change in the Midst of Conflict, The Proceedings of the Combat Studies Institute 2005 Military History Symposium* (Fort Leavenworth, KS: Combat Studies Institute Press, 2006), 193.

24. Coalition Provisional Authority Order No. 1, "De-Baathification of Iraqi Society" (16 May 2003), http://www.cpa-iraq.org/regulations/20030516_CPAORD_1_De-Ba_athification_of_Iraqi_Society_.pdf (accessed 14 Mary 2006); Coalition Provisional Authority Order No. 2, "Dissolution of Entities" (23 May 2003), http://www.iraqcoalition.org/regulations/20030823_CPAORD_2_Dissolution_Of_Entities_with_Annex_A.pdf (accessed 14 September 2006).

25. Benson, "'Phase IV' CFLCC Stability Operations Planning," in De Toy, ed., *Turning Victory Into Success,* 188–189.

26. Lieutenant General William G. Webster, interview by Contemporary Operations Study Team, Fort Leavenworth, KS, 11 December 2007, 22–23.

27. L. Paul Bremer III, *My Year in Iraq: The Struggle to Build a Future of Hope* (New York, NY: Simon & Schuster, 2006), 39.

28. Webster, interview, 11 December 2007, 23.

29. Colonel Marc Warren, interview by Contemporary Operations Study Team, Fort Leavenworth, KS, 15 March 2007, 7–8.

30. Office of the Staff Judge Advocate, US Army V Corps, *Agreement to Disavow Party Affiliation,* 1 May 2003.

31. Garner, "Iraq Revisited," in De Toy, ed., *Turning Victory Into Success,* 260.

32. Peter Slevin, "Wrong Turn at a Postwar Crossroads? Decision to Disband Iraqi Army Cost US Time and Credibility," *Washington Post* (20 November 2003), A01, http://www.washingtonpost.com/ac2/wp-dyn/A63423-2003Nov19?language=printer (accessed 12 April 2006).

33. Bremer, *My Year in Iraq,* 39.

34. Bremer, *My Year in Iraq,* 42.

35. CPA Order No 1 (appendix A).

36. For the lack of coordination between CPA and V Corps, see Warren interview, 15 March 2007, 8–9.

37. Bremer, *My Year in Iraq,* 39.

38. CPA Order No 2 (appendix B).

39. Garner, "Iraq Revisited," in De Toy, ed., *Turning Victory Into Success,* 265.

40. Webster, interview, 11 December 2007, 10.

41. Webster, interview, 11 December 2007, 10.

42. Webster, interview, 11 December 2007, 10.

43. Webster, interview, 11 December 2007, 10.

44. Webster, interview, 11 December 2007, 11.

45. Bremer, *My Year in Iraq,* 54.

46. Jon Lee Anderson, "Letter From Iraq: Out on the Street," *The New Yorker,* 15 November 2004, http://www.newyorker.com/printables/fact/041115fa_fact (accessed 8 November 2004).

47. Colonel Don C. Young, interview by Contemporary Operations Study Team, Fort Leavenworth, KS, 10 April 2006, 15.

48. Michael R. Gordon and General Bernard E. Trainor, *Cobra II: The Inside Story of the Invasion and Occupation of Iraq* (New York, NY: Pantheon, 2006), 491.

49. General William S. Wallace, interview by Contemporary Operations Study Team, Fort Leavenworth, KS, 22 May 2006, 12–13.

50. Wallace, interview, 22 May 2006, 12–13.

51. Ahmed S. Hashim, *Insurgency and Counter-insurgency in Iraq* (Ithaca, NY: Cornell University Press, 2006), 69.

52. Lieutenant General David H. Petraeus, interview by Contemporary Operations Study Team, Fort Leavenworth, KS, 17 February 2006, 11.

53. Petraeus, interview, 17 February 2006, 12; Ambassador L. Paul Bremer III, interview by Contemporary Operations Study Team, Chevy Chase, MD, 20 April 2006, 4.

54. Bremer, *My Year in Iraq,* 261.

55. Petraeus, interview, 17 February 2006, 12.

56. Hashim, 96.

57. Major Susan Arnold, interview by Operational Leadership Experiences Project Team, Combat Studies Institute, Fort Leavenworth, KS, 25 January 2006, 13.

58. Coalition Provisional Authority, *Press Release, 23 June 2003 (PR No. 006),* "Good News for Iraqi Soldiers," 1–2, http://www.iraqcoalition.org/pressreleases/23June03PR6_good_news.pdf (accessed 30 January 2008).

59. Coalition Provisional Authority, *Public Service Announcement, 6 July 2003*, 1.

60. 3d ACR, *Desert Rifles Newsletter*, Issue 11, 18 July 2003, 4.

61. 101st Airborne Division, *AO North Brief 3*, 21 January 2005, slide 87.

62. Coalition Provisional Authority, *Iraqi Seized and Vested Assets*, April 2004.

63. CPA Order No. 2, 3. The 23 June 2003 CPA Press Release that announced the stipend program also announced the beginning of a recruiting drive for the New Iraqi Army (NIA). See CPA, *Press Release, 23 June 2006 (PR No. 006)*, 1.

64. Mr. Walter B. Slocombe, interview by Contemporary Operations Study Team, Fort Leavenworth, KS, 12 September 2006, 2–3.

65. Wallace, interview, 22 May 2006, 12.

66. Wallace, interview, 22 May 2006, 12.

67. Colonel (Retired) Paul Hughes, interview by Contemporary Operations Study Team, Fort Leavenworth, KS, 1 March 2006, 9–10.

68. Mao Zedong's most important works on revolutionary warfare can be found in *Selected Military Writings of Mao Tse-tung* (Peking: Foreign Language Press, 1972). To see an example of the influence of Mao's ideas on insurgency/counterinsurgency theorists, see David Galula, *Counterinsurgency Warfare: Theory and Practice* (St. Petersburg, FL: Hailer Publishing, 2005), first published in 1964.

69. JP 1-02, 213.

70. Anderson; Hashim, 21.

71. Andrew Krepinevich, "The War in Iraq: The Nature of Insurgency Warfare" (*First in a Series*), Center for Strategic Budgetary Assessments (2 June 2004), 3; Hashim, 20–21.

72. "In Their Own Words: Reading the Insurgency," International Crisis Group, Middle East, Report No. 50 (15 February 2006), 6; Hashim, 33.

73. Colonel Derek J. Harvey, "A 'Red Team' Perspective," in McGrath, ed., *An Army at War,* 193.

74. "In Their Own Words," ICG, Report No. 50, 6.

75. Hashim, 115.

76. Hashim, 116.

77. "DOD News Briefing—Mr. Di Rita and Gen. Abizaid," *DefenseLink,* 16 July 2003, http://www.defenselink.mil/transcripts/2003/tr20030716-0401.html (accessed 29 August 2006).

78. "In Their Own Words," ICG, Report No. 50, 7.

79. Harvey, "A 'Red Team' Perspective," in McGrath, ed., *An Army at War,* 193.

80. US Government Accountability Office, GAO Report GAO-05-431T, *Rebuilding Iraq: Preliminary Observations on the Challenges in Transferring Security Responsibilities to Iraqi Military and Police*, 14 March 2005, 10.

81. "In Their Own Words," ICG, Report No. 50, 10–11.

82. Hashim, 37.

83. Kevin M. Woods et al., *Iraqi Perspectives Project: A View of Operation Iraqi Freedom From Saddam's Senior Leadership* (Norfolk, VA: US Joint Forces Command, 2005), 48–72, http://www.cfr.org/publication/10230/Iraqi_perspectives_project.html (accessed 12 September 2006).

84. Woods et al., 96–98.

85. Harvey, "A 'Red Team' Perspective," in McGrath, ed., *An Army at War*, 201.

86. Harvey, "A 'Red Team' Perspective," in McGrath, ed., *An Army at War*, 210; Hashim, 155.

87. Hashim, 157.

88. Hashim, 123.

89. Harvey, "A 'Red Team' Perspective," in McGrath, ed., *An Army at War,* 208.

90. Hashim, 122.

91. General George W. Casey Jr., interview by Contemporary Operations Study Team, Fort Leavenworth, KS, 27 November 2007, 4.

92. Amatzia Baram, *Who Are the Insurgents? Sunni Arab Rebels in Iraq*, United States Institute of Peace, Special Report No. 134 (April 2005), 3.

93. Baram, 3.

94. Baram, 3.

95. Baram, 16.

96. Michael Eisenstadt and Jeffrey White, "Assessing Iraq's Sunni Arab Insurgency," *Military Review* 3, May–June 2006, 34.

97. Hashim, 79.

98. Baram, 4; Hashim, 84.

99. Baram, 4.

100. Baram, 4.

101. Hashim, 89.

102. Baram, 4.

103. Baram, 4.

104. Baram, 6.

105. Baram, 6.

106. Baram, 6.

107. Hashim, 104.

108. Baram, 6.

109. Baram, 7.

110. Baram, 7.

111. Hashim, 29.

112. Baram, 7.

113. Baram, 7.

114. Baram, 11.

115. Baram, 12.

116. Baram, 12.

117. Baram, 12, 14.

118. Hashim, 270.

119. Giles Trendle, "Young Radicals on the Rise," *Middle East*, Issue 41, January 2004, 28–30.

120. Trendle, 28–30.

121. Hashim, 248–249.

122. "NBC News' Meet the Press," Transcript for 26 September 2004, http://www.msnbc.msn.com/id/6106292/ (accessed 1 September 2006).

123. Michael E. O'Hanlon and Nina Kamp, "Iraq Index: Tracking Variables of Reconstruction and Security in Post-Saddam Iraq," The Brookings Institution, 10 April 2006, www.brookings.edu/iraqindex (accessed 11 April 2006).

124. "NBC News' Meet the Press," Transcript for 26 September 2004.

125. "In Their Own Words," ICG, Report No. 50, 1–2. Loretta Napoleoni, *Insurgent Iraq: Al Zarqawi and the New Generation* (New York, NY: Seven Stories Press, 2005), 123.

126. Napoleoni, 78–79; Mary Anne Weaver, "The Short, Violent Life of Abu Musab Al-Zarqawi," *The Atlantic Monthly*, July/August 2006 (edited for the Web 8 June 2006), http://www.theatlantic.com/doc/print/200607/zarqawi (accessed 9 June 2006).

127. Mark Mazzetti and Josh Meyer, "The Conflict in Iraq; In a Battle of Wits, Iraq's Insurgency Mastermind Stays a Step Ahead of US," *Los Angeles Times*, 16 November 2005, A.1; Napoleoni, 56, 79.

128. "In Their Own Words," ICG, Report No. 50, 1–2.

129. "In Their Own Words," ICG, Report No. 50, 1–2.

130. Hashim, 209–210.

131. Hashim, 178.

132. "Big Iraq Ambush was Bank Heist," *BBC News,* 1 December 2003, http://news.bbc.co.uk/2/hi/middle_east/3253236.stm (accessed 1 September 2006).

133. Ready First Combat Team, 1st Armored Division, *Command Brief,* 19 October 2003, slide 10.

134. O'Hanlon and Kamp, 9.

135. Colonel Karl Reinhold, *A Paradigm for the System of Systems Countering Asymmetric Enemy Kinetic Attacks* (Carlisle Barracks, PA: US Army War College, 2005), 1.

136. Lisa Rose Weaver, "Iraq Promises More Suicide Bombings," *CNN.com*, http:www.cnn.com/2003/WORLD/meast/03/29/sprj.irq.car.bomb/index.html (accessed 6 July 2006).

137. Michael E. O'Hanlon and Andrew Kamons, "Iraq Index: Tracking Variables of Reconstruction & Security in Post-Saddam Iraq," The Brookings Institution, 29 June 2006, 19, http://www.brookings.edu/fp/saban/iraq/index20060629.pdf (accessed September 2006).

138. GAO-05-431T, *Rebuilding Iraq: Preliminary Observations*, 10.

139. Reinhold, 1.

140. "DOD News Briefing—Mr. Di Rita and Gen. Abizaid."

141. "DOD News Briefing—Mr. Di Rita and Gen. Abizaid."

142. Lieutenant General R. Steven Whitcomb, interview by Contemporary Operations Study Team, Fort Leavenworth, KS, 7 June 2006, 6.

143. Whitcomb, interview, 7 June 2006, 6.

144. Lieutenant Colonel Wesley R. Odum Jr., interview by Contemporary Operations Study Team, Fort Leavenworth, KS, 17 March 2006, 11.

145. 1st Armored Division, *Command Brief*, 3 December 2003, slide 12.

146. Lieutenant Colonel Brian J. McKiernan, interview by Contemporary Operations Study Team, Fort Leavenworth, KS, 29 April 2006, 8, 14–15.

147. S3, Task Force 1-22 IN, *03 September 2003 Briefing*, 5.

148. Roger Trinquier, *Modern Warfare: A French View of Counterinsurgency*, trans., Daniel Lee (New York, NY: Frederick A. Praeger, 1961), 8.

149. Galula, 87. See also US Army Field Manual (FM) 100-20, *Military Operations in Low Intensity Conflict* (Washington, DC, 1990), E-2, E-22.

150. Galula, 89.

151. Petraeus, interview, 17 February 2006, 3.

152. Petraeus, interview, 17 February 2006, 3–4.

153. Major George H. Sarabia, interview by Operational Leadership Experiences Project Team, Combat Studies Institute, Fort Leavenworth, KS, 22 September 2005, 6.

154. Sarabia, interview, 22 September 2005, 6.

155. 2d Squadron, 3d Armored Cavalry Regiment, *Sabre Squadron AO Robertson Update for 2 BDE, 3 ID*, 31 May 2003, slide 41.

156. Coalition Provisional Authority, *CPA Vision Statement*, 13 July 2003, 5.

157. *CPA Vision Statement*, 13 July 2003, 9–11. The CPA would issue a more detailed plan titled *Achieving the Vision to Restore Full Sovereignty to the Iraqi People* in the fall of 2003. That plan included five core foundations that were very similar to the operational directions in the July 2003 Vision Statement: security, essential services, governance, economy, and strategic communications. See Coalition Provisional Authority, *Achieving the Vision to Restore Full Sovereignty to the Iraqi People,* 15 October 2003.

158. V Corps and CJTF-7, *V Corps and CJTF-7 Transition and Challenges* Briefing, 30 September 2004, slide 5.

159. Odum, interview, 17 March 2006, 4–5. For details on the V Corps planning for Phase IV operations, see V Corps, *V Corps Update Briefing—V Corps Commander's Conference*, 16 May 2003, slides 1–9.

160. Odum, interview, 17 March 2006, 7.

161. JP 3-0, *Doctrine for Joint Operations* (Washington, DC, 2006), IV-9.

162. Odum, interview, 17 March 2006, 14.

163. FM 3-0, *Operations* (Washington, DC, June 2001), 5-37.

164. *V Corps and CJTF-7 Transition and Challenges* Briefing, 30 September 2004, slide 4; Odum, interview, 17 March 2006, 11–12.

165. Odum, interview, 17 March 2006, 4–6.

166. Lieutenant General Ricardo Sanchez, interview by Contemporary Operations Study Team, Fort Leavenworth, KS, 18 August 2006, 17.

167. TF *All American, America's Guard of Honor* Briefing, 1 April 2004, slides 6 and 7.

168. TF *All American, America's Guard of Honor* Briefing, slide 7.

169. 4th Infantry Division, *Lessons Learned: Executive Summary* (17 June 2004), 6.

170. See Gordon and Trainor, 445–448; Thomas E. Ricks, *Fiasco: The American Military Adventure in Iraq* (New York, NY: The Penguin Press, 2006), 142–144, 235–239.

171. Michael R. Gordon, "To Mollify Iraqis, US Plans to Ease Scope of Its Raids," *New York Times*, 7 August 2003.

172. "Major General Odierno Videoteleconference from Baghdad," DOD News Transcript, 18 June 2003, 2, http://merln.ndu.edu/merln/pfiraq/archive/dod/tr20030618-0281.pdf (accessed 25 October 2007).

173. Lieutenant Colonel Troy D. Perry, interview by Contemporary Operations Study Team, Fort Leavenworth, KS, 11 May 2006, 11, 16, 18.

174. Perry, interview, 11 May 2006, 10.

175. Lieutenant Colonel Greg Reilly, Initial Operational Assessment (September 2003), 3–4.

176. Reilly, Initial Operational Assessment, 3–4.

177. Major General Thomas G. Miller, interview by Contemporary Operations Study Team, Fort Leavenworth, KS, 23 August 2006, 7.

178. Miller, interview, 23 August 2006, 7.

179. Miller, interview, 23 August 2006, 6.

180. Major General Peter W. Chiarelli and Major Patrick R. Michaelis, "Winning the Peace: The Requirement for Full Spectrum Operations," *Military Review*, July–August 2005, 7.

181. Colonel Stephen R. Lanza et al., "Red Team Goes Maneuver: 1st Cav Div Arty as a Maneuver BCT," *Field Artillery*, May–June 2005, 11.

182. Lieutenant General Peter Chiarelli, interview by Contemporary Operations Study Team, Fort Leavenworth, KS, 8 May 2006, 5.

183. Martin Rodriguez, Andrew Farnsler, and John Bott, *Constructive Engagement: A Proven Method for Conducting Stability and Support Operations*, Land Power Essay No. 07-1, February 2007. Association of the United States Army, Institute of Land Warfare, 2–5, http://www.ausa.org/pdfdocs/LPE07-1.pdf (accessed 25 October 2007).

184. Rodriguez, Farnsler, and Bott.

185. Casey, interview, 27 November 2007, 3.

186. Casey, interview, 27 November 2007, 8–9.

187. Colonel William Hix, e-mail interview by Contemporary Operations Study Team, Fort Leavenworth, KS, 1 November 2006, 5.

188. Hix, e-mail interview, 1 November 2006, 5.

189. Kenneth W. Estes, "Command Narrative: 1st Armored Division in Operation Iraqi Freedom, May 2003—July 2004," Unpublished study, 39–41.

190. Estes, 39–41.

191. McKiernan, interview, 29 April 2006, 2.

192. Colonel Stephen Lanza, interview by Contemporary Operations Study Team, Fort Leavenworth, KS, 2 November 2005, 4.

193. Petraeus, interview, 17 February 2006, 8–9.

194. Petraeus, interview, 17 February 2006, 8–9.

195. Petraeus, interview, 17 February 2006, 8.

196. Petraeus, interview, 17 February 2006, 7.

Part II

Transition to a New Campaign

Chapter 4

Leading the New Campaign: Transitions in Command and Control in Operation IRAQI FREEDOM

To understand any military campaign, one must first recognize how the military forces involved organized themselves and led their Soldiers. This is, perhaps, more important to comprehending modern military campaigns because of the remarkable growth in the size and complexity of armies over the last two centuries, and the corresponding increase in the headquarters and supporting elements that command and control these massive organizations. Command relationships and structures, especially in the modern period, have always affected the military's ability to execute and achieve the overall objectives of a campaign or a war. Awareness of the Coalition's military command structure in Iraq after May 2003 as well as how that command evolved and, in turn, affected operations is essential to any study of Operation IRAQI FREEDOM (OIF).

The US Central Command (CENTCOM), based at MacDill Air Force Base in Florida, commanded all the Coalition forces that launched OIF in March 2003. Faced with this responsibility and simultaneously commanding ongoing operations in Afghanistan, the CENTCOM commander, General Tommy Franks, tasked subordinate headquarters with responsibility for various portions of the OIF campaign. Thus, US Third Army, an operational-level headquarters under the command of US Army Lieutenant General David McKiernan, served as the Combined Forces Land Component Command (CFLCC) and had responsibility for planning and conducting land operations in Iraq. Similarly, Franks allocated responsibility for all air operations to the Combined Forces Air Component Command (CFACC) under US Air Force Lieutenant General T. Michael Moseley. Special Operations Forces (SOF) found themselves under the command of the Combined Forces Special Operations Component Command (CFSOCC) under Brigadier General Gary L. Harrell.

CENTCOM and CFLCC commanders and planners understood this command structure would change once the Coalition defeated the Saddam regime. In its ECLIPSE II plan, CFLCC made rudimentary plans for Phase IV or postconflict operations once the regime was toppled, and then, after a relatively brief period, to transition with a follow-on headquarters, known first as Combined Joint Task Force–Iraq (CJTF-Iraq) and then as Combined Joint Task Force–7 (CJTF-7) (see chapter 2). Neither the US Department of Defense (DOD) nor CENTCOM, however, developed the actual structure for this follow-on headquarters until after the land campaign began in March 2003. Thus, when the Baathist regime fell in April, most of the planning for this transfer of responsibility had been left undone.

This difficult transition in command, explained in detail throughout this chapter, was only the most visible challenge the US Army faced in its effort to reorganize and reorient for a new type of campaign. Just as important were the evolving relationships between the Coalition's military headquarters and its political command, the Coalition Provisional Authority (CPA). The emergence of Iraqi governing bodies and Iraqi security force commands further complicated the establishment of a clear, well-functioning system of command and control that could establish and maintain unity of command and unity of effort in Iraq.

Phase III to Phase IV of Operation IRAQI FREEDOM

On 9 April 2003 when Sergeant Kirk Dalrymple and other US Marines pulled down Saddam Hussein's statue in Baghdad's Firdos Square, the headquarters of CENTCOM oversaw the war in Iraq from its location in Florida. Its warfighting forward command post directed operations out of the Gulf nation of Qatar. CFLCC led the ground war from Camp Doha in Kuwait. Under CFLCC's supervision, British forces were consolidating their occupation of southern Iraq around the city of Basrah. Meanwhile the US 1st Marine Expeditionary Force (1st MEF) had occupied Baghdad east of the Tigris River. The US Army's main tactical headquarters, V Corps, was still south of Baghdad while the 3d Infantry Division (3d ID), the spearhead of the V Corps attack into Baghdad, consolidated in Baghdad and its environs to the south, west, and north. Simultaneously, the 101st Airborne Division (101st ABN) and the 2d Brigade of the 82d Airborne Division (82d ABN), having fought hard in An Najaf, Karbala, and Al Hillah to destroy Iraqi forces along the V Corps' lines of communication back to Kuwait, established their forces in the Shia cities south of Baghdad.

During this phase of the war the US military chain of command operated according to joint doctrine, leading directly from the President to the Secretary of Defense to CENTCOM and then on to the CFLCC. McKiernan's headquarters issued orders to the 1st MEF, V Corps, and British forces that then conducted the fighting to accomplish their tactical and operational objectives. Unity of command ensured unity of effort during the fighting in accordance with traditional military practice. What would happen after Coalition forces toppled the Saddam regime was less clear. As chapter 2 has illustrated, great uncertainty existed about the nature of postwar Iraq, about the political and military leadership in Iraq once Saddam was toppled, and about which military headquarters would be tasked with the mission of turning the military victory into political success. The Coalition and CENTCOM Commander, General Franks, believed by mid-April that it was time to transition Phase IV operations and put a new Iraqi Government in place. During his first visit to Baghdad on 16 April 2003, Franks tacitly acknowledged this transition in his "Freedom Message" to the Iraqi people:

> I, General Tommy R. Franks, Commander of Coalition Forces, do hereby proclaim that: Coalition forces have come as liberators, not conquerors. . . . The Coalition is committed to helping the people of Iraq heal their wounds, build their own representative government, . . . Iraq and its property belong to the Iraqi people and the Coalition makes no claim of ownership by force of arms.[1]

As the Coalition's ground force commander during the invasion, Lieutenant General McKiernan also had responsibility for the conclusion of Phase III combat operations and the start of Phase IV operations. But based on prewar planning assumptions in the DOD and at CENTCOM, CFLCC was counting on the Office of Reconstruction and Humanitarian Assistance (ORHA), the State Department, Iraqi expatriates, the Iraqi Government, and international organizations to eventually take the lead after regime change. CFLCC's deputy commander, Major General William Webster, recalled how these assumptions shaped the overall land component command's planning for what came after the removal of the Saddam regime:

> There was seriously not anything but a skeleton of Phase IV until very late. We had assumptions given to us by CENTCOM that said that the Office of Reconstruction and Humanitarian Assistance (ORHA) or the State Department

was going to come in early and perform all Phase IV operations. Our requirement would be to stand up the Iraqi Army again, get them training and organized and back on their feet, and to provide security. All along, General Franks said that the Secretary of Defense wanted us to quickly leave and turn over post-hostilities to international organizations (IOs) and nongovernment organizations (NGOs) led by ORHA. That was the notion.[2]

Thus, on 16 April 2003 as Franks arrived in Baghdad to make his address, the impact of incomplete and uncoordinated prewar planning was about to set in with significant negative effects on the US Army, OIF, and Iraq.

As April ended, the makeup of US Army combat forces in Iraq was rapidly changing. Some units were still moving into Iraq while others had their deployments canceled and some were ordered home. V Corps headquarters was moving to consolidate in and to the north of Baghdad itself. The 4th Infantry Division (4th ID) was just entering Iraq via Kuwait after Turkey denied access to its territory. The 2d Armored Cavalry Regiment (2d ACR) was ordered to deploy in late March, and on 8 April 2003 it began securing the lines of communication (LOCs) extending northward out of Kuwait.[3] The 3d Armored Cavalry Regiment (3d ACR) was deploying into Kuwait and by late April would initially be sent to operate in Al Anbar province in western Iraq, which had yet to be occupied by Coalition forces.

The two Germany-based brigades of the 1st Armored Division (1st AD) received orders to deploy on 28 February 2003, after having been shelved from the plan entirely the month before. Their new mission was to secure the LOCs from Kuwait into Iraq and to be prepared for further operations as needed.[4] Two battalions of the 3d Brigade, 1st AD, had earlier deployed from Fort Riley, Kansas, to Kuwait, and fought under three different divisions before being reunited with the 1st AD in late May. The 1st AD loaded its equipment at the European ports of Bremerhaven, Rotterdam, and Antwerp in April. Once they arrived in theater in early and mid-May, the Soldiers of the Old Ironsides Division began replacing the 3d ID in Baghdad on 19 May 2003, completing the process on 5 June 2003.[5]

It was unclear what role American forces were to play in Iraq once Saddam's regime had been removed from power. At CFLCC, the assumption, based on guidance from CENTCOM and higher authorities, was that Coalition troops would not become involved in major law enforcement operations across Iraq. Major General Webster remembered fielding queries from Iraqi leaders about the possibilities of the Coalition declaring martial law and recalled McKiernan responding, "The President and the Secretary of Defense have said that we will not declare martial law. We are not going to put our military in a position of enforcing Iraqi laws."[6] At the tactical level, unit commanders were unsure about their role in maintaining law and order. Major General David Petraeus, commanding the 101st ABN, thought initial guidance on operations after regime removal lacked specific details on tasks and purpose.[7] Leaders in the 3d ID, which was busy conducting operations in Baghdad, were also unsure of their missions, not entirely convinced that imposing law and order in Baghdad was their responsibility. It is important to note that even if CENTCOM or CFLCC had formally tasked the 3d ID, the 101st ABN, or any other subordinate units with this mission—those units had very limited capability to carry out comprehensive law enforcement operations across Iraq. There simply were not enough American troops in Baghdad, a city of 5.5 million people, after 9 April 2003 to impose order. The troops who did find themselves in Baghdad lacked the resources and preparation necessary for any formal organized response to the breakdown of order or for more ambitious operations designed to begin reconstruction of Iraqi infrastructure and governance. In April and May 2003 American Soldiers did what they could, arriving at their own solutions to the most obvious and demanding problems. However, neither a consistent approach nor an overarching policy emerged in those very early days.

During his first visit to Baghdad in mid-April, Franks gave his commanders guidance that made the difficult transition to Phase IV even more challenging. He told his commanders to "be prepared to take as much risk departing as they had in their push to Baghdad."[8] Later that same day, a video teleconference (VTC) with the President and Secretary of Defense Donald Rumsfeld reinforced Franks' directive for a quick redeployment. This guidance had a major impact during this critical period, and came as a surprise to McKiernan and his chief of staff, Marine Major General Robert Blackman.[9]

The staffs at CENTCOM Forward command post (CP) and CFLCC immediately began planning for their redeployments back to the United States and for the rapid drawdown of US forces in Iraq. The 3d ID and the 1st MEF were ordered to begin their movement out of theater. At this point in the campaign, CENTCOM anticipated reducing Coalition forces rapidly from 140,000 to around 30,000 by September, less than 7 months away. V Corps and 1st AD issued similar orders in mid-April.[10]

During the last week of April, the DOD canceled the deployment of the 1st Cavalry Division (1st CAV) to Iraq. The 1st CAV was one of the two Army divisions called for in the CFLCC plan to deploy to Iraq following the start of Phase III. This decision followed a series of queries from Rumsfeld to the Chairman of the Joint Chiefs of Staff and the CENTCOM commander about limiting the flow of follow-on forces into Iraq if Saddam's military quickly collapsed.[11] Franks has taken responsibility for the decision:

> Rumsfeld presented [the cancellation of the 1st CAV] to me as an idea. I initially said, 'No. We need to continue to flow the 1st CAV Division.' His response to that was, 'Maybe so, general, tell me why?' I talked to Dick Myers, the Chairman, Pete Pace, the Vice Chairman, and my own people, and over the course of a few days to a week I convinced myself. Rumsfeld didn't convince me, Rumsfeld didn't brow beat me, . . . the right thing to do was to terminate the flow with the idea that if we were not able to bring a sense of stability in there then we will turn the flow on again.[12]

Despite Franks' confidence at the time, he suggested in a 2006 interview that he has reconsidered this critical decision, "Had I to do it again, based on the fact that I'm a lifelong learner, I would have said, 'By comparison, Mr. President, by comparison, Mr. Secretary, keep it flowing, put the 1st CAV in and then we will adjust and decide.'"[13] General John Keane, the acting Chief of Staff of the Army, supported the decision to stop the deployment of the 1st CAV. His explanation illustrated the general assumptions among senior military and civilian leaders about the security situation in post-Saddam Iraq: "I thought Iraq was going to be Bosnia on steroids and that we were going to be there, I told Rumsfeld, 8 to 10 years minimum with some measure of force. So I was immediately concerned about rotations and I didn't want the 1st CAV to deploy."[14] Keane noted that he did not anticipate the emergence of an armed opposition in Iraq, "I think if we thought that an insurgency was a realistic option and we had [the 1st CAV] in the queue, we probably would have deployed the 1st CAV."[15]

In his memoirs, Franks claims that in late April and early May, "Phase IV was going about as I had expected—*not* as I had hoped—but as I expected."[16] The decision to cancel the 1st CAV's deployment was consistent with his thinking about the entire campaign, especially the imperatives of keeping troop levels low, the idea of the "running start" to the ground war, and the idea of adjusting forces in Phase IV based on the Iraqi reaction to the fall of Saddam. That thinking implied an analysis of various courses of action. The decision to maintain, increase, or decrease the force flow would have to be made once the regime was toppled and Coalition troops took stock of what they found.[17] It is a stretch to think that a precise assessment of the nature of post-Saddam Iraq was possible in late April 2003, with the Baathist dictator still on the run and much of the country still unoccupied. During this critical transition period, however, it is questionable whether leaders at the DOD, CENTCOM, and CFLCC conducted a thorough, coordinated, and realistic evaluation of the probable force levels required for Phase IV based on the realities of the new Iraq that were emerging in front of them.

President George W. Bush, General Franks, and "Mission Accomplished"

Soon after Saddam's statue was pulled down in Baghdad, Franks called Secretary of Defense Rumsfeld and suggested that President Bush make a public acknowledgment of the success of the Coalition and US troops. Franks wanted to recognize them for their stunning military success, to send a signal that major combat operations or Phase III operations were over, and that it was time for international aid to begin flowing to rebuild Iraq.[18] In a display of bravado that has been criticized ever since, the President landed aboard the USS *Abraham Lincoln,* festooned with a "Mission Accomplished" banner, as it prepared to enter the harbor of San Francisco after returning from its tour in the Persian Gulf.

President Bush's speech on the aircraft carrier that day serves as a useful benchmark for the CENTCOM transition to Phase IV operations:

> Major combat operations in Iraq have ended. In the Battle of Iraq, the United States and our allies have prevailed. And now our Coalition is engaged in securing and reconstructing that country. We have difficult work to do in Iraq. We are bringing order to parts of that country that remain dangerous. We are pursuing and finding leaders of the old regime, who will be held to account for their crimes. We have begun the search for hidden chemical and biological weapons. We are helping to rebuild Iraq, where the dictator built palaces for himself, instead of hospitals and schools. And we will stand with the new leaders of Iraq as they establish a government of, by, and for the Iraqi people. The transition from dictatorship to democracy will take time, but it is worth every effort. Our Coalition will stay until our work is done. And then we will leave—and we will leave behind a free Iraq.[19]

In his memoirs, Franks claimed that as early as December 2001, as he contemplated operations in Afghanistan, he realized that Phase IV in general "might prove more challenging than major combat operations."[20] That realization seems to have been forgotten in late April 2003 when the CENTCOM commander recommended that the President make an address that sounded to both the US audience and the international community like a victory speech. Franks later lamented the law of unintended consequences for the immense criticism that the President's speech in front of the "mission accomplished" banner generated. It is important to note that Bush did not use the phrase "mission accomplished" during his 1 May speech, and that he noted the "difficult work" that lay ahead. In fact, Major General Webster and other CFLCC leaders convinced key ORHA and State Department officials in Iraq to replace the "mission accomplished" statement in the president's draft manuscript with the phrase "major combat operations in Iraq have ended" because they already realized that more fighting lay ahead.[21] The president's cautionary note, however, was lost in the public euphoria over the quick military victory.[22]

Lieutenant General William Wallace, the commander of V Corps, did not believe the declaration in Bush's speech had any practical impact on the Soldiers of his Corps: "The term didn't even resonate much I don't think, at least with me, because the mission was not accomplished. The regime was gone, certainly. The Iraqi Army was defeated, certainly. But there were still mission requirements with regard to prewar positioning of Coalition forces throughout the width and depth of the country that still had to be done."[23] The announcement did, however, contribute to an unfortunate rush to hand off responsibility for postwar Iraq from CFLCC to CJTF-7.

From CENTCOM and CFLCC to V Corps and CJTF-7

In late April 2003, Major General Ricardo Sanchez, commander of the 1st AD, which was still deploying its troops from Germany to Kuwait, found that the Army had nominated him for his third star and planned for him to replace Wallace as commander of V Corps. By 1 May he was in Baghdad with the V Corps headquarters preparing for the transition, while the remainder of his division was debarking in Kuwait.[24] At that time CFLCC, however, was still designated as the headquarters for the next phase of OIF. The two chief US political and military entities in Iraq were the ORHA under Lieutenant General (Retired) Jay Garner and the CFLCC under Lieutenant General McKiernan. The Combined Joint Task Force–IV (CJTF-IV) headquarters, which had arrived in Kuwait in early March, had by this time become an abortive undertaking that CENTCOM appears to have never seriously considered as a viable option for leading Phase IV of OIF.

Prior to May 2003 nearly everyone in the senior levels of the military and civilian chains of command expected military operations in Phase IV to be very short-lived, a belief derived from assumptions made at the very earliest stages of planning for OIF.[25] The initial campaign plan developed by the staff of the 1st AD, for example, envisioned a short period of combat operations to destroy remnants of the regime, followed by a turnover of authority to an Iraqi Government and its security forces, and then redeployment back to Germany by December 2003.[26] Soon, however, reality rendered prewar assumptions and the mid-April euphoria obsolete. Indeed, the 1st AD would not redeploy home to Germany until July 2004, after a period of intense combat operations in the spring against the Shia forces of Muqtada al-Sadr, actions that extended the division's tour of duty beyond one year.

The belief in a curtailed Phase IV led General Franks to direct Lieutenant General McKiernan and CFLCC to leave Iraq. After his retirement, Franks stated that the reason he rapidly redeployed CFLCC out of theater was to use the move as a lever with the Armed Services and the DOD to get leaders in those organizations to rapidly insert a combined joint headquarters into Iraq to work alongside ORHA and later with the CPA. In a 2006 interview, Franks explained his thinking:

> I look at military services, the Army included, as force providers. I look at Washington, DC, as a force provider. I thought it was sufficient to tell Don

Rumsfeld and [Chairman of the Joint Chiefs of Staff] Dick Myers, 'Here is what we are going to do in Iraq. Here is what we need in Iraq. We need a joint headquarters, a CJTF. You [guys] figure it out. I don't care whether the Army convinces you to bring a headquarters out of Europe or whether the Air Force convinces you to bring a headquarters from Shaw Air Force Base.'... So that is a task that [CENTCOM Commander] John Abizaid and I very simply laid on Washington and said, 'Figure it out. Do it fast. Get me a joint headquarters in here. We have a lot of work to do and [CPA Administrator] Jerry Bremer has a lot of responsibility and he needs help.'[27]

As Major General Steve Whitcomb, the CENTCOM chief of staff, recalled, Franks and others were interested in lowering the size of the military footprint in Iraq in line with the prewar planning for a very brief period of military operations after toppling Saddam Hussein.[28] The CFLCC staff, as well as parts of the CENTCOM staff, had been deployed to Qatar and other places in the Persian Gulf region since late 2001 when Operation ENDURING FREEDOM (OEF) began in Afghanistan. They had planned and conducted two major and very successful military campaigns in that time. It was not totally unreasonable to believe that a new headquarters was needed to direct long-term operations in Iraq. However, the attempt at leverage did not work as General Franks had anticipated.

General Franks ultimately decided to make V Corps the senior headquarters in Iraq. The decision to replace CFLCC with V Corps surprised the Army's Vice Chief of Staff, because it seemed to contradict assumptions about which headquarters would lead Phase III and Phase IV of OIF. General Keane remembers,

> I was directly involved in making certain that [CFLCC Commander] Lieutenant General McKiernan, at the behest of the Chief of Staff of the Army [General Erik Shinseki], got absolutely the best possible team that we could put together for him for this invasion. When it came to that same headquarters taking the fight to Iraq, we decided to put together the absolutely hands-down best team we could. Franks and his guys called them the 'Dream Team.'[29]

Keane and the Army leadership chose to do this because they envisioned that CFLCC would direct Phase IV of OIF, not just Phase III.

Keane was therefore surprised and upset when he was told about Franks' decision to turn over Phase IV to V Corps during the daily Pentagon briefing sometime in mid-May 2003. His reaction that day etched strong memories:

> The brief had talked about the CFLCC headquarters moving to Kuwait. Well, I got a hold of the G3 who was [Lieutenant General Richard A.] Cody and I said, 'What the [hell], over? What is going on here? Why are these guys going south?' He said, 'Sir, I don't know. That's the plan.' I said, 'Well, who the hell is going to be running Phase IV?' He said, 'Well, the plan is to keep the corps headquarters.' So I said, 'Let me get this right. We are going to take the last arriving division commander, who just got here a couple weeks ago, and we are going to put him in charge of the war in Iraq. That is what we are going to do?'... so I got Abizaid on the phone and I said, 'What the [hell], over?' He said, 'Sir, this was hashed out by McKiernan and Franks.... Franks thinks this is okay so we are going to turn this over to Sanchez.'[30]

Keane explained that the decision made little sense to him: "I flipped. I said, 'Jesus Christ, John, this is a recipe for disaster. We invested in that headquarters. We have the experience and judgment in that headquarters [CFLCC].' So I had a lot of concern about it and I was upset about it to say the least, but the decision had been made and it was a done deal."[31] For Keane, the passage of time has not made him less critical of the decision to replace CFLCC with V Corps. In a 2006 interview, he stated:

> I still remain very disappointed by it because I think we did not put the best experienced headquarters that we had in charge of that operation. That operation, in terms of dealing with Phase IV, with an insurgency, was going to be one of the most challenging things the Army had ever taken on and we just needed absolutely the very best people involved in it. It took us months, 6 or 7 or 8 months, to get some semblance of a headquarters together so Sanchez could at least begin to function effectively.[32]

Keane was not the only senior experienced official to view the decision in this light. In Baghdad, Jay Garner, the ORHA chief, had a similar reaction:

> I tell you what, I thought that the [CFLCC] staff he had was probably the best staff I had ever seen in my life. You had [CFLCC Chief of Intelligence US Army Brigadier General James] 'Spider' Marks, [CFLCC Deputy Commander US Army Major General William] 'Fuzzy' Webster, and [CFLCC Chief of Operations US Army Major General James D.] Jay Thurman. Those guys were magnificent and they could make anything happen. . . . they had a ton of talented colonels and lieutenant colonels working for them and they had been working this problem for a year and a half.[33]

Garner questioned the wisdom of replacing CFLCC with a headquarters that had a dearth of senior officers and far less experience in the region: "All of sudden, overnight, you pick them up and move them out of there and you stick the V Corps staff in there, where many of their principals were lieutenant colonels and in some cases colonels, not many, with Sanchez as the [commanding general]." The decision created a wide gap, in Garner's opinion, between the staggering scope of the American project in Iraq and the assets chosen to implement that project. He stated, "We took the junior three-star in DOD and put him in charge of the greatest problem in the nation."[34]

V Corps was an odd choice to assume the duties of the postconflict military headquarters. Prior to the invasion, the command had focused solely on the tactical level of war and did almost no planning or training to prepare itself to become the senior military headquarters in Iraq.[35] As Lieutenant General Wallace stated in 2006, "I don't recall ever being given the indication that V Corps would assume the [joint task force] mission until after we crossed the line of departure [the Kuwait-Iraq border]."[36] It was not until late April, as Wallace was planning to move his headquarters north to Tikrit to locate it where he thought would be the center of V Corps' geographic area of responsibility in Iraq for Phase IV, did he begin to get word of the new mission. In response to the new guidance, Wallace established the V Corps main command post (CP) at Camp Victory near the Baghdad International Airport, and ordered his Deputy, Major General Walter Wojdakowski, to move the Corps logistical assets and rear CP to the new base (Logistics Support Area [LSA] Anaconda) at Balad, Iraq.[37]

Soon after the decision was made to replace CFLCC with V Corps, the role of personalities appears to have affected decisions about who would command in Iraq. Sometime in early May, the CENTCOM commander and the Defense Secretary decided to replace Wallace as commander of V Corps with Major General Sanchez (still in command of 1st AD and at the time arriving in Iraq), and Lieutenant General McKiernan told Wallace that General Franks wanted both Wallace and McKiernan out of theater in as little as 10 days. Wallace was not given the reasoning behind either of these decisions, though he delayed his departure until 14 June 2003 to conduct a transition with Sanchez.[38] After the meeting in which these decisions were made, the CFLCC deputy, Major General Webster, asked McKiernan why CFLCC was being pulled out and Wallace was being replaced at V Corps. McKiernan replied only that he and Wallace "were not in favor of the change."[39] As Webster stated in early 2007, "It just seemed a crazy decision to make while the fight was still on, to change horses in mid-stream. I was looking around at my fellow generals as staff officers there and we were kind of saying to each other, 'Well, they must know something we don't know.'"[40] Despite the urgency felt at the senior levels of DOD about the need to alter the Coalition military leadership, the changes in commanders and command structure would significantly complicate what was already a difficult transition for US forces in Iraq.

Around 17 May 2003 Sanchez was officially notified that the V Corps headquarters would transform itself into CJTF-7 and serve as the Coalition's senior military command in Iraq. The change was scheduled to take effect on 15 June 2003. Sanchez did not believe the extraordinarily complex transition was done with the care and planning that it deserved, contending, "There was not a single session that was held at the command level [in April or May] to hand-off or transition anything from the CFLCC to the Corps."[41] In his words, the CFLCC staff had already begun its movement out of theater in a "mad dash home."[42] With typical Soldier irreverence, some on the V Corps planning staff dubbed CFLCC's redeployment plans "Operation Shag Ass."[43]

This judgment may be too harsh. V Corps planners had begun to get indicators of the impending transition in late April when Major General Sanchez was still the 1st AD commander, and they participated in a coordination session with the CFLCC staff planners on 14 May. Between 6 and 10 June 2003, the CFLCC staff visited the V Corps staff at Camp Victory to exchange staff products, to finalize the table of distribution and allowances (TDAs), and other issues relating to the transfer of authority (TOA).[44] Major General Webster and Brigadier General Daniel A. Hahn, the V Corps chief of staff, met several times during this period to plan the transition.[45] The rapid TOA and the level of coordination, however, reflected the general mood in Iraq in the aftermath of the invasion's success. As Major General Wojdakowski noted, "They [CFLCC] still had a big function back in Kuwait, so it was not a real clean, comprehensive transfer, and I think the primary reason was that most everybody thought the war was over."[46] Wojdakowski himself claimed to have fallen victim to this optimistic view of the situation in Iraq, stating, "I am not chastising anybody for that because I will tell you personally that I thought it was more or less over myself."[47]

As CENTCOM Forward CP, CFLCC, and the 1st MEF began their redeployments home, V Corps was left as the only ground force headquarters in theater above division level. Franks' gambit to have the DOD bring in a new headquarters to serve as the CJTF in Iraq did not succeed. Perhaps worse was that the transition process did little to prepare the new commander and his staff for their role as a CJTF with responsibility for operations across the theater-strategic, operational, and tactical spectrum of warfare in Iraq. Not until mid-September 2003 did the CENTCOM CJ3 send a staff element back to Qatar and Baghdad to work with CJTF-7 and the CPA in shaping the new campaign.[48]

V Corps, a European-based headquarters with a purely tactical mission during the invasion of Iraq and on the verge of gaining a new commander, would now have to develop the staff, knowledge, and experience to take over for CFLCC, an organization whose focus since 1990 had been Iraq. To further complicate this transition, on 13 May 2003 the CPA replaced the ORHA. In preparation for the new mission and the requirement to work at the theater-strategic level, Lieutenant General Wallace located the V Corps Tactical CP inside the Green Zone with the CPA headquarters and kept the main CP outside the city at Camp Victory to conduct tactical and operational missions.[49]

It was clear to McKiernan, Wallace, and Sanchez in mid-May that combat operations were not over. Law and order in Baghdad were tenuous. By early May 2003, for example, Major General Buford Blount, the 3d ID commander, reported to the CFLCC deputy commander that he did not even have enough troops to guard the specific installations that he had been directed to protect from looters.[50] Sporadic attacks on US troops increased daily. While the 3d ID consolidated its hold on Baghdad, the 101st ABN was just moving into Nineveh province in northern Iraq where previously only a small Marine force had been operating with small units from US Special Operations Forces (SOF). Additionally, the 173d Airborne Brigade held a small area of northern Iraq after parachuting into the country near the town of Irbil. The 2d Brigade of the 82d ABN and the 3d ACR were moving west from Baghdad into the heart of Sunni territory. To the north of Baghdad around the city of Tikrit, the 4th ID had replaced the Marines of 1st MEF and was finding former Baathist forces that had not been defeated or captured during the invasion.

The rapidly changing command structure in May 2003 created confusion about which phase of the OIF campaign plan Coalition forces were conducting. Much more than a semantic difference, this issue had significant affects at all levels. The phase of the operation influenced the task organization, the type of missions the US forces would conduct, and the rules of engagement (ROEs) under which US forces would operate. It appeared that CENTCOM had declared an end to Phase III after General Franks' 16 April 2003 visit to Baghdad, though Franks himself is not sure if an order was issued to that effect.[51] The President's "mission accomplished" speech on 1 May 2003 contributed to the perception of transition.

Meanwhile, V Corps continued to execute its operations under the orders issued at the start of Phase III. When 4th ID arrived to replace the redeploying Marines of 1st MEF in the area around Tikrit, they took an aggressive posture in the heavily Sunni region to destroy what were then being called "dead enders" and former regime elements (FRE). In fact, before 16 June 2003 Lieutenant General Wallace never issued an order formally transitioning V Corps to Phase IV operations, though the Corps mission did change. The new mission statement, issued in mid-May, directed the Corps' subordinate units to conduct offensive operations and "stability operations that support the establishment of local government and economic development" concurrently.[52] This statement signaled V Corps' recognition that full spectrum operations in Phase IV in Iraq might become far more complex than the transition phases of previous campaigns.

As CENTCOM and CFLCC started moving out of Iraq, Sanchez began communicating directly with Franks' replacement, Lieutenant General John Abizaid, then serving as the deputy commander of CENTCOM and designated to take the reins of that command in early July 2003. As the date for the CENTCOM and V Corps changes of command drew near, both men had concerns about the security situation in Iraq. After a meeting in Baghdad in late June, Sanchez recalled,

> We both knew, even by that point, that we had a couple of major issues. We had an issue with the sourcing for the V Corps/CJTF-7 staff and we had an issue with the operational environment that was unfolding. The war was not over. It wasn't as benign an operating environment as everybody thought. We were continuing to have attacks, even though at a low rate, but we recognized very early on, by the first couple of weeks of July 2003, that we were in a continuation of Phase III [of OPLAN COBRA II]. We were still fighting and all indications were that we probably had an insurgency on our hands. We weren't quite sure at this point. We figured it was elements of Saddam's regime but we did not know yet exactly what this thing looked like.[53]

Sanchez's understanding of the postinvasion situation articulated the widening realization that there would be no clean break between Phase III and Phase IV and that Army units would have to conduct combat and stability and support operations simultaneously.

In July Abizaid made his concerns about the security environment crystal clear. In his first Pentagon press conference as the new CENTCOM commander on 16 July 2003, Abizaid stated his belief that the US faced "a classical guerrilla type campaign" in Iraq.[54] He had been in command of CENTCOM only 8 days and one of his first official statements appeared to run counter to public comments from Secretary Rumsfeld and his deputy, Paul Wolfowitz, and some commanders on the ground.[55] Abizaid's statement was a sobering recognition that turning military victory into strategic success was going to be neither easy nor quick. The hopes for a peaceful turnover of power to a new Iraqi Government followed by a rapid withdrawal of US forces had essentially disappeared.[*]

Political-Military Relations I: The Short Reign of ORHA

On 1 April 2003 Lieutenant General (Retired) Jay Garner and his ORHA team had been in Kuwait for about 2 weeks, its staff still assembling as the fighting moved rapidly northward toward Baghdad. Since 20 January 2003 ORHA had served as the US Government's organization designated to lead postwar Iraq until Iraqis could form a new government. When that moment arrived, ORHA planned to hand off its mission to a new diplomatic entity or embassy in as little as a few months.[56] CENTCOM and CFLCC prewar plans assumed that military forces would receive strategic guidance from ORHA once major fighting ended and postconflict operations began. In the chain of command, Garner reported directly to the Secretary of

---

[*]As discussed in chapter 3, the authors of this book are using the term "insurgency" to refer to the broad mix of groups that used violence to oppose the Coalition powers and the evolving Iraqi governing bodies in 2003 and 2004. The opposition included former regime elements, al-Qaeda terrorists, regional terrorists, sectarian militias, criminal enterprises, and others.

Defense. Once he received his authority and mission from Secretary Rumsfeld, Garner and his fledgling staff developed four "pillars" to guide ORHA's work: reconstruction, humanitarian affairs, civil administration, and an expeditionary staff to handle logistics and security.

Using his connections with military and civilians in Government service, Garner had moved quickly to assemble a staff:

> I briefed Rumsfeld and he concurred with [the staff structure]. I took it to Condoleezza Rice and told her that I needed to exercise the President's Decision Memorandum and get the interagency to provide the people. So she called a deputies meeting and she brought in all the deputies of each interagency. There was Wolfowitz from Defense, Armitage from State, and so on, and I gave all of them a copy of that chart and all the functions. I briefed them on it and they asked a few questions. Then they all went back and sent me people and they all sent me absolutely superb people. I didn't get a C Team. I got an A Team.[57]

The nucleus of Garner's "A team" formed in February and early March 2003. By the time ORHA departed for Kuwait in mid-March, he had approximately 250 people on his staff. Although interagency conflict inside the Bush administration created friction in the formation of ORHA, the organization continued growing and had 400 staffers by the time it reached Baghdad in late April.[58]

As its name indicated, ORHA focused on providing humanitarian and reconstruction assistance. ORHA planners expected Saddam to blow up the Iraqi oil fields in a reprise of his actions in the 1991 Iraq War. Garner also expected massive refugee problems as people fled the fighting. That neither calamity occurred is a tribute to the stunningly rapid success of Coalition military forces and to Iraqis who refused to sabotage their country's resources.[59] Unfortunately, a series of calamities far worse than oil field fires soon engulfed Iraq.

Outside of the humanitarian and reconstruction mission, Garner had little guidance. ORHA's uncertain relationship with CENTCOM contributed to the vague planning and coordination of efforts for post-Saddam Iraq. According to Colonel Mike Fitzgerald, CENTCOM's deputy CJ5 planner:

> The only [ORHA-related] document that I ever saw was the one to two page document that said these are your essential tasks. It didn't tell him [Garner] where he was lined up in the chain of command and who he responded to. So a lot of energy was expended trying to get them embedded in planning, to understand the relationships, and to bring people together, that could have been resolved up front . . . with a document that clearly stated what their charter was, who they worked for, and what their relationship was with the CENTCOM commander.[60]

General Keane had similar concerns about Garner's authority in the spring of 2003 when DOD formed ORHA. After a briefing from Garner at the Pentagon, Keane recounted, "I asked him who he was working for and he said that he was working for Secretary Rumsfeld. I said, goddamn it, Jay, that is the wrong answer. Every damn time we don't have unity of command. You should be working for one guy and one guy only, and that is Franks."[61] Garner suggested to the Chairman of the Joint Chiefs of Staff, General Richard Myers, that ORHA should fall under the command of a sub-unified military headquarters in Iraq that would function alongside a diplomatic mission under Ambassador Zalmay Khalilzad. The civilian DOD leadership did not agree, though in June 2004, the Coalition created a military/political command that followed this recommended structure.[62]

When ORHA began deploying to Kuwait in March 2003, just days before the invasion began, it was clear to many senior staff officers that Garner's organization was not in a position of leadership. ORHA personnel were not provided housing or offices at Camp Doha where CFLCC had its headquarters. In Kuwait, ORHA staffers, CFLCC planners, and the soon to be disbanded CJTF-IV, found themselves uttering a collective "who the hell are you guys," according to one member of Garner's team.[63] Major General Webster, the CFLCC deputy commander, echoed that sentiment, noting that CFLCC did not have a formal relationship with the ad hoc CJTF-IV staff, which arrived in Kuwait in early March. The US Joint Forces Command had sent CJTF-IV to support CENTCOM's Phase IV planning effort, not CFLCC's planning. Similarly, within a day of Garner's arrival in Kuwait, Webster met with Garner and recalled that the ORHA chief said he did not need any significant assistance from CFLCC at the time. Garner thought he would have the time to get ORHA organized in Kuwait and establish relationships with international organizations and leading Iraqis long before US forces reached Baghdad. Webster also knew that Garner and ORHA reported directly to DOD and coordinated with CENTCOM and General Franks.[64] Thus, ORHA and CFLCC did not develop a close relationship. Even if Garner had sought tighter coordination with CFLCC concerning Phase IV operations, in February and March 2003 McKiernan's staff was consumed with planning and preparing for the impending invasion of Iraq, trying to get all their forces into theater, and fending off incessant requests for changes to the deployment schedule from DOD.[65]

No one in the US Government ever envisioned that ORHA would become the headquarters of an occupying power—with the responsibilities inherent in that term as defined in the Hague and Geneva Conventions—for anything but the briefest period of time. Garner and his senior staff certainly did not view ORHA's responsibilities in this light. Instead, they defined their organization as an adjunct agency that would briefly deal with anticipated humanitarian issues and assist the Iraqis in quickly taking responsibility for their own affairs.[66] Accordingly, one of Jay Garner's first moves once he arrived in Iraq was to hold a meeting with representatives of various Iraqi tribes, ethnic groups, and religious leaders at the ruins of the Biblical city of Ur, a few miles from An Nasiriyah, on 15 April 2003. He had previously dispatched a team to Basrah on 27 March to work with forces from the United Kingdom (UK) in the south, and sent a team on 7 April 2003 to Irbil in northern Iraq to coordinate with Kurdish leaders.[67]

After personally asking General Franks for transportation and a security escort, Garner arrived in Baghdad on 21 April 2003. Along with Presidential Envoy Zalmay Khalilzad, Garner made plans to host a second conference in Baghdad. On 22 April 2003 Garner flew north to As Sulaymaniyah and met with Kurdish leader Jalal Talabani, head of the Patriotic Union of Kurdistan. The following day he met in Irbil with Massoud Barzani, leader of the Kurdistan Democratic Party. After the ORHA chief arranged safe passage for the Kurdish leaders, they met on 28 April in Baghdad with expatriate Shia leader Ahmed Chalabi, expatriate Sunni leader Adnan Pachachi, the secular Shia expatriate Ayad Allawi, and Supreme Council for the Islamic Revolution in Iraq (SCIRI) leader Ayatollah Muhammad Bakr al-Hakim. In the background, sporadic fighting still echoed throughout the city while looters methodically dismantled nearly every unoccupied manifestation of the former government.

The series of meetings with Iraqi leaders, however, generated neither a functioning government in April 2003 or even an agreement on how to form one. Talabani himself blamed the failure on Iraqi leaders bent on dividing the spoils of war. Other problems surfaced as the expected aid and military forces from other nations did not immediately materialize. A British official confidentially warned Prime Minister Tony Blair in early May that the Coalition was losing popular support.[68] ORHA's staff of 400 finally made it to Baghdad on 24 April 2003, and on that very day, the Secretary of Defense notified Garner that he was replacing ORHA with the CPA led by Ambassador L. Paul Bremer III. Bremer would arrive in May with much greater authority than ORHA and a much different mandate for the future of Iraq.

Despite the unexpected news, Garner continued to work in Baghdad. ORHA had planned to restart almost all of the ministries in the Iraqi Government as they existed under Saddam, with the exceptions of the Ministries of Propaganda and Intelligence. But in late April and early May, with most ministry buildings looted or destroyed and Iraqi society in chaos, he and his staff were reduced to roaming the streets of Baghdad with military escorts provided by V Corps looking for anyone who had been part of the Iraqi Government. Like most Americans involved in the planning of OIF, Garner vastly overestimated the condition of Iraq's infrastructure.[69] The buildings had been destroyed by bombing, looted down to the bare walls, and the employees had nowhere to work and no one to whom they could report.[70] ORHA immediately set out to get food supplies moving again, restore electricity, and reestablish the destroyed telecommunications network in Iraq.

Garner also met with both Lieutenant General McKiernan and Lieutenant General Wallace in Baghdad, and the two military leaders agreed to provide ORHA with military escorts and security for its headquarters because of the continued fighting in Baghdad. V Corps focused on eliminating pockets of resistance in Baghdad, expanding its control out to the vast stretches of Iraq which it had not occupied, and moving its still arriving forces from Kuwait to Iraq. ORHA and CFLCC developed good initial working relationships, and both CFLCC and V Corps provided as much support as they could to ORHA. Garner and McKiernan agreed to match key ORHA staff members with CFLCC general officers and staff sections.[71] Despite their initial understanding, CFLCC's support to ORHA slowed once McKiernan and his staff received orders to deploy out of Iraq in May. By that time ORHA had begun thinking about redeploying to make way for Bremer and the CPA.

In retrospect, it was clear to many that ORHA and its mission had several serious flaws. Wallace recalled that ORHA was simply too small and lacked sufficient resources, explaining, "They showed up and had no capability. Jay Garner is a wonderful guy and [ORHA chief of staff] Jerry Bates is a wonderful guy . . . but they had no capability to do anything."[72] The lack of interagency planning behind the ORHA effort also appeared obvious. Wallace noted, "When Jay Garner and his folks showed up, it wasn't the US State Department, it wasn't Department of Agriculture, and it wasn't the Treasury Department, it was just a bunch of former military guys trying to bridge from military to something."[73] This was not an auspicious start for the Coalition effort in Iraq. Although Wallace's comments overlooked the ORHA staffers who came from other departments of the US Federal Government, they capture the essential problem with this aspect of prewar planning. CENTCOM and CFLCC were consumed with deploying forces to Kuwait and planning the invasion of Iraq. CJTF-IV, ORHA, and later CPA all lacked the capacity to plan for or conduct the occupation that would follow the toppling of the Saddam regime. When conditions in Iraq proved to be wildly out of synch with prewar assumptions, the effect on US military forces was immense.

Political-Military Relations II: From ORHA to the CPA and the Iraqi Governing Council

In mid-April 2003 Vice President Richard Cheney's Chief of Staff, I. Lewis "Scooter" Libby, and Deputy Secretary of Defense Paul Wolfowitz contacted former Ambassador Bremer to serve as the senior American official in Iraq. Bremer would replace Garner and Khalilzad in leading Coalition efforts to help shape the new Iraq. President Bush publicly announced the decision on 6 May 2003, 17 days after Garner arrived in Baghdad as the head of ORHA.[74] The CPA's stated mission was to "restore conditions of safety and stability, to create conditions in which the Iraqi people can safely determine their own political future, and facilitate economic recovery, sustainable reconstruction and development."[75] The US Government never issued a formal order dissolving the ORHA. Some of its staff members joined the CPA, and Garner returned to civilian life.[76]

Creation of the CPA signaled to the world that the United States was going to assume responsibility as an occupying power over Iraq under the Hague and Geneva Conventions until a new government could be formed. Though reluctant to use the phrase "occupying power" because of its cultural connotations in the Middle East, the United States and the United Kingdom registered their intentions in an 8 May 2003 letter to the United Nations (UN) Security Council.[†] The new Coalition political headquarters symbolized an American commitment that was far greater than that assumed when policymakers offered their initial visions of OIF. In his initial meeting with President Bush, the Vice President, Secretaries of State and Defense, and National Security Advisor Condoleezza Rice, Bremer insisted on unity of command in Iraq. He recounted that after the meeting, "The message was clear. I was neither Rumsfeld's nor Powell's man. I was the President's man."[77] Bremer believed he reported directly to the President and noted that some began calling him the "American viceroy" in Iraq.[78] Officially, however, the CPA chief was subordinate to the Secretary of Defense, as were US military forces in Iraq.[‡]

Bremer arrived in Baghdad on 12 May 2003 after meeting with Garner the night before in Kuwait. On the morning of 13 May 2003, the CPA and Bremer formally replaced ORHA and Garner, 4 months after ORHA was created and only 22 days after it had entered Baghdad. Bremer immediately put his stamp on the nature of post-Saddam Iraq and on the relationship between the CPA and US military forces in Iraq. He issued CPA Regulation No. 1 on 16 May 2003, which stated:

> The CPA shall exercise powers of government temporarily in order to provide for the effective administration of Iraq during the period of transitional administration, to restore conditions of security and stability, to create conditions in which the Iraqi people can freely determine their own political future. . . . The

---

[†]Security Council Resolution 1483, 22 May 2003, recognized the United States and the United Kingdom as occupying powers in Iraq.

[‡]As will be discussed later in this chapter, the CPA was removed from the DOD's chain of command in November 2003 and began reporting directly to the National Security Council.

> CPA is vested with all executive, legislative and judicial authority necessary to achieve its objectives.[79]

This declaration and others regarding law and order and administration of Iraq were in compliance with international law governing military occupations, which required an occupying power to take certain measures to establish a safe and secure environment for all persons under its control. International law also requires the civilian population to behave peacefully, to take no part in continuing hostilities, and to not interfere with the operations of the occupying power.[80]

The regulation also underlined the CPA's limited authority over military forces in Iraq and the resources they controlled: "As the Commander of Coalition Forces, the Commander of US Central Command shall directly support the CPA by deterring hostilities; maintaining Iraq's territorial integrity and security; searching for, securing and destroying weapons of mass destruction; and assisting in carrying out Coalition policy generally."[81] Thus, with Regulation No. 1, Bremer established an ambitious set of objectives and a broad set of responsibilities for the CPA. But his organization was utterly lacking in people, organization, and resources for the mission. The interagency process of the US Government was simply not prepared to support the CPA in May 2003 with the personnel and expertise required by the situation in Iraq. Nor did the CPA have authority over the military instrument of national power in Iraq, the most important means of achieving the CPA's mandate in the absence of other national resources.

Security in Iraq was on Bremer's agenda from the very first day. As early as 14 May 2003, Bremer had begun discussing the need for CFLCC forces to take a more active role in restoring law and order with Lieutenant General McKiernan and Lieutenant General Abizaid. Both men promised to change the ROE that governed the actions of American Soldiers and Marines in Iraq and have US forces take the appropriate measures.[82] CFLCC had already issued an order for US forces to stop the looting on 1 May 2003, but the ROE had not been fully developed and US forces were focused on deploying into Iraq, spreading out into the country, and conducting sporadic combat operations.

Bremer wasted no time in establishing his relationship with military forces. Unlike the informal relationship between ORHA and CFLCC, the CPA was the preeminent US authority in Iraq. The future military headquarters in Iraq, CJTF-7, reported directly to CENTCOM headquarters, with the mission of providing direct support to the CPA, which reported to DOD. This dual chain of command understandably caused friction—some personal and some functional—between the staffs of the CPA, ORHA, CFLCC, and V Corps as they tried to sort out their respective roles, relationships, and priorities in the midst of continued fighting and the collapse of Iraqi governance between mid-April and late May.[83]

Some of this friction stemmed from the earliest days of the CPA. According to some parties present, the first thing Bremer said at V Corps headquarters in Baghdad was, "You all work for me."[84] Sanchez, though not present at the time, heard credible accounts of this blunt statement and believed it set a particular tone, "So it started out fairly rough and it didn't help that he completely cut out McKiernan and Wallace when he said, 'I don't want to deal with you guys. I want to deal with Sanchez.'"[85] While this was realistic recognition of the command hierarchy with whom he would have to work, Bremer's demeanor further increased the divide between the CFLCC staff—who were beginning to redeploy—and V Corps whose units were still fighting and whose staff was preparing to take over all military operations in Iraq.

Despite the frosty introduction between Bremer, McKiernan, and Wallace in May 2003, Sanchez and Bremer would forge a reasonable working relationship in Iraq. They would have frequent disagreements about policy decisions over the next year. However, on a personal level, they got along well during and after their time in Iraq.[86] Sanchez understood that the principal role of CJTF-7 was direct support of the CPA. This was a major change from the original guidance from CENTCOM, which directed the military's postconflict headquarters to provide only limited assistance to the CPA in post-Saddam Iraq. Recalling the initial CENTCOM guidance, Sanchez noted that he took a different approach based on how he understood the overall military mission in Iraq: "In reading the direct support mission that had been issued to [CJTF-7], I changed that [from limited support]; the implied task was to make CPA successful and, therefore, we pumped significant amounts of resources into the CPA."[87]

CPA's late creation, small size, short-term staff rotations, and fragmented arrival into Iraq meant that Bremer did not have the capacity he needed to function as the headquarters of an occupying power. One result of its late creation and lack of planning capacity was that rather than arriving in Baghdad with the equivalent of a campaign plan, Bremer and his staff took over a month to create a vision statement that contained the broad outlines and objectives of the CPA mission.[88] The CJTF-7 staff was also underresourced, but by virtue of its units and Soldiers, it had the type of presence across the country that the CPA dearly sought. That reach also meant, however, that US Army units faced daily problems, which required decisions and actions. Confronted with the lack of CPA staff presence and specific policy guidance in the many provinces of Iraq, some Soldiers began to dismiss the CPA as irrelevant outside the environs of Baghdad. This judgment was perhaps unfair; but in the spring and summer of 2003, the reach of the CPA did not extend much beyond the Iraqi capital.

The informal culture and lack of formal staffing processes within the CPA also clashed directly with the disciplined military decision-making process (MDMP) of the Army. Sanchez and his staff felt continually frustrated by what they perceived to be arrogant and informal staffing of key issues by CPA officials, many of whom came from the State Department and other agencies outside the DOD community. One officer who served with CJTF-7 in 2004 described some CPA meetings between former ambassadors and their staffers as being "more akin to professors having a discussion with graduate students than anything resembling the [MDMP]."[89] Military officials tended to see the CPA process as shallow and lacking in the understanding of the full range of actions needed to prepare, implement, and monitor the effects of major policy issues. While CJTF-7 would begin integrating its staff with that of the CPA in June 2003, it is clear that a cultural gap continued to divide the two organizations. As one military officer attached to the CPA put it, "State is from Venus and DOD is from Mars."[90] An exception to this general culture clash appears to have been the linkage between division commanders and regional CPA officials who worked closely together in the country's provinces later in 2003. Still, military officials tended to view the CPA as lacking in the resources required to make significant change in Iraq. Sanchez later noted, somewhat uncharitably, that CPA had all the authority in Iraq, but little responsibility for and no capacity to carry out its policy decisions.[91]

The very real limitations of the CPA shaped the manner in which the Coalition approached many issues. Perhaps the best example was the CPA's program for establishing new Iraqi

Security Forces (ISF) that would include an army and police forces. The issue of training the ISF emerged as a major point of contention between CJTF-7 and the CPA. Bremer and the CPA were keenly interested in having Coalition military forces establish law and order in the country, but did not plan to have them involved in creating the ISF. Despite the severe lack of capacity to create the ISF, Bremer retained complete responsibility for those functions until a major policy change in the spring of 2004, refusing offers by CJTF-7 to take over those missions or even to assist. As later chapters will show, CJTF-7's forces took certain actions out of necessity that ran counter to this official division of labor.[92]

The United States: An Occupying Power

During the initial invasion of Iraq in late March and early April 2003, both Secretary of State Colin Powell and National Security Advisor Rice had publicly stated that the United States intended to rapidly turn over power to the Iraqis once Saddam was overthrown. Prewar plans had assumed no more than a 2 or 3 month period before this transition occurred. Garner had taken steps to do just that when he arrived in Iraq. Bremer, however, brought a radically different view with him, one that he maintains was approved by the Secretary of State and the President.[93] Once in Baghdad, Bremer quickly rejected Garner's intentions to convene a meeting in late May of Iraqi leaders to form a new Iraqi Government. He instead opted for a more methodical approach that he thought necessary to ensure the government enjoyed support from both the population and institutions of civil society that he called "shock absorbers."[94] As with Bremer's policies on the de-Baathification of Iraqi society and the dismantling of Iraq's security forces discussed in chapter 3, his decision to launch a slow, deliberate transition to Iraqi sovereignty would have a tremendous impact on the Army's mission in Iraq.

Ultimately, in mid-July 2003, the CPA formed the Iraqi Governing Council (IGC), a body solely advisory in nature, as a quasi-partner until free and fair elections could elect a truly representative Iraqi Government. The IGC replaced the self-appointed Iraqi Leadership Council (ILC), which Iraqi exiles in London had created in December 2002, and entered Iraq in late April 2003. The 25-member IGC included 13 Shia, 5 Sunni Arabs, 5 Sunni Kurds, 1 Sunni Turkoman, and 1 Assyrian Christian.[§] The transition to a sovereign Iraqi Government would take another 11 months, ending on 28 June 2004 when the Interim Iraqi Government (IIG) assumed political authority from the CPA.

As the previous chapter recounted, the first two orders issued by the CPA in May 2003—the policy of de-Baathification and the dissolution of the Saddam-era military, security, and intelligence institutions—had significant and long-lasting impacts on Iraqis and on US forces in Iraq. Taken together, these two orders marked the official end to the Saddam regime. Unlike in Afghanistan, however, where an internationally approved interim Afghan leadership took power immediately after the fall of the Taliban in the spring of 2002, in Iraq, these and other CPA decisions demonstrated that the Coalition would function as an occupying power for an indefinite period. Unfortunately, US military forces and the US Government had not prepared for that mission. That lack of preparation had enormous influence on events after May 2003.

[§]Among its most prominent members were Ahmed Chalabi, Adnan Pachachi, Massoud Barzani, Muhammad Bakr al-Hakim, Ghazi Mashal Ajil al-Yawer (the first Interim President of Iraq), Jalal Talabani (the first permanent President), Ayad Allawi (the first Interim Prime Minister of Iraq), and Ibrahim al-Jaafari (the second Interim Prime Minister). Three of the council members were women.

V Corps Becomes CJTF-7

In May 2003 Generals Sanchez and Abizaid began considering the magnitude of the challenges facing them and their Soldiers as the situation in Iraq evolved. Key among those challenges would be transitioning V Corps into a CJTF. Recognizing that direct support to the CPA was perhaps the most important of his roles, Sanchez decided to locate himself and a small command element in Baghdad with the CPA. Sanchez's deputy, Major General Wojdakowski, directed the CJTF-7 main CP from its location in Camp Victory near the Baghdad International Airport on the western outskirts of the capital. Given the rapidly changing military command structure in Iraq, and the changing nature of US strategic policy for postwar Iraq, deciding where to place critical command elements was just the first task in what would become a Herculean effort.

Army doctrine in 2003 indicated that a corps headquarters like V Corps could serve as a joint task force (JTF) or combined joint task force (CJTF) if properly augmented with personnel and resources. A corps headquarters was the Army's highest tactical headquarters and normally functioned at the tactical and operational levels of war. Once it became a CJTF, however, the corps had to operate at the tactical, operational, and theater-strategic levels of war. Once augmented, Army doctrine also held that the corps might have responsibility to create a campaign plan if one does not exist.[95] CENTCOM, which retained authority for strategic matters throughout the Middle East and parts of Central Asia, also had the responsibility for augmenting the V Corps staff so that it could carry out its missions in Iraq at all three levels of war.

General Franks' guidance to quickly redeploy the CENTCOM Forward CP in Qatar and the CFLCC headquarters in Doha, Kuwait, made the huge task of transitioning V Corps to CJTF-7 even more problematic. The confusion was so great that a week before turning over command of V Corps, Lieutenant General Wallace notified the CFLCC commander that the transition would have to be delayed unless CENTCOM finalized and fleshed out the Corps' Joint Manning Document (JMD), the table of organization that authorized the positions on the joint staff. The temporary solution was to leave selected CFLCC personnel behind to augment V Corps. This move increased V Corps' manning levels from 50 percent to 70 percent of the JMD by 15 June 2003.[96] But the numbers were still small, the personnel were often rather junior in rank, and no command expected the CFLCC augmentees to remain in theater beyond 45 days. Even before they took over, it was clear to Sanchez and his deputy, Wodjakowski, that the V Corps staff would not have the proper structure, size, or sufficient rank to fully handle its role as a CJTF. For Wojdakowsi, one of the most glaring gaps was the absence of general officers in the principal staff positions. He explained the problem in the following way:

> To put it in perspective, I think the Combined Forces Land Component Command (CFLCC) had six general officers in it. When [CFLCC] left on 15 June 2003, there was one general officer in the [CJTF-7] command post and that was me. When I left there on 1 February 2004, we had a little get-together a couple nights before we left and there were 19 general officers there. . . . So we had to elevate the corps staff up to a CJTF staff.[97]

The V Corps staff eventually grew from its initial strength of some 280 officers and noncommissioned officers (NCOs) to nearly 1,000 by early 2004. But this expansion occurred slowly.

The initial JMD, completed by CFLCC, provided V Corps with only three general officers—the normally assigned three-star commander, two-star deputy, and one-star chief of

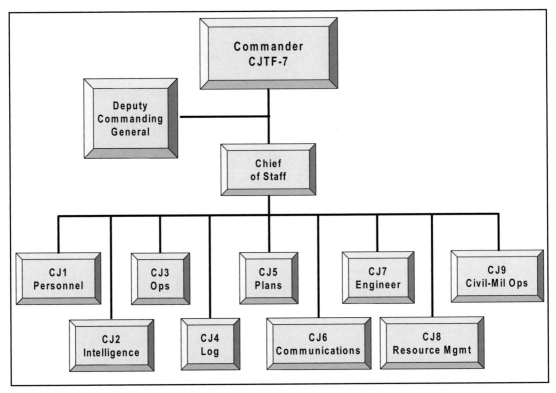

Figure 35. Combined Joint Task Force–7 Staff Structure.

staff. This contrasted sharply with CFLCC, which had general officers as the principals in most of its staff sections. As the new command emerged and it became clear that he would need senior staff officers, Sanchez reached out to the Coalition partners for assistance and recalled that some of the best thinkers and planners in the early days of CJTF-7 were the dozen or so officers who joined his staff from the British, Canadian, and Australian Armies.[98] Still, there was a shortage of staff officers, a weakness that Lieutenant General Wallace had recognized and tried to address before he left command of V Corps in June 2003. Wallace requested a team from the Joint Warfighting Center (JWFC) in Suffolk, Virginia, to do an assessment of the CJTF-7 JMD.[99] While that team eventually assisted in the expansion and refinement of the JMD, CJTF-7 would continue to experience difficulties in obtaining the authorized number and type of staff officers throughout 2003 and well into 2004.[100]

By mid-June 2003 it was clear to the V Corps commander that the numbers of billets on the JMD and the rank of officers assigned were only the most obvious challenges facing CJTF-7. The new command also had to assemble the proper mix of capacity, capability, and collective experience required for its staff to serve competently as a Coalition headquarters and to operate at the tactical, operational, and theater-strategic levels of war. Sanchez recalled one glaring example of the obstacles the Corps faced in finding experienced planners for the Corps CJ5 Plans section:

> Within 2 days after I took over as the CJTF-7 commander, I asked the C5 [Plans section] to 'Bring me your roles and functions for review.' Now this was a theater strategic headquarters and the Chief came back and told me

'Well, we do future [military] plans.' That was it! At this point we had to go back and completely rework the staff structures over the summer months to be able to document the skills necessary to handle the normal functions of a C5 at the theater-strategic level. This included strategy and policy, force generation, Coalition operations, political-military affairs and all other aspects of a combined, joint theater strategic headquarters.[101]

The initial CJTF-7 JMD called for a 21-person CJ5 Plans staff; on 7 June it was filled with only 9 personnel, lacking the full colonel to lead it and a number of other key positions. The JMD also called for only a two-person planning staff to liaise with the CPA in the Green Zone, anticipating that the CPA's capability for planning would be far more robust than turned out to be the case.[102] In addition, the V Corps staff had no strategic communications cell, nor was there a strategic communications plan at CENTCOM for V Corps to use as guidance for its own operations.[103] The staff was also heavily weighted with Army personnel instead of being truly joint. The initial JMD, for example, did not include a Coalition Air Operations Center (CAOC) to handle the complexity of joint air operations in Iraq.[104]

CJTF-7 began working with CFLCC and CENTCOM to amend the JMD, adding general officers and staff positions to meet the demands placed on the new headquarters. CJTF-7 started this assessment in early July 2003 and submitted its first written requests to upgrade the JMD to CENTCOM in August 2003. The DOD and the Armed Services, however, reacted slowly to approve and fill the personnel requirements of that new manning structure. Major General Thomas Miller, who became the CJTF-7 Chief of Operations (CJ3) in July 2003, stated his staff was "understaffed rather significantly and in a state of constant personnel instability" through 2003 and early 2004.[105] The instability that Miller noted was partly a result of joint and Coalition staff officers arriving on short tours:

> I would say that the healthiest that [the CJ3 Operations staff] ever got was probably at about the 50 percent mark, but you never sustained that more than 30 to 40 days because of the turnaround ratio you had amongst the various services. As an example, the Air Force [colonels] that served as the C3 Air, in a year I had 7 of them. They were all great officers, don't get me wrong, but they were only there for 60 days, some even 30 days, or some 120 days. It was very, very difficult, in my opinion, to deal with that turbulence.[106]

Miller concluded, "The JMD, in my opinion, never matured fully until about the spring of 2004" when CJTF-7 was on the verge of transitioning to a completely new command structure.[107]

CJTF-7's Intelligence staff section (CJ2) had its own challenges, some of which were related to the larger JMD issues. The V Corps Intelligence staff was designed for the conventional war the Coalition had just fought. It lacked a Joint Intelligence Center, which has the capacity to conduct human intelligence (HUMINT) collection and analysis, a "Red Team," and other key assets that are necessary to conduct intelligence operations at the operational and strategic levels of war. Many of these agencies and resources had left when CFLCC pulled out of Iraq. Major General Barbara Fast, who became the chief of the CJTF-7 Intelligence staff section in July 2003, described the situation that summer:

> When CFLCC departed, the Defense Intelligence Agency (DIA) HUMINT assets and the US Army Intelligence and Security Command (INSCOM) assets

departed, as well. The remaining DIA assets were part of the Iraqi Survey Group (ISG) and designated to find WMD [weapons of mass destruction]. These were the designated, experienced assets on which we rely for some of our more sophisticated HUMINT operations. This left only CIA assets, also limited initially in number, and our tactical HUMINT assets which were not as capable in numbers or experience.[108]

Sanchez recalled that his intelligence officers were very smart and dedicated, but "their instinct, their forte . . . what we had trained these kids for was to go out and fight a conventional fight and they were pretty damn good at it. But now we were completely lost in a totally different operational environment and we were really struggling."[109] The V Corps intelligence staff was accustomed to building briefings that used red unit icons to precisely depict conventional enemy formations such as those they faced during the drive on Baghdad. As CJTF-7 intelligence work progressed, the briefings to Sanchez would soon use overlapping circles and amorphous clouds to imprecisely depict shadowy insurgent groups, terrorists, criminal gangs, and sectarian militias.[110] This type of analysis took time to learn and perfect.

More problematic for the longer campaign was that like the CJ3 section, the CJ2 staff never grew to meet the operational demands for information and analysis. Major General Fast continued to have a difficult time filling the positions in her section throughout the first year of the campaign: "We didn't have an adequate number of people to begin with for intelligence operations in general. We built a Joint Manning Document (JMD) in the early fall of 2003, but even as I left Iraq in 2004, we were still only at about 50 percent strength. So we never had the assets that we required."[111] The CJ2 staff also spent considerable time addressing security and classification considerations, to include training, for intelligence personnel from 19 Coalition countries. These tasks diverted the officers on the staff from more pressing operational requirements.

The shortage of personnel in the summer and early fall of 2003 meant that the CJTF-7 staff would often have to cease work on one project to shift effort in reaction to an emerging crisis or opportunity. Major General Miller, the CJ3, noted that given his small staff, he made the choice to spend little time on the theater-strategic and operational-level issues, concentrating instead on the tactical level:

> Quite frankly, the day-to-day fight, the turmoil of transition . . . and all the other unforeseen tasks (Iraqi Civil Defense Corps, Police, Iranian Mujahedin-e Khalq forces, etc.), and then the enormous task of orchestrating a force rotation OIF I to OIF II, completely consumed the undermanned staff (CJ3). So as a result of that, I would have to say that the tactical situation and associated current operations tasks received the bulk of our attention, especially within the CJ3.[112]

Miller also noted that some of the critical cells within the CJ3 could not focus on their mission because unanticipated taskings sometimes pulled them away from their core requirements. For example, in the summer and fall of 2003, Miller essentially had to shut down the CJ3 Effects cell so the officers who made up that cell could concentrate on coordinating the training of the Iraqi Civil Defense Corps (ICDC) and Iraqi police forces. As Miller later stated, "There was not anyone else to do [the Iraqi police/ICDC mission]."[113] The other staff sections within CJTF-7 had similar problems simultaneously working at all three levels of war.

By July 2003 Sanchez had convinced the Acting Army Chief of Staff, General Keane, to provide major generals for the CJ2, CJ3, CJ4, and CJ5, along with supporting staff officers. However, those decisions took time to implement. Sanchez noted that adding the general officers to the staff did not address all of the critical shortcomings in his organization, "You would get the general officer, but the skill sets underneath them, the staff officers underneath them, didn't have the experience or the capacity to be able to work the actions that were so critical during those periods. That doesn't really evolve to a point where I would say you are near effective until the late spring of 2004."[114] Again, turnover of key personnel made the situation even more difficult. Lieutenant Colonel Wesley Odum, a V Corps plans officer, recounted that he worked for six different chiefs in the CJ5 Plans section between July and November 2003, some of whom were American and others who were from the Coalition nations.[115]

CJTF-7 and the Planning of the New Campaign

In the 18-month period covered by this study, three different Coalition military commands developed and used four separate campaign plans to direct the military effort in Iraq. These four plans existed at the operational and theater-strategic levels of war and did not include the tactical-level plans generated by brigades and divisions, which were part of the Coalition command in Iraq. The campaign plan was the single most important document used by the US Army to provide direction and to set objectives for its units to accomplish. Its overarching purpose is to turn military actions into favorable strategic outcomes for the United States. The timing, purpose, and general content of these plans are integral to understanding the overall approach and effectiveness of the Coalition effort in Iraq. This section will briefly describe the first two plans and focus on the third plan created by CJTF-7 in the summer of 2003. A subsequent section will cover the fourth plan issued by Multi-National Force–Iraq (MNF-I) in August 2004.

COBRA II was the first of these campaign plans. Written before the war by CFLCC, COBRA II guided the conventional operations that toppled the Saddam regime in March and April 2003. The ECLIPSE II plan, also written by CFLCC but published only after the war began, served as the blueprint for operations in Iraq after the fall of Saddam. Its life span, however, was very short because of CFLCC's transfer of responsibilities to CJTF-7 in mid-June 2003. Moreover, CFLCC planners had made important assumptions about the amount of stability in post-Saddam Iraq. As stability and security decreased in the spring and early summer, the conditions on the ground made ECLIPSE II essentially irrelevant. (Chapter 2 discusses these plans in greater detail.)

CJTF-7 created the third plan, releasing it in draft form in August 2003. That plan, which remained nameless, served as the overarching guidance for Coalition military operations until January 2004 while being constantly modified as the political and military situation in Iraq fluctuated. That this plan remained a work in progress throughout the summer and fall of 2003 has led to the erroneous conclusion that CJTF-7 failed to have a campaign plan in 2003. In fact, the CJTF-7 CJ5 Plans section began work on documents that articulated guidance and vision for the Coalition military campaign just days after the JTF headquarters was created on 15 June 2003.[116]

Though the CJTF-7 commander and his planners had not inherited a fully developed plan for the postconflict phase of OIF from CFLCC or from CENTCOM, and while CPA certainly lacked any kind of comprehensive plan at this stage in its development, the CJTF-7 staff was not planning in a vacuum. Even before the decision to make V Corps the lead military headquarters in Iraq, Corps planners worked to ensure their operations were nested within the existing CENTCOM, CFLCC, and CJTF-Iraq (as CJTF-7 was then called) briefings. CENTCOM's planning envisioned seven logical lines of operation in their Phase IV planning: unity of effort, security, rule of law, civil administration, relief and resettlement, governance, and economic development. By late June the CPA had developed five lines of operations with the assistance of CJTF-7 planners: security, essential services, governance, economy, and strategic communications. General Abizaid would add more guidance to the planning efforts after he took over CENTCOM in July 2003, introducing what he called the "Five I's" to guide US military operations: Iraqization, improvement of intelligence, development of infrastructure, internationalization, and information operations. Abizaid believed these five priorities were critical to success, stating, "If we can dominate those five I's, we can win the campaign."[117] From this pool of documents, briefings, and concepts, CJTF-7 began its own planning effort.

Working with planners from the divisions and other subordinate Coalition commands, the CJTF-7 CJ5 staff completed a working draft plan and a set of briefing slides that described the direction and goals for the military effort in Iraq. The role of this draft plan has been somewhat misunderstood, primarily because it continued to evolve in reaction to the changing political and military conditions in Iraq between August 2003 and January 2004 when it was finally published as a complete operation order (OPORD). Another complicating factor was that the Coalition was conducting operations while the plan was being developed, which required commanders to act on drafts and briefings as well as on verbal and written fragmentary orders. Additionally, while it completed the draft plan in the summer of 2003, the CJTF-7 staff still had to coordinate with and seek approval for the plan from the CPA, CENTCOM, DOD, and other parts of the US Government.

In setting down the basic foundation of the plan, the CJTF-7 staff faced significant difficulties. To what degree, for example, would they rely on COBRA II and ECLIPSE II? In the minds of the plans officers in CJTF-7, a wholly new campaign plan was needed in the summer of 2003, one that essentially served as a replacement for CFLCC's ECLIPSE II plan for Phase IV of OIF which no longer matched reality on the ground.[118] Between June 2003 and January 2004, however, Lieutenant General Sanchez, the CJTF-7 commander, chose to employ aspects of the original CFLCC COBRA II plan. This decision stemmed from the fact that in the summer of 2003, Coalition leaders understood the Iraqi insurgency as primarily composed of former regime elements loyal to Saddam. In Sanchez's view, the Saddam regime was not yet fully dismantled and the security situation on the ground too tenuous for a transition from COBRA II's emphasis on offensive operations (Phase III) to a new phase that focused on stability and support tasks (Phase IV). For this reason, he frequently stated that the Coalition remained in Phase III throughout 2003. To Sanchez, it appeared logical to modify that plan to support emerging CPA and US Government decisions. As he later explained, "The mission statement for us at this point in time is that we know we have to continue to conduct offensive operations across the country in order to be able to defeat these noncomplying [former regime element] forces that are out there."[119] He also wanted to send the message inside and outside of CJTF-7 that combat was not over, that the Saddam regime had not been entirely eliminated, and that OIF was not yet transitioning to the kind of stability and support operations that were employed in the Balkans and that would allow for the rapid drawdown of US and Coalition forces in Iraq. In fact, General Abizaid and Lieutenant General Sanchez were working feverishly in the summer of 2003 to reverse those redeployments already underway, and to plan for the extended occupation of Iraq.[120]

Throughout 2003, the CJTF-7 staff thus categorized their OPORDs and fragmentary orders as extensions of the Phase III of the original COBRA II plan. While Sanchez emphasized the offensive aspect of CJTF-7's effort, his planners continued to develop the new plan and, while that plan retained its status as a draft, it served as important guidance for division planning and operations. The CJTF-7 Plans section continued to update and issue briefing packets to subordinate commands as the situation on the ground changed and as US strategy for Iraq evolved.[121]

Despite the volatile conditions, some critical elements of the plan remained unchanged throughout 2003. CJTF-7 directed its forces to act along four lines of operations: security, essential services, governance, and economy—essentially the same as those used by the CPA. CJTF-7 integrated a fifth line of operation, information operations, into the other four lines of operation. The new plan contained four phases—Phase III, Offense; Phase IVa, Stability; Phase IVb, Support; and Phase IVc, Deterrence—each with its own triggers, objectives, and military and political end states, and all centered on the idea that the Coalition would reduce levels of military forces and operations as the campaign progressed.[122] Though offensive combat operations were dominant in Phase III of the plan, this phase also included stability and support operations that were to be carried out simultaneously by Coalition forces. The same mix of operations would also characterize the phases that followed. The plan's mission statement captured this important concept:

> Conduct offensive operations to defeat remaining noncompliant forces and neutralize destabilizing influences in the AO in order to create a secure environment in direct support of the Coalition Provisional Authority. Concurrently conduct stability operations to support the establishment of government and economic development in order to set the conditions for a transfer of operations to designated follow-on military or civilian authorities.[123]

The mission statement, with its simultaneous emphasis on combat and stability operations, expressed CJTF-7's understanding that the military effort in Iraq required full spectrum operations. Equally important was the plan's identification of the Iraqi people as the center of gravity for the campaign. To be successful, CJTF-7 planners believed Coalition forces had to enable the CPA to gain and retain the popular support of the Iraqi people for the Coalition's efforts to create a new Iraqi Government.

The new CJTF-7 campaign plan provided its units with broad guidance within which they were to conduct a combination of offensive, defensive, stability, and support operations suited to their particular region of Iraq. In this way, the plan empowered commanders at the tactical level to tailor operations as they saw fit. As Major General Miller, the CJTF-7 chief of operations (CJ3), noted:

> The campaign plan provided what I would call a very broad framework [lines of operation] and little specific direction—or specific when warranted. It was descriptive not prescriptive—and rightfully so. In some cases though—it was

Braille warfare to put it bluntly. . . . You just sorted some things out on the fly—and that is OK—you adapt. . . . So the whole nature of this operation was decentralized and driven by the campaign plan.[124]

It must be recalled that as this plan was being developed, the enemy situation in Iraq was changing as other religious, sectarian, and international terrorist forces joined the resistance to the Coalition, and as the Iraqi and international political situation evolved.

By September 2003, barely a month after the first draft was completed, it was becoming evident to Coalition military leaders that security was not soon going to be established, that the resistance consisted of more than former Saddam loyalists, and that Phase IV would take much longer to reach. This reality forced further revisions to the plan, delaying its publication as a fully-fledged operation order (OPORD), though it continued to serve as general guidance for CJTF-7's subordinate units. In what Lieutenant General Sanchez later described as a "tectonic plate shift," the decision made by the Bush administration and Bremer to hand over power to an IIG in June 2004, well before popular elections could be held and far earlier than originally envisioned by Bremer, forced the CJTF-7 staff to make further revisions to the plan.[125]

The resolution to hand over sovereignty to an Iraqi Government did not mesh with the conditions-based timelines in existing CPA and CJTF-7 plans, both of which envisioned the Coalition implementing major political changes only after sufficient security had been established in Iraq. This decision drove CJTF-7 to continue its focus on offensive combat operations while at the same time the CPA prepared for and conducted the transition to Iraqi sovereignty, making the mission even more complex. In January 2004 Sanchez issued the final version of CJTF-7's campaign plan as a fully constituted and finalized OPORD.[126] This OPORD remained in effect until the staff of MNF-I published a new plan in August 2004, after new political and military realities forced the Coalition to reconsider how its military operations should support a newly sovereign Iraqi Government. In explaining how he viewed the campaign in 2003 and 2004, Sanchez contended that throughout his tenure in command in Iraq, his forces remained in Phase III of first the COBRA II and later the CJTF-7 campaign plan, conducting full spectrum operations focused on establishing a sufficient amount of security so the campaign could fully transition to Phase IV.[127]

CJTF-7 in Retrospect

Despite the many shortcomings of his command's organization, Sanchez remained extremely proud of what his staff and subordinate commanders were able to accomplish in those early weeks and months, believing they prevented a bad situation from becoming disastrous by their determination, hard work, and patriotism. Three years after that long summer, Sanchez reflected on their contribution: "As ugly as it was and as difficult as it was, it was their individual efforts, their ingenuity, their adaptability, and it was the leadership that just went out and said, 'hey, this has got to be done. We will figure it out.'"[128]

It is clear V Corps was not properly augmented to serve as a CJTF on 15 June 2003 when it assumed responsibility as CJTF-7. Initially a tactical headquarters from March to May 2003, by June V Corps found itself faced with the tasks of transforming into a joint and combined task force, developing a new campaign plan, planning force levels for what would become known as OIF II, and conducting operations at all three levels of war. Making matters more difficult was that all of these missions had to be done while working with an evolving CPA organization and with the IGC which had no clear vision for the future of Iraq. Looking back on this period in 2006, Wojdakowski, the CJTF-7 deputy commander, summarized his thoughts, "Although the Corps did a great job, I think, on converting to a CJTF staff . . . we lost something in the translation from the day we took over until we reached our full capability in running such an immense operation."[129]

By late spring of 2004 Lieutenant General Sanchez felt he had the staff structure and experienced personnel in place to perform most of these tasks at an acceptable level. But in reality, it was not until the creation of MNF-I in late spring of 2004 that the Coalition resolved the mismatch between the command structure and the enormity of the military requirements in Iraq. Several years later, General McKiernan, commander of CFLCC during the invasion of Iraq, noted the debilitating impact of the changes in command structure as well as the shortcomings of the CJTF-7 organization and concluded that they resulted from a larger failure—a lack of planning: "We had all these transitions of organizations and command and control [CENTCOM, CFLCC, and V Corps] on top of a transition in the campaign, Saddam to post-Saddam. That is not how we would plan normally."[130] From this experience, McKiernan drew the obvious but salient conclusion, "What is the lesson learned out of all that? You have to put as much effort into the back end of the campaign as you do into the front end."[131]

Boots on the Ground in Iraq: The Coalition Military Command and the Issue of Troop Strength

In the summer of 2003, the DOD faced the issue of determining whether there would be a requirement for a second rotation of US forces in Iraq, an "OIF II" as it would later be called. CENTCOM and CJTF-7 planners immediately had to determine how long forces would remain in theater. Given the uncertain security environment that was developing that summer, the first decision was to stop the hemorrhaging of units leaving Iraq. In a series of meetings in late June, Sanchez and Abizaid decided to halt the flow of forces out of Iraq.[132] The new policy stated that units did not leave until their replacements were in place. Therefore, he and Abizaid succeeded in halting the redeployment of the 3d ID and having the 82d ABN headquarters, one of its maneuver brigades, its aviation brigade, and other organic supporting units deploy to Iraq to increase troop strength on a temporary basis. Both of those decisions caused significant difficulties for the Army. This was to be a stopgap measure until CJTF-7 had time to develop a comprehensive plan for the forces that would be needed for OIF II.[133] Abizaid announced this new stance after he assumed command of CENTCOM on 8 July 2003.

Later that month, the Army announced its "one year boots on the ground" policy in recognition of the long-term nature of the mission.[134] This major policy announcement required units and Soldiers to spend 1 year in Iraq itself, plus whatever time it took to train and deploy into and out of the country. A 1-year rotation would give units and Soldiers time to develop situational awareness, experience, and connections with Iraqis—all critical to operations in the new campaign in Iraq. After the yearlong deployment of the Implementation Force (IFOR) to Bosnia in December 1995, the Army had used a 6-month rotation policy for units and for individual personnel for its deployments. This decision to create an OIF II rotation based on 1-year rotations put tremendous pressure on the Army as an institution, on the Reserve Components in particular, and on commanders and Soldiers personally.

OIF II did help CJTF-7 plan for troop levels in the future. But in considering the situation in mid-2003, Coalition leaders could not expect to gain any significant increase in troop strength. Still, Lieutenant General Sanchez believed he had sufficient forces to accomplish the military missions charged to CJTF-7 at that time:

> Given what we knew in that period, during the June, July, and August time-frame, the missions that we were assigned, the missions that were evolving during that timeframe and expanding or threatening to expand, and the uncertainty of the operational environment, I thought we had sufficient forces to do what we had to do, but then very quickly we got to the point where we had to start making tradeoffs.[135]

Political and military developments in Iraq clearly forced Sanchez to compromise and shift efforts from event to event. CJTF-7, for example, had no operational reserve force in 2003 and 2004. If a situation developed that required more troops in a certain area or for a certain operation, forces had to be shifted away from another part of Iraq. Wojdakowski, the CJTF-7 deputy commander, echoed his commander's comments about shifting forces around to deal with changing requirements:

> What we did was we shifted other forces around and used the forces like any prudent commander would and took risk in the areas where we needed to take risk. Face it, you never have a perfect solution, but you get paid to shift forces around, you get paid to decide where you are going to take risk and where you are going to put your effort, and we did those things and I guess history will determine whether we took the right risks or not.[136]

In mid-summer 2003, Coalition military leaders grew concerned about the size of their formations, the type of units required for the new campaign, and the missions they had to perform. As Wojdakowski stated in 2006:

> As a corps, we certainly had enough force to take down the regime and we had enough forces at corps to execute what our Phase IV plan was if we had executed it. We ended up not doing that because we took on the mission of the entire country. It became pretty obvious to General Sanchez and me by about 1 July 2003 that we would need at least as much force, maybe more than we had, in order to continue operations without beginning to get behind on countering this insurgency, and we started making that known.[137]

Given the Army's total force structure in the Active and Reserve Components, there was considerable tension within the US Army concerning the need to keep force levels at a sustainable rate for the long term. Other pressures came from the evolving nature of the military tasks, the differing roles of the CPA and CJTF-7, and the increasing Iraqi opposition to Coalition rule and military forces.

As the summer wore on and as new security challenges developed, the CJTF-7 commander's judgment changed. "As major events started to unfold," Sanchez stated, "it was very clear that additional forces would be required, but at all levels of command it was acknowledged that there were no additional forces available. The existing forces were either deployed and [in Iraq], just recently redeployed such as the 3d ID and a couple of other units, or they were already scheduled for deployment as part of OIF II."[138] The CJTF-7 commander and his deputy knew the Army did not have the force structure to indefinitely maintain its peak strength of the equivalent of six divisions in the country. In response, the top military decisionmakers began the practice of delaying some unit redeployments out of Iraq during rotation windows to temporarily generate greater troop capacity. Wojdakowski noted another example of the issues posed by overall troop levels, this one dealing with the composition of specific capabilities in Iraq:

> I mean, we had about three-fourths of the MPs in the Army in the country and we were told they were all going to leave and we knew that we needed three-fourths of the Army's MPs to replace the three-fourths we already had, ... So we knew we had some force structure issues and we told the Army that and they began training artillerymen to be MPs. They started converting artillery batteries to do infantry tasks.[139]

He added, "So it was a huge challenge just replacing what we had for OIF I with the right force for OIF II."[140]

As noted earlier, Sanchez found himself compelled to take risks with his forces. Many US units in mid-summer 2003 were beginning to deal with the mounting insurgency that threatened the fundamental objectives of postconflict operations. However, the CPA and CJTF-7 recognized that new tasks, such as securing borders, securing and destroying the massive number of ammunition dumps around Iraq, and guarding key Iraqi infrastructure, were emerging at the same time. US units diverted resources to meet these requirements. Sanchez described the situation:

> You begin to very rapidly accept risk and make tradeoffs. From my perspective as the ground commander, what I was doing was to identify what forces were necessary to accomplish the mission . . . and the strategic, operational and tactical risks associated with the diversion of forces [to the emerging tasks], should that be required. I would provide that assessment to higher headquarters stating that I'd be glad to accomplish the mission with assigned forces, if ordered. This meant that the decisionmaker would have to accept the risks identified in our assessment.[141]

Clearly by the fall of 2003, the demands of the worsening security situation, as well as those of the other lines of operation, forced CJTF-7 leaders and units to prioritize their tasks and take significant risks.

Other factors contributed to the formal position held by Sanchez on the force-level issue. First, it was the CPA, not CJTF-7, that maintained the responsibility for standing up the ISF in 2003 and early 2004. This program was consistent with the belief that the Iraqis themselves had responsibility in the security situation. Any great influx of US troops had the potential to decrease the Iraqis' sense of urgency to accept responsibility for security tasks. Second, the United States was attempting to secure more troops from the "Coalition of the willing," an effort that might have been undermined by sending more US troops to Iraq. It is also reasonable to have believed in the summer of 2003 that a significantly greater Coalition and US troop presence would alienate Iraqis who had remained neutral up to that point. Sanchez maintained a delicate balance between all these competing interests during his tenure as the commander. The evolving situation in Iraq required CJTF-7 to conduct an expanding set of missions that overwhelmed the manpower assets available to the Coalition headquarters. As other commanders have done in other conflicts, the CJTF-7 commander continued to execute the mission while pushing for more Coalition forces and pushing the CPA to more rapidly build the new ISF.

Critical to the understanding of the troop strength issue is that, as the senior US official in Iraq, the CPA Chief had the final say over US policy in Iraq. Bremer at times expressed displeasure to Coalition military leaders about the inadequate security situation and its relation to troop levels. Those concerns, however, did not persuade him to significantly change the CPA-led programs to train new Iraqi police and military forces or to agree that Iraqi military forces should have a role in internal security matters. Ultimately, neither Sanchez nor Bremer had the final word on troop levels. That authority rested inside the Pentagon. Bremer remembered that the al-Sadr uprising and Sunni attacks of April 2004 conclusively demonstrated to him that Coalition troops were stretched too thin and that led him to send a written request for one or two more divisions—25,000 to 45,000 troops—to Secretary of Defense Rumsfeld.[142] The CPA chief confirmed that in mid-May 2004 Rumsfeld received the request and that the Secretary of Defense passed it on to the Service Chiefs. According to Bremer, he never received an official response to his request.[143]

Closely related to the issue of force size was the matter of force structure and equipment. Sanchez and his commanders spent a great deal of time trying to determine the right mix of units and equipment. It quickly became apparent that US Soldiers could not perform all of the missions required by the new campaign with the Abrams tanks, the Bradley Fighting Vehicles (BFVs), and the other heavy equipment that had been decisive in swiftly defeating the Saddam regime. American units needed a greater number of wheeled vehicles and aerial platforms. In addition, as improvised explosive devices (IEDs) and other threats increased, the armor on those vehicles would have to be increased to protect the vehicle and to protect the Soldiers inside. CJTF-7 incrementally increased its requirements for equipment as they were identified and as enemy tactics evolved. In retrospect, Sanchez admits he was slow to communicate this to CENTCOM, and by extension, to the Army. "We made a mistake in not just putting a blanket requirement [for additional equipment] out there for the Army."[144]

Given the worsening security environment in mid-2003 and the very real need to increase Iraqi forces, CJTF-7 began to get involved in the mission to train Iraqi police and paramilitary units. However, as chapter 11 of this study will show, the CPA held formal responsibility for this program and Bremer strenuously resisted attempts by CJTF-7 to assist with the training mission. Between June 2003 and early 2004 Sanchez questioned that decision, arguing that the construction of the new Iraqi military and police forces should be assigned to CJTF-7. He even channeled multiple appeals to the Secretary of Defense and the National Security Council (NSC) asking for authority over the program.[145] In Sanchez's view, CPA programs were too limited and the actual rate of progress far too slow to deal with the rising security problems in Iraq. Coalition units, on the other hand, dealt with security issues on a daily basis and had, in theory, the rudimentary training and capacity to form the type of security forces needed immediately to quell the growing instability.

Technically in violation of CPA policy, but with Bremer's reluctant acknowledgment and later his support, the CJTF-7 commander took matters into his own hands and directed his subordinate commanders to form Iraqi Civil Defense Corps (ICDC) battalions. These hastily formed paramilitary units provided some much needed local and regional security assistance to Coalition forces until they were incorporated into the Iraqi Army in late 2004. Similarly, CJTF-7 supported the efforts of its subordinate units to use their MP forces to help train and mentor local police forces, in coordination with the program being run by the CPA. The ICDC and police programs clearly illustrated the disconnect between the policies of the two major US organizations in Iraq in the summer of 2003. However, that the Coalition moved ahead with the program also demonstrated the way in which the CPA and CJTF-7 often compromised to achieve some semblance of unity of effort.

The Coalition's challenges with force levels continued after the CJTF-7 and CPA were dissolved in 2004. In the spring, summer, and fall of 2004, Lieutenant General Thomas Metz, the commander of MNC-I, also believed he had sufficient forces to perform the missions assigned to him. But MNC-I lacked a reserve force, requiring Metz to accept risk in certain areas of the country when concentrating Coalition forces for an offensive operation or when reacting to enemy uprisings. In the fall of 2004, Metz requested and received two battalions of the 82d ABN from the United States. For Operation AL FAJR, the second battle of Fallujah in November 2004, MNC-I was able to employ the CENTCOM reserve, the battalion-size 31st Marine Expeditionary Unit.[146] As already mentioned, US planning for the elections of January 2005 included timing the rotation of forces between OIF II and OIF III so as to increase force levels during that critical period.

Beginning with the planning efforts in 2002 and the start of combat operations in early 2003, OIF has engendered a serious debate about the troop strength required for the Coalition to attain its objectives in Iraq. Partisans on one side of the issue argued that troop numbers were too low given the scope of Phase IV requirements. The other side suggests that the Coalition's troop presence generated the very resistance that the Coalition confronted. Arguments on both sides often referred to past campaigns that featured stability operations or counterinsurgency efforts, hoping that these cases could offer accurate benchmarks for the proper troop levels

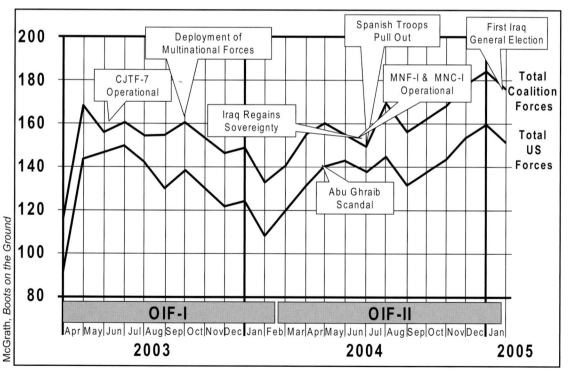

Figure 36. Troop strength.

169

required for campaigns of this type. Generating ideal troop levels from historical cases is complex and any accurate analysis depends on how the analyst calculates the size of friendly forces and the size of the host nation's population.[147]

In the case of OIF, Coalition troop strength in Iraq in the immediate aftermath of the invasion in May 2003 was roughly 168,500, with the US contingent numbering roughly 142,500. Total Coalition troop strength in Iraq declined to around 145,000 by December 2003 after the Army's 3d ID and the 1st MEF left Iraq, though many Coalition nations provided additional forces in the summer and fall of 2003. Force levels in Iraq reached a low of 131,000 in January 2004, the smallest number attained between May 2003 and January 2005. Troop numbers then rose to more than 160,000 between January and May 2004 during the rotation of US forces from OIF I to OIF II and as some US forces were extended in Iraq during the outbreak in Shia and Sunni violence that spring. Over the summer of 2004, Coalition force numbers fluctuated between 150,000 and 165,000. Troop strength then rose and peaked at 184,500 troops (160,000 US) in January 2005 to coincide with the Iraqi elections and the rotation of US forces to Iraq for the OIF III deployment. As of this writing, 184,500 remains the peak Coalition troop strength employed during OIF.[148]

To make use of troop levels in the calculation of the ideal size of security forces for occupation or counterinsurgency campaigns, analysts often employ a "troop density ratio." This statistic, usually expressed as the ratio of security forces per thousand inhabitants of the host nation, provides a tool for the comparison of troop levels in diverse historical cases. For example, troop density of British Army and Malaysian security forces during the Malayan Emergency (1948–60), a campaign often cited as the most effective counterinsurgency effort conducted by a 20th century Western power, reached a peak figure of 24.7 troops per 1,000 residents.[149] A more recent example of troop density during the NATO occupation of Kosovo in 1999 shows peak force levels attaining a ratio of 21.1 troops per 1,000 residents. NATO employed some 15 troops per 1,000 residents during the IFOR phase of the Bosnia mission in 1995–96.[150] Both missions in the Balkans attained relative success, though neither mission is complete and their outcomes are not fully known. Together, these cases support the argument that higher troop density ratios are critical to achieving strategic goals in campaigns that feature peacekeeping and other stability operations.

In contrast, US troop density during the successful Philippines counterinsurgency at the beginning of the 20th century peaked at only 9.8 soldiers per 1,000 residents. US force levels in post-World War II Japan were even lower at only 6.2 troops per 1,000 inhabitants. Troop density in occupied Germany was only slightly higher at 10.8 troops in the first year, and fell to 6.38 troops per 1,000 after only 2 years of occupation.[151] Both of those occupations are considered stunningly successful. It is important to keep in mind, however, that both Japan and Germany had been devastated by 4 or more years of "total" war.

Using the figures cited above for Coalition forces in Iraq, the troop density ratio in May 2003 was 6.6 Soldiers per 1,000 Iraqi inhabitants. The ratio varied between that date and January 2005 when it reached a peak of 10.3 troops per 1,000 Iraqi inhabitants.[152] Within Iraq's provinces, however, troop density varied significantly, achieving higher densities in Baghdad and lower ones in the extreme south and in the Kurdish north. Including ISF in these calculations for this 18-month window further complicates the analysis because of concerns about accurate numbers and types of forces that qualified as operational units. Clearly, in May 2003,

Iraq had no viable military or police units. Their numbers show a slow upward trend in 2004 as the CPA began building a new Iraqi police force and army, and as CJTF-7 began creating ICDC units. Multi-National Security Transition Command–Iraq (MNSTC-I), which began operations in May 2004, made a sharp reduction in the number of Iraqi police reported as "on duty" after an evaluation of their effectiveness in September 2004. Still, even after this correction, strength figures for the ISF in January 2005 show some 87,900 trained and equipped troops in the Iraqi police, National Guard, and Army. By including those forces with the number of Coalition troops in Iraq in January 2005, a new troop density ratio of 13.74 emerges.[153]

This analysis generally supports the argument that Coalition troop density in Iraq in 2003 and 2004 was too low, certainly in comparison to the ratios found in the Malayan and Balkan examples cited earlier. They are higher than the ratios found in postwar Germany and Japan, however, which many believed Ambassador Bremer used as a model for Iraq. What is missing from this analysis are the intangible factors unique to each historical case. Terrain and population density, population diversity and ethnic divisions, postwar physical and demographic factors, cultural issues, and the question of when peak troop density should be reached, among others, render it impossible to make simple and direct conclusions from studies of troop densities.

Still, the statistic is a useful tool for assessing the size of a military force needed in complex campaigns. In the case of OIF, this type of analysis helps make several important points about Coalition force levels. In the immediate aftermath of the regime collapse in April 2003, Coalition troop density was at the very low end of the range of the aforementioned historical cases. Since the US did not anticipate the collapse of Iraqi society and governance, nor a large-scale insurgency after Saddam was overthrown, this should not be surprising. By the summer and early fall of 2003, when CJTF-7 leaders realized a complex insurgency had emerged and that Iraq needed far more reconstruction and support than anticipated, force levels did not rise to match the new reality. The inability of Coalition forces and the Iraqi Government to provide security across all of Iraq and to control Iraq's borders are two examples of where more forces could have been employed in 2003 and 2004.[154] Though nearly every senior commander stated that he had sufficient forces on hand, they were constantly required to shift forces and adjust priorities, leaving some regions with few units to meet unexpected security challenges. The ISF during this period of the war were too few and not yet ready to meet the demands of the complex insurgency in Iraq. It is at least arguable that greater troop strength during the critical window of time in the late spring, summer, and fall of 2003 would have prevented the rise of an insurgency or at least greatly diminished its scope, though that conclusion is far from definitive.

From CJTF-7 to MNF-I: Change under Adversity

Over the course of 2003, Lieutenant General Sanchez and General Abizaid began to reevaluate Secretary Rumsfeld's and General Franks' original decision to turn Coalition operations in Iraq over to CJTF-7, in essence an augmented three-star corps headquarters. The Coalition command structure for OEF had provided a precedent for this decision. In Afghanistan, the XVIII Airborne Corps headquarters served as the core of CJTF-180, which provided command and control for US and Coalition operations in the country. CENTCOM did not establish that CJTF, however, until mid-2002, 7 months after combat operations had begun. Additionally, CJTF-180 operated alongside the NATO-led and UN-approved International Security Assistance Force (ISAF) in Kabul, and in support of the Bonn Agreement, which had legitimized Hamid Karzai as the interim leader of Afghanistan. Both Sanchez and Abizaid had served together in Kosovo and had seen the incredible complexity of Coalition and stability and support operations firsthand. In particular, they understood the challenges facing a single headquarters in conducting Coalition operations at the tactical, operational, and theater-strategic levels of war in a complex and uncertain political environment.[155] Abizaid was convinced as early as October 2003 that in Iraq "we were going to have to go to a four-star command . . . in order to deal with the myriad of tasks that were necessary."[156]

Abizaid and Sanchez sought to address the inherent weaknesses of CJTF-7 and gradually developed a plan to transition to a sub-unified four-star command in Iraq that would report to CENTCOM. This joint command structure was not unusual; it would be similar to the United States Forces Korea (USFK) headquarters in South Korea that served under the US Pacific Command (PACOM) and commanded US and Korean forces within the PACOM area of responsibility. A four-star command in Iraq would handle Coalition theater-strategic and operational-level issues leaving CJTF-7 or a new command to focus on the tactical fight. A new command of this type, however, would require the Armed Services to make a major effort to create, equip, and man a large headquarters staff and support structure.

When they first introduced the concept in the fall of 2003, Abizaid and Sanchez were met with opposition from the Secretary of Defense and the Armed Services. The Services and the US Government were already struggling to fill the ever-expanding manning needs for CJTF-7, the CPA, and other commands operating in Iraq. Planning was well underway for sourcing the next rotation of US forces in OIF II. CJTF-180, the US command in Afghanistan, was also demanding increased resources in support of OEF. Abizaid wrestled with setting up the command and control structure for multiple operations in the CENTCOM area of responsibility—CJTF-7 in Iraq, CJTF-180 in Afghanistan, Joint Task Force–Horn of Africa in east Africa—and decided to keep his main headquarters at MacDill Air Force Base in Tampa to oversee a range of operations not envisioned in prewar planning. Given all of these national level requirements, it appears that DOD leadership and the National Security Council (NSC) members were reluctant to support the extended commitment to a longer occupation that a four-star command would represent.[157] For all these reasons, the decision about creating a sub-unified command in Iraq was deferred.

Abizaid continued to make the case at DOD for a new command structure and in December 2003, the CENTCOM commander finally gained approval. Adding urgency to the military changes was the 15 November 2003 decision to transfer sovereignty to the Iraqis in the summer of 2004, well ahead of the multiyear plan first envisioned by the CPA just a few months earlier. Initially, the CENTCOM concept was to bring the CFLCC headquarters back to Iraq. But CFLCC also served as the Army Service Component Command (ASCC) for CENTCOM, with Title X responsibilities across the Middle East that would suffer if it focused solely on Iraq. That option was eventually discarded in the spring of 2004 in favor of creating a new command.[158]

The new headquarters for US and Coalition military operations in Iraq would become known as Headquarters, Multi-National Force–Iraq (MNF-I). It would provide theater-strategic and operational-level command and control for all Coalition forces in Iraq and would provide direct support to the Coalition political authority as well as to the emerging Iraqi Government and institutions. In general, MNF-I's most important functions were to coordinate, synchronize, and deliver security, economic, diplomatic, and information operations with the US Embassy and the new Iraqi Government, leaving tactical combat operations to its subordinate headquarters.[159]

The commander of MNF-I would report to the commander of CENTCOM, freeing Abizaid to spread his efforts over the entire CENTCOM area of responsibility. In turn, MNF-I would command two, three-star headquarters—Multi-National Corps–Iraq (MNC-I), which would control tactical-level military operations, and MNSTC-I, which would have authority over the programs that were organizing, equipping, training, and advising the ISF, as well as rebuilding Iraq's Ministry of Defense and other military infrastructure. MNF-I would also have operational oversight over the US Army Corps of Engineers Gulf Region Division, which was heavily involved in the reconstruction of Iraq and would enjoy the support of Combined Joint Special Operations Task Force–Arabian Peninsula (CJSOTF-AP).

The actual transition from CJTF-7 to MNF-I took place in several steps in the spring and summer of 2004; a number of factors, to include enemy actions, complicated it. The DOD conducted the massive OIF I and OIF II rotation of forces between January and April 2004. This rotation involved the replacement of the V Corps headquarters with the III Corps headquarters to serve as the nucleus of CJTF-7 staff, and replacing hundreds of units and over 100,000 US Service members. Toward the end of the force rotation in late March and April, Sunni and Shia insurgent forces burst out in defiance of the Coalition and the IGC. CJTF-7 temporarily halted the rotation to deal with the attacks, and delicate shifts in command and control responsibilities were needed. The 1st AD, partially located in Kuwait at the time, was called back to Iraq and did not redeploy until June 2004. It must be remembered that the Coalition and CPA were in the process of preparing to turn over sovereignty to an IIG through this entire period. The challenges were immense.

III Corps Replaces V Corps

The first transition took place on 1 February 2004 when Lieutenant General Thomas F. Metz and III Corps raised their colors at CJTF-7 headquarters replacing the V Corps headquarters, which had invaded Iraq in March 2003 and had formed the core of CJTF-7 since June 2003. The Army's Forces Command notified Metz and III Corps of the impending mission in early September 2003 and they had been preparing since. Metz recalled that Abizaid told him, "What I need you to do is to go in and take over the tactical fight for Lieutenant General Sanchez and I need Sanchez to focus on the strategic fight."[160] As late as August 2003, the III Corps commander and his staff had been focused on their contingency plans for Korea. After notification of the deployment to Iraq, III Corps went through a series of predeployment site surveys of Iraq, Battle Command Training Program (BCTP) exercises, and Joint Forces Command seminars to prepare for the mission.[161] The same preparation was taking place across the Armed Forces as units prepared for the first of what would become yearly rotations of forces in and out of Iraq.

The III Corps staff replaced their V Corps counterparts across CJTF-7. This transition was not a one-for-one process because CJTF-7 was far larger than a corps headquarters, having been augmented with personnel from around the US Armed Services. Metz took Major General Wojdakowski's position as Sanchez's deputy commander, and was able to focus more on operations than on force sustainment issues. CJTF-7 was still a unified headquarters, albeit physically divided between downtown Baghdad where the chief of staff and CJ5 sections worked with the CPA, and Camp Victory near the Baghdad airport where the majority of the CJTF-7 (III Corps) was located.

The transition anticipated the creation of MNF-I. Metz's chief of staff, Brigadier General William Troy, oversaw the planning for the separation of CJTF-7 into MNF-I and MNC-I scheduled for 15 April 2004. Metz tasked Brigadier General Richard P. Formica to begin the planning to turn the ICDC into a true military force prior to the planned activation of MNSTC-I in June. Though MNC-I was formally stood up in mid-April as scheduled, it was not until the end of July 2004 that Metz had reconstituted his III Corps staff under the MNC-I flag and consolidated them at Camp Victory.[162] Still, between April and the creation of MNF-I, some of the CJTF-7's staff sections were split based on their roles in the future command structure. For example, Major General Fast began focusing on intelligence at the operational- and theater-strategic levels in preparation for the establishment of MNF-I, while her deputy became the CJ2 for tactical operations anticipating the formal creation of MNC-I.[163]

Throughout his tour as MNC-I commander, Metz's command style was fairly decentralized as an operational commander. Given the vast differences between unit areas of responsibility (AORs) across Iraq, Metz saw his role this way: "You have to work what the mission, enemy, terrain, weather, and troops and time available required in your area. What are the resources you need that I can give you as the corps commander? I have often said, at that level, it becomes much more that you are a resource provider as a corps commander more than tweaking the tactical level."[164] III Corps did not develop its own campaign plan, because as the operational arm of CJTF-7 and later of MNF-I, they implemented the campaign plans of CJTF-7 and MNF-I.[165] Metz gave each multinational division and separate brigade commander broad discretion to implement those plans in a way suitable to their particular AORs. On several occasions, however, Metz took a more direct hand in tactical operations during critical periods. In February and March, CJTF-7 began planning for Operation VALIANT SABER, designed to take advantage of the short-lived lull in violence after December 2003 and the capture of Saddam. After exploiting the high-level intelligence gained from Saddam's capture, Lieutenant General Sanchez wanted to stay on the offensive against insurgent groups by fighting for more intelligence. The operation required moving units and assets from across Iraq to targeted areas; thus, Metz took a more direct hand than he would have done with an operation that was wholly within a single area of responsibility. VALIANT SABER's goal was to select areas of Iraq, beginning with Mosul in the north, where Coalition forces would concentrate their efforts to defeat the last remnants of opposition and turn it over to local rule by Iraqis. The April uprisings in Fallujah and in the Shia corridor effectively ended the initiative.[166] In April, May, and June, Metz turned to close coordination of the operations of Coalition units in their efforts to defeat the Sunni and Shia uprisings in Fallujah, Samarra, Al Kut, and An Najaf.

The second Battle of Fallujah in November 2004 was the most traditional or conventional operation that MNC-I conducted during Metz's tenure. Operation AL FAJR, or New Dawn, was launched in early November after a long period of military, humanitarian, and political preparations were put in place to destroy the Sunni insurgents that took over the town of Fallujah in April. Metz worked with MNF-I, Coalition military units, units of the new Iraqi Army, and the new IIG to put together the right tactical forces and reconstruction assets to make AL FAJR a long-term success.[167] As Metz recalled, "My career did not prepare me for irregular warfare and a counterinsurgency. My career prepared me for conventional ops, to bring all the combat power to bear that you can in a synchronized coordinated way. That was why Fallujah, to me, was the highlight of a career—because I was trained."[168]

Supporting the first free elections in Iraq in January 2005, on the other hand, was a very nontraditional mission for which Metz had never been trained. Yet he stated, "By far, it was one of the finest moments in my life."[169] In the summer of 2004, MNF-I and MNC-I did an analysis and selected 15 major cities that were key to a successful national election. Throughout the fall and winter, MNC-I implemented a Coalition and Iraqi security plan and an elections support plan to make that possible.[170] Planning for polling station locations, voter registration, the delivery of ballots, and the counting of ballots, also involved international organizations. Throughout it all Metz had to resist the temptation to have American leaders or units take over the preparations when progress seemed to be too slow. As he described it:

> An Iraqi 80 percent solution beats our 99 percent solution every time, so we have to let them do it. So, as reports would come in and as we were track-ing things getting ready and they weren't pretty, city by city and districts and provinces, there was a lot of angst. But I said, 'They have to do it. You have to make them do it.' But, boy, that was hard. But, in my opinion, it was successful because they ran the polling stations, they secured them.[171]

Metz's biggest fear was that the enemy would attempt a dramatic operation to interfere with the elections and cause a strategic defeat for the Coalition and Iraq, similar to the role the 1968 Tet Offensive played during the Vietnam war. He and General George W. Casey Jr., the MNF-I commander, convinced the IIG to cancel all leaves and passes so the ISF could have the maximum number of forces in place for the election.[172] The XVIII Airborne Corps headquar-ters under Lieutenant General John Vines was in place in Iraq before the elections began. They replaced III Corps in MNC-I after the January elections, but were present to increase overall troop levels and to learn about the process for the follow-on elections, which they would over-see throughout their rotation in 2005 and 2006. When he gave up command of MNC-I, Metz was optimistic that a successful outcome to the elections would lead to better intelligence and other forms of cooperation from an elected government.[173]

The Creation of MNSTC-I

In their recommendations to DOD about the structure of MNF-I, General Abizaid and Lieutenant General Sanchez had urged the creation of a second three-star headquarters to take on a new task assigned to MNF-I in March 2004—the mission to train, equip, and advise the ISF. (The overall history of the Coalition's programs to train the ISF in 2003 and 2004 is told in greater detail in chapter 11.) In January 2004 the NSC decided to increase the scope and pace of ISF training. This decision was in response to two factors. First, by early 2004 it was clear that Coalition and Iraqi forces faced a complex and growing threat from terrorists and Sunni and Shia insurgents. OIF was going to take many years and require a much larger Iraqi military and police force to defeat the growing threats to the emerging nation.[174] Second, after a January 2004 assessment of the CPA-led effort to train the ISF, conducted by Major General Karl Eikenberry, the NSC decided to take the mission away from the CPA and turn it over to CJTF-7. Abizaid and Sanchez had been urging the DOD leadership to turn the ISF training mis-sion over to the military since the fall of 2003 and to greatly increase the scope of that program. In Sanchez's view, the CPA was not properly resourced and lacked the correct vision of what was needed in Iraq. He told DOD, "There are tremendous challenges here and we are not making any progress. You need to give the ISF mission to CJTF-7."[175]

The CPA and Bremer initially disagreed, urging instead a slower approach to train a professional military focused only on external threats. This thinking was in line with the original policy guidance that Bremer issued in May 2003.[176] Sanchez and others wanted to stand up the armed forces and the police more rapidly, and focus them on internal as well as external threats. The January 2004 assessment validated those concerns.[177] The decision to turn over political power from CPA to an interim government in June 2004 also meant that CPA was going to be dissolved and the ISF program would need to be transferred. The new organization, Multi-National Security Transition Command–Iraq (MNSTC-I), would follow the newer vision for the ISF. Major General Petraeus, who had commanded the 101st ABN during the invasion of Iraq in March 2003, was selected and promoted to be the first three-star commander of MNSTC-I, taking command on 6 June 2004. It then took a number of months for that new organization to develop its initial staffing requirements and to get them filled.

The Creation of MNF-I

Lieutenant General Sanchez became the first MNF-I commander on 15 May 2004. Little changed on the day that CJTF-7 was deactivated and MNF-I came into existence. MNC-I had begun commanding the tactical and operational aspects of the command the month prior. Sanchez remained the senior US and Coalition military commander, though he now had a more robust headquarters and could focus on the strategic issues of the campaign. The mission statement for the new command also resembled CJTF-7's mission in its focus on offensive operations:

> Multi-National Force–Iraq conducts offensive operations to defeat remaining noncompliant forces and neutralize destabilizing influences in Iraq in order to create a secure environment. Multi-National Force–Iraq organizes, trains, equips, mentors, and certifies credible and capable Iraqi security forces in order to transition responsibility for security from Coalition forces to Iraqi forces. Concurrently, conducts stability operations to support the establishment of government, the restoration of essential services, and economic development in order to set the conditions for a transfer of sovereignty to designated follow-on authorities.[178]

During the 6 weeks of his tenure, however, Sanchez did begin the process of changing the G-staff type organization of CJTF-7 to a functional staff more appropriate to a theater-strategic level command.

On 1 July 2004, Lieutenant General Sanchez relinquished command of MNF-I to General Casey. For Sanchez, the appointment of Casey was critical in that it showed the DOD's commitment to providing the right mix of senior leadership, manpower, and other resources to the campaign in Iraq.[179] The more robust structure and staffing of MNF-I's subordinate commands that followed Casey's posting to Iraq were of particular importance. They gave the Coalition's new theater-strategic headquarters in Iraq the type of capacity and capabilities that CJTF-7 had never enjoyed.

In preparation for taking command of MNF-I, Casey emphasized that his most concrete direction came from UN Resolution 1546, which sanctioned the end of the Coalition's occupation of Iraq, directed the creation of an IIG, set a schedule for a series of elections beginning in late 2004, and called on Iraqis and all other nations to recognize the legitimacy of the new government. The political timeline entailed by the UN Resolution served as the point of departure for the new campaign plan his staff began to write in July 2004. Of course Casey and his key staff met with Sanchez and the existing MNF-I staff in Iraq. These talks acquainted the incoming MNF-I staffers with the campaign plan as it existed in late spring 2004.

Figure 37. MNF-I Commander Lieutenant General Ricardo Sanchez (left), Chief of Staff (CS) Iraqi Armed Forces General Amer Bakr Hashemi (center), and MNC-I Lieutenant General Thomas Metz salute the new flags for the MNC-I.

Casey took command 2 days after the CPA was dissolved and Iraq became a sovereign state. Roughly 30 days later, Casey's command had finalized a new campaign plan whose subtitle, "Partnership: From Occupation to Constitutional Elections," revealed the Coalition's emphasis on both political timelines and on closely assisting the Iraqis on a path toward self-determination and self-sufficiency.[180] This was the fourth campaign plan employed by Coalition forces during the 18 months between the overthrow of the Saddam regime and the first Iraqi elections of January 2005. While this new plan retained some of the concepts developed by Sanchez and his staff in CJTF-7 documents, Casey's campaign plan reflected new realities in Iraq. Issued on 5 August 2004, the MNF-I plan recognized that the Coalition was no longer an occupying power but instead supported the IIG and sought to implement the goals contained in the UN vision for Iraq. In the opening sentence of the new mission statement, MNF-I acknowledged these critical relationships:

> In partnership with the Iraqi Government, MNF-I conducts full spectrum counter-insurgency operations to isolate and neutralize former regime extremists and foreign terrorists, and organizes, trains and equips Iraqi security forces in order to create a security environment that permits the completion of the UNSCR 1546 process on schedule.[181]

This statement revealed two other critical aspects of Casey's conception of the military effort in Iraq. First, it introduced the term "full spectrum counterinsurgency operations" to replace "offensive operations" and "stability operations" used in the CJTF-7 plan and first MNF-I mission statement. This phrase reflected Casey's belief, developed even before he took command of MNF-I, that the Coalition's main obstacle in Iraq was a complex insurgency and that the focus could no longer be on offensive operations. Second, the mission statement clearly committed MNF-I to establishing the ISF. As discussed in chapter 3, Casey believed

177

the new mission statement, especially the use of the term "full spectrum counterinsurgency operations" was critical because it clearly articulated that MNF-I was engaged in a new campaign, not just the final stages of the original COBRA II plan that guided the invasion and its aftermath. Full spectrum counterinsurgency operations emphasized the simultaneous conduct of offensive, defensive, and stability operations (already long underway) in support of a new Iraqi Government.[182]

In the new plan, the MNF-I staff modified the four lines of operations as developed by CJTF-7. They retained security, governance, and economic development, the latter now including all efforts to restore essential services to the Iraqi population. Casey also re-titled CJTF-7's information operations LOO, changing it to communicating and emphasized the importance of making the Coalition military effort visible to Iraqis as well as to an international audience. The new plan stated that the main effort for the next 18 months was to make the series of elections in 2005 viable and legitimate by neutralizing the insurgency. MNF-I would focus on safe havens where insurgent groups had found refuge to plan and launch operations against Iraqi and Coalition forces. Casey specifically wanted to target the insurgents' safe havens that had developed in the cities of An Najaf, Fallujah, Samarra, and the Baghdad neighborhood of Sadr City. Overall, MNF-I would focus on securing the capital and 14 other key cities, controlling Iraq's borders, and preparing the ISF to support the elections. The key to defeating the insurgent enemy, Casey believed, was to drive a wedge between the insurgents and the Iraqi people by demonstrating the effectiveness of the new IIG.[183]

Casey and his planners identified two centers of gravity (COGs) in their campaign. At the strategic level, the COG was Coalition public opinion in support of the mission. Addressing that COG would give Coalition military leaders the time and resources necessary to attain their objectives in Iraq. At the operational level, the COG was the Iraqi Government, more specifically the amount of legitimacy and responsibility it held. As Casey explained:

> The easy thing to say is, in counter-insurgency, the center of gravity must be the population. I took a little different view in saying that yes, the population is ultimately the one that has to be brought around, but it's the perception of a sovereign Iraqi Government that is more likely to bring the population around than [were] our forces. . . . Throughout this whole campaign, demonstrating to the Iraqi people that this was a sovereign Iraqi Government was critically important.[184]

The concept of creating a sovereign secure Iraqi state was paramount in Casey's vision for the campaign. The MNF-I commander and his staff saw the campaign moving toward a point where Iraq had become a fully independent and stable state that could defend itself from both internal and external enemies and was not a threat to its neighbors. Reaching this point defined success in the overall Coalition campaign. The 2004 MNF-I campaign plan articulated this objective in the following end state: "Iraq at peace with its neighbors, with a representative government that respects the human rights of all Iraqis and security forces sufficient to maintain domestic order and to deny Iraq as a safe haven to terrorists."[185] This definition of the end state received tacit approval from senior officials in the US Government. However, some months after the publication of the campaign plan, an adjustment was made to the above statement, changing the opening phrase to read, "Iraq at peace with its neighbors *and an ally in the War on Terror* [emphasis added]."[186] This expression of MNF-I's objective remained the Coalition's end state for the next 2 years.

To align the MNF-I staff to implement the new plan, Casey significantly altered the structure of his headquarters. To begin with, the MNF-I commander had three deputies who shared command responsibilities: one British deputy, one US deputy, and a deputy for detainee operations—a position that was critical after the Abu Ghraib incidents became public in the spring of 2004. Seven deputy chiefs of staff replaced the traditional G-staff sections found in a corps headquarters. Special staff sections for strategic communications, Coalition coordination, and civil-military operations augmented the more conventional sections that oversaw intelligence, logistics, and engineer operations. MNF-I also delegated authority by directing US divisions and Coalition units to report to the three-star, MNC-I headquarters, instead of reporting directly to the MNF-I commander.

Casey also reorganized the MNF-I staff to align with the creation of a sovereign Iraqi Government and the establishment of the US Embassy. He used the phrase "one team/one mission" to describe the close conceptual and practical working relationship he and Ambassador Negroponte had agreed on before assuming their respective positions. In fact, Casey felt so strongly about the military and political leadership being closely linked that he placed his office next to the ambassador's office. After just a few weeks in command, Casey and Negroponte realized that close collaboration with the IIG meant they had to add Iraqi Prime Minister Ayad Allawi to the one team/one mission mix and began to forge very close relationships with Allawi and his ministers.[187] One of MNF-I's deputy commanders as well as the chiefs of strategic plans and operations, political-military-economic affairs, and strategic communications staff sections operated with the Embassy and the IIG in the International Zone, while the remainder

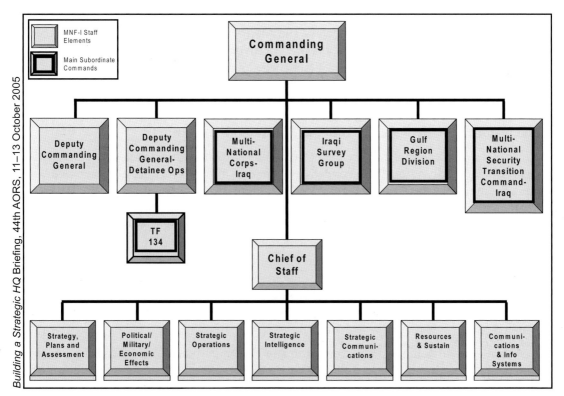

Figure 38. Multi-National Force–Iraq staff organization, January 2005.

of the MNF-I staff operated at Camp Victory South at the Baghdad International Airport on the western outskirts of the city.

A later revision to the MNF-I structure renamed and realigned some of the staff sections along functional lines to more closely match the strategic lines of operation and to better coordinate with the functions of the US Embassy and the Iraqi Government. For example, the reorganization created several new staff sections under deputy chiefs of staff, including one for strategy, plans and assessment; one for political, military and economic effects coordination, which worked closely with the US Embassy and the IIG; and one called strategic operations that focused on security effects and force requirements.[188] MNF-I also created Task Force 134, an organization headed by the deputy commanding general for detainee operations, to oversee Coalition detainee operations and coordinate with the Iraqi Government on matters concerning detainee policy and practices. MNF-I had by early 2005 become a genuine theater-strategic headquarters.

Despite the growing capability of the Coalition military headquarters and the overall military effort in Iraq, Casey believed that MNF-I units had to resist the temptation to do everything for the Iraqis. Based on his Bosnia experiences in the 1990s, Casey felt it would be self-defeating to succumb to the American tendency to do immediately what should be accomplished by local leaders and citizens, even if they took longer and were less efficient. Casey sought opportunities in each MNF-I line of operation for "the Allawi government to come together and have success in something" and to put an Iraqi face on everything the Coalition did.[189] To assess progress toward meeting the campaign objectives, Casey and the MNF-I planners developed a system of goals in each line of operation and a series of metrics or measurable items for each. He established bimonthly and monthly assessment briefings to assess progress and make adjustments. The MNF-I commander tried to integrate the US Embassy and the IIG into this process, but that endeavor moved slowly. By late 2004, however, MNF-I had matured to the point where it launched a 6-month assessment aimed at revising the campaign plan for the remainder of 2005 and the key elections that would dominate that year's effort.[190]

Conclusion: The Struggle for Unity of Command and Effort

Since the 19th century, military theory has emphasized the importance of vesting all decisionmaking authority in one commander. By adhering to this principle, a concept known as unity of command, a force can better direct all actions toward one overarching goal. Despite the importance of unity of command, US joint doctrine recognized that during stability operations and counterinsurgencies, the primacy of US, host nation, and Coalition governments makes that principle impossible to achieve. In these cases, doctrine calls for the creation of unity of effort (a principle closely related to unity of command) between the military instrument of power and the other elements of national power (diplomatic, information, and economic) through the establishment of processes, policies, and working relationships.[191] While both of these principles are deceptively simple in concept, historically they have proven to be extremely difficult to implement.

Actual unity of command between the senior US military commander and the senior US civilian representative on the ground in a foreign country is not strictly possible given existing US law. Since the passage of the Goldwater-Nichols Act in 1986, the military chain of command flows from the President, to the Secretary of Defense, to a geographic combatant commander (such as the US CENTCOM commander), and then to the deployed commander (usually a JTF or CJTF commander). The ambassador, the senior civilian US representative to a foreign country, reports through the State Department to the President. While the ambassador has primacy, it is often *pro forma* rather than actual when a sizable military force is conducting operations in the country. In some cases, this division of command has led to apparent difficulties. Critics assailed the US performance during the 1990s in the Balkans, and more recently in Afghanistan, for allowing this division of authority to obstruct unity of effort. The President's decision in January 2003 to place the DOD in charge of postwar Iraq can be seen as an initiative to improve unity of effort by providing for unity of command.

Unity of effort in OIF was severely handicapped, however, by constantly changing command relationships in 2003 and 2004. DOD, CENTCOM, and CFLCC had taken formal control of the planning for all phases of OIF, but the overwhelming majority of their effort was focused on Phase III of the plan, the invasion of Iraq. The plans that did exist offered little for the Phase IV operations in Iraq and were based on the belief that an amorphous mix of other US Government entities, international organizations, and new Iraqi leaders would quickly take over responsibility from CENTCOM once Saddam was overthrown. The ORHA reported directly to DOD, not to CENTCOM, and it was not created until late January 2003. General Garner did not arrive in the Mideast with his skeleton staff until just days before the invasion began, leaving Coalition leaders almost no time to confer before launching their attack. The military and political shortcomings inherent in these arrangements were quickly apparent to everyone involved in April and May 2003 as Iraqi governance collapsed. The decision to replace the ORHA with the CPA in May further complicated the situation for Coalition military forces. US Army units found themselves with far too many tasks to accomplish and with radically shifting postinvasion guidance with which to operate. The decision to redeploy CFLCC back to the United States and hand over its responsibilities to V Corps in mid-June further complicated the military situation.

Between May and December 2003 unity of command in the US Government did exist because both the CPA and CENTCOM reported to DOD. On the ground in Iraq, however, CJTF-7 and CPA essentially operated in parallel chains of command without a headquarters in Iraq to direct their efforts. CPA Chief Bremer reported directly to Rumsfeld, although, as he has stated in his memoirs, he also believed he had a direct line of authority from the President. Lieutenant General Sanchez and CJTF-7 were in direct support of the CPA, but reported to General Abizaid and CENTCOM in Tampa, Florida. All of this meant that unity of effort depended on cooperation between CJTF-7 and the CPA. Questions of policy, coordination, and priorities of effort in 2003 could only be resolved by the Secretary of Defense. Complicating this arrangement was the presence of Coalition forces from many nations, and the lack of an Iraqi Government with which to work. By the middle of 2004 these unexpected realities in Iraq would drive US military leaders to devise a wholly new command and control structure and campaign plan, not to wrap up the loose ends of the invasion but to fight and win a new type of campaign.

The 15 November 2003 agreement to transfer sovereignty to Iraq by the summer of 2004 heralded a significant change in the structure of decisionmaking. In December 2003 President Bush directed the CPA Chief to report to Condoleezza Rice, his National Security Advisor.[192]

This decision moved the unifying authority between the Armed Forces and the CPA further "up" the US Government's chain of command. It did, however, bring decisionmaking more directly into the purview of the President's interagency body, the NSC. Additionally, the IGC and other Iraqi leaders participated directly, if informally, in decisionmaking before the turnover of sovereignty in June 2004.

These important relationships changed again after 28 June 2004 and the restoration of Iraqi sovereignty. John Negroponte became the first US Ambassador to the new Iraqi Government and became responsible for the policy oversight and coordination of all US Government programs in Iraq. General Casey and the MNF-I staff worked closely with Negroponte, creating their campaign plan and coordinating operations with the US Embassy to ensure integration of the civil-military efforts; however, the military chain of command still reported to the President through the Secretary of Defense. Finally, with the establishment of Iraqi sovereignty on 28 June, US agencies and military forces were then in the position of operating in Iraq at the invitation of the new IIG, giving the Iraqis authority over US operations in Iraq. The challenges of those complex partnerships would open up a new chapter in OIF in 2005.

Senior civilian and military leaders struggled throughout 2003 to establish unity of effort and to implement a campaign plan that fit changing policy objectives in post-Saddam Iraq. Only in mid-2004 with the establishment of the MNF-I did the United States create a military command structure that was adequately organized and resourced for the campaign in Iraq. Casey's assumption of command of MNF-I symbolized the end of a yearlong process focused on creating the proper structures for the Coalition's military campaign in Iraq. General William Wallace, in retrospect, viewed MNF-I as the culmination of a very difficult transition, "Those divisions [of labor between the US Embassy, MNF-I, and MNC-I] were aligned appropriately, I think, but not until after we went through the pain and agony of realizing that a single headquarters couldn't do it."[193]

In retrospect, Lieutenant General Sanchez, the CJTF-7 commander, felt that despite the US Government's effort to plan and coordinate for OIF, his command was left to face almost insurmountable obstacles while reinforcements and resources were slow in arriving. To further explain his viewpoint, Sanchez drew a historical analogy between that first year in Iraq and the experience of *Task Force Smith,* an unprepared and underequipped American battalion that suffered high casualties after being hastily deployed to South Korea in the summer of 1950 to repel invading North Korean forces.

> I used the term *Task Force Smith* all over again to describe our efforts during the first 14 months—the summer of 2003 through June 2004. We had great American Soldiers and leaders on the ground who were working their hearts out with the resources available to accomplish an impossible task. In the end, I believe, when you do a very thorough analysis that throws CPA into that overall *Task Force Smith* construct, we will find that the American Soldier, our Divisions, our leaders and the CJTF headquarters were what kept the Iraq mission from being a catastrophic failure.[194]

Some may view Sanchez's analogy as inaccurate or even bordering on hyperbole. The comparison drawn by the CJTF-7 commander, however, reveals the visceral disappointment he felt as he considered what might have been accomplished in Iraq had the transitions in command been accomplished differently.

It is not yet possible to determine with any certitude how big a role the initial inadequacies of the military command and control structure played in the rise of the insurgency as well as religious and ethnic conflict between May 2003 and June 2004.[195] Certainly some of those tensions were going to be released as soon as Saddam Hussein's ironclad grip on Iraqi society was destroyed, regardless of Coalition military or political actions. That those tensions, once released, would unleash extreme political centrifugal forces and generate severe violence exceeded even the pessimists' darkest fears. Nevertheless, it is clear that the United States did not sufficiently plan for nor effectively employ all the instruments of national power in post-Saddam Iraq to deal with these tensions as well as the myriad other tasks inherent in occupying and rehabilitating a country such as Iraq. It is reasonable to believe, however, that had better military planning for Phase IV of OIF been accomplished before the war, had a more robust and effective command and control structure been rapidly put in place during the summer of 2003, and had a larger number of military forces been on the ground in 2003, the Army would have been better able to contribute to the creation of a new Iraq.

Notes

1. General Tommy Franks, *American Soldier* (New York, NY: Harper Collins, 2004), 528.

2. Lieutenant General William Webster, interview by Contemporary Operations Study Team, Fort Leavenworth, KS, 18 December 2007, 6.

3. COL Gregory Fontenot, US Army Retired, LTC E.J. Degen, US Army, and LTC David Tohn, US Army, *On Point: The US Army in Operation Iraqi Freedom* (Fort Leavenworth, KS: Combat Studies Institute Press, 2004), 219.

4. Kenneth W. Estes, "Command Narrative: 1st Armored Division in Operation IRAQI FREEDOM, May 2003—July 2004," Unpublished study, 16.

5. Estes, 18–20, 28–30.

6. Webster, interview, 18 December 2007, 17.

7. Lieutenant General David H. Petraeus, interview by Contemporary Operations Study Team, Fort Leavenworth, KS, 17 February 2006, 2.

8. Michael R. Gordon and General Bernard E. Trainor, *Cobra II: The Inside Story of the Invasion and Occupation of Iraq* (New York, NY: Pantheon Books, 2006), 459.

9. Gordon and Trainor, 459.

10. Estes, 25–26.

11. Gordon and Trainor, 460–462.

12. General (Retired) Tommy Franks, interview by Contemporary Operations Study Team, Fort Leavenworth, KS, 23 June 2006, 8.

13. Franks, interview, 23 June 2006, 8.

14. General (Retired) John Keane, interview by Contemporary Operations Study Team, Fort Leavenworth, KS, 29 June 2006, 6.

15. Keane, interview, 29 June 2006, 6.

16. Franks, *American Soldier*, 531.

17. Franks, interview, 23 June 2006, 6.

18. Franks, *American Soldier,* 524.

19. "President Bush Announces Major Combat Operations Have Ended: Remarks by the President from the USS *Abraham Lincoln* At Sea Off the Coast of San Diego, California." *Whitehouse.gov*, 1 May 2003, http://www.whitehouse.gov/news/releases/2003/05/20030501-15.html (accessed 23 October 2006).

20. Franks, *American Soldier,* 352.

21. Webster, interview, 18 December 2007, 12–13.

22. Peter Baker, "The Image Bush Just Can't Escape," *Washington Post,* 4 May 2007, 21. The President later used the phrase during a 5 June speech to US troops in Kuwait: "American sent you on a mission to remove a grave threat and to liberate an oppressed people, and that mission has been accomplished."

23. General William S. Wallace, interview by Contemporary Operations Study Team, Fort Leavenworth, KS, 22 May 2006, 4.

24. Lieutenant General Ricardo Sanchez, interview by Contemporary Operations Study Team, Fort Leavenworth, KS, 14 August 2006, 4.

25. US CENTCOM briefing slides, http://www.gwu.edu/~nsarchiv/NSAEBB/NSAEBB214/index.htm (accessed 20 February 2007).

26. Estes, 46–47.

27. Franks, interview, 23 June 2006, 12.

28. Major General Steve Whitcomb, interview by Contemporary Operations Study Team, Fort Leavenworth, KS, 7 June 2006, 3–4.

29. Keane, interview, 29 June 2006, 6–7.

30. Keane, interview, 29 June 2006, 7–8.

31. Keane, interview, 29 June 2006, 7–8.

32. Keane, interview, 29 June 2006, 7–8.

33. Lieutenant General (Retired) Jay Garner, interview by Contemporary Operations Study Team, Fort Leavenworth, KS, 6 June 2006, 6.

34. Garner, interview, 6 June 2006, 6.

35. See Colonel Marc Warren, interview by Contemporary Operations Study Team, Fort Leavenworth, KS, 15 March 2007. The V Corps Staff Judge Advocate and V Corps leaders knew they would be responsible to act in accordance of the Hague and Geneva Conventions in the immediate aftermath of military operations and planned accordingly. But that planning was very minimal and the term "occupation" was not used since it implied long-term responsibilities in Iraq.

36. Wallace, interview, 22 May 2006, 5.

37. Major General Walter Wojdakowski, interview by Contemporary Operations Study Team, Fort Leavenworth, KS, 24 August 2006, 2.

38. Wallace, interview, 22 May 2006, 5, 9.

39. Webster, interview, 18 December 2007, 13.

40. Webster, interview, 18 December 2007, 14.

41. Sanchez, interview, 14 August 2006, 6.

42. Sanchez, interview, 14 August 2006, 5.

43. Lieutenant Colonel E.J. Degen, written comments provided to Contemporary Operations Study Team, Fort Leavenworth, KS, 20 December 2006. LTC Degan was a member of the V Corps staff during this period.

44. Degen, written comments, 20 December 2006.

45. Webster, interview, 18 December 2007, 14.

46. Wojdakowski, interview, 24 August 2006, 4.

47. Wojdakowski, interview, 24 August 2006, 4.

48. Colonel (Promotable) James Boozer, interview by Contemporary Operations Study Team, Fort Leavenworth, KS, 24 January 2006, 4–5.

49. Wallace, interview, 22 May 2006, 6.

50. Webster, interview, 18 December 2007, 16.

51. Franks, interview, 23 June 2006, 14.

52. US V Corps, *V Corps Update Briefing—V Corps Commander's Conference*, 16 May 2003, slide 5.

53. Lieutenant General Ricardo Sanchez, written comments provided to Contemporary Operations Study Team, Fort Leavenworth, KS, 15 February 2007; see also, General John Abizaid, interview by Contemporary Operations Study Team, Fort Leavenworth, KS, 10 January 2007, 11.

54. Gordon and Trainor, 489.

55. See, for example, Mr. Rumsfeld's comments on 30 June 2003 at a DOD press conference. "DOD News Briefing—Secretary Rumsfeld and General Meyers," *Defense Link,* http://www.defenselink.mil/transcripts/2003/tr20030630-secdef0321.html (accessed 23 October 2006).

56. Garner, interview, 6 June 2006, 2.

57. Garner, interview, 6 June 2006, 4.

58. Garner, interview, 6 June 2006, 4. Various works have focused on the issue of interagency conflict. See, for example, Gordon and Trainor, 157-159; see also Thomas E. Ricks, *Fiasco: The American Military Adventure in Iraq* (New York, NY: Penguin Press, 2006), 101–107.

59. Jay Garner, "Iraq Revisited," in Brian M. De Toy, ed., *Turning Victory Into Success: Military Operations After the Campaign* (Fort Leavenworth, KS: Combat Studies Institute Press, 2004), 257; see also, Gordon and Trainor, 193.

60. Colonel Michael Fitzgerald, interview by Contemporary Operations Study Team, Fort Leavenworth, KS, 10 January 2006, 4.

61. Keane, interview, 29 June 2006, 8.

62. Garner, interview, 6 June 2006, 5.

63. Colonel John R. Martin, interview by Contemporary Operations Study Team, Fort Leavenworth, KS, 18 May 2006, 12.

64. Webster, interview, 18 December 2007, 7.

65. Webster, interview, 18 December 2007, 5–6.

66. Garner, interview, 6 June 2006, 2.

67. Garner, "Iraq Revisited," in De Toy, ed., *Turning Victory Into Success,* 253–256.

68. Gordon and Trainor, 471–472.

69. Garner, interview, 6 June 2006, 16.

70. Martin, interview, 18 May 2006, 15; Colonel (Retired) Paul Hughes, interview by Contemporary Operations Study Team, Fort Leavenworth, KS, 1 March 2006.

71. Garner, interview, 6 June 2006, 6 and 19.

72. Wallace, interview, 22 May 2006, 8, 15.

73. Wallace, interview, 22 May 2006, 8, 15.

74. L. Paul Bremer III, *My Year in Iraq: The Struggle to Build a Future of Hope* (New York, NY: Simon & Schuster, 2006), 5–7.

75. Elaine Halchin, *The CPA: Origins, Characteristics and Institutional Authorities* (Washington, DC: Congressional Research Service, 29 April 2004), 4.

76. Halchin, 5–6.

77. Bremer, *My Year in Iraq,* 12.

78. Bremer, *My Year in Iraq*, 4.

79. Coalition Provisional Authority Regulation Number 1, http://www.cpa-iraq.org/regulations/20030516_CPAREG_1_The_Coalition_Provisional_Authority_.pdf.

80. See Field Manual 27-10, *The Law of Land Warfare* (Washington, DC, July 1956).

81. CPA Regulation Number 1.

82. Bremer, *My Year in Iraq,* 30–31.

83. Martin, interview, 18 May 2006, 15.

84. Sanchez, interview, 14 August 2006. Lieutenant General Sanchez recalls this from some of the after-action reports and comments from V Corps staff officers who were present at the meeting.

85. Sanchez, interview, 14 August 2006, 12; see also Wallace, interview, 22 May 2006, 9.

86. Sanchez, interview, 14 August 2006, 12. Lieutenant General Sanchez has stated, "The very first contact I had with him was in Kuwait when he flew in, literally when he flew into the country from the United States. He flew in there and I spent about 10 to 15 minutes with him. My relationship with him throughout, to this day, is still a good relationship. The challenges that we faced in the professional relationship were at times fairly significant and that is kind of what blows around the press about this real bad relationship."

87. Sanchez, interview, 14 August 2006, 12.

88. Coalition Provisional Authority, *CPA Vision Statement*, 13 July 2003. According to a memorandum appended to the vision statement, the CPA had circulated a draft of the statement before 10 July 2003 and had received comments from CPA staffers. The vision statement included a mission statement, end state, assumptions, and objectives.

89. Christopher M. Schnaubelt, "After the Fight: Interagency Operations," *Parameters,* Winter 2005/2006, 53–54.

90. Schnaubelt, 52.

91. Sanchez, interview, 18 August 2006, 4, 11.

92. Sanchez, interview, 14 August 2006, 13.

93. Bremer, *My Year in Iraq*, 43. Douglas J. Feith, *War and Decision: Inside the Pentagon at the Dawn of the War on Terrorism* (New York, NY: Harper, 2008), 435–441.

94. Bremer, *My Year in Iraq*, 42–44.

95. FM 100-15, *Corps Operations* (Washington, DC, 1996), 1-3, 1-4.

96. Wallace, interview, 22 May 2006, 7.

97. Wojdakowski, interview, 24 August 2006, 3.

98. Sanchez, interview, 14 August 2006, 7.

99. Wallace, interview, 22 May 2006, 7.

100. Sanchez, written comments, 15 February 2007.

101. Sanchez, interview, 14 August 2006, 7.

102. Degen, written comments, 20 December 2006. The Corps C5 staff had been divided into two parts—the main portion operating at Camp Victory with the Corps/CJTF headquarters and a two-person team collocated with the CPA headquarters in the Green Zone.

103. Boozer, interview, 24 January 2006, 7.

104. Sanchez, interview, 25 August 2006, 19.

105. Major General Thomas Miller, interview by Contemporary Operations Study Team, Fort Leavenworth, KS, 25 August 2006, 3.

106. Miller, interview, 25 August 2006, 4.

107. Miller, interview, 25 August 2006, 3.

108. Major General Barbara Fast, interview by Contemporary Operations Study Team, Fort Leavenworth, KS, 27 March 2006, 3.

109. Sanchez, interview, 14 August 2006, 8.

110. Sanchez, interview, 25 August 2006, 19.

111. Fast, interview, 27 March 2006, 4.

112. Miller, interview, 25 August 2006, 4.

113. Miller, interview, 25 August 2006, 10.

114. Sanchez, interview, 14 August 2006, 6.

115. Lieutenant Colonel Wesley Odom, interview by Contemporary Operations Study Team, Fort Leavenworth, KS, 17 March 2006, 6.

116. Odom, interview, 17 March 2006, 4–6. Odom's fellow planners were Lieutenant Colonel Dan Stempniak, Major Dan Soler, and Major Charlie Costanza. Already in the CJ5 Plans Branch were Australian Lieutenant Colonel Dave Allen and British Wing Commander Martin Heath, though they departed relatively soon after. Between July and November a succession of officers led the CJ5—Lieutenant Colonel Allen, Wing Commander Heath, followed by Army Lieutenant Colonel (Promotable) Mike Alexander, Lieutenant Colonel Butch Botters, Marine Colonel Dan Welch, and finally Army Brigadier General Dan Keefe when the situation stabilized.

117. Abizaid, interview, 10 January 2007, 12.

118. Odom, interview, 17 March 2006, 5–7.

119. Sanchez, interview, 18 August 2006, 17.

120. Sanchez, interview, 18 August 2006; see also, Wojdakowski, interview, 24 August 2006, 4.

121. Odom, interview, 17 March 2006, 16.

122. Odom, interview, 17 March 2006, 5, 11–12

123. V Corps and CJTF-7, *V Corps and CJTF-7 Transition and Challenges* Briefing, 30 September 2004.

124. Miller, interview, 23 August 2006, 6–7.

125. Sanchez, interview, 18 August 2006, 18.

126. Odom, interview, 17 March 2006, 7, 16. This OPORD remained in place until August 2004 when MNF-I issued a new plan.

127. Sanchez, interview, 14 August 2006, 11.

128. Sanchez, interview, 25 August 2006, 19.

129. Wojdakowski, interview, 24 August 2006, 14.

130. General David McKiernan, interview by Contemporary Operations Study Team, Fort Leavenworth, KS, 10 October 2006, 9.

131. McKiernan, interview, 10 October 2006, 9.

132. Sanchez, interview, 14 August 2006, 15.

133. Sanchez, interview, 14 August 2006, 15.

134. Kathleen T. Rhem, "Officials Announce Plans for Iraqi Troop Rotations into 2004," *DefenseLink,* 24 July 2003, http://www.defenselink.mil/news/newsarticle.aspx?id=28683 (accessed 17 December 2007).

135. Sanchez, interview, 14 August 2006, 16.

136. Wojdakowski, interview, 24 August 2006, 12.

137. Wojdakowski, interview, 24 August 2006, 11.

138. Sanchez, written comments, 15 February 2007.

139. Wojdakowski, interview, 24 August 2006, 12.

140. Wojdakowski, interview, 24 August 2006, 12.

141. Sanchez, written comments, 15 February 2007.

142. Bremer, *My Year in Iraq*, 357; L. Paul Bremer III, interview by Contemporary Operations Study Team, Fort Leavenworth, KS, 20 April 2006, 7.

143. Bremer, interview, 20 April 2006, 7. In an interview with the Contemporary Operations Study Team, Bremer stated that after sending the request to Mr. Rumsfeld, "The Secretary passed the memo on to the Chiefs and asked them for their view and they came back and said, 'We think we have enough troops.' I just had a different view."

144. Sanchez, interview, 14 August 2006, 20.

145. Sanchez, interview, 25 August 2006, 9.

146. Lieutenant General Thomas F. Metz, interview by Contemporary Operations Study Team, Fort Leavenworth, KS, 8 June 2007, 7.

147. The issue is complex because one must account for US and Coalition nation troop numbers, some supporting Iraqi operations from Kuwait and other locations, a wide range of missions, the roles and capabilities of various types of still-emerging Iraqi forces, and a host of other factors. Some details of troop deployments also remain classified. For a study that uses a consistent methodology to examine some half-dozen conflicts to include OIF, see John McGrath, *Boots on the Ground: Troop Density in Contingency Operations* (Fort Leavenworth, KS: Combat Studies Institute Press, 2006).

148. McGrath, *Boots on the Ground*, 126. Even after the troop surge of the spring and summer of 2007, US force levels will be slightly below those in January 2005.

149. McGrath, *Boots on the Ground*. In Iraq, this ratio would have required some 640,000 troops, or more than three times the number of Coalition forces available in May 2003.

150. McGrath, *Boots on the Ground*, 105. Although NATO rapidly drew down to a ratio of only 7.9 troops per 1,000 for the second year under the Stabilization Force (SFOR).

151. McGrath, *Boots on the Ground,* 105.

152. McGrath, *Boots on the Ground,* 137.

153. McGrath, *Boots on the Ground,* 126, 130, 137.

154. The controversy over troop levels continues as of the date of publication, inside and outside the military. A GAO report (GAO-07-639T) released on 22 March 2007, for example, concluded that the US had too few troops to secure the vast number of munitions sites in Iraq.

155. Sanchez, interview, 25 August 2006, 15.

156. Abizaid, interview, 10 January 2007, 4.

157. Abizaid, interview, 10 January 2007, 4–5; see also Sanchez, interview, 25 August 2006, 16.

158. Sanchez, interview, 25 August 2006, 16–17.

159. Chief, Commander's Initiatives Group, *Multi-National Force–Iraq, Building a Strategic Headquarters: Operations Research Support to the Theater Commander* Briefing, 44th AORS, 11–13 October 2005, slide 7.

160. Metz, interview, 8 June 2007, 2.

161. Metz, interview, 26 August 2006, 3.

162. Metz, interview, 26 August 2006, 2–4.

163. Metz, interview, 26 August 2006, 8; Metz, interview, 7 June 2007, 4–5.

164. Metz, interview, 8 June 2007, 5.

165. Metz, interview, 8 June 2007, 14.

166. Metz, interview, 8 June 2007, 8, 10–11; Metz, interview, 26 August 2006, 11.

167. For a study of this operation, see Matt Matthews, *Operation AL FAJR: A Study in Army and Marine Corps Joint Operations* (Fort Leavenworth, KS: Combat Studies Institute Press, 2006).

168. Metz, interview, 7 June 2007, 9.

169. Metz, interview, 15 December 2005, 10.

170. Metz, interview, 8 June 2007, 14, 20–21.

171. Metz, interview, 8 June 2007, 20.

172. Metz, interview, 15 December 2005, 10.

173. Metz, interview, 8 June 2007, 21.

174. Sanchez, interview, 25 August 2006, 9.

175. Sanchez, interview, 25 August 2006, 9.

176. Major General (Retired) Paul Eaton, interview by Contemporary Operations Study Team, Fort Leavenworth, KS, 3 August 2006, 4.

177. Sanchez, interview, 25 August 2006, 9–10. The CPA leadership was also concerned that the quality of the New Iraqi Army would be compromised by the inclusion of the ICDC forces that CJTF-7 had created to handle local security issues.

178. MNF-I Mission Statement. Dr. Alexander Cochran, Historical Advisor to Chief of Staff of the Army, e-mail correspondence with authors, 12 February 2008.

179. Sanchez, interview, 25 August 2006, 17.

180. Multi-National Force–Iraq, *MNF-I Framework OPORD Rev 01 Nov 05 Link Index*, 2005.

181. Multi-National Force–Iraq, *MNF-I Framework OPORD Rev 01 Nov 05 Link Index*, 2005.

182. General George W. Casey Jr., interview by Contemporary Operations Study Team, Fort Leavenworth, KS, 27 November 2007, 3.

183. See Casey, interview, 27 November 2007, 4. Events in 2005 and 2006 would later cause him to change his understanding of the main threat to Iraq and to MNF-I.

184. Casey, interview, 27 November 2007, 13.

185. Cochran, e-mail to author, 12 February 2008.

186. Cochran, e-mail to author, 12 February 2008.

187. Casey, interview, 27 November 2007, 3.

188. *MNF-I, Building a Strategic Headquarters* Briefing, slide 11.

189. Casey, interview, 27 November 2007, 4–5, 9.

190. Casey, interview, 27 November 2007, 10–11.

191. The Army's new counterinsurgency manual dedicates an entire chapter to this issue, placing far more emphasis on the relationships between the Army and the other branches of the Federal Government, allies, and NGOs. See FM 3-24, *Counterinsurgency Operations* (Washington, DC, 15 December 2006), chapter 2.

192. Bremer, *My Year in Iraq*, 245.

193. Wallace, interview, 22 May 2006, 15.

194. Sanchez, interview, 25 August 2006, 19.

195. Abizaid, interview, 10 January 2007, 4–5. In the interview, General Abizaid wondered whether a unified civilian-military chain of command in 2003 would have been a better method.

Chapter 5

Intelligence and High-Value Target Operations

In November 2003 Task Force (TF) *Baghdad*, consisting of the 1st Armored Division (1st AD) and its supporting elements, began conducting Operation IRON HAMMER across the Iraqi capital. In the middle of this operation, the task force commander, Brigadier General Martin Dempsey, stated, "Fundamentally, here in Baghdad we do two things: We're either fighting for intelligence or we're fighting based on that intelligence."[1] Indeed, Dempsey suggested that one of the key purposes of IRON HAMMER was to gather information that would facilitate immediate follow-on operations against the insurgents. The operation would progress in a number of directions based on what type of information the Soldiers of the 1st AD gathered. When asked whether he had enough Soldiers to conduct his mission in Baghdad, Dempsey replied, "The answer is absolutely yes." But, he then added, "The larger issue is how do I use them and on what basis? And the answer to that is intelligence."[2] For Dempsey, American success in Baghdad would depend primarily on how well his Soldiers gathered, analyzed, and used information.

For military commanders throughout history, information has been critical to success on the battlefield. This was certainly true for the US Army in the latter half of the 20th century, which, as an institution, tended to view intelligence as an enabler of operations. Field Manual (FM) 34-1, *Intelligence and Electronic Warfare*, the capstone military intelligence manual that served the Army in 2003, clearly established the relationship between intelligence and operations in stating, "Intelligence shows where the commander can apply combat power to exploit threat vulnerabilities or capitalize on opportunities with minimum risk."[3] The manual added, "Commanders use [intelligence] support to anticipate the battle, understand the battlefield framework, and influence the outcome of operations."[4] Thus, intelligence allowed the commander to understand the battlefield and the enemy and make decisions at all levels of war about centers of gravity, decisive points, objectives, task organization, directions of attack, and a myriad of other elements that govern operations. In other words, intelligence facilitated operations—information was not the objective of military operations but their enabler.

By the middle of 2003 US Army units had found that the requirements of the operating environment in Iraq stood the relationship between intelligence and operations on its head. As Dempsey stated, his forces conducted many operations in Baghdad in order to collect intelligence. In a large percentage of operations in 2003 and 2004, American Soldiers planned raids, cordons and searches, and other types of operations with the objective of gathering better information. This rather dramatic shift in the focus of operations resulted from a number of factors, the most important of which was the Coalition's efforts to adapt and augment its traditional intelligence assets and methods so that tactical units could act in a decisive way.

For US forces in Iraq in 2003, the basic inability to provide what has been labeled "actionable intelligence"—that is, intelligence that is of current value and will allow a unit to conduct significant operations immediately—forced a second shift in the Army's traditional approach to operations. Rather than relying on the standard Cold War era military intelligence (MI) systems and procedures that gathered information at levels above the brigade and then pushed that information down to the tactical level, in Iraq battalion- and even company-size units began conducting their own intelligence operations. This development ran counter to doctrine, and

MI professionals expressed concern about the lack of specialized training within the infantry, armor, and other battalions that were busy creating their own intelligence. However, tactical commanders had little choice. They and their Soldiers lived and operated in their assigned areas of responsibility (AORs) and required accurate and timely information if they were to achieve their objectives, which meant, after the summer of 2003, engaging a growing insurgency.

This chapter examines the evolution of the intelligence effort in Operation IRAQI FREEDOM (OIF) from May 2003 through the elections of January 2005. It will first look at the assumptions about the type of intelligence required for the campaign and how those assumptions affected the types of intelligence operations the US Army conducted as the postinvasion phase of operations began. Critical to this part of the discussion will be an understanding of how decisions about missions and command structure at the operational and strategic levels affected the intelligence architecture and capabilities in Iraq. Then the discussion will shift to the sudden demand for human intelligence (HUMINT) within units and how that requirement led Soldiers at the tactical level to begin conducting their own intelligence collection and analysis, including interrogation operations, while working in an alien culture.* Finally, the chapter will focus on high-value target (HVT) operations, missions that were intertwined with intelligence operations and often took on strategic importance in the campaign after May 2003.

Intelligence and the Transition to Full Spectrum Operations

When the Saddam regime fell in early April 2003, the US Army had a large number of MI assets in Iraq. In addition to the robust intelligence capabilities in each US Army and Marine division involved, the Coalition enjoyed the support of national intelligence resources, the strategic assets at US Central Command (CENTCOM) and V Corps, to include the latter command's 205th MI Brigade. In addition, Combined Forces Land Component Command (CFLCC) brought the resources of the 513th MI Brigade, the US Army Intelligence and Security Command's contingency force, to bear on the mission in Iraq. Magnifying the strength of the 513th and the 205th were the US Army Reserve and National Guard MI battalions—several of which were dedicated to the collection of HUMINT—added to their structure in the weeks before the invasion. In addition to these forces, a Utah Army National Guard HUMINT unit, the 142d MI Battalion, reinforced the 75th Exploitation Task Force, which began the official search for Saddam's weapons of mass destruction (WMD) in April 2003. CENTCOM had also gained the support of US European Command's J2 section, which greatly assisted Coalition commanders in understanding the situation in northern Iraq. Thus, between January and April 2003, Coalition forces enjoyed the support of 17 MI battalions and a variety of other MI assets.

The large majority of these units were part of an MI structure designed to win a campaign against a conventional enemy like Saddam Hussein's army. The majority of the Soldiers and systems in these battalions collected signals intelligence (SIGINT) and imagery intelligence (IMINT). Only about 25 percent of the assets in these units collected HUMINT. Once the Coalition pushed Saddam out of power and the transition to full spectrum operations began, the importance of SIGINT and IMINT diminished in relation to HUMINT in their capacity to

---

*For reasons of operational security, this chapter will focus primarily on HUMINT and only touch on signals intelligence (SIGINT), imagery intelligence (IMINT), measurement and signature intelligence (MASINT), and counterintelligence (CI) methods and operations.

impact the campaign. To be sure, the systems that provided SIGINT and IMINT continued to play a role in 2003 and 2004. Their capabilities, in any event, could not meet the demand for the most important type of information required to support full spectrum operations, especially those focused on an insurgent enemy: HUMINT.

Before anyone in the Coalition had a chance to understand the situation they faced in Iraq, a series of important decisions about the Coalition's military command structure radically altered the number and type of MI assets available for operations. As chapter 4 of this study has shown, the Department of Defense (DOD) decided in May 2003 to designate the United States (US) V Corps headquarters as the core staff of the follow-on joint task force, known as Combined Joint Task Force–7 (CJTF-7). For those who assumed CFLCC would form CJTF-7, this decision was a surprise. When CFLCC and CENTCOM pulled many of their assets back to Kuwait, Qatar, and Florida in June, Coalition intelligence capabilities in Iraq suddenly decreased. Major General Barbara Fast, who became the senior intelligence officer (CJ2) in CJTF-7 in late July 2003 noted, "When CFLCC departed, the Defense Intelligence Agency (DIA) HUMINT and US Army Intelligence and Security Command (INSCOM) assets departed, as well."[5] Fast added that there were some national and strategic assets that remained in Iraq that first summer, but they were assigned to missions other than assisting CJTF-7 understand the situation in post-Saddam Iraq: "The remaining DIA assets were part of the Iraqi Survey Group (ISG) and designated to find WMD. These were the designated, experienced assets on which we rely for some of our more sophisticated HUMINT operations. This left only CIA [Central Intelligence Agency] assets, also limited initially in number."[6]

Within CJTF-7 these departures left the staff with very limited capacity to work with operational- or strategic-level intelligence. The V Corps G2 section, which now served as the foundation of CJTF-7's CJ2, was designed and manned to conduct collection and analysis of tactical-level intelligence. For Lieutenant General Ricardo Sanchez, the V Corps commander who became the CJTF-7 commander in June 2003, CFLCC's exit left the Corps' Intelligence staff without the experience or expertise to work at the higher levels required in Iraq. Sanchez stated:

> What was missing was the capacity to be able to think through those problems, to be able to address the problems with a structure that was much more robust than in a corps G2. The seniority of experience, the ability to tap into some sort of operational level and theater and strategic level experience, which is what [CFLCC] had been doing for almost 8 months at that point, all of that went away and you were now left with . . . young captains and lieutenants and warrant [officers] and sergeants that had no idea what it is all about to be talking strategic intelligence and operational level intelligence and counterinsurgencies.[7]

Sanchez emphasized that these MI Soldiers were exceptionally competent at conducting intelligence operations in support of a conventional campaign at the tactical level. "Their instinct, their forte, of course by training, what we had trained these kids for," Sanchez noted, "was to go out and fight a conventional fight and they were pretty damn good at it."[8] However, the CJTF-7 commander remarked that after May 2003, the US Army and the Coalition were no longer concerned with the conventional fight, "Now we were completely lost in a totally different operational environment and we were really struggling."[9]

The HUMINT Gap

The struggle to which Sanchez referred was not solely caused by the CJTF-7 CJ2's inability to think and conduct analysis at the operational- and theater-strategic levels. It also resulted from a more fundamental lack of HUMINT capacity. The decision to pull CFLCC out of Iraq left the 205th MI Brigade, a V Corps unit, and the MI elements that belonged to each division, regiment, and brigade as the main providers of intelligence to CJTF-7. While this support might have been adequate in a more stable environment, the situation in Iraq in the summer of 2003 was growing less secure and more complex. As a nascent insurgent opposition coalesced in Iraq, it was clear to many within CJTF-7 that they lacked a basic understanding of what was occurring and that HUMINT was the best means of creating better situational awareness.

The ability to collect and analyze HUMINT, however, was precisely what Coalition forces most sorely lacked. The 205th MI Brigade and the MI units organic to the divisions and other subordinate units did indeed have HUMINT capabilities. In fact, the Army had augmented the 205th MI Brigade with three Reserve Component MI battalions that had counterintelligence, interrogation, and other HUMINT assets. The 205th MI Brigade and the MI units that belonged to the divisions, armored cavalry regiments, and separate brigades employed their HUMINT assets mostly in the form of Tactical HUMINT Teams (THTs), groups of three to six MI Soldiers who specialized in HUMINT collection (including interrogation) or counterintelligence (CI) and who might also speak Arabic or another language. The 101st Airborne Division (101st ABN), for example, had 10 organic THTs, each of which had a CI Soldier, a HUMINT collector, and an Arabic or Kurdish linguist.[10] The THTs were small in number and in high demand across Iraq. There was simply an overwhelming absence of HUMINT that first summer and increasing requirements from units of all types and at all levels for the type of information that could only be gathered by talking to Iraqis.

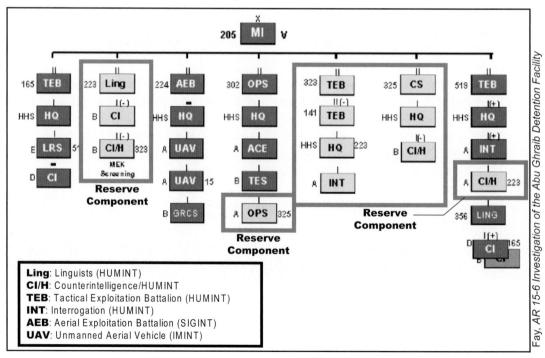

Figure 39. 205th MI Brigade task organization, August 2003.

Lieutenant General Sanchez recognized this lack of HUMINT as one of the central problems facing the CJTF-7 staff in 2003. "The human intelligence piece was just flat out not there," Sanchez stated. "We had no concept what a CJ2X [HUMINT staff officer] was. I mean literally we had no idea. . . . We didn't have Red Cells . . . we had none of the interagency there, there was no National Intelligence Council (NIC) capacity that had been left behind."[11] Major General Fast suggested that issues with the Army's HUMINT capabilities in Iraq began before May 2003:

> Even prior to hostilities, we lacked sufficient HUMINT capacity to have a proper understanding of the situation within Iraq. It required HUMINT on the ground as opposed to just the technical collection capabilities that we have . . . it became imperative once we were in Iraq to establish a strong HUMINT capability to understand the situation on the ground, but we lacked the numbers and some of the skills required in order to be as successful as we needed to be.[12]

The summer of 2003 would bring only gradual improvement as MI assets that augmented CJTF-7's ability to gather and analyze HUMINT arrived in Iraq.

Significant change came once Fast arrived to begin work as the CJ2. One of Fast's first tasks was to assess CJTF-7's intelligence capabilities and then create a comprehensive set of requirements for MI assets that was sent up the chain of command to CENTCOM and the Pentagon. This assessment as well as her experience and rank allowed Fast in the late summer and fall of 2003 to build CJTF-7's capacity to do collection and analysis at the operational and strategic levels. She enhanced the CJ2X, the staff section that focused solely on HUMINT collection and analysis, and built a Red Team, an organization that studied the insurgent network to help the commander understand the enemy's goals, methods, and intent. By October 2003 she had managed to construct an intelligence fusion center in which the various intelligence agencies, services, and activities working in Iraq would share their information and coordinate analysis and action. By late 2003 the center brought together the CJTF-7 CJ2 with US Special Operations, ISG, Criminal Investigative Task Force, National Security Agency, Defense Intelligence Agency, National Imagery and Mapping Agency (NIMA), US Department of the Treasury, US Customs, Federal Bureau of Investigation (FBI), Iraqi Police Service, International Criminal Police Organization (INTERPOL), and other organizations.[13] Fast used a similar approach to construct a Joint Interagency Task Force (JIATF) that focused on the insurgent networks and, specifically, on the finance support structures that enabled insurgent activities.

This sharing of information meant that by the end of the year CJTF-7 had a better understanding of the situation in Iraq at the strategic and operational levels. And it was better prepared to gather intelligence from tactical units, synchronize it with other reports, and create a more comprehensive, detailed, and nuanced picture of the security environment to push down to the tactical level. To facilitate this coordination process, Major General Fast introduced daily video teleconferences (VTCs) that brought together MI analysts from CJTF-7 with intelligence analysts at the tactical level. Fast complemented these conferences with her own VTCs three times a week in which she and the senior intelligence officers in the divisions (G2) shared information and discussed the overall situation in Iraq.[14]

Still, improving processes did not address all of the gaps in the Coalition's understanding of post-Saddam Iraq. The alien nature of the Iraqi culture was perhaps the most important obstacle to full comprehension of the world in which Coalition forces were operating. Understanding this, Fast created a Coalition Analysis Control Element (CACE), a team consisting of Coalition officers on her staff who specialized in collecting and analyzing information on specific problems.[15] One group focused on the role of religion in Iraq and looked closely at Salafist groups and at the role of imams in the insurgency. Another group collected information on Iraqi tribal structure and created a database for use by the Coalition. And, because Coalition forces arrived in Iraq without a detailed understanding of the state of the Iraqi economy and infrastructure, Fast tasked other Coalition officers to begin collecting intelligence on the electrical grid, gas and oil pipelines, and other parts of the Iraqi economy. All of these subjects were far outside the traditional focus on enemy military units, which had dominated V Corps' planning for the invasion of Iraq.

In January 2004 the CJ2 furthered its reach by establishing formal ties with Iraqi intelligence agencies from five groups: the Iraqi National Congress (INC), the Iraqi National Accord (INA), the Kurdistan Democratic Party (KDP), the Patriotic Union of Kurdistan (PUK), and the Supreme Council for Islamic Revolution in Iraq (SCIRI).[16] About the same time, Fast also began meeting with the newly-established Iraqi Government's National Security Advisor, Minister of Defense, Minister of the Interior, and Chief of the National Intelligence Service three times per week to coordinate information and actions.[17] The meetings gave the Coalition channels through which they could gain intelligence and vet conclusions. But these new relationships were also important in a symbolic sense—helping pave the way for the Iraqi Government and its various parties to take full political sovereignty in mid-2004.

These improvements and progress in CJTF-7's ability to deal with HUMINT and intelligence in general at the operational- and strategic-levels were significant. It is important to note, however, that throughout CJTF-7's life, its CJ2 section never had more than half of the personnel the Joint Manning Document (JMD) stated it required. Officers like Fast were attempting to build an organization that conducted collection and analysis at all three levels of war with a staff that was short of resources. The CJ2 also had to find a way to integrate the Coalition partners and eventually the Iraqis into its operations and do so while under severe pressure to understand a growing insurgency.

Tactical Intelligence: The Paradigm Shifts

Overall, most of the progress in intelligence collection, analysis, and dissemination at the CJTF-7 level had a relatively small impact on the operations at battalion-level and below. It is clear that at times intelligence products within CJTF-7 did provide key information that allowed tactical units to act in their AORs. Fast noted that the CJ2 did fill in information gaps for tactical units; analyzed enemy activities that crossed unit boundaries; and tasked operational-, strategic-, and national-level IMINT and SIGINT assets to fill priority intelligence requirements (PIR) at critical moments in tactical operations.[18] This type of top-down dissemination of intelligence was particularly important in the efforts to locate and capture HVTs. The CJ2 also empowered tactical units through its JIATF which focused on the structure and funding of the insurgent network. Relying on a number of intelligence disciplines, the JIATF helped disrupt insurgent groups in Baghdad, Mosul, and other cities by interrupting the flow of financial support to enemy networks.

The tactical units themselves—the companies, battalions, and brigades—collected and analyzed the bulk of the intelligence they used to drive operations against insurgent organizations or other threats. The intelligence brigades and battalions within CJTF-7 and its subordinate units had little choice but acquiesce to this new manner of information gathering and analysis. The enemy situation was so fluid and so local in character that the US Army intelligence system designed to push down information from division to brigade and then to battalion became increasingly irrelevant. This is not to say that the division G2s and the division-level MI battalions ceased operations. However, their traditional functions and processes were less important than lower-level efforts in the Army's new campaign.

The ascending role of tactical HUMINT in OIF should not surprise anyone familiar with counterinsurgency warfare. Put simply, the counterinsurgent's task is to disrupt and destroy the insurgent network while maintaining the support of the population. If the counterinsurgent force commander determines that this is only possible through violent action, he must know who, when, and where to attack. To do otherwise, to attack too broadly or hit the wrong targets, risks alienating the people he hopes to attract to the side of the host-nation government. Still, accurate and focused attacks are impossible without actionable intelligence. One recent study of counterinsurgency warfare described the situation facing the counterinsurgent this way: "Without good intelligence, a counterinsurgent is like a boxer flailing at an unseen opponent. With good intelligence, a counterinsurgent is like a surgeon cutting out the cancers while keeping the vital organs intact."[19] In 2004 the staff of the 1st Battalion, 24th Infantry (Stryker Brigade Combat Team [SBCT]) operating in Mosul, restated this concept in a more emphatic if simpler way: "Intel drives maneuver in a Counterinsurgency (COIN)—period!"[20]

As noted earlier, while operations evolved in the summer of 2003, commanders at brigade and battalion levels quickly assessed the nature of the security environment in their AORs and initiated intelligence operations using their own Soldiers and systems. This was a major shift in practice. US Army doctrine gave MI Soldiers and units the formal authority to gather, analyze, and disseminate intelligence. The US Army's tactical units, nevertheless, had only a handful of MI Soldiers serving on the staffs of battalions and brigades. The MI officers and noncommissioned officers (NCOs) at these levels did little of their own collection and, other than the armor and infantry battalion S2 sections that could employ organic scout platoons to locate and watch enemy activity, had few assets to do collection. Instead, the Army had designed the MI system to push information from corps and division levels down to brigade and battalion levels where the S2 would make that intelligence relevant for the commander.

To make tactical-level MI assets more capable, many units in Iraq in 2003 and 2004 reorganized their intelligence (G/S2) sections. At division-, brigade-, and in some cases battalion-level, this transition usually involved the creation of a G2X or S2X—an officer or NCO who would focus solely on the collection and analysis of HUMINT. Unlike the Stryker Brigade Combat Teams that deployed to Iraq in the latter part of 2004, S2 sections in tactical units, by standard organization, did not contain this position. However, as it became evident that HUMINT was critical to success in Iraq, commanders often decided to appoint an officer as the S2X. The 1st Cavalry Division Artillery (DIVARTY), a brigade-size unit that before deployment to Iraq in 2004 converted from a fire support element to a maneuver unit and took the title 5th Brigade Combat Team (BCT), provides a good example of this innovation.[21] In conventional operations, the DIVARTY S2 section consisted of five Soldiers who assisted in identifying and locating enemy targets for artillery strikes. The operational demands in Baghdad required Colonel Stephen Lanza, the DIVARTY commander, to augment his S2 section through the creation of an S2X team that gathered HUMINT by conducting interrogations of detainees, coordinating the attached THTs, and collaborating with Special Operations Forces (SOF) and other agencies involved in the collection of HUMINT. Ultimately, the commander charged the S2X with the task of creating actionable intelligence that could enable his operations against the insurgents active in his AOR.[22]

The 101st ABN tackled the difficulties in collecting and analyzing HUMINT in a similar way. Lieutenant Colonel D.J. Reyes, the division G2, not only created a G2X in 2003, but sought to expand the reach of its HUMINT operations by creating a JIATF. The JIATF was not a doctrinal organization but an innovation that brought together all of the American and Iraqi agencies in northern Iraq involved in HUMINT collection and analysis. The task force mission statement succinctly explained its purpose: "The AO North Joint Inter-Agency Task Force (JIATF) gathers intelligence, coordinates and synchronizes intelligence operations, and coordinates conventional/special operations in order to identify and neutralize hostile individuals and groups and their support networks in Northern Iraq."[23] Periodic meetings, coordinated by the 101st ABN G2, brought together the division's intelligence officers with representatives from the FBI, American Special Operations Forces, CIA, Iraqi Security Forces, and the intelligence organization that belonged to the KDP and the PUK. Reyes also integrated representatives from national-level IMINT and SIGINT agencies, such as the National Security Agency, into the task force. Certainly, other American units established informal collaborative relationships with SOF and CIA teams in their AORs to share intelligence. The JIATF in AO North, however, created a more formal forum in which the various agencies exchanged and vetted information.

Initially, much of the intelligence generated by the JIATF focused on enabling cordon and search operations and other combat missions directed at destroying hostile organizations and individuals. As a result, Reyes noted that eventually the JIATF added the division's Targeting and Integrated Effects Working Groups to its organization and thus became involved in information operations as well. Success in a number of critical operations validated the task force's capabilities. In June 2003 the JIATF identified a terrorist camp in Al Anbar province near the Syrian border, a target that US forces destroyed in a lightning raid. One month later, the task force developed the information that led to the killing of Uday and Qusay Hussein, the sons of Saddam Hussein, in the city of Mosul. This chapter will examine both of these operations below.

The 101st ABN's creation of the JIATF was a significant innovation. At lower levels, operational and organizational change was often equally dramatic. The experience of the 4th Battalion, 27th Field Artillery (4-27th FA) of the 1st AD provides an excellent example of how intelligence operations came to dominate unit tactical-level activities in OIF. Lieutenant Colonel Brian McKiernan, the commander of the 4-27th FA, pointed out that his unit gave up its traditional fire support mission in May 2003 and became a maneuver unit responsible for full spectrum operations in the Al Karkh district of Baghdad. McKiernan explained that his unit's situation in Baghdad required him to create his own information:

> I would . . . say that [the situation] is exactly the opposite of major combat operations in terms of producers and consumers of intelligence. I would say that in major combat operations, typically the tactical units are consumers of intelligence and less producers of intelligence. In other words, intelligence in many respects is being collected, processed, and turned into actionable

intelligence at the division level and then acted on and used to drive the brigade and below missions or the execution of their missions. I think it is quite the opposite in this environment where if you don't have the ability as a battalion commander or as a battalion formation to go out and create that intelligence and you are waiting for the brigade to hand you a target and all of the information that is required to execute that target, then you are probably not going to find yourself executing very much in the way of offensive operations.[24]

Believing that his unit had to mount focused combat operations to disrupt and destroy the insurgent networks active in his AOR, the 4-27th FA began to conduct its own intelligence operations. McKiernan stated:

You literally have to go out and create the information and turn it into intelligence which you can then act on yourself. Even some of the division targets that got passed to brigade, that got tasked to my organization, didn't have enough specificity to allow me to conduct a raid. But rather than saying, 'We don't have enough information,' and just basically telling your higher headquarters, 'Here are the following requests for information (RFIs) so that I can go ahead and execute this mission,' our approach was more, 'This is what I know. What can I do to fill in these other gaps in intelligence using my network, using my assets?'[25]

Noting that the requirement for tactical units to conduct their own intelligence operations represented a major shift away from standard procedures, McKiernan stated, "For most [Soldiers] I think that was probably a significant mindset change."[26]

This was an understatement. As McKiernan suggested, the environment in Iraq forced the doctrinal paradigm to shift. In the brigades and battalions, S2 sections began to create aggressive collection plans because, as many units found, they rarely received actionable intelligence from higher echelons. Situations changed too quickly and most information pushed down became outdated quickly. Nevertheless, at the tactical level, the information needed was HUMINT and neither battalions nor brigades had trained HUMINT assets organic to their organizations. MI organizations and doctrine did allow the divisional MI battalion commander to assign a small number of THTs to brigades. However, as noted earlier, these teams were small in number and limited in manpower. Even when they were augmented with THTs, tactical units often expressed hunger for more intelligence.

The 4-27th FA is one example of a unit that made this transition to operations designed to gather and exploit intelligence. There are many others. The 2d Battalion, 503d Infantry (2-503d IN), operating near the city of Kirkuk as part of the 173d Airborne Brigade (173d ABN), made several significant changes in organization to meet the demand for intelligence. The battalion command stated its stance on conducting intelligence operations in this way: "Treat information as your most valuable weapon. . . . Real life, unfortunately, is not like Ranger school, in that there's no [Ranger instructor] to tell you where the enemy is. You usually have to figure that out for yourself."[27] To gather this critical information, the 2-503d IN used their companies and platoons to establish relationships with local leaders and ask questions. To organize and analyze the intelligence gleaned from missions in neighborhoods, the battalion's companies created their own intelligence section out of their fire support teams.[28] These innovations were critical, the battalion believed, to collecting the key bits of information that would allow the unit to move quickly to catch insurgents who were often on the move.

The 1st Battalion, 24th Infantry (1-24th IN), a Stryker-equipped unit that conducted operations in Mosul in late 2004, launched a more radical transformation in its attempt to collect actionable intelligence. The battalion commander and his staff determined that the S2 section was by doctrine and organization simply unable to meet the demand for actionable information.[29] The unit then decided to expand the small S2 section into a much more muscular organization with 25 Soldiers, mostly drawn from elsewhere in the unit. The new S2 section included a plans cell, an operations cell, and a detainee operations cell. This reorganization integrated the attached THTs into the detainee operations cell, and information from that cell moved through the plans cell where Soldiers coordinated it with intelligence from other sources, to give the battalion the ability to conduct analysis and targeting.[30] The battalion recognized IMINT and SIGINT as "enablers," but believed that "HUMINT is the COIN of the Realm."[31] To back up this assertion, the unit integrated the attached THTs into all operations in their AOR. The battalion also began working closely with the Iraqi Security Forces (ISF) to target the enemy more precisely. This reorganization, the unit stated, led to tangible improvements in security in its AOR. Attacks decreased by 80 percent over the battalion's 12 months in Mosul, and the battalion captured or killed most of the identified terrorists in the area.[32]

This shift in the MI paradigm was quite visible to leaders at higher levels. Major General Fast, the CJTF-7 CJ2, watched as this transition occurred. She believed the overall operation was very HUMINT-centric, with approximately 95 percent of the intelligence used at the tactical level generated by tactical units themselves.[33] Having said that, Fast contended that some units were better than others in conducting intelligence operations. She singled out the 2d BCT of the 1st AD as one unit that had successfully transformed its intelligence system.

Colonel Ralph Baker, the commander of the 2d BCT, arrived in Baghdad in May 2003 and quickly realized he would have to develop his own intelligence. This revelation meant creating a new system that would be accepted and adopted fully by his subordinate units. Baker first tripled the size of the brigade S2 section and added an S2X to its staff.[34] He also directed the expansion of the S2 sections within his battalions and then charged his maneuver units to actively collect information by developing sources among the Baghdad population. The brigade took the innovative step of giving Global Positioning Systems (GPS) to Iraqi informants to assist in pinpointing insurgent locations in the complex urban terrain of the capital city.[35]

Figure 40. Staff Sergeant Camron Cook, 2d BCT, and a translator seek information from local Iraqis about a rocket launcher discovered in a Baghdad neighborhood.

DOD Photo by SGT Vernon Freeman

To synchronize these HUMINT collection efforts and ensure unity of effort, Baker empowered the brigade S2 to track all the Iraqi contacts acquired by subordinate units and develop the HUMINT it received into cogent analytical products that enabled the maneuver elements to act decisively.[36]

Successful intelligence operations bred additional success. Numerous Soldiers in OIF have described how HUMINT led them to conduct a raid on a particular location or, in some cases, a cordon operation that isolated and searched larger areas. Once on the objective, the unit—usually a squad or platoon—would identify targeted individuals, confirm their identities, and remove them for questioning and possibly detention. Tactical questioning on the objective, a method of asking Iraqi citizens simple direct questions about identity, locations, and recent events often gave Soldiers critical information. In addition, many units also developed sensitive site exploitation (SSEs) teams, which included THT personnel and other MI Soldiers when they were available, who accompanied the operation to interrogate individuals and collect documents, computers, forensic evidence, and any other information or materials that might prove valuable. In many cases, analysis of that material led to subsequent raids or other operations. This method proved the key to disrupting insurgent cells before they had a chance to flee the AOR.

The Muhalla 636 Operation

One operation conducted by the 2d BCT, 1st AD, serves as an excellent example of how tactical-level units used intelligence operations to make a significant impact on the security environment in their AOR. In a high profile attack on 26 October 2003, insurgents fired 30 rockets at the Al Rasheed Hotel in northern Baghdad, a large building on the edge of the

Figure 41. US Army Lieutenant General Ricardo Sanchez, Commander, CJTF-7, and US Deputy Defense Secretary Paul Wolfowitz listen to a reporter's question during a press conference following the attack on the Al Rasheed Hotel.

DOD Photo by SSgt David Bennett

International Zone and the temporary home of diplomats and members of the press. The attack killed Army Lieutenant Colonel Charles H. Buehring and wounded a number of others. However, most of the occupants, including Deputy Secretary of Defense Paul Wolfowitz who was visiting Baghdad, remained uninjured. The hotel was within the 2d BCT's AOR, and Colonel Baker immediately ordered the Iraqi sources and contacts developed by the brigade's subordinate units to begin collecting information about the attack.

Within 5 days, HUMINT pointed at an insurgent cell located in Muhalla (neighborhood) 636 in western Baghdad. After further developing its sources and information, the brigade had identified 22 individuals who were likely involved in the cell and determined their locations in the city.[37] Baker then arranged for non-US personnel to confirm these locations, fearing the sudden appearance of Americans in the neighborhood would cause the alleged insurgents to flee. On 8 November, once surveillance confirmed locations and identities, the 2d BCT sent the Soldiers of two infantry companies, a cavalry troop, the brigade reconnaissance troop, and a battalion headquarters to raid 15 target sites. An FBI team accompanied the brigade units on these raids to gather critical materials, as did a brigade SSE team that included female Soldiers to search the Iraqi women who might be present on the objectives.

The 8 November operation yielded 36 suspected insurgents, 30 computers, and more than 100 boxes of documents that included fake passports and other identification cards. Brigade Soldiers also found weapons and materials to make improvised explosive devices (IEDs). After

---

New Roles for the New Campaign
Female Search Teams in OIF

Female Soldiers in Operation IRAQI FREEDOM took on an unprecedented set of missions once full spectrum operations began in Iraq. As the Army became attuned to the cultural norms of the Iraqi population, the role of female Soldiers in cordon and search and traffic control operations became especially critical. Arab cultural norms forbid a male touching a woman who is not related to him, especially another man's wife. To maintain cultural sensitivity and facilitate cooperation between Iraqis and Coalition forces during operations, many units added female Soldiers to the teams that searched houses and vehicles. For example, the leaders of the 1st Battalion, 67th Armor Regiment, which operated in the Sunni Triangle in 2003 and early 2004, integrated females from their forward support company into the teams that went into Iraqi homes looking for insurgents and weapons caches. In 2004, units such as the 1st Infantry Division and the 2d Brigade, 2d Infantry Division continued this practice, finding that including their women Soldiers on searches of Iraqi houses often defused tension by making the female inhabitants feel more at ease. These types of operations placed female Soldiers alongside their male comrades in infantry, armor, and other combat arms units. Such novel use of female Soldiers illustrates the dramatic ways in which the US Army reinvented its tactics and techniques to meet the requirements of the full spectrum campaign.

Captain Donald Stewart, Captain Brian McCarthy, and Captain James Mullin,
"Task Force Death Dealers: Dismounted Combat Tankers,"
Armor, January-February 2004, 12.
Erin Solaro, "Lionesses of Iraq,"
Seattle Weekly, 6 October 2004.

detention and questioning, brigade leaders determined that the operation had netted 7 members of the cell leadership, 7 Iraqis involved in financing the cell, 4 suppliers and recruiters, and 12 operators.[38] In the 3 weeks that followed the raid, the brigade S2 section concentrated solely on interrogating the detained suspects, translating and analyzing the collected documents, and using link analysis—a proven police and intelligence technique of developing information on organized crime and insurgent organizations—to construct a picture of the insurgent cell and its relationships with external figures and agencies. Employing its organic intelligence Soldiers, an attached mobile interrogation team from the division, and daily coordination with the FBI and CIA, the brigade identified 12 additional alleged members of the cell.[39] These suspects were picked up and further collection and analysis led the 2d BCT to determine that local businesses and mosques in the AOR had played a significant role in the activities of the insurgent network. A subsequent raid on one mosque, the Umm Tubal Mosque in Baghdad, yielded bomb-making material, insurgent financial records, and individuals suspected of having important roles in the insurgency.[40]

This intelligence operation, which essentially lasted for months following the initial attack on the Al Rasheed Hotel, had a significant impact on the security environment in Baghdad. The disruption of the cell led to an immediate decrease in IED and mortar attacks on American forces in Muhalla 636. In the long term, the operation greatly improved the 1st AD's understanding of the organization, financing, and operations of insurgent networks in Baghdad. Colonel Baker's Soldiers had accomplished these effects not with large-scale cordon and sweeps or other combat operations, but through their own carefully designed and synchronized intelligence operations.

The New Paradigm's Growing Pains

Operations like the one described above demonstrate how tactical units met the demand for intelligence by going beyond the MI assets assigned and tasking all Soldiers to become collectors of information. This practice was widespread and often effective, but it did not always please the US Army MI community in Iraq. By doctrine, regulation, and training, MI Soldiers were the only individuals and units allowed to conduct most intelligence activities. According to the MI community, missions such as working with a source network and interrogation of detainees were delicate and complex and required careful planning and proper training. When battalion and brigade commanders assigned these operations to maneuver units whose Soldiers were essentially untrained, some problems surfaced. According to a report by the Department of the Army Inspector General's Office, MI Soldiers in the 4th ID noted that one tactical unit they had worked with was "running their own sources, and otherwise acting like a group of 'James Bonds,' overstepping any rules as they saw fit."[41] A 2004 report from the 519th MI Battalion echoed this complaint and described how many tactical units were conducting "do-it-yourself HUMINT collection" in Iraq and recognized that although this was done "for the best reasons," the efforts were "sometimes counterproductive."[42] The Soldiers in the 519th emphasized the nuanced and patient approach required for these operations, stating that a trained HUMINT Soldier "develops relationships of trust in order to penetrate the inner circles of the enemy. He uses discretion and unconventional tactics, techniques and procedures to prevent the compromise of his operation while safeguarding the source's identity."[43] The report then warned that without proper training, the amateur HUMINT Soldier might make the Iraqi informant vulnerable to threats or actual violence.

As tactical units increased their intelligence collection activities, tension between them and the MI community did rise. Lieutenant Colonel McKiernan, commander of the 4-27th FA in Baghdad, noted that at the beginning of his deployment, MI officers expressed concern when the battalion began intelligence operations:

> There was some discomfort initially with the tactical units engaging in HUMINT collection. There was definitely some friction, I think, between the MI community and I would say my brigade commander, definitely, about what was allowable and what wasn't in terms of sources and informants and things like that. I want to be clear here . . . we were definitely collecting information. I was not running sources, but that may be a fine line.[44]

McKiernan described that once MI Soldiers realized how large the demand was for actionable intelligence in Iraq, they tended to relent and eventually coordinated their activities with tactical units like the 4-27th FA:

> The brigade . . . had the ability to collect information across the brigade zone because we started patching things together, but it started at our level. If somebody had information, by God, we had to be ready to take it. The THTs, when we first started this, said, 'Hey, that is our job. What are you doing? You are not allowed to talk to these guys.' Then they realized, I think pretty quickly, that there were more people than they could possibly talk to. So what they would do, and there was a lot of cooperation, if there was somebody new who we felt had information of value, we would ask the THTs to talk to him to see if this was somebody the THT wanted to run or the THT would say, 'Hey, S2 down there in the battalion, why don't you just go ahead and use this guy as a source of information for you because we don't think he is somebody we need to take on.'[45]

What emerged then between 2003 and 2004 in OIF was a new and innovative process that combined the experience and training of MI professionals with the capacity and willingness of tactical-level units to collect information.

Interrogation Operations

As the success of the 1st AD's Muhalla 636 operation demonstrated, effective interrogation of detainees was perhaps the most critical mission in the larger HUMINT campaign in Iraq. Interrogations often occurred within the broader scope of detention operations, although the two types of operations were distinct. By doctrine, the US Army had assigned these two closely related missions to different branches of the force. At the time of the campaign, FM 3-19.40, *Military Police Internment/Resettlement Operations*, published 1 August 2001, established the authority for the US Army Military Police Corps to detain and hold enemy prisoners of war (EPWs), civilian internees, and criminals in time of war.[46] Once these individuals entered military police (MP) custody, whether in a camp or a temporary facility, they would be screened for intelligence value and possibly interrogated. However, these two missions—screening and interrogating—belonged to the MI Corps who operated inside the EPW camps and detention facilities run by the MPs. FM 34-52, *Intelligence Interrogation*, established the MI Corps' authority for interrogation operations and codified the US Army's policy on the authorized techniques for questioning EPWs, internees, and criminals. This section will examine interrogation operations in 2003 and 2004, focusing on the role of interrogators in the larger intelligence system. (The next chapter will address detainee operations more closely.)

Understanding that detainee operations—and the interrogations directly related to detentions—would become an integral element in the Iraq campaign, in the summer of 2003 Lieutenant General Sanchez sought to assert clear rules that established how Coalition soldiers would treat those Iraqis and others they detained and questioned. To do so, the CJTF-7 commander and his staff reviewed the policies established before the initial invasion of Iraq. In February 2003 the V Corps staff had established guidelines for the treatment of EPWs as well as those Iraqis who had been detained but did not clearly meet the legal definition of EPWs. Colonel Marc Warren, the V Corps Judge Advocate General, determined that the basis for the Corps' policy would be the Fourth Geneva Convention, which in 1950 had established norms for the protection of civilians in wartime.[47] Warren then added other measures such as magistrate review of detainees and oversight mechanisms used by the US Army during operations in Haiti and the Balkans.[48]

Warren, who in June 2003 became the CJTF-7 Judge Advocate General, believed the policies developed for the invasion had to form the basis for Coalition detainee operations after the Saddam regime had fallen. Sanchez, in agreement with his top lawyer, issued a CJTF-7 fragmentary order (FRAGO) in late June 2003 explicitly directing all Coalition units to ensure their detention activities met the regulations of the Fourth Geneva Convention concerning the legal status and treatment of civilian internees and criminal detainees.[49] A lengthier order in late August, which later became widely known as the "Mother of all FRAGOs," gave greater detail on how Coalition forces must conduct detainee operations and reiterated the requirement for all Coalition soldiers to adhere to the strictures of the Geneva Convention concerning their behavior toward detainees.[50] Thus, Sanchez established the Geneva Conventions as the legal norm for all operations, including interrogations, that involved Iraqi detainees.

The setting of clear legal guidelines became critical as the demand for intelligence increased in 2003. Under this pressure, the relatively small number of interrogators in Iraq came under increasing stress to screen and interrogate the large number of Iraqis detained by Coalition forces. Most of the HUMINT Collectors (Military Operational Specialty 97E), the MI Soldiers who were trained to conduct interrogations, served on the THTs. Even when these Soldiers were augmented in their interrogation activities by counterintelligence specialists (Military Operational Specialty 97B), there were still not enough THTs to conduct the type of interrogation operations that would produce actionable intelligence for all tactical units. Major General Raymond Odierno, the commander of the 4th Infantry Division (4th ID), which operated in the Sunni Triangle, contended that in the summer of 2003 his division simply did not have enough interrogation assets:

> At first we had no interrogators basically, so our ability to interrogate and get information at the brigade and division level was extremely limited. So what we would do is try to take our most important [detainees] and forward those to a higher level that had the assets. But they were so overwhelmed that they did not, in my mind, provide us with the information we needed.[51]

The situation was not much better in Baghdad. Colonel Michael Tucker, the commander of the 1st BCT of the 1st AD, noted that in 2003 he had only three interrogators in support of his entire unit.[52] While the number of THTs would slowly increase and most units had at least some interrogation capability by 2004, tactical units still commented on the shortfall of interrogators. The 2d Brigade, 2d Infantry Division (2d ID), which began operations in Al Anbar province in the fall of 2004, asserted that they did not have enough interrogators and had to contract civilian interrogators to fill the gap.[53]

One of the reasons why tactical units felt they lacked interrogator support was that since June 2003 the number of Iraqis detained by Coalition forces had increased dramatically. In May 2003 one estimate stated that the Coalition held a total of 600 detainees.[54] Many operations brought in small handfuls of detainees, but a large-scale multi-brigade operation like the 4th ID's PENINSULA STRIKE in June 2003 detained hundreds of Iraqis, all of which had to be screened by qualified MI Soldiers and, if determined to have valuable intelligence, questioned by trained interrogators. By November 2003 Coalition forces had processed over 30,000 Iraqi detainees with roughly 10,000 still in custody.[55] As the number of detainees rose in 2003, units constructed an increasing number of detention facilities to house them and provide the setting for interrogations. All divisions had facilities and many brigades built their own camps. The 1st Infantry Division (1st ID), for example, had a division facility and a facility for each of its four brigades.[56] Detention and interrogation became so important to the collection of HUMINT that some units began running facilities at the battalion level. After the 3d Brigade, 2d ID, left the Samarra area in December 2003 and moved to northern Iraq, two of its battalions began operating small collection points in Mosul where they detained Iraqis and conducted interrogations.[57] (The next chapter will examine the devolution of detention facilities to these lower tactical levels in greater detail.)

The broadening nature of detainee operations partly resulted from the drive for quick interrogations near the point of detention. As the US Army's *Inspector General Report on Detainee Operations* noted in 2004, most of the S2s and G2s (division-level intelligence officers) reported a severe shortage of interrogators near the points of capture and at the company and battalion detainee collection points.[58] Many MI Soldiers felt the same way. Two young interrogators in the 4th ID, for example, contended that if a unit wanted to gather actionable intelligence, it had to include interrogators on every raid it conducted to identify the detainees with the highest intelligence value.[59] The biggest obstacle to this procedure was the lack of trained personnel. Their consensus was, "There were too many interrogations and not enough interrogators."[60] This shortfall in interrogators even plagued the division-level facilities where commanders concentrated many of their HUMINT assets. In the 4th ID's division-level detainee facility, the chief of interrogations noted that he had only six military interrogators.[61] Although he received augmentation in the form of civilian contractor interrogators, who were often well-trained ex-military men, his team could not satisfy the demand for interrogations. The chief felt that he required 20 to 30 interrogators on his staff to meet the division's need for actionable intelligence.

Interrogation Operations in the Abu Ghraib Prison[62]

The demand for accurate and meaningful intelligence affected the entire MI community in Iraq. At the level of CJTF-7, this desire for information led to the creation of the Joint Interrogation and Debriefing Center (JIDC), which resided in one portion of the Baghdad Central Confinement Facility (BCCF), better known as the Abu Ghraib Prison—its name under the Saddam regime. The mission inside the JIDC involved MI Soldiers conducting interrogations of security detainees and the analysis of the information derived from those interrogations. These operations were separate from the confinement operations conducted by the MP Soldiers in the prison. Because of the doctrinal divide between the detention mission and interrogation operations, this study has divided its discussion of the operations at Abu Ghraib and the incidents of abuse that occurred there. This section will focus primarily on the role of the MI units and Soldiers who operated the JIDC, interrogated Iraqis in the facility, and, in a very small number of cases, took part in the abuse of detainees. The next chapter will look closely at the MP operations in the prison and examine how the breakdown in detainee operations played a decisive role in the incidents.[63]

The cases of abuse at Abu Ghraib by no means serve as a microcosm of how the large majority of US Soldiers conducted detainee and interrogation operations throughout Iraq in 2003 and 2004. The vast majority of Soldiers assigned to detention facilities or involved in interrogations performed their duties with honor and in accordance with international standards of decency. A review of the history of the JIDC and the incidents of abuse that occurred there, however, can improve the understanding of the challenges facing the US Army in its drive for strategic intelligence and in dealing with the deteriorating security environment.

By early summer 2003 Lieutenant General Sanchez and the staff of CJTF-7 had decided that the need for actionable intelligence required the establishment of a central interrogation facility where detainees suspected of having critical information could be held and questioned. Coalition forces had set up two other major detention facilities, the first at Camp Bucca near the southern port city of Umm Qasr for the general detainee population, and the second at Camp Cropper on the Baghdad Airport complex for the detention and interrogation of HVTs. For logistical and operational reasons, neither of these camps were a suitable site for a central interrogation center. That fact induced Sanchez on 6 September 2003 to consolidate operations and direct Colonel Thomas Pappas, the commander of the 205th MI Brigade, to establish a JIDC at Abu Ghraib and to take command of the interrogation operations there.[64] While the US Armed Forces had established JIDCs in previous campaigns and operated one at the Guantanamo Naval Base in Cuba, the DOD had no doctrine that governed the structure and operations of a JIDC. Partly because of this lack of doctrine and partly because of the demands placed on the MI community as the security environment worsened, the manning and procedures of the center changed frequently. Indeed, the 205th MI Brigade created a JMD for the JIDC only after the facility began operations in the fall of 2003.[65]

The US Army had initiated interrogation operations at Abu Ghraib 6 weeks before the establishment of the JIDC. In July 2003, 14 interrogators from Alpha Company, 519th MI Battalion, a unit that had recently conducted interrogation operations in Afghanistan, began working at the prison. At that time, Abu Ghraib held less than 100 security internees, a classification that separated civilian detainees suspected of acting against the Coalition from other detainees. Coalition forces then placed some of these security internees into a group labeled "MI Hold." This term was not a category of detainee recognized by either the Fourth Geneva Convention or US military doctrine, and its use by the Coalition did not establish a new term that superseded or contravened CJTF-7's commitment to adherence to the Geneva Conventions. Instead, the term originated in the rules of engagement developed by CENTCOM for OIF to identify those detainees who had been screened by Coalition soldiers, identified as persons likely having information of critical importance, and placed in a hold status until they could be formally interrogated by the small number of interrogators in the country.[66] By moving detainees to Abu Ghraib and placing them in the MI Hold status, Coalition forces separated these civilian internees, making them available to the experienced interrogators assigned there. The number of MI Hold detainees increased in August, and the small contingent of MI Soldiers at the prison continued to conduct interrogations. It was not long before the members of Alpha Company began to have difficulties gaining actionable intelligence. One officer in the company recalled that at this point, and on her own initiative, she directed interrogators to introduce some of the techniques the unit had used in Afghanistan, such as placing detainees in uncomfortable positions (stress positions) or reversing sleep cycles (sleep adjustment), to break down the resistance of those detainees the interrogators believed held critical information about the developing insurgency.[67]

Lieutenant General Sanchez's directive ordering the establishment of a JIDC significantly expanded interrogation operations at Abu Ghraib begun by Alpha Company, 519th MI Battalion. Around 10 September 2003 Colonel Pappas sent one of his officers to the prison to establish the JIDC. The brigade had no interrogators within its original structure, but created a composite unit of 45 interrogators and 18 linguists and translators from a number of different MI battalions and groups to run the JIDC.[68] Later in the fall, contract civilian interrogators arrived to augment the Soldiers in the JIDC. By doctrine, it was these MI Soldiers and authorized contractors who conducted the interrogations in the facility. Before and after the interrogation, the detainee came under the control and authority of the 320th MP Battalion, a unit subordinate to the 800th MP Brigade, whose officers and Soldiers served as confinement specialists. The MI and MP Soldiers came under increasing stress to gather actionable intelligence as the fall progressed and as the number of detainees increased at Abu Ghraib. By the end of November, the entire detainee population at the prison numbered approximately 10,000. The number of MI Hold detainees had also grown, from 400 around the end of September to 900 by Thanksgiving.[69]

As the number of detainees increased in the early fall, the Soldiers in the JIDC felt greater pressure to produce results. Pappas asserted that in this period he sensed the urgency to make the interrogations in the JIDC yield critical information.[70] Sanchez, the CJTF-7 commander, agreed that this pressure was indeed palpable within his command.[71] Internally, the Soldiers in

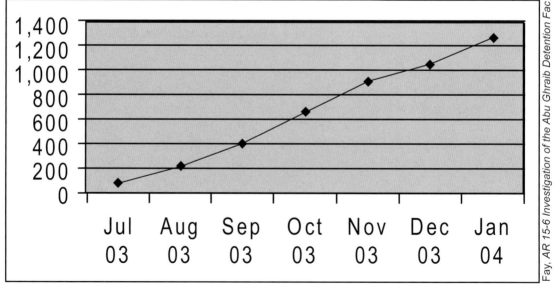

Figure 42. MI Hold population at Abu Ghraib Prison.

the JIDC worked to understand the rules, procedures, and policies that governed the operations the Coalition had come to view as critical to success. When CJTF-7 stood up in June 2003, it did not inherit any cogent set of guidelines or clear policies that established which counter-resistance techniques could be used in interrogations. Although the CJTF-7 commander and staff recognized this and sought to rectify the situation in mid-summer 2003 by requesting assistance from CENTCOM, the Army, and the DOD, help would be slow in arriving. In the meantime, for guidance on interrogation techniques MI units in Iraq relied on policies and rules from other campaigns or from FM 34-52, *Intelligence Interrogation*, the Army's 1992 manual that gave a great deal of freedom to the interrogator for decisions concerning interrogation approaches and counterresistance techniques.[72]

CJTF-7's efforts to fill the gap created by the dearth of interrogation policy began to gather steam in the summer when Major General Fast arrived to become the CJ2. In making her assessment of the joint task force's intelligence requirements, she reinforced the need for assistance visits from training teams composed of experts in interrogation techniques. In the late summer, these appeals began to produce results. As early as May 2003 senior DOD officials had begun to support Coalition forces in Iraq with training and guidance on interrogation and detainee operations. During that month, the senior intelligence officer (J2) on the Joint Staff had initiated discussions about these requirements with Major General Geoffrey Miller, the commanding general of Joint Task Force–Guantanamo Bay (JTF-GTMO) who had accumulated a great deal of experience in detaining unlawful combatants captured by Coalition forces in Afghanistan.[73] Secretary of Defense Donald Rumsfeld ordered the Joint Chiefs of Staff to task Miller to travel to Iraq with a team from JTF-GTMO to assist CJTF-7, the ISG, and a special operations task force in improving their collection and analysis of intelligence. Miller arrived with his 17-man team in late August 2003 and visited a number of locations, including the Abu Ghraib Prison. In the report that capped the visit, Miller stated that CJTF-7 "did not have authorities or procedures in place to affect a unified strategy to detain, interrogate, and report information for detainees/internees in Iraq"—a conclusion that Sanchez and many of his senior staff had already reached.[74] Based on his team's observations of the capabilities and procedures of CJTF-7, Miller made a series of recommendations to Sanchez and his staff. These suggestions included improving the integration and synchronization of the various intelligence organizations working for CJTF-7, especially those involved in HUMINT.

The Miller Report also focused on interrogations in general, finding that while interrogation operations at the tactical level were satisfactory, CJTF-7's MI organizations needed to recognize the difference between tactical questioning techniques and interrogations conducted to answer the task force commander's strategic and operational intelligence requirements. The report acknowledged that CJTF-7 had already taken an important step toward the improvement of these operations by establishing the JIDC at the Abu Ghraib Prison. However, the report continued, CJTF-7 should take additional measures to make the JIDC more effective, such as introducing interrogator-analyst "Tiger Teams" modeled on similar teams active at Guantanamo and establishing an interrogation and counterresistance policy to serve as the guidelines for interrogations in the JIDC. Most important, the Miller Report contended, was the need to create close working relationships between the Soldiers who confined the Iraqi security internees, those who conducted the interrogations, and those who analyzed the information derived from the interrogations. In interrogations at the strategic level, the Miller team argued, cooperation between the MP and MI interrogators was paramount. Based on its experience in Guantanamo, the team recommended to CJTF-7 that in interrogation centers like the JIDC, "it is essential that the guard force [MPs] be actively engaged in setting the conditions for successful exploitation of the internees."[75] The report stressed the role of the MPs in successful interrogations stating, "Detention operations must be structured to ensure detention environment focuses the internee's confidence and attention on their interrogators."[76] However, the report offered no detail on what form the MP cooperation should take. (Chapter 6 will examine the role played by those MPs supporting the JIDC in the fall of 2003 in the interrogation of some MI Hold detainees in Abu Ghraib.) In addition to his recommendations, Miller agreed to send a training team from Guantanamo to the JIDC. The team arrived in October 2003 and stayed at Abu Ghraib for 2 months to help the interrogators improve their basic interrogation skills.[77]

While the Miller team visited, Sanchez decided to address the lack of clearly defined guidance for interrogation operations by directing his staff to develop detailed guidelines for interrogators in Iraq. When CJTF-7 began operations in June 2003, the US Government had just completed a series of significant revisions to the interrogation policy of the Armed Forces that had begun more than a year earlier. In the wake of the terrorist attacks of 9/11, the Bush administration began to reshape its approach toward detainee and interrogation operations, driven by the fact that al-Qaeda, the enemy that attacked the United States, was not a country but a confederation of international terrorist organizations. Expertly waging war against an unorthodox, shadowy enemy who wore no uniform and thought nothing of killing innocent civilians to attain its goal presented a number of challenges and posed several very important questions. Perhaps the most critical of these questions was how the US Government and its military should treat those who fought on the side of al-Qaeda given that the terrorist group was not a state, had not signed the conventions that governed the treatment of combatants in wartime, and generally refused to acknowledge constraints grounded in international law. Resolution of this question would remain an issue into 2002, but the Bush administration had obtained broad unspecified powers from Congress to deal with those responsible for 9/11.[78] It will be necessary to examine some of these policy debates and decisions to understand which guidelines governed the actions of US forces in Iraq.

Of immediate concern to the administration was a perceived lack of actionable intelligence that could be used to drive antiterrorist operations. The placement of agents within al-Qaeda had proven next to impossible. One very promising means of gaining intelligence was the interrogation of those detainees captured by US forces in Afghanistan and elsewhere in late 2001 and early 2002 and in detention at the US Naval Base at Guantanamo Bay, Cuba. Officials within the Bush administration asked the Department of Justice (DOJ) and the DOD to identify interrogation counterresistance techniques capable of being legally used on the detainees suspected of terrorist activities.[79]

After robust debate both within and outside the Government, the Bush administration moved decisively to implement new approaches in dealing with al-Qaeda and Taliban detainees.[80] Definitions became significant in the arena of interrogation, particularly as the Bush administration attempted to classify the nature and parameters of acceptable counterresistance techniques in light of the limited success in gaining actionable intelligence from the detainees at Guantanamo. In a 1 August 2002 memorandum from the DOJ to Alberto Gonzales, Counsel to the President, the distinction between torture, discomfort, and intimidation became less than clear.[81] This memorandum and other guidance from the Office of Legal Counsel in the DOJ became the basis for discussion of various interrogation techniques within the DOD.

By October 2002 the continued lack of success in interrogations of HVTs detained at Guantanamo led Major General Michael E. Dunlavey, commander of Joint Task Force (JTF) 170, to ask General James T. Hill, Commander, US Southern Command (SOUTHCOM), for the use of 19 techniques not listed in FM 34-52 to counter the resistance mounted by some detainees.[82] On 2 December 2002 Secretary of Defense Rumsfeld approved the use of the milder methods, known as Category I and II techniques, that Dunlavey had requested. Rumsfeld also reviewed the harsher Category III techniques proposed by Dunlavey, but approved only the methods that allowed noninjurious physical contact with the detainee.

However, on 15 January 2003 Rumsfeld rescinded his previous approval of these new techniques. This decision originated partly in the reservations expressed by Alberto J. Mora, the General Counsel of the Department of the Navy, and uniformed lawyers serving in the Pentagon, and partly from the recent deaths and poor health of certain detainees in Afghanistan and Guantanamo.[83] Rumsfeld decided that the DOD needed to more carefully explore the various options and limitations associated with approach methods used in detainee interrogation. To do so, in January 2003 William J. Haynes II, the DOD General Counsel, appointed US Air Force General Counsel Mary Walker to convene a group of policy, legal, and technical experts to examine these issues. During deliberations, this working group was not allowed to deviate from the legal guidance set out in a draft DOJ Office of Legal Counsel opinion on interrogation.[84] After meeting for 2 months, Walker's group issued a report on 3 April 2003 to Rumsfeld recommending the approval of 35 techniques designed to break down the resistance to interrogation offered by detainees. The DOD General Counsel subsequently reviewed this list and recommended to Rumsfeld that he approve 24 of the 35 techniques.[85] The Secretary agreed and communicated his approval of these 24 techniques to General Hill in a 16 April 2003 memorandum.[86] The memorandum tagged each technique with identifying alphabetic character designations (A through X), and caveats accompanied several of them. Technique B, for example, reads as follows:

> Incentive/Removal of Incentive: Providing a reward or removing a privilege, above and beyond those that are required by the Geneva Convention, from detainees. [Caution: Other nations that believe that detainees are entitled to POW protections may consider that provision and retention of religious items (e.g., the Koran) are protected under international law (see, Geneva III, Article 34). Although the provisions of the Geneva Convention are not applicable to the interrogation of unlawful combatants, consideration should be given to these views prior to application of the technique.][87]

Four of the 24 techniques included cautionary notes on potential conflict with laws and treaties with other countries, and how their courts viewed those respective interrogation approaches.[88]

Rumsfeld attempted to build fail-safes into the process to prevent abuses. While authorizing the commanding general of SOUTHCOM to implement the techniques, he prescribed guidance relative to specific circumstances and locations: "The purpose of all interviews and interrogations is to get the most information from a detainee with the least intrusive method, always applied in a humane and lawful manner with sufficient oversight by trained investigators or interrogators."[89] Moreover, in the memorandum, Rumsfeld directed that these techniques applied only to interrogations of detainees in the Guantanamo facility.[90] Despite this qualification about limiting the techniques to those being held at Guantanamo, the methods approved in the memorandum for use in Guantanamo Bay soon would come to influence policy in the JIDC at Abu Ghraib.

With no single document governing interrogation operations in Iraq in the summer of 2003, the dilemma facing the CJTF-7 commander and staff was how to use the available body of doctrine, laws, and policy, including the Secretary of Defense's 16 April memorandum, to fashion a comprehensive set of rules for their interrogators. Colonel Warren, the CJTF-7 Staff Judge Advocate (SJA), and the 205th MI Brigade Command Judge Advocate looked closely at the Army's FM 34-52, which listed a set of approaches or techniques available to the interrogator for use in inducing a POW or detainee to give information. However, neither officer believed the manual contained enough detail or established sufficient control measures for the proper and lawful conduct of interrogations.[91] Seeking more definitive guidance, they consulted other DOD policies and doctrine, and then began working with other staff members and commanders to create a new policy. Ultimately, the new set of rules, developed in August and issued in September 2003, called the CJTF-7 Interrogation and Counter-Resistance Policy (ICRP), importantly asserted that the Geneva Conventions applied to all operations in the Iraqi theater of war, directed that Coalition forces "treat all persons under their control humanely," and stated that the guidance pertained to "detainees, security internees, and enemy prisoners of war under the control of CJTF-7."[92] The ICRP then authorized the use of the 24 counterresistance techniques listed in the 16 April 2003 Rumsfeld memorandum.[93] For example, the policy copied almost verbatim Technique B—"Incentive/Removal of Incentive" from the Rumsfeld memorandum. To remind Soldiers involved in interrogation operations that they had a duty to respect the rights of the detainees, the CJTF-7 policy contained an enclosure titled "General Safeguards," which stated that interrogators held responsibility for the safety of the detainees and that "the purpose of all interviews and interrogations is to get the most information from a security internee with the least intrusive method, applied in a humane and lawful manner with sufficient oversight by trained investigators or interrogators."[94]

Following the creation of the draft ICRP, the CJTF-7 staff circulated the policy to several units involved in interrogation operations for comments. At the end of that process, five techniques—the presence of military working dogs; deception; sleep management; the use of yelling, light control, and loud music; and stress positions—that had not been listed in the 16 April Rumsfeld memorandum appeared in an updated draft of the ICRP.[95] The CJTF-7 Staff Judge Advocate then sent the policy to the CJTF-7 Intelligence (CJ2) and Operations (CJ3) Sections as well as to the commander of the 205th MI Brigade. By 14 September CJTF-7 had finalized an ICRP that allowed interrogators in the JIDC to use the 24 techniques sanctioned in the April 2003 Rumsfeld memorandum and the 5 methods added in the staffing process.[96] Additionally, the policy stated that the 205th MI Brigade commander held the responsibility for issuing "specific implementation guidelines" for these techniques. In the ICRP, Lieutenant General Sanchez retained the right to approve the interrogators' use of six specific approaches on "enemy prisoners of war," including the use of stress positions (Technique CC) and the presence of military working dogs (Technique Y), on a case-by-case basis.

On 14 September 2003 the CJTF-7 commander signed the ICRP and directed that the new policy become active immediately. At the same time, CJTF-7 sent the ICRP to CENTCOM for approval.[97] In the letter of transmittal that accompanied the new policy to CENTCOM, Sanchez stated clearly that CJTF-7's ICRP was "modeled on the one implemented for interrogations conducted at Guantanamo Bay."[98] However, Sanchez asserted in the letter that he and his staff had "modified [the CJTF-7 policy] for applicability to a theater of war in which the Geneva Conventions apply," emphasizing that his command was unequivocal in the view that operations in Iraq were subject to the laws established in the Geneva Treaties. At CENTCOM, some concerns developed among the staff about the use of specific counterresistance techniques listed as approved approaches.[99] Colonel Warren, the CJTF-7 SJA, agreed with this assessment and began amending the ICRP to include greater constraints on interrogators. Warren contended, "The September policy, in my view, did comply with the Geneva Conventions when applied with all the appropriate safeguards."[100] Even so, he sought to place more control measures on the interrogation process. To do so, the CJTF-7 staff changed the wording of the memorandum making the revised ICRP applicable only to those detainees categorized as security internees, and reiterated the rights afforded to these internees by the Fourth Geneva Convention that confirmed protections on civilians in the time of war. The new version of the ICRP then listed the counterresistance approaches authorized by the CJTF-7 commander, a set of 17 techniques that did *not* include the presence of military working dogs, sleep management, and stress positions. These three approaches and nine others that were removed from the ICRP were no longer automatically approved for use.[101] Any interrogator who wished to use a technique not listed in the policy now had to send a written justification to CJTF-7 where the CJ2 and SJA reviewed it before sending it to Sanchez for final approval. The amended version of the ICRP also contained a new paragraph that firmly placed responsibility for the interrogation and its setting on the interrogator. To help interrogators give the detainee the impression that they had complete authority over the detainee's situation, the ICRP granted the interrogator the ability to change the environment in the interrogation room as well as the quality of the detainee's clothing, food, and shelter, as long as these changes did not go below the threshold of the requirements in the Geneva Conventions.[102] CJTF-7 issued this new version of the policy on 12 October 2003.

Lieutenant General Sanchez viewed both versions of the ICRP as placing greater control measures on interrogation operations that initially seemed to lack constraints. In his opinion, the doctrine established in FM 34-52 simply did not go far enough in creating safeguards. Sanchez contended, "Our FM [34-52] was grossly deficient because it did not require any approval by anyone in the chain of command for the use of any interrogation approach."[103] While the ICRPs certainly offered detailed guidance, they also appear to have caused some confusion. In 2004 the Fay–Jones' AR 15-6 investigation into the 205th MI Brigade's Interrogation Operations at Abu Ghraib noted that between August and mid-October "interrogation policy in Iraq had changed three times."[104] In the JIDC at Abu Ghraib, the interrogators tried to reconcile the changes. In September and October one interrogation officer made charts that used three columns to list (1) the counterresistance methods contained in FM 34-52 that had been approved for use by the CJTF-7 commander, (2) additional methods that required approval from the JIDC officer in charge (OIC), and (3) approaches that required the CJTF-7 commander's authorization before implementation.[105] The officer also required all interrogators to read and acknowledge in writing both CJTF-7's ICRP and a memorandum that mandated humane treatment for all detainees.[106] While this officer took significant steps to ensure Soldiers in the JIDC understood their interrogation constraints, Army investigators looking into JIDC operations contended that the charts were incomplete and did not list all of the counterresistance techniques actually in use by the interrogators at the time, such as removal of clothing; forced grooming; and use of loud music, yelling, and light control.[107]

Three years later, reflecting on the events in the fall of 2003, Lieutenant General Sanchez recognized that there might have been uncertainty about the CJTF-7 interrogation policy at Abu Ghraib: "When we published those memorandums, is there confusion? I think we have to accept that there probably is some confusion because you are going into a totally unconstrained environment and are now imposing standards and approval and oversight mechanisms."[108] Despite the potential for uncertainty, Sanchez contended that the modifications of the interrogation guidelines were critical to the establishment of a clear and enduring policy for MI Soldiers in Iraq that met international legal standards of decency:

> We do eliminate a couple [*sic*] of approaches [in the September 2003 ICRP] that the CJTF-7 lawyers firmly believed were within the Geneva Convention authorities but higher headquarters lawyers were debating. The other key change is that we elevate the approval authority from one memorandum to the next and force the review and approval of any interrogation plans that include the [unlisted] approaches to go to my level . . . [the approved approaches] get validated multiple times afterward as being within the Geneva Conventions.[109]

The best assessment of the confusion over interrogation policy can be found in the Fay–Jones AR 15-6 Report that stated there was uncertainty in the JIDC about which interrogation approaches CJTF-7 had approved, but that this ambiguity had multiple causes, including the changes in the ICRP: "Confusion about what interrogation techniques were authorized resulted from the proliferation of guidance and information from other theaters of operation; individual interrogator experiences in other theaters; and the failure to distinguish between interrogation operations in other theaters and Iraq."[110] The report added that changing policies about interrogation approaches "contributed to the confusion concerning which techniques could be used, which required higher level approval and what limits applied to permitted techniques."[111] Another important finding in the Fay–Jones Report documented that the interrogators in the JIDC requested CJTF-7 approve the use of techniques other than those listed in the 12 October ICRP on only a few occasions. Sanchez had established himself as the approving authority for such requests, and he recalled that throughout his time in command, he only received and approved requests for use of the isolation approach in which the detainee would be placed in a cell by himself.[112] Thus, the documented incidents of abuse in the JIDC did not occur because the CJTF-7 commander approved the use of abusive techniques.

Problems with the leadership of the JIDC more directly affected the policies and environment at Abu Ghraib. Colonel Pappas, commander of the 205th MI Brigade, commanded the JIDC yet had not established his brigade headquarters at Abu Ghraib. The 205th MI Brigade conducted missions across Iraq and the commander constantly traveled between his units and activities. In early September Pappas had sent one of the majors on his staff to help set up the JIDC. However, a shortage of officers in his brigade led Pappas to ask the CJTF-7 for a more senior officer who could supervise interrogation operations at Abu Ghraib. On 17 September 2003 the CJTF-7 CJ2 section sent Lieutenant Colonel Steven Jordan to the prison to serve as the director of the JIDC. Jordan served as the senior MI officer at the prison, and the reports and organization charts of the period acknowledge him as the officer in charge (OIC) of the JIDC.[113] Conversely, Jordan stated that while he believed he had "at times" held the title of director or chief of the JIDC, he considered himself to be a liaison officer who worked temporarily for the 205th MI Brigade at Abu Ghraib and thus had no clear authority over interrogation operations.

According to Jordan, his unclear understanding of authority and duties persisted throughout the fall of 2003.[114]

Jordan had been an MI officer in the past, but by 2003 he had been serving in the Army's Civil Affairs branch for a decade.[115] Although he had no experience in conducting or supervising interrogations, given his senior rank, his MI background, and the extreme shortage of officers at CJTF-7, Jordan was the best candidate to become the OIC of the JIDC at the time. Despite the need for senior leadership in the JIDC, Jordan stated that he chose to focus his time on improving the living conditions for his Soldiers and worked conscientiously to deal with the force protection issues at Abu Ghraib. Security of the Abu Ghraib Prison complex had become a major issue by early fall 2003, after mortar attacks became commonplace.[116] In fact, on 20 September, 3 days after Jordan's arrival at Abu Ghraib, a mortar barrage killed 2 Soldiers and wounded 11 others; Jordan was one of the wounded. According to his own testimony, Jordan left supervision of the interrogation operations in the JIDC to other commissioned and warrant officers who were involved in the routine operations of the JIDC, including the approval of interrogation plans in which interrogators recorded the techniques they planned to use to gain information from a detainee. As knowledgeable and competent as they were, the officers in this group could not be present during all interrogations. In the US Army, the overall enforcement of discipline, standards, and policies, such as the ICRP in organizations like the JIDC, traditionally falls to the NCOs. Unfortunately, the center had a shortage of trained senior MI NCOs who otherwise might have instilled a uniform understanding of standards and rules.[117]

As CJTF-7 and the 205th MI Brigade increased pressure on the JIDC to create actionable intelligence in the fall of 2003, a very small number of MI Soldiers began employing unauthorized practices that constituted detainee abuse. The Army investigators who looked into thousands of interrogations at Abu Ghraib found 22 cases in which evidence pointed to MI Soldiers using abusive techniques (such as placement of detainees in isolation cells, removal of clothing, and the use of military working dogs) or witnessing abuses and failing to stop them or report the incidents to the chain of command.[118] The Fay–Jones investigation also found that outside the sphere of interrogation operations, MI Soldiers were involved in one incident of violent assault and were present in several cases when MPs committed sexual abuses.[119] These documented abuses began in September 2003, soon after the JIDC began operations and continued sporadically through the next 3 months. As early as October, officers in the JIDC became aware of some of these abuses and chose to discipline the perpetrators using nonjudicial punishment under the Uniform Code of Military Justice (UCMJ), counseling, and removal from interrogator duties.[120]

Why did a few MI Soldiers at Abu Ghraib in the fall of 2003 commit these abuses? The Fay–Jones investigation looked at a number of factors in attempting to answer this question and found that at least part of the answer lay in the changing policies that governed interrogation techniques. As stated above, the report found that the "proliferation of guidance" had contributed to the confusion among the interrogators about authorized approaches and at the time that some of the abusive incidents occurred, some of the Soldiers "may have honestly believed that the acts were condoned."[121] However, the Fay–Jones investigation linked this confusion only "to the occurrence of some of the non-violent and non-sexual abuses," not to the incidents of physical or sexual abuse at Abu Ghraib.[122] Straightforward criminal misconduct, according to the investigation, was the primary cause of abuse of a sexual or violent nature.[123]

The Fay–Jones Report also focused on leadership in both the JIDC and the 205th MI Brigade. According to the investigation, the 205th never established a clear chain of command that could provide an unambiguous interpretation of the CJTF-7 ICRP or offer detailed oversight of interrogation operations in the JIDC. The report also contended that the 205th MI Brigade failed to coordinate with the 800th MP Brigade to delineate the boundaries between MI and MP duties, and was unable to train Soldiers to policy and regulatory standards or effectively discipline Soldiers who failed to meet those standards.[124]

When the photographs of abuse became public in the spring of 2004, worldwide attention fell on the US Army in Iraq and the Soldiers at Abu Ghraib specifically. The photographs documented incidents that took place not in the JIDC but on Tier 1 of the prison where a small group of MPs had begun abusive practices. (Chapter 6 will discuss these abuses.) Despite the fact that MI Soldiers were not responsible for the incidents in the photographs, those images led to detailed investigations of both detention *and* interrogation operations. These examinations revealed how a convergence of problems in leadership, policy, and personal character had generated a series of incidents that severely damaged the Coalition's efforts in Iraq and the reputation of the US Army throughout the world. While the Army, the American public, and the international audience understandably focused on the photographs of abuse, many overlooked the fact that most of the MI Soldiers who worked in the JIDC had performed professionally within a very difficult environment.

The Fay–Jones AR 15-6 Investigation Report characterized the service of these Soldiers in the following way:

> While some MI Soldiers acted outside the scope of applicable laws and regulations, most Soldiers performed their duties in accordance with the Geneva Conventions and Army Regulations. . . . MI Soldiers operating the JIDC at Abu Ghraib screened thousands of Iraqi detainees, conducted over 2,500 interrogations, and produced several thousand valuable intelligence products supporting the war fighter and the global war on terrorism. This great effort was executed in difficult and dangerous conditions with inadequate physical and personnel resources."[125]

The recognition of the professionalism of these Soldiers was unfortunately overshadowed by the excesses and in some cases, criminal acts, of those few who had lost their moral compasses at Abu Ghraib.

Even before the abuses at Abu Ghraib became public, the Coalition's leadership had begun to address the overall challenges of detainee and interrogation operations and began to issue unambiguous statements of policy about the proper treatment of all Iraqi citizens. In November 2003, for example, Lieutenant General Sanchez issued "CJTF-7 Rules for Detainee Operations," which demanded that all Soldiers "treat all persons with dignity and respect."[126] In May 2004 the CJTF-7 commander reiterated this basic mandate in a statement titled "Proper Conduct During Combat Operations."[127] For US Army interrogators, more guidance arrived on 13 May 2004 in a new CJTF-7 interrogation policy. The new guidelines kept intact the list of officially approved techniques found in the 12 October ICRP; however, the policy differed in the prohibition of specific techniques even if approval was requested through the chain of command.[128] This set of rules governed Coalition interrogation operations until 27 January 2005 when General George W. Casey Jr., commander of Multi-National Force–Iraq, issued a new policy that added safeguards and reduced the number of approved techniques interrogators could use to counter the resistance of detainees they suspected of holding critical information.[129]

Language and Culture

Magnifying the obstacles in the intelligence gathering efforts at all levels were the barriers posed by the differences in language and culture. These barriers posed challenges for almost all types of operations in Iraq. On a very basic level, the American Soldier's inability to speak with Iraqi citizens made building relationships difficult. With the help of a linguist or inter-

Figure 43. Interpreter with 308th Civil Affairs Brigade (right) converses in Arabic with local townspeople about their various concerns.

preter, the Soldier could converse with Iraqis, but the differences in culture remained powerful and prevented full comprehension or even caused offense and alienation. Throughout 2003 and 2004, language and culture played significant roles in shaping the Army's new campaign.

US Army Regulation (AR) 350-20, *Management of the Defense Foreign Language Program,* charged the Army to serve as the executive agent for the Defense Foreign Language Program. The Army tasked the MI Corps to provide language support to Army operations and trained many of its HUMINT and SIGINT collectors as linguists. These Soldiers were spread throughout the MI battalions in the Active Component and found in HUMINT linguist battalions in the Reserve Component. Once the planning for OIF began, the Army prepared to include most of its Arabic linguists in the initial deployment, which later created a problem. Major General Fast noted, "We frontloaded our Arabic linguists for the invasion of Iraq, as you would expect. A great many of the Arabic linguists had reached the culminating point of their tours, so we began to get fewer and fewer who were fluent Arab speaking linguists."[130] However, even if the Army had been able to retrain all of its linguists to speak Arabic—an almost impossible task—it still would not have been able to meet the needs on the ground in Iraq. Understanding this, the Army contracted with Titan Corporation and other companies to provide native Arabic speakers living in the West who could provide a variety of linguist support services to troops in OIF.

This action helped fill part of the gap, but the demand for linguists remained high. Just about all US Army units, including the MI Soldiers in the JIDC at Abu Ghraib, complained that they did not have enough interpreters and linguists throughout their tours in Iraq. Many units hired local Iraqis to serve as interpreters, but this did not always solve the problem. If units wanted to have their local interpreters provide support for sensitive missions on Coalition

---

The Death of One Iraqi Interpreter

On 20 September 2004, Sarah Latiff, an Iraqi translator for Company A, 3d Battalion, 153d Infantry Regiment, 39th Brigade Combat Team (Arkansas Army National Guard) was murdered. The Soldiers in the company had developed great respect for Sarah's attitude and courage. Private First Class Jimmy Harris recalled, "Nothing ever seemed to really get her down too much. She would gladly go on any mission we asked her to." Latiff's death devastated the company.

By 2004, Iraqi interpreters had become key players in the Coalition's full spectrum campaign. Understanding this, the insurgent network targeted those Iraqis who worked closely with US forces, helping them negotiate the new culture in which they found themselves. Violence against translators and their families made the hiring of qualified interpreters far more difficult.

After Sarah's death, the Soldiers of Company A, 3-153 IN, decided to take action. They began working with her relatives and friends to gather information about the people involved in the murder. Eventually, local sources provided enough intelligence to focus the Soldiers' attention on a small group of houses close to the unit's base. The company then mounted a nighttime cordon and search that led to the apprehension of five men and the capture of a small arms cache.

Sergeant First Class Floyd Herron, the company first sergeant, asserted at the time of the raid, "We'll start questioning them and figure out exactly their involvement in Sarah's death, maybe even find the trigger puller. So maybe we can bring some justice to Sarah's family and make the neighborhood a little bit safer for its residents."

Benjamin Cossel,
"One for Sarah: Tracking Down a Killer,"
Defend America News (4 November 2004): 1-2.

---

bases or elsewhere, they had to have these Iraqis vetted. The S2 of the 2d SBCT, 2d ID, a unit that had deployed to Iraq with Korean linguists, stated, "The number of linguists to support a BCT is significant. They are critical to the combat unit's ability to communicate and interact with the local population. Obtaining [vetted] linguists to perform tasks alongside maneuver battalions and other actions on the FOB [forward operating base] was difficult and overall affected intelligence gathering."[131] There were worse problems than clearances. In the Mosul area in 2004, the 3d BCT, 2d ID could not hire enough Arabic speakers, stating in a report that linguists "quit because of threats to them or their family from Anti-Iraqi Forces (AIF). Keeping interpreters employed and alive was a key issue with the brigade."[132] The lack of linguists not only affected combat operations and intelligence collection but reconstruction efforts as well. Sergeant Major Stephen Kammerdiener of the 326th Engineer Battalion, which supported the 101st ABN, stated that working with local contractors was a challenge, even if a unit had a linguist:

> We did hire some translators and we generally tried to get a trusted translator to go out with a new translator for a while just to get an idea of how trustworthy they really were. We had the initial vetting process and then we would never send them out alone. Plus, our military people, we had a lieutenant that was an Arab linguist and a couple times we would catch a contractor speaking with a translator and they would be brokering a [unauthorized] deal.[133]

Major General Fast believed the attempts to increase linguist support were inadequate for the support of intelligence operations. She asserted, "During my tenure in Iraq . . . even with contracting local nationals, civilian linguists, and heritage speakers, we often could only support about a quarter of the requirements for linguists. In the case of intelligence, the need for cleared linguists exacerbated the shortages."[134] Major Kenneth Cary, the Brigade S2 for the 1st BCT, 1st CAV, pointed out the gap in understanding between Americans and Iraqis was large and summed up its importance on the overall campaign in the following way: "If all our Soldiers spoke Arabic we could have resolved Iraq in 2 years. My point is that language is obviously an obstacle to our success, much more so than cultural. Even a fundamental understanding of the language would have had a significant impact on our ability to operate."[135]

Figure 44. Sergeant James Knoeller and Sergeant Meghan Kelly, Bravo Company, 325th MI Battalion, elicit information in Tikrit, Iraq. Knoeller, a CI special agent and Kelly, an Arab linguist, consult with a local business owner to gather vital information for force protection of US and Coalition forces in the area.

Cary's comments noted the cultural gap that divided Iraqis and American Soldiers. On the most basic level, the cultural gap prevented US Soldiers from comprehending the situation around them and especially hindered their ability to understand the insurgent enemy as it emerged in the summer of 2003. When left unaddressed, this divide had a larger impact, critically disabling the Army's ability to engage Iraqis in the campaign to win support for the Coalition's cause and in some cases, alienating those who were "sitting on the fence."

Lieutenant General Sanchez believed that the US Army's inability to understand Iraqi culture resided in its general unwillingness to prepare in a serious way for that understanding. Sanchez stated:

> It was a very cursory effort that we applied to try and get cultural awareness. We did the country studies that we normally are accustomed to. There was no real extraordinary effort other than some young sergeant or some young officer or some guy that you got out of a higher headquarters S2 shop that came down and did the briefing as part of your individual training right before you deployed. But the effectiveness of that was marginal at best and I would say the impact that it had on our Soldiers on the ground was almost nonexistent.[136]

The experience of the 1st Battalion, 506th Infantry (1-506th IN), which deployed to Al Anbar province in 2004, serves to illustrate Sanchez's point. In their predeployment training, the unit's Soldiers received briefings and a booklet on Arab culture but, "Once we hit the ground in Iraq, we found that much of the information in the cultural briefings and booklets was misleading. In many cases, the information did not apply to the province we were operating in, or were characteristics or traits of Muslims in different countries."[137] In retrospect, the unit wished it had received more information about Al Anbar province, especially intelligence about the clan, tribal, and religious relationships in the region.[138]

Sanchez believed the negative aspects of this lack of cultural awareness became evident early in the campaign:

> Very quickly, we started to learn that we had some major problems because during the cordon and searches we were starting to get the feedback, not just in the units at the tactical level but I started to get the feedback at the task force level from the Iraqis that we were interfacing with, that we did not understand what we were doing in terms of the way we were handling the Iraqis when we were either arresting them or isolating them or entering their homes.[139]

These problems went far beyond the level of the Iraqi street, as Sanchez contended: "All aspects of the conduct of our operations were being questioned by Iraqis at multiple levels and when the [Iraqi] governing council was put into place I had multiple discussions with them about this specific issue."[140] At the tactical level, unit leaders realized how the lack of cultural awareness affected their ability to achieve their goals. One company commander in the 1st Battalion, 503d Infantry (1-503d IN), stated, "I believe we deployed unprepared to understand the very foreign culture of Iraq. It took the entire deployment for most of us to connect with the locals with any effect. Especially in an insurgency, understanding the people is absolutely essential."[141] He then asserted, "I am convinced that if we had understood even a small portion of the subtle [cultural] clues only perceptible to the highly experienced, we would have seen much more success."[142]

CJTF-7 and many of its subordinate units did attempt to improve the Soldiers' understanding of the Iraqi culture and how to treat Iraqis in various situations. Sanchez recalled:

> Once we realized this huge gap in cultural understanding we immediately went about trying to fix it. First of all, we started by putting out some very basic guidance directing that every person deserved to be treated with dignity and respect. I will call it dignity and respect guidance because over the course of the year there are multiple memorandums that come out of the CJTF reiterating

the standards for the treatment of all people not just detainees. We also rapidly start learning that some of the actions that we took as commonplace or second-nature to us were actually pretty insulting in the Iraqi culture. The sandbagging of a detainee and arresting them in front of their families was pretty insulting to the honor of an Iraqi and in our culture we just do it.[143]

Subordinate units and forces that deployed subsequently built on this foundation. One excellent example was the 1st CAV. In the months before deploying to Iraq in the spring of 2004, Major General Peter Chiarelli, the division commander, began preparing his leaders by flying many of them to Jordan to become acquainted with Arab culture.[144] Chiarelli followed that trip with a training deployment to the Joint Readiness Training Center at Fort Polk, Louisiana, where 1st CAV Soldiers began to work with Arab role players. Once his unit was in Iraq, Chiarelli then ensured his Soldiers continued to receive cultural awareness training.

Many units had more abrupt cultural training: they learned by making mistakes. One unit experienced the shock of breaking a cultural taboo and paid a high price for its lack of aware-ness of the status and proper treatment of women in Iraqi culture. The 1-503d IN, operating in the city of Ramadi in Al Anbar province, detained women on two occasions, actions that caused angry crowds of thousands to gather.[145] The unit found that these detentions provoked even those Iraqis who had proven to be supporters of the Coalition. After the events, they concluded that the insurgent organizations had likely induced them to make the detentions to cause riots and decrease the support for US programs in the city. Whatever the root cause of the events, had the unit been better prepared to deal with sensitive cultural issues such as treatment of women, its Soldiers would have avoided alienating those whose support they were trying to win. Having received a painful lesson on cultural differences, the 1-503d IN warned other units, "Don't touch the women! If women must be detained, use the senior Sheiks to discipline her (*sic*). If you must protect women, do so with men present at their homes. Do not bring women into the [Coalition Forces] perimeter."[146] Despite the best intentions of American Soldiers and the constant attempts to explain the beneficial aspects of the Coalition's vision for Iraq, clashes like this one in Ramadi during the first 18 months of the new campaign likely eroded much of the hard-earned progress made by the US Army in places like Al Anbar province.

The Contributions of SIGINT and IMINT

While HUMINT became the centerpiece of intelligence operations in OIF, Soldiers con-ducting SIGINT and IMINT operations made significant contributions to the Coalition cam-paign. At the operational level, theater and even national SIGINT and IMINT assets at times played decisive roles. An operation against a major terrorist facility in June 2003 provides a good illustration of this critical use of both intelligence methods. As Coalition units established themselves across Iraq in the summer of 2003 and began conducting full spectrum operations, they had less than a clear understanding of the threats in Iraq. Often, HUMINT provided the best means of detecting and identifying threats in the built-up areas in which many American units began operating. Indeed, HUMINT assisted the 4th ID in locating and attacking a con-centration of former regime loyalists on a heavily-populated peninsula northeast of the city of Balad in mid-June 2003. (Chapter 8 will discuss this operation in detail.)

Threats located in remote areas of the country were more difficult to locate using HUMINT. In early June 2003, national-level SIGINT and IMINT were critical in identifying what appeared to be enemy activity northwest of the city of Haditha in Al Anbar province. The location was less than 50 miles from the Syrian border and greatly concerned Coalition leaders. Lieutenant Colonel D.J. Reyes, the G2 of the 101st ABN, leveraged the collection assets that were part of the AO North JIATF to develop a better picture of the threat in this location and quickly identified the target as a terrorist camp.[147] When Major General David Petraeus, the commander of the 101st ABN decided to mount a combat operation against the camp, Reyes began using the Joint Surveillance and Targeting Attack Radar System (JSTARS)—a theater-level IMINT asset—to gain a detailed and near contemporaneous picture of enemy strength and activity at the site.

On 11 June 2003, after indicators strongly suggested that the terrorists in the camp were planning an imminent assault against Coalition forces, V Corps ordered US aircraft and the Rangers of the 2d Battalion, 75th Regiment to conduct a quick night strike against the facility.[148] The plan also directed the 101st ABN to conduct an air assault the next day to relieve the Ranger force. Armed with a clear and deep understanding of the enemy facility as well as the strength and armament of the terrorists, US forces mounted a lightning attack that caught the enemy off guard. Although the terrorists resisted the Rangers, by daylight on 12 June US Soldiers had control of the camp and found over 37 enemy killed in action (KIA) as well as a large cache of weapons that included small arms, artillery rounds, and 87 SA-7 manportable, shoulder-fired antiaircraft missiles.[149]

The employment of SIGINT and IMINT, especially the use of unmanned aerial vehicles (UAV), at the tactical level gave commanders key information in critical situations. SIGINT assets, for example, helped the 3d Armored Cavalry Regiment (3d ACR), operating in Al Anbar province, locate and destroy an insurgent cell in the town of Rawa near the Syrian border that helped foreign fighters enter Iraq from other

Figure 45. A Shadow 200 unmanned aerial vehicle lands at FOB Warhorse, Baqubah, Iraq.

DOD Photo by SPC James B. Smith Jr.

Arab countries.[150] As the campaign progressed, MI Soldiers began operating Tactical UAVs (TUAV), such as the Shadow and the Raven, at division level and below. These aerial platforms carried various types of cameras that provided real-time video feeds to MI Soldiers and commanders. The 2d BCT of the 4th ID, for example, used its TUAV to locate insurgent mortar crews while they were setting up their weapons for a strike against US forces.[151] Based on the information from the TUAV, the brigade directed artillery fire or other types of countermortar fire to prevent the enemy crew from launching rounds at American targets. The 1st ID began using its TUAVs in the summer of 2004 to gain a better understanding of the enemy situation in the city of Samarra in Salah ad Din province north of Baghdad. In June senior leaders in the

1st ID watched video of 90 insurgents attacking an American Special Forces compound in the city, intelligence that helped shape their response as the summer progressed and the violence in Samarra increased.[152]

Perhaps the most dramatic examples of the use of SIGINT and IMINT at the tactical level are found in Operation AL FAJR, the Coalition assault on insurgents in the city of Fallujah in November 2004. By the summer of 2004, Sunni Arab insurgent forces had taken over Fallujah and transformed it into a fortress from which they launched attacks against Coalition forces. The Coalition, working with the new Interim Iraqi Government (IIG), developed a plan to destroy insurgent forces in the city and reassert official Iraqi control over Fallujah in preparation for the first Iraqi elections in January 2005. (Chapter 8 of this study will examine AL FAJR in greater detail.) The plan for AL FAJR called for an assault involving US Marines,

---

Eyes in the Sky

DOD Photo by CPT Ryan M. Rooney

SPC Robert Everheart of A/1-7 launches a Raven UAV for an early-morning reconnaissance mission.

Unmanned aerial vehicles (UAV) of various types played a critical role in US Army operations in Iraq. Units used vehicles like the Predator and the RQ-7 Shadow 200 to gain information about enemy activity and to literally see over the horizon. Most of the time, these UAVs remained under the control of division and brigade headquarters.

In 2003 and 2004, the Army fielded a new tactical UAV to battalion-size units in Iraq. The Raven, as this vehicle was known, weighed 5 pounds, had a wingspan of 5 feet, and was transportable in three small cases. Soldiers placed either optical or infrared cameras on the Raven, using them to download real-time video from the vehicle. The UAV had a ceiling of 300 meters and could stay aloft over an area of interest for 60 minutes.

Some units, like Task Force (TF) 1-7 of the 1st Infantry Division, employed their Raven to provide overwatch of main supply routes and other critical infrastructure. Other battalion-size units used the vehicle to provide immediate intelligence during conventional combat operations. For example, during Operation Al Fajr, the November 2004 assault on Fallujah, TF 2-7 of the 1st Cavalry Division utilized its Raven to locate enemy positions on their routes of advance. Captain Michael Erwin, TF 2-7's assistant S2, stated that the UAV provided "a pretty key piece of real-time intelligence. We were able to help save Soldiers' lives by determining where the enemy was before we got there, instead of spotting them with our eyes."

1st Infantry Division News,
September 2006.

US Soldiers, and the ISF. In the fall as the Coalition and the IIG slowly built up forces around Fallujah, commanders began to gather and analyze intelligence on the insurgent positions, weaponry, and intent. By November 2004 the Marine units in Fallujah had been flying a considerable number of UAVs over the city for months and had developed a deep understanding of the enemy and their defenses in Fallujah.[153] As the time for the assault phase of the operation loomed, IMINT and SIGINT became critical. Captain Natalie Friel, the Assistant S2 for Task Force 2-2 Infantry, an Army mechanized unit sent to assist the Marines in the assault, noted that there was very little HUMINT coming from the insurgent-dominated city.[154] She and other Army MI Soldiers began to rely heavily on the imagery provided by both their own UAVs and the video feeds they received from the Marine UAVs. Friel remembered that IMINT quickly located the enemy:

> Just the imagery and the UAV coverage were incredible and, for this type of fight, that was really the most important [intelligence] we could have had. Just to be able to see all the defensive positions they set up, the location of weapons on tops of roofs, seeing people set up daisy-chained IEDs or vehicles that were rigged to explode—we could see all of that through UAV feeds.[155]

While the IMINT identified enemy locations, Friel stated that SIGINT gave them details on who the enemy was and provided information that helped US forces distinguish Iraqi insurgents from foreign elements inside Fallujah.[156] Still, it was the IMINT provided by the UAVs that made a huge difference in how the assault forces operated inside Fallujah. Captain Michael Erwin, the Assistant S2 for Task Force 2-7 Cavalry, the second Army mechanized unit that joined the Marines in AL FAJR, summed up the importance of tactical IMINT in the following way:

> If you're able to work those UAVs and prepare them and have a good route for them, you can really see how they can save lives by sending real-time pictures of the battlefield to your soldiers and your commander. We were able to keep people informed about what was going on one or two kilometers ahead of them, and I think that made a difference in terms of our soldiers being prepared.[157]

Erwin added, "It wasn't just, 'Hey, I think the enemy might be here.' We were able to say, 'We know where the enemy is.'"[158]

High-Value Target Operations

Directly linked to the Coalition's intelligence operations were the operations focused on the capture or killing of the leadership of Saddam's regime who had gone into hiding. These individuals soon became known as HVTs and attracted a great amount of resources and energy from Coalition forces. Removing these figures was critical to the Coalition campaign to assure the Iraqi population that the Baathist regime was destroyed and had no chance of returning to power. It was also important to winning the support of the Kurds and the Shias, both of whom had been repressed by the Sunni Arab dominated Baath Party.

The main force behind the campaign to eliminate these men was Task Force (TF) 20, an organization manned by American Special Operations Forces. That unit, however, was empowered in many cases by the intelligence collection and analysis of the Army's divisions and brigades in Iraq. This section will briefly describe the HVT operations that quickly captured or killed several key members of the Saddam regime, including Saddam's sons Uday and Qusay. Then it will recount the major events that led to the capture of Saddam Hussein in December 2003, emphasizing the role of the 4th ID's intelligence operations.

On 11 April 2003, as the Saddam regime was beginning to implode, Brigadier General Vincent Brooks, CENTCOM's Public Affairs Officer (PAO), introduced the first set of Iraqi personality identification playing cards that had been developed by the DIA. The cards were printed by the DOD and sent to personnel in Iraq to help Soldiers identify the most-wanted

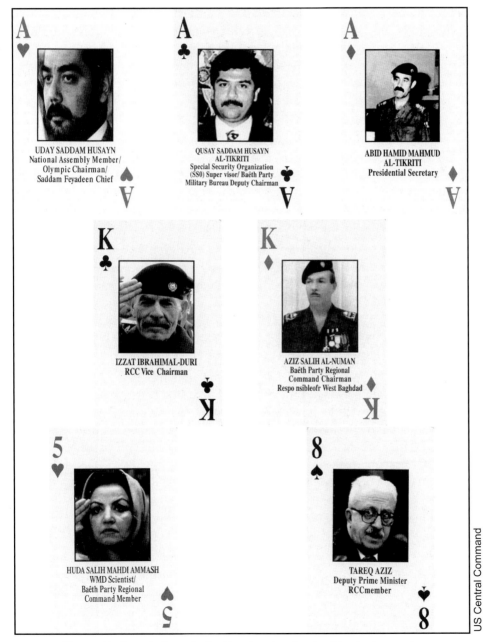

Figure 46. Sample from deck of Iraqi regime leadership playing cards.

225

members of Saddam Hussein's government. On the cards were the high-ranking Baath Party members or members of the Revolutionary Command Council.[159] The cards combined elements of wanted posters, playing cards, and trading cards. They contained the photo of the wanted person, if available, their name and any aliases they used, and their job descriptions in Saddam's regime.[160] The highest-ranking cards, starting with aces and kings, were used for the people at the top of the most-wanted list. The ace of spades was Saddam Hussein, and the aces of clubs and hearts were his two sons, Uday and Qusay.[161]

One day after CENTCOM introduced the HVT playing cards, the first target surrendered. The seven of diamonds portrayed former Iraqi Lieutenant General Amir Hamudi Hasan al-Saadi; the Iraqi science advisor and special weapons chief gave up to Coalition forces in Baghdad on 12 April 2003 after learning he was on the list.[162] The five of clubs, Barzan Ibrahim Hasan Al Tikriti, the former director of the Mukhabarat, Saddam's notorious intelligence service, was the first to be taken by force. Special Operations troops captured Al Tikriti, a half-brother and advisor to Saddam Hussein, in Baghdad on 16 April 2003.[163] The eight of spades, Tareq Aziz, Saddam's deputy prime minister, surrendered to Coalition forces on 24 April 2003.

Others remained in hiding into the summer. US forces took the ten of diamonds, Vice-President Taha Yassin Ramadan, known as Saddam's enforcer, into custody on 18 August 2003. He was accused of involvement in the occupation of Kuwait, taking part in the brutal repression of Shia Muslims in 1991, and the killing of thousands of Kurds in Halabja with poisonous gas in 1988. On 21 August 2003 Coalition forces also captured Ali Hassan Majid, known as "Chemical Ali," for his alleged role in the use of poisonous gas against the Kurds also in 1988.[164]

Saddam's sons were more difficult to locate. As Coalition forces approached Baghdad, the dictator and his sons fled to the countryside of Iraq. Staying in various hiding places, they settled in Ramadi on 11 April 2003.[165] When the building next to their safe house was bombed, Saddam and his sons fled once again and finally decided to split up to increase their chances of survival. Uday and Qusay criss-crossed western Iraq, possibly making their way to Syria.[166] On 20 July 2003, the two brothers, Qusay's 14-year-old son Mustafa, and a bodyguard were on the move again. They ended up at a relative's house in the city of Mosul.

Around 1000 on 21 July an Iraqi sheik walked into the 101st ABN's Civil-Military Operations Center (CMOC), located at the Mosul Airfield, and began giving information about Uday and Qusay's presence in the house to an MI NCO serving on a THT.[167] While there had been multiple tips about the location of the brothers in the past, the US Army National Guard Soldiers on the THT judged the sheik's story as credible. Once the THT passed this information to the 101st ABN headquarters, Lieutenant Colonel D.J. Reyes, the G2, used the AO North JIATF to coordinate a meeting between the Iraqi informant and representatives from the CIA and TF 20. The Americans listened to the story, administered a polygraph test that the sheik failed, but ultimately assessed the Iraqi's information as valid. By 2200 the 101st ABN had completed gathering information and created a concept for an operation that would capture the brothers.

At 1000 on 22 July 2003 the men of TF 20 and Soldiers from the 101st ABN surrounded the house in which Uday and Qusay were hiding. Brigadier General Frank Helmick, the 101st Assistant Division Commander for Operations (ADC-O), and Colonel Joseph Anderson, the 2d BCT commander, immediately moved to the site.[168] As Helmick recalled:

Colonel Joe Anderson . . . and I were the senior guys on the ground during that operation. Actually, Major General Petraeus was out at the Syrian border at the time when this whole thing was going down. He approved the operation the night before. We, truthfully, didn't know if those were the right guys or not. But we knew there were bad guys in there and so we had to get a lot of help from the SOF to come in and do that operation. It was a very tenuous situation.[169]

Helmick and Anderson strengthened the cordon around the area and had time to prepare for the operation. At 1000 Special Forces Soldiers knocked on the door and asked to enter the residence; they received no response. Ten minutes later, the troops entered the building and as they climbed the stairs were met by AK-47 fire. Three of the Special Forces Soldiers were wounded inside, and one of the 101st ABN Soldiers was wounded outside, so the troops withdrew and paused so the force could be substantially augmented.[170] An intense firefight ensued as the brothers and the others inside the house used grenades and assault weapons, and the American troops responded with .50-caliber machineguns and fire from two Kiowa Warrior helicopters. Around noon Soldiers attempted to re-enter the house, but again were stopped by AK-47 fire. In the early afternoon, the US forces surrounding the target added 17 tube-launched, optically-tracked, wire-guided (TOW) missiles to the fire they directed at the target.[171] Helmick had a radio conversation with Petraeus as he flew back to Mosul, and they decided to "put TOW missiles right into the window" of the building.[172]

Around 1300 Soldiers again entered the residence. They found Uday, Qusay, and a body-guard dead. But Qusay's son, Mustafa, returned fire at the Americans while hiding under a bed. After pouring more rounds into the room where Mustafa hid, US troops secured the building. By this time a considerable crowd had gathered in the area, leading Petraeus to direct CA Soldiers and engineers into the area to assess the damage and raze the half-destroyed house.[173] By 1500 Soldiers of the 101st ABN's TF *Neighborhood* went through the area surrounding the target house to identify and fix broken windows or any other damage caused by the operation. Observers wondered why Uday and Qusay were not taken alive so they could be interrogated and put on trial, but American commanders and Iraqi leaders doubted the two brothers would have allowed themselves to be captured.

Figure 47. Major General Odierno, commander of the 4th ID, discusses Operation RED DAWN and the subsequent capture of Saddam.

The killing of Saddam's sons did not defuse the growing insurgency. In fact, organized violence against the Coalition grew in the late summer and fall of 2003. Dismayed by this trend,

CENTCOM and Coalition leaders pinned their hopes on the capture of Saddam as the event that would put the final stake in an insurgent movement many of them still viewed as the dying gasp of the defeated Baathist regime. Locating Saddam as he moved in the Sunni-dominated area of north-central Iraq around his hometown of Tikrit had already become a frustrating endeavor. After separating from his sons in April 2003, Saddam had continued to run from Coalition forces.[174] His whereabouts between April and December 2003 are still unknown, but numerous sightings of him occurred in a variety of areas. Almost all of the sightings, which increased exponentially after the United States posted a $25 million reward for his capture, were false alarms.

As TF 20 collected and analyzed these leads, MI Soldiers in the 4th ID, the unit responsible for the Sunni Triangle, conducted link analysis and constructed complex diagrams that displayed in graphic form the network of individuals related to Saddam by blood, tribe, or political association.[175] According to Lieutenant Colonel Brian Reed, the Operations Officer (S3) for the 1st BCT, 4th ID, "We sort of fingered these guys through some old fashioned methods of looking at pictures and things like that. You look at all these pictures of people that appear with Saddam and you start putting names to them: 'Okay I know that guy, I know that guy. Wait a minute, I don't know this guy, but he's part of this family.' And you start putting this network together."[176] This analysis led forces to the lower-level, highly-trusted relatives, clan members, and associates who might be harboring Saddam or helping him move around the country. Using intelligence gathered from all over Iraq, two MI officers in the 1st BCT, First Lieutenant Angela Santana and Chief Warrant Officer 2 Bryan Gray, developed a database that held a core group of over 250 names, but linked over 9,000 names to that core group.[177] From that database, the 1st BCT created a diagram based on link analysis methodologies used by police departments and counterterror organizations to uncover organizational structures of crime gangs or terrorist groups. Gray described the link diagram in the following way:

> We had this huge chart, probably three foot by three foot, and we probably had about 100 to 150 people on it. We had Saddam Hussein right in the center of it and we just went from there like a tree. This was his brother, this was his cousin, this is this guy's wife, she talks to so and so, and she gave money to him. It just was a big tree, but we knew if we worked from the outside in, we could finally catch Number One.[178]

According to Colonel James Hickey, commander of the 1st BCT, 4 ID, "We built this [link diagram] together as a team effort. We maintained it in the brigade headquarters. That template got refined and developed from week to week and month to month, but it never changed in its truthfulness, and it led directly to our understanding of who had to be captured and who would lead us to Saddam."[179] Patterns started to emerge on the link diagram and US intelligence officials were able to detain and question more and more people with intelligence related to Saddam's whereabouts. American Special Operations Soldiers captured a key figure on the diagram, Muhammad Ibrahim Omar al-Musslit, on 12 December 2003 in Baghdad.[180] After a transfer to Tikrit the next day and a subsequent interrogation, al-Musslit broke down and, according to Hickey, "blurted Saddam's location."[181] According to al-Musslit, Saddam was hiding on a farm compound in one of two farmhouses near Ad Dawr, south of Tikrit.

Once the 1st BCT intelligence section identified the farm's location using satellite imagery, US forces planned and launched Operation RED DAWN to capture the dictator. Just before

Figure 48. Farmhouse on compound where Saddam Hussein was captured in December 2003.

2000 on 13 December, a convoy of more than 30 vehicles and close to 600 troops from the 1st BCT, along with members of TF 20, surrounded the Ad Dawr area. According to Reed, the 1st BCT's Operations Officer who planned RED DAWN:

> We just weren't going to have a repeat of what happened up in Mosul [when Uday and Qusay were killed]. If there was any resistance, we were going to level the place. Saddam Hussein, he had a pistol with him, that's pretty well known. And if he had done anything, if he had brandished that pistol in the face of the assault team, if there had been any gunfire on the objective, we wouldn't be dealing with a trial or anything like that. It would have been over.[182]

Prepared for the worst, the Soldiers established an inner cordon to enable SOF to kill or capture Saddam.[183] The 1st BCT also established an outer cordon to prevent any enemy reinforcement and to make sure Saddam did not escape. A screen was also established on the far side of the Tigris River to prevent the possible escape of Saddam outside of the cordon.[184] The Soldiers of TF 20, using explosive charges to enter the compound, immediately secured the two objectives—Wolverine 1 and Wolverine 2—which were the two farmhouses inside the inner cordon. The SOF Soldiers then began searching the houses. Initially, they captured the owner of the farm and his brother, but could not find Saddam. Alerted that the area contained tunnels, TF 20 had begun a thorough search of the area around the houses when one SOF Soldier noticed a carpet on the ground that looked out of place. Pulling that up, the Soldier discovered a block of Styrofoam and then the vertical crawlspace below which led to the space in which

Saddam was hiding. The Soldier was ready to toss a grenade into the hole when a disheveled head appeared.

Saddam's Hiding Place

Hole that Saddam was found hiding in

Op RED DAWN, 1st BCT, 4th ID, *Baylor Bears Brief*

Figure 49. Saddam's hiding place.

According to most sources, the man raised both hands and declared in English, "I am Saddam Hussein, I am the president of Iraq, and I am willing to negotiate."[185] Colonel Hickey remembers that although armed with a pistol, "Saddam was completely surprised when we found him and he gave up like a coward. He couldn't give up fast enough, and he should thank his lucky stars that the Soldiers that captured him were disciplined, honorable men. We could have killed him on the spot, but they were disciplined."[186] Saddam was then covered with a hood and showed no resistance when he was put on a helicopter for transport. Hickey described the operation to capture Saddam as an "effort of American Army Soldiers from various parts of our Army working together as a team."[187]

After his capture, US forces hurried Saddam off to Camp Cropper, the high-value detention center at the Baghdad Airport for examination and interrogation. Finally, on 14 December 2003, Ambassador L. Paul Bremer announced the capture of Saddam to Iraq and the world. The apprehension of the former dictator represented a major Coalition triumph as well as a victory for the efforts of the Soldiers in TF 20 and CJTF-7 that had begun aggressively conducting intelligence operations in the summer of 2003.

DOD Photo by SSGT David Bennett

Figure 50. A member of the 4th ID's 1st BCT lifts a Styrofoam lid covering the hole where former Iraqi President Saddam Hussein was discovered hiding in the village of Ad Dawr.

Saddam's capture did not end the insurgency, but it did serve as a milestone that the Iraqis and the Coalition could use to mark the true end of the Baathist regime.

Figure 51. Colonel Hickey, Commander, 1st BCT, 4th ID, with staff after capture of Saddam Hussein.

Conclusion

When the US Army entered Iraq in May 2003, its intelligence operations were the domain of a relatively small group of well-trained officers and Soldiers who employed a system based on sophisticated signals and imagery technology to locate and analyze a conventional enemy. With the shift to full spectrum operations in May 2003, all American Soldiers entered a new world, complete with a different language and an incomprehensible set of rules and expectations. Unprepared for this new situation, they had limited means to help them make sense of what they faced, especially when it came to the elusive insurgent enemy. Out of the need to understand their environments, most of the Army's tactical units in Iraq began to conduct sophisticated intelligence missions on a scale that was unprecedented. While the MI Corps may not have been amenable to this development at the outset of the new campaign, MI Soldiers quickly realized they were too few to make a significant impact in understanding the environment and the emerging enemy. Once this became clear, the MI community began developing policy and training to help tactical units sharpen their abilities to collect and analyze intelligence. The Army's introduction of the "Every Soldier is a Sensor" program, a 2004 training initiative designed to instill basic MI skills in all Soldiers, was perhaps the most direct result of recognition of these critical changes.

This discussion has shown how, from the commander of CJTF-7 down to the tactical-level, Soldiers began to collect and use HUMINT as the primary means of making sense of Iraq. This shift to a dependency on HUMINT was almost as dramatic and surprising as the transition from a top-down intelligence system to one that gathered intelligence at the tactical level and slowly pushed it up to higher echelons. No one expected the Army's relatively small set of HUMINT assets to become so important when Coalition forces crossed into Iraq in March 2003. Additionally, no infantryman, tanker, or artilleryman expected to be involved with complex intelligence networks when they deployed to Iraq.

These transitions were difficult, and as the demand for more and better information increased in mid-2003, the pressure led a few to put their values aside and mistreat Iraqis. Most Soldiers took on the role of intelligence collector and analyst with great success however. Their experiences in 2003 and 2004 serve to highlight the enduring importance of low-level HUMINT in full spectrum operations, especially those that face complex insurgencies. In campaigns like OIF, intelligence serves as much more than an enabler of military operations. It often becomes the objective for those operations.

Notes

1. "Brigadier General Dempsey Briefs on 1st Armored Division Operations in Iraq," *DefenseLink,* 20 November 2003, http://www.defenselink.mil/transcripts/2003/tr20031120-0893.html (accessed 21 July 2006).

2. "Dempsey Briefs on 1st Armored Division."

3. FM 34-1, *Intelligence and Electronic Warfare* (Washington, DC, 1994), 4–1.

4. FM 34-1, 4–1.

5. Major General Barbara Fast, interview by Contemporary Operations Study Team, Fort Leavenworth, KS, 27 March 2006, 3.

6. Fast, interview, 27 March 2006, 3.

7. Lieutenant General Ricardo Sanchez, interview by Contemporary Operations Study Team, Fort Leavenworth, KS, 14 August 2006, 7–8.

8. Sanchez, interview, 14 August 2006, 8.

9. Sanchez, interview, 14 August 2006, 8.

10. Colonel D.J. Reyes, e-mail interview by Contemporary Operations Study Team, Fort Leavenworth, KS, 17 January 2007, 4.

11. Sanchez, interview, 14 August 2006, 8.

12. Fast, interview, 27 March 2006, 3.

13. Sanchez, interview, 21 August 2006, 11–12.

14. Fast, interview, 27 March 2006, 18.

15. Fast, interview, 27 March 2006, 10.

16. Fast, interview, 27 March 2006, 10.

17. Fast, interview, 27 March 2006, 19.

18. Fast, interview, 27 March 2006, 13, 16.

19. Eliot Cohen et al., "Principles, Imperatives, and Paradoxes of Counterinsurgency," *Military Review,* March–April 2006, 50.

20. 1-24 Infantry (SBCT), *Adapting in Combat: Reorganizing to Fight a Counter-insurgency* Briefing, slide 3.

21. Colonel Stephen R. Lanza et al., "Red Team Goes Maneuver: 1st Cav Div Arty as a Maneuver BCT," *Field Artillery,* May–June 2005, 13.

22. Lanza et al., 13.

23. Colonel D.J. Reyes, 101st Airborne Division, *JIATF Mission Statement* Slide.

24. Lieutenant Colonel Brian McKiernan, interview by Contemporary Operations Study Team, Fort Leavenworth, KS, 29 April 2006, 11.

25. McKiernan, interview, 29 April 2006, 11.

26. McKiernan, interview, 29 April 2006, 11.

27. 173d Airborne Brigade, *After Action Review* Briefing, 22 January 2004, slide 8.

28. 173d ABN Bde, *AAR,* slide 7.

29. 1-24 Inf (SBCT), *Adapting in Combat,* slide 3.

30. 1-24 Inf (SBCT), *Adapting in Combat,* slide 6.

31. 1-24 Inf (SBCT), *Adapting in Combat,* slide 8.

32. 1-24 Inf (SBCT), *Adapting in Combat,* slide 9.

33. Fast, interview, 27 March 2006, 12.

34. Colonel Ralph Baker, interview by Contemporary Operations Study Team, Fort Leavenworth, KS, 1 November 2005, 7.

35. Baker, interview, 1 November 2005, 7.

36. Fast, interview, 27 March 2006, 9.

37. 1st Armored Division, *The 636 Insurgent Cell: The Gift that Keeps on Giving* Briefing, slide 9.

38. 1st AD, *636 Insurgent Cell*, slide 17.

39. 1st AD, *636 Insurgent Cell*, slide 26.

40. 1st AD, *636 Insurgent Cell*, slide 50.

41. LTC [name redacted], CONUS Team, Department of the Army Inspector General, *Memorandum for Chief, Inspections Division. SUBJECT: 4th Infantry Division Detainee Operations Assessment Trip Report*, no date. (Memorandum based on interviews conducted by CONUS Team between 5–8 April 2004.), 395, http://action.aclu.org/torturefoia/released/091505/15937.pdf (accessed 11 January 2006).

42. 519th MI Battalion, 525th MI Brigade, *Operation Iraqi Freedom: Lessons Learned*, 29 March 2004, 9.

43. 519th MI Bn, 525th MI Bde, *OIF: Lessons Learned*, 9.

44. McKiernan, interview, 29 April 2006, 13.

45. McKiernan, interview, 29 April 2006, 13.

46. FM 3-19.40, *Military Police Internment/Resettlement Operations* (Washington, DC, 2001), chapter 1.

47. Colonel Marc Warren, Statement to US Army Preliminary Screening Inquiry, 29 November 2004, 6. (Used with permission of Colonel Warren.)

48. Warren, Statement to US Army Preliminary Screening Inquiry, 29 November 2004, 6.

49. Colonel Marc Warren, e-mail correspondence with author, 5 March 2007. The specific contents of these FRAGOs remain classified as of this writing.

50. Colonel Marc Warren, interview by Contemporary Operations Study Team, Fort Leavenworth, KS, 15 March 2007, 11.

51. Lieutenant General Raymond Odierno, interview by Contemporary Operations Study Team, Fort Leavenworth, KS, 14 December 2005, 13–14.

52. Brigadier General Michael Tucker, interview by Contemporary Operations Study Team, Fort Leavenworth, KS, 20 January 2006, 8.

53. 2d Brigade, 2d Infantry Division, *After Action Review: Operation Iraqi Freedom 04–06* Briefing, 5 December 2005, slide 240.

54. Lieutenant General Anthony R. Jones, *AR 15-6 Investigation of the Abu Ghraib Prison and the 205th Military Intelligence Brigade*, 9.

55. Major General Donald Ryder, *Assessment of Corrections and Detention Operations in Iraq*, 6 November 2003, 4, 8.

56. Major General John Batiste, interview by Contemporary Operations Study Team, Fort Leavenworth, KS, 20 April 2006, 12.

57. "Stryker Brigade Combat Team 1, 3d Brigade, 2d Infantry: Operations in Mosul, Iraq," *Initial Impressions Report* (Fort Leavenworth, KS: Center for Army Lessons Learned, 21 December 2004), 54.

58. Department of the Army, The Inspector General, *Detainee Operations Inspection*, 21 July 2004, 33.

59. LTC [name redacted], CONUS Team, DA IG, *Memorandum. SUBJECT: 4th ID Detainee Operations Assessment Trip Report*, 394.

60. LTC [name redacted], CONUS Team, DA IG, *Memorandum, SUBJECT: 4th ID Detainee Operations Assessment Trip Report*, 394.

61. LTC [name redacted], CONUS Team, DA IG, *Memorandum, SUBJECT: 4th ID Detainee Operations Assessment Trip Report*, 380–381.

62. This section on interrogation operations at Abu Ghraib is intended as a summary of the key events and decisions that surround the abuses at the prison. Because of the complexity of the issues involved, the authors of this study encourage all readers to look into the key primary sources, which are available to the public, to gain a deeper understanding of the origins and characteristics of operations at the prison. Those sources, most importantly the AR 15-6 investigations into the 800th MP Brigade and the 205th MI Brigade, are identified in the endnotes below.

63. *The Taguba Report* and the AR 15-6 Investigations led by Lieutenant General Anthony Jones and Major General George Fay, which contain the details, recount the story of the abuses in a complete fashion and are available to the public. See Major General Antonio M. Taguba, *Article 15-6 Investigation of the 800th Military Police Brigade (The Taguba Report);* IG, *Detainee Operations Inspection,* 21 July 2004. See also Jones, *AR 15-6 Investigation;* and Major General George Fay, *AR 15-6 Investigation of the Abu Ghraib Prison and 205th Military Intelligence Brigade.*

64. Fay, *AR 15-6 Investigation,* 41. The AR 15-6 asserted that Colonel Pappas had command authority over the JIDC. See page 31 of Fay report.

65. Fay, *AR 15-6 Investigation,* 42.

66. Fay, *AR 15-6 Investigation,* 39.

67. The officer directing the use of stress positions and sleep adjustment claimed in a sworn statement that while conducting interrogations in Afghanistan in 2002, these techniques received approval from the Coalition military headquarters on a case-by-case basis. See "Sworn Statement of CPT [redacted], 519th MI BN, Annex to Major General George Fay, *AR 15-6 Investigation of the Abu Ghraib Prison and the 205th Military Intelligence Brigade,* http://www.aclu.org/torturefoia/released/030905/DOD565_615.pdf (accessed 16 January 2007), DOD 000602 and DOD 000603.

68. Taguba, Annex 46, "Testimony of Colonel Thomas Pappas, Commander, 205th MI Brigade," to *The Taguba Report,* 9 February 2004, 1, http://www.aclu.org/torturefoia/released/a46.pdf (accessed 16 January 2007).

69. Fay, *AR 15-6 Investigation,* 39.

70. IG, *Detainee Operations Inspection,* 21 July 2004, 45.

71. Fay, *AR 15-6 Investigation,* 76.

72. For use of guidance from other campaigns, see "Sworn Statement of CPT [redacted], 519th MI BN, Annex to Fay, *AR 15-6 Investigation,* http://www.aclu.org/torturefoia/released/030905/DOD565_615.pdf (accessed 16 January 2007), DOD 000602 and DOD 000603.

73. Fay, *AR 15-6 Investigation,* 59.

74. Taguba, Annex 20, "The Miller Report" to *The Taguba Report,* 2.

75. Taguba, Annex 20, "The Miller Report" to *The Taguba Report,* 6.

76. Taguba, Annex 20, "The Miller Report" to *The Taguba Report,* 6.

77. Fay, *AR 15-6 Investigation,* 18.

78. US Congress, Joint Resolution, 107th Cong., 1st sess. (14 September 2001): SJ23ES. It stated: "That the President is authorized to use all necessary and appropriate force against those nations, organizations, or persons he determines planned, authorized, committed, or aided the terrorist attacks that occurred on September 11, 2001, or harbored such organizations or persons, to prevent any future acts of international terrorism against the United States by such nations, organizations or persons."

79. Karen J. Greenberg and Joshua L. Dratel, eds., *The Torture Papers: The Road to Abu Ghraib* (Cambridge, MA: Cambridge University Press, 2005), xxi.

80. President George W. Bush, *Memorandum, Subject: Humane Treatment of al-Qaeda and Taliban Detainees,* 7 February 2002, http://www.pegc.us/archive/White_House/bush_memo_20020207_ed.pdf (accessed 26 October 2006).

81. Office of the Assistant Attorney General, Memorandum for Alberto R. Gonzales, Counsel to the President, Re: *Standards of Conduct for Interrogation under 18 U.S.C. 2340-2340A,* 1 August 2002. The memo reads in part: "We [the authors] conclude below that Section 2340A proscribes acts inflicting, and that are specifically intended to inflict, severe pain or suffering, whether mental or physical. Those acts must be of an extreme nature to rise to the level of torture within the meaning of Section 2340A and the Convention. We further conclude that certain acts may be cruel, inhuman, or degrading, but still not produce pain and suffering of the requisite intensity to fall within Section 2340A's proscription against torture. We conclude by examining possible defenses that would negate any claim that certain interrogation methods violated the statute."

82. Vice Admiral Albert T. Church, Unclassified Executive Summary, "The Church Report," *DefenseLink,* February 2005, http://www.defenselink.mil/news/Mar2005/d20050310exe.pdf (accessed 14 July 2005), 4.

83. Church, "The Church Report," 4.

84. This legal guidance, issued in March 2003 by the Office of Legal Counsel (OLC) in the US Department of Justice remains classified as of this writing. However, Jack Goldsmith, the head of the OLC in late 2003 and 2004, acknowledged its existence and its authority in relation to the DOD Working Group. Jack Goldsmith, *The Terror Presidency: Law and Judgment Inside the Bush Administration* (New York, NY: W.W. Norton & Company, 2007), 143.

85. Church, "The Church Report," 5.

86. Church, "The Church Report," 5.

87. Secretary of Defense, Memorandum for the Commander, US Southern Command, Subject: Counter-Resistance Techniques in the War on Terrorism, 16 April 2003, http://www.gwu.edu/~nsarchiv/NSAEBB/NSAEBB127/03.04.16.pdf (accessed 17 July 2006), 1.

88. Secretary of Defense, Memorandum, Subject: Counter-Resistance Techniques, 5.

89. Secretary of Defense, Memorandum, Subject: Counter-Resistance Techniques, 5.

90. Secretary of Defense, Memorandum, Subject: Counter-Resistance Techniques, 1.

91. Fay, *AR 15-6 Investigation,* 24.

92. Combined Joint Task Force–7, *CJTF-7 Interrogation and Counter-Resistance Policy*, 14 September 2003, 1, http://www.aclu.org/FilesPDFs/september%20sanchez%20memo.pdf (accessed 2 March 2007).

93. *CJTF-7 Interrogation and Counter-Resistance Policy*, 14 September 2003, 1.

94. *CJTF-7 Interrogation and Counter-Resistance Policy*, 14 September 2003, 1.

95. The sources are unclear about the origins of these added techniques. The Fay–Jones Report suggests that A Company, 519th MI BN, recommended the techniques. Fay, *AR 15-6 Investigation,* 25. However, the individual testimonies of an officer in A Company, 519th MI BN, and the Staff Judge Advocate assigned to the 205th MI Brigade present a more complex staffing process. See "Sworn Statement of CPT [redacted], 519th MI BN, Annex to Fay, *AR 15-6 Investigation,* http://www.aclu.org/torturefoia/released/030905/DOD565_615.pdf (accessed 16 January 2007), DOD 000603 and DOD 000604. See also Statement of person in 1st Armored Division Office of the Staff Judge Advocate, who was attached to 205th MI Brigade. Annex to Fay, *AR 15-6 Investigation,* http://www.aclu.org/torture-foia/released/030905/DOD565_615.pdf (accessed 16 January 2007), DOD 000848. Further clarification about additional recommended techniques: the Secretary of Defense's 16 April 2003 did approve sleep adjustment as a technique, but defined it as the reversal of sleep schedules, not the reduction of a detainee's sleep.

96. Fay, *AR 15-6 Investigation,* 25.

97. Sanchez, interview, 25 August 2006, 5.

98. *CJTF-7 Interrogation and Counter-Resistance Policy*, 14 September 2003, 1.

99. Warren, interview, 15 March 2007, 13.

100. Warren, interview, 15 March 2007, 13.

101. The 12 techniques removed were the presence of military working dogs; sleep management; sleep adjustment; yelling, loud music, and light control; stress positions; deception; isolation; false flag; environmental manipulation; dietary manipulation; change of scenery up; and change of scenery down. The General Safeguards section of the 12 October 2003 ICRP did allude to the possibility that military working dogs might be approved for security purposes during interrogations, but that they were to be muzzled and under handler's control at all times.

102. Taguba, Annex 94, "Headquarters, Combined Joint Task Force Seven, CJTF-7 Interrogation and Counter-resistance Policy" to *The Taguba Report*, 1.

103. Sanchez, interview, 25 August 2006, 5.

104. Fay, *AR 15-6 Investigation,* 28.

105. "Sworn Statement of CPT [redacted], 519th MI BN, Annex to Fay, *AR 15-6 Investigation,* http://www.aclu.org/torturefoia/released/030905/DOD565_615.pdf (accessed 16 January 2007), DOD 000603 and DOD 000604.

106. "Sworn Statement of CPT [redacted], 519th MI BN, Annex to Fay, *AR 15-6 Investigation,* http://www.aclu.org/torturefoia/released/030905/DOD565_615.pdf (accessed 16 January 2007), DOD 000603 and DOD 000604.

107. Fay, *AR 15-6 Investigation,* 28.

108. Sanchez, interview, 25 August 2006, 5.

109. Sanchez, interview, 25 August 2006, 5.

110. Fay, *AR 15-6 Investigation,* 5.

111. Fay, *AR 15-6 Investigation,* 22.

112. Fay, *AR 15-6 Investigation,* 92; Sanchez, interview, 25 August 2006, 6.

113. Major General Barbara Fast, comments in 6 March 2007 e-mail to author, 4.

114. Taguba, Annex 53, "Testimony of LTC Steve Jordan, Director, Joint Interrogation and Debriefing Center," to *The Taguba Report,* 21 February 2004, 2–5, http://www.aclu.org/torturefoia/released/a53.pdf (accessed 17 January 2007).

115. Fay, *AR 15-6 Investigation,* 43.

116. Taguba, Annex 53, "Testimony of LTC Steve Jordan" to *The Taguba Report,* 21 February 2004, 107.

117. Fay, *AR 15-6 Investigation,* 46.

118. Fay, *AR 15-6 Investigation,* 96–109.

119. Fay, *AR 15-6 Investigation,* 96–99.

120. Fay, *AR 15-6 Investigation,* 91. This report documented Colonel Pappas' use of UCMJ (Field Grade Article 15) to discipline three Soldiers who had been suspected of sexually assaulting a female detainee on 7 October 2003. Before deciding to use UCMJ, Pappas had ordered an Army CID investigation which ended inconclusively. The 205th MI commander also removed them from interrogation operations. See page 72 of the Fay Report.

121. Fay, *AR 15-6 Investigation,* 92; Sanchez, interview, 25 August 2006, 16.

122. Fay, *AR 15-6 Investigation,* 92; Sanchez, interview, 25 August 2006, 6.

123. Fay, *AR 15-6 Investigation,* 16.

124. Jones, *AR 15-6 Investigation,* 16–17.

125. Fay, *AR 15-6 Investigation,* 119.

126. IG, *Detainee Operations Inspection,* 21 July 2004, 21.

127. Kathleen T. Rhem, "Commanders in Iraq ordered Humane Treatment of Detainees," *DefenseLink,* 20 May 2004, http://defenselink.mil/news/May2004/n05202004_200405206.html (accessed 25 October 2006).

128. Vice Admiral A.T. Church III, *Review of Department of Defense Detention Operations and Detainee Interrogation Techniques (The Church Report),* 7 March 2005, 8. As of this writing, the details of the May 2004 Interrogation Policy remain classified.

129. Church, *Review of Department of Defense Detention Operations,* 8.

130. Fast, interview, 27 March 2006, 4.

131. 2d Bde, 2d ID, *AAR: OIF 04-06,* 5 December 2005, slide 249.

132. "Stryker Brigade Combat Team 1, 3d Brigade, 2d Infantry: Operations in Mosul, Iraq," 86.

133. Sergeant Major Stephen Kammerdiener, interview by Contemporary Operations Study Team, Fort Leavenworth, KS, 11 April 2006, 13.

134. Fast, interview, 27 March 2006, 4.

135. Major Kenneth Cary, interview by Contemporary Operations Study Team, Fort Leavenworth, KS, 7 December 2005, 9.

136. Sanchez, interview, 25 August 2006, 3.

137. 2d Bde, 2d ID, *AAR: OIF 04–06,* slide 112.

138. 2d Bde, 2d ID, *AAR: OIF 04–06,* slide 113.

139. Sanchez, interview, 25 August 2006, 3.

140. Sanchez, interview, 25 August 2006, 3.

141. 2d Bde, 2d ID, *AAR: OIF 04–06,* slide 301.

142. 2d Bde, 2d ID, *AAR: OIF 04–06,* slide 301.

143. Sanchez, interview, 25 August 2006, 3.

144. Colonel J. Mike Murray, interview by Contemporary Operations Study Team, Fort Leavenworth, KS, 8 December 2005, 14.

145. 2d Bde, 2d ID, *AAR: OIF 04–06,* slide 262.

146. Headquarters, 2d Brigade, 2d Infantry Division, Memorandum for Record, SUBJECT: OIF 04–06 After Action Review for 2d BCT, 2d ID, 5 December 2005, slide 262.

147. Colonel D.J. Reyes, e-mail interview, 17 January 2007, 2.

148. Charles H. Briscoe et al., *All Roads Lead to Baghdad: Army Special Operations in Iraq* (Fort Bragg, NC: US Army Special Operations Command History Office, 2006), 427.

149. Colonel D.J. Reyes, *OBJ SNAKE, 12 JUN 03,* slide, in Briscoe et al., *All Roads Lead to Baghdad,* the authors state that US forces killed 70 enemy at the terrorist camp on 12 June 2003. See page 434.

150. Colonel David Teeples, interview by Contemporary Operations Study Team, Fort Leavenworth, KS, 4 November, 8–9.

151. Headquarters, 2d Brigade Combat Team, *Memorandum, Subject: 2d Brigade Combat Team's Service in Operation Iraqi Freedom.* 25 August 2004, 6.

152. 1st Infantry Division, *Operation Iraqi Freedom–Samarra: An Iraqi Success* Briefing, 4 October 2004, slide 23.

153. Captain Michael S. Erwin, interview by Operational Leadership Experiences Project Team, Combat Studies Institute, Fort Leavenworth, KS, 19 April 2006, 5.

154. Captain Natalie Friel, interview by Operational Leadership Experiences Project Team, Combat Studies Institute, Fort Leavenworth, KS, 28 July 2006, 6.

155. Friel, interview, 28 July 2006, 6.

156. Friel, interview, 28 July 2006, 6.

157. Erwin, interview, 19 April 2006, 9.

158. Erwin, interview, 19 April 2006, 9

159. "About Iraqi 55 Most Wanted Regime Leader Cards," *Iraq's 55 Most Wanted Playing Cards,* http://www.streetgangs.com/iraq/ (accessed 20 March 2006); "U.S. Distributes Most-Wanted List," *Fox News,* 11 April 2003, http://www.foxnews.com/story/0,2933,83894,00.html (accessed 20 March 2006).

160. Tom Zucco, "Troops Deal an Old Tool," *St. Petersburg Times,* 12 April 2003, http://www.sptimes.com/2003/04/12/news_pf/Worldandnation/Troops_dealt_an_old_t.shtml (accessed 20 March 2006).

161. Zucco.

162. "Iraq's Most Wanted," *BBC News,* 11 November 2005, http://news.bbc.co.uk/go/pr/fr/-/2/hi/middle_east/2939125.stm (accessed 20 March 2006); "Another Saddam Relative Nabbed," *CBS News,* 14 April 2003, http://www.cbsnews.com/stories/2003/04/18/iraq/main549930.shtml (accessed 22 March 2006).

163. "Iraq's Most Wanted"; "Another Saddam Relative Nabbed."

164. "Iraq's Most Wanted."

165. Michael R. Gordon and General Bernard E. Trainor, *Cobra II: The Inside Story of the Invasion and Occupation of Iraq* (New York: Pantheon Books, 2006), 435.

166. Gordon and Trainor, 435.

167. Reyes, e-mail interview, 17 January 2007, 2–3; Lieutenant General David H. Petraeus, interview by Contemporary Operations Study Team, Fort Leavenworth, KS, 17 February 2006, 14.

168. Petraeus, interview, 18 March 2006, 3.

169. Brigadier General Frank Helmick, interview by Contemporary Operations Study Team, Fort Leavenworth, KS, 15 February 2006, 6.

170. Petraeus, interview, 17 February 2006.

171. Petraeus, interview, 17 February 2006, 15.

172. Petraeus, interview, 18 March 2006, 14.

173. Petraeus, interview, 18 March 2006, 3.

174. Gordon and Trainor, 435.

175. Robert O. Babcock, *Operation Iraqi Freedom I: A Year in the Sunni Triangle* (Tuscaloosa, AL: St. John's Press, 2005), 185.

176. Lieutenant Colonel Brian Reed, interview by Operational Leadership Experiences Project Team, Combat Studies Institute, Fort Leavenworth, KS, 26 October 2005, 12–13.

177. Babcock, 185–86.

178. Chief Warrant Officer Bryan Gray, interview by Operational Leadership Experiences Project Team, Combat Studies Institute, Fort Leavenworth, KS, 17 November 2005, 10.

179. Colonel James Hickey, interview by Contemporary Operations Study Team, Fort Leavenworth, KS, 15 February 2006, 6.

180. Babcock, 186, 188.

181. Babcock, 186, 188

182. Reed, interview, 26 October 2005, 14.

183. 1st Brigade Combat Team, 4th Infantry Division, "Operation RED DAWN, Baylor Bears Brief," slides 6 and 7.

184. 1st BCT, 4th ID, "Operation RED DAWN," slides 6 and 7.

185. Babcock, 192.

186. Hickey, interview, 15 February 2006, 11.

187. Hickey, interview, 15 February 2006, 10.

Chapter 6

Detainee Operations

As Coalition military forces began to conduct postconflict operations in the summer of 2003, they gradually became aware of the low-level insurgency coalescing around them. In reaction, many units began conducting operations designed to remove threats by detaining Iraqis suspected of involvement in insurgent activity or having information about the insurgent network. In some cases in this early period, Coalition forces like the 4th Infantry Division (4th ID) executed large cordon and searches, like Operation PENINSULA STRIKE in June 2003, that focused on breaking up concentrations of ex-Baathist fighters and detaining members of that enemy force. Operation PENINSULA STRIKE resulted in the detention of 400 Iraqis, several of which were high-level Baathist military officials. Many of these Iraqis, and others detained in subsequent operations, were sent to hastily-organized centralized holding facilities. Few within the Coalition forces had any practical experience with detainee operations on this scale. The Coalition had established Combined Joint Task Force–7 (CJTF-7), its military headquarters, without giving it comprehensive and clearly defined guidance on how to conduct these operations, apart from that found in United States (US) joint doctrine and the guidelines issued by Combined Forces Land Component Command (CFLCC) and V Corps in their operations and fragmentary orders in March and April 2003.[1] To give subordinate units guidelines for these missions, Lieutenant General Ricardo Sanchez and his staff began developing their own rules and policies in the summer of 2003. While the initial lack of guidance was problematic, more debilitating was that as detention requirements increased throughout 2003, they overwhelmed the US Army Military Police (MP) units in Iraq—the forces designated by Army doctrine to conduct detainee operations.

Despite the lack of preparation and capacity for large-scale detentions, Coalition forces could not avoid interning Iraqis. While CJTF-7 largely curtailed major cordon and search operations like PENINSULA STRIKE after the summer of 2003, the nature of the new full spectrum campaign in Iraq mandated that Army units at the tactical level would become involved in detainee operations. Most campaigns that focused on defeating insurgencies in the past have included the apprehension of suspected insurgents, their sympathizers, and criminals who took advantage of the unstable security environment that accompanied insurgencies. Detention often disrupted insurgent networks and, in many cases, provided intelligence to the counterinsurgent force. However, in counterinsurgency operations, gaining and maintaining the population's political support for the host nation government and its programs serves as the paramount principle that guides operations. If the counterinsurgent's detainee operations disaffect the civilian population, induce civilians to aid the insurgents, or drive civilians to take up arms on their behalf, then those operations will likely prove counterproductive in the final assessment. Balancing the need to detain Iraqis with the larger requirement of winning and maintaining the support of the population was a delicate task that would vex Coalition forces throughout 2003.

Beginning in the summer of 2003, the increasing demand for actionable intelligence magnified the importance of detainee operations. With violence against Coalition troops escalating and relatively little information arriving from traditional military intelligence collection and analysis methods, pressure built within CJTF-7, US Central Command (CENTCOM), and the Department of Defense (DOD) to find new means of gathering the type of information that would lead to effective operations against the insurgent forces. On the ground, this demand fell on the relatively small number of trained military interrogators who had the task of drawing actionable intelligence from a detainee population that was swelling on a daily basis and overcoming the Coalition's MP assets. But when the demand for actionable intelligence could not be met by detainee operations conducted along doctrinal lines by MP and Military Intelligence (MI) units, maneuver forces such as infantry, armor, and artillery units began conducting their own detainee and interrogation operations. In doing this, unit commanders were making innovations that allowed them to unravel and engage the growing insurgent networks in their areas of responsibility (AORs). But the adoption of the detention mission also meant that by the fall of 2003, a large number of Soldiers had become involved in capturing, screening, and detaining suspected insurgents without the benefits of training or experience in these operations.

This chapter examines the challenges in policy and practice faced by US forces attempting to deal with detainee operations in the larger context of the full spectrum campaign in Iraq. While recognizing that detainee operations are in most cases linked closely with interrogation operations, they are by doctrine and regulation separate operations and conducted by different types of units—MP Soldiers responsible for the former, MI Soldiers for the latter. This discussion will look specifically at how the detainee mission evolved and how units at both the operational and tactical levels innovated in the face of that challenge.

US Army Detainee Operations in Iraq: Planning, Invasion, and the Transition to the New Campaign

When planners at CENTCOM and CFLCC began thinking about designing a campaign aimed at the toppling of the Saddam regime, they considered requirements for Coalition forces to deal with enemy prisoners of war (EPWs), but did so using previous conventional operations like DESERT STORM as their templates. Because of this assumption, planning for EPW operations in Operation IRAQI FREEDOM (OIF) focused on accommodating large numbers of surrendering Iraqi soldiers who would be classified as EPWs. Looking back, Major General Barbara Fast, who was serving as the senior intelligence officer (J2) on the staff of US European Command (EUCOM) when OIF began and became CJTF-7's senior intelligence staff officer (CJ2) in the summer of 2003, described how the planners saw this aspect of the campaign: "Those who made the predictions were betting on units surrendering in place so there wasn't as much attention paid to really having a plan as there should have been. . . . We were, as a force, much more prepared for prisoners of war and the idea that at the end of major hostilities, in accordance with the Geneva Conventions . . . prisoners are released."[2]

Driven by these assumptions, in the early days of the invasion Coalition forces made plans for the use of two facilities, one at Camp Bucca in southern Iraq near the city of Umm Qasr and the second at Camp Cropper in the Baghdad International Airport complex.[3] The success of the initial invasion and the corresponding belief by US Soldiers that a rapid redeployment was in the future also significantly affected the early stages of detainee operations. In May 2003 Soldiers of the 800th MP Brigade, a US Army Reserve (USAR) unit that was one of the key CFLCC units designated to deal with EPWs, held only 600 prisoners. By organization and doctrine the brigade could operate as many as 12 EPW facilities, and plans called for this unit and others that held EPWs to transition the Iraqis from Coalition control to Iraqi authorities soon after the cessation of hostilities. However, because the Coalition did not empower a new Iraqi political authority in the wake of the toppling of the Saddam regime, this transition did not happen. Exacerbating the problems created by this situation was that some of the MP units originally slated in the CENTCOM plan to deploy to Iraq remained at home when the regime collapsed in April 2003. The 800th MP Brigade remained the Coalition's main asset to deal with detainees, and as the insurgency increased in magnitude that summer, the large numbers of detainees brought under US control overwhelmed the brigade.[4] Simply put, no one in the Coalition had foreseen these developments. Fast stated, "We stopped having prisoners of war when the [1 May 2003] declaration of the cessation of hostilities occurred. Everything after that constituted a civilian internee or a criminal." She added that after May, "We had to put things into place from scratch."[5]

Figure 52. Sergeant John-Paul Kilanski, 822d MP Company, does his best to deal with Iraqi civilians outside the Reserve-run EPW internment facility near Umm Qasr, Iraq.

Lieutenant General Sanchez, the CJTF-7 commander, and his staff began work on establishing a new system of detainee procedures and facilities. Beginning in June and continuing through the fall of 2003, CJTF-7 issued a series of fragmentary orders (FRAGOs) and policy statements, and held a number of detention summits, all focused on the establishment and enforcement of rules and procedures for Coalition detainee operations. Early in this process, however, Sanchez realized that he and his command faced one overwhelming challenge in the arena of detainee operations: MP resources available in Iraq were far too few to handle the growing set of detainee tasks. Although he had tactical control of the 800th MP Brigade, that unit belonged to CFLCC and had multiple missions across Iraq. In fact, the 800th MP Brigade's single largest responsibility had nothing to do with the escalating insurgency, but instead dealt with the internment of the Mujahedin-e Khalq (MEK), a military force of approximately 4,000 well-trained and well-equipped Iranians who opposed the government in Tehran. Supported by the Saddam regime because of its hostility to the Iranian Government, by 2003 the MEK had become an elite element in the Iraqi Army and had fought against Coalition forces in March and April of that year. After capitulating to Special Operations Soldiers of the Joint Special Operations Task Force–North (JSOTF-North), the MEK leaders agreed to move to Camp Ashraf, a large internment facility 60 miles northeast of Baghdad. The 530th MP Battalion, one of the units in the 800th MP Brigade that had experience with internment of EPWs and civilian internees, was charged with the mission of detaining the Iranian soldiers for the next year.

The variety and scale of the military police mission across the country weakened the 800th MP Brigade's ability to focus on detainee operations.[6] In addition to being overstretched, only a portion of the 800th MP Brigade's Soldiers had trained to conduct detainee operations. The majority of the Soldiers in the brigade had trained to execute other MP missions such as law and order and securing lines of communication. Brigadier General Janis L. Karpinski, commander of the 800th MP Brigade, claimed her chain of command in CFLCC understood the brigade had neither the assets nor the training for the detainee confinement mission in Iraq.[7] Additionally, Sanchez noted that he and his staff realized in mid-2003 that "there is no MP unit in the country, and probably within the Army, that has the experience or that has ever been involved with this level of detainee operations."[8] Still, the experience and training of the 800th MP Brigade made them the unit best prepared for the detainee mission.

While the CJTF-7 staff attempted to assist the 800th MP Brigade by finding resources, establishing facilities, and creating processes and procedures, the number of detainees and the overall scale of the detainee problem mounted. Sanchez recognized this, stating:

> In the June/July timeframe it becomes very clear that what we have is a burgeoning number of detainees that is growing exponentially. The problem manifests itself across the entire command. A central collection point [Baghdad Central Confinement Facility] is established and we begin to move the detainees from our cordon and search operations to Baghdad. The divisions are trying to move the detainees out of their sectors as quickly as possible as the numbers continue to grow. This creates major challenges with handling procedures at all levels and strains the facilities.[9]

With the detainee population growing and MP assets quickly overwhelmed, tactical units began playing a much larger role in detainee operations. Although this was not how Army doctrine dictated the handling of detainees, there was little choice on the ground. Combat arms units in the US Army did not have the mission of detaining and holding prisoners for any length of time. Neither did they have authority or training to conduct interrogations. Certainly, none of the planners of OIF expected tactical units to be heavily involved in detainee operations. What they did assume is that each brigade would maintain a collection point where subordinate units would bring in EPWs and detainees and drop them off for a short time, not to exceed 72 hours. Next, the detainees would be moved "up the chain" to a division collection point, and remain there for no longer than 96 hours before being taken to their final destination—a semipermanent detention facility staffed by qualified MP and MI personnel. The timeframe for moving prisoners out of the areas where combat actions were ongoing presumed that detainees' continued presence in those areas represented a burden to commanders and their Soldiers. The combat unit's primary mission was to close with and destroy or capture the enemy. The Soldiers in these units traditionally viewed detainee matters as a distraction from the mission.

In Iraq in the summer of 2003, however, detainee operations became a critical mission for almost every tactical unit. As the previous chapter noted, the need for actionable intelligence at the tactical level led companies, battalions, and brigades to create tactics, techniques, and procedures (TTPs) that secured detainees and established facilities for questioning and interrogations. An early example of this type of improvisation was found in an area near the town of Bayji in the Sunni Triangle where the 1st Battalion, 508th Infantry (1-508th IN), a unit belonging to the 173d Airborne Brigade (173d ABN), created a new concept called the "hasty detention facility." Lieutenant Colonel Harry Tunnell IV, the battalion commander, described the origins of the idea:

> Whenever we conducted raids or operated with extended lines of communication, we needed the means to secure and interrogate captured and detained personnel for short periods of time. It seemed to us that the brigade headquarters already had its hands full and could not realistically offer much assistance. It was not resourced to maintain detainees for extended periods, and it had to establish its own ad hoc procedures for a facility, the rules of detaining people, and the criteria for their release.[10]

Tunnell recognized that his Soldiers were not trained to conduct detainee operations. Nevertheless, the situation demanded that he and his chain of command adapt established TTPs to meet the requirements of the situation on the ground:

> Even though we, like most battalions, did not have the training and expertise to establish an enemy prisoner of war holding cage, we knew how to conduct noncombatant evacuation operations (NEO). The establishment of a control cell to search, inspect, and process NEO evacuees parallels some of the functions necessary to control detainees. During combat operations we modified the NEO task and the Headquarters and Headquarters Company established an area (with concertina [wire,] guards, etc.) that was used to sort out detainees. This arrangement was called the battalion's 'hasty detention facility.'[11]

Tunnell then described how his unit used the improvised detention facility:

> We normally kept the hasty detention facility at the OSB [operational support base] and brought it forward during raids. In the middle of an operation, a company simply turned detainees over to the battalion facility and continued fighting. During extended operations, the facility was established near the battalion CP [command post] and trained military intelligence personnel conducted field interrogations. This process allowed battalion leaders to determine which suspects should be immediately released because they were of no intelligence value (they were in the wrong place at the wrong time), who should be held briefly (curfew violation, etc.), and who was of intelligence value and should be sent to a higher echelon for further exploitation.[12]

As it became more evident to leaders like Tunnell that US Soldiers were faced with an insurgency, intelligence became increasingly important and commanders at all echelons realized detainees were critical sources of information and thus a major focus of their operations.

Still, there was a challenge that accompanied the growing involvement of combat units in interrogation and detainee operations. To be actionable at the tactical level, intelligence had to be current. The longer it took to interrogate a detainee, the less likely the intelligence gathered from that detainee would be of value to a commander looking for ways to make an immediate impact in his AOR. Yet the Army had not trained infantrymen, artillerymen, and other Soldiers in tactical units to conduct interrogations. By doctrine, the MI Soldiers responsible for interrogations worked at echelons above the battalion level. Movement of detainees to facilities where formal interrogations could take place required time; thus, doctrinal procedures reduced the likelihood that detainees could provide actionable intelligence to tactical units.

As the number of detainees increased sharply in the summer of 2003, several significant problems with detention procedures and intelligence requirements emerged. Lieutenant Colonel Frank Rangel, an MP officer who served in Iraq from June 2003 to March 2004 as executive officer for the 720th MP Battalion in Tikrit, provided an MP's perspective on how the increase in detentions clashed with established procedures and assumptions made during the planning for OIF:

> Now, doctrinally, how the detention system was set up was for collecting points in the BCTs [Brigade Combat Teams], about 72 hours max you want to keep them there. Then you want to move them up to the division collecting point, there for no more than 96 hours. It never worked out that way, though. If you were at a FOB [forward operating base] and you had an MP element there, it was closer to working out that way; but if you were doing it as a battalion, then you were evacuating to your own battalion [collection point]. Infantry unit[s] and those guys were playing loosey-goosey with some of the [detainees].[13]

(The term "loosey-goosey" described the tendency for tactical units to retain a detainee for periods of time longer than the prescribed 72 hours.)

If indeed, as Rangel phrased it, combat arms units were acting "loosey-goosey" in their conduct of detainee operations, they did so for a good reason: the increasing need for accurate and timely tactical intelligence. Lieutenant Colonel Troy Perry, who served as a battalion and brigade operations officer in the 4th ID, emphasized that detainee operations often fulfilled this need:

> The challenge for the battalions was they wanted to keep the detainees for as long as they could to do as many things as they could with them, meaning if they could peck away at getting some intelligence because they knew the specific intelligence they needed. Once you get higher, they can ask questions, but it may not be how are you tied to this specific guy, or family members come and now you have another source where you can say, 'It is interesting that you are here to see so and so. By the way, we are not going to release him, but what do you know about X, Y, and Z.' So you have this natural tension of the battalion wanting to keep them as long as possible.[14]

Tunnell, commander of the 1-508th IN, echoed these concerns, suggesting that valuable human intelligence (HUMINT) was lost if battalions and brigades relinquished control of detainees to higher echelons:

> Unfortunately, we soon lost access to any useful information the further up the detention chain a suspect would climb because there were not any feedback loops to update us with information from subsequent interrogations. Realizing

that this type of information is perishable, the results of the initial interrogations at the higher level would still have been useful.[15]

This imperative to collect actionable intelligence became so evident even the MPs could agree tactical units needed to adapt Army doctrine to the realities of the new campaign in Iraq. Lieutenant Colonel Rangel conceded, "You lose continuity of the effort of interrogation when you evacuate [detainees] to different levels, because now you have different handlers along the way. And there were *so many* of them that you just can't hand off the key issues and how to work them [to Soldiers at the higher levels]."[16] The attitudes displayed by Tunnell, Perry, and many others at battalion and brigade levels betray the biases of tactical leaders interested in information that could immediately affect their operations. They were less interested in the strategic-level intelligence that a longer, more deliberate interrogation at upper levels could produce. While the views of these tactical-level officers might seem somewhat myopic, they reflect the widespread hunger for intelligence at the lower state of the tactical-level of operations.

The Growing Detainee Challenge

In the summer of 2003, many Coalition leaders began to see the nature of the campaign in Iraq changing. Major General Fast, the CJTF CJ2, recalled that the growing insurgency had a critical impact on Coalition detainee operations:

> [CJTF-7] truly began to see and appreciate that we had the beginnings of, as Lieutenant General Sanchez would call it, low-intensity conflict. Others would call it an insurgency. We knew at that point that we had a nontraditional, irregular set of conditions on our hands and offensive operations began pretty much in earnest. I know that in one 2-week period we increased by 4,000 detainees at the Internment Facility [BCCF] based on division-level operations. Our system was never set up from point of capture, through a brigade facility, through a division facility, and into an internment facility, to handle those kinds of large numbers so it took awhile to really get it organized as a JTF."[17]

The sheer volume of detainees generated by cordon and search and other operations became a formidable challenge. Lieutenant Colonel Steven Bullimore, the commander of 1st Battalion, 6th Field Artillery recalled that the 4th ID unit which preceded his battalion had apparently detained all the most likely insurgents in the AOR: "I took over the AO in March 2004. We completed our relief in place (RIP) with the 4th Infantry Division. What the unit did prior to me arriving was they hit every potential actionable target there was. Anything that was remotely decent on the target list, they hit it, they conducted the operation. So when I took over, I had a blank sheet of paper." Bullimore recognized that the large-scale detentions conducted by some 4th ID units created other issues: "There were problems in that. I mean [Iraqis] had been detained, they were all over the place, and we didn't see them until 6 months later when all these detainees were released from Abu Ghraib and other places and we had nothing on the record as to why they were detained and who detained them."[18]

The swelling of the detainee population brought on ancillary problems, especially that of accountability. Doctrine directed that each detainee processed must be identified, cared for, and tracked throughout the system. All this is necessary to preclude creating "ghost detainees," people who are detained but for whom no records exist, rendering them "invisible" to the accountability system. Accountability was essential if Coalition forces hoped to create a functioning system that reviewed detainee status, provided for release of detainees in accordance with the Geneva Conventions, and complied with commonly accepted international standards that afford detainees the opportunity to communicate with family members.

By late June 2003, the CJTF-7 commander and staff had realized they needed to assert greater control over a system that was developing in an uncoordinated fashion. One of Sanchez's first steps was to issue a FRAGO on 28 June explaining the legal status of civilian internees and criminal detainees, and mandating that all detention facilities adhere to the Third and Fourth Geneva Conventions that defined protections for EPWs and civilians, respectively, in time of war.[19] Sanchez assigned overall responsibility for the detainee mission—to include training and planning—to the 800th MP Brigade and gave the commander of the 205th MI Brigade similar oversight over interrogation operations. Sanchez also began delegating supervisory responsibility for various aspects of the detainee mission to his staff. Major General Walter Wojdakowski, the deputy commanding general, took authority for prisons and other facilities where Coalition forces detained Iraqis and oversaw the establishment of procedures for the accounting of detainees. The CJ1 Personnel officer, CJ2 Intelligence officer, CJ3 Operations officer, CJ7 Engineer officer, and the Staff Judge Advocate (SJA) became involved in oversight of other parts of the detainee mission. Normally, the joint task force provost marshal staff section, which would have included the senior law enforcement officer on the staff, would have also become a critical asset in creating greater control over detention operations. However, in the summer of 2003, CJTF-7 did not have a senior MP officer who could serve as provost marshal, and although Sanchez requested that DOD provide an officer with the required experience and rank, that position was not filled until much later in 2003.[20]

In July CJTF-7 gave additional guidance to its subordinate units involved in detainee operations. Two additional FRAGOs directed specific rules on the handling and treatment of detainees. The CJTF-7 staff also formed the Detention Working Group that was chaired by the SJA, Colonel Marc Warren, and met weekly to deal with the growing detainee problem. Warren and the CJTF-7 staff lawyers had become involved in an overwhelming number of demanding missions by the middle of the summer. They had begun sorting out the legal status of the MEK, a problem caused by the US Government's 1997 classification of the group as a terrorist organization. After a year of internment, questioning, and continuing deliberations, the DOD decided to grant the MEK members at Camp Ashraf status as "protected persons" under the Fourth Geneva Convention, because of concerns that Iranian agents in the region would act against them. Warren's section had also launched initial efforts to put the Iraqi justice system back together. They worked closely with the Coalition Provisional Authority (CPA) to reestablish the Central Criminal Court of Iraq (CCCI), a project that became critical due to Saddam Hussein's decision to grant a general amnesty in November 2002 that flooded Iraq with convicted criminals. After 1 May 2003, US and Iraqi forces arrested many of these criminals and sent them to sites such as Abu Ghraib where they swelled the number of detainees.

To help deal with the growing burden of the detainee problem, the Detention Working Group held three Detention Summits between July and December 2003, meetings which gathered representatives from MP units, division staffs, and all other units that had a "stake" in detainee operations to share experiences, discuss policies, and implement proper practices. During the Detention Summit held on 19 August 2003, for example, participants from the 800th MP Brigade, the CJTF-7 CJ2 section, and the CJTF-7 SJA presented information on detainee record databases, detention facilities, and a new detention review process that standardized the system of evaluating a detainee's legal status and provided for appeal and release.[21]

The CJTF-7 staff took the rules and policies discussed at this meeting and formalized them in what Warren called "The Mother of all FRAGOs," a long directive that the joint task force issued on 25 August 2003.[22] By far the most comprehensive and detailed guidance on detainee operations up to that point, this order legally defined the status of all detainees and reiterated the mandate that all Coalition forces provide the protections established by the Geneva Conventions, including the establishment of a new magistrate status review process and an appeal and review board.[23] To facilitate the status review called for by the Fourth Geneva Convention, Warren created the first magistrate cell at Camp Cropper and then another at the Baghdad Central Confinement Facility (BCCF), a site better known by its original name—the Abu Ghraib Prison. By the end of the summer, CJTF-7 had assigned 10 Soldiers from its legal staff to Abu Ghraib in an attempt to ensure all detainees had a review of their legal status within 72 hours of arrival at the facility.[24] Major General Fast, the CJTF-7 CJ2 in late July 2003, became involved in the review and appeal process for those detainees classified as security internees. Fast stressed the role of this board in meeting the legal requirements of periodic review called for by the Geneva protocols:

> We set up the Security Detainee (*sic*) Appeal and Release Board because we had to have something in place in order to be consistent with the Geneva Conventions. All of our detainees were subject to the Geneva Conventions. So we had to have a mechanism in place to meet Article 78 requirements [in Fourth Geneva Convention] for being able to adjudge within 72 hours what their status was and then at a minimum at the 6 month point to be able to review their case.[25]

The "Mother of All FRAGOS" also explained the accountability system and issued specific guidelines on how tactical units would handle detentions. While stating that MP units would take the lead on many detainee missions, the order directed all Coalition units train to conduct these operations. With this FRAGO, CJTF-7 set the critical procedural foundation for the many Coalition units that in the late summer of 2003 found themselves conducting detainee operations.

Recognizing that CJTF-7 required additional expertise and training on detainee operations, Sanchez requested teams of detention and interrogation experts from the DOD to help train his units. As described in the previous chapter, in late August 2003 DOD dispatched Major General Geoffrey Miller and a team from Joint Task Force–Guantanamo Bay (JTF-GTMO) to provide guidance and training in interrogation operations to CJTF-7, a special operations task force, and the Iraqi Survey Group.[26] Miller's team visited a number of sites where CJTF-7's subordinate units conducted detainee operations, including the Abu Ghraib Prison. Although primarily concerned with assessment of interrogation practices, Miller and his team did discuss the relationship between MPs and MI interrogators and made recommendations about the establishment of a Joint Interrogation and Debriefing Center (JIDC), a facility that would empower CJTF-7 to conduct more efficient questioning of detainees suspected of having strategic intelligence.

In October, another assistance team, headed by Major General Donald Ryder, the Army's Provost Marshal General, arrived in Iraq to focus specifically on the Coalition's detainee operations. Ryder's team conducted visits to numerous prisons and division-level detention facilities. The group then made recommendations to CJTF-7 on the detainee system's command and control structure, its prisoner accountability databases, and methods of providing legal processes and healthcare to the detainee population. Overall, Ryder found that detainee operations in the fall of 2003 presented an uneven picture. The team's report stated: "There is a wide variance in standards and approaches at the various detention facilities."[27] Ryder found that while not all units were conducting detainee operations efficiently or strictly in accordance with doctrine, his assessment team "did not identify any military police units purposely applying inappropriate confinement practices."[28] Ryder's report did single out several units for doctrinally correct and effective detainee operations. The 800th MP Brigade units working with the 101st Airborne Division (101st ABN) in the Mosul area had "superb operations" and the 4th ID EPW Collection Point was "equally impressive."[29] Ryder and his team asserted that based on their inspections, the key to successful detainee operations were clear policies and standing operating procedures (SOPs) that gave direct guidance to Soldiers involved with this difficult mission.

Figure 53. A Soldier from the 101st Pathfinder Company, 101st Airborne Division, escorts detainees to a CH-47 Chinook helicopter in southwestern Iraq. The detainees were apprehended during a raid on a suspected terrorist training camp.

Detainee Operations at the Tactical Level

As CJTF-7 developed its detainee policies and SOPs in the summer of 2003, tactical-level units were taking the initiative and making significant changes to their organizations and missions to deal with the increasing number of Iraqis detained. By September 2003 many units were conducting their own detainee operations much like those run by the 1-508th IN in the middle of the summer. The commander of the 2d Armored Cavalry Regiment (2d ACR), for example, directed his Regimental Support Squadron (RSS) to establish and run a detention facility called the Regimental Holding Area (RHA). This order essentially tasked the support squadron, which was normally focused on logistics operations, to build and operate a prison. The squadron leadership eventually issued guidance based on the orders issued by CJTF-7 that established proper methods and procedures for the handling and securing of detainees.[30] This policy set SOPs for guards, schedules for detainee meals, and other details necessary to make the RHA function smoothly. Most importantly, the guidance echoed CJTF-7's statements of policy, unequivocally charging the RHA guards to "treat all detainees with dignity and respect" and added that "no form of abuse, physical or mental (including the use of abusive language), will be directed at the detainees."[31] The squadron commander concluded his guidance by stating, "While in the RHA, the detainee will be treated within the guideline established under international humanitarian law and through military channels" and then noted that Soldiers found guilty of abuse would be subject to disciplinary actions under the Uniform Code of Military Justice (UCMJ).[32]

The operations of the 2d ACR's RHA became part of the larger detainee system established by the 1st Armored Division (1st AD) in September 2003.[33] Based on CJTF-7's guidance concerning legal status of detainees, the 1st AD's SOP for this system set definitions for the three types of detainees: criminals, security detainees, and detainees of intelligence value.[34] Security detainees posed direct threats to Coalition forces, and detainees of intelligence value warranted careful interrogation from MI Soldiers. The system also established the proper flow of detainees from squadron (battalion) to the division detention facility. That flow allowed for screening and perhaps questioning of the detained Iraqi for 8 hours at the battalion level.[35] If information gained from that questioning determined the Iraqi was suspected of criminal activity, the SOP ordered his transfer to the Iraqi police. If Soldiers at the battalion level believed he was likely guilty of insurgent activity and had intelligence value, they arranged for his transfer to a regimental-level (brigade-level) detainee holding facility. The 2d ACR's RHA was an example of this type of facility. The details of that transfer process followed CJTF-7's guidance concerning the creation of a system that could track the detainees and included the requirement that the detaining unit complete a CPA Apprehension Form, two sworn statements from Soldiers involved in the detention, and a summary interrogation report that provided basic information on the detainee's identity and knowledge.[36] The proper completion of these documents was critical to the process, and commanders instructed Soldiers working in these facilities to refuse to accept detainees if they arrived without the proper paperwork.[37] Interrogators at the regimental-level facility then conducted formal interrogations, and if the detainees were found to likely have important information about the insurgent network, the unit transferred them to the 1st AD's Division Interrogation Facility (DIF) for further interrogation. Ultimately, the MI Soldiers at division level used the interrogations to determine whether the detained Iraqi should be released or classified as a security detainee. If designated as a security detainee, the DIF sent the detained Iraqi to the Abu Ghraib Prison.

Even with detailed guidance from higher headquarters, units faced significant difficulties in establishing detainee operations in their AORs. In the summer of 2003, for example, the 1st Brigade Combat Team (BCT) of the 4th ID directed its main combat service support element, the

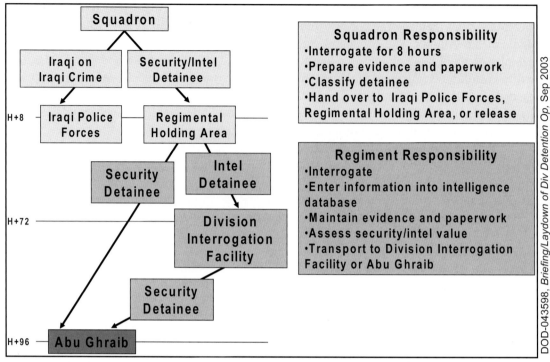

Figure 54. 2d Armored Cavalry Regiment detainee flow chart.

4th Forward Support Battalion (FSB), to establish a detainee collection point at FOB Packhorse near the city of Tikrit. The small temporary facility housed Iraqis detained by the maneuver battalions during operations in the Tikrit area. With little space available, the 4th FSB used a small building on the FOB to secure the detainees. The facility, described as makeshift by one member of the unit, had a capacity of 50 detainees, no isolation cells other than the bathrooms that were converted for that function, and only a single strand of concertina wire as the physical barrier that prevented detainees from escaping.[38] The 4th FSB chain of command supervised the operation but its operations officer (S3) described the facility as suffering from too little space, too few interpreters, and a lack of guards. By September the FSB had begun relying on the brigade's maneuver battalions to provide a constantly changing set of Soldiers as the guard force for the collection point.[39]

In early September the weaknesses of the facility's physical layout, procedures, and personnel became unequivocally clear. Late in the night on 11 September a guard shot and killed a detainee who appeared to be attempting to escape by reaching across a strand of concertina wire.[40] The preliminary Army investigation that ensued found no conclusive evidence the detainee had intended to escape and recommended the command initiate a criminal investigation into the incident.[41] Investigating officers further found that the 4th FSB had operated its collection point without the type of clear guidance that might have prevented the incident.[42] One investigator stated that the leadership of the facility had issued no written instructions to the guards, had no SOP for its operations, and had conducted no rehearsals or drills.[43] Instead, the leadership had only given verbal guidance about the use of force and rules of engagement to the guard force. The investigation noted that the leadership of both the 1st BCT and the 4th FSB had regularly inspected the collection point. However, the investigating officer emphasized the inadequate guard force as well as the absence of clearly defined procedures as the main causes of the shooting of the detainee.

Despite the problems tactical units experienced in the establishment of detainee facilities and the manning of those sites with trained and knowledgeable Soldiers, the importance of generating actionable intelligence led many battalion- and even company-size units to conduct their own detainee operations. The scale of this nondoctrinal approach to detainee operations became abundantly clear in 2004 when the US Army ordered its Inspector General (IG) office, led by Lieutenant General Paul Mikolashek, to mount an investigation into the US Army's detainee operations in Iraq, Afghanistan, and Guantanamo Bay. The IG's team then conducted 650 interviews with Soldiers in a variety of ranks and positions. At the tactical level, the IG investigators found that by early 2004 half of the company leaders interviewed in Iraq stated their units had set up their own detainee collection points at which detainees were held for periods varying from 12 hours to 3 days and sometimes interrogated by non-MI Soldiers.[44] More significantly, 77 percent of the battalion leaders interviewed in Iraq acknowledged that their units had established battalion collection points.[45] Like those facilities at the company-level, battalion detainee collection points kept Iraqis for varying lengths of time, and all units investigated conducted tactical questioning or interrogations at the sites. The officers who initiated these operations were simply reacting to the requirements for greater information about the security environment in their AORs. Nevertheless, in setting up these facilities and, in some cases, conducting questioning or formal interrogations, these Soldiers had moved outside the parameters of US Army doctrine and training.

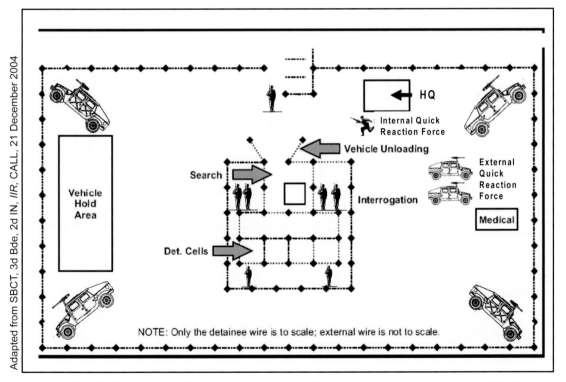

Adapted from SBCT, 3d Bde, 2d IN, IIR, CALL, 21 December 2004

Figure 55. SBCT transfer facility. Detainee transfer facility established by C Company, 1-37th Field Artillery near the city of Samarra in December 2003. Capacity of the facility was 100 detainees.

The Issue of Abuse in US Army Detainee Operations in Iraq

The case of the shooting at the 4th FSB collection point illustrated the types of problems units faced in 2003 when they transitioned to conducting nondoctrinal missions for which their Soldiers and leaders were untrained and unprepared. Without clear policies, established standards, and effective training, units experienced difficulties in adapting to detainee operations. In a very small number of cases, American Soldiers did not meet the standards of international decency and committed abuses of Iraqi detainees. The Department of the Army (DA) IG investigation into detainee operations in Iraq and Afghanistan found that as of June 2004, there were 94 cases of confirmed or possible abuse out of approximately 50,000 cases of detention. While the IG investigation team stressed that "even one case of abuse is unacceptable," it concluded that the large majority of US Soldiers conducted detainee operations "humanely and properly."[46]

What led this small contingent of American Soldiers to mistreat Iraqi detainees? The previous chapter recounted the events and conditions that allowed or caused MI interrogators in the JIDC at the Abu Ghraib Prison to commit abuses. This section will shift the focus to examine the causes of the abuses that occurred during detention operations at Abu Ghraib. Some of the factors that led the MI Soldiers in the JIDC to mistreat detainees were also responsible for the abuses elsewhere in the US Army's detainee system in Iraq. As noted earlier, the Army assigned the mission of interrogation of EPWs and detainees to Soldiers in the MI branch. Field Manual (FM) 34-52, *Intelligence Interrogation,* provided doctrinal procedures for this mission. The confinement of EPWs and civilian internees was the responsibility of MP Soldiers who used Army Regulation (AR) 190-8, *Enemy Prisoners of War, Retained Personnel, Civilian Internees, and Other Detainees* (1997), and FM 3-19.40, *Military Police Internment/ Resettlement Operations* (2001), as their regulatory and doctrinal guidelines.

In OIF, as in almost all other combat operations or campaigns, MPs were not the Soldiers on the scene at the beginning of the detention process. That role usually fell to the infantry and other combat arms Soldiers who conducted cordon and searches, raids, patrols, and other missions that brought them into close contact with the Iraqi population. Detentions occurred during these operations at an initial stage known as the "point of capture," the instance where the US Soldier first made physical contact with the individual. The capture often occurred after firefights or other incidents in which Soldiers were attacked, wounded, or killed. It was in this setting that Soldiers committed most of the documented abuses. The DA IG's *Detainee Operations Inspection* found that of the 94 confirmed or possible cases of abuse recorded up to mid-2004, 48 percent occurred at the point of capture.[47] The best explanation for these abuses was Soldier's uncertainty in very unpredictable situations. The IG report stated: "The point of capture is the location where most contact with detainees occurs under the most uncertain, dangerous, and frequently violent circumstances."[48] Major General Fast, the CJTF-7 CJ2, offered a similar perspective:

> There has been a lot of looking back and particularly with the abuse cases both on the detention side and point of capture. The majority were really point of capture abuses. That is very, very difficult and that is part of the training we are giving to our Soldiers now. One minute you are in a fire fight and maybe your best buddy has been killed, but certainly a guy is trying to kill you. The next minute you are holding the guy in your hands. Your adrenaline is flowing

and it takes every ounce of discipline to suddenly treat this guy under the new rules as he is now a detainee in your custody and you have to treat him differently.[49]

As Fast noted, the treatment of detainees in the midst of or just after combat required an extraordinary amount of personal control, and the rough handling of known insurgents and even suspected enemies was not unprecedented. As in other military operations, especially counterinsurgency campaigns that featured an elusive enemy that did not wear a uniform and hid within the civilian population, the uncertain nature of the security environment in Iraq sometimes led to cases where American Soldiers mistreated Iraqis as they took them into custody.

After capture, the detainee would be taken to a central collecting point normally run by division- or brigade-size units. Twenty percent of the possible or confirmed abuses happened at these sites where Soldiers unfamiliar with detainment procedures often served on guard forces. The final level in the detention system, the internment or detention facility, served as the setting for 22 percent of the possible or confirmed abuses.[50] This statistic included the abuses committed by MPs at Abu Ghraib Prison in 2003. Abusive practices at this stage in the process begs another question: Why did MPs—the Soldiers assigned to the confinement mission by doctrine and ostensibly trained to conduct detainee operations—participate in the mistreatment of detained Iraqis? To help answer this question, the following discussion offers a brief overview of detention operations in support of the JIDC at Abu Ghraib, focusing on the critical factors that generated an environment in which Soldiers could commit abuses.[51]

In the summer of 2003 Abu Ghraib, Saddam's most notorious prison, became the site where the Coalition held criminal detainees. By late summer the prison complex had also become the site where Coalition forces confined criminals as well as detainees considered high security risks or having critical intelligence value. CJTF-7 gave the 800th MP Brigade responsibility for running the prison; but because the brigade had missions across Iraq, Brigadier General Karpinski assigned only one unit, the 320th MP Battalion, to conduct confinement operations at the prison. This unit had trained as an internment/resettlement (I/R) battalion, the type of MP unit that performs confinement operations, and earlier that summer it had conducted detainee operations at Camp Bucca near the port city of Umm Qasr. However, the subordinate companies that made up the battalion changed over the course of 2003 and some of the companies in the battalion had neither the training nor the experience for the confinement mission. In August the Soldiers of the 320th MP Battalion had moved into Abu Ghraib and begun the confinement mission there. By early fall there were approximately 4,000 criminal and security internees inside the main prison building and several smaller tent compounds that made up the Abu Ghraib Prison complex. This number of detainees overwhelmed the battalion's Soldiers. The executive officer of the 320th MP Battalion stated that given the numbers of detainees, proper confinement operations required two I/R battalions.[52]

In early September the 320th MP Battalion began confinement operations in support of the newly established JIDC. CJTF-7 established the JIDC inside the prison complex and assigned cellblocks located on Tier 1 of the hardened main prison building to house prisoners considered MI Holds, or those suspected of having critical information that could create actionable intelligence. As noted in the previous chapter, the term "MI Hold" did not denote a category of detainee and was not recognized by the Fourth Geneva Convention. The Coalition adopted the use of the term to create a grouping of detainees who after having been screened by Soldiers were identified as likely holding intelligence of critical value and were awaiting interrogation. CJTF-7's use of the MI Hold category simply served to assist in managing the increasing number of detainees who could offer key details about the growing insurgency.

On the surface, the addition of the JIDC meant a simple expansion of MP confinement duties on the complex. Nothing about the MI mission in the JIDC should have affected how the MPs did their job, which was to confine the MI Hold detainees and escort these detainees to and from the JIDC where MI Soldiers had responsibility for them. MP doctrine mandated this narrow set of duties for MP Soldiers when working in close proximity to interrogation operations. The 2001 version of FM 3-19.40, the MP doctrine that governed detainee operations, recognized that interrogation operations might take place inside EPW or confinement facilities. However, doctrinal guidelines did not go beyond directing MP officers to coordinate generally with MI personnel stationed inside the facility and at times offer updates to MI Soldiers on the condition and mood of individual detainees. Likewise, nothing in the 1992 version of FM 34-52, *Intelligence Interrogation*, stated that MI units integrate or employ MPs in ways other than confinement and escort duties.

Despite the norms established in both MP and MI doctrine, within weeks of the introduction of the JIDC, the MPs working on Tier 1 had moved far beyond these specific missions. Indeed, records gathered in the Army's 2004 AR 15-6 Investigation of the 800th MP Brigade reveal that in September MPs assisted MI operations by forcing detainees who were not cooperating during interrogation to remove their clothing—an act designed to humiliate and wear down resistance to interrogation. For example, MPs from the 72d MP Company, the unit that provided the guards on Tier 1 in September 2003, noted in their daily journal that on 15 September 2003 a detainee was "stripped down per MI. He is neked (*sic*) and standing tall in his cell."[53] This practice apparently expanded because when the 372d MP Company arrived at Abu Ghraib on 1 October 2003 to take over confinement operations on Tier 1, the company commander recalled that he was surprised to see so many of the detainees partially stripped of their clothing or naked in their cells. He claimed that when he asked why, other Soldiers responded that the removal of clothing was an MI technique used to make the detainee uncomfortable.[54]

From these two examples, it is clear that by mid-September counterresistance techniques not formally authorized by the 14 September CJTF-7 Interrogation and Counter-Resistance Policy (ICRP) were in use by MPs as part of their confinement operations on Tier 1. Further, Colonel Thomas Pappas, the commander of the 205th MI Brigade who had authority over the JIDC, acknowledged that MI Soldiers in the facility employed the MP guard force to enforce "management plans" for detainees who were uncooperative. Pappas noted, "It was understood that the specifics of management plans, let's say, for example, like sleep management plan, would be executed by the MPs."[55] Like the forced removal of clothing, the use of sleep management or interrupting a detainee during their sleep was designed to make the detainee more compliant during interrogation.

The decisionmaking process that led the MPs on Tier 1 to become so heavily involved in managing detainees remains opaque. Some observers of the Abu Ghraib incidents have attempted to link the September 2003 visit by Major General Miller and his team from the Guantanamo Bay Detention Facility to this decision. After spending a week visiting various detention sites, including Abu Ghraib, Miller made recommendations to the CJTF-7 commander that directly addressed the role of the MPs in interrogation operations. In the Executive Summary of his report, Miller asserted, "The detention operations function must act as an enabler for interrogation."[56] The report elaborated on this concept in a later section, recommending that CJTF-7 "dedicate and train a detention guard force subordinate to the JIDC Commander that sets the conditions for the successful interrogation and exploitation of internees/detainees."[57]

The Miller Report, however, did not provide any detailed explanation of how MPs could help enable or set conditions for interrogations. The US Army and DOD investigations that looked closely at the Abu Ghraib incidents found no evidence Miller intended the MPs to enforce "sleep management plans" or other means of making the detainees less resistant to interrogation. One investigation chaired by James R. Schlesinger asserted that Miller's recommendation about MP involvement in setting conditions for interrogations in the JIDC was essentially a suggestion to use MP officers as passive intelligence collectors on the cellblock, informing interrogators on the moods of individual detainees and the incentives that appeared to work most effectively for each. MPs had served in this function at Guantanamo Bay and Miller, according to the Schlesinger Report, believed it was a critical element in successful interrogations.[58]

While the origins of MP involvement in preparing detainees for interrogations remain unclear, what is evident is that these practices began in the middle of September and continued throughout the fall. The 372d MP Company, the unit that provided the guard force for the MI Hold detainees after 1 October 2003, had not trained for confinement operations and simply followed the practices of their predecessors by working with MI interrogators in managing detainees. In November, after becoming concerned about the potential liability of his Soldiers in assisting with these practices, the commander of the 372d began forcing MI Soldiers to put their requests for sleep management and other techniques in writing to have documentation in case a detainee suffered serious injuries.[59] Despite his concerns, however, the commander maintained the close cooperation between his MPs and the interrogators.

Other practices by the MP guards on Tier 1 that constituted abuse were not related to the process of managing the detainees for the interrogation mission. In late October five MPs stripped three Iraqi detainees of their clothing and subjected them to physical and sexual humiliation.[60] In early November several of the same MP guards forced a non-MI Hold detainee to stand on a box with a hood over his head while the Soldiers attached wires to his fingers. The detainee was told that if he fell off the box, he would be electrocuted.[61] Three days after this incident, the same group of MPs ordered seven non-MI Hold detainees to strip off their clothes, physically abused them, and forced the men into sexually humiliating positions.[62] As the Fay–Jones AR 15-6 Investigation noted, these abuses resulted from the criminal propensities of a small number of MPs serving on Tier 1.[63] Soldiers involved in these three incidents captured the abuses with photographs and distributed them to others in the 372d MP Company. Eventually, a concerned Soldier in the 320th MP Battalion made copies of the photos and turned them over to the Army Criminal Investigation Division (CID), which used them as evidence in a formal inquiry into the abuses at the prison. These photos were the images that ultimately found their way to the media in the spring of 2004 and shocked many in the US military, the American public, and the international community.

The Army's CID was just the first agency to investigate the detention operations on Tier 1 of the Abu Ghraib Prison. That investigation served as the catalyst for a series of broader investigations that expanded the scope of the inquiry. In January 2004 Lieutenant General Sanchez, the CJTF-7 commander, requested that CENTCOM look into the operations of the 800th MP Brigade. The result was the AR 15-6 Investigation, headed by Major General Antonio Taguba, completed in early March 2004. At the end of March Sanchez appointed Major General George Fay to investigate the operations of the 205th MI Brigade, which was responsible for operations in the JIDC. In June 2004 the Army folded that inquiry into an investigation headed by Lieutenant General Anthony Jones into higher-level MI policies and practices in Iraq. The Secretary of the Army in February 2004 also directed the IG's office to conduct the aforementioned investigation of the Army's detainee operations in the Global War on Terrorism that encompassed Afghanistan, Guantanamo Bay, and Iraq.

The Taguba AR 15-6 Investigation into the 800th MP Brigade and the Fay–Jones AR 15-6 Investigation offer the most detailed data and analysis of the operations in the Abu Ghraib Prison and in the JIDC. Using evidence from the CID investigation as well as its own interviews, the Fay–Jones investigation contended that between September 2003 and January 2004 there was significant evidence suggesting at least 20 incidents of abuse involving MPs in addition to those noted above.[64] Most of the violent and sexually-oriented abuses, the team noted in its report, "occurred separately from scheduled interrogations and did not focus on persons held for intelligence purposes."[65]

The interviews and documents gathered in the process of conducting these investigations help answer the question posed earlier in this section: Why would MPs participate in practices that constituted the abuse of detainees? The report of the AR 15-6 Investigation into the 800th MP Brigade found three critical factors that help explain these abuses: weakness in MP training, poor leadership in the MP units at Abu Ghraib, and lack of clear procedures and policies at the prison complex. The Army investigators who focused on the MPs found that the lack of training for the confinement mission was a major issue. While the mission of the 800th MP Brigade included the establishment of internment and resettlement camps, its subordinate units were not all trained to conduct those operations. In particular, the 372d MP Company that took over the detention mission on Tier 1 in October 2003 had trained for MP law and order operations. This meant the company arrived at the prison without any extensive knowledge of proper confinement procedures or doctrine, a fact that forced the company commander to rely on Soldiers who in civilian life had experience in corrections or law enforcement. Although recognizing that his Soldiers lacked the basic understanding of confinement operations, the company commander did not find the means to give the MPs working at Abu Ghraib training in the fundamentals of those operations.[66]

Leadership deficiencies, from company through brigade level, also contributed to the potential for abuse. The most debilitating failure was the inability or unwillingness of any of the officers involved directly or indirectly with operations on Tier 1 to determine who had authority for what occurred on that cellblock. As noted in the previous chapter, the 205th MI Brigade officers who oversaw interrogation operations did not believe Tier 1 was their responsibility. On the other hand, the commander of the 372d MP Company, who understood he had responsibility for the detention operations in that part of the prison, allowed the interrogators to employ his Soldiers in managing detainee sleep plans and clothing removal, although he believed these practices unorthodox. More revealing was that the MP lieutenant in charge of Tier 1 told Army investigators he believed MI Soldiers had control of that tier, and he was responsible only for his MPs and the basic accountability and care of the detainees.[67] In this environment where understanding of authority and responsibilities on Tier 1 was less than clear, none of the MPs questioned the practice of managing the detainees. Major General Taguba, in his report, emphasized the failure to establish clear spheres of command authority for the detainee operations on Tier 1 and the significant leadership deficiencies among the senior NCOs and officers with direct responsibility for these operations. His report recommended that eight of the MP officers involved in the detainee operations on Tier 1 be relieved from their duties.[68]

The blurred understanding of the command hierarchy on Tier 1 might have been clarified. In November, after most of the abuses in the prison occurred, Sanchez made a decision about the chain of command at the Abu Ghraib Prison. Because leaders at Abu Ghraib had not managed to create a real security plan for Abu Ghraib even though attacks against the prison complex increased through the fall, Sanchez appointed Colonel Pappas, commander of the 205th MI Brigade, as commander of the FOB at Abu Ghraib on 19 November 2003. CJTF-7's two-sentence order making this change stated, "Effective immediately commander 205 MI BDE assumes responsibility for the Baghdad Central Confinement Facility (BCCF) and is appointed the FOB commander. Units currently at Abu Ghurayb (BCCF) are TACON [under tactical control] to 205 MI BDE for security of detainees and FOB protection."[69] The first sentence gave Pappas a broad mandate to take responsibility for operations at Abu Ghraib. The second sentence, using the term TACON or tactical control, meant that Pappas had authority to direct the actions of non-MI units at the prison to establish "security of detainees and FOB protection." Joint organizations like CJTF-7 used the term TACON to designate the command association between units that did not have a formal relationship. In this case, up until 19 November 2003, the 205th MI Brigade did not have formal command authority over the disparate non-MI units located at the Abu Ghraib Prison complex. Normally, a unit that has TACON of another unit has command authority over that organization for execution of specific missions or tasks.[70]

Pappas focused on the second sentence of this FRAGO, interpreting the order as a directive to take charge of the *security* of the entire complex.[71] In fact, he quickly moved one of his MI battalions into Abu Ghraib to help with the force protection mission. This fact notwithstanding, Pappas never interpreted the order from CJTF-7 as a mandate to assert his authority into all operations on the prison complex, including the MP detention operations on Tier 1 and elsewhere in the facility.[72] Pappas contended that he had wanted to take command of the MPs on Tier 1, but had been rebuffed by Brigadier General Karpinski, the 800th MP Brigade Commander.[73] However, in his investigation into the 800th MP Brigade, Taguba found that Pappas did not communicate the requirements of this new TACON relationship to either Karpinski or to the commander of the 320th MP Battalion, the MP unit located at the prison. Indeed, the CJTF-7 FRAGO did nothing to alter the way detainee operations at the prison were conducted, and the overall confusion about who was in charge of Tier 1 continued.

Closely connected to the leadership problems was an overall lack of policy and procedures on Tier 1. On the most basic level, the MPs from the 372d MP Company who worked in these areas of the prison had no official SOPs to guide their detention operations. Their chain of command at the battalion and brigade level had not provided them with this essential guidance.[74] Eventually, the Soldiers created their own procedures, but having had no training in confinement operations, these guides were rudimentary at best. The company commander also stated his Soldiers had neither requested nor were furnished copies of the Geneva Convention; according to Pappas, the MI officers in the JIDC never gave copies of either version of the

CJTF-7 ICRP to the MPs. Without the ICRP, the MPs would not have known whether sleep disruption, removal of clothing, and other detainee management techniques employed on the tier had received official sanction.

Ultimately, these three factors—lack of training, poor leadership, and a deficiency of policy and procedures—helped create an environment in which poorly disciplined Soldiers could perpetrate abuses. As stated earlier, the investigations into the incidents on Tier 1 acknowledge that the criminal propensities of a few Soldiers contributed to the abuses. However, it is hard to imagine how those Soldiers would have been able to perpetrate multiple incidents of abuse in an operation that had strictly defined procedures and was closely supervised by both junior and senior leaders.

A number of Soldiers involved in these incidents were punished for their misconduct in Abu Ghraib. As a result of the criminal and administrative investigations, the US Army court-martialed 12 Soldiers, including 1 officer, for their roles in the detainee abuses. In 2005 a general court-martial convicted Corporal Charles A. Graner Jr., 372d MP Company, of conspiracy to maltreat detainees, maltreatment of detainees, and assaulting detainees, and sentenced him to 10 years confinement and a dishonorable discharge. Private First Class Lynndie England, an administrative clerk in the 372d MP Company who had appeared in many of the Abu Ghraib pictures, including the image of her holding a leash tied to a prisoner's neck, was also convicted by a general court-martial in September 2005. She was found guilty of conspiracy to maltreat detainees, maltreatment of detainees, and committing an indecent act, and was sentenced to 3 years of confinement and a dishonorable discharge. Lieutenant Colonel Steven Jordan, the officer who served as the director of the JIDC in the fall of 2003, went before a court-martial in the summer of 2007, but was acquitted of all charges related to the mistreatment of detainees. (The court did convict Jordan of disobeying a lawful order to not discuss the investigation into the Abu Ghraib incidents given to him by Major General Fay. However, this criminal conviction was administratively dismissed by Major General Richard J. Rowe in January 2008.) Other senior leaders, including Brigadier General Karpinski, received adverse administrative actions, such as relief of command for cause, reprimands, and reductions in grade.

The Consolidation of Detainee Operations

Even as the abuses were occurring at Abu Ghraib and before they became known outside the walls of Abu Ghraib, CJTF-7 began creating a more orderly detainee system by adapting its staff structure and augmenting its earlier statements of policy, rules, and procedures. This consolidation of detainee operations, which would last well into 2004, began with the Coalition headquarters issuing more explicit guidance about the correct treatment of all Iraqis. In October 2003 and again in January 2004 Lieutenant General Sanchez sent out a memorandum titled "Proper Treatment of Iraqi People During Combat Operations," which established fundamental standards for dealing with Iraqi citizens for all CJTF-7 Soldiers.[75] Sanchez directed that subordinate commanders ensure these memorandums were disseminated down to platoon level and reinforced by the chain of command. In November 2003 Sanchez issued the "CJTF-7 Rules for Detainee Operations" that unequivocally charged Soldiers to "treat all persons with dignity and respect" and set other standards as well.[76] In May 2004 he reinforced this basic concept of proper treatment of Iraqis in a policy memorandum titled "Proper Conduct During Combat Operations," which stated in part, "Respect for others, humane treatment of all persons, and adherence to the law of war and rules of engagement is a matter of discipline and values. It is what separates us from our enemies. I expect all leaders to reinforce this message."[77]

It is impossible to say with any certitude to what degree American Soldiers internalized these fundamental behavioral concepts in their interaction with Iraqis in general and detainees specifically. However, the policies and procedures within several commands provide an indication that CJTF-7's basic guidance for detainee operations did reach the individual Soldier level. In early 2004 Task Force (TF) *Olympia*, the unit that replaced the 101st ABN in the north of Iraq, issued a new policy for the operation of detainee collection points. The SOP gave clear rules on how to process detainees into the camp, how to classify them, and how to release them to Iraqi authorities or send them to other detainee facilities. More importantly, the policy directly addressed proper treatment of the detainees while in the collection points, stating that no guard had the right to mistreat the Iraqis in custody: "Guard Force members must understand that inhumane treatment, even if committed under the stress of combat and with deep provocation, is a serious offense and is a punishable violation under National Law, International law, and the [Uniform Code of Military Justice]."[78]

On the other side of Iraq, near the city of An Najaf, Camp Duke, located at FOB Duke, began holding detainees in 2004 and was normally manned by non-MP personnel throughout 2004. To provide the untrained Soldiers specific guidelines for general operations and treatment of detainees, the leadership of the facility issued the "Camp Duke Detainee Facility S.O.P." in

DOD Photo

Figure 56. The mother of an Iraqi man taken into custody during an operation in An Najaf, Iraq, pleads with officer to release her son.

June 2004.[79] The first sentence of the SOP echoed Sanchez's statement in his November 2003 "Rules for Detainee Operations" almost exactly: "Detainees will be treated with respect and dignity."[80] The document continued, "No personnel will be allowed to humiliate any of the inmates. The guards will refrain from using inappropriate language toward the detainees. . . . There will be no physical, mental, or verbal abuse directed toward any of the detainees."[81] The guidance established standards for uniforms, schedules for both guards and detainees, administrative procedures to process detainees, and other routine matters required to govern a detention facility. It also mandated that Soldiers afford the detainees the right to practice their religion and would be given a Koran and a prayer rug if Muslim or a Bible if Christian. The SOP also established a procedure for detainees to file complaints and, toward the end of the document, mandated that the Sergeant of the Guard maintain a copy of the Geneva Convention for both reference and instructional purposes.[82]

By early 2004 units at the tactical level began reporting close adherence to the CJTF-7 guidelines for detainee operations by accounting for each detainee using databases, digital photos, and placing an identification bracelet with a tracking number on the detainee's wrist. Soldiers paid careful attention to the requirement to inventory the detainee's personal property and to the proper completion of forms that listed pertinent information about the detainee and the circumstances of his detention. This paperwork created greater accountability within the system and assisted the intelligence screening process. One form in particular, the CPA Apprehension Form, became so critical that units could not transfer detainees to higher-level facilities without it. Soldiers in the 4th ID's 1st Battalion, 22d Infantry, for example, stated that if the form was not filled out with careful attention to detail, the MPs who ran the brigade and higher-level detention facilities would not accept a detainee and might release him into the civilian population.[83] Some divisions actually added more requirements to the CJTF-7 standards, leading some Soldiers in tactical-level units to complain in 2004 that they spent up to 4 hours completing the paperwork for each detainee. This increased administrative burden had the effect of making at least some units more selective in deciding who to detain, not wanting to waste their time and resources processing paperwork for detainees who did not appear to be insurgents or criminals.[84] Other improvements to detention facilities arrived as units learned how to use the Commander's Emergency Response Program (CERP) and other funds to purchase materials such as cots and blankets for the detainees and to contract with local Iraqis to build safer and more secure detainee collection points and holding areas.[85]

The command also sought to standardize and improve practices at detention facilities by arranging for training teams to visit Iraq. One of the most effective teams was composed of MP confinement experts from the United States Disciplinary Barracks at Fort Leavenworth, Kansas, who traveled to all of the major detention facilities in Iraq to conduct a 40-hour course on basic detention procedures.[86] Major Charles Seifert, an MP officer who monitored detainee operations at Abu Ghraib in 2004, emphasized another change that was critical in the wake of the abuse scandal at the Abu Ghraib Prison. Seifert noted that in 2004 the MP and MI commands at Abu Ghraib had reasserted the doctrinal and regulatory line that separated the duties of the MI and MP Soldiers. The MPs no longer had any role inside the prison other than escorting the detainee to the JIDC and returning them to their cells at the end of the interrogation.[87]

As the detainee mission expanded in 2003, the DOD and the Army attempted to give assistance to CJTF-7 in the form of additional MP support. However, because all of the Army Active

Duty or Reserve Component MP units were serving in Iraq or Afghanistan or scheduled to deploy to these theaters in 2004, senior Army commanders had to look for innovative solutions to the problem caused by the insufficient number of MPs on the ground in Iraq. They responded by directing contingents of Army National Guard Soldiers to retrain as military police before deploying in support of OIF. Between October 2003 and January 2004, approximately 3,700 National Guard Engineer, Armor, Cavalry, Artillery, and Air Defense Artillery Soldiers from 9 states mobilized and traveled to Fort Dix, New Jersey, where they began the transition to MP duties.[88] After the 40-day training program at Fort Dix, the Soldiers earned the designation "provisional MPs" and were reorganized into "in lieu of MP" companies.

These "in lieu of" companies were responsible for a variety of MP missions including convoy escort and route security. Still, most of these provisional MPs played a significant role in CJTF-7's detainee operations. The Pennsylvania Army National Guard Soldiers of Bravo Battery, 1st Battalion, 107th Field Artillery, for example, deployed to Iraq in February 2004 and spent the next 12 months serving as guards at Camp Bucca near the southern city of Umm Qasr.[89] In that period the new MPs dealt with detainee riots, escapes, and other more mundane duties involved in running an internment facility. The Soldiers of 2d Battalion, 103d Armor, also belonging to the Pennsylvania Army National Guard, had a similar experience conducting detainee operations in Baghdad as a unit subordinate to the 89th MP Brigade.[90] All of these citizen Soldiers worked and fought alongside their Active Duty colleagues, sometimes without the Active Component headquarters realizing they were "provisional" MPs.[91] Although they lacked experience in the field of MP operations, the 20 "in lieu of" MP companies that deployed to Iraq in 2004 gave the CJTF-7 and Multi-National Force–Iraq (MNF-I) commanders the equivalent of a third MP brigade in theater, thus making a significant contribution to the Coalition's detention mission.

It was above the tactical level, in any case, that the Coalition made the most significant changes in detainee practices and policies. By January 2004 Paul Bremer, the CPA chief, had come to view the large number of detainees as a serious impediment to creating stability and progress in Iraq. One CPA report estimated that Coalition military forces detained 80 Iraqis on an average per day and contended that this rate was overwhelming the detention system.[92] Additionally, the transition to Iraqi sovereignty loomed just 6 months away and the Coalition's legal basis for continuing detention operations after 30 June 2004 was unclear. Bremer had repeatedly pressured CJTF-7 to release as many detainees as possible without handicapping the intelligence effort or threatening security.[93] On 7 January he delivered a public address, imploring Iraqis to reconcile their differences and offering to help that process by releasing those detainees who renounced violence and could find an individual willing to guarantee their conduct.[94] Bremer also promised to improve communication between detainees and their families.

The speech was just the first step in a concerted effort by the CPA and CJTF-7 to reduce the detainee population and consolidate the Coalition's methods of conducting detention operations. CJTF-7 shared the concerns about the potential legal implications for Coalition detainee operations after Iraq became sovereign, but other more pressing issues forced the command's leadership to look for ways to change procedures. On 25 January 2004 CJTF-7 reported holding 9,754 detainees, of which 7,000 had been placed in the categories of MI Hold or Security non-MI Hold. The large majority of the remaining detainees were criminal offenders.[95] By

February a CJTF-7 paper titled "Strategy for Addressing Detention Issues" contended that if processes did not change, by 30 June 2004 there would be 10,000 security or MI Hold detainees under their control, a figure that greatly concerned those in the military command involved in these matters.[96]

Coalition leaders introduced two important measures to begin addressing the problems created by the rising detainee population. First was the public listing of Iraqis under detention. The CPA mounted this action in response to Iraqi complaints about their inability to find out if a family member was interned by Coalition forces. By February 2004 the CPA had created a publicly accessible Web site that listed in English and Arabic the names and other key information of all Iraqis detained.[97] In March 2004 CJTF-7 took the additional step of constructing a reception trailer at the Abu Ghraib Prison where Coalition staff could work with Iraqis to confirm information about family members who were under detention in the prison or in other facilities.[98]

The Coalition's second measure focused on the review and appeal process and the related criminal prosecution of selected detainees. CJTF-7 had established the review and appeal system in 2003 as one of the requirements of the Fourth Geneva Convention. The process worked through the military's magistrate cell and a review and appeal board composed of senior Coalition military officers who met periodically to verify the official status of a detainee and to decide whether there were legal or operational grounds for continued detention. The board could recommend continued internment for intelligence or security reasons, initiation of civil legal prosecution, or release of the detainee.

USMC Photo by LCpl Benjamin J. Flores

Figure 57. Soldiers from 391st MP BN, Sergeant First Class Curtis A. Austin (center) and Major Jim B. Wescott (right), watch as a former inmate, recently released from Abu Ghraib Prison, prepares to sign his freedom papers.

By early 2004 it was clear to CPA officials that the board could not keep pace with the influx of detainees into the system. To help remedy this problem, Lieutenant General Sanchez directed the creation of a standing review and appeal board whose only duty was to ensure the Coalition provided timely due process to all Iraqi detainees.[99] This decision resulted almost immediately in an increased rate of review and release. In mid-March 2004, according to one CPA report, the review and appeal board was reviewing the cases of 100 detainees per day, 80 percent of which were approved for release.[100] By 3 April 2004, CJTF-7 reported to the CPA that the review and appeal board had selected a total of 2,600 detainees for release.[101]

While the review and appeal board increased the number of Iraqis slated for release, the CJTF-7 SJA and his staff focused on prosecuting detainees for crimes before the CCCI. This initiative, designed to provide due process and avoid consigning detainees to months languishing in confinement without resolution of their cases, faced many obstacles when it started in the middle of 2003. CJTF-7 had to reestablish the Iraqi legal system, a monumental task that included finding judges willing to serve in an unstable security environment. As the process gathered steam, other problems emerged including the collection of evidence in combat zones and gathering testimonies from witnesses from the Coalition armed forces who had redeployed back to their home countries. By mid-2004, however, the CJTF-7 SJA had restarted the system and had Coalition military lawyers working closely with Iraqi prosecutors as they carefully shepherded cases through the CCCI.

The entire process of resuscitating the Iraqi criminal court received a boost in the spring of 2004 when the DOD sent a group of lawyers, paralegals, and investigators, collectively called the Joint Services Law Enforcement Team (JSLET), to Iraq. The CJTF-7 staff broke the team up into smaller units and placed them at division headquarters across the country.[102] By July 2004 the staff of MNF-I reported that the introduction of the JSLETs had led to the convening of 95 hearings and 37 trials for 55 defendants, 5 of which were acquitted.[103] Colonel Marc Warren, the CJTF-7 SJA who had started the CCCI initiative, believed that while difficult at times, the collaboration with the CCCI was critical for the establishment of the rule of law in Iraq because it created a system of due process in which the Iraqis had a stake.[104]

Perhaps the most important organizational change to CJTF-7's detainee operations came in the spring of 2004 when Major General Geoffrey Miller deployed to Iraq to serve as CJTF-7's deputy commanding general for detention operations, a position that did not exist prior to Miller's arrival. Miller had commanded JTF-GTMO in 2002 and had led the JTF-GTMO Assessment Team to Iraq in late August 2003. At the time Miller's team made that visit, the commander and staff of CJTF-7 had recommended to higher headquarters that detainee operations should be under the authority of a general officer whose responsibilities were focused on oversight of all the processes and policies related to detention. Eight months later Miller began serving in that role, and, after CJTF-7 transitioned to MNF-I, he created a support organization, Task Force (TF) 134, to assist him in the oversight of Coalition detainee operations.

The new TF ensured that once the new Iraqi Government became a sovereign power, all Coalition detainee operations continued under the controls established in the Fourth Geneva Convention. Miller's staff also had the responsibility for close coordination with the Interim Iraqi Government (IIG) and collaboration with Coalition agencies on matters of policy. The TF also gained significant authority over MI and MP units in an effort to synchronize the critical assets involved in detainee operations.

Figure 58. Just released from the Baghdad Central Confinement Facility (Abu Ghraib Prison), Iraqis board vehicles for Fallujah and Ramadi.

Over the summer of 2004, Miller and the new detainee TF enjoyed some success in reducing the number of detainees held by the Coalition. In May 2004 CJTF-7 had reported to the CPA that it was holding 7,819 security internees.[105] By July that number had dropped to 5,514.[106] Miller also reported a reduction in the number of detainees held in tactical-level internment facilities for long periods of time.[107] In May 2004 CJTF-7 units had documented 240 Iraqis who had been in these facilities for more than 14 days. By August 2004 Coalition units reported less than 30 detainees in this category.

Much of this improvement could be attributed to the review and appeal process and MNF-I's work with the IIG and the CCCI. In fact, 6 weeks after Iraq became a sovereign state, General George W. Casey Jr., the MNF-I commander, and Major General Miller created a new entity called the Combined Review and Release Board, which included two Iraqi members from each of the Ministries of Justice, Interior, and Human Rights, along with three officers from the Coalition forces.[108] Nevertheless, the review and release procedures still had weaknesses. Earlier in 2004 the Coalition's senior military leaders had wrestled with creating a release process that balanced their desire to reduce the number of detainees with the very real security concerns of military commanders at the tactical level. In the spring of 2004, the system allowed for tactical-level commanders and staff to have input into the Review and Appeal Board's recommendation, and place a hold on the release if they believed there were grounds for keeping the detainee interned. This measure had led to slowdowns in the release process.

However, when Miller took over detainee operations in May, he gained authority to make the final decision about releases. This move appears to have provided greater impetus to the system and over the course of the 4-month period between April and July 2004, 3,700 detainees were released. This number represented over half of the total detainees released since the Coalition had begun interning Iraqis in the spring of 2003.[109] As the IIG and MNF-I moved toward the elections in early January 2005, they continued to adjust the system. In retrospect, it appears the scrutiny caused by the incidents of abuse at Abu Ghraib and the Coalition's increased emphasis on due process and releases had led to more orderly, efficient, and disciplined operations that served the security and intelligence interests of Iraqi and Coalition soldiers while also attempting to prevent the disaffection of the Iraqi people.

Conclusion

After April 2003 the full spectrum campaign in Iraq placed unprecedented demands on US Army units to identify those acting against Coalition and Iraqi authorities, detain as many of these individuals as possible, and interrogate those suspected of having critical information to satisfy the insatiable appetite for actionable intelligence. The result of these imperatives was the Army's mounting of detainee operations on a massive scale. This chapter has documented that most tactical units and even some MP units lacked general preparation and training for this type of operation. Like many missions suddenly thrust on the US Army in the full spectrum campaign, the detention of Iraqis became a widespread requirement that many units at the tactical level were compelled to fill. While infantry, armor, field artillery, and other units had almost no training in how to conduct these missions, they nevertheless improvised and in most cases, did so effectively.

The consolidation of the US Army's detainee operations occurred steadily over the course of late 2003 and 2004. Colonel Warren, CJTF-7's SJA who had been heavily involved in laying the regulatory foundation for the detention mission, recalled that over time, the Coalition military headquarters learned which regulations, staff and organizational structures, and control measures were necessary to provide the proper legal environment for detainee operations.[110] In retrospect, it is clear that in May 2003 the US Armed Forces were not prepared to conduct detainee operations on the scale that was required in Iraq. The abuses at the Abu Ghraib Prison were perhaps the most visible symptom of that lack of preparedness. However, problems with facilities, training, equipment, and administrative processes also hindered the system. Warren contended that the Coalition's progress toward an orderly and effective detention process was slow, recalling, "It was not like we realized there was a problem and it was all fixed. It was very much an iterative process that required constant vigilance and refinement to get improvement."[111]

The US Army in Iraq had little choice but to take on this deliberate process of improvement and oversight. An effective and lawful detainee system removed suspected and confirmed insurgents from areas of operation while avoiding the unnecessary alienation of the local population. Detentions also offered the possibility of interrogations, which held the promise of generating the critical HUMINT required for full spectrum operations focused on creating a more stable environment. Over the course of the 18 months that followed the fall of the Saddam regime, tens of thousands of Soldiers became involved in the operations that became an integral component in the new campaign. With very few exceptions, the men and women who conducted the Coalition's detainee operations in this period did so with professionalism and honor.

Notes

1.   Both COBRA II and ECLIPSE II contained annexes that give guidance about handling EPWs. In addition, V Corps issued FRAGO 006 in the spring of 2003 that foresaw the likelihood of US forces dealing with Iraqis who did not fit into the legal category of EPWs and established methods for working with them. The contents of these orders remain classified at the time of this writing. See Colonel Marc Warren, Statement to US Army Preliminary Screening Inquiry, 29 November 2004, 6. (Used with permission of Colonel Warren.)

2.   Major General Barbara Fast, interview by Contemporary Operations Study Team, Fort Leavenworth, KS, 27 March 2006, 22.

3.   Fast, interview, 27 March 2006, 22.

4.   Lieutenant General Anthony R. Jones, "Executive Summary," *AR 15-6 Investigation of the Abu Ghraib Prison and 205th Military Intelligence Brigade,* 24 August 2004, 9.

5.   Fast, interview, 27 March 2006, 22.

6.   Major General Antonio M. Taguba, *Article 15-6 Investigation of the 800th Military Police Brigade (The Taguba Report),* Annex 45, "Interview with Brigadier General Janice L. Karpinski," to *The Taguba Report,* 15 February 2004, 23, http://www.aclu.org/torturefoia/released/a45.pdf (accessed 23 January 2006).

7.   Taguba, Annex 45, "Interview with Brigadier General Janice L. Karpinski," to *The Taguba Report,* http://www.aclu.org/torturefoia/released/a45.pdf (accessed 12 March 2007).

8.   Lieutenant General Ricardo Sanchez, interview by Contemporary Operations Study Team, Fort Leavenworth, KS, 23 August 2006, 11.

9.   Sanchez, interview, 23 August 2006, 11.

10.   Lieutenant Colonel Harry D. Tunnell IV, *Red Devils: Tactical Perspectives from Iraq* (Fort Leavenworth, KS: Combat Studies Institute Press, 2006), 25.

11.   Tunnell, 25.

12.   Tunnell, 25–26.

13.   Lieutenant Colonel Frank Rangel, interview by Operational Leadership Experiences Project Team, Combat Studies Institute, Fort Leavenworth, KS, 26 October 2005, 12.

14.   Lieutenant Colonel Troy D. Perry, interview by Contemporary Operations Study Team, Fort Leavenworth, KS, 11 May 2006.

15.   Tunnell, 26.

16.   Rangel, interview, 26 October 2005, 12.

17.   Fast, interview, 27 March 2006.

18.   Lieutenant Colonel Steven Bullimore, interview by Contemporary Operations Study Team, Fort Leavenworth, KS, 18 May 2006, 6.

19.   Colonel Marc Warren, e-mail correspondence with authors, 5 March 2007. The specific contents of these FRAGOs remain classified as of this writing.

20.   Sanchez, interview, 23 August 2006, 12; see also, Warren, Statement to US Army Preliminary Screening Inquiry, 29 November 2004, 33.

21.   CJTF-7, Agenda for CJTF-7 Detention Summit—Camp Victory—19 AUG 03, 1; see also, Fast, interview, 27 March 2006.

22.   Colonel Marc Warren, interview by Contemporary Operations Study Team, Fort Leavenworth, KS, 15 March 2007, 11.

23.   Warren, interview, 15 March 2007, 11.

24.   Warren, interview, 15 March 2007, 10–11.

25.   Fast, interview, 27 March 2006.

26.   Major General George Fay, *AR 15-6 Investigation of the Abu Ghraib Prison and 205th Military Intelligence Brigade,* 57.

27.   Taguba, Annex 19, "The Ryder Report," to *The Taguba Report*, Executive Summary.

28.   Taguba, Annex 19, "The Ryder Report," to *The Taguba Report*, Executive Summary.

29.   Taguba, Annex 19, "The Ryder Report," to *The Taguba Report*, Executive Summary.

30.   Regimental Support Squadron, 2d Armored Cavalry Regiment, *RSS/RHA Detainee Holding Area Guidance* Memorandum, 18 December 2003.

31.   *RSS/RHA Detainee Holding Area Guidance* Memorandum, 18 December 2003, 1.

32.   *RSS/RHA Detainee Holding Area Guidance* Memorandum, 18 December 2003, 3.

33.   2d Armored Cavalry Regiment, *Laydown of Division Detention Operations/Detainee Process* Briefing, September 2003.

34.   *Laydown of Division Detention Operations/Detainee Process*, slide 4.

35.   *Laydown of Division Detention Operations/Detainee Process*, slide 6.

36.   *Laydown of Division Detention Operations/Detainee Process*, slide 9.

37.   See, for example, *RSS/RHA Detainee Holding Area Guidance* Memorandum, 18 December 2003, 1.

38.   1st Brigade Combat Team, 4th Infantry Division, Sworn Statement from Unnamed Soldier (name redacted), D Company, 4th FSB, Exhibit A, Report by AR 15-6 Investigating Officer On Shooting Death of Iraqi Detainee, FOB Packhorse, Tikrit, Iraq, 11 September 2003, http://www.aclu.org/projects/foiasearch/pdf/DOD044873.pdf (accessed 14 December 2006).

39.   4th Forward Support Battalion, 1st Brigade Combat Team, 4th Infantry Division, AR 15-6 Investigation Conducted by officer (name redacted), 4th FSB, Exhibit K, Sworn Statement from 4th FSB Operations Officer (name redacted), 13 September 2003, http://www.aclu.org/projects/foiasearch/pdf/DOD044873.pdf (accessed 14 December 2006).

40.   1st BCT, 4th ID, Report by AR 15-6 Investigating Officer On Shooting Death of Iraqi Detainee, FOB Packhorse, Tikrit Iraq, 1.

41.   1st BCT, 4th ID, Report by AR 15-6 Investigating Officer On Shooting Death of Iraqi Detainee, FOB Packhorse, Tikrit Iraq, 1

42.   1st BCT, 4th ID, Report by AR 15-6 Investigating Officer On Shooting Death of Iraqi Detainee, FOB Packhorse, Tikrit Iraq, 3

43.   1st BCT, 4th ID, Report by AR 15-6 Investigating Officer On Shooting Death of Iraqi Detainee, FOB Packhorse, Tikrit, Iraq, 4.

44.   The Inspector General, *Detainee Operations Inspection*, 21 July 2004, 53.

45.   IG, *Detainee Operations Inspection*, 21 July 2004, 54.

46.   IG, *Detainee Operations Inspection*, 21 July 2004, 14.

47.   IG, *Detainee Operations Inspection*, 21 July 2004, 17. The IG Report defined point of capture as detainee operations that occurred at battalion-level or below.

48.   IG, *Detainee Operations Inspection*, 21 July 2004, iv.

49.   Fast, interview, 27 March 2006.

50.   IG, *Detainee Operations Inspection*, 21 July 2004, iv. Location of remaining 10 percent of the cases could not be determined.

51.   This section on detention operations at Abu Ghraib is intended as a summary of the key events and decisions that surround the abuses at the prison. Because of the complexity of the issues involved, the authors of this study encourage all readers to look into the key primary sources, the large majority of which are available to the public, to gain a deeper understanding of the origins and characteristics of operations at the prison. Those sources, most importantly the AR 15-6 investigations into the 800th MP Brigade and the 205th MI Brigade, are identified in the endnotes below.

52.   Taguba, Annex 60, "Testimony of MAJ Michael Sheridan, S3, 320th MP BN," to *The Taguba Report*, 14 February 2004, 7, http://www.aclu.org/torturefoia/released/a60.pdf (accessed 30 January 2007).

53.   Taguba, Annex 37, "Excerpts from Log Books, 320th MP BN (15 September 2003 entry)," to *The Taguba Report,* http://www.aclu.org/torturefoia/released/t37.pdf (accessed 30 January 2007).

54. Taguba, Annex 63, "Testimony of CPT Reese, Commander, 372d MP Company," to *The Taguba Report*, http://www.aclu.org/torturefoia/released/a63.pdf (accessed 30 January 2007).

55. Taguba, Annex 46, "Testimony of Colonel Thomas Pappas, Commander, 205th MI Brigade," to *The Taguba Report,* 9 February 2004, 3, http://www.aclu.org/torturefoia/released/a46.pdf (accessed 16 January 2007).

56. Taguba, Annex 20, "Assessment of DOD Counterterrorism Interrogation and Detention Operations in Iraq," to *The Taguba Report*, 9 February 2004, 1, http://www.aclu.org/torturefoia/released/a20.pdf (accessed 9 March 2007).

57. Taguba, Annex 20, "Assessment of DOD Counterterrorism Interrogation," to *The Taguba Report*, 9 February 2004, 5, http://www.aclu.org/torturefoia/released/a20.pdf (accessed 9 March 2007).

58. James R. Schlesinger, Chairman*, Final Report of the Independent Panel to Review DOD Detention Operations*, August 2004, 72–73.

59. Taguba, Annex 63, "Testimony of CPT Reese, Commander, 372d MP Company," to *The Taguba Report*, 45, http://www.aclu.org/torturefoia/released/a63.pdf (accessed 30 January 2007).

60. Fay, *AR 15-6 Investigation,* 72.

61. Fay, *AR 15-6 Investigation,* 77.

62. Fay, *AR 15-6 Investigation,* 77–78.

63. Fay, *AR 15-6 Investigation,* 9.

64. Fay, *AR 15-6 Investigation,* 96–108.

65. Jones, *AR 15-6 Investigation of the Abu Ghraib Prison and the 205th Military Intelligence Brigade,* 4.

66. Taguba, *The Taguba Report*, 46.

67. Taguba, Annex 71, "Testimony of 1LT Lewis C. Raeder, Platoon Leader, 372d MP Company," to *The Taguba Report*, 3, http://www.aclu.org/torturefoia/released/a71.pdf (accessed 1 February 2007).

68. Taguba, *The Taguba Report*, 44–47.

69. CJTF-7, FRAGO 1108 to CJTF-7 OPORD 03-036, 19 November 2003. Order reproduced in Taguba, *The Taguba Report*, 38.

70. For complete definition, see Department of Defense Joint Publication 1-02, *DOD Dictionary of Military and Associated Terms*, 12 April 2001 (as amended through 5 January 2007), 525.

71. Taguba, Annex 46, "Testimony of Colonel Thomas Pappas," to *The Taguba Report*.

72. Taguba, Annex 46, "Testimony of Colonel Thomas Pappas," to *The Taguba Report*.

73. Taguba, Annex 46, "Testimony of Colonel Thomas Pappas," to *The Taguba Report*.

74. Taguba, Annex 63, "Testimony of CPT Reese, Commander, 372d MP Company" to *The Taguba Report*, 13, http://www.aclu.org/torturefoia/released/a63.pdf (accessed 30 January 2007).

75. Colonel Marc Warren, *V Corps/CJTF-7 Document Extract* (as of 1 October 2005), 1.

76. IG, *Detainee Operations Inspection,* 21 July 2004, 21.

77. Kathleen T. Rhem, "Commanders in Iraq ordered Humane Treatment of Detainees," *DefenseLink*, 20 May 2004, http://defenselink.mil/news/May2004/n05202004_200405206.html (accessed 25 October 2006).

78. Headquarters, MNB-North, *Memorandum for Record, Subject: Standing Operating Procedures for all MNB-N Detainee Collection Points*, 27 January 2004, 1.

79. Camp Duke Detainee Facility S.O.P., 1 June 2004, http://www.aclu.org/projects/foiasearch/pdf/DOD045995.pdf (accessed 25 February 2008).

80. Camp Duke Detainee Facility S.O.P.

81. Camp Duke Detainee Facility S.O.P., 1.

82. Camp Duke Detainee Facility S.O.P., 7.

83. Task Force 1-22 IN, Point Paper: Operation IRAQI FREEDOM—Handling of Detainees.

84. LTC [name redacted], CONUS Team, Department of the Army Inspector General, *Memorandum for Chief, Inspections Division. SUBJECT: 4th Infantry Division Detainee Operations Assessment Trip*

Report, no date. (Memorandum based on interviews conducted by CONUS Team between 5–8 April 2004.), 36, http://action.aclu.org/torturefoia/released/091505/15937.pdf (accessed 9 March 2007).

85. *Memorandum, Subject: 4th Infantry Division Detainee Operations Assessment Trip Report*, 7.

86. Major Charles Seifert, interview by Contemporary Operations Study Team, Fort Leavenworth, KS, 3 May 2006, 9.

87. Seifert, interview, 3 May 2006, 16.

88. Jon Myatt, "Air Defenders Become MPs for Duty in Afghanistan," 15 March 2004, *Defend America,* http://www.defendamerica.mil/articles/mar2004/a031504e.html (accessed 14 March 2007).

89. Staff Sergeant Matthew Claycomb, B Btry, 1/107th Field Artillery, Pennsylvania Army National Guard, *Memorandum, SUBJECT: Operation Iraqi Freedom II Report from Bravo Battery 1st Battalion, 107th Field Artillery, October 2003 to February 2005.*

90. Company History for C CO FWD, 2/103 AR, 2.

91. Captain David E. Beveridge, "New Jersey National Guard Soldiers Earn Right to Proudly Wear Brassard," *Military Police Bulletin*, April 2005, http://www.wood.army.mil/mpbulletin/pdfs/April%2005/Beveridge-In%20Lieu%20of%20MP.pdf (accessed 14 March 2007).

92. Dobie McArthur, Senior Advisor for Detainee and Prisoner Issues, CPA, Memorandum for the Administrator, Subject: *Analysis of Detention Operations*, 22 March 2004, 3.

93. L. Paul Bremer, *My Year in Iraq: The Struggle to Build a Future of Hope* (New York, NY: Simon & Schuster, 2006), 264, 288.

94. Coalition Provisional Authority, "Conditional Release Announcement," 7 January 2004, 2–3, http://www.cpa-iraq.org/transcripts/Jan7Bremer_Conditional.htm (accessed 2 November 2007).

95. CJTF-7, *Interrogation Operations* Brief (25 January 2004), "Detainees Population & Release" slide. The numbers given here do not reflect the 3,855 Mujahedin-e Khalq (MEK) detainees under detention at Camp Ashraf.

96. Coalition Provisional Authority, Memorandum, Subject*: Strategy for Addressing Detention Issues*, 69.

97. McArthur, Memorandum, Subject: *Analysis of Detention Operations*, 22 March 2004, 1.

98. McArthur, Memorandum, Subject: *Analysis of Detention Operations*, 22 March 2004, 1.

99. Taguba, *The Taguba Report*, 38.

100. McArthur, Memorandum, Subject: *Analysis of Detention Operations*, 22 March 2004, 3.

101. McArthur, Memorandum, Subject: *Analysis of Detention Operations*, 3 April 2004, 3.

102. Warren, Statement to US Army Preliminary Screening Inquiry, 29 November 2004, 24.

103. MNF-I, *Detainee Operations, Commander's Conference Update* Briefing, 13 August 2004, slide "Referral to Iraqi Legal System," http://www.aclu.org/projects/foiasearch/pdf/DOD044828.pdf (accessed 8 November 2007).

104. Warren, Statement to US Army Preliminary Screening Inquiry, 29 November 2004, 24–25.

105. CJTF-7, *Coalition Detainee Operations Strategy* Briefing (30 April 2004), slide "CJTF-7 Detainee Status."

106. MNF-I, *Detainee Operations, Commander's Conference Update*, slide "Security Internees—Disposition of Detainees Based on Risk."

107. MNF-I, *Detainee Operations, Commander's Conference Update*, slide "MSC Detention Facilities Length of Detention."

108. MNF-I, *Detainee Operations, Commander's Conference Update*, slide "Combined Review and Release Board."

109. Headquarters, United States Central Command, "News Release: Detainee Release Board Takes on Iraqi Partners," 16 April 2004.

110. Warren, interview, 15 March 2007, 16.

111. Warren, interview, 15 March 2007, 15.

Chapter 7

Fighting the Battle of Ideas in Iraq

On 29 January 2005, the day before the first democratic elections in Iraq were to be held, a rocket landed near the American Embassy in Baghdad's International Zone killing two Americans and wounding five others. Soldiers in an aviation unit from the 1st Cavalry Division (1st CAV) caught the launch of the rocket on an airborne video camera and recorded seven insurgents leaving the launch site and traveling to a building in the southeastern part of the capital. Soldiers from the 1st CAV then moved into the neighborhood and detained the seven men.[1] This attack, launched on the eve of the elections, was clearly intended to lash out at the Coalition as well as create the impression in Iraqi minds that the Coalition, regardless of its military strength, could not create a secure environment in which to hold elections for the Iraqi National Assembly. The insurgents hoped to plant fear in the population and thus prevent them from going to the polls. Major General Peter Chiarelli, the commander of the 1st CAV, viewed the attack as potentially having adverse strategic effects on the overall Coalition effort. Chiarelli immediately directed that the videotape of the launch and the detention of the insurgents be declassified and given to Iraqi media outlets so that it could calm the concerns caused by news of the attack that had already begun spreading among Baghdad's population.[2] The public release of that videotape, which occurred within hours of the attack, demonstrated the Coalition's efficiency in dealing with threats and its resolve to maintain secure conditions for the elections that were held successfully the next day in the capital and across the country. Chiarelli's use of the Iraqi media to help protect the security of the elections also serves as an excellent illustration of how after 18 months of conducting full spectrum operations, the US Army had come to understand and employ information in its overall campaign in Iraq.

The action taken by the 1st CAV commander and his Soldiers was just one engagement that US Soldiers fought in an extremely difficult and critical "battle of ideas" in Iraq. This battle was of paramount importance, and Army leaders had understood its significance from the inception of Operation IRAQI FREEDOM (OIF). When Coalition military commanders articulated their understanding of the campaign during 2003 and 2004, they often defined the center of gravity (COG) of the campaign as the Iraqi people. If the Coalition hoped to be successful, it needed to convince the citizens of Iraq that its goals were in their best interests and its actions in support of these goals were effective and sincere. Military leaders also had to counter propaganda from forces opposed to the Coalition. If this battle of ideas was successful, commanders believed most Iraqis would willingly embrace the Coalition's efforts to provide security and remake Iraq into a unified, stable, prosperous, and free nation.

The Army's chief means of fighting the battle of ideas was a group of related actions and processes, collectively called information operations (IO). Army doctrine in 2003 defined IO as a set of activities taken to attack or defend information and information systems to gain information superiority and to affect decisionmaking of both friendly and enemy forces.[3] IO thus included operations designed to militarily attack enemy automation systems and defend friendly automation systems, particularly those providing command and control to military units. This so-called "hard" aspect of IO played a prominent role during the actual invasion of Iraq in March and April 2003, and it continued throughout the period in this study at a lesser intensity.

The aspect of IO doctrine used by Chiarelli on the eve of the elections included another set of activities designed to win the ideological struggle for ideas. During the full spectrum campaign that followed the invasion of Iraq, most US leaders believed this "soft power" side of IO was more important than the "hard" side because it had the potential to win over the Iraqi population and the international community. The concepts and terminology involved were very complex, and synchronizing them with other forms of operations was a delicate task. It was also difficult to assess the results of IO, because it dealt not just with observable actions, but also with the hearts and minds of the Iraqi people.

Parallel to and often intertwined with this battle of ideas in Iraq was the Army's diligent effort to tell its story to the American people. Army public affairs (PA) offices and public affairs officers (PAO) provided command information to the media and facilitated media access to US units. Like the soft power aspect of IO, PA also dealt with the intangible realm of ideas. These two missions were by doctrine quite distinct. IO is one of the tools used to conduct military operations; its purposes are to protect one's own information systems, attack the enemy's systems, and use information to achieve certain results with targeted audiences. The mission of PA, however, is to provide truthful information to the American people, and by extension to the international community, about the Army's operations. Army leaders during this period of OIF were faced with the doctrinal, organizational, and sometimes ethical tension between manipulating information to achieve specific military objectives and providing accurate information to tell the Army story. This tension became acute because most of the Army's efforts in the battle of ideas occurred within a complex non-Western culture.

Using information to support the new campaign in Iraq was an extremely challenging task in 2003 and 2004. Many Department of Defense (DOD), Army, and civilian leaders somewhat complicated the task by using the terms "strategic communications" and "strategic effects" in conjunction with and synonymous with IO. The conflation of terms, and creation of various staff agencies to use information in support of military operations, made understanding and directing IO that much more difficult.[*] This chapter will first briefly examine the concepts and doctrine underlying the use of information and then cover the conduct of IO to include its use by Iraqi insurgents during OIF. The discussion will then shift to the relationships between the Army and the media in providing PA support to the campaign. Finally, the chapter will examine the work of Army PA Soldiers in Iraq, including their efforts in relation to the Iraqi media.

Information Operations: Definitions and Doctrine

While IO is a relatively new term in the Army, the fundamental concept behind IO is not novel. The Army has a long history of using information as a tool or a "weapon" to influence the outcome of its campaigns. One of the more famous examples of IO was Operation QUICKSILVER, a deception operation undertaken in support of the D-Day invasion during World War II. For the deception, the Allied military headquarters in Great Britain created a fictional Army group in England that appeared to be poised for the invasion of France at the Pas-de-Calais. American troops used a variety of tactics to deceive the German High Command

---

[*]This chapter will use the term "information operations" in its broadest sense, meaning the use of information and information systems in support of military operations. Where necessary, the distinctions between particular doctrinal and operational terms will be discussed more broadly.

about the intent of this force and location of the primary invasion, thus keeping German reserves away from the actual landing sites in Normandy.[4] Although IO has changed over the years, especially with the advent of the information age, some of its basic concepts such as deception have remained the same.[5]

IO is a term and a concept with which the Army, the Services, and DOD have grappled with since the 1990s when it emerged and served to combine previously disparate activities into a whole. The Army's IO doctrine prior to 2003 was encapsulated in Field Manual (FM) 100-6, *Command and Control Warfare*, and then in the 1996 version of FM 100-6, renamed *Information Operations*. IO in the FM 100-6 construct was directed toward attacking an enemy's command, control, and communications systems and abilities while protecting one's own. This concept of IO as an integrated set of tools to be wielded in support of a campaign is similar to how a commander would employ maneuver, fires, or logistics to achieve the objectives. With the US advantages in technology and systems integration, its proponents saw IO as a way to prevent adversaries from degrading US capabilities while exploiting enemy weaknesses in the information age. Army planners expected to need these capabilities if the United States found itself fighting an enemy with its own information-age capabilities.

Photo by PFC Jason Phillips

Figure 59. Sergeant Jason McGinn, 361st PSYOP Company, listens as a local man discusses his concerns in Al Fallujah, Iraq, in May 2003.

The Army's new IO doctrine published in late 2003 as FM 3-13, *Information Operations: Doctrine, Tactics, Techniques, and Procedures,* built on this definition of IO, defining these operations as "the employment of the core capabilities of electronic warfare (EW), computer network operations (CNO), psychological operations (PSYOP), military deception (MILDEC), and operations security (OPSEC), in concert with specified supporting and related capabilities, to affect or defend information and information systems, and to influence decision-making." These five core capabilities of IO were complemented by six "supporting capabilities" that would provide additional affects: physical destruction, information assurance, physical security, counterintelligence, counterdeception, and counterpropaganda.[6] The 2003 manual placed responsibility for conducting these operations in the G7 IO cell on staffs at division and higher level to synchronize the various core and supporting capabilities into a unified whole. These capabilities and missions had previously been divided among a number of separate staff sections.[7] In the 1990s the Army also created an IO career field for officers who would be trained to integrate this disparate range of activities into a whole.[8]

Alongside the predominant understanding of IO as offensive and defensive actions to destroy or protect information systems, proponents supported a complementary aspect of IO—the use of information itself, in part through the use of traditional PSYOP and MILDEC methods—to affect enemy behavior. MILDEC and PSYOP are well-established techniques used to gain a military advantage over one's enemy. In recent years, IO targets were expanded to include nonmilitary audiences in host nations and the international community. To distinguish this aspect of IO from its other functions that were more closely related to conventional combat operations, military leaders began referring to it as "soft-power." In this construct, the purpose of IO was to "influence the behavior of target decision-makers or audiences through the use of information and information systems."[9] The goal was to encourage others to act in ways favorable to US forces. In the 2003 version of FM 3-13, this aspect of IO doctrine included three related capabilities: PA, civil-military operations (CMO), and defense support to public diplomacy.[10]

In this concept, information itself could be used to influence neutral or hostile audiences to support US forces and host nation authorities, an effort that was often articulated as "winning hearts and minds." Most counterinsurgency theory views information as particularly important in trying to sway public opinion against insurgents, terrorists, or other opposing forces, thus isolating these opposition groups from the general population of the host nation. Based on this assumption, military commanders could use a combination of themes and messages delivered by PSYOP units and practical steps undertaken by civil affairs (CA) units to demonstrate the credibility and effectiveness of the counterinsurgent force and the host nation government. Surrounding these actions was the continual PA mission to inform the American public of Army operations. It is important to note that the creation or use of information for a particular purpose could be segmented within a military organization, but once disseminated it was to become unified into a whole that would have a particular outcome.

In the information age, even the most isolated or technologically primitive target audiences have access to a wide variety of news sources. Military planners and commanders had to compete in this information environment to get their messages heard and to counter false messages launched by other outlets, including adversaries. Therefore, IO doctrine held that PA measures taken to spread US and host nation messages, themes, and objectives via the media could also be used in support of military operations.[11] It was this nexus, the juncture of IO and PA, that has presented Army planners with doctrinal, organizational, and ethical challenges since the 1990s.

The role and mission of PA will be discussed later in this chapter; briefly, Soldiers involved in PA are charged with providing accurate and truthful public information in support of US operations. The distinction between IO, which is focused on manipulating an enemy or neutral host nation audience, and PA operations, which are directed at US (and international) audiences, at times made for uneasy relations between those Soldiers and units performing these related activities. In turn, commanders struggled with how to organize their staffs and how to assign responsibility for the many core and related capabilities that defined IO. The issue of subordinating PA staff officers to the IO staff cell was contentious and, as will be shown later, was addressed in different ways by US Army units as OIF progressed.

These dual aspects of the doctrinal basis of IO, and the relationship between IO and PA, evolved during the 1990s and greatly influenced the US Army's planning and operations during OIF. This chapter will focus on the "soft power" side of IO for two reasons. First, the offensive and defensive use of information systems and other weapons is both highly classified and technically complex. Second, though the US Army extensively employed various EW and IO systems in the invasion of Iraq and, to a lesser degree, continued to do so once the new campaign began, the primary focus of IO and PA in Iraq since May 2003 has been on the use of information in the public sector. The following section will briefly examine how the Army employed the soft-power aspect of IO in the Balkans before turning to events in Iraq between 2003 and 2005.

Information Operations before Operation IRAQI FREEDOM: The Balkans

The Army's use of IO in the Balkans during the 1990s was a formative experience for many Soldiers and served as a useful precedent for those who later deployed to Iraq in 2003 and 2004. For the US Army, the experience in the Balkans began in 1995 after the Dayton Peace Agreement ended years of civil war inside the former Yugoslavia. Some 28,000 US troops led the NATO Implementation Force (IFOR) into Bosnia on 16 December 1995. The mission of the 60,000 NATO and Russian soldiers in the IFOR, and later the Stabilization Force (SFOR), was to "ensure continued compliance with the cease-fire" and to "ensure the withdrawal of forces from the agreed cease-fire zones of separation back to their respective territories, and ensure the separation of forces."[12]

As soon as US and NATO troops entered Bosnia and Yugoslavia, commanders and planners spent considerable time and effort on the soft power aspect of IO to support their overall campaign. In Bosnia, commanders directed IO to help communicate their intentions to the local population and win their support for the IFOR and the SFOR missions. At the same time, IO was utilized to deter the former warring factions from violating the Dayton Agreement and to discourage those factions from attacking NATO forces.[13]

For Soldiers in the IFOR, IO consisted of two main efforts. According to one study by the National Defense University (NDU), the first effort was designed to establish IFOR's "credibility with the international media to gain international support of the operation."[14] This part of the campaign was largely successful because of widespread international approval for the operation. The second element was a PSYOP campaign designed to "shape the local population's perception in favor of IFOR troops and activities."[15] Products included posters, magazines, newspapers, and radio station programs. The PSYOP effort, despite some initial setbacks, was also considered a success. However, too many of the products produced in the first months, especially the printed posters, reflected an orientation toward American culture rather than European culture. The later products that had a European feel, such as the teenage magazine *MIRKO*, proved much more successful.[16] The Army quickly learned the importance of cultural understanding as a critical component of IO.

One significant and decidedly low-tech factor in the success of PSYOP in Bosnia was the individual actions of US commanders and Soldiers. The NDU study of IO in Bosnia contended, "The success of the IFOR mission as a whole rested largely on their individual abilities to persuade the FWF [former warring factions] that peace was the only alternative."[17] This was largely accomplished with one of the oldest PSYOP techniques in the book—face-to-face communications. The ability of commanders and Soldiers of all ranks to sit down in coffee houses, restaurants, or private homes and talk with the local population allowed the Soldiers to speak to people in real terms and build rapport. These interactions distributed the PSYOP message quickly, and the impact of that message was assessed immediately from the response of the target audience.[18]

Four years later, the US and NATO employed IO during the 1999 NATO-led occupation of Kosovo to stop the humanitarian disaster and ethnic warfare between Serbians and ethnic Albanians. During the 78-day bombing campaign, IO targeted offensive and defensive weapons systems to support air strikes and other military operations. When the threat of a NATO ground invasion forced withdrawal of Serbian troops in June 1999, NATO's Kosovo forces (KFOR) entered a region without an effective central government and with two ethnic groups bent on revenge. The Serbs, though small in number, had held all political and economic power under the regime led by Slobodan Milosevic. After years of perpetrating abuses on the ethnic Albanian population, which made up the majority of Kosovo's population, the Serbs found themselves the target of Albanian retribution. Kosovo soon became a three-way information struggle between KFOR, the Serbian Government, and Kosovo Albanians for the attention of the civilian population.

To fight the battle of ideas in Yugoslavia and Kosovo, KFOR used PA, CA, and both offensive and defensive IO. Defensively, IO countered misinformation and propaganda, especially that distributed by local and regional media. By circulating KFOR's perspective regarding events and issues, IO limited, and even neutralized, the effects of provocative rhetoric and anti-KFOR misinformation.[19] Offensively, KFOR Soldiers and leaders actively engaged important Albanian and Serbian leaders and organizations. US forces used PSYOP loudspeaker operations, handbills, radio broadcasts, press releases, media events, medical assistance programs, reconstruction and short-term employment projects, face-to-face meetings, and force presence to achieve their goals in the information environment.[20]

Assessing the success of IO in Kosovo proved difficult. Army officers tried to determine the effectiveness of specific efforts by determining trends within their areas of responsibility (AORs) using unit and media reporting assessments. Most commands tried to determine whether an incident generally resulted in a positive effect—one that supported KFOR's mission, or had a negative effect—one that went against KFOR's mission.[21] Though the campaign dragged on without a solution to Kosovo's status as a political entity, most US commanders deemed IO in Kosovo as successful because neither side turned against NATO and negotiations continued relatively peacefully.

For many Soldiers who served in the Balkans, their experience in IFOR and KFOR validated the importance of the soft-power aspect of IO doctrine and at the same time revealed many shortcomings in its practice. Though the Balkan deployments generated debate about how to implement IO in concert with overall campaign plans, nearly all leaders internalized the principle that IO was integral to the overall campaign in Bosnia and Kosovo. Unlike Iraq in mid-2003 and 2004, however, the Balkans did not present the Army with a determined insurgent and terrorist enemy, or with the degree of cultural and religious separation between the occupier and the general population.

Information Operations in Support of Operation IRAQI FREEDOM: The Overall Effort

From the inception of planning for operations in Iraq, US commanders and their planners ensured that IO became integral in the structure of OIF. The deception, EW, and CNO aspects of the IO plan in support of OIF remain classified. Nevertheless, some details of the PSYOP portion of COBRA II, the plan for ground operations in Iraq, are available and establish that the planning for this IO element began more than 3 months before the invasion. Teams within the 8th PSYOP Battalion of the 4th PSYOP Group at Fort Bragg, North Carolina, which supported CENTCOM, began leaflet and broadcast operations, targeting Iraqi Armed Forces and the Iraqi population in December 2002.[22] Some of their success could be seen in the number of Iraqi units that did not resist the Coalition invasion and in the generally positive reception afforded to Coalition troops by most Iraqis in March and April 2003.[23]

The nature of full spectrum operations in Iraq after May 2003 presented Coalition leaders with a set of challenges not found in the conventional phase of OIF. The invasion of Iraq moved with obvious logic, speed, and a visible outcome from its start in Kuwait to its end in Baghdad. The new campaign that began in May 2003, however, was more complex and featured economic, political, and other lines of operation for which progress was slow and difficult to measure. The creation of a new Iraq, like the development of the United States, did not happen in a brief time and did not move linearly from start to a logical end. Developing an IO plan to support the overall campaign and communicating progress to multiple audiences was thus extremely difficult.

In mid-May 2003, during the transition from decisive combat operations to Phase IV operations and the change of command within CENTCOM, both Combined Forces Land Component Command (CFLCC) and V Corps (soon to become Combined Joint Task Force–7 [CJTF-7]) made IO a line of operation in their campaign plans. The focus of these operations switched from undermining Iraqi military morale in support of the invasion to encouraging Iraqi support for the Coalition's political objectives. V Corps initially labeled this part of the plan "perceptions," a category of tasks intended to "integrate and leverage Coalition efforts to establish a secure and stable environment" and "positively influence the Iraqi population in support of Coalition initiatives and aggressively counter destabilizing influences."[24] This objective included four major subtasks: inform the Iraqi people about progress toward forming *their* new government, neutralize anti-Coalition elements, neutralize anti-Coalition propaganda, and influence Iraqis to support Coalition efforts to build a new Iraqi Government.[25]

Army and Marine units at nearly every level in CJTF-7 also included IO in their subordinate planning efforts. Naturally they supported the Coalition's broad efforts, tailoring them to their specific AORs. The 4th Infantry Division (4th ID), for example, spent considerable effort developing and executing a plan to communicate its rules of engagement to local Iraqi leaders to prevent misunderstandings as it hunted down former regime elements in the summer of 2003.[26] Putting these IO plans into action, as previously mentioned, was difficult. The environment included severely fractured Iraqi audiences competing for their share of power in a post-Saddam Iraq. Terrorist and insurgent groups opposed any Coalition efforts, and international opinion and domestic public opinion were ambivalent at best.

One detailed study of the effectiveness of IO in OIF completed in 2005 by a student at the US Army School of Advanced Military Studies (SAMS) revealed four sets of shortcomings. First, the author of the study concluded that doctrine was not sufficiently clear with regard to the proper linkages between IO and PA regarding how to legally influence domestic, enemy, and neutral audiences. Second, the study found that Army units at division and lower echelons lacked sufficient staff and other resources to carry out IO. Third, it concluded that insufficient intelligence support was used in developing and carrying out the IO plan. Finally, the study claimed, "Commanders, staffs and IO officers did not understand how to integrate IO with all the tools (CA, PA, maneuver, fire support, logistics, etc.) available to them to shape the information environment in which they would operate."[27] These four issues reoccur repeatedly when examining IO in OIF.

The problems created by lack of staff and other resources should have surprised no one. When the CFLCC staff redeployed out of Iraq in May and June 2003, it took with it the Army's main IO assets, including the Joint Psychological Operations Task Force (JPOTF) that had been created for the initial invasion. Thus, once DOD and CENTCOM established CJTF-7, Lieutenant General Ricardo Sanchez and his staff had no theater-strategic and operational-level PSYOP resources and had to rely on support from the IO units within the US Army Civil Affairs and Psychological Operations Command (USACAPOC) located at Fort Bragg.[28] This delayed and complicated the provision of high-level technical support, making it almost impossible to quickly or effectively react to insurgent IO. According to the SAMS study, "What this meant in practical terms for the CJTF-7 was that it could not produce its own operational-level PSYOP products locally and tactical units had to rely upon their assigned tactical PSYOP organizations for more and more support."[29]

At such a critical time in the summer of 2003, IO support for operations in Iraq was completely inadequate for the needs of CJTF-7 and the Coalition Provisional Authority (CPA). The SAMS study contended that the "CPA could not compete against the Iraqi rumor mill, partisan Iraqi media outlets, or even foreign satellite broadcasts such as *Al Jazeera*" and to complicate matters further, "leaders in CPA had no understanding of the capabilities and limitations of the [military] assets at its disposal."[30] According to an Army analysis of IO at the tactical level of the campaign in Iraq, almost all brigades lacked trained IO personnel and had limited IO capability. The authors of this analysis stated succinctly, "The brigades lack[ed] the resources to win the IO fight."[31] Many of these problems did not begin to improve until late 2003, when CENTCOM redeployed the JPOTF to Iraq.

Neither the Office of Reconstruction and Humanitarian Assistance (ORHA) nor the CPA had any real capability to execute IO when they arrived in Iraq. The CPA proclaimed freedom of the press and assembly on assuming power in May 2003, but it had limited media resources of its own to disseminate the Coalition's major objectives or to explain its particular decisions. The CPA also failed to rapidly create or support fledgling Iraqi media outlets that could compete in the "marketplace of ideas" and fill the vacuum that opened after Saddam Hussein was deposed. This was perhaps most damaging to the efforts to publicize the work of the Iraqi Governing Council (IGC), which enjoyed the support of no media outlets in the summer of 2003. The lack of planning for sophisticated and dedicated media support to these important organizations was a critical shortcoming that could not be made up for by highly effective military IO, had it existed.

There was a direct connection between the level of popular support enjoyed by the Coalition and the Coalition's ability to improve the quality of life, physical security, and stability in Iraq. Army doctrine stated that IO supported other lines of operation—military, economic, and political—and that principle became critical in the new campaign in Iraq. Soldiers had to use IO to tell the story of how the Coalition was making significant improvements in sewage projects, water treatment plants, and the creation of a new education system. Otherwise, most Iraqis would remain essentially ignorant of the Coalition's overall effort to improve the country.[32] Success or failure in IO could buttress or undermine the overall success in building Iraqi support for the Coalition and the new Iraqi Government.

Many participants in OIF viewed the inability to fully address Iraqi expectations and needs as one of the chief failures of the Coalition IO effort. Colonel Ralph O. Baker, commander of the 2d Brigade Combat Team (BCT), 1st Armored Division (1st AD) in Baghdad during 2003 and 2004, stated that the biggest issues he faced were the "credibility challenges we encountered among the Iraqis . . . a consequence of the initial mismanagement of Iraqi expectations before we ever crossed the berm into Iraq."[33] Perception management was a constant problem; Iraqis had enormously unrealistic expectations and perceptions about how quickly life would improve after Saddam was ousted. These expectations were inflated by Coalition pronouncements before the war that the average Iraqi would be much better off when Saddam and his regime were out of power. Baker asserted, "The concept of 'better' proved to be a terrible cultural misperception on our part because we, the liberators, equated better with not being ruled by a brutal dictator. In contrast, a better life for Iraqis implied consistent, reliable electricity, food, medical care, jobs, and safety from criminals and political thugs."[34] The cultural gap between expectations of both groups was exacerbated by the proclivity of some Iraqis to believe in conspiracy theories. Some American Soldiers encountered this problem in the form of the man-on-the-moon analogy. Colonel Baker recalled repeatedly hearing the following form of that complaint: "If you Americans are capable of putting a man on the moon, why can't you get the electricity to come on? If you are not turning the electricity on, it must be because you don't want to and are punishing us."[35] Most explanations about problems with antiquated infrastructure and time required to ship in new equipment did little to regain the confidence of distrustful Iraqis.

Assessing the effectiveness of PSYOP techniques presented another challenge. During the summer of 2003 tactical units received IO products from higher headquarters containing messages that were often too broad to resonate with the diverse population in Iraq. As the Army had learned in the Balkans, to be effective IO themes and messages had to be tailored to the specific audience. Colonel Baker emphasized this point stating, "IO planners at commands above division level appeared to look at the Iraqis as a single, homogeneous population that would be receptive to centrally developed, all-purpose, general themes and messages directed at Iraqis as a group."[36] To address some of those weaknesses and lack of capability, CJTF-7 contracted with private firms in late 2004 to begin producing PSYOP products and news stories in support of the IO line of operations plan. The use of those stories in Iraqi media outlets, despite their truthfulness, generated some controversy in 2005.[37]

The Army's 2004 tactical IO analysis noted an additional problem. Across Iraq in 2003 and early 2004, commanders did not or could not ensure synchronicity of the messages and effects. The report stated, "A vertically integrated, horizontally synchronized IO campaign simply did not appear to exist" in Iraq.[38] CJTF-7 did steadily increase its IO capacity as it revamped its staff from a tactical to a theater-strategic headquarters in the late summer and fall of 2003. IO plans then improved over time and commanders increasingly incorporated IO into all their operations. By the time CJTF-7 transitioned authority to Multi-National Force–Iraq (MNF-I) and Multi-National Corps–Iraq (MNC-I) in the summer of 2004, US commanders had learned key lessons about IO. The first MNC-I commander, Lieutenant General Thomas Metz, became a particularly forceful proponent for IO in Iraq, arguing that strategic and operational commanders needed to become as aggressive and offensive-minded with IO as they were with other elements of warfighting.[39] General George W. Casey Jr., who took command of MNF-I in July 2004, held a similar attitude toward IO, introducing the idea that Coalition forces had to communicate a "drumbeat of steady progress" to the Iraqi population to win their support.

Signs of the improvement in IO could be seen in the Coalition's preparations for and responses to the creation of the Interim Iraqi Government (IIG) in June 2004, the AL FAJR operation against the insurgents in Fallujah in November 2004, and the Iraqi elections of 2005. But as the 2005 study noted, a critical window of time had passed in the summer of 2003. MNF-I and MNC-I corrected many of the IO problems first encountered in 2003, "but the CPA and CJTF-7 had lost the opportunity to shape Iraqi perceptions of the Coalition."[40]

The Practice of Information Operations at the Tactical Level

When the Coalition invaded Iraq in March 2003, US Army units at battalion and brigade level did not have dedicated IO assets in their organizations. As CJTF-7 transitioned to full spectrum operations in the summer of 2003, tactical units dearly missed this capability. However, Soldiers quickly adapted and improvised solutions to this problem. During that summer many units tasked the IO mission to the field artillery (FA) Soldiers on their staffs. After major combat operations ended in April 2003, the primary FA mission to provide indirect fire support to ground maneuver units for the most part disappeared. Of course FA units continued to perform some traditional missions. They routinely conducted counterfire missions to defeat insurgent mortar and rocket attacks on Coalition forces and provided indirect fire support to Coalition units conducting large-scale attacks on insurgent strongholds. As demonstrated elsewhere in this study, many artillery units also became maneuver forces, conducting patrols, searches, and raids.

Fire support officers and staffs also changed missions. Many were tasked by their commanders to lead the IO planning for their units. IO at the lower tactical level required the integration of existing EW, deception, PSYOP, PA, and civil-military staff sections into a comprehensive whole. For many units, fire support officers and fire support coordination cells filled that niche. These ad hoc staff sections became known as "effects cells" or "IO cells." Some of the staff processes and training for FA officers involved with targeting and planning artillery missions loosely lent themselves to the "targeting processes" involved in IO. Artillery doctrine described the outcome of their mission in terms of "effects" inflicted on the enemy, and part of IO doctrine similarly used the effects concept in measuring the impact of IO activities on neutral audiences and hostile forces. Because of this connection, many artillery officers, such as Lieutenant Colonel Chuck Hardy, the Division Fire Support Officer for the 82d ABN in 2003 and 2004, were tasked to coordinate "nonlethal effects" and IO for their commands.[41] The 1st ID and 4th ID took similar steps to implement their own IO plans.

Not all tactical units coordinated their IO efforts in this way. Some brigades created ad hoc IO planning and coordination cells out of their various staff sections. The 173d Airborne Brigade (173d ABN), for example, created two working groups—one that met twice a month to develop long-term IO strategy and a second that met twice a week to coordinate more short-term IO targeting.[42] Battalion representatives at the latter meeting shared their experiences and

Figure 60. Examples of leaflets used by Coalition forces in Iraq.

http://www.psywar.org/

Figure 61. Sergeant First Class Dain Christensen, 9th PSYOP Battalion (right) places antiterrorists flyers over graffiti in Mosul, Iraq, as a fellow service member holds materials.

requested resources. For this brigade, coordination was critical because of the short supply of IO Soldiers and resources. In fact, the 173d ABN conducted most of its IO with the lone attached PA team, while providing the team with modest resources to conduct their operations. The brigade combined practical steps, such as visits of the Medical Civic Action Program (MEDCAP) to villages in its AOR with public information messages, in an "attempt to alter the Iraqi perception of Coalition forces."[43]

In most tactical units, PSYOP units provided the only dedicated means of conducting the operations planned by the IO and effects cells at the brigade and division level. In 2003 and 2004, each US Army division in Iraq enjoyed the support of a single PSYOP company composed of a number of tactical PSYOP teams (TPTs) that could be attached to brigades and even battalions. These TPTs provided the primary products for disseminating tailored information directly to the Iraqi population in an AOR. TPTs supported operations at the tactical level by producing "loudspeaker scripts, handbills, posters and booklet[s] for everything from curfew announcements to the CJTF-7 rewards program to information about Transitional Administrative Law."[44] However, these TPTs were too few in number and capability for the immensity of the task in a nation of 26 million people.

Many local commanders developed their own products with themes and messages specifically tailored to the population in their AOR. Early in the new campaign, Captain Charles O'Brien, commander of A Company, 3d Battalion, 69th Armor Regiment, part of the 1st BCT, 3d ID, recalled that in the summer of 2003, IO initiatives often emerged among those

Soldiers that were closest to the Iraqi population, "As far as IO and themes and talking points, etc., initially we developed those at the company level."[45] Commanders knew what themes and messages were likely to work in their AORs and could get those messages distributed in the fastest manner possible. The requirement for speed in the production of IO was the most important lesson learned by Lieutenant Colonel Wayne Swan during his time in Mosul as the information officer for the 3d Stryker Brigade, 2d Infantry Division (2d ID). Swan recalled, "Probably what I learned most, and I knew this from history, 431 BC with the Peloponnesian Wars, Thucydides is quoted [stating] . . . that people pretty much believe the first message they hear and they don't look into any of the details. That was reinforced [in Iraq] . . . so we had to get the message out first."[46] In the Iraqi culture in which word of mouth and the messages spread by imams in the mosques were more important than print or television media, the need to "get the word out on the street" was vital. US forces did not excel at that skill.

In addition to supporting the reconstruction efforts and other so-called nonkinetic operations in the full spectrum campaign, PSYOP Soldiers played significant roles supporting traditional combat operations. In Mosul during 2004, the 3d Brigade, 2d ID (Stryker) made effective use of PSYOP loudspeaker teams during cordon and search operations. As the brigade's Soldiers cleared neighborhoods, the PSYOP team informed the local population about what to expect when US troops entered their homes.[47] In November 2004

Figure 62. An Iraqi man reads signs posted by Soldiers with the 321st PSYOP Company, attached to the 3d ID in Fallujah, Iraq. The posters displayed Coalition efforts for Iraqi improvement.

Coalition forces integrated IO into the plan for Operation AL FAJR, the assault on the city of Fallujah by two US Marine Corps regimental combat teams and two US Army mechanized task forces. Unlike previous attacks on large insurgent strongholds that did not make good use of IO, AL FAJR employed IO initiatives from the IIG, MNF-I, and Marine and Army tactical units involved in the operation.

For Lieutenant General Metz, the MNC-I commander in 2004, AL FAJR illustrated the right method of IO coordination and the proper use of the core elements of IO to support the tactical fight. Soldiers from the 2d PYSOP Group used multiple OPSEC and deception measures to conceal the buildup of Marine and Army forces north of the city of Fallujah, the Coalition's position from which the main attack was to be launched.[48] The Coalition command combined this effort with other OPSEC, deception, and combat actions to focus the enemy's attention to the south of the city. (Some of these measures involved the controversial use of PA activities by US Marines and will be discussed later in this chapter.) PSYOP teams encouraged noncombatant civilians to leave the city and to persuade insurgents to surrender. These

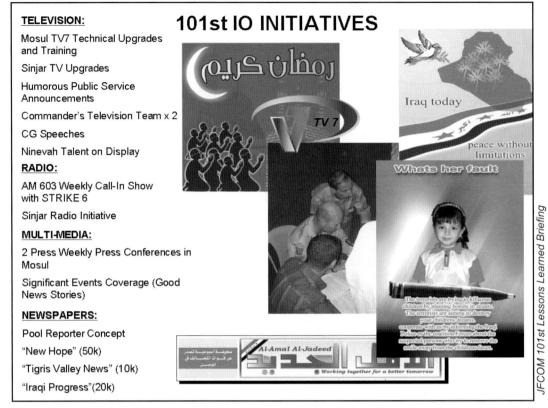

Figure 63. Summary of IO initiatives made by 101st Airborne Division in MND-North, May 2003–February 2004.

operations were effective; estimates show that approximately 90 percent of the noncombatants fled Fallujah.[49] Complementing this objective were the Coalition's well-publicized promises to conduct major humanitarian and reconstruction operations designed to provide relief and support to the residents of Fallujah after the insurgents were destroyed. On the eve of the attack and during the tough fighting in the city that continued for weeks, electronic warfare (EW) emerged as perhaps the most important element of the Coalition's IO effort by restricting the enemy's access to select communications and monitoring the communication channels the insurgents were able to use for intelligence.

The use of IO during AL FAJR was not an isolated case. The 2d PSYOP Group's Soldiers, for example, also participated in Operation BATON ROUGE, the 1st ID's assault on insurgents in the city of Samarra in October 2004. The successful employment of IO in AL FAJR, BATON ROUGE, and other discrete operations appears to have been more productive than the efforts to build widespread Iraqi support for the overall Coalition effort. As such, these operations suggest that US forces made significant advances in tactical IO by mid-2004. However, success at the strategic and operational levels was harder to document. One critical reason was the lack of preparation for IO in the immediate aftermath of regime change, which allowed many different voices to define the Coalition's purpose and objectives for Iraq. The IO challenges at these levels were partly a result of a broad political landscape in which the disparate ethnic and sectarian groups set their own agendas and mounted their own IO, sometimes in opposition to the Coalition's vision for Iraq.

Insurgent Information Operations

Clashing with friendly messages were the opposition's ideas and propaganda. A large number of insurgent and terrorist groups in Iraq proved to be adept at using all types of media to further their cause and to discredit the Coalition and the Iraqi Security Forces (ISF). By 2005 the insurgent's successful use of IO led Brigadier General G. Donald Alston, the spokesperson for MNF-I, to argue that the media had become a vital force multiplier for the insurgents: "What I mean by that is that [the insurgents] attempt to use the media to appear more capable than they really are and to intimidate others with attack videos and Web site postings."[50] Bruce Hoffman, a noted counterinsurgency expert, agreed with this assessment, adding that what makes "the insurgency in Iraq so different from previous ones is the insurgents' enormous media savvy."[51] From the perspective of Soldiers on the ground, the enemy's IO capabilities could be confounding. The Soldiers of the 1st Battalion, 503d Infantry Regiment (1-503d IN), operating in the city of Ramadi in 2004 described the enemy's IO as "far more responsive and effective than [Coalition forces'] IO efforts. We found the enemy could print and post flyers/posters detailing their version of an event inside of 24 hours."[52] The report from the 1-503d IN continued by pointing out the sophisticated means used to reinforce the insurgent message, "The enemy will also pass rumors supporting the posters and flyers and make physical threats to repress people who know the truth."[53]

According to Lieutenant General Metz, insurgent organizations were adaptive, relentless, and technologically capable.[54] Metz stated the Iraqi insurgent "recognizes that the global information network is his most effective tool for attacking what he perceives to be our [Coalition forces'] COG: public opinion, both domestic and international."[55] Like Coalition forces, the insurgents understood the power of integrating information-based operations into other missions and often used mass media in these efforts. Lieutenant Colonel Swan, the information officer for 3d Brigade, 2d ID in 2004, found this out firsthand in Mosul, and asserted, "[the insurgents] understand how valuable media is and the psychological value and that is the only weapon they have so that is why they are so good at getting videos out and getting them out ahead of us."[56] The local population in Mosul and elsewhere turned almost exclusively to Arab media and insurgent outlets for their news; consequently, they had little information about any of the positive activities of the Coalition forces.

Figure 64. Sergeant Bill Whittaker, 361st PSYOP Battalion, 24th Infantry Regiment, 1st Brigade, 25th Infantry Division (Stryker Brigade Combat Team), hands out literature and shakes hands in Mosul.

This basic failure to win the tactical battle of ideas became apparent to senior leaders in the US Government. Secretary of Defense Donald Rumsfeld commented on this enemy capability, stating that Islamic extremist groups, including the insurgents in Iraq, have "poisoned the Muslim public's view of the United States" through its "deft use of the Internet and other modern communications methods" that the American Government, including the military, has failed to master.[57] Lieutenant Colonel Stephen Boylan, who served as the director of MNF-I's Combined Press Information Center (CPIC) in 2004, recognized the insurgents' ability to use the media for their own purposes:

> I think there were some spectacular attacks that were done to ensure that they were seen by the media to help foster the terrorist organizations' information operations roles of publicizing their events. They did a great job of getting their information out on the web and they did a great job of getting it out on our TV networks. . . . In fact, I would say that they are much better at information operations, if you will, than we are, and they are more timely, because they don't have to rely on the truth whereas we do. They can lie, cheat, and steal and we can't so they can beat us to the punch almost every time.[58]

Insurgents often had a cameraman at the site of a car bombing, and within minutes of the explosion, the images appeared on the Internet without having to be vetted in any approval process and with little regard for the distinction between news and propaganda. Countering this type of instant "news" in Iraq, as Boylan noted, was almost impossible. The insurgents also used dozens of Web sites to wage a propaganda war and pass on the latest tactics to defeat Coalition forces to other insurgents.[59] The audience for most of the insurgent's propaganda was the Iraqi public, but more and more the insurgents targeted Muslims all over the world. According to one study of tactics used by the Iraqi insurgency, the insurgents employed propaganda to "garner sympathy from the Iraqi population for their 'struggle,' while keeping the international media spotlight on the American-led occupation of Iraq."[60]

One of the most gruesome propaganda tools used by insurgents in Iraq involved videos of executions. Jon Alterman, director of the Middle East program at the Center for Strategic and International Studies in Washington, argued that graphically violent videos were part of "a calculated set of actions and images directed toward influencing a mass audience. In this way, the audience was often more important than the action itself, and the symbolism was inseparable from the strategy."[61] Insurgent groups intended these videos to serve as a warning to Iraqis helping the government or Coalition forces and to demoralize public opinion in Coalition countries.[62] The capture and beheading of Western hostages showed the Iraqi population that the Coalition forces were unable to provide them security, and concurrently served as a recruiting tool for young Muslims around the world interested in joining the insurgent effort.

The vast cultural divide between Western nations and most parts of the Muslim world exacerbated the Coalition's difficulties with IO. Insurgent and terrorist propaganda leveraged their close familiarity with Iraqi, Arab, and Muslim norms and values while IO officers at all levels struggled to understand the basic elements of the culture with which they were trying to communicate. To a great degree, the larger clash of Western and Arab Muslim cultures hampered the Coalition IO effort in Iraq. Every action and every message launched by the Coalition was interpreted within the context of Iraqi conditions as well as in terms of the international, ideological, and religious conflict.

Public Affairs and Operation IRAQI FREEDOM

As noted earlier, US military doctrine separated IO and PA, defining them by different functions and limitations. Yet, these two activities often had to be synchronized, and commanders and staff officers alike struggled to combine them into a comprehensive whole without violating the boundaries between manipulating target audiences in Iraq and providing truthful information to the American people. During OIF the Army believed it had a positive story to tell, and providing the media easy access to operations would assist in telling that story.

While difficult to define with great precision, the mission of Army PA is to "fulfill the Army's obligation to keep the American people and the Army informed, and to help establish the conditions that lead to confidence in America's Army and its readiness to conduct operations in peace, conflict, and war."[63] Army doctrine in FM 3-61.1, *Public Affairs Tactics, Techniques and Procedures*, requires Army leaders to integrate PA into the planning process and synchronize PA operations with other facets of their operations. This allows commanders to better communicate their perspective and "achieve a balanced, accurate, credible information presentation."[64] US Army leaders at every level in OIF realized the vital importance of PA to their operations in Iraq, as well as to American and international public opinion. While commanders in Iraq may have differed on specific goals and methods, they and the US Army as an institution valued the PA missions and had long abandoned previously held antagonisms toward the press and accepted media coverage of its operations.

As mentioned earlier, according to joint and Army doctrine, PA operations are related to but not doctrinally a part of IO. According to joint doctrine published in 2005, PA had the additional mission of contributing to IO by "providing truthful, accurate and timely information, using approved DOD public affairs guidance to keep the public informed about the military's missions and operations, countering adversary propaganda, deterring adversary actions, and maintain trust and confidence of the US population, and our friends and allies."[65] DOD policy and Army doctrine require PA offices to provide truthful and accurate information in support of their commands. This guidance states, "Propaganda or publicity designed to sway or direct public opinion will not be included in Department of Defense PA programs."[66] IO was focused on affecting the enemy's decisionmaking capacity while protecting one's own; as such, it included the manipulation of enemy morale and public opinion. PA operations, on the other hand, focused on providing truthful information to the American people about their Army and its operations.

As the US Army became involved in Iraq, commanders were faced with the challenge of maintaining this philosophical and doctrinal divide between PA and IO while synchronizing them to win the battle of ideas. This created a natural friction between the two functions that required some nuanced understanding and delicate balancing of activities. Because of the conceptual tension between IO and PA, commanders struggled to create the proper mix of assets when employing their IO staff to simultaneously attack insurgents and terrorists, influence Iraqi public opinion, and provide a truthful and complete picture of US operations to the American public. On a practical level, commanders encountered significant difficulties in 2003 and 2004 to organize these staffs so that their operations were synchronized yet did not violate the separation between the missions.

Another key element complicating both PA and IO in OIF was the so-called "CNN effect."[67] Soldiers at all levels in Iraq operated in a "24/7" news market broadcasted on a global scale, and they fully understood that their actions and words could have an immediate impact on this broad stage. The powerful result of 24/7 media coverage was first coined "the CNN effect" when President George H.W. Bush decided to send troops to Somalia after seeing media coverage of starving refugees in that country. Similarly, President William (Bill) Clinton ordered the withdrawal of US troops from Somalia after the abortive raid to capture a rebel leader led to pictures of dead American bodies being shown on television.[68]

This real-time news coverage generated immediate public awareness and analysis of strategic decisions and military operations as they developed on the ground. One senior military officer, US Marine Corps Commandant General Charles C. Krulak, argued that every service member's actions could impact the strategic policy of the United States, because of the immense power of public media to spread and magnify his or her actions.[69] Krulak introduced the term "strategic corporal" to capture this concept. That term described a young Soldier or Marine whose actions or words at the lowest tactical level could be captured on tape and quickly broadcast around the world, thus potentially having a strategic effect on the outcome of a campaign. According to Krulak, the impact of the strategic corporal is enormous:

> World War II, Korea, and Vietnam, the young Marine could be the world's greatest hero, but he really had no strategic impact. In future wars, the tremendous capability and lethality will be in the hands of the young corporal. Combine that with the immediate 'CNN effect,' and it turns some of those actions into strategic actions. That young NCO needs to be highly trained because what he does or fails to do may literally impact on national policy.[70]

This was proven repeatedly in OIF, in both positive and negative ways. The photos taken at the Abu Ghraib Prison are only the most infamous example. "A wrong decision in the glare of the media," warned Colonel Paul Maillet, a former Canadian Director of Defense Ethics, "can have far-reaching consequences that can affect peace-keeping mandates and strategic and national policies and aims."[71] During 2003 and 2004 the US Army directed a large number of resources to deal with IO and the CNN effect.

Embedded Reporting

Perhaps the best known and most successful PA innovation during OIF was the embedding process. Embedding reporters with the military is a practice that has its modern origins in the Crimean War between Great Britain and Russia in the 1850s when the *London Times* dispatched William Howard Russell to report on the war. In the United States the relationship between the military and the press has evolved slowly. The interactions between the media and the military has swung back and forth from adversarial to cooperative, with a recent trend toward much greater cooperation. In the American Civil War, censorship by the Government and opposition from military leaders prevented much of the criticism of military leadership, though reporters on both sides of the war, using new technology such as the camera and the telegraph, still managed to report "from the front" even if they were not "embedded."[72]

This adversarial relationship became more cooperative in World War I. During that conflict, British authorities banned reporters completely from the war zone, while the Americans inducted reporters into the US military and gave them access to the front while censoring what they published. The US policy of inducting military reporters continued in World War II, though President Franklin D. Roosevelt imposed strict censorship. Ernie Pyle and Joe Rosenthal are only two examples of many journalists whose work became famous throughout the war. The Roosevelt administration also practiced IO, targeting domestic morale with multiple programs. The Army's own publications, such as *Stars & Stripes* and *Yank* and its radio stations, provided news to servicemen for the same purpose.

The media-military relationship turned decidedly hostile during the Vietnam war. The Government imposed little in the way of battlefield censorship while reporters had almost unrestricted access in Vietnam. For the first time the media used television to report directly to the American people. The experience profoundly affected both the media and the military. Most media organizations saw this as the "standard" approach that ought to be used. Many within the Government, the military, and the American public saw the media coverage differently, blaming it for undermining the war effort.

Figure 65. Katherine M. Skiba from the *Milwaukee Sentinel Journal,* in a UH-60 Blackhawk helicopter, was embedded with the 101st Airborne Division's aviation brigade during Operation IRAQI FREEDOM.

This conflict shaped official policy in the decades following the Vietnam war. The US Government prevented all media access to operations during the 1983 invasion of Grenada, much to the dismay of the media though without much public outcry. In response to the media outrage, a military commission created the idea of the military press pool. Under the pool concept, selected members of the media would be allowed to travel to the war zone under conditions tightly controlled by the military, but with the goal of providing them much greater access than before. For some in the military, the press pools presented an important means of telling the American public about its all-volunteer force created after Vietnam.

The first use of the press pool concept took place during the US invasion of Panama in 1989. The media deemed it a failure because reporters were not given access to operations in real time and they had difficulties getting their stories released quickly. Despite these concerns, the press pool policy continued during Operations DESERT SHIELD and DESERT STORM in 1990–91 on an expanded scale. Instead of the pool of 8 journalists used in Panama in 1989, the Gulf War pool consisted of 1,500 journalists.[73] General Norman Schwarzkopf, Commander of CENTCOM, made famous by his iconic approach to media briefings, wrote in his autobiography that he believed it was crucial not to "repeat the mistake we made in Grenada, where the military had stonewalled [the media]."[74] The Army had indeed succeeded in preventing the media from leaking any information about its audacious sweeping attack around the main Iraqi defenses in Kuwait by limiting pool reporters' access to certain units. However, many officers argued that the Army had actually suffered from this decision because it caused a serious dearth of stories about the skill and heroism of its Soldiers in battle.

New technology and new realities coming out of the Gulf War opened a new era in military–media relations. Live war coverage had made its debut during that conflict as reporters made use of satellite coverage for the first time, a major milestone that heralded a new era in war reporting during the information age. US and international media organizations had the ability to report on conflicts in real time, with or without military assistance. The satellite era, combined with the rise of many non-US media organizations in the developing world and in Muslim countries in particular—some friendly to US interests but many who were not—created an environment in which the US military would have to "compete" to get its version of the story to a broad audience. The US Army sought coverage of its operations because it rightly believed its Soldiers were performing well in the service of their country. The US Government likewise began to realize that, in the information age, information itself was an increasingly important if not critical component of US power.

Military operations in Bosnia and Kosovo in the late 1990s saw the first use of the term "embedded press," describing reporters who "were assigned to a unit and lived with the unit through operations" usually for about a month.[75] Though some feared the security risks of media being present before and during operations, most media figures proved responsive to the imperatives of OPSEC. However, far outweighing those risks was the belief inside the military that the more the American public knew about Soldiers' missions and performance, the greater their support would be. By the time the US Government began planning for OIF, the DOD and the Army understood the importance of news coverage in supporting military objectives, and believed that providing the media easy access to military units during operations was the proper approach.

Preparing Embedded Reporters and the Army for Each Other

During the invasion of Iraq in 2003, close to 700 media representatives from all over the world were embedded with military units. To put this in perspective, in World War II 600 journalists were assigned to cover the entire South Pacific, and only 30 reporters covered the invasion of Normandy.[76] In OIF, the "embed" program gave journalists unparalleled access to the battlefield and allowed reporters to file uncensored views of the action as it happened. DOD guidance issued before the invasion provided the logic for the embed program in terms of its affect on the success of the overall mission: "The Department of Defense (DOD) Policy on media coverage of future military operations is that media will have a long-term, minimally restrictive access to US air, ground and naval forces through embedding. Media coverage of any future operation will, to a large extent, shape public perception of the national security environment now and in the years ahead."[77] The guidance then stated that the embedding program would likely affect audiences outside the United States:

> This holds true for the US public; the public in allied countries whose opinion can affect the durability of our Coalition; and publics in countries where we conduct operations, whose perceptions of us can affect the cost and duration of our involvement. Our ultimate strategic success in bringing peace and security to [the Middle East] will come in our long-term commitment to supporting our democratic ideals.[78]

In clear recognition of the Army's dual goals in granting this level of access to the media, leaders in the 3d ID stated that the reasons for the embed program "were several, including the desire to have media tell the Soldiers' story, but also to have the ability to counter the Iraqi propaganda machine."[79]

In preparation for embedding media within their ranks, prior to the start of the invasion embedded reporters received some military training. Most of the media members in the program found this helpful in preparing them with basic survival skills they would need in Iraq. According to Amy Schlesing, a reporter for the *Arkansas Democrat-Gazette* who was embedded in 2004 with the 39th Infantry Brigade, Arkansas National Guard, attached to the 1st CAV, "We learned how to stack up on doors, we learned how to take cover, and we learned how to keep an eye on fields of fire."[80] This training, and the reporter's response to it, helped commanders and Soldiers feel more comfortable with media in their ranks.[81] Schlesing stressed it was imperative that reporters be properly trained for their dangerous missions:

> I had nothing but a pen. I could throw it if I needed to, but that was about it. So we are a liability. We are something else for them to worry about and that is why it is important for us as embeds to get training and it is also our job to seek it out ourselves and not to expect it. So it is important to remember we are a liability. No matter how invisible we try to be, we are not invisible.[82]

Given the conditions in Iraq, many reporters displayed great courage in accompanying Coalition and Iraqi forces on operations such as AL FAJR. During those operations, these men and women were certainly visible.

US Army Perspectives on the Embed Program

Most Army leaders understood the benefits offered by the embedded media program. Colonel Baker, commander of the 2d BCT, 1st AD, observed that Soldiers also needed to talk to the media to make sure their message got out. "Trying to ignore the media by denying them access or refusing to talk," Baker argued, "can result in the press reporting news that is inaccurate, biased, and frankly counterproductive to the mission."[83] He recognized that the media will get their story somehow, so it was better if the media was embedded and hearing the Army's side.[84] Baker and his team prepared the Soldiers for how to deal with the media in a systematic and deliberate manner. They discovered the types of information reporters needed to know about an incident and quickly provided them basic data. At the same time, they released messages and related stories they thought were important to the media.[85] This made it much easier for the press to report the successes in the brigade AOR that might have otherwise gone unnoticed.

Colonel Stephen Lanza, a 1st CAV brigade commander, also supported the embed program, believing that the Soldier was the Army's best spokesperson in Iraq:

> My attitude was, at the end of the day, the Soldiers are going to tell the story. And the story is going to be good. And you've got to accept a little, that there's going to be things that are going to happen . . . but at the end of the day it tells the story about the Soldiers. So, I'm a big fan of embedded media. If you don't let them in, you know what, they're going to tell the story anyway.[86]

Colonel Michael Tucker, brigade commander of the 1st BCT of the 1st AD, agreed, "If you do not wrap your arms around the media, then you will no longer be able to influence the media. I am a firm believer that if you don't control the media, it will control you."[87] Tucker asserted that the embedded media actually helped his mission "because, again, I was trying to get the message out. I was trying to send the message that we are not an occupying Army. . . . Having the media with you also gets your Soldiers' coverage, which is read by their loved ones back home. . . . They told it right."[88]

Colonel David Perkins, commander of the 2d BCT of the 3d ID, the unit that executed the "Thunder Runs" into Baghdad in early April 2003, also supported the embedded media program for a variety of reasons, but "the biggest reason is because the story of the American Soldier is a good story. The more in-depth you can talk about the Soldier and the more accurate you can be about it, I'm convinced it is going to be a good story. I just have faith in it. Yes, some knuckleheads are going to do bad things, but the more complete story you can tell about the Soldier, the better it is."[89] Lieutenant General William Wallace, commander of the US Army V Corps in 2003, felt that "embedded media told the story of the Soldier to the nation. Otherwise it would not have been told. The stories filed by the embedded media gave the public something to hold onto at the 'mom and pop' level. The embeds gave the people back home the 'Willie and Joe' of OIF."[90] Major General John Batiste, the commander of the 1st ID, concurred with these sentiments and added that media involvement was critical to the national war effort, "I was always looking for press to embed and bring on the team because I think it is important that the American people know the truth. The Army does not go to war, America goes to war and the press is the glue which holds it all together."[91] During OIF, the Soldier's story became so compelling that *Time* magazine named "The American Soldier" as the 2003 person of the year.

The Army found the embedded media program beneficial in another way. Embedded reporting could, to some degree, counter the false reports being broadcast by certain Arab media outlets.[92] However, this type of reporting had to be independent or it would lose all credibility.[93] When an inaccurate story was broadcast, the Coalition could not always offer an immediate verification or denial of the account. Using the operational chain of command, it took time for commanders to counter the disinformation and provide the facts. If a false story was released soon after an event and the US military's verification or denial took hours or days to be released, Iraqis, and often the international and American media, had already accepted the original "false" version of events. Frequently, timely reporting of the facts came from the embedded reporters and photojournalists. Another PA officer stated, "Any propaganda was nullified when an incident was thoroughly reported by the embeds, which included the background and context for what happened."[94]

It was evident to most Soldiers that the program worked well. The media told firsthand accounts of the Soldiers fairly and accurately. In retrospect, the leaders of the 3d ID agreed that the embed program was an overall success:

> Neither mission accomplishment nor the integrity of the media was compromised. . . . Embedded media had a more realistic understanding and were more optimistic in their accounts than media who were reporting from the Pentagon, from (CENTCOM) in Qatar, or from Coalition Forces Land Component Command (CFLCC) in Kuwait. . . . In sum, the embedded media balanced the negative press from reporters outside Iraq.[95]

Army leaders and Soldiers were eager to have their story told and were particularly pleased with that coverage.

Criticisms of Embedding and the "Embed Effect"

Most media organizations and journalists were also satisfied with the results of the embedded program, but some journalists voiced concerns about their embedded experience. The majority of the criticisms focused on two issues: narrow reporting and objectivity. While both issues received extensive coverage inside the media, neither issue had much resonance with Soldiers serving in OIF. Although embeds were hugely successful in providing accurate and detailed reports of the units to which they were attached, their reports obviously focused on single units and isolated events in time. Phil Bronstein, editor of the *San Francisco Chronicle*, discerned other related problems with perspective, stating, "You're going to have the famous fog of war. If you're in a unit, you'll get to see combat in that particular moment in that square mile of the world. But we don't have any mechanism for seeing the larger picture."[96] Paul Slavin, executive producer of ABC's *World News Tonight*, offered a useful metaphor that described the media's concerns about embed reporting: "We were looking at the battlefield through 600 straws. It was difficult to contextualize it."[97] Certainly, embedded reports lacked a comprehensive view of the OIF campaign from the strategic and operational levels.

Some reporters feared that by embedding with Army units they would appear "too close" to Soldiers and therefore lose their reputation for impartiality. Amy Schlesing warned that as a reporter "you could never think of yourself as one of them and never think of yourself as fighting that war because you are not. . . . You are writing for your readers at home and it is vital to remain objective." Schlesing continued, "I guess my gauge was if I ever wondered if I should write a story because of what these Soldiers would think, then, I needed to go home."[98] *Los Angeles Times* reporter John Hendren saw how easily reporters could be influenced. "When you're living in tents with these guys and eating what they eat and cleaning the dirt off the glasses, it's a whole different experience. You definitely have a concern about knowing people so well that you sympathize with them."[99]

These criticisms have some merit. That embedded journalists saw only a narrow view of a story is an accurate characterization of much of the embed reporting in OIF. The reverse, however, is also true. Reporting from the safety of a rear headquarters or the center of Baghdad can lead to a distorted and filtered view of complex events in the rest of the country. The concept that comprehensive understanding of any military issue requires multiple sources and sound analysis is hardly a "journalistic revelation," or an excuse to avoid embedded journalism. The often-expressed media fear of losing one's impartiality struck many Soldiers and a good number of Americans as misplaced. Accurate and timely reporting need not be considered biased merely because it was positive and supported US policy objectives, or because journalists came to understand the Soldiers with whom they lived and who protected them from danger.

The Challenges of Embedded Reporting in the New Campaign

As noted earlier, at the height of major combat operations during OIF nearly 700 journalists were embedded with the military in Iraq. After the fall of Baghdad, that number quickly dropped, and by December 2004, only 35 journalists were reporting as embeds.[100] There were many reasons for this steep decline in the numbers of embedded reporters. The dramatic fall of Baghdad on 9 April 2003 signaled a shift in the intensity of events to be reported. In some cases, financial concerns of media organizations led to the decision to pull out journalists, especially those from smaller news outlets. Other news organizations believed the story changed to

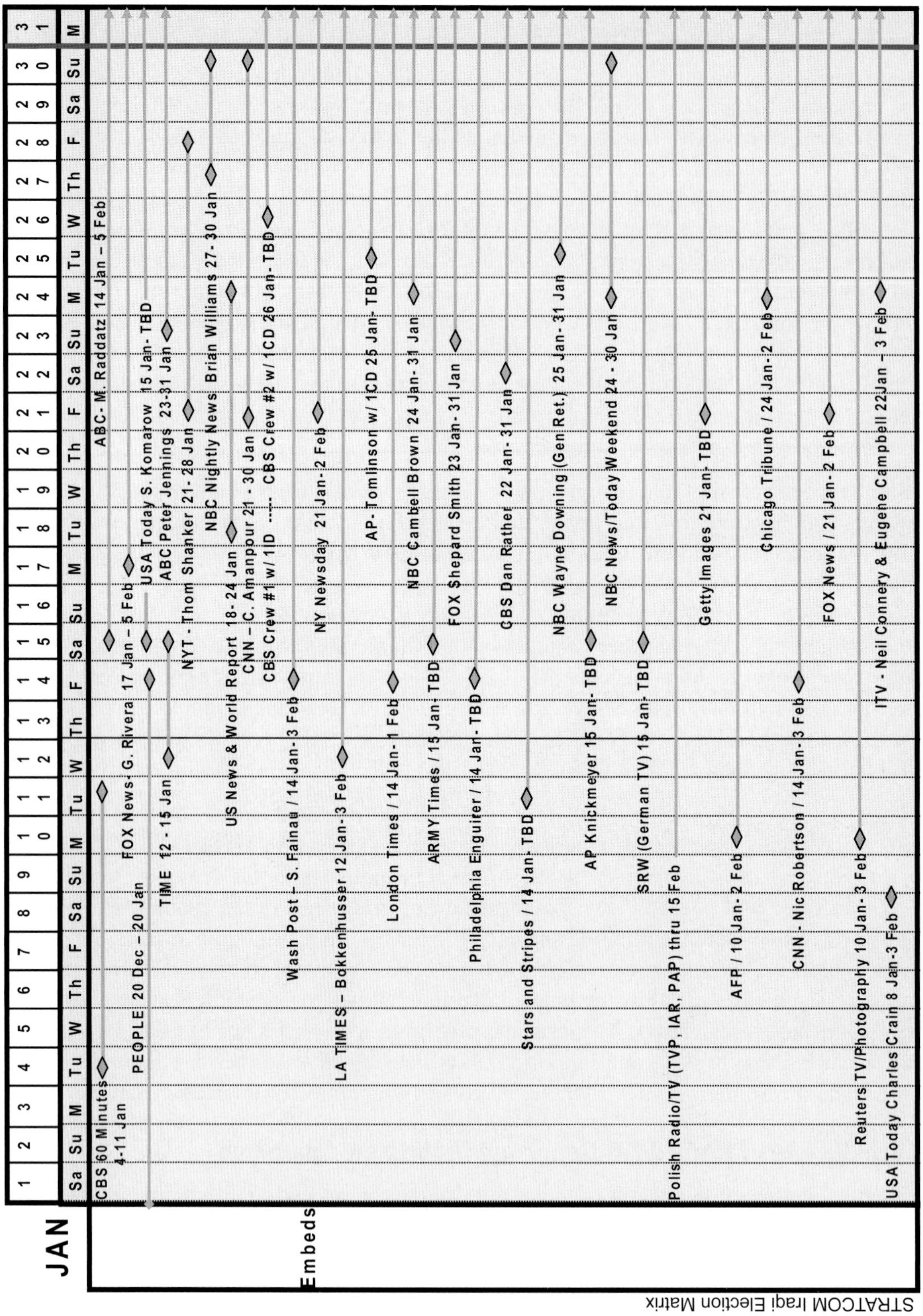

JAN

Embeds

CBS 60 Minutes 4-11 Jan
USA Today Charles Crain 8 Jan-3 Feb
Reuters TV/Photography 10 Jan-3 Feb
PEOPLE 20 Dec – 20 Jan
AFP / 10 Jan- 2 Feb
CNN - Nic Robertson / 14 Jan- 3 Feb
TIME 12 -15 Jan
FOX News- G. Rivera 17 Jan - 5 Feb
SRW (German TV) 15 Jan- TBD
Polish Radio/TV (TVP, IAR, PAP) thru 15 Feb
AP Knickmeyer 15 Jan- TBD
Stars and Stripes / 14 Jan- TBD
Philadelphia Enquirer / 14 Jan- TBD
ARMY Times / 15 Jan- TBD
London Times / 14 Jan- 1 Feb
LA TIMES – Bokkenhusser 12 Jan- 3 Feb
Wash Post - S. Fainaa / 14 Jan- 3 Feb
US News & World Report 18 - 24 Jan
NY Newsday 21 Jan- 2 Feb
FOX News / 21 Jan- 2 Feb
AP - Tomlinson w/ 1CD 25 Jan- TBD
NBC Campbell Brown 24 Jan- 31 Jan
FOX Shepard Smith 23 Jan- 31 Jan
CBS Dan Rather 22 Jan- 31 Jan
NBC Wayne Downing (Gen Ret.) 25 Jan- 31 Jan
NBC News/Today Weekend 24 - 30 Jan
Getty Images 21 Jan- TBD
Chicago Tribune / 24 Jan- 2 Feb
USA Today S. Komarow 15 Jan - TBD
ABC Peter Jennings 23-31 Jan
NYT - Thom Shanker 21- 28 Jan
NBC Nightly News- Brian Williams 27 - 30 Jan
CNN – C. Amanpour 21 - 30 Jan
CBS Crew #1 w/ 1ID ..... CBS Crew #2 w/ 1CD 26 Jan- TBD
CBS Crew #2 w/ 1CD 26 Jan- TBD
ITV - Neil Connery & Eugene Campbell 22 Jan - 3 Feb
ABC- M. Raddatz 14 Jan – 5 Feb

Figure 66. Sample of journalists embedded with Coalition units as of 31 January 2005.

the rebuilding of Iraq and to Iraqi politics after Saddam. The best way to get these stories was to talk with Iraqis themselves, something better accomplished by unattached reporters.[101] The number of embedded reporters after May 2003 tended to wax and wane in concert with major military or political events in Iraq. The fighting around Fallujah and other locations in the fall of 2004 created a surge in embedded reporters; their numbers fell again to roughly 35 by the end of the year. Then the number rose again in advance of the Iraqi elections, with 164 reporters embedded with US and Coalition units on 30 January 2005, the day before the elections.[102]

As terrorists and insurgents began to target civilians in Iraq, some media outlets judged reporting in the country as too dangerous. After the fall of Baghdad in May 2003, reporters were able to walk the streets, visit shops and restaurants, and talk directly to Iraqis.[103] Captain Joseph Ludvigson of the 139th Mobile PA Detachment (MPAD) noted that between late April and June 2003, Western media could rent cars with Iraqi drivers and "drive around on their own to see stuff. . . . By about early summer, that stopped. Nobody was moving anywhere unless they were moving with [the military]."[104] Most journalists agreed that by August 2003 the security situation for reporters in Iraq had changed significantly. Kidnappings began, reporters started altering their identities, and some of the larger news agencies hired security teams and armored cars.[105]

The kidnappings and deaths forced journalists in Iraq to work differently. Reporters lived outside the Green Zone in a few heavily armed compounds. To get the news outside their compound, they were forced to plan trips protected by armed escorts.[106] Ludvigson noted, "Other than embedding with us, it was very hard to get their own people out on the ground, so they were very limited."[107] Many reporters chose to "work the phones" from their hotels, calling hospitals, morgues, and police stations to get stories.[108] This was far from a perfect solution, so many news outlets started to rely on Iraqi "stringers"—part-time or freelance correspondents who traveled across Iraq to gather information and help report on the story.[109]

More effort and nuance was required in the reporting of full spectrum operations in Iraq than was needed for the more straightforward nature of conventional operations in March and April 2003. The slow progress toward economic and political goals during most of 2003 and 2004 did not lend itself to quick sound bites and video clips. According to Colonel Daniel Allyn, commander of the 3d BCT, 3d ID, "The slant toward sensationalism also made it very hard to get them [reporters] out there to cover the more routine activities . . . stabilization operations are a steady, often not glamorous, ongoing activity."[110] Although the media offered many good news stories about reconstruction and successful security operations, the bad news stories captured the public's attention and were often picked up by the primetime news.[111]

In defense of the practice, Nic Robertson of CNN argued that while there was a lot of what could be called "bad" news coming out of Iraq, this was what he labeled "the dominant information. It's the prevailing information."[112] Amy Schlesing explained:

> I wrote countless stories about what civil affairs was doing with the schools,
> how they were picking contractors, that they were using Iraqi contractors to
> rebuild the economy, and the state of the electricity and what they were doing
> to increase electricity in the city, which involved all the contractors at the elec-
> tric plants . . . [these stories] would still get front page play, but they wouldn't

get as high a play as an explosive day. This is just my opinion, but I think those stories about rebuilding are considered more feature stories and actions stories always get better play. Now, is that the right thing to do? Not necessarily, but I think that is the reality that we are in right now. If Soldiers are hurt or injured or Iraqis are killed, human life trumps anything.[113]

Part of the problem with the types of stories covered after the toppling of the Saddam regime stemmed from the decreasing number of journalist in Iraq who were increasingly confined to secure locations such as the International or Green Zone in Baghdad. By the end of 2004 most routine reporting of OIF came from journalists near the Green Zone relying on official Coalition news sources and Iraqi stringers. Very few journalists dared to venture unescorted into the most dangerous parts of Iraq occupied by US and Iraqi troops; some who did paid with their lives. Army commanders and PA officers lamented coverage that seemed to focus too much on US and Iraqi casualties or on slow progress and setbacks in building a new Iraq. They rightly pointed to the many positive steps being taken by US Soldiers in Iraq that would be better covered if only more reporters would embed themselves for more than a few hours "outside the wire." Neither side was fully satisfied with the reporting of military operations during the Coalition's new campaign, suggesting that as in the past, new approaches will be tried in the future.[†]

Telling the Story "Back Home"

Like those involved in IO, Army PA Soldiers after May 2003 faced their own challenges in Iraq. As discussed in chapter 4, the full manning of the CJTF-7 staff took some time, and during the critical summer of 2003, Army PA manning levels were inadequate to support the mission at nearly every level of command. The Coalition did take an important step in enabling PA operations in July 2004 when it established the Combined Press Information Center (CPIC). However, even that organization was undermanned, initially receiving only one of five PA officers and none of the additional Mobile Public Affairs Detachments (MPADs) requested.[114]

Developing a PA plan to support the overall campaign and clearly communicating it to multiple audiences was extremely difficult. PA operations were traditionally divided into three functions: community relations, command information, and media relations. In OIF, community relations were primarily the purview of CA and PSYOP units. In Iraq, command information involved internal Army communications, such as a monthly print publication called the *Coalition Chronicle* [later called *The Scimitar*], the *Armed Forces Network*, and the *Armed Forces Radio and Television Service*. Media relations involved working with the various American and international media outlets.[115] In Iraq, PA units inherited a new and rather unique mission—assisting Iraqis in developing a media establishment suitable to a free society. This section examines PA efforts in support of the command information and media relations missions.

In support of domestic community relations, PA units kept Soldiers' families updated on events in Iraq in a variety of ways. PA units contacted local hometown newspapers and released stories about Soldiers' activities. They conducted live interviews with Soldiers to be released

---

[†]The debate over whether media coverage of the war in Iraq is biased in favor of bad news has escalated sharply over time. It is closely tied to US domestic politics and is beyond the scope of this book.

to hometown television stations. They also created and maintained a Web site and posted a weekly newsletter for Soldiers and their families. The PA units produced and published weekly newsletters for the Soldiers in a specific AOR that contained stories about unit activities and operations. PA officers also made memorial videos to send to the unit and to families of Soldiers who lost their lives in Iraq. These communications provided Soldiers in Iraq an opportunity to honor their fallen comrades.[116]

The PA mission at each level of command in OIF was to enact and support the commander's strategic communications plan. As was the case with IO assets, Army units at brigade and lower levels lacked organic PA capability. Units above the brigade found that their PA staffs were too small for the myriad tasks they inherited. As the PA chief for the 139th MPAD during its tour in support of Task Force *Olympia* during 2004, Captain Angela Bowman explained that the success of any PA plan depended heavily on the task force, brigade, or division commander's support of the plan "because if that commander is not supportive of PA, you are going nowhere fast."[117] Because of the complexity of the full spectrum campaign after May 2003, PAOs, many of whom came from the US Army Reserve or Army National Guard, found themselves briefing busy commanders to educate them about the potential uses of PA concepts in support of their overall operations.[118]

New technology aided the ability of PA units to get the story in Iraq out to the American public. In 2004 the Army launched the Digital Video and Imagery Distribution System (DVIDS), which allowed the MPADs using the system in Iraq, Kuwait, or Afghanistan to send text, photos, and video footage to a teleport in Atlanta.[119] In the United States, DVIDS users "ranging from the civilian media to military personnel seeking to acquire information from the field" acquired the "real-time, broadcast-quality products from a centralized, archived database via the satellite feed."[120] This system especially helped to quickly publicize Soldiers' activities and commanders' objectives, and assisted in providing an imagery resource for media markets to use in reporting news from Iraq. In addition, the DVIDS allowed MPADs to conduct live press briefings or interviews with officials in Iraq to be broadcast anywhere in the world. Lieutenant Colonel Will Beckman, a senior PA officer in Iraq, considered the speed of the system to be the critical factor in its effectiveness: "The speed is the critical thing . . . there's nothing new in this, we can just do it much, much faster and at greater quality."[121]

PA/IO Tension in the New Campaign

When General George W. Casey Jr. assumed command of MNF-I on 1 July 2004, he expanded the role of IO and PA to improve the Coalition's efforts to win the battle of ideas in Iraq. He also increased the resources devoted to that line of operations. Realizing that MNF-I had to compete with the graphic television and video images that highlighted the visual imagery of violence in Iraq, he created a concept called "the drumbeat of steady progress." Casey wanted MNF-I to publicize in a very emphatic manner the steady march toward the Iraqi assumption of responsibility for every aspect of their political, economic, and military lives. The most salient indication of self-rule was, of course, the elections for an Iraqi National Assembly scheduled for January 2005—only 7 months from the creation of the interim government in late June 2004 and the main effort for the Coalition in the second half of 2004.[122]

To better synchronize IO and PA efforts within his headquarters, Casey created the Directorate of Strategic Communications within the operations staff of the MNF-I. The mission of the directorate was to increase public support for the Iraqi Government and the Coalition

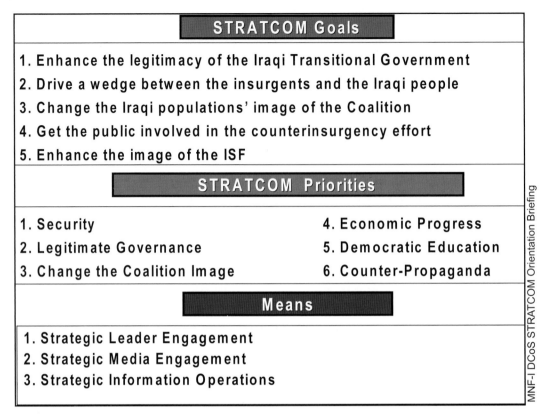

Figure 67. STRATCOM goals, priorities, and means.

while reducing support for the insurgents and terrorists. The STRATCOM‡ office, as the directorate was often called, defined its mission in the form of five goals, which included "driving a wedge" between the Iraqi population and the insurgents (see figure 67). Understandably, the staff in the directorate viewed the Iraqi people as their primary target audience, but considered the US and Coalition audiences as important secondary audiences. Using surveys conducted by an Iraqi organization, the STRATCOM staff determined that 70 to 80 percent of the Iraqi people received their news from satellite or ground-based television, while only 10 to 15 percent used newspapers, and 3 to 5 percent got their news from posters and fliers.[123] MNF-I used this analysis to prioritize their efforts in 2005.

The STRATCOM office merged the previously separate functions of PA and IO into a single staff section under Air Force Brigadier General Erwin F. (Erv) Lessel who had served as the IO Officer for MNF-I. Lessel was assisted by a Navy deputy, a deputy for PA, and a deputy for PSYOP. The office consisted of five divisions: plans and effects, current operations, assessment, a liaison cell with MNC-I, and the CPIC, each led by a lieutenant colonel.[124] For the 6 months following its inception in September 2004, the STRATCOM office reported to the MNF-I Deputy Chief of Staff for Strategic Operations. In January 2005 Lessel and his staff directed one of the biggest IO efforts of the campaign when it orchestrated 121 media

---

‡The term STRATCOM is unofficial and should not be confused with the United States Strategic Command (STRATCOM), which is a unified command responsible for the nation's nuclear forces.

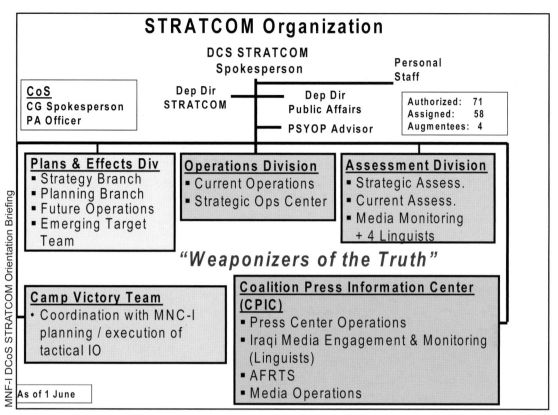

Figure 68. STRATCOM organization as of 1 June 2005.

interviews, 19 media trips, and 10 press conferences; hosted 164 embedded reporters; and facilitated 36 Iraqi media events in support of the Iraqi elections.[125] In the spring of 2005, the STRATCOM office within the MNF-I headquarters was again elevated, making Lessel one of seven deputy chiefs of staff reporting directly to General Casey.[126] Despite its increasing visibility and importance, the STRATCOM office experienced difficulties in filling its entire staff; as late as June 2005 the office had filled only 62 of 71 authorized positions.[127]

The conceptual tension between IO and PA, which was centered on the issue of how to use information as both a weapon in operations against the enemy and as a means of providing truthful information about the Army to the American public, caused IO and PA Soldiers in OIF to constantly adjust and coordinate their efforts. It was impossible for PA officers and commanders to avoid any linkage between PA and IO operations. It was also impossible for them to subordinate PA, with its requirement for truthfulness, to IO that targeted various audiences to advance Coalition objectives. No one wanted to mix the two disciplines too closely; it was unethical and risked returning military–media relations to the nadir they reached at the end of the Vietnam war. Commanders and PA officers in OIF resolved the dilemma by coordinating the two efforts where useful while maintaining a barrier between them to preserve the supremacy of truthfulness in PA.

According to Colonel Jill Morgenthaler, a PA officer for CJTF-7 and MNF-I in 2004, maintaining conceptual and legal distance between IO and PA functions required constant vigilance the entire time she served in Iraq.[128] Colonel William Darley, a PAO for CJTF-7, recalled that there was pressure to put a positive slant on information. However, Darley felt that he and his team remained objective and unbiased when working with the media. Darley stated, "The view that I took and the view I tried to impart to the people who were working for me directly was that we were there as PA officers, military PA officers, and we try to be as apolitical as possible."[129] Captain Ludvigson, of the 139th MPAD, also strived to maintain a separation between IO and PA even while coordinating activities within the IO strategy:

> Now, did we synchronize our messages with IO? Yes, absolutely. If IO had the intent of trying to build up a particular area, let's say Tall Afar, if they had the intent of trying to convince the people of Tall Afar that things were getting better and the terrorists were doing bad things, there was nothing wrong with us getting a hold of some of the Tall Afar media and saying, 'hey, would you like to come and look at some of the water wells that have been built in the outlying towns? Would you like to see the hospital that has been built?' Again, we were telling the truth, but it just so happened to nest with the IO.[130]

The attitudes of Ludvigson, Darley, and Morgenthaler were illustrative of the PA community's commitment to keeping that barrier between its mission and IO strong.

As mentioned earlier, the MNF-I staff had designed the STRATCOM office to better integrate all IO and related activities by creating unity of effort and command within one staff section. This organizational move, nevertheless, also created a potentially dangerous merging of the two disciplines of PA and IO. It is clear that MNF-I and the STRATCOM office created and maintained an organizational "firewall" between its IO functions and its media operations/PA agencies (see STRATCOM functional lay down). However, the actual processes used on a routine basis involved sending guidance and feedback across that "firewall," rendering it less than insurmountable.[131]

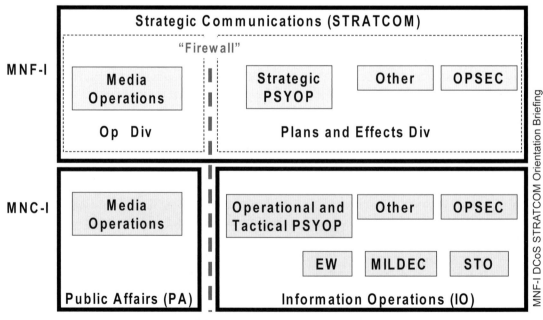

Figure 69. STRATCOM functional lay down, 21 November 2004.

Soon after MNF-I created the STRATCOM office, Chairman of the Joint Chiefs of Staff General Richard B. Myers issued a memo to all joint commands warning that combining IO and PA staffs into one section "[has] the potential to compromise the commander's credibility with the media and the public."[132] The message cautioned commanders to be careful; it was not, as some media reports indicated, a prohibition of the practice. Though he acknowledged that "it drove the public affairs guys absolutely crazy," General Casey believed that better coordination did not compromise the PA function. Casey asserted, "I believe that we are sophisticated enough to have IO and PA in the same organization. We can operate in that mode without people rushing over trying to influence the international media."[133]

Fewer than 2 months after the creation of the MNF-I Directorate of Strategic Communications headquarters in Baghdad, the Coalition began preparations to attack the Sunni insurgents who had taken control of the city of Fallujah. As part of their overall plan of operations, Marine leaders created very close linkages between PA and IO in support of Operation AL FAJR. Marine and Army commanders used a variety of IO activities, PSYOP, and EW to shape the battlefield before the Marine and Army forces launched their main ground attack on the city.[134]

On 14 October 2004, 3 weeks before the main attack began, US Marine First Lieutenant Lyle Gilbert spoke live to CNN reporter Jamie McIntyre from a location on the outskirts of the city. In the midst of other remarks, Gilbert stated, "Troops crossed the line of departure. We had artillery fire, prep fire going out . . . aircraft have been moving through the area all day, helicopters providing transport. It's been a pretty uncomfortable time. It's going to be a long night."[135] In fact, the assault phase of AL FAJR had not begun, and later that day CNN reported they had been misled. General Casey later acknowledged that this was a case where the lines might have been improperly blurred, but that decentralized execution of strategic communications was necessary. At the same time he noted the tremendous success of the overall IO effort against the insurgents' tactical operations, and even insurgent leaders admitted they lost the battle for ideas in Fallujah.[136]

Subsequent reporting by the media asserted that Gilbert's comments were carefully worded to create the impression the attack was beginning, to deceive the insurgents as to the time and location of the main attack, and to lure them into exposing their positions and plans. As such, it was a classic use of a military deception (MILDEC) operation, one that apparently assisted Coalition forces to pinpoint insurgent locations in Fallujah. Media outlets and others in and outside of the Government also criticized the Marines and the MNF-I Directorate of Strategic Communications (though it was not involved in this incident) for improperly blurring the lines between PA and IO.[137] This incident and the ensuing controversy illustrated the difficulty in maintaining the boundaries between the various activities falling under the umbrella of IO in particular situations in Iraq. It is exceedingly difficult to prevent MILDEC and PSYOP activities on the battlefield from spilling over into normal media processes in the information age, particularly when the media is part of the battlefield itself. In this case, while they proved beneficial, PA activities were improperly used in support of an overall IO plan.

The cardinal principle that PA operations must remain faithful to the truth, even if coordinated with other IO activities focused on influencing the enemy, was reinforced after this incident. Darley succinctly and cogently summarized the principle:

> The foremost role of public affairs is to protect the integrity of the military as an institution overall by ensuring that it is recognized as the most reliable source for official military information among all other competing sources. To accomplish its mission, the only arrows in the public affairs quiver are exercising the simple virtues of telling the truth and facilitating access by outside observers to confirm the truth of what is elsewhere officially asserted. Where neither access nor truth is appropriate, public affairs is not appropriate.[138]

As a result of the Fallujah incident and other pressures, DOD reinforced the existing principle of the primacy of truth in PA operations with new joint doctrine published in 2006, which unequivocally stated that specified IO activities are directed against *adversaries*, not domestic US audiences or the media.[139]

Working with Arab Media

PA Soldiers worked with media outlets from around the world, spending as much as 40 percent of their effort with Arab outlets. The Iraqi media were a critical component of the international press pool as both the fledgling and more experienced outlets established themselves in a new era of free press and free speech in Iraq. Professional Arab journalists received the same access and consideration as American or other international journalists, including the opportunity to embed with American forces.[140] Some Arab outlets such as *Al Jazeera* earned a reputation for being biased and, because they seemed to have a propensity for being in the area when an insurgent attack occurred, were sometimes suspected of colluding with the anti-Iraqi enemy.[141] Colonel Morgenthaler and her PA team made a concerted effort to track false stories about the Coalition in the Arab media and subsequently approached representatives from *Al Jazeera, Al Iraqia,* and *Al Arabiya* to review their findings. They pointed out the stories containing lies or partial truths, and they identified the correct accounts based on factual reporting as amounting to only 5 percent of the total. Morgenthaler and her team enjoyed some short-term wins, but no long-term success.[142] However, Colonel Darley found that the journalists from *Al Jazeera* also covered good news stories. He noted, "We would send out these media releases to various things like school openings or power station openings and that sort of thing and you could count on *Al Jazeera* being there."[143]

In Baghdad, Colonel Baker, a brigade commander in the 1st AD, viewed the Arab press as important to the success of his brigade and developed a successful working relationship with journalists from across the Arab community. To engage the Arab press, Baker developed the biweekly brigade-level news huddle.[144] This roundtable meeting met every 2 weeks at his headquarters. In preparation for the meeting, one of Baker's PAOs drafted talking points and a speech that began each meeting. Then Baker opened the floor to questions from the press.[145] In an effort to focus the brigade's hard work and to determine where the Iraqis received their news, the brigade conducted public opinion surveys and discovered which newspapers Iraqi citizens read and which television programs they watched.[146] Baker additionally hired two Iraqis to be the brigade's press agents, recalling, "Their main jobs were to facilitate attendance at our press roundtables and to promote the publication of our messages."[147] The press agents visited Arab newspapers and invited Arab reporters to the roundtables. Because of the work of these two Iraqis, Baker had from 8 to 10 newspaper reporters, to include representatives from *Al Jazeera, Al Arabiya,* and one of the Lebanese satellite television stations, regularly attending the roundtable meetings. After the roundtable, Baker usually made himself available for offline interviews with Arab satellite stations.[148]

Baker and the brigade also developed a good working relationship with *Al Jazeera* and *Al Arabiya*. As noted earlier, both stations suffered from a bad reputation inside the Coalition because of their biased reporting, but Baker contended, "The fact is they report to the audience we need to influence, so why not develop a rapport with them so that maybe we can get some of our messages across to the Iraqi public?"[149] Initially, when *Al Jazeera* reporters came to the brigade's press huddles, they were distant. However, according to Baker, "After three or four meetings they began warming up to us and later, they became just as friendly as any of the other reporters attending."[150] Baker believed if a unit was willing to put some effort into it, it was possible to develop a working relationship with almost any reporter just as long as the units are honest, adding that the Arab media "cannot help but respect us for that and, much of the time, respect is rewarded with fairer and more balanced news accounts because reporters know they can trust what we are saying."[151] According to Baker, it would have been a mistake not to engage *Al Jazeera* and other Arab media simply because of their biased reporting. He argued, "We cannot just censor them, deny them access, or fail to respect them because, ultimately, they talk to Arab peoples in their own language and are the most likely to be believed. Not to engage them or work with them is to miss tactical and strategic opportunities."[152]

Developing a Free Press in Iraq

As part of the Coalition's efforts to create a new Iraq, Army units worked with the Iraqis to assist in the development of a media culture and media organization suited to a free society. Under Saddam's dictatorship, the Iraqi media was little more than a propaganda arm of the regime; every aspect of their work was tightly controlled. In mid-April 2003, Iraqi media outlets and figures suddenly found themselves without experience or even a conception of the role of the media in a democracy. In many cases, the Iraqi media network had become rundown or had been knocked out by Coalition operations at the beginning of OIF. The 101st Airborne Division (101st ABN) used Commander's Emergency Response Program (CERP) funds to help television and radio stations get back on the air in the north of the country. Those funds bought equipment for Iraqi reporters and even underwrote the production of simple public service announcements for local governing councils broadcasted on television networks.[153] PA units offered more specialized assistance to fledgling Iraqi media organizations. The operations of the 139th MPAD, composed of 20 military specialists in broadcast and print journalism from the Illinois and Wisconsin Army National Guard, provide one excellent example of this initiative. The 139th MPAD supported the 101st ABN, Task Force (TF) *Olympia*, and other units in the Mosul area from January 2004 to January 2005. The unit set up a process to send press releases in Arabic to local media outlets and brought local media representatives into training sessions to do Arabic briefings and broadcast live interviews with local civic and religious leaders. The 139th and TF *Olympia* conducted press conferences with local Iraqis, including local leaders, in briefings by military leaders. Over time, the PA Soldiers in the 139th developed personal relationships with Iraqi reporters who facilitated the growth of a new type of media in Iraq. Captain Angela Bowman and other officers in the 139th trained the local Iraqi media personnel in Western-style journalism, emphasizing the special responsibility journalists have in a democracy to present accurate and objective accounts of the news. The most imposing challenge was showing Iraqis how to gather, write, edit, and package stories for television without governmental direction. When Iraqi journalists requested more information on ethics and standards of the profession, PA officers offered classes on those subjects. They also trained local leaders on the role of media spokespersons in government.[154]

This process of establishing the new Iraqi media culminated with the creation of the CPIC within MNF-I in the summer of 2004. The CPIC represented all branches of service and operated 24 hours a day, 7 days a week in Baghdad. Lieutenant Colonel Stephen Boylan, who served as the director of CPIC, found that as the Iraqi Government and military stood up, a significant part of his mission involved teaching the Iraqis about the role of PA, public communication, and strategic communication. PA Soldiers in the CPIC created a program of instruction similar to that of the US Defense Information School so Iraqis could learn skills such as press desk operations, media monitoring, and media escort. Senior leaders were taught the basics of media engagement and press conferences. Iraqi PA officers worked with Boylan's Soldiers in the CPIC to receive hands-on training in preparation for establishing the Iraqi Government Communications Division. In fact, the CPIC PA personnel included the IIG in its PA planning for the January 2005 elections. In the 30 days prior to the 31 January elections, the CPIC facilitated 36 separate IIG media events with Iraqi and international media as part of the overall MNF-I strategic communications plan.[155]

Conclusion

Using information as an enabler in the broader campaign was by no means a new concept for US Army commanders and planners during OIF. However, the imperative of merging the various core and related components of IO into a unified whole during the campaign presented a serious obstacle to the US Army and Coalition forces. As such, the battle of ideas in Iraq in 2003 and 2004 can be viewed as one of the most daunting operations in the history of the US Army. As was the case with other aspects of the transition to full spectrum operations after April 2003, US civilian and military commands in Iraq were not fully prepared to implement a synchronized IO strategy after the regime change. Both the CPA and CJTF-7 struggled to find suitable organizational structures, resources, and personnel to conduct effective IO activities in support of their political, economic, and security objectives.

Army IO doctrine and practice continued to evolve over time to adapt to the reality of postinvasion operations in an unfamiliar culture. Army units at every echelon in CJTF-7 and MNF-I devised ad hoc methods to conquer those challenges and those techniques became increasingly integrated into the Coalition's campaign by mid-2004, progress that was best demonstrated by the tactical-level IO successes in support of military operations in Fallujah and Samarra. PA specialists also made important contributions to the creation of an independent media that could provide significant assistance to the Iraqi Government's fledgling PA efforts. All of these efforts, however, took the better part of a year to develop. At the theater-strategic level of war, US commanders tried various means to organize and integrate the activities of IO in their headquarters to improve their ability to persuade the fence sitters in the Iraqi population to support the Coalition's efforts to create a new Iraq. MNF-I's establishment of the Directorate of Strategic Communications represented one such attempt. Nevertheless, the Coalition's general lack of preparation for the campaign that began in May 2003 meant that IO at this upper level struggled to find the right mix of messages that could win over Iraqis in an increasingly unsecure environment.

Telling the Army story to the American people was equally challenging. Army PA officers can be proud of the introduction of the embed program—a particularly successful effort that shined during the invasion of Iraq as well as during the elections of 2005. With the acceptance of embedded media, the Army decisively resolved the sharp historical oscillation between unfettered and tightly controlled media access to military operations in favor of openness during OIF. America's Army had a positive story to tell as it performed its role in support of the nation's foreign policy, and needed and wanted the media to help it communicate with the American public and other audiences. After the invasion of 2003 and as the security situation deteriorated in 2004, US media outlets decreased the use of embedded reporting and relied more on other means of gathering information. This change created a significant obstacle to objective and comprehensive reporting about the Army's involvement in a complex and dangerous campaign that featured few signs of progress and almost no dramatic victories.

Whether well-prepared and wholly-integrated IO and PA programs launched immediately after the fall of the Saddam regime in April 2003 would have significantly altered the 18-month period under study is questionable. Iraqis themselves were heavily divided about their vision of the political, economic, and social future of Iraq after Saddam. Terrorists and insurgents competed with the Coalition and the Iraqi Government for the loyalty of ordinary Iraqis. No single vision put forth by the Coalition, the US military, or the emerging Iraqi Government could command the loyalty of all or even most Iraqis. The fact that most Sunni Arab Iraqis boycotted the January 2005 elections is evidence of this fundamental challenge. While Coalition forces could rightly claim a number of IO successes in 2003 and 2004, these were just individual engagements in the larger battle for ideas in Iraq. As Iraqis went to the polls in early 2005, that battle still raged and the Coalition could at best be described as conducting a holding action.

Notes

1.   "Insurgents Caught After Attack on US Embassy in Iraq," *DefenseLink*, 30 January 2005, http://www.defenselink.mil/news/newsarticle.aspx?id=24225 (accessed 20 February 2008).

2.   Major General Peter Chiarelli and Major Patrick R. Michaelis, "Winning the Peace: The Requirement for Full-Spectrum Operations," *Military Review*, July–August 2005, 15.

3.   Field Manual (FM) 3-13, *Information Operations: Doctrine, Tactics, Techniques, and Procedures* (Washington, DC, 28 November 2003), 1-13.

4.   Sergeant Major Herb Friedman (Retired), "Deception and Disinformation," http://www.psy-warrior.com/DeceptionH.html (accessed 12 July 2006).

5.   US Army War College, Department of Military Strategy, Planning, and Operations, "Information Operations Primer: Fundamentals of Information Operations," January 2006, 1, http://www.carlisle.army.mil/usacsl/publications/IO-Primer-AY06.pdf (accessed 12 July 2006).

6.   FM 3-13, 1-13 to 1-14.

7.   FM 3-13, 1-21.

8.   Colonel Curtis D. Boyd, "Army IO is PSYOP: Influencing More with Less," *Military Review*, May–June 2007, 67.

9.   US Army War College, "Information Operations Primer," 1.

10.   FM 3-13, 1-16, and 2-21 to 2-26.

11.   FM 3-13, chapter 2.

12.   Larry Wentz, *Lessons from Bosnia: The IFOR Experience* (Washington, DC: National Defense University, Institute for National Strategic Studies, 1997), 26.

13.   Wentz, 168.

14.   Wentz, 168.

15.   Wentz, 168.

16.   Wentz, 205.

17.   Wentz, 209.

18.   Wentz, 208–229.

19.   Major Marc J. Romanych and Lieutenant Colonel Kenneth Krumm, "Tactical Information Operations in Kosovo," *Military Review*, September–October 2004, 58, http://www.au.af.mil/au/awc/awcgate/milreview/romanych.pdf (accessed 20 July 2006).

20.   Romanych and Krumm, 59.

21.   Romanych and Krumm, 61.

22.   4th Psychological Operations Group, Annual Historical Review for 2005. Unpublished manuscript.

23.   As the authors of the first *On Point* concluded, assessing the effectiveness of EW and CNO is difficult. Assessing the effectiveness of PSYOP and MILDEC in the phases of OIF is even more problematic. See COL Gregory Fontenot, US Army Retired, LTC E.J. Degen, US Army, and LTC David Tohn, US Army, *On Point: The United States Army in Operation Iraqi Freedom* (Fort Leavenworth, KS: Combat Studies Institute Press, 2004), 419–422.

24.   V Corps Briefing, *Nested Lines of Operation & V Corps' Objectives*, 18 May 2003.

25.   V Corps Briefing, *Nested Lines of Operation & V Corps' Objectives*, 18 May 2003.

26.   4th Infantry Division, "Lessons Learned Executive Summary," 18 June 2004.

27.   Major Joseph L. Cox, "Information Operations in Operations Enduring Freedom and Iraqi Freedom—What Went Wrong?" US Army School of Advanced Military Studies Monograph, United States Army Command and General Staff College, Fort Leavenworth, KS, AY 2005–06, 1–2.

28.   Cox, 44.

29.   Cox, 44.

30.   Cox, 45.

31. Chapter 2, "Civil-Military Operations," *CALL Newsletter 04-13: Operation Iraqi Freedom (OIF), CAAT II Initial Impressions Report (IIR)* (Fort Leavenworth, KS: Center for Army Lessons Learned, May 2004), 22.

32. Colonel Ralph O. Baker, "The Decisive Weapon: A Brigade Combat Team Commander's Perspective on Information Operations," *Military Review*, May–June 2006, 19.

33. Baker, 19.

34. Baker, 19.

35. Baker, 19.

36. Baker, 16.

37. Mark Mazzetti and Borzou Daragahi, "The Conflict in Iraq: US Military Covertly Pays to Run Stories in Iraqi Press," *Los Angeles Times,* 30 November 2005, A1.

38. Chapter 2, "Civil-Military Operations," *CALL Newsletter 04-13,* 1.

39. Lieutenant General Thomas F. Metz et al., "Massing Effects in the Information Domain: A Case Study in Aggressive Information Operations," *Military Review*, May–June 2006, 5.

40. Cox, 75.

41. Brigadier General James Huggins, interview by Contemporary Operations Study Team, Fort Bragg, NC, 11 May 2006, 7.

42. 173d Airborne Brigade, *After Action Review* Briefing, 22 January 2004, slides 34–35.

43. 173d Airborne Brigade, *After Action Review* Briefing, 22 January 2004, slide 36.

44. Cox, 71.

45. Major Charles O'Brien, interview by Operational Leadership Experiences Project Team, Combat Studies Institute, Fort Leavenworth, KS, 24 February 2005, 21.

46. Lieutenant Colonel Wayne Swan, interview by Contemporary Operations Study Team, Fort Shafter, HI, 19 July 2006, 10.

47. "Stryker Brigade Combat Team 1, 3d Brigade, 2d Infantry: Operations in Mosul, Iraq," *Initial Impressions Report* (Fort Leavenworth, KS: Center for Army Lessons Learned, 21 December 2004), 31.

48. Metz et al., 8.

49. Metz et al., 8.

50. "Briefing with Brigadier General Donald Alston, US Air Force, Spokesperson for Multinational Force Iraq," Coalition Press Information Center, 30 October 2005, http://www.mnf-iraq.com/Transcripts/051030a.htm (accessed 5 June 2006).

51. Brian Ross, "Staying Strong: The Insurgency in Iraq: Many Media Savvy Groups Make for Tough Opponents," *ABC News,* 20 March 2006, http://abcnews.go.com/WNT/print?id=1748161 (accessed 30 May 2006).

52. 2d Brigade, 2d Infantry Division, *After Action Review: Operation Iraqi Freedom 04-06* Briefing, 5 December 2005, slide 305.

53. 2d Brigade, 2d ID, *AAR: OIF 04-06,* 5 December 2005, slide 305.

54. Metz et al., 4–5.

55. Metz et al., 5.

56. Swan, interview, 19 July 2006, 10–11.

57. "Rumsfeld says extremists winning media war," *USA Today On-Line Edition*, posted 2/17/2006, http://www.usatoday.com/news/washington/2006-02-17-rumsfeld-media_x.htm (accessed 5 June 2006).

58. Lieutenant Colonel Steve Boylan, interview by Contemporary Operations Study Team, Fort Leavenworth, KS, 9 August 2006, 7.

59. Ross.

60. Ibrahim Al-Marashi, "Iraq's Hostage Crisis: Kidnappings, Mass Media and the Iraqi Insurgency," *Middle East Review of International Affairs,* Volume 8, No. 4, Article 1, December 2004, http://meria.idc.ac.il/journal/2004/issue4/jv8no4a1.html.

61.   Al-Marashi.

62.   Al-Marashi.

63.   FM 3-61.1, *Public Affairs Tactics, Techniques and Procedures* (Washington, DC, 1 October 2000), iv.

64.   FM 3-61.1, 1-1.

65.   Joint Publication (JP) 3-61, *Public Affairs* (Washington, DC, 9 May 2005), xi.

66.   FM 3-61.1, A-1.

67.   Margaret H. Belknap, "The CNN Effect: Strategic Enabler or Operational Risk?" Strategy Research Project (Carlisle Barracks, PA: Army War College, 30 March 2001), 1.

68.   Belknap, 1.

69.   Lieutenant Colonel Arthur P. Brill Jr., USMC (Retired), "A Defining Moment in Marine Corps History," *Sea Power, Navy League of the United States*, http://www.navyleague.org/seapower/krulak_interview.htm (accessed December 2007).

70.   Brill.

71.   Lieutenant Colonel Bernd Horn, "Command and Control Complexity Squared: Operating in the Future Battlespace," 3 July 2004, http://worldaffairsboard.com/showpost.php?p=20409&postcount=38 (accessed 24 July 2006).

72.   Brendan R. McLane, "Reporting from the Sandstorm: An Appraisal of Embedding," *Parameters,* Spring 2004, 77–88. The overview of media–military relationships in the following paragraphs is based on this article.

73.   McLane, 83.

74.   Douglas J. Goebel, "Military–Media Relations: The Future Media Environment and Its Influence on Military Operations" (Maxwell, AL: Air University and Air War College, 1997), 22.

75.   Christopher Paul and James J. Kim, *Reporters on the Battlefield: The Embedded Press System in Historical Context* (Santa Monica, CA: RAND Corporation, 2004), 49.

76.   McLane, 81.

77.   Office of the Secretary of Defense, "Public Affairs Guidance on Embedding Media During Possible Future Operations/Deployments in the US Central Command's (CENTCOM) Area of Responsibility (AOR)," 10 February 2003.

78.   Sec of Defense, "Public Affairs Guidance on Embedding Media."

79.   3d Infantry Division (Mechanized), After Action Report, Lessons Learned, Chapter 6: Embedded Media, 40–44.

80.   Amy Schlesing, interview by Contemporary Operations Study Team, Fort Leavenworth, KS, 12 June 2006, 7.

81.   3d ID, AAR, Lessons Learned, Chapter 6: Embedded Media, 40–44.

82.   Schlesing, interview, 12 June 2006, 6.

83.   Baker, 18.

84.   Chapter 2, "Civil-Military Operations," *CALL Newsletter 04-13,* 11.

85.   Baker, 18–19.

86.   Colonel (Promotable) Stephen Lanza, interview by Contemporary Operations Study Team, Washington, DC, 2 November 2005,17.

87.   Brigadier General Michael Tucker, interview by Contemporary Operations Study Team, Washington, DC, 20 January 2006, 9–10.

88.   Tucker, interview, 20 January 2006, 9–10.

89.   Brigadier General David Perkins, interview by Contemporary Operations Study Team, Washington, DC, 25 January 2006 20.

90.   Colonel Glenn T. Starnes, "Leveraging the Media: The Embedded Media Program in Operation Iraqi Freedom," Strategy Research Paper, Volume S04-06, Center for Strategic Leadership, US Army War College, July 2004.

91. Major General (Retired) John R. Batiste, interview by Contemporary Operations Study Team, Rochester, NY, 20 April 2006.

92. Starnes.

93. Richard K. Wright, "Assessment of the DOD Embedded Media Program," Institute for Defense Analysis Joint Warfighting Program, IDA Paper P-3931, September 2004.

94. Wright.

95. 3d ID, AAR, Lessons Learned, Chapter 6: Embedded Media, 40–44.

96. Howard Kurtz, "Media Weigh Costs, Fruits of 'Embedding:' News Outlets Stretch Budgets for Chance to Witness Iraq War From Front Lines," *Washington Post*, 11 March 2003, A.15.

97. Howard Kurtz, "For Media After Iraq, A Case of Shell Shock: Battle Assessment Begins For Saturation Reporting," *Washington Post*, 28 April 2003, A.01.

98. Schlesing, interview, 12 June 2006, 9.

99. Lieutenant Colonel Tammy L. Miracle, "The Army and Embedded Media," *Military Review*, September–October 2003, 44–45.

100. Steve Ritea, "Media Troop Withdrawal," *American Journalism Review*, December/January 2004, http://www.ajr.org/Article.asp?id=3477 (accessed 30 May 2006).

101. Joe Stupp, "Newspapers Pull Reporters From Embed Slots," *Editor and Publisher*, 28 April 2003.

102. MNF-I Directorate of Strategic Communications, *STRATCOM January 05 Iraqi Election Matrix* Briefing, 31 January 2005; Lieutenant Colonel Steve Boylan, Chief of the Coalition Press Information Center in 2004 and 2005, written comments.

103. Mark Memmott, "Reporters in Iraq under fire there, and from critics," *USA Today*, 2 August 2006, http:www.usatoday.com/news/world/iraq/2006-03-22-media-critisism_x.htm (accessed 2 August 2006); Jennifer Senior, "The Baghdad Press Club," *New York Magazine*, 22 May 2006, 38.

104. Captain Joseph Ludvigson, interview by Contemporary Operations Study Team, Fort Leavenworth, KS, 12 June 2006, 6.

105. Senior, 38–39.

106. Memmott; Senior, 39–40.

107. Ludvigson, interview, 12 June 2006, 6; Major Edward L. English, "Towards a More Productive Military-Media Relationship," US Army School of Advanced Military Studies Monograph, US Army Command and General Staff College, Fort Leavenworth, KS, AY 2004–05, 38.

108. Memmott; Senior, 105.

109. Ludvigson, interview, 12 June 2006, 5–6.

110. Colonel (Promotable) Daniel B. Allyn, interview by Contemporary Operations Study Team, Washington, DC, 4 November 2005, 10.

111. Colonel William Darley, interview by Contemporary Operations Study Team, Fort Leavenworth, KS, 8 August 2006, 11.

112. Memmott.

113. Schlesing, interview, 12 June 2006, 10.

114. Darley, written comments, 4 December 2006, 1.

115. Darley, interview, 8 August 2006, 1–2.

116. Captain Angela Bowman, interview by Operational Leadership Experiences Project Team, Fort Leavenworth, KS, 7 February 2006, 4, 10.

117. Bowman, interview, 7 February 2006, 14.

118. Lieutenant Colonel Paul Hastings, interview by Operational Leadership Experiences Project Team, Fort Leavenworth, KS, 10 March 2006, 12.

119. Justin Ward, "Army sends Media Imagery from Iraq at Push of Button," *Army News Service*, 21 June 2004; Hastings, interview, 10 March 2006, 6.

120. Ward; Hastings, interview, 10 March 2006, 6.

121. Ward.

122. General George W. Casey Jr., interview by Contemporary Operations Study Team, Fort Leavenworth, KS, 27 November 2007, 11–12.

123. MNF-I Headquarters, *MNF-I, Deputy Chief of Staff for Strategic Communications Orientation* Briefing, 14 June 2005.

124. *MNF-I, Deputy Chief of Staff for Strategic Communications Orientation* Briefing, 14 June 2005.

125. *STRATCOM January 05 Iraqi Election Matrix* Briefing, 31 January 2005.

126. *MNF-I, Deputy Chief of Staff for Strategic Communications Orientation* Briefing, 14 June 2005.

127. *MNF-I, Deputy Chief of Staff for Strategic Communications Orientation* Briefing, 14 June 2005.

128. Colonel Jill Morgenthaler, interview by Contemporary Operations Study Team, Fort Leavenworth, KS, 12 June 2006, 2.

129. Darley, interview, 8 August 2006, 5.

130. Ludvigson, interview, 24 May 2006, 8.

131. *MNF-I, Deputy Chief of Staff for Strategic Communications Orientation* Briefing, 14 June 2005.

132. Tom Shanker and Eric Schmitt, "Pentagon Weighs Use of Deception in a Broad Arena," *New York Times,* 13 December 2004, http://www.nytimes.com/2004/12/13/politics/13info.html?ex=1260594 000&en=d83314fc17eb65d5&ei=5090&partner=rssuserland (accessed 5 January 2007).

133. Casey, interview, 27 November 2007, 11.

134. Lieutenant General Thomas F. Metz, interview by Contemporary Operations Study Team, Fort Leavenworth, KS, 13 December 2005, 6.

135. "Pentagon Debate Rages Over 'Information Operations' in Iraq," *CNN*, http://edition.cnn. com/2004/US/12/12/pentagon.media/ (accessed 3 January 2007).

136. Casey, interview, 27 November 2007, 11.

137. Mark Mazzetti, "The Nation; PR Meets Psy-Ops in War on Terror; The use of misleading information as a military tool sparks debate in the Pentagon," *Los Angeles Times*, 1 December 2004, A1.

138. Colonel William M. Darley, "Why Public Affairs is not Information Operations," *Army*, January 2005, Volume 55, Issue 1.

139. See JP 3-13, *Information Operations* (Washington, DC, 13 February 2006).

140. Darley, interview, 8 August 2006, 7.

141. Darley, interview, 8 August 2006; Schlesing, interview, 12 June 2006.

142. Morgenthaler, interview, 12 June 2006, 8.

143. Darley, interview, 8 August 2006, 7.

144. Baker, 27.

145. Baker, 27.

146. Baker, 27.

147. Baker, 27.

148. Baker, 27.

149. Baker, 27.

150. Baker, 27.

151. Baker, 27.

152. Baker, 27.

153. Lieutenant General David H. Petraeus, interview by Contemporary Operations Study Team, Fort Leavenworth, KS, 18 March 2006.

154. Bowman, interview, 7 February 2006, 10.

155. *STRATCOM January 05 Iraqi Election Matrix* Briefing, 31 January 2005; Boylan, written comments.

Chapter 8

Combined Arms Operations in Iraq

In March 2003 the Coalition launched a campaign designed to overthrow the Saddam regime by using mechanized land forces conducting large-scale offensive operations with significant air support against an enemy that used comparable forces in a similar manner. The campaign in Iraq that spring was a contest, however uneven, between conventional military forces. Once Baghdad fell and the Saddam regime crumbled, the nature of operations changed radically. Beginning in May 2003 Coalition forces began dealing with an unconventional enemy that engaged in asymmetrical warfare in many different settings, including complex urban areas. These insurgents employed a variety of means to attack Coalition forces, and the US Army responded using full spectrum operations to win the support of the Iraqi population and counter the growing threat. The new campaign included an array of actions designed to gather intelligence, seize key members of insurgent networks, and assist in rebuilding Iraqi governance and infrastructure. Most of these missions were mounted by tactical-level units, ranging in size from squad- to battalion-size elements, and fell outside the range of operations that most American Soldiers had prepared for before Operation IRAQI FREEDOM (OIF) began.

US Army units, nevertheless, did plan and conduct missions in this period that were much closer on the spectrum of conflict to conventional combat. The most common of these operations were the counter-improvised explosive devise (IED) and countermortar operations that units conducted on a routine basis. Infantry, armor, and other maneuver companies, or their subunits, most often mounted these operations, but routinely did so with assistance from combat support elements such as engineer and field artillery batteries. While small in scale, these missions were critical to US commanders because they granted American units the freedom to maneuver and the ability to retain the initiative in the campaign. The 4th Infantry Division (4th ID) in 2004 classified these actions as "enabling operations" that allowed the unit to "conduct its decisive operations."[1]

Contrasting sharply with these routine albeit dangerous missions were the large-scale operations that focused the combat power of brigade-size units on areas where insurgents and militia forces had concentrated. After the summer of 2003, Combined Joint Task Force–7 (CJTF-7) and its subordinate units became less inclined to conduct large-scale offensive operations such as the 4th ID's Operation PENINSULA STRIKE, because of concerns that these broad assaults might be alienating the general populace and preventing Iraqis from supporting the Coalition effort against the insurgency.[2] Despite these fears, in 2004 major offensive actions by insurgent forces compelled the Coalition to reconsider the use of large-scale combat operations of its own. The April 2004 uprising of Muqtada al-Sadr and his militia forces, the Sunni Arab insurgent takeover of the city of Samarra in late summer 2004, and the creation of a formidable insurgent enclave in Fallujah that same summer constituted the most serious threats to stability and progress in Iraq. In each of these cases, Coalition forces chose to employ large combat formations in conventional offensive operations to destroy those threats.

This chapter will first examine the more common counter-IED and countermortar operations that characterize how US Army units attempted to create security in their areas of responsibility (AORs). The discussion will then shift to the large operations the Coalition felt were required to defeat major insurgent offensives and concentrations. US Army units conducted hundreds of company-, battalion-, brigade-, and division-level operations between May 2003 and January 2005. For example, between June 2003 and March 2004, the 1st Armored Division (1st AD) alone mounted 11 major operations in the city of Baghdad, all of which featured the division's subordinate brigades and battalions conducting raids, cordon and searches, and other offensive-oriented missions in their AOR.[3] In that same period, the 4th ID executed 10 offensive operations in the Sunni Triangle to the north of Baghdad.[4]

Rather than attempt to describe and analyze even a small portion of these actions, this chapter will examine four of the largest combined arms offensive operations as a means of providing insight into how the Army conducted combat missions in 2003 and 2004. These four operations are Operation PENINSULA STRIKE in which the 4th ID conducted a large-scale cordon and search against a Sunni Arab insurgent stronghold in June 2003; the April 2004 "extension campaign" that focused the 1st AD and other US Army units against the Shia militia forces in An Najaf, Al Kut, and other towns to the south of Baghdad; the 1st Infantry Division's (1st ID) Operation BATON ROUGE, which pitted US and Iraqi Security Forces (ISF) against Sunni insurgents in the city of Samarra in October 2004; and Operation AL FAJR, the November 2004 joint and combined assault that directed US Marine forces, US Army combined arms task forces, and ISF against the insurgent bastion in the city of Fallujah. These actions forced units to shift quickly from decentralized stability and support operations to the planning and conduct of complex, large-scale combined arms operations that featured intensive combat actions against a resolute enemy.

Counter-IED and Countermortar Operations

For the US Army in Iraq in 2003 and 2004, the most constant threat to American Soldiers was the IED.[*] The IED was not a new weapon. In the 20th century, guerrilla forces in a number of conflicts had used IEDs against their opponents. Soviet partisans employed IEDs against German trains during World War II and Viet Cong insurgents had used similar devices to attack American vehicles and Soldiers during the Vietnam war. In the last decade, Hezbollah forces have used IEDs against Israeli conventional forces in southern Lebanon, and Chechen rebels similarly targeted Russian army units in Chechnya. In Iraq the most common type of IED consisted of an explosive charge, a detonator, and a variety of trigger mechanisms. In a number of cases, insurgents obtained 155-mm artillery shells and antitank mines from the numerous weapons caches across the country and used them to create a shrapnel-laden explosion; however, any type of explosive could be used. Early in 2003 some IEDs even employed gasoline or diesel fuel as an explosive charge. Iraqi insurgents often placed IEDs along roadsides where they could best attack passing Coalition convoys. To prevent Coalition forces from finding the devices, the insurgents normally hid the IEDs in trash that accumulated along the curbs and medians of the roads, sometimes placing the weapon inside the carcass of a dead animal.

IED attacks increased in the summer and fall of 2003, and in response CJTF-7 and its subordinate units gradually developed tactics, techniques, and procedures (TTPs) to counter the threat. Commanders disseminated information about the IEDs, the insurgent's techniques of emplacing them, and the TTPs to use to defeat the devices throughout their formations. For

---

[*]The discussion of IEDs in this section is limited based on the 24 April 2006 memorandum from Gordon England, Deputy Secretary of Defense, regarding the "Policy on Discussion of IED and IED-Defeat Efforts in Open Sources."

Figure 70. A Buffalo vehicle belonging to the Army Reserve's 467th Engineer Battalion uses its hydraulic arm to probe a trash pile thought to contain an IED.

example, CJTF-7 headquarters began issuing TTPs for countering the IED threat in December 2003 in the form of "Smart Cards" that a Soldier could easily place in his or her pocket. The Smart Cards showed pictures of IEDs and described how to identify their firing mechanisms and how to defeat them or move past them safely.[5] Other commands distributed information and TTPs through PowerPoint briefings, which could be easily shared through digital networks.[6] Insurgents favored emplacing IEDs on the sides of roads and highways, and because the large percentage of US Soldiers moved by vehicle on a regular basis to conduct all types of operations, all American Soldiers trained on the TTPs and, by necessity, became involved in these operations.

The IED became a daily threat to US Soldiers. Between May 2003 and March 2004, statistics collected by the Department of Defense (DOD) suggested that there were an average of 20 attacks per day on Coalition forces. After April 2004, these attacks had increased to an average of between 40 and 60 incidents per day.[7] IEDs accounted for many if not most of these attacks. For the Soldiers of the 1st AD located in Baghdad, a "normal" day consisted of approximately 10 attacks across the division's AOR, half of which came from IEDs and indirect (mortar and rocket) fire.[8] These statistics did not include the IEDs discovered before they could be detonated.

While commanders in Iraq expected every Soldier to be aware of the IED threat during routine operations, the growth of the IED problem in 2003 and 2004 led many US units to adopt overt tactics focused on countering the threat. If units did not develop effective countermeasures, they risked ceding the initiative to the insurgents and the freedom to maneuver in their AOR. The counter-IED tactics and operations were diverse and tailored for the threat in a particular area. However, most involved active measures designed to frustrate the insurgent's ability to emplace and detonate the IED.

315

For the 1st AD, the most effective tactic was unit presence on the streets of Baghdad. The division's official history states that 1st AD Soldiers quickly decided "that only a very aggressive and energetic patrolling effort kept the routes reasonably clear. Repeated experiences taught the Soldiers how to spot unusual and suspicious objects and increasing knowledge of the tactics and techniques of IED employment gradually reduced their effectiveness."[9] Other units stressed changing routes and departure or arrival times to avoid establishing patterns that could be discerned and taken advantage of by insurgent bombers. In 2004 Soldiers in vehicular patrols and convoys would get technological assistance in the form of electronic jammers that rendered IEDs with electronic triggering devices, such as garage door openers, ineffective. Still, insurgents used a variety of firing techniques, not all of which were vulnerable to electronic interference.

Some units developed a broad, combined arms approach to the IED problem. In the 4th ID, unit commanders initially responded to the IED threat with engineer assets that could destroy any detected device in a safe manner. The division's official after action review (AAR) characterized these early tactics as "simplistic," and its subordinate units gradually built a more sophisticated set of techniques and procedures designed to eliminate the insurgent infrastructure.[10] As the division stated in its AAR, "Wherever there was an IED, there was a bomber, a bomb maker, a cache, and someone funding the operation."[11] Once leaders and staff officers in the division realized this, they began to use a combination of intelligence, combat, and combat support units to defeat the threat. By the spring of 2004 the division had integrated these elements into a broad counter-IED campaign that included the following types of operations: route reconnaissance, route sweeping to include trash removal, information operations (IO), traffic control points, and snipers. Division leaders felt so strongly about this broad approach that they contended, "Commanders must resist technical or functional solutions to tactical situations. The nature of Iraqi Freedom did not and will not lend itself to cookbook solutions. Continual pressure through a multi-BOS [battlefield operating systems] and combined arms approach is the only sure way to success."[12]

The evolution of the Army's response to the mortar threat was similar to its reaction to IEDs. Beginning in mid-2003 insurgents began to attack Coalition static sites with indirect fire using weapons and ammunition left over from Saddam's army. Quickly, indirect fire became the insurgents' second most effective form of attack, producing American casualties at a rate second only to the IED.[13] Most popular among the insurgents in Iraq were 60-mm, 82-mm, and 120-mm mortar systems for which there was an ample supply of rounds. Higher commands issued broad guidance and developed some TTPs to deal with this threat. The most common of these tactics was counterbattery fire operations—involving the conventional tactic of locating the "shooter" and destroying it with indirect counterfire from US mortars, artillery, and aircraft. Counterbattery fire required target acquisition radar systems such as the Q36 Firefinder and the light countermortar radar (LCMR) to detect the incoming mortar or artillery round. These systems then calculated the round's point of origin (POO), which became the target for US 120-mm mortars and 155-mm howitzers, often located on forward operating bases (FOBs) with the target acquisition radar systems. In many cases, American units began hitting enemy mortar POOs while the insurgents were loading their second or third rounds.

Some units developed more comprehensive countermortar operations. In the 2d Brigade Combat Team (BCT) of the 4th ID, for example, brigade positions began to take fire from enemy mortars once its units began operating in Diyala province in mid-2003. The brigade's commander and staff responded by using the intelligence preparation of the battlefield (IPB) process to locate likely enemy mortar sites. The brigade's maneuver units then established temporary sites from which they could survey these enemy sites, while its own fire support units stood by to provide immediate counterfire. At times, the brigade integrated its tactical unmanned aerial vehicle (TUAV) into the effort and conducted a supporting IO campaign that communicated with sheiks and farmers in the province about the American use of counterfire, its damaging effect on farmland, and the importance of preventing the use of their property by enemy mortar crews.

For some units, particularly those in larger cities, countermortar fire was not the best solution for the situation in their AOR. The 3d Stryker BCT of the 2d Infantry Division (2d ID) began operations in the densely populated urban terrain of the city of Mosul in January 2004. Although the brigade, located on a series of FOBs in the city, became a target of insurgent indirect fire, the brigade commander greatly restricted the use of countermortar fire fearing the likelihood of damage to civilian infrastructure. US counterfire would likely have been effective, but the price in terms of decreased Iraqi support for the unit's overall campaign would have been too high in the commander's estimation. The brigade's joint fires and effects cell (JFEC) determined that the best way to defeat enemy indirect fire was to use imagery intelligence (IMINT), UAVs, human intelligence (HUMINT), and analysis of both target acquisition radar data and actual mortar craters to determine the most likely enemy mortar positions. The analysis was used to build a database that was then disseminated to subordinate units through the brigade-wide digital network.

Once analysis yielded likely POOs within the AOR, the brigade used a variety of maneuver and support units to establish countermortar observation posts and provide immediate reaction to find and destroy insurgent mortar teams. In one action in September 2004, a military police (MP) platoon attached to the brigade occupied an observation post overlooking potential insurgent firing points.[14] That platoon observed four insurgents firing a 60-mm mortar from a vehicle, engaged the insurgents with their weapons and, with the help of another platoon that moved to the site, killed one insurgent and wounded the other three. The brigade often made small adjustments to their operations to ensure the insurgents were constantly off balance. However, the JFEC, as well as the brigade commander, came to believe that the best means of defeating insurgent indirect fire in Mosul was not countermortar *fire* but countermortar *maneuver*.

Major Combined Arms Operations

All US Army maneuver units in Iraq in 2003 and 2004 participated in large-scale operations. The majority of these operations, however, consisted of raids, cordon and searches, and other counterinsurgent-type operations coordinated to occur simultaneously across numerous AORs throughout much of Iraq. Put more simply, most of the large-scale operations were synchronized in time but not in space. Operations such as DESERT SCORPION, which began on 15 June 2003 and continued for 2 weeks, consisted of a series of raids on suspected insurgent sites and follow-on stability operations conducted simultaneously in many parts of the country. DESERT SCORPION included the 1st AD in Baghdad, the 4th ID in the Sunni Triangle, the 101st Airborne Division (101st ABN) in Mosul, and the 3d Armored Cavalry Regiment (3d ACR) in Al Anbar province. Operations at division level often shared these characteristics. In Baghdad, for example, the 1st AD launched Operation IRON HAMMER on 12 November 2003 in response to increased insurgent attacks during the Muslim holy month of Ramadan.

During IRON HAMMER, the division directed its subordinate units to conduct an increased number of patrols, IO, intelligence-gathering missions, and raids throughout the city as a way of blunting the attacks and demonstrating to the population that Coalition forces would not allow the insurgent network to grow unimpeded.[15] Operations like DESERT SCORPION and IRON HAMMER put a great deal of pressure on insurgent networks across specific areas. However, in reaction to the dispersed and elusive nature of the insurgent network, these operations did not normally focus the combat power of brigade-size elements on any one limited geographic objective.

Still, at critical times in 2003 and 2004, Army commanders decided to launch large-scale combined arms combat operations, usually in response to the concentration of insurgent forces in specific cities. These cases are important to the full understanding of how Coalition forces managed the shift between stability and major offensive actions, the type of transition that is fundamental to the concept of full spectrum operations. The operations described below are examples that demonstrate how the Army attempted to wield its advantages in training, fire-power, and technology against an irregular enemy and offer important insights into how the Army integrated information warfare, stability operations, and reconstruction efforts into what was often very intensive combat.

Operation PENINSULA STRIKE: Cordon and Search in the Sunni Triangle, June 2003

Soon after the fall of the Saddam regime, US Army units began conducting operations designed to find members of the Baathist networks they suspected of planning and mounting sporadic attacks against Coalition forces. Often, these actions took the form of cordon and searches—operations in which military forces isolated specific geographic areas and conducted forced entries into houses and buildings to find insurgents and weapons. Although US Army doctrine assigned this type of mission to infantry units, cordon and search became a standard operation for armor, cavalry, and other maneuver units in 2003 and 2004 as the security environment worsened. When the threat was considered low, Soldiers conducted "cordon and knock" missions, a variation of the cordon and search in which units firmly announced their arrival before entering homes and generally used more gentle methods of entering and searching homes. Both types of operations enabled US units to capture key members of insurgent networks and collect critical intelligence that led to further operations. In fact, by the fall of 2003 many units had begun bringing sensitive site exploitation teams, often composed of military intelligence (MI) Soldiers and other specialists, on cordon and searches to exploit the documents and other materials found during these missions.

Cordon and searches became a staple of operations at the platoon, company, and battalion levels. Even so, in several significant instances, larger tactical formations employed these actions to clear major areas of insurgent activity. PENINSULA STRIKE, a multi-brigade cordon and search that integrated infantry, armor, aviation, field artillery, and combat support units serves as an excellent example of how the US Army conducted this type of mission in the summer of 2003. In May and June of that year, Coalition military forces found themselves on the receiving end of multiple attacks from shadowy forces that many believed were remnants of the old regime. In the Sunni Triangle north of Baghdad, the Soldiers of 4th ID became targets of a number of enemy assaults that featured IEDs, rocket-propelled grenades (RPGs), and small arms. Sunni Arabs densely populated this part of Iraq, consisting primarily of Diyala and Salah ad Din provinces. It was also the traditional stronghold of the Baathist Party and contained the city of Tikrit, Saddam Hussein's birthplace. In the initial campaign to depose Saddam's regime, Coalition forces had not conducted major combat operations in the triangle, and the regime's military, paramilitary, and intelligence organizations, essentially still intact, had gone underground. By late May CJTF-7 and Major General Raymond Odierno, the commanding general of the 4th ID, decided to gain control of the region by identifying the locations of former Baathist officers, soldiers, and intelligence agents and using a cordon and search operation to capture these men.

The idea for Operation PENINSULA STRIKE emerged in early June after intelligence reports indicated a relatively large group of Baathist leaders had gathered in a crowded urban area located on a peninsula of the Tigris River northeast of the city of Balad. The 4th ID staff also believed this area served as the likely safe haven for enemy forces that had launched a series of ambushes on American Soldiers the previous month. The division, working with the CJTF-7 staff, began planning an operation whose purpose was to "clear paramilitary and Baath Party forces along the Tigris River vic[inity] Balad."[16] The plan's concept centered on the use of two BCTs and other divisional units in a two-phase operation that would rely on the principles of surprise and mass. The division would unexpectedly insert a large force of close to 4,000 Soldiers into the 10-square kilometer peninsula area to locate and arrest high-ranking members of the former Saddamist regime, thereby disrupting the enemy networks based in the area.

In the first phase, elements of two BCTs would cordon off the peninsula—the 2d BCT to the south on the other side of the Tigris River and the 3d BCT north of Duluiyah, a town located on the northern end of the peninsula. To ensure the tightness of the cordon, the division added units belonging to the 555th Engineer Group (Combat) to its own 4th Engineer Battalion to establish riverine checkpoints along the Tigris River. These positions would help interdict any escape attempts by the Iraqis who lived and kept boats along the banks of the river. Prior to these units taking their positions, the 3d BCT planned to send Task Force (TF) *Gauntlet*, a composite group of MP and MI Soldiers, into the heavily-populated urbanized area of the peninsula to gather information and pinpoint targets, if possible.[17]

In the second phase of the operation, the 3d BCT in the north, supported by field artillery and attack aviation, would enter the peninsula area with two battalions. The 2d Battalion, 503d Infantry (2-503d IN), an airborne infantry battalion from the 173d Airborne Brigade under the operational control of the 3d BCT for PENINSULA STRIKE, would move a reinforced company with helicopters to three landing zones just south of the town of Duluiyah where it would establish three checkpoints to further isolate the peninsula. The 1st Battalion, 8th Infantry (1-8th IN), would then move its companies equipped with Bradley Fighting Vehicles (BFVs) southward on the single major road through the town of Duluiyah, to seize Objective CARTHAGE, an area that made up the southern two-thirds of the peninsula. Once 1-8th IN approached the peninsula, Lieutenant Colonel Dominic Caracillo, the battalion commander of the 2-503d IN planned to use wheeled vehicles to move the remainder of his forces through Duluiyah and then turn south and southeast to seize areas that US intelligence believed served as havens for Saddamist elite.[18]

Once they reached the designated areas, the infantrymen in both battalions would conduct searches of all the buildings on their objectives, first securing and searching the sites that intelligence reports suggested served as sanctuaries for key members of the Saddam regime.[19] Clearly expecting a large number of detainees as a result of these actions, 4th ID headquarters established several enemy prisoner of war (EPW) collection sites along the edges of the cordoned area as well as a temporary holding facility at the Balad airfield to the southwest of Duluiyah that could accommodate as many as 200 people. To get the detainees to the facility safely, the division ordered MP units to plan for escorting these Iraqis along ground routes and arranged for helicopters to remove the detainees from the objective area.[20]

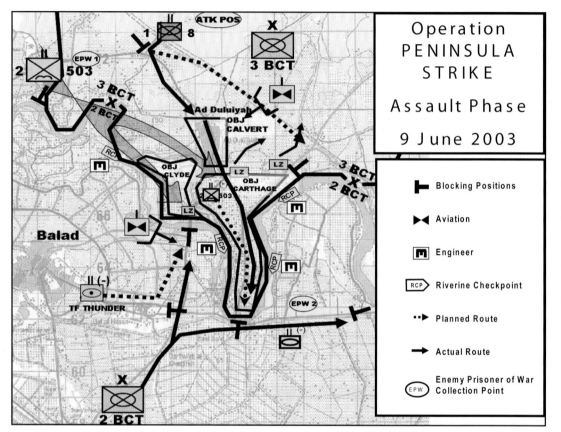

Figure 71. Operation PENINSULA STRIKE.

In the first week of June, after the 2d and 3d BCT commanders and staffs had completed planning and rehearsals, Major General Odierno gave the green light to begin the operation. On 4 June the MP and MI Soldiers of TF *Gauntlet* moved into the area south of Duluiyah. Once they had completed gathering intelligence and confirming locations of specific targeted individuals, the 3d BCT initiated the next phase of the operation. Around midnight on 9 June the reinforced company from the 2-503d IN loaded into helicopters and flew to the three landing zones where they established checkpoints. At roughly the same time, the BFVs of 1-8th IN began traveling in column south through Duluiyah toward Objective CARTHAGE. With maneuver space for the BFVs limited to the narrow road running south through the peninsula, the battalion dismounted its infantrymen at key intersections and they fanned out to assigned sectors using their night vision goggles to locate and search the buildings where the elite members of the Saddam regime were thought to be located. The BFVs then drove to the southern tip of the peninsula where they served as a quick reaction force in case the infantrymen on foot met violent organized opposition.

Fortunately, the BFVs and their heavy weapons remained idle that night. With one dramatic exception, the Soldiers of 1-8th IN conducting the searches did not meet resistance as they entered the homes on the peninsula. One of the houses was believed to harbor a high-ranking member of the Baathist regime, and when the infantrymen entered that property, an Iraqi inside greeted them with a shotgun blast at close range that caught one Soldier in the chest.[21] Only the Soldier's body armor (Small Arms Protective Inserts [SAPI]) prevented this attack from becoming fatal. A small number of Iraqis did attempt to evade US forces by using boats to escape on the Tigris River; however, the engineer Soldiers manning the riverine checkpoints apprehended them.[22] Lieutenant Colonel Philip Battaglia, the commander of 1-8th IN, attributed the lack of Iraqi resistance to the 4th ID's decision to launch the operation in the middle of the night, a move that caught most Iraqis in the area by surprise.[23]

The 2-503d IN rolled through Duluiyah not long after 1-8th IN had rumbled past. By that time, the enemy was more alert. Gunfire from a building on the southern edge of Duluiyah hit a HMMWV belonging to the battalion's scout platoon. First Sergeant John Bagby, who was riding in the column, recalled, "I heard and saw tracer rounds from the top of the roof of what was later determined to be a police station."[24] The ambush wounded five Soldiers in the vehicle, but did not deter the battalion from moving onto their objectives. Once they arrived, the paratroopers immediately located the houses suspected of harboring members of Saddam's paramilitary and intelligence organizations. They met relatively little resistance as they looked for those suspected of running the networks in the peninsula area.

Once the sun rose and all of the houses of the most critical targets had been secured and searched, both battalions began systematically clearing all the buildings on their objectives. Battaglia recalled that the 120-degree heat and humidity made the Soldiers' tasks even more difficult. The hard work, nevertheless, paid immediate dividends. At the end of the first day on the peninsula, the infantrymen had seized large caches of small arms weapons and ammunition and captured additional Iraqis they believed had connections to Saddam's paramilitary and intelligence organizations. The patrolling and searches continued for the next 3 days, ultimately resulting in the detention of close to 400 men.[25] MI Soldiers screened the detainees, found that 30 had likely connections to the Baath Party or to the suspected insurgent activities, and released the other detainees. Of those captured, the most important figures were Major General Abul Ali Jasmin, the Secretary of Saddam's Defense Ministry and his brother, Brigadier General Abdullah Ali Jasmin, the head of the Iraqi Military Academy, both of whom turned themselves in to US forces on the first day of the operation.[26]

PENINSULA STRIKE was only the first of several large-scale combined arms operations mounted by Coalition forces in the summer of 2003. Based on the success of the 4th ID's actions on the peninsula, especially the ability of such actions to round up large numbers of suspected insurgents, CJTF-7 planned and conducted a series of similar operations across much of Iraq in June and July. Operation DESERT SCORPION, which followed on the heels of PENINSULA STRIKE, featured 2 weeks of raids on Baathist and insurgent targets in Baghdad, the Mosul area, and the Sunni heartland around the city of Tikrit. During this operation, American Soldiers detained hundreds of Iraqis suspected of cooperating with the emerging insurgent network. In July Coalition forces launched another series of raids in a coordinated operation called SODA MOUNTAIN. Once again, the cordon and searches netted a large number of weapons and approximately 611 detainees, of whom 62 were identified later as leaders in the Saddam regime.[27]

By early August, however, evidence emerged that these large-scale operations were in some ways counterproductive. Instead of generating widespread support for the capture of those connected to the Saddam regime, Coalition forces found that their tactics fostered resentment within segments of the Iraqi population, specifically among Sunni Arabs who were fearful of their future in Iraq after Saddam. The fledgling Iraqi Governing Council (IGC) suggested to Coalition leaders that the intrusive searches and other aggressive tactics of the cordon and searches were not building support for the Coalition. Lieutenant General Ricardo Sanchez, the commander of CJTF-7, stated that by June 2003 he realized "there was a noncompliant element out there that was very willing to conduct [operations] against us to kill us and therefore we had to go out there and do these big sweeps."[28] But, according to Sanchez, operations like SODA MOUNTAIN created problems, "I started to get multiple indicators that maybe our iron-fisted approach to the conduct of [operations] was beginning to alienate Iraqis. . . . I started to get those indications from a variety of sources all the way from the Governing Council on down to the average people."[29] Worse was the suggestion that these large-scale operations were not only alienating some Iraqis but also inducing those who might not be disposed to insurgent activities to use violence against the Coalition. About this effect, Sanchez stated, "Unquestionably, I think, we created in this culture some Iraqis that then had to act because there were casualties on their side and also because of the impact on their dignity and respect."[30]

Coalition forces continued to mount raids against suspected insurgent objectives after August 2003. However, because many Coalition military leaders came to see their mission focused on generating support from the population for the Coalition, in most cases, these actions were small, no longer the massive type of combined-arms operation that swept into the Tigris peninsula in June 2003. From the fall of 2003 into 2004, Coalition leaders attempted to plan operations that were focused on specific insurgent or terrorist targets in a specific geographic area rather than multi-brigade searches through large areas. More importantly, leaders increasingly took a balanced full spectrum approach to their operations, one that included aggressive action against a suspected insurgent objective, civic actions that tried to win the support of the Iraqis in the affected neighborhood or village, and IO to explain what Coalition forces were doing and why it was necessary to create a secure environment in that area.

The 1st Armored Division's Extension Campaign: April–May 2004

The general cessation of large-scale combined arms operations in the summer of 2003 did not prevent the Coalition from mounting major offensive actions when faced with enemy forces intent on fighting Coalition units and disrupting the overall Coalition project in Iraq. In 2004 threats of this type emerged, taking the form of Sunni Arab insurgent groups and Shia militia forces that asserted political and military authority over specific cities or geographic areas and thus challenged the power of the Coalition and the Iraqi Government. To suppress these serious dangers, the US Army, working with its joint counterparts, other Coalition forces, and the nascent ISF, mounted large offensives that featured combined arms operations. In doing so, the Army displayed its ability to transition quickly from stability missions to high-intensity conventional combat operations that allowed US units to muster all of their advantages in technology, training, and firepower.

The first of these major military challenges arose in April 2004 when the radical Shia cleric Muqtada al-Sadr launched a general insurrection by his militia force called the Mahdi Army and its related organizations, hereafter referred to as Sadrist forces. This revolt began simultaneously in eastern Baghdad in the Shia neighborhood of Sadr City, and in the Shia-dominated cities of south-central Iraq—Karbala, An Najaf, Kufa, and Al Kut. Al-Sadr's rise to power began after the toppling of the Saddam regime. In the chaos that followed, al-Sadr had set up his own power structure in Sadr City, filling the governmental vacuum. At various times in 2003, the cleric had spoken openly about establishing his own theocratic government in the huge slum. Beginning in the summer of 2003, the Coalition had forged an uneasy truce with al-Sadr, although Coalition leaders had come close to arresting al-Sadr in August 2003 for complicity in the April 2003 murder of rival cleric Abd-al-Majid al-Khoei.

The fragile truce began unraveling on 10 October 2003 when a large group of al-Sadr's supporters ambushed a unit from the 2d ACR in Sadr City, killing two American troopers and wounding several others. This attack caused a standoff between Coalition forces and the Mahdi Army, but the conflict slowly cooled over the next several months. However, in the spring of 2004, when al-Sadr's forces began taking over mosques in An Najaf and Kufa, leaders in the Coalition Provisional Authority (CPA) and CJTF-7 lost their remaining patience. In this tense environment, al-Sadr personally called for civil disorder and when his newspaper, *al-Hawza,* reprinted the appeal, Coalition authorities shut it down and on 3 April 2004 arrested one of al-Sadr's senior aides, Mustafa al-Yacoubi. This arrest sparked violence in Sadr City and attacks by Mahdi Army militiamen on local Iraqi Government buildings, Iraqi police stations, and CPA offices in An Najaf province.

The already tense relations between the Mahdi Army and Coalition forces had crossed an invisible line. Despite US intentions, many Shia Iraqis had, by the spring of 2004, began to believe the Americans had stripped them of the freedoms they had been promised. The resulting frustration, anger, and resentment spilled over into open revolt. Major George Sarabia, who served in Sadr City in April 2004 as the executive officer of 2d Squadron, 2d ACR, described this climate:

> You had the crackdown on the newspaper, the *al-Hawza* newspaper, so it cannot be produced. . . . Then we arrested Mustafa al-Yacoubi, one of the key lieutenants of Muqtada al-Sadr, with perhaps the intent of going after Sadr himself. Who knows? Certainly, Sadr didn't know. But there's the perception, and the perception becomes the reality. So now, Sadr looks like he's getting fenced in. His newspaper's been shut down; one of his key lieutenants has been arrested. Who knows what this lieutenant is saying in terms of this indictment against Muqtada al-Sadr for the killing of the [al-Khoei]. . . . And so tensions are rising.[31]

The tensions boiled over on 4 April 2004 when Mahdi Army militiamen attacked an American convoy in Sadr City, killing 7 Soldiers from the 1st Cavalry Division (1st CAV), 1 Soldier from the 1st AD, and wounding 52 others. At the same time, Sadrist forces surrounded the CPA compound in An Najaf and demanded the release of Mustafa al-Yacoubi. Mahdi Army militiamen also moved against Coalition forces far to the south in An Nasiriyah, took control of a radio station in Al Kut, and began assembling in the town of Karbala. To Paul Bremer, the CPA chief, it appeared that Muqtada al-Sadr was making a "straight-forward power grab."[32]

In response, Bremer and Lieutenant General Sanchez began moving decisively. The multi-national units that had responsibility for the southern Shia cities—the Spanish, Salvadorans, and Ukrainians—were few and not prepared to act quickly against the uprising. Sanchez determined that these forces needed assistance from the heavier and more powerful US Army and tasked the 1st AD to respond. In many ways, the timing of the uprising occurred at a bad moment for the 1st AD. The division had begun the redeployment process and approximately one-third of its force had already been cycled out of Iraq with some units already in Kuwait and Germany. The units from 1st AD that remained in Iraq were on the verge of transferring authority for their AORs to their replacements. This was especially important for operations in tumultuous Sadr City where the 2d ACR, a unit subordinate to the 1st AD, had been in charge.

After receiving a warning order from CJTF-7 on 4 April, the division commander, Major General Martin Dempsey, acted immediately by ordering Colonel Ralph Baker, the commander of the 1st AD's 2d BCT, to reinforce Coalition forces facing the Sadrist threat to the south of Baghdad. Baker responded by tasking the 2d Battalion, 6th Infantry (2-6th IN), the brigade reconnaissance troop, and the brigade forward command post to move to An Najaf and support the multinational troops in their defense of Coalition sites in the city. The move of this force represented the first tactical step in the 1st AD's campaign to suppress the Sadrist revolt in the Shia cities.

As the 2d BCT moved south, Dempsey met with his staff to plan the division's next move. Without being told explicitly, Dempsey and his staff officers realized Sanchez intended to use their division as the main effort in the destruction of the Sadrist insurrection.[33] They based this assumption on the fact that, in April 2004, the 1st AD was Sanchez's de facto operational reserve. The unit had already begun transferring authority for its AORs and was preparing to leave Iraq, meaning the impressive combat power of the 1st AD was not committed at the time and was the only force available for the campaign.

After declaring the Mahdi Army a hostile force—a term that empowered Coalition forces to engage and destroy Sadrist foces—on 6 April 2004, Sanchez officially halted the 1st AD's redeployment, ordering the division to move against the Sadrist revolt and to create a theater reserve force to respond to further uprisings that Coalition intelligence feared would arise. Dempsey ordered his commanders to cease all redeployment operations and prepare for combat operations against Sadrist forces.[34] This decision entailed the return of Soldiers and equipment from Germany and elsewhere to Iraq, where they could be committed to the new operation. The division commander projected that the campaign against the Sadrist insurrection would take approximately 4 months, and on 9 April Dempsey formally announced to his Soldiers they would remain in Iraq for another 120 days. He told them, "I know you are eager to get home. I am too. But not if it means allowing one thug to replace another. We've worked too hard here to watch that happen."[35]

With time critical, the 1st AD could not wait to begin operations until all of its forces had returned to Iraq. Dempsey and his staff began to plan for immediate action with the units he had available in early April. In this early stage the division commander established the outline for a broad, multifaceted campaign against the Sadrist revolt based on four lines of operation: combat operations, IO, reestablishment of the ISF, and stability and reconstruction operations. The division would pursue these lines of operation in a "deliberate, patient, and methodical" manner at the operational level. However, at the tactical level, 1st AD's units would be "aggressive and tenacious" when situations required combat operations.[36] These guidelines were the product of 12 months of experience in Baghdad and the critical realization that methodical campaign tempo allowed time for Iraqi political and military authorities to deal with Muqtada al-Sadr and his forces in their own way before the Coalition had to use force.

With little intelligence to help flesh out the campaign plan, Dempsey ordered the division into action with the expectation that his units would develop the situation, gather information, and assist him and his staff in creating a more detailed operational plan. The division published that plan, Operation IRON SABRE, 8 days after the uprising began. 1st AD's operations would become part of the larger Coalition plan called RESOLUTE SWORD. In the interlude during which these plans were finalized, the units of 1st AD traveled great distances with little preparation and entered the fight against a determined foe.

TF Striker *in Al Kut: 4–11 April 2004*

The vanguard of the 1st AD in IRON SABRE was its 2d BCT. The first elements of this vanguard, the brigade forward command post, TF 2-6th IN—consisting of elements from a mechanized infantry battalion combined with cavalry and antitank units—and the brigade reconnaissance troop departed Baghdad on 4 April and arrived on the outskirts of An Najaf by the morning of 5 April 2004. These elements spent the next 2 days preparing to defend the CPA installations and mounting opposition to Sadrist moves focused on taking over the city. By 7 April the 1st AD staff had received numerous reports of Sadrist forces threatening to take control of Al Kut, a city located approximately 100 miles to the northeast of An Najaf. Al-Sadr's militia had forced Ukrainian units and the CPA staff out of the CPA compound in Al Kut and had occupied police headquarters and the television and radio station in the city.[37] The Ukrainian battalion, Iraqi police, and employees of the private security company Triple Canopy had not been strong enough to hold off the Shia militia. The Ukrainians, in particular, were not armed with heavy weapons and in the skirmishing with Sadrist forces, had run low on ammunition for their small arms.[38]

On 7 April Major General Dempsey assessed the threat in Al Kut to be more dire than the threat in An Najaf and ordered Colonel Baker, the commander of the 2d BCT, to move his forces in An Najaf to a tactical assembly area on the outskirts of Al Kut. Baker's force, now designated TF *Striker*, still consisted of a mechanized infantry battalion, the brigade reconnaissance troop, a cavalry troop, and other support units. This TF arrived at Camp Delta on the western edge of Al Kut on 8 April, placing the Americans on the fringes of a city whose large Shia-dominated population of approximately 380,000 was located in a relatively small geographic area inside a horseshoe-shaped bend of the Tigris River. In fact, as Baker and his staff looked east from Camp Delta toward the heart of Al Kut, they found that the Tigris River separated them from the center of the city, which held the CPA compound and the other locations that would become major objectives in the upcoming action. To cross this major obstacle, the Soldiers of TF *Striker* would have to make use of the five bridges that led into Al Kut or find another way into the city. The TF staff went to work immediately to make plans to clear the city of Sadrist forces, starting with the recapture of the CPA compound on the western edge of the city, which they called Objective BETTY. The mission statement for the operation made it clear that TF *Striker* sought not only to seize the CPA compound but also to eliminate the Sadrist threat in Al Kut: "2d BCT attacks to seize Objective BETTY (CPA compound) [to] restore order to the city of Al Kut. [On order], continues offensive operations to destroy remnants of Mahdi's Army (*sic*)."[39]

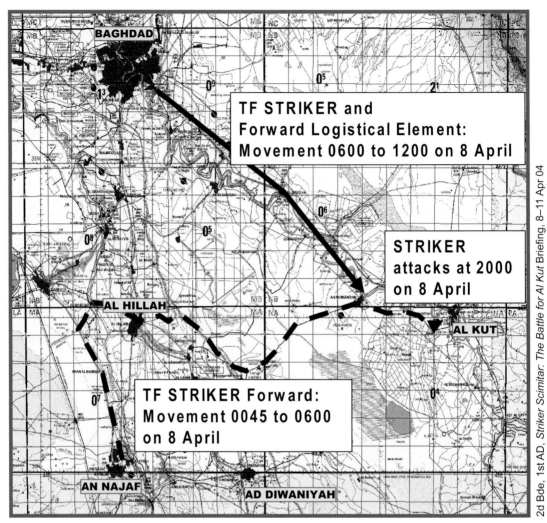

Figure 72. Staging 2d BCT, 1st AD to strike Al Kut, 7 April 2004.

2d Bde, 1st AD, *Striker Scimitar: The Battle for Al Kut Briefing, 8–11 Apr 04*

As the TF staff began to assess the situation in Al Kut, reconnaissance elements reported that Sadrist fighters had clustered near two bridges northeast and east of the city. The TF commander, hoping to avoid these concentrations, planned to send K Troop, 3d Squadron, 2d ACR, to seize and hold three bridges on the west of the city, a move that would place US forces close to the CPA compound. But among the staff, questions arose over whether or not these bridges could support the weight of the heavy armored vehicles in 2-6th IN, the unit designated to be the main effort in the attack. Lieutenant Colonel T.C. Williams, the commander of 2-6th IN, decided to circumvent these bridges completely by entering the city from the northwest and thus catching the Sadrist militiamen occupying the CPA compound by surprise. To do so, however, he had to find an alternative route into that side of Al Kut. After doing a careful analysis of the city and the surrounding area, Williams decided to send Team Dealer, a mechanized company reinforced with M1 Abrams tanks, 21 miles to the west—away from the city—to a bridge that crossed the Tigris River in the town of Namaniyah. Once on the opposite side of the river, the Soldiers in the BFVs and Abrams tanks hoped to find the road leading southeast into Al Kut open and the

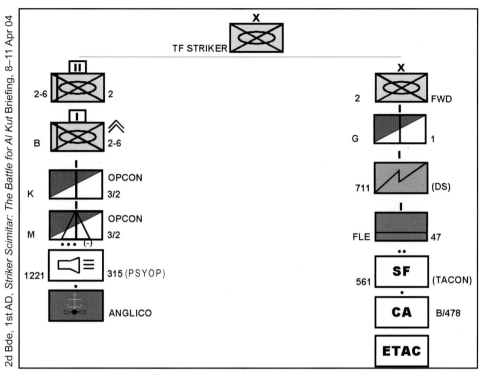

Figure 73. TF *Striker*, task organization, 8 April 2004.

enemy unaware of their envelopment. To divert the attention of the Sadrist forces from Team Dealer's approach, Baker planned to use close air support to attack the Sadr Bureau, the enemy headquarters located on the southern side of Al Kut, away from the CPA compound.

The operation to recapture Al Kut began in the middle of the evening on 8 April when Team Dealer left Camp Delta, crossed the Tigris River, and approached the city.[40] Once this team was in place just before 0200, TF *Striker* began its assault by directing two AH-64 Apaches to fire a pair of Hellfire missiles at the Sadr Bureau headquarters. An AC-130 Gunship followed this salvo with multiple volleys from its 105-mm cannons. This attack on the enemy's command and control center confused the Mahdi Army forces and enabled 2-6th IN to surprise the Sadrist forces on Objective BETTY and secure the CPA compound without much opposition. At roughly the same time, K Troop, 3/2 ACR attacked to seize the three southern bridges over the Tigris. Two of the bridges fell quickly, but enemy fighters offered a tenacious defense on the third. Williams sent M1 tanks and BFVs from the CPA compound to that bridge to overwhelm the Sadrist defenders.[41] However, even the firepower of this force did not break the enemy resistance, and Baker decided to call in the AC-130 gunship to destroy the Sadrist forces mounting the defense. While some Shia fighters remained in the city and continued to engage the American units with small arms and RPGs, by dawn these unorganized centers of resistance had been cleared by a combination of direct and indirect fire.[42]

That morning Coalition forces appeared to have seized the initiative in the city. US forces had recaptured the CPA compound and destroyed the Sadrist headquarters. The Mahdi Army in Al Kut was in disarray and not effectively resisting the Coalition's overwhelming force. TF

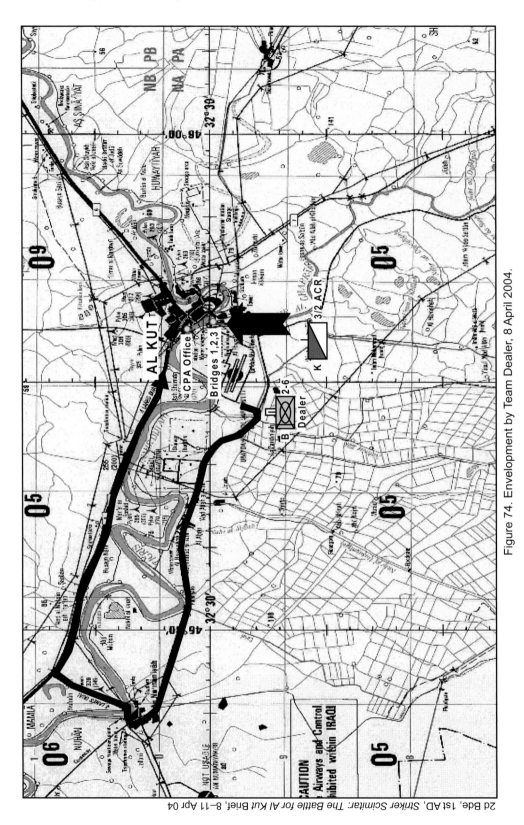

Figure 74. Envelopment by Team Dealer, 8 April 2004.

2d Bde, 1st AD, *Striker Scimitar: The Battle for Al Kut Brief,* 8–11 Apr 04

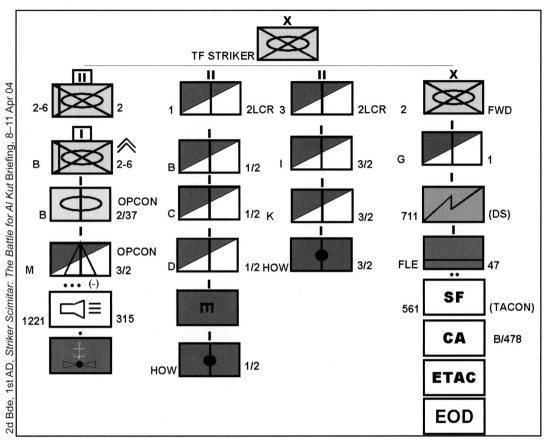

2d Bde, 1st AD, *Striker Scimitar: The Battle for Al Kut Briefing*, 8–11 Apr 04

Figure 75. Task organization, 9–11 April 2004.

Striker estimated they inflicted approximately 50 casualties in the action on the previous night. To keep the pressure on the enemy, the TF commander directed 2-6th IN to seize Objective CAROL, the television and radio station north of the CPA compound, and Objective ELLEN, the local municipal government building. These targets fell quickly, denying the Mahdi Army a means of distributing its propaganda and preparing the way for the Coalition to reestablish the basic economic and governmental infrastructure of the city.[43]

As 2-6th IN accomplished these tasks, Colonel Baker received some welcome reinforcements. 1st and 3d Squadrons of the 2d ACR, which had spent the previous 12 months conducting operations in the Sadr City section of Baghdad, had left the capital and arrived in the Al Kut area. The addition of these two battalion-size units gave Baker the combat power to eliminate the Sadrist presence in Al Kut. Before the sun set on 9 April, these units had begun operations to secure the bridges over the Tigris River. First Lieutenant Nathaniel Crow, who served as a company executive officer in the 1st Squadron, 2d ACR, recalled that after arriving in the city, the cavalry troopers barely paused before closing with the enemy, "We literally moved from Baghdad to Al Kut, stopped on Camp Delta to refuel, and rolled into the attack. Phil Sheridan probably stood up in his grave and cheered—it was classic cavalry."[44] His squadron cleared an enemy position on the southern edge of Al Kut known as Objective FRAN, and seized the Dawa building, the headquarters of an important Shia political party, which had been taken over by Sadrist forces.

On 10 April, the final day of the operation, TF *Striker* secured several other buildings in the city and then assessed the results. In 3 days of combat, the American unit had seized control of Al Kut while suffering only a small number of casualties with minor wounds. This did not mean the fighting had not been serious. Crow described the combat as "up close and personal" and noted that the Soldiers of the US cavalry and mechanized infantry units in Al Kut often dismounted from their vehicles to enter buildings and go "nose to nose" with a well-organized enemy.[45] Crow summed up his experience in Al Kut by stating, "It alternated between terrifying and inspiring."[46] As determined as the Sadrist fighters were, they relied on hit and run tactics that featured small arms, IEDs, mortars, and RPGs. US forces routinely countered with heavier weapons that included the "Ma Deuce" .50-caliber machinegun and the MK-19 40-mm grenade launcher. When these weapons failed to neutralize the enemy, TF *Striker* called on fire support from AC-130 gunships, AH-64 Apache Attack Helicopters, and OH-58D Kiowa Warrior Helicopters. In the 4 days of offensive operations that regained Al Kut for the Coalition, Baker relied on the seasoned combat veterans and superior firepower of his TF to destroy the Mahdi Army in the city. The quick and violent assault on Sadrist forces in Al Kut resulted in 33 militiamen killed, 16 wounded, and 93 prisoners.[47]

Containing al-Sadr: TF Duke *in An Najaf, 13–22 April*

When the Sadrist uprising began, CJTF-7 began work on a plan to coordinate units and actions in the Shia-dominated area south of Baghdad. The plan, called Operation RESOLUTE SWORD, became operational on 8 April and imposed order on a confusing command picture in the area of operations, allowing 1st AD and other Coalition units to operate efficiently.[48] CJTF-7 created four Joint Operating Areas (JOAs) in the south: JOA SWAMP in the vicinity of Al Kut, JOA IRON between Baghdad and the town of Musayyib, JOA STRIKER around An Najaf, and JOA READY around the city of Karbala. The operation also called for the reinforcement of the 1st AD with units from other areas of Iraq. This decision, which redirected American Soldiers from Mosul and the Sunni heartland to the south, signaled the great amount of concern the Coalition had about the Sadrist threat. As part of the larger operational plan, after TF *Striker* defeated Sadrist forces in Al Kut on 11 April, Major General Dempsey ordered the force to return to Baghdad, complete its transition of authority with the 1st CAV, and prepare for future combat operations. The 1st and 2d Squadrons of the 2d ACR remained behind in Al Kut to maintain stability.

Although the Coalition had recaptured Al Kut, the situation in An Najaf remained dangerous. An Najaf was a large sprawling city with a population approaching 500,000. As the burial site of the Imam Ali bin Ali Talib, the Fourth Caliph and a key figure in the history of Shiism, the city had served for centuries as the spiritual center for Shia Muslims of all nationalities. Dominating the geography of the city are the Imam Ali Mosque, which houses the shrine to Ali, and the Wadi as-Salam, the largest cemetery in the Islamic world, which covers approximately 6 square kilometers. The smaller city of Kufa, several miles to the northeast of An Najaf on the banks of the Euphrates River, also contains several important Shia shrines and over the centuries became an important center of Islamic scholarship. Given the religious importance of the An Najaf and Kufa, the Coalition could not afford to cede control of this urban complex to Muqtada al-Sadr and his forces.

Lieutenant General Sanchez tasked the 1st ID to send a BCT to An Najaf to reinforce the Honduran battalion, El Salvadoran battalion, and Spanish company there. Major General John

Batiste, the 1st ID commander, chose his 3d BCT, then operating near the city of Baqubah in the Sunni Triangle, to be the main force in what the division called Operation DANGER FORTITUDE. The 3d BCT staff finalized the plan for the operation on 9 April, and the brigade immediately began preparing for movement of Soldiers, supplies, and vehicles to An Najaf.[49]

Batiste assigned the 3d BCT the mission to conduct "offensive operations to defeat [anti-Coalition forces], capture or kill Muqtada al-Sadr, and reestablish order in An Najaf."[50] The 1st ID commander could not commit the entire 3d BCT to that mission, however. Increasing violence in the Sunni Triangle made that course of action impossible. Instead, Batiste worked with CJTF-7 to create a composite brigade-size force called TF *Duke,* which was built around the 3d BCT headquarters and included TF 2d Battalion, 2d Infantry (TF 2-2), a mechanized battalion TF equipped with BFVs that was normally assigned to the 3d BCT. TF *Olympia,* the reinforced brigade-size force that had responsibility in the north of Iraq around the city of Mosul provided two more battalions—the 1st Battalion, 14th Infantry (1-14th IN), a light infantry unit attached to *Olympia* from the 2d Brigade, 25th Infantry Division, and TF *Arrow,* a battalion-size composite unit made up of Stryker-equipped companies from the 5th Battalion, 20th Infantry (5-20th IN), 2d Battalion, 3d Infantry (2-3d IN), and 1st Battalion, 23d Infantry (1-23d IN). In addition, the BCT would deploy to An Najaf with an engineer company, a cavalry troop, an MP company as well as military intelligence, special forces, and logistics detachments.[51] The BCT, now rechristened TF *Duke,* moved by road and air to FOB Duke, approximately 20 kilometers northwest of An Najaf, and prepared to reassert Coalition control over the city.[52]

The commander of TF *Duke,* Colonel Dana Pittard, recalled that the movement to An Najaf was a significant challenge. Not only did TF units have to move over 100 miles to reach FOB Duke, but they also faced constant attacks along their route and had to deal with insurgents destroying key bridges across the Tigris and Euphrates Rivers on their route.[53] Despite the long distances and constant attacks, the move took only 40 hours. Providing critical security during this phase of the operation were the Soldiers of TF *Arrow,* which escorted the soft-skinned vehicles of the 201st Forward Support Battalion (FSB). During this mission, the battalion encountered blown bridges, land mines, IEDs, and two ambushes, actions which wounded two 1st ID Soldiers and killed a third. The Stryker companies, strategically situated at front, rear, and key points in the middle of the convoy serials, used their vehicular firepower and Force XXI Battle Command, Brigade and Below (FBCB2) digital command and control systems effectively, demonstrating Stryker adeptness in providing convoy security. They proved so effective in this role that the convoy-security support requirement subsequently evolved into a longstanding mission for the 5-20th and other Stryker units.[54]

On arrival at FOB Duke, TF *Duke* along with a contingent of Spanish soldiers began isolating and containing Sadrist forces in An Najaf and the nearby city of Kufa. Over the course of the next 10 days, TF *Duke* suppressed Sadrist attacks and successfully contained al-Sadr's forces, including Muqtada al-Sadr who had isolated himself and his close advisors in several of the shrines of An Najaf and Kufa. While the TF had prepared plans to enter the city and destroy al-Sadr's forces, CJTF-7 never ordered the unit to do so. Instead, a standoff ensued as the Coalition gave Iraqi leaders time to solve the crisis without bloodshed. In those 10 days of impasse, Coalition soldiers operated on the periphery of the city, and far away from the religious shrines to avoid fostering unnecessary tension.[55]

In this period, TF *Duke* patrolled the outskirts of An Najaf and Kufa, restricting Sadrist fighters to the core areas of the cities. Usually the patrols were sufficient to contain the

Ghost Riders—Stryker Vehicles in Iraq

Operation IRAQI FREEDOM was the first opportunity for the US Army to test its new Stryker family of vehicles in full spectrum operations. The lightly armored, wheeled vehicle served in a multitude of roles between October 2003 and January 2005. Although the Stryker family included a number of versions of the vehicle, the first Stryker Brigade Combat Team to deploy to Iraq, the 3d Brigade, 2d Infantry Division (2d ID) from Fort Lewis, Washington, arrived with the command vehicle and infantry carrier varieties.

After extensive use in patrolling in urban areas, the Stryker quickly gained a favorable reputation among Soldiers for its speed, maneuverability, and relatively quiet operation, making it uniquely suitable for surprise raids and cordon-and-search operations. In fact, some Iraqis in the city of Mosul began calling the Stryker Soldiers "Ghost Riders" because the vehicles were so quiet. However, the Stryker also revealed its vulnerabilities in the face of improvised explosive devices and attacks with rocket propelled grenades. The slat-armor countermeasure, called the "catcher's mask" for its cage-like appearance around the perimeter of the vehicle, proved to be an adequate solution.

The 3d Brigade, 2d ID also took advantage of the Force XXI Battle Command Brigade and Below (FBCB2) digital network that linked all Stryker vehicles. Leaders passed photos, maps, graphic overlays, and other information across that network allowing, for example, enemy positions to be marked on digital maps and disseminated. These capabilities radically reduced the amount of time required to react to information and intelligence. In one case in 2004, the staff of the 1st Squadron, 14th Cavalry (1-14 CAV), a Stryker-equipped unit operating near Mosul, received intelligence that a high-value target had been seen in their area of responsibility. Within 10 minutes of receiving this information, the staff used the network to send the mission and operational graphics to one of the squadron's companies which in turn began a cordon and search operation 30 minutes later. Major Joseph Davidson, the executive officer of the squadron in 2004, noted the advantages of the digital network that connected the Strykers, "FBCB2 is a great system. It allows us to dynamically change our mission on the go. A process that would normally take up to an hour or two, I'm doing it in minutes. It's a very powerful capability for tactical planning and execution."

DoD photo by Jeremiah Johnson

Mark J. Reardon and Jeffery A. Charlston, *From Transformation to Combat: The First Stryker Brigade at War*, 2007. Grace Jean, "Styker Wins Over Skeptics," *National Defense Magazine,* October 2005.

Soldiers dismount a Stryker Infantry Carrier Vehicle with slat armor to conduct a patrol in Mosul, Iraq. The Soldiers are assigned to Company C, 1st Battalion, 23rd Infantry Regiment, Stryker Brigade Combat Team.

militiamen, but occasionally there were firefights between the two sides. On 16 April, for example, elements of the 1st Battalion, 14th Infantry landed in a 5-hour engagement with Sadrist militiamen near the Kufa Bridge that spanned the Euphrates River on the eastern side of the city of Kufa. Captain Chris Budihas, commander of Alpha Company, 1-14th IN, recalled that the enemy his Soldiers faced that day was disciplined and organized into small, five-man teams. Only after directing the fire of his crew-served weapons and calling in approximately 400 mortar rounds on the enemy positions did the militiamen retreat from the bridge and return to Kufa.[56]

Soon after this engagement, political negotiations defused the crisis and CJTF-7 pulled TF *Duke* out of the An Najaf area, replacing the brigade-size unit with TF 2-37 Armor, a smaller battalion-size TF. On 20 April, just before TF *Duke* began redeploying its forces to their various AORs in the north, Lieutenant General Sanchez explained to the Soldiers of the TF why he had decided against sending them into the Sadr-controlled urban complex, "The problem is that if we launch you into the city of An Najaf and we get you into a major firefight . . . and if we get into destroying the holy shrines it will create a backlash."[57] TF *Duke* departed the area with the knowledge that its Soldiers had intervened in an explosive situation in An Najaf, contained the insurrection there, and prevented the further spread of the Sadrist uprising.

Operation IRON SABRE

The operations of TF *Striker* and TF *Duke* at Al Kut and An Najaf demonstrated the US Army's stunning ability to rapidly shift forces at the operational level and quickly conduct combat operations in new and distant areas. What is more striking is that in a few short days, in the midst of a brewing Iraqi political crisis over the Marine assault on Fallujah, CJTF-7 and the 1st AD had completed new campaign plans, RESOLUTE SWORD and IRON SABRE respectively, which viewed the operations around Al Kut as simply the first tactical step in a longer, more complex effort. Those plans restructured the entire architecture of the Multi-National Division–Central South (MND-CS) area, creating the JOAs mentioned earlier. On 18 April Sanchez took another decisive step, giving Major General Dempsey, the commander of the 1st AD, tactical control of all the units conducting operations in these areas.[58]

As described earlier, after the recapture of Al Kut, CJTF-7 moved 1st ID's TF *Duke* to An Najaf to relieve the 2d BCT of 1st AD. This move released the 1st AD to do several important things. First, the 2d BCT returned to Baghdad from Al Kut and completed its transition of authority with the 1st CAV. The brigade then moved to the Baghdad International Airport (BIAP) to refit and prepare for future combat missions in the south. Dempsey also directed the 2d ACR to move to JOA SWAMP, the area just south of Baghdad, while sending its 3d Squadron to An Najaf to replace TF *Duke*. By the end of April, the division's 1st BCT had shifted to the city of Karbala where it worked with Polish forces to isolate Sadrist forces while a political solution was sought there as in An Najaf.

Between 20 April and the end of May, 1st AD units were involved in several more significant combined arms operations in An Najaf, Karbala, and other cities in the Shia south. These operations, aimed at hemming in Sadrist forces, were demanding urban-combat missions, which featured the widespread and synchronized use of all weapons systems available

The Tank in the Concrete Jungle

There has always been debate about the utility of armored vehicles in urban terrain. In the summer and fall of 2004, armor units in Iraq adapted to the needs of the new campaign by developing tactics and technology that allowed the tank to become a critical weapon system in urban operations. In August of that year, Muqtada al-Sadr and his militia forces threatened to take control of Sadr City and An Najaf. To prevent these areas from becoming enemy sanctuaries, Multi-National Force-Iraq and the Interim Iraqi Government (IIG) took decisive action.

In August, the 1st Battalion, 5th Cavalry (1-5th CAV), operating as part of the 1st Cavalry Division in the Baghdad area, deployed to An Najaf and prepared to begin mounted operations against the militia enemy. 1-5th CAV's M1A2 Abrams tanks were equipped with the System Enhancement Package (SEP), a series of technological improvements that gave the gunner and the tank commander their own independent sights. This innovation became critical in the close quarters of an urban fight when enemy fighters could simultaneously approach from a variety of directions. The greater situational awareness provided by the SEP allowed the unit's Soldiers to move through the area more effectively while "buttoned up" (all hatches closed).

As 1-5th CAV began operations inside An Najaf and in the huge cemetery that made up part of the battlefield, the unit created new formations that enabled its Soldiers to penetrate deeply down the alleys of the city. The new formations featured tanks with Bradley Fighting Vehicles (BFV) and dismounted Soldiers that slowly moved in unison. This moving "box" of armored vehicles thus provided its own interior and flank protection and individual gunners could concentrate on identifying and destroying insurgent targets before the insurgents had time to react. This technique was also employed by the Soldiers of 2d Battalion, 5th Cavalry who called it the "Sadr City Box" after using it successfully in that neighborhood.

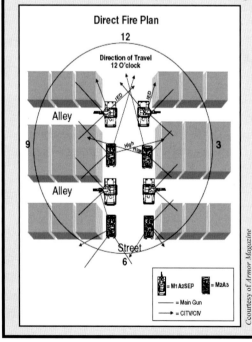

In the fall of 2004, tanks and BFVs proved effective in Operations BATON ROUGE and AL FAJR, both of which took place in complex urban terrain. The success of those missions suggested strongly that when called on to go into battle in towns and cities, the mechanized combined arms team can survive and even serve as the decisive force.

MG Peter Chiarelli, MAJ Patrick Michaelis,
and MAJ Geoffrey Norman,
"Armor in Urban Terrain: The Critical Enabler,"
Armor, March-April 2005, 7-12.

Moving block by block, the patrol would travel at extremely slow speeds to allow for acquisition of targets in the alleyways and proper handoff to subsequent vehicle gunners.

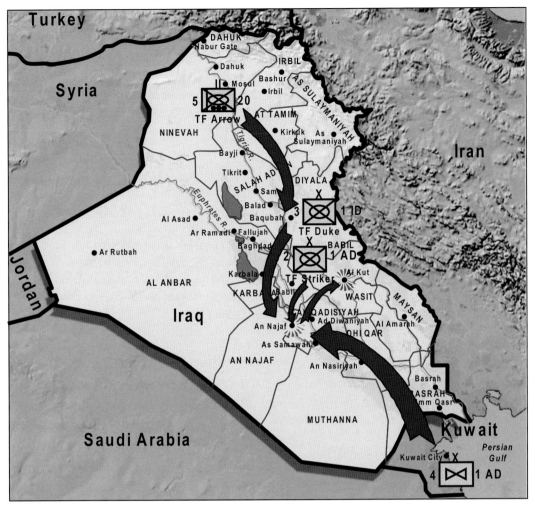

Figure 76. CJTF-7 operational maneuver, 4–15 April 2004.

to the Soldiers of the division. At various times, 1st AD leaders employed M1 Abrams tanks, M2 BFVs, 81-mm and 120-mm mortars, howitzers, C-130 gunships, Apache helicopters, and a wide variety of crew-served weapons and small-arms. Lieutenant Colonel Pat White, the commander of TF 2-37 Armor, which served in An Najaf, claimed that of all these systems, the most precise weapon in his unit was the M1A1 Abrams tank because its combination of machinegun and main gun gave Soldiers a choice and the ability to use pinpoint fire at ranges that prevented effective counterfire from the enemy. The logistics efforts to support the sustained urban-combat operations in this period were remarkable. In fact, the division created an air bridge, dubbed the "Iron Eagle Express," which featured UH-60 and CH-47 helicopters for the ferrying of 250 tons of rations, ammunition, and other critical supplies from Baghdad to Karbala and An Najaf.[59]

It would be a mistake, however, to focus solely on the combat aspect of Operation IRON SABRE. Equally important was that commanders in the 1st AD viewed operations in An

Najaf, Karbala, and the other towns through a full-spectrum lens. In his original guidance to the division, Major General Dempsey had stressed the need for four lines of operations that included stability operations, reestablishment of the ISF, and IO. The operations conducted before and after the publication of IRON SABRE followed this guidance. In Al Kut, An Najaf, and Karbala, US units reached out to the Iraqi Civil Defense Corps (ICDC) and police units that had crumbled in the face of al-Sadr's militiamen. The remaining Iraqi forces often proved very useful in dealing with the local population and in the hunt for weapons caches that Sadrist forces hid in mosques. ICDC counterterrorist teams in An Najaf were especially effective in these missions.[60]

Major General Dempsey had originally envisioned the 1st AD's extension campaign as a "deliberate, patient, and methodical" operation that would contain Sadrist forces, wear down their fighting capacity and overall effectiveness with full spectrum operations, and grant time for a political settlement. There is no doubt that for the Soldiers in this campaign, patience was the last thing that came to mind when they engaged in tough urban combat in the streets of Karbala and An Najaf. In any event, Dempsey's approach proved successful. American forces had proved too strong for the Mahdi Army to defeat and gradually its manpower and fighting capability was worn down by unrelenting Coalition operations. By late May the last of the fighting in Karbala was over, and in June Muqtada al-Sadr announced a cease-fire, allowing the Coalition and Iraqi forces to reestablish authority over the Shia south.

An Najaf, August 2004: The Elimination of the First Safe Haven

Between June and August 2004, Muqtada al-Sadr spent a great deal of time in An Najaf while Iraqi police, small in number, tried to exert authority over the shrine city. Tensions rose as the summer progressed and culminated on 31 July when US and Iraqi forces arrested Mithal al-Hasnawi, one of al-Sadr's deputies in Karbala. Demonstrations protesting the arrest broke out in An Najaf, leading to the detention of a number of al-Sadr's followers. In response, Sadrist groups kidnapped several Iraqi policemen in An Najaf. Other attacks on police stations followed, leading the governor of An Najaf province to request military assistance from ISF and Coalition military units. On 2 August tensions rose again when Sadrist elements opened fire on a Coalition patrol near a clinic in northern An Najaf. Suddenly, An Najaf looked to be on the verge of exploding again in violence, imperiling much of what the Coalition had been trying to achieve in the months since the transition to Iraqi sovereignty. As noted previously, General George W. Casey Jr., commander of Multi-National Force–Iraq (MNF-I) after 1 July 2004, had focused Coalition military efforts on facilitating Iraq's move toward elections based on the schedule developed by United Nations (UN) Resolution 1546. To make sure the path to elections was clear, senior Coalition and Iraqi leaders had decided to target areas that militia forces and insurgents used as safe havens. While MNF-I had already begun looking toward insurgent safe havens in the Sunni-dominated cities of Samarra and Fallujah, al-Sadr's breaking of the cease-fire made An Najaf a more immediate target.

The Coalition responded by sending elements of the 11th Marine Expeditionary Unit (MEU) against Mahdi Army locations in An Najaf on 5 August. On 9 August the Marines of the 11th MEU, reinforced by Soldiers from 1st Battalion, 5th Cavalry (1-5th CAV), 2d Battalion, 7th Cavalry (2-7th CAV), and 1st Battalion, 227th Aviation Regiment (1-227th AV) re-engaged the Shia militia forces in northern An Najaf near the Wadi as-Salam Cemetery and in the residential areas of southern An Najaf. In addition to the Coalition units, the 405th Iraqi National

Guard (ING) Battalion, the 404th ING Battalion, and the 36th Iraqi Commando Battalion also participated in this operation. While Coalition forces conducted the initial assaults, the ISF were instrumental in helping to secure cleared areas and in conducting operations against militia forces located in sensitive sites. Indeed, as the Coalition's military operations in An Najaf took their toll on the Sadrist forces, most of the militiamen gradually withdrew to the city's most sensitive site—the Imam Ali Shrine. As the cordon tightened around the shrine, the Iraqi Government decided to put its security forces on the front lines in case an assault on the militia inside became necessary. On 27 August, after 3 weeks of intense fighting, Grand Ayatollah Ali al-Sistani brokered an agreement between Iraqi Government officials and Muqtada al-Sadr that disarmed al-Sadr's forces still in the city and turned authority for An Najaf over to the Iraqi Government. In exchange, US military forces withdrew from the city and Muqtada al-Sadr retained his freedom.

Once the agreement went into effect, Coalition efforts immediately shifted to restoring services and rebuilding An Najaf, with a considerable amount of effort spent on ensuring the Iraqi Government received credit for the improvements. Initial concerns focused on clearing the remaining ordnance and weapons caches in the city. While this work was ongoing, Civil Affairs (CA) personnel from the Marine Corps and the Army worked with the governor's office to identify future projects and critical services requiring restoration after the conflict that had devastated much of An Najaf. Hundreds of local Iraqis were hired to clean up the area around the Imam Ali Mosque and the Old City, which resulted in visible improvement to the area and provided a much-needed stimulus to the local economy. As early as 29 August, the local government established a claims office to begin taking claims for death, injury, and loss of residence. The idea behind these efforts was to demonstrate the IIG and Coalition's commitment to improve the lives of Iraqis by initiating immediate efforts to rebuild areas disrupted by violence. While small in scope, by November 2004 the US Department of State reported that 226 projects worth more than $53 million had been started in An Najaf or were scheduled to begin in the near future.[61]

For senior Coalition military leaders, the actions against al-Sadr in An Najaf were a formative experience. General Casey recalled that MNF-I's response to al-Sadr's challenge included three key elements the Coalition would use in upcoming operations against insurgent safe havens.[62] The first of these elements was the role of the Iraqi Government in legitimizing Coalition military operations. The second element was the inclusion of the ISF in the actual military operations. Although the number of Iraqi units was limited in An Najaf, they did play a key role in demonstrating the IIG's resolve to enter the Imam Ali Shrine to deal with Muqtada al-Sadr decisively. The final element was the integration of reconstruction efforts into the larger operation. When joined together, these three elements created a model that Casey and his senior commanders would follow as they planned major operations against insurgent concentrations elsewhere.

Operation BATON ROUGE: The Full Spectrum Engagement of Samarra

As the Sadrist threat lessened during the early fall of 2004, the Coalition leadership's attention focused on the armed Sunni Arab opposition that posed serious obstacles to Iraq's stability. Faced with the entrenchment of insurgent forces in two cities dominated by Sunni Arabs—Samarra and Fallujah—and preparing for national elections in January 2005, the new Interim Iraqi Government (IIG) and the Coalition began planning measures to remove the insurgent control of these two cities as part of a larger campaign to prepare for the elections. To allow both Samarra and Fallujah to remain under insurgent domination was an unacceptable admission of impotence and threatened the viability of the elections.

Operation BATON ROUGE was a direct response to the sudden increase in anti-Coalition and anti-Iraqi violence in and around Samarra in mid-2004. Located on the Tigris River in Salah ad Din province, Samarra had a population of approximately 200,000, the large majority of which were Sunni Arab. Even though most of its citizens were Sunni, Samarra was a significant religious center for both Sunni and Shia Muslims. At one time, the city had been the capital of the Abbasid caliphate, and its al-Askari Mosque, also known as the Golden Mosque, became the site of the tombs of Ali al-Hadi and Hasan al-Askari, the 10th and 11th Shia Imams. The mosque also holds a monument to Muhammad al-Mahdi, known as the 12th and final Imam or Hidden Imam of the Shia. Many Shia believe that at the funeral of his father, al-Mahdi disappeared, was hidden by Allah, and would someday return. Because of these sites, many Sunnis who revere these figures of Islamic history view Samarra with special significance. The presence of such religious sites in the city placed critical constraints on the operations of Coalition units.

Since the arrival of Coalition forces in 2003, Samarra had been a bastion of Sunni Arab intransigence, and by early 2004, a mix of insurgent, criminal, and tribal organizations struggled to gain dominance over the city, despite the presence of Coalition forces in the area and their attempts to win over the population with reconstruction programs and other civic projects.[63] The increase in insurgent power in late 2003 in Samarra did not go unnoticed by Coalition forces. To combat the insurgency, the 4th ID reinforced its 3d BCT and sent it into Samarra in December 2003. In an operation called IVY BLIZZARD, the brigade attempted to eliminate the insurgent presence in the city and hand responsibility for Samarra's security over to the newly constituted ISF.

While American leaders initially saw IVY BLIZZARD as a success, they soon discovered that insurgent leaders had received notification of the operation before it was launched and had escaped. Because of requirements elsewhere, at the end of January 2004 the 4th ID directed most of the elements in the 3d BCT to return to their own AORs, leaving one mechanized task force and a US Army Special Forces detachment in the city. This decision made the return of insurgents possible, and by February Samarra was once again falling under the sway of Sunni Arabs who opposed the Coalition and its vision for Iraq.[64]

In March 2004 the 1st ID replaced the 4th ID in and around Samarra. During the Shia uprisings in Sadr City and An Najaf in April, attacks on Coalition and Iraqi forces in the Samarra area tripled from 5 to 15 per week. The escalation in violence forced the 1st ID to respond with Operation SPADER STRIKE, an offensive by the 1st Battalion, 26th Infantry (1-26th IN) in May 2004 designed to flush out and kill or capture insurgents in the city. While enjoying some success, SPADER STRIKE also encountered a significant amount of armed resistance inside Samarra, an indication that insurgent forces had consolidated and strengthened in the city since the 1st ID had taken charge.

Following SPADER STRIKE, conditions in Samarra rapidly worsened. Between May and July, the city council president resigned only to be replaced with a citizen council sympathetic to the insurgency. The ISF charged with the mission of maintaining peace and stability in Samarra largely disappeared, with some members even joining the insurgency. Not surprisingly, die-hard

Baathists, foreign and domestically recruited al-Qaeda operatives, and other insurgent groups flocked to the city. The nadir in Samarra came on 8 July 2004 when insurgents attacked the 202d ING Battalion headquarters located on the western outskirts of the city with small-arms fire, mortars, and a vehicle-borne improvised explosive device (VBIED). The attack killed 5 US Soldiers from the 1-26th IN and wounded 20 others, all of whom were working with the Iraqis at the facility. The ISF lost three soldiers and suffered four wounded. The suicide bomber had driven an Iraqi police car and worn a police uniform.[65]

This assault on both American and Iraqi forces compelled the leaders of the 1st ID to look for a permanent solution to the problems in Samarra. The division commander, Major General John Batiste, and his division staff began planning Operation BATON ROUGE, a brigade-size combined arms operation that would wrest control of Samarra from the insurgents, reestablish the ISF in the city, and set conditions so the insurgency could not return. From the inception of their planning, however, the leadership of the 1st ID attempted to fit the operation into the broader campaign planning of MNF-I, which had established four lines of operation: governance, communications, economic development, and security. BATON ROUGE's objective was not solely to clear out insurgents but to direct operations along all four lines to create a stable city with a legitimate Iraqi Government and robust security forces willing and able to defend the new order. Further, the 1st ID planners hoped the Iraqi Government and its security forces would lead all of these operations as a way of creating greater legitimacy for that order within the city.

Thus, as the plan evolved in July, BATON ROUGE came to resemble a template for an extended full spectrum operation rather than a plan featuring massed mechanized formations in a large-scale assault on the city. In fact, in its final form, BATON ROUGE included only a brief "kinetic" period that included an abbreviated combined-arms assault that *might* be used against those insurgents, terrorists, and criminals that proved intractable in their opposition. Rather than begin with a determined preparation for an assault on Samarra, the 1st ID staff, working with the division's 2d BCT, crafted the operation to begin with Phase I—Set Conditions, Reconnaissance, and Preparation. This phase would begin in late July or August and use focused attacks on insurgent targets to disrupt enemy organizations and eventually allow the ISF and civil government to establish control of Samarra.

Success in this first phase of BATON ROUGE would lead directly to Phase IV, the decisive part of the operation that the leaders of the 1st ID called Transition Operations. During Phase IV, the Soldiers of the 2d BCT "would continue to support the ISF and civil authorities in and around Samarra to ensure irreversible momentum toward self-government."[66] The 1st ID commander and his staff envisioned that this phase would include reconstruction projects, IO, the establishment of a legitimate and popularly-supported government, and the placement of well-trained security forces in the city. Only when Batiste felt that these conditions had been met and the city would not revert to insurgency control would the operation end.

If the 2d BCT and local authorities did not succeed in Phase I in setting the proper conditions for an Iraqi solution to Samarra's problems, Colonel Randall Dragon, the brigade commander, was prepared to execute Phase II, Isolation of the City, and Phase III, Search and Attack. The latter phase of the operation called on the BCT, reinforced with other US units as well as the ISF, to enter Samarra, locate and destroy insurgent forces, and secure key sites within the city.[67] This was the large-scale combined-arms assault that the 1st ID hoped to avoid.

The 1st ID began Phase I, Set Conditions, Reconnaissance, and Preparation, in late July. As part of this phase, in August the 2d BCT launched three operations—CAJUN MOUSETRAP I, II, and III—that used the brigade's mechanized battalion task forces, Army attack helicopters, and US Air Force close air support to mount raids into Samarra.[68] Although these attacks were limited and the brigade's Soldiers did not hold areas of the city, the three actions yielded tangible results. Sergeant Major Ron Pruyt, the operations sergeant major for 1-26th IN which participated in the missions, described how the shaping operations forced the enemy to reveal their intentions, "We attacked into the city and secured a few objectives and held them for a short period of time. This allowed us to determine how they would defend the city when we conducted the actual mission. They were great operations."[69] Pruyt also noted that the three "mousetraps" lured the insurgents into pitched battles with the tanks and mechanized infantry of the 2d BCT, actions that allowed US forces to focus their considerable advantage in firepower on identifiable enemy forces. During CAJUN MOUSETRAP III, which ran for 3 days between 13 and 15 August 2004, the Soldiers of the 2d BCT killed approximately 45 insurgents who had resisted the brigade's entry on the edge of Samarra.[70]

While the 2d BCT mounted these initial raids, the 1st ID staff directed IO at political and religious figures in the city, clearly articulating the four conditions in which the Coalition would end the isolation of Samarra and enter the city peacefully to begin important reconstruction projects. Those conditions were the selection and seating of a new mayor and city council,

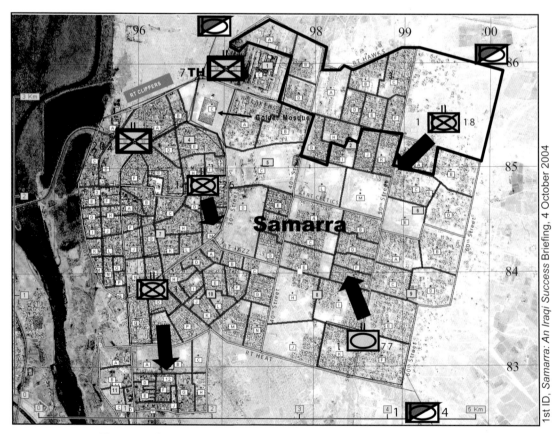

Figure 77. Operation BATON ROUGE, Phase III, H-hour to 011700C.

installation of a police chief capable of creating a stable security environment, termination of insurgent activity, and safeguarding access to the entire city for US forces and ISF.[71] This message and other promises, it was hoped, would drive a wedge between the insurgent groups on one side and the tribal and political leaders in the city who chose a peaceful solution to Samarra's problems on the other. It almost worked. By 10 September the city had established an acceptable city council and established enough security to allow US and Iraqi forces to enter unscathed.[72] It appeared that Major General Batiste and the 1st ID had avoided the large-scale combat operations of Phase III and moved directly to Phase IV of Operation BATON ROUGE.

Unfortunately, this transition was premature. Pro-stability politicians and ISF inside Samarra proved too weak to maintain the forward momentum toward a peaceful solution. On 10 September 2004 insurgent groups renewed their attacks on American and Iraqi units in the city in earnest. Six days later insurgent threats forced the Samarra police chief to resign. These incidents forced leaders in the Coalition military command and 1st ID to consider more forceful action. After recognition that more drastic measures were required for stabilizing the city, on 28 September the decision was made to go ahead with the isolation of Samarra (Phase II) and the assault on enemy forces (Phase III) in the city.

The third phase of BATON ROUGE, Search and Attack, began on 1 October. For this operation the 1st ID committed the 2d BCT, which at the time of the assault consisted of 1-26th IN and 1-18th IN, both of which were mechanized battalions equipped with BFVs; 1-14th IN, a light infantry battalion equipped with armored M1114 high-mobility multipurpose wheeled vehicles (HMMWVs); 1-77th Armor, a battalion equipped with M1 Abrams tanks; elements of the 2-108th IN, an air assault infantry battalion from the New York Army National Guard that served as light infantry; and 1-4th CAV, a mechanized squadron armed with a variety of equipment and weapons. The BCT also controlled six battalions of the ISF, including the 36th Commando Battalion. Batiste further reinforced the effort with intelligence assets, artillery, and close air support. The assault that began on 1 October was the largest single offensive action by Coalition forces to date since the initial invasion in the spring of 2003.

The 2d BCT commander planned to hit the enemy in Samarra from multiple directions to keep them off balance and unable to mass their forces. At midnight that attack began with 1-26th IN entering the city from the west. Simultaneously, 1-18th IN came in from the northeast, 1-77th Armor assaulted from the southeast; and elements of 1-4th CAV operating on the north, northeast, and southeast edges of Samarra. The Iraqi battalions would follow the 2d BCT units as the latter fought their way into the neighborhoods on the fringes of the city. Despite the operations aimed at eroding the insurgents and their combat capabilities in the 6 weeks leading up to the assault, the enemy met American units with small-arms fire, RPGs, mortars, and IEDs. The greatest resistance was found on the southeastern edge of the city and in the northwestern quadrant where the Golden Mosque was located. In most areas, the enemy operated in small groups. In the southeast portion of the city, however, US forces found larger enemy concentrations soon after the attack began and called in AC-130 gunfire to destroy them.[73] As dawn approached, the Soldiers of the 2d BCT were still involved in clearing insurgent fighters from neighborhoods on the perimeter of Samarra.

Just before sunrise, 2d BCT ordered a sixth battalion, 1-14th IN, into the fight. The light infantrymen of this unit had arrived on 30 September, the day before Phase III began, from the city of Kirkuk where it normally operated as part of the 2d Brigade, 25th Infantry Division. Many of 1-14th IN's Soldiers were on leave when Major General Batiste ordered the battalion to participate in BATON ROUGE. Although equipped with M1114 up-armored HMMWVs armed with heavy crew-served weapons, Colonel Dragon decided to increase 1-14th IN's combat power by attaching to it two BFV-equipped platoons and one M1A2 tank platoon from 1-26th IN. Once the fight began, the light infantry platoons and the HMMWVs worked closely with the BFVs, tanks, and other combined arms to push their way deeper into the city.

The mission of 1-14th IN was critical. In the opening hours of the assault, 2d BCT had secured footholds on the perimeter of Samarra. To secure those lodgments and prepare for deeper penetrations into the city, Dragon directed 1-14th IN to pass through 1-26 IN's position on the northwestern edge of the city and turn south to clear insurgents from roughly 2 square kilometers on the western edge described by one member of 1-14th IN as "dense urban sprawl."[74] Once the unit secured the western flank of Samarra, Dragon would direct 1-26th IN to continue the attack east into the city center.

As the companies of 1-14th IN worked their way south between dawn and the afternoon of 1 October, they operated as combined arms teams that moved gradually through the neighborhoods of southwest Samarra, making contact with small insurgent groups and using mortars, heavy machineguns, and in a few cases, attack helicopters to suppress enemy fire.[75] Around noon on the eastern side of 1-14th IN's zone, the light infantrymen, engineers, and HMMWVs of Charlie Company, 1-14th IN, met up with the tanks and BFVs of Apache Company, 1-26th IN, and advanced south together down a major avenue. The M1A2 Abrams tanks led the way in this maneuver, relying on the dismounted infantry to secure their flanks and rear. Insurgent teams equipped with small arms and RPGs shadowed the company's progress, moving in a maze of alleyways parallel to the avenue. The American infantry prevented this enemy force from setting up ambushes that might have deterred the unit's advance.[76]

When the formation arrived at its objective—a multistory building that dominated the surrounding neighborhoods, the tanks and M1114s surrounded the site while the light infantry and engineers entered the building, cleared it, and established a command post in its vicinity. The position then came under persistent enemy fire, which only gradually decreased as the infantrymen sought out and destroyed those insurgent threats in the area. As the sun went down, the infantrymen of Charlie Company regrouped around their command post. In the 12 hours of almost continuous combat that helped secure the western edge of the city, the company had suffered 1 Soldier wounded in action and had killed approximately 24 insurgents.[77] They would continue to mount patrols, cordon and searches, and other operations in this part of Samarra for the next week.

The 1-14th IN's movement south allowed 1-26th IN to penetrate more deeply into Samarra. By 0700 on 1 October, the battalion's BFVs and tanks had reached the area surrounding the Golden Mosque, approximately 1 kilometer east from their point of entry into the city. By the end of the day, they had pushed another 1,000 meters toward Samarra's center. Like their counterparts in 1-14th IN, the Soldiers of 1-26th IN met continuous resistance and used combined arms teams to suppress enemy fire. The presence of insurgents in the Golden Mosque, however, posed a unique challenge to the battalion's leadership. Preferring to have Iraqis enter the religious shrine, Dragon tasked the soldiers of the Iraqi 36th Commando Battalion to force their way into the mosque and eliminate the enemy threat. At around 1100 that morning, after

Soldiers from 2-108th IN emplaced a cordon around the mosque compound, the Commandos blew open the front doors of the main building and secured the site, detaining 25 insurgents in the process.[78] The 36th Commando Battalion would later capture 50 suspected insurgents while securing the city hospital. Other Iraqi units, advised by members of US Army Special Forces, followed the American units, holding the neighborhoods taken by US forces as they moved toward the center of Samarra.[79]

By the end of 1 October, the Soldiers of the 2d BCT had secured all of their major government and religious objectives. Offensive operations continued for the next 2 days to engage known insurgent targets and locate weapons caches. After 3 days of intense combat in Samarra, the 2d BCT had seized control of the city, killed over 127 insurgents, wounded 60, and detained 128.[80] In taking back the city from the grips of the insurgency, the brigade had suffered one fatality and eight Soldiers wounded.[81] A combat operation involving a reinforced brigade and set on urban terrain might have become an extended fight. Nevertheless, Major General Batiste believed that careful preparation and focused firepower from the combined arms teams and other sources allowed his division to avoid the type of debilitating urban combat that might have produced higher casualties on both sides. The 1st ID commander contended:

> [Phase III] was over so quickly for several reasons. We had good intelligence and a well developed and rehearsed plan. We attacked from the march to overwhelm the insurgency in a 360-degree fight with the right kind of fire control measures. . . . In addition to employing artillery and mortars in urban operations, we employed lots of CAS with F-18s, 16s and 14s; our own Kiowa and Apache helicopters were in this fight the entire time. We employed AC-130s every time we could get them.[82]

After 3 days of combat, the 2d BCT had neutralized the enemy presence in Samarra, killing or driving out almost all of the insurgent forces in the city. Some small pockets of resistance remained behind in the city, laying low and re-emerging in the weeks that followed to harass American units and ISF. Despite their continued presence, Phase III of Operation BATON ROUGE had set the stage for creating lasting stability in Samarra.

On the afternoon of 3 October, Colonel Dragon directed the Coalition forces in the city to once again shift to Phase IV, Transition Operations. Overnight, the 2d BCT's emphasis switched to reconstruction operations. Major Barrett Bernard, the assistant operations officer for the brigade, noted that Dragon and his subordinate commanders immediately began projects of all types to help rebuild Samarra and reestablish the Iraqi Government and the ISF in the city. Bernard recalled that the reconstruction efforts included "everything from making a trash dump to sewer systems, water, bridge, hospital repair, rebuilding the doors to the Golden Mosque—there was a litany of them."[83] In the minds of many Soldiers in Samarra, the most important projects were those that had an immediate impact by employing Iraqis who might have otherwise gravitated toward the insurgency. Using the 9th Engineer Battalion and teams from the 415th CA Battalion to oversee the projects and infantry units to conduct raids and other operations that kept insurgent groups from interfering with the rebuilding effort, Dragon restored a semblance of stability to Samarra. The Soldiers on the streets of Samarra noted that the attitude among the populace had changed dramatically. With the insurgent threat neutralized, many of the city's residents felt free to interact with the Americans. In the days following the transition to Phase IV of BATON ROUGE, Lieutenant Greg Longo, a platoon leader in 1-14th

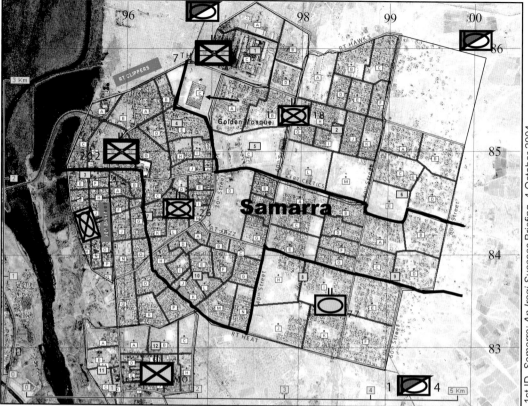

Figure 78. Phase IV, 030800C–032300COCT04.

IN, remarked that the reconstruction and security operations had achieved their desired effect: "We're winning over those folks that may have been borderline before. . . . It's night and day as far as their reception toward us now and before."[84]

Unfortunately, the stability that emerged in Samarra in October did not become permanent. In the days before Operation AL FAJR began in Fallujah in November 2004, some of the insurgents located in that city fled to Samarra and began operating against the ISF established after BATON ROUGE. The enemy presence compelled US and Iraqi forces that remained in Samarra to mount focused intelligence operations and raids to keep the insurgent organizations from gaining the initiative. As 2005 began and Iraq approached its first democratic elections, Samarra still had not become completely pacified. BATON ROUGE had revealed the potential that full spectrum operations offered to a commander intent on defeating an intransigent insurgent force and setting the conditions for stability and self-government. However, the operation also highlighted the difficulties in forging lasting changes in those communities where the insurgents chose to contest the Coalition.

AL FAJR: The Liberation of Fallujah

At 1900 on 8 November 2004 the US forces massed on the northern edge of the city of Fallujah began pouring fire into buildings just inside the wall that surrounded the city. As this fire forced insurgent groups to seek cover, other US units approached the wall that surrounded the city and prepared to create two breaches through which American Soldiers and Marines would invade Fallujah and put an end to the insurgent regime there. By midnight on that first day of the operation, the tanks and BFVs of two Army mechanized battalions had struck deep into the core of the city, eliminating insurgent positions with fire from the 120-mm main guns on the M1A2 Abrams tanks and the 25-mm chain guns on the BFVs. This quick and lethal advance disrupted insurgent command and control and forced enemy groups to seek refuge far from the marauding Army task forces.

Figure 79. Planning Operation AL FAJR.

With this violent and rapid assault, Operation AL FAJR ("New Dawn" in Arabic) began. The 1st Marine Division (1st MARDIV) planned the operation, originally called PHANTOM FURY, to free Fallujah from the grips of the insurgency and rees-tablish an enduring Iraqi governmental presence in the city in preparation for elections in January 2005. In terms of forces involved on both sides and intensity of combat, AL FAJR surpassed BATON ROUGE as the largest combat operation in Iraq since April 2003. The decisive assault that began on 8 November was led by two US Marine Corps regimental combat teams, reinforced by two US Army mechanized battalions, multiple Iraqi Army battalions, and numerous fire support platforms. This formidable force met the deter-mined resistance of approximately 4,500 insurgents defending a fortified Fallujah that had been in their hands since April 2004. AL FAJR came to epitomize the type of full spectrum operations the US military had gradually learned to conduct in response to the insurgency. As a broad-based operation, AL FAJR included shaping actions that relied heavily on the use of IO, violent combined arms operations that defeated the insurgents in Fallujah, and stability opera-tions that returned the city to normalcy and reasserted Iraqi authority.

Fallujah became a problem for the Coalition long before November 2004. Known for both its large number of mosques and its support of the Baathist government during Saddam's regime, the city sits on the Euphrates River 43 miles west of Baghdad in the Sunni Arab-dominated Al Anbar province. Its approximately 250,000 inhabitants resided in a densely packed area of about 5 square miles. Concrete apartment buildings and two story houses, many with courtyard walls, dominated the geography of the city. Although Fallujans traveled primarily by the narrow roads and alleyways that separated the city's dwellings, they also made use of several wider boulevards, the largest of which was Highway 10, the six-lane corridor that bisected the city from east to west. The city's industrial area lay to the south of this highway.

Fallujah emerged as a flashpoint soon after the overthrow of the Saddam regime. On 28 April 2003 Soldiers from the 82d Airborne Division (82d ABN) shot into a crowd of Iraqis when a demonstration against the American presence turned violent. A number of Iraqis were killed and wounded as a result, although the actual figures never became clear. That event began the city's slow transition into a center of anti-Coalition sentiment and insurgent activity. By early 2004 a myriad of insurgent and terrorist groups found a safe haven in Fallujah. The trigger that caused the Coalition to unleash its first military assault against the insurgent concentration in the city was the murder on 31 March 2004 of four American contractors working for the Blackwater Corporation. The killings became macabre after the insurgents mutilated and burned the bodies and eventually strung up two of the corpses from a bridge across the Euphrates River for millions of horrified television viewers to witness.

The first sign that the Coalition intended to forcefully respond to what was clearly a significant provocation came from the very top. Two days after the event, CPA Chief Paul Bremer declared:

> Yesterday's events in Fallujah are a dramatic example of the ongoing struggle between human dignity and barbarism. Five brave Soldiers were killed by an attack in their area. Then, two vehicles containing four Americans were attacked and their bodies subjected to barbarous maltreatment. The acts we have seen were despicable and inexcusable. They violate the tenets of all religions, including Islam, as well as the foundations of civilized society. Their deaths will not go unpunished.[85]

The 1st Marine Expeditionary Force (MEF) spearheaded the Coalition's attack on Fallujah on 7 April in an operation called VIGILANT RESOLVE. Four Marine battalions reinforced by a small number of tanks and various forms of air and artillery support entered the city and began making slow progress against the insurgents who made effective use of the urban terrain. To deal with the resistance, the Marines called in artillery and fire from AC-130 gunships. The amount of destruction in Fallujah raised protests from the IGC, which had opposed VIGILANT RESOLVE and almost collapsed over opposition to this Marine operation. The political pressure from the IGC forced the United States to halt military operations in Fallujah and declare a unilateral cease-fire on 9 April 2004.

After the announcement of the cease-fire, the Marines attempted to resolve the security situation in Fallujah by putting it in the hands of Iraqi forces. At the end of April, the Marines turned over the city to the so-called Fallujah Brigade, an ad hoc unit of local forces led by General Muhammad Latif, a former Saddam Hussein crony, who was both ineffective and openly hostile toward the Coalition. This agreement left the insurgents largely in place and able to claim a victory over the United States. By mid-2004 the insurgents in the city had co-opted the Fallujah Brigade, introduced Sharia law to the city, and used that code to impose harsh behavioral limitations on Fallujah's populace. As it became increasingly isolated from Coalition influence, Fallujah's insurgent leaders such as Sheik Abdullah Janabi, the head of the Mujahideen Shura (Council), became emboldened. More importantly, the city became a magnet for other radical Islamist leaders like Abu Musab al-Zarqawi and ex-Baathist fighters who viewed Fallujah as an excellent bastion behind whose walls they could plan and launch operations against targets in other parts of Iraq. Between May and late October 2004 the flow of insurgents into the city increased their number to 4,500. As the summer progressed, much of the activity of these groups focused on strengthening the city's defenses in expectation that the Coalition forces would try once again to gain control of Fallujah. Coalition intelligence would later conclude that the enemy force in the city constructed 306 defensive strongpoints, most of which were reinforced with IEDs.[86]

The Distinguished Service Cross
For Extraordinary Heroism in Action
Army NCOs in Fallujah

Master Sergeant Donald R. Hollenbaugh and Staff Sergeant Daniel A. Briggs each received the Distinguished Service Cross for their actions on 26 April 2004 during operations in Fallujah, Iraq. While assigned to the US Army Special Operations Command and operating in support of the United States Marine Corps, Hollenbaugh and Briggs prevented approximately 300 enemy fighters from overrunning the platoon of Marines to which they were attached. Occupying a forward observation point approximately 300 meters forward of friendly forces, the Marine platoon faced isolation and destruction as enemy forces advanced along the narrow streets and alleys threatening to cut it off from the main element. After another team took casualties during the initial contact, Briggs crossed a street under intense small arms fire to render aid to the wounded and organize defensive operations. At approximately the same time, enemy fire wounded a large number of Marines located at the platoon's original position. Hollenbaugh began directing the platoon's defense, constantly moving around his team's perimeter and engaging enemy personnel so that the enemy came to believe they faced a much larger force. His success in delaying the enemy's advance bought the Marine platoon enough time to evacuate their casualties and withdraw to a more secure position. Of the 37 Marines in the platoon, 25 were wounded (11 required litter evacuation) and 1 was killed in action. In receiving the Distinguished Service Cross, Staff Sergeant Briggs was cited for "repeatedly subjecting himself to intense and unrelenting enemy fire in order to provide critical medical attention to severely injured Marines" and "preventing enemy insurgent forces from over-running the United States Force's position." For his award, Master Sergeant Hollenbaugh was recognized for demonstrating "the highest degree of courage and excellent leadership through his distinguished performance as Team Leader while engaged in Urban Combat Operations. His heroic actions throughout one of the most intensive firefights of the Operation Iraqi Freedom campaign were directly responsible for preventing enemy insurgent forces from overrunning the United States Force."

Kevin, Maurer, "Courage Under Fire,"
Fayetteville Observer, 23 June 2005.

This insurgent assumption about an impending attack was correct. In the summer of 2004 Coalition leaders began crafting a plan for an operation that would liberate the city. As in April, the Marines would lead the assault on the insurgents in Fallujah. Major General Richard Natonski, the commander of the 1st MARDIV, stated that his overall intent for the operation was to do three things: eliminate insurgent activity, set the conditions for local control in the city, and support the MNF-I effort to secure approaches to Baghdad.[87] The plan consisted of four phases and would require several months to execute. Phase I, Preparation/Shaping, brought together a variety of efforts to stage the forces that would conduct the assault and "shape the battlefield," which included gathering intelligence on the enemy strength, preparations, methods, and tendencies. Information on the insurgents in Fallujah indicated they would not be surprised by a US-led attack on the city. Nevertheless, that did not mean the insurgents knew when the attack would take place or which avenue of approach Coalition forces would use to enter the city. Marine planners did have intelligence that suggested insurgents within Fallujah had constructed most of their fighting positions to defend against an attack into the southeast corner of the city, the direction used by the Marines in April during VIGILANT RESOLVE. Marine planners took steps to reinforce that belief. In November, however, the assault would come from a different direction. Further, Marine commanders verified that insurgent and terrorist groups were using 33 of the 72 mosques in Fallujah for military purposes and pinpointed specific buildings in the city used as safe houses by the insurgents.[88] Coalition forces then began targeting these sites to disrupt the enemy before the actual assault began.

AL FAJR planners also used Phase I to conduct an aggressive information campaign aimed at decreasing the legitimacy of the insurgent network and keeping the insurgent network off balance. The Marines relied on special operations forces to conduct raids and feints, especially on the southern edge of Fallujah, as part of the overall deception plan to confirm enemy assumptions that Coalition forces would attack from that direction.[89] Psychological operations (PSYOP) teams also used leaflets and other means to communicate to the population how the widespread insurgent activity prevented the Coalition from investing up to $30 million in building up Fallujah's economic infrastructure. These information offensives also emphasized what most inside Fallujah already knew: the insurgent network did not offer a political goal that most or even many Iraqis endorsed. Instead, the network was made up of disparate groups, unified only in their desire to defeat and expel the Coalition. The most important PSYOP message to the Fallujah population was to leave immediately because the Coalition was planning to enter. A significant majority, probably close to 80 percent of the population, heeded the call of the Americans and actually departed.[90]

In preparation for the battle, the Marines built Camp Fallujah southeast of the city where they could create a supply and training base. The camp became the site of large stocks of ammunition, fuel, food, and other supplies, with the objective of building a 15-day supply of critical materials in a secure spot near the battlefield. This decision made Coalition forces less

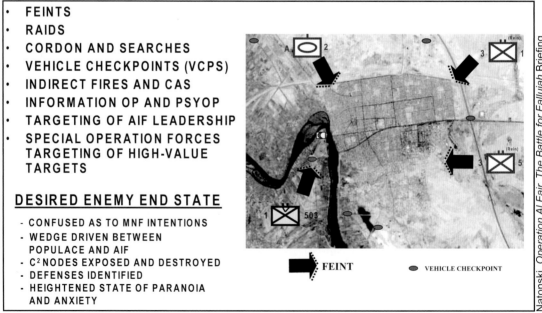

- **FEINTS**
- **RAIDS**
- **CORDON AND SEARCHES**
- **VEHICLE CHECKPOINTS (VCPS)**
- **INDIRECT FIRES AND CAS**
- **INFORMATION OP AND PSYOP**
- **TARGETING OF AIF LEADERSHIP**
- **SPECIAL OPERATION FORCES TARGETING OF HIGH-VALUE TARGETS**

DESIRED ENEMY END STATE

- CONFUSED AS TO MNF INTENTIONS
- WEDGE DRIVEN BETWEEN POPULACE AND AIF
- C² NODES EXPOSED AND DESTROYED
- DEFENSES IDENTIFIED
- HEIGHTENED STATE OF PARANOIA AND ANXIETY

➤ **FEINT**   ● VEHICLE CHECKPOINT

Natonski, Operation Al Fajr, The Battle for Fallujah Briefing

Figure 80. Phase I, Shaping.

vulnerable to supply shortages caused by the potential insurgent interdiction of lines of communication as had happened during the April uprisings.[91] Camp Fallujah also became a base for the training and integration of the Iraqi Army battalions that would participate in later phases of the operation. Additionally, in the days before the assault on Fallujah, the base became the firing position of an Army artillery battery that would provide critical fire support to the Soldiers, Marines, Airmen, Sailors, and ISF who were about to enter the fortified city.

Phase I, Preparation and Shaping, began in September 2004 and continued through October as the Coalition waited for the proper military and political conditions that would allow for the transition to the assault phase of the operation. Before the assault could begin, Marine planners decided to add a short phase that featured the final actions designed to set the battlefield and gain critical advantages. During Phase II, Enhanced Shaping, Coalition forces, including the 2d BCT, 1st CAV (Black Jack Brigade), would take up positions to the south and east of Fallujah, securing bridges and other entryways into the city to contain the insurgents that remained inside. Other units began moving into attack and blocking positions to the west and north of the city. To place the insurgents under pressure, the 1st MARDIV planned to use snipers, raids, feints, and searches in the Fallujah area, actions which Major General Natonski would later describe as leaving the ranks of the insurgents in the city in a "heightened state of paranoia and anxiety."[92] On the eve of the operation, Natonski planned to send the Iraqi 36th Commando Battalion to seize the Fallujah Hospital on the western fringe of the city. To support this attack, the Marine 3d Light Armored Reconnaissance Battalion, reinforced by

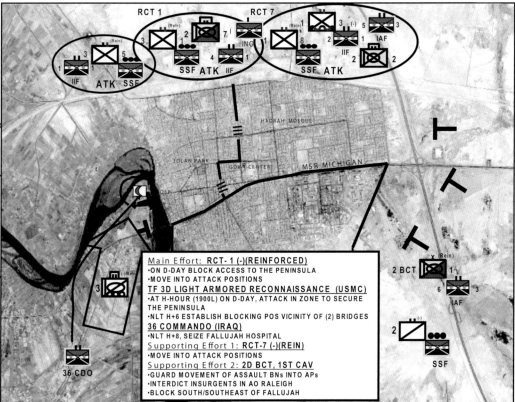

Figure 81. Phase II, Enhanced shaping.

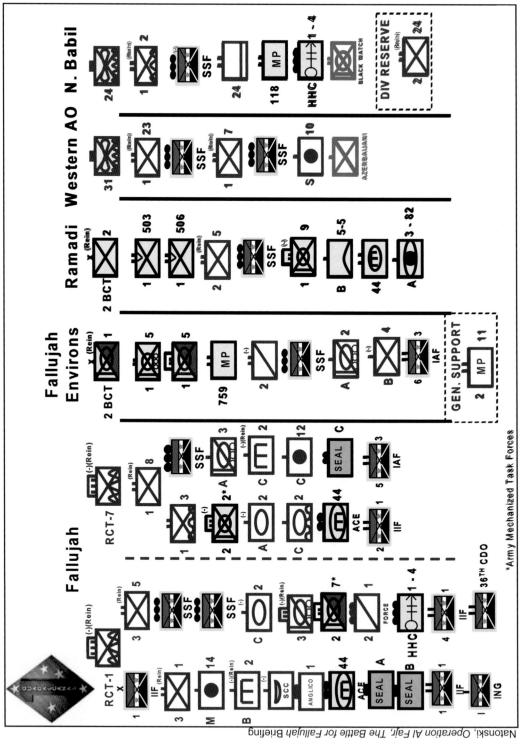

Figure 82. Task organization, AL FAJR.

a company from the Army's 1st Battalion, 503d Infantry, would secure the bridges near the hospital. During VIGILANT RESOLVE, insurgent groups had used the hospital as a platform to distribute propaganda and effectively turn public opinion against the Coalition. The US and Iraqi operation to secure the hospital would deny the insurgents the possibility of repeating that success.

Phase III of the operation would be the decisive piece of AL FAJR. Natonski established a straightforward mission for his forces in this phase: attack "to destroy anti-Iraqi forces in Fallujah to establish legitimate local control."[93] He and his staff then divided the phase into two subphases: IIIA—assault; and IIIB—search and attack.[94] To achieve their objectives once Phase III began, the Marines planned to conduct a rapid penetration of the city using shock, firepower, and mobility of an armored force. Natonski believed a heavier and more mobile force would help overcome some of the problems encountered by the Marines during the April VIGILANT RESOLVE debacle.

Based on intelligence that revealed the formidable strength of the insurgent defenses in Fallujah, the Marines believed they did not have enough tanks and heavy infantry fighting vehicles to quickly penetrate the outer defenses and spearhead the assault. By doctrinal organization, the two United States Marine Corps (USMC) regimental combat teams (RCT-1 and RCT-7) that served as the assault force had only a small number of tanks. Recognizing the need for more heavily armored firepower, Natonski pushed a request for US Army mechanized forces up through the chain of command.[95] The requirement reached the commander of MNC-I, Lieutenant General Thomas Metz, who eventually decided to attach two Army mechanized battalions—2d Battalion, 2d Infantry (from the 1st ID) and 2d Battalion, 7th Cavalry (from the 1st CAV)—to the 1st MARDIV for the direct assault on Fallujah.[96] Lieutenant General John Sattler, the commander of the 1st MEF, described these two Army units as the penetration forces that would punch through insurgent positions and drive deep into the city, thus disrupting the enemy's ability to mount both defensive operations and counterattacks.[97]

Natonski's joint Marine and Army TF would attack with additional units, taking on a true joint and combined character. The assault force would include six Iraqi Army battalions that were to follow the Marine and US Army units into the city. Further, the British Black Watch Battle Group assisted with the isolation of the Fallujah area. The RCTs would gain joint assistance in the form of US Navy Seal teams and Air Force Enlisted Terminal Attack Controllers (ETACs) who would coordinate the use of US Air Force (USAF) aircraft for close air support. Moreover, Natonski's force took the idea of jointness one step further by integrating the Army and Marine units at company level and below. In one case, 2-2d IN received a Marine Light Armored Vehicle (LAV) company for operations. In another, Army commanders detached tank and BFV sections to Marine reconnaissance companies.[98] All told, the Coalition forces involved in AL FAJR numbered close to 12,000, of whom approximately 10,000 would enter the city at some point in the operation.

As the end of October approached, Coalition military authorities believed the first phase of AL FAJR was nearing completion. Most of the required forces were in place and the great majority of civilians in Fallujah had followed the Coalition's recommendations and left the city.[99] What remained was the final decision to launch the assault. On 30 October a terrorist with a bomb in his car killed eight US Marines and wounded nine others outside of Fallujah. This incident prompted Iraqi Prime Minister Ayad Allawi to announce on 7 November that a

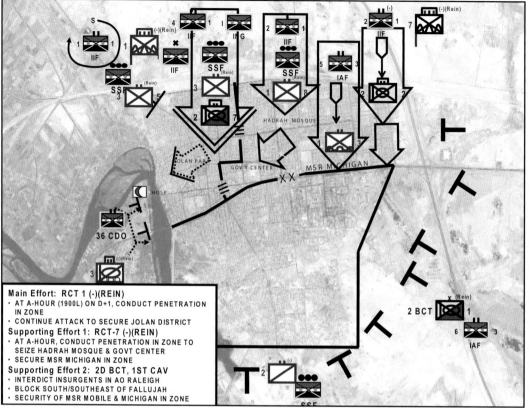

Natonski, *Operation Al Fajr, The Battle for Fallujah Briefing*

Figure 83. Phase IIIA.

State of Emergency existed across Iraq (except for the Kurdish-controlled north), which would allow for curfews and other measures designed to curb the insurgency. Allawi also stated he believed the situation in Fallujah could no longer be solved by peaceful means and he had given his approval for an attack on the city.[100] This endorsement of a new offensive operation against the insurgents in Fallujah was critical in the wake of VIGILANT RESOLVE, when political pressures from the Iraqi Government had forced the Coalition to halt its April attack arguably transforming that operation from a tactical stalemate into a strategic victory for the insurgency. With Allawi's approval, the Marines and the Iraqi 36th Commando Battalion began Phase II, Enhanced Shaping Operations, at 1900 on 7 November. Once this combined force seized and secured the city hospital, Natonski directed the main assault to begin the next day.

The attack on the hospital deceived the insurgent defenders. Thinking that this small action was the vanguard of the main assault force, enemy commanders began moving their small units toward the fighting, thus revealing their locations, tactics, and techniques.[101] However, the main effort for Phase III was on the opposite side of the city. The two reinforced RCTs of the 1st MARDIV stood ready to begin the main attack on 8 November by making two breaches in a railroad embankment and the city wall on the northern edge of the city. The holes would allow the RCTs to move into Fallujah on parallel axes with RCT-1 on the western axis and RCT-7 on the eastern side of the city. Leading the penetrations would be the M1 Abrams tanks and BFVs of the 2-7th CAV and 2-2d IN.

At 1900 on the night of 8 November, after an artillery preparation by 155-mm howitzers hit the neighborhoods in the northwest corner of the city, Alpha Company, 2-2d IN approached the wall that surrounded Fallujah. The engineers attached to the battalion fired a Mine Clearing Line Charge (MCLC), an explosive device used to clear minefields, and made a breach large enough to accommodate the unit's powerful armored vehicles. The MCLC immediately set off six IEDs that had been placed on or near the wall to disable any invading force. Concerned about the presence of other IEDs, Captain Sean Sims, the company commander, led the way through the breach with two Abrams Plow tanks, M1A2s configured with a large blade on the front used to clear mines and other obstacles. Once inside the city, Alpha Company pushed south making way for Alpha Company, 2-63d Armor, a tank company attached to 2-2d IN, to expand the foothold that US forces had established in Fallujah. For the next 3 hours, these two companies were in constant contact with the enemy. Dismounted insurgents, moving in the open on the streets and rooftops, engaged the Soldiers with small arms fire, RPGs, and IEDs hidden in buildings and road barriers.[102] Staff Sergeant David Bellavia, a squad leader in Alpha Company, 2-2d IN, described encountering very sophisticated defensive positions in the buildings close to the breach site: "During the day, you could see the way these insurgents were dug in; and without that relentless 155-millimeter barrage, we would've taken massive casualties. The front four buildings we were going into, which were completely pancaked—there were little spider trails and you could see fighting positions everywhere: dug in, overhead cover, even [grenade] sumps on the bottom."[103] The Soldiers of 2-2d IN also found entire buildings that had been filled with C4 explosives and converted into huge IEDs.

In the almost total darkness of that first night, the enemy discovered that the Soldiers could combine their night vision capabilities with the powerful weapons on their armored vehicles

Natonski, Operation Al Fajr, The Battle for Fallujah Briefing

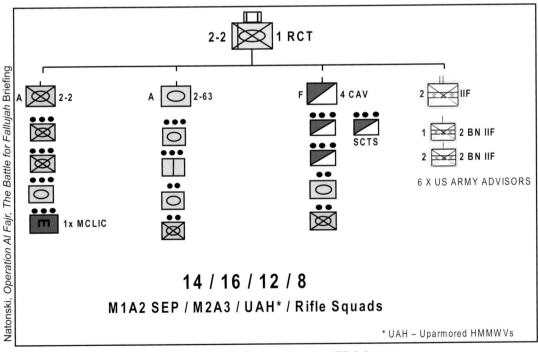

Figure 84. Task organization, TF 2-2.

to create lethal fires that collapsed buildings and killed insurgents. Despite this fact, as the lead units of 2-2d IN made their way slowly to the south, the insurgent resistance reacted by retreating from building to building using tunnels or moving across rooftops, while maintaining its small arms and grenade fire on US forces. Bellavia recalled that the Soldiers in the tanks and BFVs easily identified the groups that tried to halt the American advance and engaged them in a very direct and effective manner: "You would actually hear insurgents challenging [Alpha Company's] tanks with AK-47 fire and then, *Boom!* Silence."[104] Using these tactics, the Soldiers of 2-2d IN, the lead element on the eastern axis of the assault, pushed deeply into the city and by dawn were overlooking their objective, Highway 10, the main east-west corridor through Fallujah, also known as main supply route (MSR) Michigan to US troops. They had traveled approximately 1 mile through a complex urban environment, but their assault had been so rapid and violent that many of the insurgents in the northeastern part of the city had begun streaming away from 2-2's advance into the western half of Fallujah.[105]

On the western axis, RCT-1, AL FAJR's main effort, was behind schedule. Difficulties with the breaches of the embankment and the wall had slowed the Marines' progress. However, by 0200 on 9 November, the Marine combat team was on the move and had conducted a passage of lines allowing 2-7th CAV to take the lead into Fallujah. The tanks of Alpha Company, 2-7th CAV, the lead element in the assault, quickly began moving down one of the city's streets toward Jolan Park, an antiquated amusement park that was the unit's first objective. When they met insurgent resistance, the Soldiers of the TF called on the Marines for close air support or used the main guns on their tanks and BFVs to quickly suppress enemy defensive positions. Lieutenant Colonel James Rainey, the commander of 2-7th CAV, directed the tanks of Alpha Company to sweep through the park, after which the infantrymen in the BFVs would dismount to clear the objective of any insurgents that might remain. Rainey contended that the rapidity

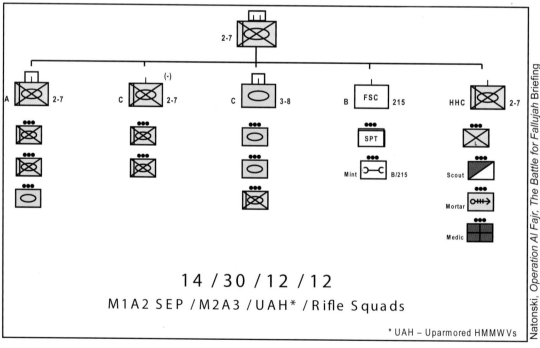

Figure 85. Task organization, TF 2-7.

and lethality of this tactic "totally devastated the enemy . . . they were still trying to get out of the way of the tanks and BFVs and our infantry squads were on top of them."[106] As the sun rose on 9 November, the Soldiers of 2-7th CAV had seized Jolan Park and were prepared to pass 3d Battalion, 1st Marine Regiment through their position as the Marines continued to attack.

Marine planners for AL FAJR envisioned that the Army's mechanized spearheads would require 4 or 5 days to seize and secure central Fallujah. But those mechanized battalions had made short work of the insurgents' defenses and denied them the time to reestablish a solid defense. Instead of the 72-to-96 hours anticipated for the capture of the central city, lead elements of RCT-7 crossed Phase Line Fran, the control measure that denoted that central spot, in a mere 43 hours. Adjusting their prebattle plans, Marine commanders decided to have RCT-1 in the west continue its southward assault as RCT-7, with 2-2d IN on the left flank, would swing around to the southwest.

By the second day the mission for most maneuver units was "search and attack in zone," which included a great deal of intense street combat and house-to-house fighting. Many of the remaining insurgents were hardened fighters who knew how to use their small arms and RPGs. Captain Chris Brooke, commander of C Company, 2-7th CAV, described the enemy as initiating contact from alleyways and fortified buildings with sequential salvos of RPGs.[107] Initially, he ordered his platoons to maneuver on these enemy locations; but by the first night, Brooke and his subordinate leaders were suppressing the insurgent positions with 25-mm fire from their BFVs while the company fire support officer (FSO) called in fire from 120-mm mortars or 155-mm howitzers or even from aircraft that dropped 500-pound bombs. "We engaged with the largest size ordnance the FSO could achieve clearance for," Brooke stated and added, "This proved to be highly successful."[108]

After the first 5 days of "search and attack operations," enemy contact became more sporadic and the insurgent enemy became more willing to surrender. The two Army battalions remained with the RCTs for the next 8 days as the city was gradually cleared and the 1st MARDIV began preparing for a transition to the next phase of AL FAJR. While both RCTs had made better than expected progress in AL FAJR, problems emerged in the coordination between US Army and Marine units. The most disruptive was the speed at which the Army mechanized task forces moved through the city. Although this capability had unhinged enemy command and control, the quick Army maneuver often left the Marine infantry units behind, causing gaps and insecure flanks as the Marines carefully cleared buildings before moving forward. At times, Marine commanders directed the Army battalions to cease movement while the Marine units caught up.[109] The difference in rates of advance reflected the difference between the Army mission to penetrate the defenses and seize key terrain in the city, and the Marine units who had to methodically clear every building in Fallujah. Problems with communications, coordinating close air support, and sharing of intelligence also created some obstacles in the joint operation.[110]

These challenges were relatively minor flaws in an operation that was highly successful from the joint perspective. The Marines, the Army, and other joint and Coalition elements had come together and created a plan for the operation that synchronized their systems and command structures to leverage the capabilities of each service. For the Marine and Army units, tactical interoperability and integration reached a level unseen since World War II. Marine rifle companies, for example, had called in Army tanks and BFVs to suppress enemy fortified

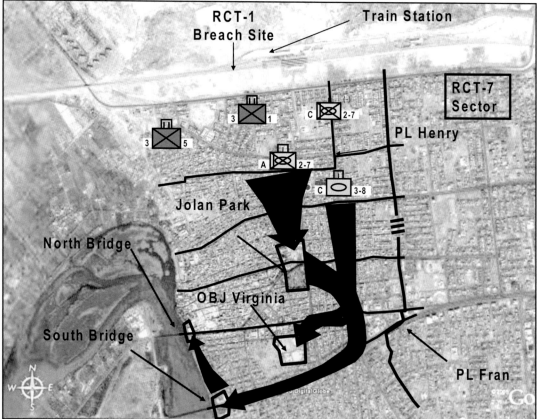

Figure 86. RCT-1/TF 2-7, 8–10 November 2004.

positions before their assaults. The Marines, for their part, attached their engineer demolition teams to the 2-7th CAV's platoons where they proved particularly effective in making large holes in concrete walls for the battalion's infantry to use in clearing a market in the Jolan Park area of Fallujah.

Despite the issues of coordination that at times made some aspects of the operation problematic, the operation's leaders were impressed by the effectiveness of the Marine-Army teams. Rainey stated he was humbled by "the selflessness and lethality of the American fighting man: Marine and Soldier, tanker and infantryman . . . to watch these guys look at a building full of bad guys that they know are in there, to watch them look at their buddy and look at their team leader and go, 'Hell yeah, we can do this.' They went building after building, block after block and won every single fight."[111] The commander of RCT-1, Colonel Michael Shupp, believed that at the tactical level Soldiers and Marines worked very well together, "It really was one team, one fight."[112]

The integration of Iraqi Army units also went smoothly. In marked contrast to April 2004 when an Iraqi unit had refused to fight during VIGILANT RESOLVE, in November most Iraqi soldiers performed well. The six battalions that entered the city in the assault cleared assigned buildings and neighborhoods, attacked and cleared sensitive targets such as mosques, and helped gather and process intelligence. They played a particularly important role in taking detainees and screened these prisoners to determine whether or not they were combatants.

Perhaps most impressively, the 2d Iraqi Army Battalion, the unit that had balked at combat in Fallujah in April, returned for AL FAJR and fought competently beside the Soldiers and Marines.[113]

Success in AL FAJR came at a high price. In the period between 7 November and 31 December 2004 when sporadic resistance ceased, 82 Americans lost their lives in the fighting in Fallujah and over 600 were wounded.[114] The majority of the casualties were Marines who bore the brunt of the house-to-house clearing operations. Those operations led to the deaths of 76 Marines. The two Army task forces suffered the loss of six Soldiers, five in 2-2d IN and one in 2-7th CAV. The

DOD Photo by SSGT Michael Nasworthy

Figure 87. US Army Soldiers from the 2d Battalion, 7th Cavalry Regiment move along a wall as they clear buildings around their main objective in Fallujah, Iraq, during Operation AL FAJR (New Dawn) on 9 November 2004.

fighting in AL FAJR wounded another 72 Soldiers.[115] Iraqi Army units suffered as well. At the end of the first 2 weeks of combat inside the city, the Iraqis had lost 6 killed and 55 wounded.[116] Of the approximately 4,500 insurgents in Fallujah, the Coalition forces killed 2,000, taking another 1,200 as prisoners.[117] These casualty figures are striking, but given the historical record of battles in urban terrain, the numbers, especially for Coalition forces, are relatively light.

Of course the Soldiers' and Marines' use of heavy firepower helps explain the difference between friendly and enemy casualties. During AL FAJR, Coalition forces directed thousands of artillery shells, mortar rounds, and bombs at targets in the city. Urban combat against a defender willing to fight hard has historically driven the attacker to use massive amounts of firepower; the second Battle for Fallujah was no exception. However, this reliance on firepower, especially indirect fire and close air support, created a different problem once the battle was over. How would the Coalition deal with the destruction it caused in Fallujah and avoid creating more insurgents out of those who had fled the city and lost their property?

MNF-I and the Marines had anticipated the great damage caused by the Coalition assault and had tried to avoid hitting key infrastructure, such as the electrical grid, the bridges over the Euphrates River, and the water supply.[118] More importantly, the Coalition planned a fourth phase to follow the attack. Phase IV, Transition, made use of a huge stockpile of food, water, and medical supplies accumulated outside the city in Camp Fallujah. CA teams and US Navy Construction Battalions (Seabees) also moved into the city to establish a civil-military operations center and clear the streets of rubble. Other Marine teams cleared unexploded ordnance from buildings and began repairing the damage to electrical lines.[119] The Iraq Reconstruction Management Office (IRMO), which served as part of the US Embassy, had also set aside $12 million to cover the cost of longer-term reconstruction in Fallujah.[120]

Finally, 6 weeks after the assault began, the Marines allowed some of Fallujah's citizens to return. When they arrived, the Coalition gave them $2,500 as a form of compensation and condolence for their losses and suffering. Strict access controls imposed by the Coalition and the Iraqi Government prevented insurgents from infiltrating back into the city. These were some of the many steps in a much larger effort to rebuild a city and its population that began after the end of AL FAJR. As Iraq prepared for elections in January 2005, Fallujah stood as a symbol of the Coalition's and the IIG's resolve to remove all obstacles from the path of political progress.

Conclusion

When the Coalition arrived in Baghdad in April 2003 and deposed the Saddam regime, it seemed likely to most—both civilian and military—that high intensity combat operations had come to an end. The US Army, which had honed its combat capabilities to a sharp edge, began the transition to stability operations and redeployment in May. Yet, as early as mid-June the 4th ID was planning and conducting Operation PENINSULA STRIKE, a complex combined arms action that was larger and longer than some of the major engagements in the first 6 weeks of the war.

By late summer, Coalition military leaders had begun to see operations like PENINSULA STRIKE, though necessary to defeat Saddamist forces in the immediate aftermath of the invasion, as counterproductive to the overall effort to win the support of the population in an environment that was becoming increasingly insecure. After the summer of 2003, however, units continued to conduct small combined arms operations, such as raids and counter-IED and countermortar missions, that required Soldiers to behave less like nation-builders and more like warriors. Some critics have emphasized that stability operations in general and counterinsurgency operations specifically require the minimization of violence so as to avoid making more enemies. This concept drove the Coalition's decision to cease large-scale combat operations in August 2003. But this did not remove all requirements for combat operations. As units struggled to gain control of their AORs so they could mount reconstruction, governance, and other stability operations, they were often compelled to use combat actions to suppress insurgent IEDs and mortar attacks.

What is striking is that during OIF, the US Army showed a marked ability to shift smoothly from low-level stability operations to a quickly-planned, large-scale combat operation such as the 1st AD's Extension Campaign in April 2004. As impressive was the Army's evolving capacity to look at a problem, such as the insurgent network in Samarra, in a holistic way, viewing combat operations as only one means of achieving objectives. In the case of Operation BATON ROUGE, the 1st ID displayed a refined ability to plan deliberately and across the full-spectrum so as to avoid high-intensity urban combat. That operation also showed the division's lethal ability to conduct tough street fighting when the situation required.

As in many of the other chapters in this study, this discussion returned repeatedly to the flexibility and agility of US Soldiers and their use of weapons and equipment. Not only could units transition quickly from stability to offensive operations, but they could also make that shift without undertaking major changes in their organizations or armament. Most Soldiers found that their vehicles and weapons could be adapted for a variety of situations across the spectrum of conflict. The best examples of this were the M1 Abrams tank and the M2/3 BFV, designed for high-intensity conflict in open areas but adapted for use on traffic control points and employed with great effectiveness in urban areas such as Al Kut, An Najaf, and Fallujah. Perhaps more significantly, AL FAJR showed that without a great deal of preparation, the Army could make the transition to combat operations that involved joint and Coalition partners.

For the American Soldier, the 18 months in Iraq between May 2003 and January 2005 were filled with great uncertainty. Out of this period, however, one key principal emerged. Regardless of the situation in which they find themselves, American Soldiers need to be able to combine lethal combat operations with a variety of nonlethal operations at all levels to be successful. The experience of the US Army in Iraq suggests that this capability remained one of the strengths of the force even after it transitioned to the full spectrum campaign.

The previous five chapters, Part II, of this study have focused on the US Army's establishment of command structures and operations directly involved in creating a secure environment in Iraq. The following chapters that comprise Part III, Toward the Objective: Building a New Iraq, describe the US Army's participation in rebuilding the country. For the Coalition, success meant more than just defeating the insurgency. To create a stable Iraq ruled by a representative government, US Soldiers became heavily involved in reconstructing the physical and economic infrastructure of the nation, introducing new institutions of governance to Iraqi life, and fostering the type of security forces supportive of the new state. The US Army was not alone in these monumental projects. In 2003 and much of 2004, the Coalition's political headquarters had authority for the reconstruction, governance, and ISF programs. Additionally, nonmilitary organizations made significant contributions to these aspects of the campaign. During the 18 months that followed the toppling of the Saddam regime, however, it was the Coalition's military forces, with their manpower and organizational capacities, that formed the solid core of these efforts to remake Iraq.

Notes

1. 4th Infantry Division (Mechanized), *Lessons Learned: Executive Summary,* 17 June 2004, 66.
2. Michael R. Gordon, "US Re-evaluates 'iron-fisted' Strategy in Iraq," *New York Times*, 7 August 2003, A1.
3. Kenneth W. Estes, "Command Narrative: 1st Armored Division in Operation IRAQI FREE-DOM, May 2003–July 2004," Unpublished study, 78. These operations were IRON DIG, SCORPION STING, IRON MOUNTAIN, IRON BOUNTY, LONGSTREET, CROSSBOW, IRON HAMMER, IRON JUSTICE, IRON GRIP, IRON RESOLVE, and IRON PROMISE.
4. Robert O. Babcock, *Operation Iraqi Freedom I: A Year in the Sunni Triangle* (Tuscaloosa, AL: St John's Press, 2005), 279. These operations were PENINSULA STRIKE, DESERT SCORPION, SIDEWINDER, IVY SERPENT, IVY NEEDLE, IVY FOCUS, IVY TYPHOON I and II, IVY CYCLONE, IVY BLIZZARD, and IVY TYPHOON III.
5. CJTF-7, *OIF Smart Card 1* (20 December 2003) and *OIF Smart Card 4* (2 January 2004). These documents remain classified as For Official Use Only (FOUO) as of the writing of this study.
6. See, for example, the briefing entitled 3d Corps Support Command, *Enemy Tactics, Techniques and Procedures (TTP) and Recommendations* created in 2004. This document remains classified FOUO as of the writing of this study.
7. US Government Accountability Office, GAO Report GAO-05-431T, "Rebuilding Iraq: Preliminary Observations on the Challenges in Transferring Security Responsibilities to Iraqi Military and Police," 14 March 2005, 10; Estes, 124.
8. Estes, 125.
9. Estes, 55.
10. 4th ID (Mech), *Lessons Learned: Executive Summary*, 68.
11. 4th ID (Mech), *Lessons Learned: Executive Summary*, 68.
12. 4th ID (Mech), *Lessons Learned: Executive Summary*, 69–70.
13. Captain Roger M. Stevens and Major Kyle J. Marsh, "3/2 S BCT and the Countermortar Fight in Mosul," *Field Artillery,* January–February 2005, 36.
14. Stevens and Marsh, 36.
15. Estes, 87.
16. 173d Airborne Brigade, *The AMB PENINSULA STRIKE* Briefing, 6 June 2003, slide 15.
17. 173d ABN, *AMB PENINSULA STRIKE* Briefing, slide 15.
18. Colonel Dominic Caracillo, Commander, 2-503d Airborne Infantry Regiment, excerpts from personal journal, 8–13 June 2003 entry.
19. 173d ABN, *AMB PENINSULA STRIKE* Briefing, slide 15.
20. 173d ABN, *AMB PENINSULA STRIKE* Briefing, slide 15.
21. Colonel Philip Battaglia, interview by Contemporary Operations Study Team, Fort Leavenworth, KS, 13 December 2006, 10.
22. Battaglia, interview, 13 December 2006, 12.
23. Battaglia, interview, 13 December 2006, 10.
24. Sergeant First Class Todd Oliver, "Soldiers attacked While on Operation Peninsula Strike," *USAREUR Public Affairs*, 18 June 2003, http://www.hqusareur.army.mil/htmlinks/Press_Releases/2003/Jun2003/18Jun2003-01.htm (accessed 20 February 2007).
25. Caracillo, journal excerpts concerning Operation PENINSULA STRIKE. See also, "4th Infantry Division and Task Force 'Ironhorse' Conclude Operation Peninsula Strike," *Defend America*, 14 June 2003, http://www.defendamerica.mil/iraq/update/june2003/iu061703.html (accessed 13 October 2006).
26. "4th ID and TF 'Ironhorse' Conclude Operation Peninsula Strike."
27. Kathleen T. Rhem, "Pentagon Leaders Describe Offensive Operations in Iraq," *DefenseLink*, 29 July 2003, http://www.defenselink.mil/news/Jul2003/n07292003_200307295.html (accessed 13 October 2006).

28.   Gordon, "US Re-evaluates 'iron-fisted' Strategy in Iraq," A1.

29.   Gordon, "US Re-evaluates 'iron-fisted' Strategy in Iraq," A1.

30.   Gordon, "US Re-evaluates 'iron-fisted' Strategy in Iraq," A1.

31.   Lieutenant Colonel George Sarabia, interview by Operational Leadership Experiences Project Team, Combat Studies Institute, Fort Leavenworth, KS, 25 September 2005, 28.

32.   L. Paul Bremer III, *My Year in Iraq: The Struggle to Build a Future of Hope* (New York, NY: Simon & Schuster, 2006), 319.

33.   Estes, 131.

34.   Estes, 131.

35.   Estes, 134.

36.   Estes, 137.

37.   2d (IRON) Brigade Combat Team, 1st Armored Division, *Striker Scimitar: The Battle for Al-Kut, 8 April 04–11 April 04* Briefing, slide 3.

38.   David Stokes, "Taking stock," *Middle Eastern Quarterly*, http://www.meforum.org/pf.php?id=669 (accessed 22 June 2006).

39.   *Striker Scimitar: The Battle for Al-Kut, 8 April 04–11 April 04*, slide 6.

40.   *Striker Scimitar: The Battle for Al-Kut, 8 April 04–11 April 04*, 1–2.

41.   Terry Boyd, "Bronze Star Recipient Led to Stunning Victory," *Stars & Stripes, European Edition*, 14 June 2005, http://www.estripes.com/article.asp?section=104&article=28917&archive=true (accessed 28 February 2007).

42.   *Striker Scimitar: The Battle for Al-Kut, 8 April 04–11 April 04*, 1–2.

43.   *Striker Scimitar: The Battle for Al-Kut, 8 April 04–11 April 04*, 1–2.

44.   Captain Nathaniel Crow, e-mail interview by Contemporary Operations Study Team, Fort Leavenworth, KS, 4 December 2006, 3.

45.   Crow, e-mail interview, 4 December 2006, 3.

46.   Crow, e-mail interview, 4 December 2006, 3.

47.   *Striker Scimitar: The Battle for Al-Kut, 8 April 04–11 April 04*, slide 18.

48.   "Coalition Working to Pacify Fallujah, Destroy Sadr Militia," *DefenseLink,* 8 April 2004, http://www.defenselink.mil/news/Apr2004/n04082004_200404081.html (accessed 19 October 2004).

49.   3d Brigade Combat Team, 1st Infantry Division, *FRAGO 1 to 3 BCT OPORD 04-13*, 09 April 2004.

50.   3d BCT, 1st ID, *FRAGO 1 to 3 BCT OPORD 04-13*, 09 April 2004.

51.   Task Force *Danger*, *Operation DANGER FORTITUDE* Briefing, 12 April 2004, slide 7.

52.   3d BCT, 1st ID, *FRAGO 1 to 3 BCT OPORD 04-13*, 09 April 2004.

53.   Colonel Dana Pittard, interview by Contemporary Operations Study Team, Fort Leavenworth, KS, 22 February 2006, 8–9.

54.   Pittard, interview, 22 February 2006, 50–51.

55.   Major Chris Budihas, interview by Operational Leadership Experiences Project Team, Combat Studies Institute, Fort Leavenworth, KS, 31 January 2006, 7.

56.   Budihas, interview, 31 January 2006, 8.

57.   Quoted in Alistair Lyon, "Tension Eases in Two Iraqi Flashpoint Cities," *Reuters*, 20 April 2004, http://www.strykernews.com/archives/2004/04/20/tension_eases_in_two_iraqi_flashpoint_cities.html (accessed 20 October 2006).

58.   Estes, 141.

59.   Estes, 145.

60.   Estes, 141.

61.   US Department of State, "Najaf/Samarra Reconstruction Effort, Questions Taken at November 12, 2004," *Daily Press Briefing*, http://www.state.gov/r/pa/prs/ps/2004/38162.htm (accessed 8 January 2008).

62. General George W. Casey Jr., interview by Contemporary Operations Study Team, Fort Leavenworth, KS, 27 November 2007, 5–6.

63. Major General John R.S. Batiste, and Lieutenant Colonel Paul R. Daniels, "The Fight for Samarra: Full-Spectrum Operations in Modern Warfare," *Military Review,* May–June 2005, 15, http:// usacac.leavenworth.army.mil/CAC/milreview/English/MayJun05/MayJun05/bat.pdf (accessed 14 May 2007).

64. 1st Infantry Division, *Operation Iraqi Freedom-Samarra: An Iraqi Success* Briefing, 4 October 2004, slide 23; Batiste and Daniels.

65. 1st ID, *OIF—Samarra: An Iraqi Success* Briefing, 4 October 2004, slide 24; Batiste and Daniels, 15.

66. 1st ID, *OIF—Samarra: An Iraqi Success* Briefing, 4 October 2004, slide 17.

67. 1st ID, *OIF—Samarra: An Iraqi Success* Briefing, 4 October 2004, slide 17.

68. Sergeant First Class Chuck Joseph, "'Duty First' Soldiers Conduct Cajun Mousetrap III in Iraq," *USAREUR Public Affairs News Release,* 16 August 2004, http://www.hqusareur.army.mil/htm-links/Press_Releases/2004/Aug2004/16Aug2004-02.htm (accessed 14 May 2007).

69. Sergeant Major Ron Pruyt, interview by Operational Leadership Experiences Project Team, Combat Studies Institute, Fort Leavenworth, KS, 25 August 2006, 17.

70. 1st Infantry Division, *Task Force Danger Press Release,* 15 August 2004, 3, http://www.1stid. org/about/pressreleases/tfdanger_pr081504.pdf (accessed 22 May 2007).

71. Batiste and Daniels, 19.

72. Batiste and Daniels, 19.

73. 1st ID, *OIF—Samarra: An Iraqi Success* Briefing, 4 October 2004, slide 30 and notes pages.

74. Major James L. Anderson, 2d Brigade Combat Team, 25th Infantry Division (Light), *OIF Historical Account Submission #35,* 10–16 October 2005, 2.

75. Anderson, 2d BCT, 25th ID (Light), *OIF Historical Account Submission #35,* 10–16 October 2005, 5.

76. Major James L. Anderson, 2d Brigade Combat Team, 25th Infantry Division (Light), *OIF Historical Account Submission #44a (Samarra Supplemental),* 2–3.

77. Anderson, 2d BCT, 25th ID (Light), *OIF Historical Account Submission #44a (Samarra Supplemental),* 4–5.

78. "U.S., Iraqi Troops Strike Samarra Insurgents," *American Forces Press Service,* 1 October 2004, http://www.defenselink.mil/news/newsarticle.aspx?id=25169 (accessed 1 June 2007).

79. Sergeant Major Cory McCarty, interview by Operational Leadership Experiences Project Team, Combat Studies Institute, Fort Leavenworth, KS, 24 May 2006, 10.

80. Batiste and Daniels, 13.

81. 1st Infantry Division DTAC, *Samarra OPSUMs,* 02–04 October 2004.

82. Patrecia Slayden Hollis, "Task Force Danger in OIF II: Preparing a Secure Environment for the Iraqi National Elections," *Field Artillery,* July–August 2005, 4–5.

83. Major Barrett Bernard, interview by Operational Leadership Experiences Project Team, Combat Studies Institute, Fort Leavenworth, KS, 26 January 2006, 14.

84. Sergeant W. Wayne Marlow, "Samarra Adjusts to Life After Insurgents," *Danger Forward,* Volume 1, Issue 8 (November 2004), 13, http://www.1id.army.mil/1ID/Danger_Forward/Documents/ Danger_Forward_Nov.pdf (accessed 6 July 2007).

85. "Coalition Provisional Authority, Police Academy Commencement, Baghdad, April 1, 2004," *CPA Official Web site,* http://www.iraqcoalition.org/transcripts/20040401_bremer_police.html (accessed 5 July 2006).

86. Lieutenant General John F. Sattler and Lieutenant Colonel Daniel H. Wilson, "Operation AL FAJR: The Battle of Fallujah—Dousing the Bright Ember of the Insurgency," *Marine Corps Gazette,* July 2005, 14.

87. Major General Richard Natonski, *Operation Al Fajr: The Battle for Fallujah* Briefing, slide 10.

88. Sattler and Wilson, 14.

89. Lieutenant General Thomas F. Metz et al., "Massing Effects in the Information Domain: A Case Study in Aggressive Information Operations," *Military Review,* May–June 2006, 8.

90. Metz et al., "Massing Effects in the Information Domain," 8.

91. Sattler and Wilson, 14.

92. Matt M. Matthews, *Operation AL FAJR: A Study in Army and Marine Corps Joint Operations* (Fort Leavenworth, KS: Combat Studies Institute Press, 2006), 40.

93. Natonski, *Operation Al Fajr: The Battle for Fallujah* Briefing, slide 9.

94. Natonski, *Operation Al Fajr: The Battle for Fallujah* Briefing, slide 15.

95. Matthews, 14.

96. Matthews, 14.

97. Sattler and Wilson, 21.

98. Matthews, 2.

99. Official estimates suggested that less than 500 civilians, less than 1 percent of the city's population, remained in Fallujah when the assault began in early November. Sattler and Wilson, 16.

100. Casey, interview, 27 November 2007, 7–8. See also, Jim Garamone, "Iraqi, US Troops Begin 'Al Fajr' Operation in Fallujah," *DefenseLink*, 8 November 2004, http://www.defenselink.mil/news/Nov2004/n11082004_2004110805.html (accessed 23 October 2006).

101. Sattler and Wilson, 18–20.

102. Lieutenant Colonel Peter A. Newell, interview by Operational Leadership Experiences Project Team, Combat Studies Institute, Fort Leavenworth, KS, 23 March 2006, 11.

103. Staff Sergeant David Bellavia, interview by Operational Leadership Experiences Project Team, Combat Studies Institute, Fort Leavenworth, KS, 27 July 2006, 13.

104. Bellavia, interview, 27 July 2006, 14.

105. Matthews, 45.

106. Matthews, 64.

107. Captain Chris Brooke, interview by Operational Leadership Experiences Project Team, Combat Studies Institute, Fort Leavenworth, KS, 1 May 2006, 9.

108. Brooke, interview, 1 May 2006, 10.

109. Matthews, 48.

110. Matthews, 49–51, 79–80.

111. Lieutenant Colonel James Rainey, interview by Operational Leadership Experiences Project Team, Combat Studies Institute, Fort Leavenworth, KS, 19 April 2006, 21.

112. Quoted in Matthews, 83.

113. Sergeant Jared Zabaldo, "MNSTC-I's ASTs Led Way, Training in Iraqi Fight for Fallujah," *The Advisor,* 27 November 2004, 6.

114. Lieutenant General Richard F. Natonski, e-mail correspondence with Matt Matthews, Combat Studies Institute, Fort Leavenworth, KS, 12 February 2007.

115. Natonski, e-mail correspondence, 12 February 2007.

116. Zabaldo, "MNSTC-I's ASTs Led Way," 7.

117. Patrecia Slayden Hollis, "Second Battle of Fallujah: Urban Operations in a New Kind of War, Interview with Lieutenant General John Sattler," *Field Artillery*, March–April 2006, 4.

118. Hollis, "Second Battle of Fallujah: Urban Operations in a New Kind of War," 9.

119. Hollis, "Second Battle of Fallujah: Urban Operations in a New Kind of War," 9.

120. Donna Miles, "Fallujah Reconstruction Effort to Begin Soon," *DefenseLink*, 19 November 2004, http://www.defenselink.mil/news/Nov2004/n11192004_2004111909.html (accessed 24 October 2006).

Part III

Toward the Objective: Building a New Iraq

Chapter 9

The US Army and the Reconstruction of Iraq

When Coalition military forces entered Iraq in March 2003 they did not come prepared to rebuild, in a literal sense, the country they hoped to liberate. The US Army had trained its Soldiers to defeat Saddam's army and ensure the dictator's regime fell so they could assist with the installation of a new representative government in Iraq. To be sure, the Soldiers in the Coalition forces understood they would be asked to perform missions after combat operations were completed to help stabilize Iraq; but few commanders made the assumption that stabilization meant involvement in major reconstruction projects designed to deliver basic services to the Iraqi population.

At the upper echelons of the US force, commanders knew that the US Department of Defense (DOD) had created the Office of Reconstruction and Humanitarian Assistance (ORHA) to address major civil crises after the toppling of the Saddam regime as well as to initiate efforts to establish new governance and reconstruction projects. The Combined Forces Land Component Command's (CFLCC's) plans for Operations COBRA II and ECLIPSE II reinforced the notion that ORHA would oversee the initial reconstruction efforts and that CFLCC forces would hand responsibility for the large-scale stabilization campaign to the follow-on joint task force, designated first as Combined Joint Task Force–Iraq (CJTF-Iraq) and then as Combined Joint Task Force–7 (CJTF-7). This guidance was passed down to lower echelons where it shaped tactical commanders' attitudes about the need to focus planning and training on the initial combat operations that would depose the Saddam regime. One critical example of these assumptions as they pertained to reconstruction was the guidance given to Colonel Gregg F. Martin, the commander of the 130th Engineer Brigade, the engineer unit that directly supported V Corps operations. Martin contended that before the invasion began, he was told that ORHA would supervise the entire reconstruction effort and Jay Garner and his staff would rely primarily on American contractors and Iraqi labor to do the work. The plan, according to Martin, was for military engineer units to provide support for civil reconstruction "only under emergency circumstances."[1]

When US Central Command (CENTCOM) designated V Corps headquarters as the headquarters for CJTF-7 and directed Coalition land forces to remain in Iraq to serve as the forces for the new Combined Joint Task Force (CJTF), all assumptions about the US Army's role in post-Saddam Iraq, including those concerning responsibilities for the reconstruction of the country, were swept away. In fact, in late April and May 2003, as Soldiers transitioned to the new campaign and began serving as the chief agent of stabilization, the Army in Iraq rather quickly began conducting a wide variety of reconstruction operations. For most units in Iraq, this mission—normally referred to as reconstruction but at times using the broader term "nation-building"—encompassed activities that built or improved aspects of Iraq's economic and physical infrastructure. Not surprisingly, the transition to these efforts was difficult. The US Army units that traditionally conducted reconstruction missions—civil affairs (CA) and engineer construction battalions—were few in number and did not have the capacity to conduct reconstruction on the scale required in Iraq.

To fill the yawning gap between capacity and need, Soldiers from a wide variety of units became heavily involved in projects that ranged from clearing trash from neighborhood streets to rehabilitating large fertilizer plants. By the end of 2003 almost all units had assumed aspects of the reconstruction mission. American Soldiers worked with Iraqis and the Coalition Provisional Authority (CPA) to make the best of the limited resources available in the early stages of the new campaign. The most important tool in this effort became the Commander's Emergency Response Program (CERP), an improvised method of funding projects at the unit level. By the end of 2004 American units had completed or facilitated projects such as the building and refurbishing of schools, the repair of water treatment plants, the establishment of waste removal systems, the repair and improvement of the electrical grid, and the creation of economic opportunities through small business grants and other means.

For the US Army, reconstruction was not a mission that was entirely unprecedented. In the latter half of the 20th century, American Soldiers had been involved in rebuilding infrastructure in Germany, Japan, and Vietnam. More importantly, in the decade before Operation IRAQI FREEDOM (OIF), the Army had conducted reconstruction efforts in Bosnia and Kosovo. However, the US Government had limited the role of its Armed Forces in the Balkans, mandating that Army engineers and other forces provide only minor reconstruction assistance and that CA units work through nongovernment organizations (NGOs) to meet the larger reconstruction objectives of those campaigns. Behind this decision was great concern that a more robust reconstruction initiative would lead US forces into larger efforts in the Balkans from which they might find it difficult to extricate themselves.[2]

DOD Photo by Thomas O'Hara

Figure 88. US Army Corps of Engineers Soldiers and civilians focused on large-scale infrastructure projects such as the electrical grid near the city of Bayji, Iraq.

The reconstruction mission in Iraq was far more ambitious than those in Bosnia and Kosovo. Indeed, one DOD official who visited Iraq in May 2003 to assess the size and nature of the reconstruction project wrote that the United States faced "a much more difficult problem than a traditional postconflict reconstruction challenge" and added, "the CPA is confronting the equivalent of both a defeated Germany in 1945 and a failed Soviet Union in 1989."[3] Such a massive undertaking would consume a great deal of resources and effort from American commanders and their Soldiers. Nevertheless, as the security environment worsened in 2003 and gaining the support of the Iraqi population became more critical, most US units recognized that the reconstruction of the country was not just a well-intentioned effort to improve the lives of Iraqis. US Soldiers found that for Iraqi citizens, having essential services (electricity and clean water) were second only to being safe and secure. If Coalition forces could provide basic services, they would make significant progress toward securing what many commanders viewed as the campaign's center of gravity (COG)—the support of the population for the Coalition. Major General Peter W. Chiarelli, commander of the 1st Cavalry Division (1st CAV) which arrived in Baghdad in March 2004, adopted this view, contending "that public works projects [like electricity and water] may be more effective than guns in deciding the future of Iraq" and defeating the insurgency.[4] Thus, reconstruction became a critical factor in winning over "fence sitters," those Iraqis who gave active support to neither the Coalition nor the insurgency but were instead waiting to see which side would prevail. Reconstruction then became a key element in the campaign plans of CJTF-7 and Multi-National Force–Iraq (MNF-I) as well as in the plans of their subordinate units. This chapter examines how American Soldiers adapted the reconstruction mission, overcoming major cultural, political, and financial barriers in the process.

The Context for Reconstruction Operations: Coalition Goals and US Army Capabilities

In the wake of the fall of the Saddam regime and the departure of ORHA, the CPA took over all authority for the reconstruction campaign in Iraq. In the July 2003 CPA Vision Statement, Ambassador Paul Bremer articulated the critical nature of the Coalition reconstruction mission as an imperative: "As a top priority, urgently restore physical and social infrastructure and public utilities."[5] In the list of areas that needed the most attention, Bremer placed water, power, sewage, and health infrastructure as well as the oil industry and the country's school network.[6] Given the dilapidation of the Iraqi economy and infrastructure, Bremer and the CPA sought to focus first on the large-scale reconstruction projects that would provide key benefits to Iraqi society at large. To do this, in the spring of 2003, the CPA worked with the US Army Corps of Engineers to establish two task forces—*Restore Iraqi Oil (RIO)* and *Restore Iraqi Electricity (RIE)*—that would help get the country's oil and electricity flowing again. Bremer set the date of 1 October 2003 as the date on which Iraq's electricity and oil output would be restored to prewar levels. The CPA administrator set other goals as well. By the fall of 2003, the Coalition planned to renovate 1,000 schools and reopen Iraq's 240 hospitals.[7] In addition, the CPA hoped to replace the currency of the old Iraqi Dinar, the symbol of Saddam's economy. In August 2003 representatives from the World Bank told Bremer that the estimated cost of the Coalition's overall reconstruction project in Iraq would be between $55 and $75 billion.[8]

The US Army had only a peripheral role in the largest of the CPA's reconstruction programs. The Army Corps of Engineers did supervise the two task forces to restore the oil sector and electrical services, but most of the workers in these efforts were civilian contractors from the United States, Iraq, and elsewhere. The requirements for the restoration of electricity and the oil industry overwhelmed the CPA staff and the organization's capacity. Thus, reconstruction at levels below these national projects largely became the responsibility of Coalition military units although the large majority of US Army units and other Coalition forces were untrained and unprepared for these types of operations.

In 2003 the DOD did have doctrine that described and defined the military's role in reconstruction operations. Joint Publication 3-57, *Joint Doctrine for Civil-Military Operations*, published in 2001, addressed reconstruction missions but did so broadly, stating that all joint force commands had to be prepared to conduct civil-military operations (CMO), the term that encompassed physical and economic reconstruction.[9] As a set of missions, CMO encompassed all types of activities that enhanced the military command's ability to achieve its objectives by improving relationships with a civilian community in an area of operation. CMO also included actions and programs that the commander was obligated to pursue to meet legal and moral obligations. Joint doctrine then suggested that all units could contribute to this broad set of operations that comprised missions such as Foreign Humanitarian Assistance and Military Civic Action.[10] However, by doctrine and training, CA, engineer, and health services units were the type of organizations best suited to achieve the commander's CMO goals.

DOD Photo by Jim Gordon

Figure 89. Iraqi subcontractors lay concrete tiles at a school play yard renovation project outside of Irbil, Iraq.

For the US Army in 2003, the units best prepared for the reconstruction mission were its CA battalions and its engineer units. Despite its small size, the CA Branch of the US military has had a significant influence on US campaigns since the end of the Cold War when campaigns in Haiti, the Balkans, and elsewhere required reconstruction and other CMO missions.* In Iraq after April 2003 the expertise of these CA Soldiers quickly became a priceless commodity. Organized in small elements that could be detached to brigade-size maneuver units, many CA Soldiers served in Civil Affairs Teams–Alpha (CAT-A) that assessed needs, planned projects, provided liaison to local authorities and NGOs, and supervised CMO. Other members of CA units were organized in functional specialty teams that gave assistance on specific types of projects such

---

*The entire US military CA component comprises only 6,000 total Army and Marine CA Soldiers, or less than ½ of 1 percent of the total force.

as public works and utilities and public health. These teams did not actually do the physical work involved in the reconstruction projects. Their role was to plan the projects; coordinate with other military units, US agencies, NGOs, local authorities, and contractors, to get the job started; and then provide oversight and quality control. In 2003, 96 percent of all CA Soldiers served in the Army Reserve and were individuals with experience and skills in areas such as administration, public health, legal systems, public education, and public works and utilities. This base of experience and knowledge could not easily be found in the ranks of the Active Army and were invaluable when coordinating postconflict reconstruction efforts.[11]

Four CA brigades deployed to Iraq in the spring of 2003 and initially became involved with humanitarian assistance operations. Then, after the regime fell and the situation appeared to stabilize, most CA assets became absorbed into the massive reconstruction effort at various levels. Because the CPA lacked staff members experienced in reconstruction activities, many CA Soldiers became part of Bremer's headquarters in Baghdad.[12] Most CA teams, at that point, married up with tactical units and began conducting CMO missions throughout Iraq. Using their experience, skills, and connections with local maneuver units and US organizations such as the US Agency for International Development (USAID), CA teams facilitated the refurbishing of schools and hospitals, repairing of bridges and irrigation systems, and other improvements to the Iraqi infrastructure.

Army engineers were also integral to CMO in general and the reconstruction effort specifically. At the national level, the US Army Corps of Engineers (USACE) led Task Force (TF) *Restore Iraqi Oil* (*RIO*) and TF *Restore Iraqi Electricity* (*RIE*), both of which were under the auspices of the CPA. However, even before the invasion began, both civilian and military Army engineers arrived in Kuwait to begin assessing the broader engineering challenges in OIF. Corps of Engineer planners designated teams to target anticipated oil and electricity projects, and immediately following the fall of the regime, Forward Engineering Support Teams (FESTs) operated throughout Iraq assessing projects, developing courses of action, and initiating contracts.[13] On 25 January 2004 all engineering efforts were consolidated under one command with the formation of the Gulf Region Division (GRD). This gave the USACE control of all activities of the Pentagon's Project and Contracting Office (PCO), which would become a key agency in the summer of 2004.

Below the level of the Corps of Engineers, military engineer units in Iraq played a significant role providing force protection, collecting and destroying enemy ordnance, and working with CA and other units to complete reconstruction projects.[14] When the US Army V Corps entered Iraq in March 2003, it enjoyed the support of approximately 4,000 Engineer Soldiers, most of whom supported combat operations at the tactical level.[15] By June 2003, however, the engineer force supporting CJTF-7 had grown dramatically to 19,000 Active Duty, Reserve, and National Guard Soldiers serving in a wide variety of engineer units. About one-third of these Soldiers served in units that were organic to divisions like the 82d Airborne Division (82d ABN) in Al Anbar province. The other two-thirds served in echelons above division (EAD) units, which could be allocated across Iraq to support the reconstruction missions the CJTF-7 commander believed were critical to achieving his objectives. These EAD units included combat heavy battalions that specialized in vertical (buildings) and horizontal (roads) construction, multi-role bridging companies, topographical engineer detachments, well drillers, and even divers. The CJTF-7 CJ7 Engineer staff section packaged these EAD assets to support specific tactical operations at the division level.

By May 2003 all of these units became directly involved in reconstruction operations even though many were not trained or equipped for the types of projects that the Iraqi communities most needed. The best example of this mismatch in capabilities was the 130th Engineer Brigade that had been organized and trained to conduct the demolition of obstacles, the digging of defensive

Figure 90. US Army Engineers work through the night in Iraq. October 2003

fortifications, and the bridging of rivers in support of the V Corps combat operations. Once the Saddam regime came to an end, the 130th had to remake itself into a brigade focused on construction. This was a painful transformation, partly because the brigade lacked construction management detachments that were critical to the type of missions required after 1 May 2003.[16] Engineer units at the division level had the same challenge. Once the full spectrum campaign began, the engineers at the tactical level did not have the organic assets that would enable them to manage large-scale construction projects.

Despite the initial disparity between capabilities and needs, all types of engineer units became involved in the local efforts to rebuild the infrastructure and worked closely with CA teams and maneuver brigades to repave roads; reinforce bridge structures; dig wells; and construct schools, clinics, airfields, and roadways.[17] In Baghdad, for example, the 1st Armored Division's (1st AD's) Engineer Brigade conducted a large-scale road construction project in Sadr City. Colonel Lou Marich, who took command of the brigade in the summer of 2003, stated the purpose of the project was "just to improve the quality of life."[18] Marich emphasized that the project had an immediate beneficial impact on the area, "We could see it as we did this road. Shops started opening up and the whole area came back to life."[19]

Army engineers also filled gaps in the reconstruction campaign by focusing construction resources on Iraqi communities outside the areas targeted by US maneuver brigades and other units. One excellent example of this type of CMO mission was conducted by TF *Able*, an engineer group made up of Active and Reserve Component engineer battalions from across the United States. Between 2003 and early 2004, TF *Able* supported the 4th Infantry Division's (4th ID's) operations in the Sunni Triangle. The 4th ID had directed its brigades to focus operations on the cities and larger towns in their area of responsibility (AOR), leaving the smaller towns and villages largely untouched. To help improve the lives of these smaller communities, the engineers in TF *Able* began working with local authorities to assess, plan, and complete key construction projects.[20] While focusing on basic infrastructure requirements, such as road repair and water distribution systems, the task force's battalions also repaired schools and mosques and improved soccer fields and police stations. One of these units, the Mississippi Army National Guard's 223d Engineer Battalion, not only refurbished the schools in the villages of Al Hamra and Al Mahazim near the city of Tikrit, but also worked with its Family Readiness Group (FRG) in Mississippi to collect school supplies for the Iraqi children in these areas.[21]

CJTF-7's combat engineer units were well prepared for one critical mission: destroying captured Iraqi ammunition. Ridding the country of unexploded tank and artillery ordnance promised to create a more secure environment that would foster reconstruction and stability. However, the job was massive in scale. Colonel Don C. Young, the commander of the 1st AD's Engineer Brigade in May 2003, recalled the scope of the unexploded ordnance (UXO) mission for his unit, "When I drove into Baghdad, I was overwhelmed with . . . the amount of ordnance just lying around. You would drive through the middle of Baghdad and you would look over into a median and it would be littered with artillery rounds and rockets just lying there."[22] Young explained that the demands of disposal of weapons caches became so overwhelming for his unit's Explosive Ordnance Detachments that the V Corps reinforced the engineers in that effort, tasking the V Corps Artillery Brigade to assist with ammunition removal.[23]

For the engineer and CA units, one of the largest obstacles in the reconstruction effort was the lack of an overall Coalition plan for the reconstruction of the country. By doctrine, CMO take shape and direction from the commander's plan and vision for a campaign. Coalition civil and military authorities had entered Iraq in March 2003 without an overarching plan for reconstruction, and both the CPA and CJTF-7 required time before they could establish a detailed concept for reconstruction. Bremer did articulate a set of important goals for the restoration of key services and infrastructure. But, according to US Army researchers who studied CMO in Iraq in 2003 and early 2004, the CPA never translated this vision into detailed guidance that was then passed on to Coalition military forces. According to the 2004 report:

> The common perception throughout the theater is that a road map for the rebuilding of Iraq does not exist. There is not a plan that outlines priorities with short, medium, and long-term objectives. If such a national plan exists with the CPA, it has not been communicated adequately to Coalition Forces. Task force staff at all levels of command reiterated that there is no clear guidance coming from Baghdad.[24]

This report continued with the contention that in the eyes of many Soldiers, the lack of a "road map" was a symptom of the Coalition's overall failure to plan for postconflict operations and the lack of coordination between the CPA in Baghdad and the units conducting CMO on the ground. The major result of these shortcomings was that tactical units were forced to create their own plans for reconstruction based on the priorities of the communities in their AORs, in spite of the fact that their staffs had no assurance that the projects in these plans contributed to achieving the Coalition's larger goals. Moreover, the absence of an overall plan initially meant a severe shortage of resources. The many brigades and battalions that began to conduct CMO in the late spring and early summer of 2003 were significantly handicapped by a lack of funds. Money to pay for Iraqi laborers and construction materials, as this chapter will show, became available only gradually and through a system invented in its entirety by Soldiers on the ground in Iraq.

"Everyone Must Do Nation-Building": Broadening Reconstruction Operations

Figure 91. Major Lawendowski, Alaskan National Guard, assembles a swing set for Iraqi children living in an impoverished neighborhood in Al Hillah, Iraq.

Given the scope of the reconstruction mission and the devolution of that mission to the tactical level, there were simply not enough CA units or engineers to perform all the CMO adopted by Coalition forces. In an environment in which reconstruction became one critical part of the larger full spectrum campaign, all Soldiers had to become CA officers and many became engineers. Most were not trained to manage even the smallest reconstruction project. Yet they often embraced their new role as nation-builders. While serving as the commander of the 101st Airborne Division (101st ABN) based in Mosul, Major General David H. Petraeus came to grips with the nature of postconflict operations and focused on the key role of reconstruction in that type of mission. Recalling his experience in dealing with the full spectrum campaign in northern Iraq in 2003–2004, Petraeus argued that "civil affairs are not enough when undertaking huge reconstruction and nation-building efforts . . . *everyone must do nation-building* . . . [When] undertaking industrial-strength reconstruction on the scale of that in Iraq, civil affairs forces alone will not suffice; every unit must be involved [emphasis in original]."[25]

Early in the new campaign, not all Soldiers were convinced that tactical units like the 101st ABN were the right instruments for reconstruction and nation-building. Petraeus explained that in 2003 there were "two or three infantry battalion commanders [in the 101st] who were either not that comfortable with the nation-building aspect of things, or really weren't that enthusiastic about it"[26] Petraeus continued:

> When that happened, we sat down with the [assistant division commanders] and the brigade commanders and said, 'you know, you need to go put your arm around that guy and make sure he realizes the importance of this, and also, frankly, realizes this is not an option and to get on with it, and that I will come out in a few days to confirm the excellence of his plan for nation-building in his particular area.' So they got it. Everybody did it. Even aviation battalion commanders were given civil-military areas of responsibility.[27]

For the US Army in Iraq in 2003, every Soldier had to be a nation-builder. There was simply no other agency that had the resources, organization, manpower, or willpower to even consider attempting the overall task of reconstruction.

At times, the adoption of CMO by a wide variety of units such as aviation battalions did lead to problems in coordination. Major Chris Bentch, a CA officer who served in 2003 as the Civil Affairs Staff officer (S5) for the 3d Brigade Combat Team (BCT), 4th ID, noted in his journal that by late June 2003, CMO in the Sunni Triangle lacked coherency. Bentch described the situation as "a CA nightmare as everyone is doing CA and no one knows what everyone else is doing."[28] Bentch and staff officers like him in the brigades and battalions took on the task of channeling this energy and the resources available into directions they believed would benefit the Iraqi people and further the Coalition project in Iraq. However, the Coalition's lack of an overarching plan for reconstruction meant that all of these early efforts remained essentially local initiatives not implicitly tied to larger strategic goals.

The single most important resource in the reconstruction campaign was money. Because of the failure to plan for CMO, US units arrived in their initial AORs in April and May 2003 without any means of funding even the smallest reconstruction projects. Indeed, in early June, 2 months after the fall of the Saddam regime, some brigades still had no means of obtaining money to support their CMO plan. In the first week of that month, Bentch expressed his discontent with the funding situation in his journal:

> The Brigade Commander is as frustrated as I am that there is no money to do anything with. We have assessed things to death, but at some point all we have accomplished is to figure out what is wrong. We still haven't done anything to fix it. It is unconscionable that no one knows how to access the money yet. We have been operating since early May with no way of impacting our areas.[29]

Cognizant of the need for funding at the tactical level, CJTF-7 took a significant step forward in June 2003 in its development of the Commander's Emergency Response Program (CERP), a new source of funds that would directly affect tactical-level reconstruction efforts. According to Colonel Michael Toner, CJTF-7's Chief of Resource Management (CJ8), the driving idea behind the CERP was "to enable commanders to respond to urgent humanitarian relief and reconstruction requirements within their areas of responsibility, by carrying out programs that will immediately assist the Iraqi people."[30] The origins of CERP lay in a fortuitous accident. Soon after Saddam's regime fell, Soldiers in the 3d Infantry Division (3d ID) found $700 million (US) hidden in a hole in the wall of one of the Iraqi dictator's palaces.[31] Toner and a group of innovative staff officers then reasoned that because CJTF-7 had no immediate funds available for reconstruction, part of the money discovered in the palace should be used to support projects at the local level. After verifying that the cash was not counterfeit, Lieutenant General Ricardo Sanchez, the CJTF-7 commander, asked Bremer for permission to use the funds for local reconstruction. Bremer agreed, and CERP began with approximately $178 million.

The program was designed to function just like the Federal Acquisition Regulation (FAR) for small purchases. This allowed CJTF-7 to push money down to the commanders, but balanced the need for quick action with the requirement for strict accounting and distribution measures. The new improvised system allowed a unit, for example, to assess a local need such as a school requiring repairs and to immediately obtain an estimate from a local contractor for those repairs. Once CJTF-7 staff officers received the estimate and approved it, the unit withdrew the needed cash. To prevent the omnipresent problems of kickbacks, theft, and fraud, the CJTF-7 CJ8 developed a set of control measures and verification procedures.[32]

Initially, the program managers at CJTF-7 allowed brigade commanders a total of $25,000 and the ability to spend up to $2,500 on any single project.[33] By late summer 2003 CJTF-7 raised the threshold to $10,000 per project, then up to $50,000, and eventually higher.[34] Since CERP was one of the few programs in which tangible physical results became swiftly visible, the initiative expanded at a rapid rate. Toner noted that the virtues and visibility of the program made it increasingly powerful:

> A lot of the projects just take a long time to build. [CERP] was something where we could go in and buy a generator for this town and give them some electricity right then. It might not fix the whole big problem that they have across the country, but it got results right there. We could go in and fix a water pump that did the irrigation for the town. We could fix their school. . . . So as the program grew and as everybody saw good results, and as many of the other programs that CPA was doing were slow in seeing results, we got more and more funding put into this.[35]

The beneficial results were so apparent that the US Congress supported and then extended the program. In September 2003, when the seized money started running out, the Army received

---

Reconstructing Iraq's Medical Knowledge

In May 2003, when 4th Infantry Division surgeon Dr. (Lieutenant Colonel) Kirk Eggleston entered the Tikrit Medical College Library in the city of Tikrit, he became immediately aware of the great need to modernize the Iraqi medical system. Eggleston recalled, "When I first toured the library, it was neat and tidy, but had very little recent medical literature." Most of the materials were 10 to 20 years out of date. Medical innovations move very fast and even a few months away from the mainstream of medical knowledge can leave a physician behind. Ten years of missing knowledge can severely impede a doctor's ability to treat patients. Word of the plight of the medical library made it back to Dr. David Gifford, a part-time physician at Darnall Army Community Hospital at Fort Hood. He decided that helping the Tikrit medical library would be his part in the reconstruction of Iraq. Gifford put the word out and Dr. Susan Yox responded with a posting on www.medscape.com, an online international nursing education bulletin board. The response was "amazing," according to Dr. Gifford. Donations began

flooding in from all over the country. Thousands of textbooks and journals, worth close to half a million dollars, were shipped to Iraq and just 1 year later, the Tikrit Medical College Library was filled with current medical texts and journals along with 18 new computers that could connect with the Internet. Gifford stated, "These donations will dramatically improve the quality of the delivery of health care in Iraq."

Mollie Miller, "Fort Hood Doctor Helps
Bring 21st Century to Iraqi Health System"
Defend America, 1 July 2004

US Soldiers look through recently arrived book donations with the dean of the Tikrit Medical College. In total, the college has received nearly 15,000 medical textbooks and 5,000 medical journals.

notification from Congress authorizing "the DOD for operation and maintenance, not to exceed $180,000,000 . . . to fund the CERP . . . and fund a similar program be established to assist the people of Afghanistan."[36] By January 2004 division and brigade commanders had expended approximately $126 million in CERP funds.[37] Then, when the appropriated dollars dried up, the Army received funds from the Development Fund for Iraq (DFI). The United Nations (UN) had created the DFI to administer proceeds from the export sales of Iraq's oil, funds remaining from the UN Oil-for-Food Program, and any other assets seized from the regime. The US Government placed the DFI under the control of the CPA, which transferred an additional $453 million into CERP.[38]

American units used CERP funds for humanitarian relief and reconstruction projects that provided immediate assistance to Iraqi communities. Projects included civic clean-up, education, electricity, food production and distribution, health care, irrigation, rule of law and governance, telecommunications, water, and sanitation. According to one report on the program, most of these efforts were "quick, small-scale projects—minor repairs of sewage systems, rubbish collection, refurbishing youth centers and mosques—that relied principally on local labor and were designed to 'win the hearts and minds' of ordinary Iraqis."[39] The CERP money had an immediate impact on the reconstruction operations of many units. The 3d Brigade, 4th ID, for example, had been hamstrung by the lack of funds, and in its first 6 weeks in Iraq, had not been able to initiate any reconstruction work. By the middle of July, however, its units had begun 60 projects using $1.2 million.[40] As of 2 October 2004 Coalition military units had spent over $578 million in CERP funds on approximately 34,500 different projects across Iraq.[41]

From the perspective of the US military, CERP funding was one of the biggest success stories in Iraq because the projects made possible by the funding program often appeared to have a direct impact on their ability to achieve campaign objectives. One 2006 study that examined the effects of the CERP asserted that many commanders noticed a direct correlation "between CERP funded projects and improved stability and security in their sector."[42] Lieutenant Colonel Brian McKiernan, the commander of 4th Battalion, 27th Field Artillery, 1st AD, used the number of attacks against Coalition forces and the number of actionable tips or information received from the civilian population as a metric for determining if progress was being made on reconstruction in a community.[43] If attacks were down and tips were up, McKiernan then assessed ongoing reconstruction projects as successful.

This direct correlation between reconstruction projects and support from the local Iraqi population became very apparent in September 2003. It was in this month that a delay in approving additional funding in the US Congress allowed the CERP to lapse. Iraqi unrest followed on the heels of this decision. One unit reported, "The battalion had spent considerable time building trust and faith with the local interim government . . . much of this 'good faith' was destroyed when the CERP funds were no longer available to the battalion commander."[44] Many Soldiers came to agree that although CERP funds increased during the duration of OIF, commanders were still underfunded in their reconstruction endeavors. In just 4 months in 2003 the CERP distributed $23 million, but that was less than $1 for each Iraqi.[45] According to Major George H. Sarabia, who served with the 2d Squadron, 2d Armored Cavalry Regiment (2d ACR), "If we had more money, then we would have been able to do more projects geared toward not just goodwill . . . but geared toward local leaders that were supporting us."[46] Colonel Frederick Rudesheim, commander of the 3d BCT, 4th ID believed "money was 'the' most powerful method we had to reach the people; it was leveraged more than combat power.[47] Major General

Petraeus summarized all of these statements in a shorter adage, "In an endeavor like that in Iraq, money is ammunition."[48]

All Reconstruction is Local: The US Army Rebuilds Iraq

The Army's campaign to reconstruct and refurbish Iraq began even before the CPA and CJTF-7 had taken over the Coalition effort in Iraq. In the days just following Saddam's fall, Lieutenant General William S. Wallace, the commander of V Corps, and his staff decided to reach out to Iraqis and demonstrate the Coalition's intent to serve as more than just an occupying force. Accordingly, V Corps units across Iraq launched TF *Neighborhood*. This effort was actually an operation that provided community improvement for local Iraqis by focusing on small projects intended to make a difference in everyday life. Many of the projects centered on cleaning up the trash and debris from the neighborhoods damaged by the war and looting. Major General Buford Blount, the commander of the 3d ID, explained, "Every day, a neighborhood section will get a full-court press of support that will include garbage pickup, medical assistance, ordnance cleanup, and anything else we can do in a day to help the neighborhoods."[49] Blount's Soldiers became heavily involved in a variety of reconstruction projects including hauling tons of garbage, making repairs to schools and police stations, and providing medical resources.[50]

Figure 92. An Iraqi laborer finishes the concrete footings for an Iraqi Army barracks complex at a new Iraqi Army base near Kirkuk, Iraq.

As the Iraqi summer began, the 1st AD focused on reconstruction projects in the sprawling Iraqi capital city. Because there was no overall Coalition plan for reconstruction, commanders in the division sought to address the most pressing and obvious local needs first. Initial work focused on cleaning streets by concentrating engineering resources, utilizing CA, and working with local Iraqis.[51] Once CERP became available, the 1st AD launched a variety of infrastructure projects to repair sewer lines, water systems, and the electrical grid.[52] Colonel Ralph O. Baker, commander of the 2d BCT, 1st AD, recalled that he created the acronym SWEAT, which stood for sewer, water, electricity, academics and trash, as a device to focus his Soldiers' efforts in the reconstruction part of the new campaign. Baker explained the importance of pursuing *academic* projects: "Academics were repairing schools because the school year was getting ready to start and there is no faster way to win over parents than to do something for their children. We also knew that education and trying to influence the young population was an important component of our information operational strategy anyway."[53]

This basic principle of channeling funding to simple projects that could markedly and immediately improve communities drove the reconstruction efforts of other units as well. Major General Raymond Odierno, commander of the 4th ID, described the objective of his reconstruction campaign in 2003 as "our ability to put money, specifically the CERP money we were given to do critical projects that would show the community we were first trying to make their lives better and we were trying to normalize what was going on. This went from building schools, to sewers, to water, and to electricity."[54] Odierno also arranged for economists from the US Military Academy at West Point to serve as consultants to the new government in the city of Kirkuk to help that city create a development plan to coordinate the local CERP-funded initiatives.[55]

Colonel Frank Rudesheim also used reconstruction programs for small improvements to the infrastructure. He viewed these works as a means of fostering the legitimacy of the local government officials, another key objective within the new campaign. Rudesheim noted that he became very conscious of ensuring the city council in Samarra, a key city in the Sunni Triangle, received credit for projects that were often collaborations between Iraqi leaders and US Soldiers. Like other commanders, Rudesheim tried to employ as many Iraqis in these efforts as possible for several reasons. First, employment in reconstruction helped prevent local Iraqis, especially young men, from joining insurgent groups for economic reasons. Second, the use of Iraqi labor placed an Iraqi face on the overall effort, legitimizing the post-Saddam political order and demonstrating the Coalition's role as a partner with that new order.[56]

In northern Iraq in 2003, the 101st ABN placed great emphasis on the potential effects of its reconstruction efforts. Believing that the Iraqis needed a general sense of normalcy for their economy and society to begin recovery, the 101st ABN concentrated on infrastructure and schools, but also spent time opening swimming pools, restaurants, and even worked with a company to open a hotel in Mosul.[57] Engineers attached to the 101st ABN taught former Iraqi soldiers basic construction skills to help them find employment. The Iraqis learned and honed their skills in the Village of Hope project that provided homes for displaced families in Mosul.[58] Reconstruction projects that employed local Iraqis became a priority because of their ability to stimulate the economy.

To the west of the 101st ABN's AOR, in Al Anbar province, the 82d ABN also accomplished a broad set of reconstruction projects. By the time the division left Iraq in 2004, its units had spent more than $40.4 million in funding 2,436 projects.[59] Within the province, the division concentrated these projects on four decisive services essential to improving the quality of life for the Iraqi people: power production, health care, education, and water and sanitation.[60] The 82d ABN used CERP to contract with local Iraqis for the repair of 431 schools and invested over $3.2 million to reconstruct the provincial education system. The division also funded Iraqi efforts to refurbish over 300 mosques in the province.[61] Because water was so important in this hot arid region of Iraq, division leaders made a concerted effort to increase the amount of drinking water that was available to the Iraqi population. To help garner support for the Coalition in the unstable city of Fallujah, Major General Charles H. Swannack Jr., the division commander, directed the purchase of water purification units and had his engineer units set them up in the city. The division also used its quartermaster units to create more potable water for smaller communities by using their reverse osmosis water purification units (ROWPUs).[62]

Some of the US Army's projects targeted specific types of economic activity. In the city of Ramadi in 2003, Soldiers in the 1st Battalion, 124th Infantry Regiment, Florida Army National

Figure 93. Private First Class Denegro, Charlie Battery, 1st Battalion, 9th Field Artillery Regiment, 3d Infantry Division, unloads medical supplies at a clinic in Kandari, Iraq, 3 July 2003.

Guard, helped local fishermen regain their livelihood and provide food for their families by contributing new nets and other fishing equipment.[63] Similarly, in 2004 Soldiers from the 1st CAV became involved in making improvements in agricultural production. Soldiers in the 5th BCT, 1st CAV, created a farmer's co-op and provided seed and assistance with irrigation for farmers in their AOR.[64] The division's 1st BCT also became involved in helping Iraqi farmers through the use of their CERP money to buy wheat and barley seed as well as fertilizer. Second Lieutenant Brendan Tarpey, a platoon leader in the brigade, explained the long-term benefits that the seed program promised, "It's not so much that it's us handing out free stuff. It's that this is something we can give the farmers so that they can have a leg-up in this next planting season."[65]

The leaders of the 1st CAV and other units that made up the OIF II rotation—those divisions and brigades that deployed to Iraq in the first half of 2004—enjoyed an advantage over the commanders of units that had deployed in 2003: the time and information required to adequately train and prepare for full spectrum operations. Once notified of the 1st CAV's future deployment, Major General Chiarelli and his staff gathered intelligence about the AORs the division's units would occupy and prepared for missions in those areas. In 2003 during the division's training for OIF, Chiarelli insisted that his engineer units work with civilian planners, administrators, and engineers in the cities of Austin and Killeen, Texas, to gain a basic understanding of how cities function.[66] This preparation paid off when the 1st CAV took over responsibility for the city of Baghdad. Chiarelli's engineers immediately established an interagency effort with the US Department of State and the USAID to coordinate reconstruction projects through the University of Baghdad so that the division's projects would benefit Iraqi contractors and the local government as much as possible.

According to Chiarelli, the leaders of the 1st CAV placed paramount importance on reconstruction missions, making it the line of operation in the division's campaign plan that was the "first among equals."[67] Initially, the unit's reconstruction efforts focused on funding and facilitating large projects, such as water treatment plants and landfills, with the expectation that other agencies would initiate the improvements to connect these major sites to neighborhoods in Baghdad. Yet, when funding issues jeopardized the efforts to make the connections to local levels, the 1st CAV partly reoriented its operations

Figure 94. Specialist Andy Weekley, 86th Dive Team, 1st CAV, resurfaces from the Tigris River after cleaning out intake valves at a water treatment plant.

toward projects that provided essential services—water, electricity, sewer—along the "First Mile," the division's term for the neighborhood level where making signs of visible progress was critical.[68]

In some cases, the 1st CAV was able to complete large-scale projects that had an immediate local impact. In May 2004, for example, the 5th BCT, 1st CAV, worked with the CPA and its contractor, FluorAmec, to build a large landfill in southern Baghdad.[69] However, rather than having the contractor do most of the work with sophisticated machinery, the division and brigade leadership coordinated with the CPA and the contractor to ensure the project made the widest possible use of local Iraqi suppliers, craftsmen, and laborers. By adding such a provision to the terms of the contract, both the military and the civilian headquarters sought to employ the greatest possible number of local Iraqis in the shortest time possible.[70] The 5th BCT worked with local sheiks and ultimately put 4,000 Iraqis from southern Baghdad neighborhoods to work on the landfill project. Chiarelli viewed projects like this as vital to demonstrating the Coalition's ability to make visible improvements in Iraqi life. Moreover, Chiarelli believed that by employing 4,000 local men, the project was actually supporting these workers, their extended families, and others in service-oriented firms that might indirectly gain from the injection of wages from the landfill construction. This large group, potentially 60,000 Iraqis in Chiarelli's estimation, had been positively affected by a single project and perhaps dissuaded from joining the insurgency as a result. Thus, for the 1st CAV leadership, reconstruction operations became another way of eroding the pool of disaffected Iraqis from which insurgent leaders recruited their followers.[71]

Other units used different means of maximizing Iraqi involvement in reconstruction operations. The 1st Infantry Division (1st ID), operating in the Sunni Triangle in 2004, established an Iraqi engineer group within their division staff to design and direct a number of their projects. As members of local communities, these engineers were invaluable for their input

Figure 95. Iraqi laborers clean the turbine housing of a power generator plant in Bayji, Iraq, in 2004.

DOD Photo by Mitch Frazier

and help in finding reputable contractors. The division's leaders also met with provincial governors on a weekly basis to decide where reconstruction money should be spent. The 1st ID staff followed up these efforts by ensuring that Iraqi politicians received credit for all of the improvements to the infrastructure and economy.[72] According to Master Sergeant Luis Jackson, a noncommissioned officer (NCO) in the 1st Battalion, 18th Infantry (1-18th IN) which was part of the 1st ID's 2d BCT, the division and its subordinate units attempted to conduct reconstruction projects jointly with the Iraqis at all times. Jackson's unit dispatched joint Iraqi and American CA patrols that surveyed Tikrit three times a week to help decide priorities for reconstruction efforts.[73] Like the leaders of the 1st CAV, Colonel Dana Pittard, commander of 1st ID's 3d Brigade, stressed the importance of hiring locals to do the projects and set as his goal the employment of 50,000 Iraqis. Through its coordination with the local Labor Directory, the division matched contractors with unemployed citizens in the Diyala province.[74] Using this method, the division facilitated the rebuilding of the Bayji Power Plant with the help of the Corps of Engineers and local contractors, employing over 2,000 civilians in the process.[75]

US Army units tackled a broad array of small projects in a wide variety of settings. The 3d Brigade, 2d Infantry Division (2d ID), made great efforts in 2004 to bring fresh water to the people in the northwest reaches of Iraq. First Sergeant Richard Gano Jr., who served with the 1st Squadron, 14th Cavalry Regiment, recalled drilling water wells and building irrigation lines for the people of Tall Afar.[76] Units throughout the brigade's AOR worked on small projects, such as individual wells, and on larger projects in coordination with the Army Corps of Engineers and the Iraqi Reconstruction Management Office (IRMO), the US Embassy agency that after June 2004 directed the overall reconstruction effort in Iraq. Other units focused on humanitarian efforts designed to relieve suffering. In Baghdad in 2004, Soldiers of the 2d BCT, 10th Mountain Division conducted Operation WINDY CITY to distribute fleece blankets to an impoverished sector of Baghdad that had historically been ignored by the Saddam regime.[77] Projects such as these were small compared to the programs focused on infrastructure improvements, but helped meet the immediate needs of Iraqi citizens and allowed Soldiers to engender good will and support for their missions.

By the middle of 2004 all of these efforts had made a large impact on the physical infrastructure of Iraq. One estimate completed by the CJTF-7 staff asserted that between June 2003 and May 2004, the Soldiers, Sailors, Marines, and Airmen of the joint task force refurbished

Figure 96. Contractor Janene Van Deroef and Captain Rodrick Pittman of the 40th Engineering Battalion make a site inspection at the Baghdad South power plant.

USAID Photo by Thomas Hartwell

and opened 240 hospitals; 2,200 health clinics; and 2,300 schools, technical institutes, and universities.[78] They cleared more than 15,000 kilometers of clogged canals and completed numerous water distribution improvements. Overall, CJTF-7 forces conducted roughly 13,000 reconstruction missions worth over $8 billion. All of the US Army's projects, large and small, demonstrated the Coalition's resolve to improve the lives of Iraqis.

A Success in Al Anbar: Rebuilding the State Company for Phosphate Plant

Much of the US Army's reconstruction effort focused on small projects that could be funded by CERP and promised to have a direct benefit on local populations. As noted earlier, the larger projects that addressed the national infrastructure, such as the electrical grid, remained the responsibility of the US Army Corps of Engineers and the contractors working for the Corps. In a number of cases, however, the Army's maneuver units became involved in larger projects that had beneficial results at the national, provincial, and local levels.

One excellent example of this type of project was the renovation of the State Company for Phosphate (SCP), Iraq's largest industrial chemical fertilizer plant, located in the city of Al Qaim, in Al Anbar province. The Belgian firm Syberta had designed the plant in 1977 and its construction was completed in 1982.[79] A five-stage processing plant that manufactured high-quality fertilizer, SCP employed 2,000 Iraqis at its peak and produced enough fertilizer to satisfy Iraqi consumers and provide exports to neighboring countries. When US Soldiers from the 3d Armored Cavalry Regiment (ACR) arrived in the province in the spring of 2003, the plant was rundown, employed only 50 people, and was not producing any fertilizer.[80] UN sanctions during the 1990s had led to the shutting down of most of the plant's production lines and cannibalization of its equipment.[81] To make the situation worse, the plant required 40 megawatts of electricity to restart and 20 megawatts to sustain production, but was receiving only 10 megawatts of electricity when Coalition forces entered Iraq.[82] The company had four turbine generators capable of producing 7.5 megawatts of power each, but only one of them was working by mid-2003.

Early assessments by the CA team attached to the 3d ACR noted that returning the SCP plant to production promised to employ thousands of Iraqis while producing a key resource for a rehabilitated Iraqi economy. Initial efforts by the CA and 3d ACR Soldiers in the fall of 2003 used $50,000 in CERP funds to restore the power supply and market the inventory of fertilizer

---

Restoring the Lives of the Marsh Arabs

After a rebellion by the Shia Marsh Arabs at the end of the Gulf War in 1991, the Saddam regime largely drained and thus destroyed the Mesopotamian Marshlands. Located between the Tigris and Euphrates Rivers, the 8,000 square mile marsh area, roughly twice the size of the Florida Everglades, was once among the world's oldest wetlands. The marshes were renowned for their biodiversity, full of a wide variety of birds, fish, and plant species. Saddam's wrath displaced 150,000 Marsh Arabs and by 1999 the marshlands were reduced to 7 percent of their original state. This meant the catastrophic loss of wildlife as well as the destruction of a natural filter system for those people living in southern Iraq. In November 2003, the Army Corps of Engineers, the US Agency for International Development (USAID), and the Iraqi Ministry of Water Resources developed a water management system that aided efforts to reconstruct the water flow system and restore the marshlands. A 5-year program began to restore the marshlands to 75 percent of pre-1991 levels.

Nani Gould, "Army Engineers Helping Restore Iraqi Wetlands,"
Army News Service, 4 August 2004.

SSG James Sherrill, "Work Continues to Restore Iraqi Marshlands,"
Defend America, 7 June 2006.

SCP had as inventory, a decision that generated approximately $5 million in capital.[83] These first steps allowed the SCP to hire 1,000 workers and produce up to 700 metric tons of fertilizer per day.[84] As fall progressed, the CA officers became more ambitious, connecting experts from the 82d ABN, the 432d and 490th CA Battalions, and members of TF *RIO* with Iraqi stakeholders from the Ministries of Industry and Minerals, Transportation, Agriculture, and Oil to expand the renovation and increase production.

Eventually, leaders in the 3d ACR and the 82d ABN made possible the purchase of four new electric generators and helped retrofit the plant's natural gas conversion burners. Other key machinery received much needed maintenance and repair parts. To get the fertilizer to markets, American Soldiers worked with Iraqis to repair trucks that served the plant, restore rail lines, and plan the use of railcars to ship the product.[85] Perhaps most important was the fact that by February 2004 the project employed 3,000 Iraqi workers, managers, and administrators.[86] Reestablishing a labor force of this size and renovating a major production facility in the midst of a region beset by insurgent violence, on the other hand, created new concerns. To safeguard the investment in the plant, the CA team involved in the SCP project coordinated for the establishment of a police academy on the complex to provide security for the facility. Eventually, Coalition forces used the academy to train 322 security officers and first responders to support the SCP.[87]

As the SCP project began to bear fruit, the Coalition and Iraqi authorities started to look for ways to make it more successful. Soon after the plant began producing fertilizer, the CPA and the Iraqi Ministry of Industry and Minerals committed an additional $5 million to continue the repairs.[88] After further success in marketing, sales, repairs, and production, USAID, the UN, and the World Bank together committed an additional $27 million in February 2004 for continued rehabilitation of the entire complex.[89] In addition to the plant's contribution of fertilizer and other products to the Iraqi economy, the economic effects of the SCP project had a direct impact on Iraqi quality of life. One summary estimated that the rebuilding of the SCP created 45,000 jobs in a variety of sectors, including trucking, distribution, agriculture, mining, and other related industries.[90]

The Coalition's focused effort on SCP serves as an excellent illustration of how US Army units, working with local Iraqis, the CPA, and the fledgling Iraqi Government integrated reconstruction operations into the full spectrum campaign. In scale and scope, the project was beyond the doctrinal capability of the CA units assigned to the region. Moreover, none of the maneuver units that operated in the province had any preparation or training for mounting a project of any size, much less one as large as this one. Nevertheless, the CA team initially on the ground recognized that SCP could have far-reaching benefits. Perhaps more importantly, the commanders of the tactical units that operated in the region—the 3d ACR and the 82d ABN—understood the critical role of projects such as the SCP in achieving their larger campaign objectives in Al Anbar province and made the necessary investments in personnel, money, and time to help reach their potential.

Obstacles on the Path to a New Iraq

Despite the US Army's effort to help Iraqis rebuild their country, its reconstruction mission still encountered significant problems. Any balanced approach to examining the Army's role in Iraqi nation-building must consider that Soldiers were often operating in a dangerous environment, in a culture with which they were unfamiliar, and with Iraqis who, quite often, did not share the Coalition's vision for their country. While a myriad of large and small obstacles complicated the Army's efforts in the full spectrum campaign, this section discusses the most crippling ones impeding Soldiers in their day-to-day reconstruction tasks. A decrepit infrastructure, the worsening security situation, sabotage, corruption, and the 1-year rotation cycles of US Army units all posed serious, real-time challenges to the Soldiers engaged in their mission to rebuild Iraq.

In May 2003 the most obvious difficulty facing the reconstruction effort was the state of the Iraqi infrastructure. Coalition planners had not anticipated Iraq to be so devoid of basic, functioning systems. Major Kris Arnold, who worked closely with the CFLCC intelligence staff section and moved into Baghdad in April 2003, noted this problem: "We really didn't have a good understanding of how deteriorated the infrastructure was, and that caused us to underestimate how much reconstruction would be required. . . . I think the level of effort that would be required was gravely underestimated."[91] Indeed, when Saddam's regime fell and the US Army emerged as the chief agent of stabilizing and rebuilding Iraq, Soldiers scrambled to immediately assess and comprehend the situation on the ground. What they discovered was that much of Iraq's infrastructure was being held together with something akin to "chewing gum and bailing wire."[92] When the CPA replaced ORHA, also in May, approximately 40 percent of Iraqis had no access to drinkable water, 70 percent of Iraq's sewage-treatment plants were in disrepair, and, of Iraq's 25,000 schools, 80 percent could only supply one book for every six students.[93] This level of unexpected dilapidation, coupled with the lack of preparation most Soldiers had upon embarking on this overwhelming, complex nation-building mission, made it impossible for the Coalition, and the US Army in particular, to conduct quick repairs to any of Iraq's infrastructure.[94]

Throughout Baghdad, arguably the Iraqi city with the best functioning essential services yet still one debilitated by "un-maintained and un-synchronized systems," the Army faced such things as broken sewer lines excreting raw sewage into the streets and often directly into the rivers.[95] Lieutenant Colonel Wes Gillman, who served in the 3d ID as battalion commander for 1st Battalion, 30th Infantry, remembered being shocked to witness large piles of garbage collecting outside villages and cities, and goats grazing off the refuse.[96] Often, US Soldiers were forced to focus most of their energy on merely keeping existing systems from collapsing, rather than on improving them. Coalition attempts, in the fall of 2003, to boost electricity production to the same levels of operation in existence before the invasion overstressed Iraq's old machinery. At the Baghdad South power station, troops successfully restarted six outdated generators for the first time in years. This achievement was short-lived, however; station manager Gazi Aziz stated, "We worked like crazy, but it was all too much. . . . It fell apart in five days."[97]

Conditions outside of Baghdad were often much worse. Henry Ensher, a 22-year veteran of the State Department, served as a CPA representative in the Iraqi province of Qadisiyah in southern Iraq from the fall of 2003 to June 2004. There he encountered a population more isolated from world progress and development than he had witnessed in more than 10 years of experience in the region:

> I had expected that infrastructure would be widespread but in bad repair and would need a lot of work to bring it up to reasonable standards. In fact, infrastructure was not at all widespread. That is to say that even in the capital of [Qadisiyah], there were entire neighborhoods and entire quarters that had no access to the basics. They had no electricity and no water.[98]

Much of this had to do with the way in which the Saddam regime ruled Iraq. Ensher noted that local Iraqis told him the lack of infrastructure was "an indication of Saddam's desire to punish the south and to keep the Shia down."[99]

The US Army's ability to reconstruct Iraq was also severely hampered by the unexpected widespread instability following the overthrow of Saddam Hussein. Initially, the chief problem was looting. In the electrical, sewage, and oil sectors, sabotage and looting caused extensive damage to key electrical buildings and transmission lines, ruined the critical resources needed to activate water treatment facilities across the country, and wreaked over $900 million of havoc on Iraq's oil systems.[100] Reports in May of that year described thousands of government cars being stolen from unguarded police stations as well as fires erupting daily in public buildings.

Worse problems emerged in the summer of 2003 when a full-fledged Iraqi insurgency began to emerge. The single most debilitating assault on the Coalition's reconstruction effort was the suicide attack on the UN compound in Baghdad in August. After leaving Iraq before OIF began in March 2003, most aid agencies, including the United Nations (UN), World Health Organization (WHO), World Food Programme (WFP), and Oxfam International, returned to the country in early May 2003 to help with the reconstruction effort. While the violence escalated in the early summer of 2003, the UN and the other aid organizations remained committed to their work in Iraq. Yet, the truck bomb that exploded in the United Nations compound in Baghdad and killed the UN special representative in Iraq, Sergio Vieira de Mello, and 22 others deeply damaged the consensus about whether or not to continue the reconstruction effort in Iraq.

Though de Mello and the other UN employees murdered on that day were not the first UN members to be killed in Iraq, the vicious and purposeful assault on the United Nations signaled that the insurgency was becoming more organized and entirely willing to attack any institution or individual associated with the Coalition, even unarmed civilian aid workers. Soon after the bombing, aid organizations started pulling workers out of Iraq and significantly cutting back on staff. Even the International Committee of the Red Cross (ICRC), the humanitarian organization well known for never leaving the most dangerous conflict zones, departed Iraq. In response to the bombing, other countries in the international community decided to reconsider sending troops to aid reconstruction in Iraq because of the questionable security conditions.

This security concern on the part of aid organizations and Coalition countries intensified after a second bombing occurred outside the UN headquarters in Baghdad on 22 September 2003. This second attack prompted the UN and other relief organizations to withdraw more staff and continue to cut back in their work in Iraq. Other aid agencies followed suit including Doctors without Borders. With more and more relief organizations and experts leaving Iraq, the burden of reconstruction fell increasingly on the US military.

The deteriorating security situation affected aid agencies' ability to provide services and affected the activities of private security contractors working on reconstruction projects. In November 2003 the US Army Corps of Engineers and Kellogg, Brown, and Root (KBR) suspended oil industry work in northern Iraq after a KBR engineer was killed. Washington Group International, a large engineering firm, halted work just north of Baghdad after two subcontracted workers were killed.[101] By mid-December 2003, 18 contractors had been killed in Iraq, and contractor deaths from attacks temporarily halted at least 2 subsequent reconstruction projects.[102] These increased attacks on private security contractors forced companies opting to continue work amid these worsening conditions to redirect resources away from the critical reconstruction projects to the new demands of heightened security at worksites. As of 31 December 2004, a Government Accountability Office (GAO) report on rebuilding Iraq found that, of the 15 reconstruction contracts that were reviewed, 8 of them spent as much as 15 percent of contract costs on either obtaining security providers or purchasing needed equipment for security purposes or both. Many reconstruction projects had been canceled outright due to the poor security.[103]

Iraq's worsening security environment affected every aspect of the reconstruction effort. Earlier chapters of this study have already documented that the average number of attacks on US and Coalition forces during the summer of 2003 was around 500 per month. However, by May 2004 the number of attacks had reached approximately 2,000 per month.[104] Mirroring the increase in attacks were the increased incidences of sabotage to and vandalism of many parts of Iraq's infrastructure, as well as to reconstruction projects themselves in various stages of completion.[105] Additionally, insurgents launched aggressive attacks on Iraqi personnel and civilians; by 1 January 2004 over 700 soldiers from the Iraqi security forces had been killed as well as hundreds of Iraqi civilians.[106] By the spring of 2004 the Sunni insurgency and the Shia uprising had led to a marked increase in overall violence and the kidnapping and killing of non-Iraqis as well.[107] By the end of April 2004, two of the largest contractors in Iraq, Siemens and General Electric, had suspended their operations because of the lack of security.

Sabotage also damaged reconstruction efforts. Another symptom of the deteriorating security situation in Iraq, sabotage most often occurred when poor Iraqis sought means of supplementing meager incomes. Often, Iraqis sabotaged a facility or worksite with the intent of finding materials that could be sold on the black market. Copper became a highly prized product sought after by Iraqis for sale, and high-voltage transmission lines were an excellent source for extracting it. The sabotage against these critical transmission lines exacted massive amounts of damage to the country's electrical grid, while also stopping the progress of reconstruction endeavors across Iraq to repair the lines. Missing copper wire posed severe difficulties for US Army reconstruction efforts involved in refurbishing oil facilities as well; yet, a greater challenge resulted from increased insurgent strikes against pipelines in attempts to siphon oil for personal use or resale on the black market.[108] At the end of 2004, Iraq's oil production had not yet risen above pre-OIF levels and had actually decreased when compared with the end of 2003. Department of Defense and Department of State assessments attributed this decline in production primarily to insurgent assaults.[109]

By mid-2003 insurgent attempts to thwart the Coalition's overall campaign in Iraq had come to include direct attacks on reconstruction projects, contractors, workers, and supplies. These attacks against the Iraqi infrastructure rose steadily in 2003 and early 2004, with sharp spikes occurring between April 2004 and January 2005. In August 2004 insurgents launched nearly 3,000 attacks on various parts of Iraq's infrastructure.[110] Enemy groups assaulted trucks carrying supplies to job sites and at times killed or kidnapped truck drivers. They attacked contractors working on projects either at the worksites or during travel to and from the sites. In early 2005 these types of attacks temporarily prevented contractors from completing the 1st CAV-sponsored south Baghdad landfill project mentioned earlier in this chapter.[111] US Soldiers often grew extremely frustrated by the directed attacks against newly finished reconstruction projects. Major General John Batiste, Commander of the 1st ID, explained that often his Soldiers would have just completed the ribbon cutting ceremony celebrating the completion of a project "and the next day it would be blown up. . . . We got to the point

USAF Photo by SSgt James A. Williams

Figure 97. An Iraqi electrical worker repairs damaged power lines outside the northern city of Kirkuk, Iraq. Many of the lines were damaged or stolen by looters shortly after the beginning of OIF.

where we didn't even announce when we were going to be done because if we made a big deal out of it then that just drew the wrong kind of attention."[112]

In some places, the insurgents mounted a concerted campaign to deter all Coalition rebuilding plans. In 2004, for example, insurgent forces launched a coordinated effort to end all rebuilding in the town of Abu Ghraib, located about 10 miles west of Baghdad. The 2d Battalion, 14th Infantry (2-14 IN), a unit that operated in western Baghdad as part of the 2d Brigade, 10th Mountain Division, had begun work with contractors on a number of local projects designed to improve quality of life and economic prospects for the citizens of Abu Ghraib. In August 2004 leaders in 2-14 IN invested $72,000 in renovating a local business center; but only 3 days after the facility was opened, an insurgent group blew it up. Major John Allred, executive officer of 2-14 IN told an American journalist at the time, "Anything we're involved with, [the insurgents] want to see it fail. Anyone involved with us they want to kill."[113] Major Russ Harper, a CA officer attached to the battalion, added that since the unit arrived, $10 million in reconstruction projects had been completed in the Abu Ghraib area. However, insurgents had described five of the biggest projects through sabotage or by threatening and killing contractors. Harper stated, "Unfortunately, the terrorists have been pretty successful here."[114]

Corruption served as another type of obstacle hindering the Coalition's effort to reconstruct the country. In Iraq, corruption was widespread and complex. One particular type was endemic to authoritarian countries like Iraq under Saddam Hussein where the government becomes the integral part of the economic system.[115] These problems were worse in Baathist Iraq which had a cash system that led to an economy based on patronage networks rather than market imperatives. To get anything done in pre-war Iraq, one had to bribe the right people, usually those within Saddam's circle. During the decade of UN sanctions when everything was scarce, ordinary people were forced to resort to illegal economic activities, especially bribery of officials, just to survive. Not surprisingly, this legacy carried over to post-Saddam Iraq. Colonel Mike Murray, commander of the 3d BCT, 1st CAV, witnessed the role of corruption in Iraq, stating, "What we call corruption had become a way of life for the Iraqi society."[116] For many Iraqi officials and those trying to do business with them, the environment in post-Saddam Iraq did not change much. According to a report by the International Crisis Group (ICG) on the reconstruction environment in Iraq, Ministry officials in the Iraqi Governing Council and Interim Iraqi Government operated on a "business-as-usual basis, asking for presents and privileges. . . . It's the same culture as under Saddam. . . . Nothing has really changed."[117]

Two other types of corruption emerged in Iraq in this period. The first involved the sudden rise of political parties. Given the Coalition's emphasis on establishing new governance, 2003 became a critical time in terms of creating political parties and finding financial support for them. Without established procedures to finance political parties and political activities, corruption spread widely. One Iraqi quoted in the ICG report on reconstruction stated, "The political parties took everything they could get hold of."[118] The second was typical of a country transitioning from a command economy to one based on market forces. This transition period typically offers major opportunities for corruption because of the major influx of economic aid that usually accompanies it. That type of financial influx occurred in Iraq after the fall of the Saddam government. Some arrived in the form of Iraq's own oil revenues or recovered stockpiles of hidden money, others in the form of financial aid from the United States or other international donors.

After May 2003 corruption directly related to the aid flowing into the country flourished. Businessmen routinely complained about the need to resort to bribery when dealing with the

Iraqi Government.[119] The problems became so large that the CPA Inspector General assisted the Iraqi Governing Council in the creation of an Iraqi Inspector General that focused on corruption.[120] By September 2004 the Interim Iraqi Government took another step, forming the Iraqi Anti-Corruption Council (IACC).[121] In reports submitted in 2004, the CPA Inspector General and the US Special Inspector General for Iraqi Reconstruction (SIGIR) documented numerous cases of corruption of various types in Iraq and noted that US agencies such as the Defense Criminal Investigative Services (DCIS) were conducting investigations into these cases.[122]

The final obstacle—lack of continuity in personal relationships—affected not just reconstruction operations, but the entire Coalition military effort in Iraq. It quickly became clear that 1-year troop rotation cycles adversely affected the Army's abilities to make sustainable progress. Many Army leaders commented on the general momentum they had created by establishing the close personal relationships valued by Iraqis. When units rotated home or moved to new AORs, this momentum often ceased. For many Soldiers, fostering close and enduring personal relationships to meet professional goals was a new experience. Leaders in the US Army relied more on knowledge of duty positions than on establishing personal relationships with individuals. Colonel David Perkins, commander of the 2d BCT, 3d ID, noted that in Iraqi culture, personal ties were the foundation of social, political, and economic life. Perkins believed this to be one of the friction points between Iraqi society and the world of the American military: "If I go to a battalion and I want to talk to the sergeant major, I really don't care who it is. I want to talk to the sergeant major because I know what his job is and I know if I talk to him he will get the first sergeants in line."[123] That was not how the Iraqis operated. According to Perkins, "They know Joe; they want to talk to Joe. They really don't care what his job is; he is the guy with whom they have worked."[124]

In 2003 and 2004 US Army units served in Iraq on 1-year rotations and often changed AORs during those 12 months. But the Iraqi officials and Iraqi contractors involved in reconstruction projects largely remained in place. When a new Soldier transitioned into an AOR, he or she would begin building a relationship with the Iraqis from scratch. Perkins explained that this also occurred when working with American civilians. In terms of his relationship with the Coalition political authorities, Perkins stated, "We go by position. They don't. I would learn to work with Ms. X, and then she would rotate out. Someone else came in and you had to develop this personal relationship again. It was all based on personal relationships."[125]

Colonel Dan Allyn, commander of the 3d BCT, 3d ID, also found that personal relationships created transition problems with the Iraqi population. Allyn recalled, "Asking the Iraqi people to take people they had been working with for a couple of months and, just at the snap of a finger, transfer loyalties is really stretching the bounds for a people who, for a lot of good reasons, are suspect."[126] Colonel Joseph Anderson, commander of the 2d BCT, 101st ABN, concurred with Allyn. During his tour in northern Iraq, Anderson learned quickly how critical knowing the key Iraqi players was to achieve results: "If you [didn't] understand who you engage for what purpose on the political front, on the public works and ministry front, and on the security front, you [were] going to have problems."[127]

Because Soldiers understood the importance of both establishing and keeping personal relationships with their Iraqi counterparts, many of them ensured their transfer of authority with the next rotating unit included cordially meeting with key individuals. According to Colonel Michael Linnington, commander of the 3d Brigade, 101st ABN, he and his staff took great pains to ensure the units coming in to replace his Soldiers started off on the right foot with the local Iraqis:

> We introduced our replacements to the important tribal and religious leaders in our sector, showed them projects we were engaged [with], and warned of potential issues that might be raised after our departure. We spent an inordinate amount of time on transferring personal relationships, as this was the most critical to our success, and the area that was of the greatest concern to those we had befriended.[128]

Linnington added that as his Soldiers prepared to leave Iraq in early 2004, many of the Iraqis in his area began to dread their departure. Ultimately, despite their Iraqi counterparts emphatic entreaties to stay, the 3d Brigade departed, passing the responsibility for reconstruction projects and relationships to a new group of American Soldiers.[129]

Refocusing the Reconstruction Effort: July 2004–January 2005

In the summer of 2004 the Coalition began to modify its overall political and military campaign in Iraq. The most visible sign of this was the transition of sovereignty to the IIG, a change that was complemented by the establishment of the US Embassy and MNF-I as replacements for the CPA and CJTF-7, respectively. When the CPA dissolved in June 2004, the US Embassy took over authority for the American reconstruction efforts in Iraq and created the Iraqi Reconstruction Management Office (IRMO) to oversee these operations. In addition, the new US Ambassador to Iraq had supervision of the PCO, a DOD agency staffed by the US Army Corps of Engineers that focused on acquisition and management of US-funded reconstruction projects.[130] These two offices worked closely with the UN and other Coalition organizations, such as the United Kingdom's Department for International Development, to coordinate the Coalition initiatives to improve Iraq's infrastructure.

While the IRMO and PCO made use of Iraqi and foreign contractors as well as US governmental organizations such as the USAID, Coalition military forces remained heavily involved in reconstruction. For the senior leaders of US forces, this was largely by choice. When General George W. Casey Jr. took over as commander of MNF-I in July 2004, he ensured that reconstruction became a critical element in his economic line of operation. Moreover, as Casey began moving forward on his plan to reduce the insurgent and militia safe havens in preparation for the January 2005 elections, he found reconstruction activities a key role in stabilizing those cities targeted as safe havens. By rebuilding destroyed infrastructure and enabling local economic activity, reconstruction projects promised to win over and retain the support of the local populations in these former insurgent safe havens.

As mentioned earlier in this study, Casey viewed the Coalition's assault on the Mahdi Army forces in An Najaf in August 2004 as a model to be followed in the reduction of other safe havens.[131] One of the critical elements in the Coalition attack on An Najaf was the immediate introduction of reconstruction activities in the aftermath of the fighting that had done great damage to the city and its economic sectors. Major operations that followed the An Najaf assault adopted this template to include reconstruction operations as a significant part of the overall plan. The best examples of this emphasis on reconstruction were the commitment of military forces and other resources for the final phases of the operations against insurgents in Samarra and Fallujah in the fall of 2004. In the plans for both actions, military operations terminated with civil-military missions designed to restore essential services to the cities. Thus, reconstruction became an integral element in the overall operation rather than a follow-on action subject to the availability of scarce engineer and CA units and rebuilding funds.

Of course the inclusion of reconstruction efforts in larger operations in Iraq was not exactly new. In the summer of 2003, for example, units in the 4th ID had planned for CMO to follow their major combined arms operations in the Sunni Triangle. On a smaller scale, in the operation that killed Uday and Qusay Hussein, the leaders of the 101st ABN had immediately cleaned up and repaired the area of Mosul where the brothers had been found.[132] In the summer of 2004, however, it appears that US Army forces began to place fresh emphasis on reconstruction and viewed these operations as critical to achieving their tactical, operational, and strategic goals in Iraq. Perhaps the best example of this attitude was the approach taken by the units of the 1st CAV in 2004. As noted earlier, the division commander, Major General Chiarelli, had deployed to Iraq believing that restoring essential services to Iraqis was critical to winning the support of those Iraqis who were "sitting on the fence." While in Iraq, Chiarelli and his subordinate leaders had an "epiphany" about the additional power of reconstruction operations, concluding that when projects aimed at restoring essential services gave jobs to unemployed Iraqi men, attacks on Coalition soldiers and Iraqi security forces decreased.[133] Especially convincing to Chiarelli was the division's experience in Sadr City in the fall of 2004 when new funding allowed his units to employ young Shia men in infrastructure projects that directly benefited the neighborhood. According to the division, these operations reduced attacks on US forces in Sadr City from a high of 160 per week in early October 2004 to an average of less than 10 per week by early November.[134] For Chiarelli, this evidence supported the critical concept of using low-level reconstruction projects not only to show the Iraqis how committed the Coalition was to improving their lives, but also to defuse the threats that the insurgency and other violent actors posed to Coalition forces.

At about the same time that the Soldiers of the 1st CAV were confirming the salutary effects of facilitating low-level infrastructure projects in a place like Sadr City, the US Embassy was reassessing its overall reconstruction campaign and, for a variety of reasons, came to a conclusion similar to that reached by the 1st CAV. Since the spring of 2004, US officials involved in the reconstruction campaign had recognized the effectiveness of low-level projects funded by CERP. In April 2004 the Office of Management and Budget, an agency that assessed the CPA and conditions in Iraq for the US President, asserted in its quarterly report, "Some of the most important reconstruction efforts are occurring at local levels through the Commander's Emergency Response Program."[135] The same agency reiterated the strength of these types of unit-level efforts in its July 2004 report, stating, "The CERP continues to be a highly effective program enabling quick responses to urgent humanitarian relief and reconstruction requirements which has built trust and support for the United States at the grassroots level."[136]

This belief about the value of low-level projects combined with concerns about the sustained insurgency in Iraq forced the US Government to shift some of the resources in its reconstruction campaign away from the large-scale efforts designed to rebuild the oil sector and the electrical grid. Stuart Bowen, the Special Inspector General for Iraqi Reconstruction (SIGIR), documented this change, stating in his January 2005 report to Congress that the new policy began in September 2004 with a reallocation of $3.4 billion away from large-scale water and electrical projects.[137] Within 3 months, the US Embassy in Iraq had given a large portion of

Project Type	Number of Projects	Amount Disbursed ($M)
Education	5,484	$78.5
Electricity	937	$17.5
Health	1,862	$34.5
Other Public Services	5,944	$84.8
Police/Security	4,586	$124.2
Reconstruction	3,142	$54.7
Rule of Law/Government	1,678	$27.3
Social Programs	925	$10.8
Transportation	422	$11.7
Water/Sewer	2,770	$48.5
Other Projects	5,868	$35.9
Total	33,618	$528.4

US Dept of State, Quarterly Update to Congress, 2207 Report, October 2004

Figure 98. Status of CERP Projects and Funding (through 11 September 2004).

these funds to programs aimed at increasing Iraqi employment rates in the cities of An Najaf, Samarra, Sadr City, and Fallujah, many of which were run by US Army units like the 1st CAV. Bowen noted that this was a "significant change in US spending priorities" driven by the desire "to address the need for improved security, to improve Iraq's economic and political environment, and to create jobs for Iraqis."[138] In addition to the shift of these funds, in the fall of 2004 US Army leaders at the tactical level gained access to a new source of funds called the Commander's Humanitarian Relief and Reconstruction Projects (CHRRP). Modeled on the CERP and loaded initially with $86 million, the new program was designed to empower commanders to make major strides in key areas such as Baghdad, Samarra, Ramadi, and North Babil province.[139] More important was that by creating the CHRRP, US Government representatives were reinforcing the perceived success of the CERP and essentially recognizing the effectiveness of the Army's efforts to make a difference in Iraqi lives.

Conclusion

The Coalition's reconstruction efforts in Iraq in 2003 and 2004 were monumental in scale. Even though the US Government had conducted relatively limited planning and resource allocation for this effort before hostilities began in March 2003, in a short time the CPA initiated a major program that attempted to coordinate funds, agencies, contractors, and Iraqi needs. According to the January 2005 SIGIR report to Congress, by the end of 2004 the Coalition had overseen the influx of $60.3 billion into Iraq for humanitarian relief and reconstruction of the country.[140] This money was provided by Iraqi funds and other donor nations, with the

United States appropriating $24.1 billion.[141] In 2003 and early 2004 most of this money went into the reconstruction of the oil sector, the electrical grid, and other large-scale projects. But because of the emergence of a lethal insurgency and other systemic problems, these efforts had achieved relatively minimal gains, especially given the amount of resources invested. At the end of 2004, Iraq's oil production remained below the prewar level, and electricity flow, while increased across the country, was still sporadic in places because of the grid's age and its vulnerability to insurgent attacks. By early 2005 Coalition spending on reconstruction had already met the estimate given to Paul Bremer in the summer of 2003 by the World Bank, and the Coalition was still far from achieving its goals in Iraq.

Within this larger effort, the American Soldier played an important role. Although unprepared and largely untrained for reconstruction activities, the US Army in OIF assumed that mission as readily as it adopted the other key operations that comprised the new full spectrum campaign. As this chapter has shown, Soldiers became involved in reconstruction in numerous ways. They secured reconstruction sites and became project managers, coordinating funds with contractors and Iraqi officials. Their ingenuity was perhaps best demonstrated by the development of the CERP at CJTF-7 and its rapid employment at the unit level. It is at least arguable that their efforts to rebuild sewage plants, refurbish schools, and generally improve conditions in their AORs had a greater impact on the overall campaign than the larger projects managed by the CPA and IRMO. Certainly Soldiers saw the beneficial impact of employing Iraqis and showing the Iraqi population that the Coalition intended to make their lives better.

The Army's experience in OIF suggests strongly that US forces will be involved to some degree in reconstruction efforts in future campaigns. In accordance with the Army's doctrine for full spectrum operations, units and leaders will have to prepare to conduct basic reconstruction efforts. Still, beyond doctrinal imperatives, the participation of Soldiers in future reconstruction operations seems likely for one simple reason: the US military is the only agency with the logistical, administrative, organizational, and manpower resources required for reconstruction in situations where security had not been fully established. Thus, the Soldier becomes the major provider of the reconstruction effort in these types of conflicts. If OIF is a model, it probably best represents how well American Soldiers can adapt to missions of this type and how determined they can be in their attempts to improve the lives of others even in environments where resources, training, and guidance are less than adequate.

Notes

1. Colonel Gregg F. Martin, "Victory Sappers: V Corps/CJTF-7 Engineers in Operation Iraqi Freedom. Part 2: Since the Liberation. . . ." *Engineer,* October–December 2003, 6.

2. See Garland H. Williams, *Engineering Peace: The Military Role in Postconflict Reconstruction* (Washington, DC: United States Institute of Peace, 2005).

3. L. Paul Bremer III, *My Year in Iraq: The Struggle to Build a Future of Hope* (New York, NY: Simon & Schuster, 2006), 114.

4. Scott Wilson, "A Different Street Fight in Iraq; U.S. General Turns to Public Works in Battle for Hearts and Minds," *Washington Post,* 27 May 2004, A01.

5. Coalition Provisional Authority, *CPA Vision Statement*, 13 July 2003, 9.

6. *CPA Vision Statement*, 13 July 2003, 9.

7. Bremer, *My Year in Iraq*, 115.

8. Bremer, *My Year in Iraq*, 117.

9. Joint Publication (JP) 3-57, *Joint Doctrine for Civil-Military Operations* (Washington, DC, 8 February 2001), 1-1.

10. JP 3-57, viii.

11. Sandra I. Erwin, "As Demands for Nation-Building Troops Soar, Leaders Ponder Reorganization," *National Defense*, May 2005, Volume 89, Issue 618, 20; Ariana Eunjung Cha, "Soldiering On to Rebuild Iraq; Civil Affairs Takes on Tough Task," *Washington Post*, 12 February 2004, A13.

12. Chapter 2, "Civil-Military Operations," *CALL Newsletter 04-13: Operation Iraqi Freedom (OIF), CAAT II Initial Impressions Report (IIR)* (Fort Leavenworth, KS: Center for Army Lessons Learned, May 2004), 22.

13. Army Corps of Engineers, Gulf Region Division, http://www.grd.usace.army.mil/divisioninfo/GRDbrochure4_26.pdf.

14. Robert B. Flowers, "Army Engineers: Supporting the Warfighters and Reconstruction Efforts," *Army*, October 2004, Volume 54, Issue 10, 185.

15. Martin, "Victory Sappers," 4–5.

16. Martin, "Victory Sappers," 8.

17. Keith A. Dotts, "The 420th Engineer Brigade: Builders in Battle," *Engineer*, April/June 2005, Volume 35, Issue 2, 24.

18. Colonel Lou Marich, interview by Contemporary Operations Study Team, Fort Leavenworth, KS, 10 April 2006, 4.

19. Marich, interview, 10 April 2006, 4.

20. 555th Combat Engineer Group, *555 History Main Body*, 18 February 2004, 13–14.

21. *555 History Main Body*, 18 February 2004, 14.

22. Colonel Don C. Young, interview by Contemporary Operations Study Team, Fort Leavenworth, KS, 10 April 2006, 3.

23. Young, interview, 10 April 2006, 3.

24. Chapter 2, "Civil-Military Operations," *CALL Newsletter 04-13*.

25. Lieutenant General David H. Petraeus, "Learning Counterinsurgency: Observations from Soldiering in Iraq," *Military Review*, January–February 2006, 6.

26. Lieutenant General David H. Petraeus, interview by Contemporary Operations Study Team, Fort Leavenworth, KS, 17 February 2006, 7.

27. Petraeus, interview, 17 February 2006, 7.

28. Major Christopher Bentch, *CA Journal Entries by Major Christopher Bentch, 3BCT S-5*, 28 June 2003, entry 14.

29. Bentch, *CA Journal Entries, 3BCT S-5*, 3 June 2003, entry 9.

30.　Colonel Michael Toner, interview by Contemporary Operations Study Team, Fort Leavenworth, KS, 24 May 2006, 3; CJTF-7, *C8 Resource Management, Commander's Emergency Response Program (CERP)* Briefing, slide 3.

31.　Toner, interview, 24 May 2006, 2; CJTF-7, *C8 Resource Management, CERP* Briefing, slide 10.

32.　Toner, interview, 24 May 2006, 4.

33.　Toner, interview, 24 May 2006, 3; CJTF-7, C8 *Resource Management, CERP* Briefing, slide 13.

34.　Toner, interview, 24 May 2006, 3; CJTF-7, *C8 Resource Management, CERP* Briefing, slide 13; Draft Coalition Provisional Authority Memorandum, Subject Commander's Emergency Response Program (CERP), undated.

35.　Toner, interview, 24 May 2006, 4.

36.　Public Law 108-106, Section 1110—6 November 2003, 117 Statute 1215, http://www.export.gov/iraq/pdf/public_law_108-116.pdf.

37.　Brigadier General David Blackledge, 352d Civil Affairs Command, "Department of Defense Press Conference Transcript," *DefenseLink,* 14 January 2004, http://www.defenselink.mil/transcripts/2004/tr20040114-1144.html (accessed 9 October 2006).

38.　Toner, interview, 24 May 2006, 4–5; Philippe Le Billion, "Corruption, Reconstruction, and Oil Governance in Iraq," *Third World Quarterly,* 2005, Volume 26, No. 4–5, 696; and CJTF-7, *C8 Resource Management, CERP* Briefing, slide 15.

39.　"Reconstructing Iraq," International Crisis Group, Middle East, Report No. 30, 2 September 2004, 18.

40.　Bentch, *CA Journal Entries, 3BCT S-5*, 18 July 2003, entry 18.

41.　Office of the Inspector General, Coalition Provisional Authority, *Report to Congress,* 30 October 2004, 69.

42.　Major Robert S. Widmann, "The Commander's Emergency Response Program, Part II," in *OnPoint: A Counter-Terrorism Journal for Military and Law Enforcement Professionals,* http://www.uscav.com/uscavonpoint/Print.aspx?id=169 (accessed 27 April 2006).

43.　Lieutenant Colonel Brian McKiernan, interview by Contemporary Operations Study Team, Fort Leavenworth, KS, 29 April 2006, 10.

44.　Widmann, "The Commander's Emergency Response Program, Part II."

45.　George Packer, *The Assassins' Gate: America in Iraq* (New York: Farrar, Straus and Giroux, 2005), 241; "Reconstructing Iraq," ICG, Report No. 30, 18.

46.　Lieutenant Colonel George Sarabia, interview by Operational Leadership Experiences Project Team, Combat Studies Institute, Fort Leavenworth, KS, 23 September 2005, 19.

47.　Colonel Frederick Rudesheim, interview by Contemporary Operations Study Team, Fort Leavenworth, KS, 4 November 2005, 8.

48.　Petraeus, "Learning Counterinsurgency," 4.

49.　"3d Infantry Division Live Briefing from Iraq," *DefenseLink,* 15 May 2003, http://www.defenselink.mil/transcripts/2003/tr20030515-0184.html (accessed 5 September 2006).

50.　Staff Sergeant Marcia Triggs, "3ID Winning Hearts with TF Neighbor," *Army News Service,* 19 May 2003.

51.　Major Gerald H. Green, interview by Contemporary Operations Study Team, Fort Leavenworth, KS, 12 April 2006, 3.

52.　Colonel Russell Gold, interview by Contemporary Operations Study Team, Fort Leavenworth, KS, 25 January 2006, 10.

53.　Colonel Ralph Baker, interview by Contemporary Operations Study Team, Fort Leavenworth, KS, 1 November 2005, 14.

54.　Lieutenant General Raymond Odierno, interview by Contemporary Operations Study Team, Fort Leavenworth, KS, 14 December 2005, 9.

55. Odierno, interview, 14 December 2005, 9.

56. Rudesheim, interview, 4 November 2005, 8.

57. Petraeus, interview, 18 March 2006, 14; Brigadier General Frank Helmick, interview by Contemporary Operations Study Team, Fort Leavenworth, KS, 15 December 2006, 12.

58. Specialist Joshua Hutcheson, "Engineers Teach Construction Projects to Former Iraqi Soldiers," *Iraqi Destiny—101st Airborne Newsletter,* 25 September 2003, Volume 1, Issue 41.

59. Major General Charles Swannack, 82d Airborne Division Closure Report, Summation of Dollars Spent.

60. Swannack, 82d ABN Closure Report, Summation of Dollars Spent.

61. Major General Charles H. Swannack Jr., interview by Contemporary Operations Study Team, Fort Leavenworth, KS, 6 September 2006, 10.

62. Swannack, interview, 6 September 2006, 9.

63. Sergeant First Class Gary L. Qualls Jr., "Guardsmen Give Iraqi Fishermen Means to 'Net' Long Forbidden Treasure," *Desert Rifles,* Issue 2, 16 May 2003.

64. Colonel Stephen Lanza, interview by Contemporary Operations Study Team, Fort Leavenworth, KS, 2 November 2005, 11.

65. Quoted in Specialist Erik LeDrew, "Artillery Troops Plant Seeds of Reconstruction in Iraq," *DefenseLink,* October 2004, http://www.defendamerica.mil/articles/oct2004/a101504d.html (accessed 12 September 2006).

66. Major General Peter Chiarelli and Major Patrick R. Michaelis, "Winning the Peace: The Requirement for Full-Spectrum Operations," *Military Review,* July–August 2005, 10.

67. Chiarelli and Michaelis, 10.

68. Patrecia Slayden Hollis, "1st Cav in Baghdad: Counterinsurgency EBO in Dense Urban Terrain. Interview with Major General Peter W. Chiarelli," *Field Artillery,* September–October 2005, 5.

69. Office of the Special Inspector General for Iraqi Reconstruction, *Baghdad Municipal Solid Waste Landfill*, SIGIR PA-06-067, 19 October 2006, 9–10, http://www.sigir.mil/reports/pdf/assessments/PA-06-067_Baghdad_Landfill.pdf (accessed 8 December 2007).

70. Chiarelli and Michaelis, 11.

71. Chiarelli and Michaelis, 12.

72. Major General John Batiste, interview by Contemporary Operations Study Team, Fort Leavenworth, KS, 20 April 2006, 9.

73. Master Sergeant Luis Jackson Jr., interview by Contemporary Operations Study Team, Fort Leavenworth, KS, 25 January 2006, 7.

74. Brigadier General Dana Pittard, interview by Contemporary Operations Study Team, Fort Leavenworth, KS, 22 February 2006, 18.

75. Specialist Ismail Turay Jr., "1st Infantry Division Boosts Power Plants' Output, Local Economy," *Danger Forward,* Volume 1, Issue 7, October 2004.

76. First Sergeant Richard Gano Jr., interview by Contemporary Operations Study Team, Fort Leavenworth, KS, 26 January 2006, 6.

77. Major Webster M. Wright III, "Soldiers Blanket Iraqis in Operation Windy City," *DefenseLink,* November 2004, http://www.defenselink.mil/news/Nov2004/n11022004_2004110206.html (accessed October 2006).

78. These statistics can be found in MNC-I/MNF-I History Office, *History of CJTF-7*, Executive Summary, 5.

79. Lieutenant Colonel Gregory Reilly, e-mail interview by Contemporary Operations Study Team, Fort Leavenworth, KS, 23 June 2006; Major Chris Dantoin, e-mail interview by Contemporary Operations Study Team, Fort Leavenworth, KS, 28 April 2006; 432d Civil Affairs Battalion, *For CG, Iraq's State Company For Phosphate (SCP) Al Qa'im, Iraq*, 25 January 2004, 1.

80. Reilly, e-mail interview, 23 June 2006.

81. 432d CA Battalion, *For CG, Iraq's State Company For Phosphate (SCP), Al Qa'im,* 30 January 2004, bullet comments, 1.

82. Reilly, e-mail interview, 23 June 2006.

83. Dantoin, e-mail interview, 28 April 2006.

84. Reilly, e-mail interview, 23 June 2006; Dantoin, e-mail interview, 28 April 2006.

85. 432d Civil Affairs Battalion, *SCP Rail Projection,* undated document.

86. Reilly, e-mail interview, 23 June 2006; Dantoin, e-mail interview, 28 April 2006.

87. Dantoin, e-mail interview, 28 April 2006.

88. Dantoin, e-mail interview, 28 April 2006.

89. Dantoin, e-mail interview, 28 April 2006.

90. 3d Armored Cavalry Regiment, *SCP Progress/Update Brief,* 28 February 2004, Rifles Base, slide 8.

91. Major Kris Arnold, interview by Operational Leadership Experiences Project Team, Combat Studies Institute, Fort Leavenworth, KS, 1 April 2005, 11–12.

92. Thomas F. Armistead et al., "Reviewing Markets: Oil, Water and More in Practically Every Sector, the Lack of Security Hampers Reconstruction Efforts," *ENR,* 9 June 2003, Volume 250, Issue 22.

93. Stuart W. Bowen Jr., Office of the Coalition Provisional Authority Inspector General, *Report to Congress*, 30 March 2004, 5.

94. Sergeant Major Kevin Gainey, interview by Contemporary Operations Study Team, Fort Hood, TX, 9 December 2005.

95. Chiarelli and Michaelis, 11. Chiarelli and Michaelis also explain that, due to overpopulation, rapid urban growth, and intentional neglect by Saddam Hussein, many parts of Baghdad proper never had existing basic services.

96. Lieutenant Colonel Wes Gillman, interview by Contemporary Operations Study Team, Washington, DC, 7 December 2005.

97. Neil King Jr., "Power Struggle: Race to Get Lights on in Iraq Shows Perils of Reconstruction," *Wall Street Journal* (Eastern Edition), 2 April 2001, A1.

98. Henry Ensher, interview by Contemporary Operations Study Team, Washington, DC, 26 January 2006.

99. Ensher, interview, 26 January 2006.

100. Joseph A. Christoff, Director, International Trade Division of the Government Accountability Office (GAO), testimony before the Senate Committee on Foreign Relations, "Rebuilding Iraq: Enhancing Security, Measuring Program Results, and Maintaining Infrastructure Are Necessary to Make Significant and Sustainable Progress," 18 October 2005, 8.

101. Thomas F. Armistead, Glen Carey, and Gary Tulacz, "Contractor Fatalities Prompt Suspension of Work in Iraq," *ENR,* 8 December 2003, Volume 251, Issue 23, 18.

102. Armistead, Carey, and Tulacz, 18.

103. Christoff, testimony before the Senate Committee on Foreign Relations, 14–15.

104. United States Government Accountability Office, GAO Report GAO-05-43T, *Rebuilding Iraq: Preliminary Observations on Challenges in Transferring Security Responsibilities to Iraqi Military and Police*, 14 March 2005, 10.

105. Steven M. Kosiak, "Iraq Reconstruction: Without Additional Funding, Progress Likely to Fall Short, Undermining War Effort," Center for Strategic and Budgetary Assessments, 27 February 2006, 3.

106. State Department, Section 2207: Report on Iraq Relief and Reconstruction, Executive Summary, October 2004, 14.

107. Between April 2003 and January 2005, 157 civilian contractors were killed in Iraq according to http://icasualties.org/oif/Civ.aspx; Michael E. O'Hanlon and Adriana Lins de Albuquerque, "Iraq Index:

Tracking Variables of Reconstruction & Security in Post-Saddam Iraq, Updated April 18, 2005," The Brookings Institution, www.brookings.edu/iraqindex (accessed 18 December 2006).

108. Armistead et al., 18.

109. US Special Inspector General for Iraqi Reconstruction, *Quarterly Report and Semiannual Report to Congress*, 30 January 2005, 59.

110. Christoff, testimony before the Senate Committee on Foreign Relations, figure 2, 10.

111. Office of the Special Inspector General for Iraqi Reconstruction, *Baghdad Municipal Solid Waste Landfill*, SIGIR PA-06-067, 19 October 2006, 13, http://www.sigir.mil/reports/pdf/assessments/PA-06-067_Baghdad_Landfill.pdf. (accessed 8 December 2007).

112. Major General (Retired) John Batiste, interview by Contemporary Operations Study Team, Rochester, NY, 20 April 2006, 12.

113. Josh White, "Town Reflect Rising Sabotage in Iraq," *The Washington Post*, 9 December 2004, A01.

114. White, A01.

115. Le Billion, 688–689.

116. Colonel Mike Murray, interview by Contemporary Operations Study Team, Fort Leavenworth, KS, 8 December 2005, 12.

117. "Reconstructing Iraq," ICG, Report No. 30, 22.

118. "Reconstructing Iraq," ICG, Report No. 30, 20.

119. "Reconstructing Iraq," ICG, Report No. 30, 20.

120. SIGIR, *Quarterly Report and Semiannual Report to Congress*, 30 July 2004, 45.

121. SIGIR, *Quarterly Report and Semiannual Report to Congress*, 30 July 2004, 30 October 2004, 50.

122. See, for example, CPA Inspector General, *First Quarterly Report to Congress*, 30 March 2004, 44.

123. Brigadier General David Perkins, interview by Contemporary Operations Study Team, Fort Leavenworth, KS, 25 January 2006, 8–9.

124. Perkins, interview, 25 January 2006, 8–9.

125. Perkins, interview, 25 January 2006, 8–9.

126. Colonel Daniel Allyn, interview by Contemporary Operations Study Team, Fort Leavenworth, KS, 4 November 2005, 11.

127. Colonel Joseph Anderson, interview by Contemporary Operations Study Team, Fort Leavenworth, KS, 4 November 2005, 13–14.

128. Colonel Michael Linnington, interview by Contemporary Operations Study Team, Fort Leavenworth, KS, 3 November 2005, 15.

129. Linnington, interview, 3 November 2005, 15.

130. GAO Report GAO-05-431T, 4.

131. General George W. Casey Jr., interview by Contemporary Operations Study Team, Fort Leavenworth, KS, 27 November 2007, 5–6.

132. Petraeus, interview, 18 March 2006, 3.

133. Chiarelli and Michaelis, 10.

134. Chiarelli and Michaelis, 12.

135. Executive Office of the President, Office of Management and Budget, *Section 2207, Second Quarterly Report*, 5 April 2004, 11, http://www.whitehouse.gov/omb/legislative/index.html (accessed 18 January 2008).

136. Executive Office of the President, Office of Management and Budget, *Section 2207, Third Quarterly Report*, 2 July 2004, 11–12, http://www.whitehouse.gov/omb/legislative/index.html (accessed 18 January 2008).

137. SIGIR, *Quarterly Report and Semiannual Report to Congress*, 30 January 2005, 1.

138. SIGIR, *Quarterly Report and Semiannual Report to Congress*, 30 January 2005, 1

139. Paul V. Kelly, Executive Office of the President, Office of Management and Budget, *Section 2207, Quarterly Report*, Executive Summary, 5 October 2004, http://www.state.gov/s/d/rm/rls/2207/oct2004/html/ (accessed 18 January 2008).

140. SIGIR, *Quarterly Report and Semiannual Report to Congress*, 30 January 2005, 75.

141. SIGIR, *Quarterly Report and Semiannual Report to Congress*, 30 January 2005, 75.

Chapter 10

A Country United, Stable, and Free: US Army Governance Operations in Iraq

On 9 April 2003 a US Army Special Forces (SF) company belonging to the 5th Special Forces Group entered Ar Rutbah, a city near the Iraqi border with Syria and Jordan. As part of Combined Joint Special Operations Task Force–West (CJSOTF-West), these Soldiers had been searching for Saddam's Scud missiles in the western desert of Iraq. However, once they occupied Ar Rutbah, the SF teams adopted a very different mission: the establishment of a new system of governance for the city.[1] Without any guidance, preparation, or special resources, the Soldiers created a new political structure for Ar Rutbah that was responsive to the citizens of the community. In the process of overturning the old governing regime, the SF Soldiers recruited a new police force, invented their own de-Baathification process that included a pledge of allegiance to the new Iraq, made arrangements for mayoral elections, facilitated the creation of a city council, and ensured that tribal and religious leaders in the city were integrated into the new structure. When the SF teams left just 2 weeks later, the city was headed in a new political direction.

The experience of this SF company is emblematic of a particularly difficult challenge faced by many Soldiers in Iraq in 2003 and 2004. As US Army units moved into their areas of responsibility (AORs) in late spring 2003, they found cities, towns, and villages with little or no governing structure prepared to assume authority after the fall of the Saddam regime. Some of the Soldiers in Iraq that spring had deployed on contingency and peacekeeping missions to Haiti, Somalia, and the Balkans, and did have some experience in working with local governmental bodies and mediating with various political factions. Even so, like the SF Soldiers in Ar Rutbah, none of these Soldiers had any specific guidance on what the Coalition's governance objectives were and how they might help the Iraqis remake their institutions of government. Additionally, few, if any, were prepared to deal with the unique and complex cultural characteristics that shaped the Iraqi political environment. Major James Gavrilis, the commander of the SF company that worked in Ar Rutbah, recalled the improvisational nature of this task, stating, "Because we didn't receive any guidance for governance or reconstruction, and certainly not for spreading democracy, I had to make up everything as I went, based on the situation on the ground and what I remembered from my Special Forces training and a handful of political science classes."[2]

Despite its lack of preparation for the governance mission, by the middle of 2003 the US Army was heavily involved in facilitating political change at many levels in Iraq. Because developing local and regional institutions of government directly supported President George W. Bush's stated goal of fostering an Iraq that was "united, stable, and free," senior military leaders viewed governance operations as a critical part of the new full spectrum campaign.[3] After May 2003 the Combined Joint Task Force–7 (CJTF-7) and the Coalition Provisional Authority (CPA) focused a great deal of their energy on the creation of a representative government at the national level. Still, both the political and military headquarters of the Coalition believed the new national government would become more robust if it was undergirded by new political institutions at the regional and local levels. This belief and guidance from the CPA drove Lieutenant General Ricardo Sanchez in the summer of 2003 to adopt governance as one of the five lines of operation that directed CJTF-7's campaign in Iraq.[4] With this decision, Sanchez mandated that his forces at the tactical level become agents of political change. Fostering the growth of a new political system was so critical to the Coalition that even after Iraq's transition to full sovereignty in June 2004, General George W. Casey Jr., commander of Multi-National Force–Iraq (MNI-F), retained governance as one of the four lines of operation in the campaign plan he and his staff created.

In the 18 months that followed the toppling of the Saddam regime, Iraqis experienced dizzying political change. While the United States and its Coalition partners initially exerted political power through the CPA, in July 2003 Mr. L. Paul Bremer formed a 25-member Iraqi Governing Council (IGC) to begin setting the foundation for transition of sovereignty to the Iraqis. The CPA worked though the IGC and other Iraqi individuals and institutions in the fall of 2003 and winter of 2004 to gain approval of the interim constitution and the Transitional Administrative Law (TAL), which authorized the election of a Transitional National Assembly (TNA). Finally, in June 2004, the CPA restored political sovereignty to the Iraqis who established a new Interim Iraqi Government (IIG) led by Prime Minister Ayad Allawi. On 30 January 2005 more than 8 million Iraqi citizens exercised their new political rights by defying insurgent threats and going to the polls to elect representatives to the 275-member TNA.

At lower levels, the change in how Iraqi communities governed themselves was equally dramatic. This chapter examines the role of US Army units in facilitating this shift by first looking at the larger political environment in which Soldiers found themselves working and then discussing the broad variety of operations and programs devised to establish good governance in Iraq. The challenge went beyond the creation of local bodies of self-government such as school boards, neighborhood advisory councils (NACs), and district advisory councils (DACs). Soldiers also had to transform themselves into negotiators and mentors, working with multiple religious, ethnic, and tribal groups to help defuse local tensions and impart the fundamental principles of a cooperative, representative government. US Army units involved in the governance mission were not the sole agents of political change. Indeed, Soldiers worked with the CPA, the US Department of State, and other agencies in this mission. To a significant extent, however, in many of Iraq's smaller cities and towns the US Army was the only institution that represented the Coalition. Soldiers thus served on the leading edge of this political front, attempting to bring the ideals and practices of their own democratic system to a country that had for decades known little besides dictatorial rule.

A New Direction for Iraq

When US forces arrived in Iraq in 2003, Saddam Hussein had ruled Iraq for 24 years. As leader of the Iraqi Baath Party, Saddam governed as the head of an organization that proclaimed itself the political expression of the Iraqi people. Like most totalitarian regimes, however, Saddam and his small cohort of trusted advisors sought control of all aspects of political, social, and economic activity within the state. He controlled the wealth of Iraq and attempted to secure his paramount position in the political system by erecting thousands of portraits and statues of himself throughout the physical landscape of the country.[5] This cult of personality, combined with the use of state and Baath Party security organizations to suppress with ruthless brutality all those who opposed him, created a system which suppressed the collective political voice of the Iraqi population. Saddam's totalitarian rule eroded the civic infrastructure of Iraq as much as it damaged the physical infrastructure of the country.

When Coalition forces began the enormous project of nation-building and creating a new functioning representative state in Iraq, they encountered a society that was completely unfamiliar with democracy or civil society. One study of Iraq described the effects of living under totalitarian rule and noted the difficulties these societies faced in transitioning to a different political order:

> Survival in a totalitarian society is dependent on slavish devotion to those with power and on passivity when neither personal power nor the power of a patron provides protection. Fear is pervasive and paralyzing. Fairness and justice have little meaning, and individuals have difficulty distinguishing truth from propaganda or rumor because the regime controls information. Moving from the psychology of totalitarianism to the psychology of an open society, with its foundation in political initiative, consensus building, and compromise, is a long and torturous journey.[6]

While most Iraqi citizens likely desired a more representative political system, years of totalitarian rule left them unprepared for this type of system. American Soldiers found that rather than jumping into the renewal of their government, Iraqi citizens often waited for permission to act. Colonel Michael Tucker, commander of 1st Brigade Combat Team (BCT), 1st Armored Division (1st AD), explained, "We had professional and educated people, but they had difficulty understanding that the people had a voice at all. This whole concept of democracy was foreign to [the Iraqis], so it took a while."[7]

To lead the Iraqi people into a new political future, Secretary of Defense Donald Rumsfeld created the Office of Reconstruction and Humanitarian Assistance (ORHA) and made Lieutenant General (Retired) Jay Garner its head. After a brief 2 months in the Pentagon forming his team, Garner deployed his organization to Kuwait on 16 March 2003, just 3 days before the Coalition invaded Iraq.[8] ORHA conducted the Coalition's first attempts at instituting new governance in Iraq when Garner and his team directed a forum on democracy in An Nasiriyah on 14 April with 300 Iraqis.[9] The ORHA chief also began discussions with a variety of political figures—Kurds, expatriates such as Ahmed Chalabi, Sunni and Shia politicians, and members of the Baathist ministries—as an initial step in the process of choosing a transitional government that would put an Iraqi face on the Coalition's project in the country.

Soon after Garner began these deliberations, however, the Bush administration made a decision that took the political future of Iraq in a different direction. The 11 May 2003 appointment of Ambassador Bremer as Presidential Envoy to Iraq brought a more deliberate and, in some ways, radical approach to political change in the newly liberated country. One of Bremer's first priorities was the de-Baathification of Iraqi society. As described in earlier chapters, he issued CPA Order No. 1 on 16 May 2003, mandating that the four highest levels of the Baath Party be removed from their positions and prohibited from serving in the government in the future. The order also stipulated that the Coalition would investigate the many Iraqis who had held a position in the top three layers of management in every national government ministry, affiliated corporations, and other government institutions, such as university or health care systems to determine whether they had been full members of the Baath Party. If the investigations found that they were indeed full members, the Coalition would remove these bureaucrats and officials from their positions within the government.[10] This sanction prevented many individuals who had been instrumental in the workings of the old Baathist regime from being considered as the Coalition began establishing the new government.

On the same day that he proclaimed CPA Order No. 1, Bremer made an equally important decision. The CPA chief announced that the formation of a sovereign Iraqi interim government had been postponed, and that the CPA would fill this vacuum by creating an IGC as an advisory body to help the CPA govern Iraq. This decision surprised most Iraqis and angered many. Almost immediately, Grand Ayatollah Ali al-Sistani, the most important Shia leader in Iraq, called for elections to be held to form an Iraqi Government. Bremer ignored Ayatollah al-Sistani's appeals, and al-Sistani responded on 30 June with a *fatwa*—a legal announcement by an authority on Islamic law arguing that the IGC Bremer was establishing was illegitimate. As such, the plan, according to al-Sistani, was "unacceptable from the outset."[11]

Despite these threats, Bremer created the IGC on 13 July 2003. On its surface, the IGC was representative of the Iraqi population. The Council included 25 prominent Iraqis from the country's various factions and ethnic groups. The Shias held a slim majority of 13 seats, with 5 Kurds, 5 Arab Sunnis, 1 Assyrian Christian, and 1 Turkoman also serving on the council. Although the council ostensibly advised Bremer, its main role was to draft a constitution to help speed along the process of Iraqi rule and to pave the way for a democratically elected government. The establishment of the IGC was the CPA's first move toward meeting the mandate in UN Resolution 1483 for "a process leading to an internationally recognized, representative government" in Iraq. [12]

Under intense pressure from all sides to return political sovereignty to the Iraqis as soon as possible, in the fall of 2003 Bremer brokered the November 15th agreement, which imposed a number of deadlines on the IGC. By 28 February 2004 the IGC formulated a rough draft of the law that was to govern Iraq until a more formal government and constitutional process could be agreed on. This temporary governing document was called the TAL. The goal of the agreement was to return sovereignty to Iraq by 30 June 2004, and the timeline called for a multistage process with the initial stage of local caucuses held throughout Iraq.[13] These caucuses would eventually choose district, county, and provincial officials (and the province governor). Ultimately, Iraqis would elect a national assembly and then that body would elect the members who would form the transitional national government, which would take power from the CPA on 30 June 2004.[14] Bremer and the IGC would later amend the political processes established in the TAL. Nonetheless, the CPA chief saw the process as paramount: "I felt very strongly, given Iraq's recent history, it was important to get them a decent constitution to define the government structure, define what the rights were, define who an Iraqi citizen was, the very basic stuff, and I thought we needed to do that before we left. So we worked with them. It took three months of negotiations to get this TAL."[15] Despite the long and difficult process, Bremer thought the TAL was critical: "I think it is the most important legacy of the Coalition. It defined the structure of the government. It defined the political path to the elections [in 2005]."[16]

Good Governance: Another New Mission

While the CPA initiated the establishment of a representative government in Iraq at the national level, almost immediately after decisive combat ended Coalition soldiers on the ground began dealing with the realities of their new function as nation-builders. After the fall of Baghdad, Major General David Petraeus, commander of the 101st Airborne Division (101st

ABN), moved north to his AOR in Ninevah province. He described a general assumption that existed among the leaders of the US Army as they considered what would happen next: "Returning Iraqi leaders and the organization called ORHA and other US and other non-US governmental agencies would materialize and take the effort forward using those Iraqi elements that remained at their posts and continued to keep their ministries and their organizations going."[17] When it became clear those expectations would not come to fruition, US Soldiers faced the heavy responsibility of rebuilding Iraq, literally from the ground up, in the immediate postwar aftermath. This duty included implementing new governance on the provincial and local levels throughout Iraq.

The US Army was not the only organization introducing political change at the local level. The CPA eventually created regional offices that helped coordinate the overall reconstruction effort. As a part of that campaign, the CPA employed the US Agency for International Development (USAID) to administer civic education programs that taught democratic principles and organizing methods to Iraqi nongovernment organizations (NGOs).[18] The CPA also collaborated with CJTF-7 and its tactical units to establish and enable local government. However, Bremer's headquarters had a relatively limited pool of personnel and funds to assist local governance initiatives.[19] For this reason, Soldiers bore the heaviest portion of this effort in its early stages.

While not prepared to serve as political organizers, many units like the 101st ABN quickly organized their efforts to assist the Iraqis in creating a new system of governance. This emphasis began at the top of the command structure. During a May 2003 commanders conference in Baghdad, the V Corps staff presented a briefing that outlined the three key objectives the corps commander hoped to attain: create a secure environment, support economic development, and facilitate the establishment of local government.[20] The brief then further defined the last objective as the creation of "functional, moderate, and inclusive local governments" and listed a number of key governance tasks, including the establishment of bureaucracies, identification of potential leaders, the holding of meetings, and re-opening of schools.

Once V Corps became CJTF-7 in June 2003, the new Coalition military headquarters began to organize operations along five major lines, one of which was governance.[21] For much of the next year, Lieutenant General Sanchez would be involved on a daily basis with the CPA and the IGC in helping Iraq attain the goals of sovereignty and representative government. For a number of US Army divisions, this emphasis on governance led to its inclusion as a line of operation in their own campaign plans. The 4th Infantry Division (4th ID), for example, made governance one of the four pillars that structured their overall plan of operations.[22] That campaign plan defined operations within this pillar as working with all Iraqi leaders and building local councils to assist Iraq gain sovereignty. The 82d Airborne Division (82d ABN) likewise identified one of their four critical capabilities as governance, describing its requirements as assisting with rule of law, elections, the judicial system, and the de-Baathification process.[23] When units such as the 1st Cavalry Division (1st CAV) began operations as part of the OIF II rotation in early 2004, they inherited governance as a line of operation from the units they relieved.

Although governance became a key line of operation, very few units were prepared to conduct "governance operations" or had any thorough understanding initially of what these operations entailed. The exceptions were the Army's Civil Affairs (CA) battalions, each of which had governance teams. The governance mission appeared to be a very good fit for the capabilities of those teams. However, as the previous chapter has established, the Coalition had not created any coherent plan for civil-military operations (CMO) that might have provided guidance, priorities, and processes for the CA teams to follow in making changes to the system of governance in Iraq. Moreover, CA teams quickly became enmeshed in providing guidance and coordination for the physical reconstruction of Iraq. Thus, in many Army units it became apparent that, like the reconstruction mission, assisting the Iraqi shift to new systems of governance was a mission Soldiers of all types would have to adopt.

Growing Iraqi Grassroots: The US Army and Governance at the Local Level

Without a CMO plan, both the CA units and the tactical units they supported deployed to their AORs in late April and May 2003 without any understanding of how to deal with the Baathist governing institutions and what steps to take to reestablish the rule of law and proper administration. Like Major Gavrilis in Ar Rutbah, most commanders tried to make the right decisions based on what resources they had available and what courses of action seemed the most reasonable. Rarely did this mean that US Army units immediately established working democracies at the local level. Normally, the challenge was to simply reestablish Iraqi authority so that basic services and stability could be restored. In most cases, unit leaders removed Baathist bureaucrats, selected mayors and other officials to create a new administration, and organized and mentored advisory councils. In some AORs, Soldiers also facilitated local and provincial elections as a means of giving legitimacy to the new governing institutions.

The governance operations of the 2d Squadron, 3d Armored Cavalry Regiment (ACR) in May 2003 demonstrate some of the obstacles faced by Army units in the early stage of the new campaign. V Corps tasked the squadron to conduct operations in eastern Al Anbar province, and the unit focused much of its effort on Fallujah, a city of 250,000 people most of whom were Sunni Arabs. During Saddam's tenure in power, Fallujah had become known as a bastion of Baathist loyalists and had close ties to the regime in Baghdad. The cavalry squadron took authority of the city in early May from the 2d Brigade, 82d ABN whose Soldiers just days before the transition had used lethal fire in response to what they believed was enemy gunfire directed at them during a large demonstration in which a number of Iraqis were killed and wounded.

Spread thin across the AOR and hoping to avoid positioning a large concentration of American forces in Fallujah, the commander of 2d Squadron hoped to place the Iraqis back in control of the city. He asked the attached CA team to assist the Iraqis in reinstating civil administration "to pre-war state or better."[24] Ultimately, the squadron leadership sought to create a civil administration that provided those services independent of Coalition military forces.[25] To accomplish this, the squadron leadership and the CA team planned to remove Baathist officials in Fallujah, seat a new mayor in the city, foster support for the new civil administration among the sheiks and clerics, and eventually hold elections.[26] When they transitioned control of Fallujah to the 2d Brigade of the 3d ID in late May—only 30 days after taking responsibility for the city—the squadron had only managed to hire a mayor, identify a small number of other individuals for service in the new administration, and place these men on the Coalition payroll. Local government in the eastern part of Al Anbar province would grow throughout 2003, but the constant realignment of military units in the province further hindered efforts to establish good working relationships between military leaders and local or regional Iraqi leaders.

PROCLAMATION

I, COLONEL David A. Teeples, Commander of local Coalition Forces, do hereby proclaim the following:

That I endorse ABDUL KARIM BRIJAS ALRAWI as the Governor of this community known as Al Anbar province, and that under his leadership, he may decree that services, businesses, and administrative functions in this province may open and conduct business. I endorse all measures he takes to facilitate the operation of the hospitals, banks and financial institutions, public works, public and private businesses, and government administration. The Governor may remove any person from a position of authority if he determines that they are ineffective or interfering with the good order of services within the Al Anbar province. Those persons will be replaced by means of elections and appointments that the Governor will convene.

تصريح رسمي

انا، عقيد دافيد ا. تيبلس، قائد قوات الئتلاف المحلي، اصرح ان:

أيد عبد الكريم برجس الراوي كالحاكم لمحافظة الانبار وتحت قيادته قد يصدر انخدمات وأعمال تجارية ودكاكين وعملات إدارية في هذه المحاظة قد يفتح ويدبر عمليات تجارية. ايد كل اجراءيت التي قد يفعل لسهل عمليات في المستفيات والبنوك وموءسسات المالية والمرافق العامة و تجارة في قطع العام وقطع الخاص وفي إدارات الحكومية. اسمح بالمحاكم ليسخرج اي شخص من وظيفته إذا يقرر ان هذا الشخس يكون غير جيد لهذه الوظيفة وسوف يعيّنه بواسطة انتخابات او تعيين تحت إشراف الحاقم.

دافيد ا. تيبلس

عقيد، جيش امريكي

قائد قوات الئتلاف لمنطقة جدارية العنار

هذه التصريح عوض عن كل تصاريح من قبل عن هذا الموضوع.

Copy ___ of ___   Order Number 0007

Figure 99. 3d ACR commander's official endorsement of provincial governor, 2003.

Eventually, the 3d ACR and the 82d ABN were successful in establishing local and provincial bodies of government in Al Anbar.

Perhaps the largest obstacle to making good decisions about governance was a fundamental lack of knowledge of the Baathist system of government, especially at the provincial and local levels. While the Baathist Party exerted power through its own officials down to the municipal and county (*nahiah*) levels, Iraqi governance also included unofficial political authorities. In many parts of Iraq, tribal leaders held power and at times would exert their authority over the officials appointed by US units.[27] In Iraqi villages, the local headman, often referred to as the *mukhtar* or *shareef*, maintained detailed records about everyone in their village and were often revered for their services to the community. While not Baathist officials, many had been corrupted under the Baathist regime, appointed to be Saddam's "eyes and ears" at the local level.[28] Despite their unofficial status, these men held authority and became critical to the governance effort. One *mukhtar* told a CA Soldier that Coalition forces would not be successful in Iraq without the support of village officials like him. Yet, the question about their loyalties and commitment to the Coalition project in Iraq remained unanswered.

If the structure of the Baathist state was difficult to detect, the processes by which it operated were no less opaque to the recently arrived Soldiers. In fact, by the 1990s cronyism and

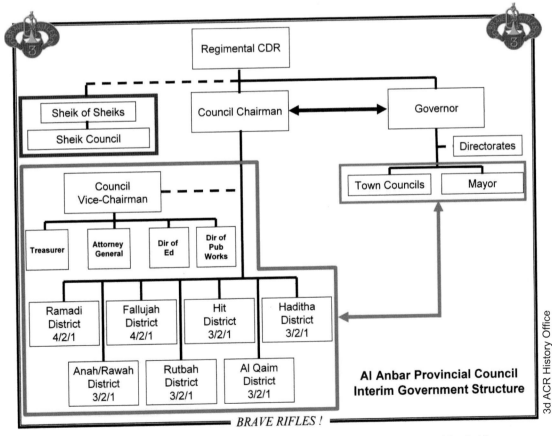

Figure 100. Al Anbar province interim provisional council structure developed by Soldiers of 3d ACR, 2003.

corruption had created a complex and byzantine system of powerful organizations and individuals who governed capriciously. Corruption based on bribes and power had worked its way into the state structure and worsened after 1991 because of the former regime's decision to freeze salaries at low levels to deal with UN sanctions. In this environment, the most powerful positions and best salaries went to those in the Baathist Party who were loyal to the regime and

Figure 101. Al Anbar province meeting announcement.

not to the most efficient administrators. This problem confronted Major Larry Shea, a CA officer involved in creating local councils, in 2003. Shea based his organizing efforts in the rural areas surrounding Baghdad and, in an attempt to simplify his work, tried to base the new system on previous regional and local governing divisions. However, the Saddam regime had not maintained a rational, well-organized system. For Shea and others, even the attempt to discern the geographic and political boundaries of *kadaas* (districts) and *nahiahs* (counties) of which they were comprised, proved difficult.[29] Major Dennis Van Wey, another CA officer working in the Baghdad area, also noted this problem: "We just had issues early on determining what the boundaries were for . . . the city of Baghdad and the *kadaas* and the DACs. Evidently, Saddam had changed boundaries several times based on who was in favor politically."[30]

In this environment where personal connection defined government far better than rational structures and processes, US forces did not always appoint the proper person to authority. Lacking any real understanding of the political culture, CA Soldiers and other units tried to wade through the huge amount of information and opinions to choose the right people to hold power and make decisions. Some of their candidates were not warmly embraced by the local population. For example, in mid-2003 the Coalition authorities chose Abdullah al-Jaburi, a Sunni, as the governor of Diyala province, an area with a Shia majority. Perhaps for this reason, many Iraqis in the province did not view him as a true representative, and in October 2003 and again in May 2004 insurgents attempted to assassinate him.[31]

Despite this lack of understanding, most US units waded into the sphere of governance with great energy and commitment. Without a great amount of guidance, CA teams and unit commanders often chose to use advisory councils as the chief vehicles of political change. These councils began sprouting up at the local, district, and provincial levels soon after the Saddam regime fell and were seen by Soldiers as the means of imparting the key concepts and practices of representative government to Iraqis. Perhaps the greatest concentration of these councils was found in the capital city. Lieutenant Colonel Joe Rice, an officer in the 308th CA Brigade, played a key role in the early formation of the city's local government. Rice served as a liaison between V Corps and ORHA and was invited to become part of the Baghdad Council's Working Group. This group initially consisted of representatives from the State Department and the USAID.[32] Rice brought practical experience to the mission of the working group. As a former mayor of Glendale, Colorado, and with 10 years experience in local government, Rice became pivotal to realizing the council's concept of establishing a system of neighborhood advisory councils (NACs), district advisory councils (DACs), and city councils in Baghdad. The CA officer, working within the group, created a system that used caucuses to select members to 88 NACs. Those bodies then chose representatives to serve in the nine DACs. The DACs then formed the base for the Baghdad City Council.

Because there were so few CA or other officers who had background in governance, Rice had to use military units to implement his council plan. He taught junior officers and noncommissioned officers (NCOs) the fundamentals of democracy on the local level, explaining how to hold caucuses and creating a guidebook for the councils explaining how the local government would operate.[33] He explained that his handbook included "things like agenda formats, a little bit about the role of the local elected official, what's in their lane and what's not in their lane, rules of procedure for a meeting" and other topics.[34] Eventually, Rice noted, the system worked quite well. However, the first steps in the plan to implement the concept were difficult because of the lack of planning before Operation IRAQI FREEDOM (OIF) began. As other

CA officers recalled, no American officials in Baghdad, military or civilian, knew how many neighborhoods there were in the capital city or understood the boundary lines between the local political divisions. And no plan assigned resources to the mission Rice and the many Soldiers in Baghdad were just beginning to conduct. Rice recalled, "We had this grand vision but, again, who was going to implement and how it was going to be implemented, the details weren't even thought of."[35]

The NACs and DACs gave Iraqis their first taste of empowerment at the local level. In June 2003, in the midst of the initial sprouting of advisory councils in Iraq, First Lieutenant Jason Beck, an Army spokesman, described the purpose of the NACs and DACs as providing "a forum where Iraqis could raise their concerns. The councils are a mechanism where residents could actively participate in rebuilding their neighborhoods as well as their hope."[36] Some of the councils in Baghdad and elsewhere began to involve themselves in local reconstruction issues. Still, Rice asserted that ORHA and the CPA never established a well-defined relationship between the councils and the Iraqi ministries that coordinated most of the major decisions about economic and social plans and policy. While critical to the US Army's initial campaign to establish new governance, Beck's statement indirectly noted one important weakness of the concept behind the NACs and DACs: they served more as forums or sounding boards than actual governing institutions that could make decisions and take action.

By establishing and fostering councils, the US Army in Iraq tried to have an immediate effect on the political lives of the Iraqis in their AORs. Clearly, this approach was heavily improvised and Rice stated that guidance for governance operations in this period could often be summarized as "Okay Captain, you're in charge of this neighborhood. Go make a council. Go make some Democracy."[37] In Sadr City, the poor and populous Shia neighborhood in the eastern portion of Baghdad, the 2d Armored Cavalry Regiment (2d ACR) did just that. Major George Sarabia of the 2d ACR explained how his unit, almost immediately after the fall of the Saddam regime, tasked low-level leaders to serve as mentors and organizers for the Iraqis:

> We divided the city into sectors for politics and those sectors mirrored the sectors that belonged to our ground-cavalry troops. So, in other words, that platoon leader who was working with Sadr 1 Neighborhood Advisory Council, for example, did his patrols every day in that area of operations. And so we really wanted to link those two, link the political with the military and the security piece.[38]

Sarabia recognized that the councils had to serve as a laboratory for the Iraqis, demonstrating how to organize and work within a new system that was foreign to their experience under Saddam:

> As far as imparting Democracy 101, I think the platoon leaders did a pretty good job of that. You do that mostly by modeling the behavior that you're trying to do. If you have a big argument, you might let the argument go on for awhile and then say, 'Okay, but how are we going to resolve this. We have limited resources. How do you, as Neighborhood Advisory Council members, wish to resolve this?'[39]

To the Soldiers of the 2d ACR, these councils showed great promise by serving as an outlet of local political energy and agendas. However, Sarabia noted that the citizens involved in Sadr City quickly wanted more authority:

You had people, once they saw how this could work, saying, 'Okay, great, we appreciate this advisory role and the chance to be at the grassroots level and see what's out there, but now give us real authority so we can make those decisions,' which the CPA was not prepared to do yet. So with my limited experience in Sadr City, the people were very well adapted and could understand these types of things and were wanting to get more power quickly—and how they would have used that is something we'll never know, because they did have that advisory role.[40]

Iraqis in some parts of the capital city did not gain their political voice immediately after the fall of Saddam. In one case, the creation of a local representative government required the involvement of energetic American officers who saw that the population in their AOR had been

---

Improvising Democracy: The 3d Battalion, 67th Armor in the City of Khalis

In 2003, the 3d Battalion, 67th Armor (3-67 AR), part of the 4th Infantry Division, found itself responsible for creating a new system of governance in the city of Khalis, 35 miles northeast of Baghdad. Like other units in the same situation, 3-67 AR faced intense pressure from local Iraqis who wanted to create new local governance after the toppling of the Saddam regime. The leaders in 3-67 AR had little or no guidance from higher Coalition authorities on what processes to use in developing new government or even what those new structures should look like. Moreover, nothing in their training had prepared the Soldiers in the unit for creating electoral processes or any of the other numerous tasks connected to the complex project of establishing local government.

Still, the officers of the battalion jumped into the mission and created a hybrid system that featured both the election and selection of local officials. 3-67 AR decided to conduct elections at the *kadaa* (district) level first to be followed by elections at the lower *nahiah* (county) level. To make the new system work in a culture where nonelected tribal and religious leaders have

traditionally held power, battalion leaders first assembled all the local leaders and from this gathering identified 40 people who agreed to serve on the *kadaa* council if elected. These names became the list of candidates from which the entire assembly of leaders subsequently chose. The 20 candidates receiving the most votes formed the council and they selected 1 individual from among themselves to serve as the mayor. While it certainly did not represent an American-style form of democratic local government, this model worked satisfactorily in the cultural and political conditions in north-central Iraq in 2003. The Soldiers of 3-67 AR took the template they had created for the *kadaa* level and used it to establish new systems of governance at the *nahiah* level.

Captain Steven Miller,
"3-16 FA, 4th ID, Conducting Elections in Iraq,"
Field Artillery, January-February 2004, 22-24.

DoD photo by SSG William Davis

A member of the Diyala Provincial Council cast his vote on 15 July 2003. The council selected a lieutenant governor and governor for the province.

overlooked, not just by the Baathist government but also by the Coalition in its initial efforts to establish a local government. In early 2004, Bravo Company, 16th Engineer Battalion, a unit that supported the 1st AD in Baghdad, began to assist the North Kadhimiya community on the northern outskirts of the capital, which the Saddam regime had isolated. The Baathist state had for decades denied the 30,000 plus residents of the area basic government services such as electricity and drinking water.[41] The engineer company began to assist the community by organizing a NAC. Soon after, the unit identified key community leaders and initiated regular weekly meetings, eventually leading the local NAC to gain a seat on the area's DAC. The unit then conducted a variety of humanitarian and reconstruction operations that repaired roads, sewers, and schools as a way of granting legitimacy to the NAC. One benefit from this governance effort was the improvement in the security environment. Captain Mike Baim, the commander of Bravo Company, believed the effort was very worthwhile stating, "Looking back on our last year in Iraq, we have truly made a positive impact on the lives of the Iraqi people living in North Kadhimiya."[42]

The Coalition's political initiatives, however, did not always include an immediate shift to representative government. In fact, in some parts of Iraq in the summer of 2003 Army leaders chose to rein in the efforts to hold caucuses that would choose mayors, governors, and local bodies of self-government.[43] In Diyala and Salah ad Din provinces in June 2003, for example, Major General Raymond Odierno chose to appoint key leaders rather than allow local elections to select those officials. Driving this decision was a larger concern within the military and the CPA leadership that anti-Coalition organizations, including insurgent groups and radical Shia militias, would hijack the electoral process and install their own candidates. These concerns led to the selection of Abdullah al-Jaburi as governor of the province, a politician who was not deemed as legitimate by many in the province. In Samarra, a city in Salah ad Din province, 4th ID leaders had selected Shakir Mahmud Mohammad, a retired Iraqi general, to continue serving as mayor rather than allow planned elections to be held.[44] Despite Iraqi concerns about the delays in the process, Coalition leaders saw these appointments as temporary measures taken to further the stabilization of Iraq and prepare the country for the national elections and the writing of a new constitution.

Even in parts of Iraq where representative government did not flourish immediately, Soldiers sought to create legitimacy for the new Iraqi political establishment. The funneling of reconstruction projects to local governments was a common means of doing this. In Samarra, the commander of the 3d Brigade Combat Team of the 4th ID, Colonel Frederick Rudesheim, made a concerted effort to use the Samarra City Council and other local bodies as the sponsors of projects that created jobs and directly improved the lives of Iraqis. Rudesheim recalled that the Samarra Council initially wanted to pass credit to the American forces in the area: "The Samarra City Council offered, 'We will tell them that you have given us this money.' And I said, 'No. We don't want credit. We want the council of city X to say they gave this money.'" For Rudesheim, this perception was closely intertwined with the governance mission, "It was important that the city council—not us—was seen as the distributors of the money and received the credit for the projects that were completed."[45]

One of the more ambitious unit efforts to create a functioning *and* representative form of government was the 101st ABN's campaign in the city of Mosul located in Nineveh province. In May and June 2003 the division leadership quickly decided to create an interim government while the CPA established its guidance and goals. Major General Petraeus, the division

commander, then initiated a process that, while improvised, led gradually to procedures that were essentially democratic. Petraeus based his actions on a strong belief that having Iraqi partners who knew the region and the ways in which the country worked was essential to gaining Iraqi support for the Coalition's vision for the new Iraq. He described the process he used to create new governing institutions in the following way: "We met very intensively all day, every day, for about not quite 2 weeks, with an ever expanding group of people. Of course, this group would bad-mouth that group and so on, as we met with various elements, but we started to get a good feel for what the elements in the society were, in a sense, in need of representation."[46] The division leadership soon discovered that standing up a representative government in a region divided along ethnic lines was a extremely complex. Petraeus stated,

> We ran a caucus, if you will, of about 270 people that were from all these different groupings, and then were broken down by categories, and they would vote either for the Kurdish members of the Province Council, the Christian member, the Yazidis, the Shbak, the Turkoman, the tribes outside the city, the tribes inside the city, and on and on. You had all these different categories, and there was an agreement already among the group that the Province Governor would be a Sunni Arab. There was no question that it would be a Sunni Arab (the majority of the province) that the Vice Governor would be a Sunni Kurd (since that was clearly the second largest grouping), and that there would be two Assistant Governors; one would be a Christian and one would be a Turkoman. Then we sorted out the rules on how all this was going to happen.[47]

This selected group of 275 delegates chose the interim executive positions of governor, vice-governor, and assistant governors as well as a provincial council with representation from across the region.[48] The system was not perfect and did not represent every constituency adequately. As Petraeus noted, this was the trial and error part of a difficult process: "Over time . . . we convinced them to add representatives from two different

Figure 102. Captain Stephen Thomas, Commander, Company A, 1st Battalion, 327th Infantry Regiment, 101st Airborne Division (Air Assault), speaks with the town mayor in al-Lazakah, Iraq, about service his unit can provide in rebuilding the town.

districts that turned out not to be adequately represented, one of which included a huge tribe that basically just lost the election. They just hadn't campaigned effectively and then they got into a snit and walked out. They were learning democracy."[49]

Once the division had established a provisional Iraqi government, its Soldiers began several large-scale programs to rehabilitate key agencies in the Mosul area by assigning staff sections and subordinate tactical units to specific institutions. Petraeus, for example, tasked the 159th Aviation Brigade to help the Iraqis reestablish Mosul University. The commanding general himself served as the political advisor to the provincial governor and the link to the two principal Kurdish leaders in the other two provinces for which the division was responsible. The 101st ABN's governance program was ambitious and largely successful. However, it had taken place in a relatively permissive security environment and had required many of the unit's resources. Still, Mosul and Nineveh province stand as an early success story in the Coalition's effort to bring representative government to post-Saddam Iraq, and the structure put in place by the 101st ABN proved quite durable, lasting essentially unchanged until the transition to Iraqi sovereignty in June 2004.

The efforts to build and strengthen representative government continued in 2004 bridging the OIF II transition that brought new forces to Iraq. The 1st CAV, which took over responsibility for operations in Baghdad from the 1st AD, continued to work with local councils in the capital. Major General Peter Chiarelli, the commander of the 1st CAV, not only included governance as one of his division's five lines of operations, but also saw the creation of legitimate and effective governing institutions that extended basic services and security to the population as a powerful tool in the fight against the insurgent's attempts to create a shadow government.[50] To help create a vibrant local government, Chiarelli created a governance support team inside his division led by the senior engineer officer and staffed with Soldiers who had experience with contracting and other governance-related jobs. In the commander's words, this team served as the "connecting tissue" that brought his subordinate leaders, US civilian officials, NGOs, and Iraqi institutions more closely together.[51] Like Petraeus, Chiarelli made personal links between his leaders and Iraqi officials in his AOR. The commanding general served as the advisor for the governor of Baghdad province, the city's mayor, and deputy mayors. The brigade commanders in the 1st CAV worked closely with district-level leaders, and the battalion commanders advised neighborhood councils, tribal leaders, and clerics.[52]

In similar fashion, the Soldiers of the 1st Infantry Division (1st ID) that took responsibility for much of the Sunni Triangle in early 2004 built on the foundation of the local government created by the 4th ID. In Diyala province, the 1st Battalion, 6th Field Artillery (1-6 FA) began conducting full spectrum operations in March 2004, focusing much of its attention on the provincial capital of Baqubah. The battalion commander, Lieutenant Colonel Steve Bullimore, inherited a governance system from the 4th ID that featured district councils and a city council that wielded authority in partnership with a mayor.[53] By the time the Soldiers of 1-6 FA moved into the area, the Iraqis had created a political system that operated efficiently with US forces. Still, the battalion's leaders served as mentors to assist the Iraqis in creating processes that vetted contracts and disbursed funds. Additionally, even though the official governance system had gained a measure of traction in the province, Bullimore found himself spending a great deal of time negotiating with tribal leaders in the area and working diligently to ensure that insurgent intimidation in the area did not prevent the growth of good governance. Ultimately, the battalion commander had become hopeful about the potential for a representative government in Diyala province and the efforts of his Soldiers along that line of operation. He recalled that the Iraqis "were looking for our example and they were very excited. The movers and shakers are very excited about this democracy thing but it is all very new to them."[54] Bullimore tempered that optimism by recalling what the mayor of Baqubah had told him, "You must be patient. You have over 200 years of experience with this and your past is not all perfect. We have no experience. This is going to take time. There will be corruption, there will be issues, but we are all going to work through this."[55]

The US Army in Kirkuk: Governance on the Fault Lines of Iraqi Society

As illustrated by the 101st ABN's efforts in Mosul, some of the most significant difficulties facing the US Army's governance operations were the ethnic and sectarian divisions in Iraqi society. Saddam's dictatorship had used repression to keep a lid on the tensions that existed along these fracture lines, but those stresses had erupted in outright violence at times, such as the Shia revolt in the south of Iraq following Operation DESERT STORM in 1991. When OIF removed the authoritarian rule of the Baathist state, those tensions once again surfaced. Although some Soldiers were aware of the ethnic and religious differences that existed in Iraq, very few were prepared to deal with them directly. Certainly, few expected to place themselves between competing groups as these groups sought ways to redress injustices that had occurred under Saddam's rule.

Perhaps the most volatile site for this type of conflict was the city of Kirkuk, located in northern Iraq approximately 150 miles north of Baghdad. The city was located in what was historically Kurdish territory, but its population had long been a mix of Kurds, Arabs, Assyrian Christians, and Turkoman. Situated in the heart of Iraq's oil fields, Kirkuk had strategic importance for much of the 20th century. Partly for that reason, in the 1970s and 1980s Saddam attempted to "Arabize" Kirkuk by forcing Kurds to leave and moving Arab groups in. The arrival of Coalition troops in the city in May 2003 opened up the possibility for the Kurdish population to take control once again over an important cultural and economic center.

The 173d Airborne Brigade (173d ABN) took responsibility for the city soon after the toppling of the Saddam regime. In May 2003 Soldiers of the brigade found themselves attempting to mediate between groups of armed Arabs moving north to ensure the Kurds did not overwhelm the city and the Kurdish groups that had begun flexing their muscles by forcibly evicting some Arabs. On 17 May this conflict became violent with firefights erupting in the streets of Kirkuk. Colonel William Mayville, the brigade commander, recalled that this event served as the "really big first lesson into, or insight into what some of the social dynamics in this community at play were."[56] He added, "If you did not address [these dynamics], the consequences could be very, very violent."[57]

Over the next 8 months, the 173d ABN mediated between the various groups to find a peaceful solution to the problem in Kirkuk. As early as May 2003, however, officers in the brigade began to understand that the creation of political stability in the city meant downplaying the Coalition's goal of creating a truly democratic process. One of the unit's reviews of the political situation in Kirkuk that month noted that the city's residents "have only a limited understanding of Western Democratic processes."[58] The report described other impediments to the establishment of a democratic form of municipal government, noting that the Patriotic Union of Kurdistan (PUK), the major Kurdish political group in Kirkuk, was a highly centralized party and the Arab tribes in the city did not view nonfamily officials as having any political legitimacy.[59] To make the overarching point more emphatic, the review stated there was no "popular mandate for immediate transition to representative government" and closed with a more direct statement: "Political Legitimacy ≠ establishing a popular democracy."[60]

Instead of finding citizens eager for democracy, the Soldiers of the 173d ABN discovered a multiethnic populace interested in removing all vestiges of Baathist power and solving the problems of Saddam's Arabization policies, while also ensuring their ethnic group retained its social, economic, and political position in the city. This presented a complex problem to the Soldiers of the brigade, the large majority of whom had no experience in politics of any type. These Soldiers found themselves in a very unusual position, and they required time to understand the interests involved and the key politicians with whom they worked. However, given the tensions surrounding the Arabization policies, the 173d ABN had to act immediately to create some type of representative government that might be able to create consensus among the competing groups.

One of the first recommendations made by brigade officers was the establishment of a multiethnic city council that could help redress the grievances of the various groups and begin moving the city forward. By the end of May 2003, less than 6 weeks after the brigade arrived in Kirkuk, Mayville and his governance team orchestrated the selection of 300 delegates from the city that in turn elected a 30-seat council, which included 6 representatives from each of the 4 ethnic groups. The new system also mandated the seating of six at-large candidates who could come from any of the ethnic groups and would be selected by the Coalition military authorities. In late May, Major General Odierno, the commander of the 4th ID, the unit responsible for the province in which Kirkuk was located, chose four Kurds, one Assyrian Christian, and one representative from a multiethnic tribe for these six seats.[61] Because Kurds held four of the at-large positions, representatives from the other groups launched immediate protests, demonstrating that the US Army's attempts to establish new governance in Kirkuk would be anything but easy.

Mayville and his Soldiers did have some successes in the summer of 2003. Working with civilian consultants from the Research Triangle Institute (RTI), the contractor who had partnered with USAID, brigade officers convinced the city council to establish a new structure that included five directorates: employment, public safety, public works, budget office, and resettlement. The employment directorate would play a direct role in enforcing the de-Baathification process and US officers hoped the resettlement office could work with both Arabs and Kurds to defuse the tensions caused by land disputes.[62] RTI consultants and CA officers also assisted the new Kirkuk budget office prepare the city's budget for 2004 and established a citizens bureau to help handle complaints from the public. However, Mayville noted that by late 2003 some in Kirkuk had begun to see the council as unrepresentative and they began to mount protests.[63] Soon, ethnic rivalries reasserted their control over politics in the city and the brigade commander had to play a more active role in persuading the local authorities to continue down a peaceful path of compromise. By that date, Mayville was unsure of how to define a successful political outcome in Kirkuk and resorted to hoping to "break even" in the city.

When the 173d ABN left Iraq in February 2004, the situation in Kirkuk was still tense. After months in the city organizing and mentoring the new government, it was unclear whether the city was any closer to a stable future than it had been after the violence in May 2003. Mayville's brigade turned the city over to the 2d Brigade, 25th Infantry Division (25th ID), a unit that served under the command of the 1st ID. The brigade commander assigned the overall mission of fostering political progress in the city to his Team Governance, a small group of Soldiers from the brigade's Judge Advocate General staff section. Led by Major Sam Schubert, the team worked with US State Department officials and the Kirkuk city and provincial councils on a daily basis in an attempt to create greater political progress.

Team Governance was not alone in conducting governance operations. Soldiers from the 1st Battalion, 21st Infantry (1-21 IN), the main maneuver element in Kirkuk, assisted the larger effort in a number of ways. Despite the creation of local representative bodies in 2003, continued grievances among the ethnic groups ensured the city remained restive throughout 2004. The discord caused peaceful protests as well as direct attacks on politicians and specific neighborhoods where ethnic groups resided. On 15 March 2004, for example, Sheik Akar, a Shia Arab city councilman, was assassinated in a drive-by shooting while he was en route to the government building in Kirkuk.

To prevent the violence from overwhelming the progress made by the Coalition in Kirkuk, Soldiers from 1-21 IN provided security for local officials and ensured street protests did not escalate into riots. Some leaders in the battalion became involved in the intricacies of the disputes in the Kirkuk region.[64] Throughout the summer of 2004, for example, the commander of the battalion's headquarters and headquarters company and his scout platoon leader met repeatedly with leaders in the nearby town of Taza where they tried to mediate a dispute between Turkoman and Arabs over land in the village of Busheir, which had been occupied by the latter group during the Arabization program.[65] As the summer ended and the conflict continued, the responsibility for ensuring negotiations continued in a peaceful manner fell to the officers of the 1st Battalion, 14th Infantry. The fact that 2004 ended with no lasting resolution to the Busheir land dispute was emblematic of the deeply-rooted political problems facing the Soldiers of the 2d Brigade, 25th ID in Kirkuk. The elections of January 2005 approached with Kirkuk and its environs still simmering with ethnic tension.

The Interim Iraqi Government and 30 January 2005 Elections

As the Coalition entered 2004, Paul Bremer and other leaders were aware of the need for national elections to help legitimize the new Iraq they had helped bring into existence. To assist with the first step, the Coalition worked with the United Nations to pave the way for the assumption of political sovereignty by the Iraqis and the establishment of an IIG. The UN Security Council issued Resolution 1546 on 8 June 2004 that endorsed the formation of an IIG and set the schedule for elections for a Transitional National Assembly (TNA) to be held in late December 2004 or January 2005.

The UN Resolution played a critical role in the development of MNF-I, which the Coalition had created in May 2004 looking forward to the day when Iraq was sovereign yet would still require Coalition forces to maintain security and safeguard its political progress. In a letter that accompanied the UN resolution, US Secretary of State Colin Powell articulated the overarching purpose of MNF-I, emphasizing the ascending role of the Iraqis in the security of their own country: "Development of an effective and cooperative security partnership between the MNF and the sovereign Government of Iraq is critical to the stability of Iraq. The commander of the MNF will work in partnership with the sovereign Government of Iraq in helping to provide security while recognizing and respecting its sovereignty."[66] That sovereignty came sooner than expected. In a surprise move, Ambassador Bremer and the CPA officially transferred sovereignty to the IIG on 28 June 2004, 2 days before the planned date to avoid potential terrorist disruptions. At a ceremony in Baghdad's Green Zone, Bremer officially ended the Coalition occupation and gave authority to Ayad Allawi, Iraq's Interim Prime Minister. He read aloud from a letter he had written that morning, concluding with, "We welcome Iraq's steps to take its rightful place of equality and honor among the nations of the world." Two hours later, Bremer left Iraq for good.[67]

During the summer and fall of 2004, the insurgency in Iraq continued to escalate. US forces and the Iraqi Government became increasingly concerned that insurgent-held areas would not be pacified prior to the January 2005 elections. Those elections had become the most important objective for both the Coalition and the IIG. General Casey unequivocally identified the goals set in UN Resolution 1546 as the most important direction he received when he took command of MNF-I. The campaign plan he and his staff developed in the summer of 2004 focused on preparing Iraq for its first set of national elections.[68] For Casey and many others, any disruption to the political timeline would be seen as a major setback for the legitimacy of the IIG and the Coalition project in Iraq. Consequently, MNF-I began a series of offensive actions to rid Iraq of militia and insurgent strongholds. In August US Army and Marine Corps units teamed with Iraqi security forces to force Muqtada al-Sadr and his militiamen out of the city of An Najaf. In early October a force of 3,000 Soldiers from the 1st ID, along with 2,000 Iraqi soldiers, launched Operation BATON ROUGE to eliminate the insurgent safe haven in the city of Samarra. In the assault, 94 insurgents were killed as Coalition and Iraqi forces reasserted control over the city. In early November 2004, in the wake of Operation BATON ROUGE, the Coalition began Operation AL FAJR, a major offensive against the Sunni insurgent stronghold in the city of Fallujah. By the end of the month, US and Iraqi forces had eradicated most of the insurgent opposition in the city. These successful attacks sent a powerful message to both insurgents and Iraqi citizens alike that the interim government would not tolerate interference with the upcoming national elections.

In further anticipation of the January elections, the Coalition took steps to increase combat power in Iraq to help maintain security. The British First Battalion Royal Highland Fusiliers deployed 400 soldiers from their base in Cyprus to southeast Iraq to provide election support.[69] In addition, 3,500 US Soldiers from the 2d Brigade, 1st CAV and 3,000 from the 1st ID had their tours extended until after the elections. The extended 1st ID forces were to remain deployed north of Baghdad in the Sunni Arab cities of Samarra, Balad, and Baquba. Shortly thereafter, two battalions from the 82d ABN were sent to Iraq to provide security for the International Zone in Baghdad, and additional troops from 2d BCT, 25th ID, along with 2,300 Marines from the 31st Marine Expeditionary Unit, stayed on in Iraq in preparation for the Iraqi elections. Thus, MNF-I increased the pre-election force in Iraq by nearly 12,000 Soldiers and Marines.[70]

In the last week of January, when insurgent violence did not abate, officials from the Independent Electoral Commission announced the closing of Iraq's international borders in an effort to tighten security. Iraq's government also proclaimed a nationwide nighttime curfew, restricted election day driving to officials only, prevented traveling between provinces, banned weapons, canceled all leave for Iraqi police and military forces, and declared 29–31 January holidays.[71]

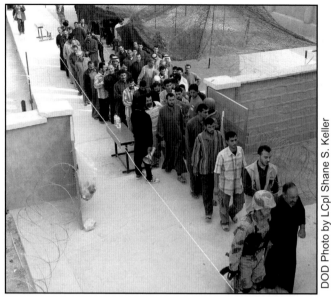

DOD Photo by LCpl Shane S. Keller

Figure 103. An Iraqi security force soldier (bottom right) leads Iraqi citizens into a voting area during elections in Rawah, Iraq.

Despite the elaborate security precautions, terrorist threats and insurgent attacks continued. On 23 January, for example, the leader of al-Qaeda in Iraq, Abu Musab al-Zarqawi, in an effort to dissuade Iraqi citizens from voting released an Internet recording declaring "a bitter war against democracy and all those who seek to enact it." He went on to denounce the IIG "as a tool used by the Americans to promote this lie that is called democracy."[72] In that final week before the elections, IED attacks and mortar barrages were met by operations mounted by both Coalition and US forces to detain suspected insurgents and uncover weapons caches. At the same time, US units moved into position to support the ISF on election day. Although Iraqi police and military forces had been assigned primary polling-site security duty, significant numbers of US troops were scheduled to patrol the streets and wait nearby, ready to provide immediate backup whenever necessary.

Before the elections, the Iraqi Electoral Commission published all of the candidates' names on their official Web site, and on 28 January Iraqi exiles and expatriates began casting their votes from special polling stations established in 14 countries to accommodate Iraqi residents. One Iraqi in a polling booth in Sydney, Australia, told a journalist, "When I look at the ink on my finger, this is a mark of freedom." Handren Marph, a Kurd voting in London, remarked: "This is a fantastic feeling. I feel hope and fear—fear because freedom might not come back, but hope because a new constitution may give us protection and opportunity for all."[73]

On 30 January 2005 the Iraqi people voted in overwhelming numbers despite repeated attempts by insurgents to disrupt the elections. By the end of the day, an estimated 8.4 million citizens had voted, representing a surprising 60 percent turnout. Along with the 275 representatives

USAF Photo by TSgt Andy Dunaway

Figure 104. An Iraqi soldier places his completed ballot into the ballot box after voting along with other Iraqi security forces in Hayji, Iraq.

Figure 105. Iraqi men proudly show their inked-stained fingers after voting in Hayji, Iraq.

who were elected from 111 political parties to the TNA, the elections established provincial councils in each of the 18 provinces and elected a Kurdistan regional assembly legislature. Two hundred thousand election workers and organizing officials had worked tirelessly at 5,200 polling places to make this historic day a remarkable success.[74] In many instances, Iraqis had to wait in long lines to cast their votes. Most were proud to do so.

In Baghdad, there was great celebration. Nuhair Rubaie, a resident of the city, explained to a reporter, "It's like a wedding. I swear to God, it's a wedding for all Iraq. No one has ever witnessed this before, no one has ever seen anything like. And we did it ourselves."[75] Another Iraqi added, "Whatever they do, I would still vote. Even if I were dead, I would still participate. The vote comes from the bottom of my heart."[76] After casting his vote, Prime Minister Allawi addressed the sense of hope that those who had voted were now feeling when he noted, "This is the starting point on the path to democracy, rule of law, prosperity, and security for Iraq and the entire region."[77]

In a show of pride, Iraqi citizens continued to display their ink-stained fingers for several days after the election. At the US State of the Union address in Washington, DC, the following week, members of Congress dyed their own index fingers purple as a show of support for the Iraqi people and their successful election. President Bush had closely followed the Iraqi election returns. He would later compliment those who had voted in the dangerous conditions. "For millions of Iraqis, it was also an act of personal courage," he said, "and they have earned the respect of us all."[78]

Not all Iraqis took part in the elections. The large majority of the country's Sunni Arabs had boycotted the process or stayed away from the polls because of fear of violence. For at least some Sunni Arabs, staying home on election day was a means of protesting or potentially undermining the new Iraqi political system that had been forced on their country by the Coalition

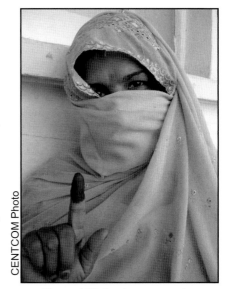

Figure 106. Iraqi woman voter.

421

and had granted preeminent power to rival groups in Iraqi society. So many Sunni Arabs stayed away that Sunni parties garnered only 17 seats in the 275-member transitional legislature.[79] The inability of the Coalition and the IIG to integrate the Sunni Arab minority more fully into the political process surely stands as the most glaring failure of the overall effort in 2003 and 2004 to remake Iraq's system of national governance.

There were other challenges for the Coalition and the IIG on election day. Insurgents mounted close to 300 attacks on polling sites and voters to prevent the elections from proceeding. These incidents represented a fourfold increase in the average number of daily attacks and led to the deaths of 1 American, 10 British Soldiers, 8 Iraqi Soldiers, and 26 civilians.[80]

Nevertheless, the IIG, the UN, and the Coalition had staged the first free elections in Iraq's modern history. This success was complemented by the fact that Coalition forces, especially the US military, managed to keep a relatively low profile as voters went to the polls. Lieutenant Colonel Bullimore, who commanded 1-6 FA, was initially skeptical that the Iraqis and their security forces could handle the elections, but was happily surprised by how the overall effort went in the city of Baqubah in the Sunni Triangle. Initially, the morning of election day had brought widespread mortar attacks in the city, but the Iraqi police and Army remained at their posts and by noon the attacks had stopped and people began going to the polls. Bullimore stated, "It was nice to see that it was working. It was nice to see some courage from the Iraqis that, 'We are going to vote.' I was very impressed with the police force, how seriously they took it, and how well it went at the polling sites. They were the ones that managed that."[81] Even in Kirkuk, the city most beset by political and ethnic tension, the elections were a success. As in Baqubah, insurgents launched a small number of mortar rounds at US targets early in the day hoping to intimidate Kirkuk's citizens and prevent them from going to the polls. However, Iraqi Security Forces and the Soldiers of 1-21 IN had mounted highly focused raids on the eve of the election, detaining a number of insurgent leaders and disrupting plans to attack polling places in the city.[82] There was only one attack on voters that election day. In the afternoon, a sniper began shooting at Iraqis in line at a poll site. Although four were wounded, the others in the queue refused to leave and voted despite the continued threat of violence.

From his vantage point at a higher level, Lieutenant General Thomas Metz, the commander of Multi-National Corps–Iraq (MNC-I), reflected on the momentous events of late January 2005:

> By far, it was one of the finest moments in my life. One thing people have to realize is that it was a very complex process. It was an Iraqi process, somewhat supported by the UN and somewhat supported by the Coalition, but we had to make it their process. That was really hard. I really felt that if there was ever really a time, like the Tet of 1968, the enemy would expend all tactical resources for a strategic win, it would have been for the election.[83]

The insurgents did not succeed in making the elections their Tet offensive, and the day was clearly the pinnacle of the US Army's efforts to build a new system of representative government in Iraq.

Conclusion

In the context of the full spectrum operations campaign, Coalition forces accepted the mission of developing Iraqi governance, understanding that their mission included the larger task of attempting to construct local, regional, and national bodies of government that represented the entire population. CA teams and functional experts were instrumental in reestablishing city, provincial, and national governments. Daily interaction with city department managers, provincial directors, and regular citizens afforded CA Soldiers the unique opportunity by virtue of their duties to interact and understand the Iraqi people and their problems. However, as this chapter has shown, CA units were not alone in this effort. Soldiers in a wide variety of units were focused on the establishment of NACs, DACs, and even the provincial-level government.

The elections of January 2005 were proof of progress toward the building of a more representative Iraqi state. The insurgent attacks and the large absence of Sunni Arab voters at the polls on that day, nevertheless, served as a reminder that not all Iraqis shared this particular political vision for their country. The challenge for Coalition forces after that joyous election day was to continue to invest legitimacy into the institutions they were growing at the local, provincial, and national levels. Success in this task, more than the momentary victory of the election, would be the real measure of how well the new Iraqi institutions of governance had set down roots.

Notes

1.   This account of the US Army Special Forces governance project in Ar Rutbah in April 2003 is from James A. Gavrilis, "The Mayor of Ar Rutbah," *Foreign Policy,* November/December 2005, 1, http://www.foreignpolicy.com/story/cms.php?story_id=3265 (accessed 22 March 2007).

2.   Gavrilis, 4.

3.   George W. Bush, "Transcript of President Bush's Address to the Nation," 19 March 2003, 1, http://www.whitehouse.gov/news/releases/2003/03/20030319-17.html (accessed 23 March 2007).

4.   V Corps and CJTF-7, *V Corps and CJTF-7 Transition and Challenges* Briefing, 30 September 2004, slide 4.

5.   Ambassador L. Paul Bremer III, interview by Contemporary Operations Study Team, Windermere, FL, 6 June 2006, 2–3.

6.   Steven Metz, "Insurgency and Counterinsurgency in Iraq," *Washington Quarterly* (Winter 2003–04): 27.

7.   Brigadier General Michael Tucker, interview by Contemporary Operations Study Team, Fort Leavenworth, KS, 20 January 2006, 5.

8.   Jay M. Garner, "Iraq Revisited," in Brian M. De Toy, ed., *Turning Victory into Success*: *Military Operations After the Campaign* (Fort Leavenworth, KS: Combat Studies Institute Press), 253.

9.   Garner, "Iraq Revisited," in De Toy, ed., *Turning Victory into Success*, 254.

10.   Coalition Provisional Authority Order No. 1, "De-Ba'athification of Iraqi Society (16 May 2003)," http://www.cpa-iraq.org/regulations/20030516_CPAORD_1_De-Ba_athification_of_Iraqi_Society_.pdf (accessed 14 March 2006).

11.   Ayatollah al-Sistani's official Web site, *Sistani.org*, http://www.sistani.org/messages/eng/ir5.htm. (accessed 17 March 2006).

12.   Larry Diamond, *Squandered Victory: The American Occupation and the Bungled Effort to Bring Democarcy to Iraq* (New York, NY: Henry Holt and Company, 2005), 41–43; Coalition Provisional Authority Regulation No. 6, "Governing Council of Iraq," 13 July 2003, http://www.cpa-iraq.org/regulations/20030713_CPAREG_6_Governing_Council_of_Iraq_.pdf (accessed 22 March 2006); UN Security Council, "Resolution 1483 (2003)," 22 May 2003, http://daccessdds.un.org/doc/UNDOC/GEN/N03/368/53/PDF/N0336853.pdf?OpenElement (accessed 22 March 2006). Bremer references section 9.

13.   Diamond, 51.

14.   Diamond, 51–52.

15.   Bremer, interview, 6 June 2006, 11.

16.   Bremer, interview, 6 June 2006, 11.

17.   Lieutenant General David H. Petraeus, interview by Contemporary Operations Study Team, Fort Leavenworth, KS, 17 February 2006, 2.

18.   Diamond, 108–111.

19.   Diamond, 115–116.

20.   US V Corps, *V Corps Update Briefing—V Corps Commander's Conference*, 16 May 2003, slides 22–23.

21.   V Corps and CJTF-7, *V Corps–CJTF-7 Transition and Challenges* Briefing, slide 4.

22.   4th Infantry Division, *Lessons Learned: Executive Summary*, 17 June 2004, 12.

23.   82d Airborne Division, *Campaign Plan Overview* Briefing, 1 April 2004, slide 7.

24.   2d Squadron, 3d Armored Cavalry Regiment, *Sabre Squadron AO Robertson Update for 2d BDE, 3 ID* Briefing, 31 May 2003, slide 28.

25.   2d Sqdn, 3d ACR, *Sabre Squadron AO Robertson*, slide 39.

26.   2d Sqdn, 3d ACR, *Sabre Squadron AO Robertson*, slide 41.

27.   Major Dennis Van Wey, interview by Operational Leadership Experiences Project Team, Combat Studies Institute, Fort Leavenworth, KS, 1 December 2005, 16.

28. Baqubah CMOC S3 Information Paper: *Muktar Data—Edited Version For Release*, 5 August 2003.

29. Major Larry Shea, interview by Contemporary Operations Study Team, Fort Leavenworth, KS, 21 October 2006.

30. Van Wey, interview, 1 December 2005.

31. Ian Fisher, "The Struggle for Iraq: Attacks North of Baghdad Kill 3 GI's, and barely miss governor of an Iraqi Province," *New York Times,* 14 October 2003; Edward Wong, "The Struggle for Iraq: The Troops; Years later, A Division Takes Stock on Different Sands," *New York Times,* 7 June 2004.

32. Lieutenant Colonel Joe Rice, interview by Benard Engel, United States Institute of Peace Association for Diplomatic Studies and Training, Iraq Experience Project, 31 July 2004, www.usip.org/library/oh/sops/iraq/sec/rice.pdf (accessed 28 November 2005).

33. Rice, interview by Engel, 31 July 2004.

34. Rice, interview by Engel, 31 July 2004.

35. Rice, interview by Engel, 31 July 2004.

36. Jason P. Beck, "Neighborhood Advisory Councils: Democracy at the Community Level," Third US Army, 22 June 2003, 1–2, http://www.arcent.army.mil/news/archive/2003_news/june/advisory_councils.asp (accessed 1 November 2006).

37. Rice, interview by Engel, 31 July 2004, 17.

38. Lieutenant Colonel George H. Sarabia, interview by Operational Leadership Experiences Project Team, Combat Studies Institute, Fort Leavenworth, KS, 23 September 2005, 9–34.

39. Sarabia, interview, 23 September 2005, 9–34.

40. Sarabia, interview, 23 September 2005, 9–34.

41. Donald Walker, "Army Engineering Battalion Helps Community Help Itself," *DefendAmerica News,* 18 March 2004, 1, http://www.defendamerica.mil/articles/mar2004/a3180d.html.

42. Walker.

43. William Booth and Rajiv Chandrasekaran, "Occupation Forces Halt Elections Throughout Iraq," *Washington Post*, 28 June 2003, A20.

44. Booth and Chandrasekaran, A20.

45. Colonel Frederick Rudesheim, interview by Contemporary Operations Study Team, Fort Leavenworth, KS, 4 November 2005, 8.

46. Petraeus, interview, 18 March 2006, 8.

47. Petraeus, interview, 18 March 2006, 8.

48. Petraeus, interview, 17 February 2006, 8.

49. Petraeus, interview, 17 February 2006, 8.

50. Major General Peter W. Chiarelli and Major Patrick R. Michaelis, "Winning the Peace: The Requirement for Full-Spectrum Operations," *Military Review,* July–August 2005, 12.

51. Chiarelli and Michaelis, 12.

52. Major General Peter Chiarelli, *Winning the Peace—USMA* Briefing, 8 March 2005, slide 46.

53. Lieutenant Colonel Steven Bullimore, interview by Contemporary Operations Study Team, Fort Leavenworth, KS, 18 May 2006, 7.

54. Bullimore, interview, 18 May 2006, 7.

55. Bullimore, interview, 18 May 2006, 7.

56. "Interview, Col. William Mayville," *Frontline: Beyond Baghdad.* 1 December 2003, http://www.pbs.org/wgbh/pages/frontline/shows/beyond/interviews/mayville.html (accessed 2 April 2007).

57. "Mayville Interview," *Frontline: Beyond Baghdad.*

58. 173d Airborne Brigade, *Operation CREATE DEMOCRACY* Briefing, 13 May 2003, slide 18.

59. 173d ABN, *Operation CREATE DEMOCRACY,* slide 18.

60. 173d ABN, *Operation CREATE DEMOCRACY,* slide 18.

61. "Row Overshadows Kirkuk Poll," *BBC News*, 24 May 2003, http://news.bbc.co.uk/1/hi/world/middle_east/2934594.stm (accessed 27 November 2007).

62. US Department of State, US Agency for International Development, *Iraq-Humanitarian and Reconstruction Assistance, Fact Sheet #35*, Fiscal Year (FY) 2003, 30 June 2003, http://www.usaid.gov/iraq/updates/jun03/iraq_fs53_063003.pdf (accessed 27 November 2007).

63. "Mayville Interview," *Frontline: Beyond Baghdad.*

64. See, for example, Major James L. Anderson, 2d Brigade Combat Team, 25th Infantry Division (Light), *OIF Historical Account Submission #19* (19–25 June 2004), 2.

65. Anderson, 2d BCT, 25th ID (Light), *Submission #19*; see also, *Submissions #22* and *#30.*

66. Colin Powell, "Annex to UN Security Resolution 1546" to UN Secretary General Kofi Annan, 5 June 2004, UN Web site, http://www.un.org/News/Press/docs/2004/sc8117.doc.htm (accessed 18 April 2006).

67. L. Paul Bremer III, *My Year in Iraq: The Struggle to Build a Future of Hope* (New York, NY: Simon & Schuster, 2006), 392–396.

68. General George W. Casey Jr., interview by Contemporary Operations Study Team, Fort Leavenworth, KS, 27 November 2007, 10.

69. Matthew Tempest, "400 More UK Troops to be Sent to Iraq," *The Guardian* (10 January 2005): 1–4.

70. Thom Shanker and Eric Schmitt, "U.S. to Increase Its Force in Iraq by Nearly 12,000," *New York Times,* 2 December 2004, 1–2.

71. Rory McCarthy, "New Curfew After 15 Iraqi Soldiers are Shot Dead," *The Guardian* (23 January 2005): 1–3.

72. "Purported al-Zarqawi Tape: Democracy a Lie," *CNN.com,* 23 January 2005, 1–3.

73. Jeremy Lennard, "Voting Begins in Iraq Election," *The Guardian* (28 January 2005): 1–4.

74. Kenneth Katzman, CRS Report for Congress, "Iraq: Elections, Constitution, and Government," 22 December 2006.

75. Anthony Shadid, "Iraqis Defy Threats as Millions Vote," *Washington Post Foreign Service* (31 January 2005): A01.

76. Shadid, "Iraqis Defy Threats," A01.

77. Shadid, "Iraqis Defy Threats," A01.

78. President George W. Bush, "State of the Union Address," 2 February 2005, http://www.whitehouse.gov/news/releases/2005/02/20050202-11.html (accessed 28 November 2007).

79. Katzman, CRS Report to Congress, 2.

80. "Can the Voters Build on Success?" *The Economist,* 5 February 2005, 43–44.

81. Bullimore, interview, 18 May 2006, 15.

82. This account based on Captain Jeremiah Cordovano, "TF 1-21 Infantry Applies the Nine Principles of War in Kirkuk: Preparing an Iraqi City for Elections," *Infantry*, January–February 2006, 37–40.

83. Lieutenant General Thomas Metz, interview by Contemporary Operations Study Team, Fort Hood, TX, 13 December 2005.

Chapter 11

Training the Iraqi Security Forces

The United States Department of Defense (DOD) and US Central Command (CENTCOM) designed Operation IRAQI FREEDOM (OIF) to be a lightning strike that would seize Baghdad and quickly overthrow Saddam Hussein's regime. This concept was the antithesis of US strategy in the European theater during World War II that employed the so-called "broad front" strategy to methodically annihilate Axis military forces. Thus, one of the expected outcomes of CENTCOM's Operation COBRA II plan was that during combat operations Coalition forces would not destroy, or even capture, most Iraqi conventional military units. Using a combination of propaganda and combat operations to restrict Iraqi command and control capabilities and movement, the Coalition's military planners sought to prevent Iraqi Army units from maneuvering freely, and even hoped that some of Saddam's forces would remain in their barracks. This concept worked well and can be credited as a key part of the overall success of the decisive phase of OIF. Many units within Saddam's army never offered more than token resistance to Coalition forces, and some remained on the sidelines during the short conventional combat phase of the campaign.

However, this successful strategy left the Coalition with a potential problem after the destruction of the regime. As a group, US and Coalition leaders believed that Iraq's security forces would need to be reshaped after Saddam was overthrown. For a democratic Iraq to develop, Iraq's military and security forces had to be reformed into a professional military force under civilian control instead of being used as an instrument of repression. Although planners at CENTCOM, the Office of Reconstruction and Humanitarian Assistance (ORHA), and the Coalition Provisional Authority (CPA) recognized this requirement, the Coalition, overall, did not have a detailed, well-coordinated plan for the reconstruction of the ISF when the regime fell in April 2003.

During the 12 months that followed, the formal responsibility for creating new security forces in Iraq fell to the CPA. Initially, the CPA viewed this mission as the construction of a national, professional army that had no role in internal security. For the CPA, the refusal to give the new Iraqi Army internal security responsibilities was part of the larger long-term and methodical project aimed at altering the cultural legacy of the ISF. As the insurgency developed over the summer of 2003 and it became clear that the CPA plan did not meet the immediate security needs of the country, Coalition units under the aegis of Combined Joint Task Force–7 (CJTF-7) began spending considerable time and resources to build and employ their own local and regional security forces to fill the immediate requirements. Thus, for the US Army the training and advising of the Iraqi Security Forces (ISF) became another critical element in the new full spectrum campaign. The division of effort that evolved between the CPA and CJTF-7 did address the obvious security needs on the ground. However, it represented another example of the lack of unity of command and effort between the Coalition's political authority and its military arm.

As a full-blown insurgency emerged in the fall of 2003, the creation of the ISF had arguably become the single most important operation in the Coalition's campaign. Despite this fact, the Coalition was only able to achieve unity of command and effort in June 2004 when the CPA's and CJTF-7's efforts to train the ISF were brought under a single Coalition command, the Multi-National Security Transition Command–Iraq (MNSTC-I). Two important events marked the next stage of building and employing the ISF. The first came on 28 June 2004 when the Interim Iraqi Government (IIG) took control of the ISF after the CPA handed over sovereignty to the Iraqi people. Iraqi forces continued to operate under the tactical control of Multi-National Corps–Iraq (MNC-I), however, and the Coalition and MNSTC-I continued to train and advise the IIG. The second event was the symbolic and very real assumption of responsibility by the ISF for the provision of a safe and secure environment during the January 2005 Iraqi Constitutional Assembly elections. This chapter is the story of the transitions that led to this important accomplishment.

Saddam Hussein's Military Legacy

During his long tenure in power, Saddam Hussein used his military and security forces as a tool to enforce his dictatorship. Promotions within the military, security, and police forces were largely based on favoritism and loyalty to Saddam rather than on competency or merit.[1] The Iraqi Republican Guard (IRG), an elite warfighting force composed of seven divisions, was the core of the military, while the Special Republican Guard (SRG) served as Saddam's praetorian guard and responded to any specific threat to his power. Although Iraq's conventional forces looked formidable in 2003, in reality they were less than an imposing threat. Despite the experience gained during the brutal war with Iran between 1980 and 1988, the Iraq military was quickly crushed by US forces in 1991. After the Gulf War, Saddam feared the military might one day rise against him, and he worked assiduously to undermine its internal cohesion and professionalism. The 12 years of United Nations (UN) sanctions that followed the 1991 defeat severely degraded this force, making it a shell of its former self. Its training was woefully inadequate, its leaders lacked professional military education, its equipment was barely operational, and its enlisted men were largely conscripts with questionable loyalty to the regime.

Saddam feared mutiny by his own military leaders and, as a result, prohibited his commanders from rigorously practicing their profession. Military leaders tended to maintain a low profile, terrified that the paranoid Saddam would reward displays of initiative with execution.[2] Lieutenant General Nasier Abadi, who served in the Iraqi Armed Forces (IAF) under Saddam, recalled, "For a dictatorship, the most vital thing for officers was to be obedient and that was the primary skill that you had."[3] The Iraqi Army was led by politically reliable Sunnis, and its ranks manned by Shia conscripts who were terribly mistreated and would often desert at the first opportunity.

Not surprisingly, officers in all of Iraq's security forces had little understanding of how to effectively train their forces or employ their equipment. Lieutenant General David H. Petraeus, former Commander of MNSTC-I, illustrated the lack of hands-on training:

> I was meeting with this superb Iraqi. . . . He hugged me as we landed there and he said, 'General, I can't thank you enough for introducing us to these revolutionary new training techniques.' We were looking at some training. What I saw, people doing basic rifle marksmanship, some that were doing slightly advanced close combat marksmanship, but again, pretty basic stuff. . . . So I asked him, 'What do you mean?' He said, 'Well, this idea of shooting live ammunition. This is really great. You can see where the round goes. You can

see whether the people are actually hitting what they are aiming at.' I said, 'Well, how did you used to do marksmanship training?' He said, 'We were only allowed three rounds a year on average.'[4]

The country's police forces also suffered from poor training, and widespread problems of illiteracy and poor physical conditioning further hindered this institution. Military analyst Anthony Cordesman contended, "The police ranked 11th out of Iraq's 11 security services, and had minimal pay, training, and equipment. They feared any form of interference with government activity, and were largely passive and station-bound. . . . Corruption, favoritism, and nepotism were endemic."[5]

Throughout his 26-year rule, Saddam made all important security-related decisions with little delegation. His elite forces, the SRG and the IRG, were the only trained and competent military and police force. Despite their inadequacies, Saddam relied on the ISF to keep the population under control, even if it meant the use of brutal techniques. Colonel Michael Tucker, the commander of the 1st Brigade Combat Team (BCT) of the 1st Armored Division (1st AD), explained that the Iraqi police under Saddam had a particularly odious legacy:

> [The police] were Saddam's foot soldiers that went out and kicked your door down and drug your father out of the house, killed him, and then drove away. These were the people who when you called them in the middle of the night and said someone was robbing your house, they responded with, 'Hey, listen, we are really busy. How much money do you have?'[6]

It was obvious to many within the Coalition that for the new ISF to become professional and capable institutions, they had to reject the legacy of Saddam's military and police forces.

The Challenges of Post-Saddam Iraq

As stated earlier, planners within the US Government envisioned the large-scale surrender of Iraqi Army units during the invasion.[7] However, they assumed that police and justice systems would remain intact, and the Coalition would adopt an advisory role to facilitate bureaucracies that would continue to function in a post-Saddam Iraq.[8] Military plans at CENTCOM and Combined Forces Land Component Command (CFLCC) called for the rapid handover of responsibility for rebuilding security forces to Iraqi civilians and would recall Iraqi officers to duty after the toppling of the regime. The Bush administration further sanctioned this concept by approving the prewar ORHA plan to recall Iraqi troops to provide security, repair roads, and tackle the various reconstruction tasks of a new Iraq. Lieutenant General (Retired) Jay Garner, the chief of the ORHA, proposed paying 300,000 to 400,000 members of the Iraqi regular army to do the reconstruction work.[9] The plans further expected all Army and security service personnel to present themselves to Coalition authorities to be registered, an act for which they would receive a $20 payment.[10]

Despite the Coalition's planning, in late May, Ambassador Paul Bremer III issued CPA Order No. 2, "Dissolution of Entities," which officially dissolved the Iraqi Army, Air Force, Navy, and other forces. This directive rendered all previous assumptions and expectations obsolete. On the ground in Iraq, Saddam's disappearance had created a vacuum of power in which most civilian institutions and entire units of the old Iraqi armed forces simply melted away. As Secretary of Defense Donald Rumsfeld and others pointed out, the army effectively disbanded itself when its officers and soldiers returned to their homes following the fall of the Saddam regime.[11] Bremer and others in the CPA had arrived in Iraq in May 2003 with no intention of keeping Saddam's military under arms, and saw no possibility of doing so even if they had sought to use it as a base for Iraq's new forces. Thus, for many in the CPA, Order No. 2 merely formalized what had already occurred.[12] For the Bush administration, the order did more than simply reflect the reality on the ground. It also served as a critical tool in the purging of the remnants of the Baath Party and the old security forces from Iraq so that a new state and society could be born.[13] As this study previously noted, many in the Coalition's leadership viewed this purge as critical to the CPA effort to gain Kurdish and Shia support for the reinvention of Iraq. Those two groups had suffered at the hands of the Baathist security forces and would not likely support any political project in which significant elements of these forces played a part.

The Coalition then made the momentous decision in May 2003 to create new military and police forces for a country with a complex society replete with multiple political, ethnic, and confessional fault lines. The story of that effort, which continued through the elections of January 2005, is also complex, reflecting the Byzantine set of organizations and processes established by the Coalition to oversee this integral part of the full spectrum campaign in Iraq. The details of this effort will be discussed in more detail later in this chapter, but a short summary of the major evolutionary steps and evolving terminology is necessary first. Former Ambassador Walter Slocombe, the CPA Senior Advisor for National Defense in 2003, led the CPA security sector reform effort. Slocombe was responsible for the creation of the defense ministry and its new armed forces, as well as coordinating for the establishment of the Iraqi police and intelligence sectors.[14] In May 2003 Slocombe and the CPA took over responsibility for building the military and police organizations that were later to become known collectively as the ISF.[15] Within the broad organization of the ISF, the conventional military forces, under the command of the Iraqi Ministry of Defense, were often referred to as the Iraqi Armed Forces (IAF) to distinguish them from organizations that had internal security roles and were controlled by the Ministry of Interior (MOI), one of three Iraqi ministries not disbanded by the CPA.

Between May 2003 and March 2004, Bremer and Slocombe organized the ISF building efforts under two commands—the Coalition Military Assistance Training Team (CMATT) under Major General Paul Eaton and the Coalition Police Assistance Training Team (CPATT), initially led by Mr. Bernard Kerik. CMATT was responsible for Iraq's military forces and CPATT for Iraq's police forces. The MOI controlled three other security organizations: the Facilities Protection Service (FPS), the Iraqi Highway Patrol (IHP), and the Department of Border Enforcement (DBE).[16]

While the CPA was busy with these major efforts, in the late summer of 2003 CJTF-7 units began forming and training their own Iraqi paramilitary units called the Iraqi Civil Defense Corps (ICDC). This was a diverse range of units that individual US divisions and brigades recruited to assist them in tasks ranging from trash cleanup and minor construction to base security, and in some cases, patrolling.

In the fall of 2003 the CPA's ISF building mission added three new forces. In September the DOD added the creation of an Iraqi Air Force and an Iraqi Coastal Defense Force to the CPA's responsibilities. Then in November the CPA tasked the Combined Joint Special Operations Task Force–Arabian Peninsula (CJSOTF-AP) under CJTF-7 to begin training the 36th Iraqi

Commando Battalion. The commander of CJSOTF-AP assigned three US Army Special Forces (SF) Operational Detachments–Alpha (ODA) to the mission.[17] More changes were ordered in the spring of 2004 as the result of the Sunni and Shia uprisings across Iraq and in anticipation of the hurriedly sped up turnover of sovereignty to the Iraqis in June 2004.

On 22 April 2004 CPA Order No. 73 transferred control of the ICDC to the Iraqi Ministry of Defense, officially making it part of the IAF. The ICDC was next redesignated as the Iraqi National Guard (ING) on 20 June 2004. In addition to these programs, the Iraqis created a special infantry division, first known as the Iraq National Task Force Division and later as the Iraqi Intervention Force (IIF), in May and June 2004 to conduct internal security operations. The Iraqis, with Coalition assistance, also created a counterterrorism unit, the Iraqi Special Operations Forces (ISOF) Brigade, which reported independently of the Iraqi Army to the Ministry of Defense.

USAF Photo by SSgt Shane A. Cuomo

Figure 107. Members of the 203d Iraqi National Guard Battalion stand at attention,
3 September 2004, at Forward Operating Base Paliwoda, Iraq, during an award ceremony
for outstanding achievement in support of building the new Iraqi National Guard.

With the transfer of sovereignty to Iraq on 28 June 2004, Iraq assumed control of all its security forces. However, the Coalition intended to play a major part in the operational employment and further development of the ISF. To do this, the Coalition centralized all of the arming, training, and advising efforts under the MNSTC-I commanded by Lieutenant General Petraeus. MNSTC-I was a military command subordinate to Multi-National Force–Iraq (MNF-I). This significant change finalized the gradual handoff of responsibility for building the ISF from the CPA to the US military that had been ongoing since the spring of 2004. In June the military arms of the ISF became known simply as the IAF, which included the Iraqi Army (IA), the IIF, the Iraqi Special Operations Brigade, the ING (made up of units from the former ICDC), the Iraqi Air Force, and the Iraqi Coastal Defense Force. The Iraqi Police, Highway Patrol, Facility Protection Service, and Department of Border Enforcement continued to report to the MOI.

The IAF were again reorganized just prior to the elections in January 2005. First, the Iraqi Government folded the ING into the Iraqi Army on 6 January 2005. Similarly, the IIF was redesignated as the 1st Division of the Iraqi Army on 12 January 2005. As the final step of this reorganization, the Coastal Defense Force was rechristened the Iraqi Navy on 20 January 2005 with subordinate naval and marine elements. As much as possible, this chapter will refer to the various elements of the ISF using the designations they had at the time.

Rebuilding Iraqi Ministries of Government

Arguably, the most important and most complicated task undertaken by the CPA was the reorganization of the civilian government departments that would administer the security forces. The leaders in the CPA felt that a fully democratic Iraq required civilian control of the military and police forces. In the fall of 2003 Walter Slocombe elaborated on the importance of this task, emphasizing the paramount concept of civilian control of the military establishment:

> In addition to creating the new Iraqi army, we will also be working with the governing council . . . on creating a law-based system for civilian oversight and control, creating the institutions and mechanisms to run the national security policies of what will be a major state in the Middle East. And that is in itself an important part of the creation of a democratic, law-based, constitutional system, which is of course our overall strategy.[18]

For this reason, the CPA began to focus on creating strong ministries that could serve as the foundation for civilian oversight. As Lieutenant General Petraeus would later explain, the eventual success of the ISF depended on strong leadership at the ministerial level, because without policies and institutional support there was potential for the security forces themselves to be weak and ineffective. Petraeus emphasized that systems were as critical as soldiers in this type of project:

> Another key factor is the ministries in the government; you've got to have advisors for them in very substantial numbers because if you can't get the top right, over time, what you build at the bottom will not be effectively used. In fact, it could be undermined. You've got to train the folks who are developing the policies, ensuring the troops are paid, performing their logistics functions, getting the fuel for them, and all the rest of that. If you can't develop those [systems], they can very much erode and undermine the development of the units.[19]

The CPA provided advisors to the Iraqi Governing Council (IGC) to help them create a transparent and efficient governmental structure—a difficult task given the decades of corrupt rule under Saddam. Every ministry within the national government, as well as those national entities that reached down to the regional and local level, required assistance for the process to be successful. The Ministry of Defense led the armed forces, while the MOI led the police and paramilitary security forces. The Ministry of Justice directed the prisons and courts and ensured rule of law. When the CPA dissolved on 28 June 2004, responsibility for advising the ministries moved to the State Department and the Iraqi Reconstruction Management Office (IRMO).*

---

*In September 2005, responsibility for advising the Ministries of Defense and Interior was turned over to the MNSTC-I.

To meet its security challenges, the CPA, in consultation with the IGC, created the Ministerial Committee for National Security (MCNS), a rough parallel to the US National Security Council. The MCNS included the ministers of Defense, Interior, Justice, Foreign Affairs, and Finance along with the senior military advisor to the government of Iraq and the director of the Iraqi Intelligence Service. Ambassador Bremer held the chair of this important committee, and between July 2003 and June 2004, the MCNS empowered the Iraqi ministers to convey their views to Bremer and Lieutenant General Ricardo Sanchez as decisions were made regarding the formation of the security forces.[20] The ministers slowly assumed the role of decisionmakers and began to interact and communicate their needs within a legitimate governmental structure months before the transfer of authority actually took place in June 2004.[21] In that month, the Iraqi prime minister took the reins of the committee. It should be noted, however, that the change of ministers and deputies and the installation of the new IIG caused a noticeable degradation in their limited capacities.

The IGC and the fledgling IIG struggled to provide effective planning and efficiency across the various levels of government. The new Ministry of Defense was built from the ground up, and most of the civilians and officers hired to lead the agency had little experience working at the ministerial level. Because the original plans for OIF called for the immediate handover of policing and internal security to Iraqi authorities, the CPA did not dissolve the MOI. Unfortunately, there were similar structural problems with that institution, and it received far less attention after the toppling of the Saddam regime. This caused problems as the CPA began to reinstate the police forces.[22] What emerged initially was a system in which the ministers of Defense, Interior, and Finance did not always coordinate their decisions and actions with each other. Further weakening the broader effort was the challenge of persuading the Shia and Kurdish factions to integrate their militias into the professional security forces. The difficulties of integrating and disbanding local and religious militias would continue to plague the CPA's campaign into 2004.[23]

The New Iraqi Army is Born

In the summer of 2003, as other offices within the CPA began reforming the Iraqi ministries and standing up the police and other security services, Major General Paul Eaton led the CMATT into Iraq and began recruiting, training, and equipping the New Iraqi Army (NIA). Eaton arrived on 13 June 2003, 2 months after the fall of the Saddam regime, with five officers. (The officers on this staff were on loan to the CPA from CENTCOM and did not plan to be in Iraq for an extended tour.) After arriving in Iraq, Eaton and the CMATT found out they would be part of the CPA and would report to Slocombe's deputy, Lieutenant General Luis Feliu of the Spanish Army. Eaton had enjoyed little time to prepare for the mission, recalling that he had received the call to leave for Iraq on 9 May 2003 from the US Army Training and Doctrine Command (TRADOC) Commander, General Kevin Byrnes, when he was at home in Georgia with his wife: "We just kind of looked at each other and I said 'it's a little late, getting this kind of notification. I would have figured the guy to do that would have been on station already.'"[24]

After rushing to Iraq, Eaton and his staff reported to CPA headquarters and found they had inherited a 24-page PowerPoint briefing and a budget of $173 million.[25] CPA's original concept for the NIA called for three divisions of light or motorized infantry to be built by September 2006—in a little over 3 years. Those numbers were arrived at by a very simple logic. The

Coalition had divided Iraq into three zones each of which would require a single division. The "rule of three" was extended downward, leading to divisional organizations that had three brigades, each of which had three battalions.[26] Thus, the new army would have an overall strength of 27 battalions. To augment the NIA, the CPA directed CMATT to form a small aviation element and a coastal defense force.[27] The NIA was designed to defend against external security threats, in contrast to its previous role as a prop for Saddam Hussein's dictatorship. One key CMATT document emphasized the defensive nature of the NIA, describing the basic set of missions of the army as "point security, convoy security, route security, foot and vehicle patrols, border patrols and other duties for territorial defense and stability operations in Iraq."[28] The plan kept the force small so as to pose no threat to Iraq's neighbors, and it would be built slowly to create a professional force under civilian control. Eaton would later call this Phase I of building the NIA.

In a major departure from military practice under Saddam's regime, the CPA decided the NIA was to be a volunteer army. Consistent with CPA Order No. 2, CMATT began accepting volunteers with service in the old regime up through the rank of lieutenant colonel and planned to promote from within to create new general officers. (A later guideline revision allowed high-ranking former officers to return.[29]) The CPA also decreed that the ISF reflect the ethnic, religious, and regional diversity of the country.[30]

Figure 108. As the sun rises over the desert, a Soldier guards the Kirkush Military Training Base in Iraq.

Among the first challenges CMATT faced was locating sites for the billeting and training of the NIA. The army would need infrastructure such as barracks, bases, training centers, and other facilities. Coalition bombing and Iraqi looting had damaged most of the old army's infrastructure beyond repair. Eaton found a partially completed set of military facilities near the town of Kirkush in the eastern part of the country. Although some structures and roads existed, the facilities did not have electricity, water, sewage, and other necessities. With the help of the 937th Engineer Group, CMATT hired an Iraqi firm to build the facilities. The Iraqis based their construction standards on the Army's well known Grafenwoehr Training Area in Germany.[31] Eaton continued this practice throughout his time in Iraq, employing Iraqis to build other garrisons and provide support services whenever possible to foster growth in the economy.[32]

Recruiting took place in Baghdad, Mosul, and Basrah as CMATT sought to create an ethnically balanced force. About 60 percent of all the recruits had prior military service, but the quality of their training varied greatly. While most officers were educated and had previous military experience, enlisted soldiers had little military training. The CPA tried to vet all recruits, and officers endured a competitive selection process which included individual interviews, questionnaires, and background checks.[33] Former members of the SRG, members of the intelligence services, senior level officials of the Baath Party, people affiliated with terrorist organizations, and anyone with human rights violations or crimes against humanity were prohibited from entering the Iraqi forces.[34] CMATT intended for all recruits to be literate, but placed more importance on the physical fitness of the new soldiers.[35] In the early phases of the effort, it took CMATT 1,000 recruits to produce an active battalion of 757 soldiers.[36]

The NIA was to be a *national* force that included all of Iraq's religious and ethnic groups. Units were purposefully staffed to ensure that Shias, Sunni Arabs, Kurds, and other groups were represented in each Army battalion. Slocombe explained, "The idea was that the units should be integrated and that you should implement blunt, no kidding, affirmative action. So that it was not coincidence that you had a battalion commander, deputy commander, and a chief of staff, one was a Shia, one was a Sunni, and one was a Kurd."[37] Further, in the spirit of creating a national army, soldiers could be deployed anywhere throughout Iraq rather than allowing a soldier to remain near his hometown.[38]

In July 2003 the US Government bolstered CMATT's effort by sending a team of contractors from the Vinnell Corporation to Iraq. Composed of retired Army and Marine Corps personnel, the contractor team was supposed to begin planning and preparations to train the new army.[39] The Vinnell contract provided planners, operations officers, unit trainers, and translators, but the US Government had not asked the company to provide drill instructors—the trainers who work directly with military recruits to instill fundamental skills and knowledge. Instead, CMATT assumed that US and Coalition forces would provide the Soldiers to serve as drill sergeants for the NIA's basic training. CENTCOM, however, never tasked that mission to CJTF-7 and the drill sergeants did not materialize until much later. At this point CMATT faced a significant problem. While its staff had grown to 18, it was still far too small to provide drill sergeants from within its own organization.[40] Assistance came from the Coalition partners. The British and Australian Army each provided four senior noncommissioned officers (NCOs) and officers to support the basic training mission. CMATT would also get seven US officers from the 3d Infantry Division (3d ID) for a 2-week period that summer. This mix of Americans, Britons, and Australians were the sum total of uniformed, military personnel available to CMATT in July 2003, and they worked tirelessly to find recruits and supplies so that training could begin.[41] Major General Eaton credits them with saving the program from collapse.

Eaton also reached out to former Iraqi leaders but enjoyed less success in this initiative. He requested 45 former Iraqi officers, identified by Coalition units around the country, to report to Kirkush as leaders of the new training program. They arrived on 15 July 2003, but Eaton had to fire them all within a week when they declined to serve as trainers, and refused to work without restoration of their former rank, increased pay, and better accommodations.[42] Despite this setback, CMATT managed to get 1,000 Iraqi recruits to Kirkush to begin the first basic training session for the NIA on 2 August 2003, actually in advance of CPA Order No. 22, "Creation of a New Iraqi Army," issued on 7 August 2003. From recruiting stations in Mosul, Basrah, and Baghdad, the new Iraqi soldiers arrived via civilian buses, escorted by Major Geoff Fuller, Major Trey Johnson, and Lieutenant Colonel Duncan Hayward of the CMATT staff.[43]

The training of the new recruits and units focused on fundamental skills, leadership, membership in a multiethnic team, and orientation to the military service. Whenever possible, CMATT used Iraqis to train Iraqis. During their initial training, soldiers learned individual tasks while units concentrated on low-level collective training featuring operations in both rural and urban terrain. The training produced recruits with basic leadership and individual skills, as well as units that could conduct a small number of tactical operations in a proficient manner.[44]

The enlisted soldiers of the first Iraqi battalion graduated from training at Kirkush on 4 October 2003, and the second battalion graduated from a rebuilt base in Taji, just north of Baghdad, on 6 January 2004, a date recognized as Iraqi Army Day. After graduation, some of the soldiers stayed at the academy to help teach while others began their careers in the NIA. By late January 2004 CMATT had trained the enlisted soldiers of the first three battalions of the NIA.

CMATT was making slow progress but its capacity was very limited. To expand and speed up its training, Eaton had to look beyond the assets available to CJTF-7, the CPA, and even CENTCOM. Toward the end of August 2003, while visiting Jordan to find much needed equipment, Eaton witnessed the country's military forces in action: "I observed the Jordanian Army and I really liked what I saw. I saw sergeants and lieutenant colonels engaging with their Vice Chairman, with very senior officers. They were talking, they were expressing their opinions, they had a dialogue going . . . so I think, 'These guys can help us.'"[45] Eaton spoke to the Jordanian Chief of Training about assisting CMATT train up to 2,000 Iraqi officers.

Figure 109. Seven hundred five recruits from the new Iraqi Army's 2d Battalion conduct a pass and review at a graduation ceremony 6 January 2004, in Baghdad, Iraq.

King Abdullah II quickly approved the request.[46] A Jordanian Princess—also a colonel in the army—provided assistance with the recruiting and training of Iraqi women, including a contingent of 75 women who trained as police officers in the Jordan police academy.[47] Colonel Kim Smith, a British Army officer, served as CMATT's liaison officer in Jordan.[48]

The initial set of Iraqi battalions did not have the capability of mounting operations because they lacked a cadre of trained officers and NCOs. The creation of this corps of officers and NCOs was occurring separately from the training of the enlisted soldiers. CMATT had screened roughly 750 Iraqi officers, from lieutenant to general, and then sent them to Jordan for training in late December. Similarly, 750 NCOs were in training at the new NCO Academy in Taji.[49] CMATT planned to form successive battalions of the NIA by taking officer–NCO cohorts from these two schools and linking them up with recruits after basic training. But funding delays at the DOD in the fall and winter of 2003/2004 prevented CMATT from meeting its plan. Eaton could not remain on schedule in the construction of more bases, and this delayed the start of basic training for the 7th Battalion of the NIA for a number of months.

From the beginning of their mission, Eaton and others at CMATT recognized that the Iraqi forces would need continued training and mentoring if they were to accomplish their missions. Out of this realization came a plan to assign a 10-man advisory team to each battalion after it completed basic training. In mid-September the CMATT staff submitted a Joint Manning Document (JMD) request to the US Joint Staff for action. Because Secretary of Defense Donald Rumsfeld had ordered the acceleration of NIA training on 5 September 2003, the CMATT JMD requested a large number of advisory

Figure 110. A platoon of the newly-formed Joint Iraqi Security Company marches to class. These Iraqi forces were trained by 2d Battalion, 44th Air Defense Artillery, 101st Airborne Division.

teams. The new plan, called Phase II, moved the deadline for the fielding of the first three divisions from September 2006 to September 2004. While DOD had accelerated the overall schedule, the US Army and Marine Corps still required 6 months to locate, train, and deploy the advisory teams. The first advisory teams were not sent to Iraq until March 2004; they joined their units 1 month later.[50] Part of the challenge of getting advisors into the CMATT program was that in June 2003, the US Armed Services had just begun to fill CENTCOM's demands for advisors to serve in Task Force (TF) *Phoenix*—the program to build a new Afghan Army. Planning for that effort had begun in the fall of 2002. The demands of Operation ENDURING FREEDOM (OEF) and OIF were putting significant strain on both the Army and the Marine Corps to sustain the ever-increasing need for personnel.

Equipping the newly-trained Iraqi soldiers created other challenges. It was both extraordinarily difficult and expensive to use Saddam-era material because most of Iraq's old equipment was outdated, broken, or stolen in the looting. CMATT had a woefully inadequate budget of $173 million in its start-up stage, and a large portion of its funds were already allocated to rebuilding the barracks and training facilities. Further, to boost the Iraqi economy, the CPA required that all purchases for the NIA be channeled through Iraqi sources. Thus, Eaton admitted, the uniforms and boots CMATT issued to the initial Iraqi soldiers were of low quality.[51]

Once CMATT trained and equipped the recruits, their battalions joined Coalition forces in the fight despite the CPA's original intent to have these units avoid internal security missions. The 4th Infantry Division (4th ID) operating in the Sunni Triangle employed the first battalion, the 1st AD in Taji employed the second battalion, while the third battalion deployed to Mosul with the 101st Airborne Division (101st ABN). Coalition leaders viewed the fielding of these initial Iraqi units as a watershed moment, one that marked the birth of a new kind of professional soldier in Iraq. At the graduation of the first battalion in October 2003, Ambassador Bremer remarked, "Gone is the brutality of the old regime. The New Iraqi Army will be responsible to its citizens and will serve to protect Iraq from external threats."[52]

CJTF-7 Creates the Iraqi Civil Defense Corps (ICDC)

While the CPA and CMATT were planning and beginning to create the NIA in the summer of 2003, Coalition units throughout Iraq were confronted with a deteriorating security situation. Faced with an increasing number of security tasks, Army commanders exercised their initiative to create ad hoc paramilitary units to deal with local and regional security problems. Lieutenant General Sanchez and General John Abizaid, the commander of CENTCOM, developed the sketchy concept for these forces that they called the ICDC. They based their design on similar programs that both leaders had overseen in Kosovo.[53] To get the program running, CJTF-7 directed each multinational division to stand up a single ICDC battalion. In early 2004 CJTF-7 massively expanded the program to one ICDC battalion in each of Iraq's 18 provinces. By late 2004 the program was expanded again to 60+ battalions that were then combined and renamed the ING.

The ICDC gave US operations an "Iraqi face," soaked up unemployed young men to keep them out of the insurgency, and increased the number of security forces available to the new government. Although the ICDC had very little capacity for independent military action and was viewed as a temporary measure, it provided crucial Iraqi involvement in operations.[54] Colonel Greg Gardner, the chief of staff for Walt Slocombe, explained:

> The idea was that these were locally recruited Iraqis, recruited from the area where that division was operating, they would stay at home at night, they would live at home, we would keep their weapons at work, and we gave them a particular type of uniform that we purchased for them. They would work during the day doing physical labor type details or security details securing physical locations. We would feed them one meal a day, and then they would go home at night.[55]

The ICDC expanded quickly in the fall 2003 as nearly every US division created its own program. The overall effort progressed from 1 battalion per division to 2 battalions for each of the 18 provinces of Iraq for a total of 36.[56] Some commanders embraced the idea while others saw it as a distraction. The leaders of the 3d Armored Cavalry Regiment (3d ACR) saw great promise in creating the paramilitary units. Using Commander's Emergency Response Program (CERP) money, the 3d ACR built the Navea Training Center, named after Specialist Rafael Navea who was killed on 27 August 2003 when an improvised explosive device (IED) struck his vehicle in Fallujah, Iraq. Located between the towns of Al Asad and Hit, the regiment's 2d Battalion, 5th Field Artillery managed the center and trained about 2,000 Iraqis, who then supported the 1st, 2d, and 3d Squadrons of the regiment.[57] Other divisions became similarly involved with the ICDC. Colonel James Hickey's 1st BCT of the 4th ID trained over 1,000 ICDC troops.[58] By 21 August 2003 the CENTCOM Commander, General Abizaid, reported that 23,000 ICDC members were working with the Coalition.[59] They served as linguists, security personnel, drivers, and humanitarian relief providers, and they participated in patrols, convoys, cordons, and checkpoints.[60]

The ICDC program initially became a source of friction between the CPA and CJTF-7, one symptom of the larger lack of unity of command and effort within the Coalition. To Bremer, the ICDC effort looked like an attempt by the military to artificially inflate the number of Iraqis engaged in security work by using poorly trained forces to substitute for US and Coalition troops.[61] He also viewed the program as a diversion from CJTF-7's primary effort of defeating the insurgency, as well as a potential diversion of funds from the CPA's own military and police building programs. Individual ICDC units also tended to be dominated by single ethnic groups or religious sects because they were drawn from specific locales. This characteristic ran counter to the CPA plan for diversity in Iraq's new security forces.

USAF Photo by SSgt Ricky A. Bloom

Figure 111. Female members of the Iraqi Civil Defense Corps learn proper drill techniques from a member of the US Army 1st Battalion, 5th Infantry Regiment, 1st Cavalry Division, at Camp Bonzai Forward Operating Base in Baghdad, 28 April 2004.

Leaders in CJTF-7 and CENTCOM strongly disagreed with the CPA's view; they felt the program complemented CPA's efforts to stand up a professional army. Both Lieutenant General Sanchez and General Abizaid saw the ICDC as a critical means of employing Iraqi men, improving the ability of US units to work with the Iraqi population, and giving Iraq greater responsibility for its own security and future. US Army units in Iraq simply could not wait 6 years, 2 years, or even 18 months for CPA programs to bear fruit. Moreover, Sanchez and Abizaid viewed the program as temporary and likely to be folded into the CPA's broader efforts in the near future.[62] In CPA Order No. 28, issued on 3 September 2003, Bremer somewhat reluctantly sanctioned the ICDC and officially made it part of the IAF alongside the NIA.[63]

Figure 112. Two new Iraqi civil defense recruits practice clearing a building alongside Staff Sergeant John Pickett, 82d Airborne Division (right), during the Iraqi Civil Defense Course (ICDC).

Many US units were proud of their ICDC units and credited them with filling a huge void that the CPA simply could not address at this point in the campaign. Lieutenant Aaron Boal, an officer in the 1st Squadron, 2d Armored Cavalry Regiment (2d ACR) operating in and around Baghdad in 2003 and 2004, was one of the pioneers in the ICDC program. As a platoon leader and later a staff officer in the 2d ACR, Boal recruited for, trained, and operated with ICDC units. Boal's squadron decided to commit precious assets to the effort, selecting officers and NCOs who had any measure of experience working with military forces from other countries. While Boal and his colleagues went into the mission with a great deal of enthusiasm, they met a number of obstacles, the most daunting of which were the lack of resources, language and cultural barriers, and uneducated and unskilled recruits.[64]

After graduating from a 1-week course in rudimentary military skills conducted at a training center established by the 2d ACR, the ICDC recruits reported to Boal and other Soldiers at the squadron level. Boal then formed them into squads or platoons and launched them into operations alongside 2d ACR units. One officer and a handful of NCOs advised the ICDC units. Over time, the squadron developed its own more extensive basic training programs that built on the 1-week program. Eventually, they chose the best and brightest Iraqi recruits to serve as NCOs and officers. Despite this selection process, Boal and his team found the instilling of discipline, initiative, and decisionmaking skills into ICDC leaders challenging.[65] ICDC soldiers and units, however, did prove adept at collecting information, which became integrated into the 2d ACR's intelligence gathering system.[66] Over time, Boal's advisors and ICDC soldiers grew to understand and respect one another. By the time of their departure from Iraq, he felt ICDC advisors were even more physically and mentally exhausted than others in the squadron because of the additional set of tasks they had performed. Yet Boal believes the ICDC program was integral to the success his squadron enjoyed in Baghdad in 2003 and early 2004.

In December 2003 CJTF-7 tasked the commander of the CJSOTF-AP to provide SF teams to assist conventional units with training the ICDC. By early 2004 SF Soldiers were working with 1st Cavalry Division (1st CAV) and 1st AD units to provide a more standardized, rigorous program of military training. Different units, however, had varying views of how best to employ the ICDC, and hence, what training was appropriate. Some wanted to continue to use the ICDC for reconstruction, static guard, and infrastructure protection. The Combined Joint Special Operations Task Force (CJSOTF) commander and others wanted to train the ICDC to take more active roles in counterinsurgency and foreign internal defense operations. While debates about the proper use of the ICDC raised tensions between conventional forces and SF, those issues were resolved without great damage to the overall effort. In one unique case, the 1st AD and SF personnel worked together to train the 36th ICDC Battalion—an ethnically and religiously integrated unit that was given specialized training and deployed to conduct counter-insurgent missions in the capital.[67]

Despite a measure of success in the initial months of the program, the ICDC program faced many obstacles. The ICDC's proficiency and effectiveness were directly tied to the type of training and equipment they received from their US partner units. In a few cases, lack of US effort led to ICDC members feeling that the Coalition did not take them seriously.[68] As US units began to employ ICDC units in patrolling and other security missions, the lack of training, equipment, and sustainment systems put them at great risk. ICDC units did not have permanent bases or support systems in most areas, situations that required their soldiers to live at home and report for duty each day. Neither police nor full-time soldiers, the ICDC existed in a dangerous gray zone between these two poles.

The Phase II Plan for the Iraqi Armed Forces

One month after the first Iraqi recruits began basic training, and in the midst of CMATT's struggles to build bases, obtain equipment, and find trainers and advisors for the NIA, Eaton received a change of mission. As noted earlier, on 5 September 2003 the DOD ordered what was labeled Phase II, the first of two major expansions of the original plan for Iraq's armed forces. Driving this expansion was the Coalition leadership's realization by early fall 2003 that a coherent insurgency was emerging in Iraq and that the ISF had to play a critical and immediate role in engaging that threat. CMATT briefings from early September 2003 reflected this shift in the understanding of the security situation. One briefing made the following assertions: "Time is not on our side in Iraq"; "Iraqi army units brought on line quicker enable Coalition units to leave sooner"; and "Iraqi army units in the field may enable friendly Arab nations to commit troops to security operations in Iraq . . . which they won't do now."[69] Thus, by the fall of 2003 the Coalition's effort to train ISF had become a strategic as well as an operational objective.

For the Iraqi Army to contribute to stabilizing the security situation, they had to be quickly trained, equipped, and fielded. Thus, Phase II of the NIA program called for the original 27 battalions and 3 divisions of the NIA to be operational by 1 September 2004—2 years earlier than the June 2003 Phase I plan. Phase II also included the creation of an Iraqi Coastal Defense Force for river and coastal patrolling, and an Iraqi Air Force, to be initially equipped with 8 C-130 transport aircraft and 12 UH-1 "Huey" helicopters.[70]

Iraq's expanded military forces would be stationed at brigade-size garrisons, at one air base, and at one naval base with supporting recruiting offices, training centers, and support facilities of all types. The plan required a major increase in US and Coalition support to include mobile training teams, embedded unit advisors, equipment fielding teams, and significantly greater military and civilian construction capability. The cost of the program ballooned from the $173 million in Phase I to just over $2.2 billion in Phase II.[71]

A New Iraqi Police Service

As noted throughout this study, the Coalition's prewar planning did not anticipate the near complete breakdown of law and order and the almost complete disruption of Iraqi governance that followed the fall of Saddam Hussein. In fact, in their planning efforts both ORHA and the CPA hoped the Iraqi MOI could be quickly reformed and put in charge of internal security and control of the borders. The security situation in Iraq after the removal of Saddam necessitated a rush to stand up police forces and related civilian security organizations, but despite the urgency of the task, the Coalition underestimated its immensity and did not adequately resource the process.[72] The CPA exacerbated the situation when it issued its de-Baathification order and, almost overnight, most of the MOI's leadership became unemployed. The Coalition's program to reestablish Iraq's police would become a struggle for resources, leadership, and direction—in many ways mirroring the efforts to create a new professional army.

On 2 May 2003 ORHA recalled to duty the Baghdad police, and Coalition commanders made similar recall announcements in secured areas outside the capital. In June 2003 the CPA issued a directive requiring all former police officers to return to work by 3 July 2003. According to a 2005 State Department Inspector General (IG) report, approximately 38,000 police officers returned, and Coalition units in the field recruited an additional 30,000.[73] At this point in the campaign, training levels and equipment were extremely rudimentary.

Figure 113. Iraqi Police Lieutenant Narseed was one of the first female officers. She was assigned to the Khabat Police Station in Irbil province.

To help improve the program, Bremer tapped Bernard Kerik, a former New York City police commissioner, to lead the CPA's effort as head of the CPATT. A British police official, Douglas Brand, arrived to serve as Kerik's deputy. The US State Department's Bureau of International and Narcotics Law Enforcement (INL) and the Justice Department's International Criminal Investigative Assistance Training Program (ICITAP) assisted in the design of the new police program and the State Department allocated $25 million to "assess" the state of Iraq's police.[74] Additional advisors arrived from the United Kingdom, Australia, Canada, and Spain and began assisting the MOI. Many of those involved in planning the new police force wanted decentralized control of the police to build a force that was representative and responsive to the needs of the local constituents. At the same time, the problem of insurgents and terrorists caused some advisors to argue that control be centralized. Ultimately, the CPA chose a hybrid model where local police chiefs had some autonomy, but were accountable to both local elected officials and the MOI.[75]

While recruiting the number of men required for the new Iraqi Police Service (IPS) was a large-scale problematic undertaking, finding quality leadership was even more difficult. Due to de-Baathification and revenge killings, the senior leadership of the police had fled or had been removed by the CPA. Many junior personnel who knew the fate of the senior leadership abandoned their posts as well. Although some of the new Iraqi senior officers were dedicated to the mission, overall professional standards were low. The leadership program was eventually modified to include a focus on management and leadership skills.[76]

Figure 114. Iraqi policemen fall into formation to begin a full day's worth of combat techniques and weapon handling.

Between mid-May and August 2003, Kerik and the CPATT struggled with finding methods, resources, and the infrastructure to train the IPS. Using US police forces as models, Kerik estimated that Iraq needed between 65,000 and 75,000 police officers. In early August 2004, the CPA estimated that only 30,000 mostly untrained, underequipped, and unmotivated officers had returned to duty. Kerik originally estimated it would take 6 years to train the police in Iraq. Bremer told him he had only 2 years, and to look for support from Hungary using the Taszar Air Base that NATO had used in support of operations in Bosnia during the 1990s. Bremer then allocated $120 million of seized Iraqi assets to fund a recruiting and training program that Kerik believed would require $750 million in the first year alone.[77]

On 31 August 2003 Bremer notified Kerik that the Hungarian option was dead; the Hungarian parliament had decided to delay the request for support until after the beginning of 2004.[78] The country of Jordan, which had agreed to train some 2,000 officers of the NIA, was identified as the next nation that might provide assistance in the CPATT effort. CPA and CPATT hoped to implement a plan to train some 25,000 police in Jordan over the next 18 months. But the program could not begin until funding was provided in the US President's supplemental budget request then working its way through Congress.[79] As a result, the first Iraqi police recruits did not begin training in Jordan until mid-November 2003.

Perhaps more debilitating than the problems in finding resources and training sites was Iraq's traditional attitude toward its police. In Iraqi cultural and historical experience, service in the police was not seen as an honorable profession. An Iraqi expression encountered by US forces explained the challenge: "If a man should fall from grace it's okay because he can still become a policeman."[80] This stereotype had deep roots. The legacy of Iraqi policing before 2003 was one of corruption, repression, and a career of last resort. The ethnic and religious

443

fractures in Iraqi society had traditionally hampered attempts to create police forces based on equal treatment under the law, and the Baathist regime had often used its police to enact revenge and suppress political adversaries.

For these reasons, Iraqi police resembled Western style police forces in name only. New and even returning recruits desperately needed comprehensive training because simple forensic procedures, such as establishing a fingerprint database, were unknown.[81] The Jordan International Police Training Center (JIPTC) and the Baghdad Public Safety Academy provided much of that rudimentary yet necessary training. The basic course included modern police methods, such as defense tactics, firearms training, and emergency vehicle operation. Recruits also learned the basic framework of constitutional democracy, use of force, human rights, gender issues, police ethics, and codes of conduct among other subjects. The first class of 456 Iraqi recruits began the new program in November 2003.[82]

CPA police advisors also designed a 3-week Transition Integration Program (TIP) to vet prospective officers and provide initial training for former police officers who had returned to duty. The course included 126 hours of instruction including the role of the IPS, prohibitions against torture, police ethics and codes of conduct, and practical training in firearms instruction. However, because the CPA's civilian police advisors were not present throughout the country, US Army Military Police (MP) units conducted much of the recruiting and training with only nominal CPA supervision.[83] Without civilian police advisors, MPs taught with limited knowledge of the culture and procedures of the Iraqi criminal justice system.

While CPATT struggled with funding and a lack of sufficient personnel to train the IPS, other Coalition military units across Iraq tried to fill the void by standing up local police units on their own. In late spring 2003 the 3d ID's 1st Battalion, 30th Infantry (1-30th IN) took matters into its own hands by opening a police station in their area of responsibility (AOR) in Baghdad. The unit's Soldiers physically went into the abandoned building, swept it out, opened the door, and placed a tank outside for protection. Battalion leaders then traveled around the city to convince former Iraqi police officers to return and accompanied Iraqi officers on their initial patrols to provide legitimacy. The leadership of 1-30th IN also conducted a limited information operation campaign in their area as they tried to convey the message that the police stations and academies were open and those interested in serving should report to the academies.[84] When the Soldiers of the 1st AD took over responsibility for Baghdad from the 3d ID in May 2003, they also supported the newly established Iraqi police departments in their neighborhoods by providing basic items such as weapons seized during house raids and traffic checkpoints, dark blue T-shirts for temporary uniforms, and Nissan Maxima cars that they had painted blue and numbered.[85]

In the north of the country, the 101st ABN conducted numerous projects to help the Iraqis reinstate their police. The division's 2d Brigade rebuilt a local police academy in Mosul from the ground up. The brigade's Soldiers began by securing funding to rebuild offices and locate furniture and computers. By late summer 2003 the 2d Brigade had established a permanent police academy overseen by a US Army Reserve MP company comprised of Soldiers who served as police officers in their civilian lives.[86] Units in the 4th ID established a similar police training program in Salah ad Din province in the summer of 2003. By August the US-trained Iraqi police had begun planning operations on their own and conducting joint missions with Soldiers from the 4th ID.[87]

Like its program to build the ICDC, CJTF-7's improvised efforts to stand up police units ran afoul of the CPA and Ambassador Bremer. In another illustration of the problems caused by lack of unity of command in Iraq, Bremer often clashed with CJTF-7 and CENTCOM over security force efforts that remained outside the CPA's control. Bremer believed that CJTF-7 was trying to inflate police numbers as a means to lessen the need for increased levels of US forces in current and future troop rotations. At one point in early October 2003, Bremer even ordered Sanchez to end the Army's police building programs.[88] Nevertheless, the program continued until April 2004 when CJTF-7 was given responsibility for building all Iraqi security forces.

The IPS effort was the least successful aspect of the entire ISF train and equip program in 2003 and 2004. The Coalition's attempts to give Iraq a professional law enforcement institution had become the victim of inaccurate assumptions about post-Saddam Iraq, a worsening security environment, and traditional Iraqi antipathy toward the profession. Simply put, neither the CPA nor CJTF-7 had the resources to give the police programs the priority they needed to surmount the historical and cultural obstacles in their way.[89] In the spring of 2004 many Iraqi police forces simply dissolved in the cities where Sunni and Shia armed groups rebelled. Not until the fall of 2004 would the IIG and the Coalition be able to revamp their police building efforts in any significant way.

Iraqi Border Security

CPA Order No. 26 created the Department of Border Enforcement (DBE) on 24 August 2003 placing it under the control of the MOI, and making it responsible for border policing, customs, passports, and immigration procedures. However, despite the creation of the DBE, border security remained an extremely thorny problem until the DBE program came under the supervision of MNSTC-I in mid-2004.[90] As a result, the Iraqi Government lost billions of dollars in potential tax revenue due to smuggling. More importantly, the routes into Iraq from Syria and Iran were plentiful and easy to infiltrate for terrorists and insurgents.

In some parts of Iraq, US forces developed their own ad hoc methods of securing the borders in their AORs. The 101st ABN conducted operations in northern Iraq near the Syrian border where foreign insurgents were able to infiltrate into the country. Brigadier General Frank Helmick, Assistant Division Commander for Operations (ADC-O) for the 101st ABN, described the border crossing sites as "a two-lane road, probably just a little bit bigger than the width of this room, and you had these big trucks crossing and there was no tariff."[91] To secure this area, the 101st ABN, particularly the 3d BCT commanded by Colonel Michael Linnington, undertook the massive project of rebuilding the border facilities, constructing a berm complex, and training the new Iraqi border police. The 2d and 3d Battalions of the 187th Infantry led the effort of rebuilding the forts, and by the time winter came, these forts consisted of covered buildings, a mess hall, sleeping accommodations, water, and vehicles. In cooperation with Iraqi and US Army Engineers, the Soldiers of the 3d BCT completed a 270-kilometer berm to inhibit smuggling and infiltrators.[92] A tariff of $10 for cars and $20 for trucks was imposed to further improve the border patrol, and the secure border allowed trade with Syria to resume, which bolstered the local economy.[93] Soon after the border opened, goods came flooding into Iraq. Automobiles, which were heavily taxed during Saddam's era, became the most popular import while Iraqi farmers exported large amounts of grain to Syria.[94]

While units of the 101st ABN stepped up their oversight, they also trained Iraqis to control the borders. Soldiers helped Iraqi Kurds in As Sulamaniyah province establish an all-female unit to help search women crossing the Jordanian border as potential insurgent couriers carrying equipment and messages for terrorists. This unit gained the attention of many Iraqis, some of whom criticized the female officers because they symbolized a break from traditional values while others applauded the initiative as a step forward for the involvement of women in the public life of the new Iraq.[95]

To the south the 3d ACR, responsible for Al Anbar province, secured the porous border with Syria, helping to deter insurgents from slipping into Iraq. Lieutenant Colonel Greg Reilly of the 1st Squadron, 3d ACR did not have enough Soldiers to secure the entire 200 kilometer border, but by focusing on the high traffic crossing areas on the Euphrates River, they achieved considerable success in halting insurgent movement.[96] In southern Iraq the 2d Squadron, 3d ACR, provided extensive training to the Iraqi Border Police, and although some initial recruits failed to report for duty, by January 2004 the squadron's G Troop had a formation of 180 Iraqi Border Police at the Al-Waleed border crossing point and thousands of Iraqi citizens were able to cross the border to Saudi Arabia for the religious pilgrimage to Mecca.[97]

The ISF at the Crossroads, January 2004

In September 2003 the Coalition had directed a major increase in the number of ISF, accelerated by 2 years the CPA's original plan to train 27 battalions of the NIA by the summer of 2006, and added an air force and maritime force to the overall Iraqi defense structure. The CPATT's efforts to train Iraqi police finally began to bear fruit when Iraqi police recruits began training in Jordan in November 2003. Nevertheless, confirming the actual state of the IPS and other police forces, including the actual numbers of trained police on duty, remained a difficult task for the Coalition at the close of 2003. By the spring of 2004, it had also become clear to senior Coalition leaders in CJTF-7, the CPA, CENTCOM, and the US Government that they faced an increasingly large and effective insurgency in Iraq. By that time, the Coalition reported it had fielded over 100,000 police, including the IPS, the FPS, 30,000 members of the ICDC, and approximately 1,200 soldiers in the NIA.[98] However, the actual quality and quantity of these forces, especially police units, were questionable.

After the Sunni and Shia uprisings in April 2004, the threat of the growing insurgency required that all ISF units add internal security tasks to their mission sets. Consequently, the Coalition had to make major improvements in training and equipping the ISF's to take on their role in internal security. "We'll stand down as the Iraqi's stand up" soon became shorthand for the goal of the security line of operation within the overall Coalition campaign plan for Iraq. Neither the CENTCOM commander nor the CJTF-7 commander, however, felt that the CPA was giving CMATT sufficient priority and related resources to handle the vastly expanded mission. To resolve the issue, Sanchez and Abizaid wanted the overall ISF mission moved from CPA to CJTF-7.[99]

By January 2004 Major General Eaton's CMATT staff had grown in size from its original 6-person team in June 2003 to slightly over 200 personnel, including the members of the advisor teams who served with ISF units. CMATT had also become a true joint and Coalition effort. Its initial headquarters JMD authorized 19 international officers, 22 Marines, 11 Sailors, and 12 Airmen among the 126 planned positions. Spain, the United Kingdom, Australia, and Poland contributed officers to CMATT and a British brigadier general, Jonathan Riley, served as CMATT's deputy chief.[100] Despite this augmentation, Eaton believed from the beginning that the

Coalition program to build the ISF had never received the attention or resources it warranted. He recalled, "Nobody wearing a DOD sticker gave [the ISF program] the importance it needed in the face of compelling evidence that the only way out of Iraq was the ISF becoming viable."[101]

The CMATT's planning efforts to create the organizational structure for training and advising the NIA were hampered by joint and Army manning processes. CPA and CMATT had contracted with the Vinnell Corporation to jump-start the process in July and August 2003. The Army and Marines provided a few individuals, as did Australia and the United Kingdom, but many involved realized that the long-term solution was to man the CMATT primarily with US military personnel. The greatest need appeared to be continued development and mentoring after units completed initial training. The 1st Battalion of the NIA, for example, began to dissolve soon after its October graduation due to poor Iraqi leadership and desertions. To instill rigor and continue the training, some US Army units began serving alongside the new Iraqi soldiers. Artillerymen from the 1st Battalion, 17th Field Artillery (1-17th FA), of the 4th ID, for example, became advisors to the Iraqi battalion in their AOR.

By early fall of 2003 one of the original members of the CMATT, Lieutenant Colonel Blaise Cornell-d'Echert, had begun to view advisors as an integral element in the effort to create a sustainable Iraqi force. Cornell-d'Echert devised the structure and personnel requirements that would truly enable CMATT to train and advise a large professional army. Working with Eaton, he designed three components to the structure—a headquarters element for CMATT; training teams to provide initial military training to new Iraqi units, NCOs, and officers; and US advisor teams to accompany those new units on operational missions. The advisors would form 10-man units initially called advisor support teams (ASTs), each of which were assigned to an Iraqi battalion. The components required different types of Soldiers with different skills suited to the particular task at hand. Those personnel were needed quickly because the next Iraqi units, manned with enlisted soldiers, NCOs, and officers, were scheduled to be activated fully and available for operations in early 2004.[102]

In early October 2003 the CMATT submitted its new structural concept to the Services via CENTCOM using the Request for Forces (RFF) process. This process allowed the requesting headquarters to ask for existing units for specified missions. In contrast, the JMD process created a list of individual positions, with required specific skills and ranks that the Services must fill. The first RFF requested 311 Soldiers, organized in teams designed to train and advise 2 division and 2 brigade headquarters, 8 battalions, and an NCO academy.[103] Cornell-d'Echert and the CMATT recommended the use of the US Army Reserve Training Support Divisions (TSDs) to fill the RFF.[104] Those units provided training to the Reserve Components and were staffed with combat arms and combat support Soldiers experienced in providing, observing, and evaluating collective training.

Many of the TSDs, however, were being used by the Army in 2004 to support the large-scale mobilization of the Army Reserve and the Army National Guard (ARNG) and were not available for service in Iraq. Instead of receiving individuals and teams that were picked and trained for the mission, CMATT, in Cornell-d'Echert's view, began to receive a mix of personnel in early 2004 who, in many cases, were not prepared for the missions they had to perform. The US Marine Corps provided some of the best-suited personnel in the initial wave of advisors to arrive in Iraq.[105] The Army provided a combination of Soldiers from the Active and Reserve Components, only some of which had the necessary background.[106] This contingent included some highly trained observer-controllers from the Combined Arms Maneuver Center at Hohenfels, Germany, who were well prepared for the mission.

Despite CMATT's efforts to remodel and improve its structure, leaders in the DOD found that the overall Coalition ISF effort needed to be revamped. In January 2004 they sent Major General Karl W. Eikenberry to assess the ISF training programs. Eikenberry had just completed more than a year in Afghanistan in command of the Coalition headquarters that oversaw the creation of a new Afghan Army. His report confirmed what both CPA and CJTF-7 already knew—providing security was the main effort in Iraq and current ISF programs were not building capacity fast enough. His most significant recommendation to the DOD was that all security force programs be consolidated for efficiency and effectiveness, and most importantly, that they be placed under the command of CJTF-7.[107] Naturally this rankled the CPA, and Ambassador Bremer did not concur with the report.[108] Nevertheless, the NSC and Secretary of Defense Rumsfeld accepted and acted on Eikenberry's report.

Iraqi Forces Join the Fight

In the spring of 2004, while the Coalition was overhauling the ISF training efforts, the NIA suffered an embarrassing failure when the Coalition sent one of the Iraqi battalions hastily into combat. On 31 March four contractors from Blackwater USA, a private company providing logistics security to the CPA, traveling in two vehicles were ambushed and killed in the Sunni Arab city of Fallujah. The killers strung up their charred corpses on a nearby bridge. The grisly scene, televised in the United States and around the world, elicited calls for a strong US response. At about the same time, Shia militia groups under the firebrand Muqtada al-Sadr rose up in defiance of the Coalition in several cities to the southeast of Baghdad. In April 2004, after a few months of relative calm and in the midst of the massive rotation of forces into and out of Iraq, the Coalition suddenly faced the greatest level of resistance to its occupation since the invasion a year before.

Over the objections of US Marine Corps commanders, who had recently taken over the sector that included Fallujah from the 82d Airborne Division (82d ABN), the CPA ordered CJTF-7 to attack Fallujah to find those responsible and destroy the growing insurgent cells in the city. In response, Lieutenant General Sanchez directed the 1st Marine Expeditionary Force (MEF) to create a plan for the assault, and the Marines launched Operation VIGILANT RESOLVE with four Marine infantry battalions, supported by significant amounts of Marine airpower and artillery, into Fallujah on 5 April 2004. US forces encountered intense enemy resistance as they entered the city.

On the first day of the offensive, CJTF-7 ordered the 2d Battalion of the NIA, then operating with the 1st AD north of Baghdad in Taji, to join the Marine operation in Fallujah. The Iraqi unit was to man checkpoints and form a cordon around the city. Of the five companies in the battalion, two were on leave. The three companies on duty boarded trucks for the move accompanied by a new 10-man CMATT advisor team from the US Marines. As they drove through a Shia neighborhood in Baghdad, a large crowd stopped them and accosted them about the immorality of attacking fellow Iraqis.[109] After shots rang out and seven Iraq soldiers were wounded, the convoy returned to camp. CJTF-7 then provided helicopters to move the Iraqi companies to Fallujah later that night.

But by that time, the unit had begun to dissolve as groups of soldiers refused to take part in an operation that would pit them against other Iraqis. Major General Eaton recalled the situation:

> At the Pickup Zone, in the dark, blades turning on several CH-47s, about 70 Iraqi Soldiers became demonstrably upset. . . . the situation was chaotic and the senior Marine, Major Chris Davis, called me to inform me of what was going on. . . . Major Davis indicated he was about to stand the unit down, and ultimately did so. I met him at dawn the next morning after a dangerous trip from Baghdad to review the situation. We dismissed the 70 Iraqi soldiers who were the greatest problem, and changed out three company commanders and the battalion commander, replacing them from within the battalion.[110]

As the situation developed, Iraqi troops began to voice the following complaint: "We enlisted to fight enemies from outside Iraq, not our own people."[111]

The 2d Battalion of the NIA was not the only Iraqi force to face serious problems in April 2004. During the uprisings of that month, many ICDC units disintegrated under contact with insurgent and militia forces, especially when left to operate on their own. The intensity of the fighting exposed the weakness of their limited military training, support institutions, and the ethnic basis on which they had been recruited. Even the specially trained multiethnic 36th Battalion, sent to Fallujah in April 2004, lost many of its Soldiers to desertion after only a few days of action. Sunni soldiers in the unit refused to engage in combat against Sunni insurgents, Shia soldiers balked at being used for offensive operations, and Kurds formed the core of those who remained. The CJSOTF pulled the battalion out of action in May and it later was reconstituted as the 36th Commando Battalion, a founding element of the Iraqi Special Operations Brigade, and eventually one of the most competent units in the ISF.[112] In mid-2004, as will be discussed later in this chapter, MNSTC-I incorporated the ICDC effort into the regular army training program recognizing that the future role of these units in Iraq would be a military one and would require the appropriate level of military training and support.

After its embarrassing refusal to fight during Operation VIGILANT RESOLVE, the NIA redeemed itself in November 2004 when it participated in Operation AL FAJR, the second battle of Fallujah. Five Iraqi infantry battalions joined the combined Marine and Army offensive that destroyed the resistance in the city. Iraqi forces secured and cleared parts of Fallujah with US forces, and conducted reconnaissance and surveillance missions around the city.[113] US Army Staff Sergeant Bryan Reed, a member of the AST working with the unit, explained that Iraqi forces were eager to return to Fallujah and demonstrate their abilities. Reed asserted, "They wanted to come back here. They had something to prove."[114] The Iraqis did prove themselves up to the demands of combat, losing 6 soldiers and taking 55 casualties in their effort. Demonstrating that CMATT advisors not only trained their Iraqi counterparts but also fought alongside them in combat, Staff Sergeant Todd Cornell was killed in action by insurgent small arms fire while fighting with his Iraqi soldiers on a rooftop in Fallujah.[115]

There were other signs of improvement in the NIA's performance in 2004. As they became better trained and equipped, as more US advisors were assigned to NIA units, and as the interim government took ownership of the ISF after 28 June 2004, the new forces became more involved in Coalition operations. One excellent example of increasing ISF capabilities was Iraqi involvement in Operation BATON ROUGE. Mounted by the 1st ID in the summer and fall of 2004, the operation's objective was to return the city of Samarra to Coalition and Iraqi control. Like Fallujah, the city had become a safe haven for Sunni insurgents after the 202d ING Battalion and Iraqi police had been driven out in the spring of 2004.

In the summer of 2004, the 2d BCT of the 1st ID began Operation BATON ROUGE, a sustained full spectrum operation in which Iraqi units played an important role. The 1st ID and the 2d BCT specifically rebuilt the 202d ING Battalion from the ground up to include training and equipping new recruits and leaders at a forward operating base (FOB) constructed by the division support command (DISCOM), the 167th Corps Support Group, and the 264th Combat Engineer Group outside the city. The 7th Battalion of the Iraqi Army also joined the division in training for BATON ROUGE at the FOB.

After 3 months of operations to encircle and isolate the city, limited strikes to kill and capture insurgent forces, and several failed negotiations, the IIG ordered an assault on 28 September 2006. In just over 2 days of combat in early October, the 2d BCT of the 1st ID, the 202d ING Battalion, and the 7th Iraqi Army Battalion killed or wounded 185 and captured 128 insurgents. Inclusion of Iraqis in this battle was imperative because it sent an important message to the Iraqi people that their own army was capable of fighting in a disciplined, professional manner. Iraqi forces also played a critical role in defusing potentially explosive cultural issues by being the only Coalition military elements allowed to enter sensitive areas such as the Golden Mosque, a shrine in the center of Samarra of great importance to both Sunni and Shia Muslims. Further, the ISF provided effective human intelligence (HUMINT) to US forces as they moved into the city.[116] While not yet ready for independent action or to take responsibility for security in parts of Iraq, the Iraqi Army, National Guard, and police forces were demonstrating their growing capabilities.

The Coalition Creates the Multi-National Security Transition Command–Iraq (MNSTC-I)

In February and March 2004 the Coalition made further revisions to its security force programs in Iraq. The US Congress had approved an expansion in funding for operations in Iraq and new mechanisms had to be devised to administer the program. At the same time, the CPA was focusing its efforts on the accelerated turnover of sovereignty to an IIG on 1 July 2004, a transition that had been announced in November 2003. These new imperatives coincided with organizational changes. On 9 March 2004 Eaton became the head of the new Office of Security Cooperation–Iraq (OSC-I), which in turn oversaw the operations of CPATT and CMATT, now both under the command of British brigadier generals. Brigadier General Nigel Aylwin-Foster led the CMATT and was responsible for the army, air force, navy, and the ICDC (which became the ING later in 2004). Brigadier General Andrew Mackay commanded the new CPATT, now responsible for the police, border troops, and FPS. In retrospect, Major General Eaton considered this as Phase III of the CPA's program to build the ISF. Eaton knew the NIA mission had its challenges, but once taking charge of the overall ISF effort, he found the police, FPS, and the border police programs to be in "absolute chaos."[117] His ability to begin addressing the turmoil was hindered because, for the first 2 months of its existence, OSC-I reported to both the CPA and the CJTF-7 in a contentious and awkward arrangement. Despite these obstacles, Eaton did manage to make an important symbolic move in mid-April. In preparation for the upcoming transfer of sovereignty to the IIG, he transferred control of the Iraqi Army from the Coalition to its new Iraqi commanders. Eaton described the simple, understated ceremony:

I sat down with the man we selected to be the Commanding General of the Iraqi Armed Forces, Lieutenant General Amer Bakr. . . . I said, 'Today, you are a lieutenant general in the Iraqi Armed Forces and you are the Commanding General of the Iraqi Armed Forces.' Then I said to Major General Daham (a 1966 graduate of the US Army Ranger School at Fort Benning), 'You are the Deputy Commanding General for the Iraqi Armed Forces.'[118]

Eaton closed the official transfer by clearly stating to the Iraqi generals how he viewed the new relationship between the Iraqi Armed Forces and the Coalition: "I am subordinate to you now and I will take your instructions on what to do with the Iraqi Army provided it does not run counter to what I believe my government wants."[119]

Soon after this transition, the Coalition transformed its military command structure in Iraq. Headquarters, MNF-I replaced CJTF-7 on 15 May 2004 with Lieutenant General Sanchez in command. MNF-I in turn replaced OSC-I on 6 June 2004 with the MNSTC-I. This new command, headed by Lieutenant General Petraeus who replaced Eaton, had the mission of coordinating the development of all ISF. (See chapter 4 for a fuller discussion of this process.) Although Eaton and his team had struggled to overcome significant hurdles and in the end had not met many of the Coalition's goals, by mid-2004 CMATT had established a solid foundation on which Petraeus could build.

Prior to taking command of the MNSTC-I, Petraeus returned to Iraq in late April 2004 at the request of General Abizaid to do an assessment of the ISF and of the program to train and equip those forces. During this visit, he attended a conference on the ICDC and assisted the CJTF-7 leaders in introducing significant changes to the program. The conference agreed on 10 principles for the ICDC (later the ING), which included the need for Iraqi soldiers to be treated as soldiers, not day laborers; the need to station them on military bases rather than requiring the soldiers to commute; and the need to have adequate and reliable pay and support.[120] These changes were important because the existing six ICDC brigades each later became the nucleus for a division of the Iraqi Army in 2004. Along with the 3 initial regular army divisions and

Petraeus, Training Iraqi Security Forces Briefing

- Firm embrace of ICDC by Coalition Forces—live, eat, and sleep with ICDC, or vice versa.
- Commanded and controlled by Coalition forces and treated like our Soldiers.
- Given doable missions—supported by and integrated with Coalition forces.
- Paid on time—accompanied by initiative to make pay same as police.
- Emphasis on ICDC Soldiers, not day laborers: transition to 3 weeks on and 1 week off—get rid of the 8-hour work day.
- Develop Regional Training Centers—Basic Training, PLDC, NCO, and leadership schools.
- Equip and build facilities with money earmarked for ICDC by supplemental.
- Show that we care—good facilities, good gear, good food, memorial ceremonies, mentoring, joint operations, solatia pay, etc.
- Daily interaction and joint operations.
- Look for and publicly recognize success.

Figure 115. Principles of ICDC.

1 mechanized division, these formations became the 10 divisions of the army fielded by Iraq and the Coalition in early 2005.[121]

In the midst of the changes in command structure, Petraeus' team developed a vastly expanded JMD for MNSTC-I headquarters to replace the relatively small OSC-I staff. By early 2005 Petraeus would have a British lieutenant general working as his deputy. Additionally, Petraeus placed US general officers in charge of CMATT and CPATT, each with unique advisory efforts, and gained an Australian brigadier as the chief of a team advising the Iraqi joint head-quarters. MNSTC-I's staff followed the traditional structure of most joint staffs, but Petraeus had reinforced the command's logistics, contracting, and engineering capacity at every level to handle the purchasing, supplying, and construction aspects of its new missions. The task in front of MNSTC-I was enormous—to build the tactical units, the training and educational base, the recruiting system, the policies and systems, and the national institutions of Iraq's entire security structure and accomplish all of this while fighting a lethal insurgency. Also, Petraeus had to coordinate his command's program with the US Embassy which oversaw the advisors who assisted the IIG's new ministries.

The realities of Iraqi sovereignty after 28 June 2004 increased the complexity of the train, equip, rebuild, and advise tasks facing the Coalition and MNSTC-I. With the IIG in control of its own future, US and Coalition forces could not simply direct or order Iraqi units and leaders as they had during the occupation from May 2003 to June 2004. As a sovereign nation, Iraq's government and ministry officials had the authority to structure and equip their forces as they

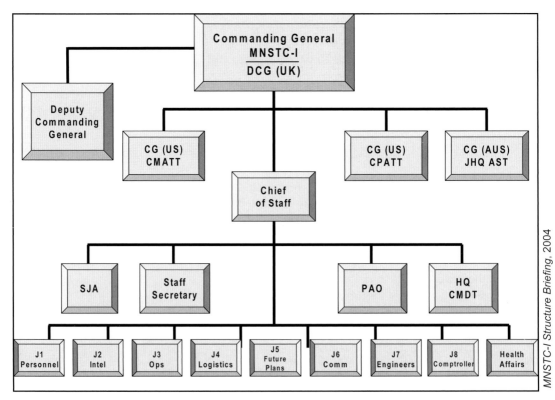

Figure 116. MNSTC-I staff.

chose. This change fit within a larger pattern of new relationships between Coalition organizations in Iraq and the Iraqi Government.

Just prior to the IIG taking power in June 2004, the CPA transferred management of the reconstruction projects and the Iraqi ministries advisory mission to the IRMO under the oversight of the US Embassy in Baghdad. The US Army Corps of Engineers Gulf Region Division and the US Army Joint Contracting Command–Iraq/Afghanistan provided construction and contracting support to IRMO and MNSTC-I. Other US agencies, such as the US Agency for International Development (USAID), administered programs funded by the Iraq Relief and Reconstruction Fund (IRRF). The MNSTC-I staff had to engage all of these organizations on a daily basis as they worked with the various security forces that reported to the MOI and the Ministry of Defense.

With the IIG in place after June 2004, Coalition political and military officials made great progress in getting Iraqi officials to take ownership and demonstrate leadership over their security forces. As Petraeus recalled, creating security forces that were self-sufficient was paramount:

> I talked about ministry capability being absolutely crucial. But it was recognized some months back that we can develop all the battalions, brigades, divisions and ground forces, and police, and so forth, in the world, but they've got to be supportable and supported by the Ministries of the Defense and Interior to ensure eventual self-reliance and transition to complete Iraqi control.[122]

Petraeus and his planners, in coordination with the new Iraqi leadership, conducted an extensive troop-to-task analysis of Iraq's security force requirements in July and August 2004. The analysis recommended increasing the strength levels of the Iraqi Army, the new ING (formerly the ICDC), police, and border police yet again. The ING, for example, grew from the original 6 battalions of the ICDC in the summer of 2003 to 65 battalions operating under 6 different Iraqi divisions by the end of 2004.[123] In a significant change from the CPA concept for the Iraqi Army, the MNSTC-I analysis also recommended that the Iraqi Armed Forces take on responsibility for Iraq's internal security threats. The new ISF analysis, which included unit sizes, end strength, and costs, underscored the need for additional funds. Ambassador John Negroponte and the new MNF-I Commander, General George W. Casey Jr., allocated another $1.8 billion to the mission in response to the findings.[124]

Measuring progress in the building of new Iraqi Security Forces generated intense controversy almost from the beginning of the program. Progress could not simply be gauged by the number of individuals enrolled, but also had to be measured by the level of equipping, training, and continued operation of those individuals. The CPA and CJTF-7 sparred over responsibilities, standards and the rate of progress in 2003 and the first half of 2004. Making this problem worse was the weak and divided Iraqi Government that struggled to emerge in the face of an unrelenting insurgency. Iraq's security forces trying to adapt professional military practices in this period were challenged by high desertion rates, a culture of corruption, infiltration by insurgent groups, and internal ethnic and religious strife.

During its first two months of existence, MNSTC-I undertook a comprehensive review of the size and reporting of the various ISF programs it had inherited. That review led to a dramatic reform in the way the Coalition measured ISF numbers and capabilities. Instead of simply reporting the number of individuals enrolled in an ISF program, MNSTC-I created the "trained and equipped" standard. Between July and September 2004, for example, this assessment removed almost 100,000 insufficiently trained, ill equipped, or nonexistent police and facility protection service officers from the MOI's rolls. In September 2004 DOD reported there were approximately 100,000 fully trained and equipped soldiers and police officers in Iraq, and another 60,000 who were in the process of training and other preparation.[125] Not surprisingly, the sharp decrease in the numbers of trained Iraqis garnered a great deal of attention within Iraq and the United States.

The new assessment system, however, marked the introduction of a more careful and deliberate approach to measuring progress in the training of the ISF. By early 2005 the numbers and capability of Iraqi Security Forces began to climb, reflecting the vastly increased size of the train and equip mission under MNSTC-I. In January 2005, on the eve of the first free national elections in Iraq in decades, MNSTC-I reported that it had assisted Iraqi authorities in the training and equipping of approximately 125,000 ISF of all kinds—Army, Navy, Air Force, National and Local Police, and Border Security Troops.[126] Petraeus and his staff also knew that in addition to an accurate accounting of numbers of individuals, a rating system was necessary to measure the effectiveness of ISF units once they became operational. Over the winter of 2004–2005 they worked with MNC-I to establish unit readiness standards similar to the criteria used by the US Army. The four-tiered system assessed each unit on six different measures of effectiveness and would become known as the Transition Readiness Assessment System when it was implemented in the spring of 2005.[127]

Some obstacles to the formation of professional and competent security forces could not be overcome with money. Perhaps the most important of these was creating a sense of commitment among those who served the country they defended. Events such as the NIA's 2d Battalion's refusal to fight in the first battle of Fallujah revealed that ISF members in 2004 did not all share a desire to defend the new Iraq regardless of the threat. Ethnic and confessional identities, of course, militated against the establishment of a national ethos of service in post-Saddam Iraq. Recruits for the ISF tended to be from Shia and Kurdish areas where citizens felt empowered to participate in the nation's future. Despite being aggressively encouraged to join the ISF, Sunni Arabs were more reluctant to participate, reflecting their fear of intimidation by aggressive Sunni insurgents, as well as the loss of privilege they enjoyed under Saddam and an emerging sense of disenchantment with the IIG, which they perceived to be biased against Sunnis. To create diversity, the ministries and the Coalition focused extensively on recruiting Sunnis with only minimal success.[128] To begin the process of instilling a sense of commitment to the new Iraq, leaders of the ISF developed a new oath of service that emphasized duty to the nation, the Iraqi constitution, and the many populations that made up the country.

NATO Training Implementation Mission–Iraq (NTIM-I)

At the request of the IIG, NATO announced a small but important contribution to the ISF training mission in August 2004. NATO's previous role had been limited to logistical support of the multinational division led by the Poles operating south and southeast of Baghdad. The new program included military personnel from Canada, Hungary, Norway, the Netherlands, and Italy and took the name NATO Training Implementation Mission–Iraq (NTIM-I).[129] As of 10 February 2005, 90 personnel were deployed in support of the mission from 10 countries.[130] Dutch Major General Carel Hilderink led the initial team and became deputy when Lieutenant

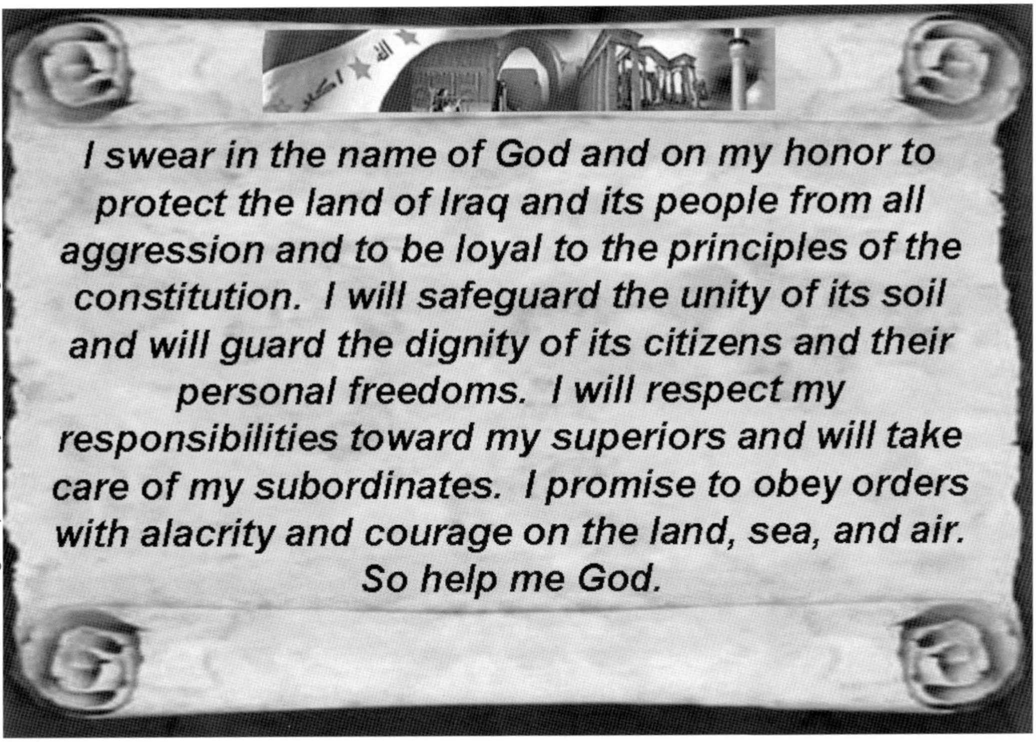

I swear in the name of God and on my honor to protect the land of Iraq and its people from all aggression and to be loyal to the principles of the constitution. I will safeguard the unity of its soil and will guard the dignity of its citizens and their personal freedoms. I will respect my responsibilities toward my superiors and will take care of my subordinates. I promise to obey orders with alacrity and courage on the land, sea, and air. So help me God.

Figure 117. Iraqi Armed Forces Oath.

General Petraeus assumed dual command of both MNSTC-I and NATO Training Mission–Iraq (NTM-I) (which had dropped the middle "I" from its name in November 2004).

NATO filled various niches in the Coalition's ISF training program. One such area was advising and mentoring the Iraqi Joint Headquarters and the Iraqi Ministry of Defense. They also advised the military, police, and National Operation Centers. Under Italian leadership, NTIM-I developed the junior and senior staff colleges and provided mentors for the Iraqi instructors. Rather than having NATO instructors teach through translators, at Petraeus' urging the Italians took the time to train the Iraqis who taught the course and provided the support staff. The NATO mission staff also ensured that Iraqis held the commandant position in each school. Some Iraqi officers attended NATO schools in Norway, Italy, Germany, and others. Instructors at the Iraqi NCO Academy, for example, traveled to the United Kingdom to be trained for their positions. Petraeus recalled, "[The ISF] had normally about 3,200 Iraqis out of the country on a given day. Now, the bulk of them, about 3,000 of those, were typically in the Jordan Police Academy, another 80 to 100 might be in the Jordan Special Operations Training Center, and then you would have anywhere from 40 to 100 or more literally sprinkled all over the world at NATO, US, and other country courses."[131]

MNSTC-I provided some of the funding that enabled the NTIM-I mission as NATO funding mechanisms proved relatively inflexible and inadequate. NATO did provide substantial equipment donations such as 30,000 vehicles and weapons delivered in January 2005 before the national elections. The most substantial gift came from Hungary in the form of 77 T-72

455

tanks after the Hungarian Prime Minister visited Iraq. Greece provided the ship to transport the tanks as well as 36 BMP armored personnel carriers.[132] The NTIM-I mission provided a way for some member countries to support Iraq's rebuilding effort without direct involvement in the military Coalition.

Beyond the NATO mission, many other countries provided training support. Jordan, as already mentioned, provided the largest contribution. Instructors for the police program came from United Arab Emirates (UAE), Spain, the United Kingdom, Australia, Poland, Canada, Sweden, Denmark, Austria, Finland, the Czech Republic, Germany, Hungary, Slovenia, Slovakia, Singapore, and Belgium.[133] The Royal Navy supported Iraq's Coastal Defense Force and the Australian Army provided officers in support of CMATT.[134] Although it did not participate in the NATO mission, Germany trained Iraqi military drivers and mechanics, provided training in the UAE and equipment for Iraqi engineering personnel, and provided military hospital equipment. And Egypt invited a company of 134 Iraqi soldiers from the 5th Infantry Division to participate in a joint training exercise.[135]

The Unit Advisory Effort Begins in Earnest

The creation of MNSTC-I marked a renewed effort to increase the size and effectiveness of the Coalition advisory effort in Iraq. From the original 350 Soldiers performing advisory duties as their sole mission in November 2003 (as opposed to Soldiers assigned to US tactical units with duty as advisors), the program grew to around 1,200 advisors by November 2004.[136] CMATT had initially filled its advisor corps with individual Soldiers and Marines hastily provided by the Services and often lacking specific preparation for serving as advisors. Many of the early advisors were volunteers; some were assigned the duty from US Army Combat Training Centers (CTCs) and some from Training Support Brigades (TSBs) which worked with National Guard tactical units. Soldiers from the CTCs and the TSBs were some of the Army's most experienced trainers and were familiar with advising US tactical units in training. The number of advisors that came from these units, however, was small because each of these organizations also needed to train the Active and Reserve Component units for future deployments to Iraq and Afghanistan.

The early advisors to the ISF faced enormous challenges and performed near miracles in sustaining themselves and advising their Iraqi counterparts in the initial months of the mission. Very few had received any training for the advisory mission, partly a result of the extremely short deployment timelines and partly because, other than its Special Forces (SF) training programs, the US Army did not have courses that trained tactical unit advisors. Further, the SF schools had limited capacity and were not prepared to teach Arabic or Kurdish to a large group of advisors headed to Iraq. Most Soldier and Marine advisors deployed without a deep understanding of the Iraqi culture and almost none could speak Iraqi Arabic.[137]

As one of the early volunteer advisors to the NIA, Major Jeffrey Allen experienced firsthand the shortcomings of the Coalition ISF program. Allen departed for Iraq from the US Army War College in August 2004 without any specific preparation for advising units. Though his advisory team was authorized 10 Soldiers, Allen had only 5, including 4 Army National Guard volunteers. Once in Iraq, Allen had difficulties securing much-needed equipment and other support for both his team and for the 18th Battalion of the NIA, the unit he was advising. The Coalition military command had not yet established the proper contracting systems, accountability of local Iraqis was nonexistent, and support from Coalition military forces including US Army units was minimal. Allen recalled that of all the problems he faced, the inability to secure basic support services was the single most pressing issue: "Culture, the threat of insurgents—all of that paled in comparison to [the lack of] any sort of logistical support."[138]

Putting Iraqis in charge of rebuilding their forces was extremely important. One method for achieving this was encouraging the newly trained Iraqis to teach classes while Coalition members served as mentors to the Iraqi trainers. Consequently, Coalition team members formed advisory support teams to coach and mentor the new Iraqi forces while Iraqi instructors provided the formal training. Allen described the guidance he received:

> My clear guidance was to coach and to mentor but not to teach. You normally say coach, teach, mentor. My job, at least in a formal environment, was not to teach. Not to stand up in front of a classroom and teach the classes: the Iraqis were to do that. What we were to do was to coach and mentor the leadership on all aspects of being a modern military, from how to organize a staff, how to prepare for and conduct training, how to take care of their soldiers—and it really became all-encompassing.[139]

Though Allen and his team faced many challenges, including the desertion or dismissal of seven battalion commanders in a span of 8 weeks before a Kurdish executive officer was chosen and proved effective, he found most junior officers and NCOs very receptive to the advice from their US advisors. He found that Kurdish soldiers were especially eager to learn. The 18th Battalion and the 3d Brigade operated in Fallujah in late 2004 and performed well. Despite the difficulties he and his team encountered, Allen called his tour as an advisor the most rewarding experience he could imagine in Iraq.[140]

Major Peter Fedak, an Army Armor officer, deployed to Iraq and CMATT from the Combat Maneuver Training Center (CMTC) in Germany in March 2004, after he and some members of his observer-controller team volunteered in December 2003. Because they were experienced observer-controllers, Fedak and his team received minimal preparation, attending several days of classes on the advisor mission, Arabic language, and Iraqi culture after they arrived at the Taji Training Center near the city of Taji, Iraq. His team was not impressed with their initial briefings or training. They were at the Taji center when the Iraqi 2d Battalion was ordered to Fallujah in early April and refused to go, leaving one member of his team, Army Captain Mike Sullivan, to remark, "We sat there scratching our heads thinking, 'What did we get into?'"[141] Fedak led a 10-man team consisting of 2 captains, 1 master sergeant, and 7 sergeants first class. They became the advisors to the 6th Battalion of the NIA, joining a Marine-led team advising the 5th Battalion and another Army-led team from CMTC that advised the 7th Battalion. On 1 April 2004 these units and their advisors moved together from Taji to Kirkush and became part of the 3d Brigade of the Iraqi Army, which was then forming.[142]

Fedak and his team first trained the officers and NCOs to prepare them for the arrival of the battalion's junior soldiers. Fedak task-organized the team, giving himself and his senior NCO the job of advising the Iraqi commander and supervising the overall team effort. The captains advised the Iraqi battalion staff officers while the sergeants first class advised each of the battalion's companies. Because the Iraqi Army historically lacked the tradition of a professional NCO Corps, it took some time for the American NCOs to earn the respect of Iraqi officers and further to convince them to give responsibility to their own NCOs. The team also found it challenging to build rapport with their Iraqi counterparts. Fedak recalled:

> It takes a lot longer in the Middle Eastern culture to establish that rapport than in America . . . I think over time we grew closer. Fast forward from forming up in April to actually rolling out to Fallujah in November 2004, which was approximately 7 months later, that core group was pretty tight. There was a high level of respect both ways. My respect grew quite a bit for the Iraqi troops and what they've gone through and understanding their cultural aspects . . . how to look at it from their point of view, versus always imposing an American point of view.[143]

In training their battalions, the initial US advisor teams could not rely on a standardized program. Indeed, in the spring of 2004, the Coalition was still developing programs of instruction and other written training. The tactics, techniques, and procedures taught by each team bore the stamp of their unique backgrounds. The Marine team relied on Marine training methods and experiences, and the two Army teams from the CMTC used their own backgrounds to set up the training programs for their Iraqi battalions. As Sullivan remembered, "You could tell who trained each battalion just by watching them."[144]

Position	Rank	Branch/MOS
Team Leader	LTC	Combat Arms
Staff Advisor	MAJ	Combat Arms
Staff Advisor	MAJ	Branch Immaterial
Staff Advisor	CPT	Combat Arms
Staff Advisor	CPT	Branch Immaterial
Advisor/Team NCOIC	SFC-MSG	Combat Arms
NCO Staff Advisor	SSG-SFC	Combat Arms
NCO Staff Advisor	SSG-SFC	Combat Arms
NCO Staff Advisor	SSG-SFC	MOS Immaterial
NCO Staff Advisor	SSG-SFC	MOS Immaterial

Clay, *Iroquois Warriors in Iraq*, CSI, 2007

Figure 118. Brigade advisor support team organization, 2004.

The US advisor team for the 7th Battalion, under Army Major Robert Dixon, followed a training schedule with their Iraqi officers, NCOs, and enlisted soldiers that was similar to that created by Fedak's team. Dixon and his Soldiers worked without any interpreters at first, relying on English speaking Iraqis. The goal was to prepare the Iraqi officers and NCOs to lead the training when their recruits reported to the battalion. They spent 4 weeks working on individual movement and marksmanship skills, then 4 weeks on squad level skills and convoy procedures. The training had to be done quickly because after graduation and personal leave, the 7th Battalion was scheduled to become operational in August 2004. They would ultimately

Position	Rank	Branch/MOS
Team Leader	MAJ	Combat Arms
Advisor	CPT	Combat Arms
Advisor	CPT	Branch Immaterial
Advisor/Team NCOIC	SFC-MSG	Combat Arms
NCO Advisor	SSG	Combat Arms
NCO Advisor	SSG	Combat Arms
NCO Advisor	SSG	Combat Arms
NCO Advisor	SSG	Combat Arms
NCO Advisor	SSG	MOS Immaterial
NCO Advisor	SSG	MOS Immaterial

Clay, *Iroquois Warriors in Iraq*, CSI, 2007

Figure 119. Battalion advisor support team organization, 2004.

take part in Operation BATON ROUGE fighting alongside Task Force 1-18th Infantry of the 1st ID. After the battle, Soldiers from the 98th Division of the USAR replaced Dixon's team in a planned rotation of US advisors.[145]

The 5th and 6th Battalions of the 3d Brigade endured their baptism of fire when they joined US Marine and Army forces in the fighting in Operation AL FAJR in and around Fallujah in early November 2004. The 5th Battalion followed Marine and Army forces into the city and took part in clearing the insurgents from the town. The 6th Battalion, with an Army advisor team, was attached to the 2d Brigade of the 1st CAV and took part in operations to cordon off the city. While the planners of AL FAJR did not assign the 6th Battalion its own sector—a decision that disappointed both the battalion's leaders and its US advisors—the unit was used to supplement US forces at key points in the cordon where contact with Iraqis was likely and it performed its mission particularly well. The battalion's chief advisor attributed the reluctance of the US planners to assign sole responsibility for a sector to the Iraqis on previous American experience working with poorly trained and equipped ICDC units.[146]

Both CMATT and CPATT advisors worked hard to overcome the culture of officer privilege, excessive centralization of decisionmaking, and unwillingness to take initiative that had debilitated the security forces under Saddam Hussein. Coalition police training teams, for example, mentored IPS cadets to reject these cultural norms.[147] The CPATT also emphasized mentoring as a way of improving police performance. Major Shauna Hauser, a MNSTC-I police planner, explained the importance of allowing Iraqi police officers to exercise initiative:

> As we move away from being in charge of operations and directing things, it becomes more important that we work with them and not direct them. And assisting doesn't necessarily mean doing it for them, but trying to give them the tools. And if they do it in a way that you wouldn't do it, but it still accomplishes what you wanted to accomplish, then that's okay.[148]

American advisors quickly learned to accept some Iraqi cultural rituals as a prerequisite for accomplishing their missions. Major Mike Sullivan, one of the US Army advisors for the 6th Iraqi Battalion recalled the "chai story" as one of the examples of learning to work within Iraqi norms. That story merits quoting at length:

> I'd never had chai before—the hot tea that the Arabs drink—and after the first week or two of basic training, we realized that chai was critical to mission success. If they didn't have their chai, things were out of whack. So the first time we were going out to the range, the battalion executive officer (XO) asked how they were going to get their chai. Well, I told him they wouldn't be getting it. We had box lunches for them and bottles of water, but we just can't bring hot tea out to the range. He basically said that if they didn't get chai, they wouldn't train. And me, being the stubborn Army guy, told them they were going to the range. They were going to the field, they had to suck it up, and I didn't care about their chai. They just insisted that they wouldn't go if they didn't get it and said they would quit. At this point, I was in a quandary because I was so frustrated thinking this would *never* happen in an American unit. Long story short, we brought out the damn chai. We got a truck and a big metal container of scalding hot chai in the 110 degree desert sun. We had chai for lunch and everybody was happy. That literally was the decisive point for that training event—not shooting their weapons or understanding the marksmanship, but whether or not they were going to have chai for lunch.[149]

Many other Army officers told similar stories about the importance of chai and conversation as preludes to serious discussions or training. Sullivan's comments are especially revealing because they describe how US advisors brought their own cultural biases into their relationship with Iraqi Soldiers, and how some Americans learned to compromise their own norms, however grudgingly, to accomplish the mission with their Iraqi counterparts. Cultural sensitivity, patience, and sheer determination became the hallmark of the CMATT, CPATT, and MNSTC-I advisory teams. In 2005 Lieutenant General Petraeus praised the performance of those units, stating, "Those 10-man teams are real heroes. Our country should be very, very proud of them. They are with every single battalion, brigade headquarters, division headquarters, ground forces headquarters, even in the ministries, the joint force headquarters and so forth, and they're helping enormously."[150]

In addition to the concentrated efforts of advisors assigned to the CPA and MNSTC-I programs, Coalition military units in Iraq continued to provide mentorship and training to the former ING battalions and to the IPS. During the Mahdi Army uprising in April 2004, the 2d ACR helped support and train the Iraqi police in the city of Diwaniyah by conducting joint dismounted patrols throughout the city.[151] The 1st CAV and 1st ID provided just over 600 of their Soldiers to serve as advisors to the ISF in the summer of 2004.[152] The 1st CAV focused on this effort throughout their mission. Colonel Stephen Lanza, commander of the 5th BCT, reported a very high rate of police recruiting through a process of working with local sheiks and imams. By involving local leadership, the Iraqis were able to take ownership of the process and insurgent attacks on the new recruits decreased.[153]

In the late summer and fall of 2004, the first group of advisors drawn from a US Army unit (as opposed to advisors drawn from individual volunteers or selectees) began to arrive in

Iraq. Most of them were from the 98th Division (Institutional Training) or DIVIT, nicknamed the "Iroquois Warriors."[154] These Army Reserve Soldiers were cadres of senior NCOs and officers who in peacetime ran training schools and individual training programs for USAR and National Guard Soldiers. Major General James Helmly, chief of the USAR in 2003 and 2004, had begun studying the idea of deploying elements of a DIVIT in the late fall of 2003. Initially, the USAR, the Army G3, and the 98th Division discussed creating an organization known as the Foreign Army-Training Assistance Command (FA-TRAC) to conduct the mission. This organization would deploy to Iraq and provide the permanent command and control structure for other units and Soldiers involved in the ISF training program. Other Soldiers would form the ASTs that would conduct the training of Iraqi soldiers and mentoring of Iraqi units.

The training of foreign forces was not the designated mission for USAR institutional training divisions, and the Army never implemented the FA-TRAC concept because the establishment of MNSTC-I made it unnecessary. But Helmly tried hard to convince leaders on his own staff as well as those in the Department of the Army that the USAR could conduct the mission.[155] The Army National Guard had assumed the mission of providing trainers for the Afghan Army training program in the summer of 2003, and Helmly admitted some institutional rivalry affected the process.[156] To move the USAR closer to the point where it could play a major role in training the ISF, in May 2004 Helmly told Major General Bruce E. Robinson, commanding general of the 98th Division, to begin preparing for the mission.

The USAR proposed the concept of employing its units to man much of the new MNSTC-I organization to Lieutenant General Petraeus in the Pentagon on 2 June 2004, just days before he took command in Iraq. Petraeus approved the concept for further study. After a mission analysis by the 98th's staff, a more complete plan was briefed to Major General Helmly on 15 June, and then to the Army G3, Lieutenant General Richard Cody, who approved it on 18 June 2004. Brigadier General Richard Sherlock, the assistant division commander of the 98th Division, and others in the USAR and 98th Division understood the mission to involve the establishment of training academies and individual training programs for the NIA at several locations. They also understood that the 98th would deploy a task-organized piece of the division that would be attached to MNSTC-I for the mission.[157] The leaders of the 98th Division, however, found that more specific information about the details of the program was hard to come by in the Pentagon, especially because the inauguration of MNSTC-I focused attention and resources elsewhere.

Without a complete understanding of their mission, senior members of the division left for Iraq hoping to begin preparations for the arrival of their Soldiers. Colonel Frank Cipolla, a commander for an engineer basic training brigade in the division, led a three-man team to Iraq a week later as the advance party. Sherlock and nine others joined them for a reconnaissance and analysis of the mission from mid-July to early August. During their trip, the 98th's leaders discovered that MNSTC-I already had a command and control structure in place and needed individuals, not units, to man that structure. They also learned that the 98th's mission would begin with training new recruits and units, but that the division's Soldiers assigned to the ASTs would stay with their Iraqi units after they graduated and became operational. This was a surprise and represented a dramatic increase in the scope of the mission for the 98th because it expanded their role from simply preparing new soldiers during their initial training to advising them in combat.[158]

Between late 2004 and late 2005 approximately 900 Soldiers of the 98th Division served in MNSTC-I as members of the command's staff, as school instructors, and as advisors to Iraqi units. Iroquois Soldiers manned 31 of the first 39 ASTs envisioned for the initial three divisions of the Iraqi Army, the others were manned by the Marines and some by Coalition nations.[159] Before deploying, these Reservists attended stateside training at Camp Atterbury, Indiana, to prepare for the mission. Many of them considered the training to be of limited value as the Army and the Atterbury trainers themselves were unfamiliar with the mission for which they were preparing the Iroquois Soldiers to perform. On arrival in Kuwait, they completed some theater-specific training before moving into Iraq; this training was more focused and useful.[160] Once part of MNSTC-I, the members of the 98th Division worked through the growing pains of becoming comfortable with the enlarged scope of their mission. Some of them also endured open skepticism from Active Duty counterparts about their ability to do the advisory mission.[161] The AST members met their new Iraqi recruits in basic training, trained with them to develop individual and unit skills, and then accompanied them after graduation on operational missions in 2005.

While they lacked the tactical experience of Soldiers from Active and National Guard combat units, Petraeus credited the Soldiers of the 98th Division with providing a much needed boost to MNSTC-I due to their expertise with building and operating the institutional training systems of a modern army. Although their experience was in training individual soldiers in a school setting, most Soldiers of the 98th Division made the transition to combat advisors successfully. They steadily developed tactical competence as they trained with their Iraqi units and then deployed with them into combat.[162] For some in the division, it was obvious they had accepted a mission for which their previous experience had not prepared them, and a few had difficulty transitioning to the demands of advising units in combat. Still, the great majority adapted and felt they had shown how the USAR Soldier could meet the complex challenges posed by the Iraqi operational environment. Indeed, a large number of advisors from the 98th Division went into combat with their Iraqi units in major operations like AL FAJR in the city of Fallujah in November 2004.[163] Command Sergeant Major Milt Newsome, who served in Iraq with the division in 2004–2005, expressed the pride felt by the Iroquois Warriors on their return, stating, "I'm very proud to be a member of the 98th Division because history will realize what the 98th Division and all those who supported us had to do, and did. . . . When all the ashes settle, you'll see the silhouette of the 98th Division and you can say it was a job well done.[164]

As a result of the lessons learned in the fall of 2004, MNF-I and MNSTC-I began making major improvements to the advisor training and support programs. These changes took place outside the timeframe of this book, but they help highlight the challenges faced by the 98th Division and other Soldiers who were part of this initial wave of advisors. One of the first steps was to improve stateside mobilization training in early 2005. MNSTC-I also established the Phoenix Academy at Taji in early 2005 to provide a 10-day course conducted by members of the 98th Division focused on the latest tactics, techniques, and procedures (TTP) used by existing advisor teams. In the spring of 2005 the Coalition also changed its term for unit advisor teams from AST to Military Transition Teams (MiTT) to better reflect their mission. Finally, MNSTC-I established the Iraqi Assistance Group in April 2005 to provide better command, control, and logistical support to US advisors working with Iraqi units after they transitioned from training under MNSTC-I control to the operational control of units in the MNC-I, the Coalition's tactical command.

Soldiers in the next wave of advisors, for which the USAR's 80th DIVIT formed the core, benefited from these improvements. But they too faced new challenges. The first wave of advisors had linked up with and trained their Iraqi units when they were first formed; thus, they were able to develop personal relationships with their Iraqi counterparts before conducting operations. Many advisors in the next wave reported to Iraqi units already in combat. Their learning curve was steep and time to build cohesion and trust was almost nonexistent. The Army continued in 2005 to find the right mix of training, personnel, techniques, and processes for advising the ISF.

Creating the Institutions of the Iraqi Armed Forces (IAF)

All modern armies require a series of training institutions to create and sustain itself and to form its cultural and doctrinal base. They also require higher level commands and organizations to plan and conduct operations. In its initial efforts to train the ISF, the Coalition built only the tactical level of the Iraqi defense establishment. CJTF-7 and the CPA worked from the bottom up in 2003 and early 2004, while largely disregarding the higher military headquarters and the institutions that characterize a professional army. Only in April 2004 did the CPA begin to construct the upper level infrastructure of the defense establishment. In that month Major General Eaton established a rudimentary Iraqi Armed Forces Joint Headquarters. Given the complete absence of this type of organization and others like it in the Saddam-era, the Armed Forces Joint Headquarters, held no real authority over its subordinate units and retained its status as a training organization into 2005.[†]

Establishing the IAF's training base also moved slowly. In June 2004 the first contingent of 843 Iraqi Army officers, including 11 female officers, graduated from the officer training course established in Jordan. On 6 July 2004 the first class of enlisted soldiers graduated from the Iraqi-run basic training program in Kirkush. The 8-week basic training at the Kirkush base included basic skills, weaponry, drill, and physical training. Marine Corps Lieutenant Colonel Kevin Foster of CMATT noted that graduation from the enlisted course marked a major Iraqi success stating, "This marks one more step in building increased capability in the Iraqi Army. It validates that the training model produces a cohesive unit with well-trained soldiers that will only increase in capability over time."[165] Taken together, these two events marked an important milestone in the development of the ISF—the establishment of an institutional training system that could sustain a professional military force. By the end of 2005, the Iraqi Army training program for new soldiers was about the same length as equivalent US training. It included a 5-week common core course followed by an 8-week course that taught specialized skills such as infantry tasks or supply procedures.[166] In addition to basic training, there were various specialty courses such as the 10-week Special Operator Course and the 4-week Commando Training Program that followed basic training.[167]

[†]Not until May 2005 would an Iraqi Ground Forces Headquarters be established, and the United States retained operational control of all Iraqi Armed Forces until September 2006.

In January 2005 the Iraqi Military Academy at Al Rustamiyah that trained officers was converted from the 3-month pilot course to a 1-year course based on a similar program at the British Sandhurst Royal Military Academy. This enabled the NIA to train its own officers rather than sending Iraqis for officer training in Jordan. The British Army had constructed the academy at Al Rustamiyah in 1924, and the introduction of the Sandhurst model in 2005 was a return of the academy to its British roots. Using infantry skills and tactics as the base for all instruction, the cadets at the academy studied arms, field craft, drill, and physical training. The academic curriculum included subjects such as international affairs, military history, and communications studies. Leadership training was a primary component of all instruction, and the course concluded with a field exercise with heavy emphasis on counterinsurgency warfare.[168] With the same motto as its British counterpart, "Serve to Lead," the school became known as "Sandhurst in the Sand."

The Iraqi Army also expanded from a pure infantry force to one that included many of the specialized units of a modern army. In late 2004 the initial elements of the 1st Mechanized Brigade stood up in Taji as the nucleus of a future, larger mechanized division. Equipped with 10 tanks and 37 MTLB armored personnel carriers (APCs), the brigade began training for its first security mission during the 30 January 2005 elections. As the equipment rolled off the trucks, Colonel David Styles, MNSTC-I's 1st Mechanized Brigade project officer, remarked, "We made history today as we assisted the Iraqi Army in returning armor to its rightful place at Taji where it has been absent for several years."[169] The first mechanized brigade was largely an Iraqi idea. The strength of the brigade reached 3,000 soldiers by June 2005 with an additional brigade training in advance of receiving tanks and APCs donated by NATO and others purchased by MNSTC-I.

Training in specialized fields was essential for the Iraqi Army to function in an integrated and effective fashion. To build critical capabilities, MNSTC-I established a signal school in Baghdad that focused on basic communication skills and advanced courses in radio operation, frequency management, and satellite communication.[170] The Coalition also helped plan for a medical corps, with a tentative force of 2,600 personnel, to include doctors, medics, technicians, and administrators. Initial training included a medical logistics course in Jordan. Among the first recruits to the new Iraqi military medical corps was a female dentist with advanced training from Harvard University.[171] To make the Iraqi Army more mobile, the fledgling Iraqi Air Force took a step closer to viability in January 2005 when the 65 members of the 23d Transportation Squadron, trained by the 6th Special Operations Squadron of the US Special Operations Command (SOCOM), took delivery of three US-donated C-130E aircraft.[172]

In 2004 the Coalition also began developing the type of focused capabilities that it and the Iraqi leadership felt would be critical to dealing with current and future internal security threats. Given the likelihood that the insurgency and terrorist groups would be active in Iraq for some time, MNSTC-I began programs to create special forces to combat these groups, tasking soldiers from SOCOM to establish and train the Iraqi Special Operations Forces (ISOF). The ISOF initially consisted of an Iraqi Counterterrorist Force (ICTF) to conduct small antiterrorist raids, and a larger commando battalion that was similar in organization and function to a US Army Ranger Battalion. By the end of January 2005, the ISOF had executed 538 combat missions, captured 431 insurgents, and recovered 1,700 weapons.[173] Among the most effective ISOF units were the ICTF and the Al Hillah Special Weapons and Tactics (SWAT) team. The

ICTF required all recruits (who volunteered from existing Iraqi units) to complete a 12-week counterterrorism course that included basic training and specialized training in the origins of terrorism, advanced weapons handling and marksmanship, sniper training, and concealment training among other topics. Trained by US Special Operations Forces and advised in late 2004 by Marines from the 24th Marine Expeditionary Unit, the Al Hillah SWAT team conducted key raids against insurgent targets in Babil province in October 2004.[174] Major Dennis Levesque, who served on the staff of the CJSOTF-AP, stated, "When [ISOF units] roll into your neck of the woods . . . and you're an Iraqi bad guy, you just back down before they even show up. We had that happen many times. Because these guys were well outfitted and well trained on good equipment, their confidence and morale was very high."[175]

The ICDC Becomes the Iraqi National Guard

Coalition units had committed a significant amount of time and resources in 2003 and 2004 to stand up the ICDC as a vital support to Coalition forces. But as the IIG assumed control of the nation in June 2004, the future of this poorly trained support force became unclear. CJTF-7 had established the ICDC units primarily to assist its forces with domestic security and reconstruction efforts, but their duties

USAF Photo by TSgt Scott Reed

Figure 120. Iraqi National Guardsmen patrol alongside their Coalition counterparts in the village of Albu Hassan, 16 July 2004.

quickly evolved to include military operations against the insurgency. In recognition of the need to provide better training and Iraqi control, on 22 April 2004 CPA Order No. 73 transferred authority of the ICDC to the Ministry of Defense. This move was part of the reorganization of the ISF and the Coalition command structure that controlled that process.[176] On 20 June 2004, with the concurrence of the IIG, the ICDC was redesignated as the Iraqi National Guard.

As the ICDC transitioned to the ING, US military units were ordered to expand their efforts to train and equip the new ING forces. The 1st ID and the 1st CAV in particular devoted a significant amount of resources to establishing these units. In the city of Tikrit, units of the 1st ID designed a 3-week course that included training on rifle marksmanship, conduct of traffic checkpoints, map reading, basic drill, and first aid. The ING soldiers continued to improve their skills as they conducted joint missions with Coalition forces. Iraqi Colonel Shaker Faris Al Azawi, commander of the 203d ING Battalion, commented, "Our relationship with the Coalition forces is very good. They give us ammunition, supplies, vehicles, and experience, and the training they've given us is very important. Because of it, we're operating at a very high level."[177] In addition to providing training to the ING, the 1st ID, with support from MNSTC-I's nascent logistics structure, was instrumental in fielding equipment to the new ING units.

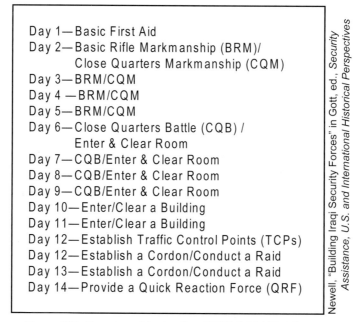

Day 1—Basic First Aid
Day 2—Basic Rifle Markmanship (BRM)/
   Close Quarters Markmanship (CQM)
Day 3—BRM/CQM
Day 4 —BRM/CQM
Day 5—BRM/CQM
Day 6—Close Quarters Battle (CQB) /
   Enter & Clear Room
Day 7—CQB/Enter & Clear Room
Day 8—CQB/Enter & Clear Room
Day 9—CQB/Enter & Clear Room
Day 10—Enter/Clear a Building
Day 11—Enter/Clear a Building
Day 12—Establish Traffic Control Points (TCPs)
Day 12—Establish a Cordon/Conduct a Raid
Day 13—Establish a Cordon/Conduct a Raid
Day 14—Provide a Quick Reaction Force (QRF)

Newell, "Building Iraqi Security Forces" in Gott, ed., *Security Assistance, U.S. and International Historical Perspectives*

Figure 121. Program of Instruction (POI). Initial Training Course, Iraqi Security Forces, Diyala Regional Training Facility, 2004.

In Baghdad the 1st CAV conducted similar ING training missions. Soldiers in the division conducted a 10-day leadership academy that taught basic combat skills, followed by a command post exercise for the battalion leadership. Colonel Mike Murray, commander of the 1st CAV's 3d BCT, recalled stressing the importance of the NCO Corps to the Iraqi officers who, as stated earlier, had little experience in delegating authority and responsibility to lower-level leaders. Murray estimated that approximately 48 US officers and NCOs from his brigade worked and patrolled with the ING on a daily basis.[178] The 2d BCT of the 1st CAV embedded a number of Soldiers with the 303d ING Battalion, and eventually the Iraqi unit became so effective in patrolling and other missions that Coalition forces assigned it a separate AOR in the capital in which it conducted operations without US advisors in 2004. Lieutenant Colonel Scott Efflandt, the XO of the 2d BCT, attributed part of the 303d Battalion's success to its commander, Colonel Mohammad, who Efflandt described as "a good guy and a good warrior."[179] But Efflandt also believed that American training and mentoring was a critical part of the formula for success with Iraqi units.

If the ING became more tactically proficient under American tutelage in 2004, many of its units remained hamstrung by equipment and supply problems caused by the lack of logistical infrastructure in the emerging Iraqi defense sector. American forces often filled the needs to make their Iraqi counterparts operational. Murray recalled spending considerable time and effort to provide vehicles, radios, weapons, ammunition, and vehicle armor.[180] The division's 2d BCT did likewise and that effort prompted Efflandt to conclude that the Iraqi nonexistent logistics base was the greatest hindrance to the ING's effectiveness. After his BCT made great effort to provide helmets and uniforms, the 303d ING Battalion began to look like and act more like professional soldiers. Efflandt recalled, "As we invested interest in them, they took off."[181]

CPATT Evolves to Meet the Enemy

While the mission of the IPS was to be a traditional civilian public safety and security agency, the force soon found itself facing a different reality, one in which its officers were on the front lines confronting a violent insurgency. The insurgent network quickly targeted the IPS with its attacks; but without proper equipment and training, the IPS forces were simply not able to counter the threat. Intimidation, fear, poor training, and lack of equipment caused many policemen to desert their posts in 2003 and 2004. IPS Sergeant Walid Hani Hamid, who served in the capital, told an American journalist in May 2004, "All the policemen are afraid. People think the Iraqi police are walking hand in hand with the Americans."[182] Iraqi Officer Maytham Talib quit his job in August 2004 and fled after a violent attack. He recounted, "Each one of them had an automatic weapon. The police, we had four rifles, but only two worked. We had seven bullets for each rifle. We ran."[183] Despite suffering significant casualties, Iraqis continued to join the IPS and often displayed tremendous courage and determination. After an attack on the town of Husseiniya in December 2003 that killed 6 Iraqi officers and wounded 15 civilians, Police Colonel Hamad Ghazan said, "It will do nothing. We won't be affected by this. We are going to serve Iraq. We are going to serve the Iraqi people."[184]

While CMATT was increasing the scope and nature of training for the Iraqi military forces, CPATT was also evolving to meet the insurgent threat. In his early assessment of the IPS, Lieutenant General Petraeus found that the police were inadequately trained and equipped for the high-level threat posed by the insurgency.[185] Building on the existing basic training, CPATT added practical survival skills, counterterrorism, and counterinsurgency techniques. As more Iraqi police completed training, an increasing number of Iraqi instructors returned to the academies in Iraq and Jordan. The increase in the number of Iraqi instructors allowed the MOI to assert ownership of the program, and the ability of these trainers to communicate in their own language enhanced efficiency and effectiveness.[186]

By mid-2004 CPATT had successfully expanded its police training to improve the leadership and flexibility of the IPS. On 7 July 2004, 80 IPS officers graduated from a special course at the Adnan Training Facility that included classes on mid-level management, basic criminal investigations, criminal intelligence, and executive leadership.[187] The CPATT added specialized courses and refresher classes to the police curriculum enabling the police to practice with their weapons, now including AK-47s and machineguns, and learn advanced techniques such as identifying IEDs. Other training included courses on human rights and treatment of detainees.[188]

After completion of the police academy, MNSTC-I placed new police officers on joint patrols with Coalition forces. Partnered with Coalition civilian police advisors or MPs, the new officers received on-the-job training with Coalition Soldiers before working independently.[189] At times, US Soldiers used some unorthodox techniques to instill leadership and pride within the ranks. These methods included the screening of Hollywood movies such as "SWAT," "Bad Boys," and the television series "Band of Brothers." While these films provided motivation for the new Iraqi policemen, they were most impressed with American technology and training. Captain Christian Solinsky noted, "As soon as they would see a movie, they would ask us when they were getting more radios, more body armor, and weapons like [those in the movie]."[190]

MNSTC-I also assisted the Iraqi MOI establish the IHP to help secure Iraq's highways and provide convoy security. Initially planned as a force of 1,500 officers, the Ministry later ordered

Distinguished Service Cross
An American Advisor and His
Iraqi Unit in Combat

On 24 August 2005, General George W. Casey Jr., commander of Multi-National Force-Iraq, awarded the Distinguished Service Cross to Colonel James H. Coffman for actions in November 2004. In the fall of 2004, Colonel Coffman was serving as the Senior Advisor to the Iraqi 3d Battalion, 1st Special Police Commando Brigade. On 14 November 2004, elements of that battalion were part of a Quick Reaction Force (QRF) that responded to help other commandos at a police station in the city of Mosul defend their position from a heavy insurgent assault. As they neared the Police Station, Coffman and the QRF came under fire from rocket-propelled grenades (RPGs), mortars, and machineguns. After relieving the besieged force at the station, the QRF fought the insurgents for the next 5.5 hours. The citation for his award described the critical role played by Coffman inside the station, "with all but one of the commando officers killed or seriously wounded by the initial enemy fire, Colonel Coffman

General George W. Casey Jr., (left) commander of Multi-National Forces-Iraq, congratulates Colonel James H. Coffman Jr. after awarding him the Distinguished Service Cross in front of a formation of Iraqi Special Police Commandos.

exhibited truly inspirational leadership, rallying the commandos and organizing a hasty defense while attempting to radio higher headquarters for reinforcements. Under heavy fire, he moved from commando to commando, looking each in the eye and using hand and arm signals to demonstrate what he wanted done."

Colonel Coffman was wounded when machinegun fire hit his shooting hand and damaged his M4 rifle. Despite his injury and the loss of his rifle, Coffman picked up ammunition and an AK-47 and fired that weapon while continuing to advise the Iraqi commandos. When other police units arrived as reinforcements, he positioned them and stayed to help prevent the station from falling into enemy hands. Only after he supervised the evacuation of Iraqi policemen wounded in the action did Colonel Coffman seek medical attention for his hand. During the battle, 12 commandos were killed and 24 were wounded. The Iraqi police and their advisor had succeeded in protecting the station and inflicted heavy losses on the insurgent enemy.

The award citation recognized Coffman for his "exceptionally valorous conduct" during the battle and emphasized that if not for the bravery of the American advisor and the one Iraqi police officer that had remained unwounded throughout the battle, the police station would have likely been overrun.

Sergeant Lorie Jewell, "Colonel receives DSC for leading Iraqi commandos," *Army News Service*, 24 August 2005.

the increase of the force to 6,300. The IHP's ability to secure roadways freed up Coalition troops and the ISF to perform other security missions. Additionally, the IHP provided much needed help discovering and disarming numerous IEDs.[191]

More important was the introduction to the IPS of paramilitary forces similar to the gendarmerie in countries of Europe. The MOI created three police commando brigades, some equipped with wheeled, armored vehicles. Initially trained by handpicked Iraqi leaders selected by the commander of the special police forces, over time a special police academy was established to train leaders of the commando units. In addition to tactical and technical subjects, the academy curriculum included focused training on safeguarding human rights.[192] Another MOI force, the so-called "public order" units were much more problematic in 2004. Recruited almost entirely from Shia neighborhoods around Baghdad and locations in southern Iraq, these units were not under MNSTC-I supervision. They were regarded by Sunnis as evidence of Shia abuse of their power as head of the MOI.

These police commando forces proved their ability to work within their own culture and engage insurgent networks. In the city of Samarra, commandos detained 200 suspected anti-Iraq forces and discovered more than 20 weapons caches before the 30 January 2005 elections. Proud of his unit's accomplishments, MOI Special Police Commando Major Ibrahim stated, "We know who the leaders are here. They are too scared to stay in Samarra because they fear the MOI Special Police Commandos. We will come to them and we will get them. We will not stop until Samarra is 100-percent safe."[193] Other special police units deployed to Mosul, after the police forces in that northern city collapsed in November 2004 in combat that saw American advisors like US Army Colonel James H. Coffman fighting alongside Iraqi police officers. The special police units helped restore order in Mosul and assisted Coalition units there to rebuild Mosul's security forces. During the months leading up to the 30 January 2005 Iraqi elections, the Commandos proved to be the most courageous and aggressive of Iraq's civilian security forces.[194]

In some parts of Iraq, the IPS did not increase in professionalism and competence. To improve and foster the IPS in these areas, CPATT developed the Provincial Police Partnership Program (P3P). Coalition military and civilian advisor teams embedded with the MOI, provincial police headquarters, and local police stations to provide hands-on mentorship to the IPS leadership. Because Iraq was a sovereign country, however, Coalition leaders needed to consult the MOI for training design and approval of programs. MNSTC-I police planner, Major Hauser, recalled the serious limitations facing the Coalition's vision for the police:

> The situation was extremely complex, because you had the Iraqi Ministry of Interior, who technically we had transferred power over to. And as they became stronger and started to act on their own accord, it was harder for us to direct operations and what they wanted. As US and Coalition forces, we had certain things we wanted to accomplish, but sometimes those wouldn't be on the same playing field as what the ministry wanted to do.[195]

Like Coalition police advisors in the field, Hauser and others working with senior MOI leaders found compromise was the best path to success in working with their Iraqi counterparts.[196]

Securing the Borders

When Iraqis regained their sovereignty in mid-2004, their country did not have any type of centralized effort to secure its borders. The CPA had established the Department of Border Enforcement (DBE) in 2003 and some Iraqi security personnel had been stationed along the borders, supplemented by Coalition forces that had created local programs to prevent terrorists, arms, explosives, and other contraband from entering the country. MNSTC-I's establishment, however, marked the beginning of a concerted effort to secure the border by working with the MOI to train and equip the DBE. The DBE assumed responsibility from Coalition forces for Iraq's borders on 1 July 2004. Once the department became operational, its leaders and the MNSTC-I advisors realized the force needed more manpower and they planned for an expansion that would increase the ranks of the border police to 32,000 by the end of 2005.[197]

As with other ISF training efforts, the country of Jordan hosted the initial border police training center with the assistance of instructors from the US Department of Homeland Security. In September 2004 the first class of 451 Iraqi students graduated from the basic training course, which included classes on border security, customs supervision, and immigration procedures. MNSTC-I then assisted the DBE to create training academies in the cities of Basrah, Al Kut, and As Sulaymaniyah, locations close to the lengthy Iraqi border with Iran.[198] MNF-I and the DBE also began a monumental construction initiative to build a series of border crossing checkpoints and fortifications from which these new forces could operate. In December 2004 only about 50 forts were operational, but the rate of progress increased rapidly in 2005.[199] The goal of the DBE was to have 300 forts along with a command and control structure, four sector headquarters, and a national headquarters in Baghdad. Modernization efforts brought needed technology to the border forces, allowing officials to scan cargo as it entered the country.[200]

Despite all of these efforts, securing Iraq's borders remained a difficult task. One area on the Iraq–Iran border illustrated the significant amount of resources required to meet this challenge. In Multi-National Division–Central-South (MND-CS), controlled by the Poles in 2004, the AOR included approximately 140 kilometers of border between Iraq and Iran, a sector that included 14 border forts, 1 point of entry (POE), and 1 denial point (DP). Up to 200 Iraqi border patrol agents under an Iraqi lieutenant colonel manned the POE. These police manned and patrolled the area using about 60 border police with 6 Jeeps at the POE itself, and about 140 personnel with 14 Jeeps conducting mounted and dismounted patrols. In addition, the POE was staffed by about 40 customs inspectors and 40 immigration inspectors. The DP was manned with 30 border police under the leadership of an Iraqi captain. Each border fort provided living accommodations and communications for about 60 border police to control their AOR.[201] Although substantial work eventually went toward securing Iraq's borders after a slow start in 2003 and early 2004, this area would remain among the most challenging of the ISF programs.

Equipment and Facilities

Problems with logistics and equipment plagued the ISF in 2003 and 2004. The Iraqi Government had not yet developed the capacity to supply its forces with the immense requirements for weapons, supplies, vehicles, uniforms, ammunition, barracks, and countless other items needed to combat the insurgency. In March 2004 the CPA's Provost Marshal's Office reported that the IPS was operating at 41 percent of authorized vehicles, 63 percent of uniforms, 43 percent of pistols, and only 9 percent of protective vests. The CPA also confirmed that the ICDC was behind schedule in body armor, uniforms, vehicles, radios, and weapons.[202] MNSTC-I's troop-to-task analysis, completed in the summer of 2004 took these reports into consideration and led the Coalition to substantially increase the size of the budget for equipping all types of ISF units. Progress took time, however, and as late as the fall of 2004 US advisors encountered the most basic shortages. Major Jeffrey Allen, an advisor to the NIA in 2004, recalled the serious implications of the equipment and supply shortages and an Iraqi logistical infrastructure still in its infancy:

> I had issues like the fact we did our first 3 weeks of basic training without socks. No socks. So you have a culture where these guys have never, most of them, worn anything but sandals in their lives—and now they're wearing combat boots, brand new combat boots that have to be broken in. After about 3 weeks, half of my soldiers either quit or were walking around in sandals conducting basic training, because their feet were bloody messes. . . . So you see the second- and third-order of effects of the broken logistical system, and if we would have had a logistical system inherent to CMATT, it could have solved a lot of these problems.[203]

Given the critical impact of these issues in creating a viable ISF, MNSTC-I prioritized the creation of a supply system and the training of Iraqi units and higher commands on logistical issues.

When notified that he was taking command of MNSTC-I, Lieutenant General Petraeus requested six contracting officers and six Class A agents from DOD to help deal with the immense logistical challenges. Petraeus additionally asked for $40 million to be reprogrammed into a Quick Reaction Fund (QRF).[204] The MNSTC-I team came to rely on the Defense Logistics Agency and the Air Force Center for Environmental Excellence to deliver quality projects on time and within budget in support of the emerging Iraqi defense establishment.[205]

If supplying US forces that supported the MNSTC-I mission was a challenge, working with the Iraqi Government was an equally formidable task. As a sovereign nation, Iraq had the responsibility, but not the capability, to equip the nation's troops. After 28 June 2004 the Staff Judge Advocate (SJA) for MNSTC-I had to ensure that IIG officials signed all contracts for the procurement of weapons and equipment.[206] Although the United States, Coalition partners, and other donor nations provided the vast majority of the funding for the ISF, MNSTC-I attempted to transfer responsibility to the IIG for the provision of its own forces. However, determining how to allocate money between the construction of new security forces, sustainment systems, and operational funds used to fight the insurgency was not an easy problem to solve. Colonel Richard O. Hatch, MNSTC-I SJA, gave an example of the funding dilemma:

> When we were sending the Special Police Commandos into Samarra and they were going to stay there for several months . . . we assumed that the sustainment costs would come out of the operations and maintenance accounts from the Iraqi Government. Well, . . . most [Iraqis] were kind of looking to us. But we said, 'If we do that, if we expend those funds for operations, we are not going to have the money to do the training or the initial supply of units that are scheduled to stand up in the future.'[207]

The choice was a difficult one between immediate needs and building future capacity; nevertheless, the MNSTC-I staff attempted to achieve compromise with its Iraqi counterparts.

Working with the new Iraqi Government to stand up the combat service support systems that would provide basic provisions for the ISF proved to be exceedingly difficult as well. The MNSTC-I staff assisted the US Embassy advisors working with Iraqi ministry officials to ensure they were purchasing the correct equipment and in the correct quantities for those systems. The Coalition assisted with the construction of a huge national depot in Taji to receive the supplies coming in from Baghdad International Airport. This facility provided the physical storage for the supplies, but the space had to be matched with a cataloging system to make it available to the ISF distribution system. Not surprisingly, the cataloging system introduced by the Coalition was new for the Iraqis and logistics personnel had to be trained to use the system.[208] But, as Major Levesque, an officer involved in establishing the ISOF logistics staff, recalled, there was a basic cultural gap between American expectations and Iraqi experience with logistical systems and record keeping: "It was the things that are common knowledge to us—things we do every day—that these guys just didn't have any concept of. We're talking about crawl, walk, run, and we were pretty much [in 2004] just at the crawl stage with these guys. The Iraqi logistics staff [for the ISOF] probably consisted of no more than three or four guys at that stage."[209] As Levesque implied, the efforts in 2004 were just the very beginning of the MNSTC-I's efforts to introduce a modern method of providing basic support services to a new professional army.

Despite the obstacles, MNSTC-I did make some early headway in arming and equipping the ISF. The Saddam regime had stored literally millions of tons of munitions, but most of its equipment was outdated or stolen by looters when Saddam's army left their barracks and depots wide open during the invasion of March and April 2003. Still available, however, were stores of AK-47 Assault Rifles, and CMATT decided to arm the security forces with AK-47s because the Iraqis were familiar with them.[210] Although police forces are not normally equipped with powerful assault rifles, the MNSTC-I leaders considered the security environment and decided to issue the IPS and other police organizations the AK-47s as well.[211] The ISF received more specialized equipment, including French armored vehicles donated by one of the Gulf States, and nonstandard tactical vehicles such as pickup trucks and Land Rovers. Over time, the IIG ordered or refurbished more wheeled and tracked armored vehicles.

In addition to the border forts, police stations, and other operational facilities, MNSTC-I had the task of coordinating the reconstruction of the basic infrastructure of the ISF. A simple but critical example was the huge kitchen facility built at the An Numaniyah Military Training Base. The new kitchen allowed the cooking staff to consolidate the satellite kitchens to provide tens of thousands of meals per day to the Iraqi trainees and staff. Not only did the kitchen facility provide for the Iraqi recruits, it also employed an estimated 1,300 Iraqis and provided a significant boost to the local economy.[212]

By January 2005 the Coalition military command had facilitated the issuing of hundreds of thousands of pistols, machineguns, vehicles, uniforms, ammunition, and other equipment to both Ministries of Defense and Interior forces. In addition, MNSTC-I provided for and supervised the renovation of hundreds of buildings including training facilities, barracks, police stations, headquarters, and border forts. The scope of MNF-I's ISF effort was staggering, and the amount of money spent on the numerous projects equally striking. During its first 2 years,

MNSTC-I expended approximately $11 billion on equipment, construction, training, weapons, salaries, and a host of other requirements.[213] Petraeus compared the scale of his work as commander of MNSTC-I with his experience leading the 101st ABN in 2003:

> The 101st Airborne Division, with all the capabilities that we had in that first year that we were up in Mosul, had $53.6 million in Commander's Emergency Response Program (CERP) funds for reconstruction. We did over 5,000 projects with that, little ones obviously. Then in MNSTC-I, we did some that were several hundred million dollars over time. These are just enormous bases that are much bigger than this place [Fort Leavenworth] and could house 15,000 Soldiers with ranges, with training areas, with their own water treatment plants, their own power generation, their own mess halls, their own security, their own barracks and offices, and their own mosques. They were little cities.[214]

The need to create the "little cities" was just one piece of that enormously ambitious plan to rebuild and reshape Iraq's defense and security establishment that few had considered when Coalition forces entered Iraq in the spring of 2003.

January 2005 Elections

On 30 January 2005 the government of Iraq planned to hold elections that would choose representatives for a 275-member Iraqi Transitional Assembly (ITA). The assembly's task was to select a transitional government and to write a Constitution for Iraq that would later be submitted to the voters for approval. The ITA was designed to exercise legislative functions until the Constitution was approved and put into effect. These elections provided the first nationwide test for the country's new security forces. For both the IIG and the Coalition, it was a test that could not be failed.

Throughout the summer and fall of 2004, the Coalition worked feverishly with the ISF to prepare them to secure Iraq during the elections to prove they could be effective, were subservient to civil authority, and had broad national support. For General Casey, the MNF-I commander, the elections were the most crucial objective of the Coalition military and political campaign in Iraq. Moreover, Casey believed that putting an Iraqi face on election security was a critical requirement, stating "We felt we had to have sufficient Iraqi Security Forces available to provide security for those elections."[215] MNF-I, the IIG, and Iraqi military commanders thus planned for the ISF to lead the effort to secure the polling sites throughout Iraq. Coalition forces would remain in the background, available in case of emergencies.

The threats to the elections were indeed real. Leaders of the insurgency, especially those that headed the major Sunni Arab insurgent organizations, vociferously opposed the elections during the months before January 2005. Terrorist organizations also promised to mount operations that would prevent peaceful voting. Abu Musab al-Zarqawi, head of al-Qaeda in Iraq, reportedly stated in a speech made available on a terrorist Web site: "We have declared a fierce war on this evil principle of democracy and those who follow this wrong ideology. Anyone who tries to help set up this system is part of it."[216] Al-Zarqawi's opposition to democracy was based on his particular interpretation of Islam. But other Sunnis opposed the elections because they feared the likely result would be a Shia-dominated government.

Beginning on 28 January 2005, 2 days before the election, Iraqi authorities implemented curfews, imposed severe restrictions on vehicular traffic, closed Iraq's borders, and banned the

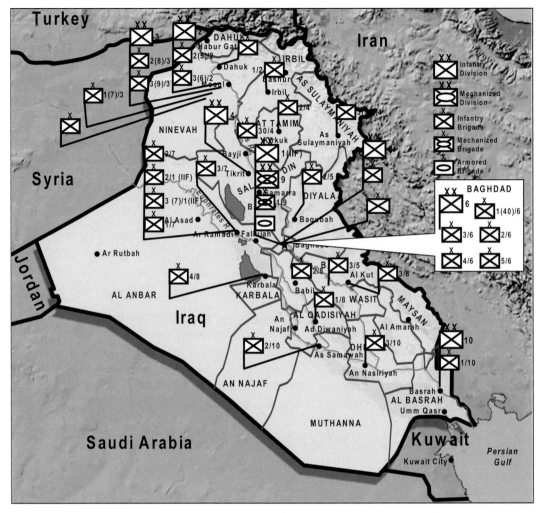

Figure 122. Location of Iraqi Army units, 2005.

carrying of weapons by civilians. Approximately 130,000 ISF personnel secured over 5,000 polling sites throughout the country for the elections.[217] In Baghdad, for example, the 303d Battalion of the NIA (formerly a National Guard battalion) secured 24 polling stations in their AOR on 30 January 2005. They provided security in the streets surrounding the polling stations as well as at the polling stations.[218]

US Soldiers and Marines played a vital but limited role supporting the Iraqi forces. For the elections, nearly 184,500 US and Coalition troops secured Iraq, a level higher than the number of forces used for the 2003 invasion. Major General John Batiste, commander of the 1st ID, spent 10 months working with the ISF north of Baghdad to prepare for the elections. US forces created Joint Coordination Centers (JCCs) staffed with US and Iraqi leaders to synchronize operations. This was the ISF's introduction to real-time command and control using 21st century technology. To help the Iraqi command deal with the scope of operations, Coalition forces and Iraqi units conducted extensive planning sessions and rehearsals. The effort paid great dividends. Batiste described the operations of the JCCs on Election Day:

We had [JCCs] in all four of our provinces and in each major city; some 21 total. Inside each JCC were all of the tools that you would need from radios to computers so that there was situational awareness and people reporting in from the field. For example, in the Diyala province, I will never forget it; there was Governor Abdullah, the brigade commander from the Iraqi Army and his staff, the provincial police chief and his staff, Iraqi emergency services, and the appropriate Coalition liaison officers. Colonel Dana Pittard was standing in the background offering suggestions. At first, the Iraqis were a little bit reticent. In their day, a command post was a desk, a map, an ash tray, and a phone. So we took them up to a new level.[219]

In this way, the elections marked a military as well as a political milestone. By placing the ISF forward, Coalition leaders were asking them to take responsibility for many of the command and control tasks that they would conduct once they became a fully independent professional army.

Lieutenant Colonel Steven Bullimore, commander of 1st Battalion, 6th Infantry, a unit serving with the 1st ID, described the role played by the ISF in Baqubah: "We never touched a ballot box ever and there were some pretty heroic things by Iraqis. We escorted the Iraqi police delivering the ballots with protection front and back, but the only things we dealt with were the materials like the tables and the ink. The ballots themselves were sacred. They held them, and they pledged them."[220]

Al-Qaeda and the other Sunni insurgent groups failed to stop the elections. Although more than 100 attacks took place across Iraq on that day killing at least 45 people (including 9 suicide bombers), the level of violence was far below expectations. In most parts of the country, the Iraqis were able to vote free of violence. Threats by opponents of the election to "wash the streets in blood" never materialized. General Casey later attributed the success of the elections to the efforts of the ISF, "The bottom line was that by the elections in January we had enough Iraqi security forces . . . to put an Iraqi face on the elections. We were out there. We set it up. We put the barriers up. We did all this stuff, but when [the elections] came out we were in the background."[221]

Conclusion

The inability of the ISF to take the lead in combating the insurgency in 2003 and 2004 was one of the greatest shortcomings of the overall Coalition and Iraqi campaign. Nearly 4 years later, as this study was prepared for publication, the ISF was still not fully prepared to engage internal and external threats to their country. Part of the reason for this slow development was that for the first 12 months of OIF, the ISF program was largely an improvisation. Though Coalition special operations forces (SOF) trained and advised Iraqis during and after the invasion of March 2003, the scale of the mission far exceeded their capacity. No American military leader entered Iraq in 2003 expecting to train, equip, or advise the entire body of security forces in a new Iraq on a multiyear basis, and to do so in the midst of an intense insurgency. Instead, Coalition military headquarters planned and made decisions based on the critical assumption that Saddam's army and police, in some configuration, would be called back into service and employed as the main security forces in a post-Saddam Iraq. The complete collapse of Saddam's armed forces in April 2003 invalidated that key assumption. The CPA's order to formally dissolve the security forces, which recognized facts on the ground, required a massive rebuilding program for which the US had not prepared. The multifaceted insurgency that evolved by late summer 2003 soon forced this mission to the forefront of the Coalition's effort.

Despite the problems created by the CPA decision, the Coalition responded quickly and resolutely in two ways. First, through CMATT and CPATT the CPA initiated the creation of professional military and police forces that would, in the long term, provide security for the new Iraqi state. Second, when the CMATT and CPATT efforts proved to be moving too slowly to address the worsening security environment in Iraq, Coalition military units began their own ad hoc programs to build the ICDC and to create local police forces to help engage the population and fight the mounting insurgency. Due to the scale and timeframe of the mission, and because the mission required building the entire set of institutions, processes, and units of a modern military, these efforts put the conventional forces of the US military in the lead for what had traditionally been a SOF mission. The results of the ISF program demonstrated the uncoordinated aspect of the overall effort and this led to a notably poor showing by both the NIA and the ICDC during the uprisings in April 2004.

The establishment of MNSTC-I in the late spring of 2004 began to place the Coalition's program on a better foundation. The decision to create this new command was critical because it placed all of the programs involved in training, equipping, and advising the ISF under one headquarters. MNSTC-I was then able to secure a massive increase in the level of resources necessary to expand the scope of the program and to speed up the timeline for training and equipping the ISF to meet the worsening security situation in Iraq. This clear articulation of command brought unity to an effort that was divided when both the CPA and CJTF-7 had conducted their own independent programs. Assisting MNSTC-I was the realization among senior leaders in the US Government of the importance of the ISF effort and the huge commitment of money, equipment, and personnel required for the Coalition to be successful in this endeavor. Only with this commitment did MNSTC-I begin to create the training and logistics infrastructure necessary for a modern and effective security establishment.

MNSTC-I, however, was not created until June 2004, more than a year after the fall of Saddam, and it took time for MNSTC-I leaders to organize their own systems to improve the performance of this program. American Soldiers charged with the task of training and advising the new Iraqi formations found their mission daunting. The Army went through several methods to find Soldiers to fill the ranks of the organizations involved in the train, equip, and advise missions. Army Reserve, National Guard, and Active Duty Soldiers struggled to perform these new missions in a complex security environment and often lacked the specific training and logistical support required to make their Iraqi units operationally effective. Cultural differences, as well, continued to contribute to the gap between American expectations and Iraqi unit performance that was in many American assessments less than adequate.

The ISF did score a number of notable successes, which demonstrated that despite shortcomings in the Coalition's initial efforts to train the Iraqi military and police formations, these forces made progress in 2003 and 2004 toward the goal of securing Iraq. By the end of 2004 the ISF not only displayed greater perseverance in the face of terrorism, insurgency, and sectarian conflict, they improved their ability to operate with Coalition forces and, in a few cases, independently. Iraqi Army and National Guard units had fought well in major operations against concentrated insurgent forces in Samarra and Fallujah, actions that suggested when properly supported and commanded by competent leaders, the ISF had the capacity to defeat threats to their country's security. Moreover, ISF operations during the elections of January 2005 demonstrated a capability and a willingness to provide their citizens with the opportunity for a new political future. This stands as the ISF's greatest success during the difficult 18 months that followed the fall of Saddam.

Notes

1.   Anthony Cordesman with William D. Sullivan, "Iraqi Force Development: Can Iraqi Forces Do the Job?" *Center for Strategic and International Studies*, Revised 29 November 2005, 19.

2.   James Zumwalt, "The Iraqi Military's Achilles' Heel Is Saddam Hussein: He's so worried about a rebellion that he has emasculated his own army," *Los Angeles Times,* 26 December 2001, B13.

3.   Lieutenant Colonel David J. Conboy, *An Interview with Lieutenant General Nasier Abadi, Deputy Chief of Staff, Iraqi Joint Forces* (Carlisle Barracks, PA: US Army War College, 2005), 7.

4.   Lieutenant General David H. Petraeus, interview by Contemporary Operations Study Team, Fort Leavenworth, KS, 8 April 2006, 24.

5.   Cordesman with Sullivan, 19.

6.   Brigadier General Michael Tucker, interview by Contemporary Operations Study Team, Fort Leavenworth, KS, 20 January 2006, 5.

7.   Major General (Retired) Buford C. Blount III, interview by Contemporary Operations Study Team, Fort Leavenworth, KS, 15 February 2006, 13; Lieutenant Colonel Rod A. Coffey, interview by Contemporary Operations Study Team, Fort Leavenworth, KS, 8 December 2005, 3; Former Ambassador to Yemen Barbara Bodine, interview by Contemporary Operations Study Team, Fort Leavenworth, KS, 15 February 2006, 5.

8.   Andrew Rathmell et al., *Developing Iraq's Security Sector, The Coalition Provisional Authority's Experience* (Santa Monica, CA: RAND National Defense Research Institute, 2005), 11.

9.   Douglas J. Feith, *War and Decision: Inside the Pentagon at the Dawn of the War on Terrorism* (New York, NY: Harper, 2008), 367–368.

10.   Colonel (Retired) Paul Hughes, interview by Contemporary Operations Study Team, Fort Leavenworth, KS, 1 March 2006, 10.

11.   "News Transcript: Secretary Rumsfeld Interview on NBC Meet the Press," *DefenseLink,* 2 November 2003, http://www.defenselink.mil/transcripts/2003/tr20031102-secdef0835.html (accessed 20 June 2006); see also "Walt Slocombe Holds Defense Department News Briefing on Rebuilding the Iraqi Police and Military," *FDCH Political Transcripts* (17 September 2003): 1–12.

12.   Mr. Walter Slocombe, interview by Contemporary Operations Study Team, Fort Leavenworth, KS, 12 September 2006, 9; see also Hughes interview, 1 March 2006, 12; and Colonel (Retired) Gregory Gardner, interview by Contemporary Operations Study Team, Fort Leavenworth, KS, 11 September 2006, 2–3.

13.   Feith, 427–435.

14.   Rathmell et al., 15.

15.   Rathmell et al., 17.

16.   Between mid-May and the end of June, Slocombe was nominally in charge of all security related issues including both CMATT and CPATT. But de facto, Bernard Kerik reported directly to Ambassador Bremer since Slocombe had no police experience, and the dual chain was soon formalized. Slocombe, interview, 12 September 2006, 3–4.

17.   Joint Center for International Security Force Assistance, unpublished briefing slides, "Training Iraqi Security Forces," Combined Arms Center, Fort Leavenworth, KS, 30 August 2006.

18.   "Walt Slocombe Holds Defense Department News Briefing," 1–12.

19.   Lieutenant General David Petraeus, *Training Iraqi Security Forces* Briefing, 8 August 2006, "Measures of Progress: Force Generation" slide.

20.   Rathmell et al., 23.

21.   Rathmell et al., 23.

22.   Rathmell et al.

23.   Cordesman with Sullivan, 28.

24.   "Iraq: Three Years, No Exit: Rebuilding Iraq Has Been Tougher Than Expected," *CBS News Online,* 13 March 2006, http://www.cbsnews.com/stories/2006/03/13/eveningnews/main1397666.shtml (accessed 14 June 2006).

25.   Major General (Retired) Paul D. Eaton, interview by Contemporary Operations Study Team, Fort Leavenworth, KS, 3 August 2006, 2–3, 13.

26.   Slocombe, interview, 12 September 2006, 8; see also Hughes, interview, 1 March 2006, 12; and Gardner, interview, 11 September 2006, 2–3.

27.   "CPA Briefing with Major General Paul Eaton, Commander, Coalition Military Assistance and Training Team, RE: Rebuilding Iraq Armed Forces, Location: Baghdad, Iraq, Wednesday, 21 January 2004," http://www.cpa-iraq.org/transcripts/Jan21_Eaton.html (accessed 21 June 2006).

28.   "DRAFT Statement of Work (SOW): New Iraqi Army Training (NIAT)," 7 June 2003, 1.

29.   Ambassador L. Paul Bremer, interview by Contemporary Operations Study Team, Fort Leavenworth, KS, 20 April 2006, 5.

30.   Rathmell et al., 33.

31.   Eaton, interview, 3 August 2006, 6–7.

32.   "CPA Briefing with Major General Paul Eaton, RE: Rebuilding Iraq Armed Forces."

33.   "CPA Briefing with Major General Paul Eaton, RE: Rebuilding Iraq Armed Forces."

34.   "NIC Brief—SECDEF Version—3 June 2003 DC with Backups," Draft PowerPoint Presentation provided to Contemporary Operations Study Team by Colonel (Retired) Greg Gardner, OSA Chief of Staff, 11 September 2006; Eaton, interview, 3 August 2006, 6–7.

35.   Eaton, interview, 3 August 2006, 11.

36.   Thom Shanker, "US Is Speeding Up Plans for Creating a New Iraqi Army," *New York Times*, 18 September 2003, A1.

37.   Slocombe, interview, 12 September 2006, 11.

38.   Slocombe, interview, 12 September 2006, 11–12.

39.   "Vinnell Corp. To Dispatch Team to Iraq Under Contract to Train Army," *CongressDaily* (26 June 2003): 13–14.

40.   Eaton, interview, 3 August 2006, 8.

41.   Eaton, interview, 3 August 2006, 9–10.

42.   Eaton, interview, 3 August 2006, 11–12.

43.   Eaton, interview, 3 August 2006, 11–12.

44.   Shanker, "US Is Speeding Up Plans for Creating a New Iraqi Army," A1.

45.   Eaton, interview, 3 August 2006, 12–14.

46.   Eaton, interview, 3 August 2006, 12–14.

47.   Eaton, interview, 3 August 2006, 23.

48.   Eaton, interview, 3 August 2006, 15.

49.   Eaton, interview, 3 August 2006, 16.

50.   Eaton, interview, 3 August 2006, 17.

51.   Eaton, interview, 3 August 2006, 9.

52.   "CPA Press Release: First Battalion of New Iraqi Army Graduates," 7 October 2003, http://govinfo.library.unt.edu/cpa-iraq/daily/archives/01October2003_index.html (accessed 20 June 2006).

53.   Lieutenant General Ricardo Sanchez, interview by Contemporary Operations Study Team, Fort Leavenworth, KS, 18 August 2006, 6–7; see also Lieutenant Colonel Wesley Odum, interview by Contemporary Operations Study Team, Fort Leavenworth, KS, 17 March 2006, 9, 13–14. The term "Iraqi National Guard" was initially rejected by the CPA because it sounded too much like "Republican Guard" from the Saddam regime, though in 2005 the ICDC was renamed the Iraqi National Guard.

54.   Rathmell et al., 38.

55.   Gardner, interview, 11 September 2006, 5.

56.   Slocombe, interview, 12 September 2006, 8.

57. Colonel David Teeples, interview by Contemporary Operations Study Team, Fort Leavenworth, KS, 4 November 2005, 14.

58. Colonel James Hickey, interview by Contemporary Operations Study Team, Fort Leavenworth, KS, 15 February 2006, 4.

59. "News Transcript: DOD Briefing—Secretary Rumsfeld and Gen. Abizaid," *DefenseLink,* 21 August 2003, http://www.defenselink.mil/transcripts/2003/tr20030821-secdef0604.html (accessed 20 June 2006).

60. Rathmell et al., 38.

61. L. Paul Bremer III, *My Year in Iraq: The Struggle to Build a Future of Hope* (New York, NY: Simon & Schuster, 2006), 175, see also 150, 168–169, and 182–183.

62. Sanchez, interview, 25 August 2006, 9–10. The ICDC was later incorporated into the NIA in the spring of 2004 when MNSTC-I was formed and the security force mission was given to CJTF-7. In 2004 the ICDC became the Iraqi National Guard, and in 2005 was made part of the Iraqi Army.

63. Coalition Provisional Authority, CPA Order No. 28, "The Establishment of the Iraqi Civil Defense Corps (3 September 2003)," http://www.cpa-iraq.org/regulations/20030903_CPAORD_28_Est_of_the_Iraqi_Civil_Defense_Corps.pdf (accessed 9 January 2008).

64. Aaron D. Boal, "On the Ground: Training Indigenous Forces in Iraq," in Brian M. De Toy, ed., *Turning Victory into Success: Military Operations After the Campaign* (Fort Leavenworth, KS: Combat Studies Institute Press, 2004), 287–306.

65. Boal, "On the Ground," in De Toy, ed., *Turning Victory into Success,* 288–289.

66. Boal, "On the Ground," in De Toy, ed., *Turning Victory into Success,* 296.

67. Colonel Mike Repass, interview by Contemporary Operations Study Team, Fort Leavenworth, KS, 29 January 2007, 11–13.

68. Cordesman with Sullivan.

69. CMATT Briefing, *The New Iraqi Army: Update and Acceleration Plan*, 5 September 2003.

70. CMATT Briefing, *The New Iraqi Army: Update and Acceleration Plan*.

71. CMATT Briefing, *The New Iraqi Army: Update and Acceleration Plan*.

72. Seth G. Jones et al., *Establishing Law and Order After Conflict* (Santa Monica, CA: RAND National Defense Research Institute, 2005), 118.

73. Inspectors General Report, US Department of State and US Department of Defense, "Interagency Assessment of Iraq Police Training," 15 July 2005, Department of State Report No. ISP-IQO-05-72, Department of Defense Report No. IE-2005-002, 19.

74. Bremer, *My Year in Iraq*, 127.

75. Jones et al., 124, 127.

76. Rathmell et al., 44–47.

77. Bremer, *My Year in Iraq*, 128–129.

78. Bremer, *My Year in Iraq*, 152.

79. Bremer, *My Year in Iraq*, 169, 182.

80. Lieutenant Colonel Blaise Cornell-d'Echert, interview by Operational Leadership Experiences Project Team, Combat Studies Institute, Fort Leavenworth, KS, 31 October 2006, 6.

81. Captain Christian Solinksy, interview by Contemporary Operations Study Team, Fort Leavenworth, KS, 5 July 2006, 4.

82. Inspectors General Report, Department of State Report No. ISP-IQO-05-72, Department of Defense Report No. IE-2005-002, 55–56.

83. Jones et al., 120.

84. Lieutenant Colonel Wesley Gillman, interview by Contemporary Operations Study Team, Fort Leavenworth, KS, 7 December 2005, 5.

85. Tucker, interview, 20 January 2006, 5.

86. Major Brian Pearl, interview by Contemporary Operations Study Team, Fort Leavenworth, KS, 8 December 2005, 5.

87. 4th Infantry Division, "Press Release #251-03-01: Task Force Iron Horse MP's and Iraqi Police Go on Joint Raid," 7 September 2003.

88. Bremer, *My Year in Iraq*, 186, see also 150, 168–169, and 182–183.

89. Rathmell et al.

90. Rathmell et al., 55.

91. Brigadier General Frank Helmick, interview by Contemporary Operations Study Team, Fort Leavenworth, KS, 15 February 2006, 9.

92. Colonel Michael Linnington, interview by Contemporary Operations Study Team, Fort Leavenworth, KS, 4 December 2005, 30.

93. Colonel Richard Hatch, interview by Contemporary Operations Study Team, Fort Leavenworth, KS, 14 February 2006, 11.

94. Linnington, interview, 4 December 2005, 12.

95. Ariana Eunjung Cha, "Female Officers Cross Cultural Frontier in Iraq; Women on Patrol Near Iran Brave Insults and Disapproval," *Washington Post,* 3 January 2004, A01.

96. Lieutenant Colonel Gregory Reilly, e-mail interview by Contemporary Operations Study Team, Fort Leavenworth, KS, 30 May 2006, 7.

97. "Significant Events of Grim Troop, 2/3 ACR during Operation Iraqi Freedom," 27 January 2004.

98. John J. McGrath, *Boots on the Ground: Troop Density in Contingency Operations* (Fort Leavenworth, KS: Combat Studies Institute Press, 2006), 130. As this work notes, the number of police originally reported was approximately 190,000, but that number was likely far too high because it did not reflect officers who had deserted, were unfit for service, or who had never existed. In mid-2004 the number of police was recalculated and discovered to be around 100,000, 129.

99. Sanchez, interview, 25 August 2006.

100. DRAFT Joint Manning Document Excel Spreadsheet, provided to Contemporary Operations Study Team by Colonel (Retired) Greg Gardner, OSA Chief of Staff, 11 September 2006.

101. Eaton, interview, 3 August 2006, 18.

102. Cornell-d'Echert, interview, 31 October 2006, 8–9.

103. Joint Center for International Security Force Assistance, "Training Iraqi Security Forces" Briefing.

104. Cornell-d'Echert, interview, 31 October 2006, 6.

105. Cornell-d'Echert, interview, 31 October 2006, 9.

106. Cornell-d'Echert, interview, 31 October 2006, 8–9.

107. Lieutenant General Karl Eikenberry, e-mail interview by Contemporary Operations Study Team, Fort Leavenworth, KS, 9 August 2006.

108. Sanchez, interview, 23 August 2006.

109. Eaton, interview, 3 August 2006, 20.

110. Eaton, interview, 3 August 2006, 20–21.

111. Eaton, interview, 3 August 2006, 20.

112. Repass, interview, 29 January 2007, 12, 15.

113. See Matt M. Matthews, *Operation AL FAJR: A Study in Army and Marine Corps Joint Operations* (Fort Leavenworth, KS: Combat Studies Institute Press, 2006), for an account of the second battle of Fallujah.

114. "MNSTC-I 'ASTs' Led the Way, Training in Iraqi Fight for Fallujah," *The Advisor,* Volume 1, Issue 12, 27 November 2004, 7.

115. "MNSTC-I 'ASTs' Led the Way, Training in Iraqi Fight for Fallujah," 8.

116. Major General John R.S. Batiste and Lieutenant Colonel Paul R. Daniels, "The Fight for Samarra: Full-Spectrum Operations in Modern Warfare," *Military Review,* May–June 2005.

117. Eaton, interview, 3 August 2006, 18.

118. Eaton, interview, 3 August 2006, 24.

119. Eaton, interview, 3 August 2006, 24.

120. Petraeus, interview, 4 March 2006, 4.

121. Petraeus, interview, 8 April 2006, 4.

122. Remarks by Lieutenant General David Petraeus, Former Commander, Multi-National Security Transition Command Iraq, to the Center for Strategic and International Studies, "Iraq's Evolving Forces," Moderator: Anthony Cordesman, 7 November 2005, 21, http://www.comw.org/warreport/fulltext/0512petraeus.pdf (accessed 8 January 2008).

123. John McGrath, "Iraq Security Forces Order of Battle," Unpublished manuscript, on file with Combat Studies Institute, Fort Leavenworth, KS.

124. Colonel Chris King, interview by Contemporary Operations Study Team, Fort Leavenworth, KS, 24 May 2006, 2.

125. Gerry J. Gilmore, "Despite Challenges, Iraqi Forces 'In the Fight'" *DefenseLink,* 29 September 2004, http://www.defenselink.mil/news/newsarticle.aspx?id=25181 (accessed 3 January 2008).

126. The 125,000 figure does not include those security forces that were still in training. Lieutenant General David H. Petraeus, *Training Iraqi Security Forces* Briefing, 8 August 2006, "Measures of Progress: Force Generation" slide. It was also true that many of these individuals were not still on the roles of active Iraqi units.

127. Lieutenant General David H. Petraeus, *Iraqi Security Forces Update as of 27 February 2006* Briefing.

128. King, interview, 24 May 2006, 2.

129. Jeremy M. Sharp and Christopher M. Blanchard, "Post-War Iraq: Foreign Contributions to Training, Peacekeeping, and Reconstruction," *CRS Report for Congress RL32105,* updated 6 June 2005, 3.

130. "NATO Expands Training Mission in Iraq," *NTM-I Fact Sheet,* 10 February 2005, http://www.afsouth.nato.int/JFCN_Missions/NTM-I/Factsheets/NATO_ExpandsTM.htm (accessed 5 July 2006).

131. Petraeus, interview, 4 March 2006, 18.

132. Petraeus, interview, 4 March 2006, 20.

133. Sharp and Blanchard, 2.

134. "Iraqi Coastal Defence Force Ready to Patrol Iraqi Waters Thanks to Navy," *Australian Government Defence Media Release*, CPA 222/04, 1 October 2004.

135. Sharp and Blanchard, 11.

136. This does not count the many thousands of Soldiers involved with IAF train and equip programs who were not strictly classified as advisors. See Joint Center for International Security Force Assistance, "Training Iraqi Security Forces" Briefing.

137. This has been a common trend in US Army history. See Robert D. Ramsey, *Advising Indigenous Forces: American Advisors in Korea, Vietnam, and El Salvador* (Fort Leavenworth, KS: Combat Studies Institute Press, 2006).

138. Major Jeffrey Allen, interview by Operational Leadership Experiences Project Team, Combat Studies Institute, Fort Leavenworth, KS, 5 December 2005, 17.

139. Allen, interview, 5 December 2005, 6.

140. Allen, interview, 5 December 2005, 19–20.

141. Major Mike Sullivan, interview by Operational Leadership Experiences Project Team, Combat Studies Institute, Fort Leavenworth, KS, 5 May 2006, 5.

142. Major Pete Fedak, interview by Operational Leadership Experiences Project Team, Combat Studies Institute, Fort Leavenworth, KS, 5 December 2005, 5.

143. Fedak, interview, 5 December 2005, 9.

144. Sullivan, interview, 5 May 2006, 21; see also, Major Robert Dixon, interview by Operational Leadership Experiences Project Team, Combat Studies Institute, Fort Leavenworth, KS, 10 October 2006, 9.

145. Dixon, interview, 10 October 2006, 10.

146. Fedak, interview, 5 December 2005, 13–14.

147. Inspectors General Report, Department of State Report No. ISP-IQO-05-72, Department of Defense Report No. IE-2005-002, 25, 15.

148. Major Shauna Hauser, interview by Operational Leadership Experiences Project Team, Combat Studies Institute, Fort Leavenworth, KS, 29 November 2005, 10.

149. Sullivan, interview, 5 December 2005, 9.

150. Remarks by Petraeus to Center for Strategic and International Studies, Former Commander, MNSTC-I, "Iraq's Evolving Forces," 7 November 2005, 5.

151. Mr. Henry Ensher, interview by Contemporary Operations Study Team, Fort Leavenworth, KS, 26 January 2006, 8–9.

152. Joint Center for International Security Force Assistance, "Training Iraqi Security Forces" Briefing.

153. Colonel Stephan Lanza, interview by Contemporary Operations Study Team, Fort Leavenworth, KS, 2 November 2005, 11–12.

154. The following section of this chapter only briefly examines the role of the US Army Reserve's 98th Division. For a thorough analysis of this unprecedented deployment of the USAR, see Steven Clay, *Iroquois Warriors in Iraq* (Fort Leavenworth, KS: Combat Studies Institute Press, 2007).

155. Major General James Helmly, interview by Contemporary Operations Study Team, Fort Leavenworth, KS, 2 December 2006.

156. Helmly, interview, 2 December 2006.

157. Brigadier General Richard Sherlock, interview by Contemporary Operations Study Team, Fort Leavenworth, KS, 16 November 2006; Colonel Frank Cipolla, interview by Contemporary Operations Study Team, Fort Leavenworth, KS, 20 November 2006.

158. Sherlock, interview, 16 November 2006; Cipolla, interview, 20 November 2006.

159. Sherlock, interview, 16 November 2006.

160. Colonel Doug Shipman, interview by Contemporary Operations Study Team, Fort Leavenworth, KS, 3 November 2006.

161. Cipolla, interview, 20 November 2006.

162. Lieutenant General David H. Petraeus, "The 2006 TRADOC/Combat Studies Institute Military History Symposium Keynote Presentation," in Kendall D. Gott, ed., *Security Assistance, U.S. and International Historical Perspectives; The Proceedings of the Combat Studies Institute 2006 Military History Symposium* (Fort Leavenworth, KS: Combat Studies Institute Press, 2006), 12.

163. Clay, 138.

164. Command Sergeant Major Milt Newsome, interview by Contemporary Operations Study Team, Fort Leavenworth, KS, 3 November 2006, 5–6.

165. "Iraq's 6th Battalion Completes Training, Activates," *DefenseLink,* 8 July 2004, http://www.defenselink.mil/news/newsarticle.aspx?id=25734 (accessed 4 April 2008).

166. Remarks by Petraeus to Center for Strategic and International Studies, Former Commander, MNSTC-I, "Iraq's Evolving Forces," 7 November 2005, 8–9.

167. Petraeus, interview, 4 March 2006, 11.

168. Jim Garamone, "Iraqis Adapt British Military Academy as Model," *American Forces Press Services* (26 May 2006), http://www.defenselink.mil/news/May2006/20060526_5249.html (accessed 9 June 2006).

169. Chief Petty Officer Joe Kane, "Iraqi Mechanized Brigade Rolls Out Heavy Equipment," *The Advisor,* Volume 1, Issue 12, 27 November 2005, 1, 11–12.

170. Technical Sergeant Andrew Hughan, "11 Graduate from First Iraqi Signals Schools," *The Advisor,* Volume 2, Issue 4, 22 January 2005.

171. Sergeant Jared Zabaldo, "Iraq Adds First Female Officer to Army's Medical Corps," *The Advisor,* Volume 2, 18 September 2004, 4.

172. Technical Sergeant Andrew Hughan, "Iraqi Mechanized Brigade Assumes Mission," *The Advisor,* Volume 2, Issue 3, 15 January 2005; Captain Tim Jeffers, "Iraqi Air Force Takes Off with Aircraft Delivery," *The Advisor,* Volume 2 Issue 3, 15 January 2005; also, General Bryan Brown, written comments provided to the Combat Studies Institute, 19 December 2006, on file at Fort Leavenworth, KS.

173. "Special Forces Produce," *The Advisor,* Volume 2, Issue 3, 15 January 2005.

174. For one publicly available record of this operation by the Al Hillah unit, see W. Thomas Smith Jr., "In Their Own Hands: An Emerging Iraqi Special-ops Force Works to Get the Bad Guys," *MilitaryPhotos.Net,* 12 October 2004, http://www.militaryphotos.net/forums/showthread.php?t=24143 (accessed 18 December 2006). The unit continues to operate in Iraq in 2006.

175. Major Dennis Levesque, interview by Operational Leadership Experiences Project Team, Combat Studies Institute, Fort Leavenworth, KS, 14 March 2006, 9.

176. Rathmell et al., 39.

177. Specialist Joe Alger, "203rd Iraqi National Guard Battalion Makes Tremendous Progress," *1st Infantry Division Public Affairs Office,* 19 December 2004, http://www.1id.army.mil/1ID/News/December/Article_18/Article_18.htm (accessed 6 July 2006).

178. Colonel J. Mike Murray, interview by Contemporary Operations Study Team, Fort Leavenworth, KS, 8 December 2005, 19.

179. Lieutenant Colonel Scott Efflandt, interview by Contemporary Operations Study Team, Fort Leavenworth, KS, 14 December 2005, 14.

180. Murray, interview, 8 December 2005, 19.

181. Efflandt, interview, 14 December 2005, 14.

182. Romesh Ratnesar and Paul Quinn-Judge, "Can Iraq Do the Job?" *Time,* no. 18 (3 May 2004): 35–37.

183. Doug Struck, "Iraqi Security has Come Far, With Far to Go; U.S.-Trained Forces Hit by Defections," *Washington Post,* 1 August 2004, A18.

184. Ian Fisher, "Attacks Go On; Bomb Kills 6 Iraqi Officers," *New York Times,* 16 December 2003, A1.

185. Lieutenant General David Petraeus, "Office of Security Cooperation" Briefing.

186. Inspectors General Report, Department of State Report No. ISP-IQO-05-72, Department of Defense Report No. IE-2005-002, 25, 15.

187. "Iraq's 6th Battalion Completes Training," 1–2.

188. Remarks by Petraeus to Center for Strategic and International Studies, Former Commander, MNSTC-I, "Iraq's Evolving Forces," 7 November 2005, 9.

189. Solinksy, interview, 5 July 2006, 8.

190. Solinksy, interview, 5 July 2006, 12.

191. Sergeant Jared Zabaldo, "Iraqi Ministry of Interior Orders Highway Patrol to 6,300 Strong," *The Advisor,* Volume 1, Issue 8, 30 October 2004.

192. Inspectors General Report, Department of State Report No. ISP-IQO-05-72, Department of Defense Report No. IE-2005-002, 13. Also, Lieutenant General David Petraeus, written comments provided to the Contemporary Operations Study Team, 9 January 2007, on file with Combat Studies Institute, Fort Leavenworth, KS. Also, US Government Accountability Office, GAO Report GAO-05-431T, *Rebuilding Iraq: Preliminary Observations on the Challenges in Transferring Security Responsibilities to Iraqi Military and Police,* 14 March 2005.

193. "Iraqi Police Commandos take Fight to Insurgents," *The Advisor,* Volume 1, Issue 16, 25 December 2004.

194. Petraeus, written comments, 9 January 2007.

195. Houser, interview, 29 November 2005, 6.

196. Hauser, interview, 29 November 2005, 6.

197. Chief Petty Officer Joe Kane, "Iraq's Border Enforcement Department Graduates First Cadets," *The Advisor,* Volume 1, Issue 4, 2 October 2004, 5.

198. Petraeus, "Keynote Presentation," in Gott, ed., *Security Assistance, U.S. and International Historical Perspectives.*

199. Petraeus, "Keynote Presentation," in Gott, ed., *Security Assistance, U.S. and International Historical Perspectives.*

200. Chief Petty Officer Joe Kane, "Iraqi Border Forts Strengthen Security at More than 300 Locations," *The Advisor,* Volume 1, Issue 5, 9 October 2004.

201. Major Lars Hyrup and Captain Piotr Siemienski (Polish Army), *MND-CS Press Release,* 28 October 2004, http://republika.pl/piomndcs/MND%20CS%20News/IBP.htm.

202. US Government Accountability Office, GAO Report GAO-04-902R, *Rebuilding Iraq: Resource, Security, Governance, Essential Services, and Oversight Issues,* 28 June 2004.

203. Allen, interview, 5 December 2005,17.

204. Petraeus, interview, 4 March 2006, 6.

205. Petraeus, interview, 4 March 2006, 25.

206. Hatch, interview, 14 February 2006, 4.

207. Hatch, interview, 14 February 2006, 10.

208. Remarks by Petraeus to Center for Strategic and International Studies, Former Commander, MNSTC-I, "Iraq's Evolving Forces," 7 November 2005, 22.

209. Levesque, interview, 14 March 2006, 5.

210. Petraeus, interview, 4 March 2006, 12.

211. Hauser, interview, 29 November 2005, 7.

212. Technical Sergeant Andrew Hughan, "Kitchen Serves Thousands of Iraqi Soldiers," *The Advisor*, Volume 2, Issue 3, 15 January 2005.

213. "Unit Responsible for Training Iraqi Forces Changes Command," *American Forces Press Service,* 8 September 2005.

214. Petraeus, interview, 8 April 2006, 26.

215. General George W. Casey Jr., interview by Contemporary Operations Study Team, Fort Leavenworth, KS, 27 November 2007, 12.

216. Jackie Spinner and Bassam Septi, "Militant Declares War on Iraqi Vote," *Washington Post*, 24 January 2005, A01.

217. "Special Defense Department Briefing on Iraq Security Forces." *DefenseLink*, 4 February 2005, http://www.defenselink.mil/transcripts/2005/tr20050204-0283.html (accessed 7 October 2006). Presenter: Lieutenant General David Petraeus, Commander, MNSTC-I.

218. Specialist Brian Schroeder, "Iraqi Troops Risk Lives for Elections, 10th Mountain Division News Release, CAMP LIBERTY, BAGHDAD, Iraq," *Defend America,* http://www.defendamerica.mil/articles/jan2005/.

219. Major General (Retired) John R. Batiste, interview by Contemporary Operations Study Team, Fort Leavenworth, KS, 20 April 2006, 7–8.

220. Lieutenant Colonel Steven Bullimore, interview by Contemporary Operations Study Team, Fort Leavenworth, KS, 18 May 2006, 13, 15.

221. Casey, interview, 27 November 2007, 12.

Part IV

Sustaining the Campaign

Chapter 12

Logistics and Combat Service Support Operations

There is an aphorism among military professionals that states, "Amateurs study tactics; professionals study logistics."* Perhaps no other army in the world has studied logistics more than the US Army. Certainly no fighting force in history has been as effective at providing its fighting Soldiers with the resources for modern warfare as the US Army. In 2003, no army in the world could dream of conducting and sustaining two military campaigns in some of the world's most remote and inhospitable regions, more than 10,000 miles from their home territory. US Army logisticians are, in this sense, without peer.

Yet, despite their undeniable skill, Army logisticians faced widespread difficulties in supporting Operation IRAQI FREEDOM (OIF). Like other parts of the Army, which were making the transition to full spectrum operations after April 2003, Army logisticians went through their own transition during OIF. The most dramatic change was mental in nature and driven by incorrect assumptions about a post-Saddam Iraq. The prewar expectations of Brigadier General Scott G. West, an experienced Quartermaster Corps officer who became the principal Combined Joint Task Force–7 (CJTF-7) Logistics staff officer (CJ4) in the summer of 2003, are representative of widely held assumptions among American logisticians:

> I expected an increasingly safe or permissive SASO [stability and support operation], with an emphasis on consolidating and reducing the logistics footprint in theater. I suspected that my biggest challenges would be in the areas of distribution and base camp development, with heavy participation by government contractors. I figured that it would not take more than about six months to get to 'steady-state' logistics. How far wrong could this Quartermaster have been?[1]

While making the required shift to long-term combat service support (CSS) operations in what would become an increasingly *nonpermissive* environment, West and other Army logisticians simultaneously introduced a new logistics doctrine called distribution-based combat service support (DB CSS). The implementation of this new system, a method that differed fundamentally from that used by the US military since World War II, had a significant effect on CSS organizations and the units they supported. This chapter focuses on CSS operations in Iraq in 2003 and 2004 to examine how Army logisticians adapted to the difficult and dangerous operational environment, to explain the effects of the new doctrine on CSS operations, and to describe how these critical operations shaped the larger campaign in Iraq.

To understand the Army's CSS operations in OIF in 2003 and 2004, it is necessary to understand the basic framework of CSS doctrine. Army doctrine divides CSS operations into 11 self-explanatory subcategories: Supply, Field Services (such as food preparation, laundry, and hygiene), Transportation, Maintenance, Ordnance and Explosive Ordnance Demolition

---

*There is much dispute as to who uttered this military maxim. It has been attributed to General Omar Bradley and US Marine Corps Commandant General Robert H. Barrow. In various other forms, it has also been attributed to Napoleon, Helmuth von Moltke, and Carl von Clausewitz. For the purposes of this study, its origin is far less important than its message.

Support, Financial Management, Legal Support, Band Support, Human Resources, Religious Support, and Health Services Support. Tied to these 11 areas, but not technically a logistics function, is engineering support to logistics, which included real estate management, contracting, construction, and repair of infrastructure such as roads, ports, and bases to support US operations.

Even before the 2003 invasion of Iraq, the Army's CSS branches and organizations were making fundamental changes in the way they operated.[†] Operations in areas of Afghanistan and Iraq took place during this transformation, a fact that added even greater complications to the Army's already challenging logistical missions. The transition from conventional offensive operations to full spectrum operations after April 2003 took place on many levels—doctrinal, organizational, and operational to name a few. Most importantly, CSS Soldiers made the transition from providing support from a relatively safe rear area to constantly operating in a war zone.

Figure 123. A (UH-60) Blackhawk with a sling load of food and water packed by Soldiers of the 101st Airborne Division (Air Assault) for the Jump Assault Command Post (JCP) in Mosul, Iraq.

DOD Photo by PVT Daniel D. Meacham

Unlike conventional military operations in which most combat takes place along relatively well-defined front lines and logistical operations are conducted in relatively safe zones behind those lines, the combat and logistics aspects of postinvasion operations in Iraq took place in an environment that had no front or rear areas. Full spectrum operations occurred with noncontiguous front lines and in a nonpermissive environment where insurgent attacks were common but almost entirely unpredictable. Delivering logistical support to units was itself often a combat operation as CSS units were forced to deal with ambushes against convoys and attacks on their logistical bases. During the invasion of March and April 2003, the primary challenge of the CSS system was to keep up with the pace of advance. As CJTF-7 transitioned to full spectrum operations, the challenge became the long-term sustainment of operations across a country the size of California that had very poor infrastructure and in an environment where insurgents acted to impede supply lines.

[†]The US Army's doctrinal term for the various types of support needed to conduct and sustain military operations is "combat service support" (CSS). The term "logistics" is actually a subset of CSS dealing with materiel support, as opposed to health services or financial services. This chapter will use CSS and logistics interchangeable in the interest of style. Where it is necessary to be precise, terms will be more explicitly used.

The speed of the deployment of US forces to the Middle East in 2003 and their brilliant campaign of maneuver in March and April could not have been accomplished by any other army in the world. No military operation is without flaws, however, and the Army has harshly judged several aspects of its logistical performance during that part of OIF, focusing on materiel management and unit communications in particular. Since the transition to full spectrum operations in May 2003, the Army has experienced other difficulties in the field of CSS. The ability to provide personal and vehicle survivability equipment suitable for the 360-degree environment of full spectrum and counterinsurgency operations was slow to develop. More fundamentally, the basic premises underlying the Army's logistics transformation underway during OIF have also been questioned. Nonetheless, the CSS community's accomplishments in operating a supply and service chain that stretches halfway across the globe have been remarkable. To understand the CSS aspect of OIF, one first needs a basic overview of the CSS system that was the legacy of the Cold War era and the transformation that sought to revamp that system in the early years of the 21st century.

Iron Mountains

Critics inside and outside the Defense community in the 1990s derisively labeled the Army's traditional logistics system as the "iron mountain" concept. To ensure Soldiers and units had all the supplies and services they needed to conduct combat operations, each echelon of command, from company to division carried with it relatively large amounts of materiel and contained relatively robust service capabilities to sustain itself in combat. A huge number of CSS units and Soldiers in the Army's so-called "tail" backed up those unit capabilities. In turn, the CSS support to the Army's "teeth" were serviced and supplied by a robust industrial plant in the United States.

The deployment of combat and combat support units into a theater in early phases of a campaign was usually preceded by the delivery of CSS units and accompanying materiel over a period of months. These supplies created the so-called iron mountains that had to be built up before combat could begin. In this way, the vast majority of combat units could arrive in theater and could fall in on the logistics infrastructure already in place. The buildup before Operation DESERT STORM in 1991 is an excellent example of how the American Army employed this concept.[2]

The start of Phase III, Decisive Operations, was thus predicated on having stockpiled sufficient materiel and CSS units to sustain the intensity of modern combat. The Army accumulated large supply stores at logistical bases, airbases, or ports, and then moved provisions toward the front line from which combat units were supplied. For the most part, units sustained themselves on the battlefield with their internal logistical assets, which were then re-supplied by convoys to and from the nearest logistical base or node. As the front lines moved, mini-iron mountains moved to keep the length of the last leg of the system from exceeding prescribed distances. In similar fashion, maintenance and other integral parts of combat units were reinforced with greater capabilities as the distance from the front lines extended.

A significant part of the combat power of the US Army rested on its extensive CSS systems. Only in extreme cases since mid-1943 have US Army units had their operations significantly limited by a lack of logistical support. This system has great appeal to combat and combat support units because they had authority over enough CSS assets to fight without counting on logistics units outside of their control. One of the hallmarks of the American way of war was the Army's ability to sustain its units in combat, which in turn allowed for an unrelenting application of combat power against enemies far less prepared for sustained operations. The system was redundant but very effective.

Critics believed this mass-based system placed too great an industrial and financial strain on the nation to sustain in peacetime, placed too much demand on the Navy and Air Force to deliver, and prevented rapid deployments and the rapid start of combat operations. Facilities to store the surplus had to be located in theater. Personnel were needed to staff and service the warehouses, while other personnel and resources were critical for moving supplies. This mass-based system had proven itself where the full energies of the United States' industrial, technological, and economic might were focused on producing weapons, materiel, and supplies to support the war effort.[3] But military thinkers who put forth theories about future conflicts in which combat would be short and decisive asked serious questions about the detrimental effects of relying on the iron mountain. The rapid defeat of Saddam Hussein's army in DESERT STORM and the huge quantities of unused materiel that remained after the conflict seemed to reinforce this point of view.

Distribution-Based Logistics

Beginning in the 1990s, the US military began to look for alternatives to the iron mountain and became very interested in the business world's ability to shorten delivery times and lessen its reliance on warehousing through the use of advanced technology. Models used by companies with their own worldwide logistical systems such as FedEx, Wal-Mart, and UPS appeared especially promising and distribution-based logistics (DBL), or as it is more commonly referred to, "just-in-time" logistics, became a new operational concept.[4] From this idea, the Army derived a new term—distribution-based combat service support (DB CSS). This innovation became part of doctrine in 2003 when the Army issued its new keystone logistical manual, Field Manual (FM) 4-0, *Combat Service Support*. This manual defined the concept, stating, "DB CSS replaces bulk and redundancy with velocity and control."[5] DB CSS promised the exact amount of a particular item to arrive at the exact location at the right time for the Soldier to use. Real-time tracking of requirements coupled with precise tracking and delivery of supplies would greatly reduce the need for combat units to carry large amounts of materiel with them into battle. DB CSS also held out the promise of vastly lowering the amount of supplies and units that needed to be put in place before combat operations could begin. And units themselves would be more mobile and able to conduct operations without the encumbrance of moving their vast logistical tail with them.

Technology was the key to making DB CSS work on the battlefield. CSS planners had to synchronize their plans to the operational scheme of the campaign to ensure they planned for the correct materiel and services to arrive at the right time. The Combat Service Support Control System (CSSCS), encompassing an array of automated computer systems used by Army logisticians, would enable this process. CSSCS was designed to interface with other combat and combat support systems under the Army Battlefield Command System (ABCS) to provide near real time visibility of CSS requirements and capabilities from the factory to the front line. Logisticians used the term "total asset visibility" to describe the highly accurate understanding of unit logistics requirements and available resources required to make DB CSS work. This knowledge provided CSS planners and operators the ability to deliver supplies and services only when and where needed, avoiding the cost, slowness, and redundancy of the iron mountain system. In theory, combat units were thus liberated from some degree of planning and executing their own CSS systems, allowing them to focus on planning and conducting operations.[6]

The Army's implementation of DB CSS accelerated after Operation DESERT STORM in the context of changing joint doctrine about the nature of future warfare.[7] The Army made changes to its organizational structure and doctrine while fielding new equipment and technology. Prime among those changes was a major reduction in the number of CSS units and Soldiers during the Army drawdown that followed the collapse of the Soviet Union. Accompanying these changes, the Army also began to make extensive use of contractor support to supplement and replace Army CSS capabilities, freeing additional Soldiers for other duties. The phrase "contractors on the battlefield" described the process and required a host of changes to operating procedures, legal issues, and treaty obligations. By the late 1990s, contractors performed key roles at all levels within the Army's logistical architecture.[8]

Some of these changes actually predate Operation DESERT STORM. With Congressional support, the Army established the Logistics Civil Augmentation Program (LOGCAP) on 6 December 1985 with the publication of Army Regulation (AR) 700-137. LOGCAP gave major commands the authority to contract for peacetime logistical services. Between 1987 and 1989 the United States conducted two military operations to safeguard oil tanker traffic in the Persian Gulf against Iranian attacks. The newly established LOGCAP was first used in 1988 to support these and future contingency operations when the Army Corps of Engineers contracted out the construction and maintenance of two petroleum pipeline systems in Southwest Asia.[9]

During Operation DESERT STORM, the Army used dozens of contractors to provide logistics support that included feeding, fuel deliveries, and the fielding of new combat systems, such as the M1A1 version of the Abrams tank to units before they deployed into battle. Contractors provided the bulk of their services within Kuwait, though some maintenance and other contractors moved with tactical units. Results were mixed. Costs and performance problems plagued the generally successful effort as both the Army and private contractors developed new techniques during actual operations.

The relatively small scale of combat operations during the various contingencies between 1991 and 2001 gave the Army the opportunity to develop its new CSS processes in relatively benign environments. LOGCAP and DB CSS were extensively used in Somalia and the Balkans to support US operations in Bosnia, Macedonia, Albania, and Kosovo. This 10-year interlude was both a blessing and a curse. Both systems provided impressive results in that decade and became an ever more important part of the Army's logistical transformation.

In response to inefficiencies in the process, the Army Materiel Command (AMC) took over centralized management of the LOGCAP in 1996. Under AMC, a single umbrella contract was awarded to a single contract firm for the sustained delivery of contractor services in peacetime and for the rapid delivery of increased levels of support during wartime. The LOGCAP contract, designed for a base year plus 9 years of optional renewals, was awarded to Kellogg, Brown and Root Services (KBR), a Houston-based subsidiary of Halliburton, on 14 December 2001. KBR was thus the major contractor in place for both Operation ENDURING FREEDOM (OEF) in Afghanistan (and elsewhere) and OIF.

DBL had its detractors. The old mass-based system placed a premium on effectiveness, meaning its success was based on combat units having all the logistical support they needed, without interruption, even if the process required a large logistical tail and mountains of supplies. DB CSS made efficiency paramount—minimum stockage levels, speed and accuracy of delivery, and reduction of forces committed to delivering CSS were major determinants of success. DBL's effectiveness and efficiency were difficult to achieve even with the most sophisticated business practices operating over highly advanced infrastructure. On the modern battlefield, DB CSS faced a host of additional and obvious challenges ranging from the harsh demands of operations in geographic and climactic extremes, to uncertain and rapidly changing natures of war and foreign policy, to catastrophic combat outcomes and attacks anywhere on the supply line from the factory to the front line.

The Army's DB CSS transformation, like the Army's overall transformation efforts, was not complete when OIF began. CSS doctrine was undergoing change in 2002 and 2003 and the Army codified this transition in August 2003 when it published FM 4-0, replacing its previous doctrine that dated from 1995. FM 4-0 did note the incompleteness and potential shortcomings of the new logistics practices during the change stating, "During this transition, some units may not be able to execute all operations 100 percent according to distribution doctrine."[10] Additionally, in the summer of 2003, OIF itself, as the title of this book suggests, was undergoing transition to full spectrum operations. It is against this evolving backdrop that CSS operations in Iraq must be understood and examined.

The CSS Structure for Operation IRAQI FREEDOM

The CSS concept of support for OIF included the linkages between the combat formations fighting at the tactical level, the theater support units at the operational level, and the national providers (such as the AMC) at the strategic level.[11] Army doctrine defines strategic level logistics as the linkage between the US economic base and military forces. Operational logistics is the linking of strategic logistics to the tactical level of war. Last, and most importantly, tactical logistics is the synchronization of all CSS assets to sustain Soldiers and their weapons systems during operations.[12]

In a theater of war, such as the US Central Command (CENTCOM) theater, Army doctrine calls for the creation of the communications zone (COMMZ), extending from the rear of the combat zone to the continental United States (CONUS), in which strategic logistics will operate. Within the COMMZ, the joint task force commander creates a theater base at which air, land, and sea lines of communications and CSS facilities can be located in relative safety to support combat operations. From this base, operational logistics links national assets to Army tactical units. The base consists of facilities such as aerial and sea ports of debarkation (APODs and SPODs, respectively), staging bases, fixed maintenance and logistics storage facilities, and some CSS unit headquarters.[13] When OIF began, Kuwait served as that base, though some CSS operations were also present in Qatar and Bahrain. Kuwait continued to serve as the main CSS base for OIF throughout 2003 and 2004, though a forward base was established near Baghdad because of the long distances involved.

The US Army was not only responsible for its own CSS, it was also required to provide certain categories of support to its US Marine Corps and US Air Force partners in theater. These "Title X" requirements, prescribed by law and regulation, are apportioned to each of the Services based on their unique capabilities for the sake of efficiency. In support of a large operation such as OIF, the senior Army force commander, Combined Forces Land Component Command (CFLCC)/Third Army in this case, made the decision to deploy a full Theater Support Command (TSC) to provide CSS support.‡ The TSC is designed to coordinate Army and national CSS assets in support of a campaign. These assets ranged from tactical CSS companies, battalions, brigades, and civilian contractors to the Army and Air Force Exchange Service (AAFES), Red Cross, AMC, Defense Logistics Agency (DLA), General Services Administration (GSA), and included host nation assistance.[14] Army logisticians also found themselves supplying the military forces provided by the two dozen plus members of the Coalition, each of whom needed logistical support in different areas. Finally, as efforts to reconstruct Iraq and rebuild Iraq's security forces ramped up in late 2003 and 2004, Army CSS operators inherited those immense responsibilities as well.

The US Army Reserve's 377th TSC coordinated the overall CSS effort for OIF. The TSC concept was developed in the 1990s in response to the shortcomings identified in Operations DESERT SHIELD and DESERT STORM. In 1998 the 377th Theater Army Area Command was redesignated as the 377th TSC, restructured with a general staff, and given the wartime responsibility to provide CSS management to CENTCOM. Made up largely of Reserve Soldiers, the 377th TSC was the Army's only deployable TSC, the others being the 21st TSC in Europe and the 19th TSC in Korea. The Army Reserve took great pride in this new mission.[15]

The Army first mobilized the 377th TSC in 2001 to support OEF in Afghanistan, and the command returned to the United States in 2002 only to be mobilized and deployed again to the Middle East for OIF in early 2003. It was commanded by Army Reserve Major General David E. Kratzer and reported to the CFLCC, Third Army, in Kuwait. From Camp Arifjan, Kuwait, it was responsible for the joint logistics support of all Coalition forces including functions such as base operations and security, transportation management, seaport and airport management, and the materiel management of all classes of military supplies.[16] Kratzer recounted how the Third Army commander, Lieutenant General David D. McKiernan, told him during an initial planning meeting, "You guys have got to make us succeed. Without you, we can't succeed. You know, CSS will not win a war, but CSS will sure lose a war."[17]

At its peak strength, the 377th TSC controlled 8 general-officer level and 13 colonel-level commands, each responsible for specific CSS functions such as personnel (3d Personnel Command), communications (335th Signal Command), financial management (366th Finance Command), area/base support (43d and 171st Area Support Groups), fuel (49th Quartermaster Group [POL]), and transportation management (3d Theater Army Movement Control Agency). Active Army units served under Reservists in the 377th TSC with Reservists making up 65 percent of the total strength of the command.

Brigadier General Sean Byrne, an Active Duty officer, commanded the Army Reserve's 3d Personnel Command (PERSCOM). Drawing on lessons learned from DESERT STORM when Soldiers became "lost" in the personnel and medical channels, for the first time personnel

---

‡This decision was made in late 2002. When V Corps then became CJTF-7 on 15 June 2003, the Third US Army reverted to its role as the Army Service Component Command (ASCC) for the entire CENTCOM area of operations to include Afghanistan, while CJTF-7 assumed responsibility for all operations in Iraq.

managers were placed under the command of a TSC instead of reporting directly back to the United States. Byrne credited that arrangement and the Army's new digital identification cards and other systems with keeping error rates well under the Army standard of 2 percent.[18]

An additional and very important benefit of accurate personnel tracking was the improved performance in delivering mail to Soldiers. Getting large amounts of mail delivered promptly to hundreds of thousands of Soldiers in thousands of units whose locations changed on a regular basis was a monumental task. A General Accounting Office report released in 2004 highlighted several problems with mail delivery in theater during the spring and summer of 2003, to include insufficient postal units and mail handling equipment. Many of the problems found were the normal result of the rapid deployment of US forces, the decision to limit CSS forces to the bare minimum, and the inevitable confusion of trying to deliver mail to units on the move from Kuwait to Iraq during Phase III and the transition to Phase IV of the campaign. In 2003 the Military Postal Service Agency and the 3d PERSCOM delivered 65 million pounds of mail to service members and contractors in Iraq, 11 million pounds in April 2003 alone, and an average of 378,000 pounds per day during the year.[19]

US Army Reserve Brigadier General Jack Stultz commanded the 143d TRANSCOM (in his civilian job, he was the logistical manager for Proctor & Gamble Corporation).[20] The 143d took advantage of changes made in 1990 and 1991 to speed up the offloading of equipment at Kuwaiti ports and airfields and the reception, staging, onward movement and integration (RSOI) of arriving units. The use of pre-positioned equipment; radio frequency identification (RFID) tags; newer and more numerous heavy equipment and tank transport trucks; and new, large, medium-speed roll-on, roll-off (LMSR) ships improved efficiency by more than 50 percent for the 143d TRANSCOM. The huge backlogs of tens of thousands of unsorted and unidentified cargo containers that clogged Saudi and Kuwaiti ports before the start of Operation DESERT STORM were mostly a thing of the past.[21] Though improved technology and management prevented the kind of backlog that literally choked supply lines in 1990 and 1991, the system was not error free. In 2004, a year after the invasion, some 30,000 shipping containers were categorized as "frustrated cargo," a term that denoted an interruption in the delivery process and meant that units did not receive the equipment and goods dispatched to them.[22]

Unlike most units that rotated into and out of Iraq on 1-year tours, the 377th TSC has remained in theater since February 2003 as CENTCOM's theater-level CSS organization. Units and individual Soldiers rotated in and out of the 377th, but the headquarters has remained. Even before the 377th TSC arrived in theater, Army civilians and contractors from the AMC began relocating and preparing pre-positioned equipment in Qatar and Kuwait. AMC was the national-level logistical command for the US Army, providing supply and maintenance support to CSS units in theater by embedding specialized teams in units from brigade to theater Army level.[23] In August 2002 Camp Arifjan was opened in southern Kuwait to handle the volume of pre-positioned equipment being downloaded off the Army Pre-positioned Sets–Afloat (APS-3) and Army Pre-positioned Sets–Southwest Asia (APS-5) fleets. Thus, equipment, ammunition, fuel, and supplies for an entire heavy division and supporting units were on the ground in Kuwait when the first units began to deploy in February 2003. Those AMC Logistical Support Elements then became part of the 377th TSC when it arrived in Kuwait to assume theater-level CSS responsibilities for CFLCC.[24]

A division of the AMC oversaw the use of the LOGCAP process that remained a critical aspect of the CSS concept for OIF. In 2004 over 24,000 contractors, one-third of them US expatriates and the remainder local national civilians, provided services to Army forces in Southwest Asia (OIF and OEF) under LOGCAP. Even larger numbers of contractors (perhaps as many as three times that number) supported the other services, the Iraqi Security Forces, the Coalition Provisional Authority (CPA), and later the State Department.[25] Some 250 Active Duty and Reserve Component Soldiers and DA civilians in AMC managed the hundreds of individual task orders under the LOGCAP umbrella contract. Those services included food service, base camp support, transportation, laundry and maintenance support, and many others.[26] The overall LOGCAP budget for the first 16 months of OIF exceeded $5.2 billion.[27] Though not a straight one-for-one substitution, the 24,000 LOGCAP employees freed critical military manpower for other duties and lessened the number of CSS Soldiers needed to support operations.

Operation IRAQI FREEDOM: The War of Movement Transitions to Full Spectrum Operations

The initial invasion of Iraq during OIF was the first test of the Army's DB CSS system during intense combat over long distances. Its performance during the invasion of Iraq in March and April 2003 was checkered. The tempo of advance maintained by US and Coalition troops from Kuwait to Baghdad was unprecedented, covering a distance of over 350 miles in less than 14 days of combat. The "running start" to combat operations dramatically altered the RSOI sequence and process. Many logistical units were not in place prior to the start of combat operations and some units, such as the 101st Airborne Division (101st ABN), began operations while still unloading units and equipment at the ports in Kuwait.

An initial historical analysis of the invasion of Iraq published in 2004 concluded, "Logistically, OIF tested the Army. The size of the theater, tempo of operations, . . . terrain, . . . paucity of logistics forces, and requirements to support other services proved daunting. Despite these difficulties, Army CSS troops turned in a heroic performance by providing 'just enough' to sustain the fight."[28] Some Army units suffered from shortages of different classes of supply such as POL; package products; repair parts; and certain types of ammunition at key points during the advance. Others had not completed uploading the prescribed 5 full days of supplies when the ground attack was kicked off 1 day early; Class I (food and water) had to be cross-leveled on day 3 as a result.[29] None of the shortages, however, significantly affected combat operations. As a historical comparison, in distance, it is further from the Kuwaiti ports to Mosul in northern Iraq than it is from the beaches of Normandy to Berlin. Armies have outrun their supply lines since biblical times. For many of these forces in the past, that error was fatal; for the US Army during March and April 2003, Soldiers quickly overcame potential mistakes with improvisation and courage.

The combat in this phase of OIF was less intense than expected as once again Saddam Hussein proved to be one of the most incompetent military commanders in history. Many Iraqi units removed themselves from the fight after they were encouraged by Coalition information operations to surrender, disband, or remain in their barracks. Iraqis did stage some attacks on vulnerable CSS units struggling to keep up with the pace of advance, and US supply convoys

DOD Photo

Figure 124. A Soldier, 2d ACR, makes emergency repairs to his HMMWV during a civil affairs mission in Baghdad, Iraq.

came under attack from both conventional and irregular Iraqi forces exposing the unguarded US lines of communication (LOCs).[30] Much as today, the LOCs were not garrisoned at every point. The 3d Corps Support Command (COSCOM), the main Army logistical unit supporting the advance to Baghdad, embedded its CSS units with maneuver formations whenever possible, only committing unescorted convoys for critical missions and only if the unit had trained in convoy live fire operations.[31] The 101st ABN fought pitched battles to destroy Iraqi forces attacking the LOCs, and the 2d Armored Cavalry Regiment (2d ACR) quickly deployed to Iraq to do the same. But the rapid collapse of Saddam's regime in early April 2003 meant that Army units quickly transitioned from a war of rapid movement to full spectrum operations by late April 2003.

Three different units shared CSS responsibilities in support of Coalition military forces in Iraq between February 2003 and January 2005. 3d COSCOM, stationed in Europe in support of V Corps, led CSS operations for CJTF-7 during 2003, to include the deployment, invasion of Iraq, and the first 7 months of operations through January 2004. The 13th COSCOM, III Corps' associated CSS command from Fort Hood, Texas, assumed responsibility for OIF logistics on 31 January 2004 in support of Multi-National Corps–Iraq (MNC-I). The 13th COSCOM in turn handed over responsibility to the 1st COSCOM from Fort Bragg, North Carolina, on 12 December 2004 as XVIII Airborne Corps assumed duties as MNC-I.

In peacetime, the 3d COSCOM consisted of two corps support groups, the 7th and 16th, and three separate battalions. The 3d COSCOM, commanded by Brigadier General Charles Fletcher, controlled about 4,000 Soldiers in three support battalions, a transportation battalion, an aviation maintenance battalion, a movement control battalion, and a special troops battalion. In February 2003 Fletcher expressed two major concerns to the V Corps Historian, Dr. Charles Kirkpatrick, before leaving Germany for Iraq in February 2003—convoy security and humanitarian aid requirements. He was concerned about congestion and security for his logistical convoys along the major roads and desert trails leading from Kuwait to Baghdad. He also was concerned about the Corps' ability to logistically deal with displaced Iraqis.[32] While the refugee crisis failed to emerge in 2003, Fletcher's comments proved eerily prescient in other ways.

Between February 2003 and the start of the war in late March, 3d COSCOM grew to include two more corps support groups, two more separate battalions, and a number of separate transportation companies. The 371st Corps Support Group of the Ohio Army National Guard also joined 3d COSCOM and took over the base camps in Kuwait when 3d COSCOM moved its units forward to Camp Anaconda in April.[33] By mid-summer of 2003 the COSCOM quadrupled its size to 17,000 Soldiers in six corps support groups, five separate battalions, and a rear operations control center. Significantly, Army Reserve and National Guard Soldiers made up between 40 and 45 percent of the COSCOM's ranks.[34] After a direct appeal from the V Corps commander, Lieutenant General William S. Wallace, to General John (Jack) Keane, Vice Chief of Staff of the Army, many of those Reserve Component Soldiers flew directly to Germany for training, bypassing their stateside

DOD Photo by SSGT Kevin Wastler

Figure 125. Soldiers of the 63d Chemical Company, 101st Airborne Division, perform an inventory and maintenance check on all their assigned equipment to ensure it is kept battle ready in Mosul, Iraq.

mobilization process.[35] Nearly every battalion and higher unit in the 3d COSCOM was made up of a mix of Active and Reserve Soldiers.

"Crossing the berm" on 21 March 2003 just behind the lead elements of the 3d ID, the 3d COSCOM possessed only 20 percent of the transportation assets it required to be fully ready to conduct operations.[36] Other units were still deploying to Kuwait or assembling in their attack positions when ground operations began. Fletcher used four command posts to control the COSCOM's operations during the invasion: a stay-behind element in Wiesbaden; some 150 Soldiers from the materiel management and movement control teams embedded with the 377th TSC at Camp Arifjan in Kuwait; a rear command post (CP) collocated with the V Corps rear CP at Camp Virginia in Kuwait; and an assault CP that would move forward with the lead elements of the corps.[37]

Between 21 March and 18 April 2003, the 3d COSCOM moved forward with the combat units of V Corps. The COSCOM established four separate logistical hubs or bases as it leapfrogged its assets forward to keep pace with the speed of combat operations. The distance traveled by the COSCOM from its start point in Kuwait to its northernmost base in Mosul, Iraq, in 4 weeks was 828 miles; by comparison, the 756 miles from Normandy to Berlin took 48 weeks to cover in World War II.[38] While the enemy situation was fundamentally different and historical comparisons are never perfectly accurate, the contrast in rates of movement is astonishing.

On 19 April 2003 the assault CP of the 3d COSCOM and lead elements of the 24th Corps Support Battalion occupied an old Iraqi airfield and base near the city of Balad, some 45 miles north of Baghdad, and established Logistics Support Area (LSA) Anaconda. LSA Anaconda became the logistical hub for operations in Iraq. This event marked the transition between conventional offensive operations and full spectrum operations for the Soldiers of 3d COSCOM.[39]

From its base at Anaconda, the 3d COSCOM, and later the 13th and 1st COSCOMs, would provide all of the CSS functions needed by the Coalition over a network of ground supply routes and air cargo deliveries. They drew on support provided by the 377th TSC at Arifjan, Kuwait, and some support directly from Europe and the United States. LSA Anaconda became a city in its own right, providing support to 13,000 Soldiers in more than 200 buildings surrounded by 13 miles of fences and 49 observation towers for base defense. The base included fuel farms, ammo bunkers, an airfield, a water treatment plant, and an asphalt plant among many other fixed facilities. The COSCOM after action report stated, "If you eat it, drive it, shoot it, move it, drink it, fly it, or wear it, it comes from LSA Anaconda."[40] Average daily deliveries made by the Soldiers of 3d COSCOM were remarkable.

Command, Control, and Communications for CSS Operations

The 3d COSCOM leaders took part in two prewar exercises while still in Germany as well as numerous rehearsals in Kuwait to prepare for OIF. Those exercises (VICTORY STRIKE and VICTORY SCRIMMAGE) proved valuable in dealing with the security challenges after March 2003. Not all of the 3d COSCOM units, however, were able to participate. Some Reserve Component units had not been mobilized in time. Coordination was also difficult because 3d COSCOM had not been given authority to directly coordinate with stateside Reserve Component units. Many Reserve Component units did not have access to the Army's classified Internet at their home stations, a major limitation that prevented them from working with planning documents. This caused numerous disconnects in theater. In one case, a POL transportation company deployed to Kuwait expecting to draw pre-positioned equipment on arrival. However, 3d COSCOM had expected them to deploy with equipment and made no plans for them to fall in on equipment in theater.[41]

Figure 126. Sergeant Ariel King, from the Stryker Brigade Combat Team, 25th Infantry Division, welds a new antenna brace for a tactical vehicle in the brigade's Forward Maintenance Company shop at FOB Marez, Iraq.

CSS units at every level did not have sufficient numbers and types of radios, satellite communication sets, and computer network systems to conduct their operations. The disparity among Active Duty 3d COSCOM units and the National Guard and Army Reserve units augmenting 3d COSCOM and assigned to the 377th TSC caused numerous communications problems.[42] The complexity of CSS logistical systems and the automation used to manage those systems is far beyond the scope of this chapter, but some general insights can be gained from the after action reviews of both 3d COSCOM and 13th COSCOM.

The limited number of tactical radios in vehicles authorized in CSS units made it difficult and dangerous to conduct widespread operations. The high threat to logistics convoys exacerbated the problem when only one of three or one of five vehicles had radio systems aboard. Before the war, Major General Fletcher, the 3d COSCOM commander, expressed hope that digital- and satellite-based cargo tracking systems would also provide an ancillary security benefit to vulnerable convoys by giving the command better visibility of where their vehicles were traveling in relation to nearby combat units. Main supply route (MSR) security, nevertheless, remained his biggest fear prior to "crossing the berm" into Iraq.[43] This same radio shortage would later hamper the ability of CSS units to supervise operations on LSAs and forward operating bases (FOBs)—equivalent in many cases to "running" a small city, a city under constant threat of attack.[44]

Digital automation systems for CSS operations were in widespread use throughout OIF as they were for combat operations. One of the premises on which the Army based its transformation of logistics from so-called iron mountains to distributed logistics was the ability to have real-time tracking of unit requirements and real-time tracking of the location and condition of all logistical supplies and services. Army doctrine labeled this as "end-to-end" visibility of items from the "factory to the foxhole."[45] With that knowledge, logistical planners could make accurate decisions about how to provide support to the end user (in combat or otherwise) precisely and in a timely manner. Despite a decade of steady automation progress since DESERT STORM, the goal remained unattained in 2003 and 2004.

The Army's CSS community did make great strides in tracking the location of supplies and equipment as they were transported into theater, packaged for shipment, and then delivered by convoy to units that needed them. The RFID tags on containers and parts fed data into various logistical tracking systems to a far greater extent than ever before. Digital automation systems tracked every category of supply from the proverbial beans to bullets. Combat units sent their requisitions by radio and computer network into multiple CSS systems, which then attempted to consolidate the needs, locate, ship, or order the necessary items.

The reality of Iraq exposed weaknesses, however, in the ability of CSS operators to make the DB CSS work effectively. Though almost all cargo containers were equipped with RFID tags to identify their contents, many CSS units lacked the digital readers to access the data. Most of the long-range communication systems used in 3d COSCOM did not work as expected. A number of the corps support groups and separate battalions did not have any communication devices that worked over extended distances, to include commercial systems purchased before the war for that purpose. General Fletcher often found himself and his assault CP staff personally locating and directing convoys and other CSS assets on the battlefield.[46] Only after the CSS infrastructure of bases and fixed communication sites was installed could information be routinely passed between units.

While CSS operators faced many challenges managing every class of supply from food to ammunition and medical equipment, most problems were sporadic and relatively quickly fixed and well managed. Incompatibility between automated systems, which managed specific classes of supplies, put great burdens on materiel management centers and transportation units.

Network connections between distant sites manned by units with differing systems added to the challenge. Managing the logistical support for the roughly 180,000 Coalition Soldiers while serving in an often dangerous environment in a Third World nation with limited infrastructure was a monumental accomplishment for which CSS leaders should take pride.

The following two examples, one negative and one positive, illustrate the various command and control challenges for CSS units. The tracking of repair parts for weapons and equipment, Class IX supplies in the Army system, remained problematic throughout 2003. One study concluded that the CSS unit infrastructure and command, control, and communications architecture in Kuwait and within 3d COSCOM were simply unable to handle the volume of requirements once combat operations began. Inadequate or incompatible communication systems plagued units of all kinds. These factors, plus the lack of transportation units and other management teams between March and July 2003 drove readiness rates for key systems to less than 70 percent.[47] These problems were greatest during the advance on Baghdad and in the months following, but they continued into the initial postinvasion operations period of OIF.

The tracking and delivery of bulk fuel supplies, classified as Class III (B), was a bright spot for logisticians. One report from 3d COSCOM succinctly stated, "Little can be said of Class III (B) operations—they were a success," and "Don't change Army doctrine or organization for Class III (B). It works."[48] Unlike boxes of food, parts, and ammunition, which were transported in varying ways, bulk fuel was a "single commodity item requiring transportation in the same container, day in and day out with dedicated transportation assets." The 49th Transportation Group (POL) had sole responsibility for managing and delivering fuel to forward units in 2003.[49]

Other issues with command, control, and communications focused on digitization within the system. The 3d COSCOM commander expressed his frustration with the Army's digital systems for maintenance and supply, and with the Corps/Theater Automatic Data Processing Service Center systems: "The STAMISs, SARSS, ULLS, CTASC [various automated CSS systems], . . . we pushed it as far as it technically could go and it is not adequate to support the modern battlefield. It takes way too much expertise, time, energy, and effort to do very, very, simple tasks like passing information."[50] An Army Logistics Whitepaper summarized this fundamental problem in December 2003: "Today's Army Logistician cannot 'see' the requirements on the battlefield. Our customers cannot see the support that is coming their way. As a result, we rely on pushing support based on our best estimate of what we think the Soldier needs. Soldiers order the same item several times because they have no confidence support is on the way."[51] Among many recommendations for action, the paper calls for expanding the use of several systems that performed well during OIF. The Movement Tracking System (MTS), a mobile, two-way, text-messaging, and Global Positioning System (GPS)-based location-tracking device, provided in-transit visibility of convoys and their supplies. RFID tags also worked well. The system's design to integrate all CSS data into a comprehensive whole, however, did not work as expected in 2003 and 2004.[52] Though much progress had been made since the mid-1990s, the command and control systems required to make DB CSS operations effective on the battlefield were not fully developed in 2003 and 2004.

Transportation: Delivering the Goods in Iraq

Between April and May 2003 Coalition operations transitioned from a war of movement to an environment where units generally operated within assigned areas throughout Iraq.

OIF logistics operations also transitioned from trying to keep pace with the rapid advance of armored columns on a narrow axis of attack toward Baghdad, to establishing a steady-state system for getting supplies distributed across the country. Army doctrine divides the distribution function into three parts: visibility, management, and transportation of resources over a network to units.[53]

Figure 127. HEMMT gun truck Battleship.

After May 2003 two major logistical bases served as the hubs for CSS operations in Iraq: Camp Arifjan in Kuwait and LSA Anaconda north of Baghdad. The 377th TSC operated the main supply base at Camp Arifjan as the theater-level logistics hub for the entire CENTCOM area of responsibility (AOR). Within the 377th TSC, the 143d TRANSCOM and 3d Theater Army Movement Control Agency were responsible for modal, terminal, and movement control operations in Kuwait. They coordinated highway transportation and movement control operations with the 3d COSCOM in Iraq. A network of MSRs and alternate supply routes (ASRs) fanned out northwest toward Baghdad, with MSR Tampa actually running all the way to the Iraq-Syrian border in northern Iraq. At LSA Anaconda, 3d COSCOM supply lines radiated outward in a pattern resembling spokes to support the units of CJTF-7. This configuration supported the regular delivery of all classes of supplies, via truck convoys, to the many FOBs on which combat units were based and from which they drew their support. 3d COSCOM also ran the airfield at LSA Anaconda.

The arrangement looked more like a layered grid system encompassing and overlaying the entire country than the trace of a front line supported by logistics elements situated to the rear. Theater and operational CSS units, mainly transportation units, carried out the mission of getting supplies and materiel into and out of Iraq, using LSA Anaconda as their main hub. Some theater-level CSS units provided area support to units within a defined area

Figure 128. HEMMT PLS gun truck.

of operation from fixed supply hubs, either directly to units operating from the same FOB or by making the relatively short runs between the FOB and tactical units nearby. Tactical CSS units from division support commands (DISCOMs) and separate brigade CSS units fanned out from the various FOBs to deliver supplies to their subordinate elements located in the hinterland. Both combat and CSS units confronted a "layered, noncontiguous, nonlinear battlefield."[54]

After the conventional phase of OIF ended in April 2003, both the 377th TSC and 3d COSCOM turned to Iraqi and American contractors to supplement the Army's internal transportation assets. Once the road networks between Kuwait and Baghdad were cleared of enemy forces during major combat operations, the threat to CJTF-7 LOCs was relatively low. As convoys moved north along the main supply route into Iraq, the risk to convoys grew in proportion to their proximity to Baghdad. Trucks in the daily SUSTAINER PUSH convoy from Kuwait pulled into Tallil and transferred their trailers to waiting tractors, which in turn continued on to LSA Anaconda in an operation that took 22 hours to complete. The system was reminiscent of the RED BALL EXPRESS of World War II. If traveling north of Baghdad, SUSTAINER PUSH convoys would remain overnight at LSA Anaconda near Balad, traveling further north to Mosul the next morning. Depending on the efficiency of the cargo transfer teams, the average convoy to and from Kuwait took from 10 to 12 days. The drivers usually had a day off and then were on the road again.[55]

Figure 129. M915 gun truck.

Still, attacks on convoys by various insurgent groups during the summer and fall of 2003 forced the 377th TSC and 3d COSCOM to dedicate some of their assets to provide protection to the convoys. Attacks on convoys rose from 9 in May to 40 in September. Drawing on lessons learned from Vietnam, transportation commanders resurrected the so-called "gun truck" method of defending convoys. Gun trucks were based on a number of platforms including HMMWVs and HEMTTs and were armed with a squad automatic weapon (SAW) or heavy machinegun. These trucks, which included improvised armoring, were largely the product of the "Skunk Works" of the 181st Transportation Battalion operating out of Camp Arifjan, Kuwait. The 181st also pioneered the "Tiger Team Concept"—two HMMWV gun trucks traveled ahead of the convoy looking for improvised explosive devices (IEDs) and making sure civilian vehicles did not pass the convoy. The prevailing ratio of security was to have one "green" military vehicle covering every three "white" (i.e., commercial trucks). The 181st, whose home station was

Mannheim, Germany, was the primary ground transportation unit delivering supplies to the Army's V Corps/CJTF-7 from June 2003 through 2004.[56]

Some combat units did not have sufficient internal transportation capacity and required assistance from nontactical units. In the case of the 3d Brigade, 2d Infantry Division (2d ID), the Army's first Stryker Brigade Combat Team (SBCT), both the nearby corps support battalion (CSB) and the brigade support battalion (BSB) were needed to truck supplies to the FOBs from which the brigade operated. However, moving supplies

Figure 130. HMMWV M998 gun truck with level 2 ring mount 7.

to any SBCT elements outside the FOB was a responsibility that belonged exclusively to the BSB. One report noted, "The issue in [the Stryker Brigade's] AO is the CSB is not capable (equipment/training) of moving through high-threat areas. The [Stryker] brigade has even had to provide back-up support to the CSB for maintenance and has pushed re-supply convoys to [non-SBCT] Corps units in the AO when the threat was too high [to run CSB vehicles]."[57]

Figure 131. Heavy metal rear of the M923 gun truck 518 GT.

Traffic management for Coalition vehicle movements presented significant challenges for the convoys and the units through whose areas they moved. Commanders found that controlling, or at least knowing, what type of military vehicle movement was taking place in their unit's area of operations (AO) was extremely difficult to manage. Tactical commanders wanted to control the movement so convoys did not accidentally wander into ongoing combat operations, and so they could quickly provide security assistance to a convoy that came under attack. While theater and COSCOM level transportation managers coordinated the dispatch and routing of convoys, that information often did not get passed in a timely manner to units that controlled the territory through which the convoys moved.[58] 3d COSCOM convoys were required to have at least one vehicle with a satellite tracking device that could be monitored by each US division and separate brigade via a logistics tracking system. Not all theater level convoys, however, had these systems and employed this technique.[59]

More than simply a matter of traffic control and delayed or lost cargo, effective transportation management was a matter of life and death for lightly armed and armored logistics convoys. Movement along supply routes through major cities such as Baghdad remained dangerous throughout this period. Despite insurgent attacks, the Army's military and civilian transporters kept CJTF-7 supplied without a significant lapse throughout 2003. The scope and complexity of planning and monitoring all Coalition military and civilian road movements in a country the size of California should not be underestimated. On an average day, approximately 130 to 140 major logistical convoys were on the roads in Iraq, consisting of roughly 1,800 to 2,200 trucks and around 4,000 personnel. Insurgents targeted these convoys, causing operation of the supply chain to be treated as a combat operation.[60] Supply areas routinely were attacked by random rocket-propelled grenade (RPG) volleys and car bombs. Stability operations, force protection missions, convoy operations, and combat operations were inextricably mixed in ways few ever expected before March 2003, as Soldiers and contractors alike fought to deliver the goods.

April 2004: A Transportation Turning Point

The simmering insurgency that opposed Coalition rule and the Iraqi Governing Council erupted into open combat in April 2004. That month stands out for Lieutenant General Ricardo Sanchez, CJTF-7 Commander, and his subordinate commanders as a turning point in OIF, clearly signaling that insurgents were determined to prevent the peaceful transfer of power to a new Iraqi Government in June of that year. The events of 31 March 2004 set an ominous tone that foreshadowed the turn of events in the following weeks. A small convoy of four civilian security guards in two vehicles, employed by the Blackwater Security Consulting firm, came under attack on entering the city of Fallujah. The contractors were killed, their bodies desecrated and hung suspended from a bridge girder over the Euphrates River.[61] Shortly after the incident, violence spread to other regions in the Sunni Triangle. Six days later, the Marines from the 1st Marine Expeditionary Force (MEF) launched Operation VIGILANT RESOLVE to destroy insurgent forces in Fallujah—the most intense combat operation since April 2003.

According to Major General Peter W. Chiarelli, commander of the 1st Cavalry Division (1st CAV) and Multi-National Division–Baghdad (MND-B) during OIF II, "Everything changed on the 4th of April" as OIF I units were literally conducting transfer of responsibilities ceremonies with their replacements in OIF II.[62] US Army Transportation Corps historian Richard Killblane has argued persuasively that this period was also a "tipping point" in the logistical support of OIF. Things were about to become significantly more dangerous in theater, especially where convoy security was concerned.[63] One day in mid-April during the Shia uprising in southern Iraq, all 122 Coalition convoys traveling the roads in Iraq were attacked.[64] Worse was the fact that for a short period in April, CJTF-7's supply lines were shut down, including MSR Tampa—the main supply route from Kuwait to Iraq.

Insurgent ambushes launched against supply convoys on Good Friday, 9 April 2004, were especially significant and notable since that date was the first anniversary of Saddam's downfall. Near Abu Ghraib, insurgents attacked a convoy from the 724th Transportation Company (POL) that was escorting civilian trucks driven by KBR contractors on an emergency fuel run from

LSA Anaconda to Camp Webster, near Al Asad.[65] The convoy included 19 military tractors, 17 of which hauled fuel, as well as two contingency bobtails that were reserved to accommodate vehicles that became disabled during the trip. The 724th had provided two gun trucks for security. At that time in OIF, any vehicle with a crew-served weapon, such as a machinegun or grenade launcher, was considered a gun truck. As Kilblane noted in his study, "There was [as yet] no requirement for armor [on gun trucks]."[66]

The ambush near Abu Ghraib on Good Friday was just one of many ambushes that day, but none of the convoys took as bad a beating as the 724th Transportation Company. Several convoys on that same route turned around and headed back. Never before had any convoy in Iraq encountered an ambush this large or intense. The enemy had taken advantage of the inexperience of many of the new units that had just arrived. Previous insurgent attacks usually

---

A Whole Different Attitude
The Transportation Corps in Full Spectrum Operations

Arguably, the realities of the full spectrum campaign had the most dramatic effect on those Soldiers involved in providing combat service support (CSS) to Coalition forces. In previous campaigns, CSS operations occurred in rear areas that were relatively protected from enemy action. In OIF, the nature of CSS operations combined with an insurgent enemy led to an overall situation in which transportation units were especially likely to be attacked. Leaders in transportation companies that specialized in trucking various classes of supplies across the country had to adapt and prepare their Soldiers for combat operations.

Realizing this, in 2004 the leaders of the 233d Transportation Company began to train their Soldiers to meet the enemy. The company first sergeant, Master Sergeant Alan Upchurch, who had served as a tank crewman earlier in his military career, found that the truck drivers were essentially unprepared for this aspect of their mission. Upchurch recalled the company's early actions against the enemy, "when trucks would be in a line and somebody took fire, people would just shoot. I said, 'Look, you are firing up at this bridge. But when it goes over the bridge, it is landing in your own convoy. You can't do that.' They had never been taught how to fix the enemy just by small-arms fire from a HET [heavy equipment transporter]." Upchurch retrained the unit to take the fight to the enemy by taking advantage of their mobility and firepower, "I taught the 5-tons [trucks] and the HMMWVs how to break contact, maneuver up the side of the vehicles, and actually engage the enemy like that. I taught them how to turn their vehicle straight to the enemy. In tanks we use frontal armor as our best asset. I taught them to use the front of their vehicle and then we had MK19s that were very effective. Just those few pieces and tidbits and not treating them as they say as 'a pogue that just sits in the back and drives a truck,' treating them as a Soldier that fights, that gave them a whole different attitude."

Upchurch made sure that his Soldiers were trained on multiple weapons systems and armed his convoys with fragmentation grenades, AT-4 antitank weapons, and extra ammunition. His company also required tank crews to ride inside their tanks while being transported by the company's HETs so that they could fire their weapons if the enemy attacked the convoy. In 2004, the 233d Transportation Company completed 260 missions, driving almost 2.5 million miles in the process, and suffered no combat casualties.

Contemporary Operations Study Team interview
with MSG Alan Upchurch, 26 January 2006.

consisted of a few mines, mortar rounds, or small arms fire that quickly disappeared after being launched. This time insurgents conducted sophisticated ambushes and sustained fire against the convoys.

In the ambush of the 724th's convoy, insurgents killed one Soldier, Private First Class Gregory R. Goodrich, and five KBR contract drivers and wounded eight Soldiers and four KBR drivers. Seven fuel tankers and one HMMWV, more than one-third of the vehicles in the convoy, were destroyed in the kill zone. Insurgents captured three KBR drivers—Tommy Hamill, William Bradley, and Timothy Bell, and two Soldiers—Sergeant Elmer C. Krause and Specialist Keith "Matt" Maupin.[67] After 27 days of captivity, one of the KBR drivers escaped when he heard the voices of US Soldiers outside the building where he was being held hostage. He bravely snuck away from his guards and ran nearly a half mile yelling "I am an American POW"; he was rescued by a passing New York National Guard unit. KBR drivers Bradley and Bell are still missing.[68] Unfortunately, Sergeant Krause and Specialist Maupin were killed by their abductors.[§]

CSS units fought back against a number of other ambushes during this period. The "Ambush at Iskandariyah" is one example.[69] On 17 April 2004 a heavy equipment transporter convoy of the 175th and the 2123d Transportation Companies was hauling Bradleys and tanks belonging to the 2d Battalion, 37th Armor of the 1st Armored Division (1st AD) from Al Kut to An Najaf, cities that were key sites of the Shia uprising that month. Near Diwaniyah, while swerving to avoid an overturned trailer, the convoy came under attack from 50 or more insurgents firing RPGs and small arms. A platoon leader of the 2123d, 1st Lieutenant Robert Henderson II, though mortally wounded, situated his HMMWV between the enemy and the convoy "while the tanks fired up their engines, broke their chains and rolled off the trailers to engage the enemy" besieging the transportation units. The ensuing fight lasted for roughly an hour in which the Americans killed approximately 30 of their attackers and suffered the loss of two American Soldiers. Henderson was posthumously awarded the Purple Heart and Bronze Star.[70]

The insurgent threat forced Coalition leaders to commit combat forces to ensure the MSR and ASRs remained safe. D Company, 2d Battalion, 108th Infantry, from the New York Army National Guard, was one such unit. Attached to the 2d Brigade Combat Team (BCT) of the 1st Infantry Division (1st ID), this unit worked out of FOB O'Ryan, in Salah ad Din province between March and December 2004. Delta Company was tasked with maintaining clearance of the MSR and ASRs in the battalion AO, including route clearance, convoy security, hasty raids, outer cordon's for battalion-size operations, and traffic control points. They also conducted missions to detect and destroy IEDs.[71]

For D Company, typical platoon patrols ranged from 8 to 10 hours and were conducted round-the-clock. The platoon would begin by conducting preventive maintenance checks and services (PMCS) on their vehicles and weapons systems some 2 hours before crossing the line of departure (LD). Platoon leaders issued their operations orders (OPORDs) and platoons practiced React to Contact and React to IED battle drills. The platoon leader would report to

---

[§]Sergeant Elmer C. Krause's remains were found in late April 2004, just weeks after being abducted. The Army did not find and identify Specialist Keith Maupin's remains until 2008; until then, the Army listed Maupin as missing in action.

the battalion tactical operations center (TOC) and turn in his "Trip Ticket"—a listing of all Soldiers participating in the patrol, along with the identification numbers of their respective vehicles—before departing the FOB for their mission. Daily, the company commander committed one platoon to FOB Security at the main entrance gate and on observation posts around the perimeter.[72] D Company used HMMWVs armed with the MK-19 grenade launcher or the .50-caliber machinegun for security. Also attached to the company were a platoon of Bradley Fighting Vehicles (BFVs) and two M1A1 Abrams tanks. The commander of Delta Company, Captain John-Michael Insetta, stated that he and his Soldiers understood the importance of the mission: "The level of danger was high throughout the entire tour. The supply convoys were the focus of the insurgent's interest. They used these attacks to loot the trucks and to try to break our spirit. It was definitely palpable."[73]

Many Soldiers did not trust the concepts behind DBL in spite of the heroic work of CSS units and Soldiers to deliver the goods and units like Delta Company to protect the transporters. They felt vulnerable and uncertain about their ability to conduct operations without ownership of their own supply "mountains" and more direct control over the process. One company commander in the 2d Battalion, 69th Armored Regiment, 3d ID summed up those feelings: "As an Army, we created a system designed to save money in the short term by delivering precisely what the trooper on the line needs just as he runs out of that item. This system forces us to live day-to-day, even during combat and stability operations."[74]

Survivability of Logistics Vehicles

Insurgent attacks on US and Coalition convoys in 2004 dramatically altered transportation planning and Army equipment fielding. Vulnerabilities inherent in manning traffic control points, patrolling, and running convoys throughout the country focused attention on the need for additional armor protection for vehicles, particularly the Army's fleet of unarmored M998 HMMWVs. When OIF began, as in every previous war the US Army has fought, logistical vehicles were largely unarmored or lightly armed. Designed to function behind the front lines of conventional operations, CSS units were not expected to need the same degree of protection and firepower as combat units. The "360-degree" Iraqi insurgency once again exposed the danger of this approach.

In 1996, in response to the need for a wheeled vehicle with some armor protection against mines and to replace tanks and armored personnel carriers on Balkan roads, the Army commissioned the development of a prototype "up-armored" HMMWV designated as the M1114. This version of the HMMWV quickly became the vehicle of choice for operations in that relatively benign AO due to its increased mobility and lowered maintenance needs relative to tracked vehicles. Requirements in Bosnia and Kosovo did not seem to require logistical and other "soft-skinned" vehicles be similarly "up-armored."

The Army units that entered Iraq in March 2003 did not employ the M1114 because it was not part of their standard equipment. Nor were any of the CSS vehicles in these units armored. With few exceptions, ground combat in Phase III of OIF was conducted with vehicles specifically designed for battle—Abrams tanks, BFVs, Paladin howitzers, etc. As units transitioned to full spectrum operations, however, the greater mobility, speed, and lower maintenance needs of wheeled vehicles made them the favored vehicle for most units. The nature of operations faced by Coalition forces meant essentially that every Soldier and vehicle had to employ some protective measures in every direction at all times. As attacks on US forces increased over the summer, CJTF-7 began to submit requirements through the Joint Staff for armored wheeled vehicles. Those numbers increased steadily and rapidly in the fall of 2003 as CJTF-7 imposed restrictions on the use of nonarmored vehicles in its operations.[75] In August 2003 CENTCOM placed urgent requests for such protection with the Department of the Army.[76] The scope of the task was immense because, by late 2003, CJTF-7 employed some 12,000 HMMWVs and 16,000 other wheeled vehicles.

The Army categorized the level of armor protection for noncombat vehicles using a three-tiered structure. Level I protection could only be achieved by vehicles manufactured with armor built into the original design of the vehicle. Level II protection was achieved by installing specially made, add-on armor plates and glass to vehicles that provided nearly the same level of protection as Level I vehicles. Level III protection was created by the ever-present ingenuity and initiative of the American Soldier and consisted of various ad hoc measures—Soldiers often called this "Hillbilly armor." Units in Iraq and Kuwait installed steel plate, sandbags, and other materiel on vehicles to fill the immediate need for protection. The "gun truck" efforts by Army transporters stand out in this regard, but nearly every US unit took matters into their own hands while they awaited the installation of Level II kits or the arrival of Level I vehicles.

Figure 132. A welder works on a new Modified Protection for an unarmored HMMWV kit in Iraq.

DOD Photo by SPC Chad D. Wilerson

The HMMWV Level II kits added between 2,000 and 4,000 pounds to the standard HMMWV, depending on the variant. The kit included steel plating and ballistic-resistant windows offering improved protection against small arms fire and shrapnel. The add-on kits did not provide protection against mines or explosives detonated under the vehicle. To meet the Level II up-armor requirement while Level I production in the US was ramped up, US Army Tank-Automotive and Armament Command (TACOM) contracted for the production of add-on armor kits for the HMMWV in October 2003. The first 15 test kits were flown to Kuwait in November 2003. The contract specifications required that the weight of the kits leave the HMMWV with a 1,000-pound payload, be easily installed in theater, and that 6,700 of them be manufactured by April 2004. Steel and protective glass manufacturers suspended commercial orders to meet the demand for materiel and the kits were produced at seven different Army depots and arsenals in the United States.[77]

Seven companies produced almost 9,000 HMMWV kits by July 2004 and produced 13,000 kits by May 2005. In late 2004 TACOM also tasked its producers to make 4,200 Level II armor

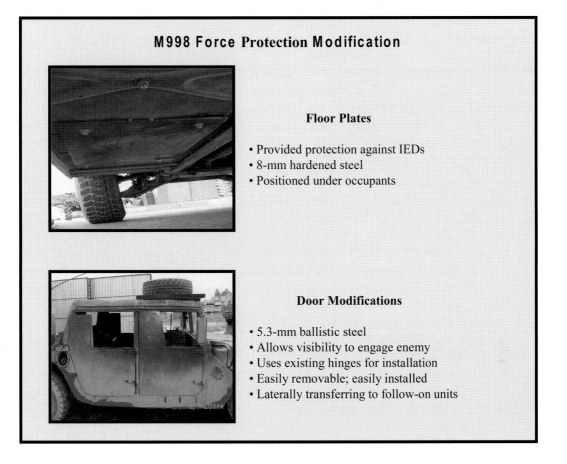

kits for the cabs of the Army's 5-ton, M939-series, cargo trucks.[78] These kits were entirely separate armored cabs that replaced the unarmored cabs.[79] In the 18 months after November 2003, TACOM supervised the production by 8 manufacturers of 20 vehicle-specific variants of add-on armor kits for 27,000 vehicles. The kits were installed in 6 different nations, at 16 separate sites in the CENTCOM AOR, by 650 Government and contract workers.[80]

The M1114 was the only armored logistics vehicle in production when OIF began. In May 2003 production lines could produce 30 M1114s per month. By December 2004 production had reached 400 per month, and by September 2005 the rate had increased to 650 per month.[81] Many variants of the up-armored HMMWV have since been produced. Though production increases were significant, they failed to keep pace with the urgency and scope of the requirements in Iraq.

While the Army stood up these programs, the issue of armor protection was being discussed in the media throughout 2004 and became a national controversy. On 8 December 2004 Army Specialist Thomas Wilson of the Tennessee National Guard asked Secretary of Defense Donald Rumsfeld at a gathering of some 2,300 Soldiers and media at Camp Buehring, Kuwait, "Why do we Soldiers have to dig through local landfills for pieces of scrap metal and compromised ballistic glass to up-armor our vehicles?"[82] Whether the story was exaggerated (scavenging for parts in wartime has never been unusual), or even planted by a hostile reporter, the question generated a firestorm of criticism of the Army for allegedly failing to protects its Soldiers.

On 9 December 2004, the day following the gathering in which Wilson raised his question, Lieutenant General R. Steven Whitcomb, Third Army and CFLCC Commander, hosted a special Defense Department briefing on the subject of armored vehicles. He explained that CENTCOM had approximately 30,000 wheeled vehicles in Iraq and Afghanistan—some 6,000 were Level I vehicles with built-in protection, 10,000 had Level II add-on protection, 4,500 had some form of ad hoc Level III protection, and roughly 8,000 had no armor protection. Many of the vehicles in the latter category did not operate outside of fixed sites or secure areas. Units had long abandoned the practice of using unarmored vehicles for tactical operations, but logistics units still had to haul supplies, fuel, and other equipment despite the lack of armor.[83]

Issues of protection also influenced the Army's first deployment of Stryker combat vehicles in its newly formed Stryker Brigade Combat Teams (SBCTs), the middleweight part of the Army's three-pronged transformation effort launched in 1999. The Army's first SBCT, the 3d Brigade, 2d ID, deployed to Iraq in December 2003 and formed the core of what would be called Task Force (TF) *Olympia*. The 8,000 Soldiers of TF *Olympia* replaced the 24,000 Soldiers of the 101st ABN in Mosul, Iraq. Though high-tech, reactive armor kits were part of the original Stryker design, they were not ready for use in 2003 or 2004. The Army equipped the Stryker fleet with an unusual add-on armor system to defeat RPG rounds in Iraq. The design had its roots in Vietnam and World War II, consisting of 2.5 tons of steel slats spaced a few inches apart surrounding the vehicle and designed to detonate the shaped charge warheads of RPGs. Though ungainly and derisively called the birdcage, it proved to be quite effective. Both the Stryker vehicle fleet and the unit design gave a good accounting of themselves. The 3d SBCT lost only two Strykers during its year in Iraq, one to a mine and one to an RPG round that detonated against the slat armor and started a secondary fire on equipment attached to the hull.[84]

These various up-armor kit programs were only a part of the Army's overall efforts to improve, field, and sustain its fleet of vehicles in OIF. Too numerous to describe or list here, the effort included new HMMWV gunner platforms, new track and road wheel designs for the Abrams and Bradley fleets, new armored versions of the light medium tactical vehicle (LMTV) and the family of medium tactical vehicle (FMTV) cargo trucks, and reactive armor kits for M113 personnel carriers. The Army also had to stand up substantial in-theater and US-based rebuild programs to repair battle losses from OIF. Even though the Army's vaunted M1A1 and M1A2 Abrams tanks proved extremely lethal and survivable in urban combat, the Tank Urban Survivability Kit (TUSK) program provided numerous upgrades to the tank commander's and loader's machinegun stations, side armor, and driver's sights, among others.[85]

In 2003 the Army's HMMWV and logistical vehicle fleets were not designed to withstand enemy attacks. The vehicles in these fleets were designed to move supplies and equipment forward from safe rear areas to front-line units along routes not under direct enemy attack. The noncontiguous front lines in full spectrum operations, however, meant that these vehicles and convoys were in great danger as soon as they departed secure sites; there were simply no areas safe from enemy attack. By late summer 2003 the worsening security environment in Iraq forced CJTF-7 and CENTCOM commanders to place significant demands on the Army to up-armor logistical vehicles. Those demands grew immensely in 2004 as commanders required every vehicle operating outside secure sites to be up-armored. The Army and the nation struggled to meet the demand for increased production of armored wheeled vehicles, add-on armor kits, and other hardened equipment throughout 2004. The Army and civilian contractors accomplished remarkable feats; still, budget limitations and national manufacturing capacity complicated their efforts. Every Soldier wounded or killed in an unarmored vehicle caused unbearable institutional pain. No plan, no matter how rapidly executed, could fill the vacuum created by decades of decisions about doctrine and equipment.

Personal Body Armor

The use of improved personal body armor by the Army and Marines during OIF has saved thousands of lives. But this success story was also not without controversy. Early versions of body armor were developed and tested in the late 1990s in the Balkans and elsewhere.[86] Given budget realities before 2001, the Army planned to issue the updated Interceptor Body Armor to its Soldiers over an 8-year period between 2000 and 2007. Initially intended only for Soldiers engaged in direct combat, the new body armor got is first test during OEF in late 2001 and 2002. Using a combination of synthetic fiber (Kevlar, as used for years in the Army's helmets) and ceramic plates called Small Arms Protective Inserts (SAPI), the body armor could stop high-powered rifle rounds, unlike its predecessors.[87] This was a revolutionary development in protection for ground forces.

When US forces crossed into Iraq in March 2003, not every Soldier had been issued the latest version of Interceptor Body Armor. Major General Walter Wojdakowski, the CJTF-7 Deputy Commander, like many of his Soldiers, wore the older style flak vest when the invasion began.[88] Based on the effectiveness of the Interceptor Body Armor, the Army accelerated its fielding during OIF. In May 2003 the Army ordered the new body armor for every Soldier in OIF, and then extended the requirement to include all DOD personnel operating in CENTCOM. These two policy decisions increased the demand more than tenfold. The Army requirement for the special plates rose from roughly 10,000 in December 2002 to 110,000 by March 2003, and then, to just over 475,000 in December 2003.[89]

The national industrial base was unable to meet the spike in demand. Two critical materials were in short supply, both for the vests and the hard ceramic plates that fit into the vest. It also took some time for material producers and manufacturers to ramp up production. DuPont Chemicals was the only domestic producer of the Kevlar fiber panels used in the vests in 2003. The DOD approved an exception under the Defense Federal Acquisition Regulations allowing vest makers to use another type of fiber panel, manufactured in the Netherlands, as a replacement for Kevlar panels. The shortfall in ceramic plates was caused by a shortage of a material called Spectra Shield, made only by Honeywell in 2003. Plate producers dealt with the shortage of Spectra Shield by manufacturing plates using Kevlar and other aramid fibers. In April 2004 DSM Dyneema, a foreign firm that produces Dyneema, a Spectra Shield equivalent, opened a production facility in the United States to meet the demand.[90]

Thus, between October 2002 and September 2004 Interceptor Body Armor was not available to every Soldier, Marine, and DOD civilian in theater who needed it. The effectiveness of the new body armor was immediately evident and many Soldiers and Marines were saved from wounds or death because of it. Some Soldiers preparing to deploy to Iraq during this period resorted to buying their own commercial body armor, because they incorrectly believed they would be forced to conduct combat operations without the latest version. The Congressional Budget Office later estimated that as many as 10,000 personnel may have purchased vests for which the Army, with Congressional support, promised to reimburse them.[91] Officials in the AMC worked with US and foreign producers and manufacturers to deliver over 100,000 additional vests and associated ceramic plates by the end of January 2004, some 8 months after major combat operations were declared over.[92] As was the case with other aspects of OIF, the benefits of this revolution in Soldier protection were obscured by controversy.

Field Services

Napoleon's observation that "an army marches on its stomach" was as true in the first decade of the 21st century as it was in the pre-industrial era of the 19th century. Delivering clean water and healthy food to units in Iraq were only two of the many field services provided to Coalition soldiers. In the spring and summer of 2003 feeding and providing water to US and Coalition forces did not go as well as expected. Brigadier General Scott West, the CJTF-7 CJ4, stated that soon after he arrived in Iraq in late July 2003:

> The most broken and contentious logistics function on this battlefield was feeding the troops. . . . This became a top priority for the staff of CJTF-7. Coupled with the feeding problem was the provisioning of bottled water and a cooling capability for the water. Soldiers will not and should not drink hot water. In the 130-degree heat of an Iraqi summer, cooling water was an imperative.[93]

Beginning in May 2003 the military's requirement for meals, ready to eat (MREs) and unitized group rations (UGRs) exceeded in-theater supplies. US commercial producers could not ramp up production fast enough to meet demand. To help alleviate the shortage of MREs and UGRs, producers placed them directly from the manufacturing plant into containers for immediate shipment. Many of the containers, however, were filled with just one type of meal, either all breakfasts, all lunches, or all dinners, and were delivered to units on the front lines unsorted. One report about OIF in this early period noted, "It was not unheard of during OIF for Soldiers to eat breakfast UGRs for all three meals for several days in a row. . . . OPTEMPO also led to instances of Soldiers subsisting solely on MREs for more than 21 days, which violated the Surgeon General's policy on MRE consumption."[94]

Some of the concerns regarding food and water, known as Class I supplies, were echoed by Lieutenant Colonel Harry Tunnell IV of the 1st Battalion (Airborne), 508th Infantry Regiment, 173d Airborne Brigade. Tunnell's unit parachuted into northern Iraq early in OIF. Tunnell noted that by day 66 of the deployment in Iraq, his Soldiers were still eating cold chow. Though lack of food was never an issue, the type of food presented a dilemma for the unit. "There are health issues because when you eat MREs for quite a while, there is a limited menu," Tunnell said. "Soldiers actually refuse to eat the right amount of food because the menu is so repetitive . . . that makes it tough on the health of the force, I think. It goes beyond a matter of convenience there because Soldiers aren't getting the right calories to perform the heavy work they have to do."[95] Military history is replete with far, far worse cases of inadequate sustenance. Thus complaints about overabundance of particular types of rations can be viewed as a somewhat backhanded compliment to the Army's logistics system.

Providing drinkable water to Soldiers in the intense heat of summer in Iraq was equally difficult. The problem was obvious: delivering enough potable water and ice to keep Soldiers hydrated in temperatures that reached 130 degrees Fahrenheit. An additional issue was the provision of clean bulk water for use in showers, laundry, cooking, and general cleaning. Bulk water was normally provided by reverse osmosis water purification units (ROWPUs) or from local water sources, delivered by pipe within bases, or trucked to units operating away from fixed locations. Further exacerbating the challenge of delivering all types of water was a general deficit in the types and sizes of military water trucks, a problem Soldiers often addressed by arranging for local contractor support.[96]

Figure 133. An Iraqi laborer grinds a plate on a metal support structure at a military training base in eastern Iraq. The structure supported a water storage tank that will soon supply the base with clean water.

Since Operation DESERT STORM, the US military has provided bottled water for its Soldiers to drink, relying less on delivering potable water in large tankers and making potable water on site by means of water purification units. For Soldiers, using bottled water made sense. Bottles are easier to store in combat vehicles and easier for Soldiers to carry into combat. Bottled water can be kept cooler much easier than bulk tankers, because ice can be used from nonpotable water purchased locally. Despite its advantages, bottled water added another burden to the transportation system.

Delivering water, however, was just the first obstacle. In the Iraqi summer, it was critical that the water be cooled. Soldiers operating in extreme heat have trouble drinking hot water despite the obvious necessity of doing so. The United States initially lacked enough refrigerated vans or reefers to deliver and cool water in the summer of 2003. Logisticians also found that many units took control of these precious assets when they arrived at base camps and did not return them to the ice and water distribution role.[97] Local purchases of water from Kuwaiti and Iraqi vendors alleviated some of the problem. Small units also lacked the cargo handling equipment to download and store large pallets of bottled water, or to store bulk water delivered by water tankers in short supply.[98]

To fix these and other problems with water and food distribution in the summer of 2003, food service personnel from the CJTF-7 logistics section began riding on ration convoys from Kuwait to the northern and western distribution hubs in Iraq to discover the sources of the problems. They found frequent double handling, lost convoys, broken refrigeration units, and "frustrated" cargo. After a variety of procedural changes that included an improvement of visibility of Class I while in transit, the CJTF-7 ration and water distribution program was functioning more smoothly by November 2003.[99]

Maintenance

The tremendous mobility and firepower of the US Army in Iraq required an equally tremendous maintenance effort to sustain. During the rapid advance on Baghdad and until the

Coalition fully established the CSS infrastructure in Iraq in the fall of 2003, maintenance suffered. Units operated with equipment that was not fully operational. This was hardly an unusual situation, and did not greatly affect combat operations. As in peacetime training, units were able to operate their equipment even with deficiencies. The 2d Battalion, 69th Armor Regiment, a unit serving with the 3d ID, fought its way into Baghdad with 29 of its 30 tanks and 13 of its 14 BFVs, despite having all 30 tanks and 7 of its 14 BFVs officially categorized as nonmission capable (deadlined) on readiness reports for one or more deficiencies. This was a very impressive figure after several weeks of combat over several hundred miles. Had Iraqi units fought harder, however, this decline in equipment readiness could have had a much greater effect on the ability of units to keep up their relentless pace.

During the advance on Baghdad, logistics priorities were for food, water, fuel, and ammunition. Units maintained their combat effectiveness by using a combination of their prescribed load list (PLL), spare parts the unit carried with it on the march to Baghdad, and by ruthless salvage operations from damaged or destroyed equipment. In October 2002 the Army had increased its funding for stocks of repair parts and supplies for its pre-positioned equipment in the Middle East. When the invasion began in mid-March, those efforts had not yet reached fruition. The Class IX parts shortage during the invasion and early in Phase IV operations was then exacerbated by the greatly extended MSRs from Baghdad to Kuwait, which were hundreds of miles long. The Class IX supply system and the maintenance system were not getting the job done in the view of the end users whose combat units wanted their equipment fully functional with no delays.[100]

The intensity of daily operations in OIF contributed to the challenges. The Army set normal peacetime mileage rates for the Abrams and Bradleys at 800 miles per year, a basis for planning annual training events, fuel costs, and required maintenance support. The 3-week attack by US forces from Kuwait to Baghdad in March and April 2003 measured more than 350 miles in straight-line distances. In October 2003 a sampling of M1A2 tanks showed monthly mileage rates in excess of 700 miles, nearly a year of use in a single month. In April and May 2004 a sample of M1A1 Abrams tanks being monitored in the program exceeded 550 miles per month.[101] While individual vehicle types and unit usage rates varied wildly from month to month, the useful service life of tanks and other Army vehicles were being rapidly expended in OIF.

In early 2005 the Congressional Budget Office reported to Congress that Army and Marine Corps equipment was being used at rates many times greater than in peacetime. In particular, Soldiers and Marines were driving trucks roughly 10 times the amount of miles per year than the average peacetime amount. Tanks and light armored vehicles were being driven at rates roughly five times those of peacetime. Additionally, Army and Marine aviators were flying helicopters at roughly twice peacetime rates.[102] Adding to the wear and tear on vehicles were the desert heat, rough terrain, and sand. As wheeled vehicles became armored in 2004, the extra weight put additional strain on drive trains, engines, and suspensions. By 2005 the Army was forced to develop a new process called "Reset," to replace, overhaul, and repair battled damaged and worn out equipment from both OIF and OEF. By fiscal year (FY) 2006, the cost of the Reset program had grown to $13.47 billion.[103]

One seemingly mundane but illustrative example of the magnitude of the increased demand on Army vehicles in 2003 and 2004 can be seen by looking at the use of track shoes, a critical part of the treads on Abrams tanks and BFVs. Anticipating the upsurge in requirements, US Army TACOM increased its monthly production order of track shoes from Goodyear Corporation from 10,000 to 17,000 per month in December 2002. Despite this increased order, the Army began to run short of track shoes by April 2003 as unit and war reserve stocks began to run out. The demand for Abrams tank and BFV track shoes in May 2003 was for 55,000 shoes, more than three times the forecasted monthly demand.[104]

The Army later raised its monthly requirement from Goodyear to 25,000 track shoes per month in July 2003. Goodyear needed between 3 and 6 months, however, to increase capacity to meet the new requirement. Budget authorization and contract timing issues also delayed production in the spring of 2003. Congress authorized the Army to make a $5.2 million investment in Goodyear's production facilities to meet the surge requirements and to maintain its track shoe manufacturing capacity into the future.[105]

To deal with the massive flow of track shoes and other repair parts into Iraq, the Army initially relied on the personnel in the relatively small Class IX warehouse operation at Camp Doha, Kuwait. Originally designed to support the regular rotation of brigades to Kuwait for exercises and staffed with Army contractors, it was overwhelmed by the demands of the war in 2003. The 377th TSC stood up a nondoctrinal theater distribution center (TDC) at Camp Doha, Kuwait, to handle the demand by drawing personnel from various CSS units in Iraq.[106]

As the high demand for spare parts became evident in the summer of 2003 and challenged the nation to produce the materiel needed to fight the war in Iraq, the Army was also learning some tough lessons about the CSS structure in its tactical units. The Army's Stryker brigades were designed to create a small logistical footprint and relied on other CSS units to augment their internal assets. The AMC created a unique logistical support element just for the Stryker brigades, because the systems were still so new that they had not been officially transferred to the Army for life cycle support purposes. AMC Stryker Forward, commanded by an Army Reserve colonel, consisted of approximately 120 civilians working in the United States and in 15-man teams deployed with each SBCT to provide maintenance expertise.[107]

The civilian logistics experts in AMC Stryker Forward were part of a much larger civilian maintenance force found driving convoys, working on FOBs, and operating within some headquarters at nearly every level of the maintenance system during OIF. In Kuwait, civilian contractors played a significant role in performing maintenance on equipment drawn from and returned to pre-positioned stocks. Contractors also performed some depot-level repairs of damaged equipment rather than transporting it all back to German or US bases for overhaul.

Maintenance issues led to a decrease in Army unit effectiveness in the immediate aftermath of the collapse of the Saddam regime and remained in decline for several months before recovering to normal levels. Put simply, combat units in this initial period lacked sufficient spare parts and other supplies necessary to keep their key equipment functional. The Army struggled to create the theater distribution network to track requirements, place timely and accurate orders into the supply system, and deliver the supplies to combat units in Iraq. Manufacturers in the United States worked overtime to increase the supply of materials and to increase their capacity to produce highly specialized equipment and parts. The production and distribution of armor for Soldiers and vehicles were particularly problematic and were not resolved until 2004, or later in the case of up-armored logistical vehicles. Nevertheless, despite sporadic shortages,

US and Coalition forces continued to conduct operations in Iraq without significant supply and maintenance limitations.

Munitions Support

In OIF, ordnance support related to munitions can be divided into three parts. The first two are doctrinal, having to do with the provision of ammunition and demolition systems to Army units and the locating and destruction of unexploded munitions on the battlefield to safeguard Army Soldiers. The third ordnance mission soon became the most visible as the insurgency developed in Iraq: the locating and defeating of IEDs and vehicle-borne improvised explosive devices (VBIEDs).

As Phase IV of OIF began, US and Coalition units began to grapple with the enormous number and variety of arms and ammunition sites located throughout Iraq. Coalition forces found over 10,000 stockpiles, ranging in size from small caches in schools, mosques, and other civilian buildings to gigantic military depots measured by the square mile including hundreds of individual bunkers. After the overthrow of the Baathist regime in April 2003, ordinary Iraqis and future insurgents alike looted many of these stockpiles. The enormity of the task soon overwhelmed the small number of unexploded ordnance demolition units in Iraq, whose time was better spent focusing on the anti-IED mission. Major General Wojdakowski, CJTF-7 deputy commander, quickly realized the task of locating, storing, and disposing these stockpiles was far beyond his command's ability to handle, and would take the limited number of explosive ordnance disposal (EOD) units away from supporting tactical operations.[108] In July 2003 the US Army Corps of Engineers (USACE) was tasked with the mission of collecting, sorting (usable stocks were provided to the Iraqi Security Forces), and destroying these huge stockpiles, estimated to total some 400,000 tons of unexploded ordnances (UXOs). The USACE awarded contracts to five civilian firms to conduct the work that began in September 2003. Some 2,600 contractors destroyed over 450,000 tons of munitions in 3 years.[109]

CJTF-7's combat units also took part in the process, particularly as they initially occupied their AOs in the summer of 2003. Every division and brigade was confronted with the tasks of finding, guarding, and turning over these stockpiles for destruction. The 1st Armored Division (1st AD) was responsible for the city of Baghdad and the surrounding areas beginning in early May 2003 and faced perhaps the largest UXO inventory in Iraq. 1st AD Soldiers encountered UXOs and weapons and ammunition caches every day of their entire 15-month stay in Iraq. But in the summer of 2003, the size and number of these caches stunned the division. The division artillery brigade formed TF *Bullet* to handle the tasks of finding and disposing of the immense stockpiles accrued by the Saddam regime. The division also launched Operations CLEAN SWEEP and IRON BULLET, which focused solely on collecting and removing the vast stores of weapons and ammunition.

During their first 12 months in Iraq, TF *Bullet* removed over 2,050 truckloads of UXOs, arms, and ammunition, totaling almost 10,000 tons. The division engineers also removed 1,113 individual UXOs and 1,265 caches of arms and weapons. In total, 1st AD disposed of more than 55 million rounds of ammunition and 1 million items of UXOs and arms. Some of the arms and ammunition were still usable and was transferred to the Iraqi Army and Iraqi Civil Defense Corps (ICDC), including 16,620 rifles and pistols; 1,935 RPG launchers; and more than 320,000 grenades, RPG, and artillery rounds.[110]

Financial Management

Operations in Iraq placed unusual and complex demands on the financial management system, another key component within the Army's larger CSS system. The extensive use of local, regional, and US-based contractors during OIF added enormous requirements to contracting and disbursing offices. More importantly, the massive economic reconstruction, government, and advisory efforts created unprecedented demands on financial assets in Iraq. The Army's doctrine divides financial management into two major parts—finance operations, which includes the disbursement of currency to Soldiers and units; and resource management, which includes the advising, policy making, and monitoring processes to track financial operations of a military command.[111]

Focusing financial assets where they could best be used was not always easy in OIF. Major General David Petraeus, who commanded the 101st ABN in 2003 and then returned to Iraq in 2004 as the commander of Multi-National Security Transition Command–Iraq (MNSTC-I), learned that "money is ammunition" in these types of full-spectrum operations.[112] He recalled firing over 110 M39 Army Tactical Missile System missiles, each of which cost $550,000, during the drive to Baghdad between March and April 2003. But in northern Iraq, the 101st ABN was initially unable to spend cash that it captured from the Iraqis or to initiate contracts for small, $10,000 projects without an excessive amount of paperwork and prior approval. Army doctrine and federal law simply did not provide mechanisms for commanders to quickly spend money on other than direct operational needs of their own units.[113]

After Soldiers in the 3d ID found $700 million (as well as large amounts of Canadian dollars and British pounds) in an abandoned Saddam palace, the cash was taken to Kuwait for counting and storage. As chapter 9 of this study described, Colonel Michael Toner, the CJTF–7 Resource Management Officer (CJ8), was struggling to provide unit commanders with a mechanism to fund small to medium projects in their areas to rebuild parts of the decrepit Iraqi infrastructure. The $700 million in cash was almost manna from heaven. While not taking sole credit for the idea, Toner and the CJTF-7 staff approached the CPA about using the captured cash. CPA had not yet gotten its funding plans or mechanisms in place, and CJTF-7 units were finding a large number of basic needs among the Iraqi population that could be addressed with relatively small funds.[114] In late May, during a visit by CPA Chief L. Paul Bremer to northern Iraq, Petraeus also broached the concept of using the captured funds.

Both Petraeus and Toner credit Bremer for breaking this financial logjam with the decision to spend the captured funds in Iraq, and with the creation of the Commander's Emergency Response Program (CERP). Together these two decisions gave US division and brigade commanders the financial "ammunition" they needed to conduct operations.[115] The CERP gave division commanders authority to fund local projects and to supervise those projects without going through the normal peacetime federal funding regulations. When the program began in early June, division commanders were given a $2,500 limit. The program was so successful the CPA expanded in steps so that by December 2003 the limit was $500,000 for division commanders and up to $200,000 for brigade commanders.[116]

These small projects satisfied immediate needs faced by Coalition units while the CPA focused on national-level priorities. Between May 2003 and January 2004 division and brigade commanders spent just over $126 million under the CERP to conduct small projects in support of operations in their AORs.[117] In 2004 and 2005 Congress then provided appropriated funds to the CERP on a regular basis—$140 million for OIF and $40 million for OEF in FY 2004; and $320 million for FY 2005.[118] CJTF-7 CJ8 personnel also drew on Iraqi funds later in 2004, once the government began to manage its own budget under the Development Fund for Iraq (DFI) program overseen by the CPA and later by the American Embassy. Colonel Toner recalls ordering and then picking up pallet loads of cash throughout the year, at $160 million per trip.[119]

Toner and his CJ8 were very concerned about accountability given the huge scope of the program and its decentralized execution. The CJ8 staff began with only 7 people and grew to 22 by December 2003. They oversaw the program while finance units and unit resource management officers administered the funds in the countryside. The Iraqi economy operated strictly on cash, so the potential for loss and theft was very high and records keeping had to be done manually. They needed three separate systems to track the program—one for captured Iraqi cash, one for US appropriated funds provided by Congress, and one for the DFI funds provided by the Iraqi Government.[120] US Marine Corps units as well as the British and Polish commanders used the CERP in their division and national sectors. In fact, Toner gives the Polish "budgeteers" of Multi-National Division–Central-South (MND-CS) credit for having the best records keeping system in all of the Coalition.[121]

The CJTF-7 CJ8 staff used the principles found in the Federal Acquisition Regulations (FAR) to create a two-person system that would satisfy the audits sure to follow. The first person, the field ordering officer (FOO), received training from the few warranted contracting agents in theater and was able to initiate projects and negotiate prices with local Iraqi contractors. Those contracts were then submitted to the local or regional finance unit for review. The second person, the Paying Agent, received training by the local finance unit, drew the actual funds, and paid the contractors when the work was completed. This two-person system lessened the possibility of fraud and met the intent of the far more complex FAR system. By late fall 2003 more contracting officers had arrived in theater to support both the CPA and CJTF-7, so projects costing more than $100,000 had to be managed by a warranted contracting officer.[122]

No one in CJTF-7 anticipated this requirement or its scope and importance. Toner credits the flexibility of resource management staff officers for the success in creating funding processes that were almost entirely unprecedented: "Overall, on the comptroller side, a lot of us are too focused on garrison. . . . Our job is to do what the commanders need and find a way to support them. We saw some of that, like I said, with CERP. I had several times where people said, 'No. We can't do that,' but we figured out how to do that."[123] Thus, the CERP became one of the most important "weapons" for CJTF-7 units and commanders in OIF.

On the tactical level, finance Soldiers made the programs like CERP work. Major Jeffery Madison's experience as executive officer for the 8th Finance Battalion, attached to the 1st AD, illustrated the role of unit-level finance personnel during OIF. He and six other members of his team were in the first two segments of 1st AD's advance parties to land in Kuwait in April 2003. His Soldiers disbursed nearly $200 million in cash—US and Iraqi—during their 15-month tour of duty in Iraq. They were responsible for the one-time stipends paid to Iraqi civil servants by the Office of Reconstruction and Humanitarian Assistance (ORHA) and CPA programs. The Finance Branch Soldiers also oversaw the Brigade Commander's Discretionary Fund program, and then the CERP.

The 8th Finance Battalion also found itself dusting off the long-forgotten manual on cash payment procedures as they set up systems to pay the Iraqis in the Iraqi Army and ICDC units in their area. By far the largest share of the 8th Finance Battalion's energy was spent on contract support to commanders, paying for real estate purchases and leases, and securing commercial vendor support for the division's logistical needs.[124] As of 10 April 2004, when 1st AD turned over control of the Baghdad area to the 1st CAV, the division had initiated $65 million of CERP projects. The division's commanders had spent roughly $45.5 million by that date to complete 3,713 of 3,994 planned projects, with the balance of funds and projects still underway and turned over to their replacements for completion.[125]

Financial management sometimes proved to be troublesome for commands at the highest levels in OIF during this period. As discussed in chapter 11, Major General Paul Eaton's ability to construct barracks for the New Iraqi Army was severely restricted in February and March 2003 while the CPA, DOD, and Congress worked out procedures to spend the huge amounts of money authorized in the FY 2004 supplemental spending bill. Perhaps more damaging was that funds in the CERP dwindled to near zero between late 2003 and spring 2004 as the CPA revised the funding sources and approval processes of the program. The efficient and effective use of reconstruction funds in Iraq, a country that lacked a modern banking system and required almost all transactions to be carried out in cash, became a major focus for the DOD and State Department, as well as the US Congress.

Providing pay and allowances to Soldiers mobilized for OIF proved to be a challenge for the DOD and Department of the Army (DA), causing at times great concern and hardship on the part of some members of the Army National Guard and the Army Reserve. The DA used multiple systems to deliver pay and allowances to Soldiers in the three components of the Army. The Army system is part of the massive Defense Finance and Accounting Service (DFAS), which provides pay and other compensation to all of the Services. In FY 2005 DFAS paid 6 million military members, civilian employees, and retirees; processed 14.2 million contractor invoices; made 7.3 million travel payments; disbursed $532 billion; and managed $70.2 billion in military pay funds.[126] When National Guard and Reserve Soldiers mobilize for Active Duty, Soldiers' records pass between multiple state and federal systems generating the potential for problems. Entire units were mobilized for OIF and individual Soldiers were mobilized as augmentees. Each method required its own pay and benefit processes, further complicating the situation.

The Army began receiving complaints soon after 11 September 2001, and they increased significantly as the subsequent mobilization of the National Guard and the Army Reserve began in earnest. Once on Active Duty, National Guard and Reserve Soldiers earn up to 50 different types of pay and allowances that vary based on rank and length of service, family status, specialized skills, and duty location. Getting each Soldier's status confirmed and their benefits accurately started in a timely manner was complex. Many Soldiers reported multiple problems with their Active Duty pay and allowances once mobilized and long delays in getting them resolved. Congress directed the GAO to examine the problem and it conducted two studies, one focused on the Army National Guard and one on the Army Reserve.

The GAO completed the National Guard study first in March 2003. The study found that almost 95 percent of National Guard Soldiers experienced at least one pay problem. Most were easily and quickly fixed with routine processes. Many problems, however, required multiple attempts to fix and took as long as a year. The GAO concluded:

> One of the primary causes for these pay problems is rooted in the complex, cumbersome processes used to pay soldiers from their initial mobilization through active duty deployment to demobilization. While not designed as such, these pay operations have evolved over time to the point that few, if any, in the department [of the Army] fully understand their breadth, scope, and inherent weaknesses.[127]

In March 2004 the Army created a special ombudsman office within its finance center in Indianapolis to respond to the rising tide of complaints from Army National Guard Soldiers. That office included 21 military and contract specialists who addressed each pay issue.[128]

By April 2004 the Army reported that it had mobilized almost 96,000 Army Reserve Soldiers since September 2001. Many of these Soldiers were mobilized in small units. Indeed, some 2,800 units had fewer than 10 Soldiers in them. The GAO's Army Reserve pay study found exactly the same problems it found in its November 2003 report about the National Guard:

> The processes and automated systems relied on to provide active duty pays, allowances, and tax benefits to mobilized Army Reserve soldiers are so error-prone, cumbersome, and complex that neither DOD nor, more importantly, Army Reserve soldiers themselves, could be reasonably assured of timely and accurate payments. Weaknesses in these areas resulted in pay problems, including overpayments, and to a lesser extent, late and underpayments, of soldiers' active duty pays and allowances.[129]

DFAS responded with a combination of temporary steps and with plans for an overhaul of the entire military pay system, which would require Congressional action as well. In testimony to Congress in July 2004, Patrick Shine, Director of Military and Civilian Pay Services at DFAS, stated, "Within the last 6 months, we have collectively made great strides in improving processes and procedures within the finance community."[130] Shine told Congress that DFAS was preparing to install a temporary pay system called Forward Compatible Payroll to resolve many of the problems caused by the existing system.

Shine also pointed out that a 1996 study called for a single integrated personnel and pay-roll system to replace the 70 different systems then in use by each of the Services. Known as the Defense Integrated Military Human Resources System (DIMHRS), the initial proposal to begin fielding it was disapproved by DOD in 2001. In 2003, however, Northrop Grumman was awarded the contract to develop the system for fielding in 2006, later delayed to 2008.[131] The demands of OEF and OIF required the unprecedented use of Reserve and Guard units and Soldiers making the Total Army concept a reality. In the same way, OEF and OIF had thus served as the catalyst for long sought after changes in the military pay system.

Band Support

Though military bands no longer serve to direct the movements of Army units on the battlefield as they once did, they are a standard part of the logistics concept of support for most military operations. Army doctrine holds that band activities should be part of public affairs, civil-military, psychological, and information operations in support of a unit's overall campaign plan. Direct support bands, those bands assigned to deployable divisions and corps, are also available to augment the local security, prisoner of war, and civilian internee operations of their assigned headquarters.[132] It was standard practice during maneuvers and exercises in the 1980s and 1990s to write in an OPORD "and the band will provide security for the division TOC." Army bands, such as those in most divisions consisted of a dozen or fewer members, played only ceremonial roles while deployed to Iraq. The 1st AD band, for example, deployed with the division in April 2003. While in Iraq, the band played at some 300 morale-boosting events, fallen Soldier ceremonies, and civil-military occasions.[133]

In a sign that the martial impact of music is more than a quaint anachronism, the New Iraqi Army insisted on having its own band. With some encouragement from Marine Colonel Albert Wey and Army Major General Eaton, a rag-tag band of Iraqi musicians began practicing on Christmas Day 2003. After additional practice, they marched and played at the graduation of the second battalion of the Iraqi Army on 6 January 2004.[134]

Troop Rotations in Operation IRAQI FREEDOM

In addition to the deployment of forces into Kuwait for the March 2003 invasion, Army logisticians planned and conducted massive operations to redeploy units and Soldiers out of Iraq and deploy their replacements into theater. In a steady flow that peaked at regular intervals, Soldiers, units, supplies, and equipment moved constantly in and out of theater between May 2003 and January 2005. Though little noticed outside CSS circles, the first major rotation of forces, constituting the transition between OIF I and OIF II in early 2004, stands as an illustration of the effort. In many ways, it is a testimony to how well Army logistics planners have conducted these rotations.

From mid-January through mid-April 2004, the DA, 377th TSC, and CJTF-7 executed one of the largest and most complex movement feats in the history of modern warfare. Nearly 260,000 personnel and more than 50,000 pieces of equipment moved into and out of Iraq during the swap of OIF I and OIF II forces. This effort included rotating forces from 32 nations, almost none of whom were self-sufficient in logistics, command and control, and force protection. Major General Wojdakowski, the CJTF-7 deputy commander, directed that Coalition forces in this rotation would enjoy the same level of support as US forces. In those cases, CJTF–7 committed to providing support functions to those Coalition forces using either US military assets or contracted support.[135] This movement took place without any pause in operations during the April 2004 uprisings. In fact, the rotation occurred during the most intense period of fighting since invasion of Iraq began in 2003. The story of how Army logisticians supported the last minute extension of 1st AD in Iraq during the rotation of OIF I and OIF II serves as an excellent illustration of the degree to which CSS operations had matured by 2004.

A Case Study in Logistical Agility: CSS Soldiers Turn 1st Armored Division Around

When the Shia militias under the leadership of Muqtada al-Sadr rose up and took control of several cities to the south and southeast of Baghdad from Iraqi and Coalition forces in April 2004, the logisticians of CJTF-7 and 1st AD performed CSS feats of Herculean proportion. After a year in Iraq, the 1st AD had spent much of March 2004 preparing to turn over responsibility for Baghdad to the 1st CAV, which had arrived as part of the OIF II rotation (after having been removed from the OIF I deployment in April 2003). This included the transfer of bases, supplies, and equipment. Many 1st AD Soldiers and thousands of pieces of equipment were moved to Kuwait to prepare the division for redeployment. This CSS operation took place in the midst of the much larger deployment and redeployment of all CJTF-7 forces for OIF II.

The transfer ceremony between 1st AD and 1st CAV took place at 0900 on 15 April 2004. On 16 April 2004 Major General Martin Dempsey, 1st AD Commander, issued OPORD 4-006, Operation IRON SABRE. Operation IRON SABRE directed the division's brigades "to defeat Anti-Iraqi Forces (AIF) threatening stability and security" in the MND-CS area of operations.[136] Ironically, the 1st AD would spend an additional 2 months conducting the traditional combat operations it had prepared for 2002–03 before its initial deployment to Iraq. This unexpected extension in theater placed heavy demands on the CJTF-7 and 1st AD logistics units who had almost completed the movement of 1st AD out of Iraq when the order was issued. The CSS operators at the 377th TSC, 3d COSCOM and 13th COSCOM, as well as those in 1st AD had to "turn off" the redeployment process, unpack, and unload equipment in Kuwait and Baghdad and prepare for combat operations in less than 1 week.[137] The division's equipment was spread widely throughout the theater—some still in Baghdad, some literally on the road being trucked south, and the remainder split between Camp Doha and Camp Arifjan in Kuwait.

Division and general support engineers constructed 10 new FOBs, as well as many rearming and refueling points for the division's heavy units. At several locations in Kuwait, CSS personnel worked nonstop to turn around the convoys coming out of Iraq and loading them with the new supplies to support the division. The insurgents had skillfully cut MSR Tampa, the Coalition's main supply route to Kuwait, by destroying bridges, culverts, and roadways. Many critically needed supplies were flown to the FOBs by heavy lift helicopters from V Corps aviation units. The helicopters of the 4th Brigade and 2d ACR had been disassembled and packed for shipment to Germany. They had to be reassembled and deferred maintenance had to be quickly completed before returning to combat. Nevertheless, twice-daily air resupply runs from the Baghdad Airport to Karbala and An Najaf, dubbed the "Iron Eagle Express," were vital to sustaining 1st AD's combat units until the land MSR was reopened. The Iron Eagle Express flew 250 tons of supplies and 1,400 passengers in more than 100 missions during the 1st AD's extension campaign.[138]

Many of the supplies, computer systems, medical stocks, repair parts, and ammunition turned over by the 1st AD to its replacements had to be reclaimed and redistributed before the division could begin operations. The DISCOM struggled to maintain a 10-day supply of rations and water at Baghdad International Airport (BIAP) and a 5-day supply at the new FOBs. Some Soldiers began referring to ammunition resupply as "an involuntary example of 'just in time' logistics," as CH-47 helicopters flew directly into unit FOBs to deliver critical stocks. The 1st AD's wheeled vehicle fleet readiness rating fell as low as 82 percent, reflecting the previous year's intensive use as well as the emergency supply and maintenance system's quick return to operations. Tracked vehicles used track and other components at much higher than normal rates due to frequent long road marches and combat operations. Ammunition, repair parts, and petroleum products remained in short supply well into May 2004.

Despite the partially severed supply lines and the half-completed process of preparing the division for redeployment, the CSS Soldiers of 1st AD and 3d COSCOM "turned the division around" in less than 10 days. Both 1st AD and 2d ACR remained in theater until early July and defeated the militia forces of Muqtada al-Sadr. Much of the credit for their success between April and July must be given to the CSS Soldiers who performed this monumental feat of logistical planning and execution.

Conclusion

Like the Soldiers in combat and combat support units, CSS Soldiers in the postinvasion phase of OIF faced unexpected and enduring challenges that required them to transition from normal procedures to an evolving and increasingly dangerous battlefield. The Army's logistical shift to the distribution based system made these challenges more difficult. Of all the aspects of CSS, delivering supplies and services to Coalition units across hundreds of miles of Iraq while fighting off insurgent attacks was the single biggest problem for planners and operators.

The so-called "running start" to the invasion of Iraq in March 2003 meant that combat operations began before the CSS system was fully in place, with many CSS units still en route to Kuwait and Iraq as the first shots were fired. The integration of Active Duty CSS units in V Corps and 3d ID, along with Reserve units in the 377th TSC and elsewhere, was hampered due to mobilization timelines, equipment disparities, and lack of prewar training and planning. The lightning speed of the US advance toward Baghdad and the rapid fall of the Saddam regime meant the CSS system did not have time to fully develop before the immense requirements of full spectrum operations and Iraqi reconstruction began. The Iraqi insurgency then threatened the ability of CSS operators to transport supplies and services to the widely dispersed Coalition and Iraqi forces. Training and equipping CSS units with survivable vehicles and systems during major operations was itself a huge undertaking. The inability of the national industrial base to ramp up production of existing equipment and to develop and build new equipment exacerbated the overall ability of the CSS system to respond to the requirements of all Soldiers in Iraq.

Most of the criticism of Army CSS operations by "end users" is directed at the theory and practice of DBL. In a 2005 paper Major Guy Jones, an Army officer who had participated in OIF I, argued that the whole concept of DBL was flawed. Jones contended, "The entire transformative process ongoing in the US Army's logistic infrastructure does not effectively fix the problem of the last 1,000 yards of the battlefield, getting the required supplies or resources to the end user."[139] He further suggested that in protracted wars such as OIF, logistics requirements will grow over time. Based on his experience with DB CSS, Jones looked ahead, asserting, "Surely, the next conflict can not be won on a reduced logistical footprint."[140]

Others in the CSS ranks supported his analysis. Reflecting on the Army's reduced military logistical capability, smaller logistics footprint, and reliance on contractor support in Iraq, Brigadier General West stated: "Whoever first had the idea of replacing the military logistics capability with a commercial-contracted application has not been to Iraq. Negotiating the long competitive lines of communication and facing an asymmetric threat in hostile urban terrain are inherently combat functions. This battlefield is the domain of warriors, not business personnel."[141]

After action reports gathered by the Army's Center for Lessons Learned (CALL) from the 1st ID, 1st AD, 3d ID, 4th ID, and numerous separate units during 2003 and 2004 rendered a mixed verdict on the effectiveness of the DB CSS concept as it affected division and smaller units. The Soldiers in these units did not reject the concept out of hand, but emphasized that its implementation did not live up to the theory. Comments generally praised the effectiveness of RFID tags, the Movement Tracking System, and various tactical satellite communication devices—but too few units were fully equipped with the latter in 2003 and 2004. Other units expressed great disappointment with the relative inability of networks and automation programs to integrate commodity-specific systems to portray the real-time status of unit needs and theater stocks. This point was particularly biting given that distributed logistics was founded on the basic premise that logisticians would have the ability to see a unit's real-time status and its needs. Too many systems were incompatible and too many units lacked sufficient communication devices. Without an accurate picture of requirements and assets, both users and logisticians were unable to make sound, prioritized decisions about the allocation of resources.[142]

These reports also expressed the belief that combat units needed greater internal capacity to sustain themselves in all areas of logistics, both in the initial period of operations before the complete CSS infrastructure was in place and during periods when enemy action disrupted the fragile logistical system. The partially transformed Army logistical structure in 2003 could not sustain the rapid deployment of units and the "running start" of OIF. Further, the extended supply lines in Iraq were vulnerable to interdiction in 2003 and 2004. Because of this concern, the 1st Marine Division created a large supply base on the outskirts of Fallujah in preparation for the Coalition assault on insurgent forces in the city in November 2004. Put simply, most units in combat wanted their "mini-iron mountains" nearby and under their control to deal with the unpredictable nature of the battlefield.

The Army's Logistics Whitepapers published since 2003 generally acknowledged these conclusions and directed further changes in four areas to make DB CSS work. The recommendations are grouped into four categories: network communications, supply chain management, force reception, and theater-level distribution.[143] The DOD initiated its own logistics assessment to examine the performance of national and joint logistics in OIF. It reached similar conclusions about the need for greater communications and network capabilities to generate an accurate logistical "picture" and the need to better integrate multiservice support.[144]

The major logistical role played by contractors in OIF has also been questioned. Tens of thousands of contractors (estimates range from 75,000 to 125,000), a force composed of US citizens, Iraqis, and third party nationals, have replaced at least an equal number of Soldiers in OIF—a major factor in the Army's ability to sustain its forces over the long duration of the operation. Outside LOGCAP, thousands of additional contractors have provided security to US, Coalition, and international organizations in Kuwait and Iraq. Unquestionably, they have performed their roles with great skill and often with bravery on the complex and dangerous noncontiguous battlefield in Iraq. Their somewhat unclear legal status on the battlefield under international law and their ability to replace military logistical support in combat have raised questions about whether the Army has come to rely too much on contracted support. Estimates vary widely, but more than 100 US contractors have been killed and many more have been wounded in Iraq since March 2003.[145] The support systems for contractors wounded or killed in Iraq are far less robust than those provided to Soldiers and are now the subject of legal action in the United States.[146] Contractors are paid substantially more than CSS Soldiers performing the same work, a fact that causes morale and related recruiting and retention challenges for the Army. These and other issues are still being debated in and outside of the Army.

DB CSS in 2003 and 2004 during OIF was a work in progress. Just before his redeployment to Germany in February 2005, Brigadier General Charles Fletcher, the 3d COSCOM Commander, commented on the effectiveness of the reality of in-transit and total asset visibility concepts in 2003 and 2004, stating, "It wasn't what we wanted it to be, but it was phenomenally better than anything the Army had ever done."[147] The goal of providing efficient CSS that was also effective in all situations on a complex battlefield remained an unattained objective. Efficiencies of cost, force structure, and time at the national and theater levels were of little interest to the Soldier in combat in need of vehicle parts, water, or ammunition. For combat units, effectiveness trumped efficiency—as it always will. It remains to be seen whether changes brought about by the continued transformation of Army logistics and the Army's modular structure will prove successful in the long run.

Yet it would be wrong to label the Army's CSS efforts in OIF a failure. In fact, the record of US Army logisticians' must be judged an overall success. Despite the many challenges of CSS operations in OIF, Brigadier General West made a simple but critical assertion: "Nothing failed due to logistics."[148] It is not perhaps the greatest of praise for the Army's CSS operations during this period of OIF, but it is a qualified victory for the many Army professionals who, to paraphrase the aphorism, have diligently studied logistics.

Notes

1.   Brigadier General Scott G. West, The Quartermaster General, "Supporting Victory in Operation Iraqi Freedom," *Quartermaster Professional Bulletin*, Autumn, 2004, http://www.quartermaster.army. mil/oqmg/Professional_Bulletin/2004/Autumn04/Quarter (accessed 21 April 2006), 2–3.

2.   The Army's own logistical doctrinal manual called it "brute force" logistics. See Department of the Army, Field Manual 100-10-1, *Theater Distribution* (Washington, DC, 1 October 1999), 3–1.

3.   Laurel K. Myers, Ph.D., "Eliminating the Iron Mountain," *Army Logistician* (July–August 2004), http://www.almc.army.mil/ALOG/issues/JulAug04/C_iron.html (accessed 6 June 2006).

4.   Myers; A RAND study described distribution-based logistics as "providing support through frequent, reliable distribution flows with focused and right-sized inventories well positioned across the supply chain to cover consumption between replenishment cycles at the point of use and to buffer against distribution disruptions (examples of what is called special cause variability) and typical variability (i.e., the amount of variability experienced when processes are in control and working to "standard" or what is called common cause variability). . . . The goal of DBL is not inventory reduction, it is improved support effectiveness and agility. Eric Peltz et al., *Sustainment of Army Forces in Operation Iraqi Freedom: Major Findings and Recommendations* (Santa Monica, CA: RAND Corporation, 2005), 1. The definition is from footnote 1.

5.   For the purposes of this study, distribution-based logistics, just in time logistics, or velocity-based logistics can be used interchangeably. The Army's doctrinal term is "distribution-based combat service support." See FM 4-0, *Combat Service Support* (Washington, DC, 29 August 2003), 1–10 and chapter 5.

6.   FM 4-0, chapter 5.

7.   For a survey of the evolution of Joint and Army doctrine in this area, see Lieutenant Colonel Victor MacCagnan Jr., "Logistics Transformation—Restarting a Stalled Process" (Carlisle Barracks, PA: US Army War College, Strategic Studies Institute, January 2005).

8.   FM 100-10-2, *Contracting Support on the Battlefield* (Washington, DC, 4 August 1999), chapter 1.

9.   The summary of the creation and evolution of the LOCGAP in this and subsequent paragraphs is taken from three sources. See Charles Dervarics, "Contractors Fill Key Role Through the Logistics Civil Augmentation Program" (Fort Belvoir, VA: US Army Materiel Command, 2004), 91–93; Charles Dervarics, "Contractors Fill Key Role Through the Logistics Civil Augmentation Program" (Fort Belvoir, VA: US Army Materiel Command, 2005), 76–81; see also FM 100-10-2, chapters 1, 2, and 3.

10.   FM 4-0, 1–10.

11.   West, 2–3.

12.   See FM 4-0, chapter 4.

13.   FM 100-10-1, 1–2.

14.   FM 100-10-1, chapter 2.

15.   Major Randolph Duke, "More Than a Name Change," *Army Logistician* (January–February 2001), Volume 33, Issue 1, http://www.almc.army.mil/alog/issues/JanFeb01/JFIndex.htm (accessed 11 October 2006).

16.   To supplement the 377th's base operations capability, the 3d COSCOM provided base support for Camps Virginia, New York, and Pennsylvania through August 2003, even after it moved north into Iraq. Brigadier General Charles Fletcher, in written comments provided to author, 2 January 2007, on file with the Combat Studies Institute, Fort Leavenworth, KS.

17.   Sergeant Frank Pellegrini, "Supporting Gulf War 2.0," *Army Magazine,* 1 September 2003, http://www.ausa.org/webpub/DeptArmyMagazine.nsf (accessed 11 October 2006).

18.   Pellegrini.

19.   US Government Accountability Office, GAO Report 04-484, "Operation Iraqi Freedom: Long-standing Problems Hampering Mail Delivery Need to Be Resolved" (Washington, DC, 14 April 2004).

20. Major General David E. Kratzer, "The Role of the 377th Theater Support Command," *Army Reserve Magazine,* Volume 49, Number 3, Spring 2003, 28–35. See also Pellegrini.

21. Kratzer, 28–35.

22. Fletcher, written comments, 2 January 2007.

23. John D. Gresham, "Army Materiel Command Logistics Support Elements" (Fort Belvoir, VA: US Army Materiel Command, 2004), 72–77.

24. Robert G. Darius, "Operation Iraqi Freedom—It Was a Prepositioned War" (Fort Belvoir, VA: US Army Material Command, October 2003), 14–21.

25. It has proven very difficult to track the number and type of contractors in OIF due to the variety of roles they have performed—logistics, security, and humanitarian. For one attempt to measure their numbers, see John McGrath, *Boots on the Ground: Troop Density in Contingency Operations* (Fort Leavenworth, KS: Combat Studies Institute Press, 2006).

26. Dervarics, 91–93.

27. West, 2–3.

28. COL Gregory Fontenot (US Army Retired). LTC E.J. Degen, US Army, and LTC David Tohn, US Army, *On Point: The US Army in Operation Iraqi Freedom* (Fort Leavenworth, KS: Combat Studies Institute Press, 2004), 408.

29. Fletcher, written comments, 2 January 2007.

30. For a more complete discussion of this issue, see Fontenot, Degen, and Tohn.

31. Fletcher, written comments, 2 January 2007.

32. Brigadier General Charles Fletcher, interview by Mr. Charles Kirkpatrick, V Corps Historian, Wiesbaden, Germany, 11 February 2003.

33. Fletcher, written comments, 2 January 2007.

34. 3d Corps Support Command After Action Review, "*History of the 3d Corps Support Command in Operation Iraqi Freedom,*" Heidelberg, Germany, January 2004, 2-1-4 to 2-1-7.

35. Fletcher, interview by Kirkpatrick, 11 February 2003.

36. 3d COSCOM AAR, 2-1-9.

37. Brigadier General Charles Fletcher, interview by Major Mark Pritchard, 3d COSCOM Historian, Baghdad, Iraq, 22 January 2004.

38. 3d COSCOM AAR, 2-1-19.

39. 3d COSCOM AAR, 2-1-10 to 2-1-14.

40. 3d COSCOM AAR, 2-1-16.

41. 3d COSCOM AAR, Executive Summary, 3-4.

42. Fletcher, interview by Kirkpatrick, 11 February 2003.

43. Fletcher, interview by Kirkpatrick, 11 February 2003.

44. "Initial Impressions Report No. 06-20, 13th Corps Support Command" (Fort Leavenworth, KS: US Army Center for Lessons Learned), April 2006, 22; see also, 3d COSCOM AAR, Executive Summary, 10–11.

45. FM 100-10-1, 3-2 and 5-6.

46. Fletcher, interview by Pritchard, 22 January 2004.

47. 3d COSCOM AAR, Executive Summary, 8. For a more detailed example of these challenges, see also Lieutenant Colonel Andrew W. Bowes, "A Corps Support Battalion's Experience in Operation Iraqi Freedom," *Army Logistician* (July–August 2004), http://www.almc.army.mil/alog/Back.html.

48. 3d COSCOM AAR, Executive Summary, 7.

49. 3d COSCOM AAR, Executive Summary, 8.

50. Fletcher, interview by Pritchard, 22 January 2004.

51. US Army Logistics Whitepaper: Delivering Material Readiness to the Army, "Connect Army Logistics" (Washington, DC: G4 Deputy Chief of Staff for Logistics), http://www.hqda.army.mil/log-web/focusareasnew.html (accessed 11 October 2006).

52.   The problem persists. The future Battlefield Command Sustainment Support System (BCS3) will tie together disparate CSS systems to provide a common operating picture to logisticians and combat commanders alike. In her 2006 article for AUSA "Green Book," the Army's Deputy Chief of Staff, G4, Lieutenant General Ann Dunwoody, lamented the lack of centralized databases and information systems. See, Lieutenant General Ann Dunwoody, "Working to Achieve Readiness for the Long Haul," *Army: 2006–2007 Green Book* (Arlington, VA: Association of the United States Army, October 2006), 201–202.

53.   FM 100-10-1, 3-4.

54.   Lieutenant Colonel Lawrence Strobel, "Common-User Land Transportation Management in the Layered, Non-Linear, Non-Contiguous Battlefield (Carlisle Barracks, PA: US Army War College Strategy Research Project, 18 March 2005), 7.

55.   Richard E. Killblane, "Transportation Corps in Operation Iraqi Freedom 2: April Uprising," Unpublished manuscript, 1–2.

56.   Mitch MacDonald, "The Art of Combat Logistics: Interview with Major Bob Curran," *DC Velocity*, Volume 3 Number 5 (May 2005), 20–24; Killblane, 1.

57.   "Stryker Brigade Combat Team 1, 3d Brigade, 2d Infantry: Operations in Mosul, Iraq," *Initial Impressions Report* (Fort Leavenworth, KS: Center for Army Lessons Learned, 21 December 2004), 101–102.

58.   See Strobel, 3–6. In 2004 the 1st Infantry Division set up its own command and control system for coordinating the movement of non-1st ID vehicles through its area of operations.

59.   Fletcher, written comments, 2 January 2007. This refers to the Joint Deployment Logistics Model (JDLM) system, which later became the Battle Command Sustainment Support System (BCS3).

60.   West.

61.   Killblane, 8. The four men killed were Scott Helvenston, Jerry Zovko, Wesley Batalona, and Michael Teague.

62.   Patrecia Slayden Hollis, "1st Cav in Baghdad: Counterinsurgency EBO in Dense Urban Terrain. Interview with Major General Peter W. Chiarelli," *Field Artillery,* September–October 2005.

63.   Killblane, 8.

64.   West.

65.   Killblane, 12.

66.   Killblane, 14.

67.   Killblane, 25

68.   "Thomas Hamill On His Iraq Escape," *CBS New,* 12 October 2004, http://www.cbsnews.com/stories/2004/10/10/earlyshow/leisure/books/main648445.shtml (accessed 5 October 2006). Official and private investigations are continuing; see T. Christian Miller, "Iraq convoy got go-ahead Despite Threat," *Los Angeles Times*, 3 September 2007, A1.

69.   Killblane, 30, 34, 38. Killblane addresses each of these events, and the individuals involved in them, in detail.

70.   Killblane, 44.

71.   Captain John-Michael Insetta, e-mail interview by Contemporary Operations Study Team, Fort Leavenworth, KS, 6 June 2006.

72.   Insetta, e-mail interview, 6 June 2006.

73.   Insetta, e-mail interview, 6 June 2006.

74.   Captain Jason A. Miseli, "The View From My Windshield: Just in time Logistics Just Isn't Working," *ARMOR Magazine*, September–October 2003, 13.

75.   Major General Walter Wojdakowski, interview by Contemporary Operations Study Team, Fort Leavenworth, KS, 24 August 2006, 11.

76. Joe Borlas, "CENTCOM Up-Armored Humvee Requirements Being Met," *Army News Service*, 6 February 2004; see also Donna Miles, "Up-Armored Vehicle Effort Progressing Full Steam Ahead," *American Forces Press Service*, 29 October 2004.

77. Scott Gourley, "Protecting our Soldiers, Armoring Vehicles" (Fort Belvoir, VA: US Army Materiel Command, 2005), 106–113.

78. Randy Talbot, "Forging the Steel Hammer: US Army Tank and Automotive Command Support to the Global War on Terrorism, 2001–2005" (Warren, MI: US Army Tank and Automotive Command, May 2006), 50–51.

79. Gourley, 106–113.

80. Talbot, 77.

81. Talbot, 80.

82. Russell Carollo and Mike Wagner, "Deadly Price Paid for HMMWV Armor Used to Protect Soldiers," *Dayton Daily News,* 11 June 2006.

83. Lieutenant General R. Steven Whitcomb, "US Department of Defense, Office of the Assistant Secretary of Defense (Public Affairs), News Transcript," *DefenseLink,* 9 December 2004, http://www.defenselink.mil/transcripts/2004/ tr20041209-1765.htm (accessed 6 October 2006).

84. Dr. Jeff A. Charlston, "The Evolution of the Stryker Brigade—From Doctrine to Battlefield Operations in Iraq," in John J. McGrath, ed., *An Army at War: Change in the Midst of Conflict, The Proceedings of the Combat Studies Institute 2005 Military History Symposium* (Fort Leavenworth, KS: Combat Studies Institute Press, 2005), 48–51.

85. The TUSK program was not funded until mid-way through FY06. See Talbot for an overview of these various Army programs.

86. In 1998 the US Army Natick Soldier Center issued the first contract to produce Interceptor Body Armor System to Point Blank Body Armor, Inc. See Program Executive Office Soldier Web site, https://www.peosoldier.army.mil/factsheets/SEQ_SSV_IBA.pdf (accessed 2 July 2007).

87. For a description of the Interceptor Body Armor System, see Program Executive Office Soldier Web site at https://www.peosoldier.army.mil/factsheets/SEQ_SSV_IBA.pdf.

88. Wojdakowski, interview, 24 August 2006, 11.

89. Government Accountability Office, GAO Report 05-275, *Actions Needed to Improve the Availability of Critical Items during Current and Future Operations* (Washington, DC, 8 April 2005), 56.

90. GAO Report 05-275, 58.

91. GAO Report 05-275, 57.

92. West, 2–3.

93. West.

94. Suzi Thurmond, "Analyzing the Lessons of OIF Distribution," *Army Logistician* (July–August 2004), 4.

95. Lieutenant Colonel Harry D. Tunnell IV, interview by Contemporary Operations Study Team, 23 January 2006, Center of Military History, Fort McNair, Washington, DC, 23 January 2006, 3.

96. "Initial Impressions Report No. 06-20, 13th COSCOM," 80.

97. Thurmond, 4.

98. "Initial Impressions Report No. 06-20, 13th COSCOM," 81.

99. West.

100. Miseli, 11–12.

101. Henry Simberg, *AMSAA Sample Data Collection Ground System Usage/Parts Replacement Analysis Operation Iraqi Freedom* Briefing, Fort Belvoir, VA: Research, Development & Engineering Command/Army Materiel Systems Analysis Activity, Army Materiel Command, August 2006, slides 14–16.

102. House Subcommittee on Readiness, Committee on Armed Services, Douglas Holtz-Eakin, Director, Congressional Budget Office, *The Potential Costs Resulting from Increased Usage of Military Equipment in Ongoing Operations*, 109th Congress, 1st Session, 6 April 2005, http://www.cbo.gov/showdoc.cfm?index=6235&sequence (accessed 9 October 2006).

103. House Committee on Armed Services, *Statement by Lieutenant General David F. Melcher, Deputy Chief of Staff G8, and Major General Jeanette K. Edmunds, Deputy Chief of Staff G4, Army Equipment Reset Program*, 109th Congress, 2d Session, 30 March 2006, 2–7.

104. GAO Report 05-275, 50–54.

105. GAO Report 05-275, 50–54.

106. Thurmond, 5–6.

107. This effort was not without precedent, having been used in World War II and Vietnam. See Christopher Prawdzik, "Support the Stryker Brigades" (Fort Belvoir, VA: US Army Materiel Command, 2005), 88–95; see also, Lieutenant Colonel Dennis Thompson, "Frontline Support of the First SBCT at War," *Army Logistician*, (July–August 2004), 15.

108. Wojdakowski, interview, 24 August 2006, 9.

109. US Army Corps of Engineers, Fact Sheet, "Coalition Munitions Clearance Program" (Huntsville, AL: US Army Corps of Engineers, June 2006), www.hnd.usace.army.mil/pao/FactShtsFY06/PAO-CMC fact sheet.pdf (accessed 15 October 2006). This work was completed in June 2006 with the demolition of 248 tons of munitions, and it has now been turned over to the Iraqi Government.

110. Kenneth W. Estes, "Command Narrative: 1st Armored Division in Operation IRAQI FREEDOM, May 2003–July 2004," Unpublished study, 71–72.

111. FM 4-0, chapter 11; see also, FM 14-100, *Financial Management Operations* (Washington, DC, 7 May 1997).

112. Lieutenant General David H. Petraeus, "Learning Counterinsurgency: Observations from Soldiering in Iraq," *Military Review*, January–February 2006, 4.

113. *CALL Newsletter 04-13: Operation Iraqi Freedom (OIF), CAAT II Initial Impressions Report (IIR)*. Fort Leavenworth, KS: Center for Army Lessons Learned, May 2004; see also, Mark Martins, "No Small Change of Soldiering: The Commander's Emergency Response Program in Iraq and Afghanistan," *Army Lawyer*, 11 February 2005, 5–6, http://www.jagcnet.army.mil/ (accessed 9 October 2006).

114. Colonel Michael Toner, interview by Contemporary Operations Study Team, Fort Leavenworth, KS, 24 May 2006, 3.

115. Lieutenant General David H. Petraeus, interview by Contemporary Operations Study Team, Fort Leavenworth, KS, 17 February 2006, 10.

116. Toner, interview, 24 May 2006, 5.

117. Brigadier General David Blackledge, 352d Civil Affairs Command, "Department of Defense Press Conference Transcript," *DefenseLink*, 14 January 2004, http://www.defenselink.mil/transcripts/2004/tr20040114-1144.html (accessed 9 October 2006).

118. Major Robert S. Widmann, USAF, "The Commanders Emergency Response Program, Part II," in *OnPoint: A Counter-Terrorism Journal for Military and Law Enforcement Professionals*, http://www.uscav.com/uscavonpoint/Print.aspx?id=169 (accessed 9 October 2006).

119. Toner, interview, 24 May 2006, 6.

120. Toner, interview, 24 May 2006, 10–12.

121. Toner, interview, 24 May 2006, 11.

122. Toner, interview, 24 May 2006, 4.

123. Toner, interview, 24 May 2006, 14.

124. Major Jeffrey Madison, "CSI Conference Roundtable Discussion," in Brian M. De Toy, ed., *Turning Victory Into Success: Military Operations After the Campaign* (Fort Leavenworth, KS: Combat Studies Institute Press, 2004), 307–309 and 315–317.

125. Estes, 67–68.

126. Defense Finance and Accounting Service Web site, http://www.dod.mil/dfas/news/2004pressreleases/pressrelease0425.html (accessed 9 October 2006).

127. General Accounting Office, GAO Report 04-89, "Military Pay: Army National Guard Personnel Mobilized to Active Duty Experienced Significant Pay Problems" (Washington, DC, 17 November 2003), http://www.gao.gov/htext/d0489.html (accessed 5 October 2006).

128. Staff Sergeant Cheryl Hackley, "New System Helps Resolve Pay Problems," *Defend America,* 28 July 2004, http://www.defendamerica.mil/articles/jul2004/a072804e.html (accessed 9 October 2006).

129. Government Accountability Office, GAO Report 04-911, "Army Reserve Soldiers Mobilized to Active Duty Experienced Significant Pay Problems" (Washington, DC, 23 August 2004), http://www.gao.gov/htext/d04911.html (accessed 5 October 2006).

130. David McGlinchey, "Defense says steps taken to fix Guard, Reserve Pay Problems," *Govexec.com*, 20 July 2004, http://www.govexec.com/dailyfed/0704/072004d1.htm (accessed 9 October 2006).

131. McGlinchey.

132. FM 4-0, 14-1 to 14-3; see also FM 12-50, *U.S. Army Bands* (Washington, DC, 15 October 1999).

133. "History of the 1st Armored Division Band," http://www.1ad.army.mil/Band/bndHistory.htm (accessed 6 October 2006).

134. Major General (Retired) Paul Eaton, interview by Contemporary Operations Study Team, Fort Leavenworth, KS, 3 August 2006, 15.

135. Wojdakowski, interview, 24 August 2006, 9–10.

136. Estes, 144.

137. The account of this operation in this and subsequent paragraphs is based on the draft 1st AD History compiled by Dr. Kenneth W. Estes. See Estes, 127–148.

138. Estes, 145.

139. Major Guy Jones, "Transformational Logistics: Solution or Shell Game?" in McGrath, ed., *An Army at War,* 345.

140. Jones, "Transformational Logistics: Solution or Shell Game?" in McGrath, ed., *An Army at War,* 353.

141. West.

142. *CALL Newsletter 04-13*; see also, Army Logistics Whitepaper: "Connect Army Logistics."

143. Army Logistics Whitepaper: "Connect Army Logistics."

144. Stephen Binova, Steve Geary, and Barry Holland, "An Objective Assessment of Logistics in Iraq," *Science Applications International Corporation*, March 2004 (Fort Leavenworth, KS: US Army Center for Army Lessons Learned).

145. The US Department of Labor tracks this data though it is based on claims for insurance benefits and medical benefits, not direct tracking of casualties in Iraq. For a nonofficial source, see Iraq Coalition Casualty Count, http://icasualties.org/oif/.

146. For one example, see Joe Sterling, "Family's Lawsuit Over Slain Contractors Stalls," *CNN International.com*; http://edition.cnn.com/2005/LAW/04/11/blackwater.lawsuit/index.html (accessed 3 April 2007).

147. Brigadier General Charles Fletcher, interview by Major Robert Smith, 305th Military History Detachment Commander, 19 May 2003, in Baghdad, Iraq.

148. West.

Chapter 13

Taking Care of Soldiers

Since the advent of the all-volunteer military in 1973, the US Army has continually, and with good reason, asserted that its Soldiers are its "greatest asset." The American way of war has traditionally included overwhelming logistics support and a high level of care for a Soldier's personal welfare, morale, and health to generate tremendous staying power and effectiveness in battle. Thus, American Soldiers have enjoyed a level of support that is the envy of every other nation in peace and in war. Additionally, the belief that while the Army may "enlist a Soldier, it retains a family" has driven the Army to extend that same level of support to Soldiers' families. The American people have also shown a great interest in the conditions in which its Soldiers live and fight.

Medical care for troops deployed during operations is, of course, the most important aspect of taking care of Soldiers. In the last half of the 20th century, high-quality food service, vaccines, routine health care, and field-sanitation practices reduced disease related deaths to almost zero. In World War I, by contrast, more US Army Soldiers died of disease and other causes than by wounds they suffered in combat. The tactical superiority of Army Soldiers and units, combined with vastly improved personal protective equipment and advanced battlefield first aid, has driven casualty rates to historic lows. US Soldiers hit by enemy fire during the first 18 months of Operation IRAQI FREEDOM (OIF) had greater than a 90-percent survival rate, and for those who reached advanced medical treatment, the survival rate was over 97 percent.[1] Advances in trauma medicine during OIF have saved many lives that just 10 years ago would have been lost. Medical treatment is indeed one of the Army's greatest accomplishments during this period of OIF.

Yet, medical care comprises only one part of a Soldier's overall well-being. The mental health of Soldiers deployed in combat—long a poorly understood issue—has recently become equally as important as their physical health, and the Army has devoted much more effort to prevent and treat these problems. In theater, the Morale, Welfare, and Recreation (MWR) programs, including the United Service Organizations (USO), helped lift Soldiers' spirits and positively affected their well-being when off duty. Soldiers' morale and mental health is also directly affected by the state of their families in the United States. Extensive family support programs, among them Family Readiness Groups (FRGs), worked alleviate domestic stressors. During OIF, the Army also focused newfound attention on helping Soldiers readjust to peace-time military life after a year-plus tour of duty in Iraq, cope with the challenge of multiple tours, and transition to civilian life at the end of their Army career.

The conduct of full spectrum operations after May 2003 created some unique challenges for those individuals and organizations charged with taking care of Soldiers. The constant threat from a shadowy insurgent fighting with unconventional and terrorist tactics, the lack of in-theater rear areas, and the difficulty in assessing progress in the overall campaign presented Soldiers in OIF with challenges that were different from those faced by troops in previous wars. This chapter will briefly address the wide range of programs and services dedicated to support-ing Soldiers as they made the transition to the new campaign in Iraq.

US Army Battlefield Medicine before Operation IRAQI FREEDOM

Since the Army's birth in the Revolutionary War, medical treatment of battlefield casualties has significantly evolved and advanced. During the American colonies' war for independence, litter bearers were often chosen from "underperforming soldiers" and were used to retrieve the wounded from the battlefield. Disease and malnutrition alone killed 10 soldiers for every 1 soldier killed in battle.[2] During the earliest phases of the American Civil War, medical care—battlefield evacuation in particular—was extremely rudimentary. It took over a week, for example, for the Union Army to evacuate its wounded from the battlefield after the Battle of Bull Run in 1861. When Dr. Jonathan Letterman was appointed as the head of Medical Services for the Army of the Potomac, he was so appalled that he overhauled the medical practices in the Army, establishing policies for treatment, evacuation, and a series of general hospitals behind the lines. His efforts later became a model for the Army Medical Corps and the US Army as a whole. Medical care in the 19th century remained primitive, however, and more than half of all wounded Soldiers died from their wounds despite treatment, primarily due to blood loss and infection. Much of this was due to the poor understanding of the causes of disease and the importance of sanitation. During the war, the Union Army lost over 140,000 Soldiers in battle, but more than 224,000 died from disease and other causes.[3] By the end of the Spanish American War in the 1890s, the "germ theory" of medicine had advanced to the point where medical personnel understood that whether or not a wounded Soldier lived was often determined by the first person to respond to the injury. Accordingly, litter-bearers were instructed on how to apply dressings in the field, both to treat the trauma of the injury or wound and to prevent infection of the wound.[4] Because of this innovation, the number of injured who died from their wounds after reaching a field hospital decreased to 19 percent.[5]

The Army made significant medical strides during World War I. New medical advances used regularly during this time included the triage concept, blood transfusions, X-rays (first

Casualty	Any person who is lost to the organization by having been declared dead; duty status—whereabouts unknown, missing, ill, or injured.
Duty Status	Whereabouts unknown, missing, ill, or injured.
Wounded in Action (WIA)	A casualty category applicable to a hostile casualty, other than the victim of a terrorist activity, who has incurred an injury due to an external agent or cause. The term encompasses all kinds of wounds and other injuries incurred in action.
Died of Wounds Received in Action (DOW)	A casualty category applicable to a hostile casualty, other than the victim of a terrorist activity, who dies of wounds or other injuries received in action after having reached a medical treatment facility.
Killed in Action (KIA)	A casualty category applicable to a hostile casualty, other than the victim of a terrorist activity, who is killed outright or who dies as a result of wounds or other injuries before reaching a medical treatment facility.
Disease and Nonbattle Injuries (DNBI)	All illnesses and injuries, not resulting from enemy or terrorist action or caused by conflict, such as disease and training or recreation accidents.
Total Casualties	KIA + DOW + WIA + DNBI
Total Hostile Deaths	KIA + DOW
Total Soldiers "Hit" by Enemy Attacks	KIA + DOW + WIA

http://www.dtic.mil/doctrine/jel/doddict

Figure 134. Medical care and casualty definitions and formulas.

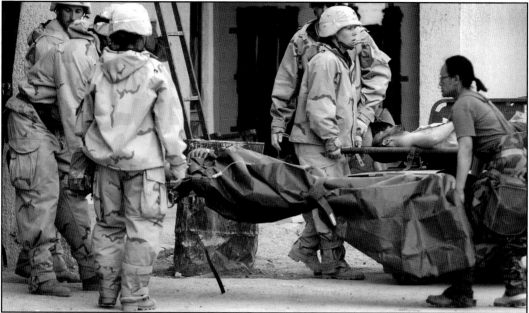

Figure 135. Wounded Soldier evacuated.

used in the Spanish American War in 1898), treatment for shock, and various reconstructive and orthopedic surgery techniques. The nature of bacteria-caused diseases was widely understood by World War I, and vaccines for smallpox and typhoid were available. Better frontline medical organizations and motorized transportation sped casualties to field hospitals. Though the Army vastly decreased the number of those who died from wounds and disease, deaths occurring from nonbattle causes still exceeded deaths caused by combat.[6]

The US Army revolutionized medical treatment in World War II. New techniques, including better field surgical care, sulfa drugs, penicillin, the use of more and better trained medics assigned to each combat unit, forward treatment centers, the use of plasma and whole blood products, greater emphasis on preventive medicine and field sanitation, as well as speedy evacuation off the battlefield dramatically lowered death rates from combat action. For the first time in US military history, the number of Soldiers lost to nonbattle injuries was lower than the number lost to combat causes.[7]

Progress in reducing casualty rates continued in the second half of the 20th century. During the Korean war, the Army used helicopters to airlift wounded Soldiers to mobile army surgical hospital (MASH) units located very close to the front lines. Only about 2 percent of Soldiers wounded in Korea who reached a MASH unit ultimately died of their wounds.[8] During the Vietnam war, medical evacuation (MEDEVAC) helicopters, or "Dustoff" missions, were commonplace on the battlefield.[*] Dustoff helicopters, piloted with incredible bravery, flew with

---

[*]Helicopters were first used in World War II for casualty evacuation in the China–Burma–India Theater, and were widely used in the Korean War. Those early medical helicopters did not have medical attendants on board who could provide en route care, so they were strictly casualty evacuation (CASEVAC) birds. Vietnam was the first use of helicopters with the ability to provide en route care that is now considered to be the definition of MEDEVAC.

DOD Photo

medics on board and provided uninterrupted treatment en route from the battlefield to rear area field hospitals. Though statistical death rates for Soldiers reaching hospital care remained about the same as the Korean war rates, many more Soldiers who would have died of their wounds on the battlefield in Korea were quickly evacuated to field hospitals in Vietnam. Rates of infection in that conflict were less than one-third the rate of World War II.[9] In the last decade of the century, continued improvements in medical treatment, deployable hospitals, dedicated ground and air MEDEVAC units, and digital links to the United States during the first Gulf War in 1991 meant that only 2 of the 356 Soldiers wounded in combat died of their wounds once reaching a field hospital. This yielded a survival rate of 99.4 percent.[10] Though almost perfect, the Army realized that the short duration and unique nature of the war should not lessen the continued efforts to improve medical treated for Soldiers.

Moving Emergency Treatment Closer to the Front Lines in Operation IRAQI FREEDOM

In October 1993 the Army Medical Department began overhauling its deployable units in a process that would evolve into the Medical Reengineering Initiative program. A post-Gulf War analysis revealed that many of the Army's medical units and equipment were too large, too slow to deploy, and lacked the mobility to keep up with the pace of offensive combat operations and the dispersed nature of unconventional operations. As a result, the Medical Reengineering Initiative imposed change in several key areas: the creation of smaller but better equipped combat support hospitals (CSHs), the adoption of new forward surgical teams (FSTs), a reorganization of combat medical skills and training, and greater emphasis on evacuation out of the theater of operations to stateside medical care.[11]

Figure 136. Members of the 447th Contingency Aeromedical Staging Facility prepare a C-141 cargo aircraft for patient transport, Camp Sather, Baghdad International Airport, Baghdad, Iraq.

FSTs, designed in 1995, were mobile units consisting of 20 medical personnel including doctors, anesthesiologists, and nurses who provided resuscitative medical care to Soldiers before their arrival at CSHs. An FST was a self-contained surgical suite or detachment that could be assembled within 60 minutes and moved directly behind the troops. The team included mobile diagnostic imaging machines, traction devices, and mobile operating rooms capable of providing life-saving trauma care to wounded Soldiers. FSTs were also equipped to handle post-operative care for up to 6 hours.[12] If Soldiers needed more than 6 hours of care, team medical personnel would first stabilize them and then arrange for transportation to the rear for further care. During the mobile operations of March and April 2003, FSTs moved forward, staying close behind the combat units to receive and treat casualties, while the CSHs initially remained in Kuwait. As Major Mark Taylor of the 782d FST explained, "If a Soldier is shot, his buddies or himself provide initial first aid. . . . Then immediately they can be brought to us by helicopter or truck. Our job is to stop the bleeding, or protect their airways so they can breathe without the assistance of a machine. If they're shot in the intestines, we stop the soilage."[13] As the campaign transitioned to full spectrum operations in May 2003, the FSTs tended to merge into the CSHs, which deployed into Iraq and established operations at selected forward operating bases (FOBs) set up by Combined Joint Task Force–7 (CJTF-7).

Following the Wounded Soldier in Iraq

A Soldier wounded in Iraq initially received what Army medical doctrine called first-response treatment, the initial stabilizing medical care rendered at the point of injury. First aid was either performed by the casualty (self-aid) or another individual (buddy aid), while enhanced first aid was provided by Soldiers who had trained to be combat lifesavers (CLS), a designation that denoted capacity to give advanced first aid and lifesaving treatment. As OIF progressed from 2003 into 2004, units increased the amount of medical training their Soldiers received, including the use of newly developed bandages containing chemical clotting agents to stop blood loss from severe wounds.

Emergency medical treatment is the first of six phases of medical care in the Army medical system. To deliver these six phases of medical care, the Army organized its medical assets into five levels of treatment facilities—Level I to Level V. The difference between phases of care and levels of care is the difference between the type of care being provided and the type of facility providing the care. Higher-level facilities are usually capable of providing multiple phases of medical care, which also (generally) makes them larger and less mobile. Lower level facilities are much more mobile, but also have a much more limited scope of treatment and are generally focused on trauma management.[14] Level I assets are those medical resources and personnel at the unit level, usually at battalion and below, such as those Soldiers trained as CLS and medics, and the physician's assistants located in the battalion aid station. Soldiers wounded in Iraq benefited tremendously from several medical advances that were employed at Level I.

Perhaps the most dramatic of these changes was the introduction of fibrin and chitosan bandages, fielded just before OIF began in 2003. Fibrin bandages were a normal pressure

Six Phases of Medical Care	Five Levels of Medical Assets
Emergency Medical Treatment	Level I (Battalion)
Advanced Trauma Management	Level II (Division)
Forward Resuscitative Surgery	Level III (Combat Support Hospital)
Theater Hospitalization	Level IV (General or Field Hospital)
Convalescent Care	Level V (CONUS Support Base/ Fixed Facilities)
Definitive Care	

FM 4-02, February 2003

Figure 137. Six phases of medical care and five levels of medical assets.

dressing impregnated with two natural blood-clotting agents (fibrin and thrombin), freeze dried, and formed into something like a thin wafer of Styrofoam. These were developed jointly by the US Army and the American Red Cross for use by Special Operations Soldiers far from second-level medical care. The second type of bandage, the chitosan bandage, was jointly developed by the Army and the Oregon Medical Laser Center. These bandages contained chitosan, a biodegradable carbohydrate found in the shells of crustaceans such as shrimp and lobsters. When applied to a wound, the chitosan in the bandage accelerates clot formation to greatly reduce the rate of bleeding.[15] Colonel John B. Holcomb, who led the development team drawn from experts at Walter Reed Army Institute of Research and the American Red Cross, called them "a revolution in hemorrhage control on the battlefield."[16]

Another critical innovation arrived in the form of a new tourniquet. At one time medical specialists viewed tourniquets in disfavor, citing them as the cause of unnecessary amputations, especially when left in place too long. Studies revealed that 7 to 10 percent of battlefield deaths in Vietnam and Somalia were caused by profusely bleeding arm or leg wounds.[17] Accordingly, the Army developed a new combat application tourniquet (CAT): lightweight, equipped with a windlass for tightening the strap, and capable of locking in place once bleeding was under control. Holcomb, who was also a surgeon with the 10th CSH, said, "There is no prehospital device deployed in this war that has saved more lives than tourniquets."[18] The CAT could be applied by one person, including the victim, and most Soldiers carried one on patrol in Iraq.

After receiving buddy-aid, possibly including the use of a tourniquet, a wounded Soldier was then attended by a medic, physician's assistant, or physician at the battalion level, the second set of Level I personnel. Though varying by unit and mission, typical Army combat medics were attached to every company of 60 to 150 Soldiers. Infantry battalions enjoyed more medics with 1 medic attached to every platoon of 30 Soldiers. The combat medic is analogous to a civilian emergency medical technician (EMT) and certified to EMT standards. Many combat medics had additionally completed sophisticated training that allowed them to provide advanced cardiac life support (ACLS) and prehospital trauma life support (PTLS) in the field and en route to treatment facilities.[19]

The Army wartime medical system differed significantly from the civilian system. Civilian physicians are accustomed to treating their patients from diagnosis to recovery. In peacetime Army physicians also see their patients through to recovery, or until transfer to another hospital for more specialized care. In wartime this paradigm changes, reflecting the various phases of the Army medical system in a combat zone that involve a variety of doctors and nurses. This longstanding practice has been continually "rediscovered" by generations of Army physicians, civilian physicians mobilized to support military operations, and the media who see it as something radically new, which it is not.[20] The Army balances mobility and capability in its hospitals and does as much forward treatment as needed. Stabilized patients are then evacuated to the rear for more care. This may be from a medic to an aid station, from a FST to a CSH, or even back to the United States if the patient is not likely to recover soon.

After receiving emergency medical treatment in the unit, wounded Soldiers were then evacuated to a Level II facility to receive the second or third phase of casualty care, advanced trauma management or forward resuscitative surgery.[21] Level II or II+ facilities included FSTs or medical clearing companies that belonged to division forward support battalions and could be located at various places in relation to combat operations.[†] If close enough to an FST, injured Soldiers were driven to the team's location by ground ambulance (GA). However, as the improvised explosive device (IED) threat in Iraq mounted in the summer of 2003, most casualties were moved by air rather than risking more lives in unarmored ambulances. The FST provided emergency surgery to save life and limb, and prepared the wounded Soldier for evacuation to the next component of casualty care. Air ambulances (AA)—MEDEVAC helicopters—then evacuated the casualty, usually by taking the Soldier directly to one of the four CSHs established in Iraq during this period. The extensive use of MEDEVAC helicopters in OIF meant that wounded Soldiers could be quickly transported to the appropriate Level II or Level III facility based on their condition, time, and distance factors.

After Operation DESERT STORM in 1991, the Army invested heavily in transforming MEDEVAC helicopters from simple transportation vehicles to flying trauma-treatment centers. Although the UH-60 Blackhawk was the Army's main utility helicopter by 1991, roughly 75 percent of the MEDEVAC helicopters used in DESERT STORM were the Vietnam-era UH-1 "Huey." The Army's MEDEVAC version of the UH-60A Blackhawk used a specially designed, rotating patient-holding system to carry up to four wounded Soldiers. The Army then fielded the improved UH-60L Blackhawk MEDEVAC helicopter in 1997.[22] In OIF, the Army largely relied on the HH-60L, a specially modified Blackhawk helicopter that contained an oxygen-generating system, an infrared radar system for locating casualties, a reserve hoist, and a litter lift. The crew of the HH-60L included a medic and on occasion a physician's assistant or doctor. Medics on board used the brief transportation time to monitor wounded Soldiers' vital signs, administer resuscitative breathing, or manage bleeding if needed, all the while recording relevant data by writing on the patient's chests, arms, or legs.[23] Typically, as standing operating procedures (SOP) dictated, MEDEVAC Blackhawks were the only helicopters to fly unescorted during combat operations in OIF. If available, Apache escort helicopters would accompany them, but if poor weather grounded the Apaches, the Blackhawks flew alone. Medical evacuations could be very dangerous missions, especially when the enemy ignored the Red Cross markings and fired on the helicopters.[24]

In OIF, because of the extensive use of MEDEVAC AAs, few wounded Soldiers were more than 30 minutes from an FST or a CSH. This proximity placed Soldiers within easy range of surgical care and almost always ensured they could get into the operating room within the "golden hour"—the period in which a trauma victim must receive basic surgical treatment to significantly improve survival.[25] On a Soldier's arrival at an FST or CSH, the AA medic updated the waiting staff on the injured Soldier's condition and wounds. At that point, the FST or CSH staff assumed responsibility for the injured Soldier. After April 2003, however, as casualties were flown directly from point of injury to a CSH, reliance on the FSTs decreased.

[†]Forward surgical teams are labeled as a Level II+ treatment facility. As the Army's modular structure was implemented starting in very late 2004, forward support battalion medical assets became an organic part of the brigade combat team.

A Doctor Volunteers for the Campaign

The events of 9/11 changed the lives of millions of people, but for Dr. Lisa Dewitt the effects of that day would alter her direction in life. An emergency room physician and head of the residency program at Mt. Sinai Hospital in Miami Beach, Dewitt felt compelled to act after 9/11. She checked into the different military services and decided that joining the Army National Guard was the best way for her to serve her country. Dr. Dewitt deployed to Iraq in October 2003, only 6 months after being commissioned. Deploying on an individual 90-day rotation program, she initially joined the 161st Area Support Medical Battalion in Camp Victory, Kuwait. A month and a half later, the 161st redeployed and Dr. Dewitt ended up in Iraq at FOB Warhorse with the 1st Infantry Division's 3d Brigade Combat Team. After 9 days, Dr. Dewitt moved to FOB Normandy where she joined the 2d Battalion, 2d Infantry Regiment aid station and eventually served with the unit during Operation AL FAJR, the assault on the city of Fallujah in November 2004. Ultimately, Dr. Dewitt would spend 16 months in Iraq.

Although female doctors do not normally serve in infantry battalion aid stations, Dr. Dewitt was happy to be there and the unit's Soldiers were glad to have her. Physician's assistant, 1st Lieutenant Gregory D. McCrum remarked that Dr. Dewitt's trauma center experience was invaluable. "She's fantastic, she really, truly brings a different dynamic that we didn't have previously." Dr. Dewitt also worked with the local Iraqi clinics and hospitals doing assess-

ments and meeting with officials. She recalled her service with great pride, stating, "Treating American Soldiers is the greatest honor I've ever had in my entire life."

Operational Leadership Experience
interview with MAJ (Dr.) Lisa DeWitt, 23 April 2006.
Sergeant Kimberly Snow, "U.S. Army Maj. (Dr.) Lisa Dewitt:
Deployed Physician Maintains Enthusiasm,
Dedication to Troops, Duties,"
Defend America, 21 October 2004.

DOD photo

Dr. Lisa Dewitt treating wounded Soldier.

The CSHs in OIF were mobile facilities transported to a theater of operations in standard military cargo containers and assembled into self-contained tent hospitals. The CSH was a Level III medical facility in the Army's five-level system, and the highest-level asset deployed for OIF. The CSH provided the third phase of Army casualty treatment—theater forward resuscitative surgery (and in selected cases they also provided phase four care or theater hospitalization).[‡] A "full-up" CSH employed some 480 medical personnel working in support of 248 beds.[26] These hospitals also assumed the burden of treating wounded Iraqi soldiers, Iraqi civilians, as well as insurgents and terrorists. (As a signatory to the Geneva Conventions, the United States provides medical care to captured enemy fighters.)

According to Colonel Casper P. Jones III, commander of the 86th CSH, the primary mission of a CSH was to stabilize wounded Soldiers before their transfer out of Iraq to receive

---

[‡]Many Army CSHs have been deployed to OIF, both Active and Reserve units. The US Air Force has also deployed its version of the CSH to OIF.

treatment unavailable in theater.[27] Jones stated that the unit's main task was "resuscitative care. . . .Our job [was] to save life, limb and eyesight, to stabilize and move the patients."[28] The CSHs in Iraq, at Mosul, Baghdad, Tikrit, and Balad Air Base, were state-of-the-art emergency centers, with some of the best trained and experienced trauma surgeons and staffs in the world, encompassing a broad spectrum of medical specialties.[29] According to Colonel John Powell, M.D., commander of the 10th CSH, "We have gynecologists, we have a dentist, we have a facial surgeon, we have people who can take care of eyes. I mean, we have

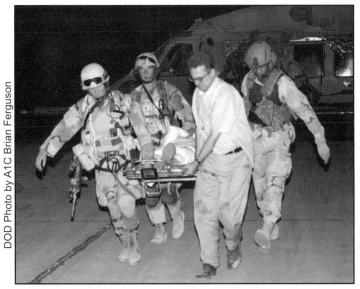

Figure 138. Pararescuemen from the 301st Expeditionary Combat Search and Rescue Squadron, Baghdad Air Base, Iraq, along with a UN paramedic and flight surgeon Major Nathaniel Russell, carry a patient from a UH-60 Pavehawk Helicopter to a waiting ambulance at Baghdad Air Base after the bombing of the UN headquarters in Baghdad.

infectious disease specialists, we have internal medicine physicians. We have to be able to do all the same things that a regular hospital does."[30]

Figure 139. Medics from 210th FSB and 303d ING Battalion carry wounded Iraqi soldiers to a helicopter.

The CSH was also capable of providing comprehensive care for Soldiers who were lightly wounded. Department of Defense (DOD) medical policy mandated out-of-theater evacuation for those Soldiers unable to return to duty quickly (within 2 to 4 days).[31] This rapid evacuation policy in OIF eliminated the need to establish a Level IV hospital in Iraq. With several in Iraq, transportation to the CSH from point of injury was extremely rapid. The availability of strategic airlift ensured wounded Soldiers were quickly evacuated out of theater directly to Level IV hospitals in Europe, and if necessary, on to Level V medical centers in the United States.

When an injured Soldier required a lengthy recovery time, the CSH transported him or her by helicopter to Balad Air Base in Iraq where they boarded aircraft and flew to Landstuhl, Germany, or to Rota, Spain, in specially equipped Air Force C-17 medical transport planes.[32]

Each plane was, in effect, a flying hospital, staffed with a doctor, nurse, medical technician, and state-of-the-art portable medical equipment.[33] This was the most sophisticated of the various forms of en route care provided to wounded Soldiers during OIF designed to hasten their trip to the next phase of medical care and the next level of medical-treatment facility.[34]

En route care was followed by the fifth and sixth phases of medical care: convalescent care and definitive care. The Army medical community designed these phases to return the Soldier to duty after recovery from illness or wounds, or if necessary, to prepare the Soldier for discharge from the Army. When a Soldier arrived at one of the US medical centers in Spain or Germany, physicians assessed the level of treatment required to determine where a Soldier would receive definitive care. If the length of stay was estimated to exceed 30 days, the Soldier was re-checked and sent to a support-base hospital or medical center in the United States. The most seriously wounded Soldiers were sent to either Walter Reed Army Medical Center in Washington, DC, or Brooke Army Medical Center in San Antonio, Texas.[35] If discharged, former Soldiers became eligible for further treatment, if necessary, via the Veterans Administration (VA).

During the Vietnam war, this journey from injury site to a stateside medical facility on average took 45 days. The medical system then in place was designed to cure as many patients as possible in Vietnam or to ensure they were fully stabilized before travel to the United States. In OIF, policy was to lower the medical "footprint" and use advanced medical technology and en route care to mitigate the travel risks for wounded Soldiers. During the first 18 months of the campaign in Iraq, the fastest recorded trip of a wounded Soldier from Iraq to the United States was 36 hours, but most averaged 4 days. For its troops in Iraq, the Army had developed a remarkable system of medical care that was the culmination of more than 150 years of progress since the US Civil War.

Personal Protection, Body Armor, and Casualty Rates

Various advances in medical care, from the point of injury to transportation and stateside medical treatment, greatly reduced casualty rates during OIF. New personal protective devices, often called body armor, played an equally important role in reducing casualties. Older style protective vests used before the mid-1990s were only useful in protecting against artillery shrapnel and low-velocity rounds. More sophisticated body armor, made from bullet-resistant Kevlar and ceramic plates, played a critical role in saving Soldiers' lives. Like the Kevlar helmet developed more than a decade earlier, the layered Kevlar vest was built to stop several shots from low velocity handgun and some high velocity rifle rounds.[36] The Interceptor vests that incorporated Kevlar covered a Soldier's torso, but not the Soldier's arms and legs. (See Chapter 12, "Logistics and Combat Service Support Operations," for an in-depth examination of the personal body armor issue.) According to Army nurse Captain Ruth M. Roettger-Lerg, "I would see shrapnel wounds on arms and they would stop right at the FLAK (*sic*) vest."[37] The body armor dramatically reduced deadly torso injuries, but legs and arms remained exposed, and many Soldiers who survived the initial blast suffered from traumatic wounds.[38]

Though body armor saved many lives from blasts and direct-fire weapons, it also compounded the treatment challenges for doctors who faced many more "polytrauma" injuries to Soldiers that historically would have died from damage to their unprotected vital organs. Captain Ed Dunton, a trauma nurse at the CSH in Baghdad, stated, "Back home, you see a car accident and it will be blunt trauma or a head injury, or single gunshot wounds . . . but here you get all that encompassed in a single patient: a head injury along with blunt trauma along with penetrating trauma."[39] Of those Soldiers involved in an IED blast who sustained head injuries, more than half sustained some neurological problems caused by skull-penetrating fragments or blows to the head.[40] Even when direct head trauma had not occurred, the concussive shock of the IED blast could cause Traumatic Brain Injury (TBI), a condition that could lead to a number of neurological problems. This particularly insidious wound was unfortunately far too common in Iraq. In 2003 the Defense and Veterans Brain Injury Center in Washington, DC, an organization affiliated with the DOD, screened 88 troops who had become blast victims in Iraq and identified 54 individuals (61 percent) with TBI.[41] According to one estimate more than 1,700 of the Soldiers wounded in Iraq during this period were diagnosed with brain injuries; of those, half were severe enough to impair thinking, memory, mood, behavior, and overall ability to work. The complexity of injuries to Soldiers was challenging not only for the medical teams at all levels of care, including postdischarge care from the VA, but also to the families of the wounded Soldiers.[42]

Improved helmets and other gear also reduced serious injuries, though not as dramatically as the new body armor. For example, the Army issued a variety of new protective safety glasses to Soldiers to reduce eye injuries. Once the Army made them more comfortable to wear with the new helmet design and more suitable to the hot, dusty conditions in Iraq, Soldiers began wearing the goggles; this sparked a corresponding reduction in eye injuries.[43] Of course, saving more lives in Iraq meant that a larger proportion of young men and women received treatment for serious injuries that affected them permanently, such as amputation and loss of vision.[44]

The wounds sustained during OIF reflect the character of the conflict. Roughly 62 percent of all US forces wounded by hostile action in OIF resulted from blast effects from artillery,

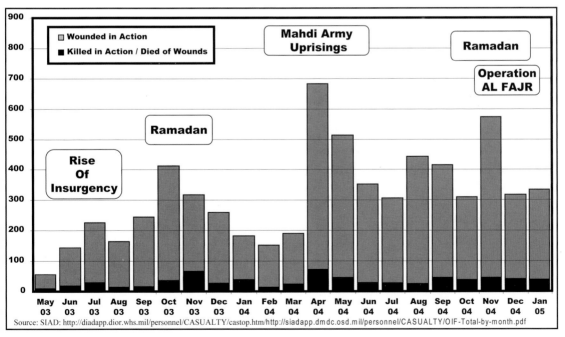

Figure 140. US Army Casualties, May 2003–January 2005.

mortars, and bombs of various types, including IEDs. Only slightly over 13 percent of US forces wounded in action were victims of small arms and other weapons.[45] According to a recent Congressional research report, which looked beyond the period covered in this study, roughly 80 percent of all Soldiers wounded in OIF suffered a single wound, while roughly 20 percent suffered multiple wounds. The same study reported 575 amputations during OIF. IEDs caused roughly 42 percent of those amputations.[46]

Statistics are a sterile way of accounting for the sacrifice of Soldiers in combat, but some empirical information is necessary for a complete understanding of the American effort in Iraq in 2003 and 2004. A brief analysis of Army casualties reveals that during the invasion of Iraq, 19 March 2003 to 30 April 2003, the US Army lost 66 Soldiers, 47 of them to hostile causes. During the period covered by this study (May 2003 to January 2005), the Army lost 885 Soldiers, 656 of them to hostile causes, while 6,636 Soldiers were wounded in action.[47] The casualty rate varied greatly from month to month based on the types of operations conducted by the Coalition, but peaked in the spring of 2004 and then again in the fall of 2004 during major operations against insurgent strongholds. Because the US Army had far more troops deployed than any other Service, it bore the brunt of the causalities, suffering roughly two-thirds of the total DOD losses during that period.[48] No statistic can capture the tragedy of even a single death or serious wound, and no historical analogy is perfect. However, this is a remarkably low casualty rate when compared to the Army's losses in conventional wars since World War II or when compared to its last major irregular conflict in Vietnam.

Because the methods of categorizing and recording casualties have changed over time, a thorough analysis of casualty statistics in various conflicts is beyond the scope of this work.[49] Nevertheless, some historical comparisons can highlight the advances made in US Army battlefield care. In World War II, roughly 4 percent of Soldiers who reached a medical treatment facility died of their wounds.[50] This ratio was lowered to around 3 percent during the Vietnam war.[51] In OIF the rate hovered just under 2.5 percent. Taken together, these figures show that medical treatment has been consistently excellent, with relatively minor improvements over time. But they are somewhat misleading because far more Soldiers injured by enemy action are now reaching a medical treatment facility to be treated in the first place. In other words, far more Soldiers are surviving being "hit" and are reaching advanced medical care than ever before.

This improvement was linked to various factors discussed in this chapter to include the widespread use of sophisticated body armor, new emergency treatment techniques, equipment used at or very near the injury site, and improved MEDEVAC methods. In World War II the survival rate for Soldiers "hit" by enemy fire has been estimated at around 70 percent, to include Soldiers killed outright (KIA) and those who later died of their wounds (DOW).[52] The survival rate for Soldiers hit by enemy fire in OIF has risen to just over 90 percent.[53] This increase is partly explained by the differing nature of combat in these two conflicts, but clearly this rate marks a significant success for the Army and for the Army medical system and its personnel.

Final Honors for the Fallen: Mortuary Affairs in Operation IRAQI FREEDOM

Although survival rates increased dramatically during OIF, some Soldiers still made the ultimate sacrifice. When a Soldier died, his or her remains were handled by Army Mortuary Affairs (MA) specialists. The 54th Quartermaster Company, the only Active Duty MA unit

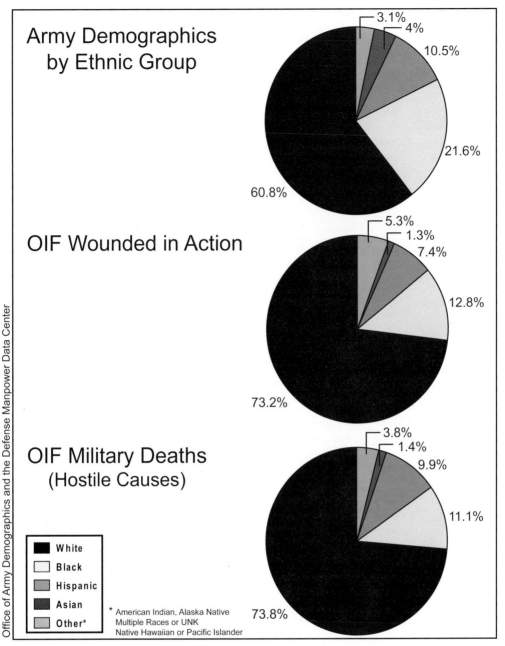

Army Demographics
by Ethnic Group

3.1%
4%
10.5%
21.6%
60.8%

OIF Wounded in Action

5.3%
1.3%
7.4%
12.8%
73.2%

OIF Military Deaths
(Hostile Causes)

3.8%
1.4%
9.9%
11.1%
73.8%

White
Black
Hispanic
Asian
Other*

* American Indian, Alaska Native
Multiple Races or UNK
Native Hawaiian or Pacific Islander

Office of Army Demographics and the Defense Manpower Data Center

Figure 141. OIF Army deaths by race/ethnicity, 19 March 2003–6 January 2007.

in the Army, operated all mortuary affairs operations in Iraq.[54] The US Army's Quartermaster Branch had the responsibility for all mortuary doctrine and training for the Armed Services. These Soldiers processed and evacuated the remains of all Soldiers from theater in accordance with the Concurrent Return Program, which stated that all US Soldiers would be returned to the United States.[55] Before the Korean war, Soldiers killed on foreign soil were usually buried in temporary graves to be disinterred after hostilities for permanent burial.[56] This created problems because the location of temporary graves was often lost. During the Korean war, the

USAF photo by MSgt James F. Bowman

Figure 142. Soldiers of a US Army disaster response mortuary affairs team bring supplies to aid the recovery process after a truck bombing at the UN headquarters building in Baghdad, Iraq.

remains of deceased Soldiers were immediately processed and shipped in refrigerated containers through Japan to the United States for internment.[57]

Soldiers lost in combat in OIF were remembered in multiple ways before being returned to the United States for burial. First, every unit would conduct a "fallen Soldier" ceremony at their base camp to render appropriate honor and respect. The unit then provided for the remains to be transported to a theater mortuary evacuation point (TMEP) facility at Camp Doha, Kuwait. At Camp Doha, a chaplain received the remains with a prayer and with Soldiers standing at attention and saluting the "angels" before they were transported back to the United States.[58]

Throughout all operations in Iraq, MA Soldiers maintained a high level of dignity and respect for the deceased Soldiers. Frederik Balfour, a journalist who gained permission to observe the MA unit, witnessed their dedication when he was in Iraq: "What truly distinguishes them as great Soldiers is the compassion and humanity they bring to their unenviable task."[59] According to Staff Sergeant Erik Thomsen, the job was a labor of love. Thomsen said, "We're the one job that nobody wants."[60] Located some distance from the frenetic activity of Camp Doha to preserve the dignity of every fallen Soldier, the MA Soldiers accepted that they were hidden from view and that their work received little public or media coverage.[61] According to Specialist Amelia Santoro, "It puts families at ease knowing somebody out there is taking care of them and that they're getting proper respect."[62] Thomsen wanted military families who lost loved ones in Iraq to know "that their loved ones, every step of the way, were treated with the full respect of the United States military. . . . To us," he said, "they're heroes."[63]

US Army Wounded Warrior Program

The impressive improvement in OIF survival rates for Soldiers with severe injuries has required changes in Army and VA medical programs to provide long-term assistance to Soldiers who would have likely died in previous conflicts. For US troops who survive their wounds, recovery can be a long, emotional, and physically trying experience for them and their families. Beginning in late 2003, the DOD and the Army introduced new measures to assist wounded Soldiers, especially those with amputations or permanently debilitating injuries. Advances in prosthetics and changes in Army policy have given Soldiers who have lost a limb or who have other permanent disabilities the opportunity to continue to serve if they desire. Many Army units detailed Soldiers from their rear detachments to assist wounded Soldiers and their families. To provide better medical and mental health support to wounded Soldiers, on 30 April 2004 the US Army announced the creation of the Disabled Soldier Support System (DS3). On 10 November 2005 the Secretary of the Army changed the name of the program to the US Army Wounded Warrior (AW2) Program. AW2 encompasses a range of programs such as medical treatment, career counseling, and options for continued military service despite disabilities, and transition training to the civilian world.

Instead of nearly automatic discharge from the Army after becoming disabled, changes in Army policy attempted to place Soldiers in other positions in which they could continue to serve if they so desired. According to General Peter Schoomaker, Army Chief of Staff, "Medical technology has advanced to the point where Soldiers injured today on the battlefield are much more likely to survive than those injured in previous wars. Soldiers enrolled in the US Army Wounded Warrior Program are also more often able to continue service to their Nation in the Army."[64] The AW2 Program included three phases: initial notification and evaluation, medical care and medical board evaluation, and either reintegration back into the Army or separation and transition to civilian employment. The program sought to closely integrate a Soldier's family into the entire process, and to include travel and lodging near Walter Reed, Brooke, and other Army medical centers during treatment.[65] Colonel Mary Carstensen, Director of AW2, stated, "Recovery is not limited to physical needs, but includes emotional, spiritual, financial, and occupational needs as well. Whatever it takes, we are committed to taking care of our own."[66]

Mental Health and Post-Traumatic Stress Disorder

Physical injuries were not the only challenges faced by Soldiers serving in Iraq. Soldiers also suffered mental health problems related to the stress of operations, the risks of death and wounds, and the death of fellow Soldiers, among other factors. As early as July 2003 the Army's Surgeon General launched what would become a series of studies on this issue. The first Mental Health Advisory Team (MHAT) visited Iraq in July 2003 to assess the scope of the mental health challenges in OIF and to recommend preventive actions and treatment. The team released its findings in December 2003. This and subsequent reports began tracking a wide number of mental health measures such as suicide rates, combat stressors, mental health treatment and evacuation rates, and post-traumatic stress disorder (PTSD) symptoms.[67] The

MHAT II report concluded that, compared to their 2003 findings, Soldiers in 2004 reported higher levels of combat stress (due to the risk of mortar, artillery, and IED attacks), but lower stress levels due to quality of life and family separation, higher individual and unit morale, lower suicide rates, fewer behavioral health problems requiring evacuation, and better access to mental health care in theater. The MHAT also noted, "Acute or post-traumatic stress symptoms remain the top mental health concern, affecting at least 10% of OIF-II Soldiers."[68] While invisible, PTSD is characterized by "depression, loss of interest in work or activities, psychic and emotional numbing, anger, anxiety, cynicism and distrust, memory loss and alienation, and other symptoms," affecting not only the Soldier, but sometimes the Soldier's family as well.[69]

The term PTSD was not adopted until 1980, but it was far from a new condition on the battlefield. In the Civil War it was sometimes called "soldier's heart." In World War I it went by other names such as shell shock, combat stress, and war neurosis. In the infancy of psychiatry and psychology, the problem was confused with malingering and cowardice. By the end of World War I, psychiatrists realized that psychiatric casualties did not suffer from physical harm inflicted from what was often labeled simple "shell shock." Psychiatrists determined that emotions, not physiological brain damage, most often caused Soldiers to reflect a wide range of symptoms.[70] Treatment used in World War II and the Korean war consisted of the fundamentals of "Proximity, Immediacy, and Expectation" (treat stress cases as close to their unit as possible, as soon as possible, and with the expectation that they will return to duty). These are still fundamental to Combat Stress Control (CSC) today.

It was the Vietnam war that propelled psychiatric issues into the limelight. The rate of PTSD among Vietnam veterans is extraordinarily complex and, like the war itself, it is also a politically charged issue. The debate includes disagreement over the symptoms of PTSD, testing methods, study timing and sample sizes, prior existing personal or family risk factors, the actual experiences of different types of veterans, and many other issues. The vast majority of Vietnam-era veterans, and those who actually served in Vietnam, reported no PTSD symptoms after their service. According to the results of the National Vietnam Veterans' Readjustment Study (NVVRS) published in 1990, an estimated 15.2 percent of male and 8.5 percent of female Vietnam era veterans were diagnosed with PTSD at one point in their lives.

PTSD is not strictly a military phenomenon; many nonmilitary causes such as personal or family crises, crime, or major accidents can trigger the symptoms of the disorder. The steady-state rate of PTSD in the general population has been estimated at between 5 and 10 percent. Civilians exposed to violent crime as victims or witnesses have been shown to incur PTSD rates as high as 24 percent.[71] Some veterans diagnosed with PTSD had preexisting or postservice risk factors in addition to their wartime service that appear to have played a role as well.[72] Seen in this light, PTSD rates for Soldiers serving in Vietnam and subsequent conflicts appear somewhat less dramatic. Nevertheless, the Vietnam war brought PTSD to the fore of Army medical preventive and postdeployment health care.

Despite the short period of combat during the Gulf War in 1990–91, studies showed a PTSD rate of between 10 and 16 percent.[73] In an attempt to better deal with psychological injuries in OIF, the Army employed mobile CSC Detachments. Operating out of six US bases across Iraq, these detachments were designed to identify combat Soldiers suffering from the early stages of PTSD.[74] According to the MHAT report, the accomplishments of the CSC Detachment fell somewhat short of expectations.[75] The survey reported that the detachments were too often overlooked and underused.[76] Following publication of the report, CSC Detachments were situated on forward support bases to better identify Soldiers exhibiting symptoms of extreme stress.[77] The forward deployment of these teams facilitated their work with Soldiers immediately following their traumatic experiences. This was an important step in reducing psychological problems both during and after deployment.[78] The 2005 MHAT report confirmed an overall improvement in mental health and well-being.[§] This was reflected in subsequent Soldier screenings that showed fewer cases of mental health problems.[79]

Medal of Honor	0
Distinguished Service Cross	3*
Silver Star	148
Distinguished Flying Cross	19
Soldier's Medal	51
Bronze Star Medal with "V" (Valor) Device	755
Air Medal for Valor	280
Army Commendation Medal with "V" (Valor) Device	2,090

*Distinguished Service Cross medals awarded in 2005 for actions in 2004.

Military Awards Branch, US Army HRC

Figure 143. Total number of decorations awarded, March 2003–January 2005.

Soldier Well-Being: Morale, Welfare, and Recreation (MWR) in Iraq

The Army spent considerable effort and resources to provide for the health and welfare of its Soldiers in Iraq in 2003 and 2004. In fact, by January 2005, living conditions for most Soldiers were idyllic compared to those experienced by the troops who fought in the World Wars. The effects of the generally comfortable conditions, however, were mitigated by the ever-present danger in a conflict without front lines and against shadowy enemy forces. During the many deployments after the end of the Cold War, the Army increasingly focused on maintaining the health and morale of its Soldiers by providing many of the comforts of home as close to the battlefield as possible. Most units operated out of bases on which they could relax and prepare for the next mission in relative safety. Providing that environment was a major effort for US commanders, combat service support units, MWR personnel, contractors, and others.

One of the Army's most important objectives was enabling the Soldier to communicate with family members. During the attack toward Baghdad in March 2003, and as units began to occupy areas within Iraq during April and May, communications systems for most tactical units were rudimentary at best. The 1st Battalion, 22d Infantry (TF 1-22 Infantry), part of the 4th Infantry Division headquartered in Tikrit, only obtained two phones for morale calls home

---

[§]Medical care for Soldiers after leaving Active Duty and as they transition to the VA medical system has received both praise and criticism. The treatment of Soldiers with nonphysical wounds has become a matter of intense scrutiny and effort in the period beyond the scope of this volume.

in August 2003, 3 months after the toppling of the Saddam regime.[80] According to Lieutenant Colonel Steve Russell, commander of TF 1-22 Infantry, even then there were obstacles because the desert heat damaged the electronic components of the satellite phones used for the calls. When the first fixed phone lines were installed on new FOBs over the summer of 2003, prices for calls were about five times the normal rate. Bowing to the demands from local commanders and the Army's senior leadership, commercial providers dramatically lowered prices. By 2004 phone calls home were routine for almost all Soldiers throughout Iraq.

Figure 144. Specialist Julio Miranda and Private First Class Eleny Guerrero unload a few of the thousands of pounds of turkey that have been shipped to troops in Iraq and Kuwait.

DOD Photo by SGM Larry Stevens

Yet, phone calls were just one avenue of communication home. The Army also established access to e-mail in August 2003 for the Soldiers of TF 1-22 Infantry and others all across Iraq. Three terminals were set up in the battalion headquarters for Soldiers to use on a rotating schedule.[81] Some units would spend their own funds to take care of their immediate needs as CJTF-7 built up its communications systems in Iraq's primitive infrastructure. In some cases, units took the initiative to construct their own link to home. The leaders of the 1st Battalion, 124th Infantry (1-124th IN), Florida Army National Guard, for example, used its own funds in 2003 to purchase a satellite terminal that provided an Internet link for their Soldiers.[82] In contrast to letters sent through the normal postal system, which could require up to 3 weeks or more to travel from the United States to units deployed in Iraq, Soldiers with Internet access could receive Web-cam pictures of family and friends in real time. This was a huge morale boost for the troops.[83] According to Staff Sergeant Jose Matias of 1-124th IN, "Before we had [the satellite], it was like being in the Dark Ages."[84] With the new satellite link to the Internet, Matias benefited from the psychological boost that came from talking with his wife and kids almost every day.[85] Eventually, most FOBs were equipped with an Internet Café; a subsequent Army study found that an overwhelming majority (95 percent) of Soldiers used these establishments to send and receive e-mail, with two-thirds using e-mail three or more times a week.[86]

Contact with home greatly enhanced morale, but the Army also provided many services at the FOBs to improve Soldiers' spirits in their down time. Unit leaders paid great attention, for example, to the quality of meals, recognizing the well-established link between food quality and Soldier health, effectiveness, and morale. The US Army has traditionally excelled in providing rations, or Class I supplies, to its Soldiers, and OIF was no exception. American Soldiers in the 1990s became accustomed to high-quality food service during the campaigns in

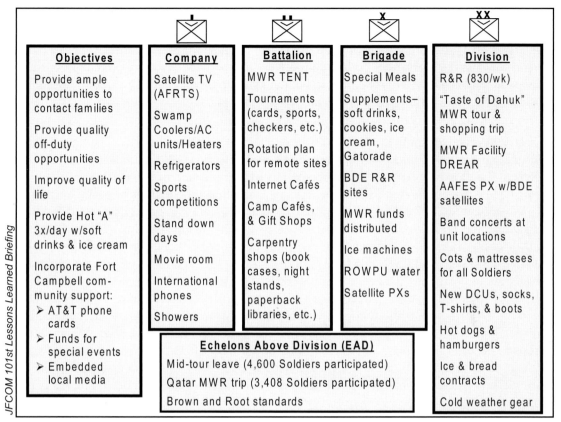

Objectives	Company	Battalion	Brigade	Division
Provide ample opportunities to contact families	Satellite TV (AFRTS)	MWR TENT	Special Meals	R&R (830/wk)
Provide quality off-duty opportunities	Swamp Coolers/AC units/Heaters	Tournaments (cards, sports, checkers, etc.)	Supplements– soft drinks, cookies, ice cream, Gatorade	"Taste of Dahuk" MWR tour & shopping trip
Improve quality of life	Refrigerators Sports competitions	Rotation plan for remote sites	BDE R&R sites	MWR Facility DREAR
Provide Hot "A" 3x/day w/soft drinks & ice cream	Stand down days	Internet Cafés Camp Cafés, & Gift Shops	MWR funds distributed	AAFES PX w/BDE satellites
Incorporate Fort Campbell com- munity support:	Movie room International phones	Carpentry shops (book cases, night stands, paperback libraries, etc.)	Ice machines ROWPU water Satellite PXs	Band concerts at unit locations
➤ AT&T phone cards	Showers			Cots & mattresses for all Soldiers
➤ Funds for special events				New DCUs, socks, T-shirts, & boots
➤ Embedded local media				Hot dogs & hamburgers

Echelons Above Division (EAD)
Mid-tour leave (4,600 Soldiers participated)
Qatar MWR trip (3,408 Soldiers participated)
Brown and Root standards

Ice & bread contracts

Cold weather gear

Figure 145. 101st Airborne Division's programs in support of Soldier morale.

the Balkans and elsewhere. After the initial problems with Class I supply during the offensive to Baghdad, packaged meals, ready to eat (MREs) were supplemented by portable mess facilities and, eventually, these in turn gave way to established dining facilities on most FOBs.[87] As FOBs became more developed over time, and smaller units were consolidated into FOBs that housed many thousands of Soldiers, food service grew even more elaborate. When the 1st Armored Division's fixed dining facilities in Baghdad opened in September 2003, they featured a wide selection of foods, including prime rib, crab legs, and baked salmon.[88] In other facilities, Soldiers could find salad bars, fast-food grills, and dessert counters featuring an array of pies, cakes, cookies, and even ice cream.[89]

The FOBs varied greatly in the quality of amenities they offered. At one extreme, some boasted swimming pools; at the other extreme, flush toilets were a much sought after luxury. The largest FOBs had well-stocked post exchanges (PXs) that resembled Wal-Mart stores, while the smallest were one-person operations with frequently barren shelves.[90] The bases also varied considerably in the recreational activities offered. Most battalions eventually established MWR tents that contained gyms and weight-lifting equipment. Some MWR tents were equipped with movie theaters, big-screen televisions, and recreation centers complete with pool, ping-pong, and foosball tables. Sports competitions and other tournaments became common as well. As in earlier conflicts, some Soldiers devoted their leisure hours to either reading books and newspapers or playing cards and board games. Most, however, brought entertainment with them in the form of DVDs (on televisions or computers), digital music, and computer games.[91]

Soldiers were also the beneficiaries of specific morale operations. Operation Slugger—established by the DHL Corporation, Louisville Slugger, USA Cares, Veterans of Foreign Wars, and the Association of the US Army (AUSA)—collected sporting goods that were assembled into sports kits then forwarded to Iraq for delivery to troops. Many other private groups conducted fundraising drives to send morale-building gifts to Soldiers in Iraq. Ambitious Soldiers also found ways to form archery clubs, jazz clubs, and bands for entertainment.[92]

Some have criticized the Army for these elaborate base camps, questioning their cost and effectiveness and claiming the Army's focus on them as misplaced priority. The financial cost of building the FOBs and providing extensive morale services is significant. The so-called "Balkan Syndrome," referring to the beginnings of this practice in the 1990s, has also been criticized because of its implications in campaigns that feature counterinsurgency operations. Significant amounts of equipment, transportation assets, command energy, support Soldiers, and contractors are devoted to sustaining the FOBs. Living on the FOB and making only occasional forays off base, so the argument goes, makes it more difficult for Soldiers to establish relationships with local Iraqis and Iraqi Security Forces (ISF) and to develop better situational awareness of conditions in specific communities. This practice also created suspicion in the minds of some Iraqis who believed the Coalition was deliberately failing to restore Iraq's decrepit infrastructure while living in virtual (and some actual) palaces. Many claimed that smaller, more numerous, and more dispersed camps would provide a more successful Coalition presence in contested areas, convincing the worried Iraqi citizens that the Coalition would sustain its commitment to protect them against the insurgents. And of course, within the US Army, the FOB lifestyle has generated a degree of divisiveness as Soldiers who routinely perform missions outside the FOB derisively refer to their FOB-bound headquarters and support Soldiers as "Fobbits."

While each of these criticisms has some merit, all must be balanced against certain benefits. The rest and relaxation provided by most FOBs was a crucial method of maintaining Soldier morale, health, and unit effectiveness during yearlong tours. In a war without rear areas, the large, well-defended FOBs provided the only safe area for Soldiers when not conducting operations. While some have maintained that US troops should have been more visible in Iraq in 2003 and 2004, others have argued that ever-present US troops exacerbated Iraqi fears of a long-term US occupation and further inflamed cultural tensions. Though beyond the timeframe of this book, during 2005 the Coalition steadily reduced the number of FOBs used by its troops and consolidated them into ever larger FOBs located outside major cities. As the ISF grew in number, this practice supported the goal of transitioning the campaign to the Iraqis.

United Service Organizations

Occasionally, Soldiering in Iraq afforded some troops an opportunity to attend one of the many variety shows that toured the country. Leading the way in entertainment for Soldiers stationed there was the 65-year old USO. Originally formed in 1941 in response to a request from President Franklin D. Roosevelt for on-leave recreational facilities that could serve a burgeoning US military establishment, the USO reached its high point in 1944 with a system of 3,000 clubs worldwide. The organization all but disbanded in 1947, but revived in 1950 with the outbreak of the Korean war. After supporting the roughly one million Soldiers deployed overseas during that conflict, the USO continued its tradition of providing entertainment throughout the 1950s and early 1960s. In 1963 the USO opened its first center to operate within a combat

Figure 146. Actor Robin Williams is surrounded by Soldiers during a holiday stop at Baghdad International Airport, Iraq.

zone in Saigon, Republic of Vietnam. In 1964 Bob Hope staged his first USO Christmas show in Vietnam, returning again and again for as long as US forces remained in theater. Throughout the closing decades of the Cold War, the USO continued to entertain troops stationed around the world. During Operations DESERT SHIELD and DESERT STORM, the USO established Mobile Canteen programs using all-terrain vehicles that USO workers drove to for-ward-deployed troops.[93]

In December 2003 the USO opened a center in Kuwait, and then opened one in Qatar in 2006.[94] Although safety, security, and logistics concerns precluded opening a full-time USO center in the Iraqi theater of operations, entertainers nonetheless brought their tours to Iraq.[95] Celebrities and entertainers who visited Soldiers in Iraq in 2003 and 2004 included the professional football cheerleaders for the Washington Redskins and Denver Broncos; comedians Robin Williams, Drew Carey, and Kathy Griffin; music stars Kid Rock, Jessica Simpson, Nick Lachey, Toby Keith, and Montgomery Gentry; entertainers from the World Wrestling Entertainment and Wayne Newton; actors Gary Sinise, James Gandolfini, Brian Dennehy, and Sean Penn; and many more. The first group, including actors Robert DeNiro and Alyssa Milano, visited Iraq with General Tommy Franks in May 2003.

Figure 147. A US Army Soldier gets a handshake and an autograph from "Stone Cold" Steve Austin, World Wrestling Entertainment, at the CPA Headquarters in Baghdad, Iraq.

Leave and Redeployment Policy

While living on most FOBs afforded Soldiers the opportunity to release the tension caused by day-to-day operations in relative safety, yearlong tours put great strain on Soldier endurance and family support. At the urging of CJTF-7 and CENTCOM, the Army mandated yearlong tours in July 2003 for reasons of practicality, but primarily because it was felt that the character of the full spectrum campaign required extended time in theater for Soldiers to understand the complex environment and make connections with their Iraqi counterparts and Iraqi citizens. This was in contrast to the 6-month rotations common in the Balkans after 1995 and in Afghanistan prior to the fall of 2003. On 25 September 2003 CENTCOM established a rest and recuperation (R&R) leave program for Service members serving in Iraq for 12 months.[96] Soldiers were flown to Europe or the United States for up to 15 days of annual leave. Every Soldier serving in OIF for a year was authorized the leave, and units developed plans to maintain unit operational tempo while simultaneously rotating Soldiers home for leave. Initially the program accommodated about 270 Soldiers daily, but by December 2003 that number had increased to roughly 480 per day. It was to be the military's largest leave program since the Vietnam war.[97]

Although the vast majority of Soldiers reported no significant or long-lasting readjustment problems, some Soldiers experienced a range of difficulties. The connection between military deployments and effects on marriage has been studied for years and has proven difficult to analyze because of the many factors involved and the wide range of personal and family relationships. Multiple deployments, especially those occurring back-to-back, predictably evoked even greater family stress levels. As one Army spouse whose husband deployed to Iraq with the 3d Armored Cavalry Regiment (3d ACR) from April 2003 to April 2004 explained, "Families are dealing with a great deal of stress and uncertainty and many children are bearing the brunt of this situation. Multiple deployments can be greatly disruptive to the normal family routine."[98] During the early stages of OIF, the institutional Army and unit support groups worked to help families adapt to the numerous complex issues that attend a deployment. The Army also created various types of screening and voluntary and mandatory programs for returning Soldiers to identify and ameliorate adjustment problems. The same spouse stated, "The Army has done a superb job of determining what challenges the families face and addressing those specific challenges by employing its various support agencies."[99] The services available to returning Soldiers and their families were invaluable in helping ease the transition from war zone to home.

Family Readiness Groups (FRGs) were another important source of support for families and Soldiers during OIF. FRGs evolved out of informal support groups common throughout the Army since its very earliest days. Commanders and noncommissioned officers' wives, supported by the unit chain of command, on an informal basis traditionally provided all kinds of assistance to families during deployments and war. By the 1990s FRGs became required programs in deployable units; some positions were filled with full-time workers, and spouse volunteers received formal training on their roles. The FRG's primary mission was to provide mutual support, offer official and accurate command information to its members, and generally reduce the stress caused by deployments.[100] Throughout the OIF rotations, the FRG network strove to support families of deployed Soldiers. The FRGs and the military pooled resources and provided families with the specific services they needed. This enabled Service members to concentrate fully on discharging duties in Iraq by relieving them from troubling preoccupations about family matters.[101] The FRG served as the primary medium for distributing information to deployed Soldiers' families. According to Dianna Emmou, the wife of Sergeant First Class Frank Emmou who deployed to Iraq with the 3d ACR, "The FRG provides information to family members regarding Soldiers, casualties, the unit, the area in which the unit was serving, recognition of media coverage for the unit, special events being held at home, meetings, and other related information."[102]

The FRG was not the only program available to families looking for support during deployments. Many Soldiers and family members relied on the Army Community Service (ACS) that provided a variety of programs from employment to parenting to family advocacy. Also available was the recently developed Military One Source, a service staffed by social workers that answered "everything, anywhere, anytime, 24/7, every day of the year."[103] The Army also initiated a Building Strong and Ready Families Program during weekend retreats to help couples develop better intrafamily communications skills during deployments. Similarly, the Strong Bonds Marriage Education Program focused specifically on issues affecting Reserve and National Guard couples.[104]

Some mobilized National Guard and Reserve Soldiers encountered unique challenges in these areas. Many Reserve Component units tended not to have active FRGs or other related programs that were extensively available to their Active Duty counterparts. Unlike Active Duty and National Guard Soldiers, Reservists often mobilized for deployment to Iraq as individuals and were attached to Active or Reserve units with which they had no peacetime connection. Such deployments made it more challenging for individually mobilized Soldiers and their families to take advantage of all the benefits available to them when they were placed on Active Duty. The experiences of Lieutenant Colonel Phil Andrews, a Reservist who served as the Information Operations Officer, Multi-National Corps–Iraq (MNC-I), explained the challenges this created: "My family had no contact with my deployed unit's FRG. I was deployed to augment the Civil Affairs rotation to OIF after they had been in Iraq for several months. The Civil Affairs unit was based in New York and my family lives in Kansas City."[105] Army National Guard (ARNG) units tended to deploy as units, though this was not universally true, and thus existing family and local support systems tended to be more effective. The ARNG and US Army Reserve (USAR) have moved rapidly to develop new solutions to support individual Soldiers and their families in this situation. Andrews believed that the Military One Source program was a step in the right direction.[106] Conversely, some Guard and Reserve units were drawn from local areas in which their social, work, and Army ties were quite strong, providing a natural support system as strong as any Active Duty unit.

Conclusion

During OIF the US Army devoted immense effort and resources to improving and sustaining its Soldiers' quality of life. The phrase "taking care of Soldiers," long a motto of the Army's Noncommissioned Officer (NCO) Corps, included a vast array of programs in OIF to protect the Soldiers' physical and mental health, to maintain their morale during off-duty periods, to sustain them over the long duration of year or year-plus tours, and perhaps most important, to treat them when they became a casualty in battle. Though sometimes criticized for the cost or for creating an occupation mentality not suited to overall campaign objectives, the effort is consistent with the gradual evolution of the Army's support for its Soldiers. Living on well-equipped FOBs provided Soldiers in this period of OIF with the only respite available from the 360-degree threat environment of full spectrum operations.

In a parallel effort, the Army has improved its programs to support the Soldiers' families before, during, and after deployments. The greatly expanded use of the ARNG and USAR exposed the need to better prepare and support those Soldiers and their families. They faced the same challenges as their Active Duty brothers and sisters, as well as challenges unique to their Reserve status. Expanded counseling programs, family support groups, the R&R leave program, and instantaneous communications via the Internet shrunk the vast distances between Soldiers in Iraq and their families at home.

The Army's greatest accomplishment in taking care of its Soldiers during this period of OIF was in the areas of emergency medical treatment and evacuation. Changes in doctrine, such as locating surgical teams further forward and rapid evacuation back to Level IV or Level V hospitals provided wounded Soldiers with more advanced care sooner than ever before. Improvements in personal protective gear and vehicle survivability, when combined with the tactical superiority of US Soldiers, kept overall casualty levels low. Improved trauma equipment such as clotting bandages and improved tourniquets saved many Soldiers who would have died of their wounds just a few years before OIF.

Advances in prosthetics and the AW2 Program allowed recovered Soldiers to continue to service in the Army with injuries that would have been grounds for discharge in previous wars. Indeed, many Soldiers wounded in OIF were determined to continue to serve the Army in whatever capacity their physical conditions would allow. In a great number of cases, Soldiers who suffered debilitating injuries saw the event as changing the nature of their service, not ending it. Unlike civilians drafted for temporary service in wartime, many volunteer Soldiers made a lifetime commitment when joining the Army. In 2003 and 2004, the Army continued and expanded on the long-standing tradition of treating its Soldiers as truly its "greatest asset."

Notes

1.   Only 2.47 percent of service members wounded in Iraq have died of their wounds after being evacuated to higher-level medical care outside of Iraq (545 of 22,057 total as of 2 December 2006). "Military Casualty Information," DOD Personnel and Military Casualty Statistics, US Department of Defense, http://siadapp.dior.whs.mil/personnel/CASUALTY/castop.htm (accessed 5 January 2007).

2.   John T. Greenwood and F. Clifton Berry Jr., *Medics at War: Military Medicine from Colonial Times to the 21st Century* (Annapolis, MD: Naval Institute Press, 2005), 5.

3.   Greenwood and Berry, 30–33.

4.   Greenwood and Berry, 50–52.

5.   David Zucchino, "Bringing Back the Wounded With Heart, Soul, and Surgery," *Los Angeles Times*, 2 April 2006, http://www.latimes.com/news/nationworld/nation/la-na-wounded2apr02,1,4738485.story?coll=la-health-medicine (accessed 15 August 2006).

6.   Greenwood and Berry, 76. A good portion of the disease related deaths were caused by the 1918 flu pandemic.

7.   Greenwood and Berry, 113–114.

8.   Greenwood and Berry, 123–126; see also, Frank A. Reister, *Battle Casualties and Medical Statistics: U.S. Army Experience in the Korean War* (Washington, DC: Office of the Surgeon General, 1986).

9.   Greenwood and Berry, 138, 140.

10.   Greenwood and Berry, 158–159. The Army also benefited from having deployed a very substantial medical care system to Iraq and having to deal with very few combat casualties during the "100-Hour War."

11.   Greenwood and Berry, 172–173. The post-Gulf War drawdown that substantially reduced the number of hospitals in the Army inventory also drove the greater emphasis on evacuation out of theater.

12.   Lawrence F. Kaplan, "America's Near-Invisible Wounded," *The New Republic*, 2 October 2003, http://www.trn.com/doc.mhtml?i=20031013&s=kaplan101303 (accessed 12 September 2006); Atul Gawande, M.D., M.P.H., "Casualties of War—Military Care for the Wounded from Iraq and Afghanistan," *The New England Journal of Medicine*, 251:24, 9 December 2004, 2472, http://content.nejm.org/cgi/reprint/351/24/2471.pdf (accessed 22 August 2006).

13.   Michael Peck, "'Golden Hour' Surgical Units Prove Worth," *Military Medical Technology Online*, Volume 7, Issue 5 (9 August 2006), http://www.military-medical-technology.com/article.cfm?DocID=176 (accessed 11 August 2006).

14.   Field Manual (FM) 4-02, *Force Protection in a Global Environment* (Washington, DC, February 2003), 1-2 to 1-3, 2-5 to 2-7, and appendix C.

15.   US Army Medical Command, "High Tech Bandages," *AMEDD Innovations Since Desert Storm*, http://www.armymedicine.army.mil/about/tl/factsbandages.htm (accessed 31 October 2006).

16.   Andrea Stone, "High-Tech Bandages Designed to Save Lives," *USA Today,* 25 February 2003, http://www.tricare.osd.mil/eenews/downloads/HighTechBandages.doc (accessed 31 October 2006).

17.   Karen Fleming-Michael, "New tourniquet named one of Army's 10 greatest inventions," *Army News Service*, 22 June 2006, http://www.globalsecurity.org/military/library/news/2006/06/mil-060622-arnews03.htm (accessed 22 August 2006).

18.   Fleming-Michael; David Zucchino, "War Brings Advances in Protection and Care," *Los Angeles Times*, 3 April 2006, http://www.latimes.com/features/health/medicine/la-na-woundedside-3apr03 (accessed 14 August 2006); "Army's new life-saving training aims to cut combat deaths," *EMS House of DeFrance*, 29 April 2005, http://www.defrance.org/artman/publish/article_1323.shtml (accessed 16 August 2006).

19. Lieutenant Commander Charles J. Gbur Jr., MC, USNR, 3/25 Battalion Surgeon, "Battalion Aid Station Support of Military Operations in Urban Terrain (BASS MOUT)," http://www.geocities.com/Pentagon/6453/bassmout.html (accessed 15 August 2006).

20. The evocative name that the public will recognize comes from the television program "M*A*S*H" and is "meatball surgery." See "The Medical Frontline of War," *CBS News*, 4 June 2006, http://www.cbsnews.com/stories/2006/06/04/Sunday/printable1680075.shtml (accessed 16 August 2006); see also, Gawande, 2473.

21. FM 4-02, 1-2.

22. US Army Medical Command, "UH-60L Medevac Helicopter," *AMEDD Innovations Since Desert Storm*, http://www.armymedicine.army.mil/about/tl/97-factsuh60l.htm (accessed 31 October 2006).

23. Staff Sergeant Gregory Givings, interview by Colonel Richard Van Ness Ginn, 20 August 2003, Falls Church, VA, AMEDD Oral History Program, Operation Iraqi Freedom, Interview OIF-067, Draft Transcripts (14 January 2004), from the Office of Medical History, Directorate of Health Care Operations, Office of the Surgeon General, US Army Medical Department, 9; Leslie Sabbagh, "Birds of Mercy," *Popular Mechanics*, October 2005, http://www.popularmechanics.com/science/defense/1894752.html (accessed 21 August 2006).

24. Sabbagh.

25. David Zucchino, "The Journey Through Trauma," *Los Angeles Times*, 3 April 2006, http://www.latimes.com/news/nationworld/nation/la-na-wounded2apr03,1,5197239.story?coll=la-health-medicine (accessed 14 August 2006).

26. FM 8-10-14, *Employment of the Combat Support Hospital Tactics, Techniques, and Procedures* (Washington, DC, 1994), 2-2, https://akocomm.us.army.mil/usapa/doctrine/DR_pubs/dr_aa/pdf/fm8_10_14.pdf (accessed 22 August 2006). This manual is currently under revision as FM 4.02-10.

27. Steven Donald Smith, "HBO Film 'Baghdad ER' Examines Combat Hospital," *American Forces Press Service*, 17 May 2006, http://www.defenselink.mil/news/May2006/20060517_5149.html (accessed 22 August 2006); FM 8-10-14, 2-1.

28. Smith.

29. Specialist Rick Rzepka, "Men and Women of Combat Support Hospital dedicate themselves to saving lives here," *MNF-Iraq.com*, 25 February 2006, http://www.mnf-iraq.com/index.php?option=com_content&task=view&id=194&Itemid=42 (accessed 22 August 2006).

30. "Life and Death in a War Zone," *PBS Airdate*, 2 March 2004, NOVA transcript, http://www.pbs.org/wgbh/nova/transcripts/3106_combatdo.html (accessed 22 August 2006).

31. FM 8-10-14, 1-1 and 2-22; Gawande, 2472.

32. Lieutenant Colonel David Vetter, interview by Major Lewis Barger, 21 May 2003, Camp Wolf, Kuwait, AMEDD Oral History Program, Operation Iraqi Freedom, Interview OIF-522, Draft Transcript (23 September 2003), from the Office of Medical History, Directorate of Health Care Operations, Office of the Surgeon General, US Army Medical Department, 9.

33. Zucchino, "Bringing Back the Wounded With Heart, Soul, and Surgery."

34. FM 4-02, 2-5 to 2-7.

35. Gawande, 2473.

36. Benny Evangelista, "Kevlar saving lives, minimizing wounds in Iraq," *San Francisco Chronicle*, 7 April 2003, http://www.sfgate.com/cgi-bin/article.cgi?file=/chronicle/archive/2003/04/07/BU275282.DTL&type=business (accessed 22 August 2006).

37. Captain Ruth M. Roettger-Lerg, interview by Mr. Ron Still, 24 July 2003, Wurzburg, Germany, AMEDD Oral History Program, Operation Iraqi Freedom, Interview OIF-046, Final Transcript (7 September 2004), from the Office of Medical History, Directorate of Health Care Operations, Office of the Surgeon General, US Army Medical Department, 16.

38. Gawande.

39.   Zucchino, "War Brings Advances in Protection and Care."

40.   Denise Grady, "Struggling Back From War's Once-Deadly Wounds, *The New York Times*, 22 January 2006, http://www/nytimes/com/2006/01/22/national/22wounded.html (accessed 22 August 2006).

41.   Defense and Veterans Brain Injury Center, "Blast Injury" Information, http://www.dvbic.org/cms.php?p=Blast_injury (accessed 19 December 2007).

42.   Michael E. O'Hanlon and Nina Kamp, "Iraq Index: Tracking Variables of Reconstruction & Security in Post-Saddam Iraq," The Brookings Institution, 30 May 2006, 6, www.brookings.edu/iraqindex (accessed 22 August 2006).

43.   Gawande, 2473.

44.   Brad Knickerbocker, "In Iraq, fewer killed, more are wounded," *The Christian Science Monitor*, 29 August 2006, http://www.csmonitor.com/2006/0829/p03s02-usmi.html (accessed 30 August 2006).

45.   DOD, "Military Casualty Information."

46.   Hannah Fischer, *United States Military Casualty Statistics: Operation Iraqi Freedom and Operation Enduring Freedom, Report RS22452*, Congressional Research Service, 8 June 2006, http://www.fas.org/sgp/crs/natsec/RS22452.pdf (accessed 19 December 2006).

47.   DOD, "Military Casualty Information."

48.   The Army generally provided more than two-thirds of the number of troops deployed to Iraq, so it may have suffered fewer casualties than its proportion of total deployed forces. This issue is outside the scope of *ON POINT II*, but it bears further study. DOD, "Military Casualty Information."

49.   Records keeping and changing terminology make direct comparisons nearly impossible. To cite one example, during World War II "battle wounds" were differentiated from "battle injuries"—wounds were caused by the enemy, e.g., getting shot, while injuries, such as breaking a wrist while diving into a fighting position during an artillery attack, were recorded separately. By Vietnam, the term "battle injury" included any physical injury incurred primarily or secondarily as a result of hostile action. For another discussion of the complexities of measuring and assessing battlefield casualties, evacuation, and treatment issues, see Colonel (Retired) Ronald Bellamy, "A Note on American Combat Mortality in Iraq*," Military Medicine*, Volume 172, October 2007.

50.   See Colonel John Lada, "Medical Statistics in World War II," in *The United States Army in World War II* (Washington, DC: Office of the Surgeon General, 1975).

51.   DOD, "Military Casualty Information."

52.   Lada; see also, Gilbert W. Beebe and Michael E. DeBakey, *Battle Casualties: Incidence, Mortality, and Logistic Considerations* (Springfield, IL: Charles C. Thomas, Pub., 1952).

53.   DOD, "Military Casualty Information"; see also Gawande, 2473.

54.   Staff Sergeant Daniel J. Seymour, "Mortuary Affairs Support In the Iraqi Theater of Operations," *Quartermaster Professional Bulletin*, Spring 2005, http://www.quartermaster.army.mil/oqmg/professional_bulletin/2005/Spring05/Mortuary%20Affairs%20Support%20in%20the%20Irai%20Theater%20of%20Operations (accessed 10 October 2006).

55.   Captain Shannon V. Stambersky, "A Lesson in Dignity in the Iraqi Desert," *Quartermaster Professional Bulletin*, Spring 2005, http://www.quartermaster.army.mil/oqmg/professional_bulletin/2005/Spring05/Mortuary%20Affairs%20Support%20in%20the%20Irai%20Theater%20of%20Operations (accessed 10 October 2006).

56.   Captain Arnd Frie et al, "Fallen Comrades: Mortuary Affairs in the US Army," *Army Mortuary Affairs History page,* http://www.qmfound.com/fallen.htm (accessed 10 October 2006).

57.   Frie et al.

58.   Frederik Balfour, "A Wartime Oasis of Selfless Compassion," *BusinessWeek Online*, 15 April 2003, http://www.businessweek.com/bwdaily/dnflash/apr2003/nf20030415_8932.htm (accessed 10 October 2006).

59. Balfour.

60. Anita Powell, "Mortuary affairs specialists perform a labor of love," *Stars & Stripes Mideast Edition*, 13 November 2005, http://www.estripes.com/article.asp?section=104&article=32152&archive =true (accessed 10 October 2006).

61. Powell; Balfour.

62. Balfour.

63. Powell.

64. Office of the Chief of Public Affairs, "US Army Wounded Warrior Program Assists Soldiers," 10 November 2005, http://www4.army.mil/ocpa/print.php?story_id_key=8185 (accessed 31 October 2006).

65. US Army Wounded Warrior Program Web site, http://www.armyfamiliesonline.org (accessed 31 October 2006).

66. Public Affairs, "US Army Wounded Warrior Program Assists Soldiers."

67. US Army Medical Department, *Mental Health Reports (OIF)*, http://www.armymedicine. army.mil/news/mhat/mhat.html (accessed 2 January 2007). Note: Since the first MHAT report, two more reports have been released—MHAT II in January 2005, and MHAT III in December 2006.

68. US Army Medical Department, *Mental Health Reports (OIF)*, Operation Iraqi Freedom Mental Health Advisory Team (MHAT-II) Report, 30 January 2005, http://www.armymedicine.army.mil/news/ mhat/mhat_ii/OIF-II_REPORT.pdf (accessed 2 January 2007).

69. Steve Bentley, "A Short History of PTSD: From Thermopylae to Hue Soldiers Have Always Had A Disturbing Reaction To War," *The VA Veteran*, March/April 2005, originally published January 1991, http://www.vva.org/TheVeteran/2005_03/feature_HistoryPTSD.htm (accessed 23 August 2006).

70. Bentley, "A Short History of PTSD."

71. Heidi S. Resnick, Ph.D., and Dean G. Kilpatrick, Ph.D., "Crime Related PTSD: Emphasis on Adult General Population Samples," National Crime Victims Research and Treatment Center and Medical University of South Carolina, US Department of Veterans Affairs, http://www.ncptsd.va.gov/ publications/rq/rqhtml/V5N3.html (accessed 31 October 2006).

72. Jennifer L. Price, Ph.D., "Findings from the National Vietnam Veterans' Readjustment Study: A National Center for PTSD Fact Sheet," US Department of Veterans Affairs, http://www.ncptsd.va.gov/ facts/veterans/fs_NVVRS.html (accessed 31 October 2006).

73. Matthew J. Friedman, M.D., Ph.D., "Acknowledging the Psychiatric Cost of War," *The New England Journal of Medicine*, 351:1, 1 July 2004, 75; and Jennifer L. Price, Ph.D., "Effects of the Persian Gulf War on US Veterans," A National Center for PTSD Fact Sheet, United States Department of Veterans Affairs, http://www.ncptsd.va.gov/facts/veterans/fs_gulf_war_illness.html (accessed 24 August 2006).

74. Jonathan Finer, "Battle-Hard G.I.'s Learn to Release their Pain," *Washington Post Foreign Service*, 14 June 2005, http://www.hws,edu/akumni/alumnews/showclip.asp?webslip=2191 (accessed 14 August 2006).

75. *Operation Iraqi Freedom (OIF) Mental Health Advisory Team (MHAT) Report*, 16 December 2003, Chartered by US Army Surgeon General, http://www.armymedicine.army.mil/news/mhat_ii/OIF-II_REPORT.pdf#search=%22Army%20Mental%20Health%20Advisory%20Team%20survey%202003 %22 (accessed 24 August 2006).

76. T. Trent Gegax, "Wartime Stress: Poor morale and high suicide rates point to big problems for troops in Iraq," Web Exclusive, *Newsweek*, *MSNC.com*, 2 April 2004, http://www.msnbc.msn.com/ id/4632956/site/newsweek/ (accessed 24 August 2006).

77. Christiane Amanpour, "Brain Rangers' Fight Iraq Stress," *60 Minutes, CBS News*, 27 February 2005, http://www.cbsnews.com/stories/2005/02/25/60minutes/main676553.shtml (accessed 24 August 2005).

78. "Combat Stress Team Helps Troops Cope," *Defend America*, 5 November 2004, http://www. defendamerica.mil/articles/nov2004/a110504e.html (accessed 24 August 2006).

79. *OIF MHAT Report*, 30 January 2005, 3-4.

80.	Lieutenant Colonel Steve Russell, Commander, TF 1-22 Infantry, Command Correspondence "Dear Family and Friends," 20 June–24 August 2003.

81.	Russell.

82.	Nick Wakeman, "Satellite communications boost troops' morale in Iraq," *Washington Technology*, 24 November 2003, http://www.washingtontechnology.com/cgi-bin/udt/im.display. printable?client.id+wtonline (accessed 25 August 2006).

83.	Wakeman.

84.	William Jackson, "Internet cafes are morale booster for troops in Iraq," *Government Computer News*, 24 November 2003, http://www.gcn.com/cgi-bin/udt/im.display.printable?client.id=gcn&story. id=24241 (accessed 25 August 2006).

85.	Jackson.

86.	Doug Swanson, "All the Comforts of War," originally published in the *Dallas Morning News*, *PE.com*, 10 June 2006, http://www/pe/com/cgi-bin/bi/gold_print.cgi (accessed 25 August 2006).

87.	"The Fight for Fallujah, TF 2-2 IN FSE AAR," *Field Artillery*, March–April 2005, 10.

88.	Kenneth W. Estes, "Command Narrative: 1st Armored Division in Operation IRAQI FREEDOM, May 2003–July 2004." Unpublished study, 105.

89.	Swanson.

90.	Swanson.

91.	James Dunnigan, "Why The Xbox is Important in the Iraq War," *www.strategypage.com*, 12 February 2005, http://www.strategypage.com/dls/articles/200521223.asp?source=send (accessed 25 August 2006).

92.	Staff Sergeant Richard Dashiell, "The Steel Snake Archery Club, Iraq," *www.texasarchery. org*, http://www.texasarchery.org/L1/IAC.htm (accessed 25 August 2006); Sergeant Enrique S. Diaz, "Troops Add Jazz to Recreation Center," *www.mnf-iraq.com*, 14 July 2006, http://www.mnf-iraq.com/ index2php?option=com_content (accessed 25 August 2006); Private First Class Sean Finch, "V Corps 'Garage Band' Revs up to Rock Soldier Morale in Iraq," Multi-National Corps–Iraq Public Affairs Office, 17 February 2006.

93.	United Service Organizations, "History of the USO," *USO.org*, http://www.uso.org/whoweare/ ourproudhistory/historyoftheuso/ (accessed 30 August 2006).

94.	"History of the USO"; Jared A. Taylor, "With No Camp in Iraq, USO Does What It Can," *Kansas City InfoZine*, 17 August 2006, http://www.infozine.com/news/stories/op/stories (accessed 25 August 2006).

95.	Taylor.

96.	"US Central Command Unveils R&R Leave Program," *CENTCOM Press Release*, 25 September 2003, http://www.centcom.mil/sites/uscentcom1/Lists/Press%20Releases/AllItems.aspx (accessed 30 August 2006).

97.	Aliza Marcus, "US leave program gets a boost, along with troops," originally published in *The Boston Globe*, *boston.com*, 2 December 2003, http://www.boston.com/news/nation/articles/2003/12/02/ us_leave-orogram-gets-a-boost/ (accessed 25 August 2006).

98.	Ms. Dianna Emmou, e-mail interview by Contemporary Operations Study Team, Fort Leavenworth, KS, 31 July 2006.

99.	Emmou, e-mail interview, 31 July 2006.

100.	*Army Commander's Guide to Family Readiness Group Operations*, 1-2, http://www.hooah-4health.com/deployment/familymatters/24Sept05_CDRsGuide.doc (accessed December 2007).

101.	"Make the Most of Family Readiness Groups," *U.S. Army HOOAH 4 HEALTH.com.* http:// www.hooah4health.com/4life/hooah4family/frg.htm# (accessed December 2007).

102.	Emmou, e-mail interview, 31 July 2006.

103.	Ms. Ann Soby, interview by Contemporary Operations Study Team, Fort Leavenworth, KS, 31 July 2006.

104. Donna Miles, "Reducing the Military Divorce Rate," *American Forces Press Service*, 13 June 2005.

105. Lieutenant Colonel Phil Andrews, e-mail interview by Contemporary Operations Study Team, Fort Leavenworth, KS, 1 September 2006.

106. Andrews, e-mail interview, 1 September 2006.

Part V

Conclusion

Chapter 14

Implications

The first, the supreme, the most far reaching act of judgment that the statesman and commander have to make is to establish . . . the kind of war on which they are embarking, neither mistaking for, nor trying to turn it into, something that is alien to its nature.

        *   *   *   *   *   *   *

No one starts a war—or rather, no one in his senses ought to do so—without first being clear in his mind what he intends to achieve by that war and how he intended to conduct it.

—Carl von Clausewitz[1]

The writing of *On Point II* was partly driven by the need to begin establishing the historical record of the United States Army in Operation IRAQI FREEDOM (OIF). That story is one centered on audacity, courage, and selfless service to the nation. Like previous generations of American Soldiers, today's Soldiers have earned a place in the pantheon of American heroes. Recording an early account of their actions and sacrifices was a paramount goal of this study.

To be sure, many of the events and complex operations described in this study were captured by journalists and other observers who offered the most immediate accounts of the Army's experience in Iraq. Over the longer term, the US Army Center of Military History and professional military historians in the academic community will offer interpretations of OIF that are the products of lengthier, more deliberate research and of perspectives sharpened by the passage of time. *On Point II* has been written to provide a preliminary understanding of OIF that exists somewhere between the journalistic accounts and the scholarly histories.

A more important reason for undertaking this project is to attempt to meet the charge posed by historians since the time of Herodotus and Thucydides some 3,000 years ago—to discern insights from the past that will cast a light, however bright or dim, that might guide today's leaders into an uncertain future. The challenges in discerning those insights, with so little historical perspective about what are on-going events, are immense. Yet some insights have emerged from this study and the Army must capitalize on them.

The stunningly successful destruction of the Saddam regime fundamentally changed the nature of the Coalition military campaign. Securing the peace and achieving US strategic goals in Iraq, however, required types of military operations that differed from those that had led to the toppling of the Baathist dictatorship. At the strategic level of national policy, this transition also required a different combination of and a greater contribution by nonmilitary elements of national power—diplomatic, economic, and informational. Turning military success into strategic success takes time and is exceedingly difficult, even in the best of situations; Iraq in 2003 was not the best of situations. The rapid military deployment, the early start of the attack, and the quick end of Saddam's regime precluded the kind of long preparation that, for example, assisted the US Army in the early stages of World War II. Additionally, the tailoring of ground forces to the minimum believed necessary to achieve relatively limited military objectives provided no flexibility for an uncertain and unpredictable environment in Iraq following the attainment of these objectives. Finally, Iraq proved to be less than fertile ground for the planting of new social, economic, and political ideas, which were fundamental tenets of the Coalition's vision for the post-Saddam order.

The subtitle of *On Point II—Transition to a New Campaign*—was not idly chosen. Not only does the phrase "transition to a new campaign" accurately capture the Army's experience in Iraq between May 2003 and January 2005, it embodies what the authors believe is the most significant insight provided by the historical record. That observation looks beyond the rather obvious lesson that military forces must be prepared for the operations that follow success in tactical-level combat missions. The superb Soldiers of the US Army improvised and adapted to unexpected circumstances in Iraq as they have in similar situations for more than 200 years. Far more critical is the planning and preparation that civilian leaders and military commanders must conduct for the transition to operations that follow the decisive combat phase of a campaign. If the Army's experience in Iraq in 2003 offers any single crucial insight, it is that this type of thoughtful, detailed, and deliberate planning must be done at the highest levels long before the campaign begins if military victory is to be transformed into strategic success.

The difficulty in Iraq in April and May 2003 for the Army, and the other Services, was that the transition to a new campaign was not well thought out, planned for, and prepared for before it began. Additionally, the assumptions about the nature of post-Saddam Iraq on which the transition was planned proved to be largely incorrect. Thus, as the US Armed Forces transitioned in April and May 2003 from Phase III, Decisive Operations, to what was essentially a new campaign that featured full spectrum operations, they did not have the benefit of policies and plans that fully envisioned the transition to guide their operations. CENTCOM's planned transition to Phase IV operations included only the final destruction of Saddam's military and paramilitary forces, the search for weapons of mass destruction (WMD), the hunt for terrorists, and limited support to the humanitarian and reconstruction efforts of the Office of Reconstruction and Humanitarian Assistance (ORHA), all in the context of a rapid turnover of sovereignty to a new Iraqi Government. As late as May 2003 the CENTCOM commander planned for the rapid withdrawal of US and Coalition military forces by September as responsibility for Iraq was turned over to the ORHA, to the new joint task force, to international organizations, and to a new Iraqi Government. In line with that thinking was the CENTCOM decision to unexpectedly turn over responsibility for Phase IV of OIF to the V Corps headquarters, designated as Combined Joint Task Force–7 (CJTF-7), and to withdraw its land forces component command, Third Army, from the theater. General Tommy Franks also decided to retire during this time, believing his military service to the nation had been accomplished, much as he believed CENTCOM's mission to depose Saddam Hussein was at a close.

CENTCOM and Third Army did only the barest planning for Phase IV of OIF. The CFLCC plan for this phase was not formally issued until the start of the ground invasion of Iraq. Few if any commanders at all levels had any idea what their missions in Phase IV were to encompass. Lieutenant General (Retired) Jay Garner and the ORHA, created 20 January 2003, barely had time to build a staff and do a limited analysis of its tasks before it deployed to Kuwait in late March. US civilian and military planning and preparation, even for what was assumed to be a relatively easy and short Phase IV, was inadequate. Though essentially a joint planning process, the Army, as the Service primarily responsible for ground operations, should have insisted on better Phase IV planning and preparations through its voice on the Joint Chiefs of Staff.

It is an open question whether senior US civilian and military leaders should have known their optimistic assumptions about the nature of post-Saddam Iraq would prove to be flawed. Many have pointed to official and unofficial prewar studies and predictions of chaos and conflict in Iraq after Saddam was overthrown. Others have pointed to voices in the US Armed Forces and Department of Defense (DOD) who questioned the relatively small number of troops planned for the postconflict phase of OIF. Historians have even questioned the assumption that the Iraqi nation-state was viable, noting its history under Ottoman, British, and Baathist rule as obscuring the underlying sources of friction and disunity—a sort of Middle Eastern version of the former Yugoslavia. It appears that most senior civilian and military leaders failed to review the historical records of military occupations and of Middle Eastern or Iraqi history, and also failed to listen and evaluate outside views about potential weaknesses with their planning assumptions. The intense desire to continue DOD's transformation to smaller and lighter forces, to implement a perceived revolution in military affairs in the information age, and to savor the euphoria over seemingly easy successes in Afghanistan using those techniques seemed to outweigh searching through the past for insights into the future.

The oft-stated goal of *regime change* implied some degree of postwar steps to build a new Iraqi Government in place of the Saddam regime. *Regime removal* might have been a more accurate description of the goal that the design of OIF was best suited to accomplish. The military means employed were sufficient to destroy the Saddam regime; they were not sufficient to replace it with the type of nation-state the United States wished to see in its place. It will also never be known what the course of events might have been had the United States and its Coalition partners simply carried out their plans to quickly leave Iraq. Four key events and decisions made those prewar plans impossible. First, the decrepit state of Iraq's physical infrastructure was far worse than expected, requiring massive rebuilding to prevent a humanitarian disaster. Second, the collapse of Iraq's civil governing structures in April and May 2003 placed enormous demands on ORHA, then on the Coalition Provisional Authority (CPA) and the Coalition to govern and provide security in Iraq, tasks for which they were unprepared. Third, Iraqi political, ethnic, and religious disunity after the removal of the Saddam regime made the rapid creation of a unity government nearly impossible in the summer of 2003.[2] Fourth, the decision in early May to create the CPA, and to have it function for an indefinite period as an occupying power under international law fundamentally changed the political dynamics in Iraq, in the United States, and in the international community.

The CPA's dissolution of the Baath Party and Iraq's military and security forces decisively signaled to all Iraqis that the Baathist Sunni domination of Iraq was over. In that sense, the decision successfully generated critical support from the Shia and Kurdish populations in Iraq. Unfortunately, many Sunni Arabs saw CPA Orders No. 1 and 2, and in particular the actual implementation of those orders by a Shia-dominated Iraqi Governing Council (IGC), as signs that they had few prospects for power in a new Iraq. Taken together, these unplanned for "realities" fundamentally changed the nature of the transition required by US and Coalition military forces. By the fall of 2003 Coalition soldiers faced civil chaos, crime, Baathist revanchism, terrorist violence, political disunity, and varying types of ethnic resentment. These decisions and events changed the always complex transition from combat operations to securing the nation's strategic goals, into a transition from conventional war (and a planned rapid withdrawal) to a multiyear occupation and full spectrum operations.

The practical steps that needed to be taken on the ground by Soldiers and commanders faced with unexpected realities occurred simultaneously or often ahead of the intellectual or planning steps that were required to provide those units with direction and resources. The situation facing Coalition forces in the spring of 2003 evoked the aphorism "if you don't know where you are going, any road will get you there." US Army units, commanders, and Soldiers reacted to the varying realities of Iraq based on doctrine and experience. Beginning in late March 2003, they took immediate steps to establish local governance, provide security, begin reconstruction, and seek local support for their actions. US Army commands tailored their operations—ranging from large-scale combat operations and antiterrorist strikes to a wide variety of stability operations—to the particular situations in the various provinces of Iraq. In large measure those reactions were appropriate, at least in terms of their immediate circumstances.

What Coalition forces lacked, however, were the overarching operational and strategic visions appropriate to the new Iraq and the myriad national resources to carry out those visions. The last minute creation, ad hoc manning, and inadequate planning by both the ORHA and the CPA made it more difficult for CENTCOM (and later, CJTF-7) to nest and to coordinate their military operations with the other elements of US national power. The limited involvement by the other departments of the US Government in the difficult work of constructing a new Iraq distorted the postconflict rebuilding effort, placing too much reliance on the military element of power. In this sense, the early 21st century version of the mid-20th century concept of "a nation at war" was tested and found wanting. The hasty changes in the military command and control structure within CENTCOM between April and June 2003, along with the decision to halt the flow of units scheduled to deploy to Iraq, added other transitional challenges to those already underway.

Even before they took command of their respective organizations, the new CJTF-7 commander and the incoming CENTCOM commander clearly recognized that the situation in Iraq did not match prewar assumptions. Army and Marine units throughout Iraq faced unexpected chaos and increasing resistance to US and Coalition objectives, particularly in Baghdad and the Sunni Arab areas of Iraq. In fact, that resistance began to emerge within a few weeks of the toppling of the Saddam statute on 9 April in Firdos Square in Baghdad. Sunni Arab Iraqis staged a protest march against US occupation of Baghdad on 18 April. On the same day, Shia leaders, still in exile in Iran, called for Iraqis to resist the US occupation. Not to be forgotten was the emergence of al-Qaeda terrorists in Iraq—operating independently with their own agenda, but cooperating with former Baathists, Sunni Arab, and Shia insurgents whenever their tactical aims coincided. When Lieutenant General Ricardo Sanchez took command of CJTF-7 on 15 June and General John Abizaid took command of CENTCOM on 8 July, they were well aware that they faced rapidly escalating and multifaceted resistance to US and Coalition forces.

From this point in the summer of 2003 forward, the story of the US Army in Iraq is that of leaders and Soldiers rapidly making adjustments to accomplish the tasks now required during a complex period of multiple transitions. The institutional Army also needed to "ramp up" to support the ever-expanding demands of the new campaign. The Army launched and is continuing a massive effort to collect, analyze, and distribute lessons learned from its experiences to the recruiting, educating, training, and operating components. *On Point II* has chronicled this record of transition and change in Iraq. The remainder of this chapter attempts to draw historical insights of immediate use from that record.

Unity of Effort and Unity of Command

The absolute necessity for unity of effort and command stands as one of the clearest lessons to emerge from the historical record of this period of the war in Iraq. Placing great weight on the imperative of unity of command and effort is hardly an original insight; military commanders and theorists through the centuries have emphasized that principle and it is currently a major tenet of US Joint and Army doctrine. Despite that fact, the principle was not well practiced during the first year in Iraq. The US civilian and military chains of command struggled through difficult changes during the critical transition from Phase III to the full spectrum campaign. US unity of command and effort, and hence overall effectiveness, suffered during what was a very important time in OIF.

The difficulties in prewar planning and in the coordination of operations within the interagency effort of the US Government have been chronicled in other studies. Those challenges are not part of the purview of *On Point II*, except to assess their impact on military operations. The December 2002 decision to give the DOD the lead role in postwar Iraq was in part an attempt to avoid the lack of unity of effort that critics had pointed out in previous US missions in the Balkans and Afghanistan. The potential benefits of that decision, however, were not realized due to interagency friction and to lack of coordination within the DOD. The DOD did not create ORHA until 20 January 2003. The level of prewar coordination between ORHA, other agencies in the US Government, CENTCOM, CFLCC/Third Army, and Combined Joint Task Force–IV (CJTF-IV) was therefore minimal. Garner and his staff secured the eager cooperation of Lieutenant General David McKiernan and the CFLCC/Third Army, but not until *after* Baghdad was captured. ORHA barely had time to open its offices in Baghdad before it was replaced by the CPA, whose chief had a strikingly different mandate for the US mission in post-Saddam Iraq than that set forth in the limited prewar planning effort.

The Coalition did not announce the creation of the CPA, the sovereign political power for Iraq, or the naming of Ambassador L. Paul Bremer III as its chief until 6 May 2003. Bremer and his advance party arrived in Iraq about a week later and had to take the normal bureaucratic steps to set themselves up as an organization. The CPA had to establish and promulgate numerous policies as an occupying power, and create mechanisms to bring competing Iraqi exile groups and local parties into the political process. At the same time, the CPA needed to coordinate its operations with the operations of the Army's V Corps (soon to become CJTF-7) headquarters, as that military organization was undergoing its own transition. It was no surprise that the CPA and Coalition military forces in Iraq were not prepared to effectively deal with the enormous problems of post-Saddam Iraq.

The DOD also reconfigured the military chain of command during the middle of this most crucial period. Between April and July 2003, the CENTCOM commander retired and that command pulled the designated land component command for the Middle East (Third Army) out of theater, replacing it with V Corps, a headquarters that had made few preparations for the mission. To add greater complexity to this set of command transitions, V Corps underwent a change of command on 14 June. These new commands had to literally "create" their organizations, establish themselves in their new roles, and grapple with the unexpected emergence of resistance to the Coalition that had fundamentally changed their mission. When it was created in June 2003 as a sub-unified command of CENTCOM, CJTF-7 lacked significant interagency assets, and its relationship with CPA was not clearly understood. The DOD and the Army were arguably too slow in providing CJTF-7 with the additional staff and resources it needed for its responsibilities in Iraq. With the ORHA to CPA transition having just occurred in May 2003, CJTF-7 did not have a fully functioning interagency organization in Iraq with which to synchronize its efforts in June. CJTF-7 also had to assume the additional tasks of integrating the forces of more than 30 nations, each with their own capabilities and limitations, into the new campaign in Iraq. CENTCOM and CJTF-7 ultimately did not have a robust political headquarters with which they could partner and together conduct the coordinated nation-building efforts required in Iraq. Not until June 2004, more than a year later, did the United States put in place the civilian and military leadership structure in Iraq commensurate with the strategic challenge.

The failure to ensure unity of command and effort in the early stages of OIF offers several critical insights for future campaigns. Most important is retaining key commanders and key commands in place during the transition between phases of an operation to prevent the inefficiencies and ineffectiveness seen during the spring and summer of 2003. The Army teaches noncommissioned officers (NCOs) and junior officers never to use terrain that includes an avenue of approach as a dividing line between different commands lest an enemy exploit the fact that no single unit is responsible for the terrain. Similarly, command and control of operations should not be handed off to the nearest available command during the transition between Phase III and Phase IV. The United States should also develop mechanisms to establish unity of command between the senior military headquarters and the senior civilian organization in a theater or country during Phase IV operations. Though they are outside the purview of the Army, these new mechanisms should include new interagency policies and procedures. Both sets of changes should have as their goal the effectiveness, efficiency, and unity of effort needed to turn battlefield success into strategic success.

Phase III and Phase IV Operations[*]

While planning and preparation for what in 2003 was called Phase III, Decisive Operations, of a joint campaign will always tend to have primacy for Joint and Army planners, it is time to increase the importance of what is now known as Phase IV, Stabilize. Sustained and decisive ground combat is the sine qua non of the US Army. The Army's operational record from Phase III of OIF, though not without flaws, is superlative. Phase III military operations may be the most intense and dangerous within a campaign, and without a military victory in Phase III, strategic success is impossible. At the same time it must be remembered that the purpose of military operations is to achieve a specific strategic or political objective. As OIF has shown, this phase of operations is ultimately more important than Phase III in securing the end for which military operations were initiated. In spring 2003, however, the DOD and the Army lacked a coherent plan to translate the rapid, narrow-front attack that avoided populated

---

[*]The 2006 version of Joint Publication 5-0, *Joint Operations Planning*, includes six campaign phases that should alleviate the artificial distinction of the previous four-phase model. They are shape, deter, seize the initiative, dominate, stabilize, and enable civil authority.

areas whenever possible, into strategic success. Soldiers and commanders at nearly every level did not know what was expected of them once Saddam Hussein was deposed and his military forces destroyed.

Clearly the Coalition lacked sufficient forces on the ground in April 2003 to facilitate, much less impose, fundamental political, social, and economic changes in Iraq. Troop density ratios were on the low end of previous US occupation experiences, much lower than many of the prewar plans for the invasion of Iraq and far lower than previous US and Western counterinsurgency campaigns. These factors were in line with prewar planning for a quick turnover of power to Iraqis and a quick withdrawal of US forces, leaving Iraqis to determine their own political future—options that proved impossible to execute. While CENTCOM and the US Army might not have been expected to plan for a full-blown insurgency of the type that emerged by late 2003, the historical record should have indicated that many more troops would be needed for the post-Saddam era in Iraq.[†] Key decisionmakers ignored cautionary warnings about the paucity of troops, both official and unofficial, without giving them sufficient review. The Coalition's inability to prevent looting, to secure Iraq's borders, and to guard the vast number of munitions dumps in the early months after Saddam's overthrow are indicative of the shortage. US commanders found it difficult to balance increasing requirements with the units available throughout 2003 and 2004. Furthermore, by the time the Saddam regime fell, most Iraqis had yet to see a Coalition soldier. Unlike Axis military forces and their citizenry in 1945, who had no doubts about their utter defeat and who accepted the imposition of far-reaching political and social changes by the victorious Allies, Iraqis not favorably inclined toward the Coalition's postconflict goals had much less reason to passively accept fundamental change.

It is too early to pass definitive judgment on the wisdom of the strategic decisions in mid-2004. In that period, the Coalition decided to rely on the Interim Iraqi Government (IIG) to implement a federal solution to Iraq's political and economic problems and to keep US force levels relatively steady while rapidly building up Iraq's security forces so they could tackle the internal security problems. By mid-2006, however, it appeared that the dysfunctional qualities of the nascent Iraqi political process, the chronically slow rise in effectiveness by Iraq's security forces, and the incredibly violent sectarian strife undermined the hopes generated by the success of the Iraqi elections of January 2005 that serve as the end point of this study. What is not open to dispute is that deposing the Saddam regime was far easier than imposing or fostering a new political order in Iraq. One simple explanation is that the Coalition directed far more resources and energy into planning for the former objective than it put into planning for the latter goal.

The concepts concerning postconflict operations are not new to military history or to US military doctrine. Joint and Army commands, nevertheless, have over recent decades rather consistently shown a tendency to ignore them in practice. Joint and Army planning doctrine and processes must be changed to more specifically include planning and preparation for the inevitable transition to Phase IV and the achievement of strategic objectives. The transition to

---

[†]Most senior US commanders, though not all, believed they had sufficient forces in Iraq throughout 2003 and 2004 to accomplish their missions. As this study has shown, this often meant concentrating forces for particular operations in specific regions while accepting risk in other areas and deploying additional forces to Iraq for temporary periods.

stability operations should begin before the end of major combat operations. Thus, planning must occur nearly simultaneously. Force level or troop density calculations must not simply be an exercise in minimalist thinking based on an alleged revolution in military affairs. Planning must also include an analysis of Phase IV force level requirements at every phase of a campaign. The doctrinal military decision-making process (MDMP) should make this explicit and prevent the sharp division between those phases that allow commands to relegate Phase IV planning to another day or to a follow-on command. Planners must also take into account the historical, cultural, and political factors that will affect national strategy and military operations, particularly Phase IV operations. The Army's education system must emphasize these principles beginning at the Command and General Staff College (CGSC) and the School of Advanced Military Studies (SAMS), and continue it through the Army War College. Army training programs, such as the Battle Command Training Program (BCTP), should include Phase IV planning and operations in their exercises and simulations—not as an afterthought, but as a primary exercise goal.

Mission Requirements and Force Rotations

In some ways, CENTCOM conducted the new campaign in 2003 and 2004 with the resources the Army and the other Services could sustain over time (in terms of types and numbers of units), and not necessarily with what was needed in Iraq to accomplish the mission. It is now common to hear concurrence with prewar estimates that postconflict operations in Iraq would require several hundreds of thousands of troops. Generals Sanchez and Abizaid took steps in June and July 2003 to delay the redeployment of the 3d Infantry Division (3d ID) out of Iraq while they revised the campaign plan and reviewed the issue of force size and composition. In the late summer and early fall, CJTF-7 and CENTCOM coordinated with the Joint Staffs and the Services to determine the size of the OIF II force rotation. Given the Army's inability to sustain the size of the original OIF I force, much less to increase it, both commanders resorted to selective tour extensions, temporary force size increases for particular operations or events, and the creation of security force capability outside the CPA's army and police building programs to generate greater numbers of forces. The decisions by the Bush administration in late 2006 to modestly increase troop levels in Iraq in 2007, to change commanders, and to increase the overall size of the Army and Marine Corps could be seen as belated recognition of the problems created by the mixing of roles between the regional combatant commanders and the Services.

The Goldwater-Nichols Act of 1986 placed responsibility for the conduct of military operations on DOD's regional combatant commanders and removed the Service chiefs from direct involvement in planning and conducting operations. The Act was drawn up to address many of the inefficiencies and interservice rivalries so evident in US military operations of the late 1970s and early 1980s. One result of the Act was that regional combatant commanders became responsible for planning operations, determining requirements, and conducting operations, while the Services provide forces and other resources as required. Yet, in this case the size and composition of the nation's ground forces and force rotation policies appear to have overridden operational requirements.

It may be time for the Army and the nation to examine the very idea of force rotations as the default solution for extended campaigns. The Army's post-Cold War experience of quick military victories, such as Operation DESERT STORM, and longer peace operations, as seen in the Balkans, has left a legacy with at least three negative side effects. The first is a belief that military campaigns can be conducted without extensive planning for and commitment to the operations that follow successful combat actions. The second is the concept of force levels that attempt to balance operational requirements with troop rotations deemed sustainable over time within existing resource levels. The third is a belief that military operations can quickly achieve national strategic objectives. If extended campaigns are necessary, the ascendant approach suggested that they could be managed as a series of rotational force deployments designed to limit the institutional effects on the Army and the nation while awaiting a political solution followed by a so-called exit strategy.[3]

While a national mobilization of the sort seen in World War II is unlikely to be needed in the future, the demands placed on the Army and the nation in OIF (and the Global War on Terrorism) call into question whether a military campaign ought to be planned and conducted in a way that does not take full advantage of the total resources of the US military, the US Government, and the nation. In 2003 the military forces were optimized for high-intensity, relatively short duration, conventional military campaigns. Waging protracted irregular war places quite different demands on military forces, and meeting those demands is emerging as one of the key strategic challenges for the United States in the early 21st century. Changes may include the longer deployment of larger portions of the Armed Forces, an increase in the size of the Armed Forces, and a greater national commitment of resources. Deploying military and nonmilitary resources for the duration rather than by rotation would put more resources on the ground, would involve a truly national commitment to victory, and paradoxically, could lead to quicker success.

Related to this issue of troop levels and warfighting requirements are the extensive mobilizations of the Army National Guard and Army Reserve. Both Reserve Components have shouldered a very heavy portion of the load in OIF. The ghosts of 1990–91, when some National Guard units were deemed unready to deploy for Operations DESERT SHIELD and DESERT STORM, have been exorcised. Guard and Reserve Soldiers have amply demonstrated that they are a fully capable, and indeed, an absolutely essential part of the Army. The Active Duty Army cannot conduct operations for any length of time without participation by the Reserve and the Guard. The price paid by reservists and communities to sustain the long and repetitive mobilizations, however, may not be sustainable in the future.

The prewar paradigm for use of the Reserves was characterized as "mobilize–train–deploy." Inherent in this model was the assumption that after mobilization, time would be available for bringing personnel, equipment, and training up to necessary levels before the Reserves were committed. The new construct is now often called "train–mobilize–deploy." This assumes well-manned, well-equipped, and fully-trained Reserve forces are ready for combat after a rapid mobilization and only limited refresher training. Before 2001 the Reserve Components were often conceived of as a "strategic reserve," implying occasional use in national emergencies; since 2003 they have been referred to as an "operational force," implying regular use in all conflicts. The differences between these two paradigms and the implications for the nation are significant. The Congress and the Army will have to provide much more of many things to rely on the Reserve Components in the future—more Soldiers, more modern equipment, more funding, more medical and educational benefits, more support to families, and more ways to support communities and businesses during mobilization periods. The practice of using individual Guard and Reserve Soldiers as augmentees to understrength Active and Reserve units rather than as cohesive units has proven quite problematic and is now avoided wherever possible.‡ Whether the Army, and the country, can continue to rely on its part-time Soldiers to perform frequent, long-duration deployments is an issue with which the military and civilian leadership must grapple. This burden is more difficult to bear in a time during which the vast majority of citizens are called on to do little in support of the war effort.

Doctrine and Training

One of the most positive changes resulting from the US Army's experience in OIF during this period is the overhauling of the Army's key doctrinal concepts in light of the current operational environment. Since 2004 the Army has spent considerable resources to update its doctrinal manuals as well as its education and training programs to catch up with realities encountered in Iraq and elsewhere in the war on terror. Two efforts stand out among many. FM 3-24, *Counterinsurgency*, updated this critical and neglected aspect of the Army's doctrinal hierarchy when it was released in December 2006. This manual directs Army leaders to use a mix of offense, defense, and stability operations which are tailored to provide security for the population and establishing the legitimacy and effectiveness of the host nation's government and security forces. The Army's Combined Arms Center at Fort Leavenworth, Kansas, developed the manual using a process that included input from a wide variety of military and nonmilitary experts.

The 2008 version of the Army's capstone doctrine, FM 3-0, *Operations*, employed the context of the Army's recent experience in Iraq and Afghanistan to offer a more complete and clearly-defined concept of full spectrum operations. The new field manual articulated the idea of full spectrum operations by stating, "Army forces combine offensive, defensive, and stability or civil support operations simultaneously as part of an interdependent joint force to seize, retain, and exploit the initiative, accepting prudent risk to create opportunities to achieve decisive results."[4] The 2008 version of FM 3-0 also called for the synchronized use of lethal and nonlethal actions that are proportional to the mission and the operational environment. This concept eliminated the old, incorrect division between fighting and "everything else," which in previous doctrine was too sharply delineated. Furthermore, the new version of FM 3-0 clarified the meaning of key concepts such as the spectrum of conflict, explained how operational themes such as irregular warfare assist in setting the basic foundations for campaigns, and established the paramount importance of information operations. Combined with Joint Publication 5-0 that established a revised joint planning process, these key documents demonstrate how the Army has integrated its experiences in Iraq into its overall theory and practice. The improvements to Army and Joint doctrine must now be matched by changes in US Government interagency processes. As both of the key manuals repeatedly state, the military instrument of national power must operate in a broader and well supported strategy if national objectives are to be achieved after battlefield success.

---

‡In December 2004 the Chief of the Army Reserve, Lieutenant General James Helmly, issued a strong cautionary note about the way many USAR Soldiers had been deployed. He decried their use as individual fillers instead of deploying them in cohesive units caused detrimental effects on the long-term readiness of the Army Reserve. The USAR and the ARNG are now undergoing fundamental changes in the way Soldiers are recruited and trained and how units are deployed.

In response to the unexpected realities of operations in Iraq and Afghanistan, the Army began revamping its training programs in late 2003 and early 2004. Training at the Army's Combat Training Centers (CTCs) has been changed to reflect operations in both Iraq and Afghanistan. The BCTP has been similarly revised. The US Army Training and Doctrine Command (TRADOC) and Forces Command (FORSCOM) have radically revised individual and unit training programs to conform to the demands of OIF and Operation ENDURING FREEDOM (OEF). They now include anti-improvised explosive device (IED), countersniper, convoy ambush, and a host of other programs designed in response to current battlefield demands. Units deployed to Iraq for OIF II had little if any time to take advantage of what were the still emerging changes in this area. Since OIF II, however, the record of those programs is much improved. The Joint IED Defeat Organization (JIEDDO), formed in late 2004 and by 2006 a 300+ person organization with a multi-billion dollar budget, is an example of these efforts. Today, JIEDDO's three pronged approach—defeat the device, attack the network, and train the force—illustrates the broad-based approaches developed during this transition.[5] The "Road to Deployment" concept, developed by the Combined Arms Center at Fort Leavenworth, Kansas, is a good model to prepare units for the full spectrum environment. The model provides a systematic process of education and full spectrum training to lead units from notification to deployment and to ensure the Army provides the most current support available. It should be made part of the Army's new training management doctrine, but it must remain flexible enough to be modified in light of future missions.

The demands of preparing for operations in Iraq have reduced the time available for training on the full range of individual and collective skills. Understandably, many Soldiers and units have not maintained their expertise in the collective tasks required by conventional operations. When the operational tempo for OIF (and OEF) slows down, the Army will have to restore its proficiency in the areas that have been neglected. Given its commitment to the concept of full spectrum operations, the Army must avoid becoming too heavily focused on one part of the spectrum of conflict, because the future tends to deal harshly with military forces whose expertise is one dimensional and backwards looking.

Intelligence Operations

As units began conducting full spectrum operations in Iraq, most leaders at the tactical level found that the gathering and analysis of information became a critical mission for all Soldiers. The Army's legacy intelligence system, primarily designed for the top-down dissemination of information on a conventional battlefield, became only an adjunct to new processes developed during OIF. The new paradigm that emerged in 2003 and 2004 featured tactical units developing their own actionable intelligence that would then enable other types of operations such as cordon and searches or reconstruction projects. While the Army adapted its signals intelligence (SIGINT) and imagery intelligence (IMINT) systems to the insurgent threat and the noncontiguous battlefield, it was human intelligence (HUMINT) that became the critical source for information that allowed tactical units to attain the objectives in their areas of responsibility (AORs).

This study has demonstrated that in May 2003 the US Army was not prepared to gather or analyze HUMINT on any meaningful scale. HUMINT assets were few in number and resided mainly in the Tactical HUMINT Teams (THTs) spread across Iraq. Pushing these scarce teams down to brigade or battalion level provided some assistance to tactical commanders, but because those teams normally consisted of only three to six Soldiers, their effectiveness was limited. Exacerbating the problems in the formal HUMINT collection process was the barrier posed by language and culture. Almost all units examined noted that the severe lack of Army or contracted civilian linguists created huge obstacles to gathering information.

Given the nature of the Global War on Terrorism, it is highly likely that HUMINT will continue to be the key means of gathering actionable intelligence in the campaigns on the horizon. Since 2003 the Army has revisited its HUMINT doctrine and incorporated lessons from Iraq and Afghanistan in an effort to better prepare military intelligence (MI) Soldiers for future campaigns. The newest version of the Army's HUMINT doctrine, Field Manual (FM) 2-22.3, *Human Intelligence Collector Operations* (2006), emphasizes the role of HUMINT managers and coordinators, such as the 2X staff officer and offers guidance and procedures for the THTs working on a noncontiguous battlefield. In 2003 and 2004 HUMINT operations almost always involved interrogations of detainees. In response to the detainee and interrogation abuses in this period, the new doctrine asserts the primacy of the Geneva Convention in establishing norms for the treatment of detainees, adheres to the standards set in the 2005 Detainee Treatment Act, and dictates to collectors the only legal interrogation techniques available for use. FM 2-22.3 also affirms the line that demarcates the roles of MI and military police (MP) Soldiers in interrogation operations, clearly stating that MP Soldiers have no role in preparing detainees for interrogations.

The Army should continue to revise and develop its HUMINT doctrine, including new concepts on the structure and manning of HUMINT teams at the tactical level, the role of the HUMINT (2X) officer and the structure of the intelligence staff section at various levels, and means of addressing the chronic shortage of linguists and interpreters. On a broader front, the Army recognized the role all Soldiers played in gathering vital information in Iraq and in 2005 began training Soldiers for this task through its *Every Soldier Is A Sensor* program. This initiative is an excellent start to what will hopefully become a systemic approach to training all Soldiers and units in the fundamentals of intelligence collection and analysis.

Detainee Operations

During OIF, in a setting where full spectrum operations became the norm, detainee operations quickly became one of the most common missions performed by Army units. This study has shown how, as the need for actionable intelligence rose, many tactical units reacted by attempting to gain information from Iraqis soon after they detained them. In fact, by 2004 many leaders at the tactical level had acknowledged that their units established and staffed detainee facilities where they often conducted interrogations. However, this approach did not fit into the Army's doctrine, which clearly assigned the enemy prisoner of war (EPW)/confinement mission to the MP Corps. Simply put, the demand for information at the tactical level and the shortage of dedicated assets to gather that information rendered doctrine irrelevant. Additionally, the large number of detainees swamped a formal system set up to handle a limited amount of EPWs on a conventional battlefield.

The use of nondoctrinal detainee facilities led to a number of serious problems. As the scale of detainee operations in Iraq grew, it was clear that most Soldiers involved did not have proper training and often lacked clear guidance on how to treat detained Iraqis. In a few cases, this led to situations in which US Soldiers mistreated Iraqis. Most of the confirmed cases of mistreatment occurred at the point of capture, often in the heat of combat. However, a significant portion of the incidents happened at confinement facilities at the brigade, division, or combined joint task force (CJTF) level. The abuses in the Joint Interrogation and Debriefing Center (JIDC) at the Abu Ghraib Prison fit into this category. As the case at Abu Ghraib demonstrated, in environments where Soldiers lack relevant training, policies are unclear, and leadership uncertain, even dedicated mission-oriented Soldiers can lose their moral compass.

The detainee system that evolved in Iraq in 2003 and 2004 has serious implications for the US Army. If detainee operations of this type are considered part of full spectrum operations, then the Army's training and education systems must broadly address this mission. The doctrinal division of effort between detention and interrogation, between the MP and MI interrogators, must be maintained. If the detention and confinement mission rests solely with the MP Corps, other issues arise. In a campaign such as OIF, can the US Army field enough trained MP units to handle the large number of detainees that will likely result? The Army has begun expanding the size of the MP branch and establishing more Internment/Resettlement Battalions, which have the doctrinal mission of running detainee facilities. However, any recasting of the MP branch and detainee operations doctrine must deal with the need for actionable intelligence at the tactical level by units conducting operations and having constant interaction with combatants and noncombatants.

The means of preventing further detainee mistreatment appears to be more straightforward. The keys are proper training, clear policies, and the presence of leadership that will enforce established standards. As noted above, in the relatively small number of confirmed cases of detainee abuse these elements were missing. Solid training on the basics of EPW/detainee treatment and enforcement from junior leaders will help prevent abuses at the point of capture. New policy, from the 2005 Detainee Treatment Act to FM 2-22.3, gives Soldiers clear parameters for detainee operations, especially those beyond the point of capture. To ensure these standards are met, commanders should consider selecting senior officers to oversee detainee operations. In 2004 Multi-National Force–Iraq (MNF-I) appointed a major general as the deputy commander for detainee operations and gave him resources to provide oversight of those operations. The formal establishment of similar command or staff positions at lower echelons within Army formations would further strengthen supervision of this critical mission.

Though not a function for which the Army is the lead arm of the US Government, national policymakers and joint commanders must plan for the interface between battlefield operations that generate detainees, and the host nation security forces, judicial process, and civilian detention systems. Soldiers must operate within a legal and doctrinal system of regulations when dealing with detained persons, but they must also work within an operational set of policies, guidelines, and host nation laws specific to the mission. The collapse of the Iraqi Government's infrastructure in April 2003 meant Coalition forces had no partner in dealing with these thorny issues. In 2002 Saddam threw open the prison system in Iraq, releasing thousands of criminals that added yet another complicating factor to the problem. These challenges are yet another example of many that must be prepared for in advance of the start of military operations.

Training Indigenous Forces

Prior to OIF and OEF, few Soldiers in the conventional Army considered the training of indigenous forces one of their missions. The US Army's Special Forces have long had this task as a core function. However, as OEF demonstrated in early 2003, even before OIF began, the potential scope of this mission exceeds the capacity of Special Operations Forces. Training and advising foreign soldiers in basic and small unit combat skills is difficult. The experience of the CPA and the Multi-National Security Transition Command–Iraq (MNSTC-I) with training and equipping the Iraqi Security Forces (ISF) makes it clear that the mission to rebuild a host nation's military units, security forces, and infrastructure requires an extremely large and robust program that is supported by many agencies of the US Government. Not until late 2004 did the DOD and the US Government create and begin to resource a program that met Iraq's security requirements.

DOD's unit advisory efforts were similarly lacking. The performance of the ISF in 2004 indicates that the size of the Advisor Support Teams (ASTs) were too small to provide the necessary degree of coaching, mentoring, and battlefield determination. Some of the Soldiers assigned to this mission did not have the requisite tactical experience to advise ground units in combat. Training for these teams in late 2003 and 2004 was inadequate, despite improvements made at US training centers and in Kuwait and Iraq. Not until mid-2005 was a comprehensive training program put in place under FORSCOM and MNSTC-I to prepare Soldiers and teams for this most important and dangerous task. Tactical, logistical, and medical coordination between US advisors, their Iraqi units, and US units in Iraq was inadequate during much of 2004. US advisors frequently found themselves without critical aspects of support despite operating near or with US and Coalition forces. These problems were not unprecedented and could have been foreseen. Indeed, these deficiencies in supplies and coordination would have been familiar to Soldiers and Marines who served as military advisors in Vietnam in the 1960s. Still, only in 2005 did MNSTC-I establish the Iraqi Assistance Group to provide coordination between US units and US advisors assigned to Iraqi units operating under the control of Multi-National Corps–Iraq (MNC-I).

The history of the security training programs in Iraq suggest that the Army needs to maintain a core of cadre, doctrine, and training programs of instruction for advising indigenous forces that can be expanded when needed. Special Operations Forces will continue to perform this mission on a regular basis in peace and in war. But when the requirement is to train, equip, and advise the armed forces of an entire nation, the conventional Army must be able to more quickly take on that mission. This is especially true when the strategic goals include fundamental societal change in the region of conflict. The conventional Army has had extensive experience with this mission since the end of World War II; signs suggest that it will be even more prevalent in the future. The establishment in 2006 of the Joint Center for International Security Force Assistance at Fort Leavenworth, Kansas, is a step in the right direction. The Foreign Security Forces Training Program, run by the 1st Infantry Division at Fort Riley, Kansas, is another positive step—although the use of the cadre of a modular brigade combat team is only a stopgap measure. The Army National Guard and Army Reserve have shouldered much of this burden in OIF (and OEF); they might be well suited to take on this mission and maintain a surge capacity on a permanent basis. Consideration should be given to creating a standing organization with the mission to be prepared to conduct these kinds of large-scale training, equipping, and advising functions.

The "M" in DOTMLPF—Materiel

Operations in Iraq have put an end to the age-old distinction between the front lines and rear echelons. The Army's equipment must reflect this new reality. The contemporary operating environment includes a 360-degree enemy threat. That threat requires every Soldier and every system to be survivable while performing their primary mission, regardless of how far remote from combat it may be anticipated. The days of unarmored command and logistics vehicles are over. This is not to suggest that every system have the survivability of the M1 Abrams tank, but they must be able to survive a mine strike, artillery shrapnel, and small arms fire. And in the future, units in the Army Reserve and National Guard will need the same level of protection for their equipment as the Active force. The cost in peacetime will be considerable; the cost of not doing so will be unbearable in wartime.

It may be hard to envision another conflict in which the arsenal of democracy will be required to expand production as it did in World War II. It is apparent, however, that the national industrial base must be capable of expanding in critical areas more rapidly. The Army Materiel Command, Army depots, and commercial manufacturers need greater reserve capacity to produce ammunition, personal equipment, vehicles, and other supplies for any campaign lasting more than a few weeks. Their repair capacity must also be expanded. This will require far greater resources in peacetime than Congress has historically been willing to provide.

Command and Control

The vastly increased use of new command, control, communications, computers, and intelligence (C4I) systems in OIF is one of many successes for the Army. The Army Battlefield Command System (ABCS [version 6.4 as of this writing]) encompasses a dazzling array of technologies that is constantly evolving—the Force XXI Battle Command, Brigade and Below (FBCB2) System; Blue-Force Tracker; new single channel ground and airborne radio system (SINCGARS); integration of Global Positioning System (GPS) data; and the Command Post of the Future (CPOF) are but a few. Commanders from battalion to corps have credited these systems with a large part of their ability to command and control larger than normal units (some divisions have commanded the operations of seven or more brigades at times) over vast distances. These technologies have reduced fratricide rates to new lows. The use of unmanned aerial vehicles (UAVs) is another success story. Though originally developed for intelligence gathering, the Army quickly adapted UAVs for battle command, and in the case of armed UAVs, to conduct attacks. At the tactical level of war, the Army has successfully harnessed the information age to improve its battlefield performance and should continue to expand those efforts.

Many outside the Armed Forces are unaware of the very restrictive rules of engagement that control the use of deadly force by US troops when engaging enemy fighters. At least some observers would also be surprised about the incredible restraint used by US forces to limit noncombatant casualties and to limit collateral damage to Iraq's physical infrastructure. Images and stories from Iraq on US operations too often focus on the loss of life and destructive nature of combat. The number of cities destroyed by fighting has been very small, and primarily the fault of insurgents. Part of the failure to understand this must be laid on the Army's public affairs programs. These efforts by the Army ought to be acknowledged. Nonetheless, more than a few celebrated cases of airstrikes and artillery missions that missed their targets or hit noncombatant targets indicate potential over-reliance on firepower and too much disregard for its imprecision and potential for collateral damage. Increasing precision continues to reduce the likelihood of error, but in stability and counterinsurgency operations, a more careful weighing of costs and benefits is imperative.

The Battle of Ideas

The record of the US Army in the battle of ideas during OIF has been mixed. Perhaps the biggest success has been the use of embedded reporters. A reasonable balance between operational security and media access seems to have been reached after decades of contention since the 1970s. Embedded reporters almost without exception provided accurate news and followed operational security requirements. Their reporting was also generally positive and with a balanced view showed the American people what their Army does in conflict. Nearly every segment of the US population, as well as political leaders from local to national levels, has remained solidly in support of the Army's Soldiers regardless of their support for operations in Iraq. The Army should work harder with media outlets and journalists, however, to reap the benefits of embedded reporting in full spectrum campaigns like OIF. The complex and often frustrating nature of these operations requires better understanding and communications on both parts.

The Army has not been as successful with its information operations (IO) or public affairs (PA) operations in Iraq. A military force must never underestimate the importance of IO, particularly during Phase IV of a campaign. The proper personnel and plans should be in place before Phase III begins so IO can be used to set the conditions for the inevitable transition. IO considerations should also be made an explicit doctrinal part of all postconflict operations. During the planning process, thought must be given to the potential positive outcomes that can be exploited, and to potential mitigation measures should the operation cause unintended negative effects. Most Army units in this period of OIF have already learned the importance of this practice.

The Army should exploit the IO potential of civil affairs (CA) projects to a greater degree. Simply doing "good things" for the host nation is not enough; those good things must be quickly and widely made known among the general population. Every Army unit at battalion and higher levels must have an organic IO capability. The Army must "grow" officers and NCOs with IO education and experience during peacetime; IO skills are not quickly learned or mastered. The CTCs and the BCTP should make these operations part of every exercise. The rank structure of staff officers in PA, psychological operations (PSYOP), CA, and IO cells in higher-level commands should be examined to ensure those disciplines are properly represented in planning and in operations. The Army placed responsibility for IO doctrine and training on the Combined Arms Center in June 2005, and in December 2005 the US Army IO Proponent (USAIOP) office was created. As of this writing, the best way to organize the work of various IO activities, PA operations, and strategic communications and effects within Army units and commands continues to be debated.[6]

The intellectual firewall between PA and IO must be restored and maintained. The distinction often made between "white" and "black" special operating forces and their missions may be useful in the case of PA and IO. If the spectrum of IO runs from PA and truth telling, to military deception and falsehoods, or from white to black, then the line beyond which PA personnel are allowed to operate must be well short of where that spectrum begins to blur into gray. The credibility of the Army requires that its PA personnel and pronouncements are known to be accurate and truthful. If a commander decides to synchronize efforts by uniting the PA and IO functions under a common staff element, such as an office of strategic communications, then the commander and his strategic communications advisor must preserve the integrity of the PA part of that office.

Combat Service and Soldier Support

The record of insights from this area, now called "sustainment" in emerging doctrine, are a mix of positives and negatives. The Army deserves credit for improvements to casualty care made before and during OIF. Those improvements include success in training, equipment, and doctrine. Soldiers and medics at the point of injury have access to new blood clotting agents and bandages, tourniquets, and pain drugs. Every Soldier now undergoes more and better training for first-line treatment of casualties. The combat support hospital (CSH) concept has proved itself a life-saving measure. Forward surgical teams and aero medical evacuation (MEDEVAC) from the point of injury to the CSH via the HH-60 Blackhawk has brought better trauma care much closer to the front lines than at any point in history. Combined with the rapid out-of-theater evacuation policy, wounded Soldiers in OIF have a far better chance of surviving their injuries than ever before.

The Army has already recognized the shortfalls in its Combat Service Support Control System (CSSCS)—a suite of communications and automation devices to process and track logistics requirements. Too few combat service support (CSS) units had the GPS-enabled systems needed to provide the total asset visibility required to make distribution-based logistics work. These shortfalls were most evident during the rapid move from Kuwait to Baghdad and beyond, but they persisted. Since the transition to Phase IV, CSS operations have functioned better using the forward operating base system, hub-and-spoke distribution road network, and improved convoy processes. However, the potential benefits of distribution-based logistics have not been fully realized.

Another insight that seems clear is that supplying and transporting the goods on the full-spectrum battlefield is itself a combat operation. CSS units need better communications and automation systems to keep pace with the advances made in battle command and to support units on the full-spectrum battlefield. Without the earlier division of ground operations into the front lines and the rear echelon, logistics units need the ability to plan and conduct combat operations on their own. This requires more survivable equipment, more radios, more GPS enabled C4I systems in more robust headquarters, more armament, and more redundancy in each of those areas. CSS units will have to spend more time training to use this equipment and on their combat tasks than ever before. This will put increased strain on CSS units, which have been made fewer and smaller since the start of the Army transformation efforts in 1999. Combat units also need greater self-sustainment capabilities during rapid mobile operations characteristic of Phase III, and even in less maneuver intensive stability operations.

The Army has made extensive use of contractors in OIF during, and after, the period under study in this book. The sheer size and complexity of the contractor force makes it impossible to give an accurate number of US contractors in Qatar, Kuwait, and Iraq, a problem that is one of the sources of attacks leveled against their use. However, it would not be an exaggeration to state that without civilian contract firms and their workers, the Army could not have conducted OIF. Their roles in preparing equipment for use prior to deployments; in maintaining equipment; in delivering supplies; in operating some command, control, and communications and automation equipment; and even in advising the ISF have allowed the Army to keep its military force levels lower than would otherwise be the case. (Some have even argued that the use of contractors makes is easier for the United States to go to war because it lessens the need to call up even larger numbers of Active and Reserve units.) There is little doubt that the tens of thousands of contract workers, many of them retired military personnel, have performed superbly in OIF. Despite the loss of life and operating with far less support for their families, contractors continue to serve very effectively in the most dangerous assignments.

Among the issues raised by this heavy reliance on contractors is cost (including the potential for waste, fraud, and abuse). The Congress and its investigative arm, the Government Accountability Office (GAO), have launched numerous investigations into charges of waste, fraud, and abuse connected with private contractors. Some Army contracting officers have been charged with abusing their positions to steer contracts toward specific firms. Some critics have also challenged the use of armed security contractors, primarily used by the CPA and Department of State, on grounds of effectiveness, control, and law of war principles. Iraqis make little distinction between the conduct of US military personnel and private security forces whose actions may not be conducted in accordance with stated military objectives, greatly complicating Coalition efforts to preserve unity of effort. The concept of the military as an exclusive profession has been called into doubt in light of the widespread use of contractors on the battlefield. Large salaries offered by contract firms have lured military personnel out of uniform. The impact of all these factors on morale and retention for Soldiers working alongside contractors performing the same or related duties for vastly greater salaries is hard to measure, but real nonetheless.

The amount of effort and resources devoted to the morale and welfare of the Army's Soldiers in Iraq is considerable. Tours that last 12 months or more take a huge toll on physical fitness, mental health, and personal and family morale. The combat actions in OIF may lack some of the intensity of the Army's more famous battles; but the constant danger, the nature of combat against unseen foes not fighting in accord with the rules of war, and the difficulty of measuring progress place demands on today's Soldiers at least as heavy as if not heavier than those born by their predecessors. However, the mid-tour morale leave program has proven to be a success in sustaining Soldier morale and effectiveness, and the many amenities provided by well-equipped forward operating bases (FOBs) provide some relief from the constant strain and danger.

These large FOBs, despised by some Iraqis as American oases in a troubled Iraq, may run counter to operations and counterinsurgency doctrine, which calls for extended interaction with local inhabitants and security forces. Another potential drawback to the immense support provided to American Soldiers is the ever lower "tooth-to-tail ratio" that it causes. The number of Soldiers who operate outside the bases in Kuwait and outside the FOBs in Iraq is much smaller than total deployed force levels would indicate. While the force protection and cultural sensitivity benefits of large FOBs are advantageous, they may well be counterproductive to the overall campaign. (Changes to US basing and operating methods in 2007 may present the opportunity to better evaluate this issue.) The Army must carefully weigh the benefits accrued from its extensive support to Soldiers' living conditions against the potential loss of effectiveness in these types of operations.

Army Education

Operations in Iraq since April 2003 indicate that Army education, as opposed to individual task-specific training, should place more emphasis on the humanities, especially on those disciplines that relate to the understanding of other cultures. The term "cultural awareness" has now emerged as a key imperative for the Army as a result of the relative lack of cultural understanding of American Soldiers in the Middle East and Iraq. The Army, and in particular the officer corps, must be better educated about the non-Western world. Precommissioning academic requirements should include required courses in history, international relations, macro-economics, culture, religion, and geography. Every Army officer should be required to speak a second language, with incentives to direct them toward languages from regions of the world deemed most important or most dangerous to US national interests. Beyond the obvious benefit of being able to converse with others, the mental agility and discipline gained from learning another language pays secondary and tertiary benefits. Language proficiency should be considered a prerequisite for commissioning of all new officers, and required over time for serving officers before being promoted to the next grade.

The Army must foster a greater contrarian spirit within the officer corps to avoid group think and naive susceptibility to the latest fads in military affairs. The creation of the so-called Red Team University at Fort Leavenworth, Kansas, to provide the Army with a core of officers trained to think like an uncooperative enemy, and to challenge plans before they are issued, is a good first step. The use of 360-degree performance evaluations will also help in creating an officer corps more aware of its leadership strengths and weaknesses. Army promotion and selection process must advance those NCOs and officers who demonstrate proficiency at full spectrum operations. The Army should push the rest of the Government to increase the professional schooling and assignment opportunities for Soldiers and civilians to serve in nonmilitary governmental agencies to foster better planning and operational effectiveness.

Soldiers: The Army's Greatest Asset

The most positive insight to emerge from this study has been the consistently superb combat and noncombat performance of US Army Soldiers and units. Despite all of the challenges and difficulties noted throughout *On Point II*, the US Army Soldier emerges again and again as the most flexible, determined, and resourceful element in the Army's arsenal. The bravery, ingenuity, and tactical skill of Soldiers, and the sustained tactical excellence of units in the US Army, are testimony to the soundness of the Army's recruiting, training, education, and leadership practices. This record of success has been marred somewhat by the dishonorable actions of a tiny, well publicized, fraction of the Soldiers who have served in Iraq. It is to the Army's credit that those incidents have been or are still being investigated, and that those found guilty of criminal misconduct are being punished. Clearly, much was done right to prepare the Army for its mission in what has become an extended campaign in Iraq. The high level of public support for the Army's Soldiers from every side of the political spectrum is ample evidence of their well earned respect. The Army must do more to put forth the names and faces of its greatest assets to maintain that level of public support.

The Army's recent emphasis on inculcating the Warrior Ethos is a positive reaction to the reality of 21st century military operations and shortfalls discovered during the march to Baghdad. The Warrior Tasks and Drills, which are now part of the Initial Entry Training (IET), the Noncommissioned Officer Education System (NCOES), and the Officer Education System (OES) should remain part of the individual training program. The 360-degree threat environment of the contemporary operating environment should put an end to that time-worn epithet for Soldiers whose missions were performed in the rear echelons of the linear battlefield. Every Soldier, regardless of military occupation specialty or rank must be a master of personal and small unit offensive and defensive combat skills.

Conclusion

Few mental exercises are more arrogant, and few have a higher risk of being just plain wrong, than hasty historical judgments about on-going military operations. At the same time, critics often accuse military leaders of fighting the last war, having missed the signs of impending change that will make the future unlike the past. Alongside this (usually exaggerated) criticism is one that accuses hidebound military leaders of planning to fight the next war in a way that they wish it to occur, not as it turns out to be. This chapter of *On Point II*, indeed the entire study, is an attempt to render those criticisms mute. Military conflicts are rarely, if ever, conducted like their predecessor, nor like the futurists predict they will be conducted. In 1973 the dean of living military historians, Michael Howard, famously stated that it may not matter what doctrine military leaders are working on for they are rarely correct about the future. He continues, "I am tempted to declare that it does not matter that they have got it wrong. What does matter is their capacity to get it right quickly once the moment arrives."[7] It is this mental flexibility, rooted in history but aware of constant change and prepared to quickly adapt to new conditions that must be cultivated in the Army. The US Army has a remarkable history of getting it right over time, and it is in that spirit that *On Point II* has been written.

Notes

1.   Carl von Clausewitz, *On War*, eds. Peter Paret and Michael Howard (Princeton, NJ: University Press, 1976), 88, 579.

2.   See Ali A. Allawi, *The Occupation of Iraq: Winning the War, Losing the Peace* (New Haven, CT: Yale University Press, 2007), 91–95, 133–146, 460. As one Iraqi politician has concluded, "The Iraqi political class that inherited the mantle of the state from the Baathist regime was manifestly culpable in presiding over the deterioration of the conditions in the country."

3.   For a recent example of this critique, see Brigadier General (Retired) Mitchell M. Zais, "U.S. Strategy in Iraq," *Military Review*, March–April, 2007, 105–108; see also, Richard Hart Sinnreich, "For Military Leaders, It's Déjà vu All Over Again," *Army*, June 2007, 9–10.

4.   See Field Manual 3-0, *Operations* (Washington, DC, 28 February 2008), chapter 3.

5.   "Head of Anti-IED Agency Says it's Been Effective," *Army Times*, 21 May 2007, 24.

6.   See Colonel Curtis D. Boyd, "Army IO is PSYOP: Influencing More with Less," *Military Review*, May–June 2007, 67–75.

7.   Sir Michael Howard, "Military Science in an Age of Peace," Chesney Memorial Gold Lecture, given on 3 October 1973, published in the *Journal of the Royal United Services Institute for Defense Studies*, 119, 1 March 1974, 7.

Epilogue

The US Army in Operation IRAQI FREEDOM
May 2003 to January 2005

There were reasons for great optimism among US Soldiers in Iraq on 30 January 2005. Eight million Iraqis—roughly 60 percent of the electorate—had just voted in the first truly democratic elections in the nation's history. The US Army had helped make that event possible. By January 2005 approximately 250,000 American Soldiers had served or were serving in Iraq. Much of their effort had been directed at this day. US Army units that assisted in establishing good governance had helped establish a foundation on which the Iraqis built the electoral system. The Iraqi Security Forces, which American Soldiers had helped equip, train, and advise, provided most of the front-line security for those elections. And American Soldiers, along with other US and Coalition forces, had set the proper conditions for the elections by destroying insurgent safe havens and suppressing the insurgent network overall so the polls could operate on that January day. General George W. Casey Jr., commander of Multi-National Force–Iraq, told Coalition Soldiers they had "shaped history" and that their "presence and preparations allowed the Iraqi people to defy terrorism and to embrace democracy as a way ahead for the nation of Iraq."[*]

The optimism at the beginning of 2005 also stemmed from the advances made by the Coalition over the previous 18 months. Having arrived in Iraq in 2003 with almost no preparation for conducting postconflict operations, the Coalition had by January 2005 established a broad, full spectrum campaign designed to assist with the reconstruction of the country, facilitate the generation of representative forms of government, and provide the new Iraqi state with loyal and effective security forces. While there had been significant difficulties in 2003 in initiating this new campaign, by mid-2004 the Coalition had passed full sovereignty to the Iraqis and created a new political-military command structure that featured a theater strategic military headquarters designed and manned to assist the new Iraqi state on its path to greater political and social stability.

In the same period, and without great fanfare, American Soldiers had begun a journey down a new road. It is no exaggeration to state that during 2003 and 2004, the US Army reinvented itself. The US Army had entered Operation IRAQI FREEDOM (OIF) in March 2003 as a force that had mastered high intensity combat operations as part of the joint team. By the end of 2003, the Army had transformed itself into an organization that conducted full spectrum operations in which conventional combat was only one mission and, arguably, of less importance than other missions within that spectrum.

Driving this transformation were the realities on the ground in Iraq. With major gaps in planning for the postconflict phase of OIF and without a large influx of resources from non-Department of Defense (DOD) agencies and nongovernment organizations (NGOs), Soldiers as well as US Marines and Coalition counterparts were left with the tasks of remaking much

---

[*]John D. Banusiewicz, "Commander in Iraq Thanks Troops Who 'Shaped History,'" *American Forces Information Service*, 3 February 2005, http://defenselink.mil/news/Feb2005/n02032005_2005020304.html (accessed 4 November 2006).

of Iraq's physical and political infrastructure and establishing the country's security forces. Considering the lack of preparation, guidance, and resources, it is striking how quickly and professionally American Soldiers began the rebuilding process. Indeed, the story of the 12 months that followed the fall of the Saddam regime is dominated by tactical units improvising, finding ways to enact a broad-based campaign focused on simultaneously defusing a mounting insurgency and building popular support for the Coalition's program in Iraq. The creation of the Commander's Emergency Response Program (CERP) and the neighborhood advisory councils (NACs) and district advisory councils (DACs) that units rapidly established in the post-Saddam political vacuum are only two dramatic examples of Soldiers' willingness to find innovative means to give Iraqis a chance for a new future. Privates, sergeants, junior officers, and senior officers from every branch of the Army extended the reputation for the inventiveness and flexibility earned by their predecessors in conflicts of the past. Difficult in any circumstances, the type of campaign the US Army began in May 2003 was complicated further by halting efforts at levels far above the Soldier where the Coalition Provisional Authority (CPA) and Combined Joint Task Force–7 (CJTF-7) struggled to create unity of command and unity of effort and where the Coalition grappled with the divisive, and at times violent, realities of Iraqi politics.

While the Army's transformation in Iraq was striking, the American Soldiers' efforts to deal with Iraqi realities were not enough by themselves to achieve the Coalition's objectives for Iraq. No one—neither Soldier nor civilian, neither American nor Iraqi—could look at Iraq in early 2005 and see a nation that fully enjoyed the prosperity and security that was at the heart of the Coalition vision for the country. On several occasions and in multiple areas of Iraq during 2004, Sunni insurgents and Shia militias had risen up in open defiance of the emerging Iraqi Government. And while the Coalition militarily defeated their actions, both elements continued to mount opposition to Iraqi and Coalition forces. The large majority of Sunni Arabs, feeling threatened by a new political system in which they would lose their historical control over matters of state, refused to participate in the January elections. Worse was that even with the Iraqi police and military forces securing much of the country, there were close to 300 terrorist attacks on Election Day, resulting in 45 deaths and many other casualties. These were the realities that diminished the optimism of that day, and they made it clear that the journey on which the new Iraq had just embarked remained arduous.

Because of the obvious challenges in Iraq's security environment, it was clear in January 2005 that the US Army would remain in the country for some time. As of this writing, American Soldiers and their Coalition and Iraqi counterparts are still in the midst of the campaign to secure Iraq. In 2007, in fact, President George W. Bush reinforced the American commitment to Iraq by deploying an additional five brigade combat teams to establish greater security in Baghdad and its environs. With the Coalition project in Iraq unfinished, this study is not in the position to offer any final historical judgment on the US Army's efforts in the country. The authors of this work have always recognized that this proximity to actual events in Iraq was a limitation on their ability to completely understand the context in which political leaders made decisions and Soldiers took actions. They also recognize that in the interest of providing a history of this early part of the campaign in Iraq in an expeditious manner, they may have made mistakes of fact, interpretation, and omission. For example, for reasons of classification, most of the sources that reveal the actions of US Special Operations Soldiers in this period of OIF were not available, leaving that important element of the campaign's story essentially untold. However, the authors have balanced these concerns with their desire to provide the Army a study of its operations in Iraq that will highlight the past actions of its Soldiers and hope that it will become an early discussion in a historical dialogue about OIF that will continue for many years.

Final comments in a history of this type should be dedicated to the hundreds of thousands of American Soldiers who served in Iraq between May 2003 and January 2005. OIF became the central mission of the US Army after May 2003. In the 18 months that followed, close to a quarter of a million Soldiers served in Iraq, and the Army began to focus its training, education, finances, and other resources on achieving victory in that nation. Fighting with and working alongside Soldiers were tens of thousands of Marines, Airmen, Sailors, DOD civilians, and American contractors. Their story is not told in this book, but without their courageous service, the Army could not have accomplished what it did. The same is true of the millions of Iraqis who, in partnership with Coalition forces, tried in the face of incredible hardships to build a new future for their country. For American Soldiers in this period, professional and private lives began to focus on Iraq as most units began to rotate into Iraq for 1-year deployments to be followed by another year spent at home station preparing to redeploy to Iraq once again. This study is a tribute to the hard work and commitment of these Americans, and especially to those who were wounded or lost their lives in Iraq.

On Point II is also a testament to the things these Soldiers created while participating in the campaign. After deposing a tyrannical regime, these men and women began rebuilding Iraq for the benefit of its population. Through this effort, the Soldiers of OIF became the heirs of the millions of American Soldiers who helped liberate Europe and Japan during World War II and then remained in those places to reconstruct economies, governments, and societies. From the vantage point of 30 January 2005, American Soldiers in Iraq could look back with a great deal of pride in their work that had similarly focused on establishing prosperity, stability, and a representative government. While most recognized that the road ahead was not certain and that there were still significant challenges remaining to the creation of a new Iraqi state, they could take satisfaction from how they had transformed the Army and made it the force that remained *on point* in America's continuing campaign in Iraq.

Appendix A

COALITON PROVISIONAL AUTHORITY ORDER NUMBER 1

DE-BA`ATHIFICATION OF IRAQI SOCIETY

Pursuant to my authority as Administrator of the Coalition Provisional Authority (CPA), relevant U.N. Security Council resolutions, and the laws and usages of war,

Recognizing that the Iraqi people have suffered large scale human rights abuses and depravations over many years at the hands of the Ba`ath Party,

Noting the grave concern of Iraqi society regarding the threat posed by the continuation of Ba`ath Party networks and personnel in the administration of Iraq, and the intimidation of the people of Iraq by Ba`ath Party officials,

Concerned by the continuing threat to the security of the Coalition Forces posed by the Iraqi Ba`ath Party,

I hereby promulgate the following:

Section 1
Disestablishment of the Ba`ath Party

1) On April 16, 2003 the Coalition Provisional Authority disestablished the Ba`ath Party of Iraq. This order implements the declaration by eliminating the party's structures and removing its leadership from positions of authority and responsibility in Iraqi society. By this means, the Coalition Provisional Authority will ensure that representative government in Iraq is not threatened by Ba`athist elements returning to power ant that those in positions of authority in the future are acceptable to the people of Iraq.

2) Full members of the Ba`ath Party holding the ranks of 'Udw Qutriyya (Regional Command Member), 'Udw Far' (Branch Member). 'Udw Shu'bah (Section Member), and 'Udw Firqah (Group Member) (together, "Senior Party Members") are herby removed from their positions and banned from future employment in the public sector. These Senior Party Members shall be evaluated for criminal conduct or threat to the security of the Coalition. Those suspected of criminal conduct shall be investigated and, if deemed a threat to security or a flight risk, detained or placed under house arrest.

3) Individuals holding positions in the top three layers of management in every national government ministry, affiliated corporations and other government institutions (e.g., universities and hospitals) shall be interviewed for possible affiliation with the Ba`ath Party, and subject to investigation for criminal conduct and risk to security. Any such persons detained to be full members of the Ba`ath Party shall be removed from their employment. This includes those

and risk to security. Any such persons determined to be full members of the Baath Party shall be removed from their employment. This includes those holding the more junior ranks of 'Udw (Member) and 'Udw 'Amil (Active Member) as well as those determined to be Senior Party Members.

4) Displays in government buildings or public spaces of the image or likeness of Saddam Hussein or other readily identifiable members of the former regime or of symbols of the Baath Party or the former regime are hereby prohibited.

5) Rewards shall be made available for information leading to the capture of senior members of the Baath party and individuals complicit in the crimes of the former regime.

6) The Administrator of the Coalition Provisional Authority or his designees may grant exceptions to the above guidance on a case-by-case basis.

Section 2

Entry into Force

This Order shall enter into force on the date of signature.

5/16/03

L. Paul Bremer, Administrator
Coalition Provisional Authority

Appendix B

COALITION PROVISIONAL AUTHORITY ORDER NUMBER 2

DISSOULUTION OF ENTITIES

Pursuant to my authority as Administrator of the Coalition Provisional Authority (CPA), relevant U.N. Security Council resolutions, including Resolution 1483 (2003), and the laws and usages of war,

Reconfirming all of the provisions of General Franks' Freedom Message to the Iraqi People of April 16, 2003,

Recognizing that the prior Iraqi regime used certain government entities to oppress the Iraqi people and as instruments of torture, repression and corruption,

Reaffirming the Instructions to the Citizens of Iraq regarding Ministry of Youth and Sport of May 8, 2003,

I hereby promulgate the following:

Section 1
Dissolved Entities

The entities (the "Dissolved Entities") listed in the attached Annex are hereby dissolved. Additional entities may be added to this list in the future.

Section 2
Assets and Financial Obligations

1) All assets, including records and data, in whatever from maintained and wherever located, of the Dissolved Entities shall be held by the Administrator of the CPA ("the Administrator") on behalf of and for the benefit of the Iraqi people and shall be used to assist the Iraqi people and to support the recovery of Iraq.

2) All financial obligations of the Dissolved Entities are suspended. The Administrator of the CPA will establish procedures whereby persons claiming to be the beneficiaries of such obligations may apply for payment.

3) Persons in possession of assets of the Dissolved Entities shall preserve those assets, promptly inform local Coalition authorities, and immediately turn them over, as directed by those authorities. Continued possession, transfer, sale, use, conversion, or concealment of such assets following the date of this Order is prohibited and may be punished.

Section 3
Employees and Service Members

1) Any military or other rank, title, or status granted to a former employee or functionary of a Dissolved Entity by the former Regime is hereby cancelled.

2) All conscripts are released from their service obligations. Conscriptions is suspended indefinitely, subject to decisions by future Iraq governments concerning whether a free Iraq should have conscription.

3) Any person employed by a Dissolved Entity in any form or capacity, is dismissed effective as of April 16, 2003. Any person employed by a Dissolved Entity, in any from or capacity remains accountable for acts committed during such employment.

4) A termination payment in an amount to be determined by the Administrator will be paid to employees so dismissed, except those who are Senior Party Members as defined in the Administrator's May 16, 2003 Order of the Coalition Provisional Authority De-Ba`athification of Iraqi Society, CPA/ORD/2003/01 ("Senior Party Members") (See Section 3.6).

5) Pensions being paid by, or on account of service to, a Dissolved Entity before April 16, 2003 will continue to be paid, including to war widows and disabled veterans, provided that no pension payments will be made to any person who is a Senior Party Member (see Section 3.6) and that the power is reserved to the Administrator and to future Iraqi governments to revoke or reduce pensions as a penalty for past or future illegal conduct or to modify pension arrangements to eliminate improper privileges granted by the Ba`athist regime or for similar reasons.

6) Notwithstanding any provision of this Order, or any other Order, law, or regulation, and consistent with the Administrator's May 16, 2003 Order of the Coalition Provisional Authority De-Ba`athification of Iraqi Society, CPA/ORD/2003/01, no payment, including a termination or pension payment, will be made to any person who is or was a Senior Party Member. Any person holding the rank under the former regime of Colonel or above, or its equivalent, will be deemed a Senior Party Member, provided that such persons may seek, under procedures to be prescribed, to establish to the satisfaction of the Administrator, that they were not a Senior Party Member.

Section 4
Information

The Administrator shall prescribe procedures for offering rewards to person who provide information leading to the recovery of assets of Dissolved Entities.

Section 5
New Iraqi Corps

The CPA plans to create in the near future a New Iraqi Crops, as the first step in forming a national self-defense capability for a free Iraq. Under civilian control, that Corps will be professional, non-political, militarily effective, and representative of all Iraqis. The CPA will promulgate procedures for participation in the New Iraqi Corps.

Section 6
Other Matters

1) The Administrator may delegate his powers and responsibilities with respect to this Order as he determines appropriate. References to the Administrator herein include such delegates.

2) The Administrator may grant exceptions any limitations in this Order at his discretion.

Section 7
Entry into Force

This Order shall enter into force on the date of signature.

[signature] 5/23/03

L. Paul Bremer, Administrator
Coalition Provisional Authority

ANNEX

COALITION PROVISIONAL AUTHORITY ORDER NUMBER 2

DISSOLUTION OF ENTITIES

Institutions dissolved by the Order referenced (the "Dissolved Entities") are:

The Ministry of Defence
The Ministry of Information
The Ministry of State for Military Affairs
The Iraqi Intelligence Service
The National Security Bureau
The Directorate of National Security (Amn al-'Am)
The Special Security Organization

All entities affiliated with or comprising Saddam Hussein's bodyguards to include:

-Murafaqin (Companions)
-Himaya al Khasa (Special Guard)

The following military organizations:

-The Army, Air Force, Navy, the Air Defence Force, and other regular
 military services
-The Republican Guard
-The Special Republican Guard
-The Directorate of Military Intelligence
-The Al Quds Force
-Emergency Forces (Quwat al Tawari)

The following paramilitaries:

-Saddam Fedayeen
-Ba`ath Party Militia
-Friends of Saddam
-Saddam's Lion Cubs (Ashbal Saddam)

Other Organizations:

-The Presidential Diwan
- The Presidential Secretariat
-The Revolutionary Command Council

-The National Assembly
-The Youth Organization (al-Futuwah)
-National Olympic Committee
-Revolutionary, Special and National Security Courts

All organizations subordinate to the Dissolved Entities are also dissolved.

Additional organizations may be added to this list in the future.

Appendix C

Unit Areas of Responsibility, 2003–2004

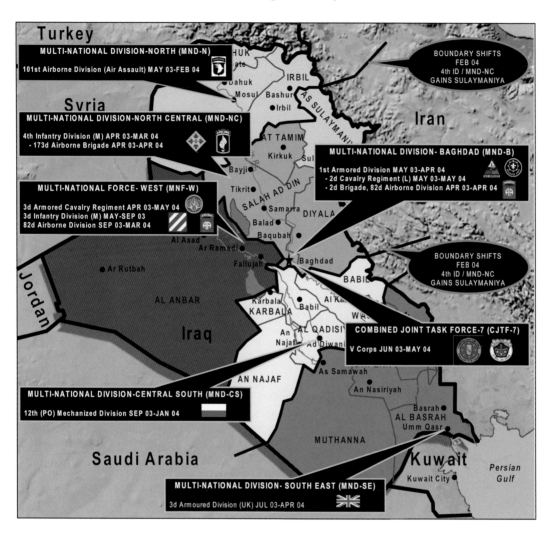

Appendix D
Theater Structure, 2003–2005

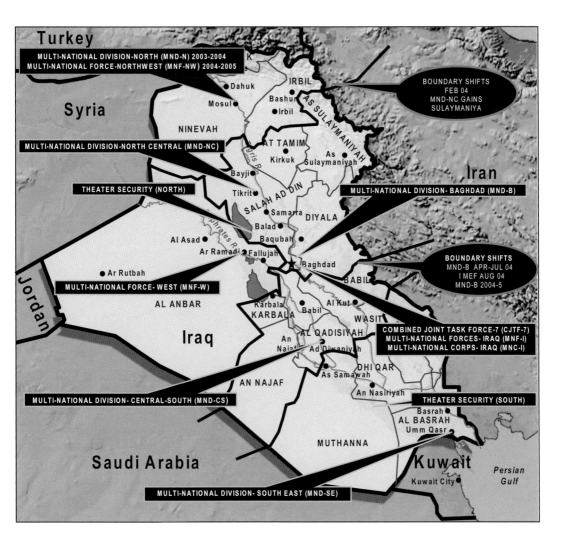

603

Appendix E
Unit Areas of Responsibility, 2004–2005

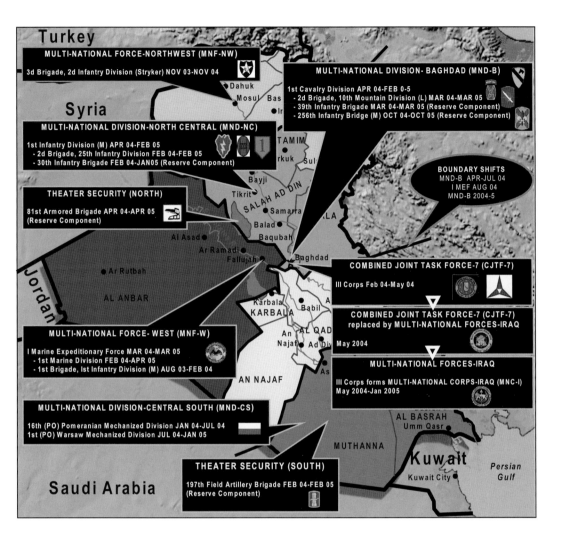

Appendix F

US Army Units in Operation IRAQI FREEDOM
Order of Battle: May 2003–January 2005

The following order of battle depicts the US Army units at battalion level and above that participated in Operation IRAQI FREEDOM (OIF) between May 2003 and January 2005. This 18-month period included two major troop rotations—OIF I and OIF II; accordingly, this order of battle is divided into two sections. Not all unit deployments fit neatly into these two rotation periods. Task Force *Olympia*, for example, deployed to Iraq in late 2003; however, that unit is placed in the OIF II portion of this order of battle. Units that arrived in Iraq between November 2004 and January 2005 as part of the troop reinforcement for the national elections are not included in this order of battle.

Task organization of Army formations in OIF during this period was dynamic, particularly at division echelon and below. This order of battle captures *habitual* command relationships, but recognizes headquarters often shifted battalions and brigade combat teams to meet immediate operational requirements. At times, company-level units from two or more divisions were joined together to form ad hoc task forces—those temporary organizations are not included.

OIF I

CJTF-7
(Combined Joint Task Force–7, built around V Corps Headquarters, replaced CFLCC as Coalition military headquarters in Iraq on 15 June 2003)

V Corps
V Corps Artillery
- 41st Field Artillery Brigade
  - 2-18th Field Artillery
  - 1-27th Field Artillery
- 17th Field Artillery Brigade
  - 1-12th Field Artillery
  - 5-3d Field Artillery
  - 3-18th Field Artillery
  - 6-27th Field Artillery
31st Air Defense Artillery Brigade (-) (OPCON)
- 5-52d Air Defense Artillery (-)
- 6-52d Air Defense Artillery (-)
12th Aviation Brigade
- 2-228th Aviation Battalion (-)
- 3-158th Aviation Battalion
- 5-158th Aviation Battalion
11th Attack Helicopter Regiment
- 6-6th Attack Helicopter Squadron
130th Engineer Brigade
- 168th Engineer Group
- 265th Engineer Group

937th Engineer Group
    724th Engineer Battalion
        1092d Engineer Battalion
        54th Engineer Battalion
        565th Engineer Battalion (Provisional)
    864th Engineer Battalion
        142d Engineer Battalion (-)
        94th Engineer Battalion
        878th Engineer Battalion
205th Military Intelligence Brigade (-)
    1st Military Intelligence Battalion
    302d Military Intelligence Battalion
    165th Military Intelligence Battalion) (-)
    223d Military Intelligence Battalion (Linguist)
    224th Military Intelligence Battalion
    323d Military Intelligence Battalion (-)
    325th Military Intelligence Battalion (-)
    519th Military Intelligence Battalion (-)
220th Military Police Brigade (-) (OPCON) (Feb 03–Feb 04)
    118th Military Police Battalion
    504th Military Police Battalion
    607th Military Police Battalion
    1-293d Infantry (-)
800th Military Police Brigade (Internment and Resettlement) (OPCON)
    115th Military Police Battalion
    320th Military Police Battalion
    324th Military Police Battalion
    400th Military Police Battalion
    530th Military Police Battalion
    724th Military Police Battalion
    744th Military Police Battalion
22d Signal Brigade (OPCON)
    17th Signal Battalion (-)
    32d Signal Battalion (-)
    440th Signal Battalion
    51st Signal Battalion (-)
    234th Signal Battalion
3d Ordnance Battalion (OPCON)
79th Ordnance Battalion (OPCON)
352d Civil Affairs Command
    308th Civil Affairs Brigade
335th Theater Signal Command (TACON)
    86th Signal Battalion
    63d Signal Battalion
    504th Signal Battalion
    151st Signal Battalion

40th Signal Battalion

    9th Psychological Operations Battalion

2d Chemical Battalion

18th Service Support Group

    90th Personnel Services Battalion

        24th Personnel Services Battalion

        546th Personnel Services Battalion

        208th Finance Battalion

3d Infantry Division (Mar 03–Sep 03)

    1st Brigade, 3d Infantry Division

        2-7th Infantry

        3-7th Infantry

        3-69th Armor

        1-41st Field Artillery

        11th Engineer Battalion

        3d Forward Support Battalion

    2d Brigade, 3d Infantry Division

        3-15th Infantry

        1-64th Armor

        4-64th Armor

        1-9th Field Artillery (-)

        10th Engineer Battalion (-)

        26th Forward Support Battalion

        211th Military Police Battalion

    3d Brigade, 3d Infantry Division

        TF 1-15th Infantry

        TF 1-30th Infantry

        TF 2-69th Armor

        1-10th Field Artillery

        121st Engineer Battalion

        317th Engineer Battalion

        203d Forward Support Battalion

    4th Brigade, 3d Infantry Division (-)

        1-3d Aviation (AH-64D) (-)

        603d Aviation Support Battalion

        3-7th Cavalry

        2-3d Aviation

    3d Division Artillery (DIVARTY)

        1-39th Field Artillery

        1-41st Field Artillery

        1-3d Air Defense Artillery

    3d Division Support Command (DISCOM) (-)

        703d Main Support Battalion

    103d Military Intelligence Battalion (-)

    123d Signal Battalion (-)

4th Infantry Division (Apr 03–Mar 04)

1st Brigade, 4th Infantry Division
    1-22d Infantry
    3-66th Armor
    4-42d Field Artillery
    720th Military Police Battalion
    299th Engineer Battalion (-)
    4th Forward Support Battalion
2d Brigade, 4th Infantry Division
    2-8th Infantry
    1-67th Armor
    3-67th Armor
    3-16th Field Artillery
    588th Engineer Battalion
    204th Forward Support Battalion
3d Brigade, 4th Infantry Division
    1-12th Infantry
    1-8th Infantry
    1-66th Armor
    1-68th Armor
    3-29th Field Artillery
    4th Engineer Battalion (-)
    64th Forward Support Battalion
4th Brigade, 4th Infantry Division
    1-4th Aviation (-)
    2-4th Aviation (-)
    1-10th Cavalry (-)
    1-17th Field Artillery
    404th Aviation Support Battalion
4th Infantry Division Artillery
    2-20th Field Artillery (-)
    5th Engineer Battalion
4th Division Support Command (DISCOM)
    704th Main Support Battalion (-)
1-44th Air Defense Artillery (-)
104th Military Intelligence Battalion (-)
124th Signal Battalion (-)
230th Finance Battalion (-)
502d Personnel Services Battalion
173d Airborne Brigade (Attached)
    1-508th Infantry
    2-503d Infantry
    1-12th Infantry
    1-63d Armor (-)
    2-15th Field Artillery (-)
    404th Civil Affairs Battalion (-)
    201st Forward Support Battalion

555th Engineer Group (Combat)
  14th Engineer Battalion (-)
  223d Engineer Battalion (-)
  244th Engineer Battalion
402d Civil Affairs Battalion
418th Civil Affairs Battalion (-)
1st Armored Division (May 03–Apr 04)
  1st Brigade, 1st Armored Division
    1-36th Infantry
    3-124th Infantry (-)
    1-37th Armor
    2-3d Field Artillery
    16th Engineer Battalion (-)
    501st Forward Support Battalion
  2d Brigade, 1st Armored Division
    1-6th Infantry
    2-6th Infantry
    1-35th Armor
    3d Squadron, 2d Cavalry Regiment
    4-27th Field Artillery
    40th Engineer Battalion
    47th Forward Support Battalion
  3d Brigade, 1st Armored Division
    1-325th Infantry
    1-13th Armor
    2-70th Armor
    4-1st Field Artillery
    70th Engineer Battalion
    125th Forward Support Battalion
  4th Brigade, 1st Armored Division
    1-501st Aviation
    2-501st Aviation
    127th Area Support Battalion
  2d Armored Cavalry Regiment (ACR) (-)
    1st Squadron, 2d Armored Cavalry Regiment
    2d Squadron, 2d Armored Cavalry Regiment
    2-37th Armor
    4th Squadron, 2d Armored Cavalry Regiment
    3-321st Field Artillery
    Support Squadron, 2d Armored Cavalry Regiment (-)
  2d Brigade, 82d Airborne Division
    2-325th Infantry
    3-325th Infantry
    1-1st Cavalry (-)
    2-319th Field Artillery (-)
    439th Engineer Battalion

        407th Forward Support Battalion (-)
    1st Armored Division Artillery
        1-94th Field Artillery
        1-4th Air Defense Artillery
    Division Support Command (DISCOM)
        123d Main Support Battalion
    1st Armored Division Engineer Brigade
        1457th Engineer Battalion (-)
        493d Engineer Group
        389th Engineer Battalion
        203d Engineer Battalion
    141st Signal Battalion
    8th Finance Battalion (-)
    55th Personnel Services Battalion (-)
    501st Military Intelligence Battalion
    18th Military Police Brigade
        519th Military Police Battalion
        709th Military Police Battalion
        168th Military Police Battalion
        716th Military Police Battalion
    354th Civil Affairs Brigade
        422d Civil Affairs Battalion
        490th Civil Affairs Battalion (-)
        414th Civil Affairs Battalion
101st Airborne Division (Air Assault) (May 03–Feb 04)
    1st Brigade, 101st Airborne Division
        1-327th Infantry
        2-327th Infantry
        2-320th Field Artillery
        3-101st Aviation
        5-101st Aviation
        426th Forward Support Battalion
    2d Brigade, 101st Airborne Division
        1-502d Infantry (-)
        2-502d Infantry
        3-502d Infantry
        3-327th Infantry
        2-17th Cavalry (-)
        9-101st Aviation
        1-320th Field Artillery
        877th Engineer Battalion
        526th Forward Support Battalion
        503d Military Police Battalion
    3d Brigade, 101st Airborne Division
        1-187th Infantry (-)
        2-187th Infantry (-)

3-187th Infantry
2-101st Aviation
3-320th Field Artillery
626th Forward Support Battalion
101st Aviation Brigade
  1-101st Aviation
  6-101st Aviation
159th Aviation Brigade
  7-101st Aviation (-)
  4-101st Aviation (-)
Division Artillery (DIVARTY)
  1-377th Field Artillery
  2-44th Air Defense Artillery (-)
Division Support Command (DISCOM)
  801st Main Support Battalion (-)
  8-101st Aviation (-)
326th Engineer Battalion (-)
311th Military Intelligence Battalion (-)
501st Signal Battalion (-)
101st Finance Battalion (-)
101st Soldier Support Battalion
926th Engineer Group
  52d Engineer Battalion
  37th Engineer Battalion
52d Engineer Battalion
431st Civil Affairs Battalion
404th Civil Affairs Battalion (-)
3d Armored Cavalry Regiment (ACR) (Attached to 82d Airborne Division in Sep 03)
  1st Squadron, 3d Armored Cavalry Regiment
  2d Squadron, 3d Armored Cavalry Regiment
  3d Squadron, 3d Armored Cavalry Regiment
  4th Squadron, 3d Armored Cavalry Regiment
  Support Squadron
  16th Signal Battalion
82d Airborne Division (Sep 03–Mar 04)
  3d Brigade, 82d Airborne Division
    1-505th Infantry
    3-505th Infantry
    1-504th Infantry
    1-32d Infantry, 10th Mountain Division
    1-319th Field Artillery
    82d Forward Support Battalion
  1st Brigade, 1st Infantry Division
    1-16th Infantry
    1-34th Armor
    1-124th Infantry

1-5 Field Artillery Battalion
1st Engineer Battalion
101st Forward Support Battalion
82d Aviation Brigade
    1-17th Cavalry
    1-82d Aviation Battalion
    2-82d Aviation Battalion
    82d Aviation Support Battalion
Division Support Command (DISCOM)
    782d Main Support Battalion (-)
    3-4th Air Defense Artillery
2-5th Field Artillery
313th Military Intelligence Battalion (-)
307th Engineer Battalion (-)
82d Signal Battalion (-)
82d Soldier Support Battalion
304th Civil Affairs Brigade
    432d Civil Affairs Battalion (-)
3d Corps Support Command (COSCOM) (May 03–Feb 04)
    16th Corps Support Group
        142d Corps Support Battalion
        485th Corps Support Battalion
        541st Ordnance Battalion
    7th Corps Support Group
        71st Corps Support Battalion
        90th Personnel Support Battalion
        413th Supply & Services Battalion
        181st Transportation Battalion
        418th Quartermaster Support Battalion
        692d Quartermaster Water Support Battalion
        7-159th Aviation Maintenance Battalion
    371st Corps Support Group
        321st Ordnance Battalion
        345th Corps Support Battalion
        548th Corps Support Battalion
        692d Corps Support Battalion
    64th Corps Support Group
        544th Corps Support Battalion
        553d Corps Support Battalion
        180th Transportation Battalion
    101st Corps Support Group
        561st Corps Support Battalion
        548th Corps Support Battalion
    171st Area Support Group
        189th Corps Support Battalion

       260th Quartermaster Battalion

       346th Transportation Battalion

       362d Quartermaster Battalion

       394th Quartermaster Battalion

       399th Movement Control Battalion

    371st Corps Support Group

       18th Corps Support Battalion

       292d Corps Support Battalion

       345th Corps Support Battalion

       546th Personnel Support Battalion

   19th Area Support Group (Provisional)

       27th Movement Control Battalion

30th Medical Brigade

   93d Medical Battalion (-)

   172d Medical Battalion

1st Medical Brigade

   21st Combat Support Hospital

   28th Combat Support Hospital

   31st Combat Support Hospital

   56th Medical Battalion

62d Medical Brigade

   109th Area Support Medical Battalion

18th Service Support Group

V Corps Troops

   Main Command Post

   V Corps Special Troops Battalion

       1138th Engineer Battalion

   Rear Detachment–Kuwait

       371st Corps Support Group

          345th Corps Support Battalion

          292d Corps Support Battalion

          18th Corps Support Battalion

          546th Personnel Support Battalion

Combined Joint Special Operations Task Force–Arabian Peninsula (in support of CJTF-7)

5th Special Forces Group

10th Special Forces Group

2d Battalion, 75th Ranger Regiment (-)

160th Special Operations Aviation Regiment (-)

Other unidentified Special Operations Forces (SOF) units

OIF II

III Corps (Feb 04–Apr 05)

(III Corps staff replaced V Corps as core of CJTF-7 in February 2004. Multi-National Force–Iraq/Multi-National Corps–Iraq replaced CJTF-7 on 15 May 2004.)

III Corps Artillery
- 197th Field Artillery Brigade
    - 2-147th Field Artillery Battalion
    - 1-201st Field Artillery Battalion
    - 4-178th Field Artillery Battalion
    - 2-130th Field Artillery Battalion

185th Aviation Brigade
- 1-106th Aviation
- 1-244th Aviation

420th Engineer Brigade
- 84th Engineer Battalion
- 980th Engineer Battalion

504th Military Intelligence Brigade
- 303d Military Intelligence Battalion
- 202d Military Intelligence Battalion

89th Military Police Brigade
- 759th Military Police Battalion

16th Military Police Brigade
- 95th Military Police Battalion
- 391st Military Police Battalion
- 160th Military Police Battalion
- 1103d Military Police Battalion

3d Signal Brigade
- 57th Signal Battalion
- 29th Signal Battalion
- 711th Signal Battalion

63d Ordnance Battalion

350th Civil Affairs Command
- 478th Civil Affairs Battalion
- 425th Civil Affairs Battalion
- 489th Civil Affairs Battalion

1st Infantry Division (Apr 04–Feb 05)
- 2d Brigade, 1st Infantry Division
    - 1-26th Infantry
    - 1-77th Armor
    - 2-108th Infantry
    - 1-18th Infantry
    - 1-7th Field Artillery (-)
    - 9th Engineer Battalion (-)
    - 299th Forward Support Battalion

3d Brigade, 1st Infantry Division
    2-2d Infantry
    2-63d Armor
    1-6th Field Artillery
    82d Engineer Battalion
    201st Forward Support Battalion
2d Brigade, 25th Infantry Division
    1-21st Infantry
    1-14th Infantry
    1-27th Infantry
    2-11th Field Artillery
    225th Forward Support Battalion
30th Infantry Brigade (North Carolina Army National Guard)
    1-150th Armor (-)
    1-252d Armor
    1-120th Infantry
    1-113th Field Artillery (-)
    105th Engineer Battalion
    230th Forward Support Battalion
4th Aviation Brigade, 1st Infantry Division
    1-1st Attack Helicopter Battalion
    2-1st Aviation Battalion
    8-229th Aviation
    601st Aviation Support Battalion
1st Division Artillery (DIVARTY)
    1-33d Field Artillery
1st Engineer Brigade
    264th Engineer Support Group
    216th Engineer Battalion
    141st Engineer Battalion
Division Support Command (DISCOM)
    701st Main Support Battalion
1-4th Cavalry Squadron
4-3d Air Defense Artillery
101st Military Intelligence Battalion
121st Signal Battalion
38th Personnel Services Battalion (-)
106th Finance Battalion (-)
415th Civil Affairs Battalion
1st Cavalry Division (Apr 04–Feb 05)
    1st Brigade, 1st Cavalry Division
        2-5th Cavalry
        2-8th Cavalry
        1-12th Cavalry
        1-82d Field Artillery

    20th Engineer Battalion

    115th Forward Support Battalion

2d Brigade, 1st Cavalry Division

    1-5th Cavalry

    2-12th Cavalry

    3-82d Field Artillery

    91st Engineer Battalion

    15th Forward Support Battalion

3d Brigade, 1st Cavalry Division

    1-9th Cavalry

    3-8th Cavalry

    1-153d Infantry

    1-161st Infantry

    3-325th Infantry

    1-206th Field Artillery

    8th Engineer Battalion (-)

    2-82d Field Artillery

    215th Forward Support Battalion

    112th Military Police Battalion

5th Brigade (Provisional) [DIVARTY]

    1-8th Cavalry

    1-7th Cavalry (-)

    1-21st Field Artillery

    2-24th Marines

    515th Forward Support Battalion (Provisional)

2d Brigade, 10th Mountain Division

    2-14th Infantry

    4-31st Infantry

    1-69th Infantry

    1-41st Infantry

    2-15th Field Artillery

    4-5th Air Defense Artillery

    210th Forward Support Battalion

256th Brigade Combat Team (Louisiana Army National Guard)

    1-156th Armor

    2-156th Infantry

    3-156th Infantry

    1088th Engineer Battalion

    199th Forward Support Battalion

39th Infantry Brigade (Arkansas Army National Guard)

    3-153d Infantry

    2-162d Infantry

    2-7th Cavalry

    39th Forward Support Battalion

4th Aviation Brigade

    1-227th Attack Helicopter Battalion

2-227th Attack Helicopter Battalion
615th Forward Support Battalion
1-25th Attack Battalion
103d Field Artillery Brigade (Rhode Island Army National Guard)
1-303d Armor (-)
1-141st Field Artillery
Division Support Command (DISCOM)
27th Main Support Battalion
Engineer Brigade, 1st Cavalry Division
353d Engineer Group
411th Engineer Battalion
612th Engineer Battalion
312th Military Intelligence Battalion (-)
13th Signal Battalion (-)
443d Civil Affairs Battalion (-)
15th Finance Battalion (-)
15th Personnel Services Battalion (-)
TF OLYMPIA (Nov 03–Nov 04)
HQ, TF Olympia
3-17th Cavalry (OH-58D)
503d Military Police Battalion
310th Military Intelligence Battalion (-)
115th Signal Battalion
416th Civil Affairs Battalion (-)
133d Engineer Battalion
44th Support Battalion (-)
3d Brigade, 2d Infantry Division (Stryker)
2-3d Infantry
1-23d Infantry
5-20th Infantry
1-14th Cavalry
1-37th Field Artillery
296th Forward Support Battalion
276th Engineer Battalion
Theater Security North
81st Armored Brigade (Washington Army National Guard) (Apr 04–Apr 05)
1-161st Infantry
1-303d Armor
1-185th Armor (California Army National Guard)
898th Engineer Battalion
181st Forward Support Battalion
Theater Security South
197th Field Artillery Brigade (New Hampshire Army National Guard) (Feb 04–Feb 05)
1-197th Field Artillery
2-197th Field Artillery
3-197th Field Artillery

US Army Units Attached to Marine Forces
 2d Brigade, 2d Infantry Division (Aug 04–Aug 05) (Attached to II MEF)
  1-503d Infantry
  1-506th Infantry
  1-9th Infantry
  2-17th Field Artillery
  44th Engineer Battalion
  2d Forward Support Battalion
13th Corps Support Command (Feb 04–Dec 04)
 593d Corps Support Group
  185th Corps Support Battalion
  298th Corps Support Battalion
  515th Corps Support Battalion
 172d Corps Support Group
  319th Corps Support Battalion
  7th Transportation Battalion
  1-142d Aviation Intermediate Maintenance Battalion
 167th Corps Support Group
  44th Corps Support Battalion
  232d Corps Support Battalion
  835th Corps Support Battalion
 300th Area Support Group
  357th Corps Support Battalion
  369th Corps Support Group
 Special Troops Battalion
 126th Finance Battalion
 50th Finance Battalion
 4th Corps Materiel Management Center
 138th Personnel Services Battalion
 292d Corps Support Battalion
2d Medical Brigade
 226th Medical Logistics Battalion
 31st Combat Support Hospital (-)
 67th Combat Support Hospital
 118th Area Support Medical Battalion
 429th Medical Battalion
163d Personnel Services Battalion
Combined Joint Special Operations Task Force–Arabian Peninsula (in support of CJTF-7/MNF-I)
5th Special Forces Group
10th Special Forces Group
160th Special Operations Aviation Regiment (-)
Other unidentified Special Operations Forces (SOF) units

Appendix G

Chronology

Operation IRAQI FREEDOM
Major Events, September 2001 to January 2005

2001

16 February	The United States (US) and United Kingdom (UK) launch air strikes on Iraqi air defense installations near Baghdad.
23 May	Iraq threatens to halt oil exports if the United Nations (UN) adopts a US and UK proposed Security Council Resolution recommending a new program of sanctions.
30 August	US warplanes launch new attacks against Iraqi air defense targets.
11 September	Two planes hit the World Trade Center towers in New York City, one plane hits the Pentagon, and one is forced down in rural western Pennsylvania. Al-Qaeda hijackers are responsible for killing several thousand Americans.
7 October	Operation ENDURING FREEDOM begins with air strikes against al-Qaeda and Taliban forces and installations in Afghanistan.
27 November	Saddam Hussein rejects an appeal by US President George W. Bush to let UN weapons inspectors back in Iraq. An Iraqi representative states that Iraq would only allow weapons inspectors back in if the UN removed sanctions and the no-fly zones in northern and southern Iraq were removed.

2002

27 January	US Central Command (CENTCOM) begins work on revising plan for campaign to topple Saddam regime.
29 January	In his State of the Union speech, President Bush declares that North Korea, Iraq, and Iran constitute an "axis of evil" because of their support of terrorism.
13 February	Iraq again states that it will not permit UN arms inspectors in the country. The Bush administration implies that it is considering options if inspectors are not allowed re-entry.
1 June	At West Point graduation ceremony, Bush announces his doctrine of "pre-emptive action" to destroy threats before they fully materialize.
12 September	President Bush travels to UN and in speech makes case for military action against Iraq.
16 September	Iraq announces it will allow return of UN weapons inspectors.
16 October	President Bush signs the "Authorization for the use of Military Force Against Iraq Resolution of 2002."
20 October	Saddam Hussein announces amnesty for all those held in Iraqi prisons.

8 November	UN adopts Resolution 1441 that stated Iraq's noncompliance with previous resolutions concerning weapons of mass destruction (WMD) proliferation constituted a threat to peace and international security.
18 November	UN weapons inspectors return to Iraq to restart inspections.
December	Combined Forces Land Component Command (CFLCC) finalizes Operation COBRA II, the plan for ground forces in the invasion of Iraq.
	US Army 3d Infantry Division (3d ID) begins to deploy to Kuwait.

2003

January	President Bush places the responsibility for toppling of the Saddam regime as well as stability and reconstruction of Iraq under the Department of Defense. Lieutenant General (Retired) Jay Garner is placed in charge of the Office of Reconstruction and Humanitarian Assistance (ORHA).
22 January	US Army 4th Infantry Division (4th ID) receives order to begin deployment to Southwest Asia.
27 January	US Army V Corps begins exercise VICTORY SCRIMMAGE in Germany. Exercise scenario closely resembles invasion of Iraq.
5 February	US Secretary of State Colin Powell addresses UN providing what he called evidence that Iraq has WMD.
6 February	US Army 101st Airborne Division (101st ABN) begins deployment to Kuwait.
17 March	US attempts to kill Saddam Hussein right before war starts.
	President Bush issues ultimatum to Saddam and his sons ordering them to leave Iraq.
	UN orders all UN personnel out of Iraq.
19 March	Coalition air campaign against Iraq begins with air and cruise missile strikes.
20 March	US and Coalition land forces enter Iraq.
22 March	Because of Turkish opposition, Coalition headquarters decides to direct the 4th ID to Kuwait.
23 March	Coalition land forces begin attack against Baghdad.
26 March	US Army 173d Airborne Brigade conducts airborne assault into northern Iraq at Bashur Airfield.
2 April	US Army 3d ID attacks through Karbala Gap.
4 April	3d ID seizes Baghdad International Airport.
5 April	3d ID launches first "Thunder Run" into Baghdad.
8 April	Second "Thunder Run" into Baghdad.
9 April	US forces topple Saddam statute in Baghdad.
	Coalition asserts control over city.
	US Army 1st Armored Division (1st AD) begins deployment from Germany to Kuwait.

21 April	Garner, chief of ORHA, arrives in Baghdad. His staff of 400 arrives 3 days later.
28 April	Soldiers in the 1st Battalion, 325th Airborne Infantry Regiment, 82d Airborne Division in the city of Fallujah shoot and kill a number of Iraqis after violence breaks out during a protest.
30 April	4th ID establishes headquarters in city of Tikrit and begins conducting full spectrum operations in Sunni Triangle.
1 May	In speech, President Bush declares an end to major combat operations in Iraqi.
6 May	Bush announces the appointment of L. Paul Bremer, former ambassador and counterterrorism director, as the administrator of the Coalition Provisional Authority (CPA), the new political authority that would replace ORHA and begin overseeing all Coalition operations in Iraq.
15 May	In one of the first major operations since the fall of the Saddam regime, the 1st Brigade Combat Team of the 4th ID launches Operation PLANET X, a brigade-size cordon and search operation in the vicinity of Ad Dawr and Al Dur (approximately 11 miles south of Tikrit) to seize Baath Party members and other militants. The results of the operation included the capture of Adil Abdallah Mahdi Al Duri Al-Tikriti (a Baath Party District Chairman who was Number 52 on the "most wanted" list) and 260 other individuals.
16 May	CPA issues Order No. 1 ordering the de-Baathification of Iraqi society and government.
22 May	UN Security Council passes Resolution 1483 which explicitly recognizes the US and Britain as "occupying powers" and calls on US and UK to promote the welfare of Iraqis and govern them so that they could determine their future. UN lifts economic sanctions against Iraq.
23 May	CPA issues Order No. 2, "The Dissolution of Entities," which officially disbands the Iraqi Army and other Baathist security forces.
26 May	1st AD begins mission in Baghdad.
1 June	CPA implements a weapons turn-in program to take arms off the streets. Program runs through 14 June 2003.
9–12 June	3d Brigade, 4th ID, along with elements of the 173d Airborne Brigade and the 3-7th CAV, 3d ID, launch Operation PENINSULA STRIKE.
11 June	Elements of the 2d Battalion, 75th Ranger Regiment and the 101st ABN attack a terrorist camp near Rawah (approximately 30 miles east of the Syrian border).
13 June	CPA begins program to establish New Iraqi Army (NIA).
14 June	Lieutenant General Ricardo S. Sanchez takes command of V Corps.

15 June	Combined Joint Task Force–7 (CJTF-7) built around the V Corps headquarters replaces CFLCC as Coalition military headquarters in Iraq.
15–29 June	US combat units in Baghdad, Mosul, Al Anbar province, and the Sunni Triangle mount Operation DESERT SCORPION, a combination of raids on suspected Baathist leaders' locations and reconstruction operations.
29 June–7 July	On the heels of the previous operation, 4th ID launched Operation SIDEWINDER to curtail Baathist attacks against Coalition and local traffic in Sunni Triangle.
7 July	General John Abazaid succeeds General Tommy Franks as the CENTCOM commander.
12–17 July	CJTF-7 conducts Operation SODA MOUNTAIN, an Iraq-wide operation that included over 140 raids focused on disrupting enemy operations and detaining insurgents.
13 July	CPA forms the Iraqi Governing Council (IGC).
16 July	General Abizaid calls attacks on Coalition troops a "guerrilla-type campaign" and says US troops may be deployed for up to 1 year.
18 July	Muqtada al-Sadr announces plan to form a militia separate from the Iraqi Army to challenge the US and the IGC.
22 July	Coalition forces kill Saddam's sons Uday and Qusay in Mosul.
7 August	A car bomb explodes outside the Jordanian Embassy in Baghdad, killing 11 Iraqis and wounding dozens.
19 August	A truck bomb explodes outside the UN headquarters building in Baghdad, killing Sergio Vieira de Mello, head of the UN mission to Iraq.
21 August	Coalition forces capture General Ali Hassan al-Majid ("Chemical Ali").
29 August	An explosion at an An Najaf mosque kills Ayatollah Muhammad Bakr al-Hakim along with 94 other Iraqis. The Ayatollah was the leader of the Supreme Council for Islamic Revolution in Iraq (SCIRI).
30 August	Operation MCCLELLAN. 101st ABN attacks terrorists in the vicinity of western Al Anbar province.
2 September	IGC names 25 ministers responsible for day-to-day affairs.
20 September	Terrorists shoot Dr. Aqila al-Hashimi, the only female member of the IGC. She dies 5 days later.
4 October	First battalion of the New Iraqi Army (NIA) completes Coalition training program.
5 October	National Security Director Dr. Condoleezza Rice establishes the Iraqi Stabilization Group to coordinate reconstruction and transition activities.
10 October	Militia forces in Sadr City ambush elements of the 2d Armored Cavalry Regiment (ACR) effectively ending the fragile truce between al-Sadr's forces and the Coalition.

25 October	Corporal Charles Graner takes pictures of US Soldiers abusing Iraqi detainees in the Abu Ghraib Prison.
23–24 October	International donors attend a conference in Madrid to address Iraq's future reconstruction.
	80 countries pledge $13 billion in addition to the $20 billion pledged by the United States.
30 October	UN withdraws all of its non-Iraqi personnel from Baghdad.
2 November	Insurgents shoot down a Chinook transport helicopter near Fallujah resulting in the deaths of 16 US Soldiers.
7 November	Turkey says it will not send troops to Iraq.
12 November	Operation IRON HAMMER. 1st AD conducts offensive operations to disrupt enemy operations in Baghdad.
15 November	CPA and IGC sign an agreement to draft an interim constitution by 28 February 2004 and transfer sovereignty to Iraq by 1 July 2004.
13 December	Coalition forces capture former Iraqi dictator Saddam Hussein near Tikrit.
17 December	Operation IVY BLIZZARD. 4th ID and Iraqi Security Forces (ISF) conduct offensive operations near Samarra to isolate and eliminate former regime elements and other anti-Coalition forces.

2004

14 January	Approximately 30,000 followers of Ayatollah Ali al-Sistani march through the city of Basrah to support Sistani's demands for direct elections.
19 January	Lieutenant General Sanchez requests that commander CENTCOM appoint officer to investigate military police operations at Abu Ghraib Prison.
	Tens of thousands of Shias protest in Baghdad demanding direct elections to choose a new government.
28 January	David Kay, former head of the Iraq Survey Group, testifies before Senate Armed Services Committee that no WMD have been found in Iraq.
1 February	US Army III Corps Soldiers replace much of V Corps personnel as staff of CJTF-7.
2 March	Five bombs kill 270 people and wound over 500 others in the cities of An Najaf and Karbala during Shia religious ceremonies marking Ashura.
8 March	IGC adopts the Transitional Administrative Law (TAL).
31 March	Insurgents in Fallujah ambush and kill four US contractors working for Blackwater Security Consulting. Their bodies are later mutilated.
3 April	Coalition forces arrest Mustafa al-Yacoubi, a key deputy of Muqtada al-Sadr, in An Najaf.
4 April	Mahdi Army militiamen in Sadr City ambush Soldiers from the 2d Battalion, 5th Cavalry, a unit that was part of the 1st Cavalry Division (1st CAV). In

the attack and the actions that followed, 7 Soldiers from the 1st CAV and 1 Soldier from the 1st AD were killed and over 60 others were wounded. Militiamen take over key sections of An Najaf, Al Kut, and Karbala, prompting Coalition forces to begin planning operations to quell the Sadrist uprisings.

4 April   Operation VIGILANT RESOLVE. Coalition forces begin offensive operations focused on the city of Fallujah to detain or destroy insurgent elements responsible for the killing of four American security contractors on 31 March 2004.

5 April   An Iraqi judge issued an arrest warrant for Muqtada al-Sadr for the 2003 killing of rival cleric Sayed al Khoei.

6 April   Lieutenant General Sanchez cancels the redeployment of 1st AD and extends the division for 120 days. Elements previously redeployed to Germany are recalled. Planning for 1st AD's "Extension Campaign" begins.

7 April   Sadrist forces launch attacks against Coalition forces in cities of Kufa, Karbala, An Najaf, and Al Kut.

8 April   Operation RESOLUTE SWORD. CJTF-7 begins operation involving 1st AD and other units to impose order in the Multi-National Division–Center-South (MND-CS) area and destroy Sadrist forces.

9 April   CPA announces cease-fire in Fallujah after two members of the IGC resign in protest of US military actions.

11–17 April   3d Brigade, 1st ID launches Operation DANGER FORTITUDE, offensive operations to defeat Mahdi militia forces in An Najaf and capture or kill Muqtada al-Sadr. The augmented brigade was designated Task Force *Duke*.

22 April   Ambassador Bremer announces the reinstatement of thousands of teachers who had been removed from their jobs in the May 2003 CPA order that directed the de-Baathification of Iraqi society.

22 April   Coalition forces transfer command of the Iraqi Civil Defense Corps (ICDC) to the Iraqi Ministry of Defense.

30 April   US military makes public photos of some of the abuses that occurred at Abu Ghraib Prison.

1 May   US troops withdraw to the outskirts of Fallujah and are replaced by 200 Iraqi soldiers from the so-called Fallujah Brigade.

11 May   A video depicting the murder of kidnapped US contractor Nicholas Berg surfaces on a militant Web site.

15 May   Coalition replaces CJTF-7 with Multi-National Force–Iraq (MNF-I).
Lieutenant General Sanchez, commander of CJTF-7, becomes commander of MNF-I.

17 May   A suicide bomber assassinates Izzedin Salim, the president of the IGC.

27 May	US forces and Mahdi Army forces reach a truce after 7 weeks of fighting in An Najaf.
8 June	UN Security Council adopts Resolution 1546 that mandates the political road map for the new sovereign state of Iraq.
20 June	Iraqi Government changes name of Iraqi Civil Defense Corps (ICDC) to Iraqi National Guard.
28 June	CPA transfers political sovereignty to Iraqi Interim Government (IIG).
1 July	US Army General George W. Casey Jr. takes command of MNF-I.
1 July	Coalition transfers Saddam Hussein to Iraqi custody.
	Iraqi Government formally charges Saddam.
5 August	Coalition units begin operations against Mahdi Army forces in An Najaf.
27 August	Agreement between Iraqi Government and Muqtada al-Sadr brings end to standoff in An Najaf.
1 October	Operation BATON ROUGE. 1st ID conducted operations near Samarra to wrest control of the area from the insurgents, reestablish the ISF in the city, and set the conditions so that the insurgency could not return. Included "kinetic" operations but also heavily emphasized "nonkinetic" operations in an effort to establish long-term results.
4 October	Coalition forces take control of Samarra.
8 November	Operation AL FAJR (originally called PHANTOM FURY). Coalition forces attack anti-Coalition forces near Fallujah to destroy insurgent combat power and reestablish an enduring Iraqi governmental presence in the city.
16 November	Main fighting in Fallujah is over. Coalition forces continue smaller actions to secure city.
18 November	US military reports 51 US Soldiers and 1,200 insurgents killed in Fallujah fighting.
26 November	Sunni Arab and Kurdish political factions request a delay in elections scheduled on 30 January 2005.
	President Bush and Prime Minister Ayad Allawi reject the request.
5 December	Insurgents halt a bus of unarmed Iraqis working for Coalition forces and kill 17.
	Insurgent attacks killed 80 Iraqis from 2–5 December.
21 December	A suicide bomber enters a US military dining facility in the city of Mosul and kills 22 people, including 18 US military.
31 December	The Iraqi Government announces the capture of Fadil Hussain Ahmed al-Kurdi, a suspected member of Abu Musab al-Zarqawi's terrorist organization.

2005

2 January	A suicide bomber kills 18 Iraqi National Guardsmen and a civilian in Balad.
12 January	US officials confirm that the Iraq Survey Group (ISG) has ended the search for WMD in Iraq.
14 January	Approximately 30,000 followers of Ayatollah Ali al-Sistani march through city of Basrah to support Sistani's demands for direct elections.
18 January	Iraqi officials announced that the government will close its borders from 29–31 January 2005 in an effort to prevent terrorist attacks on Election Day.
26 January	31 US Marines are killed when their CH-53 helicopter crashes near Ar Rutbah in Al Anbar province.
30 January	Iraq holds its first free national elections in 50 years. Voter turnout is higher than projected, but most Sunnis boycott. Nine suicide bombers and insurgents firing mortars kill 26 Iraqis and wound over 100 in election-related violence.

Glossary

A

AA	air ambulance
AAFES	Army and Air Force Exchange Service
AAR	After-Action Review
ABCS	Army Battlefield Command System
ABN	airborne
ACLS	advanced cardiac life support
ACR	armored cavalry regiment
ACS	Army Community Service
AD	armored division
ADA	Air Defense Artillery
ADC-O	Assistant Division Commander for Operations
AEB	aerial exploitation battalion
AEG	Air Expeditionary Group
AEROEVAC	US Air Force Medical Transport Plane
AFRTS	Armed Forces Radio and Television Station
AIF	Anti-Iraq Forces
AMC	Army Materiel Command
AO	area of operation
AOR	area of responsibility
APC	armored personnel carrier
APOD	aerial port of debarkation
APS-3	Army Pre-Positioned Sets-Afloat
APS-5	Army Pre-Positioned Sets-Southwest Asia
AR	Army Regulation
ARNG	Army National Guard
ARVN	South Vietnamese Army
ASAS	All Source Analysis System
ASCC	Army Service Component Command
ASR	alternate supply route
AST	Advisor Support Team
AT	antitank
atk	attack
ATLS	advance trauma life support
AUSA	Association of the United States Army
AW2	US Army Wounded Warrior program

B

BBC	British Broadcasting Corporation
BCCF	Baghdad Central Confinement Facility
BCS3	Battlefield Command Sustainment Support System
BCT	brigade combat team
BCTP	Battle Command Training Program
BDE	brigade
BFV	Bradley Fighting Vehicle
BIAP	Baghdad International Airport
BN	battalion

BOS	battlefield operating system
BSB	brigade support battalion

C

C2	command and control
C4I	command, control, communications, computers, and intelligence
CA	civil affairs
CAC	Combined Arms Center
CACE	Coalition Analysis Control Element
CALL	Center for Army Lessons Learned
CAOC	Coalition Air Operations Center
CAS	close air support
CASEVAC	casualty evacuation
CAT	combat application tourniquet
CAT-A	Civil Affairs Team-Alpha
CAV	cavalry
cbt	combat
CCCI	Central Criminal Court of Iraq
CENTCOM	US Central Command
CERP	Commander's Emergency Response Program
CF	Coalition Forces
CFACC	Combined Forces Air Component Command
CFLCC	Combined Forces Land Component Command
CG	commanding general
CGSC	Command and General Staff College
CHRRP	Commander's Humanitarian Relief and Reconstruction Projects
CI	counterintelligence
CIA	Central Intelligence Agency
CID	Criminal Investigation Division
CJ1,	Personnel Section at Combined Joint Staff
CJ2	Intelligence Section at Combined Joint Staff
CJ3	Operations Section at Combined Joint Staff
CJ4	Logistics Section at Combined Joint Staff
CJ5	Plans Section at Combined Joint Staff
CJ6	Communications Section at Combined Joint Staff
CJ7	Engineer Section at Combined Joint Staff
CJ8	Resource Management Section at Combined Joint Staff
CJ9	Civil-Military Operations Section at Combined Joint Staff
CJ2X	HUMINT staff officer at Combined Joint Staff
CJSOTF	Combined Joint Special Operations Task Force
CJSOTF-AP	Combined Joint Special Operations Task Force–Arabian Peninsula
CJSOTF-North	Combined Joint Special Operations Task Force–North
CJSOTF-West	Combined Joint Special Operations Task Force–West
CJTF	combined joint task force
CJTF-7	Combined Joint Task Force–7
CJTF-IV/CJTF-4	Combined Joint Task Force–IV/4
CJTF-Iraq	Combined Joint Task Force–Iraq
Class III B	petroleum, oil, lubricants (POL)
Class IX	repair parts for weapons and equipment
CLS	combat lifesavers

CMATT	Coalition Military Assistance Training Team
cmd	command
CMH	Center of Military History
CMO	civil-military operations
CMOC	Civil Military Operations Center
CMTC	Combat Maneuver Training Center
CNA	computer network attack
CNN	Cable News Network
CNO	computer network operations
COG	center of gravity
COIN	counterinsurgency
COMCAM	combat camera
COMMZ	communications zone
COMSEC	communications security
CONPLAN	concept plan
CONUS	continental United States
CORDS	Civil Operations and Rural Development Support program
COS	chief of staff
COSCOM	Corps Support Command
COST	Contemporary Operations Study Team
CP	command post
CPA	Coalition Provisional Authority
CPATT	Coalition Police Assistance Training Team
CPIC	Combined Press Information Center
CPOF	Command Post of the Future
CSB	corps support battalion
CSC	Combat Stress Control
CSCT	Combat Stress Control Team
CSH	combat support hospital
CSI	Combat Studies Institute
CSS	combat service support
CSSCS	Combat Service Support Control System
CTASC	Corps Theater ADP Service Center
CTC	Combat Training Center
CWO	chief warrant officer

D

DA	Department of the Army
DAC	district advisory council
DAHAC	Department of the Army Historical Advisory Committee
DB CSS	distribution-based combat service support
DBE	Department of Border Enforcement
DBL	distribution-based logistics
DCIS	Defense Criminal Investigative Services
DFAS	Defense Finance and Accounting Service
DFI	Development Fund for Iraq
DHL	Dalsey, Hillblom and Lynn
DIA	Defense Intelligence Agency
DIF	Division Interrogation Facility
DIMHRS	Defense Integrated Military Human Resources System

DISCOM	division support command
div	division
DIVARTY	division artillery
DIVIT	division institutional training
DLA	Defense Logistics Agency
DNBI	disease and nonbattle injuries
DOD	Department of Defense
DOE	Department of Energy
DOJ	Department of Justice
DOS	Department of State
DOTMLPF	doctrine, organization, training, materiel, leadership and education, personnel, and facilities
DOW	died of their wounds
DP	denial point
DREAR	division rear
DS3	Disabled Soldier Support System
DSPD	defense support to public diplomacy
DTAC	Digital Training Access Center
DVIDS	Digital Video and Imagery Distribution System

E

EAD	echelons above division
EMT	emergency medical technician
EOD	explosive ordnance disposal
EPW	enemy prisoner of war
eSB	enhanced separate brigade
ETAC	Enlisted Terminal Attack Controller
etc.	and so forth
EUCOM	US European Command
EW	electronic warfare

F

FA	field artillery
FAR	Federal Acquisition Regulation
FA-TRAC	Foreign Army-Training Assistance Command
FBCB2	Force XXI Battle Command, Brigade and Below
FBI	Federal Bureau of Investigation
FCS	Future Combat System
FEST	Forward Engineering Support Team
FLE	forward logistics element
FLN	Algerian National Liberation Front
FLP	Foreign Language Program
FM	field manual
FMTV	family of medium tactical vehicles
FOB	forward operating base
FOO	field ordering officer
FORSCOM	Forces Command
FOUO	For Official Use Only
FPS	Facilities Protection Service

FRAGO	fragmentary order
FRE	former regime elements
FRG	Family Readiness Group
FSB	forward support battalion
FSO	fire support officer
FST	forward surgical team
fwd	forward
FWF	former warring factions
FY	fiscal year

G

G2	Intelligence Section at Corps and Division Staff
G3	Operations Section at Corps and Division Staff
G5	Plans Section at Corps and Division Staff
G6	Communications Section at Corps and Division Staff
G7	Information Operations Section at Corps and Division Staff
GA	ground ambulance
GAO	General Accounting Office/Government Accountability Office
GFAP	General Framework Agreement for Peace
GPS	Global Positioning System
GRD	Gulf Region Division
GSA	General Services Administration
GTMO	Guantanamo Bay, Cuba
GWOT	Global War on Terrorism

H

HHB	headquarters and headquarters battery
HHC	headquarters and headquarters company
HMMWV	high-mobility multipurpose wheeled vehicle
HQ	headquarters
H.R.	House Resolution
HUMINT	human intelligence
HVT	high-value target

I

IA	Iraqi Army
IACC	Iraqi Anti-Corruption Council
IAF	Iraqi Armed Forces
ICDC	Iraqi Civil Defense Corps
ICG	International Crisis Group
ICITAP	International Criminal Investigative Assistance Training Program (JOD)
ICRC	International Committee of the Red Cross
ICRP	Interrogation and Counter-Resistance Policy
ICTF	Iraqi Counterterrorist Force
ID	infantry division
i.e.	that is
IED	improvised explosive device
IET	initial entry training
IFOR	Implementation Force

IG	inspector general
IGC	Iraqi Governing Council
IHP	Iraqi Highway Patrol
IIF	Iraqi Intervention Force
IIG	Interim Iraqi Government
ILC	Iraqi Leadership Council
IMIE	International Mission for Iraqi Elections
IMINT	imagery intelligence
IN	infantry
INA	Iraqi National Accord
INC	Iraqi National Congress
ING	Iraqi National Guard
INL	Bureau of International and Narcotics Law Enforcement (DOS)
INSCOM	US Army Intelligence and Security Command
int	interrogation
INTERPOL	International Criminal Police Organization
IO	information operations
IPB	intelligence preparation of the battlefield
IPS	Iraqi Police Service
I/R	internment/resettlement
IRG	Iraqi Republican Guard
IRMO	Iraqi Reconstruction Management Office
IRRF	Iraq Relief and Reconstruction Fund
ISAF	International Security Assistance Force
ISF	Iraqi Security Forces
ISG	Iraqi Survey Group
ISOF	Iraqi Special Operations Forces
IT	information technology
ITA	Iraqi Transitional Assembly
ITG	Iraqi Transitional Government

J

J2	Intelligence Section at Joint Staff
J3	Operations Section at Joint Staff
J4	Logistics Section at Joint Staff
J5	Civil Affairs Section at Joint Staff
JCC	Joint Coordination Center
JCC-I	Joint Contracting Command–Iraq
JCP	Jump Assault Command Post
JDLM	Joint Deployment Logistics Model
JFEC	joint fires and effect cell
JIATF	Joint Interagency Task Force
JIDC	Joint Interrogation and Debriefing Center
JIEDDO	Joint IED Defeat Organization
JIPTC	Jordan International Police Training Center
JMD	Joint Manning Document
JOA	joint operating areas
JPOTF	Joint Psychological Operations Task Force
JRTC	Joint Readiness Training Center

JSLET	Joint Services Law Enforcement Team
JSOTF	Joint Special Operations Task Force
JSOTF-North	Joint Special Operations Task Force–North
JSTARS	Joint Surveillance and Targeting Attack Radar System
JTF	joint task force
JTF-GTMO	Joint Task Force–Guantanamo Bay
JWFC	Joint Warfighting Center

K

KBR	Kellogg, Brown, and Root
KDP	Kurdistan Democratic Party
KFOR	Kosovo forces
KIA	killed in action

L

LAV	(Marine) light armored vehicle
LCMR	light countermortar radar
ling	linguists
LD	line of departure
LIC	low-intensity conflict
LMSR	large medium speed roll-on, roll-off
LMTV	light medium tactical vehicle
LOC	line(s) of communications
LOGCAP	Logistics Civil Augmentation Program
LOO	line of operation
LSA	logistics support area
LSB	logistic support base
LTG	lieutenant general

M

M113	armored personnel carrier
M114	command and reconnaissance carrier
M1A1	Abrams tank
M1A2	Abrams tank
M2/3	Bradley Fighting Vehicle (BFV)
MA	Mortuary Affairs
MACV	Military Assistance Command, Vietnam
MARDIV	Marine Division
MASH	mobile army surgical hospital
MASINT	measurement and signature intelligence
MCLC	Mine Clearing Line Charge
MCNS	Ministerial Committee for National Security
MDMP	military decision-making process
MEDCAP	Medical Civic Action Program
MEDEVAC	medical evacuation
MEF	Marine Expeditionary Force
MEK	Mujahedin e-Khalq (mujahedeen)
MEU	Marine Expeditionary Unit
MFO	Multinational Force and Observers

MHAT	Mental Health Advisory Team
MI	military intelligence
MILDEC	military deception
MiTT	Military Transition Team
MNC-I	Multi-National Corps–Iraq
MND-B	Multi-National Division–Baghdad
MND-CS	Multi-National Division–Central-South
MND-NC	Multi-National Division–North Central
MND-North	Multi-National Division–North
MND-NW	Multi-National Division–Northwest
MND-SE	Multi-National Division–Southeast
MND-W	Multi-National Division–West
MNF-I	Multi-National Force–Iraq
MNSTC-I	Multi-National Security Transition Command–Iraq
MOI	Ministry of the Interior
MOOTW	military operations other than war
MOS	military occupational specialty
MP	military police
MPAD	Mobile Public Affairs Detachment
MPF	Maritime Pre-Positioning Force
MPS	Maritime Pre-Positioning Squadron
MRE	meal, ready to eat
MRX	mission rehearsal exercise
MSC	Major Subordinate Command
MSR	main supply route
MTLB	USSR designed armored personnel carrier (APC)
MTN	mountain
MTS	Movement Tracking System
MWR	Morale, Welfare, and Recreation

N

NAC	neighborhood advisory council
NATO	North Atlantic Treaty Organization
NBC	nuclear, biological, and chemical
NCO	noncommissioned officer
NCOES	Noncommissioned Officer Education System
NCOIC	noncommissioned officer in charge
NDU	National Defense University
NEO	noncombatant evacuation operations
NGO	nongovernment organizations
NIA	New Iraqi Army
NIB	National Information Bureau
NIC	National Intelligence Council
NIMA	National Imagery and Mapping Agency
NLT	not later than
NPR	National Public Radio
NSC	National Security Council
NSD	National Security Directive
NTIM-I	NATO Training Implementation Mission–Iraq

NTM-I	NATO Training Mission–Iraq
NVVRS	National Vietnam Veterans' Readjustment Study

O

OBJ	objective
ODA	Operational Detachment–Alpha
OEF	Operation ENDURING FREEDOM
OIC	officer in charge
OIF	Operation IRAQI FREEDOM
OP	operation
OPCON	operational control
OPLAN	operation plan
OPORD	operation order
OPSEC	operation security
OPSUM	operational summary
OPTEMPO	operations tempo
ORHA	Office of Reconstruction and Humanitarian Assistance
OSB	operational support base
OSC-I	Office of Security Cooperation–Iraq

P

P3P	Provincial Police Partnership Program
PA	public affairs
PAO	public affairs officer
PACOM	US Pacific Command
PCO	Project and Contracting Office
PD	Public Diplomacy
PERSCOM	US Army Personnel Command
PH IV	Phase IV
PIR	Priority Intelligence Requirement
PL	phase line
PLDC	primary leadership development course
PLL	prescribed load list
PM	prime minister
PMCS	preventive maintenance checks and services
PMO	Provost Marshal Office
PO	Polish
POE	points of entry
POI	Program of Instruction
POL	petroleum, oil, lubricants
POL-MIL	political-military
POO	point of origin
POW	prisoner of war
PRT	Provincial Reconstruction Team
PSYOP	psychological operations
PTLS	prehospital trauma life support
PTSD	post-traumatic stress disorder
PUK	Patriotic Union of Kurdistan
PX	post exchange

Q

QM	quartermaster
QRF	Quick Reaction Fund

R

RCT	regimental combat team
REQ	required
RFF	request for forces
RFI	request for information
RFID	radio frequency identification
RHA	Regimental Holding Area
RIE	*Restore Iraqi Electricity*
RIO	*Restore Iraqi Oil*
RIP	relief in place
RO/RO	roll on/roll off
ROE	rules of engagement
ROTC	Reserve Officer Training Corps
ROWPU	reverse osmosis water purification unit
RPG	rocket-propelled grenade
R&R	Rest and Recuperation
RSOI	reception, staging, onward movement, and integration
RSS	Regimental Support Squadron
RTE	route
RTI	Research Triangle Institute

S

S2	Intelligence Section at Brigade and Battalion Staff
S2X	HUMINT Officer, Intelligence Section at Brigade and Battalion Staff
S3	Operations Section at Brigade and Battalion Staff
S5	Civil/Military Section at Brigade and Battalion Staff
SAMS	School of Advanced Military Studies
SAPI	Small Arms Protective Inserts
SARSS	Standard Army Retail Supply System
SASO	stability and support operations
SAW	squad automatic weapon
SBCT	Stryker Brigade Combat Team
SCIRI	Supreme Council for Islamic Revolution in Iraq
SCP	State Company for Phosphate
SEP	System Enhancement Package
SF	Special Forces
SFOR	Stabilization Force
SIAD	Statistical Information Analysis Division
SIB	separate infantry brigade
SIGACT	significant action
SIGINT	signals intelligence
SIGIR	Special Inspector General for Iraqi Reconstruction
SINCGAR	single-channel ground and airborne radio system
SJA	staff judge advocate

SOCOM	US Special Operations Command
SOF	special operations forces
SOP	standing operating procedure
SOUTHCOM	US Southern Command
SPA	Strategy, Plans, and Assessment
SPOD	sea port of debarkation
SRG	Special Republican Guard
SSE	sensitive site exploitation
STAMIS	Standard Army Management Information System
STRATCOM	Directorate of Strategic Communications (unofficial)
SWAT	Special Weapons and Tactics
SWEAT	sewer, water, electricity, academics, and trash

T

TACOM	Tank-Automotive and Armaments Command
TACON	tactical control
TACSAT	tactical satellite
TAL	Transitional Administrative Law
TBI	Traumatic Brain Injury
TDA	table of distribution and allowances
TDC	theater distribution center
TEB	tactical exploitation battalion
TF	task force
THT	Tactical HUMINT Team
TIP	Transition Integration Program
TMEP	theater mortuary evacuation point
TNA	Transitional National Assembly
TOA	transfer of authority
TOC	tactical operations center
TOW	tube-launched, optically-tracked, wire-guided missile
TPFDL	time-phased force and deployment list
TPT	tactical PSYOP team
TRADOC	US Army Training and Doctrine Command
TRANSCOM	Transportation Command
TRAS	Transition Readiness Assessment System
TSB	Training Support Brigade
TSC	Theater Support Command
TSD	Training Support Division
TTP	tactics, techniques, and procedures
TUAV	tactical unmanned aerial vehicle
TUSK	Tank Urban Survivability Kit

U

UAE	United Arab Emirates
UAV	unmanned aerial vehicle
UCMJ	Uniform Code of Military Justice
UGR	unitized group rations
UH-60L	Blackhawk
UK	United Kingdom

ULLS	Unit Level Logistics System
UN	United Nations
UNSCOM	United Nations Special Commission
US	United States
USA	United States Army
USACAPOC	US Army Civil Affairs and Psychological Operations Command
USACE	US Army Corps of Engineers
USAF	United States Air Force
USAID	United States Agency for International Development
USAIOP	United States Army Information Operations Proponent
USAR	United States Army Reserve
USCENTCOM	US Central Command
USFK	United States Forces, Korea
USMC	United States Marine Corps
USO	United Service Organizations
USS	US ship
UXO	unexploded ordnance

V

VA	Veterans Administration
VBIED	vehicle-borne improvised explosive devise
VFW	Veterans of Foreign Wars
VIC	vicinity
VTC	video teleconference

W

WFP	World Food Programme (UN)
WHO	World Health Organization
WIA	wounded in action
WMD	weapons of mass destruction

X

XO	executive officer

Bibliography

Interviews, Discussions, Notes, and e-mail Correspondence

Honorable Richard L. Armitage
Ambassador L. Paul Bremer III
Secretary of State, General (Retired) Colin Powell

General John Abizaid
General Bryan Brown
General George W. Casey Jr.
General (Retired) Tommy Franks
General (Retired) John Keane
General David McKiernan
General William S. Wallace

Lieutenant General Peter Chiarelli
Lieutenant General Keith Dayton
Lieutenant General Karl Eikenberry
Lieutenant General (Retired) Jay Garner
Lieutenant General Thomas Metz
Lieutenant General Richard F. Natonski
Lieutenant General Raymond Odierno
Lieutenant General David H. Petraeus
Lieutenant General (Retired) Ricardo Sanchez
Lieutenant General William G. Webster
Lieutenant General R. Steven Whitcomb

Major General (Retired) John R. Batiste
Major General (Retired) Buford C. Blount III
Major General (Retired) Paul D. Eaton
Major General Barbara Fast
Major General James Helmly
Major General Thomas G. Miller
Major General Stephen Speakes
Major General (Retired) Charles H. Swannack Jr.
Major General Walter Wojdakowski

Brigadier General Charles Fletcher
Brigadier General Carter Ham
Brigadier General Frank Helmick
Brigadier General James Huggins
Brigadier General Mark Kimmitt
Brigadier General David Perkins
Brigadier General Dana Pittard
Brigadier General Al-Kocher Ramadhan
Brigadier General Richard Sherlock
Brigadier General Michael Tucker

Colonel Robert Abrams
Colonel (Promotable) Daniel B. Allyn

Colonel (Promotable) Joseph Anderson
Colonel Ralph Baker
Colonel Philip Battaglia
Colonel Kevin C.M. Benson
Colonel (Promotable) James Boozer
Colonel (Promotable) Robert Brown
Colonel Francis Caponio
Colonel Dominic Caracillo
Colonel Frank Cipolla
Colonel William Darley
Colonel Peter DeLuca
Colonel Patrick Donahue
Colonel (Retired) Michael Fitzgerald
Colonel (Retired) Gregory Gardner
Colonel Gregory Gass
Colonel Russell Gold
Colonel (Promotable) William Grimsley
Colonel Toby Hale
Colonel Dyfierd Harris
Colonel Richard Hatch
Colonel James Hickey
Colonel William Hix
Colonel (Retired) Paul Hughes
Colonel Frank Hull
Colonel Mark Hurley
Colonel John D. Johnson
Colonel Chris King
Colonel (P) Stephen Lanza
Colonel (Retired) David Lawrence
Colonel (P) Michael Linnington
Colonel Richard Longo
Colonel Lou Marich
Colonel (Retired) John R. Martin
Colonel Theodore Martin
Colonel David Martino
Colonel (P) Bradley May
Colonel (P) James McConville
Colonel Mark Milley
Colonel Michael Moody
Colonel Jill Morgenthaler
Colonel J. Mike Murray
Colonel (P) Curtis Potts
Colonel Mike Repass
Colonel D.J. Reyes
Colonel (P) Frederick Rudesheim

Colonel Doug Shipman
Colonel Kevin Stramara
Colonel Richard Swengros
Colonel David Teeples
Colonel (Retired) Scott Thein
Colonel Michael Toner
Colonel Thomas Torrance
Colonel Robert Valdivia
Colonel Steve Ward
Colonel Marc Warren
Colonel Thomas Weafer
Colonel Roberta Woods
Colonel Mark Yenter
Colonel Don Young

Lieutenant Colonel Phil Andrews
Lieutenant Colonel (P) Steven Boylan
Lieutenant Colonel (P) Steven Bullimore
Lieutenant Colonel John Bullion
Lieutenant Colonel Rod A. Coffey
Lieutenant Colonel Blaise Cornell-d'Echert
Lieutenant Colonel Diane Cummins-Leffler
Lieutenant Colonel E.J. Degen
Lieutenant Colonel Scott Efflandt
Lieutenant Colonel Wesley Gillman
Lieutenant Colonel Paul Hastings
Lieutenant Colonel (P) L. Barrett Holmes
Lieutenant Colonel Mark Jones
Lieutenant Colonel Scott Kendrick
Lieutenant Colonel Steven Landis
Lieutenant Colonel (P) Sharon Leary
Lieutenant Colonel Shane Lee
Lieutenant Colonel (P) Brian McKiernan
Lieutenant Colonel Peter A. Newell
Lieutenant Colonel Wesley Odum
Lieutenant Colonel Troy D. Perry
Lieutenant Colonel Chris Prigge
Lieutenant Colonel James Rainey
Lieutenant Colonel Frank Rangel
Lieutenant Colonel Brian Reed
Lieutenant Colonel Gregory Reilly
Lieutenant Colonel Joe Rice
Lieutenant Colonel Steve Russell
Lieutenant Colonel George Sarabia
Lieutenant Colonel Jeffrey Sanborn
Lieutenant Colonel Wayne Swan
Lieutenant Colonel (P) Rodney Symons II
Lieutenant Colonel Michael Tetu
Lieutenant Colonel (P) Harry D. Tunnell IV
Lieutenant Colonel David Vetter

Major Jeffrey Allen
Major Kris Arnold
Major Susan Arnold
Major Barrett Bernard
Major Christopher Boyle
Major Chris Budihas
Major (Promotable) William Burke
Major Kenneth Cary
Major Christopher Dantoin
Major Robert Dixon
Major Pete Fedak
Major Gerald Green
Major Shauna Hauser
Major Matt Kinkaid
Major Dennis Levesque
Major Greg Nardi
Major Charles O'Brien
Major Brian Pearl
Major (P) Nancy Quintero
Major Darryl Rupp
Major Charles Seifert
Major Larry Shea
Major Mike Sullivan
Major Dennis Van Wey
Major John White

Captain Angela Bowman
Captain Keith Bragg
Captain Chris Brooke
Captain Richard Cotte
Captain Nathaniel Crow
Captain Michael S. Erwin
Captain Natalie Friel
Captain Michael Fowler
Captain (P) Damon Harris
Captain Matthew Hofmann
Captain John-Michael Insetta
Captain (P) Joseph Ludvigson
Captain Bill Meredith
Captain (P) Timothy Payment
Captain Ruth M. Roettger-Lerg
Captain (P) Sam Rogers
Captain Christian Solinsky
Captain (P) Warren Sponslor
Captain Jon Trolla

First Lieutenant Tyson Arnold
First Lieutenant (P) Jerry England

Chief Warrant Officer 3 Bryan Gray

Command Sergeant Major Tito Ortiz-Torres

Command Sergeant Major Milt Newsome

Sergeant Major Kevin Gainey
Sergeant Major (P) Stephen Kammerdiener
Sergeant Major Cory McCarty
Sergeant Major Ron Pruyt

First Sergeant Richard Gano Jr.

Master Sergeant Luis Jackson Jr.
Master Sergeant (P) Robert Ochsner
Master Sergeant Alan Upchurch

Sergeant First Class Pedro Marrero
Sergeant First Class James Prosser
Sergeant First Class Larry Scott
Sergeant First Class Erika Strong

Staff Sergeant Ronald Banner
Staff Sergeant David Bellavia
Staff Sergeant Gregory Givings
Staff Sergeant Steven Jackson
Staff Sergeant (Promotable) Jared Sargent

Sergeant Jason Bell
Sergeant Norman J. Herb
Sergeant Christopher Roe

Specialist Adrian Andrews
Specialist Seth Paul Burford
Specialist Joshua Navarra
Specialist Stephen Rockhold
Specialist (Promotable) Jondelle Romero
Specialist Brooks Vandekeere

Private Jonathan Fiore

Former Ambassador to Yemen Barbara Bodine
Former Ambassador James Dobbins
Dr. Joseph Collins (Colonel, Retired)
Dr. Alexander Cochran
Mr. David Drummond
Ms. Dianna Emmou
Mr. Henry Ensher, State Department
Mr. Jay Hines
Ms. Herro Mustafa, State Department
Dr. Michael O'Hanlon
Dr. Gordon Rudd
Ms. Amy Schlesing
Mr. Walter Slocombe
Ms. Ann Soby

Group Interviews

Interview with Chemical School students and officers at Fort Leonard Wood, Missouri, on 12 April 2006.

Interview with Operation IRAQI FREEDOM 4th Infantry Division, Commanding General, Lieutenant General Odierno, including Colonels Hickey, Moody, Rudesheim, and Stramara at the Pentagon on 14 December 2005.

Coalition Provisional Authority

Coalition Provisional Authority. *Achieving the Vision to Restore Full Sovereignty to the Iraqi People,* 15 October 2003.

———. "Conditional Release Announcement," 7 January 2004. http://www.cpa-iraq.org/transcripts/Jan7Bremer_Conditional.htm (accessed 2 November 2007).

———. *CPA Vision Statement.* 13 July 2003.

———. *Iraqi Seized and Vested Assets.* April 2004.

———. Memorandum, Subject*: Strategy for Addressing Detention Issues.*

———. Order No. 1, "De-Ba'athification of Iraqi Society (16 May 2003)." http://www.cpa-iraq.org/regulations/20030516_CPAORD_1_De-Ba_athification_of_Iraqi_Society_.pdf (accessed 14 March 2006).

———. Order No. 2, "Dissolution of Entities (23 May 2003)." http://www.iraqcoalition.org/regulations/20030823_CPAORD_2_Dissolution_of_Entities_with_Annex_A.pdf (accessed 14 September 2006).

———. Order No. 28, "The Establishment of the Iraqi Civil Defense Corps (3 September 2003)." http://www.cpa-iraq.org/regulations/20030903_CPAORD_28_Est_of_the_Iraqi_Civil_Defense_Corps.pdf (accessed 9 January 2008).

———. *Press Release, 23 June 2003 (PR No. 006).* "Good News for Iraqi Soldiers." http://www.iraqcoalition.org/pressreleases/23June03PR6_good_news.pdf (accessed 30 January 2008).

———. *Public Service Announcement, 6 July 2003,* 1

———. Regulation Number 1. http://www.cpa-iraq.org/regulations/20030516_CPAREG_1_The_Coalition_Provisional_Authority_.pdf.

———. Regulation Number 6, "Governing Council of Iraq (13 July 2003)." http://www.cpa-iraq.org/regulations/20030713_CPAREG_6_Governing_Council_of_Iraq_.pdf (accessed 22 March 2006).

"Coalition Provisional Authority, Police Academy Commencement, Baghdad, April 1, 2004." http://www.iraqcoalition.org/transcripts/20040401_bremer_police.html (accessed 5 July 2006).

"CPA Briefing with Major General Paul Eaton, Commander, Coalition Military Assistance and Training Team, RE: Rebuilding Iraq Armed Forces, Location: Baghdad, Iraq, Wednesday, 21 January 2004." http://www.cpa-iraq.org/transcripts/Jan21_Eaton.html (accessed 21 June 2006).

"CPA Press Release: First Battalion of New Iraqi Army Graduates," 7 October 2003. http://govinfo.library.unt.edu/cpa-iraq/daily/archives/01October2003_index.html (accessed 20 June 2006).

Draft Coalition Provisional Authority Memorandum, Subject Commander's Emergency Response Program (CERP), undated.

McArthur, Dobie. Senior Advisor for Detainee and Prisoner Issues, CPA. *Memorandum for the Administrator, Subject: Analysis of Detention Operations,* 22 March 2004.

Office of the Inspector General, Coalition Provisional Authority, *Report to Congress,* 30 October 2004.

US Military

Briefings

US CENTCOM Briefing. http://www.gwu.edu/~nsarchiv/NSAEBB/NSAEBB214/index.htm (accessed 20 February 2007).

CJTF-7. *C8 Resource Management, Commander's Emergency Response Program (CERP)* Briefing.

CJTF-7. *Coalition Detainee Operations Strategy* Briefing, 30 April 2004.

CJTF-7. *Interrogation Operations* Brief, 25 January 2004.

V Corps Briefing. "Nested Lines of Operation & V Corps' Objectives," 18 May 2003. Unpublished briefing.

V Corps. *V Corps Update Briefing—V Corps Commander's Conference,* 16 May 2003.

V Corps and CJTF-7. *V Corps—CJTF-7 Transition and Challenges* Briefing, 30 September 2004.

1st Armored Division. *Operations Overview* Briefing, 3 December 2003.

1st Armored Division. *The 636 Insurgent Cell: The Gift that Keeps on Giving* Briefing.

1st BCT, 1st Armored Division. *Command Brief,* 19 October 2003.

2d (IRON) BCT, 1st Armored Division. *Striker Scimitar: The Battle for Al-Kut, 8 April 04–11 April 04* Briefing.

1st Infantry Division. *Operation Iraqi Freedom–Samarra: An Iraqi Success* Briefing, 4 October 2004.

2d Brigade, 2d Infantry Division. *After Action Review: Operation Iraqi Freedom 04-06 Briefing,* 5 December 2005.

Headquarters, 2d Brigade, 2d Infantry Division. Memorandum for Record, SUBJECT: OIF 04–06 After Action Review for 2d BCT, 2d ID, 5 December 2005, slide 262.

1st BCT, 4th Infantry Division. "Operation RED DAWN, Baylor Bears Brief."

1-24 Infantry (SBCT). *Adapting in Combat: Reorganizing to Fight a Counter-insurgency* Briefing.

2d Armored Cavalry Regiment. *Laydown of Division Detention Operations/Detainee Process* Briefing, September 2003.

3d Armored Cavalry Regiment. *SCP Progress/Update Brief,* 28 February 2004, Rifles Base.

2d Squadron, 3d Armored Cavalry Regiment. *Sabre Squadron AO Robertson Update for 2d BDE, 3 ID* Briefing, 31 May 2003.

82d Airborne Division. *Campaign Plan Overview* Briefing, 1 April 2004.

101st Airborne Division. *AO North Brief* 3, 21 January 2005.

Colonel Stephen R. Reyes. 101st Airborne Division, JIATF Mission Statement Slide.

173d Airborne Brigade. *After Action Review Briefing,* 22 January 2004.

173d Airborne Brigade. *Operation CREATE DEMOCRACY* Briefing, 13 May 2003.

173d Airborne Brigade. *The AMB PENINSULA STRIKE* Briefing, 6 June 2003.

MNF-I. *Detainee Operations, Commander's Conference Update* Briefing, 13 August 2004.

MNF-I, Directorate of Strategic Communications. *STRATCOM January 05 Iraqi Election Matrix* Briefing, 31 January 2005.

MNF-I, Headquarters. *MNF-I, Deputy Chief of Staff for Strategic Communications Orientation* Briefing, 14 June 2005.

Task Force 1-22 Inf. *03 September 2003* Briefing.

Task Force *All American. America's Guard of Honor* Briefing, 1 April 2004.

Task Force *Danger. Operation DANGER FORTITUDE* Briefing, 12 April 2004.

Chief, Commander's Initiatives Group. *Multi-National Force–Iraq, Building a Strategic Headquarters: Operations Research Support to the Theater Commander* Briefing, 44th AORS, 11–13 October 2005.

CMATT Briefing. *The New Iraqi Army: Update and Acceleration Plan,* 5 September 2003.

Joint Center for International Security Force Assistance. Unpublished briefing, "Training Iraqi Security Forces." Combined Arms Center, Fort Leavenworth, KS, 30 August 2006.

Chiarelli, Major General Peter. *Winning the Peace—USMA* Briefing, 8 March 2005.

Natonski, Major General Richard. *Operation Al Fajr: The Battle for Fallujah* Briefing.

Petraeus, Lieutenant General David H. *Iraqi Security Forces Update as of 27 February 2006* Briefing.

———. *Training Iraqi Security Forces* Briefing, 8 August 2006.

———. *Office of Security Cooperation* Briefing.

Simberg, Henry. "AMSAA Sample Data Collection Ground System Usage/Parts Replacement Analysis Operation Iraqi Freedom" Briefing, Fort Belvoir, VA: Research, Development & Engineering Command/Army Materiel Systems Analysis Activity, Army Materiel Command, August 2006.

Documents

3d Corps Support Command After Action Review. *History of the 3d Corps Support Command in Operation Iraqi Freedom.* Heidelberg, Germany.

3d Corps Support Command. *Enemy Tactics, Techniques and Procedures (TTP) and Recommendations.* Created in 2004. This document remains classified as For Official Use Only (FOUO) as of the writing of this study.

1st Infantry Division, 135th Military History Detachment. "Stryker Scimitar: The Battle for Al Kut, 8 April 04–11 April 04." CD. Fort McNair, Washington, DC: US Army Center of Military History.

1st Infantry Division DTAC. *Samarra OPSUMs*, 02–04 October 2004.

1st Infantry Division. ICDC Report, 20 May 2004.

1st Infantry Division. *Task Force Danger Press Release,* 15 August 2004. http://www.1stid.org/about/pressreleases/tfdanger_pr081504.pdf (accessed 22 May 2007).

3d Brigade Combat Team, 1st Infantry Division. *FRAGO 1 to 3 BCT OPORD 04-13*, 09 April 2004.

3d Infantry Division (Mechanized). *After Action Report, Lessons Learned.*

4th Infantry Division. *Lessons Learned: Executive Summary*, 17 June 2004.

4th Psychological Operations Group. Annual Historical Review for 2005. Unpublished manuscript.

432d Civil Affairs Battalion. *For CG, Iraq's State Company For Phosphate (SCP) Al Qa'im, Iraq*, 25 January 2004.

432d Civil Affairs Battalion. *SCP Rail Projection* document, undated.

519th MI Battalion, 525th MI Brigade. *Operation Iraqi Freedom: Lessons Learned,* 29 May 2004.

555th Combat Engineer Group. *555 History Main Body*, 18 February 2004.

AMEDD Oral History Program. Operation Iraqi Freedom, Interview OIF-067, Draft Transcripts (14 January 2004). From the Office of Medical History, Directorate of Health Care Operations, Office of the Surgeon General, US Army Medical Department.

Anderson, Major James L. 2d Brigade Combat Team, 25th Infantry Division (Light). *OIF Historical Account Submission #19,* 19–25 June 2004; *Submission #35*, 10–16 October 2005; *Submission #44a (Samarra Supplemental).*

Army Commander's Guide to Family Readiness Group Operations. http://www.hooah4health.com/deployment/familymatters/24 Sept05_CDRsGuide.doc (accessed December 2007).

Army Corps of Engineers, Gulf Region Division. http://www.grd.usace.army.mil/divisioninfo/GRD brochure4_26.pdf.

Baqubah CMOC S3. Information Paper: *Muktar Data—Edited Version For Release*, 5 August 2003.

Bentch, Major Christopher. *CA Journal Entries by Major Christopher Bentch, 3BCT S-5.*

Camp Duke Detainee Facility S.O.P., dated 1 June 2004.

CJTF-7. Agenda for CJTF-7 Detention Summit—Camp Victory—19 August 2003.

CJTF-7. Interrogation and Counter-Resistance Policy, 14 September 2003. http://www.aclu.org/FilePDFs/september%20sanchez%20memo.pdf (accessed 2 March 2007).

CJTF-7. *OIF Smart Card 1* (20 December 2003) and *OIF Smart Card 4* (2 January 2004). These documents remain classified as For Official Use Only (FOUO) as of the writing of this study.

Claycomb, Staff Sergeant Matthew. B Btry, 1/107th Field Artillery, Pennsylvania Army National Guard. *Memorandum, SUBJECT: Operation Iraqi Freedom II Report from Bravo Battery 1st Battalion, 107th Field Artillery, October 2003 to February 2005.*

Company History for C CO FWD, 2/103 AR.

DRAFT Joint Manning Document Excel Spreadsheet, provided to COST by Colonel (Retired) Greg Gardner, OSA Chief of Staff. Received 11 September 2006.

"DRAFT Statement of Work (SOW): New Iraqi Army Training (NIAT)," 7 June 2003.

Headquarters, 2d Brigade Combat Team. *Memorandum, Subject: 2d Brigade Combat Team's Service in Operation Iraqi Freedom*, 25 August 2004.

Headquarters, MNB-North. *Memorandum for Record, Subject: Standing Operating Procedures for all MNB-N Detainee Collection Points*, 27 January 2004.

Headquarters, United States Central Command. "News Release: Detainee Release Board Takes on Iraqi Partners," 16 April 2004.

Headquarters, US Army Europe. *Joint Guardian After Action Report*, 2000.

Headquarters, US Army Europe. *KFOR 3 After Action Report, June 2001–May 2002*, 2003.

"History of the 1st Armored Division Band." *1st Armored Division Band*. http://www.1ad.army.mil/ Band/bndHistory.htm (accessed 6 October 2006).

LTC [name redacted]. *Memorandum for Chief, Inspections Division, Subject: 4th Infantry Division Detainee Operations Assessment Trip Report*, 5–8 April 2004. http://action.aclu.org/torturefoia/ released/091505/15937.pdf (accessed 9 March 2007).

MNC-I/MNF-I History Office. *History of CJTF-7, Executive Summary*.

Multi-National Forces–Iraq. *MNF-I Framework OPORD Rev 01 Nov 05 Link Index*, 2005.

"NIC Brief—SECDEF Version—3 June 2003 DC with Backups." Draft PowerPoint Presentation provided to COST by Colonel (Retired) Greg Gardner, OSA Chief of Staff, received on 11 September 2006.

Office of the Assistant Attorney General. Memorandum for Alberto R. Gonzales, Counsel to the President, Re: *Standards of Conduct for Interrogation under 18 U.S.C. 2340-2340A*, 1 August 2002.

Office of the Staff Judge Advocate, US Army V Corps. *Agreement to Disavow Party Affiliation*, 1 May 2003.

Press Release #251-03-01: Task Force Iron Horse MP's and Iraqi Police Go on Joint Raid. 4th Infantry Division, 7 September 2003.

Regimental Support Squadron, 2d Armored Cavalry Regiment. *RSS/RHA Detainee Holding Area Guidance* Memorandum, 18 December 2003.

Reilly, Lieutenant Colonel Greg. Initial Operational Assessment (September 2003).

Secretary of Defense. Memorandum for the Commander, US Southern Command. Subject: Counter-Resistance Techniques in the War on Terrorism, 16 April 2003. http://www.gwu.edu/~nsarchiv/ NSAEBB/NSAEBB127/03.04.16.pdf (accessed 17 July 2006).

"Significant Events of Grim Troop, 2/3 ACR during Operation Iraqi Freedom," 27 January 2004.

Swannack, Major General Charles H., Jr. 82d Airborne Division Closure Report, Summation of Dollars Spent.

Task Force 1-22 Inf. Point Paper: Operation IRAQI FREEDOM—Handling of Detainees.

Task Force 2-5 CAV. *Peace Support Operations*, 1998.

The Inspector General. *Detainee Operations Inspection*. Washington, DC, 21 July 2004.

Unit Campaign History of Tactical Psychological Operations Battalion. 324th Support of the Global War on Terror.

US Army Corps of Engineers. Fact Sheet, "Coalition Munitions Clearance Program." Huntsville, AL: US Army Corps of Engineers, June 2006. www.hnd.usace.army.mil/pao/FactShtsFY06/PAO-CMC fact sheet.pdf (accessed 15 October 2006).

US Army Logistics Whitepaper: Delivering Material Readiness to the Army. "Connect Army Logistics." Washington, DC. http://www.hqda.army.mil/logweb/focusareasnew.html (accessed 11 October 2006).

US Army Medical Command. "High Tech Bandages." *AMEDD Innovations Since Desert Storm*. http:// www.armymedicine.army.mil/about/tl/factsbandages.htm (accessed 31 October 2006).

———. "UH-60L Medevac Helicopter." *AMEDD Innovations Since Desert Storm*. http://www. armymedicine.army.mil/about/tl/97-factsuh60l.htm (accessed 31 October 2006).

———. *Mental Health Reports (OIF)*. http://www.armymedicine.army.mil/news/mhat/mhat.html (accessed 2 January 2007).

US Army War College, Department of Military Strategy, Planning, and Operations. "Information Operations Primer: Fundamentals of Information Operations," January 2006. http://www. carlisle.army.mil/usacsl/publications/IO-Primer-AY06.pdf (accessed 12 July 2006).

"US Army Wounded Warrior Program Assists Soldiers." Office of the Chief of Public Affairs, 10 November 2005. http://www4.army.mil/ocpa/print.php?story_id_key=8185 (accessed 31 October 2006).

US Army Wounded Warrior Program Web site. http://www.armyfamiliesonline.org (accessed 31 October 2006).

"US Central Command Unveils R&R Leave Program." *CENTCOM Press Release*, 25 September 2003. http://www.centcom.mil/sites/uscentcom1/Lists/Press%20Releases/AllItems.aspx (accessed 30 August 2006).

Wallace, General William S. Memorandum for Director, Combat Studies Institute. Subject: Review of On Point II Draft Manuscript, 20 December 2006.

Joint Publications, Field Manuals, and Army Regulations

Joint Chiefs of Staff. Joint Publication (JP) 1-02, *DOD Dictionary of Military and Associated Terms*. Washington, DC, 12 April 2001.

———. JP 3-0, *Doctrine for Joint Operations*. Washington, DC, 10 September 2001.

———. JP 3-0, *Joint Operations*. Washington, DC, 17 September 2006.

———. JP 3-13, *Information Operations*. Washington, DC, 13 February 2006.

———. JP 3-57, *Joint Doctrine for Civil-Military Operations*. Washington, DC, 8 February 2001.

———. JP 3-61, *Public Affairs*. Washington, DC, 9 May 2005.

———. JP 5-0, *Joint Operations Planning*. Washington, DC, 26 December 2006.

Headquarters, Department of the Army. Field Manual (FM) 1, *The Army*. Washington, DC, 14 June 2005.

———. FM 3-0, *Operations*. Washington, DC, 14 June 2001.

———. FM 3-0, *Operations* (Initial Draft), Washington, DC, June 2006.

———. FM 3-07, *Stability Operations and Support Operations*. Washington, DC, 20 February 2003.

———. FM 3-13, *Information Operations: Doctrine, Tactics, Techniques, and Procedures*. Washington, DC, 28 November 2003.

———. FM 3-19.40, *Military Police Internment/Resettlement Operations*. Washington, DC, 4 September 2007.

———. FM 3-24, *Counterinsurgency Operations*. Washington, DC, 15 December 2006.

———. FM 3-61.1, *Public Affairs, Tactics, Techniques and Procedures*. Washington, DC, 1 October 2000.

———. FM 4-0, *Combat Service Support*. Washington, DC, 29 August 2003.

———. FM 4-02, *Force Health Protection in a Global Environment*. Washington, DC, 13 February 2003.

———. FM 8-10-14, *Employment of the Combat Support Hospital Tactics, Techniques, and Procedures*. Washington, DC, 29 December 1994.

———. FM 12-50, *U.S. Army Bands*. Washington, DC, 15 October 1999.

———. FM 14-10, *Financial Management Operations*. Washington, DC, 7 May 1997.

———. FM 27-10, *The Law of Land Warfare*. Washington, DC, July 1956.

———. FM 31-23, *Stability Operations*. Washington, DC, 1972.

———. FM 34-1, *Intelligence and Electronic Warfare*. Washington, DC, 27 September 1994.

———. FM 34-52, *Intelligence Interrogation*. Washington, DC, 28 September 1992.

———. FM 100-20, *Military Operations in Low-Intensity Conflict*. Washington, DC, 1990.

———. FM 100-5, *Field Service Regulations—Operations*. Washington, DC, 1962.

———. FM 100-5, *Operations of Armed Forces in the Field*. Washington, DC, 1968.

———. FM 100-5, *Operations*. Washington, DC, June 1993.

———. FM 100-10-1, *Theater Distribution*. Washington, DC, 1 October 1999.

———. FM 100-10-2, *Contracting Support in the Battlefield*. Washington, DC, 4 August 1999.

———. FM 100-15, *Corps Operations*. Washington, DC, 1996.

Headquarters, Department of the Army. Army Regulation 350-20, *Management of the Defense Foreign Language Program.* Washington, DC, 15 March 1987.

Books, Articles, and Reports

"3d Infantry Division Live Briefing from Iraq." *DefenseLink,* 15 May 2003. http://www.defenselink.mil/transcripts/2003/tr20030515-0184.html (accessed 5 September 2006).

"4th Infantry Division and Task Force 'Ironhorse' Conclude Operation Peninsula Strike." *Defend America,* 14 June 2003. http://www.defendamerica.mil/iraq/update/june2003/iu061703.html (accessed 13 October 2006).

"About Iraqi 55 Most Wanted Regime Leader Cards." *Iraq's 55 Most Wanted Playing Cards.* http://www.streetgangs.com/iraq/ (accessed 20 March 2006).

"Abu Ghraib Timeline." *Associated Press*, 7 May 2004. http://www.scvhistory.com/scvhistory/signal/iraq/abughraib-timeline.htm (accessed 16 August 2006).

"Abu Ghraib Timeline." *CBC News*, updated 18 February 2005. http://www.cbc.ca/news/background/iraq/abughraib_timeline.html (accessed 16 August 2006).

Alger, Specialist Joe. "203rd Iraqi National Guard Battalion Makes Tremendous Progress." *1st Infantry Division Public Affairs Office,* 19 December 2004. http://www.1id.army.mil/1ID/News/December/Article_18/Article_18.htm (accessed 6 July 2006).

Allawi, Ali A. *The Occupation of Iraq: Winning the War, Losing the Peace.* New Haven, CT: Yale University Press, 2007.

Al-Marashi, Ibrahim. "Iraq's Hostage Crisis: Kidnappings, Mass Media and the Iraqi Insurgency." *Middle East Review of International Affairs*, December 2004.

Amanpour, Christiane. "Brain Rangers' Fight Iraq Stress." *60 Minutes*, CBS News, 27 February 2005. http://www.cbsnews.com/stories/2005/02/25/60minutes/main676553.shtml (accessed 24 August 2005).

Anderson, Jon Lee. "Letter From Iraq: Out on the Street." *The New Yorker,* 15 November 2004. http://www.newyorker.com/printable/fact/041115fa_fact (accessed 8 November 2004).

Andrade, Dale, and Jim Willbanks. "CORDS/Phoenix: Counterinsurgency Lessons from Vietnam for the Future." *Military Review,* March–April 2006.

"Another Saddam Relative Nabbed." *CBS News*, 14 April 2003. http://www.cbsnews.com/stories/2003/04/18/iraq/main549930.shtml (accessed 22 March 2006).

Armistead, Thomas F., Glen Carey, and Gary Tulacz. "Contractor Fatalities Prompt Suspension of Work in Iraq." *ENR.com*, 8 December 2003.

Armistead, Thomas F., Tom Sawyer, Sherine Winston, Andrew G. Wright, and Aileen Cho, with Kate Dourian and Jason Benham. "Reviewing Markets: Oil, Water and More in Practically Every Sector, the Lack of Security Hampers Reconstruction Efforts." *ENR.com*, 9 June 2003.

"Army's new life-saving training aims to cut combat deaths." *EMS House of DeFrance*, 29 April 2005. http://www.defrance.org/artman/publish/article_1323.shtml (accessed 16 August 2006).

Ayatollah al-Sistani's official Web site. *Sistani.org.* http://www.sistani.org/messages/eng/ir5.htm (accessed 17 March 2006).

Babcock, Robert O. *Operation Iraqi Freedom I: A Year in the Sunni Triangle.* Tuscaloosa, AL: St. John's Press, 2005.

Baker, Colonel Ralph O. "The Decisive Weapon: A Brigade Combat Team Commander's Perspective on Operations." *Military Review*, May–June 2006.

Baker, Gerard, and Stephen Fidler. "The Best-laid Plans? How Turf Battles and Mistakes in Washington Dragged Down the Reconstruction of Iraq." *Financial Times*, 4 August 2003.

Baker, Peter. "The Image Bush Just Can't Escape." *Washington Post,* 4 May 2007.

Balfour, Frederik. "A Wartime Oasis of Selfless Compassion." *BusinessWeek Online*, 15 April 2003. http://www.businessweek.com/bwdaily/dnflash/apr2003/nf20030415_8932.htm (accessed 10 October 2006).

Banusiewicz, John D. "Commander in Iraq Thanks Troops Who 'Shaped History.'" *American Forces Information Service*, 3 February 2005. http://defenselink.mil/news/Feb2005/n02032005_2005020304.html (accessed 4 November 2006).

Baram, Amatzia. *Who Are the Insurgents? Sunni Arab Rebels in Iraq.* United States Institute of Peace, Special Report No. 134, April 2005.

Batiste, Major General John R.S., and Lieutenant Colonel Paul R. Daniels. "The Fight for Samarra: Full-Spectrum Operations in Modern Warfare." *Military Review,* May–June 2005.

Baumann, Robert F., George H. Gawrych, and Walter E. Kretchik. *Armed Peacekeepers in Bosnia.* Fort Leavenworth, KS: Combat Studies Institute Press, 2004.

Baumann, Robert, Lawrence A. Yates, and Versalle F. Washington. *My Clan Against the World.* Fort Leavenworth, KS: Combat Studies Institute Press, 2004.

Beck, Jason P. "Neighborhood Advisory Councils: Democracy at the Community Level." Third US Army, 22 June 2003. http://www.arcent.army.mil/news/archive/2003_news/june/advisory_councils.asp (accessed 1 November 2006).

Beebe, Gilbert W., and Michael E. DeBakey. *Battle Casualties: Incidence, Mortality, and Logistic Considerations.* Springfield, IL: Charles C. Thomas, Pub., 1952.

Belknap, Margaret H. "The CNN Effect: Strategic Enabler or Operational Risk?" Strategy Research Project. Carlisle Barracks, PA: Army War College, 30 March 2001.

Bellamy, Colonel (Retired) Ronald. "A Note on American Combat Mortality in Iraq." *Military Medicine,* Volome 172, October 2007.

Bentley, Steve. "A Short History of PTSD: From Thermopylae to Hue Soldiers Have Always Had A Disturbing Reaction to War." *The VA Veteran*, March/April 2005, originally published January 1991. http://www.vva.org/TheVeteran/2005_03/feature_HistoryPTSD.htm (accessed 23 August 2006).

Berenson, Alex. "Car Bombing Outside U.N. Mission in Baghdad Kills at Least One and Injures Others." *New York Times*, 22 September 2003, Late Edition.

Berkshire Newsletter (8 August 2004). http://icberkshire.icnetwork.co.uk/0100news/nationalnews/ tm_objectid=14508590&method=full&siteid=50102&headline=nato-begins-training-iraqi-forces-name_page.html (accessed 13 June 2006).

Beveridge, Captain David E. "New Jersey National Guard Soldiers Earn Right to Proudly Wear Brassard." *Military Police Bulletin*, April 2005. http://www.wood.army.mil/mpbulletin/pdfs/April%2005/Beveridge-In%20Lieu%20of%20MP.pdf (accessed 14 March 2007).

"Big Iraq Ambush was Bank Heist." *BBC News*, 1 December 2003. http://news.bbc.co.uk/2/hi/middle_east/3253236.stm (accessed 1 September 2006).

Binova, Stephen, Steve Geary, and Barry Holland. "An Objective Assessment of Logistics in Iraq." Science Applications International Corporation. Fort Leavenworth, KS: Center for Army Lessons Learned, March 2004.

Birmingham, Specialist Crista M. "MNC-I: Training Wheels for Iraqi Government." *Soldiers On-line*, 10 August 2004. http://www4.army.mil/soldiers/view_story.php?story_id_key=6247 (accessed 20 December 2005).

Birtle, Andrew J. *US Army Counterinsurgency and Contingency Operations Doctrine, 1860–1941.* Washington, DC: Center of Military History, 1998.

Black, Major Mark. *Military Support to Elections: The Balkans Experience and the Implications for Future Planning.* Fort Leavenworth, KS: Center for Army Lessons Learned, 27 February 2004.

Blackledge, Brigadier General David, 352d Civil Affairs Command. "Department of Defense Press Conference Transcript." *DefenseLink,* 14 January 2004. http://www.defenselink.mil/transcripts/2004/tr20040114-1144.html (accessed 9 October 2006).

Bodansky, Yossef. *The Secret History of the Iraq War*. New York: ReganBooks, 2004.

Boot, Max. *The Savage Wars of Peace, Small Wars and the Rise of American Power.* New York, NY: Basic Books, 2002.

Booth, William. "Ad-libbing Iraq's Infrastructure; U.S. Troops Face Daily Scramble in 'Bringing Order to Chaos.'" *Washington Post*, 21 May 2003.

Booth, William, and Rajiv Chandrasekaran. "Occupation Forces Halt Elections Throughout Iraq." *Washington Post*, 28 June 2003.

Borlas, Joe. "CENTCOM Up-Armored Humvee Requirements Being Met." *Army News Service*, 6 February 2004.

Bowes, Lieutenant Colonel Andrew W. "A Corps Support Battalion's Experience in Operation Iraqi Freedom." *Army Logistician*, July–August 2004. http://www.almc.army.mil/alog/Back.html.

Boyd, Colonel Curtis D. "Army IO is PSYOP: Influencing More with Less." *Military Review*, May–June 2007.

Boyd, Terry. "Bronze Star Recipient Led to Stunning Victory." *Stars & Stripes, European Edition*, 14 June 2005. http://www.estripes.com/article.asp?section=104&article=28917&archive=true (accessed 28 February 2007).

"Bremer Brands Moqtada Sadr an Outlaw." *Middle East OnLine*. http://www.middle-east-online.com/english/?id=9514 (accessed 30 August 2006).

Bremer, L. Paul, III. *My Year in Iraq: The Struggle to Build a Future of Hope*. New York, NY: Simon & Schuster, 2006.

"Briefing with Brigadier General Donald Alston, US Air Force, Spokesperson for Multinational Force Iraq." *Coalition Press Information Center*, 30 October 2005. http://www.mnf-iraq.com/Transcripts/051030a.htm (accessed 5 June 2006).

"Brigadier General Dempsey Briefs on 1st Armored Division Operations in Iraq." *DefenseLink*, 20 November 2003. http://www.defenselink.mil/transcripts/2003/tr20031120-0893.html (accessed 21 July 2006).

Brill, Lieutenant Colonel Arthur P., Jr., USMC (Retired). "A Defining Moment in Marine Corps History." *Sea Power, Navy League of the United States*. http://www.navyleague.org/seapower/krulak_interview.htm (accessed December 2007).

Briscoe, Charles H., Kenneth Finlayson, and Robert W. Jones Jr. *All Roads Lead to Baghdad: Army Special Operations Forces in Iraq*. Fort Bragg, NC: US Army Special Operations Command History Office, 2006.

Broeckelman, Melissa. "K-State Professor and Retired Colonel Discusses the Effects of Deployments on Military Families." Manhattan, KS: K-State Media Relations & Marketing, 3 July 2003.

Byman, Daniel L. "Building the New Iraq: The Role of Intervening Forces." *Survival*, Summer 2003.

Bush, President George W., "Transcript of President Bush's Address to the Nation, 19 March 2003." http://www.whitehouse.gov/news/releases/2003/03/20030319-17.html (accessed 23 March 2007).

———. "State of the Union Address, 2 February 2005." http://www.whitehouse.gov/news/releases/2005/02/20050202-11.html (accessed 28 November 2007).

———. *Memorandum, Subject: Humane Treatment of al-Qaeda and Taliban Detainees,* 7 February 2002. http://www.pegcus/archive/White_House/bush_memo_20020207_ed.pdf (accessed 26 October 2006).

"Can the Voters Build on Success?" *Economist,* 5 February 2005.

Carollo, Russell, and Mike Wagner. "Deadly Price Paid for HMMWV Armor Used to Protect Soldiers." *Dayton Daily News*, 11 June 2006.

Cha, Ariana Eunjung. "Female Officers Cross Cultural Frontier in Iraq; Women on Patrol Near Iran Brave Insults and Disapproval." *Washington Post*, 3 January 2004.

———. "Soldiering on to Rebuild Iraq; Civil Affairs Takes on Tough Task." *Washington Post*, 12 February 2004.

Chapter 2, "Civil-Military Operations," *CALL Newsletter 04-13: Operation Iraqi Freedom (OIF), CAAT II Initial Impressions Report (IIR).* Fort Leavenworth, KS: Center for Army Lessons Learned, May 2004.

Chiarelli, Major General Peter W., and Major Patrick R. Michaelis. "Winning the Peace: The Requirement for Full-Spectrum Operations." *Military Review,* July–August 2005.

"Chronology: From DESERT STORM to DESERT FOX." *DefenseLink.* http://www.defenselink.mil/specials/desert_fox/timeline.html (accessed 20 April 2006).

Church, Vice Admiral Albert T., III. *Review of Department of Defense Detention Operations and Detainee Interrogation Techniques (The Church Report),* 7 March 2005.

———. Unclassified Executive Summary. "The Church Report." *DefenseLink,* February 2005. http://www.defenselink.mil/news/Mar2005/d20050310exe.pdf (accessed 14 July 2005).

Clarke, Jeffrey J. *Advice and Support; The Final Years, 1965–1973.* Washington, DC: US Army Center of Military History, 1988.

Clay, Steven. *Iroquois Warriors in Iraq.* Fort Leavenworth, KS: Combat Studies Institute Press, 2007.

"Coalition Working to Pacify Fallujah, Destroy Sadr Militia." *DefenseLink,* 8 April 2004. http://www.defenselink.mil/news/Apr2004/n04082004_200404081.html (accessed 19 October 2004).

Cohen, Eliot, Lieutenant Colonel (Retired) Conrad Crane, US Army, Lieutenant Colonel Jan Horvath, US Army, and Lieutenant Colonel John Nagl, US Army. "Principles, Imperatives, and Paradoxes of Counterinsurgency." *Military Review,* March–April 2006.

"Combat Stress Team Helps Troops Cope." *Defend America,* 5 November 2004. http://www.defendamerica.mil/articles/nov2004/a110504e.html (accessed 24 August 2006).

Conboy, Lieutenant Colonel David J. *An Interview with Lieutenant General Nasier Abadi, Deputy Chief of Staff, Iraqi Joint Forces.* Carlisle Barracks, PA: US Army War College, 2005.

Congress. House. Report 107, "Authorization for Use of Military Force Against Iraq Resolution of 2002," 7 October 2002. http://www.iraqwatch.org/government/US/Legislation/hirc-hjres114report-100702.pdf.

Congress. House. *Statement by Lieutenant General David F. Melcher, Deputy Chief of Staff G8, and Major General Jeanette K. Edmunds, Deputy Chief of Staff G4, Army Equipment Reset Program.* 109th Congress, 2d Session, 30 March 2006.

Congress. House. *The Potential Costs Resulting from Increased Usage of Military Equipment in Ongoing Operations.* 109th Congress, 1st Session, 6 April 2005. http://www.cbo.gov/showdoc.cfm?index=6235&sequence (accessed 9 October 2006).

Cordesman, Anthony H. *The Iraq War: Strategy, Tactics, and Military Lessons.* Washington, DC: Center for Strategic Studies, 2004.

Cordesman, Anthony, with William D. Sullivan. "Iraqi Force Development: Can Iraqi Forces Do the Job?" *Center for Strategic and International Studies,* revised 29 November 2005.

Cordovano, Captain Jeremiah. "TF 1-21 Infantry Applies the Nine Principles of War in Kirkuk: Preparing an Iraqi City for Elections." *Infantry,* January–February 2006.

"Corps Issues Task Orders to Restore Iraq's Electric System." *ENR,* 13 October 2003.

Cox, Major Joseph L. "Information Operations in Operations Enduring Freedom and Iraqi Freedom— What Went Wrong?" US Army School of Advanced Military Studies Monograph, United States Army Command and General Staff College, Fort Leavenworth, KS, AY 2005–06.

Crane, Conrad C., and W. Andrew Terrill. *Reconstructing Iraq: Insights, Challenges, and Missions for Military Forces in a Post-Conflict Scenario.* Carlisle Barracks, PA: Strategic Studies Institute, 2003.

Croll, Scott, and Sean Shockey. "Advances in Battlefield Pain Control." *American Society of Anesthesiologists Newsletter,* March 2006. www.asahq.org/Newsletters/2006/03-06/croll01_06.html (accessed June 2006).

Darius, Robert G. "Operation Iraqi Freedom—It Was a Prepositioned War." Fort Belvoir, VA: US Army Materiel Command, October 2003.

Darley, Colonel William M. "Why Public Affairs is not Information Operations." *Army*, January 2005.

Dashiell, Staff Sergeant Richard. "The Steel Snake Archery Club, Iraq." *texasarchery.org*. http://www. texasarchery.org/L1/IAC.htm (accessed June 2006).

De Toy, Brian M., ed. *Turning Victory into Success: Military Operations After the Campaign.* Fort Leavenworth, KS: Combat Studies Institute Press, 2004.

Defense and Veterans Brain Injury Center, "Blast Infury" information. http://www.dvbic.org/cms. php?p=Blast_injury (accessed 19 December 2007).

Dervarics, Charles. "Contractors Fill Key Role Through the Logistics Civil Augmentation Program." Fort Belvoir, VA: US Army Materiel Command, 2004, 2005.

Dexter, Specialist Derek. "Weapons Seized, Four Soldiers Hurt During Operation Peninsula Strike." *Army News Service*, 16 June 2003. http://www4.army.mil/ocpa/read.php?story_id_key=1687 (accessed 12 October 2006).

Diamond, Larry. *Squandered Victory: The American Occupation and the Bungled Effort to Bring Democracy to Iraq.* New York, NY: Henry Holt and Company, 2005.

Diaz, Sergeant Enrique S. "Troops Add Jazz to Recreation Center." *mnf-iraq.com*, 14 July 2006. http:// www.mnf-iraq.com/index2php?option=com_content (accessed 25 August 2006).

"DOD News Briefing—Mr. DiRita and Gen. Abizaid." *DefenseLink*, 16 July 2003. http://www. defenselink.mil/transcripts/2003/tr20030716-0401.html.

"DOD News Briefing—Secretary Rumsfeld and General Meyers." *DefenseLink.* http://www.defenselink. mil/transcripts/2003/tr20030630-secdef0321.html (accessed 23 October 2006).

Dotts, Keith A. "The 420th Engineer Brigade: Builders in Battle." *Engineer*, April/June 2005.

Duke, Major Randolph. "More Than a Name Change." *Army Logistician*, January–February 2001. http:// www.almc.army.mil/alog/issues/JanFeb01/JFIndex.htm (accessed 11 October 2006).

Dunnigan, James. "Why The Xbox is Important in the Iraq War." *www.strategypage.com*, 12 February 2005. http://www.strategypage.com/dls/articles/200521223.asp?source=send (accessed 25 August 2006).

Dunwoody, Lieutenant General Ann E. "Working to Achieve Logistics Readiness for the Long Haul." *Army: 2006-2007 Green Book*. Arlington, VA: Association of the United States Army, October 2006.

Eckholm, Erik, and James Glantz. "Reality Intrudes on Promises in Rebuilding of Iraq." *New York Times* (Late Edition), 20 June 2004.

Eisenstadt, Michael, and Jeffrey White. "Assessing Iraq's Sunni Arab Insurgency." *Military Review,* May–June 2006.

Engel, Bernard. "Lieutenant Colonel Joe Rice Interview." United States Institute of Peace Association for Diplomatic Studies and Training, Iraq Experience Project, 31 July 2004. www.usip.org/ library/oh/sops/iraq/sec/rice.pdf (accessed 28 November 2005).

English, Major Edward L. "Towards a More Productive Military-Media Relationship." US Army School of Advanced Military Studies Monograph, United States Army Command and General Staff College, Fort Leavenworth, KS, AY 2004–05.

Erwin, Sandra I. "As Demands for Nation-Building Troops Soar, Leaders Ponder Reorganization." *National Defense*, May 2005.

Estes, Kenneth W. "Command Narrative: 1st Armored Division in Operation IRAQI FREEDOM, May 2003—July 2004." Unpublished study.

Evangelista, Benny. "Kevlar saving lives, minimizing wounds in Iraq." *San Francisco Chronicle*, 7 April 2003. http://www.sfgate.com/cgi-in/article.cgi?file=/chronicle/archive/2003/04/07/BU275282. DTL&type=business (accessed 22 August 2006).

Executive Office of the President, Office of Management and Budget. *Section 2207, Second Quarterly Report*, 5 April 2004. http://www.whitehouse.gov/omb/legislative/index.html (accessed 18 January 2008).

———. *Section 2207, Third Quarterly Report*, 2 July 2004. http://www.whitehouse.gov/omb/legislative/index.html (accessed 18 January 2008).

Eyre, Major Michael, Captain David Albanese, Sergeant First Class John Stockton, and Sergeant First Class Colleen Burrows. "Civil Affairs (CA) Integration at the JRTC." CTC Bulletin 98-12. Fort Leavenworth, KS: Center for Army Lessons Learned, 1998.

Fay, Major General George. *AR 15-6 Investigation of the Abu Ghraib Prison and the 205th Military Intelligence Brigade.*

Feith, Douglas J. *War and Decision: Inside the Pentagon at the Dawn of the War on Terrorism.* New York, NY: Harper, 2008.

Filkins, Dexter. "Attack on Sheik is Blow to City that Has Plan for Iraqi Police." *New York Times*, 21 November 2003.

Finch, Private First Class Sean. "V Corps 'Garage Band' Revs up to Rock Soldier Morale in Iraq." Multi-National Corps–Iraq Public Affairs Office, 17 February 2006.

Finer, Jonathan. "Battle-Hard G.I.'s Learn to Release their Pain." *Washington Post Foreign Service*, 14 June 2005. http://www.hws,edu/akumni/alumnews/showclip.asp?webslip=2191 (accessed 14 August 2006).

———. "Iraq's Insurgents: Who's Who." *Washington Post,* 19 March 2006.

Finer, Jonathan, and Omar Fekeiki. "Tackling Another Major Challenge in Iraq: Unemployment." *Washington Post*, 20 June 2005.

Fischer, Hannah. *United States Military Casualty Statistics: Operation Iraqi Freedom and Operation Enduring Freedom, Report RS22452*. Congressional Research Service, 8 June 2006. http://www.fas.org/sgp/crs/natsec/RS22452.pdf (accessed 19 December 2006).

Fisher, Ian. "Attacks Go On; Bomb Kills 6 Iraqi Officers." *New York Times*, 16 December 2003.

———. "The Struggle for Iraq: Attacks North of Baghdad Kill 3 GI's, and Barely Miss Governor of an Iraqi Province." *New York Times,* 14 October 2003.

Fleming-Michael, Karen. "New tourniquet named one of Army's 10 greatest inventions." *Army News Service*, 22 June 2006. http://www.globalsecurity.org/military/library/news/2006/06/mil-060622-arnews03.htm (accessed 22 August 2006).

Flowers, Robert B. "Army Engineers: Supporting the Warfighters and Reconstruction Efforts." *Army*, October 2004.

Fontenot, COL Gregory, US Army Retired, LTC E.J. Degen, US Army, and LTC David Tohn, US Army. *On Point: The United States Army in Operation Iraqi Freedom*. Fort Leavenworth, KS: Combat Studies Institute Press, 2004.

Franks, General Tommy. *American Soldier*. New York, NY: Harper Collins, 2004.

Freedman, Lawrence, and Efraim Karsh. *The Gulf Conflict 1990–1991: Diplomacy and War in the New World Order*. Princeton, NJ: Princeton University Press, 1993.

Frie, Captain Arnd, Captain Thomas Moody, Captain Garth Yarnall, Captain Jamie Kiessling, Captain Benett Sunds, Captain Gerard L. McCool, and Captain Robert Uppena. "Fallen Comrades: Mortuary Affairs in the US Army." *Army Mortuary Affairs*. http://www.qmfound.com/fallen.htm (accessed 10 October 2006).

Friedman, Matthew J., M.D., Ph.D. "Acknowledging the Psychiatric Cost of War." *The New England Journal of Medicine*, July 2004.

Friedman, Sergeant Major (Retired) Herb. "Deception and Disinformation." http://www.psywarrior.com/DeceptionH.html (accessed 12 July 2006).

Galula, David. *Counterinsurgency Warfare: Theory and Practice*. St. Petersburg, FL: Hailer Publishing, 2005.

Garamone, Jim. "Casey: Elections will be Triumph of Democracy Over Tyranny." *American Forces Press Service*, 26 January 2005.

———. "Iraqi, US Troops Begin 'Al Fajr' Operation in Fallujah." *DefenseLink*, 8 November 2004. http://www.defenselink.mil/news/Nov2004/n11082004_2004110805.html (accessed 23 October 2006).

———. "Iraqis Adapt British Military Academy as Model." *American Forces Press Services,* 26 May 2006. http://www.defenselink.mil/news/May2006/20060526_5249.html (accessed 9 June 2006).

Gates, John M. *Schoolbooks and Krags: The United States Army in the Philippines, 1898–1902.* Westport, CT: Greenwood Press Inc., 1973.

Gavrilis, James A. "The Mayor of Ar Rutbah." *Foreign Policy,* November/December 2005. http://www.foreignpolicy.com/story/cms.php?story_id=3265 (accessed 22 March 2007).

Gawande, Atul, M.D., M.P.H. "Casualties of War—Military Care for the Wounded from Iraq and Afghanistan." *The New England Journal of Medicine*, December 2004. http://content.nejm.org/cgi/reprint/351/24/2471.pdf (accessed 22 August 2006).

Gbur, Lieutenant Commander Charles J., Jr., MC, USNR. "Battalion Aid Station Support of Military Operations in Urban Terrain (BASS MOUT)." http://www.geocities.com/Pentagon/6453/bassmout.html (accessed 15 August 2006).

Gegax, T. Trent. "Wartime Stress: Poor morale and high suicide rates point to big problems for troops in Iraq." Web Exclusive, *Newsweek, MSNBC.com*, 2 April 2004. http://www.msnbc.msn.com/id/4632956/site/newsweek/ (accessed 24 August 2006).

Ghosh, Aparisim. "A Vote for Hope." *Time,* 14 February 2005.

Gilmore, Gerry J. "Despite Challenges, Iraqi Forces 'In the Fight.'" *DefenseLink,* 29 September 2004. http://www.defenselink.mil/news/newsarticle.aspx?id+25181 (accessed 3 January 2008).

Goebel, Douglas J. "Military-Media Relations: The Future Media Environment and Its Influence on Military Operations." Maxwell, AL: Air University and Air War College, 1997.

Goldsmith, Jack. *The Terror Presidency: Law and Judgment Inside the Bush Administration.* New York, NY: W.W. Norton & Company, 2007.

Gordon, Michael R., "To Mollify Iraqis, US Plans to Ease Scope of Its Raids." *New York Times,* 7 August 2003.

———. "US Re-evaluates 'iron-fisted' Strategy in Iraq." *New York Times*, 7 August 2003.

Gordon, Michael R., and General Bernard E. Trainor. *Cobra II: The Inside Story of the Invasion and Occupation of Iraq*. New York, NY: Pantheon Books, 2006.

Gott, Kendall D., ed. *Security Assistance, U.S. and International Historical Perspectives; The Proceedings of the Combat Studies Institute 2006 Military History Symposium.* Fort Leavenworth, KS: Combat Studies Institute Press, 2006.

Gourley, Scott. "Protecting our Soldiers, Armoring Vehicles." Fort Belvoir, VA: US Army Materiel Command, 2005.

Grady, Denise. "Struggling Back From War's Once-Deadly Wounds." *New York Times*, 22 January 2006. http://www/nytimes/com/2006/01/22/national/22wounded.html (accessed 22 August 2006).

Gray, Anthony, and Maxwell Manwaring. *Panama: Operation Just Cause.* Washington, DC: National Defense University Press, 2001.

Greenberg, Karen J., and Joshu L. Dratel, eds. *The Torture Papers: The Road to Abu Ghraib.* Cambridge, MA: Cambridge University Press, 2005.

Greenwood, John T., and F. Clinton Berry Jr. *Medics at War: Military Medicine from Colonial Times to the 21st Century.* Annapolis, MD: Naval Institute Press, 2005.

Gresham, John D. "Army Materiel Command Logistics Support Elements." Fort Belvoir, VA: US Army Materiel Command, 2004.

Grimmet, Richard F. "Instances of Use of United States Armed Forces Abroad, 1789–2004." Congressional Research Service Report RL30172, as posted by the Naval Historical Center. http://www.au.af.mil/au/awc/awcgate/crs/rl30172.htm (1 of 41) (accessed 16 April 2005).

Hackley, Staff Sergeant Cheryl. "New System Helps Resolve Pay Problems." *Defend America,* 28 July 2004. http://www.defendamerica.mil/articles/jul2004/a072804e.html (accessed 9 October 2006).

Halchin, Elaine. *The CPA: Origins, Characteristics and Institutional Authorities.* Washington, DC: Congressional Research Service, 29 April 2004.

Harris, Share. "The Slog of Reconstruction." *Government Executive*, January 2005.

Hashim, Ahmed S. *Insurgency and Counter-insurgency in Iraq.* Ithaca, NY: Cornell University Press, 2006.

Hawkins, Steven R., and Gordon M. Wells. "Nation Building in Mesopotamia: U.S. Military Engineers in Iraq." *Army*, February 2005.

"Head of Anti-IED Agency Says it's Been Effective." *Army Times*, 21 May 2007.

Healy, Sergeant Joe. "Iraq Police Provide Secure Border for Pilgrims During Hajj." *Defend America*, 23 January 2004.

Hoge, Charles W., M.D., Jennifer L. Auchterloine, M.S., and Charles S. Milliken, M.D. "Mental Health Problems, Use of Mental Health Services, and Attrition From Military Service After Returning from Deployment to Iraq or Afghanistan." *The Journal of the American Medical Association*, March 2006.

Hollen, Patrick, Thomas Mundell, Dean Nilson, and Mark Sweeney. "Pre-Planning and Post-Conflict CMOC/CIMIC Challenges." National Defense University. Norfolk VA: Joint Forces Staff College, 5 September 2003. http://www.jfsc.ndu.edu/current_students/documents_policies/documents/jca_cca_awsp/Pre-Planning_and_Post-Conflict.doc (accessed 1 June 2006).

Hollis, Patrecia Slayden. "1st Cav in Baghdad: Counterinsurgency EBO in Dense Urban Terrain. Interview with Major General Peter W. Chiarelli." *Field Artillery,* September–October 2005.

———. "Second Battle of Fallujah: Urban Operations in a New Kind of War, Interview with Lieutenant General John Sattler." *Field Artillery*, March–April 2006.

———. "Task Force Danger in OIF II: Preparing a Secure Environment for the Iraqi National Elections." *Field Artillery*, July–August 2005.

Horn, Lieutenant Colonel Bernd. "Command and Control Complexity Squared: Operating in the Future Battlespace," 3 July 2004. http://worldaffairsboard.com/showpost.php?p=20409&postcount=38 (accessed 24 July 2006).

Howard, Sir Michael. "Military Science in an Age of Peace." Chesney Memorial Gold Lecture given on 3 October 1973. Published in the *Journal of the Royal United Services Institute for Defense Studies*, March 1974.

"H.R. 4655 Iraq Liberation Act of 1998." http://www.iraqwatch.org/government/US/Legislation/ILA. htm (accessed 27 February 2006).

Hughan, Technical Sergeant Andrew. "11 Graduate from First Iraqi Signals Schools." *The Advisor,* 22 January 2005.

———. "Iraqi Mechanized Brigade Assumes Mission." *The Advisor*, 15 January 2005.

———. "Kitchen Serves Thousands of Iraqi Soldiers." *The Advisor*, 15 January 2005.

Hutcheson, Specialist Joshua. "Engineers Teach Construction Projects to Former Iraqi Soldiers." *Iraqi Destiny—101st Airborne Newsletter*, 25 September 2003.

Hyrup, Major Lars, and Captain Piotr Siemienski (Polish Army). *MND-CS Press Release*, 28 October 2004. http://republika.pl/piomndcs/MND%20CS%20News/IBP.htm.

Ilfeld, Brian M., M.D., and F. Kayser Enneking, M.D. "Continuous Peripheral Nerve Blocks for Patients at Home." *American Society of Anesthesiologists Newsletter*, May 2005. http://www.asahq.org/Newsletters/2005/05-05/ilfeld05_05.html (accessed 13 October 2006).

"In Their Own Words: Reading the Insurgency." International Crisis Group, Middle East, Report No. 50, 15 February 2006.

"Initial Impressions Report No. 06-20, 13th Corps Support Command." Fort Leavenworth, KS: Center for Army Lessons Learned, April 2006.

Inspectors General Report, US Department of State and US Department of Defense. "Interagency Assessment of Iraq Police Training," 15 July 2005. Department of State Report No. ISP-IQO-05-72. Department of Defense Report No. IE-2005-002.

"Insurgents Caught After Attack on US Embassy in Iraq." *DefenseLink*, 30 January 2005. http://www.defenselink.mil/news/newsarticle.asp.?id=24225 (accessed 20 February 2008).

"Intelligence BOS." *CTC Trends 98-20.* Fort Leavenworth, KS: Center for Army Lessons Learned, 1998.

"Interview, Col. William Mayville." *Frontline: Beyond Baghdad,* 1 December 2003. http://www.pbs.org/wgbh/pages/frontline/shows/beyond/interviews/mayville.html (accessed 2 April 2007).

Iraq Coalition Casualty Count. http://icasualties.org/oif/.

"Iraq Liberation Act of 1998." Public Law 105-338—Oct. 31, 1998. *www.FINDLAW.com.* http://news.findlaw.com/hdocs/docs/iraq/libact103198.pdf (accessed 12 September 2006).

"Iraq: Three Years, No Exit: Rebuilding Iraq Has Been Tougher Than Expected." *CBS News Online,* 13 March 2006. http://www.cbsnews.com/stories/2006/03/13/eveningnews/main1397666.shtml (accessed 14 June 2006).

"Iraq's 6th Battalion Completes Training, Activates." *DefenseLink,* 8 July 2004. http://www.defenselink.mil/news/newsarticle.aspx?id=25734 (accessed 4 April 2008).

"Iraq's Most Wanted." *BBC News,* 11 November 2005. http://news.bbc.co.uk/go/pr/fr/ /2/hi/middle_east/2939125.stm (accessed 20 March 2006).

"Iraq's Security Void." *Economist.com/Global Agenda,* 27 August 2003. http://proquest.umi.com/pqdweb?did=391615061&sid=1&Fmt=3&clientid=5094&RQT=309&VName=PQD (accessed 13 June 2006).

"Iraqi Coastal Defence Force Ready to Patrol Iraqi Waters Thanks to Navy." *Australian Government Defence Media Release.* CPA 222/04, 1 October 2004.

"Iraqi Elections, January 30, 2005." US State Department Web site. http://www.state.gov/r/pa/scp/2005/41206.htm (accessed 4 September 2006).

"Iraqi Police Commandos take Fight to Insurgents." *The Advisor,* 25 December 2004.

Jackson, William. "Internet cafes are morale booster for troops in Iraq." *Government Computer News,* 24 November 2003. http://www.gcn.com/cgi-bin/udt/im.display.printable?client.id=gcn&story.id=24241 (accessed 25 August 2006).

Jay, Adam. "Iraq to Close Borders During Elections." *The Guardian* (18 January 2005): 1–4.

Jeffers, Captain Tim. "Iraqi Air Force Takes Off with Aircraft Delivery." *The Advisor,* 15 January 2005.

Jones, Lieutenant General Anthony R. *AR 15-6 Investigation of the Abu Ghraib Prison and the 205th Military Intelligence Brigade,* 24 August 2004.

Jones, Seth G., Jeremy M. Wilson, Andrew Rathmell, and K. Jack Riley. *Establishing Law and Order After Conflict.* Santa Monica, CA: RAND National Defense Research Institute, 2005.

Josar, David. "Mail flow to Kuwait and Iraq is Improving, Says General." *Star and Stripes,* 22 April 2003. http://www.stripes.com/article.asp?section=104&article=15044 (accessed 29 July 2006).

Joseph, Sergeant First Class Chuck. "'Duty First' Soldiers Conduct Cajun Mousetrap III in Iraq." *USAREUR Public Affairs News Release,* 16 August 2004. http://www.hqusareur.army.mil/htmlinks/Press_Releases/2004/Aug2004/16Aug2004-02.htm (accessed 14 May 2007).

Kane, Chief Petty Officer Joe. "Iraq's Border Enforcement Department Graduates First Cadets." *The Advisor,* 2 October 2004.

———. "Iraqi Border Forts Strengthen Security at More than 300 Locations." *The Advisor,* 9 October 2004.

———. "Iraqi Counterterrorism Force Graduates Class in Jordan." *The Advisor,* 4 December 2004.

———. "Iraqi Mechanized Brigade Rolls Out Heavy Equipment." *The Advisor,* 27 November 2005.

———. "Iraqi National Guard Graduates New Round of Recruits: 358 Troops Complete Training Developed by 1st Infantry Division." Multi-National Transition Command—Iraq Public Affairs, 17 September 2004.

Kaplan, Fred. "The Flaw in Shock and Awe: Rumsfeld's Theory of Warfare Isn't Working, At Least So Far." *Slate*, 26 March 2003. http://www.slate.com/id/2080745/ (accessed 12 September 2006).

Kaplan, Lawrence F. "America's Near-Invisible Wounded." *The New Republic*, 2 October 2003. http://www.tnr.com/doc.mhtml?i=20031013&s=kaplan101303 (accessed 12 September 2006).

Keegan, John. *The Iraq War*. New York, NY: Alfred A. Knopf, 2004.

Kelly, Paul V. Executive Office of the President, Office of Management and Budget. *Section 2207, Quarterly Report*. Executive Summary, 5 October 2004. http://www.state.gov/s/d/rm/rls/2207/oct2004/html/ (accessed 18 January 2008).

Khalil, Peter, Thomas Hammes, and Sevan Lousinian. "Securing Iraq." Interview by Ray Suarez. *Online NewsHour*, 13 December 2004. http://www.pbs.org/newshour/bb/middle_east/july-dec04/iraq_12-13.html (accessed 8 June 2006).

Killblane, Richard E. "Transportation Corps in Operation Iraqi Freedom 2: April Uprising." Unpublished manuscript.

King, Neil, Jr. "Power Struggle: Race to Get Lights on in Iraq Shows Perils of Reconstruction." *Wall Street Journal* (Eastern Edition), 2 April 2001.

Knickerbocker, Brad. "In Iraq, fewer killed, more are wounded." *The Christian Science Monitor*, 29 August 2006. http://www.csmonitor.com/2006/0829/p03s02-usmi.html (accessed 30 August 2006).

Kosiak, Steven M. "Iraq Reconstruction: Without Additional Funding, Progress Likely to Fall Short, Undermining War Effort." Center for Strategic and Budgetary Assessments, 27 February 2006.

Kratzer, Major General David E. "The Role of the 377th Theater Support Command." *Army Reserve Magazine*, Spring 2003.

Krepinevich, Andrew. "The War in Iraq: The Nature of Insurgency Warfare." Center for Strategic Budgetary Assessments, 2 June 2004.

Kretchik, Walter E., Robert F. Baumann, and John T. Fishel. *Invasion, Intervention. "Intervasion:" A Concise History of the US Army in Operation Uphold Democracy*. Fort Leavenworth, KS: Combat Studies Institute Press, 1998.

Kurtz, Howard. "For Media After Iraq, A Case of Shell Shock: Battle Assessment Begins for Saturation Reporting." *Washington Post*, 28 April 2003.

———. "Media Weigh Costs, Fruits of 'Embedding:' News Outlets Stretch Budgets for Chance to Witness Iraq War From Front Lines." *Washington Post*, 11 March 2003.

Lacey, James G., Williamson Murray, Michael R. Pease, and Mark E. Stout. *Iraqi Perspectives Project: A View of Operation Iraqi Freedom from Saddam's Senior Leadership*. Joint Center for Operational Analysis. http://www.cfr.org/publication/10230/iraqi_perspectives_project.html (accessed 12 September 2006).

Lada, Colonel John. "Medical Statistics in World War II," in *The United States Army in World War II*. Washington, DC: Office of the Surgeon General, 1975.

Lanza, Colonel Stephen R., Major Robert L. Menti, Captain Luis M. Alvarez, and First Lieutenant Michael R. Dalton. "Red Team Goes Maneuver: 1st Cav Div Arty as a Maneuver BCT." *Field Artillery,* May–June 2005.

Le Billion, Philippe. "Corruption, Reconstruction, and Oil Governance in Iraq." *Third World Quarterly*, 2005.

LeDrew, Specialist Erik. "Artillery Troops Plant Seeds of Reconstruction in Iraq." *Defend America,* October 2004. http://www.defendamerica.mil/articles/oct2004/a101504d.html (accessed 12 September 2006).

Leepson, Marc. "Most USAID personnel in Vietnam, including State FSOs, labored in obscurity; here are some of their stories." *American Foreign Service Association*. http://www.afsa.org/fsj/apr00/leepson.cfm (accessed 6 February 2006).

Lennard, Jeremy. "Voting Begins in Iraq Election." *The Guardian*, 28 January 2005.

"Life and Death in a War Zone." *PBS Airdate*, 2 March 2004, NOVA Transcripts. http://www.pbs.org/wgbh/nova/transcripts/3106_combatdo.html (accessed 22 August 2006).

Linn, Brian M. *Guardians of Empire: The U.S. Army and the Pacific, 1902–1940.* Chapel Hill, NC: University of North Carolina Press, 1997.

Loeb, Vernon. "Clan, Family Ties Called Key to Army's Capture of Hussein." *washingtonpost.com*, 16 December 2003. www.washingtonpost.com/ax2/wp-dyn/A3075-2003Dec15 (accessed 29 March 2006).

Luhnow, David. "Pace of Iraq's Reconstruction Frustrates US—Restoring Power to Capital Proves Surprisingly Hard." *Wall Street Journal,* 13 May 2003.

Lyon, Alistair. "Tension Eases in Two Iraqi Flashpoint Cities." *Reuters*, 20 April 2004. http://www.strykernews.com/archives/2004/04/20/tension_eases_in_two_iraqi_flashpoint_cities.html (accessed 20 October 2006).

MacCagnan, Lieutenant Colonel Victor, Jr. "Logistics Transformation—Restarting a Stalled Process." Carlisle Barracks, PA: US Army War College, Strategic Studies Institute, January 2005.

MacDonald, Mitch. "The Art of Combat Logistics: Interview with Major Bob Curran." *DC Velocity*, May 2005.

MacFarquhar, Neil. "Amid Blood and Rubble, A Sense of Helplessness." *New York Times* (Late Edition), 20 August 2003.

"Major General Odierno Videoteleconference from Baghdad." *DOD News Transcript*, 18 June 2003. http://merln.ndu.edu/merln/pfiraq/archive/dod/tr20030618-0281.pdf (accessed 25 October 2007).

"Make the Most of Family Readiness Groups." *U.S. Army HOOAH 4 HEALTH.com.* http://www.hooah4health.com/4life/hooah4family/frg.htm# (accessed December 2007).

Marcus, Aliza. "US leave program gets a boost, along with troops'." *The Boston Globe*, 2 December 2003. http://www.boston.com/news/nation/articles/2003/12/02/us_leave-orogram-gets-a-boost/ (accessed 25 August 2006).

Marlow, Sergeant W. Wayne. "Samarra Adjusts to Life After Insurgents." *Danger Forward,* Volume 1, Issue 8 (November 2004). http://www.1id.army.mil/1ID/Danger_Forward/Documents/Danger_Forward_Nov.pdf (accessed 6 July 2007).

Martin, Colonel Gregg F. "Victory Sappers: V Corps/CJTF-7 Engineers in Operation Iraqi Freedom. Part 2: Since the Liberation. . . ." *Engineer,* October–December 2003.

Martins, Mark. "No Small Change of Soldiering: The Commander's Emergency Response Program in Iraq and Afghanistan." *Army Lawyer*, February 2004. http://www.jagcnet.army.mil/ (accessed 9 October 2006).

Matthews, Matt M. *Operation AL FAJR: A Study in Army and Marine Corps Joint Operations.* Fort Leavenworth, KS: Combat Studies Institute Press, 2006.

Mazzetti, Mark, and Borzou Daragahi. "The Conflict in Iraq: US Military Covertly Pays to Run Stories in Iraqi Press." *Los Angeles Times*, 30 November 2005.

Mazzetti, Mark, and Josh Meyer. "The Conflict in Iraq; In a Battle of Wits, Iraq's Insurgency Mastermind Stays a Step Ahead of US." *Los Angeles Times*, 16 November 2005.

Mazzetti, Mark. "The Nation; PR Meets Psy-Ops in War on Terror; The use of misleading information as a military tool sparks debate in the Pentagon." *Los Angeles Times*, 1 December 2004.

McCarthy, Rory. "New Curfew After 15 Iraqi Soldiers are Shot Dead." *The Guardian*, 23 January 2005.

———. "US Forces Battle for Iraqi Rebel City." *The Guardian*, 2 October 2004.

———. "US Marines Put On Alert as More Die and Polling Stations Bombed." *The Guardian,* 28 January 2005.

McGlinchey, David. "Defense Says Steps Taken to Fix Guard, Reserve Pay Problems." *Govexec.com*, 20 July 2004. http://www.govexec.com/dailyfed/0704/072004d1.htm (accessed 9 October 2006).

McGrath, John J. *Boots on the Ground: Troop Density in Contingency Operations.* Fort Leavenworth, KS: Combat Studies Institute Press, 2006.

———. "Iraq Security Forces Order of Battle." Unpublished study. On file with Combat Studies Institute, Fort Leavenworth, KS.

McGrath, John J., ed. *An Army at War: Change in the Midst of Conflict, The Proceedings of the Combat Studies Institute 2005 Military History Symposium.* Fort Leavenworth, KS: Combat Studies Institute Press, 2006.

McLane, Brendan R. "Reporting from the Sandstorm: An Appraisal of Embedding." *Parameters*, Spring 2004.

Memmott, Mark. "Reporters in Iraq Under Fire There, and From Critics." *USA Today*, 2 August 2006. http:www.usatoday.com/news/world/iraq/2006-03-22-media-critisism_x.htm (accessed 2 August 2006).

Metz, Lieutenant General Thomas F., with Lieutenant Colonel Mark W. Garrett, Lieutenant Colonel James E. Hutton, and Lieutenant Colonel Timothy W. Bush. "Massing Effects in the Information Domain: A Case Study in Aggressive Information Operations." *Military Review,* May–June 2006.

Metz, Steven. "Insurgency and Counterinsurgency in Iraq." *Washington Quarterly*, Winter 2003–04.

Miles, Donna. "Fallujah Reconstruction Effort to Begin Soon." *DefenseLink*, 19 November 2004. http://www.defenselink.mil/news/Nov2004/n11192004_2004111909.html (accessed 24 October 2006).

———. "Reducing the Military Divorce Rate." *American Forces Press Service*, 13 June 2005.

———. "Up-Armored Vehicle Effort Progressing Full Steam Ahead." *American Forces Press Service*, 29 October 2004.

"Military Casualty Information." DOD Personnel and Military Casualty Statistics. http://siadapp.dior.whs.mil/personnel/CASUALTY/castop.htm (accessed 5 January 2007).

Miller, T. Christian. "Iraq Convoy got go-ahead Despite Threat." *Los Angeles Times*, 3 September 2007.

Miracle, Lieutenant Colonel Tammy L. "The Army and Embedded Media." *Military Review,* September–October 2003.

Miseli, Captain Jason A. "The View From My Windshield: Just in Time Logistics Just Isn't Working." *Armor Magazine*, September–October 2003.

"MNSTC-I 'ASTs' Led the Way, Training in Iraqi Fight for Fallujah." *The Advisor,* Volume 1, Issue 12, 27 November 2004.

Moore, Robin. *Hunting Down Saddam: The Inside Story of the Search and Capture.* New York, NY: St. Martin's Press, 2004.

Murray, Williamson, and Robert H. Scales Jr. *The Iraq War: A Military History.* Cambridge, MA: The Belknap Press of Harvard University Press, 2003.

Myatt, Jon. "Air Defenders Become MPs for Duty in Afghanistan." *Defend America,* 15 March 2004. http://www.defendamerica.mil/articles/mar2004/a031504e.html (accessed 14 March 2007).

Myers, Laurel K., Ph.D. "Eliminating the Iron Mountain." *Army Logistician*, July–August 2004. http://www.almc.army.mil/ALOG/issues/JulAug04/C_iron.html (accessed 6 June 2006).

Napoleoni, Loretta. *Insurgent Iraq: Al Zarqawi and the New Generation.* New York, NY: Seven Stories Press, 2005.

National Commission on Terrorist Attacks Upon the United States. *The 9/11 Commission Report: Final Report of the National Commission on Terrorist Attacks Upon the United States.* Washington, DC, 2004.

"NATO Expands Training Mission in Iraq." *NTM-I Fact Sheet,* 10 February 2005. http://www.afsouth.nato.int/JFCN_Missions/NTM-I/Factsheets/NATO_ExpandsTM.htm (accessed 5 July 2006).

Neal, Terry M. "Bush Backs into Nation Building." *Washington Post*, 26 February 2003. http://www.washingtonpost.com/ac2/wp-dyn/A6853-2003Feb26?language=printer (accessed 27 September 2006).

"NBC News' Meet the Press." Transcript for 26 September 2004. http://www.msnbc.msn.com/id/6106292/ (accessed 1 September 2006).

"News Transcript: DOD Briefing—Secretary Rumsfeld and Gen. Abizaid." *DefenseLink,* 21 August 2003. http://www.defenselink.mil/transcripts/2003/tr20030821-secdef0604.html (accessed 20 June 2006).

"News Transcript: Secretary Rumsfeld Interview on NBC Meet the Press." *DefenseLink,* 2 November 2003. http://www.defenselink.mil/transcripts/2003/tr20031102-secdef0835.html (accessed 20 June 2006).

Office of the Secretary of Defense. "Public Affairs Guidance on Embedding Media During Possible Future Operations/Deployments in the US Central Command's (CENTCOM) Area of Responsibility (AOR)." 10 February 2003.

Office of the Special Inspector General for Iraqi Reconstruction. *Baghdad Municipal Solid Waste Landfill.* SIGIR PA-06-067, 19 October 2006. http://www.sigir.mil/reports/pdf/assessments/PA-06-067_Baghdad_Landfill.pdf (accessed 8 December 2007).

O'Hanlon, Michael E., and Adriana Lins de Albuquerque. "Iraq Index: Tracking Variables of Reconstruction & Security in Post-Saddam Iraq, Updated April 18, 2005." The Brookings Institution. http://www.brookings.edu/fp/saban/iraq/index20050418.pdf (accessed 18 December 2006).

O'Hanlon, Michael E., and Andrew Kamons. "Iraq Index: Tracking Variables of Reconstruction & Security in Post-Saddam Iraq." The Brookings Institution, 29 June 2006. http://www.brookings.edu/fp/saban/iraq/index20060629.pdf (accessed September 2006).

O'Hanlon, Michael E., and Nina Kamp. "Iraq Index: Tracking Variables of Reconstruction & Security in Post-Saddam Iraq." The Brookings Institution, 10 April 2006. www.brookings.edu/iraqindex (accessed 11 April 2006).

Oliver, Sergeant First Class Todd. "Soldiers attacked While on Operation Peninsula Strike." *USAREUR Public Affairs*, 18 June 2003. http://www.hqusareur.army.mil/htmlinks/Press_Releases/2003/Jun2003/18Jun2003-01.htm (accessed 20 February 2007).

Operation Desert Storm: Ten Years After. National Security Archive. http://www.gwu.edu/~nsarchiv/NSAEBB/NSAEBB39/ (accessed 22 February 2006).

"Operation Enduring Freedom." http://www.globalsecurity.org/military/ops/enduring-freedom.htm (accessed 23 February 2006).

Operation Iraqi Freedom (OIF) Mental Health Advisory Team (MHAT) Report, 16 December 2003. http://www.armymedicine.army.mil/news/mhat_ii/OIF-II_REPORT.pdf#search=%22Army%20Mental%20Health%20Advisory%20Team%20survey%202003%22 (accessed 24 August 2006).

Packer, George. *The Assassins' Gate: America in Iraq.* New York, NY: Farrar, Straus and Giroux, 2005.

Paul, Christopher, and James J. Kim. *Reporters on the Battlefield: The Embedded Press System in Historical Context.* Santa Monica, CA: RAND Corporation, 2004.

Payne, Kenneth. "The Media as an Instrument of War." *Parameters*, Spring 2005.

Peck, Michael. "'Golden Hour' Surgical Units Prove Worth." *Military Medical Technology Online*, Volume 7, Issue 5 (9 August 2006). http://www.military-medical-technology.com/article.cfm?DocID=176 (accessed 11 August 2006).

Pellegrini, Sergeant Frank. "Supporting Gulf War 2.0." *Army Magazine*, 1 September 2003. http://www.ausa.org/webpub/DeptArmyMagazine.nsf (accessed 11 October 2006).

Peltz, Eric, Marc Robbins, Kenneth J. Girardini, Rick Eden, John Halliday, and Jeffrey Angers. *Sustainment of Army Forces in Operation Iraqi Freedom: Major Findings and Recommendations.* Santa Monica, CA: RAND Corporation, 2005.

"Pentagon Debate Rages Over 'Information Operations' in Iraq." *CNN.com.* http://edition.cnn.com/2004/US/12/12/pentagon.media/ (accessed 3 January 2007).

Petraeus, Lieutenant General David H. "Learning Counterinsurgency: Observations from Soldiering in Iraq." *Military Review,* January–February 2006.

Phillips, David L. *Losing Iraq: Inside the Postwar Reconstruction Fiasco.* Boulder, CO: Westview Press, 2005.

Phillips, R. Cody. *Bosnia-Herzegovina: The US Army's Role in Peace Enforcement Operations, 1995–2004*. Washington, DC: US Army Center of Military History, 2004.

"Plans for Latvian Operations in Iraq Disrupted by UN Security Situation." *BBC News*, 4 September 2003.

Pollack, Kenneth M. "After Saddam: Assessing the Reconstruction of Iraq." *foreignaffairs.org*, 12 January 2004. http://www.foreignaffairs.org/20040103faupdate83175/Kenneth-m-pollack/after-saddam-assessing-the-reconstruction-of-iraq.html (accessed July 2006).

Powell, Anita. "Mortuary Affairs Specialists Perform a Labor of Love." *Stars & Stripes Mideast Edition*, 13 November 2005. http://www.estripes.com/article.asp?section=104&article=32152&archive=true (accessed 10 October 2006).

Powell, Colin. "Annex to UN Security Resolution 1546" to UN Secretary General Kofi Annan. UN Web site, 5 June 2004. http://www.un.org/News/Press/docs/2004/sc8117.doc.htm (accessed 18 April 2006).

Prawdzik, Christopher. "Support the Stryker Brigades." Fort Belvoir, VA: US Army Materiel Command, 2005.

"President Announces Military Strikes in Afghanistan." *GlobalSecurity.org*, 7 October 2001. http://www.globalsecurity.org/military/library/news/2001/10/mil-011007-usia01.htm (accessed 23 February 2006).

"President Bush Announces Major Combat Operations Have Ended: Remarks by the President from the USS *Abraham Lincoln* At Sea Off the Coast of San Diego, California." *Whitehouse.gov*, 1 May 2003. http://www.whitehouse.gov/news/releases/2003/05/20030501-15.html (accessed 1 February 2006).

"President Delivers the State of the Union Address." *Whitehouse.gov*, 29 January 2002. http://www.whitehouse.gov/news/releases/2002/01/20020129-11.html (accessed 23 February 2006).

Price, Jennifer L., Ph.D. "Effects of the Persian Gulf War on US Veterans." A National Center for PTSD Fact Sheet, US Department of Veterans Affairs. http://www.ncptsd.va.gov/facts/veterans/fs_gulf_war_illness.html (accessed 24 August 2006).

Price, Jennifer L., Ph.D. "Findings from the National Vietnam Veterans' Readjustment Study: A National Center for PTSD Fact Sheet." US Department of Veterans Affairs. http://www.ncptsd.va.gov/facts/veterans/fs_NVVRS.html (accessed 31 October 2006).

Program Executive Office Soldier Web site. https://www.peosoldier.army.mil/factsheets/SEQ_SSV_IBA.pdf (accessed 2 July 2007).

Public Law 108-106, Section 1110—6 November 2003, 117 Statute 1215. http://www.export.gov/iraq/pdf/public_law_108-116.pdf.

"Purported al-Zarqawi Tape: Democracy a Lie." *CNN.com*, 23 January 2005.

Qualls, Sergeant First Class Gary L., Jr. "Guardsmen Give Iraqi Fishermen Means to 'Net' Long Forbidden Treasure." *Desert Rifles*, 16 May 2003.

Ramsey, Robert D. *Advising Indigenous Forces: American Advisors in Korea, Vietnam, and El Salvador*. Fort Leavenworth, KS: Combat Studies Institute Press, 2006.

Rathmell, Andrew, Olga Oliker, Terrence K. Kelly, David Brannan, and Keith Crane. *Developing Iraq's Security Sector, The Coalition Provisional Authority's Experience*. Santa Monica, CA: RAND National Defense Research Institute, 2005.

Ratnesar, Romesh, and Paul Quinn-Judge. "Can Iraq Do the Job." *Time*, 3 May 2004.

"Reconstructing Iraq." International Crisis Group, Middle East, Report No. 30, 2 September 2004.

Reinhold, Colonel Karl. *A Paradigm for the System of Systems Countering Asymmetric Enemy Kinetic Attacks*. Carlisle Barracks, PA: US Army War College, 2005.

Reister, Frank A. *Battle Casualties and Medical Statistics: U.S. Army Experience in the Korean War*. Washington, DC: Office of the Surgeon General, 1986.

Remarks by Lieutenant General David Petraeus, Former Commander, Multi-National Security Transition Command Iraq, to the Center for Strategic and International Studies. "Iraq's Evolving Forces."

Moderator: Anthony Cordesman, 7 November 2005. http://www.comw.org/warreport/fulltext/0512petraeus.pdf (accessed 8 January 2008).

Resnick, Heidi S., Ph.D., and Dean G. Kilpatrick, Ph.D. "Crime Related PTSD: Emphasis on Adult General Population Samples." National Crime Victims Research and Treatment Center and Medical University of South Carolina. US Department of Veterans Affairs. http://www.ncptsd.va.gov/publications/rq/rqhtml/V5N3.html (accessed 31 October 2006).

Rhem, Kathleen T. "Commanders in Iraq Ordered Humane Treatment of Detainees." *DefenseLink*, 20 May 2004. http://defenselink.mil/news/May2004/n05202004_200405206.html (accessed 25 October 2006).

———. "Officials Announce Plans for Iraqi Troop Rotations into 2004." *DefenseLink,* 24 July 2003. http://www.defenselink.mil/news/newsarticle.aspx?id=28683 (accessed 17 December 2007).

———. "Pentagon Leaders Describe Offensive Operations in Iraq." *DefenseLink,* 29 July 2003. http://www.defenselink.mil/news/Jul2003/n07292003_200307295.html (accessed 13 October 2006).

Richey, Warren. "To Restore Peace, US Hires Iraqi Looters." *Christian Science Monitor*, 9 May 2003.

Ricks, Thomas E. *Fiasco: The American Military Adventure in Iraq.* New York, NY: The Penguin Press, 2006.

Rieff, David. "Who Botched the Occupation?" *New York Times Magazine,* 2 November 2003.

Rigsby, Captain Robert S. "Kosovo Bound." *Army Logistician*, July–August 2001.

Ritea, Steve. "Media Troop Withdrawal." *American Journalism Review*, December/January 2004. http://www.ajr.org/Article.asp?id=3477 (accessed 30 May 2006).

Rodriguez, Martin, Andrew Farnsler, and John Bott. *Constructive Engagement: A Proven Method for Conducting Stability and Support Operations.* Land Power Essay No. 07-1. Association of the United States Army, Institute of Land Warfare. http://www.ausa.org/pdfdocs/LPE07-1.pdf (accessed 25 October 2007).

Rogers, Rick. "Some Troops Headed Back To Iraq Are Mentally Ill." *San Diego Union-Tribune*, 19 March 2006. http://www.signonsandiego.com/news/military/20060319-9999-1n19mental.html (accessed 8 August 2006).

Romanych, Major Marc J., and Lieutenant Colonel Kenneth Krumm. "Tactical Information Operations in Kosovo." *Military Review,* September–October 2004.

Ross, Brian. "Staying Strong: The Insurgency in Iraq: Many Media Savvy Groups Make for Tough Opponents." *ABC News*, 20 March 2006. http://abcnews.go.com/WNT/print?id=1748161 (accessed 30 May 2006).

"Row Overshadows Kirkuk Poll." *BBC News*, 24 May 2003. http://news.bbc.co.uk/1/hi/world/middle_east/2934594.stm (accessed 27 November 2007).

Rubin, Debra K., Sherie Winston, and Andrew G. Wright. "Contractors Tailoring Protection to Projects." *ENR*, 9 February 2004.

Rumsfeld, Donald. *War on Terror* Memorandum, 16 October 2003. http://www.usatoday.com/news/Washington/executive/Rumsfeld-memo.htm (accessed 9 March 2006).

"Rumsfeld says extremists winning media war." *USA Today On-Line Edition*, posted 2/17/2006. http://www.usatoday.com/news/washington/2006-02-17-rumsfeld-media_x.htm (accessed 5 June 2006).

Russell, Lieutenant Colonel Steve. TF 1-22 Infantry. Command Correspondence, "Dear Family and Friends," 20 June—24 August 2003.

Ryder, Major General Donald. *Assessment of Corrections and Detention Operations in Iraq,* 6 November 2003.

Rzepka, Specialist Rick. "Men and Women of Combat Support Hospital Dedicate Themselves to Saving Lives Here." *MNF-Iraq.com*, 25 February 2006. http://www.mnf-iraq.com/index.php?option=com_content&task=view&id=194&Itemid=42 (accessed 22 August 2006).

Sabbagh, Leslie. "Birds of Mercy." *Popular Mechanics*, October 2005. http://www.popularmechanics.com/science/defense/1894752.html (accessed 21 August 2006).

Sattler, Lieutenant General John F., and Lieutenant Colonel Daniel H. Wilson. "Operation AL FAJR: The Battle of Fallujah—Dousing the Bright Ember of the Insurgency." *Marine Corps Gazette*, July 2005.

Schifferes, Steve. "US Names 'Coalition of the Willing.'" *BBC News*, 18 March 2003. http://news/bbc. co.uk/2/hi/Americas/2862343.stm (accessed 13 September 2006).

Schlesinger, James R., Chairman. *Final Report of the Independent Panel to Review DOD Detention Operations*, August 2004.

Schnaubelt, Christopher M. "After the Fight: Interagency Operations." *Parameters*, Winter 2005/2006.

Schroeder, Specialist Brian. "Iraqi Troops Risk Lives for Elections," 10th Mountain Division News Release, CAMP LIBERTY, BAGHDAD, Iraq. *DefenseLink*. http://www.defendamerica. mil/articles/jan2005/.

Senior, Jennifer. "The Baghdad Press Club." *New York Magazine*, 22 May 2006.

"Senior UN Relief Officials Return to Iraq After Six-Week Absence." *UN News Centre,* 1 May 2003. http://www.un.org/apps/news/storyAr.asp?NewsID=6919&Cr=iraq&Cr1=relief (accessed 13 June 2006).

Seymour, Staff Sergeant Daniel J. "Mortuary Affairs Support in the Iraqi Theater of Operations." *Quartermaster Professional Bulletin*, US Army Quartermaster Center and School, Fort Lee, VA, Spring 2005. http://www.quartermaster.army.mil/oqmg/professional_bulletin/2005/Spring05/Mortuary%20Affairs%20Support%20in%20the%20Iraqi%20Theater%20of%20Operations.htm (accessed 10 October 2006).

Shadid, Anthony. "Iraqis Defy Threats as Millions Vote." *Washington Post Foreign Service*, 31 January 2005.

———. *Night Draws Near: Iraq's People in the Shadow of America's War.* New York, NY: Henry Holt and Co., 2005.

Shanker, Thom. "Pentagon Extends Tours of Duty for About 6,500 U.S. Soldiers." *New York Times*, 29 October 2004.

———. "US Is Speeding Up Plans for Creating a New Iraqi Army." *New York Times*, 18 September 2003.

Shanker, Thom, and Eric Schmitt. "Pentagon Weighs Use of Deception in a Broad Arena." *New York Times*, 13 December 2004. http://www.nytimes.com/2004/12/13/politics/13info.html?_r=1 &ex=12605940000&en=d83314fc17eb65d5&ei=5-90&partner=rssuserland&oref=slogin (accessed 5 January 2007).

———. "U.S. to Increase Its Force in Iraq by Nearly 12,000." *New York Times*, 2 December 2004.

Sharp, Jeremy M., and Christopher M. Blanchard. "Post-War Iraq: Foreign Contributions to Training, Peacekeeping, and Reconstruction." *CRS Report for Congress RL32105,* updated 6 June 2005.

Sinnreich, Richard Hart. "For Military Leaders, It's Déjà vu All Over Again." *Army*, June 2007.

Slevin, Peter. "Wrong Turn at a Postwar Crossroads? Decision to Disband Iraqi Army Cost US Time and Credibility." *Washington Post*, 20 November 2003. http://www.washingtonpost.com/ac2/wp-dyn/A63423-2003Nov19?language=printer (accessed 12 April 2006).

Smith, Steven Donald. "HBO Film 'Baghdad ER' Examines Combat Hospital." *American Forces Press Service*, 17 May 2006. http://www.defenselink.mil/news/May2006/20060517_5149.html (accessed 22 August 2006).

Smith, W. Thomas, Jr. "In Their Own Hands: An Emerging Iraqi Special-ops Force Works to Get the Bad Guys." *MilitaryPhotos.Net*, 12 October 2004. http://www.militaryphotos.net/forums/showthread.php?t=24143 (accessed 18 December 2006).

"Special Defense Department Briefing on Iraq Security Forces." *DefenseLink*, 4 February 2005. http://www.defenselink.mil/transcripts/2005/tr20050204-0283.html (accessed 7 October 2006).

"Special Forces Produce." *The Advisor,* 15 January 2005.

Spinner, Jackie. "After Threats, Iraqi Election Board Resigns." *Washington Post*, 10 January 2005.

———. "A Push for More Power at Iraqi Plant; Residents Grow Impatient as Engineers Struggle With Failing Equipment." *Washington Post,* 25 August 2004.

Spinner, Jackie, and Bassam Septi. "Militant Declares War on Iraqi Vote." *Washington Post*, 24 January 2005.

St. George, Donna. "Home but Still Haunted: Md. Iraq Veteran and Thousands Like Her Are Coping With Post-Traumatic Stress." *Washington Post*, 20 August 2006.

Stambersky, Captain Shannon V. "A Lesson in Dignity in the Iraqi Desert." *Quartermaster Professional Bulletin*, US Army Quartermaster Center and School, Fort Lee, VA, Spring 2005. http://www.quartermaster.army.mil/oqmg/professional_bulletin/2005/Spring05/Mortuary%20Affairs%20Support%20in%20the%20Irai%20Theater%20of%20Operations (accessed 10 October 2006).

Stammer, Captain Mark. "Peace Support Operations Rehearsals at the CMTC." *Stability and Support Operations Newsletter 98-11*. Fort Leavenworth, KS: Center for Army Lessons Learned, 1998.

Starnes, Colonel Glenn T. "Leveraging the Media: The Embedded Media Program in Operation Iraqi Freedom." Strategy Research Paper, Volume S04-06, Center for Strategic Leadership. Carlisle Barracks, PA: US Army War College, July 2004.

Sterling, Joe. "Family's Lawsuit Over Slain Contractors Stalls." *CNN International.com*. http://edition.cnn.com/2005/LAW/04/11/blackwater.lawsuit/index.html (accessed 3 April 2007).

Stevens, Captain Roger M., and Major Kyle J. Marsh. "3/2 S BCT and the Countermortar Fight in Mosul." *Field Artillery*, January–February 2005.

Stokes, David. "Taking stock." *Middle Eastern Quarterly*. http://www.meforum.org/pf.php?id=669 (accessed 22 June 2006).

Stone, Andrea. "High-Tech Bandages Designed to Save Lives." *USA Today*, 25 February 2003. http://www.tricare.osd.mil/eenews/downloads/HighTechBandages.doc (accessed 31 October 2006).

Strobel, Lieutenant Colonel Lawrence. "Common-User Land Transportation Management in the Layered, Non-Linear, Non-Contiguous Battlefield." Carlisle Barracks, PA: US Army War College Strategy Research Paper, 18 March 2005.

Struck, Doug. "Iraqi Security has Come Far, With Far to Go; U.S.-Trained Forces Hit by Defections." *Washington Post*, 1 August 2004.

"Stryker Brigade Combat Team 1, 3d Brigade, 2d Infantry: Operations in Mosul, Iraq." *Initial Impressions Report.* Fort Leavenworth, KS: Center for Army Lessons Learned, 21 December 2004.

Stupp, Joe. "Newspapers Pull Reporters From Embed Slots." *Editor and Publisher*, 28 April 2003.

Swanson, Doug. "All the Comforts of War." Originally published in the *Dallas Morning News*, *PE.com*, 10 June 2006. http://www/pe/com/cgi-bin/bi/gold_print.cgi (accessed 25 August 2006).

Taguba, Major General Anthony M. *Article 15-6 Investigation of the 800th Military Police Brigade (The Taguba Report),* 21 July 2004. http://www.aclu.org/torturefoia/released/a45.pdf.

Talbot, Randy. "Forging the Steel Hammer: US Army Tank and Automotive Command Support to the Global War on Terrorism, 2001–2005." Warren, MI: US Army Tank and Automotive Command, May 2006.

Taylor, Jared A. "With No Camp in Iraq, USO Does What It Can." *Kansas City InfoZine*, 17 August 2006. http://www.infozine.com/news/stories/op/stories (accessed 25 August 2006).

Tempest, Matthew. "400 More UK Troops to be Sent to Iraq." *The Guardian*, 10 January 2005.

"Thailand Might Cancel Deployment of Forces to Iraq following UN HQ Bombing," *Al Bawaba*, 21 August 2003.

"The Desert War—A Kind of Victory." *BBC Radio 4*, 16 February 1992.

"The Fight for Fallujah TF 2-2 IN FSE AAR." *Field Artillery,* March–April 2005.

"The Iraqi Liberation Act: Statement by the President," 31 October 1998. http://www.library.cornell.edu/colldev/mideast/libera.htm (accessed 27 February 2006).

"The Medical Frontline of War." *CBS News*, 4 June 2006. http://www.cbsnews.com/stories/2006/06/04/Sunday/printable1680075.shtml (accessed 16 August 2006).

"The Torture Question." *Frontline Interview with Bradford Berenson*, 14 July 2005. http://www.pbs. org/wgbh/pages/frontline/torture/interviews/berenson.html (accessed 14 July 2006).

Thomas, Evan, and John Barry. "Anatomy of a Revolt: What made a chorus of ex-generals call for SecDef's head? The war over the war—and how Rumsfeld is reacting." *MSNBC/Newsweek*, 24 April 2006. http://www.msnbc.msn.com/id/12335719/site/newsweek/ (accessed 12 September 2006).

Thomas, Evan, and Rod Nordland. "How We Got Saddam." *Newsweek*, 22 December 2003.

"Thomas Hamill On His Iraq Escape." *CBS News*, 12 October 2004. http://www.cbsnews.com/ stories/2004/10/10/earlyshow/leisure/books/main648445.shtml (accessed 5 October 2006).

Thompson, Lieutenant Colonel Dennis. "Frontline Support of the First SBCT at War." *Army Logistician*, July–August 2004.

Thurmond, Suzi. "Analyzing the Lessons of OIF Distribution." *Army Logistician*, July–August 2004.

Transitional Administrative Law. http://www.cpa-iraq.org/government/TAL.html (accessed 11 December 2006).

"Translators Dying by the Dozens." *USA Today*, 21 May 2005.

Trendle, Giles. "Young Radicals on the Rise." *Middle East*, January 2004.

Triggs, Staff Sergeant Marcia. "3ID Winning Hearts with TF Neighbor." *Army News Service*, 19 May 2003.

Trinquier, Roger. *Modern Warfare: A French View of Counterinsurgency*. Translated by Daniel Lee. New York, NY: Frederick A. Praeger, 1961.

Tunnell, Lieutenant Colonel Harry D., IV. *Red Devils: Tactical Perspectives from Iraq*. Fort Leavenworth, KS: Combat Studies Institute Press, 2006.

Turay, Specialist Ismail, Jr. "1st Infantry Division Boosts Power Plants' Output, Local Economy." *Danger Forward*, October 2004.

UN Security Council, "Resolution 1483" (22 May 2003). http://daccessdds.un.org/doc/UNDOC/GEN/ N03/368/53/PDF/N0336853.pdf?OpenElement (accessed 14 September 2006).

UN Web site. "Resolution 686." http://www.un.org/DOCS/scres/1991/scres91.htm (accessed 12 September 2006).

UN Web site. "Resolution 687." http://daccess-ods.un.org/TMP/7258258.htm (accessed 12 September 2006).

US Special Inspector General for Iraqi Reconstruction. *Quarterly Report and Semiannual Report to Congress*, 30 July 2004, 30 October 2004, 30 January 2005.

"Unit Responsible for Training Iraqi Forces Changes Command." *American Forces Press Service*, 8 September 2005.

United Service Organizations. "History of the USO." *USO.org*. http://www.uso.org/whoweare/ ourproudhistory/historyoftheuso/ (accessed 30 August 2006).

US Department of Defense. Defense Finance and Accounting Service Web site. http://www.dod.mil/ dfas/news/2004pressreleases/pressrelease0425.html (accessed 9 October 2006).

US Department of State. "Najaf/Samarra Reconstruction Effort, Questions Taken at November 12, 2004." *Daily Press Briefing*. http://www.state.gov/r/pa/prs/ps/2004/38162.htm (accessed 8 January 2008).

US Department of State. "Transitional Justice Working Group." *The Future of Iraq Project*. Washington, DC, 2003.

US Department of State. US Agency for International Development. *Iraq-Humanitarian and Reconstruction Assistance, Fact Sheet #35*, Fiscal Year (FY) 2003, 30 June 2003. http://www. usaid.gov/iraq/updates/jun03/iraq_fs53_063003.pdf (accessed 27 November 2007).

"U.S. Distributes Most-Wanted List." *Fox News*, 11 April 2003, http://www.foxnews.com/ story/0,2933,83894,00.html (accessed 20 March 2006).

US Government Accountability Office. GAO Report 04-484, *Operation Iraqi Freedom: Long-standing Problems Hampering Mail Delivery Need to Be Resolved.* Washington, DC, 14 April 2004.

———. GAO Report 04-89, *Military Pay: Army National Guard Personnel Mobilized to Active Duty Experienced Significant Pay Problems.* Washington, DC, 17 November 2003. http://www.gao.gov/htext/d0489.html (accessed 5 October 2006).

———. GAO Report GAO-04-902R, *Rebuilding Iraq: Resource, Security, Governance, Essential Services, and Oversight Issues,* 28 June 2004.

———. GAO Report 04-911, *Army Reserve Soldiers Mobilized to Active Duty Experienced Significant Pay Problems.* Washington, DC, 23 August 2004. http://www.gao.gov/htext/d04911.html (accessed 5 October 2006).

———. GAO Report 05-275, *Actions Needed to Improve the Availability of Critical Items during Current and Future Operations.* Washington, DC, 8 April 2005.

———. GAO Report GAO-05-431T, *Rebuilding Iraq: Preliminary Observations on Challenges in Transferring Security Responsibilities to Iraqi Military and Police.* Washington, DC, 14 March 2005.

"U.S., Iraqi Troops Strike Samarra Insurgents." *American Forces Press Service,* 1 October 2004. http://www.defenselink.mil/news/newsarticle.aspx?id=25169 (accessed 1 June 2007).

"US Names 'Coalition of the Willing.'" *BBC News,* 18 March 2003. http://news.bbc.co.uk/2/hi/americas/2862343.stm (accessed 13 September 2006).

US National Defense University. "Iraq: Looking Beyond Saddam's Rule." *Workshop Report.* Washington, DC: Institute for National Strategic Studies, 2002.

"US Secretary of State Colin Powell Addresses the UN Security Council." *Whitehouse.gov.* http://www.whitehouse.gov/news/releases/2003/02/20030205-1.html (accessed 27 February 2006).

"Vice President Speaks at VFW 103d National Convention." *Whitehouse.gov,* 26 August 2002. http://www.whitehouse.gov/news/releases/2002/08/20020826.html (accessed 12 September 2006).

"Vinnell Corp. to Dispatch Team to Iraq Under Contract to Train Army." *CongressDaily,* 26 June 2003.

Waghelstein, John D. "Post-Vietnam Counterinsurgency Doctrine." *Military Review,* May 1985.

———. "What's Wrong in Iraq or Ruminations of a Pachyderm." *Military Review,* January–February 2006.

Wakeman, Nick. "Satellite communications boost troops' morale in Iraq." *Washington Technology,* 24 November 2003. http://www.washingtontechnology.com/cgi-bin/udt/im.display.printable?client.id+wtonline (accessed 25 August 2006).

Walker, Donald. "Army Engineering Battalion Helps Community Help Itself." *Defend America,* 18 March 2004. http://www.defendamerica.mil/articles/mar2004/a3180d.html.

"Walt Slocombe Holds Defense Department News Briefing on Rebuilding the Iraqi Police and Military." *FDCH Political Transcripts,* 17 September 2003.

Ward, Justin. "Army sends Media Imagery from Iraq at Push of Button." *Army News Service,* 21 June 2004.

Wathen, Alexander M. "The Miracle of Operation Iraqi Freedom Airspace Management: How the Skies were Kept Safe . . . and what we need to do to keep them that way." *Air & Space Power Journal, Chronicles Online Journal.* http://www.airpower.maxwell.af.mil/airchronicles/cc/wathen.html (accessed 13 September 2006).

Weaver, Lisa Rose. "Iraq Promises More Suicide Bombings." *CNN.com.* http:www.cnn.com/2003/WORLD/meast/03/29/sprj.irq.car.bomb/index.html (accessed 6 July 2006).

Weaver, Mary Anne. "The Short, Violent Life of Abu Musab Al-Zarqawi." *The Atlantic Monthly,* July/August 2006. (Edited for the Web 8 June 2006.) http://www.theatlantic.com/doc/print/200607/zarqawi (accessed 9 June 2006).

Weigley, Russell F. *The American Way of War; A History of United States Military Strategy and Policy.* Bloomington, IN: Indiana University Press, 1973.

Wentz, Larry. *Lessons from Bosnia: The IFOR Experience*. Washington, DC: National Defense University, Institute for National Strategic Studies, 1997.

West, Brigadier General Scott G. "Supporting Victory in Operation Iraqi Freedom." *Quartermaster Professional Bulletin*, Autumn 2004. http://www.quartermaster.army.mil/oqmg/Professional_Bulletin/2004/Autumn04/Quarter (accessed 21 April 2006).

Whitcomb, Lieutenant General R. Steven. "US Department of Defense, Office of the Assistant Secretary of Defense (Public Affairs), News Transcript." *DefenseLink,* 9 December 2004. http://www.defenselink.mil/transcripts/2004/ tr20041209-1765.htm (accessed 6 October 2006).

White, Josh. "Town Reflect Rising Sabotage in Iraq." *Washington Post*, 9 December 2004.

Widmann, Major Robert S. "The Commanders Emergency Response Program, Part II," in *OnPoint: A Counter-Terrorism Journal for Military and Law Enforcement Professionals*. http://www.uscav.com/uscavonpoint/Print.aspx?id=169 (accessed 9 October 2006).

Williams, Daniel. "Sad, Defiant Farewell to U.N. Envoy." *Washington Post*, 23 August 2003.

Williams, Garland H. *Engineering Peace: The Military Role in Postconflict Reconstruction*. Washington, DC: United States Institute of Peace, 2005.

Wilson, Jamie. "Attacks Halt Rebuilding of Iraq: Disaster Facing Power Network as Contractors Pull Out: Attacks Halt Rebuilding of Iraq." *The Guardian*, 27 April 2004. http://www.guardian.co.uk/print/0,3858,4911034-103550,00.html (accessed October 2006).

Wilson, Scott. "A Different Street Fight in Iraq; U.S. General Turns to Public Works in Battle for Hearts and Minds." *Washington Post*, 27 May 2004.

Wong, Edward. "The Struggle for Iraq: The Troops; Years Later, A Division Takes Stock on Different Sands." *New York Times,* 7 June 2004.

Woods, Kevin M., with Michael R. Pease, Mark E. Stout, Williamson Murray, and James G. Lacey. *Iraqi Perspectives Project: A View of Operation Iraqi Freedom From Saddam's Senior Leadership*. Norfolk, VA: US Joint Forces Command, 2005. http://www.cfr.org/publication/10230/Iraqi_perspectives_project.html (accessed 12 September 2006).

Wright, Major Webster M., III. "Soldiers Blanket Iraqis in Operation Windy City." *DefenseLink*, November 2004. http://www.defenselink.mil/news/Nov2004/n11022004_2004110206.html (accessed October 2006).

Wright, Richard K. "Assessment of the DOD Embedded Media Program." Institute for Defense Analysis Joint Warfighting Program, IDA Paper P-3931, September 2004.

Yates, Lawrence A. "Panama, 1989–1999: The Disconnect Between Combat and Stability Operations." *Military Review,* May–June 2005.

———. *The US Military's Experience in Stability Operations, 1789–2005*. Fort Leavenworth, KS: Combat Studies Institute Press, 2006.

Zabaldo, Sergeant Jared. "Iraq Adds First Female Officer to Army's Medical Corps." *The Advisor*, 18 September 2004.

———. "Iraqi Ministry of Interior Orders Highway Patrol to 6,300 Strong." *The Advisor*, 30 October 2004.

———. "MNSTC-I's ASTs Led Way, Training in Iraqi Fight for Fallujah." *The Advisor*, 27 November 2004.

Zais, Brigadier General (Retired) Mitchell M. "U.S. Strategy in Iraq." *Military Review*, March–April 2007.

Zedong, Mao. *Selected Military Writings of Mao Tse-tung*. Peking: Foreign Language Press, 1972.

Ziemke, Earl F. *The US Army in the Occupation of Germany*. Washington, DC: US Army Center of Military History, 1989.

Zucchino, David. "Bringing Back the Wounded With Heart, Soul, and Surgery." *Los Angeles Times*, 2 April 2006. http://www.latimes.com/news/nationworld/nation/la-na-wounded2apr02,1,4738485.story?coll=la-health-medicine (accessed 15 August 2006).

———. "The Journey Through Trauma." *Los Angles Times*, 3 April 2006. http://www.latimes.com/news/nationaworld/nation/la-na-wounded2apr03,1,5197239.story?coll=la-health-medicine (accessed 14 August 2006).

———. "War Brings Advances in Protection and Care." *Los Angeles Times*, 3 April 2006. http://www.latimes.com/features/health/medicine/la-na-woundedside3apr03,1,5223720.story?coll=la-health-medicine (accessed 14 August 2006).

Zucco, Tom. "Troops Deal an Old Tool." *St. Petersburg Times*, 12 April 2003. http://www.sptimes.com/2003/04/12/news_pf/Worldandnation/Troops_dealt_an_old_t.shtml (accessed 20 March 2006).

Zumwalt, James. "The Iraqi Military's Achilles' Heel Is Saddam Hussein: He's so worried about a rebellion that he has emasculated his own army." *Los Angeles Times*, 26 December 2001.

Index

T

US Army Corps of Engineers (USACE), 368–369, 371, 383, 387, 391, 518, 522, 647

US Army Infantry School, Fort Benning, GA, 63

US Army Intelligence and Security Command (INSCOM), 159, 192–193

US Army Reserve (USAR), 59, 192, 242, 299, 444, 447, 459, 461–463, 483, 495–496, 557, 576

US Army War College, 88, 112, 130, 134, 308, 310, 456, 478, 528, 530, 647, 652, 659, 662, 665

US Customs, 195

US Defense Information School, 306

US Department of Agriculture, 152

US Department of Homeland Security, 470

US Disciplinary Barracks, Fort Leavenworth, KS, 262

US Institute of Peace, 105–106, 133, 395, 425, 650, 653, 668

US Marine Corps (USMC), 30, 51, 102, 127, 264, 266, 285, 290, 310, 345, 351, 443, 447–448, 489, 494, 520, 651

US Military Academy, West Point, NY, 379

US Navy (USN), 50, 100, 351, 357

US Transportation Command (TRANSCOM), 496, 503

US Treasury Department, 152

USS *Abraham Lincoln,* 9, 19–20, 143, 184, 662

Upchurch, Alan, MSG, USA, 507, 643

V

V Corps, 14–17, 19, 28–30, 38, 47, 68, 77–79, 85, 93–94, 96, 118–119, 131, 134–135, 140–142, 144–149, 152, 154, 157–162, 164–165, 173, 181, 185–187, 192–194, 196, 205, 222, 241, 268, 270, 279, 308, 367, 371–373, 378, 395, 405–406, 410, 424, 495, 498–499, 505, 524, 529, 563, 568, 571, 607, 615–616, 622–625, 644, 647, 654, 659

Valdivia, Robert, COL, USA, 642

Van Wey, Dennis, MAJ, USA, 410, 424–425, 642

Vandekeere, Brooks, SPC, USA, 643

vehicle-borne improvised explosive devise (VBIED), 111–112, 339, 518

Vetter, David, LTC, USA, 560, 642

VICTORY SCRIMMAGE Exercise, 78, 500, 622

VICTORY STRIKE Exercise, 500

Vietnam war, 49, 54–55, 62–64, 175, 291, 301, 314, 537, 544, 546, 550, 556

Vinnell Corporation, 435, 447, 479, 667

W

Waghelstein, John D., 59–60, 82–83, 667

Wahhab, Muhammad Ibn 'Abd al-, 109

Wahhabism/Wahhabi, 105, 108–109, 115

Walker, Mary, USAF, 211

Wallace, William S., LTG, USA, 1, 2, 8, 47, 85, 131–132, 152, 154, 182, 184–187, 189, 641, 648

   V Corps combat operations, 14–15, 19, 28, 93, 96, 98, 144, 146, 148, 294, 378, 499

   change of command, 28–30, 144, 147, 155, 157–158

   Phase IV planning, 78–79

Walter Reed Army Medical Center, Washington, DC, 540, 544, 549

Ward, Steven, COL, USA, 642

Warren, Marc, COL, USA, 85, 93, 131, 185, 205, 212–213, 234, 236, 248–249, 265, 267–268, 270-271, 642

Washington Group International, 387

Washington, DC, 8, 19, 21, 81–82, 130, 134–135, 144, 186, 189, 233–234, 308, 310–312, 395, 398, 421, 528, 531–533, 544–545, 559–560, 587, 647–649, 660, 666–667

water treatment, 280, 368, 381, 386, 473, 500

Weafer, Thomas, COL, USA, 642

weapons of mass destruction (WMD), 9, 11–14, 32, 73–74, 89, 154, 160, 192–193, 568, 622, 625, 628

Webster Jr., William G., MG, USA, 72, 84, 131, 141, 144, 146–147, 151, 184–186, 641

   Phase IV planning, 72, 93, 140, 147

   recalling Iraqi Army, 94–95

Weinberger, Casper, Secretary of Defense, 56

West, Scott G., BG, USA, 489, 514, 525, 527–531, 533, 668

Wey, Albert, COL, USMC, 523

Whitcomb, R. Steven, LTG, USA, 114, 134, 145, 184, 512, 531, 641, 668

White, John, MAJ, USA, 642

White, Pat, LTC, USA, 335

Widmann, Robert S., MAJ, USA, 396, 532, 668